Windsor-Chair Making in America

WINDSOR-CHAIR MAKING
IN AMERICA

FROM CRAFT SHOP TO CONSUMER

Nancy Goyne Evans

University Press of New England   HANOVER AND LONDON

Published by University Press of New England,

One Court Street, Lebanon, NH 03766

www.upne.com

© 2006 by Nancy Goyne Evans

Printed in China

5   4   3   2   1

Library of Congress Cataloging-in-Publication Data

Evans, Nancy Goyne.

  Windsor-chair making in America : from craft shop to consumer / Nancy Goyne Evans.

      p.   cm.

  Includes bibliographical references and index.

  ISBN-13: 978–1–58465–493–3 (cloth : alk. paper)

  ISBN-10: 1–58465–493–7 (cloth : alk. paper)

  1. Windsor chairs—United States. 2. Furniture making. I. Title.

  TS6.5.C45 2006

  749'.32'0973—dc22   2005014157

Photography funded in part by the National Endowment for the Humanities.

Contents

Color plates follow pages 144 and 288.

Preface and Acknowledgments

When I first began my quest for information about the craft of Windsor-chair making in America and its products, I was uncertain where the road would lead and just how long the journey would take. Early on, I discovered that the repositories and resources to be investigated—libraries, historical societies, museums, private holdings, and public and organizational records—held a plethora of appropriate material. The complexity of the subject, which soon became manifest, dictated that the material be mined deeply if a comprehensive picture of the craft were to be developed. Skimming the surface would not produce a valid study.

Like many other research projects in the decorative arts, completion of a broad investigation of the materials well exceeded estimates of the time required to finish this phase of the work. Although the task was a lengthy one, the research yielded a body of extraordinary information, which through analysis has served to illuminate this vernacular craft—its artisans, practices, and products.

Whereas my previous books on the subject of Windsor furniture, *American Windsor Chairs* and *American Windsor Furniture: Specialized Forms*, explore design sources, pattern chronology, regional characteristics, and design transmission, *Windsor-Chair Making in America: From Craft Shop to Consumer* is a study of craft practice. Discussed in contexts that often focus on the minutiae of daily life are shop structure and organization, tools and equipment, workmen and products, methods of doing business, and the nature of the consumer market. Records indicate that eighteenth- and early-nineteenth-century craftsmen entertained many of the same hopes and fears concerning the success of their businesses and the well being of their families as workers in modern society, as this volume will demonstrate.

The presentation of this study in rich detail, both verbal and visual, has been possible because of the cooperation and assistance of many individuals, institutions, and organizations. Colleagues in the field of American decorative arts and students in the Winterthur Program in Early American Culture passed along valuable citations and other references to little known works. Private collectors, dealers, and institutions made their collections available for study and, in many cases, accessible for photography. Many of these individuals are identified in the chapter notes and photographic credits.

Special thanks go to George Fistrovich, former photographer at the Winterthur Museum, for his excellent work in the studio and the field. His photographs have added a special visual dimension to this study. I am grateful to John D. Alexander, Jr., for taking valuable time from his own demanding schedule to read the sections of this manuscript dealing directly with craftsmanship and to offer critical comment and insights. Susan Randolph of the Winterthur Museum staff shared her knowledge of the publication process and offered encouragement and advice at the start of this critical phase of the work. As the manuscript moved toward production, Wendell Garrett's critical commentary of the study was especially valuable in the process of fine tuning the text, and his assessment of the manuscript as a whole offered particular encouragement. I also extend thanks to Elton W. Hall, executive director of the Early American Industries Association, for his encouragement in the task of bringing this volume to a broad, interested audience.

Prologue

Windsor seating furniture was introduced to America from England during the 1720s, although another two decades passed before domestic production began at Philadelphia in the mid-1740s. Whereas the English Windsor remained an important influence on its American counterpart through the end of the century, formal and rush-bottom chairs of local origin were equally significant design sources as American craftsmen developed a distinctive product. Well before the Revolutionary War knowledge of Windsor-chair making, which was disseminated from Philadelphia through the export trade and the migration of craftsmen, encouraged the development of small chairmaking centers at New York City and Newport, Rhode Island. As the craft spread after the war, idiosyncrasies of local design became increasingly part of the form. Today these so-called regional characteristics facilitate identification of chairs from many areas.

The American Windsor came into its own during the 1790s as this inexpensive, painted chair achieved a broad market and sales surpassed those of all other chairs combined, vernacular and formal. Windsors were used everywhere—in the home, in the business world, by social clubs and organizations, and in public institutions. Standard-chair production was augmented by specialized forms: settees, children's furniture, writing and rocking chairs, stools, and stands. After 1800 sculptural emphasis in design, which was so prominent in the eighteenth century, was supplanted by almost total reliance on bright paint and flat, ornamented surfaces as Windsor-chair design entered a new phase of development. By the mid-nineteenth century innovation had run its course in the craft shop, and factory production took over.

Introduction

Windsor-Chair Making in America: From Craft Shop to Consumer is a comprehensive study of the day-to-day activity and operation of the furniture-making shop in preindustrial America. Although focused on vernacular-chair making, the text is relevant to the furniture craft as a whole and supports a broader application to the business lives of all craftsmen, regardless of trade.

The material of this nuts-and-bolts study has been drawn largely from manuscripts and published sources produced principally in the late colonial and federal periods in America, with background and interpretive information supplied as necessary. The manuscript database alone is substantial, consisting of business accounts and papers of furniture craftsmen, private individuals, firms, and organizations; population and manufacturing census records; court and legal records; customhouse and private shipping papers; real estate and personal property records, including those of more than 120 chairmakers and turners. Other information derives from period publications: travel accounts, journals, diaries, and reminiscences; local histories; technical and statistical commentary; price and design books; city directories; and more than 225 newspapers published in the eastern part of the country. This large body of material serves well to illuminate daily life in early America, providing, in particular, insights into the business affairs, management skills, and human experiences of a sizable group of vernacular-chair makers who worked, and sometimes struggled, in a society that lacked the benefit and compensation programs of our modern age.

The five chapters comprising this volume are subdivided into many sections, each linked to the next and together providing an in-depth exploration of shop operation, personnel, facilities, products, marketing practices, and a diverse consumer market. Carefully chosen illustrations amplify the text and provide a level of interpretation that words alone cannot always achieve.

From the introduction of Windsor-chair making in America, many craftsmen labored in one-man shops, often while pursuing a supplementary occupation. In nonurban locations this work frequently was farming. Journeyman help in shops that contracted for additional labor usually was of short duration and filled specific needs. Piecework payment was considerably more common than a fixed daily or weekly wage. A chairmaker whose trade was limited was more likely to take an apprentice than to hire a journeyman. The length of the apprenticeship term varied. Some bonds were for three years or less, although the most common training period was about five years. Some master-apprentice relationships proved stormy, leading the apprentice to abscond and the master to advertise for his return. The usual method of identifying a truant apprentice was by his dress, which often was detailed in notices of runaways. Supplemental data from other sources describe the typical master's costume.

Following the Revolution woodworkers, other craftsmen, and businessmen residing in urban and semiurban locations sometimes banded together to form mechanic and manufacturing societies for protection against cheap imported goods and to provide beneficence to families of members in times of need. Disasters of all types, from fires to insolvencies, were commonplace, and workmen had little protection. During the second quarter of the nineteenth century prison reform, which embraced a work ethic designed to defray the costs of incarceration, proved a boon to some chairmaking entrepreneurs who negotiated contracts for prison work. To other craftsmen whose trade suffered from the competition of cheap labor, it represented a hardship.

Shop location often was critical to success in business. Facility size and equipment determined the extent of production. On occasion the material of the physical structure reflected a local building preference, although wood frames were ubiquitous. Hand tools, as identified in inventories and other records of chairmakers, are grouped and discussed according to their general function, such as cutting, surface shaping, and boring. Because the raw materials used in chair production varied somewhat from region to region, wood selection, especially that for the seat, can provide insights into the geographic origin of furniture irrespective of pattern. Regional preferences in material selection remained prominent even during the early nineteenth century when many craftsmen began to specialize in producing turned chair stock, which they supplied to framers scattered over a broad area. This division of labor became economically feasible only after waterpower replaced human power as the source of shop energy and permitted individual production levels to rise substantially.

Sufficient material exists in documents to piece together a reasonably accurate picture of construction practices, costs, and profit in the chairmaking shop of the postrevolutionary period. From a historical point of view, handcrafting chairs was both similar and dissimilar to modern practice using hand tools. In shops that had a brisk trade chairmakers filled orders from stockpiled parts produced efficiently in batches. The craftsman who operated a small shop or also pursued the cabinetmaking trade was more likely to build chairs a set at a time from start to finish upon receipt of an order. Records permit a reasonable estimate of the time required to complete a set of Windsor chairs. In supplement to income from building new furniture, the early American chairmaker realized a substantial part of his livelihood from repairing and altering used seating.

Over time chair patterns and influences changed. A heavy reliance on English Windsor prototypes in the eighteenth century gave way in the nineteenth century to patterns that were more reflective of formal European design, transmitted principally through design books and emigrating craftsmen. Patterns were simplified in America and reinterpreted to accommodate painted surfaces, which then as earlier consisted of a primer coat, one or two oil-base finish coats, and a protective varnish coat. Nineteenth-century chairs were further enhanced with painted decoration.

From the introduction of the craft of Windsor-chair making in America in the 1740s until the postwar years, verdigris green was the surface finish available to consumers. The color range broadened substantially following the Revolution, as demonstrated in chart 1, and remained diverse through the rise of factory production about seventy-five years later. Contemporary paint recipes provide insights on the exact hues represented by the colors named on the chart. Applied to the painted surfaces were the principal ornaments, stripes, bands, vines, sprigs, arabesques, and scrolls that comprise the lexicon of design motifs executed in paint and stencils on the plain and imitative-wood grounds of vernacular chairs.

An innovation dating from just before 1800 was the introduction of soft, resilient materials to the tops of Windsor seats to form fixed cushions, or stuffed seats. Rudimentary plank shaping and the presence of nail holes usually are indications that a plank was originally stuffed.

Chairmakers tapped one or more markets when merchandising their products, depending on location. A coastal urban situation provided the greatest potential. In supplement to local business some craftsmen turned to overland commerce and developed regional contacts and outlets in the surrounding countryside. Water routes utilizing regional bays, rivers, and streams broadened access to the interior. The coastal trade offered a wealth of opportunity to the enterprising craftsman willing to set his sights beyond regional markets. Venture cargoes could be consigned to merchant houses and sea captains, and in time a craftsman could develop his own business contacts in distant places. The entire coastal South was a lucrative market for northern entrepreneurs. A trade in Windsor chairs also opened with New Orleans before the city became an American port of entry.

Farther afield a thriving trade in chairs developed with the islands of the Caribbean. At any given time destinations depended on the state of political affairs in Europe, as most islands were colonies of European powers. A nascent commerce in Windsor chairs to the Caribbean emerged as early as the 1750s, within a few years of the craft's establishment in America. The size of the trade in the postrevolutionary period can be gauged by a few statistics. When the Spanish islands finally opened to general commerce in the late 1790s, records indicate that nearly 10,000 chairs entered the port of Havana in a four-year period from Philadelphia alone. The Virgin Islands in the Leeward group formed an important chair market in the southern Caribbean from as early as 1783. Thirty-seven percent of the chair trade to the lower Caribbean was concentrated in this area. The momentum of the Caribbean trade continued into the early 1800s. By then other markets had been developed in the wine islands of the eastern Atlantic, and small markets were being nurtured in Central America and along both the eastern and western coasts of South America. Occasionally, cargoes were landed in South Africa, the East Indies, and other Eastern markets. A few personal cargoes and orders reached Europe. On the North American continent Canadian chairmakers suffered increasingly by the early 1800s from encroachments by American chairmaking interests, both along the Atlantic coast and across the inland lakes.

The vehicles of trade were varied. For land journeys carts, wagons, and sleds were employed, depending on the route and season. Sailing vessels of all sizes, from the single-masted sloop to the three-masted ship, carried Windsors to coastal and overseas markets. The introduction of steam power to water transportation revolutionized the distribution of goods in the domestic market. Entrepreneurs developed new avenues of commerce, penetrating eastern rivers previously inaccessible and opening the vast new western region beyond the Appalachians. Canals made other inland regions accessible by water. The Erie Canal, preeminent among artificial waterways, created a veritable boomtown across northern New York State from the Hudson River to Lake Erie, with painted chairs an important commodity in the trade that developed. Toward the end of the handcrafted-chair era, railroad transportation opened still more distant domestic markets.

American consumers registered their satisfaction with Windsor furniture as early as the 1750s. Based on economy, durability, and plain good looks the Windsor secured the market in vernacular seating even before the Revolution. By the 1790s the popularity of the product had reached a groundswell. There were no class distinctions. From the day laborer to the statesman, the Windsor seated all.

The domestic setting was the early venue for the Windsor. From the front entry to the library, the Windsor met household needs, no matter how humble or grand the surroundings. A practical and popular function of the Windsor was as seating around a dining table. The compact design of the side chair, particularly the bow-back Windsor of the 1790s and the square-back styles of the early nineteenth century, served to conserve space at the table, an important consideration in a society whose average family size was large. On occasion Windsors were carried out of doors to provide seating in gardens and on piazzas. The study of Windsor furniture in the home is multifaceted: it provides a focus on the use of household space, on the similarities and differences of locality, and on change over time.

Windsor seating served social and cultural groups at functions ranging from intimate tea parties to public balls and dinners. Whether used indoors at theaters and lecture halls or out of doors in public gardens, Windsors were a reliable choice. Accommodation via Windsor seating extended to clubs and fraternal organizations. Furniture from two Masonic lodges, one in Pennsylvania and one in New Jersey, is included in this study (figs. 5-38 to 5-41).

Travelers and local residents were likely to encounter Windsor furniture wherever they lodged or dined. From neighborhood barrooms to well-appointed public houses, tavernkeepers gravitated to the Windsor as a practical and attractive choice to furnish their establishments. The emergence of large urban and resort hotels in the early nineteenth century was a boon to the Windsor-chair maker. Instead of purchasing seating furniture by the dozens, proprietors placed orders in the hundreds. Patrons often were similarly accommodated on shipboard, especially after the steamboat replaced the sailing vessel as the popular mode of transport.

The business community also was well served by Windsor furniture. From the long-legged stool of the countinghouse to the swivel chair of the mid-nineteenth-century office, Windsor construction was the usual selection. Shops and stores placed stools and chairs at counters for the use of patrons, and other seats were scattered about the premises for workmen. William Spangler, tobacconist of York, Pennsylvania, seated his "working hands" on Windsor stools around a large table where in 1811 they rolled tobacco leaf into cigars (fig. 5-55).

Institutional use of Windsor furniture was broad, including libraries, religious groups, schools, and government facilities. Members of the newly formed Massachusetts Historical Society voted in 1791 to acquire green Windsor armchairs for their library. One chair still is in the Society's possession (fig. 5-61). When the national library at Washington was burned in 1814 by the British during the War of 1812, the government drew plans to house the facility in temporary quarters. Congress authorized the purchase of Thomas Jefferson's private library, and John Bridges, a local chairmaker, supplied six Windsor chairs and a matching settee to furnish the reconstituted Library of Congress (fig. 5-60). Until the early nineteenth century many public schools were furnished sparingly with make-do furniture; however, as boarding schools supplemented day schools, needs expanded proportionally. Lewis Bancel, proprietor of a substantial school in New York City in the 1820s, furnished the premises with an astounding number of seats — 354 in all. Some were long benches to hold several persons; others were single wood-seat stools. The full complement of Windsors exceeded 150 chairs.

Government structures, particularly courthouses and statehouses, consumed quantities of Windsor seating, and given the nature of public facilities, local chairmakers were assured of continuing calls for repair work and new seating for expanded quarters. Sometime after Isaac Weld, a touring Englishman, described a visit to the local courts in York, Pennsylvania, in the mid-1790s, Lewis Miller, chronicler of his native town, drew a picture of the court of quarter sessions, complete with its row of green-painted bow-back Windsor chairs beyond the bar (fig. 5-66). Less clear is what seating was in place in the Pennsylvania Statehouse (Independence Hall) at Philadelphia in 1776 when the Continental Congress voted independence.

One of the underlying goals of this study has been to explore the persona of the chairmaker working in preindustrial America, using both written and material sources to create flesh-and-blood individuals who interacted daily with life. By having the opportunity to look closely at these artisans and their environment, the reader stands to gain a better understanding of the inner workings of the furniture trade and a greater appreciation of the cultural forces that shaped life in early America. The potential audience for this book is broad. Students and interpreters of American material culture and life will find an abundance of new material organized and presented to provide comprehensive insights on craft life and product distribution. Information on raw materials as an aid to object identification and an in-depth discussion of painted surfaces and ornament will be of particular interest and value to collectors and curators, including those with an interest in folk art. Membership organizations that focus on early American trades and crafts or on preindustrial technology as well as practicing and amateur furniture craftsmen stand to gain a better understanding of shop equipment and practices in an era when furniture was crafted by hand.

Part One

THE CRAFT OF THE CHAIRMAKER

CHAPTER 1

The Craftsman

The labor scene represented within the framework of *Windsor-Chair Making in America* is one of considerable scope and substantial change in which the pendulum realized full swing. Small chair-shops of the 1750s and later were occupied by one, occasionally more, skilled craftsmen who filled orders for "bespoke" work for named customers. The typical facility of the 1840s and 1850s, by contrast, was a large impersonal factory complex that produced thousands of chairs annually and employed numbers of semiskilled workmen, or "hands," who performed repetitive tasks, never dealing with the consumer and frequently limited in ability to the single job assigned. Certain constants did not change, however: the hours of labor were long, the work was physically taxing, and the wages were only moderate, although earnings generally were higher in America than in England, since the supply of skilled labor was seldom equal to demand until the early nineteenth century. The craftsman's standard of living gradually rose through the late eighteenth century, but by the 1820s it was on the decline again. Still, working conditions were better in America than in Great Britain.

The new nation realized tremendous population growth in the early nineteenth century. Between 1820 and 1860 collective increases of nearly 800 percent occurred in urban centers, large and small. New York, the largest American city in 1820, already had doubled its population, up from 60,000 in 1800 to 123,000 in 1820. Its craft community stood at 14,000, an increase of 10,000 in the thirty years since 1790. Whereas many urban craftsmen in earlier years had owned their homes, often as a combined residence and business, most now were renters. Many dwellings housed several families. Rural America, however, still accounted for more than 80 percent of the nation's population. Here craftsmen still enjoyed reasonable independence in a town facility or a homestead shop near a community center.[1]

The Master

An individual skilled in a trade—that is, the owner and master of a set of tools who used them in a professional manner to perform specialized tasks for his own account or in a supervisory capacity—was termed a craftsman or artisan, or in the language of the postrevolutionary period, a "mechanic." The successful master was a good manager, businessman, and entrepreneur as well. Frequently his household was sizable, consisting of a wife, children, apprentices, and perhaps a journeyman or two, whose health, well-being, education, and moral welfare were his responsibility. He fulfilled his contractual obligations in the shop by carefully supervising and training his apprentices, keeping a sharp eye on production levels and quality, and offering incentives for diligent performance. Edward Jenner Carpenter, an apprentice to cabinetmakers in Greenfield, Massachusetts, noted in the 1840s that his masters gave him "a stint to make a bureau with a double Ogee top drawer in eight days." Beginning on Monday, Carpenter noted day-to-day progress in his journal and by

Saturday wrote, triumphantly: "I finished my stint this afternoon about 3 o'clock & gained till next Tuesday night."[2]

The master also dealt with finance—making a periodic reckoning of debits and credits based on daybook records. During some periods currency fluctuated rapidly, and in the late 1700s the American monetary system converted from the British pound to a decimal base. Seldom did debits and credits balance, thus eliciting remarks such as that written in 1811 by Silas Cheney of Connecticut when crediting Daniel Burnham: "By puting up Chairs agread this Day Ballanced all accompts." Several craftsmen produced summaries or forecasts of their business dealings or net worth, including Thomas Boynton of Windsor, Vermont:

amount of income for the year 1816	$1234.23
amount of expense for the same	806.14
nominal net gain for the same time	$ 428.09

. . . appropriated partially as follows Viz	
for interest on debts	100.00
" my own Clothing	100.00
" Contingent expenses	50.00
" losses discounts &c.	50.00

A dozen years later in 1828 at Weymouth, Massachusetts, Enos White, a versatile woodworker, estimated the "Property now in my possesion all of whitch I have Earnt by the sweat of the Brow without the asistance of any one" (fig. **1-1**):

the first Cost of one half of the House, the Shop and Land	
that they stand on was	$ 800.00
the Expence . . . in repairing them is	115.00
Furniture on hand in the Shop	600.00
Stock on hand in the Shop	50.00
Tools, Benches, &c.	50.00
Cash on hand	50.00
Notes on hand	100.00
Cash paide for Cloths to Day	70.00
	$1835.00
all my Debts . . . amount to	70.00
	$1765.00
the House, Shop & Land . . . I Consider to be worth	
as they are now 1000.00 which is $85 more than they	
Cost me Consequently I Consider my self to be worth	$1850.00

This accounting preceded by one day White's union "with Miss Jane Humphrey in happy Wedlock."[3]

A more detailed look at the chair business is provided by Josiah Prescott Wilder's forecast of sales and expenses for 1837 made in New Ipswich, New Hampshire:

			Dolls cts
Common Chairs	2000 at	23 cts	460.00
Double Back do	300	35	105.00
Banister do do	150	35	52.50
Fancy Back do	150	38	57.00
Rocking Chairs	150	1.00	150.00
Amounting to 2750 Chairs			$824.50

The above will make 24 one-horse loads

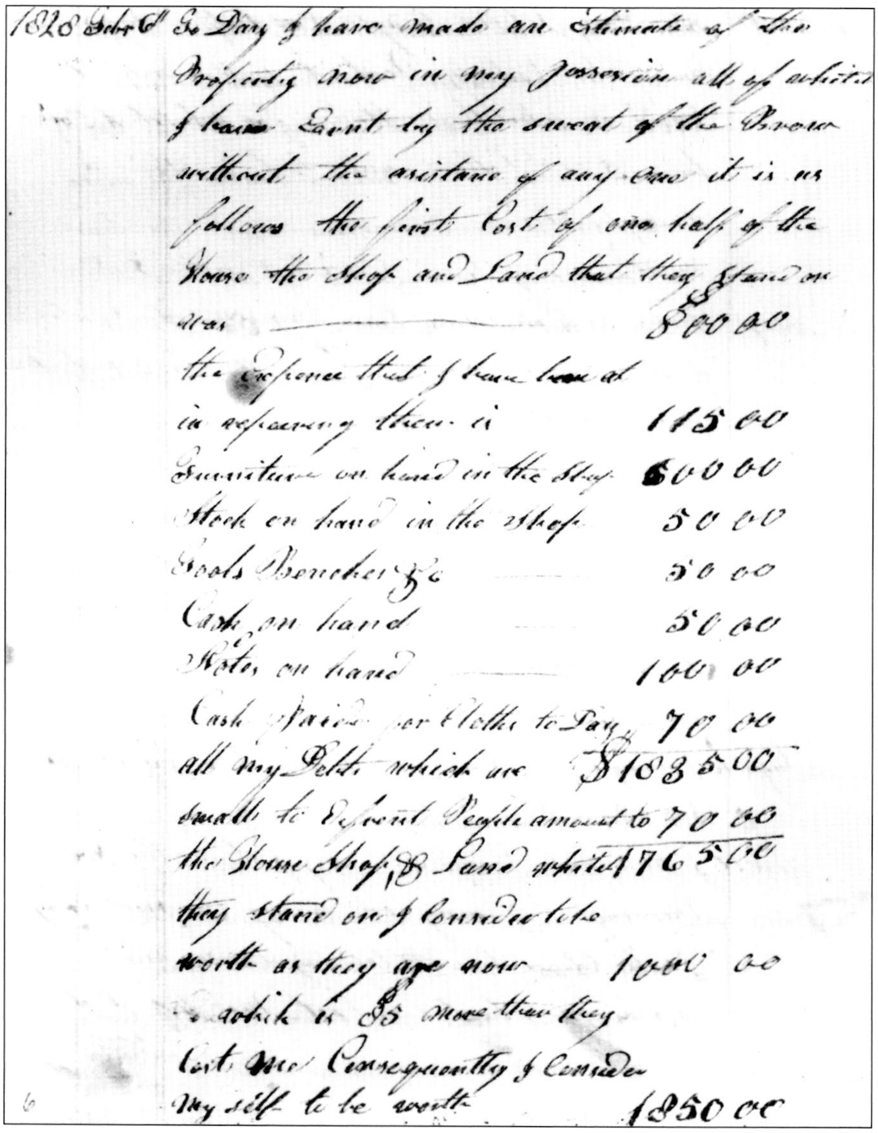

1828 Febr 6 To Day I have made an Estimate of the
Property now in my possession all of which
I have Gent by the sweat of the Brow
without the asistance of any one it is as
follows the first Cost of one half of the
House the Shop and Land that they stand on
was _____ 800 00

the Expence that I have been at
in repairing them is   115 00
Furniture on hand in the Shop 600 00
Stock on hand in the Shop   50 00
Tools Benches &c   50 00
Cash on hand   50 00
Notes on hand _____   100 00
Cash for ____ or Cloths to Pay 70 00
all my Debts which are $1835 00
owed to different People amount to 70 00
the House Shop & Land whilst 765 00
they stand on I consider to be
worth as they are now   1000 00
which is 85 more than they
Cost me Consequently I consider
my self to be worth   1850 00

FIG. 1-1 Estimate of property, Enos White journal, Weymouth, Mass., February 6, 1828. *(Winterthur Library, Winterthur, Del.)*

expenses on the road	68.00
for Plank	100.00
Hard wood timber	30.00
Rock[ing] Chair Back & rockers	7.50
Com[mon] Backs	7.00
for Glue 50# & Sand paper	9.00
16 Groce screws	4.50
for hired Labor	60.00
[subtotal]	286.00
other estimated expenses	
viz Grain & Flour	50.00
Tea & Coffee	5.00
sugar & Molases	7.00
Taxes	15.00
Tools	15.00
Cloth and Clothing	70.00
Incidentals	50.00
Amount [of total expenses]	498.00
Leaving for liquidation of old debts and interest	326.[50]
	$824.[50]

Although Wilder's business was just two-thirds that of Boynton's, there are close financial parallels. Beyond normal expenses for labor and materials, both accounts provide for debt liquidation, clothing purchases, and contingency expenses. As Boynton was still single, his living expenses were counted as part of the business.[4]

The master chairmaker functioned as a manager, maintaining sufficient raw materials, prepared parts, and, as appropriate, completed stock in the shop and wareroom for production and sale. At his manufactory in Newark, New Jersey, David Alling contracted on a regular basis with local and New York suppliers for turned and sawed stuff to frame and finish in the shop. Some chairmakers and shop owners acquired a portion of their stock already framed. Henry W. Miller patronized local suppliers in Worcester County, Massachusetts, some of whom also sent chairs down the Connecticut River to Philemon Robbins at Hartford. Robbins had similar business dealings with chairmakers Lambert Hitchcock and Edward Shepard of Connecticut. The Holcomb brothers of Otsego County, New York, supplied seating to Chauncey Strong in exchange for painting supplies and hardware.[5]

Several contracts describe work supplied by one master to another. Justus Dunn and Billie R. Thurston agreed at Cooperstown, New York, in 1831 that the latter would furnish paint and "role top" chairs for Dunn to finish and merchandise, the sale proceeds to be divided equally. Sometimes a master contracted to supply a retailer or entrepreneur. James Stabler of Sandy Spring, Maryland, struck a bargain with Joshua Stewart and Company in 1817 to make 100 spinning wheels for joint sale at $2.40 per wheel. Stewart supplied the "bands," and Stabler furnished the rest of the materials. Another document contains a comprehensive record of furniture ordered for the Sans Souci Hotel at Ballston Spa, New York, a resort facility owned and promoted by Nicholas Low, a New York City merchant. On November 24, 1803, Low's agent contracted with Elihu Alvord of neighboring Milton to construct 50 beds and Windsor seating described as: "One Hundred round Backed Chairs of the best Wood, strong, neatly finished & well painted at Seven Shillings & six pence each." The furniture was to be delivered to the new hotel by June 1 following.[6]

Occasionally a master woodworker supplemented furniture sales by renting unused shop space to another master who produced furniture on his own account. This was a good way for a young beginner to obtain a modest start without the substantial expense of renting or owning a facility. Stephen Whipple, a cabinetmaker and chairmaker of the Boston area, rented shop space and obtained board from one Jonathan P. Pollard from April 1804 to August 1805. Silas Cheney specified the terms of an agreement made at Litchfield, Connecticut, on June 12, 1808: "This Day Mr Russel Com [came] to worke in my shop for the Concidation of twelve Dollars The yeare. Said Russel is to have the fifth Part of the Chamber." Russel's last day was February 18, 1809.[7]

Christian Nestell, possibly fresh from his native New York, rented shop space from the Proud brothers of Providence in 1820. The first quarter-year's rent was recorded in the Proud accounts for February, and the last was posted on November 17: "This Day Setteled all acp [accounts] Too Shop Rent with C M Nestell Cash Reced for in full By Saml Proud $34.37." At Weymouth, Massachusetts, Enos White gave up cabinetmaking temporarily in 1830 and "let the Shop to Mr Warren Clark," a one-time apprentice, "for 30 Dollars/oo per Year with the tools." Joel Pratt, Jr., and John May of Sterling, Massachusetts, made a limited arrangement. On many occasions in the early 1820s May rented time at Pratt's lathe at the rate of 16¢ per day, apparently for the purpose of producing his own turned stock in lieu of purchasing it from a supplier. Circumstances suggest that May was a relative newcomer to the trade and as yet had not the resources to set up his own lathe.[8]

At times a craftsman served in the dual capacities of employee and master within a shop, as described by Thomas Hodgkins of Salem, Massachusetts, when billing Jacob Sanderson in 1803: "To my time and services Ceping [keeping] your tools and superintending your apprentices and Business in your absents from the Shop as Pr Power given me up to this date. $21." Planning to pursue other business in 1818, Hastings Warren, cabinetmaker of Middlebury, Vermont, engaged Horace Nichols to manage his shop. The arrangement lasted fourteen years, until Nichols opened his own facility. Henry W. Miller, hardware merchant of Worcester, Massachusetts, engaged Smith Kendall as foreman of his new "Chair Factory" in 1827. Kendall's duties included framing and painting chair stock purchased from suppliers in Worcester County, serving as shipping and receiving clerk, and supervising the activities of additional factory workmen.[9]

Once a craftsman had organized his shop, hung out his shingle, and begun production, it was time to develop merchandising outlets. Word of mouth, public notices, labels and brands, auctions, and often shop location all played a part. The chances of the industrious and knowledgeable craftsman getting ahead in the New World were far greater than in Europe. In the absence of restrictive guilds and a rigid class system, American artisans found incentive to improve their station in life. Many were moderately successful, although among the chairmakers there were no superstars like Duncan Phyfe. During a long career through 1855, David Alling of Newark, New Jersey, probably came closest to exemplifying the successful chairmaker. By contrast, Lambert Hitchcock's star rose swiftly, faltered, then rose again before descending rapidly. By a curious twist of fate, however, the embers never completely flickered and died, and Hitchcock's name, like Phyfe's, is better known to modern householders than it ever was in his own lifetime. For every craftsman who knew modest success, however, there were many who had difficulty making a living. This was especially true among artisans in urban areas and, as the nineteenth century progressed, among "workmen." Even the rural craftsman who was close to the land had his apprehensions. Enos White of Weymouth, Massachusetts, who trained in a family of craftsmen, confided his fears to his journal in 1829: "the Deploreable State that I have Considerd My Fathers Circumstances to be in together with the view of the Misfortunes of My Brothers and the Drad of Poverty Myself with all its inconvieniences has induced Me to make a slave of Myself Since I was of age to work."[10]

The Apprentice

Apprenticeship was a method of learning by doing — an exchange of work for an education. A master craftsman taught his young charge the "mysteries" of his trade, and when the boy became proficient, the master reaped the benefits until the indenture expired. The training system provided reasonable assurance that those who followed the trade were competent. Following European precedent, most apprenticeships began with a formal indenture, a legally binding instrument signed by the parties involved and duly registered. In signing the document, the main parties — the master and the apprentice — officially recognized their obligations as stated in the document, and the consenting party, usually the child's father or guardian, signified his agreement with the provisions of the contract (fig. 1-2). Many a father or guardian breathed a sigh of relief when completing an indenture with a reputable master. Like Joseph Bartlett of Maryland's Eastern Shore, most responsible adults knew all too well "the importance of watching over the slippery paths of youth." Although wording and provisions varied, the basic obligations remained fairly constant. The master agreed to teach the apprentice his trade and to provide board and lodging, adequate clothing, laundry services, and schooling sufficient to develop basic skills in reading and writing and, frequently, "cyphering." The apprentice agreed to be loyal, obedient, and morally upstanding, precepts established in the Middle Ages and still published as "Advice to the Young Apprentice" in the *London Tradesman* of 1747.[11]

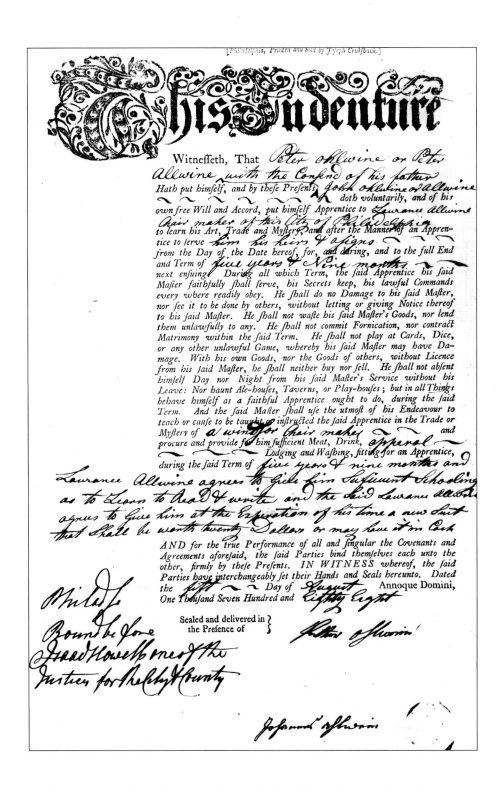

The apprenticeship indenture of Peter Allwine (fig. 1-2) is one of two documents signed in 1788 by sons of John Allwine, Sr., to serve Lawrence Allwine, a Philadelphia Windsor-chair maker. Whereas the contractual periods vary, the terms are similar except for a clause in John, Jr.'s, contract permitting him to "Go to Sacrament." This provision probably was not unusual among boys of German background. A contract drawn in 1819 in New England binding Elisha Harlow Holmes to Amos Denison Allen and Frederick Tracy of Windham, Connecticut, made provision to furnish the apprentice with "sufficient Medicine and Medical aid in case of sickness," to mend his clothes, and "to find him a gun, catridge [*sic*] box, bayonet, Catriges & balls for Ironing & mustering." Holmes probably was one of five apprentices reported in the Allen shop in the 1820 manufacturing census.[12]

The importance attached to providing an apprentice with some formal education is documented in early New England laws that required parents and masters to teach children "to read and understand the principles of religion and the capital laws of the country." In due course requirements were broadened "to teach children to writte and keep accounts" to better meet the needs of society, and schoolmasters began to provide instruction such as was required by law. Peter Allwine's indenture called for "Suficuent Schooling as to Learn to Read & write" (fig. 1-2). Other documents specified the term, as for example, "One quarter Schooling" each winter during the period of the contract. Jacob Sanderson of Salem, Massachusetts, paid Daniel Parker $6 for six weeks' instruction of four young men in March 1803. Several years later Asa Flanders charged Sanderson "for his apprentices tuition at evening school . . . four dollars per quarter." In New Hampshire, John Dunlap's sons used Daniel Adams's *Scholar's Arithmetic*, a volume that contained a sample indenture, suggesting its general use among apprentices. Other provisions for schooling are identified by Nathan Cleaveland of Franklin, Massachusetts, whose two apprentices went "home to school" for periods of seven and eleven weeks, respectively, during the winter of 1813.[13]

The apprentice's living conditions are little described in records. Lodging and dining within the master's house as a family member probably was the common practice. On this subject the *London Tradesman* cautioned the apprentice to "interfere as little as possible in . . . domestic Concerns" but rather to "keep close to . . . Business, and mind nothing else." Above all the apprentice should "avoid tattling . . . or carrying Stories" and ought to be "ready to do his Mistress all the good Offices in his Power." In the 1840s Edward Jenner Carpenter and another apprentice lived at the Miles and Lyons cabinet shop (probably in a loft) in Greenfield, Massachusetts, and took their meals in the Miles home nearby. Other documents suggest that this living arrangement was common. Eli Wood's estate recorded in Connecticut itemizes a "Shop Bedstead," and Benjamin Love's inventory drawn in Pennsylvania describes a "Cott in [the] Shop Cockloft," or upper story.[14]

Many masters were responsible for outfitting their young wards, and they often provided a new suit of clothes at the end of the training period, although clothing is seldom described in apprenticeship indentures. Public notices seeking runaway boys usually are explicit on this subject, however. A coat, coatee, or jacket served as an outer garment, frequently over a waistcoat (vest) that partially covered a shirt (figs. 2-4, 2-5, 3-32). Cotton coats were common; wool served in cool weather. Trousers, often referred to as pantaloons, frequently were of similar fabrics. Suit colors of blue and brown were popular, although gray and "bottle green" are mentioned along with stripes. Waistcoats appeared in an array of bright colors, and patterned fabrics provided additional enlivenment. Many runaway apprentices wore a hat, frequently made of felt. Shoes and stockings are mentioned occasionally, although these articles were not critical for identification. Records indicate that many apprentices had both working and dress clothes. For instance, John Lamson's apprenticeship indenture with cabinetmaker Elijah Sanderson of Salem, Massachusetts, stipulated that he was to have "decent & comfortable clothing, both for labor & to attend public worship."[15]

The apprenticeship term was variable. Originally the period was seven years, or from age fourteen to twenty-one, but long before the 1750s this rigid system was modified and four- to seven-year periods became common in America. Chairmaking indentures of less than four years were unusual unless a boy began his training with another master who had died, abused his young charge, become incapacitated, or moved away. It was to a master's advantage to secure the services of an apprentice for a maximum period because the longer the young man trained, the more productive and valuable he became. Chairmakers seeking apprentices almost always stipulated a period of from five to seven years. Town officers had the power to bind out children of the poor and orphans who seemed likely to become public wards. At the expiration of an apprentice's indenture, usually on his twenty-first birthday, he was entitled to compensation, generally termed "freedom dues." This took several forms, of which the most common was a new suit of clothes, often called a "Freedom suit." The Allwine boys were to have their choice of a suit or $20 in cash. A contract made in New England between Amos Denison Allen and Ebenezer Tracy, Sr., stipulated that in each indenture year Allen was to have 20s. worth of cloth or clothes and 20s. (about $3.33) in cash.[16]

During the indenture period the apprentice was expected to work industriously to acquire the skills of his trade, although related work was required of him. Edward Jenner Carpenter of Massachusetts described two common woodworking chores. When a fellow apprentice was busy carrying boards, Carpenter had "to kick [turn] the lathe in his place." John Woodhull Stedman of Hartford, Connecticut, recalled bringing in fuel and feeding "the old-fashioned box stoves with four-foot wood." If the master lived on a farm, there were outdoor chores twice a day. A master was not expected to abuse his privileges, however. The indenture of Elisha Harlow Holmes was explicit: "And sd Allen & Tracy will not cause sd Apprentice to work at any business foreign to the Cabinetmaking business more than twenty days per year — excepting ordinary chores."[17]

Proper supervision on the job also was important, especially in a large shop, both for the boys' welfare and the integrity of the business. Rhodes G. Allen of Providence, Rhode Island, carefully noted that he had "in his employ eight journeymen, good workmen, and only one apprentice, who all work under his inspection." When Joseph Bartlett considered placing his brother with a woodworker in Baltimore, he was pleased to learn that the master enjoyed a brisk business, thus providing his brother with "a better opportunity of advancing himself in practice & receiv[ing] more instruction." American records identify at least two dozen young men who successfully negotiated the paths of apprenticeship and became chairmakers in their own right.[18]

Unlike Edward Jenner Carpenter, apprentices seldom kept journals; thus how they spent their free time, short as it was, is to some extent speculative. Many enjoyed the close company of their master's family; some enjoyed reading. Skating and sleighing were popular in winter; summer brought swimming and fishing. Attendance at church services, while not a pastime, was a change of pace. Social events occurred from time to time. Carpenter reported attending a dancing school and an occasional informal musical evening. Barn and house raisings always drew a crowd of workers and onlookers. By the second quarter of the nineteenth century evening lecture programs were popular, some series directed specifically to apprentices.[19]

On the other side of the coin, tragedy struck in the lives of some apprentices. Among those injured in a fire at Philadelphia in 1803 was an apprentice of chairmaker Thomas Mason. A decade earlier David Evans, cabinetmaker of the same city, made a coffin for an apprentice of Windsor-chair maker William Cox. Then there was the inevitable friction between some masters and their apprentices, compromising career training if not ending it altogether.[20]

Colonial and federal-period newspapers are filled with notices announcing runaways. Some masters seemed almost relieved by their "misfortune." Most advertisements describe the errant apprentice and add a cautionary statement against "harbouring, employing or assisting" the runaway. Notices issued at seaports frequently include a directive to "masters of vessels" lest they "carry" the runaways to sea. Sometimes rewards were offered, ranging from a substantial sum to a token amount. Wesley Whitaker of Raleigh, North Carolina, proposed a "One Cent Reward, but no thanks." Most descriptions are general. Of individual nature are those that identify a boy who was "very much knock knee'd" and an apprentice with a "remarkable . . . walk" due to the "suppleness of his joints." Matthew McColm's redheaded runaway at Baltimore was "much addicted to swearing and stealing," although his match existed in a fellow at Buffalo, New York, of "quarrelsome disposition, [who] kn[e]w more than anybody else, [and was] a great liar and tatler." William Augur of New Haven, Connecticut, announced one solution to the problem: "He will have no apprentices!"[21]

Many masters who persevered did what preliminary "screening" they could. Grant and Jemison of Kentucky called for "smart Boys." Other common prerequisites were "respectable connections," "good moral principles," "habits of industry," and "absti[nence] from the use of ardent spirits." Urban masters often called for a "boy from the country," equating this background with innocence and upstanding character but overlooking the possibility that lads unused to city life could be more vulnerable to moral corruption than local boys who had weathered the storm and came "well recommended" (fig. **1-3**). All in all the balance was favorable. In Baltimore, where 163 individuals were apprenticed to the chairmaking trade between 1784 and 1823, only a handful went astray.[22]

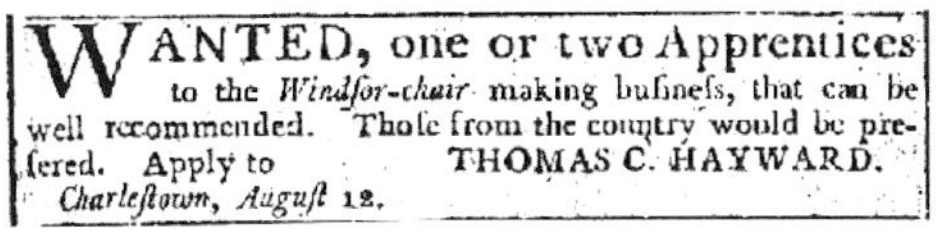
WANTED, one or two Apprentices to the *Windfor-chair* making bufinefs, that can be well recommended. Thofe from the country would be prefered. Apply to THOMAS C. HAYWARD. *Charleftown, Auguft* 12.

FIG. 1-3 Advertisement of Thomas Cotton Hayward. From *Columbian Centinel*, Boston, August 26, 1801.

The Journeyman

Upon completing an apprenticeship or comprehensive training period, a young man (or, infrequently, a young woman) was free to set up as a master on his own account. The cost, though not extraordinary, was prohibitive to some. The exact figure depended on location and whether the young man owned a complete set of hand tools, had access to or could rent a structure suitable for a shop, and possessed adequate cash or credit to acquire a workbench, raw materials, and possibly a lathe. In rural areas raw materials sufficient to begin sometimes were obtained from a local landholder with a stand of timber in exchange for a set of chairs. If the cost of a new or used lathe was prohibitive at the outset, turned stock could be secured from another craftsman in exchange for labor, a quantity of framed chairs, or other barter material. Still some men were not prepared by inclination or financial status to set up on their own, and they became journeymen, working for a daily wage or at piecework rates. With good labor in short supply until the 1820s, a journeyman usually had little difficulty finding work, especially if he was free to move about. Contemporary newspapers abound with notices of master woodworkers seeking hired labor. Isaiah Steen willingly gave "generous wages and constant employment . . . to a complete workman at the windsor chair making business" in western Pennsylvania. In the east a craftsman of Chester County sought a man "who understands both Rush and Windsor work." Some employers had more specific needs. Samuel J. Tuck of Boston sought a shop foreman in 1803 (fig. **1-4**). Some years later Jacob Batcheler of East Arlington, Vermont, was eager to hire two men "that have the use of Joiner's tools, to work on the Tops and Slats, and tend the Shop Saw-mill; also one Chair Turner."[23]

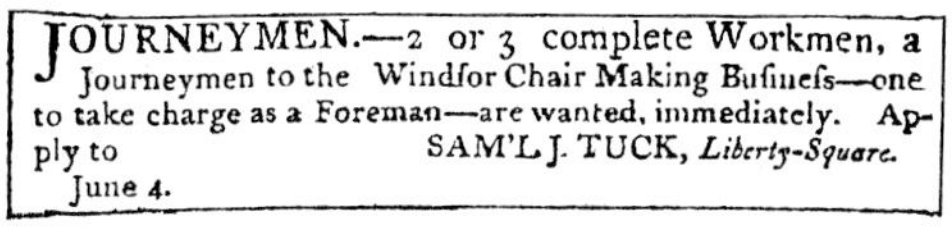
JOURNEYMEN.—2 or 3 complete Workmen, a Journeymen to the Windfor Chair Making Bufinefs—one to take charge as a Foreman—are wanted, immediately. Apply to SAM'L J. TUCK, *Liberty-Square.* June 4.

FIG. 1-4 Advertisement of Samuel Jones Tuck. From *Columbian Centinel*, Boston, June 4, 1803.

Economic depressions could alter circumstances temporarily, placing the journeyman in a position of soliciting work, as described in a letter to Silas Cheney of Litchfield, Connecticut:

> North Haven February 20th 1814
> Mr Cheney Sir
> I would inform you that I am now in want of imployment at the Cabinet makers Business for the tearm of one year—if I Could Light of a Chance where I Could have Stedy work for that time I would try my utmost to give Satisfaction. I want a place where I Can have a Room to Live with my wife and one Child ten years old. I would be willing to Live in a family—if you want to hire and Can provide me a Room I would Come immediately. I am about engaging myself to work at farming and if I Dont heer from you Soon Shall be engagd Elsewhere—yours with Respect,
> Jacob Thompson[24]

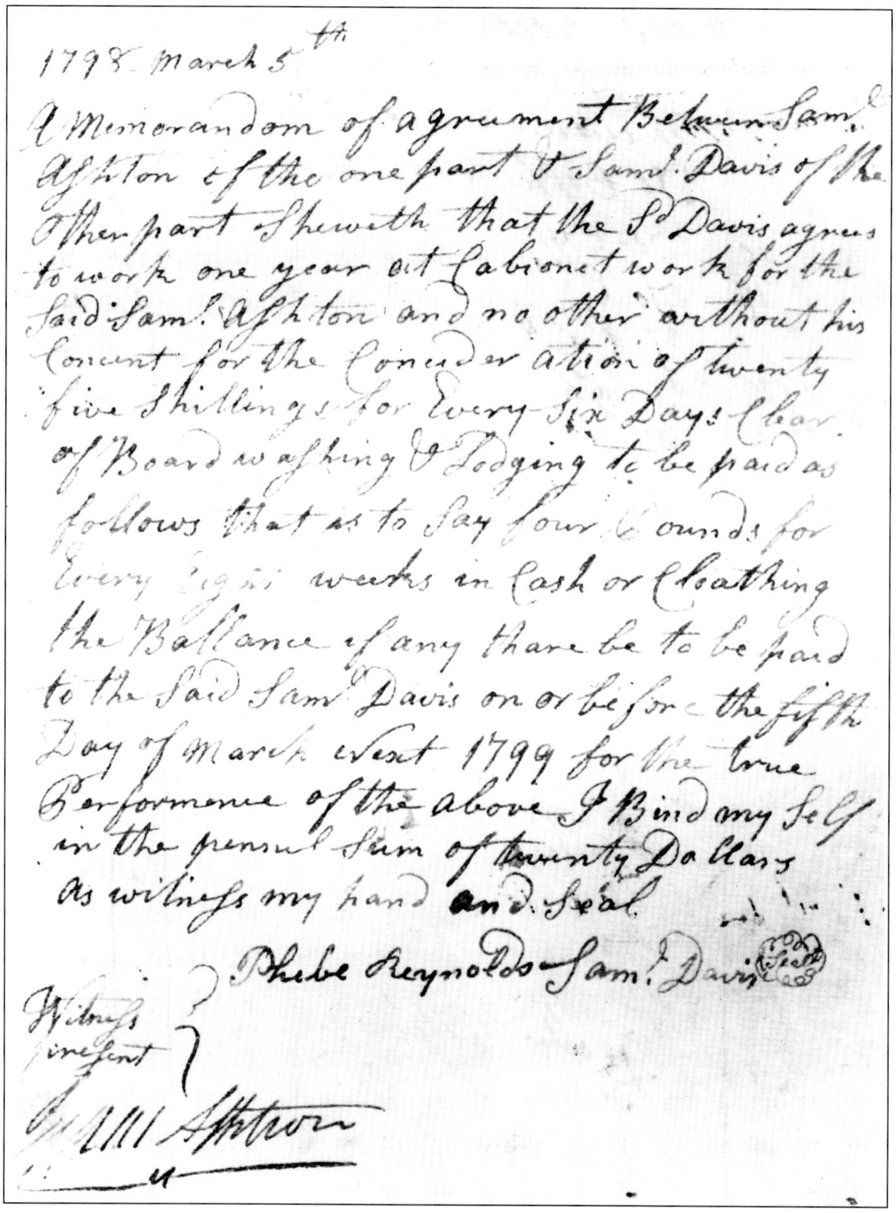
1798 March 5th

A Memorandom of agreement Between Saml Ashton of the one part & Saml Davis of the Other part Sheweth that the Sd Davis agrees to work one year at Cabinet work for the Said Saml Ashton and no other without his Consent for the Consideration of twenty five Shillings for every Six Days Clear of Board washing & Lodging to be paid as follows that is to Say four Pounds for every Eight weeks in Cash or Cloathing the Ballance if any thare be to be paid to the Said Saml Davis on or before the fifth Day of March Next 1799 for the true Performence of the above I Bind my Self in the penal Sum of twenty Dollars As witness my hand and Seal

Phebe Reynolds } Witness present

Saml Davis

Saml Ashton

FIG. 1-5 Agreement between Samuel Ashton and Samuel Davis, Samuel Ashton account book, Philadelphia, March 5, 1798. *(Winterthur Library.)*

Once a bargain was struck between master and journeyman, terms could be reaffirmed in writing. An agreement made at Philadelphia on March 5, 1798, between cabinetmakers Samuel Ashton and Samuel Davis provides insights (fig. **1-5**). Davis agreed to work for Ashton for a year at the rate of 25*s.* for a six-day week. In addition, the journeyman was to receive a stipend to cover or defray the costs of room, board, and laundry services. Davis's pay with "fringe benefits" was almost $1 a day, a typical urban wage for the period. Country pay often was less, and few agreements called for bonds. Working periods generally were shorter in rural areas, where a man may have tended the family farm part of the year and local shops often needed only temporary help. Even at Hartford when John I. Wells sought "an active Man, to assist in preparing Stuff for Windsor and other Chairs" in 1800, it was "for a few months" only.[25]

In contrast to fixed *term* contracts were agreements drawn for *piecework* labor. Typical is a contract of 1789 made at Boston between master chairmaker Joseph Adams and journeyman Robert McKeen:

> This may certify that I have this day agree'd with Robert McKine to pay Him for Seventy two Winsor Chairs that shall be made in a Workmanlike manner & compleatly

painted after the rate of Two Dollars for Every Six Chairs — I likewise agree to procure Him Sutable Stuff & in Season to make the Sd Chairs — also to be at the expense for all the turn'd Work & provide the Sticks for the number above mention'd. Witness My Hand this fourth day of Septr 1789.

Joseph Adams

Apparently there were several similar agreements between the two men along with others for work by the month or day, although if written, they no longer exist. A further provision of the working relationship was Adams's verbal agreement to "find and provide . . . suitable board, victuals, drink & lodging" for McKeen. "Notes of hand" dating several decades later and listed in the estate inventory of Gilson Brown of Sterling, Massachusetts, include one executed by Nathaniel Silsbee for $174. The balance remaining in 1834 was to "be paid in Labour or Framing Chairs within two years." Nelson Talcott of Nelson, Ohio, noted a workman credit in his accounts for 1841: "By Making chairs as pr contract up to this date."[26]

Daniel Carteret, Jr., a Windsor-chair maker of Philadelphia, spent almost two years during the difficult war period of 1812 to 1813 working primarily as a piecework journeyman for fellow chairmaker Charles C. Robinson. The business relationship began in April 1812 when Robinson paid Carteret's rent. Thereafter Robinson kept track of "Cash Paid him for making Windsor Chairs" at intervals of from two to seven days through the end of the year and into 1813. Several account entries dating in 1812 read "for work in the Shop," suggesting that Carteret usually constructed the chairs in his own establishment then delivered the framed or finished product to Robinson.[27]

Further insight into the nature of journeyman chairwork and contracts extends to Newark, New Jersey, where David Alling, a substantial consumer of chair parts in the early 1800s, employed full-time framers. Although the framers' activity is not recorded in Alling's extant accounts, his records illuminate the work of Moses Lyon, an ornamental painter, who gilded, silvered, bronzed, grained, tipped, striped, and generally decorated hundreds of chairs. Allen Holcomb, a successful woodworker of Otsego County, New York, was variously employer and employee. When he was a young shop master in western Massachusetts, he engaged one Reuben Joy to work by the month, provided him with a hammer, and duly recorded his production of turned work and his lost time due to a "fast Day." After moving to New York State about 1809, Holcomb himself worked for a time in Troy as a journeyman for Simon Smith before migrating westward. Holcomb's work in Troy sometimes involved making cross-back and bell-seat chairs from start to finish (fig. 3-32 top). At other times he concentrated on framing, painting, and ornamenting. Once settled in Otsego County, Holcomb again occasionally employed temporary help.[28]

Records originating in Connecticut describe chairmaking businesses where short-term journeyman labor was an essential component. During the 1820s James Gere of Groton frequently employed James Pettit of Norwich to make chair parts — seats, frets, and rolls — or to frame and seat chairs on a piecework basis. Pettit boarded with Gere once in December 1822 for fifteen days at the rate of 10s. per week. The late eighteenth-century records of chairmaker Solomon Cole describe how Elijah W. Webster worked in Cole's shop at Glastonbury for eleven months in 1795 and 1796. His time overlapped with that of Azel Peirce, another journeyman. Somewhat the same pattern prevailed in Silas Cheney's active shop at Litchfield, where versatile short-term workers handled any phase of production, from getting out parts to framing, finishing, and seating. The men often worked in tandem with Cheney or each other, and practically all compensation was at piecework rates.[29]

Almost from the start of his career in 1816 as a cabinetmaker and chairmaker at Barre, Massachusetts, Luke Houghton acquired finished chair stock and parts from outside suppliers in Worcester County. Few men who interacted with Houghton appear to have been journeymen in the true sense, except during brief periods. For example, Ephraim Wilder of Barre was credited by "1 month work" at $20 in January 1819, and later that year he made 100 chairs, presumably in Houghton's shop, for which Houghton supplied the seats. Wilder later moved to Templeton and settled into the role of supplier only. Between 1819 and 1840 records document Houghton's interaction with no less than thirty-one regional woodworking craftsmen, including cabinetmakers, chairmakers, turners, and a painter.[30]

Westal Rose worked in Henry F. Dewey's shop at Bennington, Vermont, full-time or intermittently between March 1839 and March 1841, primarily as a chair framer at piecework rates. Three other men supplied turned parts and plank, and a fourth provided "flag" for fancy chair seats. Nelson Talcott of Portage County, Ohio, followed a similar mixed business pattern. Some workmen supplied framed seating or parts outside the shop, and others worked on the premises. In another arrangement Edwin Cadwell rented shop space and acquired finished seating from Talcott; in return he painted chairs under contract. Sylvester Taylor, Jr., a supplier of seating furniture, worked in his own shop most of the time, except perhaps when he "made" seating by contract for Talcott and painted chairs for Edwin Cadwell. On November 18, 1839, Edwin Whiting began to work for Talcott for a daily wage, performing varied tasks that included framing chairs, hauling plank, general labor, clearing the kiln, bending stock, turning, and running errands to other communities.[31]

Other documents provide more detailed glimpses at the nature and dimension of journeywork. In his journal of the mid-1840s Edward Jenner Carpenter described the work of "Uncle Jo" Frost, a coffin specialist at the cabinet shop of Miles and Lyons in Greenfield, Massachusetts. When several deaths occurred at one time, the apprentices and even the proprietors had to help out, as embalming the dead still was little practiced. At haying time it was not uncommon for Uncle Jo to take off a few days. A part-time workman in the same shop was a Mr. Wilson of neighboring Colrain who came only when there were chairs to be painted. Once Carpenter noted the presence for a day or two of a German cabinetmaker from New York City who was visiting a relative in the area and apparently jobbed about to pay for the trip. Temporary workmen were available on call in many areas, as further suggested in a notice originating at Lewisburg, West Virginia, in 1852: Thomas Henning, Sr., advised that he could fill orders for from 300 to 600 chairs a month by advance notice sufficient "to enlarge his business." Clearly, he was able to engage journeymen or suppliers as needed. An unusual document in the papers of woodworker David Pritchard of Connecticut is a journeyman's guarantee signed by Lambert Hitchcock before he occupied his own shop:

> Waterbury 18 June 1814
> Now in case the Cheirs that I have making for David Pritchard Jr which is one hundred dining Cheirs and one hundred Citching Cheirs and twenty four rocking Cheirs Should fail I will make them good.
>
> Lambert Hitchcock

Hitchcock and Pritchard were brothers-in-law, and Hitchcock probably served his apprenticeship in Pritchard's shop.[32]

A complement to individual business accounts of master craftsmen that describe the particulars of journeywork are federal records documenting the widespread practice of employing journeymen. The 1820 Census of Manufactures, although of incomplete geographic spread and limited concentration within surveyed areas, probably constitutes a representative sampling and presents reasonably accurate data on the numbers employed. Ninety-seven chair shops are included in the report, of which some produced cabinetwork or spinning wheels along with chairs (table 1). Among surveyed shops, 26 percent also reported having one or more apprentices;

Table 1. The Employment of Journeymen in the
Chairmaking Trade as Reported in the
1820 United States Census of Manufactures

Number of Adult Workmen in the Shop, Including the Master	Percentage of the Chair Shops Surveyed
2 or more	62%
3 or more	34%
4 or more	13%
5 or more	8%

19 percent employed apprentices and two or more adult males. Of the eight shops employing five or more adult workmen, one was located in New England, two in the Middle Atlantic region, one in the South, and four in the up-and-coming Midwest. Only half reported having apprentices. Levi Stillman had a sizable cabinet- and chairworks in New Haven, Connecticut, where ten men and six boys found employment. Despite depressed conditions, Stillman reported good demand in the home market with some diminution in export sales.

Another large establishment surveyed was the chairmaking factory of Hugh Finlay and Company at Baltimore, the largest of any reported in the census. The business employed thirty men, thirteen boys, and twenty-five women. The workforce was engaged in making painted furniture—chairs, card and pier tables, sofas (settees), and cornices—as well as curtains. Although the proprietor sidestepped the question of product market value, he identified his capital investment as $30,000. The women in Finlay's employ may have undertaken part or all of the curtain work, and certainly they were responsible for most rushing and some caning executed on the premises.

Of the reported midwestern establishments of large size, three were located in Ohio and a fourth in Tennessee. Jonathan Young of Cincinnati, whose workforce numbered seven men, was one of only a few local chairmakers who reported good sales in 1820. Levi McDugal of Portsmouth and William McFarland of Vernon operated five-man shops. Portsmouth had an advantageous location for trade at the juncture of the Scioto and Ohio rivers, and Vernon, east of Cleveland near the Pennsylvania border, may have had reasonable access to the same waterway via small boats on the Shenango and Beaver rivers. Edmond Hunt owned a Windsor-chair manufactory in Blount County, Tennessee, on the North Carolina border and employed six men. The master learned his trade at the beginning of the century with John Oldham of Baltimore.[33]

Records contemporary with the manufacturing census provide additional statistics on the journeyman community. Henry Fearon noted in 1817 that three Windsor-chair factories at Pittsburgh employed twenty-three persons, the products valued at $42,600 annually. The *Mirror* of Middlebury, Vermont, reported a catastrophic fire in the cabinet and chair shop of Hastings Warren on January 26, 1814, an event that temporarily idled "10 or 12 workmen, which were constantly employed." Less than a decade later a similar number of hands labored in Lambert Hitchcock's turning mill and framing shop on the Farmington River in Connecticut. The existence of large rural establishments offers adequate testimony that by the early nineteenth century location was no deterrent in attracting adequate labor or finding suitable markets.[34]

Another decade brought further change. In some quarters the chair trade had entered the formative stages of industrial development. Nowhere is this more evident than in Massachusetts. A manufacturing schedule of 1832 presents rather cogent labor statistics for the northern and western parts of the state, where the develop-

Table 2. Comparison of Labor Statistics for the Furniture-Making Trades
in Northern Worcester County, Massachusetts, 1832 and 1855

Town	Chair and Cabinet Manufactories in 1832	Number of Hands		Chair and Cabinet Manufactories in 1855	Number of Hands	
		Male	Female		Male	Female
Gardner	10	95	98	14	441	
Ashburnham	9	56	85	4	250	50
Sterling	15	47		6	47	
Westminster	5	25		18	138	
Templeton	11	15	3	10	150	

From *Documents Relative to Manufactures in the United States* . . . , 2 vols. (Washington, D.C.: Duff Green, 1833) and Francis De Witt, *Statistical Information Relating to . . . Industry in Massachusetts for the Year Ending June 1, 1855* (Boston: William White, 1856). See note 35.

ment of waterpower promoted facility growth and expansion to the extent seen earlier in the Finlay establishment at Baltimore. Daniel Churchill of Stockbridge, Berkshire County, provided work for 25 men and a like number of women. Two turning and chair factories in neighboring Lee together employed 35 men, 8 women, and 4 boys. Statistics for the rising industrial communities of northern Worcester County are reported as town units (table 2), but the very nature of that data-gathering method testifies to the emerging importance of towns as manufacturing centers in contrast to single shops or manufactories. Although figures may be incomplete, five towns had already moved toward industrial status. Ten chairmaking facilities at Gardner employed 95 men and 98 women. Ashburnham followed with 56 men and 85 women at nine manufactories. Forty-seven men were employed at Sterling in fifteen chair shops, figures that represent an expansion of the labor force and a consolidation of facilities as reported in the manufacturing census of 1820 when twenty-three independent chairmakers were identified by name (fig. **1-6**). In the 1832 statistics Westminster followed Sterling with 20 men in four establishments, and Templeton provided work at ten sites for 13 men and 3 women. The 1832 figures bear comparison with statistics for the same towns reported twenty-three years later (table 2). The 1855 data list workers in cabinet and chair manufactories as one unit; therefore the earlier figures have been adjusted in the table to include cabinet workers, as appropriate. Area towns had mechanized to the extent permitted by technology and markets in the mid-nineteenth century. Of the five "manufacturing" centers on the list, only Sterling made no advances. Taking its place was the formidable newcomer Fitchburg, which employed 144 men in four facilities. Also rivaling Sterling in industrial size based on numbers of hands were Princeton (50), Hubbardston (44), and Royalston (40).[35]

The nature of the workforce also was changing. For several decades a significant body of semiskilled artisans had been developing, especially in the cities. Comprising the group were aliens, men who had not completed their training, and others drawn to the new centers in search of employment. In a manufacturing system where human know-how was giving way to machines, semiskilled workers took their places beside the skilled and all performed only limited tasks in the production of cheap goods for sale in expanding markets. Before 1850 the Hitchcocksville Company of Connecticut employed almost 200 workers. A few years later 300 men in two chair factories at Rochester, New York, produced $200,000 worth of goods annually, and George Coddington of Cincinnati grossed $120,000 through the labor of 180 men. Women, who had joined the workforce as seat weavers during the 1820s, saw that process mechanized as technology advanced.[36]

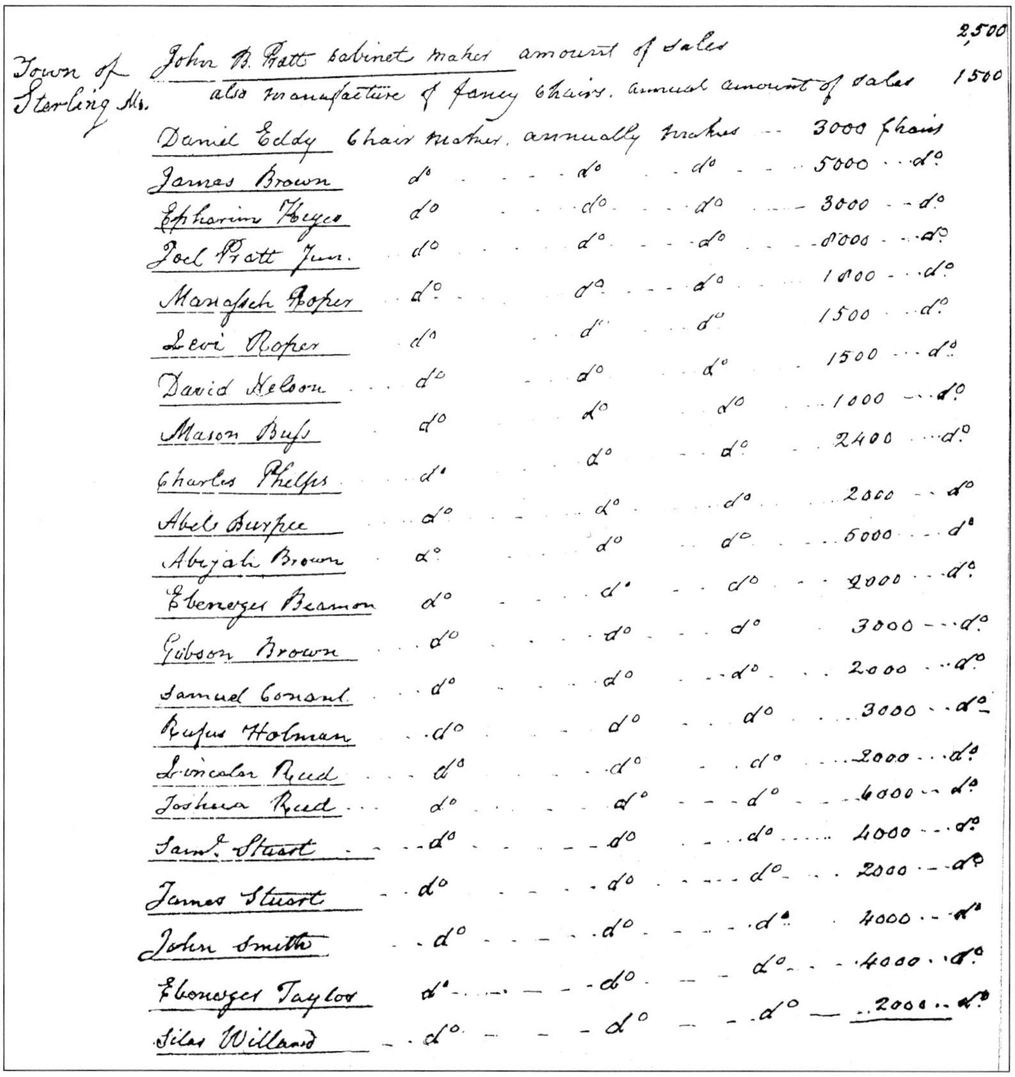

Town of Sterling Ms.   John B. Pratt cabinet maker amount of sales   2,500
                         also manufacture of fancy chairs. annual amount of sales 1500

Daniel Eddy   Chair maker, annually makes — 3000 chairs
James Brown   do   do   do   — 5000 ...do
Ephraim Heyes   do   do   do   — 3000 ...do
Joel Pratt Jun.   do   do   do   — 8000 ...do
Manassah Roper   do   do   do   — 1000 ...do
Levi Roper   do   d   do   — 1500 ...do
David Nelson   do   do   do   — 1500 ...do
Mason Buss   do   do   do   — 1000 ...do
Charles Phelps   d   do   do   — 2400 ...do
Abel Burpee   do   do   do   — 2000 ...do
Abijah Brown   do   do   do   — 6000 ...do
Ebenezer Beamon   do   d   do   — 2000 ...do
Gibson Brown   do   do   do   — 3000 ...do
Samuel Conant   do   do   do   — 2000 ...do
Rufus Holman   do   do   do   — 3000 ...do
Lincoln Reed   do   do   do   — 2000 ...do
Joshua Reed   do   do   do   — 6000 ...do
Saml. Stuart   do   do   do   — 4000 ...do
James Stuart   do   do   do   — 2000 ...do
John Smith   do   do   d   — 4000 ...do
Ebenezer Taylor   d   do   do   — 4000 ...do
Silas Willard   do   do   do   — 2000 ...do

FIG. 1-6 List of chairmakers in Sterling, Worcester Co., Mass., 1820, U.S. Census of Manufactures. (*National Archives, Washington, D.C.*)

Woodworkers other than those of the Caucasian race are little spoken of in records dating before 1840, although they were present in many communities. The skilled black workman usually labored as a journeyman. If he was not free, he received no remuneration, since he served his master directly or was hired out for the master's benefit. "TWO healthy likely NEGROE MEN . . . brought up to the Joiner's and Windsor-Chair business" were offered for sale at Philadelphia in 1780. In the South the practice of hiring out black workmen was early a cause of controversy because white journeymen were unable to compete with the low rates charged for skilled black labor. Numerous court actions ensued, and Charleston, South Carolina, enacted stopgap measures even before the Revolution to control the practice.[37]

When W. H. Hill of Wilmington, North Carolina, advertised in 1802 for his runaway Negro, John Hill, he described him as "sensible and shrewd" and knowledgeable in woodworking: "He served his time with a Cabinet-maker, and understands the business of the Windsor Chair-maker—he is very ingenious, and well acquainted with the use of the Joiner's tools. JOHN reads, and I believe can write a little." John Hill had received his training from John Nutt, a woodworker who emigrated from Charleston to Wilmington after the Revolution.[38]

Early nineteenth-century apprenticeship records from Baltimore include the indenture of Peter Jackson, a free mulatto bound to Robert Fisher to learn the trade of chairmaking for two years. Joseph Hall, a "free person of colour" at the nation's capital, received instruction in basic trade skills from Thomas Adams, and John Bridges trained Negro Benedict Jackson (or Johnson). In commenting on the death of an aged black citizen at Salem, Massachusetts, diarist William Bentley observed that only one Negro remained in town, one Jack Southward, alias Jack Lander, who had "served his time at Chairmaking with W. Lander & came from Africa." Records for New York City list a chairmaker of another race. John Williams of Frankfort Street is identified as an "aborigine," presumably a Native American.[39]

Partnerships

Of the more than 2,700 Windsor-chair makers known to have been in business through the early 1840s, at least 13 percent were involved in partnerships or related business associations. Nineteenth-century partnerships account for 89 percent of that figure, and of the remaining 11 percent, none date before the Revolution except the partnership of the cabinetmakers Daniel and Samuel Proud of Providence, although the firm did not make Windsor chairs until 1787. Among other business unions of this period, the best known is that of Thomas and William Ash (1783–94) of New York City. The short duration of most early partnerships set the stage for subsequent relationships in the trade.[40]

A partnership was an agreement, written or verbal, between two or more individuals to associate in business for a period of time that varied from a few months to several years. The association could be terminated by mutual consent at any time. To dissolve the firm, members needed only to give public notice. A representative announcement from Pennsylvania dates to 1824:

> The partnership heretofore existing between Robert Burchall and William Wickersham, under the firm of Burchall and Wickersham is this day dissolved by mutual consent: all persons, therefore, indebted to the late firm are hereby requested to call and settle their accounts; and all those that have any demands, to present them for settlement as soon as possible.

Expiration notices, such as one of 1805 from Virginia, are less common, since most partnerships never reached the previously agreed termination point: "JAMES BECK, Respectfully informs the Public, that the Copartnership between Mr. Alexander Walker and himself, in the WINDSOR-CHAIR Manufactory, having expired, he has commenced that Business in all its branches, on his own account."[41]

How partnerships were contracted and reasons for their existence would be speculative except for the survival of two documents, a reminiscence and a journal narrative, describing the early careers of two woodworkers. Charles B. Lines, who started a successful business at New Haven, Connecticut, following a five-year apprenticeship with Sherman Blair in the late 1820s, related:

> At the age of twenty I left Mr. Blair and was employed for a short time by [Levi] Stillman and then by James English, after which I could get no work. I called on [Chauncy] Treat and he offered to take me in as a partner. I had no money, and yet was restless out of work. It occurred to me that Judge Daggett, who had spoken very kindly to me at my grandmother's . . . might be interested in my case. . . . After taking an inventory, and ascertaining that it would require only $175 to pay for one-half of the entire stock, tools, and everything, Mr. Daggett . . . kindly drew a note for the amount, and when we had both signed it, he sent me to Dr. Æneas Monson [Munson], then the President of the New Haven Bank, who let me have the money. The next day the firm of Treat & Lines was organized and its colors flung to the breeze, with a capital of $350.[42]

Of quite different nature was the career and partnership of Enos White, who trained in Weymouth, Massachusetts, with his father and older brother, Lemuel. By

1829, six years after completing his training, he had purchased and improved half of his brother's house, bought his father's shop, acquired his brother's tools and stock, married, and taken several apprentices, of which one was still with him. But business was poor in Weymouth, and White had to work hard even to inch ahead. On August 10 he and Captain Stephen Salisbury became business partners. Salisbury was to "put in trade" money sufficient to balance White's stock of looking glasses, chairs, hardware, and lumber. In return Salisbury received "one half of the property Earnt by us." Annual shop rent was computed at $30 and use of the tools at $5. Salisbury's board per week was $1.50, and he was to have equal use of the apprentice, Warren Clark, toward whose wages and expenses he was to pay $8 per month, or his proportional share. White explained the move as follows: "My Object in taking a partner is not becaus I think that I shall make more money in the Cours of a Year than I have done but becaus I think I shall spend my Time much pleasantr in the Shop than I have Done for the four Years past with no one excepting an apprentice to speak too."[43]

White was pleased with Captain Salisbury, but he was not optimistic about the local business climate: "Mr Salsbury is a man of Good Sense, in my Opinion — his habits are Good — he is Industrius and Economical in all his Business and although he is a wheel wright by Trade still my Opinion is that we Shall make a Good living by persevereing although the prospects are very small at Present." Unfortunately, the "prospects" did not improve. Less than a month later White released Warren Clark from his apprenticeship noting, "I have found Business so very Dull that I have given him his Time which is about 10 weeks — he has been a steady and a faithful Boy for me." Business continued without improvement, and on March 10, 1830, White wrote: "Capt Salisbury has left me to Day after Staying with me 7 months. I have paid him 45 Dollars in Cash and he has takeing Furniture suficient to Satisfy him . . . so that we have Setled all Acounts & passed Receipts." Too often this was the small businessman's plight. Always vulnerable to fluctuations of the economy, operations such as White's often were further handicapped by a location beset with problems. In this case neighboring Boston probably siphoned off too much local business.[44]

Most partnerships began with bright prospects. At New Bedford, Massachusetts, in 1829 Cromwell, Howland, and Davis warranted their "Fancy and Windsor CHAIRS of the newest patterns . . . to be equal to any in the state." Dewey and Woodworth of Bennington, Vermont, employed "the best of workmen" and executed their work "in the most fashionable modern style" (fig. 1-7). Midwestern firms touted "Eastern" styles. In June 1817 one member of S. Williams and Company at Nashville, Tennessee, had only recently arrived from the East "in possession of the newest fashions." But expectations often withered all too soon. Thomas S. Renshaw and Company of Georgetown, District of Columbia, announced its formation on August 31, 1801, and its dissolution less than two months later. Not infrequently, a "dissolution by mutual consent" was followed by an insolvency to satisfy creditors. Few partnerships continued as long as that of Ross and Geyer of Cincinnati, Ohio, which commenced in 1830 with a third partner and continued until 1845. The misfortunes and unsatisfactory associations of craftsmen working in the colonial and federal periods have occasionally proven a boon to modern furniture-historians, however, since business connections of short duration permit accurate dating of documented products.[45]

CHAIR FACTORY.

THE subscribers inform the inhabitants of Bennington, and its vicinity, that they continue to manufacture

Fancy and Windsor Chairs,

of all descriptions.

Also—SETTEES and ROCKING CHAIRS, which they offer as low as can be bought at any shop in the country. They employ the best of workmen, and do their work in the most fashionable modern style. Those who wish to purchase are requested to call and examine for themselves.

933tf   DEWEY & WOODWORTH.
Bennington East Village, Nov. 12. 1827.

FIG. 1-7 Advertisement of Henry Freeman Dewey and Heman Woodworth. From *Vermont Gazette*, Bennington, November 13, 1827.

Migration

American chairmakers and related artisans were a mobile group: masters relocated in hopes of improving the quality of life for themselves and their families; journeymen sometimes moved from place to place to find a living; and apprentices searched

ADAM GALER,
WINDSOR CHAIR-MAKER,
(Lately from Philadelphia,)
In Little Queen Street, next door to the corner
of Great George Street, oppofite HULL's
tavern,
Makes and fells all kinds of
WINDSOR CHAIRS,
Any gentlemen or mafters of veffels may be
fupplied with a neat affortment upon reafonable
terms. 71

FIG. 1-8 Advertisement of Adam Galer. From
Rivington's New-York Gazetteer, New York, August
25, 1774.

for a bright future when their training ended, if not before. Of the more than 2,700 Windsor-chair makers known to have been working before the early 1840s, at least 7 percent can be documented as moving from one state to another at least once in their careers, and another 6 percent moved within their own area. Most men made only one move, although several exceptions are worth noting. Stacy Stackhouse started his career in New York City before the Revolution. After the war he spent a decade in Hartford, Connecticut, before completing the circle by returning to Claverack on the Hudson. Julius Barnard moved north, starting at Northampton, Massachusetts, and continuing to Hanover, New Hampshire, Windsor, Vermont, and Montreal, Canada. A northerly then westward trek was also common. Allen Holcomb, born in Granby, Connecticut, moved to Greenfield, Massachusetts, in 1808, where he remained about two years before heading west to Troy, New York, and on to New Lisbon, Otsego County. A westward migration by progressive stages is described in the career of Elihu Alvord. Born in Fairfield, Connecticut, in 1775, he worked in Saratoga County, New York, by the early nineteenth century, where he made furniture for Nicholas Low's new Sans Souci Hotel at Ballston Spa (fig. 5-49). During the next several decades four counties across the state were home to Alvord until 1837, when he left for Long Grove, Iowa. He died at Davenport in 1863.[46]

Significant resettling occurred within state boundaries. Some craftsmen moved from congested to newly developing areas; others left semirural locations for a commercial center. In another regional migration pattern craftsmen from the Middle Atlantic states relocated to the South. Even before the Revolution Windsor-chair makers migrated from Philadelphia, the early center of the trade. One craftsman left for Charleston; others removed to New York City (fig. **1-8**), bolstering production there. Removals from the city to the South continued after the war. In the late 1780s a craftsman from New Jersey resettled in New Haven, Connecticut. Already under way in New England was an extensive migration from the southern parts of the region to the north, west, and beyond. The rising town of Northampton, Massachusetts, on the Connecticut River, while attracting a number of craftsmen who settled permanently, often served as a way station for temporary residents. Massachusetts and Connecticut sustained sizable losses of craftsmen to New York State beginning in the late eighteenth century, although Maine, New Hampshire, and Vermont also made substantial gains in the early 1800s. A few American-Canadian border exchanges are recorded.[47]

Early nineteenth-century migrations from Baltimore had a notable impact on chair design in south-central Pennsylvania, Virginia, and the area that became West Virginia, although the greater exodus of workmen in this period describes an east-to-west pattern. Chillicothe, Ohio, welcomed workmen from as diverse eastern locations as Baltimore and North Yarmouth, Maine. Cincinnati, Queen City of the West, was a prime attraction. Among local chairmakers in 1825 were men with backgrounds in Maryland, New Jersey, New York, Pennsylvania, Virginia, Massachusetts, and New Hampshire. The pattern was repeated as Indiana opened to settlement, and shops in Tennessee and Kentucky had ample eastern representation. Resettlement in more distant locations placed eastern craftsmen in communities as widely scattered as Rome, Wisconsin, and Natchez, Mississippi.[48]

Working Hours, Wages, and Dress

One word describes the working hours of the colonial- and federal-period craftsman—*long*. The workweek was six days, and it is doubtful that many businesses closed earlier on Saturday than on other evenings. Daily hours varied from spring-summer to autumn-winter. Figures given in most sources probably included time off for one or two meals—breakfast at 7:30 or 8:00 A.M. and dinner at the noon hour. John Woodhull Stedman in reminiscing about his youthful days in Hartford, Connecticut, about 1830 stated that "daily hours of work were scarcely ever less than twelve, and in the winter fifteen." A twelve-hour day was also the norm at Lambert Hitchcock's establishment in Litchfield County, where fifteen men and six women were employed in 1832. At Philadelphia the journeymen chairmakers realized an eleven-hour day by 1796, although most other city craftsmen labored longer. Not for almost forty years was there a change. In 1835, a year in which almost all city trades were on strike, the skilled craftsmen finally won a ten-hour day. Still, this was the exception rather than the rule throughout the country.[49]

Some authorities describe the working day as extending from sunrise to sunset, a practice amplified in an 1833 description of the hours for unskilled workers in factories at Philadelphia: "The hours of work shall be from sunrise to sunset, from the 21st of March to the 20th of September inclusively; and from sunrise until eight o'clock P.M., during the remainder of the year. One hour shall be allowed for dinner, and half an hour for breakfast, during the first mentioned six months; and one hour for dinner during the other half year." Because working hours extended after dark in the winter months, artificial light was required. Workmen received no pay for holidays. In New England there was Fast Day in April, Independence Day in July, Muster Day in October, and likely a celebration for Thanksgiving. Christmas and New Year's Day passed unobserved in many quarters. Edward Jenner Carpenter, an apprentice in Greenfield, Massachusetts, occasionally made a coffin on a Sunday. Under those conditions he was given his choice of credit or half a day's free time.[50]

America offered encouragement to the industrious craftsman. By English standards wages were high and living costs moderate. The prerevolutionary drain on skilled labor concerned many Englishmen:

> It is well known that manufactories are already established in some of the colonies, that they have many of our artists, and it is their boast that they can procure the best workmen from England, as they can afford to give them better wages; which with the common rate of labour there, being more than double what it is here, and the provision in common not half our price, to which we may now add taxes here and freedom there, these together must do our business.

As late as the 1820s Frances Trollope commented that an English mechanic coming to "Western America" would "find wages somewhat higher and provisions . . . considerably lower" than in Europe.[51]

Direct references to daily wages of skilled woodworkers are uncommon in prerevolutionary records, although charges made by Elijah Pember, a joiner of Ellington, Connecticut, seem typical. During the mid 1760s his rate was 4s. or 5s. the day for "work at my trade." He computed the labor of his apprentice at half those sums. The difference in master rates may reflect the exact nature of the work or the day's length, a "short" versus a "long" day. Wages are more easily computed for the postrevolutionary period, when currency stabilized and the dollar replaced the British pound as the monetary unit. The rate remained constant over a long period. The dollar was equivalent to 6s. during the 1790s, the same computation employed by Thomas Boynton at Windsor, Vermont, in 1832. For comparative purposes, a set of six Windsor side chairs cost anywhere from about $4.50 to $7.50 throughout the period, depending on the quality, and the average daily "wage" of an independent master woodworker was computed in the $1 to $1.50 range, depending on location, demand, and type of work. During the 1790s both the Dominy craftsmen of East Hampton, Long Island, and the Proud brothers of Providence valued their labor at about $1.25 a day. Journeymen earned 75¢ to $1.25 and generally found board and lodging on their own. When the employer provided living accommodations as part of the employment "package," the total value realized by the journeyman fell on the low side of the range. Samuel Davis, who signed a contract with Samuel Ashton at Philadelphia in 1798, received remuneration of about 97¢ a day, including board and lodging (fig. 1-5). Apprentice labor usually was valued at about half a dollar, and the boy's "keep" probably was figured into the computation. Semiskilled workmen and factory hands were paid at the low end of the journeyman scale, or even less; women and boys not in training received wages lower than those calculated for apprentices. Piecework rates, to be discussed later, generally were comparable to the daily wage, the actual rate proportional to the skill and industry of the workman.[52]

Wages reported in other contemporary sources illuminate labor supply and demand. William Strickland found journeyman wages of the mid-1790s slightly higher in Baltimore than at Philadelphia and New York City, probably because Baltimore was emerging as a commercial center and its growth increased demand for workmen. Fluctuations in the supply of skilled labor in Virginia caused the duc de la Rochefoucauld Liancourt to comment at the same date, "The wages of white workmen, such as masons, carpenters, cabinet-makers, and smiths, amount to from one and a half dollars to two dollars a day according as they are scarce in the country." Special conditions may have prevailed at Ballston Spa, New York, about 1805 when Nicholas Low was building his Sans Souci Hotel. The area had few skilled woodworkers, which may have led Elihu Alvord to compute his wage at the unusually high rate of $1.73 a day and that of his apprentice at $1.25. John Melish reported that skilled woodworkers could earn $1 or more a day at Pittsburgh and $1 plus board at Cincinnati. Traveling in the same region, François André Michaux commented on the "scarcity of artificers in the western states" and compared earnings versus cost of living in the West to that of other areas. From Tennessee to Ohio workmen paid one-sixth of weekly wages for living expenses. In Charleston and Savannah that figure rose to one-half of earnings, and in Philadelphia and New York to two-thirds. While Michaux had no direct knowledge of conditions in New England, he was "informed" that living was "equally cheap" as in the West, but "the price of labour . . . not so high."[53]

An 1832 schedule of manufactures provides reasonably comprehensive data about New England chairmaking wages on the eve of industrialization, as the size of the shop and the workforce increased and mechanization introduced semiskilled labor trained to perform only specialized tasks in the manufacturing process. Based on data compiled for seventy-three establishments, men's daily wages varied from 62½¢ to a high of $1, excluding the Boston shops. The average rate was about 85¢. Chairmakers at Boston could earn $1.25, but undoubtedly the cost of living was higher. Women's wages were 32¢ or 33¢ a day in Massachusetts for seat caning and rushing. In western Connecticut Lambert Hitchcock paid his female employees 42¢, but the men received only 75¢. Boys earned between 36¢ and 50¢. An independent master craftsman such as Thomas Boynton of Windsor, Vermont, could still earn $1.25 a day; five years later his rate was $1.50.[54]

Uniformity characterized the dress of the woodworking craftsman and his fellow "mechanics." John Fanning Watson identified the common garment among colonial workmen and farmers as leather breeches, a close-fitting trouser extending to below the knee. To protect both breeches and cloth garments, "all such as followed rough trades . . . universally wore a leathern apron before them," a practice that continued following national independence. In a woodworking shop where sharp tools were in constant use, the leather apron protected the body as well. The inventories of three chairmakers of Connecticut enumerate this article of dress, one specifically identifying a "horse skin leather apron." Use of this garment, whether of leather or cloth, also is confirmed in visual documents (figs. 2-4, 2-7, 3-32). The practice of wearing aprons in the workplace was carried to America from Europe, where it was a tradition of long standing (fig. 2-12).[55]

Breeches remained a common garment of the craftsman for shop or dress wear

FIG. 1-9 John Lewis Krimmel, detail of *Election Day 1815*, Philadelphia, 1815. Oil on canvas; H. 16⅜", w. 25⅝". *(Courtesy, Winterthur Museum, Winterthur, Del., acc. 59.131.)*

after the Revolutionary War. Wool was suitable for winter wear, cotton or linen for summer. Ideal for rough shop work was the "pr old black Breeches" found in one inventory. Two documents from Connecticut list an unusual garment described variously as "2 pr Overalls" and "one pair Jane [jean] over Halls." Usually this garment is classified as a coverall, or smock, a piece of clothing used among British woodworkers and American porters and farmers; however, the adjective "pair" implies there were two parts, such as two legs. Indeed, one early definition describes overalls as "a kind of trowsers." As today, "jean" described a substantial cotton fabric suitable for rough use.[56]

Shortly after 1800 close-fitting pantaloons and loose trousers, both reaching to the ankles, became the common lower garments for men (fig. **1-9**). Suitable for shop wear were articles of clothing described as "1 pair Old blue Woolen pantaloons" and tow cloth trousers made of coarse linen. Shirts were loose-fitting, full-sleeved garments sometimes worn with the sleeves rolled up in hot weather (figs. 2-4, 3-32). Cotton or linen were suitable for summer; flannel and other woolens were available for winter use. In cool weather the craftsman added a vest (called a waistcoat earlier) made of plain, striped, or checked cloth (fig. 2-4). In particularly cold weather a "thick vest" was welcomed. Even with a good fire going in the shop, a coat was necessary in midwinter. A range of fabrics, weaves, and colors was available. Particularly appropriate for shop wear were the "handmade," or "homemade," coats owned by several chairmakers. When going abroad in winter the craftsman put on his greatcoat or surtout, overcoats that reached to or below the knees. It was also the season for mittens and gloves, accessories identified regularly in craft inventories. Winter hats were made of "beaver," "fur," or "wool"; for summer wear "straw" was cool. Boots were a good article for inclement weather, country use, and riding, with calfskin, "neat leather" (ox), and cowhide mentioned specifically. Lambert Hitchcock owned a pair of "India rubbers" in 1852. "Thick shoes" were ideal to guard against shop accidents. Stockings, socks, and hose were available in cotton, linen, wool, and "mixed" fibers to suit the season.[57]

For wear during leisure hours, such as they were, the craftsman owned better garments made of a variety of fabrics, light or heavy (fig. 5-28). Clothing in bright colors or special weaves, such as a crimson coat or a velvet vest, enlivened some costumes. Thomas West cut a colorful figure in New London, Connecticut, in his "Plaid Cloak." The mechanic's dress accessories after 1800 included a cravat or stock (also neckcloth) and handkerchiefs, the latter for both neck and pocket use. Whereas neck handkerchiefs for dress were made of fine fabrics, it is doubtful that woodworkers labored in any neckpiece other than a plain cloth. Lewis Miller's open shirt (fig. 2-4) probably is close to the mark for summer wear. By the 1810s suspenders had made their appearance. When dressed for social occasions, the craftsman could slip his feet into a pair of "morocco" pumps (fig. 5-28).[58]

Mechanic and Manufacturing Societies and Trade Organizations

The many mechanic and manufacturing societies that sprang up in America, principally following the Revolution, had as their central focus the promotion and protection of American industry, although benevolence within the membership was another strong interest (fig. 2-1). Organized efforts to advance domestic manufactures actually occurred in prerevolutionary days when the Sugar and Stamp Acts of 1764 and 1765 encouraged Americans to boycott British goods. Following the war the Friends of American Manufactures organized and met at Philadelphia in 1787. The group's primary purpose was to diffuse technical knowledge relating to manufacturing processes so that American manufacturers could compete successfully with European suppliers. Because foreign manufacturers possessed formidable commercial strength and expertise and frequently produced superior goods, the American promotional group eventually fell by the wayside.[59]

The next general stimuli to American manufacturing came with Jefferson's Embargo and the wartime shipping restraints of 1812. At last American industry gained a toehold. The *Niles Weekly Register* noted on May 15, 1813, that "since commerce has been embarrassed the manufactures have been increasing in the ratio of the troubles of commerce." The flood of foreign goods in the market after the conflict and the widespread depression that followed a brief postwar recovery led to a convention of the Friends of National Industry at New York in 1819. Five years later the Franklin Institute was founded at Philadelphia, and through its "annual distribution of medals and premiums to inventors, manufacturers, and mechanics" it furthered the cause of American industry. Domestic development was on track and with phenomenal speed reached full maturity in only a few decades.[60]

Concurrent with the general promotion of manufacturing were the efforts of the mechanics (skilled craftsmen) and manufacturers themselves to place American industry on a substantial footing. From 1785 these men banded together in associations to advance the manufacturing interest. The earliest recorded societies were formed in New York, Baltimore, and Boston. The General Society of Mechanics and Tradesmen, or the "New York Mechanick Society," held its first meeting on November 17 and by August 1786 had advanced sufficiently as an organization to print a membership certificate (fig. 2-1). Through correspondence the Society promoted a united effort to enact or raise duties on imported articles that competed with domestic manufactures. For their part, members of the group at Baltimore participated in a grand procession in May 1788 following ratification of the federal Constitution (fig. 1-10), and within less than a year they sent a petition to Congress containing a "List of such Articles of Home Manufactures, as may be thought worthy of the Encouragement of that honourable Body." The group at Boston passed out of existence and was replaced in 1795 by the Massachusetts Charitable Mechanic Association dedicated to promoting the mechanic arts and extending "the practice of benevolence." Paul Revere was its first president, and the organization still flourished in the mid-nineteenth century.[61]

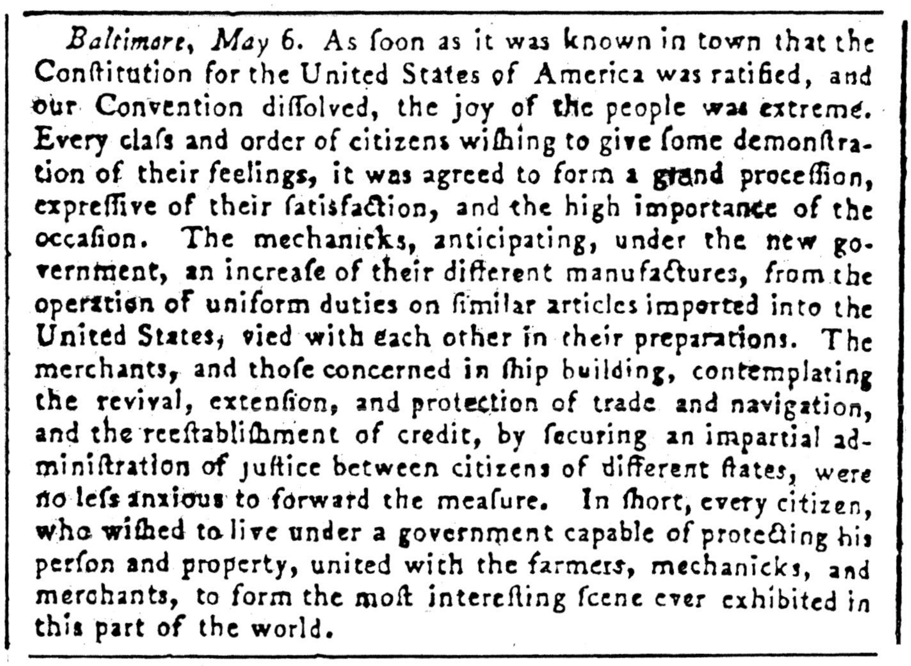

Baltimore, May 6. As foon as it was known in town that the Conftitution for the United States of America was ratified, and our Convention diffolved, the joy of the people was extreme. Every clafs and order of citizens wifhing to give fome demonftration of their feelings, it was agreed to form a grand proceffion, expreffive of their fatisfaction, and the high importance of the occafion. The mechanicks, anticipating, under the new government, an increafe of their different manufactures, from the operation of uniform duties on fimilar articles imported into the United States, vied with each other in their preparations. The merchants, and thofe concerned in fhip building, contemplating the revival, extenfion, and protection of trade and navigation, and the reeftablifhment of credit, by fecuring an impartial adminiftration of juftice between citizens of different ftates, were no lefs anxious to forward the meafure. In fhort, every citizen, who wifhed to live under a government capable of protecting his perfon and property, united with the farmers, mechanicks, and merchants, to form the moft interefting fcene ever exhibited in this part of the world.

FIG. 1-10 Introduction to a description of a grand procession in Baltimore celebrating ratification of the Constitution, May 1, 1788. From *Gazette of the State of Georgia*, Savannah, June 12, 1788.

Another group that survived into the 1800s was the Providence Association of Mechanics and Manufacturers founded in 1789 to "Promote . . . Home Manufactures, cement . . . Mechanic Interest, and . . . raise . . . a Fund to Support the Distressed." The group acquainted other associations with its "principal Objects," and at home it urged its members to patronize each other. Journeymen were admitted to membership only after producing an apprenticeship certificate or good recommendations. The subject of duties on competing imports was an early focus, and in 1799 the Association protested the practice on "National Ships" of hiring hands who were under indentures of apprenticeship. Eventually the group supported standardized apprenticeship regulations among members and the establishment of free schools in Rhode Island. The organization founded a library for members and apprentices before 1822 and later implemented a series of "chemical lectures."[62]

The General Society of Mechanics and Tradesmen at New York erected its own Mechanics' Hall on Broadway in 1802, and like the Providence group, the organization established a library for apprentices and instituted weekly lectures. Mechanic groups also were organized in smaller centers. The Providence Association records identify correspondence with societies in Trenton, New Jersey, Newport and East Greenwich, Rhode Island, Newburyport, Massachusetts, and Portsmouth, New Hampshire. The last-named society existed by 1789, and in 1823 the group established the Portsmouth Apprentices' Library. Other towns in New Hampshire represented by mechanic societies between 1790 and 1815 include Concord, Walpole, and Strafford. Recognized in the Middle Atlantic region were societies in Hudson, New York, York, Pennsylvania, and Newark, New Jersey. The last group helped to celebrate the Fourth of July in 1818 with a procession that featured many participants pursuing their trades while conveyed on horse-drawn "platforms." The cabinetmakers, "well provided with mahogany stuff and tools," constructed "a handsome breakfast table and field bedstead on their stage." Among the chairmakers there were "a number of hands busily engaged in turning stuff, bottoming chairs and painting."[63]

Southern mechanic groups were organized before 1816 in Norfolk, Fredericksburg, and Richmond, Virginia. In the last-named community Windsor-chair maker Robert McKim was appointed to a committee to draft the constitution. A constitution for the Charleston Mechanic Society in South Carolina was drawn as early as 1794. Other societies existed in Wilmington, North Carolina, and Augusta and

Savannah, Georgia. Among midwestern groups were a mechanic society formed in Nashville, Tennessee, and the Mechanicks and Manufacturers of Lexington, Kentucky, who went on record in 1810 as advocating protection of domestic manufactures. At Chillicothe, Ohio, "a company of Mechanics" drank eighteen toasts on the anniversary of Independence in July 1811 in honor of the young nation, its distinguished leaders, and its founding principles.[64]

Although the American trade union movement is recognized as beginning in the second quarter of the nineteenth century, various concerns brought skilled artisans together for concerted action during the preceding one hundred years. Trade guilds, as established in Europe, came to naught in America, although as early as 1732 the master carpenters of Philadelphia formed a Carpenters' Company to establish uniform prices for work and to standardize journeyman wages. Group action also proved an effective way to raise prices for goods and services and to control underselling.[65]

Following the Revolution changing business and political conditions dictated new approaches in the workplace. Rapidly expanding domestic and foreign markets created a demand for cheap goods. Increasingly workmen in the new republic found that low wages and long working hours left them little time to enjoy the fruits of their country's hard-won nationalism. By the early 1800s the apprentice system showed signs of deterioration, especially in large cities, as advances in industrial technology created an expanding pool of semi- and unskilled labor. The collective effect of these conditions on Windsor-chair making is well demonstrated in the product. The simulated bamboo support introduced at Philadelphia in the mid-1780s was a simple lathe-produced leg that replaced a complex baluster turning. Three decades later this profile itself give way to a cylindrical stick tapered slightly top and bottom and often embellished only with quickly applied painted lines simulating grooves. Wooden seats with finely modeled, contoured surfaces succumbed to boxy planks with hard edges and little shaping.[66]

Postrevolutionary labor/management relations in the furniture industry have been well chronicled by Charles F. Montgomery, who described the critical role of price books in this liaison. Most volumes give piecework rates for journeymen; some provide retail prices. In form and concept American price books parallel the printed volumes and rate sheets produced in England, although the earliest-known published English furniture rates date only from the 1780s. Earliest among American documents is a manuscript agreement drawn between six master cabinetmakers at Providence in 1756. Handwritten schedules of Pennsylvania origin bearing dates of 1772 and 1786 are partial copies of a recently discovered printed volume of 1772. That volume, as interpreted by Montgomery from the 1786 copy prepared by Benjamin Lehman, a lumber dealer of Philadelphia, is a dual-purpose document that provided formal agreements among furniture masters to set retail prices for walnut and mahogany furniture and between masters and journeymen to specify piecework wages. Presumably pay scales were established amicably, although the harmony ended in Philadelphia shortly after 1792, the date of a second printed American price book, a volume published at Hartford.[67]

The Philadelphia price books of 1794, 1795, and 1796 appeared during a period of turmoil in the city's furniture trade. The first volume is known only from the 1795 *Journeymen Cabinet and Chair-Makers Philadelphia Book of Prices*, identified as a "second edition, corrected and enlarged." Publication of these two volumes by the workmen rather than the masters describes a wage dispute that raged for at least two years, as confirmed by contemporary newspapers. The journeymen firmly declared they would not work on any but their own terms nor in company with workmen who were not members of their Federal Society of Journeymen Cabinet and Chairmakers. Again in 1796 the journeymen "in consequence of the rapid advance of price in every article of life" found it necessary to raise prices for their work and sub-

CABINET FURNITURE.
Journeymen Cabinet Makers'
WARE ROOMS,
NO, 48 SOUTH FIFTH STREET,
Below Walnut, Philadelphia.

The largest assortment of Furniture, of the latest and most approved designs to be found in any establishment in the United States, is constantly on hand at the above Ware-Rooms, to an inspection of which the public are respectfully invited.

The Furniture is all manufactured by the best Journeymen in the trade—apprentices and incompetent workmen being positively excluded—consequently every article sold will be warranted.

Strangers visiting the city will please make the establishment a visit, whether in the capacity of purchasers or otherwise.

N. B.—Furniture forwarded to any part of the Union, and warranted against any injury from packing.

CRAWFORD RIDDELL.

FIG. 1-11 Advertisement for the journeymen cabinetmakers' warerooms in Philadelphia. From *A. M'Elroy's Philadelphia Directory for 1839* (Philadelphia: A[rchibald] M'Elroy, 1839), n.p. *(Winterthur Library.)*

mitted a "New Book of Rates" to the masters. Rejected, the journeymen apparently staged a "turn-out," or strike, and went so far as to open a "Ware-Room in Market Street." During the several months' conflict the journeymen received support from other city groups. The outcome is suggested in the introduction to the second of two price books published by the masters in 1796. Journeymen's wages were set at a 50 percent advance on those in the 1793 London price book, and an "escalator clause" provided for rises and falls in the cost of living. In comparing the 1796 and 1795 rates Montgomery concluded the journeymen had won their case.[68]

Considerable strife marked the early 1800s. Struggles of equal magnitude between master cabinetmakers and journeymen occurred in other American cities. New York was the scene of labor troubles from 1802 to 1803, and workmen at Baltimore went through a difficult period about 1817. Between 1799 and 1840 Pennsylvania alone had at least 138 strikes in the various trades. Of these the vast majority of walkouts occurred over the question of wages, although at least 25 percent revolved around the issue of a ten-hour day, which most trades in Philadelphia achieved in 1835. In appraising this victory, the president of the National Trades' Union described the tenor of the times: "The mechanics of Philadelphia stood firm and true; they conquered, because they were united and resolute in their actions." The militancy of the period also is reflected in actions of the Philadelphia Society of Journeymen Cabinetmakers, who by the 1820s found their very jobs jeopardized by new methods of wholesale business. The master was no longer a retailer; instead he sold to a middleman who demanded low-cost goods for a highly competitive market. Journeymen found wages reduced and jobs filled by inexperienced apprentices and semiskilled labor. After five years of attempting to gain concessions from the masters, the journeymen established their own wareroom in 1834 (fig. 1-11). During this period the chairmakers also went on strike for higher wages. Declining mobility and wage instability plagued craftsmen at New York as well. When all else failed, they too replied with group action in the form of strikes, selected walkouts, and group-operated retail enterprises.[69]

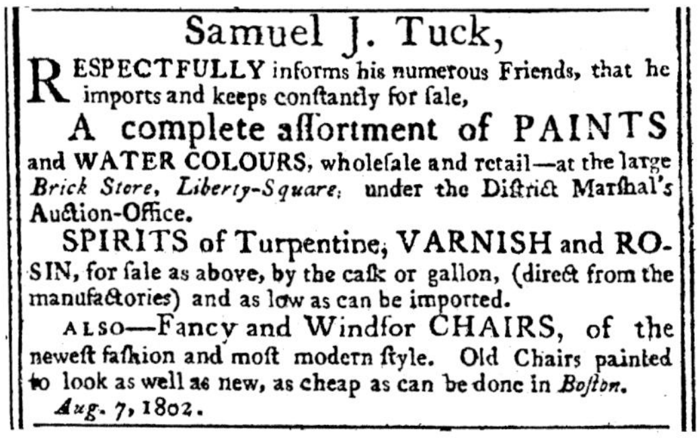

Dual and Supplementary Trades and Occupations

Few master chairmakers spent all their working hours making chairs. Most engaged in other pursuits simultaneously. These dual and supplementary occupations ranged from skilled and semiskilled trades to business enterprises undertaken with hired help or as a joint family venture. Of greatest prominence was woodworking, principally cabinetmaking. The first generation of Windsor-chair makers in Philadelphia, with the exception of Thomas Gilpin, constructed painted seating furniture as an extension of their cabinetmaking activity. Few could afford to specialize until after the Revolution, when demand in the domestic and foreign markets increased and the introduction of fancy-painted woven-bottom seating provided a supplement to Windsor production. Still opportunities for specialization were limited and confined mainly to large urban centers until the rise of the factory in the 1820s and 1830s. Rural and semirural craftsmen served a limited clientele, even in the coastal trading towns, and they had to be prepared to supply all manner of household furniture. Luke Houghton of Massachusetts and artisans Silas Cheney, Ebenezer Tracy, Sr., and his son-in-law Amos Denison Allen, all of Connecticut, represent this type of craftsman. Not until development of the steamboat and a system of canals (and later railroads) to facilitate product distribution was it practical for these artisans to specialize, and by then the nineteenth century was well under way.

The supply of parts to the chairmaking trade was a profitable sideline for some craftsmen. The manufacture of spinning wheels and reels was interrelated and proved practical in nonurban and "frontier" areas. With increasing emphasis on decorated furniture following the War of 1812, many chairmakers broadened their activity to include house, sign, and ornamental painting. Less closely allied with chairmaking was the construction of riding vehicles and wagons. Another small group of men engaged in carpentry and house joinery as a supplemental activity. Dovetailing well with craft pursuits was the preparation and merchandising of timber. Some rural artisans erected small sawmills on their properties; a few urban woodworkers stocked boards, plank, and scantling in their open lots. The manufacture and sale of paint provided additional income for some woodworkers. John B. Ackley of Philadelphia gave up chairmaking about 1807 to concentrate on that line of business, and Samuel J. Tuck pursued both occupations at Boston about the same time (fig. 1-12).[70]

With the notice "I expect my HEARSE, in a few days in compleat order, to let with a gentle Horse on Funeral occasions," Alexander Walker of Fredericksburg, Virginia, identified another income-producing activity for the cabinetmaker or chairmaker. Daniel Nields announced an expansion of the service at West Chester, Pennsylvania, in 1840, and he kept a stock of "ready made coffins, which can be had at the shortest notice." Edwin Wood of Bridgeport, Connecticut, probably advertised in the same vein, since an inventory taken at his death in 1855 lists 22 coffins. The inventory of James Renshaw drawn two years later at Phoenixville, Pennsylvania, describes the equipment required to "attend funerals": a hearse, hearse box, bier, ice boxes, and three stands (fig. 5-42).[71]

Several chairmakers plied auxiliary trades unrelated to woodworking. James Gere constructed a tan vat at Groton, Connecticut, in 1810 using chestnut plank. He prepared calfskins and deerskins for glove making. Asa Nichols engaged in similar work at Gardner, Massachusetts, where in 1829 he possessed "tools of the tan yard" and "one lot Beark [bark]." Samuel Wing pursued the allied craft of shoemaking on Cape Cod when the woodworking business was dull, and several chairmakers in Northampton, Massachusetts, turned to masonry when work was slack. Some craftsmen owned gristmills. One stood on Samuel Wing's property; others were in the possession of Stephen Shorey in New Hampshire and Hastings Warren in Vermont. Warren also operated a mill for grinding plaster, and both he and Samuel Wing owned interests in cotton factories.[72]

Samuel J. Tuck,

RESPECTFULLY informs his numerous Friends, that he imports and keeps conftantly for fale,

A complete affortment of PAINTS and WATER COLOURS, wholefale and retail—at the large *Brick Store, Liberty-Square,* under the Diftrict Marfhal's Auction-Office.

SPIRITS of Turpentine, VARNISH and RO-SIN, for fale as above, by the cafk or gallon, (direct from the manufactories) and as low as can be imported.

ALSO—Fancy and Windfor CHAIRS, of the neweft fafhion and moft modern ftyle. Old Chairs painted to look as well as new, as cheap as can be done in *Bofton.*

Aug. 7, 1802.

FIG. 1-12 Advertisement of Samuel Jones Tuck. From *Columbian Centinel*, Boston, August 7, 1802.

Retail sales were a sideline among a small group of woodworkers, probably because other family members could become involved. Thomas West sold dry goods at New London, Connecticut, and Hastings Warren had a large store at Middlebury, Vermont. Thomas Boynton may have been a partner in the firm of Hayes and Hubbard at Windsor, Vermont, as he ordered quantities of merchandise for the firm from suppliers in Boston, Cambridge, and Hartford. Groceries joined dry goods at Stephen Shorey's store in Rochester, New Hampshire, where business was good because his workmen traded there. On Cape Cod Samuel Wing sold the produce of his farm along with tea. Some chairmakers dealt in hardware. The location of William Moore's store on the "west side of the Turnpike road" in Barkhamstead, Connecticut, would appear to have been a good one for trade.[73]

Several craftsmen had interests in public facilities. Supplementing William Moore's store at Barkhamstead was a "Tavern Stand." Samuel Wing held shares in a boardinghouse on the Cape, which probably housed hired help from the local cotton factory that he partially owned. The "Large Saloon on [the] Wharf" at New London, Connecticut, listed in John French's inventory of 1848 likely identifies a hall for entertainment. French's "Bath House & appurtenances" and his "office at [the] Steam Boat Building" probably were close by. The McKim brothers owned a large double tenement in Richmond, Virginia, which they partially rented for income. Business agents Thomas Boynton and John T. Hildreth sold fire insurance in Vermont and Brooklyn, New York, respectively.[74]

When coal began to replace wood for hearth and stove, several chairmakers engaged in fuel sales as a profitable sideline, sometimes as a primary business. Philip I. Arcularius I appears to have had a sizable yard in Brooklyn during the 1830s and 1840s. John I. Wells manufactured printer's ink at Hartford as a supplement to woodworking before turning full-time to the manufacture of printing presses. In 1831 Bryson Gill of Baltimore offered "PROFESSIONAL SERVICES" at "Cupping, Bleeding and applying Leaches." A prerevolutionary "medical practice" is recorded at Leicester, Massachusetts, in the furniture accounts of Robert Crage, who performed tooth extractions on a regular basis. Other services ranged from bloodletting to midwifery and amputations.[75]

Occupational versatility permitted the craftsman to keep his head above water in the face of recession, competition, market glut, and other economic conditions over which he had little or no control. On the whole, a majority of woodworkers were successful in realizing a modest or better living. In the event of a setback those residing on farms, and there were many, could turn to land tillage and livestock breeding. Those without lands sometimes hired themselves out for limited periods as farm laborers when times were slack in the trade, as described by Jacob Thompson in a letter to Silas Cheney at Litchfield, Connecticut. Introducing diversification to general farming were several specialties. The presence of "Saptubs" among Martin Bracket's agricultural implements in Massachusetts suggests that maple sugaring was a productive, albeit limited, venture. In New Jersey some chairmakers "farmed" the coastal waters as oystermen between chairmaking stints.[76]

Business Reverses and Disasters

INSOLVENCIES AND LAWSUITS

Disaster struck the life of the American craftsman in numerous ways. In the broad range there were adverse events of national scope over which he had little or no control — wars, shipping embargoes, recessions. Closer to home community and personal calamities plagued him. Beginning with the war years in the early 1810s insolvencies struck the chairmaker's business life with considerable frequency. Often national or international events were directly responsible, and the chairmaker, like other craftsmen, merchants, and professional men, was simply caught in the groundswell. At other times the craftsman shared the blame by overextending himself. Artisans at New York were particularly hard hit by Jefferson's Embargo and the events of 1811–12 that led to war with England. Reuben Odell, James Hallet, Jr., and David Brientnall, Jr., all suffered financial reverses; the latter even was confined to jail for want of a sufficient estate to satisfy his creditors. James Whitaker of Philadelphia, who had known a brisk chair exportation business at the start of the century, went under in 1812, and the business slump of the postwar years led to additional failures. Seven more New York chairmakers succumbed during this period. The general stress of the times probably led Zenos Bronson to become "an absconding debtor" at Raleigh, North Carolina, in 1805 and William and Moses Bullock to request an insolvency hearing at Carlisle, Pennsylvania, in 1823.[77]

Several craftsmen attempted to branch out or convert their energies to mercantile pursuits. An early example is Felix Huntington of Norwich, Connecticut, who when he could not sell cabinetware and chairs during the Revolution undertook to build a vessel for the West Indian trade. But his losses at sea were heavy, and he was still struggling with the massive debt in autumn 1792 when he pleaded insolvency. In 1801 John Karnes's assignees at New York found not only Windsor chairs on their hands but "50,000 Spanish Segars" as well. Samuel Jones Tuck, a successful chairmaker and paint dealer of Boston, accumulated sufficient money to build several fine houses on Fort Hill at the start of the century. During the War of 1812 he was "deeply concerned in navigation" and "became embarrassed." The tangled financial affairs of two other chairmakers ensnared family members. When Thomas Ash II filed an insolvency petition in New York on May 11, 1811, he called himself a merchant, and records show he was extensively involved in the overseas trade. The collapse of Ash's financial world also caused the ruin of his chairmaking father, William I, who had acted as surety (fig. 1-13). Several decades later Elisha Harlow Holmes, son-in-law and former apprentice to Amos Denison Allen, forfeited his homestead farm in eastern Connecticut to satisfy his creditor, the Norwich Savings Bank. That action also brought about the attachment of the homestead farm of Allen as surety and mortgager of Holmes.[78]

The troubled financial times beginning in the late 1820s and continuing through the Panic of 1837 brought more financial woes for the chairmaker. Thomas Ash II became insolvent again along with fellow chairmaker Joseph Riley. Chairmaker David Finch of Bridgeport, Connecticut, failed in 1829, the year that Lambert Hitchcock assigned his assets for the benefit of creditors in western Connecticut. Hitchcock's failure, in turn, led to that of his neighbor William Moore, Jr. In Pennsylvania John E. Hartman turned over a business inventory worth more than $2,000 to assignees when he declared bankruptcy in 1842. The western country also had its failures. Henry Shepherd left Chillicothe when he could not meet the financial obligations of his cabinet and chair warehouse in 1835. Even the *fear* of financial reverses plagued some craftsmen, as expressed by Enos White of Weymouth, Massachusetts, in 1829.[79]

Lawsuits involving craftsmen often were interconnected with financial distress, although evidence suggests that irascible or resolute temperaments were more directly responsible for bringing some matters to a head. Francis Trumble of Philadelphia and a local shipwright disputed a piece of property on Front Street in 1765, which finally went to Trumble. Within a decade Trumble was involved in several suits for debt and an altercation with the local sheriff who, Trumble asserted, had published a levy on his property after the fine was satisfied, thus injuring his reputation. Jesse Foster of Boston claimed cause for complaint in 1798–99, naming Josiah Willard in a suit for defamation of character. Foster stated that Willard had publicly accused him of stealing a note of hand to avoid payment of a debt and further cast

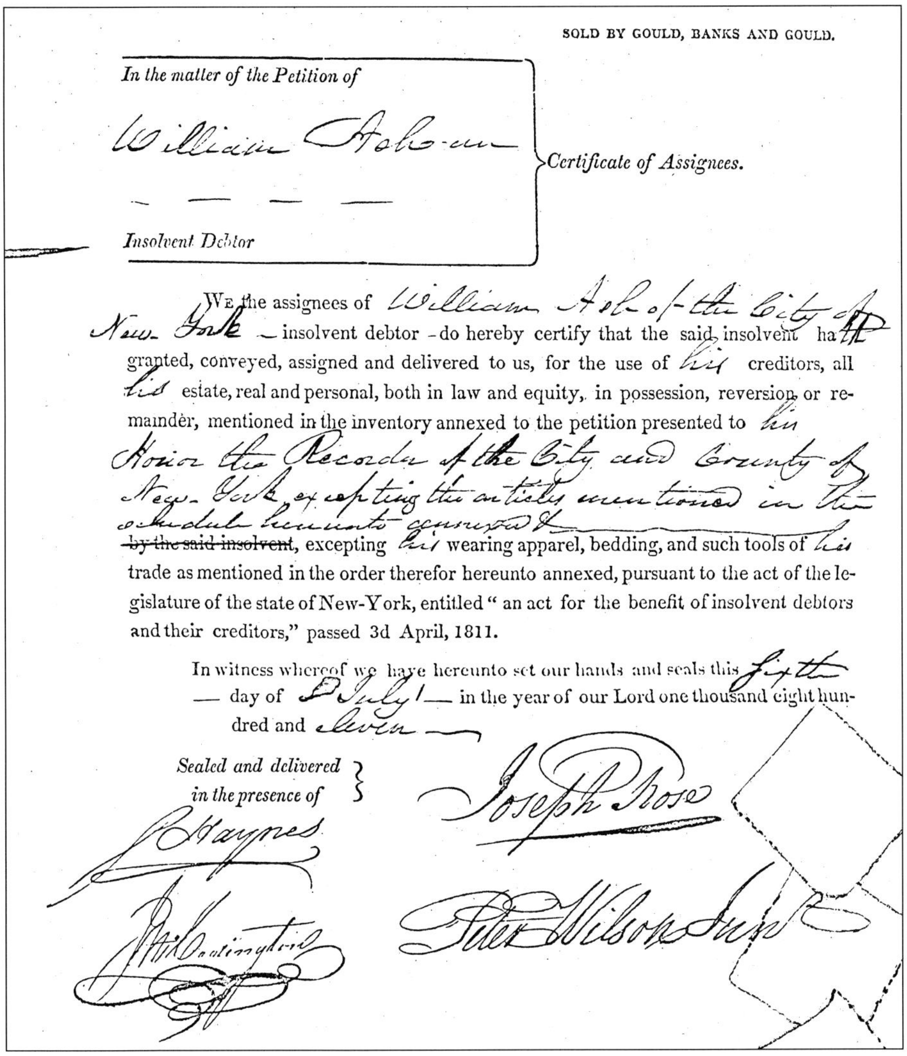
SOLD BY GOULD, BANKS AND GOULD.

In the matter of the Petition of

William Ash

Insolvent Debtor

Certificate of Assignees.

We the assignees of William Ash of the City of New York — insolvent debtor - do hereby certify that the said insolvent hath granted, conveyed, assigned and delivered to us, for the use of his creditors, all his estate, real and personal, both in law and equity, in possession, reversion or remainder, mentioned in the inventory annexed to the petition presented to his Honor the Recorder of the City and County of New York excepting the articles mentioned in the schedule hereunto annexed & ~~by the said insolvent~~, excepting his wearing apparel, bedding, and such tools of his trade as mentioned in the order therefor hereunto annexed, pursuant to the act of the legislature of the state of New-York, entitled " an act for the benefit of insolvent debtors and their creditors," passed 3d April, 1811.

In witness whereof we have hereunto set our hands and seals this first day of July in the year of our Lord one thousand eight hundred and eleven

Sealed and delivered in the presence of

Joseph Rose

Peter Wilson Jun.

FIG. 1-13 Certificate of assignees, insolvent estate of William Ash I, New York, July 1, 1811. *(Historical Documents Collection, Queen's College, Flushing, N.Y.)*

aspersions on his abilities as a chairmaker, causing the plantiff to "greatly suffer . . . in his trade." In face-saving maneuvers on both sides Foster subsequently paid the amount of the missing note and Willard stated in his receipt that the document was either "Lost or Destroyed." Joseph Adams, another chairmaker of Boston, was sued earlier by a workman to recover wages, and a similar suit at Philadelphia involved Lawrence Allwine in 1787–88. A lawsuit over debt is recorded against George W. Grimes of Raleigh, North Carolina. The plaintiff, a tradesman, claimed that Grimes denied in court his signature on a note, thereby avoiding payment.[80]

FIRES

Unquestionably, loss from fire was the second greatest financial calamity to beset the colonial and federal-period craftsman. Recognizing the importance of prevention, most major American cities embarked on energetic programs of positive action beginning in the early eighteenth century. Municipalities initiated building codes, regulated chimney sweeps, encouraged use of lightning rods and the formation of volunteer fire societies, purchased hand-pumped engines and fire buckets, and erected public water pumps. Men who served in fire companies usually were exempt from militia and other civic duties. Philadelphia established the first successful fire insurance company in America in 1752 and other cities followed, although disasters were bound to occur. Boston had a devastating fire in 1760 that destroyed more than four hundred buildings, among them the shops of many craftsmen. The Great Fire

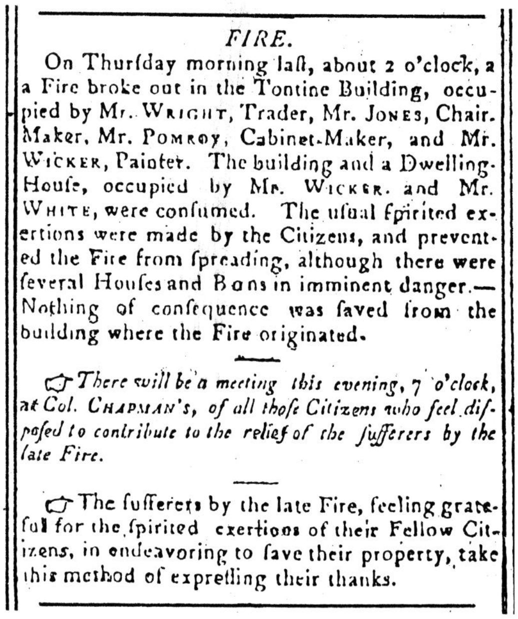
FIRE.

On Thurſday morning laſt, about 2 o'clock, a Fire broke out in the Tontine Building, occupied by Mr. WRIGHT, Trader, Mr. JONES, Chair-Maker, Mr. POMROY, Cabinet-Maker, and Mr. WICKER, Painter. The building and a Dwelling-Houſe, occupied by Mr. WICKER, and Mr. WHITE, were conſumed. The uſual ſpirited exertions were made by the Citizens, and prevented the Fire from ſpreading, although there were ſeveral Houſes and Barns in imminent danger.—Nothing of conſequence was ſaved from the building where the Fire originated.

☞ *There will be a meeting this evening, 7 o'clock, at Col.* CHAPMAN'S, *of all thoſe Citizens who feel diſpoſed to contribute to the relief of the ſufferers by the late Fire.*

☞ The ſufferers by the late Fire, feeling grateful for the ſpirited exertions of their Fellow Citizens, in endeavoring to ſave their property, take this method of expreſſing their thanks.

FIG. 1-14 Notice of a fire in the Tontine Building, Northampton, Mass. From the *Hampshire Gazette and Northampton Courier*, Northampton, October 27, 1813.

of New York occurred in 1776 just after the British occupied the city. The same year Norfolk, the most substantial town in Virginia, was reduced to rubble. Olney Winsor, a businessman of Rhode Island, reported the destruction of a third of Richmond in a letter of January 1787. When a brewery fire at Alexandria threatened Winsor's store in 1788, he wrote to his wife at Providence instructing her to send his "Bags & Bucketts" and "one Sheet of the Printed Articles of our Fire Society."[81]

Inevitably conflagrations of large scope destroyed property belonging to chairmakers. A "most dreadful fire" at Wilmington, North Carolina, in April 1786 consumed an entire square, including the house of John Nutt, a cabinetmaker who later made Windsor chairs. Detailed accounts of the great fire at Newburyport on the evening of May 31, 1811, describe the destruction of the commercial and residential center of that Massachusetts community, comprising about 16½ acres and almost 250 buildings, among which were the chairmaking shops of Samuel Dole, Joseph Noyes, and Daniel Abbot. The blaze was suspected to be the work of an incendiary, an all too common circumstance. A near disaster at Baltimore in 1805 involved the woodhouse of John Conrad, Windsor-chair maker, where "some extinguished coals were found . . . thrown in the night before with design . . . of setting fire to that and the adjoining houses, but they fell about six inches short of being lodged in some shavings and chips that would have produced the deesired [*sic*] effect." Robert McKim of Richmond suffered substantially from three fires in 1816. The first consumed his lumber house, the second his stable, and the third destroyed his chair shop and a double brick tenement across the alley containing his residence.[82]

Carelessness, thoughtlessness, and freaks of nature also took their toll. Lightning struck a house in Philadelphia rented by Francis Trumble in 1753, damaging a number of windows, furrowing brick walls, and knocking down interior plaster. Fortunately, no fire ensued, and the owner was insured. Abraham Ritter recalled the local Front Street chair manufactory of Gilbert Gaw "there already in 1795, and long after, indeed until death itself smothered his existence in the conflagration of his premises." The destruction of William and Thomas Mitchell's wooden building along with "a number of new chairs, and working tools," occurred on December 2, 1799, followed two years later by "an alarming fire" in the three-story brick building where Lawrence Allwine manufactured his "patent paints, oil, varnishes, &c." A turner's shop in Gaskell Street could possibly have been saved in February 1817 had not the "fire plugs" been frozen "from the intensity of the cold."[83]

Information from New York focuses closely on the causes of fires. A blaze in 1801 in a house occupied by John Post, an upholsterer, resulted in $1,500 damage when "one of the lads after carelessly poking the fire with a wooden stick threw it down amongst some tow and cat tails, which caught like powder, and progressed so rapidly, that it was impossible to extinguish it without the assistance of Engines." Elizabeth de Hart Bleecker, commenting on the same fire, noted that "the roof was tiled, which prevented its communicating to the adjoining House." Bleecker described another fire in the garret of a print shop, where "one of the Apprentices had carelessly thrown some ashes in a Barrel, among which were some live coals." She also spoke of fires caused by inattentive servants with lighted candles who set bed curtains and other combustibles afire. New York chairmakers John Karnes and James Hazlet were victims of a fire in September 1803 that began in a neighboring bakery and "destroyed 10 dwellings and several back buildings."[84]

New England sources describe the destruction in 1813 of the three-story wooden Tontine Building at Northampton, Massachusetts, where Asa Jones and Oliver Pomeroy had woodworking shops (fig. **1-14**). The June 1829 conflagration of the uninsured general store in Hitchcocksville, Connecticut, partially owned by Lambert Hitchcock, hastened the capitulation of the chairmaker, who already was in deep financial trouble. At New Haven Charles Lines was the victim of a fire in the 1830s that destroyed his manufactory. The woodworker, who was active in the temperance movement, suspected that the "factory was burned by emissaries of the liquor interest." Walter Corey experienced two disasters at Portland, Maine, in 1866. On June 16 his machine shop burned, although it was insured, but the loss of that building was only a prelude to what followed on July 4. A $10-million fire that swept the city left twelve thousand homeless and destroyed Corey's entire works. Upon reorganizing, Corey turned from manufacturing to distribution.[85]

Some woodworking craftsmen were perennial bad risks. High on the list is the cabinetmaker Nehemiah Adams of Salem, Massachusetts. The Reverend William Bentley noted the first fire, which destroyed Adams's shop on the Common, on April 3, 1798. Adams suspected that "defects in the hearth which the rats have repeatedly undermined" were the cause. Another fire occurred in March 1806 and a third three years later, "occasioned by the neglect of a man who worked in the upper loft of the building in boiling his varnish." Bentley recorded the last fire in the summer of 1813 and noted that by then Adams had become "a terrour to the neighbours." Adams's record was exceeded at Middlebury, Vermont, by that of Hastings Warren, who experienced six substantial fires at his cabinetmaking and chairmaking shop between 1813 and 1833, the last destroying his house as well.[86]

OTHER DISASTERS

The craftsman had little protection against natural catastrophies. When the Ohio River flooded Cincinnati and other communities along its path in 1832, shops were destroyed and goods dispersed. A cholera epidemic struck the city a second devastating blow. Years later Josiah Prescott Wilder lost his chair manufactory at New Ipswich, New Hampshire, when a spring freshet destroyed the building and dam about 1869. The loss of a hand "while engaged in firing the cannon" at a Fourth of July celebration in 1810 at Raleigh, North Carolina, was a grievous blow to David Ruth.[87]

Some chairmakers were crime victims; others committed crimes. Thomas Ash I of New York was stopped and robbed in 1774 by a pair of footpads who had terrorized other citizens. Curiously, Ash's own nephew Gabriel Leggett, a chairmaker, was imprisoned in 1791 for maintaining an illegal lottery. A Philadelphia-trained chairmaking swindler named Joseph Kerm appeared in Nashville, Tennessee, in 1813, where he fixed the names of local residents to promissory notes "which he also took the liberty to convert into ready rhino." Another chairmaker, Charles McKarahan, blew the whistle and gave public notice of the activity. Seth Sumpter, a second "wolf in sheep's clothing," appeared in Brookville, Indiana, in 1824. He boarded there for five weeks while chairmaking for a local firm and then left town without settling his accounts.[88]

Prison Work

The modern prison system had its genesis in America. Quakers in Philadelphia constituted the principal guiding force behind the reform, which occurred at the end of the eighteenth century. By official acts of 1789 and 1790 the Walnut Street Jail became the first state prison in Pennsylvania. New construction undertaken to enlarge the facility called for installation of individual cells, something unheard of at that date. The separate housing of prisoners was the first step in a plan that came to be known as the "Pennsylvania System." As explained in basic terms by Carl David Arfwedson, a European traveler in America, it called for "solitude, night and day, with labour." An alternative plan developed in the early nineteenth century in New York State eventually was called the "Auburn System" after the prison where it was first intro-

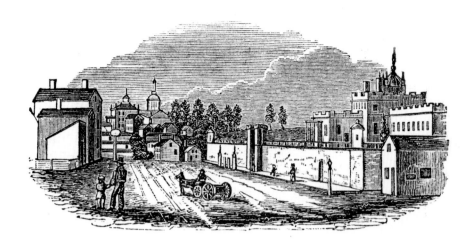

duced (fig. **1-15**). Its focus was "work together in the day-time in profound silence, and solitude at night." Under these plans prison industry had its start, generating therapeutic, but more particularly economic, benefits.[89]

Early attempts at profitable enterprise by prisons were largely unsuccessful. The technological and business knowledge of prison officials was often far from perfect. Heavy investment in raw materials put a strain on limited budgets, and prisons were little prepared to vend their own products. During a visit to the facility in Walnut Street in 1794, Dr. Benjamin Rush reported seeing individuals at activities such as sawing marble, grinding plaster, weaving, shoemaking, tailoring, spinning, chipping logwood (for dyeing), and turning. Jacob Hiltzheimer saw eighteen men cutting and heading nails several years later. By 1798 the prison had an "agent" who expedited sales. During the same decade Moreau de St. Méry observed prisoners at New York employed at "different types of work for the profit of the city." While visiting Governor's Island in Boston Harbor in 1791, the Reverend William Bentley saw "90 convicts of different ages at work in the Nail Manufactory." The inmates were "farmed by the State" to Ruggles and Company of Roxbury for this enterprise, which represents an early application of the contract labor system that became common in prisons only during the late 1820s. Beyond activity for profit, John Melish reported that convicts attended "every necessity of life" in daily prison operation: "baking, cooking, scrubbing the rooms, and so on; and every thing . . . remarkably clean."[90]

The new principles of prison governance gained momentum during the early 1800s. In Richmond, Virginia, a committee appointed to examine the "Jail and Penitentiary House" reported in 1806 that "the labour of the convicts . . . has not yet yielded a profit equal to the expenses of the institution" and made several recommendations. Among them was the proposal that the penitentiary introduce "the turners' business . . . (so far at least as the manufacture of Windsor Chairs)" was concerned, citing the cheapness and simplicity of the tools and durability of the materials.[91]

Only two years later in 1808 the state prison near Trenton, New Jersey, advertised a variety of industrial products, including a complete range of cut nails and brads, boots and shoes, fire buckets, and "RUSH-BOTTOMED CHAIRS." Shoemaking and chairmaking were still principal focuses several decades later, supplemented by weaving, and contemporary commentators reported that "the earnings of the prison now exceed the expenses." In 1809 the state prison at Windsor, Vermont, erected a workshop. Thomas Boynton, a town resident, painted "a State Prison Sign" for this facility in 1815 and altered it a year later "by order of Keeper." Possibly by that date Windsor-chair makers had begun to tap state facilities as cheap suppliers of chair parts. Certainly, there is a hint of this in 1812 at New York in the insolvency records of Reuben Odell, one of whose creditors was the "Agent of the State prison." Nathaniel

Rose's insolvency account of about a decade later names the same creditor to whom he was indebted for "chair Stuff Sold & delivered the said firm." The state prison in New York City was erected from 1796 to 1797 in a rural setting on the eastern bank of the Hudson River two miles north of City Hall on the Greenwich Road. The Doric-order stone facility had a two-story brick building at the back of the yard measuring 200 feet by 20 feet, which contained the workshops. Chairs or chair parts were first produced at the prison sometime after 1801. During a visit to the city in 1827, Mrs. Basil Hall also reported that young boys at the House of Refuge were "taught some trade . . . shoemakers, or chairmakers, or nail-makers." When released, they were "bound as apprentices or sent into the country."[92]

Increasingly through the 1810s the public mind-set became one of seeing the prisons become self-supporting. To this end the new state facility at Auburn, New York (fig. 1-15), introduced the contract labor system whereby "private entrepreneurs were to bring raw materials to the prison, pay fixed charges for the use of inmate workers, and market the finished goods at their own risk." Potential contractors were reluctant to gamble with a system not yet tried and true, however, and it was necessary for the prison to offer concessions. These took the form of low labor rates and access by contractors to prison shops to inspect the work in progress and to provide prisoners with instruction when keepers were not sufficiently knowledgeable. Direct communication with prisoners remained limited, since the prison code called for silence at all times and eyes fixed on the work. Both shop space and power were provided gratis by the prison, the Owasco River being the energy source for the turning and chairmaking shops. Positioned along the walls of the interior yard, the shops were well lighted by windows in the sides and roof. Behind them ran a narrow passage-way from which keepers could view operations through "numerous small orifices" without the prisoners' knowledge. Assistant keepers were in attendance within the shops.[93]

Contract work in chairs and cabinet furniture was under way at Auburn probably by late 1826, since Gershom Powers, "agent and keeper," listed the operation in his annual report ending October 31, 1827, noting that the workmen's pay was calculated on a piecework basis. The aggregate number of turners, chairmakers, cabinetmakers, and painters under contract at the end of 1828 was twenty-five, and seven more carpenters and turners were directly employed by the prison. The value of "tools and fixtures" in the cabinet and chair shop was calculated at $86.40.[94]

Contractors and prison agents vended their merchandise where they could, locally and at a distance. A notice in the *Rochester Daily Advertiser* for 1830 announced "AUBURN STATE Prison Cabinet Work & CHAIRS" for sale "on board the canal boat lying in Child's basin." Cheney and Seymour may have been the contractors by that date. John Seymour took over by summer 1834, as announced in the *Cayuga Patriot* and confirmed by prison reports. The prison's income from the operation had reached about $4,000 annually. A private purchase of mahogany furniture made directly from the prison agent, W. A. Palmer, in 1840 is recorded in the business papers of William S. Stow, Esq., a resident of Clyde, a small community about twenty miles distant from Auburn. Stow's purchase included 14 chairs, 2 dining tables, and a pair of footstools. Auburn's location on the Owasco River appears to have given the prison and local business establishments direct access to the Erie Canal. Along its westward course the canal communicated with Clyde.[95]

On May 20, 1843, the agent of the Auburn prison called for new and renewed proposals "for the hire and services" of a specified number of inmates, as was customary periodically. On the list were "30 to 50 convicts to be employed in the manufacture of Cabinet Ware and Chairs, for the term of five years from the first day of November next." Similar schemes were carried on at various facilities elsewhere in the state, including a new prison on the Hudson River at Sing Sing. At midcentury the Robinson firm in Rochester employed young boys from the Western House of Refuge to

FIG. 1-16 Roll-top fancy side chair, Lambert Hitchcock and Arba Alford (stencil "HITCHCOCK. ALFORD. & CO.HITCHCOCKS-VILLE.CONN./ WARRANTED."), Hitchcocksville (now Riverton), Conn., 1832–43. Birch, beech (microanalysis); H. 34⅝", W. 17⅜", D. 18⅝". *(Courtesy, Winterthur Museum, acc. 57.611.1.)*

weave cane and rush seats, a business also carried on in the county penitentiary at Syracuse for the Oswego Chair Factory. Even Canadian manufacturers, among them Richard French of Toronto, imported cane work from New York State, "where it is got up very cheaply in the Penitentiaries."[96]

A body of records for the Connecticut State Prison at Wethersfield, which operated along the lines of the "Auburn System" and received its first inmates from old Newgate Prison at Granby in 1827, describes chairmaking and related activities from the late 1820s to the 1840s. The first outside chair contractor was Lambert Hitchcock, who signed an agreement for caning chair-seat frames in March 1829 (fig. 1-16). In April Proctor Newton was made overseer, and production began on or by May 1 after the shop was organized and tools, parts, and raw materials were in place. The contract probably was intended to run for a year; however, Hitchcock's insolvency of that summer forced a change of plans. A note appended to prison records states, "This contract relinquished Jan'y 9th 1830 by assignees of Sd. Hitchcock paying a forfeiture of $250." For a while Hitchcock also had interests in the carpenter shop. A report made by prison directors to the Connecticut General Assembly in May describes what happened after Hitchcock's withdrawal: "We have been obliged during the year to commence the chair business & that a considerable sum was necessary to furnish that department with tools & stock." The actual expense was $1,811.77. Despite setbacks, the operation showed a handsome profit of $2,346 at the end of one year, with stock and tools on hand valued at another $947. In subsequent years the state continued in the capacity of contractor in the "Chair Shop," although other firms pursued related activities on the premises. During the period through 1842, daily inmate pay varied from a low of 22¢ to a high of 44¢, reflecting economic fluctuations, level of skill, or both. The pay was about half that received by workmen outside the prison. The number of men employed in the prison shop ranged from thirty-five to sixty-seven.[97]

On October 2, 1832, Smith Ely, a chairmaker of New York City, signed a bond guaranteeing his "performance and fulfilment" of a contract for chairwork with the Wethersfield Prison. A schedule of prices appended to the bond suggests that Ely shipped prepared parts for fancy chairs, fancy and "steamboat" settees, and steamboat stools to the prison shop for assembly, seating, and finishing. The work probably included bending some of the stock. This was not the first contract between the two parties, as indicated in item "No. 6 Curled Maple Seats," which states that the furniture "be made as the past year per Pattern." Ely also was a contractor in a "Cane Seating Shop" at the prison from November 1833 to July 1835. During much of the same period Lambert Hitchcock, whose financial resources had been revitalized, and then Levi Stillman of New Haven held contracts in a "Flag Seating Shop." After expiration of Ely's second contract in 1835, the work appears to have been dropped until cane seating was revived under state management in June 1837.[98]

A contract between the state and D. C. Y. Moore of Litchfield County dated June 2, 1834, describes prison management of another cane-seating shop, which apparently operated concurrently with Smith Ely's contract, although the agreement does not appear in a cumulative report prepared in 1841 by the prison warden. In June 1834 Moore agreed to deliver a quantity of material to the prison: "Stuff for Thirty Thousand Chair Seat Frames, Five Thousand to be Curled Maple agreeable to the dimentions hereunto annexed, to be well seasoned and of good materials, sawed & prepared in a workmanlike manner, to be Sawed from the same kind of wood Size &c as has been delivered by said Moore for the last year." Delivery dates and load sizes were determined by prison officials, and payment was set at $3.75 per 100 plain seat frames and $8 per 100 curled maple frames. If the prison discontinued the cane-seat manufacture, it could cancel the remaining part of the contract.[99]

From autumn 1840 through 1842 (and possibly later) as the prison continued the chair-shop operation on its own account, there existed on the premises a cabinet shop under contract to Cyrus Baldwin and James B. Cook of New York City. Beginning in January 1841 a varnishing shop was under similar direction. As described in another schedule, the work performed consisted of "making" and "varnishing chairs." The machinery that Baldwin and Cook installed for this work included a circular saw and frame, an upright saw, a boring machine, two "Tenanting Machines," and the "Shafts, drums, belts &c" necessary for their operation. The firm paid the prison $1 a day for steam power delivered from a 6-horsepower engine installed in 1833. Previous to that date power to drive machinery was supplied by "the labor of the Prisoners turning at a crank." For the year ending March 31, 1842, the prison could report a net income of $2,624.62 from the "Cabinet Shop," $1,215.70 from the "Varnishing Shop," and $7,653.37 from the production of its own "Chair Seating Shops" — not a bad profit for a public institution. The records show that the workforce in the contract shops stood at thirty-five. Eighty-two other prisoners labored in the state-run facilities: twelve individuals made seat frames; twenty worked at "Knotting, splitting & shaving cane" in the new "Cane Splitting Shop"; and fifty inmates, some possibly women, wove cane seats.[100]

As at Sing Sing Prison in New York, one of the important activities at the prison in Charlestown, Massachusetts, from its erection in 1805 across the river from Boston was stonecutting, an activity enhanced by the facility's waterside location on Lynde's Point. In the mid-1820s Anne Newport Royall described a group of enclosed shops where mechanics carried out work of "every description," including printing, engraving, and jewelry making. Newspaper and supplementary sources detail other work, which encompassed the production of hardware, nails, tools, boots and shoes, harness and leather goods, and brushes. Perhaps at Royall's visit the local Forster family of cabinetmakers had already entered into an association with the state prison, with whom it "held many contracts . . . for the employment of . . . convicts."[101]

Identifying other prison activity is a public notice dating to July 22, 1826, placed in a Frankfort newspaper by the keeper of the penitentiary in Kentucky, who announced the sale of prison-made Windsor chairs and other items. In further commentary, Mrs. Royall described the state penitentiary at Milledgeville, Georgia, in 1831 as the "best kept, and best regulated of any State Prison this side of Boston. . . . All the convicts are kept at work. . . . Those who have trades work at them." Prison products were used in state facilities and offered for public sale. A newspaper notice of 1821 itemizes the range of furniture: "tables, slabs, washstands and chests, spinning wheels, clocks, reels and looms, bedsteads, cradles, cribs and Windsor chairs."[102]

Although penal philosophy in Pennsylvania called for individual labor in prisoners' cells — basically hand weaving and shoemaking — William Chambers upon visiting the Eastern State Penitentiary, successor to the Walnut Street Prison, described one inmate who occupied a double-size cell at midcentury as "busily engaged at a bench, making chairs with carpentry tools." This type of activity must have been enlarged upon, since William J. Warren, proprietor of a chair and home-furnishing store in Philadelphia, purchased "immense quantities" of seating from the institution during the 1850s and 1860s. By that date penal institutions in Canada emulated the American system and produced furniture by contract for institutional profit. It was not always smooth sailing for the prisons or the legislatures that authorized the programs on either side of the border. Strong protests were heard from "free" workmen at an early date, as prison goods cut into and undersold their markets. Typical is that of the mechanics at Baltimore, who petitioned the state House of Delegates in 1819 to pass a law "prohibiting the manufacturing of any articles in the penitentiary at Baltimore" because this activity "interfered with the profits of their business."[103]

NOTES

1. Carl Bridenbaugh, *The Colonial Craftsman* (Chicago: University of Chicago Press, 1961), pp. 95, 127, 134; Howard B. Rock, *Artisans of the New Republic* (New York: New York University Press, 1979), pp. 14, 266; William A. Sullivan, *The Industrial Worker in Pennsylvania, 1800–1840* (Harrisburg: Pennsylvania Historical and Museum Commission, 1955), p. iii; Wendell Garrett, "Editorial," *Antiques* 114, no. 4 (October 1979): 825.

2. Bridenbaugh, *Colonial Craftsman*, pp. 3, 127; Polly Ann Earl, "Craftsmen and Machines: The Nineteenth-Century Furniture Industry," in *Technological Innovation and the Decorative Arts*, ed. Ian M. G. Quimby and Polly Ann Earl (Charlottesville: University Press of Virginia, 1974), p. 307; Rock, *Artisans of the New Republic*, p. 9; Winifred C. Gates, "Journal of a Cabinet Maker's Apprentice, Part 1," *Chronicle of the Early American Industries Association* 15, no. 2 (June 1962): 23–24.

3. Silas E. Cheney daybook, 1807–13, Litchfield Historical Society, Litchfield, Conn. (hereafter cited LHS; microfilm, Joseph Downs Collection of Manuscripts and Printed Ephemera, Winterthur Museum and Library, Winterthur, Del. [hereafter cited DCM and WL]); Thomas Boynton ledger, 1811–17, Dartmouth College, Hanover, N.H. (hereafter cited DC; microfilm, DCM); Enos White journal, 1821–51, DCM.

4. Wilder forecast quoted in Charles S. Parsons, Wilder Family Notes, Visual Resources Collection, WL (hereafter cited as VRC).

5. David Alling account book, 1801–39, and receipt books, 1824–42 and 1844–56, New Jersey Historical Society, Newark (hereafter cited NJHS; microfilm, DCM); Henry W. Miller account book, 1827–31, Worcester Historical Museum, Worcester, Mass.; Philemon Robbins account book, 1833–36, Connecticut Historical Society, Hartford (hereafter cited CHS); Chauncy Strong daybooks, 1841–52 and 1852–69, New York State Historical Association, Cooperstown (hereafter cited NYSHA).

6. Justus Dunn miscellaneous papers, 1831, NYSHA (microfilm, DCM); James P. Stabler contract with Joshua Stewart and Co., September 20, 1817, Stabler Family Account Books, vol. 2, 1817–20, Maryland Historical Society, Baltimore; Elihu Alvord memorandum to George White, November 24, 1803, Nicholas Low Collection, Library of Congress, Washington, D.C. (hereafter cited LC).

7. Stephen Whipple account book, 1803–11, Ipswich Historical Society, Ipswich, Mass.; Cheney daybook.

8. Daniel and Samuel Proud ledger and daybook, 1810–34, Rhode Island Historical Society, Providence (hereafter cited RIHS); William Mitchell Pillsbury, "The Providence Furniture Making Trade, 1772–1834" (master's thesis, University of Delaware, 1975), pp. 9,

11–12; White journal; Joel Pratt, Jr., account book, 1822–26 with additions, privately owned (microfilm, Old Sturbridge Village, Sturbridge, Mass.; hereafter cited OSV).

9. Mabel M. Swan, *Samuel McIntire, Carver, and the Sandersons, Early Salem Cabinet Makers* (Salem, Mass.: Essex Institute, 1934), p. 13; Peter M. Deveikis, "Hastings Warren: Vermont Cabinetmaker," *Antiques* 101, no. 6 (June 1972): 1038; Miller account book.

10. White journal.

11. Bridenbaugh, *Colonial Craftsman*, pp. 130–34; Robert Francis Seybolt, *Apprenticeship and Apprenticeship Education in Colonial New England and New York* (New York: Columbia University, 1917), pp. 1–21; Joseph Bartlett letter to David Brown, Jr., March 30, 1807, Talbot County Historical Society, Easton, Md. (hereafter cited TCHS; reference courtesy of Georgia Adler); R. Campbell, *The London Tradesman* (London: T. Gardner, 1747), pp. 312–17; Robert W. Symonds Papers, DCM.

12. John Allwine, Jr., apprenticeship indenture with Lawrence Allwine, November 4, 1788, DCM. By the terms of his Schuylkill County, Pa., contract, Elisha Christ was permitted to receive communion; apprenticeship indenture with Daniel Kimmel, September 9, 1825, DCM. Elisha Harlow Holmes apprenticeship indenture with Amos Denison Allen and Frederick Tracy, March 30, 1819, Antiquarian and Landmarks Society, Hartford, Conn. The *Oxford English Dictionary* defines "ironing" as the action of fitting or arming with iron. Records of the 1820 United States Census of Manufactures, state of Connecticut, National Archives, Washington, D.C. (hereafter cited NA; microfilm, DCM).

13. Seybolt, *Apprenticeship*, pp. 22–65. The term of instruction is specified in the following: Amos Denison Allen apprenticeship indenture with Ebenezer Tracy, Sr., February 5, 1790, CHS, and Lewis Case apprenticeship indenture with David Moon and Edward Prall, October 4, 1804, DCM. Swan, *Samuel McIntire*, p. 13; Charles S. Parsons, *The Dunlaps and Their Furniture* (Manchester, N.H.: Currier Gallery of Art, 1970), p. 17; Nathan Cleaveland ledger, 1810–28, OSV.

14. Campbell, *London Tradesman*, p. 314; Gates, "Journal of a Cabinet Maker's Apprentice, Part 1," p. 23; Eli Wood estate records, 1818, Barkhamstead, Conn., Genealogical Section, Connecticut State Library, Hartford (hereafter cited CSL); Benjamin Love estate records, 1821, City and County of Philadelphia, Pa., Register of Wills (microfilm, DCM).

15. John Lamson apprenticeship indenture with Elijah Sanderson, 1819, as quoted in Margaret Burke Clunie, "Salem Federal Furniture" (master's thesis, University of Delaware, 1976), p. 27.

16. Allwine, Holmes, Christ, Case, and Allen apprenticeship indentures; Philadelphia

Almshouse Indentures, books C (1804–12) and D (1812–20), City and County of Philadelphia, Archives, Philadelphia, Pa.; Philadelphia Monthly Meeting of Friends, Committee of Twelve minutes, vol. 2, 1795–1817, and treasurers' reports and receipts, 1807–18, Society of Friends, Philadelphia, Pa. (on deposit, American Philosophical Society, Philadelphia, Pa. [hereafter cited APS]).

17. Gates, "Journal of a Cabinet Maker's Apprentice, Part 1," p. 23; John Woodhull Stedman, "Hartford in 1830: Some Things I Remember about Hartford Sixty Years Ago," *Connecticut Historical Society Bulletin* 14, no. 3 (July 1949): 32; Holmes apprenticeship indenture.

18. Rhodes G. Allen, *Providence Directory* (Providence, R.I.: Brown and Danforth, 1824), p. 33; Joseph Bartlett letter to David Brown, Jr., May 20, 1807, TCHS. The best-known apprentices identified later as chairmakers include Amos Denison Allen, the Tracy brothers (Elijah and Ebenezer, Jr.), and their cousin Stephen, all of whom trained with Ebenezer Tracy, Sr., in New London County, Conn.; William Widdifield, a poor boy of Philadelphia who trained with William Cox and later gave other poor boys a start in his own shop; Isaac Covert, who served with Joseph Henzey in Philadelphia during the Revolutionary War years; Ebenezer Rose, a master chairmaker of Trenton, N.J., who bragged that he had acquired "his art from BENJAMIN LOVE at Frankfort, near Philadelphia, who is known to be much approved of in the business" (*Trenton Federalist* [Trenton], November 30, 1807); and Jacob Daley, one of several successful chairmakers who trained in the shop of Richard Sweeney at Baltimore.

19. Gates, "Journal of a Cabinet Maker's Apprentice, Part 1," p. 23, and Edward Jenner Carpenter journal, 1844–45, American Antiquarian Society, Worcester, Mass.; "Journal of the Select Committee of The Providence Association of Mechanics and Manufacturers," vol. 2, 1822–30 (and later), RIHS.

20. Fire notice, *New-York Herald* (New York), March 30, 1803, as quoted in Rita Susswein Gottesman, comp. *The Arts and Crafts in New York, 1800–1804* (New York: New-York Historical Society, 1965), p. 145; David Evans account book, 1774–82, Historical Society of Pennsylvania, Philadelphia (hereafter cited HSP; microfilm, DCM).

21. Cautionary statement in Robert McKim, *Enquirer* (Richmond, Va.), April 19, 1815, citation file, Museum of Early Southern Decorative Arts, Winston-Salem, N.C. (hereafter cited MESDA); seaport notice and apprentice with remarkable walk in Swan, *Samuel McIntire*, p. 26; once-cent reward of Wesley Whitaker, *Raleigh Register* (Raleigh, N.C.), February 23, 1809, knock-kneed apprentice of Jacob Cole, *Federal Gazette and Baltimore Daily Advertiser* (Baltimore, Md.), January 12, 1796, and redheaded apprentice of Matthew McColm,

American and Commerical Daily Advertiser (Baltimore, Md.), October 14, 1806, all three in citation file, MESDA; Oliver Pomeroy, *Gazette* (Buffalo, N.Y.), December 22, 1818, as quoted in Leigh Keno, "The Windsor Chair Makers of Northampton, Massachusetts, 1790–1820" (Historic Deerfield Summer Fellowship Program paper, Deerfield, Mass., August 1979), p. 133; Augur in *Patten's New Haven Directory, for 1843–4* (New Haven, Conn.: James M. Patten, 1843), p. 117.

22. Grant and Jemison, *Kentucky Gazette and General Advertiser* (Lexington), December 1, 1807. Apprenticeship prerequisites in the following: Alexander Walker, *Virginia Herald* (Fredericksburg), August 26, 1800, citation file, MESDA; Joseph Robinson, *Dauphin Guardian* (Harrisburg, Pa.), August 29, 1809 (reference brought to author's attention by the late William Bowers); James Meetkerke, *Reporter* (Washington, Pa.), June 3, 1811 (reference courtesy of Peter Chillingworth); George Kearns, *Martinsburgh Gazette* (Martinsburg, W.Va.), April 12, 1811, citation file, MESDA; and Lambert Hitchcock, *Connecticut Courant* (Hartford), August 17, 1831, as reproduced in John Tarrant Kenney, *The Hitchcock Chair* (New York: Clarkson N. Potter, 1971), p. 118. Country boy in Burrows Smith, *Western Spy* (Cincinnati, Ohio), May 25, 1811, as quoted in Jane E. Sikes, *The Furniture Makers of Cincinnati, 1790 to 1849* (Cincinnati, Ohio: By the author, 1976), p. 221; John Henry Hill, "The Furniture Craftsmen in Baltimore, 1783–1823" (master's thesis, University of Delaware, 1967), p. 62, appendix A.

23. Isaiah Steen, *Reporter*, March 11, 1811 (reference courtesy of Peter Chillingworth); Ezekiel White, *Chester and Delaware Federalist* (West Chester, Pa.), November 29, 1809, as quoted in Margaret Berwind Schiffer, *Furniture and Its Makers of Chester County Pennsylvania* (Philadelphia: University of Pennsylvania Press, 1966), p. 247; Jacob Batcheler, *Vermont Gazette* (Bennington), June 6, 1839, Bennington Museum, Bennington (hereafter cited Bennington).

24. Jacob Thompson letter to Silas E. Cheney, February 20, 1814, Superior Court Records, Litchfield Co., Conn., Miscellaneous Papers, CSL.

25. Charles F. Montgomery states in *American Furniture: The Federal Period* (New York: Viking Press, 1966), pp. 23, 26, that the dollar was equated with 7s. 6d. at Philadelphia in 1795; however, information from dozens of extant woodworking accounts for this and later periods clearly shows that the *usual* calculation was based on 6s. to the dollar. John I. Wells, *Connecticut Courant*, January 13, 1800.

26. Robert McKeen lawsuit vs. Joseph Adams, 1790, Colonial Court Records, Social Law Library, Boston, Mass. (hereafter cited SLL; reference courtesy of Charles A. Hammond and John T. Kirk); Gilson Brown estate

records, 1833–35, Worcester Co., Worcester, Mass., Registry of Probate; Nelson Talcott daybook, 1839–48, DCM.

27. Charles C. Robinson daybook, 1809–25, HSP.

28. David Alling ledger, 1815–18, NJHS (microfilm, DCM); Allen Holcomb account book, 1809–28, Metropolitan Museum of Art, New York.

29. James Gere ledger, 1822–52, CSL; Solomon Cole account book, 1794–1809, CHS; Silas Cheney daybooks, 1807–13 and 1813–21, and ledger, 1816–32, LHS (microfilm, DCM).

30. Luke Houghton ledgers A–C, 1816–27, 1824–51, and 1834–76, Barre Historical Society, Barre, Mass. (microfilm, DCM).

31. Henry F. Dewey account book, 1837–64, Shelburne Museum, Shelburne, Vt. (microfilm, DCM); Talcott daybook.

32. Gates, "Journal of a Cabinet Maker's Apprentice, Part 1," pp. 23–24, and Winifred C. Gates, "Journal of a Cabinet Maker's Apprentice, Part 2," *Chronicle of the Early American Industries Association* 15, no. 3 (September 1962): 35–36; Thomas Henning, Sr., *Lewisburg Chronicle* (Lewisburg, W.Va.), February 12, 1852 (reference courtesy of Anne C. Golovin); David Pritchard general family material, box 1, Mattatuck Museum, Waterbury, Conn.

33. Records of the 1820 United States Census of Manufactures, states of Vermont, Connecticut, New York, Pennsylvania, Maryland, Delaware, Virginia, Georgia, Kentucky, Indiana, Ohio, and Tennessee, NA (microfilm, DCM); Hunt apprenticeship recorded in Hill, "Furniture Craftsmen in Baltimore," p. 365.

34. Henry Bradshaw Fearon, *Sketches of America*, 2d ed. (London: Longman et al., 1818), p. 202; fire notice, *Vermont Mirror* (Middlebury), January 26, 1814, as quoted in Deveikis, "Hastings Warren," p. 1038; *History of Litchfield County, Connecticut* (Philadelphia: J. W. Lewis, 1881), p. 241.

35. *Documents Relative to Manufactures in the United States Collected and Transmitted to the House of Representatives in Compliance with a Resolution of January 8, 1832, by the Secretary of the Treasury*, 2 vols. (Washington, D.C.: Duff Green, 1833), 1:136–37, 146–47, 292–93, 492–93, 548–53, 564–65; Francis De Witt, *Statistical Information Relating to Certain Branches of Industry in Massachusetts for the Year Ending June 1, 1855* (Boston: William White, 1856), p. 601.

36. Rock, *Artisans of the New Republic*, p. 242; Kenney, *Hitchcock Chair*, p. 151; J. H. French, *Gazetteer of the State of New York* (Syracuse: R. Pearsall Smith, 1860), p. 402, n. 6; Sikes, *Furniture Makers of Cincinnati*, pp. 84–85.

37. Bridenbaugh, *Colonial Craftsman*, pp. 138–41; *Pennsylvania Packet* (Philadelphia), November 4, 1780 (reference courtesy of Barbara Soltis).

38. W. H. Hill, *Wilmington Gazette* (Wilmington, N.C.), May 13, 1802, and John Nutt,

Hall's Wilmington Gazette (Wilmington, N.C.), February 8, 1798, citation file, MESDA.

39. Hill, "Furniture Craftsmen in Baltimore," p. 375; Anne Castrodale Golovin, "Cabinetmakers and Chairmakers of Washington, D.C., 1791–1840," *Antiques* 107, no. 5 (May 1975): 914, 916; *The Diary of William Bentley*, 4 vols. (Salem, Mass.: Essex Institute, 1905), 4:361; New York City jury lists, 1819, Historical Documents Collection, Queens College, Flushing, N.Y. (hereafter cited QC).

40. A checklist of Windsor-chair makers is included in Nancy Goyne Evans, *American Windsor Chairs* (New York: Hudson Hills Press, 1996). Other early partnerships are those of Leacock and Intle and Timpson and Gillihen in New York and Freeman and Houck and Wire and Cubbin in Philadelphia. It has been suggested that the Richmond, Va., firm of Pointer and Childres was in business in the 1780s, but there is no documentation of their association before 1797; see Paul H. Burroughs, *Southern Antiques*, 2d ed. (New York: Bonanza Books, 1967), p. 163, pl. 11.

41. Burchall and Wickersham, *American Republican* (West Chester, Pa.), February 18, 1824, as quoted in Schiffer, *Furniture of Chester County*, p. 44; James Beck, *Virginia Herald*, March 19, 1805, citation file, MESDA (reference courtesy of Margaret Beck Pritchard).

42. Edward E. Atwater, *History of the City of New Haven* (New York: W. W. Munsell, 1887), p. 587.

43. White journal.

44. White journal.

45. Cromwell, Howland, and Davis, *New-Bedford Mercury* (New Bedford, Mass.), February 20, 1829, as quoted in Elton W. Hall, "New Bedford Furniture," *Antiques* 113, no. 5 (May 1978): 1119; Dewey and Woodworth, *Vermont Gazette*, November 12, 1827; S. Williams and Co., *Nashville Clarion* (Nashville, Tenn.), June 10, 1817, as quoted in Ellen Beasley, "Tennessee Cabinetmakers and Chairmakers through 1840," *Antiques* 100, no. 4 (October 1971): 621; Thomas S. Renshaw and Co., *Museum and Washington and George-town Advertiser* (Georgetown, D.C.), August 31 and October 26, 1801, as quoted in Golovin, "Cabinetmakers and Chairmakers of Washington," p. 918; Parrott and Hubbell, and Lockwood and Waite, insolvency records, 1835 and 1847, Bridgeport, Conn., Genealogical Section, CSL; Sikes, *Furniture Makers of Cincinnati*, pp. 207–8.

46. See checklist of Windsor-chair makers in Evans, *American Windsor Chairs*; Samuel Morgan Alvord, comp., *A Genealogy of the Descendants of Alexander Alvord* (Webster, N.Y.: A. D. Andrews, 1908), pp. 166–67; Nancy Goyne Evans, "The Sans Souci, a Fashionable Resort Hotel in Ballston Spa," in *Winterthur Portfolio 6*, ed. Richard K. Doud and Ian M. G. Quimby (Charlottesville: University Press of Virginia, 1970), pp. 115–17.

47. Northampton information in Keno, "Windsor Chair Makers of Northampton," pp. 6, 16, 37, 41, 50, 132, 135.

48. *Cincinnati Directory for 1825* (Cincinnati, Ohio: Samuel J. Browne, 1825); Arthur Whallon, "Indiana Cabinetmakers and Allied Craftsmen, 1815–1860," *Antiques* 98, no. 1 (July 1970): 122; Betty Lawson Walters, *Furniture Makers of Indiana, 1793 to 1850* (Indianapolis: Indiana Historical Society, 1972), pp. 205–6; Beasley, "Tennessee Cabinetmakers and Chairmakers," pp. 613, 621; Parsons, Wilder Family Notes.

49. Stedman, "Hartford in 1830," p. 32; *Documents Relative to Manufactures*, 1:1019; Montgomery, *American Furniture: Federal*, pp. 22–24; Sullivan, *Industrial Worker in Pennsylvania*, pp. 134–37. Similar conditions prevailed in England, where *The Bolton Supplement to the London Book of Cabinet Piece Prices* (Bolton, Lancashire: J. Gardner, 1802) describes "the hours of working by the day to be from six o'clock in the morning till six o'clock in the evening," as reproduced in Christopher Gilbert, *English Vernacular Furniture, 1750–1900* (New Haven, Conn.: Yale University Press, 1991), appendix 2, p. 263.

50. Sullivan, *Industrial Worker in Pennsylvania*, p. 34; Gates, "Journal of a Cabinet Maker's Apprentice, Part 1," p. 23, "Part 2," p. 35. The *Bolton Supplement* reported the "Time of Candle-Light" as beginning on October 12 and ending on February 12, as reproduced in Gilbert, *Vernacular Furniture*, appendix 2, p. 263.

51. *London Chronicle* (London, England), March 10, 1778, as quoted in Elisabeth Donaghy Garrett, ed., "Clues and Footnotes," *Antiques* 125, no. 6 (June 1984): 1400; Frances M. Trollope, *Domestic Manners of the Americans*, 2 vols. (London: Whittaker, Treacher, 1832), 1:163–64.

52. Elijah Pember account book, 1758–67, DCM; Thomas Boynton ledger, 1817–47, DC (microfilm, DCM); Charles F. Hummel, *With Hammer in Hand* (Charlottesville: University Press of Virginia, 1968), p. 235; Pillsbury, "Providence Furniture Making Trade," p. 65.

53. William Strickland, *Journal of a Tour in the United States of America, 1794–1795*, ed. J. E. Strickland (New York: New-York Historical Society, 1971), pp. 27–30; duc de la Rochefoucauld Liancourt, *Travels through the United States of North America*, 2 vols. (London: K. Phillips, 1799), 2:83; Elihu Alvord bill to George White, June 3, 1805, Nicholas Low Collection, LC; John Melish, *Travels through the United States of America*, 2 vols. (Philadelphia: By the author, 1815), 2:56, 127; François André Michaux, *Travels to the West of the Allegheny Mountains* (London: D. N. Shury, 1805), p. 124.

54. *Documents Relative to Manufactures*; Boynton ledger, 1817–47.

55. John F. Watson, *Annals of Philadelphia and Pennsylvania in the Olden Time*, 3 vols. (1830; reprint, rev. Willis P. Hazard, Philadelphia: Leary, Stuart, 1927), 1:176, 254–55; John F. Watson, *Annals and Occurrences of New York City and State in the Olden Time* (Philadelphia: Henry F. Anners, 1846), p. 257; Ebenezer Tracy, Sr., Perez Austin, and Elisha Hawley estate records, 1803, 1833, and 1843, Lisbon, Canterbury, and Monroe, Conn., Genealogical Section, CSL.

56. Old breeches in John Avery, Sr., estate records, 1794, Preston, Conn., Genealogical Section, CSL; overalls in Ebenezer Tracy, Sr., estate records, and Joel Booth estate records, 1794–95, Newtown, Conn., Genealogical Section, CSL; *Oxford English Dictionary*, s.v. "overalls"; Florence Montgomery, *Textiles in America, 1650–1870* (New York: W. W. Norton, 1983), p. 271.

57. Old blue pantaloons and homemade coats in Stephen B. Allyn estate records, 1822, Norwich, Conn., Genealogical Section, CSL, and Amasa Elwell estate records, 1814, Bennington Co., Bennington, Vt., Registry of Probate; tow pantaloons in Smith Kendall, Sr., estate records, 1824, Ashford, Conn., Genealogical Section, CSL; Kenney, *Hitchcock Chair*, p. 324. Top hats, such as those illustrated in figure 2-7, appear to have been relatively common among the "mechanic" class, although possibly they were favored more in one trade than another. Likely, top hats were not worn at all times, as some tasks would have rendered the practice awkward. John Lewis Krimmel's firsthand view of the mechanic trades in Philadelphia (fig. 1-9) suggests the practice was more an urban than a rural one.

58. Thomas West estate records, 1828, New London, Conn., Genealogical Section, CSL.

59. Tench Coxe, *An Address to an Assembly of the Friends of American Manufactures* (Philadelphia: R. Aitken and Sons, 1787).

60. Sullivan, *Industrial Worker in Pennsylvania*, pp. 6–7, including quotation from *Niles Weekly Register* (Baltimore); I. N. Phelps Stokes, *The Iconography of Manhattan Island, 1498–1906*, 6 vols. (New York: Robert H. Dodd, 1915–28), 5:1607; Edwin Wolf 2nd, *Philadelphia: Portrait of an American City* (Harrisburg, Pa.: Stackpole Books, 1975), p. 149.

61. Thomas Earle and Charles T. Congdon, eds., *Annals of the General Society of Mechanics and Tradesmen* (New York: By the society, 1882), pp. 9, 11–12; Baltimore association notices, *Maryland Gazette, or the Baltimore General Advertiser* (Baltimore), November 18, 1785, *Maryland Journal and Baltimore Advertiser* (Baltimore), November 21, 1786, and February 17, 1789, and *Gazette of the State of Georgia* (Savannah), June 12, 1788, citation file, MESDA; dissolution of Boston Association noted in "Records of the Providence Association of Mechanics and Manufacturers," vol. 1, 1789–94, RIHS; Joseph T. Buckingham, comp., *Annals of the Massachusetts Charitable Mechanic Association* (Boston: Crocker and Brewster, 1853), pp. 1, 9, 11, 14.

62. "Records of the Providence Association of Mechanics and Manufacturers," vol. 1, vol. 2 (1794–1811), journal, and circular letter, April 30, 1789, RIHS.

63. New York association discussed in Stokes, *Iconography*, 5:1392, 1612; "Records of the Providence Association of Mechanics and Manufacturers," vol. 1; New Hampshire associations discussed in Parsons, *The Dunlaps*, p. 17; Hudson, York, and Newark society notices, *Charleston Courier* (Charleston, S.C.), February 15, 1804, *Norfolk Herald* (Norfolk, Va.), June 23, 1801, and *Daily National Intelligencer* (Washington, D.C.), July 18, 1818, citation file, MESDA.

64. Norfolk and Fredericksburg society notices, *Herald and Norfolk and Portsmouth Advertiser* (Norfolk, Va.), January 24, 1795, and *Virginia Herald*, August 31, 1804, citation file, MESDA; Richmond society notice, *Virginia Argus* (Richmond), June 15, 1814, as noted in Giles Cromwell, "Andrew and Robert McKim, Windsor Chair Makers," *Journal of Early Southern Decorative Arts* 6, no. 1 (May 1980): 16. Evidence of the Charleston group appears in *The Constitution of the Charleston Mechanic Society Instituted at Charleston, South Carolina, 1794* (Charleston: G. M. Bounetheau, 1811), as cited in Bradford L. Rauschenberg and John Bivins, Jr., *The Furniture of Charleston, 1680–1820*, 3 vols. (Winston-Salem, N.C.: Museum of Early Southern Decorative Arts, 2003), 3: "Reference List," p. ii. Wilmington, Augusta, and Savannah society notices, *Cape-Fear Recorder* (Wilmington, N.C.), December 7, 1816, *Augusta Chronicle and Gazette of the State* (Augusta, Ga.), April 28, 1792, and *Maryland Journal and Baltimore Universal Daily Advertiser* (Baltimore), January 16, 1795, citation file, MESDA; Nashville, Lexington, and Chillicothe society notices, *Tennessee Gazette* (Nashville), February 11, 1801, *Kentucky Gazette* (Lexington), September 25, 1810, and *Norfolk Herald*, October 7, 1811, citation file, MESDA.

65. Bridenbaugh, *Colonial Craftsman*, pp. 144–45; Martin Eli Weil, "A Cabinetmaker's Price Book," in *Winterthur Porfolio 13*, ed. Ian M. G. Quimby (Chicago: University of Chicago Press, 1979), p. 177; Sullivan, *Industrial Worker in Pennsylvania*; Sharon V. Salinger, "Artisans, Journeymen, and the Transformation of Labor in Late Eighteenth-Century Philadelphia," *William and Mary Quarterly* 40, no. 1 (January 1983).

66. Sullivan, *Industrial Worker in Pennsylvania*, chap. 6, pp. 119–43; Kathleen M. Catalano, "Cabinetmaking in Philadelphia, 1820–1840: Transition from Craft to Industry," in *Winterthur Portfolio 13*, ed. Ian M. G. Quimby (Chicago: University of Chicago Press, 1979), pp. 81–91.

67. Montgomery, *American Furniture: Fed-*

eral, pp. 19–26; Pat Kirkham, "Introduction, Part I, Furniture-Makers and Trade Unionism: The Early London Trade Societies," in reprint of *The Cabinet-Makers' London Book of Prices, 1793* (London: London Society of Cabinet Makers, 1793), in *Furniture History* 18 (1982): 1–5; Weil, "A Cabinetmaker's Price Book," pp. 175–92; Harrold E. Gillingham, "Benjamin Lehman, a Germantown Cabinet-Maker," *Pennsylvania Magazine of History and Biography* 54, no. 4 (1930): 289–306; Lita Solis-Cohen, "Rosetta Stone for Philadelphia Furntiure," *Maine Antique Digest* (Waldoboro) 32, no. 3 (March 2004): 26-D to 27-D.

68. Montgomery, *American Furniture: Federal*, pp. 19–26, 488.

69. Montgomery, *American Furniture: Federal*, pp. 21–23; Sullivan, *Industrial Worker in Pennsylvania*, chap. 6, appendix B, pp. 119–43, 221–30; Catalano, "Cabinetmaking in Philadelphia," pp. 81–91; Rock, *Artisans of the New Republic*, pp. 243, 264–65, 272–80, 286–88.

70. Spinning wheel production data are scattered throughout the 1820 Census of Manufactures.

71. Alexander Walker, *Virginia Herald*, November 27, 1804, citation file, MESDA; Daniel Nields, *American Republican*, February 11, 1840, and James Renshaw inventory, 1857, Phoenixville, Pa., as quoted in Schiffer, *Furniture of Chester County*, pp. 169, 206; Edwin Wood estate records, 1855, Bridgeport, Conn., Genealogical Section, CSL.

72. James Gere ledger, 1809–29, CSL; Asa Nichols estate records, 1829, Worcester Co., Worcester, Mass., Registry of Probate; Henry J. Harlow, "The Shop of Samuel Wing, Craftsman of Sandwich, Massachusetts," *Antiques* 93, no. 3 (March 1968): 376; Keno, "Windsor Chair Makers of Northampton," p. 7; Shorey in Franklin McDuffee, *History of the Town of Rochester, from 1722 to 1890* (Manchester, N.H.: J. B. Clarke, 1892), as quoted in Charles S. Parsons, New Hampshire Notes, VRC; Deveikis, "Hastings Warren," p. 1038.

73. West estate records; Deveikis, "Hastings Warren," p. 1038; Thomas Boynton invoice book, 1815–25, DC (microfilm, DCM); Shorey in McDuffee, *History of Rochester*, as quoted in Parsons, New Hampshire Notes; Harlow, "Samuel Wing," p. 375; Alexander Shaw estate records, 1828, City and County of Philadelphia, Register of Wills; Joseph Jones, *Village Record* (West Chester, Pa.), December 22, 1824, as quoted in Schiffer, *Furniture of Chester County*, p. 132; William Moore, Jr., insolvency records, 1830, Barkhamstead, Conn., Genealogical section, CSL.

74. Moore insolvency records; Harlow, "Samuel Wing," p. 375; John French estate records, 1848, New London, Conn., Genealogical Section, CSL; Cromwell, "Andrew and Robert McKim," p. 6; Boynton ledger, 1817–47; Hil-

dreth in *Brooklyn Directory, for 1833–34* (Brooklyn, N.Y.: Nichols and Delaree, 1833), p. 41.

75. Arcularius in Lewis Nichols, *Brooklyn Directory, for the Years 1837–38* (Brooklyn, N.Y.: A. Spooner and Sons, 1837), p. 14; Houghton Bulkeley, "John I. Wells, Cabinetmaker-Inventor," *Connecticut Historical Society Bulletin* 26, no. 3 (July 1961): 67–72; Gill in *Matchett's Baltimore Directory* (Baltimore: [Richard J. Matchett], 1831), n.p.; Robert Crage ledger, 1757–81, OSV.

76. Thompson letter to Cheney; Martin Bracket estate records, 1840, Franklin Co., Greenfield, Mass., Registry of Probate; William H. MacDonald, *Central New Jersey Chairmaking of the Nineteenth Century* (Trenton, N.J.: By the author, 1960), p. 42.

77. James Hallet, Jr., David Brientnall, Jr., and Reuben Odell insolvency records, 1811–14, 1811, and 1812, QC; insolvency notice, James Whitaker, *Relf's Philadelphia Gazette and Daily Advertiser* (Philadelphia), February 5, 1812 (reference courtesy of Deborah D. Waters). The insolvent New York chairmakers were Michael Fassauer (1816), Nathaniel S. Rose (1821), Richard Cornwell (1817), Charles Craft (1820), William Schureman (1823), Henry Dean (1820), and John DeWitt (1819), as identified in insolvency records, QC. Sheriff's sale, Zenos Bronson, *North Carolina Star* (Raleigh), March 3, 1815, as quoted in James H. Craig, *The Arts and Crafts in North Carolina, 1699–1840* (Winston-Salem, N.C.: Old Salem, 1965), pp. 183–84, 186; insolvency notice, William and Moses Bullock, *Carlisle Gazette* (Carlisle, Pa.), December 16, 1823 (reference courtesy of the late Milton Flower).

78. Ada R. Chase, "Two 18th-Century Craftsmen of Norwich," *Connecticut Historical Society Bulletin* 25, no. 3 (July 1960): 87; insolvency notice, John Karnes, *American Citizen and General Advertiser* (New York), October 6, 1801, as quoted in Gottesman, *Arts and Crafts, 1800–1804*, p. 148; Tuck in Buckingham, *Annals*, p. 37; Thomas Ash II and William Ash I, insolvency records, 1811, QC; Allen/Holmes property attachment, 1843, Superior Court Records, New London Co., Conn., CSL.

79. Insolvency notice, Thomas Ash II, *New-York Enquirer* (New York), March 24, 1829, and Joseph Riley insolvency records, 1825, QC; David Finch insolvency records, 1829–30, Bridgeport, Conn., Genealogical Section, CSL; Kenney, *Hitchcock Chair*, pp. 100–104, 108–15; John E. Hartman assigned estate, 1842, Chester Co., West Chester, Pa., Prothonotary Office, as quoted in Schiffer, *Furniture of Chester County*, pp. 108–10; insolvency notice, Henry Shepherd, *Chillicothe Advertiser* (Chillicothe, Ohio), August 1, 1835 (reference courtesy of John R. Grabb); White journal.

80. Trumble in Nancy A. Goyne (Evans), "Francis Trumble of Philadelphia: Windsor Chair and Cabinetmaker," in *Winterthur Port-*

folio 1, ed. Milo M. Naeve (Winterthur, Del.: Winterthur Museum, 1964), p. 240; Jesse Foster lawsuit vs. Josiah Willard, 1798–99, SLL (reference courtesy of Charles A. Hammond and John T. Kirk); McKeen-Adams lawsuit; Andrew Hagerty lawsuit vs. Lawrence Allwine, 1787, DCM; nonpayment notice, George W. Grimes, *Star, and North Carolina State Gazette* (Raleigh), April 26, 1816, citation file, MESDA.

81. Carl Bridenbaugh, *Cities in Revolt: Urban Life in America, 1743–1776* (New York: Aflred A. Knopf, 1955), pp. 98–107, 292–96; New York fire in John Pintard, "Reminiscences," Papers of John Pintard, New-York Historical Society, New York; Norfolk fire in Wallace B. Gusler, *Furniture of Williamsburg and Eastern Virginia, 1710–1790* (Richmond: Virginia Museum, 1979), p. 151; Olney Winsor letters to wife, [January] 18, 1787, and February 4, 1788, Letters of Olney Winsor, 1786–88, Virginia State Library, Richmond.

82. Fire notice, John Nutt, *Gazette of the State of Georgia*, May 11, 1786, citation file, MESDA; Newburyport fire in Sarah Anna Emery, *Reminiscences of a Nonagenarian* (Newburyport, Mass.: William H. Huse, 1879), pp. 261–69, and fire notice, *Norfolk Gazette and Publick Ledger* (Norfolk, Va.), June 10, 1811, citation file, MESDA; fire notice, John Conrad, *Federal Gazette and Baltimore Daily Advertiser*, December 18, 1805, citation file, MESDA; fire notice, Robert McKim, *Virginia Argus*, February 17, 1816, citation file, MESDA, and Cromwell, "Andrew and Robert McKim," pp. 16–17.

83. Lightning damage described in William Franklin letter to Benjamin Franklin, July 12, 1753, Franklin Papers, vol. 50, APS, and Goyne, "Francis Trumble," p. 225; Abraham Ritter, *Philadelphia and Her Merchants as Constituted Fifty and Seventy Years Ago* (Philadelphia: By the author, 1860), p. 122; William and Thomas Mitchell, *Pennsylvania Packet*, December 2, 1799, as quoted in Alfred Coxe Prime, comp., *The Arts and Crafts in Philadelphia, Maryland, and South Carolina, 1786–1800* (Topsfield, Mass.: Walpole Society, 1932), p. 192; fire notice, Lawrence Allwine, *Raleigh Register and North Carolina State Gazette* (Raleigh), April 1801 (reference courtesy of Paula Welshimer Locklair); Francis Shallus, *Chronological Tables for Every Day in the Year*, 2 vols. (Philadelphia: Merritt, 1817), 1:89.

84. Fire notice, John I. Post, *New-York Gazette and General Advertiser* (New York), January 5, 1801, as quoted in Gottesman, *Arts and Crafts, 1800–1804*, p. 171; Elizabeth de Hart Bleecker diary, 1799–1806, New York Public Library, New York (hereafter cited NYPL); fire notice, Karnes and Hazlet, *Petersburg Republican* (Petersburg, Va.), September 20, 1803, citation file, MESDA.

85. Tontine fire in Keno, "Windsor Chair Makers of Northampton," pp. 17, 21, 24–25, 132; Kenney, *Hitchcock Chair*, pp. 103, 160–61; Atwa-

ter, *History of New Haven*, pp. 587–88; Earle G. Shettleworth, Jr., and William D. Barry, "Walter Corey's Furniture Manufactory in Portland, Maine," *Antiques* 121, no. 5 (May 1982): 1204.

86. *Diary of William Bentley*, 2:263, 3:219, 466, 4:182; Deveikis, "Hastings Warren," pp. 1038–39.

87. Sikes, *Furniture Makers of Cincinnati*, pp. 42, 45, 127, 142, 220. The flood at Wilder's chair manufactory occurred about 1869, Parsons, Wilder Family Notes. David Ruth, *Raleigh Register*, July 12, 1810, citation file, MESDA.

88. Ash robbery in Kenneth Scott, comp., *Rivington's New York Newspaper: Excerpts from a Loyalist Press, 1773–1783* (New York: New-York Historical Society, 1973), p. 95; Gabriel Leggett, *Boston Gazette* (Boston), May 23, 1791; swindler notice, Joseph Kerm, *Clarion and Tennessee Gazette* (Nashville), February 23, 1813, citation file, MESDA; Seth Sumpter, *Brookville Enquirer* (Brookville, Ind.), September 11, 1824, as quoted in Walters, *Furniture Makers of Indiana*, p. 19.

89. LeRoy B. DePuy, "The Walnut Street Prison: Pennsylvania's First Penitentiary," reprint, *Pennsylvania History* 18, no. 2 (April 1951): 2–5; Carl David Arfwedson, *The United States and Canada*, 2 vols. (1834; reprint, New York: Johnson Reprint Corp., 1969), 2:193.

90. DePuy, "Walnut Street Prison," pp. 11–12; Jacob Cox Parsons, ed., *Extracts from the Diary of Jacob Hiltzheimer* (Philadelphia: William F. Fell, 1893), p. 241; prison notice, *Pennsylvania Packet*, January 3, 1798, as quoted in Prime, *Arts and Crafts, 1786–1800*, p. 321; Kenneth Roberts and Anna M. Roberts, eds. and trans., *Moreau de St. Méry's American Journey, [1793–1798]* (Garden City, N.Y.: Doubleday, 1947), p. 152; *Diary of William Bentley*, 1:278; Melish, *Travels*, 1:161.

91. H. W. Flournoy, ed., *Calendar of Virginia State Papers, 1799–1807* (Richmond, 1890), 9:477–79.

92. Prison notice, *Trenton Federalist*, August 15, 1808; John W. Barber and Henry Howe, *Historical Collections of the State of New Jersey* (Newark: Benjamin Olds, 1844), p. 288; Lewis Cass Aldrich and Frank R. Holmes, *History of Windsor County, Vermont* (Syracuse, N.Y.: D. Mason, 1891), p. 321; Boynton ledger, 1811–17; Odell and Rose insolvency records; [Thomas Eddy], *An Account of the State Prison or Penitentiary House in the City of New York* (New York: Isaac Collins and Sons, 1801), pp. 17–19, 33–34; *The Aristocratic Journey: Being the Outspoken Letters of Mrs. Basil Hall*, ed. Una Pope-Hennessy (New York: G. P. Putnam's Sons, 1931), p. 21.

93. W. David Lewis, *From Newgate to Dannemora: The Rise of the Penitentiary in New York, 1796–1848* (Ithaca, N.Y.: Cornell University Press, 1965), pp. 44, 178–79, 180–86; [Gideon Miner Davison], *Traveller's Guide*, 6th ed. (Saratoga Springs, N.Y.: G. M. Davison,

1834), p. 216; *Report of Gershom Powers, Agent and Keeper of the State Prison at Auburn . . . January 7, 1828* (Albany, N.Y.: Croswell and Van Benthuysen, 1828), frontispiece, pp. 9–13.

94. *Report of Gershom Powers*, pp. 45–46; *Annual Reports of the Inspectors of the Auburn State Prison* (Auburn, N.Y.: Croswell and Van Benthuysen, 1829, 1834, 1835).

95. Prison notice, *Rochester Daily Advertiser* (Rochester, N.Y.), July 26, 1830, as quoted in Wendell Garrett, ed., "Clues and Footnotes," *Antiques* 110, no. 5 (November 1976): 1082; John Seymour, *Cayuga Patriot* (Auburn, N.Y.), March 12, 1834 (reference courtesy of Wendell Hilt); *Annual Reports of Auburn State Prison*; W. A. Palmer bill to William S. Stow, September 21, 1840, DeLancey Stow Memorial Collection, NYPL.

96. Prison notice, *Auburn Daily Advertiser* (Auburn, N.Y.), May 20, 1843 (reference courtesy of Thomas G. Eldred); Lewis, *Newgate to Dannemora*, pp. 182–83; Joan Lynn Schild, "Furniture Makers of Rochester, New York," *New York History* 37, no. 1 (January 1956): 99; W. John McIntyre, "Arms Across the Border: Trade in Chairs and Chair Parts between the United States and Upper Canada," in *Victorian Furniture: Essays from a Victorian Society Autumn Symposium*, ed. Kenneth L. Ames, published as *Nineteenth Century* (Victorian Society in America) 8, nos. 3, 4 (1982): 59–60; French in Joan Mackinnon, *A Checklist of Toronto Cabinet and Chair Makers, 1800–1865*, National Museum of Man Mercury Series (Ottawa: National Museums of Canada, 1975), p. 52.

97. Kenney, *Hitchcock Chair*, pp. 98–99, 112; "Statements and Answers of Amos Pilsbury, Warden of the Connecticut State Prison, to Sundry Questions of the Committee on the State Prison Appointed by the General Assembly of 1841," Connecticut State Prison Records, 1827–42, CSL; papers relating to the Connecticut State Prison in Wethersfield and Newgate Prison in East Granby, 1820–54, Mrs. Mary E. Welles Collection, CSL; *Report of the Directors and Warden of the Connecticut State Prison* (Hartford, Conn.: Hezekiah Howe, 1830), p. 14.

98. Smith Ely bond and schedule of work with Gurdon H. Montague, warden, Connecticut State Prison, October 2, 1832, DCM; "Statements and Answers of Amos Pillsbury," pp. 71–73, 81.

99. D. C. Y. Moore agreement with Amos Pillsbury, warden, Connecticut State Prison, June 2, 1834, DCM.

100. "Statements and Answers of Amos Pillsbury," pp. 15, 78–79, 81, 85, 94, 97, 99; papers relating to the Connecticut State Prison, Welles Collection.

101. [Anne Newport Royall], *Sketches of History, Life, and Manners in the United States* (New Haven, Conn.: By the author, 1826), p. 318; Timothy T. Sawyer, *Old Charlestown* (Boston: James H. West, 1902), pp. 57, 70, 85, 156; *Co-*

lumbian Centinel (Boston), September 5, 1810, and April 13, 1811.

102. Prison notice, *Argus of Western America* (Frankfort, Ky.), July 22, 1826, as referred to in Clement Eaton, *The Growth of Southern Civilization, 1790–1860* (New York: Harper, 1961), pp. 167–68; Anne Newport Royall, *Mrs. Royall's Southern Tour, or Second Series of the Black Book*, 3 vols. (Washington, D.C.: By the author, 1831), 2:124–25; prison notice, *Milledgeville Journal* (Milledgeville, Ga.), April 1, 1821, as quoted in *Neat Pieces: The Plain-Style Furniture of 19th-Century Georgia* (Atlanta: Atlanta Historical Society, 1983), p. 8.

103. William W. Chambers, *Things as They Are in America* (Philadelphia: Lippincott, Grambo, 1854), pp. 309–11; Warren in Page Talbott, "Cheapest, Strongest, and Best Chairmaking in 19th-Century Philadelphia, Part 1," *Early American Industries Association Chronicle* 33, no. 2 (June 1980): 30; Joan Mackinnon, *Kingston Cabinetmakers, 1800–1867*, National Museum of Man Mercury Series (Ottawa: National Museums of Canada, 1976), pp. 95–112; Sullivan, *Industrial Worker in Pennsylvania*, p. 83; Lewis, *Newgate to Dannemora*, pp. 187, 190–91; Baltimore mechanics' petition, January 14, 1819, Maryland Legislative Proceedings, House of Delegates, as reported in *Maryland Gazette* (Annapolis), January 21, 1819, citation file, MESDA.

CHAPTER 2

Facilities, Equipment, and Materials

The American craftsman came into his own during the eighteenth century. A popular symbol adopted to express "the perfect knowledge of a mechanic Art" was the "strong Arm with the Hand grasping the lifted Hammer," as featured on the membership certificate of the New York Mechanick Society (fig. 2-1). The document depicts the craftsman as the backbone of American society. Social awareness and benevolence, principal tenets of mechanic societies in the postrevolutionary years, are expressed at the upper right in concern over the welfare of deceased members' families. Opposite, the figures of Liberty and Industry face the new American nation (an Indian, or Native American), where the arts are free to flourish. The small figures of a plowman and fisherman (lower left) demonstrate the nation's bond with field and stream for sustenance. Upstream the waterwheel of a mill identifies a renewable energy source so vital to industrial stability, and the forest suggests the importance of raw materials to industrial growth. The stream winding into the interior and the ship on the stocks are oblique references to the importance of commerce, communication, and transportation in advancing the mechanic arts.[1]

Facilities and Equipment

THE SHOP

Artisans formed the second-largest occupational group in America, next to the husbandmen, until the mid-nineteenth century. Indeed, numbers of craftsmen were part-time farmers. Some chairmakers owned their home and shop. City dwellers often rented a property or leased the ground, and until the postrevolutionary period shop and dwelling frequently were combined under one roof. Rural craftsmen generally occupied a "homestead farm" where the shop and home stood apart. In the early nineteenth century simple one- or two-room shops slowly gave way to the "manufactory" followed by the factory, where ofttimes a series of buildings housed individual operations. A growing national population and widening foreign markets stimulated production. Business expansion led to development of the furniture wareroom, a small facility that stocked ready-made goods in a selection of patterns, woods, and paints.[2]

John Fanning Watson commented on business in prerevolutionary Philadelphia: "The late aged John Warder, Esq., told me that in his younger days he never knew of more than five or six persons at most, in the whole city, who did not live on the same spot where they pursued their business." Francis Trumble, cabinetmaker and Windsor-chair maker, occupied a rented house in 1753, "one of a continued Row on the West Side of Second Street." The insurance policy referred to "the Joyners business being carried on there." Indeed, even late in the century when annual trade directories were introduced, the incidence of dual addresses among chairmakers was moderate—about 50 percent at Boston and considerably less at Philadelphia and New York. In 1825 Charles Robinson still combined house and shop in one

FIG. 2-1 Membership certificate of the New York Mechanick Society, drawn and engraved by Abraham Godwin, New York, 1786 (engraved), 1791 (inscribed). Etching; H. 8½", W. 11⅛". *(Courtesy, Winterthur Museum, Winterthur, Del., acc. 58.1797.)*

frame building at Philadelphia: the workroom and kitchen occupied the first floor, family living quarters the second floor and garret. Single-room shops in the dwelling also were the rule at Ashburnham, Massachusetts, after 1800, when the chairmaking industry of northern Worcester County was in its infancy. Other records document the practice elsewhere.[3]

Urban chairmakers with separate home and business addresses usually lived in the immediate shop area. In 1809 William Ash I's residence was three blocks north of his John Street shop in lower Manhattan. Some homes and businesses stood side by side. Reuben Odell dwelt at 176 Duane Street; his shop occupied No. 178. David Alling's residence at Newark, New Jersey, stood between his two commercial properties. Robert McKim of Richmond, Virginia, resided in a brick tenement across a six-foot alley from his workshop.[4]

Young craftsmen frequently occupied rental properties. The estate of Henry Prall, victim of a yellow fever epidemic in Philadelphia in 1802, was entirely consumed by rents due. New York jury lists of the early 1800s record master chairmakers who rented along with their journeymen. Even in rural Barre, Massachusetts, chairmaker Luke Houghton rented his shop.[5]

Business papers of the Philadelphia Monthly Meeting of Friends record the lease of a 17-by-50-foot property in Front Street at Keyes Alley for almost half a century to a succession of Windsor-chair makers and provide insights into typical urban leasing practices. Joseph Henzey, the first chairmaking tenant, occupied the premises about March 1773. A lease drawn in May 1774 describes a frame tenement that served as a home and shop and rented for £12 annually. The next tenant made improvements valued at £70 for which the Friends reimbursed him in 1790. By 1791 William Love rented the premises for £40 per annum paid quarterly. He was not the best tenant, however, and by March 1798 the Committee of Twelve, which administered Meeting properties, was concerned. The chairmaker made payment but was in arrears again the next quarter, when his lease was canceled.

John B. Ackley leased the property on July 14, 1798, at the same rate. In 1808 the Committee raised the annual rent to £50 and drew new "Articles of Agreement" for the property, described as "a certain House and Frame wood shop situate in Front Street." When chairmaker Jonathan Tyson took over the lease in January 1811, the property was in need of repair. The Committee hired carpenter John Hutchinson to shingle and weatherboard, replace sills, make a cellar door, put "new posts and rails round [the] roof," and erect a new fence. The cost exceeded half the annual rent of $200 (£60). Tyson remained until September 1815, when he was followed by Daniel Teese, although Tyson returned a year later when the two men formed an association. The cycle of Windsor-chair making at the Front Street property ended in 1818 when the partnership was dissolved.[6]

Wooden framing was the most common shop construction between 1750 and 1850, although other types were sufficiently well known. Early in the period log structures occurred with some regularity throughout rural Pennsylvania. Moravian workers at Bethlehem erected a log house in 1742 for the carpenters and joiners, later occupied by the turners. Chester County log shops varied in size from 15 by 12 feet to 20 by 20 feet, one described as "part Stone part Logs." In neighboring Lancaster in the 1810s the Fetter brothers (fig. 5-38) resided on a rental property containing a "one story frame dwelling house and half lot of ground with a log shop adjoining and some brick buildings." The owner occupied the frame; the Fetters may have erected the brick buildings. The brothers were permitted "to keep and put up their lumber" on the lot.[7]

As the population moved west, the log structure moved with it. In the 1850s James Wilson, whose weatherboarded 1½-story log shop stood southwest of Pittsburgh, made chairs on the first floor and painted and decorated them in the loft, accessible by an inside ladder. He used a small rear shed for roughing out stock. David Kautz occupied a log shop at Cincinnati, and William McCracken produced Windsor chairs and spinning wheels in a similar structure in Knox County, Indiana. During a trip to the Midwest in 1835 Lambert Hitchcock, an entrepreneur-chairmaker of Connecticut, commented on the extensive use of log construction among settlers.[8]

The wood-framed shop was well known. An old cooper's shop that stood in Middlesex County, Massachusetts, probably approximates the typical woodworking establishment of the postrevolutionary period in size and appearance. The rectangular building, measuring 12 by 20 feet, had a low-gabled, shingled roof and brick chimney; several windows and a door pierced a long facade without architectural embellishment. Samuel Wing's woodworking shop on the Cape at Sandwich was attached to his clapboarded dwelling. In contrast to these simple structures was the large wooden commercial building called the Tontine erected in Northampton near the courthouse in the late eighteenth century. The 100-by-200-foot building stood three stories high. Five cabinetmakers and chairmakers worked there between 1795 and 1813, among them Oliver Pomeroy, who purchased his shop for $100. An adjacent lot probably served to store lumber.[9]

Representations of several Middle Atlantic chair shops depict wooden structures. James Chesney's dark-painted, light-trimmed building stood on State Street, Albany (fig. 2-8). In New York brick buildings flanked John Cowperthwaite's framed

NATHANIEL S. & ELIHU ROSE,
FANCY & WINDSOR CHAIR MAKERS,
NO. 5 WARREN-STREET, NEAR BROADWAY, NEW-YORK,

Where they have the most elegant assortment of Chairs, Settees, &c. of the best quality and newest fashions, constantly on hand.

N. B. Old Chairs, Toilet Tables, Wash Stands, Tea Trays, Cornices, Bedsteads, &c. repaired and repainted. Orders thankfully received and punctually attended to.

₊ Merchants and Ship-Masters, will find it particularly advantageous to call at the above store, when in want of the articles. Jan. 1817.

FIG. 2-2 Detail of facsimile advertising sheet of Nathaniel S. Rose and Elihu Rose, New York, 1817 (original). *(Collection of the late Kenneth E. Tuttle; Photo, Winterthur Museum.)*

three-story manufactory and store in Chatham Square. Across the bay David Alling's neat framed and shuttered home, shop, and store all stood in a row on Broad Street, Newark. On Long Island the Dominy family's cabinet and clock shops were extensions of their clapboarded and shingled dwelling, following New England practice.[10]

Philadelphia had its share of small frames, among them Francis Trumble's 13-by-20-foot shop in Southwark and the Mitchells's contemporary shop on Lombard Street, destroyed in 1799 by fire. With 792 square feet John Letchworth's two-story business frame on south Fourth Street had substantial working and storage space. In rural Pennsylvania the chairmaking and paint business of John Cree at Chambersburg filled a one-story frame; the craftsman stored lumber in a back lot. John Oldham's 19-by-30-foot shop in Baltimore stood two stories high, in contrast to Boteler and Donn's modest frame building located behind a grocery on Pennsylvania Avenue in the nation's capital.[11]

Information about new construction is rare, but with an entry reading "Monday the 6th day of August 1804 we began our shop in Duanesburgh," Samuel Silliman described a business venture in New York State with Sylvester Higgins, a fellow craftsman of Connecticut. Both men probably helped to erect the building, used briefly for cabinetmaking. Silliman's accounts provide insights into the appearance and fabric of the structure. Horses drew wagonloads of materials to the site, where framing took two days. The shingle-roof building had a stone foundation, and masons who received $11 "by the job" built a brick chimney. Finishing materials included "harth stones," "bench stuff," and sand and lime for plastering. Silliman ended by noting, "The whole amount of building our shop was 290 Dols 94 Cents." The cabinetmaker gave some "account of stuff to build with," itemizing pine boards, nails, shingles, bricks, lath, glass, Spanish white for paint, and an iron manteltree.[12]

Brick shops, although not as common as framed structures, were present in some number, and stone is mentioned occasionally. At Hartford John I. Wells advertised in 1806 that he had "removed his Furniture to the second and third story of JOHN DODD jun'rs Brick Store." In 1839 Edward Bulkley of New Haven lost to creditors his "four story brick building in Orange Street occupied . . . as a chair makers shop." When Edward and Francis Birge commenced business in Troy, New York, they leased a new "brick building . . . fifty [feet] wide front and rear and sixty feet deep"; it rose "four stories high above the cellar." Although touted as fireproof, brick construction did not guarantee immunity. The three-story brick paint manufactory of Lawrence Allwine at Philadelphia was consumed in only a few minutes in April 1801 when fire broke out.[13]

Depictions of craft shops on advertisements and billheads became popular during the 1820s. Frederick Starr's 3½-story establishment in Rochester, New York, is clearly delineated with a brick or dressed-stone facade (fig. 4-32). A front railing protected passersby from street traffic. Thomas Ash II's chair manufactory at New York was brick with stone lintels and sills (fig. 4-36), whereas the two-story masonry shop of Nathaniel and Elihu Rose featured a large, twenty-pane window on the ground floor (fig. 2-2). The line of chairs inverted on the roof coping above the sign may represent aggressive merchandising or simply a solution to drying paint above the street dust. In contrast are the rows of tall, vertical buildings typical of urban centers several decades later (fig. 3-33).[14]

Floor space in eighteenth-century facilities generally was modest compared to that typical of structures following the War of 1812. A small chair-shop in Philadelphia occupied by Caleb Emlen in the 1740s stood on a lot fronting only 15 feet on Chestnut Street. Half a century later Benjamin Love's chairmaking shop in Frankford outside the city contained an upper "Cockloft," or attic, adding half a story. Shop space in neighboring rural Chester County in the 1790s and later varied from as little as 180 square feet to more than 720 square feet. More spacious was the four-story establishment at Baltimore occupied in the 1810s by the Finlay brothers. The structure had a 30-foot room on each floor.[15]

To accommodate his expanding business in 1803 John Wadsworth of Hartford built a "new Factory, directly back of his old Shop." Cabinetmakers Joel Lyons and Isaac Miles had similar needs at Greenfield, Massachusetts, four decades later when they took over all the stock and three shop benches of Francis A. Birge. As noted by apprentice Edward Jenner Carpenter, they began "tearing out to make room for more hands." Soon Carpenter reported that two new journeymen, "Dick & David, have been fitting up their benches today ready to go into it tomorrow. It makes a pretty good shop full, 4 jours, 2 apprentices & 2 bosses, & they have advertised for another apprentice." The shops of bachelors Alexander Brown and Barnes and Seaton in Virginia contained "sleeping rooms."[16]

A few woodworking shops began modestly in makeshift quarters and were never improved. At his death in 1814 James Blauvelt, a cartmaker, owned a "Shop or Shed Situate in the rear of James Gridley's Blacksmith's Shop" on Walker Street, New York. A lease drawn at Boston between cabinetmakers William Fisk and Samuel Payson identifies a barn behind Payson's shop "occupied by Samuel Horton as & for a chair makers shop." Lambert Hitchcock also commenced modestly about 1818 in a small lean-to attached to a sawmill on the Farmington River in Connecticut, although he soon erected a brick building and a waterwheel. By then turning mills located at a water source were becoming common in New England. Before 1840 Daniel Foot of Lee, Massachusetts, occupied a "Turning shop & dwelling with water privilege—Dam, flume & fixed Machinery" worth $895.[17]

GROUNDS AND LOCATION

Frequently chairmakers' properties contained structures and facilities other than the shop and home. Charles Chase's town site on Nantucket Island included a barn, outbuildings, fences, and part interest in a neighborhood well. "A good stable & Smokehouse adjoining" were features of John Humes's real estate in Cincinnati. Joel Brown of Raleigh, North Carolina, enjoyed "a garden well laid out, rich and productive."[18]

Chairmaking craftsmen who resided on a rural "homestead" often occupied a shop near the dwelling, and a common auxiliary structure was a barn. Among this group was Ebenezer Tracy, Sr., of Connecticut, whose "Home Farm [of] 165 Acres" contained a dwelling, shop, barn, corn house and shed, weaving house, and the "Elijah Tracy lott & barn [of] 16 Acres." William Moore, Jr.'s, 2-acre property at Barkhamstead contained a brick dwelling, "Chair shops," and an "Acquduct," or race, that powered the apparatus driving the shop equipment. Some barns served as storage. That of Abijah Wilder at Keene, New Hampshire, contained pine and hardwood lumber, and the barnyard served for additional wood storage. Peter Willard used his "waggon house" at Sterling, Massachusetts, for the same purpose. Almon Preston had a wagon shed and "hog house" on his property at Wallingford, Connecticut.[19]

Property size varied considerably. With just a few acres New Englanders James Comee and Amasa Elwell probably maintained only kitchen gardens and animals sufficient to provide labor and a supply of dairy and meat products. Among large farms that of Amos Denison Allen in Connecticut contained 190 acres, and William Rogers resided on 228 acres in Vermont. Property advertisements provide further insights. Stephen Ross of Salisbury, New Hampshire, offered in 1815 a farm "situated on the turnpike Road between the two Meeting Houses containing twenty acres of good land, a good two story dwelling house, a good barn and a shop and stock suitable for the cabinet and chair making business." Three decades later Joseph F. Loring's estate near Sterling, Massachusetts, contained "about 70 acres of first rate land equally divided into mowing, pasturing and tillage with the Buildings thereon, a large two story House, Barn 20 feet by 30 with two Sheds. There is Water at both

House and Barn conveyed in lead pipes from a never failing spring, Likewise a Chair and paint Shop with a small Dwelling House adjoining. The buildings are all in good repair."[20]

Wooded lands provided a reliable source of inexpensive timber that the craftsman could cut and carry to the local sawmill. Joseph N. Dow's woodlot in Coventry, Connecticut, contained about 8 acres. Holdings in well-wooded Worcester County, Massachusetts, were slightly larger, and in neighboring Framingham David Haven and son Abner divided woodlots totaling 31 acres. Walter Corey secured timber for his manufactory at Portland, Maine, from lots in and around Sebago Lake, probably floating the timber down the Presumpscot River to his mill in Windham.[21]

A few craftsmen erected sawmills. A document of 1818 identifies Eli Wood's "Saw-Mill near the Dwelling House" at Barkhamstead, Connecticut, and his "Spencer Saw-Mill & Small Barn." Beginning in 1817 mills and millponds are mentioned in land records of Calvin Bedortha at Springfield, Massachusetts. At midcentury one of Solomon Rich's many tracts in Searsburg, Vermont, contained a sawmill worth $900.[22]

Shop location frequently was critical to a chairmaker's success. Directory listings in Philadelphia and New York for a forty-five-year period describe the urban patterns. In 1795 Philadelphia chairmakers were concentrated on or near three streets paralleling the docks in the seven blocks between Pine and Vine. Of the chairmakers residing beyond this area, only two seem to have had success. As members of the Society of Friends, Francis Trumble and John Letchworth had many contacts, and both were aggressive businessmen. In contrast, John Chapman, also a Quaker, gave up chairmaking to become keeper of buildings and grounds for the Friends' Monthly Meeting. By 1820 the chairmakers occupied a larger area, although the pattern had not changed significantly. Activity along the Delaware River now extended into Southwark and the Northern Liberties to form a long, shallow triangle with its apex at Eighth and Ninth streets. Central density still extended only to Third and Fourth streets. Chairmakers George C. Lentner and Charles C. Robinson, located west of the Schuylkill River, found good trade in a new residential area. The pattern in 1840 was one of greater density, with activity concentrated near the waterfront and proportionally fewer chairmakers in fringe areas. Waterborne commerce dominated commercial life in the chairmaking community.[23]

Lower Manhattan in 1795 constituted the business and population center of New York. Most chairmakers were located south of City Hall, with only a few to the northeast in a section that today contains approaches to the Manhattan and Brooklyn bridges. By 1819 chairmakers located on the island's tip were concentrated between the East River and William Street. North of City Hall, however, there had been a veritable explosion, and dozens of shops spanned the island as far north as Greenwich Village and the Bowery. Two decades later the same northern areas still housed most of the city's chairmakers, with heavy concentration in part of present-day Chinatown and northeast toward the Williamsburg Bridge. Along the Hudson the business community crept northward around Greenwich, although a brisk trade remained at the island's tip surrounding the present financial district and in lower Broad, Pearl, and Greenwich streets.[24]

Outside the large cities factors other than population shift influenced the chairmaking business. "Main Street," the major thoroughfare in smaller communities, generally attracted business. Cyrus Cleaveland and Henry Farley located advantageously on principal streets in Providence, Rhode Island, and Concord, New Hampshire. A site on the busy Vermont "highway leading from Bennington Meeting House to Safford's mill" served the firm of Dewey and Woodworth, and land in Bristol County, Massachusetts, occupied by Abraham Shove bordered on roads leading to the "new Freetown furnace," a local sawmill, and Slades Ferry. Cabinetmakers Abraham and James Bennett kept shop at Hammorton, Pennsylvania, a village located on the state and stage road from Philadelphia to Baltimore at the juncture of the Wilmington road.[25]

Close proximity to public buildings was a boon to some chairmakers. Silas Cheney located near the busy county courthouse in Litchfield, Connecticut. Once in 1819 when a neighborhood boy was rowdy he charged the boy's father 12¢ for "your boy breaking Glass out [of] Shop." Ebenezer P. Rose of Trenton, New Jersey, found an excellent site "in Second street . . . opposite the State-house." A location near the basin along the James River Canal, a busy access route to the interior, stimulated business at Robert McKim's shop in Richmond, Virginia. In New York State Thomas Kinsela's property at Schenectady backed up to the Erie Canal, and David Dexter was well situated for similar access. Dexter's mill site on the Black River in Jefferson County (fig. 2-30) communicated with Lyons Falls, where a connector canal led to the Erie. Another short water carriage through Watertown gave Dexter access to Lake Ontario and markets in Canada.[26]

SHOP SIGNS

When Brissot de Warville arrived in Philadelphia in 1788, he praised the city plan but found in its precision problems for the newcomer. Describing the difficulties of finding one's way in American communities where rapid growth negated attempts at orderly systems of building identification, he remarked, "Philadelphia is built on a regular plan; long and large streets cross each other at right angles: this regularity . . . is at first embarrassing to a stranger . . . especially as the streets are not inscribed, and the doors not numbered." Despite his annoyance, the Frenchman praised "the shops, which adorn the principal streets [as] remarkable for their neatness." In the absence of building numbers craftsmen and businessmen commonly identified their premises with a sign on the front of the building or suspended over the entrance. Many were pictorial, and the emblems often described the proprietor's occupation, since literacy still was by no means widespread. Printed signs were more common in the nineteenth century. Typical insignia might include the easy chair of an upholsterer, the tankard of a silversmith, or the chariot and phaeton of a coachmaker. So important were signs in the commercial world that even in small communities like Tisbury on Martha's Vineyard painted boards hung over shop doors "as ostentatiously as though the place contained many thousand inhabitants."[27]

Not surprisingly the most common insignia among seating specialists was the chair, as noted at Baltimore in an advertisement of John Oldham, who "removed his Shop, from the corner of Frederick and Market-Street, to the sign of the Chair, in South-Street." A "Large Chair" identified the premises at Boston of Whitney and Brown and the shop of Isaac Barton at Fayetteville, Tennessee. A painted board bearing three chairs served the firm of Gill and Halfpenny in Baltimore. Hector Sanford chose a Windsor chair to identify his shop at Chillicothe, Ohio. The eye-catching "Golden Chair" that served William Seaver and Nathaniel Frost in State Street, Boston, around 1800 was still popular when Edward Bulkley plied his trade in 1830 at New Haven. Equally bright were the red chairs marking the premises in Pennsylvania of both John Denig and Frederick Fox.[28]

To supplement the signboard some craftsmen placed samples of their work outside the shop. Aggressive salesmen could further adorn the building facade with three-dimensional specimens (fig. 2-2). Owen McGarvey of Montreal also suspended a rocking chair over his front entrance, although these "signs" were not confined to large cities. In Bethlehem, Pennsylvania, a Moravian community, Charles W. Rauch hung a rocking chair from an extended name board to attract attention (fig. **2-3**).[29]

Some craftsmen painted their own signs, although in large cities where specialization was common the chairmaker could call on an ornamental painter. George Davidson of Boston debited Reuben Sanborn's account in April 1799 for "Painting

FIG. 2-3 Anadeus Reineke, detail of *Main Street, Bethlehem*, Bethlehem, Pa., 1841, copied by Rufus A. Grider, 1856. Wash drawing; w. 4⁵/₁₆", H. 3⅞". *(Collection of Moravian Archives, Bethlehem, Pa.)*

His sine Eighteen Dolars NB gold chair." Within a month Davidson had painted a sign for chairmaker Thomas Cotton Hayward and charged him $10. Moreau de St. Méry took notice of contemporary artisans in Philadelphia who made "a specialty of painting remarkably beautiful signboards with backgrounds of different colors, speckled with gold or silver." In the late 1850s chairmaker-painter William Capen of Portland, Maine, made the "beautiful signs" ornamenting the factory of chairmaker Walter Corey. The cost of executing a sign varied with size, preparation, and ornament. In Hampden, Maine, William H. Reed furnished a cut board for 84¢; he charged another 50¢ for priming and preparation of the ground. Several layers of paint with finish coats of varnish insured weathering ability. Not all signboards hung from shop facades. Paul Jenkins of Kennebunk, Maine, charged Bryant and Worrin (Warren?) 50¢ in December 1837 for "hueing post for Sign to Shop."[30]

Insignia other than chairs identified some shops. In Front Street, Philadelphia, John B. Ackley's spinning wheel was well known. Other craftsmen adopted patriotic symbols. American eagles were the choice of Low and Damon of Concord, New Hampshire, and Mullen and Cowperthwaite of Cincinnati, Ohio. An American flag served William Sweney of West Chester, Pennsylvania. A different sign identified Joel Brown's shop in Petersburg, Virginia, in 1806: a standing, robed "figure of Hope, with a chair in her hand," was contained within a rectangle resembling a pressed-metal profile frame. The chairmaker used the same insignia in an advertisement. Representations of tools were less common among chairmakers than other woodworkers. Secondary boards adorned some premises, such as the "Gilt Sign Terms Cash" in Edward Ball's window-blind shop in New York.[31]

MAJOR EQUIPMENT

FIG. 2-4 Lewis Miller, *Self Portrait*, York, Pa., ca. 1845. Ink and watercolor on paper. *(The York County Heritage Trust, PA; Photo, Winterthur Museum.)*

The Workbench and Framing Bench
Documents supporting this study identify the workbench, lathe, and grindstone as the important large shop equipment. Basic to the operation was the bench, a horizon-

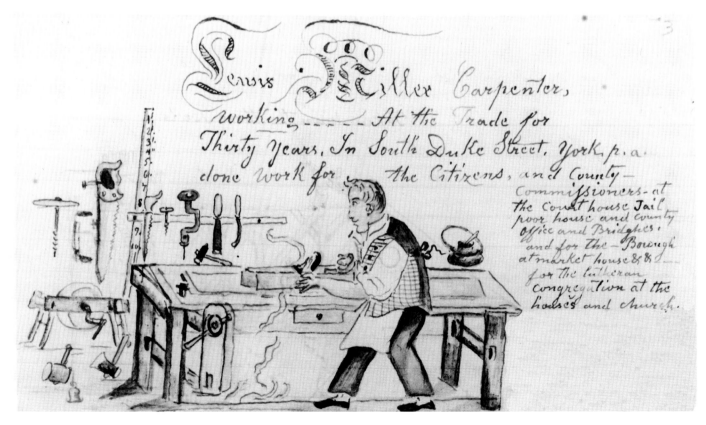

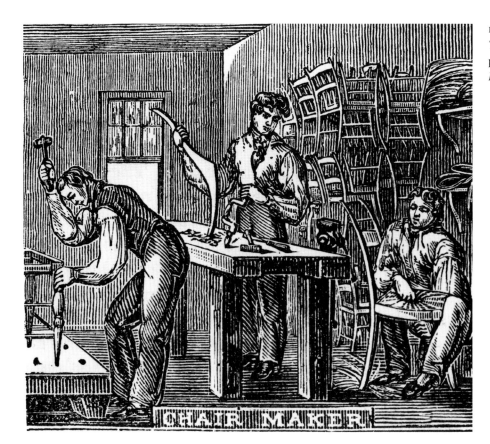

FIG. 2-5 The *Chair Maker*. From Edward Hazen, *The Panorama of Professions and Trades* (Philadelphia: Uriah Hunt, 1836), p. 226. *(Winterthur Library, Winterthur, Del.)*

tal rectangular slab supported on legs usually braced by heavy, rectangular stretchers (fig. **2-4**). Integral to most benches was a large wooden screw, or vise, its jaw fixed parallel to a front corner or vertically along one leg. This device, accompanied by a variety of wooden and metal accessories that socket into the benchtop, held the craftsman's work stationary. The Pennsylvania German carpenter Lewis Miller, who in figure 2-4 depicts himself planing a board secured by a bench stop (left end), sketched a scene familiar in cabinet- and chairmaking shops around the country. Beneath the benchtop a drawer holds small tools and finishing materials; wall racks store larger hand tools. As a benchtop became uneven from wear, it was smoothed with a plane. Windows behind the bench supplied natural light, the principal source of shop illumination.[32]

Chairmakers who pursued their trade intensively also used a low platform designated a framing bench where parts were bored and assembled into complete chairs or frames ready for seating. Early evidence of the low bench dates from prerevolutionary records. A nineteenth-century illustration pictures equipment in an urban shop of some size (fig. **2-5**), judging by the number of workmen and the job specialization. To the right of the framing bench a tall workbench carries a metal vise, the jaws probably lined with wood or leather to protect delicate chair parts.[33]

A shop survey based on about ninety-five documents, principally chairmakers' inventories dating between 1766 and 1877, provides statistics on the prevalence of the workbench: shops containing 1 bench, 24 percent; 2 benches, 36 percent; 3 benches, 11½ percent; 4 benches, 13½ percent; and 5 to 12 benches, 15 percent. Shops that ceased operation in the eighteenth century comprise 13½ percent of the sample, and most fall into the 2-workbench category. Among establishments containing 4 or more workbenches, location was an important factor in shop size. Three classifications are prominent: major cities, smaller seaport towns, and inland towns located at a manufacturing site, county seat, or near a commercial trade route.

The survey provides information on workbench value, which ranged from a low of 50¢ to a high of $14, the mean average about $2.50. Some higher-valued benches

FIG. 2-6 Pole lathe in reconstructed interior of Dominy woodworking shop, Nathaniel Dominy III or Nathaniel Dominy IV, East Hampton, N.Y., 1750–75. White oak, red oak, and ash (microanalysis), with wrought iron; H. 32⅝", L. 77⅝", D. (base) 34½". (*Courtesy, Winterthur Museum, acc. 57.26.372.*)

may have been enumerated complete with equipment. The "stuff" of a bench was described in 1808 as "White oak plank for [a] Work bench" by Robert Whitelaw at Ryegate, Vermont. Ebenezer Knowlton's shop inventory taken at Boston in 1811 specifically itemizes "6 Benches with a Screw to ea[ch]," and five benches in Jacob Cole's shop at Baltimore (1801) had "Doble screws." During the 1830s Cyrus Cleaveland of Providence found the newer "Work Bench with Tail Screw" more suited to his needs. When used with a bench stop this end vise, which was fitted to the right front bench corner and sometimes of L shape, introduced flexibility in securing boards of varying length on the benchtop.[34]

The Lathe

The chairmaker produced his round work using a pole lathe, great wheel lathe, or treadle lathe, the power supplied by human labor, a horse, water, or steam. Joseph Moxon illustrated all three machines in his *Mechanick Exercises* of 1678 and later. The simple pole lathe (fig. **2-6**) grew out of an elementary hand-powered tool known in ancient cultures. In this "machine" a foot treadle is the power source, and the delivery vehicle is a cord tied below the lathe bed to the treadle and above it to a spring pole, the center wrapped around the stock to be turned. The turner shaped his stock on the downstroke of the treadle as the work revolved toward him. Upon releasing the footboard, which was returned to a raised position by the action of the spring pole as the stock rotated away from him, the craftsman slightly reduced the pressure of the shaving tool on the work. He steadied his hands or tools on a rest in

FIG. 2-7 The *Turner*. From Edward Hazen, *The Panorama of Professions and Trades* (Philadelphia: Uriah Hunt, 1836), p. 219. *(Winterthur Library.)*

front of the work, and his implements were within easy reach in wall racks or on the lathe bed.[35]

Of prime importance in development of the lathe was the introduction of rotary motion, permitting continuous turning. This was achieved by using a great wheel or by attaching the foot treadle to a cranked axle rotating a large flywheel within the lathe framework (fig. **2-7**) or suspended overhead (figs. 2-12, 3-32). In the cranked-axle machine, a belt attached the flywheel to a mandrel in the lathe bed, which is visible in each view. The mandrel centered a metal rod that passed through the adjacent block of wood, or puppet (fig. 2-12), to the live center, which drove the work to be turned. This "state-of-the-art" one-man flywheel lathe well addressed production needs in the average shop. Of simpler mechanism and greater power was the great wheel lathe, although its cumbersome size and reliance on additional human power were substantial drawbacks. Some lathes were adapted for use with either a flywheel or great wheel (fig. 2-7). Eventually, through systems requiring special gearing, animal, water-, or steam power were utilized for lathe operation. Toward the middle of the nineteenth century variable speed was introduced through various mechanisms.[36]

The lathe's broad valuation in inventories precludes identification by type except when further described, although lathes of substantial value were not powered by poles. "Old" machines ranged from $1 to $5. About 1800 the Cole brothers of Baltimore owned lathes equipped with tool rests appraised at $25 to $36. The "Turning Lathe & apparatus" of Beza White at Boston commanded a figure of $20; it was used with a "Horse power for turning" estimated at $35. Appraisers at Lambert Hitchcock's factory in Connecticut counted six lathes in 1852, two worth about $40 together.[37]

Prices given for new lathes also are variable. About 1800 young Stephen Whipple, who worked in the Boston area, sold or mortgaged a relatively new "lathe and apparatus thereunto belonging" for $58. In rural Charlton, Massachusetts, Chapman Lee supplied cabinetmaker Samuel Thompson with a turning lathe for $15, two benches at $7, and "one set Bench tools" for $2.67. Thomas Boynton, who set up a chair factory in 1812 at Hartland-Windsor, Vermont, recorded expenditures for turning equipment between 1813 and 1827:

May 6, 1813	timber for a Lathe	$ 1.33
Nov. 1813	Manufactory Dr for lathe [metalwork] of [Mr. Gordon]	6.00
Mar. 11, 1814	mending lathe strap	—
June 1, 1814	Tools Dr for 2 turning Lathes ea 35 & 15	50.00
Oct. 18, 1815	[John Parker credit for labor of] making a Lathe	1.50
June 28, 1827	[Asa Watriss credit] fix[ing] Lathe Crank, Drill, &c.	1.00

Boynton appears to have outfitted his shop with treadle lathes. Later he supplied a customer with "a large Lathe Wheel" for $5.[38]

Other records provide more precise descriptions of the lathe. A history of Ashburnham, Massachusetts, states that from about 1805 "the early manufacture of chair stock . . . required only a small room in some part of the dwelling-house, a saw, a frow and a shave, while a foot-lathe [treadle lathe] introduced the owner to the front rank." The four "Double Geer" lathes used in a Connecticut shop before 1826 may have permitted two-speed turning. Pole lathes stood in the shops of John Lambert and Anthony Steel at Philadelphia in the 1790s, although both men also owned "wheel" lathes. In fact, the great wheel lathe is named more often than any other in American records through the mid-nineteenth century. John Avery of Preston, Connecticut, made lathes for members of the Tracy family priced from about $4.50 to $7. Items for "Lathe boxes" and sets of "Wheel Boxes," or bearings, *suggest* that the Tracys, who are known to have had a labor force of journeymen and apprentices, employed great wheel lathes.[39]

Notes on repairs and replacements amplify the picture. Straps, belts, and bands, some identified as leather, transferred power from flywheels or great wheels to the shop lathe. Gearing, cranks, and spindles are mentioned in other records. Josiah Briggs of Vermont constructed a turning lathe in 1826 that cost $8; he charged an additional 75¢ for "makeing [tool] rests." Another attachment, called a steady rest today, was anchored in the lathe bed behind the work and supported material "too long and slender to bear the action of the tool without yielding" (whipping). This brace was "brought close up" to the work to prevent it "from being bent or broken by the tool."[40]

Large shops usually owned more than one lathe. In 1806 appraisers counted seven at William Ryder's turnery in New York, each identified by location, thereby illuminating equipment placement:

1 Turning lathe in [east side?] of the shop	£9.12.0
1 Turning lathe in west side of the shop	8.0.0
1 turning lathe in front, 1 in the back side of sd shop	8.0.0
1 little turning lathe in front of sd shop	1.12.0
1 Large ditto for turning Columns in the Cellar	1.12.0
1 Ditto [for] Iron work only	10.0.0

As the appraisers detailed no energy source, power must have been supplied by human labor, using foot treadles and possibly a great wheel.[41]

Alternative power sources were already being tapped and used to advantage. By the 1830s some craftsmen successfully operated their lathes by horsepower. The power source of greatest potential, however, was water. John Peterson, a turner near Wilmington, Delaware, advertised in 1803 that "his Lathe goes by water," and during the next decade other craftsmen followed suit. Of the dozen or so woodworkers identified in the 1820 manufacturing census as using waterpower, eight were chairmakers or turners, and five of that number made Windsor chairs. Stephen Kilburn's "water privilege" was in northern Worcester County where water was already an important energy source. In the Midwest Samuel Rooker relocated in 1830 from Indianapolis to Logansport, where he "erected a Turning Lathe at Gen. Tipton's Mill." Ultimately it was the successful application of steam power to the machine that permitted shop size and production to increase to factory proportions.[42]

The Grindstone

This wheel-shape tool consisted of a finely grained sandstone pierced by an axle that suspended the stone in a wooden frame with legs; a crank provided for hand power. Some frames carried a trough, or water box, below the stone. When the trough was absent, water was poured or dripped onto the stone during use to reduce friction. In William Sidney Mount's anecdotal painting *Who'll Turn the Grindstone?* a cranked-wheel-in-frame is central to the scene, and a copper gooseneck teakettle stands nearby to provide water. Grindstones mounted in low or high frames with or without troughs are visible at the left in two woodworking scenes (figs. 2-4, 2-7). By the early 1800s some grindstones were operated by a foot treadle attached to a flywheel.[43]

The grindstone was a critical instrument in grinding the cutting bevels of edged tools common to the chairmaker's shop, including axes, drawknives, chisels, gouges, and plane blades. The tool is a common item in woodworkers' inventories, although most listings occur without further description. Valuations vary from 50¢ to $5 or more, but most fall within the $1 to $3 range. Unknown variables include size, condition, and sophistication of the apparatus. Most stones probably stood in a frame. Philip Deland, a handyman of West Brookfield, Massachusetts, described his work on a customer's stone in 1842 as "making a frame for your grindstone Hanging and turning the stone nice"; he charged $2. The reference to "turning" probably identified a stone out of round. Appraisers seldom took time to list a complete apparatus as they did in 1825 when inventorying Asa Faunce's estate in Maine, which itemizes "1 grindstone, iron crank, frame & trough" worth $4. Unusual wear and tear on his stone in 1801 prompted Silas Cheney of Connecticut to debit Charles Butler's account by about 75¢ for "the youse of my grinstone by your Joiners summer past." Two inventories suggest power sources other than the crank. John E. Hartman of Pennsylvania, who operated his turning lathes by horsepower using "long shaft straps," owned a "Grind Stone, Strap & fixtures" likely powered from the same source (1842). At Daniel Foot's turnery in Massachusetts water from a dam and flume that activated "fixed Machinery" probably also operated his "Grindstone, frame & band" (1840). Mechanization made rapid strides. In 1858 William Holgate and Son of Kingston, Ontario, occupied a new factory equipped with "a ten horsepower engine with shafting, belting, grindstones, turning lathes," mortising and planing machines, and a variety of saws.[44]

The Shaving Horse

A low combination seat-and-workbench called a shaving horse (fig. 2-12, left foreground) was an essential part of the chairmaker's equipment. This utilitarian apparatus consisted of a long, narrow or shaped plank supported on four splayed legs. The forepart had an extra wedge-shape slab, or platform, rising in elevation toward the sitter. Through a slot in the platform and bench passed a heavy wooden shaft hinged by a pin to the platform. The head of the shaft was beak- or block-like (dumbhead), and the foot had a pedal. Into the horse's jaws was inserted a square stick of wood secured when foot pressure was applied to the pedal. Using the horse and a drawknife, the chairmaker shaved bows and spindles to proper form and reduced heavier sticks to octagonal shape preparatory to turning.[45]

Records originating from New England to the South establish the shaving horse as an apparatus of utility. Its valuation was low, generally in the 25¢ range, indicat-

ing that many were crudely made or well worn when appraised. Two new horses acquired by Thomas Boynton in 1814 for his chair manufactory in Vermont cost only $1 apiece. Alternative names include drawing, spoke, and shaving bench. Francis Trumble's estate appraised at Philadelphia in 1798 contained "2 Wood horses & drawing knives," the lot valued at just over $1. In the 1850s appraisers located David Alling's "Shaving Bench in [the] shed" and his grindstone for sharpening tools under the building, suggesting their place of use in his facility at Newark, New Jersey.[46]

The Sawhorse

The sawhorse, also called a saw bench or sawbuck, probably was common, although it is mentioned infrequently because of its nominal value. The structure is that of two cross-shape end supports united by a long central brace (figs. 2-7, left, 1-9). Its purpose was to support small logs for sawing crosswise into short lengths suitable for splitting into firewood or turning stock (fig. 2-12). In figure **2-8** a sturdy sawhorse stands in front of James Chesney's chair shop on State Street, Albany, where the chairmaker had his timber sawed. The log in the foreground awaits cutting. Documents of the early nineteenth century describe a "Saw Bench" and saw valued at $1 in the possession of Ebenezer Knowlton at Boston and a "Saw & Buck" worth 50¢ in Campbell Dunham's shop in New Jersey.[47]

Steaming and Bending Equipment

Nineteenth-century boatbuilders and coopers made use of the steam chest, "a box or cupboard, generally of wood, in which timber is heated by steam to render it more supple for bending." Still earlier, Windsor-chair makers employed moist heat to prepare chair stock for bending in shapes dictated by prevailing fashion, limited only by the nature of the wood. Craftsmen used a "boiler," or "kettle," to generate steam, which then might be introduced into a long container called a steam box. Inventory entries such as "Steam kettle" (1803–1849) and "tin steamer" (1826) corroborate that exposure to steam rather than immersion in boiling water was the general method of heating chair stock. Vapor heat was adequate for bending stock in chairs fashionable through 1850.[48]

Other references enlarge the picture. When Francis Trumble, a Windsor-chair maker in Philadelphia from the late 1750s, died in 1798, appraisers identified his equipment for steam heating as an "Oblong Copper Kettle & Trivet." The kettle could be placed on the hearth or on Trumble's "Six plate Stove & pipes." Copper fabrication for steam apparatus was common, although references to "tin" and "sheet iron" (probably tinned) vessels also occur. Identification by material or heating process is supplemented by references to function. Thus there are "bow kettles," a "bending kettle," a "long boiler for Chair stuff," and a "Steam Kittle for bending." Apparently these vessels were fitted with an interior rack to elevate the bending stock above the boiling water. Entries for steam boxes appear in some records. In Vermont Thomas Boynton's accounts for 1814 describe a complete apparatus as a "steam Box and Boiler." By the 1850s steam boxes were common in Worcester County, Massachusetts.[49]

Complementing the steaming apparatus was equipment used to bend processed chair stock to form. These devices had several names, usually prefaced by "bending." Thus there are "bending moulds," racks, locks, machines, and frames, and even "bow benders." Well before Windsor craftsmen were part of the chairmaking community, rush-bottom-chair makers used bending clamps to introduce a lateral curve to slats. Some may have resembled the slat-bending clamp employed by the Dominy craftsmen of Long Island (fig. 2-9), which has fixed and adjustable end blocks that hold four precut, steamed or green-wood slats, two above and two below, against a long segmental block until dried and shaped. Windsor slats and crests (pl. 2) could have been similarly shaped, although for quantity production a rack would have been more efficient. Rush-bottom-chair makers Daniel Jones and William Savery of Philadelphia were equipped with "slatt racks." A frame of this description is illustrated in figure 2-10. Another, owned by Samuel Wing of Cape Cod, still contained bent Windsor rods, or "short bows," when found.[50]

Despite few references to bending equipment, it is apparent that these devices were common, considering the many listings for steaming equipment. When chairmaking in the "West" as a young man in 1854, Josiah Wilder, Jr., wrote from Rome, Wisconsin, to his family in New Hampshire stating that he was "making chairs of several different kinds" and had found it necessary to "make patterns and racks for bending." Allen Holcomb made "a bending machine" for Simon Smith in 1809–10

FIG. 2-9 Slat-bending clamp, Nathaniel Dominy V, East Hampton, N.Y., 1800–1810. Yellow poplar, white pine, and oak (microanalysis); H. 7½", L. 27¹⁄₁₆". *(Courtesy, Winterthur Museum, acc. 57.26.223.)*

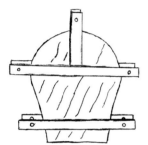

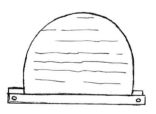

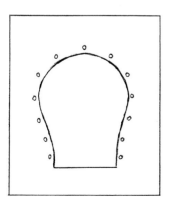

FIG. 2-11 Drawing of bending molds. *(Author's drawing.)*

while employed at Troy, New York. The form of this apparatus is uncertain, although estate records of 1842 for Charles Riley, a chairmaker of Philadelphia, provide a hint. Accounts of tool sales list "2 Bending Mechin & Kettle," further described in the inventory as "2 Bending Racks & Kettle." This equipment and the "frame for Bending Chair Stuff" owned in Connecticut by Silas Cheney in 1821 likely resembled the rack of figure 2-10. John Wilson, a chairmaker of Eatontown, New Jersey, acquired a "Clamp to Bend Backs in 1807." The apparatus may have approximated that owned by the Dominys (fig. 2-9), although Wilson's purchase of raw materials in quantity, such as a "Cord mappel wood for Chare Stuf," suggests he could have made better use of a rack. Wilson probably was bending round stock for square-back single- and double-"bow" Windsors (figs. 3-34, 3-35). Two "bow benders" listed at Baltimore in Jacob Cole's inventory of 1801 perhaps were similar, since the new square-back design already was current in Baltimore and Philadelphia.[51]

Modern craftsmen have developed a variety of rigs to introduce curves to Windsor arm rails and back bows of eighteenth-century pattern (figs. 3-64, 4-3). Their independent solutions probably have parallels in early practice. One type of apparatus employs a slab of wood, or mold, shaped to the desired curve, whether a bow-back loop or sack-back arch (fig. **2-11**, top and center). Some molds are fitted on both faces with vertical and/or cross battens that extend beyond the slab and are pierced at each end by a hole to accommodate a large pin, or dowel. Between each dowel and the bending stock the chairmaker inserts a wedge, which presses the heated flexible wood firmly against the mold until dried to form. To store a bent bow for use the base was tied or lightly nailed across the bottom with a batten. Samuel Wing of Sandwich, Massachusetts, favored battens. Other bending equipment employs a wooden mold fixed to a large backboard pierced by a row of spaced holes conforming to and bordering the forming block (fig. 2-11, bottom). Long pegs inserted into the holes hold the steamed bow in place until dried. Doubtless there are other effective methods of bending bows and arm rails curved in a single plane. A more complicated mold introduces curves in two planes to produce the continuous-bow back (fig. 3-16, center). The modern bending apparatus resembles a roughly formed chair top comprised of an arched mold mounted on a backboard accompanied by projecting side boards channeled or pegged to angle the arms forward.[52]

Thomas Boynton of Vermont mentioned "chair bending moulds" in his accounts. His record in 1814 of "3 Large" molds, five "smaller" ones, and "4 others" suggests that bending equipment of varied size and form was available in many chair shops. Prevailing chair design indicates that Boynton's molds were clamps or possibly racks. The largest mold undoubtedly was used to introduce a backward bend to chair posts. The Shakers used a clamp of this type to form the back bend in their chair frames. The mold is a long slim elliptic block of wood channeled on one narrow face to cradle the round bending stock along its curved surface. Leather bands secure the top and bottom. This also may have been the form of the "50 locks to bend Chair backs" supplied in 1840 by chairmaker Elbridge Gerry Reed of Sterling, Massachusetts, to Paul Bailey, a fellow artisan, for 75¢ the lot. A chairmaking rack used in New Jersey for bending many posts simultaneously is described as having holes at the bottom to receive the stock and rings at the top. In the trade the rack was referred to as a "crimp." After 1850 mechanical machinery began to replace hand power for bending, permitting wood of greater thickness to be shaped to form.[53]

New Mechanical Equipment

Once an energy source greater than human labor was available—horse, water-, or steam power—the potential existed for developing other mechanical equipment to lighten and speed the chairmaker's work. One innovation was the circular saw, although its early use is still the subject of speculation. European development of a powered rotary blade appears to date to the late eighteenth century. Smith's *Key*, a survey of tools and other metal goods produced in Sheffield in 1816, and a notice in the Birmingham city directory for 1821 illustrate circular saws. Smith's accompanying price schedule lists blade diameters from 4 to 36 inches. The circular saw was used in America about this time for cutting "small stuff," such as staves, shingles, clapboards, and sash stock. By 1822 Robert Eastman of Brunswick, Maine, was successfully operating a "ROTARY SAWING MACHINE" sufficiently rugged and powerful to cut house-building lumber. The entrepreneur remarked, "Though the circular saw had previously been in operation in this country, and in Europe, for cutting small stuff, it had not . . . been successfully applied to solids of great depth." Eastman implies that the circular saw could have been in use at the start of the century, and certainly by the close of the War of 1812.[54]

Reinforcing this observation is the inventory of Benjamin Bass, a furniture maker of Boston, which was compiled before September 27, 1819. Item No. 380 is a "Circular Saw" valued at $1.25. Within six years a local notice advised of the importation of "200 Groves & Son's Cast Steel patent turned Circular Saws, from 3 to 36 inches in diameter." Manufacturers in Sheffield, England, were major suppliers. Another development was the common use of leather banding "to communicate motion from one part of machinery to another," thus providing power for the saw. Before the close of the 1820s circular saws were operating in several woodworking facilities in New England and the Middle Atlantic region, some of which produced chairs.[55]

Use of the circular saw increased during the 1830s and 1840s throughout the East and the Midwest. One chairmaker owned a saw "Bench," and another craftsman had a bench and "band." James Smith described the early saw bench as a strong table "made of planks firmly braced together in the form of a joiners bench." The middle of the frame contained a longitudinal opening for the "well-tempered steel plate" rotated by means of "an endless strap from a large fly wheel, turned by horse power." As blade diameter increased to accommodate heavier work, a more powerful energy source was required. Jacques and Hay of Toronto, who before 1851 employed ninety to a hundred men in their extensive furniture factory, operated all the machinery with a 15-horsepower steam engine. Lambert Hitchcock relied on a waterwheel at his factory in Connecticut. His inventory of 1852 lists fifteen circular saws. In the 1870s William D. Herrick commented on the advanced mechanization of the chairmaking industry as he saw a "large circular saw, passing through a log with a rapidity fitted to astonish the minds of our fathers, with their grunting, spasmodic, upright saw."[56]

Among other mechanically operated blades, a "cross saw" was part of Stephen Shorey's mill equipment in New Hampshire. As a producer of 3,000 to 4,000 chairs a year in the 1840s, Shorey found the machine useful for cutting small logs into proper lengths for turning. Large and small saws of this description were used in Ontario in 1858 by Holgate and Son. The firm's ripping saw probably was the equivalent of Lambert Hitchcock's splitting saw, both used to divide wood along the grain. Mechanized whip, vertical, up-and-down, and mill saws served a like function — to saw timber into lumber. The band, or continuous-belt, saw used after 1850 had little impact on the early chairmaking industry.[57]

Mechanical equipment for drilling and mortising appears with frequency in documents dating to the 1830s and later. The "Turning & boring Machinery, Frames &c" that stood in William Moore, Jr.'s, chair shop in Connecticut was powered from his "Acquduct [sic]," or race. Mortising machines owned by other chairmakers produced rectangular slots in Windsor and fancy back posts to receive slats, frets, and stay rails. Operated by a hand or foot lever, the equipment probably was freestanding. Records of equipment sales suggest that in the 1830s $10 to $15 was an average price. Water- and steam power operated the equipment by the 1850s. Of consequence in view of their $100 and $45 valuations were Lambert Hitchcock's "Double tenanting machine" and "Squaring up mortising machine with cutters & Mandrels." Another new piece of equipment was the planer, used for smoothing board and plank surfaces and adjusting thickness. The Shakers of New Lebanon, New York, operated a water-powered planer in 1826, although the earliest use of this machinery by American chairmakers may date only to the 1830s. The machine standing in Daniel Foot's shop in Lee, Massachusetts, in 1840 was powered by his "water privilege — Dam [and] flume."[58]

HAND TOOLS

The American chairmaker frequently wore several hats. Until the 1810s, when tremendous population and territorial expansion began to permit increased specialization, few woodworkers outside the large cities could survive by producing seating furniture alone. The eighteenth-century urban chairmaker was often a cabinetmaker as well. Miscellaneous carpentry sometimes comprised a part of the chairmaker's regular work in less-populated areas. Thus before mechanization was common, the typical chairmaking shop contained a range of tools beyond those necessary for specialization, providing a choice of implements to carry out a given task. Analysis of a large group of more than 120 chairmakers' inventories augmented by estate records for several turners and spinning-wheel makers and miscellaneous accounts, advertisements, and price sheets provides a rich data bank. Some shop inventories are detailed; others group hand equipment under the titles "bench" or "chairmaker's" tools. Well into the nineteenth century many implements were crafted at the great English tool-producing centers of Sheffield and Birmingham, and competition by local blacksmiths and whitesmiths was limited. Not until the 1830s was the groundwork laid for a flourishing home industry. The 1832 federal schedule of manufactures reported that Gawen B. Newman, whitesmith of Lancaster, Massachusetts, produced 100 sets of "chair tools" a year retailing for $850. Whatever a chairmaker's source of tools, his competence was demonstrated in their use and care. As Thomas Sheraton noted, "One sure sign of a bad workman, is the ill condition in which his tools are in."[59]

The Saw

> Saws are made of plates of steel. . . . The edge in which the teeth are cut, is thicker than the back, that the back may readily follow the edge. The teeth are cut and sharpened with a triangular file, the blade of the saw being first fixed in a whetting-block or vise. After the teeth have been filed, they are set, that is, turned out of the right line, that they may make the kerf or fissure wider than the thickness of the saw-plate, and thus prevent the friction which would otherwise impede the motion of the tool. If the first tooth be bent to the left, than the next is turned to the right, and so on.

Thin blades were also desirable. To prevent buckling they were strengthened by a spine or strained in a wooden frame.[60]

LARGE AND FRAMED SAWS

Evidence of the two-man pit saw (sometimes called a whipsaw) for ripping timber lengthwise to produce board and plank is uncommon in chairmaking documents dating to the 1760s and later, since sawmilling was well established in America by that date and sawed timber was easily obtained for cash or barter. Nevertheless, in 1804 John Pinkerton, ironmonger and toolmaker of Philadelphia, stocked thirty-seven pit saws. Despite the tool name, some timber to be sawed was elevated above ground on pairs of trestles rather than placed over an open excavation. Before 1750 the pit saw had a slim blade supported in a long rectangular frame. After that date improved steel permitted the introduction of a wider, tapered, unsupported blade. Either tool had a long tiller at one end and a cross-handle at the other. The saws owned by chairmakers Silas Cheney and David Partridge in early nineteenth-century New England were fitted with frames.[61]

Another type of saw, the long, slim, unsupported crosscut saw, extends from 4 to 7 or more feet, the blade edges straight or curved. A long upright handgrip at each end identifies its two-man operation. To cut both on the push and the pull, the large, distinctive, vertical teeth often are M shape with intervening gaps to discharge sawdust. The saw was used in crosscutting logs supported on wooden horses to produce sticks of timber for conversion to boards, veneers, or square stock for hand shaping or turning. Two sawyers regularly cut logs to size outside James Chesney's chair shop at Albany, New York. In figure 2-8 their tool has vertical handles and large, prominent teeth. Joseph Smith's *Key* to the manufactories at Sheffield in 1816 lists crosscut saws of common, German, or cast steel. "Warranted" steel blades topped the line. Prices ranged from 9s. 6d. to 35s. (about $1.65 to $6). There was an additional charge when the blade was "set and sharped."[62]

Appraisers who in 1803 evaluated Ebenezer Tracy, Sr.'s, estate in Connecticut assigned a figure of $2 to the colonel's "Crosscut saw," one of a variety of shop blades. Values under $2 were common. The crosscut saw Jacob Felton sold in 1838 for $5.50 at Fitzwilliam, New Hampshire, apparently was of large size or new condition. Many craftsmen owned these saws in partnership. In Massachusetts, Merrick Wallace's "⅓ of Cross cut saw" was valued at $1.[63]

Bow saw construction is that of a thin blade stretched, or strained, within an H-shape wooden frame. End pieces, or cheeks, in small saws frequently are bellied. A bow saw hangs on the shop wall at the left in figure **2-12** in company with a two-handle drawknife. The saw's long wooden center brace rides easy in one or both end joints, depending on the construction. Connecting the upper ends of the cheeks is a twisted cord centered by a wooden toggle. Tightening, or twisting, the cord spreads the lower ends, holding the cutting blade taut. The tension is secured by "locking" the toggle against the center brace. The bow saw's principal use in Windsor-chair making was to cut seat blanks from plank. The same tool is described in some records as a "turning," frame, or framed saw. The large, griplike knobs projecting at either blade end can be loosened to permit "turning" the metal to any angle desired for cutting curved forms.[64]

Chairmakers' inventories from Massachusetts to Virginia identify bow saws, the values ranging from 17¢ to 75¢. The term *frame saw* is encountered only infrequently, although "2 little frame do [saws]" were used at Baltimore by Jacob Rahm for cutting out felloes, or rim sections, for his spinning wheels. David Judd's inventory identifies a "Turning Saw" and its "Frame" at his shop in Massachusetts. The "wood saws," or bucksaws, used in crosscutting small sticks of timber for firewood on a sawhorse, or

FIG. 2-12 Turner's shop. From Johann F. Schreiber, *30 Werkstätten von handwerkern* (Esslingen, Germany, ca. 1830–50), pl. 16. *(Winterthur Library.)*

buck, are also bow saws (fig. 1-9). Values ranged from 25¢ to $1, an indication that some saws were evaluated as a unit with their sawhorses.[65]

HAND- AND BACKSAWS

The saws discussed so far are implements for preparatory work; those that follow, the hand- and backsaws, are finishing tools. The long, triangular steel-bladed handsaw with teeth that cut on the push stroke ranged in size from the large utilitarian tool to the smaller panel, compass, and keyhole types. In America and parts of Europe it often replaced the bow saw. The characteristic wooden handgrip, represented in schematic form in the saw hanging in Lewis Miller's carpentry shop (fig. 2-4), was developed in England. The grip's slotted forward end secured the blade with rivets; the bottom was open or closed, depending on tool size.[66]

James Smith described the handsaw about 1816:

The *hand-saw* . . . is made for a single man's use; the length of the plate is about twenty-six inches, and it is generally made with about four teeth in an inch. It is used in cutting wood across, as well as in the direction of its fibres. The teeth toward the lower end of it are rather smaller than those at the upper end, or broadest part of the plate, which facilitates the working of the saw in that part of its course, when the workman has the least power upon it, and the wood [fibres] on the surface and at the sides of the kerf, particularly in cross-cutting, are not so much torn as they would be if the teeth were all of equal size.

Until about 1840 most handsaws had imported blades. An appraisal of Parrott and Hubbell's property in Bridgeport, Connecticut, made in 1835 lists:

1 Cast steel hand Saw Ibitsons Make	$1.50
1 " " " " Barber & Green	1.00
1 German " " " Spears	.75
1 " " " " " "	.62½

The substantial valuations and the short career of the partners suggest that some of these imported tools were almost new. During this period cabinetmaker Gilbert M. Lyons of Greenfield, Massachusetts, paid $2 for a "Hand saw," and general-store keeper Thomas Walter Ward II priced new saws from 88¢ to $1.37 at Pomfret, Connecticut. Most handsaws were well used, like those of carpenter David Williamson at Southold, Long Island, which were described in 1814 as "4 Handsaws, much worn some of them." Typical values ranged from 25¢ to $1. Despite wear and tear, tools were a valuable craft asset, leading James Rousham of South Carolina to offer a £5 reward for his stolen tools, noting that "one of the Hand-saws is branded upon the handle R."[67]

The panel saw, listed in sizes from 10 to 20 inches in Smith's *Key* of 1816, is smaller than the utilitarian handsaw. The serration is finer, permitting a "cleaner finish" when sawing thin boards. Many documents distinguish between panel and hand saws by using the terms "fine" and "coarse." The shop accounts of J. P. Wilder, who worked in New Hampshire, price a new fine saw from $1.25 to $1.42, probably including the handle.[68]

Among fine saws the narrow-bladed compass and smaller keyhole types have handles that attach only at the top forward corner; the grip is open below. This tool hangs in Lewis Miller's shop to the right of the measuring stick (fig. 2-4). The blade is thick at the cutting edge and thin at the top, or back, providing a "compass to turn in" when making curved and circular cuts. Many nineteenth-century tool catalogues refer to the keyhole saw as a fret saw. Indeed, its use in American chairmaking shops probably was to cut pierced work for chair backs, yet the term is uncommon. Perhaps the bow saw served as well. Daniel Clay, a woodworker and shopkeeper of Greenfield, Massachusetts, offered for sale in 1810 "Hand, Tenon, Dovetail, Sash, Compass, Fret & Keyhole" saws. About 1800 chairmakers Jacob and Godfrey Cole of Baltimore owned several compass saws apiece. Often the term was a generic one, identifying all small serrated-blade tools, including the keyhole saw.[69]

An advertisement of 1804 listing new saws for sale by William S. Wall at New Bedford, Massachusetts, is a reminder that before 1850 most tools were imported: "Lately received via New York, per ship Mercury from Hull . . . an assortment of CUTLERY, consisting of Pit, Cross-cut, Veneering, Hand and Back Saws." Hull, or Kingston upon Hull, had access to major suppliers via the Humber River, which communicated with the Don River and Sheffield, a major metals manufacturing center by the late eighteenth century. The swift rise of that city can be gauged from listings of saw-making firms in the *Local Register of Sheffield* during the early nineteenth century: in 1797 there were fourteen names; in 1821, forty-three; and in 1828, sixty.[70]

The backsaws of Wall's notice comprise the final group listed in chairmakers' inventories. Thin-bladed with fine teeth slightly set for smooth cutting, they are stiffened with a metal spine, or "back," made of iron, brass, or, later, steel to prevent buckling. The back slopes along the spine, and the grip resembles that of the handsaw. Smith's *Key* illustrates four backsaws, from a 19-inch tenon saw to a small dovetail tool. These are the two backsaws mentioned most frequently in American records. Although dovetails are uncommon in painted seating furniture, the saw's small size recommended it for cutting delicate rectangular tenons at the joints formed by arms and arm rails with posts and bows and the connections between legs and rockers. Like the handsaw, the backsaw cuts on the push stroke.[71]

Two Connecticut inventories make note of the backsaw: Stephen B. Allyn's document lists a "Brass Back fine saw" at his shop in Norwich (1822); Joel Booth of Newtown owned three brass-backed and one steel-spine saw (1795). The same metals reinforced the tenon and smaller sash saws stocked at John Pinkerton's ironmongery in Philadelphia. Chairmaking specialists generally owned one or two backsaws; the cabinetmakers in the group were equipped on a more substantial scale. Silas

Cheney of Litchfield, Connecticut, owned five sash saws (1821); Parrott and Hubbell of Bridgeport employed seven backsaws during their brief partnership of 1835.[72]

Unusual terminology revolves around the tenon saw. In Buckinghamshire, a chairmaking region of England, "tenant" and "tenanting" were common names in the eighteenth century and later. Even Joseph Moxon spoke of a "Tennant Saw" in his *Mechanick Exercises*. L. J. Mayes, historian of the chairmaking industry in High Wycombe, explained the variation by noting that the tenon, or "tongue of wood, was the 'tenant of the mortise.'" The term also was current in America.[73]

A saw in good working condition was sharpened frequently, and in most types the teeth were reset, a process described earlier. Triangular files and a saw set, or wrest, which introduced the outward rake, or "set," to the teeth, did the job. Joseph Smith illustrated the saw set in several shapes and sizes. Few references occur in American inventories, probably because the tool's small size and low monetary value caused it to be overlooked.[74]

The Axe and Related Implements

Tool historian W. L. Goodman has written that "any comprehensive study of the history of woodworking tools must . . . begin with the axe; it was not only the first, but for many years almost the only woodworking tool of any kind. . . . Its original purpose [was] the felling and preparation of timber." Preparation refers to splitting and hewing wood. From ancient times the wedge-shape axe head was standard, the wooden handle, or helve, socketed into the head through a hole, or eye.[75]

Although few axes are described by type in inventories, their number included the felling axe used to cut down trees. Since woodlots frequently formed part of a chairmaker's property, this axe was essential in securing timber for the sawmill or handwork. The felling axe's long handle is complemented by a reasonably long, frequently slim, head. In use the force of both hands coupled with a concentration of weight at the top of the axe, or poll, produces an efficient, powerful stroke.[76]

The broad axe, mentioned frequently in chairmakers' inventories, probably was a one-handed hatchet. With its broad cutting edge, either single- or double-bezeled, chairmakers and turners trimmed excess wood from square sticks, or billets, in preparation for turning. Reuben Loomis of Suffield, Connecticut, owned "2 Broad hatchets." The "shop axe" of several documents probably is the same tool. Its purpose was explained succinctly in the inventory of David Alling drawn in 1855 at Newark, New Jersey: "1 Broad Ax for chopping on Block." This operation is clearly illustrated in figure 2-7, in which the craftsman at the left is shaping split stock for lathe work. The "block" here is an upright flat-ended section of log. Prominent in the center foreground of figure 3-32 are another block and hatchet. The "Chopping & Joining block" owned by Jedidiah Johnson in Massachusetts in 1821 was worth 50¢. At Baltimore John Oldham's shop fixture was called a "Block & dubbing board."[77]

The Dominy craftsmen of Long Island employed another implement for shaping wood called a block or stock knife, which looks and operates much like a modern paper-cutter blade. The U-shape tip hooks into a metal eye at one edge of the block, permitting free movement from side to side and up and down, while securing the tool against shop accidents. Several other terms that describe this blade include the "Rounding Knife" of Adam Fizer, a Virginia resident, and the "Cutting Nife" itemized in the estate of Daniel Berger of Pennsylvania.[78]

Another tool, known among English chairmakers as a "splitting-out hatchet," served as a wedge to split wood. The process is demonstrated by the seated craftsman of figure 2-12. The splitting hatchet with its heavy, wedgelike body was positioned on the end of a short length of log supported on a block and through blows applied by a mallet or beetle was driven into the wood until it split apart. The craftsman repeated this procedure until the log section had been divided into sticks suitable for turning after further trimming with the broad hatchet or stock knife.[79]

The froe usually is cited as the implement for splitting out (riving) shingles, laths, clapboards, fence palings, and barrel staves, and the example shown in Smith's *Key* is illustrated with the cooper's tools. The froe was an essential tool of the chairmaker as well, serving to split out long stock along the wood grain, such as poles for bows and arm rails. No doubt some craftsmen employed the tool in place of the splitting-out hatchet to obtain short stock for turning and the boards that formed the crests and rails of nineteenth-century chairs. A froe blade often extended 12 to 15 inches or more in length. After the horizontal blade was embedded in the top or end of a stick of timber by the blow of a wooden club or beetle, it performed its work through a levering action using the upright wooden handle.[80]

William Davis, a rush-bottom-chair maker of Philadelphia, used an iron froe to split out stock before 1767. When John Lambert, a local Windsor-chair maker, died in 1793 at the height of his career, appraisers detailed the equipment and stock of a shop in full production. They listed the wood-splitting tools as a "Mall, Frow & Wedge." On the premises was a quantity of stock split by the froe—"Settee Bows," "Long Bows," and "Round Top arms" (rails). Supplementing the froe at James Grant's shop in New England were a beetle and wedge.[81]

Some inventories that list a beetle and wedges do not mention the froe. Although both tools split wood, iron wedges driven by a beetle usually perform heavy-duty work, such as cleaving logs, rather than the lighter work of the froe in riving sticks of wood. The beetle is a large wooden cylinder bound around near the ends with metal rings to prevent the wood from splitting during use. Between the rings a cylindrical handle pierces the head at right angles. The beetle of Samuel Loomis, a cabinetmaker of Connecticut, had seen good service by 1814 when estate appraisers listed only "1 pair beetle rings & wedge." Frequently the beetle is mentioned in conjunction with *several* wedges. The maul of other inventories probably was a beetle. These wooden striking implements protected valuable metal tools from damage.[82]

The mallet is a one-handed tool smaller than the club, beetle, or maul whose function is pounding or tapping. The seated craftsman of figure 2-12 employs this implement to strike blows on the top of his splitting hatchet. Mallet heads may be rectangular or cylindrical (fig. 2-4), but the material should be a sound, tough wood. Striking wood upon wood also minimizes damage to the handles of lightweight hand tools designed to be driven by the blows of a blunt instrument. Craft inventories list mallets either with other pounding implements or among the light bench tools. Chairmaker Cyrus Cleaveland of Providence, Rhode Island, who pursued several sidelines, mass-produced mallets, which appraisers valued at 8¢ apiece in 1837 at his death.[83]

Development of the adze paralleled that of the axe. The function of the tool in removing waste wood and trimming has changed little over the centuries. Windsor-chair makers employed the adze, and it also was common in carpentry, coopering, and shipbuilding. This long-handled implement with a hoelike head set at right angles to the helve converted plank to Windsor seats. L. J. Mayes has written of English practice:

> Much of the comfort of a good windsor comes from its shaped seat, hollowed out to fit the human anatomy, so 'bottoming,' or adzing, was a most important process. The bottomer used a curved and dished adze, razor sharp, and with the seat held firmly on the ground gripped by the sides of his feet he used this adze with a quick chopping motion, working always at right angles to the run of the grain. An amazing amount of wood was taken out of a good seat and it is not unusual to find specimens where the two-inch bottom is reduced to three-quarters or even a half-inch in the appropriate places.[84]

The large number of inventory entries for the adze confirms its widespread use in America, and several documents detail its precise function. In New Jersey David

Alling's inventory describes "2 Adse for cutting out the seats for windsor chairs," and in Virginia Adam Fizer's estate records list a "foot adze." Some tools were imported; others were of domestic manufacture. John Reynell, a Philadelphia merchant, ordered carpenter's adzes in 1760 from his English factor. In the 1790s Seth Pomeroy, a blacksmith of Massachusetts, priced an adze of his make at about $1.25. Pomeroy also new-tempered an adze for chairmaker Benjamin Alvord Edwards of Northampton.[85]

Fastening Tools

The hammer evolved with the axe and adze. A bifurcated peen, or claw, opposite the striking face facilitated nail removal. Two methods of attaching the head and handle were common: piercing the eye of the head and wedging the handle from the top, or extending metal straps from the head to grip either upper side of the handle. Although only the inventories of Jabez Gilbert and Parrett and Hubbell of Connecticut list claw hammers by name, Mercer found the wedged claw hammer the common tool in nineteenth-century America. The dozen claw hammers distributed by the mercantile Fisher family of Philadelphia probably were the "nail hammers" of other inventories. Thomas Ward II stocked nail hammers at his general store in Pomfret, Connecticut. The hammer purchased there in 1824 for 37¢ by chairmaker Zadock Hutchins probably is the one listed in 1830 in his inventory.[86]

A second hammer substituted a tapered peen for the claw. The hammer lying on Lewis Miller's workbench may be this tool (fig. 2-4). Both tapered-peen and claw hammers had a place in the chairmaking shop. In some early Windsor chairs heavy nails secure cross stretchers, three-piece arm rails, or arm and post joints. Lighter nails often attach wooden casings to the seats of fancy chairs (fig. 3-32, top).

A third hammer common to the chairmaking shop was the mallet-shape framing hammer with its slightly convex metal faces, used to drive stretchers and legs into round sockets. Lighter hammers secured the rectangular tenons and mortises in the crests and posts of nineteenth-century chairs (fig. 3-38). Framing hammers are illustrated in American shop interiors (figs. 2-5, 3-32), although few are identified in chairmakers' inventories. One-third of the shops surveyed had one unidentified hammer; the rest had two or more. Appraisers counted six hammers in the active shops of Silas Cheney and Asa Nichols in New England. At Northampton, Massachusetts, blacksmith Seth Pomeroy charged 36¢ to 75¢ in the early 1800s for a new hammer. Across the state in Franklin, Nathan Cleaveland had his hammer newly faced in 1815, paying 10¢.[87]

Screws are essential fasteners in securing the seats and tops of fancy woven-bottom chairs, and they are found occasionally in eighteenth-century Windsors. Until after 1800, however, the screwdriver, or turnscrew, was not a common tool in the shop of the vernacular chairmaker. Inventories generally list but one screwdriver; a few shops had two or three. Only businesses engaged in large-scale production would have needed more. In 1835 the shop of Parrott and Hubbell at Bridgeport, Connecticut, stocked several gross of screws in various sizes and had "1 Case of Drawers for screws &C [etc.] under the Shed." Still appraisers overlooked the shop screwdriver. Blacksmith Seth Pomeroy of Northampton, Massachusetts, charged 15¢ in 1799 for a screwdriver. Two acquired in Windsor, Vermont, in 1817 by chairmaker Thomas Boynton cost 42¢.[88]

Tools for Surface Shaping and Smoothing

DRAWKNIVES, SHAVES, AND SCRAPING DEVICES

The widespread incidence of drawknives and shaves in chairmakers' inventories attests to their common use for shaping wooden surfaces, although both tools were employed by other woodworkers. Drawknives hang in place on shop walls in figures 2-4 and 2-12. The tool consists of a long narrow horizontal metal blade with a single beveled cutting edge and ends that terminate in tangs usually bent in the direction of the cutting edge and fitted with wooden handles. A craftsman used the tool by pulling it toward him while the work was supported in a bench vise or shaving horse. With the drawknife the Windsor-chair maker prepared turning stock, formed spindles, rounded bows and arm rails, chamfered or rounded seat edges, smoothed crest pieces, and flattened the faces of back posts.[89]

Drawing knife was the popular term for the shaping tool, although "shaving knife" and "draw shave" appear in some records. A single drawknife is common to most inventories, although two and three are known; few chairmakers had more. Occasionally the tool is listed in conjunction with a shaving horse, and various accounts note the purchase of a new drawknife. Jedidiah Snowden of Philadelphia acquired several during the 1750s from a local ironmonger, and John Pinkerton stocked forty-four tools just after 1800 at his ironware store in the city. Lewis Sage patronized contemporary suppliers in Northampton, Massachusetts, paying 84¢ to $1 for drawknives. Tools of domestic manufacture were augmented by imported ones. Drawknives advertised by William Wall of New Bedford, Massachusetts, in 1804 were made in Sheffield, England.[90]

The spokeshave is a cutting iron mounted in a stock. Traditionally, it was used by wheelwrights, coopers, and post-and-rung chairmakers. In the eighteenth century it became a common tool of the Windsor-chair maker. Salaman states that English chairmakers and framers owned a straight-blade tool and many curved-iron shaves. Elbridge Gerry Reed acquired "3 english spoke Shaves" in 1832 from one of his chairmaking associates in Sterling, Massachusetts. Figure 2-16 illustrates four shaves (bottom right) from the tool kit of chairmaker Gilbert Burnett (working 1810–43) of Harrisburg, Pennsylvania. Clearly delineated in side view are the blade spines and the tapered tangs attaching them to the wooden stocks. The orifice beneath the blade permits the ejection of shavings, and the stock extensions are rounded to form handles. The cutting edge of the iron is beveled on one side only. Windsor craftsmen used the shave on seat tops to remove the marks of the adze (fig. 3-65) and to further define and smooth the contours. Seat edges, spindles, bows, and rails also were smoothed with this tool. The half-round or round shaving tool called an inshave or scorp employed by some modern Windsor-chair makers for shaping seats had little if any use.[91]

Demonstrating the close link of the shave with Windsor-chair making are the tool transactions of Jedidiah Snowden recorded during the 1750s at Philadelphia. They include the purchase of a new "Spoakshave" and irons and repairs described as "grinding a Spoakshave." The term *spokeshave* appears more often than any other in chairmakers' inventories, including the word *shave* used alone. The term *stock shave* gives emphasis to the tool's wooden part. The "Stock Shave with two Irons" owned by Joel Booth of Newtown, Connecticut, is identified by Salaman as a straight-edge tool consisting of double, or "cap," irons, giving "the Shave the properties of a Plane." Most chairmaking shops managed with one or two shaves; several had twice that number, and a few had many more. In 1842 estate appraisers at Philadelphia counted nineteen "Spoake Shaves" in Charles Riley's shop. A spokeshave drawn by John Green of Long Island in his account book delineates a form similar to those in figure 2-16 and gives the blade length as 3¾ inches "to the Shoulders," or tangs.[92]

Sometimes a craftsman acquired only a "spoke Shave Iron" and stocked the tool himself. Allen Holcomb sold a metal blade for 50¢ in 1817 at New Lisbon, New York. The expense of stocking an iron was about half that figure, as recorded by Solomon Cole of Connecticut when crediting a workman in 1803 for "stocking spoke shave ¼ of day." A chairmaker's daily wage was about $1. The cost of materials was negligible, since odds and ends of wood abounded in the shop. Local blacksmiths had a good trade in supplying woodworkers with the metalwork of simple tools. Gilbert Lyons purchased several shaves at Greenfield during the 1830s at prices ranging from 27¢ for a spokeshave (probably the iron only) to 56¢ for a stock shave. J. P. Wilder of New Hampshire, whose chair production by 1850 was substantial, re-ironed his shave about once a year for 33¢.[93]

The wood scraper is a simple tool, usually homemade from a small sheet of metal with a squared or contoured cutting edge. An old saw blade frequently supplied the material. L. J. Mayes explained the use and importance of this tool to the Windsor-chair maker:

> An adzed seat was a mass of hollows and ridges and these latter were removed and the whole seat smoothed by the use of curved spokeshaves and curved scrapers, both stocked and plain. A very fine finish could be produced by a scraper ... 'sharpened' dead square on an oil stone and its cutting edge just turned over.

The scraper removes a fine shaving without tearing the grain. A selection of round, hollow, or straight cutting blades permitted cleaning the work in any part required. Records originating in Connecticut describe Joseph C. Clark's tools by function as "3 Scrapers for Pollishing" (1799) and those of Silas Cheney by material as "6 Steel Scrapers" (1821).[94]

Few chairmakers' inventories mention the scratch stock or beader, yet this tool or a substitute was in considerable use during the period of round-back chair production to work moldings or grooves on bow faces. The explanation may lie in the fact that most devices were homemade and of negligible value; thus they were bypassed in the appraisal process. The inventory of Timothy Hanson, taken at Wilmington, Delaware, in 1798, itemizes a "Scratch beed" along with "45 Bamboo bows bent" and another 470 poles ready for bending.[95]

PLANES

The plane was an indispensable tool in the furniture maker's kit, and its presence is noted in most inventories that itemize shop implements. The tool consists of a wooden block, or stock, with a central cavity to accommodate a cutting "iron" (usually of cast steel) secured by a wooden wedge. Because many Windsor- and fancy-chair makers were also cabinetmakers or manufacturers of painted case furniture whose need for the plane was greater than that of the seating specialist, analysis of *this particular tool* concentrates primarily on the shop records of men who were chairmakers only. Many identified tools are bench planes, implements that smooth and prepare lumber for use. Some chairmakers owned as many as three to five planes. Named implements include the jointer, the jack (fore) plane, and the smoothing plane. Trying and long planes appear to be identified in the records as "large" or "long" jointers.[96]

In chairmaking records the term *jack* is favored over "fore" plane. This tool, from 14 to 16 inches long with an upright handle called a toat, has a slightly convex blade that projects through a slit in the sole, or bottom, of the stock called the mouth. The blade curve prevents the corners from tearing the wood as the tool performs its coarse work of taking off "the greater irregularities of the stuff, left by the axe, the adze, or the saw." The Windsor-chair maker used this plane more than any other. With it he dressed plank bottoms to remove the rough surface left by pit and mill saws. Figure 2-21 illustrates prominent jack plane marks. Occasionally a plank bottom was not dressed, and the saw marks remain intact (fig. **2-13**). Here the evidence appears as a series of light, spaced parallel lines at right angles to the long grain of the wood. The inventories of three early nineteenth-century chairmakers of New York

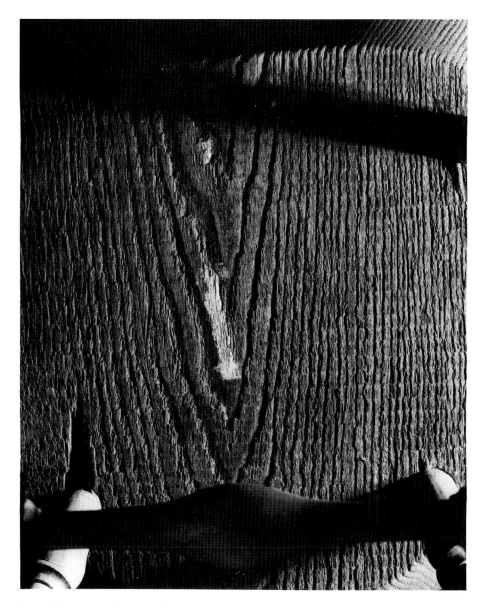

FIG. 2-13 Detail of saw marks across the long grain of the wood on the plank bottom of a fan-back Windsor side chair, Rhode Island, 1785–95. Chestnut. *(Collection of the late I. M. Wiese; Photo, Winterthur Museum.)*

list jack planes. About midcentury Josiah Prescott Wilder of New Hampshire paid 80¢ for a new tool of similar description, probably both stocked and ironed.[97]

The jointers mentioned in some inventories appear to have been trying or long planes, which exceed the jack plane in length by 4 to 10 inches and produce "a higher degree of regularity and smoothness." Samuel Chapman, a wheelwright of New York State, owned a "Jointer Trying plain for plain smoothing." The flat sole and blade of this tool evened surfaces of boards to be sawed into arm rails for low-back Windsors and a host of parts for the fancy chair, including the one-piece back post and leg. In comparing the operation of the jack and trying planes, James Smith noted that "the strokes given with the jack-plane are only within arms' length" whereas the trying plane "in taking off a shaving, is pushed along the whole length of the stuff." Lewis Miller probably uses a trying or long plane in his self-portrait (fig. 2-4). A bench stop above the vise holds the long board firm.[98]

A smoothing plane is pictured on the rear workbench of figure 2-12. The shortest bench plane, it measures 6 to 10 inches and lacks a handle; it is operated by grasping the stock in both hands. As described by James Smith, "It is the last plane used in finishing off the surface of wood." The smoothing plane performed spot work or reached surfaces not easily touched by the longer flat-soled planes. Craftsmen David Brientnall, Jr., and Michael Fassauer of New York owned both smoothing and jack

Facilities, Equipment, and Materials 69

FIG. 2-14 Chairmaker's "thumb" plane stamped "G.FAWKES" and "G.F.," England, 1800–1875. Wood and steel; L. 6⁵⁄₁₆". (Photo, the late James A. Keillor.)

FIG. 2-15 Molding planes owned by Samuel Wing of Sandwich, Mass.; England or United States, 1790–1800. Wood. (Old Sturbridge Village.)

planes. Elijah Webster of Chatham, Connecticut, possessed a complete bench kit, consisting of jack, smoothing, and jointer planes.[99]

Some chairmakers employed special-purpose planes. Michael Fassauer of New York owned a compass plane, which has a slightly convex sole from front to back for smoothing curved surfaces. The implement may have proven particularly indispensable in Fassauer's fancy-chair line, where curved backs and arms and klismos legs suggest this use (figs. 3-68, 4-28). Thomas Cotton Hayward's "Round" planes perhaps smoothed and rounded the rear surfaces of bows in his early Boston-area production. An English chairmaker's plane of hollow (concave) sole may be similar (fig. 2-14). It produces a low crowned (rounded) profile not unlike that common to bow faces in Philadelphia Windsors (fig. 3-66). Small molding planes that produced grooved surfaces were owned by Samuel Wing, a craftsman of Sandwich, Massachusetts. Two shown in figure 2-15 correspond in surface profile to shop chair bows. The plane at the right carries Wing's initials and the date "1798."[100]

Most chairmakers' bench and special-purpose planes were imported, although English-trained metalworkers Lucas and Shepard advertised domestic plane irons in 1771 at New York. By 1788 Philadelphia nurtured an infant plane-making industry numbering about nine shops, and a trade in "Joiners' Bench & Moulding Tools" developed at Providence, Rhode Island. Pressure from British interests accelerated after the war, however, as Sheffield and Birmingham became large producers of metal goods, and there was little American competition again until the 1830s. John J. Bowles of Hartford, Connecticut, manufactured "JOINERS' TOOLS" in 1840, the date of a broadside price sheet. A jack plane with a single cast-steel iron cost 96¢; when fitted with double irons the price was $1.37½. Prices were comparable at F. K. Collins's manufactory in Ravenna, Ohio.[101]

FILES

Files shaped wooden surfaces and sharpened metal tools. Two hang in a wall rack behind the seated workman in figure 2-12. Before the nineteenth century files were handmade. The forged steel was hammered into blanks and grooved with the chisel and hammer. Windsor- and fancy-chair makers used flat and round files to "clean up" tight crevices at the angles produced by rear seat extensions or in the notches of scroll-end crest rails. Other files kept saws sharp and boring bits fit for use.[102]

Chairmaker Godfrey Cole of Baltimore owned six files in 1804. Shops that also offered cabinetwork frequently possessed more. Craftsmen could choose between domestic and imported tools, many of the latter from the manufactories of Sheffield. Zadock Hutchins purchased "2 Sawfiles" in 1825 at Thomas Walter Ward's general store in Pomfret, Connecticut. Ward also sold 10-inch half-round files and flat files in 8- and 12-inch lengths at prices varying from 14¢ to 33¢. At Windsor, Vermont, Thomas Boynton paid 42¢ in 1816 for a half-round file at Green and Wardner's hardware store, and in the 1830s George Landon made good use of half a dozen flat files at his shop in Erie, Pennsylvania.[103]

Chisels and Gouges

Virtually all American Windsors contain turned work shaped with turning tools, from the baluster supports of eighteenth-century chairs to the bamboo and simple tapered sticks of later years. Views of shop interiors illustrating the lathe include a rack of turning tools within easy reach of the turner (figs. 2-7, 2-12, 3-32). Appraisers of one woodworker's estate even noted the "Goughes—Chisels in the shop Rack." Ordinarily turning tools were valued as a lot without description. When numbers are given, the tools range from as few as three to more than a dozen. Silas Cheney owned "15 Turning Gouges & Chissells," although this woodworker from Connecticut practiced both cabinet- and chairmaking and usually employed journeymen. Turning specialist Daniel Foot of Lee, Massachusetts, owned "18 Turning chissels." He, too, probably employed workmen, since his mill site was equipped with "fixed Machinery" to supply shop power.[104]

Chisels of domestic production vied with English imports. During the 1740s John Page, a Philadelphia turner, engaged ironmonger Stephen Paschall to make "4 turning tools" and repair five others. Page probably turned and fitted the handles himself. Whether these implements could be recognized as "made in this country" by their "clumsy" appearance, as said of turning tools stolen at an earlier date in the South, is unknown, although tools fabricated by the Dominys of Long Island and many of those illustrated by Henry Mercer fall into this category. About 1800 storekeeper John Breck and blacksmith Seth Pomeroy supplied chairmakers at Northampton, Massachusetts, with imported and domestic turning tools. In 1793 a chisel and gouge sold by Calvin Barstow, a blacksmith of Preston, Connecticut, to chairmaker Elisha Swan cost $1.17.[105]

Charles Tomlinson described the use of lathe tools: "The gouges are first employed for roughing out and forming the work, and the chisels for smoothing and reducing it to the required form." Turning tools generally have longer blades and handles than chisels and gouges used for other purposes. The gouge has a rounded cutting edge beveled on the outside. The chisel is squared or skewed and beveled on both sides of the cutting edge. The turner used the tip of a thin-bladed chisel to produce the grooves in simulated bamboowork, and he often scored a fine line on finished legs and stretchers to mark the drilling points for sockets. Other blades parted the work from the lathe when complete.[106]

In placing a chisel or gouge in contact with a revolving stick in the lathe, the turner held the tool with both hands steadied on an adjustable rest positioned across the front of the machine. Preparation of the turned work in an eighteenth-century Windsor consumed about one-third of production time. Short spindles as well as turned military drumsticks could be managed in the lathe with proper care. Long spindles were shaved by hand.[107]

Craftsmen employed a second group of chisels differently. Not intended for lathe work, these tools cut rectangular mortises to receive tenons of like form. In eighteenth-century Windsor work joints of this type occur at the junctures of arm posts and arm rails, top bows and arm rails (fig. 5-62), scroll arms and bows (fig. 3-12), and at the attachment of some rear seat extensions. Nineteenth-century seating utilizes the mortise and tenon to provide structural stability in the chair back. Crest rails, stay rails, and intermediate elements all tenon into narrow mortises cut into the back posts (fig. 3-47). Some vertical elements use the same construction (fig. 3-46).

Mortising chisels are distinguished from turning tools by their shorter blades and metal shoulders abutting the handles, which prevent further penetration of the tangs when struck with the wooden mallet. Tools of this type hang on the wall rack behind Lewis Miller's workbench (fig. 2-4). Mortising tools are not often itemized in shop records, although enumeration of both "chisels" and "turning tools" identifies their presence. Chisel names describe their special design and function. To begin a mortise a chairmaker scribed a rectangle then took a firmer chisel and made cuts on the long sides of the scribed form by striking the wooden handle of the tool with a mallet. Next followed a mortising chisel, its blade the width of the cavity to be formed and its cutting edge deeply canted. Waste material was removed by pounding and levering. When the mortise reached the required depth, the chairmaker cleaned the cavity by paring the sides. The paring chisel is lighter than the firmer and operates by body pressure rather than mallet blows.[108]

The carving gouge is named in several documents. An inventory of Jacob Cole's estate taken in 1801 at Baltimore lists "5 fluting gouges." Lewis Sage bought a new "carving gouge" in 1806 from John Breck, a hardware dealer of Northampton, Massachusetts. Ownership of carving tools by Zadock Hutchins in the 1820s speaks to the continuing presence of the carved channel in plank seats to define spindle platforms and front edges (fig. 3-41). The eighteenth-century chairmaker also carved crest volutes and three-dimensional handgrips (figs. 2-25, 5-62).[109]

Tools for Boring
Boring tools were essential to Windsor chair construction because round mortises, or sockets, anchor the undercarriage and most backs. The tool used by eighteenth- and early nineteenth-century chairmakers consisted of an elbow, or crank, with a revolving head, or button, and a socket at the bottom to receive a bit mounted in a wooden pad (fig. **2-16**). The illustrated tools are those of Gilbert Burnett, who practiced chairmaking in Harrisburg, Pennsylvania, from 1812 until the 1840s. The brace, possibly of American origin, is beech with a maple head. The purchased metal bits are fitted into wooden pads, probably made or acquired by Burnett over a period of years. They represent more than a dozen patterns turned from oak, ash, and maple (fig. **2-17**). Some pads are punched with numbers or incised lines on the shanks, and many bits have horizontal markings on the backs that served as depth gauges for boring. Several pad shanks are wrapped with leather, ensuring a tight fit in the brace. A turnscrew with a metal reinforcing collar on the pad at the right of the brace also was used in the stock (fig. 2-16). The blade, probably made from a file, is stamped on the shank "JAMES•[?]•CAST•STEEL." The spacing suggests the missing surname could be that of James Cam, one of only two manufacturers identified in Smith's Sheffield *Key* of 1816. The *Key* illustrates a turnscrew of similar blade along with bits without wooden pads.[110]

The word *brace* was one of two popular terms used to describe the wooden boring frame. The second and slightly more common name was *bitstock*. Braces are prominent in three shop views (figs. 2-4, 2-5, 3-32). Besides bitstocks of wood, documents occasionally identify an iron brace. In 1835 Parrott and Hubbell, Connecticut chairmakers, owned a metal tool with one bit, although they made greater use of their wooden "Scotch Brace with 38 Bitts." Joiner Robert Walker used metal and wooden stocks with "bitts and pads" in prerevolutionary Philadelphia. In early nineteenth-century Massachusetts the cost of a new wooden brace without the bits ranged from

FIG. 2-16 Chairmaker's brace, bits, turnscrew, and shaves owned by Gilbert Burnett of Harrisburg, Pa.; England and United States, ca. 1812–43. Brace: beech with maple, L. 16"; shaves: maple with steel, L. 11¼–12¼"; bits: oak, maple, ash, and other woods with steel, L. 6½"–10"; turnscrew: maple with steel, L. 11¹³⁄₁₆". *(Collection of the Historical Society of Dauphin County, Harrisburg, Pa.; Photo, Winterthur Museum.)*

about 58¢ to 75¢. Most chairmakers' probate records itemize a single bitstock; occasionally several are listed. Perez Austin of Connecticut owned thirteen. The shops of Jacob Cole (Baltimore) and Anthony Steel (Philadelphia) also were exceptional in being equipped with nine and ten stocks, respectively. In speaking of the chair framers of High Wycombe, England, L. J. Mayes noted it was the custom for each man to own "dozens of wooden stocks or braces, each with its own permanently fitted spoon-shaped bit." Whereas a few American chairmakers elected to do the same, interchanging bits was the more common practice, as demonstrated in the shop of Gilbert Burnett (fig. 2-16).[111]

Metal bits were available in a range of sizes and employed one of several methods of cutting depending on the design. Although numbers and types of bits are not usually recorded, a few chairmaking inventories develop the picture. Ownership of more than a dozen bits was common, and larger groups of two dozen and even three dozen blades are recorded. Of more modest number were the seven bits mounted in pads owned by Thomas Boynton of Vermont; two pads were made of lignum vitae and three were "lined with pewter." Thomas Kinsela of Schenectady, New York,

FIG. 2-17 Chairmaker's bits owned by Gilbert Burnett of Harrisburg, Pa.; England and United States, ca. 1812–43. Ash, maple, and unidentified wood with steel; (*left to right*) L. 7½", 6½", 8⅜", 8". (*Collection of the Historical Society of Dauphin County; Photo, Winterthur Museum.*)

numbered among his tools "3 Braces & a Sett Bitts." A "set" probably represented a variable quantity rather than a specific number. Josiah Powers of Connecticut purchased a "New bit stock with complete sett of bits" in 1827 shortly before his death. Estate appraisers, who valued the lot at $3.34, further described the items as "26 chair makes [*sic*] bits inclusive stock," focusing on both bit number and function. When hardware dealer Thomas Maule of Philadelphia offered "chair-makers bitts" for sale three-quarters of a century earlier, the principal users were the rush-bottom-chair makers, as Windsor-chair making was still in its infancy. Early in the nineteenth century appraisers at Litchfield, Connecticut, identified a "Brace & Bitts for Chairs" with Silas Cheney's Windsor- and fancy-chair-making equipment.[112]

J. Geraint Jenkins has written of the boring bits common to the English wood-seat chairmaking trade: "Traditionally the beech-stocked braces that the framer uses have permanently fixed *spoon bits* and each one is known by the type of work it is designed for. Thus a framer will have a 'legging bit,' 'a stump bit,' 'a bow bit,' and 'a stick bit,' each one being from a quarter to one inch wide. Every framing shop has a large number of these." John Breck retailed spoon, or chairmaker's, bits, probably of English manufacture, at his hardware store in Northampton, Massachusetts, during the early nineteenth century. The blades form a hollow half cylinder, or flute, the lower cutting end cupped, or "spooned," upward. Some spoon bits were slightly

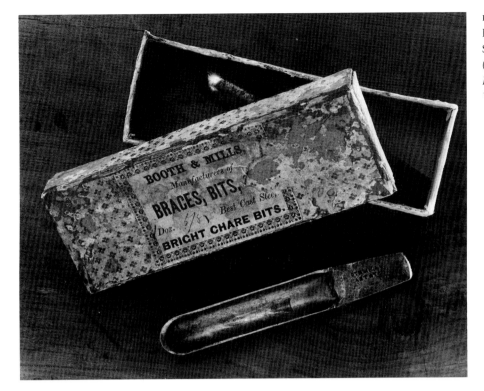

FIG. 2-18 Chairmaker's spoon bits and box, John Booth and Edward Mills, Philadelphia, 1855–70. Steel, and pasteboard with paper; L. (bit) 4⁵⁄₁₆″, (box) 5¼″. *(Collection of Monmouth County Historical Association, Freehold, NJ; Photo, Winterthur Museum.)*

wider at the cutting end. This is the bit used by Gilbert Burnett (figs. 2-16, 2-17) and the premier choice among American craftsmen for boring chair sockets. The blade cuts a round-bottom hole and readily discharges its shavings up the flute without binding. Two spoon, or "CHARE," bits of American manufacture, the remainder of a dozen in the original box, are illustrated in figure **2-18**. The manufacturer's name is on the box, and the bit tangs are stamped on the face "BOOTH MILLS / CAST STEEL." John Booth and Edward Mills, toolmakers of Philadelphia, formed a partnership in 1855 to manufacture braces and bits "and other light tools." The firm continued until 1870 under this name. Booth and Mills's charge for bits is not indicated, although in 1814 Thomas Boynton of Windsor, Vermont, valued at $2 a dozen spoon bits received in credit. Contemporary documents also record "round Bitts," perhaps an alternative term for the spoon bit. Equipment maintenance, a task critical to optimum shop production, was on the mind of Edward Mathews of Sterling, Massachusetts, in 1830 when he farmed the work of "pollishing 18 bits & sharping the same" to Elbridge Gerry Reed, a local chairmaker.[113]

Several records list the center bit. This tool of flattened, hemispherical, clawlike head, consists of a central pivot point flanked by a horizontal cutter and a sweep terminating in a scribing pin. Benno M. Forman found sockets cut with this tool in early eighteenth-century cane-seat chairs. At Philadelphia Thomas Maule offered center bits for sale to the woodworking community at midcentury. Ansel Goodrich of Massachusetts is one of several chairmakers known to have possessed center bits. Although this is not the usual tool of the Windsor-chair maker, some evidence of its use has been reported. Chairmakers probably knew greater use of this bit, however, in fancy-chair production; this type of chair utlizes straight, square-bottom holes to accommodate screw heads and to secure box-style stretchers inside almost vertical legs. Silas Cheney of Litchfield, Connecticut, recorded the sale in 1815 of "2 Senter bits" for 50¢ to Lambert Hitchcock, soon to be a substantial fancy-chair manufacturer. Four years later Cheney charged a supplier of chair parts 25¢ for "1 Center bit you brock."[114]

Other references identify the taper bit, a tool that reams a tapered hole or enlarges an existing one to that form. Eighteenth-century Windsor-chair makers used the bit

to prepare open, tapered sockets in seat planks to receive legs, arm posts, and back posts. Even after 1800 when blind sockets prevailed for leg joints, the taper bit continued in use to prepare through sockets for posts. A chairmaker probably needed no more than two taper bits since the slim, open funnel served many socket sizes. Jared Chesnut of Wilmington, Delaware, purchased a taper bit in 1800. Jacob Cole of Baltimore owned two and Adam Fizer of Virginia, three. Daniel Clay and Luther Davis of western Massachusetts purchased similar tools from local blacksmiths. The "taper rimmer" lent in 1829 by Thomas Boynton, a chairmaker of Vermont, could have been either hand or brace operated.[115]

Thomas Boynton first recorded shaping devices called "tenoning sockets" in 1811 at Boston when he sold four tools to Joseph Wilder, a chairmaker. Wilder offset half the expense by providing the "socket blocks" from which the tools were fashioned. Years later after Boynton had moved to Windsor, Vermont, he lent a fellow chairmaker "6 Chair tenoners, 2 long ones good, 4 short ones worn." What were these tools? The term does not appear in standard reference works. The implement may well be a rounder plane for making cylindrical tenons on the ends of posts. Salaman describes the process: "The stick to be rounded is held in a vise . . . ; one end is placed in the mouth of the rounder which cuts circumferentially across the grain when turned hand-over-hand." Samuel Wing owned a brace-driven tool that tapered tenons at the tops of legs somewhat on the principle of the rounder plane, the blade edge skewed to the axis of rotation. An additional cutting lip produced a shoulder. John Alexander suggests it is possible that hollow bits, or hollow augers, small tools with radial cutters that fit into a hand brace, produced shouldered cylindrical tenons of the type shown in the back post of figure **2-19**.[116]

Two small tools of the chair shop, the gimlet and the awl, are used to pierce pilot holes for inserting nails or screws into wood. The shell, or twist-blade, gimlet also drills small holes. Zadock Hutchins may have stored his four gimlets purchased at Ward's general store in Pomfret, Connecticut, in a shop wall rack, as illustrated in figures 2-4 and 3-32. The chisel-pointed brad awl perforates rather than cuts wood. Its function when twisted was to provide a hole "to admit those small slender nails, which have no head except a trifling projection on one side, . . . called brads in some parts of the country, and sprigs in other parts." This tool enabled the Windsor-chair maker to insert metal sprigs into crest pieces and other chair parts to secure the joints. Thomas Cotton Hayward's probate records list as many as thirteen awls. Perhaps several were scratch, or marking, awls that served as pencils to lay out work or mark the location of holes to be drilled (fig. 2-20).[117]

Processes normally carried out by hand, among them hole boring, were commonly mechanized during the second quarter of the nineteenth century. In 1830 chairmaker William Moore, Jr., of Barkhamstead, Connecticut, owned "Turning & boring Machinery, Frames &c" worth $14.50. An item from Lambert Hitchcock's factory inventory compiled at Unionville, Connecticut, provides a clue to the operation of some machines: "1 Mandrel for drilling, & bits." The apparatus was attached to a lathe. Although Joseph Moxon illustrated a drilling mandrel in the late seventeenth century, it was only after 1825 that the apparatus came into common use in the chair shop. Obviously, it was possible to bore only small chair-units by this method.[118]

Tools for Gripping, Measuring, and Marking
Chairmakers' inventories contain many references to the holdfast. The shaft of this angled piece of iron resembling a figure 7 fits into a benchtop hole, permitting its horizontal arm with pad tip to clamp flat work in place for sawing or planing. A knock on the holdfast with a hammer or mallet both secures and releases it. Figure 2-7 illustrates a holdfast in the right foreground anchored in a small block of wood on legs. Anthony Steel of Philadelphia owned five holdfasts. The holdfast purchased by Jedidiah Snowden in the city during the 1750s was a rugged tool weighing 6 pounds. Other named benchtop holding devices include the hook and the dog. A dog is visible at the left end of Lewis Miller's bench (fig. 2-4).[119]

Chairmakers' probate records list the vise with regularity. Some were wooden implements mounted horizontally (figs. 2-6, 2-12) or vertically (fig. 2-4) as an integral unit of the bench itself. Others were the iron tools mentioned regularly in shop inventories — from Jeremiah Cresson's "small iron bench vice" at Philadelphia to Jacob Cole's "large Smiths Vice" at Baltimore. The iron vise of figure 2-5 with its leg running to the floor is such a smith's tool, and Moxon illustrated an almost identical vise under the heading "SMITH'S WORK." Most iron vises used in eighteenth- and early nineteenth-century American chair shops were of English manufacture.[120]

References to wooden handscrews, or clamps, are common, although many chairmakers also practiced cabinetmaking. Chairmakers John Lambert and Charles Riley of Philadelphia owned half a dozen clamps apiece. The design is that of two long slim blocks, or jaws, of hardwood pierced at the center and one end by long wooden screws, each with a turned, opposing handgrip. Whereas clamps are used in woodworking shops to secure glued surfaces until they have bonded, the chairmaker is more likely to have employed the handscrew for clamping parts on a flat surface for smoothing, boring, or carving. It is impossible to positively identify the many other "clamps" and "cramps" listed in craft records. Jeremiah Cresson of Philadelphia advertised in 1779 "one large iron screw clamp for chairs," although that implement just as likely was employed in making joined chairs. Windsor-chair makers in High Wycombe, England, used a large wooden shell-like device called a donkey, which they secured in an iron vise, to hold curved chair parts in position for working.[121]

Pliers, pincers, and nippers, the latter two terms synonymous, identify general utilitarian tools associated with miscellaneous tasks such as pulling nails, bending wire, and holding small objects. Probably all were more useful in chair repair than in original construction. Thomas Boynton purchased a pair of pliers in 1817 for 28¢ at Windsor, Vermont.[122]

The square was the most common measuring device in the woodworking shop. Wood, iron, and steel are mentioned, the last a nineteenth-century material. In 1841 Thomas Walter Ward II sold steel squares at his store in Connecticut for 75¢.

Identified occasionally are "try," or fixed right-angle, squares and the bevel square, a straight stock slotted along one side to enclose a pivoting blade capable of being set to duplicate any angle. Moxon illustrated both among the joiners' tools.[123]

The rule, or ruler, likely was of two types. The first, a flat stick, or bench rule, was one to several feet long and graduated in inches and fractions. One hangs on the wall in Lewis Miller's carpentry shop at York, Pennsylvania (fig. 2-4). An "Iron Two feet rule" served Philemon Hinman at Harwinton, Connecticut. Among folding measures, there was the "Joint Rule," comprising two hinged and graduated one-foot sticks. Joseph Wetherbee of Ashburnham, Massachusetts, owned a "Box-rule," called elsewhere in his records a "Pocket rule," the name derived from the boxwood of its fabrication. Thomas Walter Ward II priced box rules in 1838 from 50¢ to $1.[124]

The marking gauge is a device "for scratching lines spaced from a fixed margin." Having adjustable or stationary parts, it consists of a wooden rod that passes through a small flat-faced block of wood. Fitted into one lower end of the rod are one or two metal spurs for marking wood. The block acts as a fence, or guide, as the tool is drawn along the edge of the chair part to be scribed. Double-spurred gauges marked parallel lines for mortise holes on back posts and other chair parts. Single- or double-spurred tools scratched lines on seat planks to indicate spindle placement (fig. **2-20**) or to lay out the ornamental grooves (fig. 3-41).[125]

Ranking second after the square and equally common as the gauge was the compass, its purpose to scribe circles and arcs and to take or transfer measurements. The straight legs of the tool are pointed at the tips and hinged at the top. Godfrey Cole of Baltimore owned nine compasses by 1803, and John Pinkerton, an ironmonger of Philadelphia, stocked eight dozen about that date. Specific uses for the tool include laying out volutes for carving crest tips and handgrips and plotting the curves of flat arm pads (figs. 5-56, 5-61) and fancy crest profiles (fig. 3-46). The calipers relate to the compass in appearance, but the legs are bowed. Several pairs hang on the shop walls of figure 2-12. This tool functions differently than the compass in measuring the diameters of round work in the lathe. Not commonly identified in records, calipers probably were lumped together with "turning" or "chairmaker's tools."[126]

Miscellaneous Tools and Equipment

After edge tools were ground to shape on the grindstone, sharpening stones of various types were used to hone the resulting cutting edge. When Richard Johns set up business in 1760, his Philadelphia agent sent to England for a set of "Joiners Tools," among which was a "Turkey Stone Clear of Knotts." The Turkey stone, mined in Asia Minor, was the standard sharpening device for small edge-tools. If the small, cut stone was not already boxed, the craftsman made a container for it. When oiled, the stone was ready for use. A boxed stone rests on the bench to the right of the turner in figure 2-7. Most establishments managed with a single sharpening stone and perhaps some slips, or splinters, to hone difficult curved surfaces. Joseph C. Clark used a single "whetstone & box" at his shop in Connecticut. Joseph Wetherbee, Jr., maintained optimum activity at his establishment in Ashburnham, Massachusetts, with several "oilstones."[127]

As demonstrated in Smith's *Key*, many woodworking tools came without handles, although wooden handgrips were available upon request. Richard Johns's English tool order of 1760 specified that "chizels & gouges be handled." Among tools of English manufacture owned by the Dominy craftsmen of Long Island, shop-made handles predominate. American woodworkers appear to have fabricated most of their own handles or acquired them through barter.[128]

Many references identify tool handles by purpose. Those for augers and shaves were most requested, although handles for drawknives and helves for axes were in demand. Handles were made by hand or in the lathe. In 1740 chairmaker Solomon Fussell of Philadelphia turned two auger handles for a customer. Almost a century later Henry DeWitt, a Shaker joiner and turner at New Lebanon, New York, noted, "I turned 15 handles 12 which are for chisels, for Hiram & myself." There were distinctions in quality, since Philip Deland of West Brookfield, Massachusetts, recorded a "pair of shave handles nice." At Thomas Walter Ward's store in Connecticut "Cheap Awl Handles" were 20¢ the dozen and those painted "Patent Black," 10¢ more. Whether handles were turned or shaved, design was critical to efficiency. Tools likely to roll were sometimes flattened, front and back, or shaved to octagonal form. The tool handles in Lewis Miller's shop are typical for the period (fig. 2-4).[129]

Most references to tool chests occur in shop inventories of deceased craftsmen. Many chests contained some, if not most, of the shop tools, and the contents often are described as "old." The new toolbox Elisha Harlow Holmes made in 1827 for a customer in Essex, Connecticut, cost about $5.50. Elaborate chests are known, the most familiar being that of Duncan Phyfe. The box is fitted with drawers, trays, compartments, and brackets to hold tools and accessories, large and small.[130]

Chairmakers used glue, as confirmed by listings for glue pots or kettles in more than twenty specialty shop inventories. Most references date after 1800, however, when the bracing in the undercarriage of the Windsor was converted from an H-plan to a box-style system. In the late 1600s Moxon directed that newly boiled glue be poured into a clean glue pot, a straight-sided vessel with a bail handle "made of good thick Lead, that by its Substance it may retain a heat the longer." In 1802 Amos Wells of Colchester, Connecticut, still used a "led glue pot." Moxon's directions for reheating hardened glue are unclear, although the lead vessel probably was set into a container of boiling water, a procedure that ultimately proved the most satisfactory.[131]

A few records describe the complete glue kettle and pot. Josiah Austin of Charlestown, Massachusetts, in petitioning to recover losses incurred during the Revolution, itemized "One join[ers] pot & glue, one iron Kittel." Chairmaker Henry Prall of Philadelphia, who died in 1802, owned "two Glewe Kettels with Potts to them." The same number were in Parrott and Hubbell's shop in Connecticut, one of copper, the other of iron. Samuel Loomis of Saybrook made do with improvised equipment described as "2 Glue pots & one old Tea Kittle." The pots fit into the kettle, the principle being that of a double boiler. A glue kettle and pot stand at the right on the

FIG. 2-21 Detail of chairmaker's brand on plank bottom of continuous-bow Windsor armchair, Walter MacBride, New York, ca. 1792–96. Yellow poplar (seat, microanalysis). *(Courtesy, Winterthur Museum, acc. 65.832.)*

FIG. 2-22 Detail of branding iron owned by Jacob Fox, Tulpehocken Township, Berks County, Pa., 1839. Wrought iron; L. 19⅝", (face) 1¾" by ⅜". *(Collection of Barbara J. and Lester P. Breininger; Photo, Winterthur Museum.)*

bench in Lewis Miller's shop (fig. 2-4). These vessels were common among English chairmakers at High Wycombe.[132]

Insights on methods of heating glue are part of several records. Appraisers at Boston evaluated Ebenezer Knowlton's "Glue pot" in company with a "Lot on fire place." The "Glue pot & furnace" of blindmaker Edward Ball at New York may describe a brazier. The "Stove & Glue Kettle" used by James Renshaw at his shop in Pennsylvania was possibly a brazier, although when the freestanding stove became a shop fixture (fig. 2-7), its flat top could accommodate the glue kettle, as in English practice. One appraiser recorded a "Brush & Glue boiler." The typical brush consisted of a "tapering round handle" with "stiff bristles bound to the thick end."[133]

The branding, or marking, iron employed to impress names, initials, numbers, or devices into wood was used widely between 1730 and 1850. Although *branding iron* is the favored term in contemporary documents, *marking iron* appears from an earlier date. Patrick Gordon, lieutenant governor of Pennsylvania in the 1730s, owned a "marking Iron PG" for personal use. Ownership of brands by merchants and businessmen for marking containers was commonplace in the rising mercantile economy of the eighteenth century. Henry Skinner, a sea captain employed by Stephen Girard, purchased a brand in 1794 for the ship *Good Friends*. Charges for 9 pounds of metal and cutting letters came to about $5.58, or the equivalent of a week's wages for a journeyman. In use, the iron was heated, though not to the point of charring surfaces. It left a smooth impression on long wood fibers, such as those under a Windsor chair seat (fig. 2-21). Stamps, applied with the blow of a blunt instrument, are more common on end grain (fig. 3-64).[134]

Brands served individuals and groups in private and public life. William Campbell, an innholder of Maine, branded tavern furnishings. After the Revolution the Carpenters' Company of Philadelphia resolved to "have a Brand Made with the words Carpenters Co. thereon and to brand the Chairs and other articles belonging to the Comp'y." Earlier, local brassfounder Daniel King had advertised "City and County" brands. Branding for purposes of identification was common enough by the early nineteenth century to support specialty businesses. James Foster of Baltimore advised in 1824 that he made "Branding Irons & Stamps For Millers, Merchants, Mechanics, Ec. [*sic*]" and illustrated his notice with crossed irons.[135]

Extensive use of the branding iron by chairmakers is manifest in their products. Bold impressed names on plank bottoms are accompanied occasionally by place-names (fig. 2-21). Aside from the impressions in wood, there are written records. David Haven of Framingham, Massachusetts, owned an iron before 1801, the year Daniel Clay purchased a "Brand" from blacksmith William Bull of Greenfield. The iron that produced John B. Ackley's diamond-pellet name impression on Windsor seating made at Philadelphia is recorded in his estate and alluded to in a ship's manifest that lists twenty-four dozen Windsor chairs "Branded J B Ackley."[136]

The usual material of the brand was iron, hence the names marking or branding *iron*. That metal was not wholly satisfactory, however, as suggested in documents from Connecticut recording Tracy family purchases of brass-headed tools and Daniel King's advertisement at Philadelphia for "all Sorts of Copper Brands . . . which far exceed Iron ones, for Neatness, and Continuance of Heat; and one Property they have beyond Iron ones, they neither burn nor scale away." A typical brand is that made for Jacob Fox of Pennsylvania dated "1839" on the head (fig. 2-22); impressions occur on the end grain of spinning-wheel planks. More common for use on end grain is the stamp with knifelike letters impressed by a blow to the tool end. When used on long grain, however, stamps "cut and distort the wood fibers." James C. Tuttle of Salem, Massachusetts, used a stamp (fig. 3-64), because close examination of his name impression on chair seats reveals torn and splintered wood.[137]

The Fox brand (fig. 2-22) is typical — a blocked head, a long slim shaft to dissipate heat, and a hanging ring. Some irons have wooden handles. Introduced in the early

nineteenth century were irons with boxlike heads accommodating "manufactured" letters or numbers in any combination. J. P. Wilder of New Hampshire appears to have acquired irons of this type in 1847, when he recorded "brands & letters $1.34," and by then steel brands were available. One heating of an iron produced several impressions. To achieve a good impression without charring the wood, the temperature was regulated carefully. In general letter size diminished from eighteenth- to mid-nineteenth-century impressions. To *suggest* that brands identified their products, chairmakers Christian Nestell and John Priest introduced initials to the seats of chairs illustrating their advertisements. Both makers' and owners' brands appear on Windsor seating.[138]

Salaman defines furniture patterns as "thin pieces of material cut to the size or profile of the finished article and used as a guide to their external shape during manufacture." Brief, though rare, insights occur in probate records. Ebenezer Allen, Jr.'s, estate, probated in 1793 in Massachusetts, contained "several wooden patrons or shapes to cut work by." Similar property belonging to Purnel Hall in Delaware was described as "all the patterns, cuting boards &c." Wooden patterns frequently were crafted from shop scraps and exhibit considerable variety. Other patterns were made of heavy paper, oiled and unoiled, or cardboard. Individual patterns for chairs were full size (fig. **2-23**) or half figure to be partially marked out then reversed. Punched holes permitted hanging. Appraisers at Newark, New Jersey, found David Alling's "lot of patterns on [the] floor." When working in Wisconsin in 1854, Josiah P. Wilder, Jr., of New Hampshire was obliged to make patterns before he could begin to make chairs.[139]

Materials and Sources

WOOD FOR CHAIRMAKING

François André Michaux, French naturalist, silviculturist, and member of the American Philosophical Society, traveled extensively in North America between 1806 and 1809, recording his observations on the properties of American plants and the uses of forest trees. In a chapter of his *North American Sylva* Michaux described the raw materials of the chairmaker. His brief observations on Windsor-chair making generally are correct:

Windsor Chairs: In all the cities of the United States, this branch of industry forms a distinct trade. Windsor chairs are in general use, and they are exported from the Northern States to the Southern, and to the West Indies.

At Hallowel [Maine], Portland, Portsmouth, etc., the seat is of Bass Wood, the lower frame of Sugar Maple, and the bow and rods . . . of White Ash.

At New York, Philadelphia, Baltimore and Richmond, the seat is of Tulip Tree, the legs of Red-flowering Maple, the rods of the back, of Shellbark Hickory, and the bow of White Oak. These species are not preferable to those in use in the more northern States, except the Tulip Tree, which is firmer and more durable than the Basswood.

In the Northern States, particularly at Boston, chairs of this sort are made wholly of

FIG. 2-24 Detail of yellow poplar seat of bow-back Windsor side chair, Michael Stoner, Harrisburg or Lancaster, Pa., 1789–1800. Yellow poplar (seat) with maple and hickory (microanalysis). *(Courtesy, Winterthur Museum, acc. 78.211.)*

White Pine [the seat only], except the bow, which is of White Oak: they are light and cheap, but easily broken. . . . In well-furnished apartments, *japanned chairs* are fashionable; they are made of Red Maple, painted, varnished and gilt; the seat is of cane or of rushes (*Tipha angustifolia*) cut in the salt-meadows.

In the country, common chairs are made of Maple, and sometimes of Hickory, with the bottom of straw.[140]

Middle Atlantic Region

Pennsylvania, the center of Windsor-chair making until the War of 1812, is a principal focus in the study of chair materials and their origin. Central to the investigation is information obtained from period records and the microanalysis of chair parts. Plank from the tulip tree (*Liriodendron tulipifera*), commonly called poplar or yellow poplar (although not actually related to the poplars of genus *Populus*), was the universal choice for seats in Pennsylvania (fig. **2-24**). At Philadelphia in 1775 Francis Trumble sought "5000 feet 2 inch poplar plank." Almost half a century later in 1817, Anthony Steel carried a stock of "9892 feet poplar plank." In western Pennsylvania Isaiah Steen advised: "The highest price given for two inch poplar plank."[141]

Michaux actually sighted the tulip tree from central New England southward and noted its preference for "deep, loamy, and extremely fertile soils." Under favorable conditions the tree grew as high as 100 feet and obtained a diameter of 3 feet or more. In the Midwest some trunks exceeded 5 feet. In consequence of its size and "perfect straightness," Michaux found the tulip tree "one of the most magnificent vegetables of the temperate zones." Aside from its use in Windsor seats, yellow poplar was employed in fancy-chair making, cabinetmaking, coachmaking, and building. The wood when aged ranges in color from deep tan in the heart to pale yellow, often greenish, in the sapwood. It is relatively free of knots. In the Philadelphia area Windsor craftsmen sometimes also used yellow poplar for sawed arm rails.[142]

Maple was the wood most favored everywhere for Windsor turnings. Following in popularity were hickory, oak, ash, and birch, subject to regional preference. Most Pennsylvania Windsors have maple legs; the same wood frequently forms the

FIG. 2-25 Detail of white oak crest of fan-back Windsor side chair, Francis Trumble, Philadelphia, ca. 1778–85. Yellow poplar (seat) with maple, black walnut, oak, and hickory (microanalysis). *(Courtesy, Winterthur Museum, acc. 71.281.)*

stretchers. Arm supports and back posts exhibit variation. Ranging from Canada to Florida, maple was highly suitable for lathe work and an excellent choice for furniture that often emphasized crisp, sharply defined turnings. Michaux identified three varieties of maple associated with Windsor-chair making in North America: red (*Acer rubrum*), sugar (*Acer saccharum*), and black (*Acer nigrum*). Of the red, he stated: "It is principally employed for the lower part of Windsor chairs." Microanalysis confirms the preference.[143]

Pennsylvania chairmakers made moderate use of ash. Jacob Bigelow described its salient features: "Ash wood is strong, elastic, tough, and light, and splits with a straight grain. It is also durable, and permanent in its dimensions." The tree ranged in its several varieties from Canada to the South. The black ash (*Fraxinus nigra*) also provided material for splint seats and baskets. Ash often supplied the turned parts for Windsor chairs and occasionally served as the material of the crest or the bent arm rail in eighteenth-century work. Craftsmen frequently shaved ash into spindles, but even in that capacity it was totally eclipsed by the hickory tree.[144]

Hickory was especially suited for spindles and served occasionally for turned work, arm rails, and bows. Pennsylvania German craftsmen selected hickory more frequently than ash for chair crests. Like ash and maple, hickory grew in most areas where Windsor production flourished. Hard, tough, and flexible, it was an excellent choice for chair backs, which depend on resilient materials for survival. Michaux in noting that hickory "is selected, in the neighborhood of New York and Philadelphia, for the back-bows of Windsor chairs" probably referred to the spindles. As spindles were fashioned easily with a drawknife, farmers and "country operatives" often enjoyed a supplemental income by providing chairmakers with "sticks." Francis Trumble of Philadelphia drew attention in 1775 to his need for "40,000 hickory sticks for Windsor chairs." Fellow craftsman Josiah Sherald paid £5 per cord for hickory wood, "the Grain of which must be Half an Inch apart, [and] must split strait and clean." He advised potential suppliers to look for the tree "about Hedges and Fences," requesting "the Butt Cut [quartered] . . . at least four and an Half or five Feet long." In this length the material was intended for bent arm rails in high-back and sack-back chairs. Trumble chose oak for this purpose, seeking "4 cords of white oak butts, clear of knots, in 4 foot lengths."[145]

Oak proved its worth in the Windsor bow and frequently provided the "stuff" of the scroll-end crest (fig. 2-25) and heavy, sawed arm rail. Some chairmakers fashioned spindles of oak; others used it in the bow-back arm structure (fig. 3-66) when not employing ash, hickory, or a fine cabinet wood. Michaux emphasized the prominence of oak in bent work, stating that "except in the District of Maine, it is always chosen for the bow or circular back of windsor-chairs." Microanalysis indicates

FIG. 2-26 *South View of Trenton, N. J.* From John
W. Barber and Henry Howe, *Historical Collections
of the State of New Jersey* (Newark, N.J.: Benjamin
Olds, 1844), facing p. 280. *(Winterthur Library.)*

that chairmakers in Pennsylvania preferred white oak (*Quercus alba*) over red oak (*Quercus rubra*). Joseph Robinson of Harrisburg paid "the highest price" in 1809 for "Poplar Plank, Maple, Hickory and White Oak." Similar materials served Windsor-chair makers throughout the greater Delaware Valley. In Philadelphia walnut and mahogany also were chosen occasionally for the sawed arm rail of high-back chairs, and both were options in the scroll elbow of the bow-back chair (fig. 3-66).[146]

Chairmakers in Philadelphia acquired their lumber from city board yards and country suppliers. Until the 1790s the lumber district was centered near the wharves on the Delaware River. Gradually, some yards moved inland. By 1859 Maule and Brother could offer 1½ million feet of seasoned lumber. Outside the city Isaac White-lock of Frankford gave up chairmaking in later life to deal in lumber and hardware.[147]

Stock was carried to the board yards from area sawmills and farther afield. In 1748 the Swedish naturalist Peter Kalm observed all the native trees identified with local Windsor-chair making still growing in the woodlands near Philadelphia. Public timber vendues on site were common. A broadside of 1821 announced the sale of "TIMBER TREES" on an 11-acre tract across the Delaware River in Burlington County, New Jersey. During a visit to Philadelphia in 1794 Henry Wansey remarked on the river where "vast rafts of timber of a quarter of a mile in length . . . float[ed] down the stream." Two rafts manned by helmsmen are depicted in a view of the Delaware River opposite Trenton, New Jersey, several decades later (fig. 2-26). Further insight on nineteenth-century timber sources comes from Thomas P. Cope, a Philadelphia merchant, who describes a passage up the Delaware in a vessel "crowded with rafts-men who reside in the State of N. York, 300 miles from Phila. & having disposed of their boards were now on their return home." By the 1850s a canal linked the resources of the Lehigh Valley with the Delaware River, opening the rich timber-lands of northeastern Pennsylvania.[148]

The rural Pennsylvania chairmaker without timberlands acquired his lumber from neighbors or local sawmills. In Lancaster County John Gormly patronized Benjamin Herr, a mill owner, purchasing "2 hors lode Bowood [for bows] haul[ed] from out lot" in 1810 and 800 feet of poplar plank the next year. The Susquehanna, like the Delaware, was an avenue of lumber transport. By midcentury Harrisburg merchandised 5 million feet annually, and Columbia and Port Deposit (Maryland) handled 100 million feet apiece, shipping half to Baltimore and half to Philadelphia. Western Pennsylvania, a land of "large and lofty" timber, had "mill seats . . . on all streams" by the early 1800s. The forested headwaters of the Allegheny River offered encouragement to lumbermen and provided access to Pittsburgh and the western lands watered by the Ohio and Mississippi. The scene illustrated in figure 2-27 suggests the potential of an advantageous location. The steam-powered sawmill owner likely resided on the prosperous farm in the background and operated the ferry on the well-traveled upstate road. Similar scenes were duplicated hundreds of times in the 1800s as settlements were established and prospered.[149]

Maryland resources duplicated those of Pennsylvania. At Hagerstown John and

FIG. 2-27 *Wardwell's Ferry*, near Warren, Pa., ca. 1870–1900. Lithograph; H. 6¹/₁₆", w. 15⅛". (*Winterthur Library.*)

George Bradshaw advertised occasionally for "a load of Poplar Plank." Chairmakers at Baltimore, profiting from the city's coastal site, imported lumber from the Susquehanna and other regions. Creamer and Son, lumber merchants, advertised "every description of ALBANY LUMBER" and pledged prompt attention to "ORDERS from a distance." Lumber was "forwarded by *Vessel* or *Rail Road*."[150]

Chairmaking materials in New York City followed the Middle Atlantic pattern. Wood analyses and written records confirm the popularity of yellow poplar for seats. The manufacturing census of 1820 identifies a fancy- and Windsor-chair-making shop that employed four men and six apprentices and produced $7,000 worth of seating annually using maple and whitewood, 1,000 bundles of flag (rush), and 5 bundles of cane. Lumber was available in board yards and at wharfside; deliveries were made in two-wheeled carts (fig. 4-43). Brodie and Dennistown advertised in 1803 a supply of "15,000 feet white wood plank suitable for coach and chair makers." The term *whitewood* as a substitute for yellow poplar also was common across the bay at Newark, where David Alling's seating furniture manufactory consumed quantities of timber. In July 1825 the chairmaker paid "for freighting a lot of white wood plank from N York to N Ark dock." In a later purchase of 4,148 feet of whitewood, a load of plank came in by steamboat.[151]

Windsors of New York origin have maple turnings. Hickory was favored for spindles, and either hickory or white oak served for the bent work. David Alling of Newark, New Jersey, recorded purchases of all three woods in the plank or log, and a stock of each was on the shop premises at his death. In neighboring Eatontown John Wilson made periodic purchases of a "Cord mappl wood for Chare Stuf." Oak and hickory grew in the vicinity of Newark and on Long Island, where Dominy family records document the use of whitewood plank.[152]

Traveling up the Hudson in 1794 William Strickland found hickory, oak, and maple plentiful, but he did not mention the tulip tree, which Peter Kalm had found of small growth near Albany. Strickland remarked on the appearance of a new tree: the white pine. Kalm had found pine abundant around Albany along with red maple. Because chairwork from Albany is unmarked, these observations suggest local use of pine for planks and red maple for turnings. Oak and hickory probably formed the back elements. Above Albany log and lumber rafting was prevalent on the Hudson. Timber from upstate woodlands and Lake Champlain was drawn by sledge to stream and river where rafts were assembled and floated to Albany. Sailing vessels and later steamboats carried the wood to New York City for distribution. Other sources highlight chairmaking materials of the Champlain region. The 1820 manufacturing census describes area consumption of birch, maple, beech, and basswood. Two travelers also noted the growth of beech and birch. The data suggest that regional Windsors had planks of basswood, occasionally pine, with turnings of maple, hickory, beech, or birch. Oak or hickory could have served for bent parts. The speculation is strengthened by the presence of basswood in the seats of two chairs made on the Vermont lakeshore.[153]

Basswood (*Tilia americana*, also linden) probably remained an important material for Windsor seats westward across New York State, based on written evidence. A fine, close-grained material, the wood is white, soft, and light in weight. Michaux stated, "In the Northern States, where the Tulip Tree does not grow, [basswood] is used for the pannels of carriage-bodies and the seats of Windsor-chairs." A low shock resistance, however, makes the wood vulnerable to splitting. The basswood, or "Lime Tree," ranges from Canada to the Allegheny Mountains of Georgia, but Michaux found it "most abundant in Genessee, which borders on lake Erie and lake Ontario." West of Albany at Schenectady Thomas Kinsela used basswood plank for Windsor chair seats. This is the only wood mentioned in his inventory of 1822 along with flag for woven seats. The accounts of several Otsego County woodworkers identify basswood in other regional shops. Allen Holcomb of New Lisbon used basswood plank in substantial quantities, often receiving it as barter from his customers. He also spoke of pine plank and maple, woods mentioned again in a Utica advertisement of Gilbert and Fairbanks. Timothy Dwight called the country around Utica "maple and bass land" and also noted the presence of beech and oak. In the Genessee Valley Mrs. Basil Hall observed hickory and basswood growth intermingled with beech, ash, and white oak. In southwestern New York chair planks likely were made of white pine. The *Western Gazetteer* of 1817 states, "The southeastern corner of the [Holland land] purchase . . . is covered with extensive groves of some of the finest white pine timber in America."[154]

New England
Regional placement of New England Windsors is far more complicated than identifying work from the Middle Atlantic states, although the material of the seat plank offers substantial clues. The range and diversity of the wood found in the northern Windsor-chair seat is described in map 1. As indicated, both white pine and basswood were common; other woods were favored locally. Particularly illustrative of the last point is activity along the Connecticut–Rhode Island border, where chairmakers selected from no fewer than ten woods for conversion to Windsor seats. Most prominent were white pine, basswood, chestnut, and yellow poplar. The remaining materials—butternut (a walnut), ash, maple, sycamore, birch, and *Populus*, the true poplar, realized only modest use, based on personal choice and availability. The selection of birch for seats appears to have occurred principally around Boston and the North Shore of Massachusetts, although white pine was still the first choice in the region. The use of beech, elm, yellow pine, and mahogany for seats was rare.[155]

Of the native New England woods white pine probably was in greatest demand and the most versatile. It provided ship masts, building timber, carving blocks, and furniture lumber. The tree thrived in the northern states. To the south its home was "in the valleys and on the declivities of the Alleghanies to their termination." With few exceptions white pine growth was limited in southern New England, but stands in the north were enormous, supplying domestic and foreign markets. Timber and lumber from Maine and New Hampshire were carried cheaply to Boston and coastal Massachusetts. Other supplies were transported to the Connecticut coast via the Connecticut River from the interior of New Hampshire and Vermont or through the Sound from New York, the entrepôt for upstate timber from as far north as Lake Champlain. By the early 1800s Michaux and others voiced concern over the rapid depletion of American forests. Timothy Dwight even speculated that "the next generation may never see a white pine of the full size."[156]

White pine lumber was common in furniture construction outside the main timber-producing areas, as confirmed by microanalysis and the records of furniture makers and sawmill owners in Massachusetts and Connecticut (fig. 2-28). Among written records are the estate inventories of Ebenezer Knowlton and Benjamin Bass (Boston), the insolvency papers of Parrott and Hubbell (Bridgeport), the shop

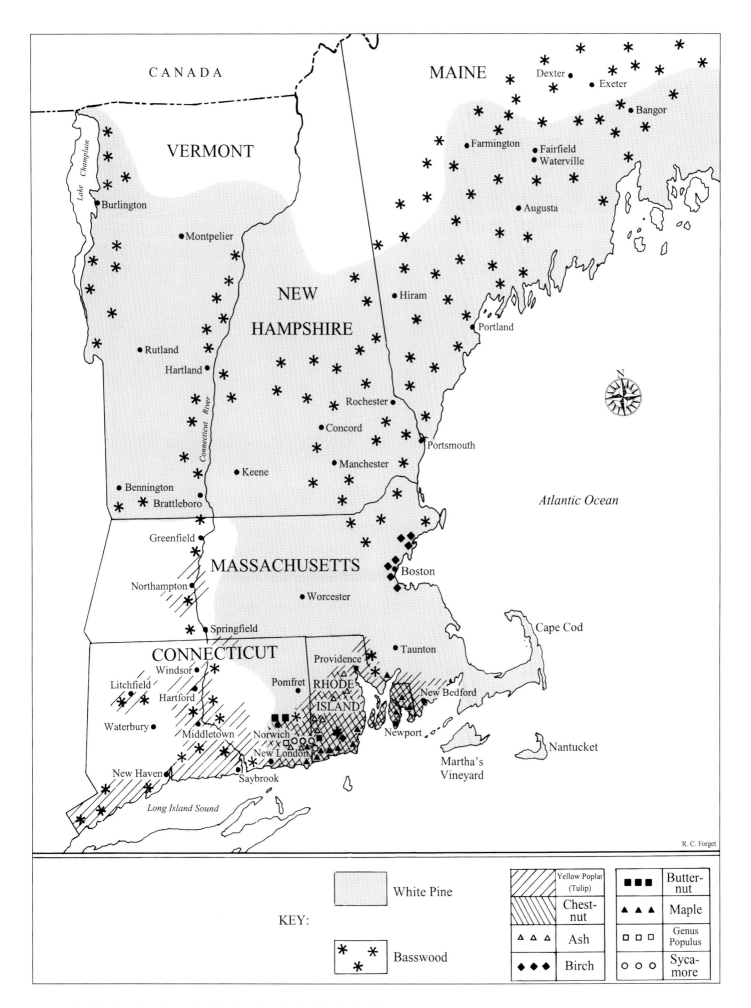

CANADA

MAINE

VERMONT

Dexter •
• Exeter

• Bangor

Lake Champlain

• Burlington

• Montpelier

• Farmington
• Fairfield
• Waterville

• Augusta

NEW

• Rutland

Hartland •

HAMPSHIRE

• Hiram

• Portland

Connecticut River

• Rochester

• Concord

Portsmouth

• Keene

• Bennington

* Brattleboro

• Manchester

Atlantic Ocean

Greenfield •

MASSACHUSETTS

Boston

Northampton •

• Worcester

Cape Cod

* Springfield

CONNECTICUT

Windsor •

Litchfield

Hartford

Pomfret

Waterbury •

Middletown •

New Haven •

Saybrook

Providence

RHODE
ISLAND

• Taunton

New Bedford

Newport

Nantucket

Norwich

New London

Martha's
Vineyard

Long Island Sound

R. C. Forget

KEY:

White Pine

Basswood

Yellow Poplar
(Tulip)

Chest-
nut

Ash

Birch

Butter-
nut

Maple

Genus
Populus

Syca-
more

MAP 1 Distribution of woods used in Windsor chair planks, New England, 1760–1840

accounts of Philemon Robbins (Hartford), and a schedule of manufactures for 1832, listing pine stock in shops throughout Worcester County, Massachusetts. Commentary by Edward Jenner Carpenter, an apprentice in a cabinet shop in western Massachusetts, provides further insight: "This forenoon, Miles went over to Montague City & got about 300 feet of the best up river pine that I ever saw; it is so good that I am afraid that I shan't have the pleasure of working much of it."[157]

Next to pine, basswood was the popular material in New England for Windsor seats. The map identifies its use from southwestern Connecticut to coastal Maine, with considerable activity along the Connecticut River and in the Champlain region. In speaking of Windsor and carriage work Michaux stated, "It is in Boston and the more northern towns that I have observed the Lime Tree [basswood] beginning to be substituted for the Tulip Tree," a statement substantiated by microanalysis of regional examples. Moderate activity also is associated with coastal New London County, Connecticut, and Rhode Island, where basswood timber may have come down the Connecticut River with the white pine. Nathan Brown and Horace Colton of Norwich, Connecticut, solicited basswood plank in their newspaper notices. Joseph Birdsey used the same material farther west in Fairfield County, as determined by microanalysis.[158]

Other evidence corroborating the widespread use of basswood in Windsor-chair seats occurs in both written and analytical form. Chairs with bass planks are documented to the shops of Samuel White and Walter Corey in Maine. In 1825 appraisers of Asa Faunce's estate at Waterville itemized 212 "Bass Chair bottoms." Basswood was equally popular in central New Hampshire from Concord north to Lake Winnipesaukee. James Chase's accounts and estate records itemize basswood plank and boards. Speaking of Vermont's forests in 1789, Jedidiah Morse commented: "Elm, black birch, maple, ash and bass wood, grow in the moist low ground." The records of Montpelier, Windsor, and Bennington chairmakers identify considerable quantities of basswood. Advertisements from central Massachusetts towns soliciting "Bass Plank suitable for Chair Bottoms" further spell out the regional preference. The inventories of David Judd and Ansel Goodrich recorded in Northampton itemize basswood plank and seats. Below Hartford, William Perkins and Matthew Noble worked basswood plank if they could not obtain whitewood. In northwestern Connecticut, Silas Cheney followed suit. The price for either timber was the same, $2 per hundred plank feet.[159]

Use of yellow poplar plank in New England Windsors was substantial although limited in region. Activity extended along the Connecticut coast to southern Massachusetts, with heavy concentration along the Connecticut–Rhode Island border, and into the Connecticut Valley as far north as Northampton. Probably most of the plank and hardwood for regional chairmaking was harvested locally. Ebenezer Tracy, Sr.'s, inventory of 1803 taken in eastern Connecticut lists a stock of 1,583 feet of whitewood (yellow poplar). Other evidence appears in public notices, such as Francis Bushnell's advertisement at Norwich seeking "2 or 3000 feet White Wood Plank, suitable for Chair Seats." New London also was a center of activity. William Harris solicited potential suppliers for whitewood plank eighteen inches wide and two inches thick. Use of the material extended to New Bedford, Massachusetts, where in 1833 appraisers accounted for "A Lot of white wood plank & Boards supposed 1200 feet" among the "Chairmaking stock and Tools" of William Russell, Jr.[160]

Records originating in the coastal region bounded by the Quinnipiac and Connecticut rivers between New Haven and Saybrook and extending inland to Hartford describe the primacy of whitewood as a chairmaking material. A distinctive Windsor recovered in the area of coastal Westbrook has a whitewood seat. Advertisements by chairmakers John Wadsworth, Jacob Norton, and Stacy Stackhouse of Hartford suggest that they preferred whitewood over other materials, an assumption further supported by a chair with a whitewood plank attributed to Stackhouse. Whitewood also was popular with chairmakers of the southern Connecticut coast. Insolvency papers drawn in Bridgeport for David Finch, Parrott and Hubbell, and Lockwood and Waite between 1829 and 1847 all list whitewood plank in quantities ranging from 269 to 1,743 feet and valued at 3¢ to 3½¢ per foot. Shaped seats in stock were worth 6¢ apiece. At his Litchfield shop in northwestern Connecticut Silas Cheney employed both basswood and whitewood for Windsor-chair construction, as did some of his colleagues up the river valley in Northampton, Massachusetts.[161]

Chestnut, which flourishes only in climates marked by cool summers and mild winters, was selected as a secondary material for cabinetwork in southeastern New England and was a frequent choice for seat plank among Windsor-chair makers along the southern Connecticut–Rhode Island border (map 1). Michaux described the wood as strong, elastic, and capable of withstanding extremes in humidity. There is little written material documenting the specific use of chestnut in Windsor-chair making, although the wood was present in *cabinet* shops from Providence westward across Connecticut and northward into Worcester County, Massachusetts, and up the Connecticut River Valley to Northampton. The inventory of Ebenezer Tracy, Sr.'s, estate in New London County, Connecticut (1803), lists 707 feet of chestnut wood valued at .007¢ the foot. Comparable valuations in the same record include pine at .01¢ the foot, whitewood at .008¢, and maple at .011¢. The Tracy family chairmakers are the largest identifiable group of craftsmen to employ chestnut plank in their Windsor work (fig. **2-29**), although they probably used as much whitewood. Their interest in chestnut was shared by other chairmakers in the border region.[162]

Of restricted selection for use in Windsor seats were five other woods — namely, maple, butternut, ash, sycamore, and genus *Populus*. Maple, a traditional American chairmaking wood, was employed in prerevolutionary Windsor work of Rhode Island. The wood frequently comprises all the major components, if not the entire

FIG. 2-29 Detail of underside of chestnut seat of sack-back Windsor armchair with maker's brand, Ebenezer Tracy, Sr., Lisbon Township, New London County, Conn., ca. 1792–1800. Chestnut (seat) with maple and oak. *(Bennington Museum, Bennington, Vermont, acc. 1978.2; Photo, Winterthur Museum.)*

chair. Following the war, maple was still chosen occasionally as the stuff of a Windsor seat.

The butternut tree is a walnut (*Juglans cinerea*) that ranged in growth from eastern Virginia to New Brunswick. General use of butternut lumber is documented in several areas of New England, although for Windsor seating it was restricted to the southern Connecticut–Rhode Island border. Microanalysis associates some use of butternut plank with chairs made by Tracy family members and craftsmen influenced by their work. A two-seat, tall-back settee of Rhode Island origin broadens the area of incidence. Extending the evidence into the nineteenth century is Nathan Brown's advertisement of 1823 from his shop in Griswold, Connecticut, requesting "a few thousand feet White Wood, Bass Wood, and Butternut Plank, suitable for Chair Seats."[163]

The ash tree, which supplied small turned and flexible parts for Windsor construction, was a limited source of plank. A popular wood with carriage makers and wheelwrights, it is durable. Of the Windsors known to have ash seats, one is a bow-back armchair of classic Rhode Island pattern with scroll arms, vase spindles, and swelled feet. A triple-back settee with design affinities to work from the Connecticut–Rhode Island border has a sizable 96-inch ash plank. A well-splayed high stool puts to the test a distinguishing property cited by Michaux — strength.[164]

Although one author has stated that the sycamore tree (*Platanus occidentalis*), also called the "Buttonwood" or "Plane" tree, was of little use beyond giving shade because "the wood is perishable, and prone to warp," the material served in a limited capacity as a furniture wood in the eighteenth century. Windsor-chair makers of southeastern New England used sycamore occasionally as seat plank. The sycamore seat in a large writing-arm chair attributed to the Tracy family is still as firm as when it left the Tracy shop. By contrast, a similar plank in a bow-back side chair from the same general area is split in several places.[165]

True poplar (genus *Populus*), also known in some varieties as cottonwood and aspen, fared no better than sycamore when rated by botanists as a furniture material. The wood is soft, and light in weight and color. Although the tree ranged from Canada to Florida, its use among chairmakers was centered primarily along the Connecticut–Rhode Island border. Features in two regional examples with poplar seats are unusual enough to suggest that use of the wood was distant from mainstream production. Two other Windsors with poplar seats exhibit Rhode Island characteristics; one has a poplar back rail as well. Another rail of poplar lends structural support to a triple-back settee.[166]

Boston-area craftsmen made considerable use of birch in furniture construction. Esther Singleton cites a Boston record of 1751 describing half a dozen black birch joiner's chairs. By the 1790s neighboring Salem had a brisk trade in painted rush-bottom "Burch Chairs," which interpret cabinetmakers' designs. The chairs sold at about Windsor prices, and the Sanderson brothers found them a good product for their Salem export business. Local appraisers counted 109 birch chairs at the shop of Samuel Phippen in 1798 and another dozen in the house. References to birch plank from eastern Massachusetts indicate its general availability. Benjamin Bass, a furniture maker of Boston, stocked birch plank along with more than 5,000 feet each of board and "joist." A Windsor settee and stool of Boston origin, both with particularly fine turnings, have birch planks as the principal construction units. In prerevolutionary Rhode Island a few chairmakers favored birch for the seats of a small group of distinctive high-back Windsors.[167]

Materials for shaved and turned work in New England Windsors varied from place to place and even within a single locale, although this diversity is characteristic of woodworking in America. A foreign traveler observed of American forests the great variety of trees "all growing close to each other, as if of the same species." With a broad selection to choose from craftsmen could experiment with different woods. A regional tabulation of materials drawn from analyses of more than seventy-five New England Windsors provides a basis for identification, especially as supplemented by chairmakers' stocks of wood and descriptions of local forest growth.[168]

Maple was preferred throughout much of New England for Windsor turnings. In New Hampshire the choice between maple and birch was about even, while the latter held an edge in Maine. Some interest in birch turnings is recorded in Massachusetts, especially around Boston, and to some extent in Worcester County. Only modest use is recorded in Vermont and Rhode Island and very little in Connecticut. Chairmakers in New Hampshire and Maine showed considerable interest in beech, although that wood was not particularly favored for Windsor work in southern New England. In Maine beech may have realized 25 to 50 percent of the combined use of maple and birch for turned work. Ash appears occasionally, usually as the wood of secondary turnings, such as stretchers. The Tracy family of eastern Connecticut used some ash in this manner. At least one nineteenth-century dealer, who obtained chairs from Joel Pratt, Jr., of Sterling, Massachusetts, expressed his dissatisfaction with ash, saying, "I do not like ash for rounds it is so open grained."[169]

Because of its elastic properties ash served better for spindles and bent parts than for turned work. Still its *overall* use in New England did not equal that of oak except in the northern areas, particularly in New Hampshire and Maine. According to Michaux, ash replaced oak "for the circular back of Windsor-chairs" in Maine chairmaking, although with little work of that description identified, the statement is not easily assessed. Rhode Island and Vermont chairmakers appear to have been about evenly divided in their use of the two materials. Hickory was of less consequence in New England Windsor-chair making, except in Rhode Island and to some extent in Connecticut.[170]

The South, Midwest, and Canada

Documentation of Windsor-chair-making materials south of Maryland is limited, as only a small body of identified work exists. Evidence points to broad use of yellow poplar (tulip) for seats, although yellow pine was readily available and perhaps served on occasion. Describing the distribution of yellow poplar, Michaux found it "multiplied . . . in the upper parts of the Carolinas and of Georgia" but comparatively rare in the corresponding maritime regions. Earlier Lord Adam Gordon had found "tulip trees . . . in great quantities" at Norfolk, Virginia. The duc de la Rochefoucauld Liancourt commented on the great height of the tulip tree "near Federal-City," where David Bates later sought "10,000 feet of 1¾ yellow poplar plank, 17 inches wide of a good quality" for his chair factory. Poplar plank was in demand at neighboring Alexandria and at Charles Town, West Virginia. A sale in 1803 at Joseph Childres's shop in Chesterfield, Virginia, offered "a parcel of Poplar Plank," a material also used in western Virginia. Moravian-made chairs have yellow poplar seats.[171]

Southern Windsors employ maple, oak, hickory, and ash for turned and bent work. In Moravian chairs of North Carolina origin the spindles and bows are hickory and the turnings, ash or maple. Artisans in these sectarian settlements discovered early that red maple was "good on a turning lathe." A sheriff's sale at Raleigh in 1815 offered chairmaker's tools and "maple stuff turned" from Zenos Bronson's shop. Earlier, Alexander Walker of Fredericksburg, Virginia, had amassed a large supply of maple, ash, hickory, and oak "by the CORD" before joining forces with James Beck to construct Windsor and fancy chairs. Lasker Smith of Wythe County also used oak. Some seacoast towns imported chairmaking wood. Cargoes from Newburyport and Boston probably represented Maine and New Hampshire timber; New York shipped Albany lumber. Pennsylvania's Susquehanna region supplied many craftsmen through the port of Norfolk.[172]

The 1820 manufacturing census presents good, though limited, information on midwestern chair wood. Ohio and Tennessee sources identify yellow poplar, maple, and hickory. Yellow poplar for seats grew abundantly in Kentucky and Indiana. At Cincinnati, where Jacob Roll used 12,000 feet of "poplar plank" annually, both poplar and "sugar tree" boards figured in his fancy production. He purchased his turned work from suppliers. In speaking of the common "Western" maple, Michaux identified the "Black Sugar Tree" (*Acer nigrum*). Use of pine was limited due to its scarcity in the Midwest. Christian Schultz wrote in 1807: "I do not recollect meeting with any white pine below Pittsburgh, nor was any pitch or yellow pines below the Falls of Ohio." Pine boards, shingles, and lumber for building came from Pittsburgh, cut from groves at the head of the Allegheny River.[173]

Insights into Canadian chairmaking materials are based on identifications made by local authors. Pine seats were used throughout the maritime provinces (Nova Scotia and New Brunswick) and Upper and Lower Canada (Ontario and Quebec). White pine was common and, according to Michaux, attained its greatest diameter around the Saint Lawrence River in Upper Canada. Basswood chair planks are rare. Maple was the common choice for turned work. Michaux's remarks on the range of the sugar maple (*Acer saccharum*) are pertinent: "It is nowhere more abundant than between the 46th and 43d degrees which comprise Canada, New Brunswick, Nova Scotia, the States of Vermont and New Hampshire, and the District of Maine." In the Maritimes chairmakers sometimes selected yellow birch as an alternative for turned work. The tree abounded in the forests of Nova Scotia, New Brunswick, and Maine. William Bentley of Salem, Massachusetts, described a heavy growth of rock (sugar) maple, birch, and ash in southern Quebec adjacent to the Vermont border. Hickory and ash provided wood for bent chair parts.[174]

WOOD PREPARATION

The chairmaker had two concerns in working the raw materials of his trade: that the moisture content of his wood was appropriate to the task and that the final product was durable and stable. To meet the varied structural requirements of a Windsor the craftsman chose several woods. The principal construction unit is the plank, for which relatively soft, moderately light, air-dried stock suited best. Wood partially dried in this manner remained easy to saw and work to saddled or saucered form, and it was less likely to split upon drying further. At Templeton, Massachusetts, Peter Pierce stored his "Lot of Chair Plank in the Shed," where it was protected from the elements while drying to the degree desired for working. Peter Willard of neighboring Sterling used his "waggon house" for the same purpose. Straight-grained hardwood was chosen for turnings. It rived and turned best when relatively "green," or of high moisture content. Ring porous hardwoods provided the flexibility and strenth required for wood bending. Green stock again was desirable for ease of riving and shaving. Preliminary to framing the chairmaker could condition his materials further by allowing steamed and bent bows to air-dry. He preserved the curve by tying the ends. Bows and turned parts also could be exposed to heat from the shop hearth or stove to achieve a state of lowered moisture content referred to in the English trade as "tenon dry."[175]

Considerable evidence documents the chairmaker's awareness of the economic benefits of using well-prepared, seasoned materials and sound construction practices. When advertising on July 19, 1787, at Providence, Rhode Island, Daniel Lawrence "warranted" his Windsor chairs "of good seasoned Materials, so firmly put together as not to deceive the Purchasers by an untimely coming to pieces." John Denig of Chambersburg, Pennsylvania, equally confident in 1822 of the quality of his materials, promised: "Any work done in my shop after this date, that comes a part by reason of unseasoned stuff, I will make as good as new, or give a new chair in its place, without any expense to the purchaser." At Nashville, Tennessee, the firm

FIG. 2-30 David Dexter and Son factory, Black River, N.Y., ca. 1866–77. From *History of Jefferson County, New York* (Philadelphia: L. H. Everts, 1878), facing p. 500.

of Samuel Williams and Company warranted their work "to stand as long as any in the western country."[176]

New construction techniques of the early nineteenth century, which replaced the H-plan stretcher system of the Windsor (fig. 3-17) with box-style braces (fig. 3-35), and an increasing demand for quantities of dry flat stock for fancy-chair production encouraged some chairmakers to introduce a kiln to their premises. A structure with a tall smokestack, probably for this purpose, stands at the extreme left of David Dexter's woodworking complex at Black River, New York (fig. **2-30**). Use of a kiln speeded drying and could reduce the moisture content of wood below that of normal air-drying, as required. A credit in the accounts of Nelson Talcott of Portage County, Ohio, suggests that some kilns were of substantial size. On February 5, 1841, Talcott noted that Edwin Whiting spent "one and half day clearing Kill and Bending 54 Dining Chairs." Even if Whiting devoted most of his time to the chairwork, the kiln appears to have held a fair amount of prepared timber. Another large kiln was the "Dry house" equipped in 1836 with an "old Stove" on Peter Pierce's property at Templeton, Massachusetts. As Pierce stored his chair plank in a shed, the kiln apparently dried turned stuff and small lumber. Later, Lambert Hitchcock's facilities in Connecticut included a "Building used as a kiln dry & stove & pipe."[177]

PREPARED CHAIR STOCK

Levels of Business
The chairmaker had three options when acquiring stock for chair assembly: to prepare it himself, to obtain hired help, or to purchase "chair stuff" from a supplier. Some shops utilized all three options. Chairmakers' accounts suggest that before the rise of mechanization in the nineteenth century many artisans, especially those located outside commercial centers, prepared their own stock in a small facility, occasionally with a partner or temporary help. An example of the small independent workman is Jonathan Cahoone of Newport, Rhode Island, who in the early 1770s supplied Windsor chairs to merchant Aaron Lopez. His report of losses from British depredations during the Revolution describes the limited production of the one-man shop: a "Number of Cheresmakers Tules of all sorts, one Dussen of Chers made, and maney more sawed out stuff for Chers I Cannot tell how much." As was common, Cahoone supplemented woodworking with other activity, since he owned "one good Boot[boat] fit for Bsenss[business]."[178]

Facilities, Equipment, and Materials 93

Limited exchanges of chair parts were normal expedients of the barter system for payment of goods and services. When in 1813 Wait Garret of New Hartford–Canton, Connecticut, sold "one set Common Chairs at 62½ cents" per chair, he accepted in payment "chair legs, bows, and ball lists [back elements] at 11 Cent pr Chair to be deliverd by the first of march nex[t]." At Suffield-Windsor Andrew Denison acquired "chair stuff turn'd" and a "clothe chest not painted" from Reuben Loomis in exchange for "ornamenting chairs one day." Titus Preston of Wallingford debited his son Almon, who occupied shop space, for "materials for 12 Chairs with the legs ready turned."[179]

Journeyman labor to fabricate parts in quantity for framing inexpensive seating furniture was part of the trade even before the introduction of Windsor furniture. Described among Windsor-chair making records is the work of journeyman Robert McKeen for Joseph Adams of Boston. Under typical shop agreements McKeen framed chairs from parts provided by Adams and painted the seating. In autumn 1789 after several of these stints McKeen replenished the turned stock:

90 Doz Legs for chairs at 7d pr Doz	£2.12.6
8 Doz short Corner pieces at 6d	0.4.0
18 Doz Long corner pieces at 8d	0.12.0
2 Doz long stretches at 5d pr Doz	0.0.10[180]

Just after 1800 Joseph Hooper worked occasionally for Silas Cheney of Litchfield, Connecticut, framing chairs and producing turned "Chare stuf" and bows. Another workman named McNiel spent "4½ Days at giting out rods." Somewhat later David Pritchard of Waterbury employed Augustus Harrison to produce "Tops and rockers." In New Hampshire John B. Wilder worked occasionally for his brother Josiah P., who in 1841 credited him with "Shaving 800 Office [chair] Pillors" and "150 Front Stretchers" and smoothing "20 Common Seats." Moses F. Weld worked for extra pay outside the terms of his general shop contract at Windsor, Vermont, in 1825 when he prepared "a lot of Chair Stuff" for Thomas Boynton. References to both day work and piecework appear in the records of Nelson Talcott, who worked in Ohio.[181]

The production of chair parts in one shop for delivery to another was extensive. Hugh O'Neal supplied Solomon Fussell with seat lists and stretchers as early as 1739–40 for his rush-bottom-chair business at Philadelphia. To maximize the skilled artisan's time Fussell employed Samuel Hurford to prepare stock "to be Turnd by Hugh Oneal." Lawrence Allwine, another local chairmaker, employed Andrew Hagerty during the 1780s to turn 1,950 "Windsor Chair Legs." François André Michaux shed additional light on the Philadelphia trade in chair stock when noting the use of red maple "for the lower part of Windsor chairs" and explaining, "The pieces are turned in the country, and so considerable is the demand, that boats laden with them arrive at New York and Philadelphia, where an extensive manufacture is carried on, for the consumption of the neighboring towns, and for exportation to the Southern States and to the West India Islands."[182]

Eighteenth-century documents from New England, where the Windsor became popular after the Revolution, provide further insights into the trade in chair parts. Elisha Hawley of Ridgefield, Connecticut, recorded the receipt of "common" and "long Chair Rounds," "Chair Bottoms," and bows. William Colgrew supplied the Proud brothers of Providence with dozens of chair bows, sticks (spindles), and a few settee bows, all split from green logs and shaved to form. The Prouds, who counted turning a specialty, produced their own round work.[183]

The New England trade in chair parts swung into high gear in the early 1800s, when it operated on several levels. Chairmakers with substantial businesses sometimes wholesaled parts to chair framers who assembled and retailed the seating in a limited neighborhood market. Rural handicraftsmen earned extra money or credit by "getting out" chair parts—seats, spindles, and dressed sticks for lathe work—with hand tools for disposal at regional shops. Turning specialists offered a variety of prepared stock, and some men built sizable businesses supplying lathe work in quantity to shops in commercial centers, large and small.

A spirit of cooperation prevailed in most areas. Competition, while inevitable, seems not to have been cutthroat and ruthless, as common in later periods. In slack times rural craftsmen could fall back on farming or on other types of woodworking activity. The real problems lay in urban centers, where frequently there were more independent operatives than local or regional commerce could support. When the going got tough some artisans moved on. Usually it was the men who lacked the commercial savvy or capital to deal effectively in a competitive market, individuals who had experienced a run of bad luck, or craftsmen whose restless spirits looked to new horizons.

Exchanges of prepared "chair stuff" among local craftsmen were common. Records for New Haven, Connecticut, show dealings between Levi Stillman and fellow chairmakers James English and Edward Bulkley. Silas Cheney of Litchfield sent "turned" and "Chair Stuff" to David Pritchard in neighboring Waterbury. Ephraim Wilder, who obtained 100 chair seats from Luke Houghton of Barre, Massachusetts, in 1818, repaid that and other debts the following year by supplying finished chairs and working for a month in Houghton's shop. From his manufactory at Windsor, Vermont, Thomas Boynton supplied William Ayres with turned work, rods, and even stuff bent to form. Boynton himself sometimes "borrowed" chair seats from Rufus Norton.[184]

Shop accounts extend the parameters of the regional trade in chair parts. Henry W. Miller of Worcester, Massachusetts, acquired "60 Grecian Posts" in 1827 from the New York firm of Tweed and Bonnell. The purchase may have served a dual purpose: to test a new pattern in the local market and to provide a model to copy if the chair was successful. Jacob Felton of Fitzwilliam, New Hampshire, had a network of regional contacts extending as far as neighboring Worcester County, Massachusetts, where he interacted with chairmakers in the towns of Ashburnham, Sterling, and Gardner. His border trade included a full complement of parts—seats, turnings, and shaved work.[185]

Sometimes local residents in other occupations who possessed a degree of handiwork skill capitalized on opportunities to earn extra cash. Versatile woodworker Samuel Davison of Plainfield, Massachusetts, supplied several area chairmakers with seats. He purchased rough planks from a country jack, partially finished them, and turned a profit in the transaction. David Pritchard and Silas Cheney of western Connecticut acquired seats for their chair trade from handymen such as Davison. Other individuals prepared stock for turning, and persons of greater skill provided limited quantities of turned work. There were, however, standards to be maintained. Cheney carefully checked the stock he received and noted on occasion "18 frunt rowns [rounds] . . . poore," or "Standards [arm posts] too Short," or seats "narrow & sum shaky" (cracked). Elizur Barnes, a craftsman of Middletown, found among "200 Sett of Windsor Cheir fraimes" supplied by Nathan Wilcox in 1822 "100 Rods wanting" and a substantial number of "verry Bad" posts and legs.[186]

Major Suppliers and Consumers

Some individuals made a livelihood of preparing chair "stuff," as described by a resident of Worcester County, Massachusetts: "Mr. Ezra Baker . . . constructed a small dam . . . securing sufficient water power to carry a turning lathe. [He] bought timber of his neighbors, partly prepared, by being sawed into suitable length and rounded somewhat upon the corners, for turning in this lathe driven by water power. . . . The stock thus turned, by Mr. Baker, was sold . . . and in this way greatly facilitated the manufacture of . . . chairs."[187]

In the bloom of his career Silas Cheney of Litchfield, Connecticut, formed business liaisons with several large suppliers of chair stock at Lee, Massachusetts. Making inquiry in April 1814, Cheney received a reply from West and Hatch on May 11:

> Sir
>
> I Receaved youer apriel the twenteyh an it informs us that You air in wont of Chair Stuff an I think that you Can have as mush as you wont for the Sam[e] as we have lat [let] Mr Wells of hartford have it, the fancy Bamboo 45 Dollers an hundred Seat [set], Bamboo winsor at 27 Dollers an hundred, an other Stuff according to the work on it. I have plain winsor Stuff on hand an if you will Com Soon I will keep it for you and you Can have Other Stuff By a Short notice.
>
> West & Hatch

During the year Cheney purchased 200 sets each of plain and bamboo Windsor stuff, 100 sets each of "Spring Back" (bent back) and "Bamboo Ball Back" stock, fancy bamboo stuff for 50 chairs, "Common Chair Stuff," and "Backs, fronts, an[d] Spindles for 12 plain fancy chairs." Total material cost was $198.10. Cheney later dealt with Daniel Foot and Company of Lee.[188]

From his coastal location in Groton, Connecticut, James Gere was a major supplier of chair parts in southern New London County. His customers included almost a dozen chairmakers in Norwich and Preston. In a quarter century of record keeping from 1809 to the 1830s Gere supplied thousands of sets of turned "Chair Stuff" and six or seven times as many miscellaneous parts. Sets were available for "small," "bamboo," "fancy," and Windsor seating, some with arms. Comprising a set were legs, "rounds" (stretchers), posts, "banisters" (spindles or cross pieces), and, at times, arms. Walnut or curled maple parts rated special note. Customers paid for materials in several ways: with cabinetwork, sets of framed chairs, native timber or mahogany, supplies of sandpaper, glue, and varnish, or by painting and performing other services.[189]

Josiah Prescott Wilder and Increase Pote represent the suppliers of northern New England. Although Wilder primarily made finished seating for a regional market that extended from southern New Hampshire to Boston, he knew a brisk trade in chair stock to New York City, where his brother Calvin was established. Shipments, which began in 1837, were directed between 1841 and 1844 to Wilder and Stewart (Edwin). Most stock was for special seating—office, sewing, rocking, and barber chairs, and camp stools. From 1824 to 1829 Increase Pote supplied chairmakers in Portland, Maine, with turned work.[190]

David Alling of Newark, New Jersey, was a substantial *consumer* of chairmaking materials throughout his career from 1800 to 1855. His stock lists form a lexicon of chairmaking terms, from "benders," or laterally curved back pieces, to "Beeded front rounds," or fancy front stretchers. When purchasing complete sets of parts, Alling recorded fancy and bamboo stuff, large rocking stuff, and Windsor stock in plain, new-fashioned, and roll-top patterns at prices ranging from 11¢ to 37¢ the set. His suppliers resided in New Jersey and New York. Sometimes Alling acquired almost 8,000 individual chair parts in one purchase.[191]

John Schroeder, a Lancaster, Pennsylvania, chairmaker, carried a supply of "dry Chair turned stuff and bows [crest pieces] at all times." In Portage County, Ohio, Nelson Talcott sometimes hired Pliny Allen to turn chair timber. Special stock included rocking and children's chairs. Jacob Roll of Cincinnati identified his source of stock in 1820: "I purchase my Turned Stuff from Persons that live and do their Turning in the Country." He and a partner, Isaac Deeds, had advertised: "Wanted, a very considerable quantity of chair stuff, for Fancy and Windsor chairs. Turners that wish a good Job, and prompt payment, are requested to call on the subscribers, at their Chair Factory, on Fourth-street . . . and get patterns. We wish to enter into contract for a regular supply."[192]

Arrangements such as these typify those made by chair manufacturers throughout the country from the early 1800s on. Edwin T. Freedley described the advantages of cooperative enterprise in a burgeoning industrial society:

> The economy which results from producing on a large scale, induces an increased demand for . . . manufactured goods; and an increased demand leads to a more minute subdivision of a manufacture into parts. When thousand of machines . . . are required, we find establishments springing up, devoted exclusively to making parts—one, the nuts and washers; another the screws; another the bolts; another the nails; and others tools and machines to facilitate making parts, and so on, each extensive in its way, and thus large establishments in the leading branches of Manufactures are the parents of other extensive concerns in minor branches. A man who has not the requisite capital to conduct a leading Manufacture where large establishments abound . . . will not benefit himself by moving away from them. His policy [should be] to remain . . . and then to accommodate his business to their operations and to his capital—that is, he will find it more profitable to be an extensive manufacturer of eyes for children's dolls in the centre of Manufactures, than a small manufacturer of machinery elsewhere.[193]

Another supply source for the chairmaker was the entrepreneur businessman who acquired chair materials at wholesale for retail in small parcels. In 1806 Ebenezer Fox, general-store keeper of Salem, Massachusetts, purchased in Boston "the stuff compleat for five hundred Bamboo Chairs & one hundred Fan-Back Ditto @ 50 cs" to retail locally. Earlier, in 1801, Simon Francis, a lumber dealer and cabinetmaker of Boston, had advertised for sale "100 dozen Windsor Chair-Bows." These likely were short, laterally "bowed" top pieces for square-back Windsors (fig. 3-34). At Baltimore Sinclair and Moore offered "about 6,000 CHAIR TOPS . . . at moderate prices" from their stand on the Pratt Street wharf. The estates of deceased or insolvent chairmakers often yielded ready stock along with tools and equipment. The Virginia sheriff who attached the shop goods of Joseph Childres placed on public sale "a vast quantity of Rounds, Sticks, &c. ready prepared for putting together." The sale in 1815 of Zenos Bronson's property at Raleigh, North Carolina, offered "Maple stuff turned . . . as well as the bottoms gotten out, for near 200 chairs." Stuff available in 1832 upon the death of N. W. Burpee at Montreal included "Turned Wood fit for 100 Chairs [and] 1300 Chair Bottoms." Particularly complete are the estates of Peter Pierce (1836) and Peter Willard (1842) of Worcester County, Massachusetts, who died in midcareer. The Pierce sale offered "Chair Stuff" comprising almost 44,000 individual pieces; the two Willard sales disposed of almost 17,000 parts.[194]

Nomenclature and Cost of Components
The nomenclature of Windsor-chair components is variable, sometimes regional, and often confusing. Frequently only collective evidence supports an identification. The survey that follows draws on more than fifty documents, originating primarily in New England and the Middle Atlantic region, to provide insights into the language of the trade.

The seat, the basic component of the Windsor, frequently was termed a *bottom* (fig. 3-17). Legs were legs, but the word *feet* often prevailed in the Delaware Valley. Leg braces were *stretchers* or, more often, *rounds*. Uprights framing structural back members were called *posts*—back posts, chair posts, long posts, or corner posts— and occasionally *long corner pieces*; *pillar* was an alternative name. By extension, low under-arm supports were *short posts*, *front posts*, *short corner pieces*, or *arm pillars*. Other terms include *stand ups* and *arm standards*, both used on occasion in New

England. *Stump* was current from Pennsylvania south. Fancy chairs and Windsor chairs with rabbeted tops were *stump-back* chairs in the same region (fig. 3-68).

Arms may have been called *elbows* only in the Delaware Valley. Various terms describe the spindles, as that specific word was not in common use. *Rod* was the popular name, although heavier back members were similarly described upon occasion. *Stick* was the leading alternative; a *flat stick* was a spindle of arrow shape or other ornamental profile (fig. 3-8). Some terms, such as *rounds for backs*, are self-explanatory. Occasionally the word *banister* referred to a spindle, but more often it was a heavy vertical or horizontal member at the center back (figs. 3-45, 3-46). *Bow* clearly describes the arched back piece of an eighteenth-century Windsor (fig. 3-16); however, the nineteenth-century use of the word is less obvious. In patterns dating after 1800 the "bow" of the cross rods (fig. 3-35) or slats (*broad bows*, fig. 3-47) produces a lateral curve more easily perceived when looking down on a chair back than facing it. The word *bow* also applied at times to the crest of an eighteenth-century fan-back chair (fig. 3-17, right).

There was no such thing as a "crest" by that name. Supplementing *bow* were the terms *top*, *top rail*, and *cap piece*; more popular by far was the word *back*. This term originated in the eighteenth century, or earlier, to describe a rush-bottom turner's chair with two, three, four, or more cross pieces, or *backs* (fig. 3-18). A substitute word was *slat*. Another term of modest use in describing the top piece was *bender*. This word was especially common in northern New Jersey and New York City in the early nineteenth century, as confirmed in David Alling's accounts. Other records describe heavy, turned tops as *rolls* (fig. 5-25). The *scroll top* was either a Baltimore-style tablet with a backward-scrolled top lip (fig. 5-27) or the crown-top crest with scroll ends common to the Boston rocker (pl. 27). For horizontal cross pieces positioned between the chair top and seat words such as *banister*, *slat*, *centerpiece*, *fret*, and *ball list* (pl. 10) describe the variety. A complete, or even partial, *set* of turned and shaved parts necessary to make a chair was designated *stuff*, *stock*, or *stand*.

Calculating the cost of individual chair parts is uncertain at best. Particular information about the components — size, elaboration, and finish — generally is lacking, and prices given even for specific items are variable. Few values are available for eighteenth-century materials, and those that appear often represent late work in the bamboo style. Thus, except for a small amount of data dating from the 1790s, the following estimates are based on figures given for early nineteenth-century work.

Large finished rocking-chair seats generally cost about 11½¢ or 12½¢. The seat price for the smaller, armless *nurse* rocking chair was about 7¢, a figure that also represented the average cost of an armchair plank. Seats for *small*, or children's, chairs are quoted from about 1½¢ to 3¼¢, leaving the range between 3¢ and 7¢ to be assigned to bottoms for side chairs. Information from the inventory of Ansel Goodrich, who died at Northampton, Massachusetts, in 1803, and the accounts of supplier Samuel Davison provides a rare opportunity to follow the development and cost of a chair seat from the timber to the finished article. Goodrich's inventory lists "Plank for 2 douzen chair seats" valued at 72¢, or 3¢ per seat. Advancing the unit value to 4¢ was a group of 120 seats probably sawed to form only, since another five dozen seats appraised at 6¢ each were described as "partly finished." Labor in the form of "hewing & dubbing 346 chair Seats" supplied by Davison the year before Goodrich's death cost the chairmaker 2¢ per plank. This unit charge, added to the value of the 4¢ sawed seat blank, produced the appraiser's "partly finished" 6¢ plank. Five dozen of Davison's seats remained in the shop at Goodrich's death. Shaving to final form probably required somewhat more time per unit than Davison's adze and drawknife work, raising the unit cost another 2½¢ or 3¢. Some finish work likely was carried out by the "Three Journeymen Chairmakers" promised "good encouragment" the summer before Goodrich's death. The valuation of Goodrich's finished seats at 8½¢ or 9¢ apiece, more than the general range suggested for side chairs, is explained by their eighteenth-century form with front pommels and highly contoured surfaces (fig. 4-18) in contrast to the simple saucered tops of nineteenth-century planks (fig. 3-49). This line of reasoning is confirmed in John Lambert's estate inventory compiled at Philadelphia in 1793, which lists "Chair Bottoms made" at 11*d*. (15¼¢) apiece and the same article "partly made" at 2*d*. less (12½¢).[195]

The cost of chair legs per unit varied from ¼¢ to about 1½¢. Items in the ¼¢ to ½¢ range usually represented "unturned" stock readied for the lathe, as reported in several inventories from New England. At Philadelphia "600 Turned Bamboo Feet" listed in John Lambert's estate of 1793 achieved a valuation of 1⅓¢ apiece. Legs turned earlier in the city for Lawrence Allwine, perhaps to a similar pattern, cost 2¢ apiece. The transaction date of 1787 falls within the baluster-and-bamboo conversion period for Philadelphia and could represent either pattern. Stretchers were of simpler form than legs and therefore cheaper. Rough stock prepared for the lathe probably cost no more than ¼¢ apiece. Prices for the finished article fell within the ½¢ to 1¢ range, except for fancy front stretchers, which brought prices of 1¢ to 3¢. Back posts were priced the same as legs when of similar pattern. Some had ornamental rings, and many were shaved on the face, a further step after turning that advanced the price. Bending stock for the bent-back styles added another price increment. Arm posts cost about a quarter less than the long, turned back members.[196]

A unit cost of ½¢ to 1½¢ was usual for common spindles. The lower figure corresponds to the individual price of "5042 Rods at 60 Cent Pr 100" itemized in 1798 in the estate of Timothy Hanson at Wilmington, Delaware. During the same decade John Lambert stocked a supply of "Turnd Bamboo Sticks" at Philadelphia, each worth 1¢ apiece. The difference in values reflects the presence of shaped segments and turned grooves in Lambert's spindles. At Providence the Proud brothers paid as much as 1¾¢ apiece for chair sticks. Specialty items such as David Alling's oval, squared, Cumberland, and organ spindles purchased from suppliers around Newark, New Jersey, in the early 1800s cost as much as 2¾¢, a price comparable to that of long rocking-chair rods quoted at 2½¢ each in the accounts of J. P. Wilder at New Hampshire from the 1830s and later.[197]

Several documents illuminate the cost of eighteenth-century Windsor bows. There are two types: an arch that anchors in the sack-back armrail and a long curved looplike bow that fastens in the seat of a bow-back side chair (figs. 5-61, 4-19). The two cannot always be differentiated in records, although there are clues. The Proud brothers of Providence paid 7¢ and 8¢ for one type and slightly more than 4¢ apiece for another, probably those described in an unpriced reference as "Littel ons" and used in the sack-back armchair. By extension, it can be surmised that Francis Trumble's "108 Bowes for Chairs (in the Ruff)" valued at 5¢ apiece at Philadelphia were for use in bow-back chairs. More particular data occur in the inventory of fellow chairmaker John Lambert, whose "Long Bows bent" were worth 7¢ apiece and "Long Bows clean'd up and Boxed," 12½¢ each. Terms used in the second reference appear to imply that the bows had been bent, patterned on the face, and secured in arched form pending use by means of a cord, stick, or clamp fastened across the open end. In the same inventory is an item for "4 Round Top arms bent," that is, arm rails for sack-back chairs, priced at 8¼¢ apiece. At Timothy Hanson's shop in Wilmington, south of Philadelphia, quantities of "Bamboo bows bent" and "unbent" were valued in 1798 at 7¢ and 2¢ apiece. Hanson also made fan-back side chairs. Stock on hand included "12 Top rails bent" worth 55¢ the dozen, or something more than 4½¢ apiece. Appraisers at Philadelphia were not as generous in evaluating John Lambert's "Fan Back top Rails bent" at only 2¾¢ apiece or Francis Trumble's stock at 2½¢ each.[198]

Laterally curved top pieces in early nineteenth-century painted seating took two forms. As described by David Alling, *round benders*, or Windsor cross rods, cost 1⅓¢ apiece. *Flat benders*, or slats, at twice the price were integral to Alling's fancy-chair production. The same *broad bows* commanded a price of only 1½¢ in Connecticut and Boston a few years later. Fancy parts for chair backs were more expensive: 4¢ for turned rolls; 5¢ and 3¢ for "Birdseye Tops" and matching banisters. Specialty items also realized extra prices. The mahogany for a pair of arms cost 14¢ in 1841, as noted by J. P. Wilder. Forward-scroll walnut arms made for bow-back seating forty years earlier by Timothy Hanson cost slightly more than half that figure, or 8⅓¢ the pair, but they were smaller in size. Some settee materials were costly. Bottoms evaluated in Anthony Steel's shop at Philadelphia reached figures of 63¢ and $1 apiece in a compilation that assigned only 4¢ to chair seats. Price was based in part on the extra log size required to provide timber of suitable breadth. Likewise, bows for eighteenth-century settees were costly, since bending required a special steam vessel of extra length or a two-stage manipulation of the bend, first one end, then the other. Thus, the 25¢ unit value of John Lambert's "4 Settee Bows bent" was not out of line.[199]

MISCELLANEOUS MATERIALS

Glue

The use of animal glue was common among American chairmakers, as indicated by the many glue pots listed in shop inventories and the number of documents containing references to the adhesive. The practice was especially prominent after 1800 when box-style stretchers were introduced to the Windsor. The manufacturing process is explained in the London *Book of Trades* (1805): "Glue . . . is made of the skins of animals, as oxen, sheep, &c. and the older the animal is, the better is the glue. Whole skins are rarely used for this purpose, but only the shavings and parings made by curriers, felt-mongers, &c. These are boiled to the consistence of jelly, and poured into flat moulds to cool; it is then cut into . . . square pieces, and hung up to dry." Joseph Moxon stated that "the clearest, driest, and most transparent Glew is the best." To achieve this state Thomas Sheraton advised adequate refining. For final air-drying glue cakes were attached to string. After purchasing glue in this form, the woodworker broke the cakes into small pieces with a hammer, placed the material in his glue pot with cold water, and set it aside to steep overnight, thus allowing it to swell and regain the consistency of jelly.[200]

Glue preparation for shop use required care to prevent sticking or burning. A wooden spatula and special boiler were requisite equipment. As described in a manual of the practical sciences, "the joiners . . . suspend the vessel containing [glue] in another vessel containing only water, which latter vessel is generally made of copper, in the form of a common tea-kettle without a spout, and alone receives the direct influence of the fire." Glue-pot double boilers are well documented in American craft records. The glue was ready for use when it achieved the consistency of an egg white. If too thick, it could be thinned by adding water, although with repeated heating glue became dark and "its qualities . . . impaired."[201]

For optimum results the glue was heated and applied promptly to wooden chair parts that were warm and dry. Both surfaces to be united required a thin brushing of adhesive, although the tenon ends of turnings could be dipped into the glue pot. A warm atmosphere also was essential while the glue hardened. To ensure satisfactory performance glue usually was heated only twice.[202]

Although "English" or "London" glue was the standard in eighteenth-century American woodworking circles, concern over lack of a native manufacture led to the erection of several American glue houses before 1800. A few facilities were located in New York by 1814 when Joseph Riley of that city promoted the qualities of "PHILADELPHIA GLUE" at his fancy-chair store. Later, when manufactories were common in many cities, one Canadian consumer considered "the best New York glue" even superior to the English product. Glue production in Philadelphia reached 12,500 barrels annually by midcentury; the barrel price was $22.[203]

From the late 1700s to the 1850s the price/evaluation of a pound of glue varied from 10½¢ to 54¢, with 23⅓¢ the average. The highest prices were recorded during the first two decades of the nineteenth century. In general, cost related directly to the quantity purchased, as recorded in eastern Massachusetts from 1803 to 1804 by Stephen Whipple: one-quarter pound cost 40¢ per pound; one-half pound, 34¢ per pound; and 100 pounds, 25¢ per pound. Small quantities could be stored in a box; a large stock required a barrel. Two chairmakers provided insights on shop consumption. One Mallery of Plattsburgh, New York, estimated in 1820 that he used 50 pounds a year; his annual production was 2,000 chairs. In a business projection for 1837, J. P. Wilder of New Ipswich, New Hampshire, set chair production at 2,750 units and glue consumption at 50 pounds.[204]

Sandpaper and Other Abrasives
In the late seventeenth century Joseph Moxon described the traditional practice of turners in smoothing work before removing it from the lathe: "Lastly, they hold either a piece of Seal-skin or *Dutch* Reeds (whose outer Skin or Filme somewhat finely cuts) pretty hard against the Work, and so make it smooth enough to polish." In 1760 "200 Fish Skins for Joiners use" were available at Philadelphia. The practice continued into the early 1800s, with "shark's skin" and "Dutch rushes" both mentioned. Of the second material, James Smith described the "flinty particles in the substance of its leaves" but cautioned that before use rushes "should be moistened a little with water, otherwise they presently break and become almost useless." Perhaps the more common practice among chairmakers was to hold a handful of shavings against the finished work rotating in the lathe.[205]

An early reference to sandpaper occurs in 1764 at New York in a notice of its importation from London. Sandpaper, like emery and glasspaper, utilized particles of hard material sieved to selected fineness and sprinkled over heavy glue-coated paper later cut to size and packaged. By the early 1800s manufactories were established in America, as attested by a Pittsburgh notice of 1819 for "Glass or Sand Paper and EMERY at the Philadelphia and Baltimore prices." The following year J. W. Mason of Cincinnati commented: "We have a Glue & Sand paper Manufactory in operation and if encourage[d] might well in a short time be of Great importance to the Western Country."[206]

Woodworkers purchased sandpaper in quantities ranging from a sheet to a quire (24 to 25 sheets) and occasionally a ream (482 to 500 sheets). As the product became more common, the price dropped. A sheet cost about 5½¢ at the start of the nineteenth century. By the 1830s it was priced at 2¢, a 64 percent reduction.[207]

Brads and Wood Screws
The brad has a headless or L-shape top with a square or rectangular shaft. Large sizes were employed in flooring and finish woodwork because with a punch they could be hammered below the wood's surface and concealed. Cabinetmakers used small brads to attach moldings, and chairmakers employed them to secure crests, bows, arm supports, and seat casings. The brad awl pierced a small hole to receive the brad, also called a sprig, and the small hammer drove it home. In figure **2-31** brads are embedded in a shaped and carved glue block forming the lower half of an arm terminal in a sack-back chair made by Sampson Barnet of Wilmington, Delaware. The combination of brads and glue generally ensured a tight joint.[208]

Records confirm the common use of metal fasteners among chairmakers in references such as "1000 brads" or a "keg of Brads." Four-penny brads bought in quantity in 1785 cost about 80¢ per thousand. By 1824 the cost of five-penny "cut Brads" was about 45¢ the thousand. The fabrication method accounted for the substantial drop

FIG. 2-31 Detail of scroll return for right arm terminal of sack-back Windsor armchair, Sampson Barnet, Wilmington, Del., ca. 1785–92. Yellow poplar (seat) with maple, oak, and hickory (microanalysis). *(Courtesy, Winterthur Museum, acc. 78.107.)*

in price: metal-cutting machines replaced hand forging. By 1789 national production was substantial. In Connecticut alone "almost every town and village" made "nails of every size" for domestic use and exportation at prices lower than European goods.[209]

Windsor-chair makers employed wood screws on occasion to attach arms to back posts, particularly in nineteenth-century work. The fancy-chair maker used this fastening device to secure joints between back posts, seat rails, and arms and to attach tablet-type crests to post faces. Initially screwmaking was a laborious hand process requiring several steps additional to nailmaking; however, mechanical operations replaced handwork by the early nineteenth century, especially through use of the mandrel lathe to cut the shaft spiral. Still it was midcentury before a point replaced the blunt screw tip and eliminated the need to bore or punch a pilot hole when using this fastener.[210]

Eighteenth-century documents describe the early use of screws in furniture, a practice that became common during the early nineteenth century. By 1820 Joseph Beck, a cabinetmaker and chairmaker of Virginia, sustained annual production with a stock of 10,000 screws. In New England David Judd kept a "Small Tub containg screws" on the shop premises, and the partners Parrott and Hubbell owned a "Case of Drawers for screws." Stock on hand in 1852 at Lambert Hitchcock's factory in Connecticut included 55 gross of screws in two sizes.[211]

Shop Energy Sources

POWER

Central to shop operation was availability of an energy source to power mechanical equipment. The early Windsor-chair-making apparatus was the pole lathe, and the power source was the human body (fig. 2-6). The treadle lathe and the great wheel increased production potential, although the latter required the services of a second workman (figs. 2-12, 2-7). Still other power sources permitted the chairmaker to work independently or to expand his operation, but again each had its price and limitations. An elementary though infrequent resource was dog power. In 1828 the New England Farmer described a dog-powered mill at Troy, New York. Somewhat later dogs supplied power to operate the lathes in a Sullivan County, Indiana, cabinet and turning shop.[212]

Horses were the usual animal resource for light industry, and documents occasionally mention oxen. In 1812 Captain William Ashley of Vermont partially covered the cost of half a dozen bent-back chairs acquired from Thomas Boynton by supplying his "oxen and horse to the lathe." Horsepower realized considerable geographic breadth in nineteenth-century America. Beza White, a turner of Boston, relied on horsepower to earn a living as did Caleb Hobart, Jr., of neighboring Hingham. Hobart's assets in 1853 included a half interest in a woodworking shop, "the machinery in said shop, and . . . whatever else is moved by the horse power therein," along with "half of the horses" and harnesses. Walter Corey manufactured chairs and cabinetware in Maine, his lathe and other machinery driven by horsepower before conversion to another energy source about 1840.[213]

Water was the more popular power source among American chairmakers, although periods of drought or flood could compromise, even jeopardize, a manufactory's operation. Erection of a milldam or pond for water storage, an essential power component, mitigated drought conditions by providing two prerequisites necessary to water-mill operation, an adequate flow and fall of water in the millrace. The weight of water times the height of its fall to the wheel within the period of one second is the measure of its "horsepower." In some cases a dam could double the power potential of a natural water site. Water forced against a wheel, whether of impact or gravity (bucket) type, gave it rotary motion, which power in turn was transmitted to the building's interior machinery. In 1828 the *New England Farmer* endorsed the use of "leather bands" to communicate power: "By adopting bands we get rid of the disagreeable noise which attends the movement of toothed machinery, and also save considerable expense in constructing and repairs." The inventory of Peter Pierce (1836), who "made chairs . . . on Pierce's Brook" in Templeton, Massachusetts, describes a "lot of Leather belts" and refers to a "Mill chamber." Maintenance of the power-transmitting machinery was essential. Josiah Prescott Wilder of New Ipswich, New Hampshire, credited an area workman in 1841 for "1 days work on Water Wheel." Earlier Thomas Boynton of Windsor, Vermont, hired out one of his workmen to another mill owner for "part of two afternoons at work on waterworks."[214]

In a comprehensive study of waterpower Louis C. Hunter remarked on the "great natural wealth" of this resource in the United States and its development "on a scale unapproached elsewhere" despite a scattered population, a predominantly rural economy, and an expanding frontier. From the 1820s until well past midcentury waterpower was of prime importance in developing the chair industry of northern Worcester County, Massachusetts, where innumerable watercourses subdivided the land and provided a host of "water privileges." The 1820 manufacturing census also identified the importance of waterpower to chair manufacturers throughout the Midwest and New York State. Sites such as Rochester on the Genessee River, with access to Lake Ontario, encouraged optimum development of resources. In the 1850s two chair factories employed three hundred men and produced chairs valued at $200,000 per annum. Lambert Hitchcock of Connecticut based his chair production on waterpower. In the 1820s he built a dam of logs and stone across the Farmington River, erected a three-story brick shop and a smaller building for turning and sawing, and installed an undershot waterwheel. The chair shop of William Moore, Jr., a neighbor to the north on Still River, was served by an aqueduct. A large waterwheel, probably of the breast or undershot type, is just visible behind a tree at the right end of Dexter's millpond in Jefferson County, New York (fig. 2-30).[215]

Steam power was not a major focus in the American furniture industry until the mid-nineteenth century because waterpower was cheap and relatively plentiful. Early references are sporadic. In 1798 a fire occurred in a wooden building in Philadelphia where a "Mr. M'Elwee had a steam-engine for the purpose of grinding paints." About 1831 John Fulton of Bank Alley in the city "erected a *Steam Engine for Turning*." The following year at Baltimore John Needles introduced steam power to his Hanover Street cabinet works to operate two turning lathes, circular and upright saws, and a tenoning machine. By the early 1840s L. M. Crane and Company of Newark, New Jersey, "CABINET MANUFACTURERS, AT THE CLINTON STEAM WORKS," advertised "Power and Rooms to let—Sawing and Turning."[216]

Activity escalated during the 1840s. Steam power provided American industry with new flexibility. On an introductory basis steam could be used at a mill site to overcome seasonal water shortages. Eventually this power source enabled industry to choose sites irrespective of waterpower. Typical of steam facilities at midcentury is the Price and Harper sawmill and fancy-chair manufactory with adjacent lumberyard at Philadelphia (fig. **2-32**). Walter Corey already had introduced a "trim little steam engine" to his facility at Portland, Maine, and at Poughkeepsie, New York, S. Chichester and Company had converted from water to steam by installing a 25-horsepower engine.[217]

Midwestern interests also looked to steam power. John Pfaff manufactured chairs by steam in 1844 in Cincinnati, and a decade later W. D. Rand advertised his "STEAM CHAIR FACTORY" at Louisville, Kentucky. Canadian manufacturers discovered the advantages of steam power. By 1851 Jacques and Hay of Toronto employed

FIG. 2-32 Advertisement of Price and Harper, drawn by William H. Reese, printed by Wagner and McGuigan, Philadelphia, 1855. Color lithograph; H. 12", W. 21½". *(The Library Company of Philadelphia.)*

a 15-horsepower steam engine that set in motion lathes, circular saws, and planing machines.[218]

HEATING, LIGHTING, AND SANITATION

Stoves are well represented in woodworkers' records, suggesting that this heat source was standard equipment in most shops from the late 1700s. Many stoves are identified by type. When Robert Walker offered his Philadelphia joiner's shop for sale in 1766, it was complete with "Benches already fixed" and "a good Cannon stove," an upright heater of cannon shape. The six-plate stove of cast iron was a contemporary shop fixture in Pennsylvania. This freestanding elevated rectangular box comprising six individual plates bolted together has a fire door and hearth at the front and a smoke pipe rising from the top. Stovepipes probably vented into the chimney flue above the fireplace, a facility of limited use once the stove became common. James Wilson's shop building erected in the 1830s near Pittsburgh relied entirely on stove heat, as did that in Massachusetts of Enos White, who commented in 1831: "I now have been at the Expense of fitting up the second story of the Shop so as to work in it the year round, the whole Cost amounts to 54.00 with the stove which cost 15.00. I have put in two windows filled it with Brick and Boarded it." Stoves had several advantages over fireplaces: they burned fuel more efficiently, were freestanding, and radiated heat in all directions.[219]

The "open" stove, or Franklin heater, listed in several Philadelphia shop inventories is a broad, hooded box open at the lower front and furnished with a rounded hearth. It was placed in the recess of a masonry fireplace. In 1811 a "Franklin" also heated William Ash I's shop at New York. A ten-plate stove served other facilities. Larger than the six-plate stove, it contains an interior oven elevated above the fuel. Before 1810 a "ten plated Stove with Pipe" stood in the shop of Michael Stoner at Lancaster, Pennsylvania.[220]

The utilitarian heater designed for shop and business was the rectangular sheet-iron stove, which stands on four legs and contains a hearth, or ledge, at the front (fig. 2-7). A metal tray protected the floor from scorching and reduced chances of accidental fire. A sheet-iron stove that heated Ziba Ferriss's shop in Wilmington, Delaware, was described in 1794 as "much worn." By the 1820s a "Cast iron box stove," such as that installed by Lambert Hitchcock at his factory in Connecticut, was common in woodworking shops. Supported on three or four legs, it is slightly larger than the sheet-iron stove. Later references to an "air tight" heater probably describe the "cylinder" stove of other documents.[221]

A heated shop provided more than just warmth for the workmen; it was essential to the craft itself. Selected chair parts required drying before framing. The inventory of Godfrey Cole's shop at Baltimore made in 1804 refers to a six-plate stove immediately following an entry for two glue pots, which likely stood on or near the heater most of the time. Large nineteenth-century manufactures commonly had several stoves. Charles Riley of Philadelphia owned six. An $8 cast-iron stove was one of five heaters in Benjamin Bass's shop at Boston. Appraisers listed three of Lambert Hitchcock's seven stoves under specific room headings.[222]

Stovepipes, or "funnels," are mentioned frequently with the heating unit. Thomas Boynton of Vermont paid $1.20 for "6 lbs Stove pipe," the cost equal to the price of one painted chair. Parrott and Hubbell's investment in heating equipment is itemized in a record of 1835 from Connecticut:

1 Large Box Stove	$3.50
1 Smaller Do	2.50
1 quite small Do	1.50
40 feet of 6 inch stove pipe at 10 [cents]	4.00
18 " 5 " " " 8	1.44
3 Elbows at 6	.18
1 Oil Can	.25

Job Danforth of Providence described a typical installation in 1792: "cutting holes in the floor and Roof of the shop for your Stove pipe."[223]

Hearth and stove required "fuel." Woodworkers often exchanged their services and products for cords of wood suitable for heating or chairmaking. In 1829 an auction notice for a chair manufactory located at the nation's capital carefully distinguished between "stove" and "chair stuff," and about this time David Alling exchanged "Sixteen dollars in Chairs for fire wood" at Newark, New Jersey. Some years later appraisers of Lambert Hitchcock's property in Connecticut took account of the "Fuel in the yard."[224]

Another fuel is identified as "Refuse Chair Stuff" in two inventories of Connecticut origin. In New Hampshire Jacob Felton's shop accounts are even more explicit in noting the sale of "Refuse stuff to burn." Whereas Felton turned his extra waste material into a merchantable commodity, John Paine of Long Island gave away a load of "chips from [the] yard." Years later when mechanization held sway, the wood chips of the factory were gathered in troughs and sent by conveyor belt to the boiler rooms to supply energy for production and heat. Smaller establishments managed with something like the "10 barrels of shavings, Kindling wood &c" stored at Luke Houghton's shop in Massachusetts. Occasionally a "Coal Stove & Pipe" is identified in shop records. At his death in 1842 Charles Riley of Philadelphia possessed four tons of coal to fuel the shop stoves.[225]

Artificial light in the shop is not easily interpreted, given the scarcity of information. Summer posed few problems, but winter days were short, and daylight ended before the working day was over. In factory practice in nineteenth-century England "each man had his own oil-lamp and bought his own lamp-oil" to light his bench. During the day shops and factories, alike, utilized natural light to the greatest extent possible, positioning work areas and mechanical equipment close to windows (figs. 2-5, 2-12, 3-32).[226]

Other records hint at prevailing practice in early nineteenth-century America. Gilbert M. Lyons, a journeyman, wrote on October 1, 1834, while in Connecticut: "Commenced working evenings, Lamp and oil found at Sixpence per week." Ten years later on March 15, 1844, Edward Jenner Carpenter, an apprentice at Greenfield, Massachusetts, provided further insights: "We quit working evenings tonight; we shall not have to work any more evenings till the 20th of next September." Several times Carpenter helped to make coffins during the hours of darkness. Once he worked from 10:00 P.M. to 3:00 A.M., and on another occasion he rose at 4:30 A.M.[227]

The accounts of several New England craftsmen list candles in contexts suggesting they were used in the shop. Charles T. West's expenses in 1812 when framing and painting chairs for Silas Cheney in Connecticut included "stuff for Chairs" and a pound of candles. Between 1814 and 1817 Thomas Boynton of Vermont itemized candles with his shop expenses; the price per pound ranged from 20¢ to 25¢. According to the *Cabinet and Chair Maker's Union Book of Prices* for 1828, employers at Philadelphia were expected "to find candles" for their workmen. A year later Elisha Harlow Holmes of Connecticut charged a customer 17¢ for "Making candlesticks for shop." An unusual fixture was the "High candle stand" in the paint shop at David Alling's chair manufactory in Newark, New Jersey. Presumably designed to hold two or more candles, the fixture probably was anchored to the floor or a bench where it shed light over a broad area, the flames out of harm's way. Because candles with open flames constituted a fire hazard, especially in a woodworking shop, prudent craftsmen might utilize a "Glass Lantern," such as that valued at 50¢ among the painting equipment itemized in 1839 at Henry Farley's shop in New Hampshire.[228]

Lamps appear in sufficient numbers in early nineteenth-century shop records to indicate they were common. In 1836 Thomas Boynton paid $1 for "a tallow lamp," a closed metal device to burn grease. References to oil lamps and apparatus are more numerous. Robert Scadin's shop at Cooperstown, New York, was lighted by five lamps in 1830, and he owned a "filler" to replenish the fuel. Appraisers of Thomas Sill's estate at Connecticut valued his "lamp filler" at 20¢ but assigned only 25¢ to his six lamps. These likely resembled the inexpensive 6¢ "Japan," or painted sheet iron, lamps in Parrott and Hubbell's shop at Bridgeport. Lewis Miller depicted an oil or burning-fluid lamp in his shop portrait (fig. 2-4): the small bell-shape article with tall wick tube and saucer base stands on the floor left of the bench. Thomas Boynton's record of lamp-oil purchases at Windsor, Vermont, pinpoints the expense of refueling lamps as 25¢ the pint. The oil likely fueled the "2 Boxes Tin Lamps" sold from his estate after his death. Greater demands for shop lighting occurred in John I. Wells's diversified operation at Hartford, as he kept a barrel of "Lamp Oil" on the premises.[229]

Shop sanitary conditions were primitive. Water was pumped or drawn from a well, and an open bucket in the shop kept a supply for drinking and washing. On the homestead farm one privy frequently served house, shop, and outbuildings. It was the rare rural woodworking establishment that had an adjoining facility. Before demolition, a farm shop near Pomfret, Connecticut, measuring about 12 by 15 feet contained a door on one wall leading to a small attached shed containing a one-hole seat. The facility would have required close regulation in summertime. Another structure attached to a building is the boxlike compartment cantilevered over the pond in the right-hand building of David Dexter's factory at Black River in upstate New York (fig. 2-30, right). This type of privy calls to mind a typical arrangement in medieval English manor houses and castles, where tower shafts carried waste to moats, water channels, or sewage pits below.[230]

Most city shops likely had a backyard privy standing amidst the piles of lumber. Offering proof is a newspaper notice of 1803 from Baltimore: "LEFT this morning, about nine o'clock, in the privy, back of Mr. Williams, chair-maker, Public-alley, a plain GOLD WATCH." Metropolitan conditions were poor. Water was easily contaminated, and manufacturing refuse often found its way into the streets, where rain washed it and other filth into nearby watercourses. Weather conditions also dictated special uses for wood shavings. Miles Benjamin of New York State recorded in May 1825 that he sold a customer "stuff &c for to throw out doors." Wood chips helped to alleviate muddy conditions common in springtime before the use of asphalt, concrete, and crushed stone.[231]

The Manufactory and the Wareroom

Commenting in 1858 on the rise of industry in Philadelphia, Edwin T. Freedley defined the word *manufacture* and noted its changed meaning: "The term *Manufacture* ... signifies — making by hand. Its modern acceptation, however, is directly the reverse of its original meaning; and it is now applied ... to those products which are made extensively by machinery, without much aid from manual labor." The word as first defined was current to the woodworking vocabulary by 1770 when John Nutt of South Carolina described "Well Manufactured Mahogany Furniture." Samuel Claphamson added a *y* in 1785 and advertised his cabinet and chair "Manufactory" at Philadelphia. The term still was in limited use in July 1788 when Thomas and William Ash "of the Windsor Chair manufactory" headed their line of march at the first Federal Procession in New York. Chairmakers first equated quantity production with manufacturing only in the late 1790s.[232]

Gradually the concept of a division of labor became part of the manufacturing experience in the chairmaking trade. The practice is well documented in chapter 1 of this book and in several interior shop views (figs. 2-5, 2-7, 3-32). Although many masters and journeymen remained sufficiently skilled to undertake any task, the tendency was to concentrate on one job to increase efficiency and maximize output. Prominent among the specialties were turning, chair framing, painting and ornamenting, and seat weaving. As production and markets expanded, the chairmaker found it necessary to enlarge his facility. Early additions were modest: expansion into a storeroom, the erection of a few sheds, or the conversion of a loft into a second-story chamber. Rhodes G. Allen of Providence eventually rebuilt his manufactory. In other facilities specialized structures complemented the main shop even before the War of 1812. A kiln (or "Dry house"), paint shop, turning shop or mill, and finishing room were part of the new facilities introduced in the trade. When United States marshals compiled the manufacturing census in 1820, Stephen Kilburn of Templeton, Massachusetts, employed "a number of hands," who produced 12,000 chairs annually using waterpower, and Hugh Finlay of Baltimore had a large workforce numbering thirty men, twenty-five women, and thirteen boys.[233]

Even before the mid-nineteenth century, the manufactory was fast becoming a factory (fig. 2-32), a facility distinguished by a large labor force, substantial space, extensive mechanical equipment, and frequently steam power. Lambert Hitchcock's factory in Connecticut stood two stories high and had a garret and basement; the warehouse was three stories. A kiln, wagon shop, and shed also had been erected on the 300-acre property. Complementing the factory lathes and circular and splitting saws were tenoning, drilling, mortising, and planing machines. David Alling's facility at Newark, New Jersey, although smaller and more compact, contained a two-story shop with front and back rooms, which probably included the "paint shop" and "Ornamental Room." The two-story woodhouse and adjacent storage barn and shed communicated with a yard. Larger perhaps was the chair manufactory of David Dexter and Son at Black River, New York (fig. 2-30), an upstate location accessible to Lake Ontario and the Erie Canal. The small building with a tall smokestack at the left probably was a kiln for seasoning timber.[234]

Rapid, cheap production marked the factory of the 1850s, when many facilities were located for direct access to rail or water transport. In Massachusetts, where chairmaking was a leading industry in Worcester County, the state's furniture production rose in value from $1.3 to $5.8 million between 1837 and 1855. Toronto's Jacques and Hay produced 15,000 Windsor chairs in 1851, a figure dwarfed by production

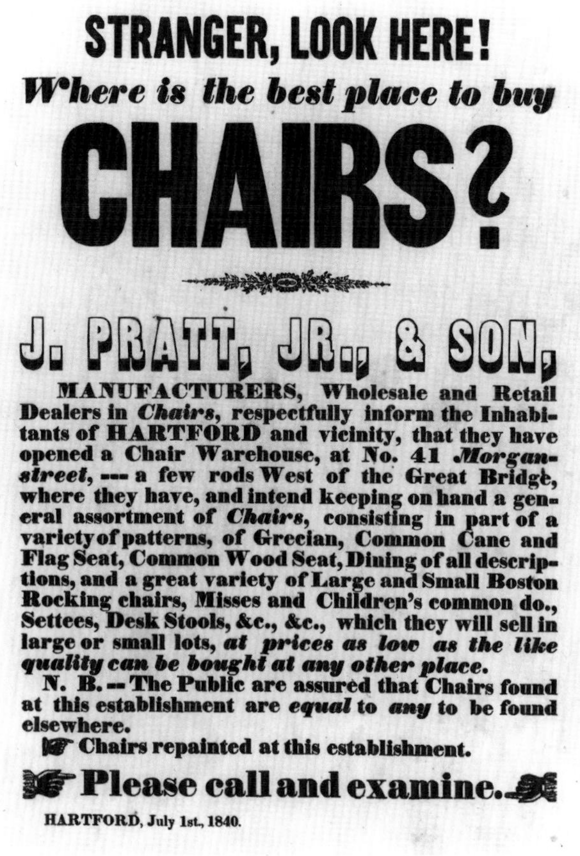

STRANGER, LOOK HERE!

Where is the best place to buy

CHAIRS?

J. PRATT, JR., & SON,

MANUFACTURERS, Wholesale and Retail Dealers in *Chairs*, respectfully inform the Inhabitants of **HARTFORD** and vicinity, that they have opened a Chair Warehouse, at No. 41 *Morgan-street*, — a few rods West of the Great Bridge, where they have, and intend keeping on hand a general assortment of *Chairs*, consisting in part of a variety of patterns, of Grecian, Common Cane and Flag Seat, Common Wood Seat, Dining of all descriptions, and a great variety of Large and Small Boston Rocking chairs, Misses and Children's common do., Settees, Desk Stools, &c., &c., which they will sell in large or small lots, *at prices as low as the like quality can be bought at any other place.*

N. B. — The Public are assured that Chairs found at this establishment are *equal* to *any* to be found elsewhere.

☞ Chairs repainted at this establishment.

☞ Please call and examine.

HARTFORD, July 1st, 1840.

FIG. 2-33 Broadside advertisement of Joel Pratt, Jr., and Son, Hartford, Conn., 1840. (*From the Collections of The Henry Ford, Dearborn, Mich.*)

at George W. Coddington's factory in Cincinnati, where 180 workmen manufactured 180,000 low- and medium-priced chairs valued at $120,000. The large manufacturing centers became public marts, attracting independent and support-type industry and drawing businessmen and agents from considerable distances.[235]

Paralleling development of the manufactory was the genesis of the wareroom or warehouse, a display and retail facility. Whereas early owners were manufacturers, the 1810s marked the rise of independent retailers who acquired their "wares" from various producers. Outlets of this type were the forerunners of the modern retail store. Thomas and William Ash of New York advertised an early merchandising facility in 1784: "They have now ready at their Ware-House, a great number of very neat Chairs and Settees." The practice of keeping finished work on hand for public view took hold somewhat slowly due to space limitations, insufficient cash reserves, and inadequate cash flow. Successful wareroom merchandising also required a well-selected location, urban or rural, that supported a reasonable level of trade. Gradually the chairmaking business prospered and warehouse retailing reached full maturity, as demonstrated in a broadside notice of Joel Pratt, Jr., and Son (fig. **2-33**).[236]

Many warerooms carried a full range of furniture. When Parrott and Hubbell of Bridgeport, Connecticut, became insolvent in 1835, they had in stock a considerable selection of cabinetwork along with a dozen Windsors, ten dozen fancy chairs and a settee, two nurse and two rocking chairs, a sewing chair, and a child's chair. Some cabinetmaking specialists also retailed chairs made by others. Rhodes G. Allen of Providence offered "Chairs of all descriptions, from the best manufactory in New-York . . . at a small advance." During an apprenticeship in the 1840s at Greenfield, Massachusetts, Edward Jenner Carpenter commented from time to time on retail sales in the shop wareroom, illuminating the operation of a small rural facility. One day a tin peddler came in and bought "a couple of rocking chairs." When a customer from neighboring Bernardston purchased wedding furniture for his daughter, Carpenter was elated that "he bought a Bureau of my make worth 13 or 14 dollars." Business was brisk. The apprentice soon reported: "I never saw so little work in the wareroom. They have but 3 or 4 Bureaus that are not sold. They have sold 80 or 90 dollars worth today; they need a jour. [journeyman] now if they ever did."[237]

NOTES

1. "Records of the Providence Association of Mechanics and Manufacturers," vol. 2, 1794–1811, Rhode Island Historical Society, Providence (hereafter cited RIHS).

2. Carl Bridenbaugh, *The Colonial Craftsman* (Chicago: University of Chicago Press, 1961), p. 6.

3. John F. Watson, *Annals of Philadelphia and Pennsylvania in the Olden Time*, 3 vols. (1830; reprint, rev. Willis P. Hazard, Philadelphia: Leary, Stuart, 1927), 1:174; William Franklin letter to Benjamin Franklin, July 12, 1753, Franklin Papers, American Philosophical Society, Philadelphia, Pa. (hereafter cited APS); minutes of directors' meetings, 1752–69, Contributionship Insurance Company of Philadelphia, Philadelphia (microfilm, Joseph Downs Collection of Manuscripts and Printed Ephemera, Winterthur Museum and Library, Winterthur, Del. [hereafter cited DCM and WL]); Charles Robinson estate records, 1825, City and County of Philadelphia, Pa., Register of Wills; Ezra S. Stearns, *History of Ashburnham, Massachusetts* (Ashburnham: By the town, 1887), p. 408.

4. *Longworth's American Almanac, New-York Register, and City Directory* (New York: David Longworth, 1809 and 1810). For David Alling's home and business complex, see Nancy Goyne Evans, *American Windsor Chairs* (New York: Hudson Hills Press, 1996), fig. 4-45. Robert McKim, *Richmond Enquirer* (Richmond, Va.), March 6, 1816, citation file, Museum of Early Southern Decorative Arts, Winston-Salem, N.C. (hereafter cited MESDA).

5. Henry Prall estate records, 1802, City and County of Philadelphia, Register of Wills; New York City jury lists, 1816 and 1819, Historical Documents Collection, Queens College, Flushing, N.Y. (hereafter cited QC); Luke Houghton ledger A, 1816–27, Barre Historical Society, Barre, Mass. (hereafter cited Barre; microfilm, DCM).

6. Philadelphia Monthly Meeting of Friends, Committee of Twelve ledgers, 1773–1800 and 1779–1817, minutes, vol. 1, 1770–95, vol. 2, 1795–1817, indenture with Joseph Henzey, May 5, 1774, and treasurers' reports and receipts, 1807–18, Society of Friends, Philadelphia (on deposit, APS).

7. Frank A. Banyas, "The Moravians of Colonial Pennsylvania: Their Arts, Crafts, and Industries" (Ph.D. dissertation, Ohio State University, 1940), p. 62 (microfilm, DCM); Hellmuth Erbe, "Bethlehem, Pa.: Eine kommunisikische hernhuter Kolonie" (Ph.D. dissertation, as published by the German Foreign Institute, Stuttgart, Germany, 1929), pp. 62–63, Archives of the Moravian Church, Bethlehem, Pa.; Margaret Berwind Schiffer, *Furniture and Its Makers of Chester County, Pennsylvania* (Philadelphia: University of Pennsylvania Press,

1966), pp. 274–75; Jacob Bitner and Jacob Fetter III, *Lancaster Journal* (Lancaster, Pa.), January 19, 1818, advertisement file, Lancaster County Historical Society, Lancaster, Pa. (hereafter cited LCHS); George F. Fainot agreement with Jacob Fetter III and Frederick Fetter, March 18, 1815, Lancaster Co., Lancaster, Pa., Registry of Deeds.

8. Donald L. Tuttle and Joyce Bauduin, "James Wilson, a Pennsylvania Chairmaker," *Chronicle of the Early American Industries Association* 32, no. 4 (December 1979): 53–57; Jane E. Sikes, *The Furniture Makers of Cincinnati, 1790 to 1849* (Cincinnati, Ohio: By the author, 1976), p. 133; Betty Lawson Walters, *Furniture Makers of Indiana, 1793 to 1850* (Indianapolis: Indiana Historical Society, 1972), p. 139; John Tarrant Kenney, *The Hitchcock Chair* (New York: Clarkson N. Potter, 1971), p. 309.

9. Stephen C. Wolcott, "A Cooper's Shop of 1800," *Chronicle of the Early American Industries Association* 1, no. 9 (January 1935): 1–2, 7. For Samuel Wing's home and shop, see Evans, *American Windsor Chairs*, fig. 6-224. Leigh Keno, "The Windsor Chair Makers of Northampton, Massachusetts, 1790–1820" (Historic Deerfield Summer Fellowship Program paper, Deerfield, Mass., August 1979), pp. 21–22; Oliver Pomeroy property records, 1803, Hampshire Co., Northampton, Mass., Registry of Deeds.

10. For Cowperthwaite's and Alling's shops, see Evans, *American Windsor Chairs*, figs. 5-46, 4-45. Charles F. Hummel, *With Hammer in Hand* (Charlottesville: University Press of Virginia, 1968), pp. 6–8.

11. United States Direct Tax of 1798, Federal Archives and Records Center, Philadelphia; William and Thomas Mitchell, *Pennsylvania Packet* (Philadelphia), December 2, 1799, as quoted in Alfred Coxe Prime, comp., *The Arts and Crafts in Philadelphia, Maryland, and South Carolina, 1786–1800* (Topsfield, Mass.: Walpole Society, 1932), pp. 198–99; Cree in John M. Cooper, *Recollections of Chambersburg, Pa., Chiefly between the Years 1830–1850* (Chambersburg, Pa.: A. N. Pomeroy, 1900), p. 21 (reference courtesy of the late William Bowers); Oldham in John Henry Hill, "The Furniture Craftsmen in Baltimore, 1783–1823" (master's thesis, University of Delaware, 1967), p. 111; Edward Dyer/Boteler and Donn, *Daily National Intelligencer* (Washington, D.C.), August 31, 1839, as quoted in Anne Castrodale Golovin, "Cabinetmakers and Chairmakers of Washington, D.C., 1791–1840," *Antiques* 107, no. 5 (May 1975): 909.

12. Samuel Silliman account book, 1804–7, New York State Historical Association, Cooperstown (hereafter cited NYSHA; microfilm, DCM).

13. John I. Wells, *American Mercury* (Hartford, Conn.), May 1, 1806 (reference courtesy of Nancy E. Richards); Edward Bulkley insolvency records, 1839, New Haven, Conn., Ge-

nealogical Section, Connecticut State Library, Hartford (hereafter cited CSL); Edward W. Birge and Francis A. Birge property records, 1846, Rensselaer Co., Troy, N.Y., Registry of Deeds; Lawrence Allwine, *Raleigh Register and North Carolina State Gazette* (Raleigh), April 1801, citation file, MESDA (reference courtesy of Paula Welshimer Locklair).

14. Starr in *King's Rochester City Directory and Register, 1841* (Rochester, N.Y.: Welles and Hayes, 1840), n.p.

15. Caleb Emlen and Benjamin Love estate records, 1748 and 1821, City and County of Philadelphia, Register of Wills; Schiffer, *Furniture of Chester County*, pp. 44, 169, 275; Finlay brothers in Hill, "Furniture Craftsmen in Baltimore," p. 112.

16. John Wadsworth, *American Mercury*, December 15, 1803 (reference courtesy of Nancy E. Richards); Carpenter journal, as quoted in Winifred C. Gates, "Journal of a Cabinet Maker's Apprentice, Part 2," *Chronicle of the Early American Industries Association* 15, no. 3 (September 1962): 35–36; Alexander Brown, *Richmond Commercial Compiler* (Richmond, Va.), December 23, 1816, and Seaton and Barnes, *Petersburg Republican* (Petersburg, Va.), August 20, 1819, citation file, MESDA.

17. James Blauvelt inventory, 1814, DCM; William Fisk indenture with Samuel Payson, September 1, 1809, DCM; Kenney, *Hitchcock Chair*, p. 43; Daniel Foot estate records, 1840, Berkshire Co., Pittsfield, Mass., Registry of Probate.

18. Charles Chase, Sr., property records, 1781 and 1811, Nantucket Co., Nantucket, Mass., Registry of Deeds; John Humes, *Western Spy* (Cincinnati, Ohio), December 25, 1805, and Joel Brown, *Star, and North-Carolina Gazette* (Raleigh), June 25, 1819, citation file, MESDA.

19. Ebenezer Tracy, Sr., and Almon Preston estate records, 1803 and 1852, Lisbon and Wallingford, Conn., and William Moore, Jr., insolvency records, 1830, Barkhamstead, Conn., Genealogical Section, CSL; Abijah Wilder estate records, 1864, Cheshire Co., Keene, N.H., Registry of Probate; Peter A. Willard estate records, 1842–43, Worcester Co., Worcester, Mass., Registry of Probate.

20. James M. Comee and Joseph F. Loring estate records, 1832 and 1845–46, Worcester Co., Mass., Registry of Probate; Amasa Elwell and William Rogers estate records, 1814 and 1812, Bennington and Windsor counties, Bennington and Woodstock, Vt., Registries of Probate; A. D. Allen in Elisha H. Holmes property attachment, 1843, Connecticut Superior Court Records, CSL; Stephen Ross, *Concord Gazette* (Concord, N.H.), November 16, 1815, as quoted in Charles S. Parsons, New Hampshire Notes, Visual Resources Collection, WL (hereafter cited VRC).

21. Joseph N. Dow estate records, 1881, Coventry, Conn., Genealogical Section, CSL;

Willard estate records; Joseph Jackson estate records, 1837, Worcester Co., Mass., Registry of Probate; David Haven estate records, 1801, Middlesex Co., Cambridge, Mass., Registry of Probate; Walter Corey property records, 1843–55, Cumberland Co., Portland, Maine, Registry of Deeds.

22. Eli Wood estate records, 1818, Barkhamstead, Conn., Genealogical Section, CSL; Calvin Bedortha property records, 1817–36, Hampden Co., Springfield, Mass., Registry of Deeds; Solomon Rich estate records, 1848, Bennington Co., Vt., Registry of Probate.

23. Edmund Hogan, *Prospect of Philadelphia* (Philadelphia: Francis and Robert Bailey, 1795); Edward Whitely, *Philadelphia Directory and Register for 1820* (Philadelphia: McCarty and Davis, 1820), and *Supplementary Directory for 1820* (Philadelphia: Robert Desilver, 1820); *A. McElroy's Philadelphia Directory for 1840* (Philadelphia: A[rchibald] McElroy, 1840).

24. William Duncan, *New-York Directory and Register for 1795* (New York: T[homas] and J[ames] Swords, 1795); *Longworth's American Almanac, New-York Register and City Directory* (New York: Jonathan Olmstead, 1819); *Longworth's American Alamanc, New-York Register and City Directory* (New York: Thomas Longworth, 1840); *New York Business Directory for 1840 and 1841* (New York: [Seth W. Benedict], 1840).

25. Cyrus Cleaveland property records, 1803 and 1812, Providence, R.I., Registry of Deeds; Henry Farley property records, 1826–35, Merrimack Co., Concord, N.H., Registry of Deeds; Dewey and Woodworth property records, 1827, Bennington, Vt., Town Clerk's Office; Abraham Shove property records, 1805 and 1821, Bristol Co., Taunton, Mass., Registry of Deeds; Abraham and James Bennett, *Village Record* (West Chester, Pa.), January 18, 1837, as quoted in Schiffer, *Furniture of Chester County*, pp. 32–33.

26. Joseph Adams deed to Silas E. Cheney, March 29, 1802, Papers of Silas E. Cheney, Connecticut Historical Society, Hartford (hereafter cited CHS); Silas E. Cheney ledger, 1816–22, Litchfield Historical Society, Litchfield, Conn. (hereafter cited LHS; microfilm, DCM); Ebenezer P. Rose, *Trenton Federalist* (Trenton, N.J.), November 30, 1807 (reference courtesy of James R. Seibert); Robert McKim, *Richmond Enquirer*, March 6, 1816, citation file, MESDA; Catharine/Thomas Kinsela property records, 1827, Schenectady Co., Schenectady, N.Y., Registry of Deeds.

27. J. P. Brissot de Warville, *New Travels in the United States of America* (Dublin: P. Byrne et al., 1792), p. 315; Watson, *Annals of Philadelphia*, 3:368; Esther Singleton, *Social New York under the Georges, 1714–1776* (New York: D. Appleton, 1902), p. 21; Robert Donald Crompton, "A Philadelphian Looks at New England—1820," *Old-Time New England* 50, no. 3 (January–March 1960): 60.

28. John Oldham, *Maryland Journal* (Baltimore, Md.), December 9, 1793, as quoted in Prime, *Arts and Crafts, 1786–1800*, p. 192; Whitney and Brown in Henry Wyckoff Belknap, *Artists and Craftsmen of Essex County, Massachusetts* (Salem, Mass.: Essex Institute, 1927), p. 77; Isaac Barton, *Western Cabinet* (Fayetteville, Tenn.), August 21, 1830, as quoted in Ellen Beasley, "Tennessee Cabinetmakers and Chairmakers through 1840," *Antiques* 100, no. 4 (October 1971): 612; Gill and Halfpenny, *Baltimore Patriot and Mercantile Advertiser* (Baltimore, Md.), October 18, 1830; Hector Sanford, *Scioto Gazette* (Chillicothe, Ohio), December 26, 1805, as quoted in John R. Grabb letter to author, December 3, 1978. For additional Seaver and Frost address information, see Nancy Goyne Evans, *American Windsor Furniture: Specialized Forms* (New York: Hudson Hills Press, 1997), fig. 2-51. The partners Seaver and Frost have been identified correctly only recently as William Seaver and Nathaniel Frost (formerly William Seaver and James Frost) in the Suffolk Co., Boston, Mass., court of common pleas docket books, 1798–1820, under the dates October 1799 and July 1804 (reference courtesy of Robert Mussey). Edward Bulkley, *New Haven Palladium* (New Haven, Conn.), March 30, 1830 (reference courtesy of Wendell Hilt); John Denig, *Franklin Repository* (Chambersburg, Pa.), July 1821 (reference courtesy of the late William Bowers); Frederick Fox, *Berks and Schuylkill Journal* (Reading, Pa.), April 26, 1845.

29. For McGarvey's warehouse facade, see Elizabeth Collard, "Montreal Cabinetmakers and Chairmakers: 1800–1850," *Antiques* 105, no. 5 (May 1974): 1136.

30. George Davidson waste book, 1793–99, Old Sturbridge Village, Sturbridge, Mass. (hereafter cited OSV); Kenneth Roberts and Anna M. Roberts, eds. and trans., *Moreau de St.-Méry's American Journey, [1793–1798]* (Garden City, N.Y.: Doubleday, 1947), p. 176; Capen in Earle G. Shettleworth, Jr., and William D. Barry, "Walter Corey's Furniture Manufactory in Portland, Maine," *Antiques* 121, no. 5 (May 1982): 1201; William H. Reed account book, 1803–48, DCM; Paul Jenkins daybook, 1836–41, DCM.

31. Ackley in Abraham Ritter, *Philadelphia and Her Merchants as Constituted Fifty and Seventy Years Ago* (Philadelphia: By the author, 1860) p. 105; Low and Damon, *New-Hampshire Patriot* (Concord), February 6, 1816, as illustrated in Donna-Belle Garvin, James L. Garvin, and John F. Page, *Plain and Elegant, Rich and Common: Documented New Hampshire Furniture, 1750–1850* (Concord: New Hampshire Historical Society, 1979), p. 149; Mullen and Cowperthwaite in *Cincinnati Directory for 1834* (Cincinnati, Ohio: E. Deming, 1834), n.p.; William Sweney, *Village Record*, February 19, 1850, as quoted in Schiffer, *Furniture of Chester County*, p. 227; Joel Brown, *Republican* (Petersburg, Va.), October 20, 1806, and *Star, and North-Carolina State Gazette*, June 25, 1819, citation file, MESDA; Edward A. Ball inventory, 1832, DCM.

32. William L. Goodman, *History of Woodworking Tools* (New York: David McKay, 1964), pp. 183–87; the vertical vise derives from a Continental form. Hummel, *Hammer in Hand*, pp. 53–56; Henry C. Mercer, *Ancient Carpenters' Tools* (Doylestown, Pa.: Bucks County Historical Society, 1951), pp. 69–73; Raphael A. Salaman, *Dictionary of Tools* (London: George Allen and Unwin, 1975), pp. 72–73; Charles Tomlinson, *Illustrations of Trades* (1860; reprint, n.p.: Early American Industries Association, 1972), pp. 46–47; Joseph Moxon, *Mechanick Exercises* (1703; reprint, New York: Praeger Publishers, 1970), pp. 64–65, pl. 4 and explanation. The author is grateful to John D. Alexander, Jr., for reading those parts of the manuscript dealing with equipment, tools, and materials and making critical comment.

33. Daniel Jones and William Davis estate records, 1766 and 1767, City and County of Philadelphia, Register of Wills. Framing benches in Windsor-chair-making records include Purnell Hall inventory, 1848, as quoted in Harold B. Hancock, "Furniture Craftsmen in Delaware Records," in *Winterthur Portfolio 9*, ed. Ian M. G. Quimby (Charlottesville: University Press of Virginia, 1974), app. 6; Robinson estate records; David Coutant estate records, 1829–30, West Chester Co., White Plains, N.Y., Surrogate Court.

34. Robert Whitelaw ledger, 1804–31, Vermont Historical Society, Montpelier; Ebenezer Knowlton inventory, 1811, Suffolk Co., Mass., Registry of Probate (microfilm, DCM; document brought to author's attention by Page Talbot); Jacob Cole inventory, 1801, as quoted in Hill, "Furniture Craftsmen in Baltimore," p. 119; Cyrus Cleaveland estate records, 1837, Providence, R.I., Registry of Probate; tail vise (screw) illustrated and discussed in Salaman, *Dictionary*, p. 73.

35. Moxon, *Mechanick Exercises*, pls. 12, 14, 17.

36. Mercer, *Ancient Carpenters' Tools*, pp. 216–24; Tomlinson, *Illustrations of Trades*, p. 48; Robert S. Woodbury, *History of the Lathe to 1850*, Monograph Series, no. 1 (Cleveland, Ohio: Society for the History of Technology, 1961), pp. 13–14, 23, 25, 31–35, 38–49, 52, 74–75; Salaman, *Dictionary*, pp. 127, 258; Hummel, *Hammer in Hand*, pp. 91–94; Moxon, *Mechanick Exercises*, pls. 12–14, 17, 18 and explanations.

37. Jacob Cole inventory; Godfrey Cole inventory, 1804, as quoted in Hill, "Furniture Craftsmen in Baltimore," p. 119; Beza White estate records, 1832, Suffolk Co., Mass., Registry of Probate (microfilm, DCM); Kenney, *Hitchcock Chair*, p. 321.

38. Stephen Whipple account book, 1803–11, Ipswich Historical Society, Ipswich, Mass.; Chapman Lee ledger, 1799–1850, OSV; Thomas Boynton ledgers, 1811–17 and 1817–47, Dartmouth College, Hanover, N.H. (hereafter cited DC; microfilm, DCM).

39. Stearns, *History of Ashburnham*, p. 408; the implication is that the pole lathe was common and the more expensive treadle lathe was considered "first rate." Thomas Sill estate records, 1826–30, Middletown, Conn., Genealogical Section, CSL; John Lambert estate records, 1793, City and County of Philadelphia, Register of Wills; Anthony Steel, *Relf's Philadelphia Gazette and Daily Advertiser* (Philadelphia), March 14, 1818; John Avery, Jr., ledger, 1780–1814, CHS.

40. Joseph Griswold ledger, 1804–13, privately owned (microfilm, DCM); James Gere ledgers, 1809–29, 1822–52, CSL; Frederick Allen estate records, 1830, Windham, Conn., Genealogical Section, CSL; David Alling estate records, 1855, Archives and History Bureau, New Jersey State Library, Trenton (hereafter cited NJSL); Jonathan Dart account book, 1793–1800, CHS; Thomas Aiken, Jr., estate records, 1805, Hillsborough Co., Nashua, N.H., Registry of Probate; Elisha Harlow Holmes daybook, 1825–30, CSL; Josiah Briggs account book, 1823–32, DCM; James Smith, *Panorama of Science and Art*, 2 vols. (Liverpool, England: Caxton Press, [ca. 1816]), 1:84.

41. William Ryder inventory, 1806, DCM.

42. John Peterson in Charles G. Dorman, *Delaware Cabinetmakers and Allied Artisans, 1655–1855* (Wilmington: Historical Society of Delaware, 1960), p. 68; records of the 1820 United States Census of Manufactures, states of New York, Pennsylvania, and Connecticut, National Archives, Washington, D.C. (hereafter cited NA; microfilm, DCM); William D. Herrick, *History of the Town of Gardner* (Gardner, Mass.: By the committee, 1878), pp. 167–68; Samuel R. Rooker, source unknown, as quoted in Arthur Whallon, "Indiana Cabinetmakers and Allied Craftsmen, 1815–1860," *Antiques* 98, no. 1 (July 1970): 123; Edwin T. Freedley, *Philadelphia and Its Manufactures* (Philadelphia: Edward Young, 1858), pp. 34, 452.

43. Mercer, *Ancient Carpenters' Tools*, pp. 283–88; Moxon, *Mechanick Exercises*, pl. 1 (bricklayers); Hummel, *Hammer in Hand*, p. 86; Salaman, *Dictionary*, p. 216. For Mount painting, see Alfred Frankenstein, *Painter of Rural America: William Sidney Mount, 1807–1868* (Washington, D.C.: H. K. Press, 1968), p. 50.

44. Philip Deland account book, 1812–46, OSV; Asa Faunce inventory, 1825, Kennebec Co., Augusta, Maine, Registry of Probate (reference courtesy of Edwin A. Churchill); Silas E. Cheney ledger, 1799–1817, LHS (microfilm, DCM); Schiffer, *Furniture of Chester County*, p. 109; Foot estate records; Joan Mackinnon, *Kingston Cabinetmakers, 1800–1867*, National Museum of Man Mercury Series (Ottawa: National Museums of Canada, 1976), p. 113.

45. Mercer, *Ancient Carpenters' Tools*, p. 16; Salaman, *Dictionary*, pp. 463–64; Goodman, *History of Woodworking Tools*, p. 184; J. Geraint Jenkins, "A Chiltern Chair Bodger," *Country Life* 118, no. 3063 (September 29, 1955): 684, 686.

46. Boynton ledger, 1811–17; Francis Trumble estate records, 1798, City and County of Philadelphia, Register of Wills; Alling estate records.

47. Salaman, *Dictionary*, pp. 441–42; Mercer, *Ancient Carpenter's Tools*, pp. 145, 148; John R. Grabb, "The Bucksaw and the Sawbuck," *Chronicle of the Early American Industries Association* 29, no. 2 (June 1976): 18–20; [Gorham Worth], "Albany Fifty Years Ago," *Harper's New Monthly Magazine* 14, no. 82 (March 1857): 452, 455; Knowlton inventory; Campbell Dunham estate records, 1837, NJSL.

48. Salaman, *Dictionary*, p. 479; Ansel Goodrich estate records, 1803, Hampshire Co., Mass., Registry of Probate; Jedidiah Johnson estate records, 1821, Essex Co., Salem, Mass., Registry of Probate; Foot, Sill, and Coutant estate records; Charles Walker, *Montreal Gazette* (Montreal, Que.), September 17, 1849, as quoted in Collard, "Montreal Cabinetmakers," p. 1146.

49. Trumble, Foot, and Coutant estate records; Alexander Rigby inventory, 1811, as quoted in Hill, "Furniture Craftsmen in Baltimore," p. 120; James Whitaker and Anthony Steel estate records, 1822 and 1817, City and County of Philadelphia, Register of Wills; Gere ledger, 1822–52; Boynton ledgers, 1811–17 and 1817–47; Herrick, *History of Gardner*, p. 177.

50. Jones estate records; William Savery inventory, 1788, as quoted in William MacPherson Hornor, Jr., *Blue Book: Philadelphia Furniture* (1935; reprint, Washington, D.C.: Highland House, 1977), p. 295. For Wing bending frame, see Henry J. Harlow, "The Shop of Samuel Wing, Craftsman of Sandwich, Massachusetts," *Antiques* 93, no. 3 (March 1968): 376.

51. Charles S. Parsons, Wilder Family Notes, VRC; Allen Holcomb account book, 1809–28, Metropolitan Museum of Art, New York; Charles Riley estate records, 1842, City and County of Philadelphia, Register of Wills (microfilm, DCM); Silas Cheney estate records, 1821, Litchfield, Conn., Genealogical Section, CSL; Wilson in George Corlies account book, ca. 1797–1816, Papers of the Corlies Family, Rutgers University Library, New Brunswick, N.J.; Jacob Cole inventory.

52. For Wing bows, see Harlow, "Samuel Wing," p. 374. Salaman, *Dictionary*, p. 128.

53. Boynton ledgers, 1811–17 and 1817–47; Shaker chair clamp at the Shaker Museum, Old Chatham, N.Y.; Elbridge Gerry Reed daybook, 1829–51, OSV; William H. MacDonald, *Central New Jersey Chairmaking of the Nineteenth Century* (Trenton, N.J.: By the author, 1960), p. 15.

54. John O. Curtis, "The Introduction of the Circular Saw in the Early 19th Century," *Bulletin of the Association for Preservation Technology* 5, no. 2 (1973): 162–63, 166–67, 171, 174; another Maine sawmill note of 1824 states that "Circular saws have long been in use." A circular saw is listed in a Lancashire chairmaker's inventory of 1815, according to Bill Cotton, "Vernacular Design: The Spindle Back Chair and Its North Country Origins," *Working Wood* (Spring 1980): 42; Joseph Smith, *Explanation, or Key, to the Various Manufactories of Sheffield, with Engravings of Each Article* (1816; reprint, South Burlington, Vt.: Early American Industries Association, 1975), p. 7 (catalogue), fig. 656; Birmingham directory reference in A. Hyatt Mayor, "Mail Orders in the Eighteenth Century," *Antiques* 108, no. 4 (October 1975): 760.

55. Benjamin Bass estate records, 1819, Suffolk Co., Mass., Registry of Probate (microfilm, DCM; document brought to author's attention by Page Talbott); Curtis, "Circular Saw," pp. 174, 176-77, 179, 182; Rand and Abbott, *New-Hampshire Patriot*, October 15, 1825, as quoted in Parsons, New Hampshire Notes; Thomas West estate records, 1828, New London, Conn., Genealogical Section, CSL; Coley and Smith account of David Pritchard, 1829, Pritchard Collection, General Family Papers, Mattatuck Museum, Waterbury, Conn. (hereafter cited Mattatuck); Asa Nichols estate records, 1829, Worcester Co., Mass., Registry of Probate; Duane Hamilton Hurd, ed., *History of Worcester County, Massachusetts*, 2 vols. (Philadelphia: J. W. Lewis, 1889), 1:830.

56. Moore insolvency records; John Barrell estate records, 1841, Worcester Co., Mass., Registry of Probate; Smith, *Panorama*, 1:98; Joan Mackinnon, *A Checklist of Toronto Cabinet and Chair Makers, 1800–1865*, National Museum of Man Mercury Series (Ottawa: National Museums of Canada, 1975), p. 82; Kenney, *Hitchcock Chair*, pp. 156, 320–21; Herrick, *History of Gardner*, p. 176.

57. Shorey data in Parsons, New Hampshire Notes; Mackinnon, *Kingston Cabinetmakers*, pp. 113–14; Kenney, *Hitchcock Chair*, p. 321; band saw in Herrick, *History of Gardner*, p. 303, and Polly Ann Earl, "Craftsmen and Machines: The Nineteenth-Century Furniture Industry," in *Technological Innovation and the Decorative Arts*, ed. Ian M. G. Quimby and Polly Ann Earl (Charlottesville: University Press of Virginia, 1974), pp. 309–11.

58. Moore insolvency records; Luke Houghton ledger B, 1824–51, Barre (microfilm, DCM); Leonard and James Proctor ledger, 1834–40, NYSHA (microfilm, DCM); Kenney, *Hitchcock Chair*, pp. 320–21; Curtis, "Circular Saw," pp. 163, 165; Foot estate records.

59. *Documents Relative to the Manufactures in the United States Collected and Transmitted to the House of Representatives in Compliance with*

a *Resolution of January 19, 1832, by the Secretary of the Treasury*, 2 vols. (Washington, D.C.: Duff Green, 1833), 1:500–501; Thomas Sheraton, *Cabinet Dictionary*, 2 vols. (1803; reprint, New York: Praeger, 1970), 1:146.

60. Smith, *Panorama*, 1:105; Goodman, *History of Woodworking Tools*, pp. 111, 115–19.

61. Salaman, *Dictionary*, pp. 426–29; Goodman, *History of Woodworking Tools*, pp. 118–19, 138–42; Mercer, *Ancient Carpenters' Tools*, pp. 21–25; Louis C. Hunter, *Waterpower in the Century of the Steam Engine*, vol. 1 of *A History of Industrial Power in the United States, 1780–1930* (Charlottesville: University Press of Virginia, 1979), p. 15; John Pinkerton estate records, 1804, City and County of Philadelphia, Register of Wills; Cheney estate records; David Partridge estate records, 1850, Worcester Co., Mass., Registry of Probate.

62. Goodman, *History of Woodworking Tools*, pp. 143–45, 156–59; Salaman, *Dictionary*, pp. 414–16; Smith, *Key*, p. 6 (catalogue).

63. Tracy estate records; Jacob Felton daybook, 1836–38, OSV; Merrick Wallace estate records, 1875, Worcester Co., Mass., Registry of Probate.

64. Salaman, *Dictionary*, pp. 408–10, 419–20; Goodman, *History of Woodworking Tools*, pp. 127–31, 152; Mercer, *Ancient Carpenters' Tools*, pp. 145, 147–55; Hummel, *Hammer in Hand*, pp. 130–31; J. Geraint Jenkins, *Traditional Country Craftsmen* (London: Routledge and Kegan Paul, 1965), p. 115.

65. Jacob Rahm estate records, 1778, Baltimore Co., Baltimore, Md., Register of Wills (microfilm, DCM); David Judd estate records, 1827, Hampshire Co., Mass., Registry of Probate; Grabb, "Bucksaw and Sawbuck," pp. 18–20.

66. Mercer, *Ancient Carpenters' Tools*, pp. 136–41; Salaman, *Dictionary*, pp. 421–23; Goodman, *History of Woodworking Tools*, pp. 141, 145–52; Hummel, *Hammer in Hand*, pp. 136–37.

67. Smith, *Panorama*, 1:106; Parrott and Hubbell insolvency records, 1835, Bridgeport, Conn., Genealogical Section, CSL; Gilbert M. Lyons account book, 1830–35, DCM; Thomas Walter Ward II inventory book, ca. 1838–45, DCM; Williamson in Dean F. Failey, *Long Island Is My Nation* (Setauket, N.Y.: Society for the Preservation of Long Island Antiquities, 1976), p. 291; James Rousham, *South Carolina Gazette* (Charleston), July 1, 1732, as quoted in Alfred Coxe Prime, comp., *The Arts and Crafts in Philadelphia, Maryland, and South Carolina, 1721–1785* (Philadelphia: Walpole Society, 1929), p. 187.

68. Salaman, *Dictionary*, p. 426; Smith, *Key*, p. 6 (catalogue), figs. 591, 598; Smith, *Panorama*, 1:106; Josiah Prescott Wilder daybook and ledger, 1837–61, privately owned, as transcribed in Parsons, Wilder Family Notes.

69. Salaman, *Dictionary*, pp. 412, 424–25; Mercer, *Ancient Carpenters' Tools*, pp. 137, 139, 141; [Raymond R. Townsend], "Eighteenth

Century Saws," *Chronicle of the Early American Industries Association* 21, no. 1 (March 1968): 15; Smith, *Panorama*, 1:107; Daniel Clay, *Greenfield Gazette* (Greenfield, Mass.), November 20, 1810, advertisement file, Historic Deerfield, Deerfield, Mass. (hereafter cited HD); Jacob Cole and Godfrey Cole inventories.

70. William S. Wall, *Columbian Courier* (New Bedford, Mass.), July 27, 1804, as quoted in Elton W. Hall, "New Bedford Furniture," *Antiques* 113, no. 5 (May 1978): 1111; Charles F. Hummel, "English Tools in America: The Evidence of the Dominys," in *Winterthur Portfolio* 2, ed. Milo M. Naeve (Winterthur, Del.: Winterthur Museum, 1965), p. 30.

71. Salaman, *Dictionary*, pp. 407, 411, 418, 431, 434; Mercer, *Ancient Carpenters' Tools*, pp. 139, 141; Smith, *Key*, p. 6 (catalogue), figs. 600, 605, 610, 615.

72. Stephen B. Allyn estate records, 1822, Norwich, Conn., Geneological Section, CSL; Pinkerton and Cheney estate records; Joel Booth estate records, 1794–95, Newtown, Conn., Genealogical Section, CSL; Parrott and Hubbell insolvency records.

73. Moxon, *Mechanick Exercises*, p. 116; Mayes's definition of "tenanting" is given in Salaman, *Dictionary*, p. 4.

74. Salaman, *Dictionary*, pp. 437–41; Mercer, *Ancient Carpenters' Tools*, pp. 291–301; Hummel, *Hammer in Hand*, p. 138; Smith, *Panorama*, 1:105; Smith, *Key*, p. 8 (catalogue), figs. 549–52.

75. Goodman, *History of Woodworking Tools*, pp. 12–38; Salaman, *Dictionary*, pp. 46–48.

76. Salaman, *Dictionary*, pp. 54–56; Mercer, *Ancient Carpenters' Tools*, pp. 1–11; Smith, *Key*, p. 3 (catalogue), figs. 260, 268–69.

77. Reuben Loomis estate records, 1860, Suffield, Conn., Genealogical Section, CSL; Alling and Johnson estate records; Moxon, *Mechanick Exercises*, p. 196, pl. 13; John Oldham estate records, 1835, Baltimore Co., Md., Register of Wills (microfilm, DCM).

78. Hummel, *Hammer in Hand*, p. 90; Adam Fizer inventory, 1838, Botetourt Co., Fincastle, Va., Registry of Probate (reference courtesy of Neville Thompson); Daniel Berger estate sale, 1814, DCM.

79. Salaman, *Dictionary*, pp. 50, 126–27; Smith, *Key*, p. 4 (catalogue), fig. 265.

80. Smith, *Key*, p. 3 (catalogue), fig. 183; Salaman, *Dictionary*, pp. 126–27; Hummel, *Hammer in Hand*, pp. 88–89; Mercer, *Ancient Carpenters' Tools*, pp. 11–15; froe technique illustrated and described in John D. Alexander, Jr., *Make a Chair from a Tree: An Introduction to Working Green Wood* (Newtown, Conn.: Taunton Press, 1978), pp. 52–53, 95.

81. Davis and Lambert estate records; James Grant estate records, 1826, Norfolk, Conn., Genealogical Section, CSL.

82. Salaman, *Dictionary*, pp. 71–72, 270;

Mercer, *Ancient Carpenters' Tools*, pp. 14, 19, 307; Samuel Loomis estate records, 1814, Saybrook, Conn., Genealogical Section, CSL.

83. Salaman, *Dictionary*, pp. 126–27, 268–69; Hummel, *Hammer in Hand*, pp. 94–95; Mercer, *Ancient Carpenters' Tools*, pp. 170–73, 268; Goodman, *History of Woodworking Tools*, p. 201; Smith, *Panorama*, 1:117; Cleaveland estate records.

84. Salaman, *Dictionary*, pp. 24–25, 126; Goodman, *History of Woodworking Tools*, pp. 13, 16, 18, 22, 24–27, 31–34, 37; Mercer, *Ancient Carpenters' Tools*, pp. 92–97; Hummel, *Hammer in Hand*, pp. 43–44; L. J. Mayes, *The History of Chairmaking in High Wycombe* (London: Routledge and Kegan Paul, 1960), p. 11.

85. Alling estate records; Fizer inventory; John Reynell letter book, 1760–62, Historical Society of Pennsylvania, Philadelphia (hereafter cited HSP); Seth Pomeroy account book, 1794–1801, Historic Northampton, Northampton, Mass.

86. Salaman, *Dictionary*, pp. 218–19; Goodman, *History of Woodworking Tools*, pp. 201–2; Smith, *Panorama*, 1:116; Mercer, *Ancient Carpenters' Tools*, pp. 264–68; Jabez Gilbert estate records, 1828, Windham, Conn., Genealogical Section, CSL; Parrott and Hubbell insolvency records; Fisher ledger entry in Hummell, "English Tools in America," p. 34; Thomas Walter Ward II account book, 1824–25, American Antiquarian Society, Worcester, Mass.; Zadock Hutchins, Jr., estate records, 1830, Pomfret, Conn., Genealogical Section, CSL.

87. Salaman, *Dictionary*, p. 221; Mayes, *Chairmaking*, p. 15; Cheney and Nichols estate records; Pomeroy account book; Nathan Cleaveland ledger, 1810–28, OSV.

88. Salaman, *Dictionary*, pp. 449–53; Mercer, *Ancient Carpenters' Tools*, pp. 268–70; Hummel, *Hammer in Hand*, p. 146; Smith, *Key*, p. 8 (catalogue), figs. 553–55; Parrott and Hubbell insolvency records; Pomeroy account book; Thomas Boynton shop account, 1817–35, DC.

89. Goodman, *History of Woodworking Tools*, p. 202; Hummell, *Hammer in Hand*, pp. 87–88; Salaman, *Dictionary*, pp. 175–76; Mercer, *Ancient Carpenters' Tools*, pp. 97, 100; shaving technique illustrated and described in Alexander, *Make a Chair*, pp. 62–63, 95.

90. Snowden purchases in Arthur W. Leibundguth, "The Furniture-Making Crafts in Philadelphia, ca. 1730–1760" (master's thesis, University of Delaware, 1964), p. 83; Pinkerton estate records; Keno, "The Windsor Chair Makers of Northampton," pp. 9, 32–33, 122; Wall, *Columbian Courier*; Smith, *Key*, p. 2 (catalogue), figs. 161–66.

91. Goodman, *History of Woodworking Tools*, pp. 202–3; Smith, *Key*, p. 2 (catalogue), fig. 159; Mercer, *Ancient Carpenters' Tools*, pp. 97–98, 101, 104, including cooper's shaves; Salaman, *Dictionary*, pp. 455–56; Reed daybook;

Hummel, *Hammer in Hand*, pp. 141–42. Early nineteenth-century publications consistently describe the inshave as a coopering tool, and indeed a cooper's inventory of 1773 lists three inshaves among the cutting tools; see Tomlinson, *Illustration of Trades*, pp. 102–3. David Gordon inventory, 1773, Fairfax Co., Va., as quoted in Alice Hanson Jones, *American Colonial Wealth*, 3 vols. (New York: Arno Press, 1977), 3:1382–83.

92. Snowden in Leibundguth, "Furniture-Making Crafts in Philadelphia," pp. 83–84; Booth and Riley estate records; Salaman, *Dictionary*, p. 455; John Green account book, 1790–1803, DCM.

93. Holcomb account book; Solomon Cole account book, 1794–1809, CHS; M. Douglas Sackman, "William Bull, Blacksmith, and Daniel Clay, Cabinetmaker," *Historic Deerfield Quarterly* 13, no. 4 (October 1974): 10; Keno, "Windsor Chair Makers of Northampton," pp. 32–34; Lyons account book; Wilder daybook and ledger.

94. Mercer, *Ancient Carpenters' Tools*, p. 135; Salaman, *Dictionary*, pp. 444–45; Mayes, *Chairmaking*, pp. 11–12; Joseph C. Clark estate records, 1799, Middletown, Conn., Genealogical Section, CSL; Cheney estate records.

95. Salaman, *Dictionary*, pp. 447–48; Timothy Hanson estate records, 1798, State of Delaware, Division of Historical and Cultural Affairs, Hall of Records, Dover. J. Geraint Jenkins writing in *Traditional Country Craftsmen*, p. 119, states that "scratch tools" similar to scrapers were employed by English chairmakers "to produce the shallow mouldings found on some chairs." Exhibits at the High Wycombe Chair Museum in Buckinghamshire include a homemade tool for patterning a bow face consisting of a piece of old narrow saw blade filed to a curved profile at one end and mounted in a small wooden block so as to project slightly from one face of an inside right angle. The cutting action occurs as the scraper is pulled along the bow stock. The side wall of the tool acts as a fence, butting up against the bow edge to ensure a uniform molded surface along the length of the bow.

96. Goodman, *History of Woodworking Tools*, pp. 40, 42, 56–57, 63, 65–70, 77, 88–90; Salaman, *Dictionary*, pp. 299–301, 305–6, 332–33, 368–69; Mercer, *Ancient Carpenters' Tools*, pp. 98–103, 105–6, 121–25, 129–33; Smith, *Panorama*, 1:107–10.

97. Goodman, *History of Woodworking Tools*, p. 102; Benjamin Branson estate records, 1831–35, DCM; Michael Fassauer and David Brientnall, Jr., insolvency records, 1816 and 1811, QC; Wilder daybook and ledger.

98. Smith, *Panorama*, 1:109; Chapman in Edward Deming Andrews and Faith Andrews, *Shaker Furniture* (New York: Dover Publications, 1950), p. 42.

99. Smith, *Panorama*, 1:110; Brientnall and

Fassauer insolvency records; Webster in Cole account book.

100. Fassauer insolvency records; Thomas C. Hayward estate records, 1845, Ashford, Conn., Genealogical Section, CSL; Salaman, *Dictionary*, pp. 315, 331–32, 367–68; Smith, *Key*, fig. 720. According to Smith, a "round" plane has a hollow sole and iron that create a rounded surface on the worked wood.

101. Lucas and Shepard and other data in Hummel, "English Tools in America," pp. 27–29, 34–35; "Records of the Providence Association of Mechanics and Manufacturers," 1790–91; John J. Bowles broadside, ca. 1839–41, OSV; Fitch K. Collins broadside, 1838, as illustrated in Larry L. Nelson, "Cabinetmaking Tools at the Ohio Historical Center," *Chronicle of the Early American Industries Association* 33, no. 2 (June 1980): 18.

102. Mercer, *Ancient Carpenters' Tools*, pp. 291–95; Salaman, *Dictionary*, pp. 194–95, 439–40; Hummel, *Hammer in Hand*, pp. 76–78; Smith, *Key*, p. 5 (catalogue), figs. 771–96.

103. Godfrey Cole inventory; Hummel, "English Tools in America," p. 30; Hutchins in Ward account book; Ward inventory book; Boynton ledger, 1811–17; George Landon account book, 1813–32, DCM, and estate records, 1834, Erie Co., Erie, Pa., Register of Wills.

104. Shop rack in Gilbert Dinese inventory, 1813, DCM; Cheney and Foot estate records.

105. Page in Leibundguth, "Furniture-Making Crafts in Philadelphia," p. 85; notice of James Rousham, *South Carolina Gazette*, July 1, 1732, as quoted in Prime, *Arts and Crafts, 1721–1785*, p. 187; Hummel, *Hammer in Hand*, pp. 69, 85; Mercer, *Ancient Carpenters' Tools*; Keno, "Windsor Chair Makers of Northampton," pp. 32–34; Calvin Barstow ledger C, 1792–1815, CHS.

106. Tomlinson, *Illustrations of Trades*, p. 48; Smith, *Panorama*, 1:67–68; Salaman, *Dictionary*, pp. 144–46; Smith, *Key*, p. 2 (catalogue), figs. 118–24.

107. Smith, *Panorama*, 1:67, 84; Moxon, *Mechanick Exercises*, p. 184; references to "turning Drum Sticks" in Philemon Hinman account book, 1804-17, Plymouth, Conn., CHS.

108. Mercer, *Ancient Carpenters' Tools*, pp. 163–70; Salaman, *Dictionary*, pp. 130–34, 138–39, 141–42; Smith, *Key*, p. 1 (catalogue), figs. 83–112; Hummel, *Hammer in Hand*, p. 68; James M. Gaynor and Nancy L. Hagadorn, *Tools Working Wood in Eighteenth-Century America* (Williamsburg, Va.: Colonial Williamsburg Foundation, 1993), pp. 12–13.

109. Jacob Cole inventory; Sage in Keno, "Windsor Chair Makers of Northampton," p. 9; Hutchins estate records; Salaman, *Dictionary*, pp. 135–37.

110. The Burnett bits could have been made for several different braces originally.

111. Parrott and Hubbell insolvency re-

cords; Robert Walker estate records, 1774, City and County of Philadelphia, Register of Wills; Griswold ledger; Houghton ledger A; Perez Austin estate records, 1833, Canterbury, Conn., Genealogical Section, CSL; Jacob Cole inventory; Steel estate records; Mayes, *Chairmaking*, p. 14.

112. Boynton ledger, 1811–17, and shop account; the pewter "lining" of the bit pads probably consisted of bands of reinforcing metal. Thomas Kinsela estate records, 1822, Schenectady Co., N.Y., Surrogate Court; Josiah Powers estate records, 1827, Middletown, Conn., Genealogical Section, CSL; Thomas Maule, *Pennsylvania Gazette* (Philadelphia), March 3, 1752; Cheney estate records.

113. Jenkins, *Traditional Country Craftsmen*, p. 119; Keno, "Windsor Chair Makers of Northampton," p. 9; Michael Dunbar, *Antique Woodworking Tools* (New York: Hastings House, 1977), pp. 183–84; Mercer, *Ancient Carpenters' Tools*, pp. 181–82; Carl E. Bopp, " 'Premium Awarded by Philadelphia and New York Institutes BOOTH & MILLS, PHILADA.," *Chronicle of the Early American Industries Association* 27, no. 3 (September 1974): 41–42, front cover; Boynton ledger, 1811–17; Austin estate records; Ward inventory book; Reed daybook.

114. Benno M. Forman, *American Seating Furniture, 1630–1730: An Interpretive Catalogue* (New York: W. W. Norton, 1987), pp. 251–53, fig. 136; Thomas Maule, *Pennsylvania Gazette*, April 5, 1748; Goodrich estate records; Cheney ledger, 1816–22; Silas E. Cheney daybook, 1813–21, LHS (microfilm, DCM).

115. Chesnut in Dorman, *Delaware Cabinetmakers*, p. 20; Jacob Cole inventory; Fizer inventory; Clay in Sackman, "William Bull," p. 10; Davis in Keno, "Windsor Chair Makers of Northampton," pp. 115, 128; Boynton ledger, 1817–47.

116. Boynton ledgers, 1811–17, 1817–47; Salaman, *Dictionary*, pp. 82, 351; Alexander, *Make a Chair*, pp. 74–75, 77, and notes to author.

117. Salaman, *Dictionary*, pp. 44–46, 208–9; Smith, *Panorama*, 1:115–16; Mercer, *Ancient Carpenters' Tools*, pp. 61, 176–77, 202–3, 205; Ward account book; Tomlinson, *Illustrations of Trades*, p. 46; Hummel, *Hammer in Hand*, pp. 48–49; Hayward estate records.

118. Moore insolvency records; Kenney, *Hitchcock Chair*, pp. 320–21; Moxon, *Mechanick Exercises*, pl. 13, fig. 2, and pl. 14 (upper right-hand corner).

119. Goodman, *History of Woodworking Tools*, p. 52; Mercer, *Ancient Carpenters' Tools*, pp. 69, 71, 79; Salaman, *Dictionary*, pp. 240–41; Hummel, *Hammer in Hand*, pp. 54–56, 87; Steel estate records; Snowden in Leibundguth, "Furniture-Making Crafts in Philadelphia," p. 83.

120. Jeremiah Cresson, *Pennsylvania Packet*, March 15, 1779, as quoted in Prime, *Arts and Crafts, 1721–85*, p. 164; Jacob Cole inven-

tory; Moxon, *Mechanick Exercises*, pl. 1 (smith); Hummel, *Hammer in Hand*, pp. 203–4.

121. Salaman, *Dictionary*, pp. 168–69, 173, 448–49, including chairmaker's donkey; Hummel, *Hammer in Hand*, pp. 70–71; Mercer, *Ancient Carpenters' Tools*, pp. 73–74, 230–31; Lambert and Riley estate records; Cresson, *Pennsylvania Packet*.

122. Salaman, *Dictionary*, pp. 295–96, 379; Boynton shop account.

123. Salaman, *Dictionary*, p. 472; Mercer, *Ancient Carpenters' Tools*, pp. 54–58, 60; Hummel, *Hammer in Hand*, pp. 142–44; Ward inventory book; Moxon, *Mechanick Exercises*, p. 4 (joiner).

124. Salaman, *Dictionary*, pp. 397–99; Mercer, *Ancient Carpenters' Tools*, pp. 62–63; Philemon Hinman estate records, 1835, Harwinton, Conn., Genealogical Section, CSL; Joseph Wetherbee, Jr., estate records, 1847, Worcester Co., Mass., Registry of Probate; Ward inventory book.

125. Mercer, *Ancient Carpenters' Tools*, pp. 60–61, 63; Salaman, *Dictionary*, pp. 201–4; Hummel, *Hammer in Hand*, pp. 80–81.

126. Goodman, *History of Woodworking Tools*, pp. 200–201; Mercer, *Ancient Carpenters' Tools*, pp. 58–59, 61, 228–30; Salaman, *Dictionary*, pp. 108–13, 153–55; Godfrey Cole inventory; Pinkerton estate records.

127. Mercer, *Ancient Carpenters' Tools*, pp. 288–91; Salaman, *Dictionary*, pp. 285–86; Johns order in Hummel, *Hammer in Hand*, p. 32; Clark and Wetherbee estate records.

128. Smith, *Key*; Hummel, *Hammer in Hand*, pp. 32, 34.

129. Solomon Fussell account book, 1738–48, Stephen Collins Papers, Library of Congress, Washington, D.C. (microfilm, DCM); DeWitt in Andrews and Andrews, *Shaker Furniture*, pp. 38, 40; Deland account book; Ward inventory book; Hummel, *Hammer in Hand*, p. 78.

130. Elisha Harlow Holmes ledger, 1825–30, CHS; Salaman, *Dictionary*, p. 487. For Phyfe tool chest, see Marshall B. Davidson, *The American Heritage History of American Antiques from the Revolution to the Civil War* (New York: American Heritage Publishing Co., 1968), p. 90.

131. Moxon, *Mechanick Exercises*, pp. 104–5, pl. 5 (joiner); Goodman, *History of Woodworking Tools*, pp. 154, 203; Amos Wells estate records, 1802, Colchester, Conn., Genealogical Section, CSL.

132. Austin in Mabel M. Swan, "Furniture Makers of Charlestown," *Antiques* 46, no. 4 (October 1944): 204; Prall and Samuel Loomis estate records; Parrott and Hubbell insolvency records. For a glue pot and kettle, see Tomlinson, *Illustrations of Trades*, p. 33. Salaman, *Dictionary*, p. 211; Mercer, *Ancient Carpenters' Tools*, pp. 262–63. Glue kettles are exhibited at the High Wycombe Chair Museum, Buckinghamshire, England; another is visible in an in-

terior view of the early twentieth-century chair shop of "Jack" Goodchild in Buckinghamshire, as illustrated in F. Gordon Roe, *Windsor Chairs* (London: Phoenix House, 1953), pl. 53.

133. Knowlton inventory; Ball inventory; Renshaw in Schiffer, *Furniture of Chester County*, p. 206; brush and glue pot in Wetherbee estate records; Salaman, *Dictionary*, p. 211.

134. Patrick Gordon estate records, 1736, City and County of Philadelphia, Register of Wills; Benjamin Price bill to Henry Skinner, October 10, 1794, Girard Papers, Board of Directors of City Trusts, Girard College History Collections, Philadelphia, Pa. (microfilm, APS).

135. Thomas Beck lawsuit vs. William Campbell, February 8, 1808, DCM; Carpenters' Company of Philadelphia account book, 1763–1834, and warden's book, 1769–1831, Papers of the Carpenters' Company (on deposit, APS); Daniel King, *Pennsylvania Gazette*, September 22, 1763; Foster in *Matchett's Baltimore Directory for 1824* (Baltimore: R[ichard] J. Matchett, 1824), n.p.

136. Haven estate records; Clay in Sackman, "William Bull," p. 10; John B. Ackley estate records, 1827, City and County of Philadelphia, Register of Wills; manifest of ship *America*, October 17, 1807, Philadelphia Outward Coastwise Entries, U.S. Custom House Records, NA.

137. Tracy purchases in Avery ledger; King, *Pennsylvania Gazette*. Copper-headed irons also were used by members of the Van Rensselaer family of New York State; see Roderick H. Blackburn, "Branded and Stamped New York Furniture," *Antiques* 119, no. 5 (May 1981): 1130–32. John R. Grabb, "Burning Brands or Marking Irons," *Chronicle of the Early American Industries Association* 31, no. 3 (September 1978): 40. For a branded Fox spinning wheel, see Evans, *Specialized Forms*, fig. 3-34.

138. Grabb, "Burning Brands," p. 40; Wilder daybook and ledger; steel brands in Freedly, *Philadelphia and Its Manufactures*, p. 340; Salaman, *Dictionary*, p. 106; Christian Nestell, *Providence Patriot* (Providence, R.I.), August 28, 1822 (reference courtesy of Robert P. Emlen). For Priest advertisement, see John Priest, *Impartial Review and Cumberland Repository* (Nashville, Tenn.), March 24, 1808, in Evans, *American Windsor Chairs*, fig. 8-30.

139. Salaman, *Dictionary*, p. 291; Allen in Hall, "New Bedford Furniture," p. 1109; Hancock, "Furniture Craftsmen in Delaware Records," p. 208; Hummel, *Hammer in Hand*, pp. 96–98, 247–48, 252–53, 256, 262; Alling estate records; Parsons, Wilder Family Notes.

140. *Dictionary of American Biography*, s.v. "Michaux, François André"; F. André Michaux, *The North American Sylva*, 3 vols. (Philadelphia: J. Dobson, 1841), 1:xiii, 3:207. Michaux's work was first published between 1810 and 1813 at Paris.

141. Francis Trumble, *Pennsylvania Ga-

zette*, December 27, 1775, as quoted in Nancy A. Goyne (Evans), "Francis Trumble of Philadelphia, Windsor Chair and Cabinetmaker," in *Winterthur Portfolio 1*, ed. Milo M. Naeve (Winterthur, Del.: Winterthur Museum, 1964), p. 239; Steel estate records; Isaiah Steen, *Reporter* (Washington, Pa.), March 15, 1813 (reference courtesy of Peter Chillingworth).

142. Michaux, *North American Sylva*, 2:143–48.

143. Gordon Saltar, "New England Timbers," in *Boston Furniture of the Eighteenth Century*, ed. Walter Muir Whitehill, Publications of the Colonial Society of Massachusetts, vol. 48 (Boston: Colonial Society of Massachusetts, 1974), pp. 258–59; Michaux, *North American Sylva*, 1:97–108. Microanalysis of the Winterthur Museum collection of Windsor furniture confirms that among maples red (soft) maple was the overwhelming choice of chairmakers for turned work.

144. Jacob Bigelow, *The Useful Arts*, 2 vols. (Boston: Thomas H. Webb, 1840), 1:103; Saltar, "New England Timbers," pp. 255–56; Michaux, *North American Sylva*, 3:106–14; George B. Emerson, *A Report on the Trees and Shrubs . . . in the Forests of Massachusetts*, 2 vols. (Boston: Little, Brown, 1894), 2:375–83.

145. Saltar "New England Timbers," p. 258; Michaux, *North American Sylva*, 1:80–82, 89–92; Trumble, *Pennsylvania Gazette*; Josiah Sherald, *Pennsylvania Gazette*, September 5, 1765, as quoted in Prime, *Arts and Crafts, 1721–85*, p. 182.

146. Saltar, "New England Timbers," pp. 259–60; Michaux, *North American Sylva*, 1:1–11; Joseph Robinson, *Dauphin Guardian* (Harrisburg, Pa.), August 29, 1809 (advertisement brought to author's attention by the late William Bowers).

147. Watson, *Annals of Philadelphia*, 1:229; Maule and Brother, *Philadelphia Ledger* (Philadelphia), January 17, 1859, as quoted in Charles E. Peterson, "Sawdust Trail," *Bulletin of the Association for Preservation Technology* 5, no. 2 (1973): 120–21; Isaac Whitelock estate records, 1848, City and County of Philadelphia, Register of Wills (microfilm, DCM).

148. Adolph B. Benson, ed., *Peter Kalm's Travels in North America*, 2 vols. (New York: Dover Publications, 1966), 1:37–39; Benjamin Hunt and Asa Matlack broadside notice, February 1, 1821, as illustrated in *Chronicle of the Early American Industries Association* 38, no. 2 (June 1985): back cover; Henry Wansey, *An Excursion to the United States of North America in the Summer of 1794*, 2d ed. (Salisbury, England: J. Easton, 1798), p. 93; Eliza Cope Harrison, ed., *Philadelphia Merchant: The Diary of Thomas P. Cope, 1800–1851* (South Bend, Ind.: Gateway Editions, 1978), p. 124; Freedley, *Philadelphia and Its Manufactures*, p. 106.

149. Benjamin B. Herr (attributed) account book, 1796–1837, private collection; Susque-

hanna trade described in Eli Bowen, *The Pictorial Sketch-Book of Pennsylvania* (1852), p. 168, as quoted in Peterson, "Sawdust Trail," p. 120; Samuel R. Brown, *The Western Gazetteer, or Emigrants Directory* (Auburn, N.Y.: H. C. Southwick, 1817), pp. 331–39; Edwin James, comp., *Account of an Expedition from Pittsburgh to the Rocky Mountains, Performed in the Years 1819 and '20*, 2 vols. (Philadelphia: H. C. Carey and I. Lea, 1823), 1:14, as quoted in Charles van Ravenswaay, "A Historical Checklist of the Pines of Eastern North America," in *Winterthur Porfolio 7*, ed. Ian M. G. Quimby (Charlottesville: University Press of Virginia, 1972), p. 207.

150. George Bradshaw and John Bradshaw, *Maryland Herald and Hagerstown Weekly Advertiser* (Hagerstown), September 13 and October 11, 1815, citation file, MESDA; Creamer in *Matchett's Baltimore Directory* (Baltimore: Baltimore Director Office, 1842), p. 11.

151. 1820 Census of Manufactures, state of New York; Brodie and Dennistown, *New-York Gazette and General Advertiser* (New York), February 18, 1803, as quoted in Rita Susswein Gottesman, comp., *The Arts and Crafts in New York, 1800–1804* (New York: New-York Historical Society, 1965), p. 199; David Alling receipt books, 1803–24 and 1824–42, New Jersey Historical Society, Newark (hereafter cited NJHS; microfilm, DCM); Alling estate records.

152. Alling receipt book, 1824–42; David Alling receipt book, 1844–56, NJHS (microfilm, DCM); Alling estate records; Wilson in Corlies account book; Henry Bradshaw Fearon, *Sketches of America*, 2d ed. (London: Longman et al., 1818), p. 75; Timothy Dwight, *Travels in New England and New York*, 4 vols., ed. Barbara Miller Solomon (Cambridge, Mass.: Belknap Press, 1969), 3:199, 212, 225.

153. William Strickland, *Journal of a Tour in the United States of America, 1794–1795*, ed. J. E. Strickland (New York: The New-York Historical Society, 1971), pp. 91, 96, 131, 134; Benson, *Kalm's Travels*, 1:333, 336–38; 2:592, 606, 618; Peterson, "Sawdust Trail", pp. 105–8; *The New Democracy in America: Travels of Francisco de Miranda in the United States, 1783–84*, trans. Judson P. Wood, ed. John S. Ezell (Norman: University of Oklahoma Press, 1963), p. 100; "Charles Carroll of Carrollton, 1776," in Roland Van Zandt, ed., *Chronicles of the Hudson: Three Centuries of Travelers' Accounts* (New Brunswick, N.J.: Rutgers University Press, 1971), p. 87; Michaux, *North American Sylva*, 3:164; 1820 Census of Manufactures, state of New York; Isaac Weld, *Travels through the States of North America*, 2 vols. (London: John Stockdale, 1800), 1:281. For the Vermont chairs, see Evans, *American Windsor Chairs*, fig. 6-255, and *Specialized Forms*, fig. 1-28.

154. Michaux, *North American Sylva*, 3:131–32; Saltar, "New England Timbers," p. 256; Kinsela estate records; Holcomb account

book; Gilbert and Fairbanks in William Richards, comp., *Utica Directory 1840–'41* (Utica, N.Y.: John P. Bush, 1840), p. 20; Dwight, *Travels*, 3:123, 4:32; *The Aristocratic Journey: Being the Outspoken Letters of Mrs. Basil Hall*, ed. Una Pope-Hennessy (New York: G. P. Putnam's Sons, 1931), p. 54. Brown, *Western Gazetteer*, p. 343; the Holland land purchase comprised the western counties of New York State.

155. The distribution of plankwood given in map 1 is based on data obtained by microanalysis and is supported by written evidence; the map is not necessarily all-inclusive. For insights into wood identification the reader is directed to R. Bruce Hoadley, *Understanding Wood* (Newtown, Conn.: Taunton Press, 1980), especially chap. 3, and *Identifying Wood: Accurate Results with Simple Tools* (Newtown, Conn.: Taunton Press, 1990). Case furniture from the Connecticut–Rhode Island border region also employs a multiplicity of woods.

156. Michaux, *North American Sylva*, 3:160–66; [Theodore Dwight, Jr.], *The Northern Traveller*, 2d ed. (New York: A. T. Goodrich, 1826), p. 265; Strickland, *Journal*, p. 147; Dwight, *Travels*, 4:10.

157. Knowlton inventory; Bass estate records; Parrott and Hubbell insolvency records; Philemon Robbins account book, 1833–35, CHS; *Documents Relative to Manufactures*; Gates, "Journal of a Cabinet Maker's Apprentice, Part 2," p. 35.

158. Michaux, *North American Sylva*, 3:132; Horace Colton and Nathan Brown, *Norwich Courier* (Norwich, Conn.), October 21, 1812, and November 19, 1823 (references courtesy of Wendell Hilt).

159. Edwin A. Churchill, *Simple Forms and Vivid Colors* (Augusta: Maine State Museum, 1983), pp. 3–5, 82–83, 88–89, 94–101; Faunce inventory; Judd, Cheney, Goodrich, and Bass estate records; James Chase inventory and account book, 1797–1812, as excerpted in Parsons, New Hampshire Notes; John Cate daybook, 1833–42, DCM; True Currier, Joseph S. Comings, and Edwin Hall account books, 1815–38, 1829–65, and 1814–18, DCM; Jedidiah Morse, *American Geography* (Elizabethtown, N.J.: Shepard Kollock, 1789), p. 470; 1820 Census of Manufactures, state of Vermont; Boynton ledgers; Henry F. Dewey account book, 1837–64, Shelburne Museum, Shelburne, Vt. (microfilm, DCM); Daniel Clay, *Greenfield Gazette*, July 27, 1801, as quoted in Peter Rippe, "Daniel Clay of Greenfield, 'Cabinetmaker'" (master's thesis, University of Delaware, 1962), pp. 62–64; William Perkins, *American Sentinel* (Middletown, Conn.), August 3, 1825, and Matthew Noble, *Connecticut Courant* (Hartford), March 27, 1797 (references courtesy of Wendell Hilt); Cheney ledger, 1799–1817; Silas E. Cheney daybooks, 1802–7 and 1807–13, LHS (microfilm, DCM).

160. Tracy estate records; notices for whitewood in *Norwich Courier*: Francis W. Bushnell,

October 1822, J. W. Coyl, December 18, 1822, and Nathan Brown and J. F. Throop, November 19, 1823 (references courtesy of Wendell Hilt); notices for whitewood in *Connecticut Gazette* (New London): William Harris, Jr., February 7, 1798, and Thomas West, February 10, 1810; William Russell, Jr., estate records, 1833, Bristol Co., Mass., Registry of Probate.

161. For the Stackhouse advertisement and the Westbrook and Stackhouse chairs, see Evans, *American Windsor Chairs*, figs. 6-186, 6-173, and 6-184. John Wadsworth and Jacob Norton, *American Mercury*, June 3, 1793, and June 29, 1789 (references courtesy of Nancy E. Richards); Parrott and Hubbell insolvency records; David Finch, and Lockwood and Waite insolvency records, 1829–30 and 1847, Bridgeport, Conn., Genealogical Section, CSL; Cheney ledgers and daybooks; Beckwith and Holman, *Hampshire Gazette* (Northampton, Mass.), February 11, 1807. A Boston Windsor described as having a "poplar" seat, an identification that is almost certainly incorrect, is illustrated in Oswaldo Rodriguez Roque, *American Furniture at Chipstone* (Madison: University of Wisconsin Press, 1984), fig. 104; the author has found no Windsors associated with the Boston area that have yellow poplar seats, and Michaux states quite clearly in *North American Sylva*, 2:146, that "the vicinity of Boston does not produce this tree."

162. Michaux, *North American Sylva*, 3:80-81;Job Danforth ledger, 1788–1818, RIHS; Oliver Avery account book, 1789–1813, DCM; Elisha Hawley account book, 1781–1800, CHS; James Gere ledgers; Jonas Green account book, 1830–40, OSV; Samuel Douglas and Son account book, 1810–58, CSL; Cheney daybooks, 1802-7 and 1807–13; Loring estate records; John B. Pratt estate records, 1855, Worcester Co., Mass., Registry of Probate; Tracy estate records.

163. Michaux, *North American Sylva*, 1:68–71; Saltar, "New England Timbers," p. 257. For the Rhode Island settee, see Evans, *Specialized Forms*, fig. 1-83. Brown, *Norwich Courier*.

164. Michaux, *North American Sylva*, 3:106. For the Rhode Island chair, see Patricia E. Kane, *300 Years of American Seating Furniture* (Boston: New York Graphic Society, 1976), fig. 190. For the settee and high stool, see Evans, *Specialized Forms*, figs. 1-82 and 3-24.

165. Bigelow, *Useful Arts*, 1:105. For the writing-arm chair, see Evans, *Specialized Forms*, fig. 1-4. For the chair with the split seat, see Barry A. Greenlaw, *New England Furniture at Williamsburg* (Williamsburg, Va.: Colonial Williamsburg Foundation, 1974), pp. 176–77, fig. 153. Another example is in the Garvan Collection; see Kane, *American Seating Furniture*, fig. 171.

166. Emerson, *Report*, 1:277; Michaux, *North American Sylva*, 2:71-72; Saltar, "New England Timbers," p. 260. For chairs with pop-

lar seats, see Evans, *American Windsor Furniture*, figs. 6-129 and 6-139. For the settee, see Evans, *Specialized Forms*, fig. 1-82.

167. Esther Singleton, *The Furniture of Our Forefathers* (Garden City, N.Y.: Doubleday, Page, 1913), p. 398; Mabel M. Swan, *Samuel McIntire, Carver, and the Sandersons, Early Salem Cabinet Makers* (Salem, Mass.: Essex Institute, 1934), pp. 5, 25; Samuel Phippen estate records, 1798, Essex Co., Mass., Registry of Probate; Michaux, *North American Sylva*, 2:181; Samuel Hendrick (Amesbury) daybook, 1816–25, DCM; Martin Sampson (Duxbury) account book, 1812–30, DCM; Bass estate records. For the Boston Windsors, see Evans, *Specialized Forms*, figs. 1–84 and 3–15. For a Rhode Island chair, see Evans, *American Windsor Chairs*, fig. 6-11.

168. Carl David Arfwedson, *The United States and Canada*, 2 vols. (1834; reprint, New York: Johnson Reprint Corp., 1969), 1:67.

169. Joel Pratt, Jr., account book, 1822–26 with additions, privately owned (microfilm, OSV).

170. Michaux, *North American Sylva*, 1:8, 3:108.

171. Michaux, *North American Sylva*, 2:143; "Journal of Lord Adam Gordon," in *Narratives of Colonial America*, ed. Howard H. Peckham (Chicago: R. R. Donnelley and Sons, 1971), p. 254; duc de la Rochefoucauld Liancourt, *Travels through the United States of North America*, 2 vols. (London: R. Phillips, 1799), 2:364; Bates in Golovin, "Cabinetmakers and Chairmakers of Washington," p. 906; Ephraim Evans, *Virginia Journal and Alexandria Advertiser* (Alexandria), October 20, 1785, Matthew Wilson, *Farmer's Repository* (Charles Town, W.Va.), October 20, 1814, and Joseph Childres, *Virginia Gazette and General Advertiser* (Richmond), August 17, 1803, all in citation file, MESDA; Adam Fizer inventory; Lasker Smith, 1820 Census of Manufactures, state of Virginia; Thomas J. Moyers and Fleming K. Rich account book, 1834–40, DCM; John Bivins, Jr., and Paula Welshimer, *Moravian Decorative Arts in North Carolina* (Winston-Salem, N.C.: Old Salem, 1981), pp. 21, 25.

172. Bivins and Welshimer, *Moravian Decorative Arts*, pp. 8, 2, 25; Zenos Bronson, *North Carolina Star* (Raleigh), March 3, 1815, as quoted in James H. Craig, *The Arts and Crafts in North Carolina, 1699–1840* (Winston-Salem: Old Salem, 1965), pp. 183–84, 186; Alexander Walker, *Virginia Herald* (Fredericksburg), March 19, 1802, citation file, MESDA; 1820 Census of Manufactures, state of Virginia; white pine sale notices in *Wilmington Gazette* (Wilmington, N.C.), January 6, 1807, and *Charleston Courier* (Charleston, S.C.), January 29, 1807, citation file, MESDA; Peterson, "Sawdust Trail," p. 105.

173. 1820 Census of Manufactures, states of Ohio and Tennessee; Fearon, *Sketches*, p. 237;

Michaux, *North American Sylva*, 1:107; 2:143; Christian Schultz, Jr., *Travels on an Inland Voyage*, 2 vols. (1810; reprint, Ridgewood, N.J.: Gregg Press, 1968), 1:24; Caleb Atwater, *The Writings of Caleb Atwater* (Columbus, Ohio: By the author, 1833), p. 215, as quoted in van Ravenswaay, "Checklist of Pines," pp. 207–8.

174. Jeanne Minhinnick, *At Home in Upper Canada* (Toronto: Clark, Irwin, 1970), p. 185; Philip Shackleton, *The Furniture of Old Ontario* (Toronto: Macmillan of Canada, 1973), p. 22; Howard Pain, *The Heritage of Country Furniture* (Toronto: Van Nostrand Reinhold, 1978), pp. 109–34; Jeanne Minhinnick, *Early Furniture in Upper Canada Village, 1800–1837* (Toronto: McGraw-Hill of Canada, 1964), p. 10; Donald Blake Webster, "The Identification of English-Canadian Furniture, 1780–1840," *Antiques* 115, no. 1 (January 1979): 179; George MacLaren, "The Windsor Chair in Nova Scotia," *Antiques* 100, no. 1 (July 1971): 125; Huia G. Ryder, *Antique Furniture by New Brunswick Craftsmen* (Toronto: Ryerson Press, 1965), p. 3; Michaux, *North American Sylva*, 1:100, 2:178, 3:107, 160; *The Diary of William Bentley*, 4 vols. (Salem, Mass.: Essex Institute, 1905), 2:331.

175. For insights on selecting and working "wet" versus "dry" wood I am indebted to John D. Alexander, Jr., and to my experience at Drew Langsner's Country Workshops in Marshall, North Carolina; see also Hoadley, *Understanding Wood*, chap. 4; Peter Pierce estate records, 1836, Worcester Co., Mass., Registry of Probate; Willard estate records. *Tenon dry* was a term used among English chairmakers, as indicated in a taped interview with a Mr. Barnes in the 1950s now on deposit at the High Wycombe Library, High Wycombe, England. Barnes was among the last group of craftsmen in Buckinghamshire to labor within a semi-industrial framework little changed from nineteenth-century practice.

176. Daniel Lawrence, *United States Chronicle* (Providence, R.I.), July 19, 1787, as quoted in Irving Whitall Lyon, *The Colonial Furniture of New England* (Boston: Houghton Mifflin, 1924), p. 181; John Denig, *Franklin Repository*, May 14, 1822 (reference courtesy of the late William Bowers); Samuel Williams, *Clarion and Tennessee State Gazette* (Nashville), June 10, 1817, citation file, MESDA.

177. Nelson Talcott daybook, 1839–48, DCM; Pierce estate records; Lambert Hitchcock estate records, 1852, Farmington, Conn., Genealogical Section, CSL.

178. Jonathan Cahoone claim of losses during Revolution, [1782], DCM.

179. Wait Garret account book, 1810–58, CSL; Reuben Loomis account book, 1796–1836, CHS; Titus Preston ledger, 1795–1817, Sterling Memorial Library, Yale University, New Haven, Conn. (hereafter cited Yale).

180. John Underwood, a Boston turner, worked on occasion during the 1730s and 1740s

in his father's shop, where he prepared materials for slat-back rush-bottom chairs; see Brock Jobe and Myrna Kaye, *New England Furniture: The Colonial Era* (Boston: Houghton Mifflin, 1984), p. 10. Solomon Fussell's Philadelphia accounts of the 1740s record William Sneed's production of a large number of chair parts, comprising slats, lists for seat rails, and stretchers; see Fussell account book and Benno M. Forman, "Delaware Valley 'Crookt Foot' and Slat-Back Chairs," *Winterthur Portfolio* 15, no. 1 (Spring 1980): 45. Robert McKeen lawsuit vs. Joseph Adams, 1790, Colonial Court Records, Social Law Library, Boston, Mass. (reference courtesy of Charles A. Hammond and John T. Kirk).

181. Cheney and Boynton ledgers, 1799–1817 and 1817–47; Silas E. Cheney court records, 1807–19, Superior Court Records, Litchfield Co., Conn., Miscellaneous Papers, CSL; David Pritchard account book, 1827–38, Mattatuck; Wilder daybook and ledger; Talcott daybook.

182. Fussell account book; Forman, "Delaware Valley Chairs," p. 45; Andrew Hagerty lawsuit vs. Lawrence Allwine, 1787, DCM; Michaux, *North American Sylva*, 1:98.

183. Hawley account book; Daniel and Samuel Proud ledger, 1782–1825, RIHS.

184. Levi Stillman account book, 1815–34, Yale; Cheney daybooks, 1802–7 and 1813–21, and ledger, 1816–22; Houghton ledger A; Boynton ledger, 1811–17.

185. Henry Wilder Miller account book, 1827–31, Worcester Historical Museum, Worcester, Mass.; Felton daybook.

186. Samuel Davison ledger, 1795–1824, HD (on deposit from the Pocumtuck Valley Memorial Association, Deerfield, Mass.); Cheney ledger, 1816–22, and daybooks; Cheney court records; David Pritchard ledger, 1800–1810, Mattatuck; Elizur Barnes account book, 1821–25, Middlesex Historical Society, Middletown, Conn. (microfilm, CHS).

187. Herrick, *History of Gardner*, p. 167.

188. Cheney daybook, 1813–21, and ledger, 1816–22; Cheney court records.

189. Gere ledgers; James Gere account book, 1809–39, CSL.

190. Wilder daybook and ledger; Josiah P. Wilder and George B. Gardner account book, 1839–41, Parsons, Wilder Family Notes; Increase Pote account book, 1824–30, Maine Historical Society, Portland.

191. David Alling account book, 1801–39, NJHS (microfilm, DCM).

192. John F. Schroeder, *Lancaster Union* (Lancaster, Pa.), February 16, 1841, LCHS; Talcott daybook; 1820 Census of Manufactures, state of Ohio; Roll and Deeds, source unknown (1818), as quoted in Donna Streifthau, "Cincinnati Cabinet- and Chairmakers, 1819–1830," *Antiques* 99, no. 6 (June 1971): 903.

193. Freedley, *Philadelphia and Its Manufactures*, p. 44.

194. William Parkhurst bill to Ebenezer Fox, December 19, 1806, Papers of Ebenezer Fox, Peabody Essex Museum, Salem, Mass.; Simon Francis, *Columbian Centinel* (Boston, Mass.), April 11, 1801 (reference courtesy of Robert Mussey); Sinclair and Moore, *Baltimore American* (Baltimore, Md.), July 16, 1829 (reference courtesy of Arlene Palmer Schwind); Joseph Childres, *Virginia Gazette and General Advertiser*, August 17, 1803, citation file, MESDA; Zenos Bronson, *North Carolina Star*, March 3, 1815, as quoted in Craig, *Arts and Crafts*, pp. 183–84; Catherine Burpee, *Montreal Gazette*, October 4, 1832, as quoted in Collard, "Montreal Cabinetmakers," p. 1138; Willard and Pierce estate records.

195. Component cost is based on figures drawn from many documents; some documents serve as sources for nomenclature as well. Goodrich and Lambert estate records; Davison ledger; Keno, "Windsor Chair Makers of Northampton," p. 9; Ansel Goodrich, *Hampshire Gazette*, ca. June 1, 1803, as quoted in Florence Thompson Howe, "The Brief Career of Ansel Goodrich," *Antiques* 18, no. 1 (July 1930): 39.

196. Wood, Pierce, and Lambert estate records; Hagerty-Allwine lawsuit.

197. Hanson and Lambert estate records; Proud ledger; Alling account book; Wilder daybook and ledger.

198. Proud ledger; Trumble, Lambert and Hanson estate records.

199. Alling account book; David Alling account book, 1836–54, NJHS (microfilm, DCM); Wood, Bass, Steel, and Lambert estate records; Lockwood and Waite, and Parrott and Hubbel insolvency records; Wilder daybook and ledger; Hanson estate records.

200. *The Book of Trades, or Library of the Useful Arts* (London, 1805), pt. 3, p. 58; Moxon, *Mechanick Exercises*, p. 104; Sheraton, *Cabinet Dictionary*, 2:237; Smith, *Panorama*, 1:120.

201. Sheraton, *Cabinet Dictionary*, 2:237–38; Smith, *Panorama*, 1:120–21; Moxon, *Mechanick Exercises*, pp. 104–5.

202. Smith, *Panorama*, 1:121; Bigelow, *Useful Arts*, 1:160.

203. "English Glew" in advertisements of John Davis, *Boston News-Letter* (Boston), April 8/15, 1736, as quoted in George Francis Dow, comp., *The Arts and Crafts in New England, 1704–1775* (1927; reprint, New York, Da Capo Press, 1967), p. 105, and James Reynolds, *Pennsylvania Chronicle* (Philadelphia), September 14, 1767, as quoted in Prime, *Arts and Crafts, 1721–85*, pp. 224–25. Notices for American glue houses in *New-York Gazette* (New York), February 17, 1766, and *New-York Journal* (New York), March 15, 1770, as quoted in Rita S. Gottesman, comp., *The Arts and Crafts in New York, 1726–1776* (1938; reprint, New York: Da Capo Press, 1970), pp. 303, 104; John Dietz, *Mercantile Advertiser* (New York), November 18, 1799,

as quoted in Rita Susswein Gottesman, comp., *The Arts and Crafts in New York, 1777–99* (New York: New-York Historical Society, 1954), p. 308; Roberts and Roberts, *Moreau Journey*, p. 154; and Joseph Riley, *New-York Evening Post* (New York), February 16, 1814. Shackleton, *Furniture of Old Ontario*, p. 36; Freedley, *Philadelphia and Its Manufactures*, p. 218.

204. Whipple account book; boxes of glue in Riley estate records and Henry Farley inventory, 1839, Merrimack Co., Concord, N.H., Registry of Probate; Ward account book; 1820 Census of Manufactures, state of New York; Wilder data in Parsons, Wilder Family Notes.

205. Moxon, *Mechanick Exercises*, p. 213; Tench Francis, ledger-invoice book, 1759–61, HSP; Smith, *Panorama*, 1:84–85.

206. William Scandrett, *New-York Gazette*, April 16, 1764, as quoted in Gottesman, *Arts and Crafts, 1726–76*, pp. 195–96; Loring McMillen, "Sandpaper," *Chronicle of the Early American Industries Association* 8, no. 2 (April 1955): 17–18; Mercer, *Ancient Carpenters' Tools*, pp. 135, 310; Thomas Bryan in J[ames] M. Riddle and M[agnus] M. Murray, *Pittsburgh Directory for 1819* (Pittsburgh, Pa.: [John B.] Butler and [J. H.] Lambdin, 1819), n.p.; 1820 Census of Manufactures, state of Ohio.

207. Cost analysis based on figures drawn from many documents.

208. Mercer, *Ancient Carpenters' Tools*, pp. 235–37.

209. John Doolittle II account book, 1816–47, DCM; Nichols estate records; four-penny brads in Samuel Wetherill and Sons ledger, 1777–88, University of Pennsylvania, Philadelphia (microfilm, DCM); Ward account book; Morse, *American Geography*, p. 217.

210. Mercer, *Ancient Carpenters' Tools*, pp. 254–57, 259, 310–11.

211. Felix Huntington account of Col. Joshua Huntington, 1775–84, DCM; Wetherill ledger; 1820 Census of Manufactures, state of Virginia; Judd and Hitchcock estate records; Parrott and Hubbell insolvency records.

212. *New England Farmer* 6, no. 37 (April 4, 1828): 293, as quoted in Curtis, "Circular Saw," p. 177; Walters, *Furniture Makers of Indiana*, p. 58.

213. Boynton ledger, 1811–17; White estate records; Caleb Hobart estate records, 1853–65, Plymouth Co., Plymouth, Mass., Registry of Probate; Shettleworth and Barry, "Walter Corey," pp. 1199–1200.

214. Woodbury, *History of the Lathe*, p. 46; Hunter, *Waterpower*, pp. 54, 64, 416, 420; Pierce estate records; *History of Worcester County, Massachusetts*, 2 vols. (Boston: C. F. Jewett, 1879), 2:402; *New England Farmer* 6, no. 30 (February 15, 1828), p. 235, as quoted in Curtis, "Circular Saw," p. 176; Parsons, Wilder Family Notes; Boynton ledger, 1817–47.

215. Hunter, *Waterpower*, pp. 37–38, 536–40; *History of Worcester County*, 2:403; Hurd,

History of Worcester County, 1:829–30; Herrick, *History of Gardner*, pp. 167–68, 171–72, 303; 1820 Census of Manufactures, states of Connecticut, New York, Pennsylvania, Ohio, and Indiana; J. H. French, *Gazetteer of the State of New York* (Syracuse: R. Pearsall Smith, 1860), p. 402; *Documents Relative to Manufactures*, 1:836–37, 854–55, 1019; Hitchcock in *History of Litchfield County, Connecticut* (Philadelphia: J. W. Lewis, 1881), p. 241; Kenney, *Hitchcock Chair*, pp. 38, 43, 91–92; Moore insolvency records.

216. Hunter, *Waterpower*, pp. 343, 413, 514, 516–17; Victor S. Clark, *History of Manufactures in the United States*, 3 vols. (1929; reprint, New York: Peter Smith, 1949), 1:472–73; John McElwee, *Pennsylvania Packet*, June 30, 1798, as quoted in Prime, *Arts and Crafts, 1786–1800*, p. 304; John Fulton, *Atkinson's Saturday Evening Post* (Philadelphia), 1831; Gregory Weidman, "The Furniture of Classical Maryland, 1815–1845," in *Classical Maryland, 1815–1845* (Baltimore: Maryland Historical Society, 1993), p. 120; Crane in *J. F. Kimball and Co.'s Eastern, Western, and Southern Business Directory* (Cincinnati, Ohio: J. F. Kimball, 1846), p. 352.

217. Hunter, *Waterpower*, pp. 287, 514; Freedley, *Philadelphia and Its Manufactures*, pp. 34, 36; Shettleworth and Barry, "Walter Corey," pp. 1199–1200; Chichester in Edwin T. Freedley, *Leading Pursuits and Leading Men* (Philadelphia: Edward Young, 1856), p. 457.

218. Sikes, *Furniture Makers of Cincinnati*, pp. 42, 46–47; Rand in *Louisville Directory and Annual Business Advertiser for 1855–56* (Louisville, Ky.: W. Lee White, 1855), p. 210; Mackinnon, *Kingston Cabinetmakers*, pp. 63, 113–14; Mackinnon, *Toronto Cabinet Makers*, pp. 81–83.

219. Robert Walker, *Pennsylvania Gazette*, June 5, 1766; Henry C. Mercer, *The Bible in Iron* (1914; rev. Horace M. Mann, Doylestown, Pa.: Bucks County Historical Society, 1941), pp. 117–21, 167; Tuttle and Bauduin, "James Wilson," p. 55; Enos White journal, 1821–51, DCM.

220. Mercer, *Bible in Iron*, pp. 140–44, 168–72; Josephine H. Peirce, *Fire on the Hearth* (Springfield, Mass.: Pond-Ekberg, 1951), pp. 39–45; William Ash I, insolvency records, 1811, QC; Michael Stoner inventory, 1810, Lancaster Co., Pa., Registry of Probate.

221. Peirce, *Fire on the Hearth*, pp. 91–103, 142–53; Ziba Ferriss inventory, May 15–16, 1794, as quoted in Hancock, "Furniture Craftsmen in Delaware Records," p. 204; Hitchcock estate records.

222. Godfrey Cole inventory; Riley, Bass, and Hitchcock estate records.

223. Boynton shop account; Parrott and Hubbell insolvency records; Danforth ledger.

224. *Documents Relative to Manufactures*, 1:475–565; Aloysius Clements, *Daily National Intelligencer*, May 12, 1829, as quoted in Golovin, "Cabinetmakers and Chairmakers of Washington," p. 910; Alling receipt book, 1824–42; Kenney, *Hitchcock Chair*, p. 321.

225. "Refuse Chair Stuff" in Cheney and West estate records; Felton daybook; John Paine account book, 1761–1815, Institute for Colonial Studies, State University of New York at Stony Brook (microcards, DCM); Nathan Rosenberg, ed., *The American System of Manufactures, 1854-55* (Edinburgh, Scotland: Edinburgh Press, 1969), p. 345; Luke Houghton estate records, 1877, Worcester Co., Mass., Registry of Probate; Russell and Riley estate records.

226. Mayes, *Chairmaking*, pp. 44–45.

227. Lyons account book; Gates, "Journal of a Cabinet Maker's Apprentice, Part 2," p. 36, and Winifred C. Gates, "Journal of a Cabinet Maker's Apprentice, Part 1," *Chronicle of the Early American Industries Association* 15, no. 2 (June 1962): 23.

228. Cheney daybook, 1807–13; Boynton ledger, 1811–17, and shop account; *The Philadelphia Cabinet and Chair Makers' Union Book of Prices for Manufacturing Cabinet Ware* (Philadelphia: William Stavely, 1828), as quoted in Charles F. Montgomery, *American Furniture: The Federal Period* (New York: Viking Press, 1966), pp. 23, 488; Holmes ledger; Alling estate records; Farley inventory.

229. Boynton ledgers and shop account; Robert C. Scadin ledger, 1829–31, NYSHA (microfilm, DCM); Sill and Wells estate records; Parrott and Hubbell involvency records; Thomas Boynton estate sale of personal property, 1849, Windsor Co., Vt., Registry of Probate.

230. Information on the Pomfret shop and privy related to the author by Russell Ward Nadeau. Mark Girouard, *Life in the English Country House* (Harmondsworth, England: Penguin Books, 1980), pp. 246–48.

231. Notice of lost watch, *Federal Gazette and Baltimore Daily Advertiser* (Baltimore, Md.), October 15, 1803, citation file, MESDA.; Miles Benjamin daybook and ledger, 1821–29, NYSHA (microfilm, DCM).

232. Freedley, *Philadelphia and Its Manufactures*, p. 21; John Nutt, *South Carolina Gazette*, August 2, 1770, and Samuel Claphamson, *Pennsylvania Packet*, January 8, 1785, as quoted in Prime, *Arts and Crafts, 1721–85*, pp. 162, 178; Federal Procession, *Impartial Gazetteer* (New York), August 9, 1788, as quoted in Gottesman, *Arts and Crafts, 1777–99*, p. 109.

233. Allen in *Providence Directory* (Providence, R.I.: Carlile and Brown, 1826), n.p.; 1820 Census of Manufactures, states of Massachusetts and Maryland.

234. Hitchcock and Alling estate records.

235. Clark, *History of Manufactures*, 1:473–74; Mackinnon, *Toronto Cabinet Makers*, pp. 81–82; Sikes, *Furniture Makers of Cincinnati*, pp. 84–85.

236. Thomas Ash I and William Ash I, *New-York Packet* (New York), October 7, 1784.

237. Parrott and Hubbell insolvency records; Allen in *Providence Directory* (1826); Gates, "Journal of a Cabinet Maker's Apprentice, Part 1," p. 24, and "Part 2," p. 35.

CHAPTER 3

Construction and Design

Construction

SEAT PREPARATION

The seat is the principal construction unit of the Windsor. Visually and structurally it ties the chair together. Following hand sawing or mill sawing the plank required preparation before seat shaping began. Chairmakers cut blanks to proper dimensions from 2-inch thick stock to receive the seat pattern, the long grain oriented from front to back for side chairs and from side to side for the large, early armchairs. William Beesley of Salem, New Jersey, credited a workman 25¢ for "½ days work at sawing off seats" in January 1831 and at another time with 16¢ for "Sawing off 50 chair seats." Figure 2-13 pictures a rare eighteenth-century seat left in a rough sawed state on the bottom surface. By contrast, a square seat of mid-nineteenth-century date bears the curved marks of a Daniel's thickness planer (fig. **3-1**), distinctive evidence that some chairmaking facilities already were taking advantage of new mechanical woodworking equipment introduced to the market. The construction is two pieces of plank butted together near the center, a technique that became increasingly common after midcentury to utilize cheaper narrow stock. Occasionally, an earlier seat is pieced out at one edge to utilize a smaller than normal plank.[1]

The chairmaker dressed his plank, top and bottom, with a jack, or fore, plane (fig. 2-4), leaving a series of shallow, parallel channels along the surface (fig. 2-21). The side chosen for the top, which ideally was clear of knots, was marked with the seat outline, using a pattern that likely was a piece of thin board or an old seat blank. The marker was a scratch awl (fig. 2-12, rear wall to right of calipers). Next, the chairmaker sawed the seat from the prepared section of plank with a framed bow saw (fig. 2-12, upper left). There followed the work of hollowing the top with an adze and shaping the edges and contours with a drawknife and spokeshaves. John Green, a woodworker of Long Island whose accounts contain a sketch of a continuous-bow Windsor (fig. **3-2**), describes a 2-inch plank hollowed to a thickness of 1 inch at the center. Ansel Goodrich, a Massachusetts Windsor-chair maker, paid handyman Samuel Davison at the rate of 2¢ apiece in 1802 to rough-shape 346 chair seats by a process he described as "hewing and dubbing." *Dubbing* is a term meaning to "trim or make smooth with an adze." In this case it referred to hollowing the seat top (fig. 3-65). Hewing is a method of removing excess wood from the plank edges to form the seat profile using a hewing hatchet. A country craftsman such as Davison may not have owned a workbench or a bow saw, but he would have had a hewing hatchet, and he could have improvised a chopping block from a vertical section of log (fig. 2-7, left rear). Holding the seat blank vertically, he hewed it to the proper exterior profile while rotating the blank on the block.[2]

Air-dried, or seasoned, plank was desirable for working sawed blanks into shaped and contoured seats. Wood not properly prepared could result in seats that quickly became "cracked & shakey [split]," as described by Silas Cheney of western Connecticut. The hollowing tool, as indicated, was the adze. With the flat plank anchored

FIG. 3-1 Detail of planer marks on pieced plank bottom of tablet-top Windsor side chair, Walter Corey (stencil), Portland, Maine, ca. 1842–55. (*Old Sturbridge Village, Sturbridge, Mass.*)

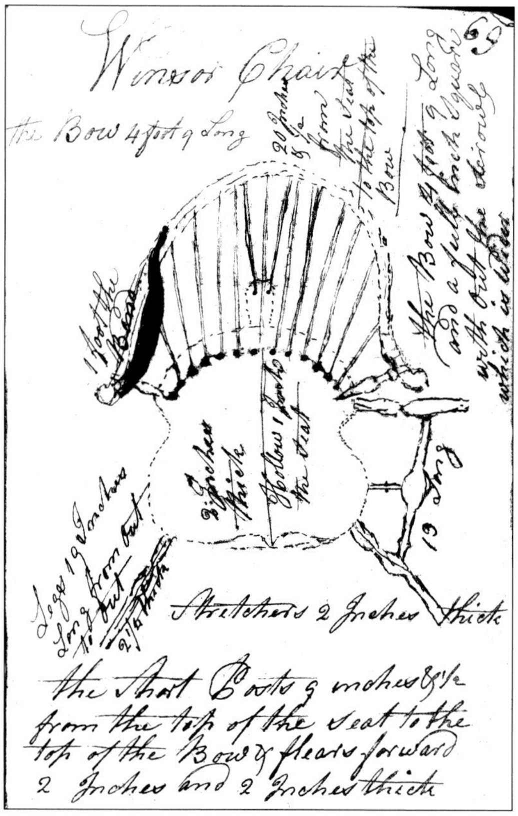

FIG. 3-2 Sketch and measurements for a continuous-bow Windsor armchair, John Green account book, Southampton, N.Y., ca. 1790–1803. (*Winterthur Library, Winterthur, Del.*)

between his feet on the shop floor, the workman removed excess wood from the center of the upper surface in a series of short chopping strokes forward of the spindle platform, allowing for the higher contours of the side and front edges. The work that followed employed the drawknife and a series of spokeshaves (figs. 2-4, rear wall second from left, 2-16, lower right), the first to form the remaining surface contours by removing wood coarsely, the second to clean up rough surfaces by removing wood finely. To smooth the hollow, the English used a convex-bladed shave called a travisher, or bottoming iron. Some American spokeshaves approximate this tool. Final smoothing was achieved with a small plane designed for the purpose or metal scrapers. The eighteenth-century seat resembles a saddle, whereas a shallow saucered surface met the requirements of most nineteenth-century work. To secure the seat plank to the benchtop while finishing the top surface and introducing a groove to the inside edge of the spindle platform, the chairmaker used either a holdfast or a bench stop, tools mentioned in period inventories (fig. 2-4, left end of benchtop). The seat was held in the bench vise to finish the edges.[3]

Upon delivering a quantity of finished "bottoms" at Litchfield, Connecticut, in 1816, Miles Hart "Recd of Silas E. Cheney nine Dollars fifteen cents for one hundred & 18 chair Seets & in part for . . . drying the same." The price per seat was about 7¾¢. Several years later Sidney Twidell got out chair bottoms at the rate of 8⅓¢ apiece, although in 1812 Cheney had paid as little as little as 6⅓¢. By the 1820s James Gere of Groton quoted prices varying from 6¼¢ to 7⅓¢ apiece. The nature of chairwork often varied from stint to stint. For instance John Parker, who built chairs on a piece-work basis at Thomas Boynton's Vermont manufactory in 1814–15, was furnished at times with seats already "spoke shaved," indicating that the edges were completely finished. On other occasions he worked up "seats from the plank." When Nelson Talcott, a chairmaker of Ohio, borrowed two dozen chair seats from Edwin Cadwell in 1839, Talcott noted that "Eliven of them . . . were shaved & spoke shaved, thirteen of them . . . were not spoke shaved." In other words, the second group had been shaped and contoured with the drawknife, but the surface needed smoothing. John B. Wilder of New Ipswich, New Hampshire, worked for his brother Josiah once in 1841 "smoothing 20 Common Seats." Nineteenth-century English records provide some account of the time involved in rough-shaping saucered-top planks. One "bot-

120   *The Craft of the Chairmaker*

FIG. 3-3 Detail of chairmakers' brand and "butterfly" wedge repair on plank bottom of bow-back Windsor armchair, William Seaver and Nathaniel Frost, Boston, 1799–1803. *(Collection of David C. Stacks; Photo, Winterthur Museum.)*

tomer" who adzed seats from elm wood could hollow and shave nine planks per hour. Another was able to complete two dozen seats before breakfast, or one every five minutes. In comparison, shaping the fully contoured eighteenth-century American Windsor chair seat was a far more complicated task. Still, even the Englishman's rate of a dozen seats per hour by hand labor during a ten-hour day in the early nineteenth century was nothing compared with the production of the industrial seat-shaping machine introduced in the late nineteenth century, which could turn out a thousand units per day.[4]

One of two final steps in producing an eighteenth-century Windsor chair seat was to carve the decorative channel or groove forward of (and sometimes behind) the spindle platform, a task accomplished with a small carving gouge. The practice continued into the next century. Late examples often have a faux-painted "channel." Occasionally a seat split after work was under way. One repaired example from the shop of Seaver and Frost at Boston survives with its original "butterfly," or dovetail key, intact (fig. **3-3**), as attested by the presence of the chairmakers' brand across the dovetail face. Most makers applied their brand to the plank bottom before the legs and stretchers were installed, a practice confirmed by the position of many impressions. The number of marked examples is small, however, compared with the vast number of chairs produced.

THE SUPPORT STRUCTURE

The production chairmaker usually made several dozen chairs at one time because preparing parts in quantity was an efficient working method. When Ebenezer Tracy, Sr., died in 1803 in eastern Connecticut, "6400 Chair rounds & legs" and "277 Chair bottoms" were stockpiled for shop use. The craftsman who did not purchase his round work turned his own legs and stretchers. After riving billets (turning blanks) from short log sections, frequently maple, he hewed them square and then removed the corners with a hatchet on the chopping block or a drawknife in the shaving horse (figs. 2-7, left, 2-12, left and right front). J. P. Wilder of New Hampshire noted on March 22, 1848, "Have been splitting and shaping chair legs today." Upon completing a leg turning in the lathe, a chairmaker carefully scored a light line to mark the point for boring a stretcher socket. Lengths and diameters were predetermined from long experience (fig. 3-2), and supports were turned longer than finish size to allow for leg joints and foot trimming. Depending on individual craft practice, stretchers were turned overlong and trimmed, or they were sawed to final length before turning. Tenons were formed by one of several methods: lathe turning, hollow augering, or whittling.[5]

To prepare for "legging up," as English craftsmen described framing the support structure, or "stooling up," as identified by Nelson Talcott of Ohio, a chairmaker

FIG. 3-4 Detail of laying-out lines on plank
bottom of bow-back Windsor armchair, area of
Jonestown, Pa., 1805–15. Yellow poplar seat.
*(Collection of the late Charlotte and Edgar Sittig;
Photo, Winterthur Museum.)*

drilled holes in a shaped seat plank, usually all the way through in pre-1800 work. Socket positions were determined by one of several methods. A common practice was to lay a pattern on the plank top through which four points were scribed with an awl. Spindle sockets could be marked at the same time. Some English chairmakers used a seat pattern with projecting points, which they pressed against the upper seat surface. An uncommon approach is illustrated in figure 3-4, a plank bottom scribed with one of several layouts in use to mark socket placement and direct the angles of boring. Several documents describe other or related methods of determining boring angles. Chairmaker Jacob Cole of Baltimore owned "3 guides for boaring," while John Lambert of Philadelphia made use of "3 Machiens for letting in feet with Propriety & Dispatch." The form of these guides, or "Machiens," is speculative, but one apparatus was likely an unshaped plank cut to profile and bored with through sockets at the correct angles. Placed over the top of a finished seat resting on the chairmaker's low framing bench (fig. 2-5) and held fast by pegs and large wedges or simple hand pressure, the guide directed the angle of boring through its sockets. When only hand pressure was used to steady the work, as was common in English practice, the force necessary for boring was directed through the chest of the crafts-man, who wore a breast bib. The bevel gauge served as a guide in other shops. This measuring device, adjustable to any desired angle, is employed even today to sight for drilling sockets in Windsor seat planks.[6]

Many seats were bored by eye, especially by experienced craftsmen engaged in quantity production. After boring one of either pair of front or back sockets, the craftsman could insert a dummy leg into the hole to use as a sighting line to direct the second boring. Because the spoon bit is likely to splinter the wood where it breaks through, most boring in the eighteenth century was done from the seat top downward. Exceptions were in following laying-out marks on the plank bottom and in drilling blind sockets that did not pierce the top surface. The latter technique was common in eastern Connecticut and parts of Rhode Island in the late eighteenth century, although by the War of 1812 the practice had become universal.

After producing through-sockets in the seat for the leg tenons, the craftsman fur-ther enlarged the holes from the underside of the plank, using a taper bit or reamer to create conical openings. Corresponding tapered tenons were worked on the leg tops, and the legs were test-inserted into the seat sockets to determine stretcher lengths. This done, the stretchers were tenoned and framed, and the legs were socketed into the seat, their tenons frequently wedged from the top surface to spread the ends and produce a tight joint. Figure **3-5** (right) illustrates a corresponding arm post with tapered tip and a wedge in place. Leg tenons for blind (internal) sockets often were treated differently. Figure **3-6** (left) illustrates an example from a chair made by a member of the Tracy family. Below the mushroom-shape cap a deeply incised circumferential notch forms a cavity to create a locking mechanism. Figure **3-6** (right), a blind leg tenon from a Rhode Island or Connecticut chair, is almost cylindrical. The top edge is chamfered to keep the tip from binding during framing. This joint may have relied on the use of glue.[7]

Legs and stretchers were stockpiled for production. Medial stretchers are longer than side stretchers and often extra-embellished with ornamental tips or rings (fig. 3-16) flanking the central swell. In the box-stretcher system the rear stretcher often is shorter than the others (fig. 3-41), although the plain cylindrical form was easily cut to length from a full-size round. Into the early nineteenth century most stretcher tenons were slightly bulbous at the tips and reduced in size at the neck (fig. **3-5**, left), the shape produced in the lathe or by hand whittling. When a tenon was driven into the blind spoon-bit socket of a leg or side stretcher, the slightly oversize bulbous tip caused a locking action at the neck. Nineteenth-century English sources make frequent mention of cutting stretchers to length and tenoning (also tenanting). Among American records only the accounts of Silas Cheney actually identify this process, although it must have been common. When working for Cheney in November 1815, Ebenezer Bryant received credit one day for "tenenting rounds for Wood seat Chairs." After tenoning, in English practice, stretchers and legs might be subjected to heat at the tenon ends until achieving a state referred to as "tenon dry." Commonly, the process involved stacking the turnings with their tips against the shop stove or placing them partially in the stove box. This was often the shop apprentice's work. Just before assembly the chairmaker bored the mortises.[8]

American Windsor-chair makers bored their round work on a low framing bench (fig. 2-5, left) in the English manner. One or two sticks at a time were held secure between pegs and wedges. The sockets were bored at lines scored on the turnings while in the lathe. The mortise diameter produced a snug fit with an oversized tenon, and a mark on the bit guided the depth of the bore (fig. 2-17). In the eighteenth century craftsmen often flattened bulbous stretcher tips slightly on opposite sides to avoid splitting the joint as the mortise shrank and the tenon swelled. In framing the understructure the chairmaker drove home the stretcher tenons with the framing hammer, a tool whose face is slightly rounded (figs. 2-5, 3-32, bottom). The assembly then was ready for attachment to the inverted seat. Again, the hammer drove the legs firmly into place.[9]

A chisel split the leg tips projecting from the seat top to receive wedges inserted at right angles to the direction of the long fibers of the plank. Some wedges extend slightly outside the tips into the seat wood itself, further securing the expanded joint. American documents are silent on wedge preparation. Insight comes from English sources in which early twentieth-century chairmakers describe splitting hardwood stock for wedges from the slab, or first cut at the sawmill, and completing the job using a shaving horse and drawknife. A modern chairmaker prepares a flat, stick-length wedge sharpened at one end, which he inserts into a leg joint, cuts off, and reuses until only a stub remains. Wedges, which must be bone dry, were placed in the chamber of the shop stove prior to use. Once the wedges were in place and the leg tops trimmed flush with the seat using the chisel or gouge, the chairmaker trimmed the leg bottoms to level the chair.[10]

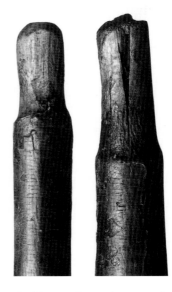

FIG. 3-5 Blind (internal) stretcher tenon (*left*) and through-tenon of arm post base with wedge in place (*right*) from Windsor armchair. (*Collection of James C. Sorber; Photo, Winterthur Museum.*)

FIG. 3-6 Blind leg tenons from Windsor side chairs, attributed to Tracy family (*left*), (*left to right*) eastern Connecticut and Connecticut–Rhode Island border region, ca. 1789–95 and 1795–1805. (*Private collection; Photo, Winterthur Museum.*)

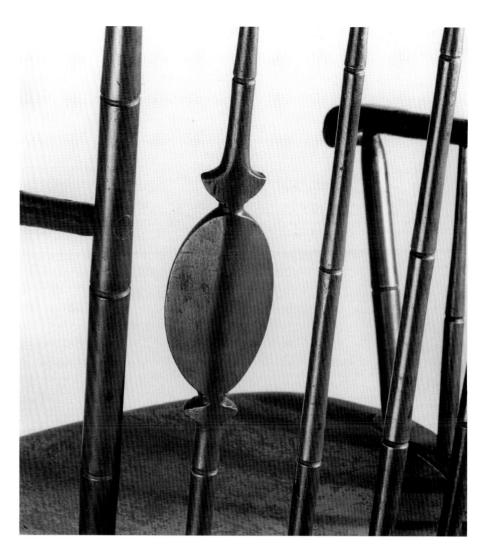

FIG. 3-7 Detail of shaved back surface of spindle medallion of the Masonic master's square-back Windsor armchair in fig. 5-38 (*center*), Frederick Fetter and Jacob Fetter III, Lancaster, Pa., 1811. *(Collection of Lodge No. 43, Free and Accepted Masons, Lancaster, Pa.; Photo, Winterthur Museum.)*

THE UPPER STRUCTURE

The Windsor side chair was simpler and cheaper to build than the armchair. For every Windsor made with arms, dozens of side chairs entered the market. Fan-back (fig. 3-17, right) and bow-back (fig. 3-64) styles prevailed in the eighteenth century. Nineteenth-century square-back designs in all their variations are simply modifications of the fan-back post-and-rail structure (figs. 3-35, 3-41). Before or after framing the undercarriage, the chairmaker bored holes in the plank top for the spindles, posts, and bows. The back posts closely duplicated the turned work of the legs, although nineteenth-century posts often were shaved to a flat face, steamed, and angled backward (fig. 3-49). At Enfield, Connecticut, Stephanus Knight occasionally undertook odd jobs such as "hueing Chare Poasts." Chairmaker James Gere of Groton paid a handyman about 33¢ in 1823 for "shaving Chair posts ⅔ of Day." In the shaving process part of the post face was reduced to a flat surface with a drawknife and spokeshave. Josiah Prescott Wilder of New Hampshire hired his brother John B. on occasion to shave both "Pillars" (posts) and ornamental front stretchers. The tapered and wedged post-and-seat joints duplicate those of eighteenth-century legs and arm supports (fig. 3-5, right).[11]

Spindles, the common structural units filling the chair back between the posts or bow ends, were rived, drawknifed, and spokeshaved to form, usually from hickory, ash, or oak. Many were shaped by hand and easily produced by semiskilled workmen outside the shop. Some ornamental sticks, such as nineteenth-century ball spindles, were turned on the lathe (fig. 3-45). The vase-shape elements common to the long sticks in early Rhode Island high-back chairs were lathe-turned before the remaining stick was shaved to slender form. "Arrow"-type spindles, sticks with flat ornamental medallions, and fancy front stretchers were prepared by one of two methods: some were turned round and finished by cutting away the wood, front and back (fig. 3-7); more commonly craftsmen sawed and hand tooled the ornamental elements to form. Rived sticks for cylindrical spindles took only a few minutes to shave (fig. 3-17). When a workman named McNiel spent "4½ Days at giting out rods" for Silas E. Cheney of Litchfield, Connecticut, in 1810, he produced anywhere from 600 to 900 sticks. Once formed, the spindles were set aside to dry. Kilns often were employed in the nineteenth century. Just prior to assembly the chairmaker shaped the lower tips that socket into the seat. Some spindle tenons were rounded and necked (fig. 3-5, left). Others were rounded and faceted with flat, longitudinal cuts to prevent their splitting the seat or rotating in the socket. This stability was particularly important in the ornamental stick with a forward orientation, as shown in figure 3-8. Other spindle tenons inserted into blind seat sockets have circumferential notches. A lock joint formed as the seat fibers expanded into the hollow neck (fig. 3-9).[12]

Chair crests either cap the back structure as tablets or are framed between the posts as slats (figs. 3-45, 3-55). All are bowed laterally. The serpentine top piece of the fan-back chair is wedge shape in section to provide a visually slim top edge and a thick base to socket posts and spindles (fig. 3-17, right). Sawed from a pattern (fig. 2-23), shaped with the drawknife and spokeshave, and bent, the curved piece was drilled in the last stage of preparation. If volute terminals were ordered, the chairmaker used the carving gouge. During assembly the spindles were angled slightly behind the crest plane as they rose from the seat. Forced forward into the top piece, the resulting light tension kept the assembly tight and produced more comfortable seating. Further joint stability was assured by inserting tiny pins from the back or the front and back of the crest. Some were wooden pegs, although small metal sprigs appear to have been more common. To guide spindle and post tips into the blind sockets of the crest, craftsmen whittled both to a slim diameter, although sometimes none too carefully, as visible tool marks attest (fig. 3-8). At his death in 1798 Francis Trumble of Philadelphia carried a stock of "75 Top Rails" for fan-back or square-back chairs. The nineteenth-century tablet-framed crests of rectangular, rounded, and stepped form surmount the sticks and posts in much the same way as in the fan-back chair (figs. 3-45, 3-46, 3-41). A small manuscript volume titled "Paints and Receipts for Wooden Work" dating to the early 1800s contains general directions for constructing backs of the stepped pattern: "for dining Chairs the Banasters [spindles and posts] are all of A length if they are scholup [scallop] top, ... the Cap to the Dining Chares 21 inches and ½ long [before bending], 2 inches and ½ in the widest Place [height]."[13]

The nineteenth-century crest formed of one or two cross rods ("bows") often is framed like the tablet-top chair, the top rod capping a through-tenon on the tip of each post (fig. 2-19). One day in 1815 Ebenezer Bryant was employed at "getting out bows for wood seat chairs" during a stint in Silas Cheney's shop in Connecticut. On another occasion he turned both the "standards" (posts) and "bows." By contrast, the roll-type crest butts against the post tops at small rabbets cut in the back faces (pls. 7, 12). Countersunk screws concealed by a composition material and paint secure the turned pieces. When Nelson Talcott of Ohio had the roll-top chair in production, one of his workmen spent several days doing nothing but turning crest pieces.[14]

Framing slat-back patterns between the back posts involved other woodworking techniques. The rectangular cross pieces are tenoned into mortises on the inner post faces. This construction has a long history in rush-bottom slat-back framing, dating at least from the Renaissance (fig. 3-18). Most slat tenons in Windsor construction are blind-mortised into the posts and frequently held fast by pegs or metal sprigs.

FIG. 3-8 "Flat sticks" from slat-back Windsor side chair, Portland, Maine, 1820–30. White pine (seat) with beech and birch; (*left to right*) L. 16¾", 16½"; light mustard yellow ground with brown and medium and dark mustard. (*Collections of Maine Historical Society, Wadsworth-Longfellow House, Portland; Photo, Winterthur Museum.*)

FIG. 3-9 Blind spindle tenons (seat level) from Windsor side chair, attributed to Tracy family, eastern Connecticut, ca. 1789–95. (*Private collection; Photo, Winterthur Museum.*)

FIG. 3-10 Detail of rectangular tenon at bow tip of bow-back Windsor side chair, William Harris, Jr., New London, Conn., 1790–1802. Yellow poplar (seat) with maple and other woods. *(Collection of Dietrich American Foundation [until 1988]; Photo, Winterthur Museum.)*

Occasionally the rectangular tenon has a small circular extension that pierces the outside post face, a construction particularly common in eastern Massachusetts. Cross slats, whether of broad or narrow depth, were sawed or, preferably, rived from timber, cut in rectangular blanks, smoothed on their broad surfaces with the drawknife and shave, and pierced with frets, if required. If sufficiently thin they were bent to form in a rack while green without steaming (fig. 2-10). The tenons were reduced in thickness on the back surface, the bevels often visible near either end. Plain cross pieces usually are referred to as *backs* or *slats* in records. One supplier of Nelson Talcott's shop in Ohio in 1840 provided "50 Rocking chair Slats" at 2¢ apiece, and he received similar credit the next year for fancy-chair slats. In comparison, pierced or fancy-profile *frets* cost 12½¢ to produce in 1819, as recorded by Silas Cheney of Connecticut. James Gere quoted that price again four years later in eastern Connecticut, although by 1832 some patterns cost only 8¢.[15]

The bow-back side chair posed a different set of construction challenges (fig. 3-64). The loop required steaming and bending in a special apparatus (fig. 2-11). White and red oak, hickory, and ash usually were chosen for this purpose. The chairmaker began by riving slim square stock from a log section in 5-foot or longer lengths, carefully maintaining a continuous run of long grain and avoiding irregularities such as knots and curls. Surface shaping using a drawknife and spokeshave carried the work to a semifinished state. After bending the bow, but prior to assembly, the chairmaker embellished the face with decorative detail using tools that varied from a small plane to a shop-made scraper. Faces are flat or crowned, beaded, grooved, molded, or channeled. Tapered cylindrical or rectangular tenons were formed at the ends, and corresponding mortises were made in the seat. Figure 3-10 illustrates a rectangular tenon at one end of a bow that probably was beaded on the face with a scraping tool. Bow tenons pierce through the seat plank and generally are wedged from the bottom surface. Some tenons are further pinned from the seat edge, as shown in figure 3-11. Other wooden pins secure the bracing spindles in the seat extension. The tenons of the bow ends form an effective stop to prevent the back from sinking into the plank. Bow-back Windsors made as armchairs usually have forward-curving scroll arms attached to the bow with a round or rectangular tenon in a conforming

FIG. 3-11 Detail of wooden pegs (pins) securing bow tip and bracing spindle in plank edge of bow-back Windsor side chair, Ebenezer Tracy, Sr., Lisbon Township, New London Co., Conn., 1790–95. Chestnut (seat) with maple and other woods. *(Collection of Dr. and Mrs. Edward Wallace; Photo, Winterthur Museum.)*

through-mortise (fig. 3-66). Figure **3-12** illustrates a detail of rectangular-mortise arm construction from a Philadelphia chair. Frequently this joint was wedged top and/or bottom (or, in a round tenon, at the center) and further secured by a through wooden pin from side to side. The armchair bow diminishes in thickness below the arms and generally is rounded in section, eliminating the patterned face.[16]

"108 Bowes for Chairs . . . in the Ruff" comprised part of Francis Trumble's stock in 1798 at Philadelphia. Bows discovered in Samuel Wing's shop at Sandwich, Massachusetts, after his death had been bent and fastened across with wooden laths to hold the shape. Other chairmakers tied the ends pending use. Bows were routinely stockpiled, at least in small quantity. When the Proud brothers of Providence recorded a "Minnet of Edward Killy work" in 1793, they noted that the journeyman pieceworker had completed half a dozen "dining" chairs "with our Bows." Before framing the chair backs, Killy smoothed the bow surfaces and patterned the faces. Test fittings with loose spindles established mortise locations on bows, which were marked and bored through. Some spindle tips were further shaved or whittled at framing to fit the mortises. Once framed, key spindles sometimes were secured in the bow by wedging the exposed tops. Metal sprigs inserted into the bow and spindles provided further stability.[17]

Like the bow-back chair, other eighteenth-century Windsors employed bent-work construction, beginning with the high-back chair and continuing through the sack-back and continuous-bow patterns. The U-shape bends of high-back and sack-back arm rails were not difficult to achieve (fig. 3-17, left). The bow, or top, of the latter usually introduces a slight lateral bend to the arch as well. The compound curves of the continuous-bow chair (fig. 3-16, center) required a complex apparatus. Arm-rail terminals in early Windsors usually are pieced to width, whether the scroll ends are flat or three-dimensional, although one-piece construction became almost standard later in the century. Scroll returns on the lower part of some terminals are exceptions (fig 2–31). The anonymous author of a short manuscript titled "Paints and Receipts for Wooden Work" provided measurements for constructing sack-type chair backs:

> flat Boes [arm rails] for winsor Chairs to be Cut fore feet long, five inches of each end to be left the [w]hole width, and the middle to be one inch and one quarter; the Banasters [spindles] for winsor Chairs: 4 Banasters 13 inches long, 2 d[itt]o 15 inches long, 2 d[itt]o 19 inches long, 2 d[itt]o 21 inches long, 1 d[itt]o 21½ inches long, and 2 frunt Banasters [arm posts] to each Chair.

The small, plain arm terminals of some sack-back and continuous-bow chairs of New York and New England origin have canted edges that contribute to the design's lightness and delicacy (fig. 3-2).[18]

In framing patterns with bent arm rails, the arm posts (also called standards or pillars) were orientation points. Inserted into tapered through-mortises drilled in the plank, the arm posts define compound angles, sloping outward and forward, that complement those of the legs. By fitting rails to posts and loosely inserting the spindles into the seat sockets, the chairmaker could check alignment and symmetry before marking and drilling the rail holes. Because rails for high-back and sack-back Windsors slip down over the long spindles to the halfway point or lower, compatibility in spindle and hole diameter was essential. The continuous-bow and sack-back bows also required preliminary fitting to adjust for small irregularities and to mark the drilling points. Once framed, key spindles, like those in bow-back chairs, often were secured in the bow by wedging the through-tips and inserting metal sprigs. Sack-back bow tips, whether round or square, were mortised through the arm rail and frequently wedged from the bottom. Many, along with the short spindles and arm posts, were secured with wooden pins or metal sprigs. Preliminary to bending

FIG. 3-12 Detail of wedged and pinned, through-mortise-and-tenon joint of arm and back bow of bow-back Windsor armchair, Joseph Henzey, Philadelphia, 1785–90. Yellow poplar (seat) with maple, hickory, oak, and ash (microanalysis). *(Courtesy, Winterthur Museum, Winterthur, Del., acc. 63.673.)*

FIG. 3-13 Detail of countersunk plank socket for arm post of low-back Windsor settee, Philadelphia, 1760–65. Yellow poplar (seat) with maple and oak (microanalysis). *(Courtesy, Winterthur Museum, acc. 82.116.)*

the continuous bow, a chairmaker thinned the wood at the points of the forward angles to reduce stress and to avoid fractures. John Green of Long Island recorded bow measurements as "1 foot [to] the Bend," 20½ inches above the seat, and 4 foot 9 inches overall (fig. 3-2).[19]

Large early Pennsylvania and Rhode Island chairs with sawed rails and high or low backs introduce other construction features (fig. 5-69). The undercarriage of early Rhode Island Windsors have crossed stretchers related in concept to those in many formal corner chairs. The double rabbet joint at the center crossing is secured by a hand-wrought nail driven from the bottom. Legs and arm posts generally socket inside the plank, a regional practice of the period. In Pennsylvania work both turnings pierce through the opposite surface; however, mortises frequently are larger at entry than at exit. Figure 3-13 provides the explanation. A countersunk hole from the entry surface (top or bottom) forms an inner ledge supporting the base (or top) of a heavy turning, preventing further penetration. With both legs and posts subject to body pressure, this technique helped to preserve the joints, although it did not prevent turned elements from backing out of their mortises unless tightly wedged on the exposed tips. Arm-rail construction also varies in Pennsylvania and Rhode Island work. The S-curved sawed arms have similar profiles, but underarm spindles in Philadelphia chairs pass through the wood and are wedged; most Rhode Island spindles have blind tenons. Often a decorative bead outlines the Pennsylvania arm. The rear joints show substantial variation. Rhode Island chair arms form the lower part of the back rail and butt together at the center, secured by the top piece. Hand-wrought nails driven in from the bottom penetrate the capping piece. Sometimes the two center back spindles are further secured with pegs or sprigs to prevent the rail from lifting off the spindles. In Pennsylvania chairs diagonal lap joints at the back corners secure the arms beneath extensions of the solid, one-piece, sawed and shaved back rail (fig. 5-69). The joints are held firm by rosehead nails or wooden pegs driven from both the top and bottom, often through the decorative lamb's-tongue tips. The spindles further strengthen the back joints in the tall chairs of both regions.[20]

CONSTRUCTION COSTS AND PROFIT

Although eighteenth-century Windsor-chair-making records are not sufficiently complete to compute cost versus retail price definitively, some early nineteenth-century documents provide insights. Despite the lack of some critical data, the ambiguity of language, and variances in time, geographic location, and production, a reasonable composite emerges. The side chair, which serves as the basis for the estimates, sold at retail for prices ranging from 50¢ to $1.50. Seating at the low end of the scale may have been sold unpainted or unadorned. At the top of the scale special decoration and gilding occasionally advanced the price beyond the quoted high.

Statistics center on square-back chairs of average or better quality and include four types: chairs with (1) straight or (2) bent cylindrical back posts, long spindles, and an inset cross slat at the top (pl. 4); seating of (3) bent-back form with shaved posts, short spindles, one cross banister (slat), and a slat or tablet crest (fig. 5-56, without arms); and seating of (4) bent-back form with two banisters, short spindles, and a roll top (pl. 12). The comparative figures in table 3 include allowances for raw materials, some journeyman labor, and the occasional purchase of prepared parts. Craftsmen who relied on their own labor and shops that approached factory production probably were able to lower their unit costs; however, the former would have served only a small market and known limited profits.

Framing costs include the expense of a workman "getting out seats" from the plank, as indicated in a manuscript "Book of Prices" dated in 1838 (fig. 3-14). Other records quote framing prices without seat cost as low as 9¾¢ for chairs represented by groups 1 and 2, all remaining parts supplied. That figure complements the 5¢

Table 3. Construction Costs of Early Nineteenth-Century Windsor Side Chairs

	(1) Cylindrical-Post Straight-Back Chair	(2) Cylindrical-Post Bent-Back Chair	(3) Bent-Back Slat/ Tablet-Top Chair	(4) Bent-Back Roll-Top Chair
Framing (including seat shaping)	16½¢	16½¢	22¢	25¢
Seat plank (material)	3¢	3¢	3¢	3¢
Legs and stretchers (8 pieces)	17¢	17¢	17¢	17¢
Posts (2 pieces)	4¢	4¢	6¢	6¢
Spindles (4 pieces)	4¢	4¢	4¢	4¢
Crest and cross pieces	1½¢	1½¢	3¢	8¢
Painting	8⅓¢	8⅓¢	8⅓¢	8⅓¢
Ornamenting	6¼¢	6¼¢	8⅓¢	8⅓¢
Varnishing	2¢	2¢	2¢	2¢
Bending		6¢		
	62½¢	68½¢	73½¢	81½¢

and 9¢ prices given for making seats and reconfirms the table estimates. The higher framing costs in groups 3 and 4 reflect the extra work of mortising the cross banisters and in the case of group 4 preparing the post tops to receive the crest roll and attaching the roll with screws. The unit figure quoted for the sets of legs and stretchers has been taken from the accounts of Silas Cheney, a craftsman of Litchfield, Connecticut. When parts are calculated individually, this allows 1¢ apiece for three plain cylindrical stretchers, 2¢ for an ornamental front stretcher, and about 3¢ for each leg, including leveling. These figures parallel prices for individual parts in other accounts.[21]

Differences in unit costs for the back posts reflect the labor involved. Posts in group 1 required turning only; those of group 2 were turned and bent. A separate item for bending at the bottom of the column also includes the spindles. Posts in groups 3 and 4 were turned, bent, and shaved. Spindles, valued at 1¢ apiece, include

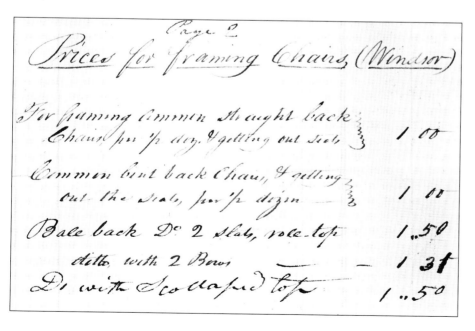

FIG. 3-14 Excerpt from James C. Helme "Book of Prices for Making Cabinet & chair furnature," Plymouth, Luzerne Co., Pa., August 30, 1838. (Winterthur Library.)

long sticks and short ornamental "half spindles." Only one group was bent, as noted. Spindles with "arrows," medallions, or fancy profiles required special work and cost more. Crest pieces in groups 1 to 3 consist of slats rived and shaved to form, then "bowed" in a rack. Inexpensively produced, they are valued at 1½¢ apiece. Cross banisters at midback are valued the same. The table makes allowances for two banisters in the roll-top chair and one in the slat or tablet-top pattern of group 3. The substantial unit cost of group 4 also reflects the special work of forming the roll top in the lathe, cutting a rabbet in either end, and creating a lateral bend. Surface finishing will be described in detail later. For present purposes each chair received two coats of paint with 1⅓¢ or more reserved for materials. The ornamenting allowance covers striping the bamboo joints and seat grooves and introducing a simple panel border in the crest without additional embellishment. An increase of approximately 2¢ in this figure for groups 3 and 4 reflects the need to ornament the cross banisters and shaved posts, which is not a consideration in the first two groups. Most decorated furniture was given a final protective coat of varnish.[22]

Middle-range seating generally retailed at $1, $1.12, $1.25, and $1.33. When compared successively with figures across the bottom of table 3, each group falls into a profit range of 60 to 70 percent. How many chairs could a single workman make in a six-day week? James Gere of Connecticut recorded a payment of $4 to journeyman James Pettit in 1841 for "framing 16 Chairs @ 1/6 2 days." Pettit's pay rate at 1s. 6d. was 25¢ per chair, suggesting that he framed bent-back side chairs, as described in groups 3 and 4. His earnings of $2 per day were substantial and probably reflect long working hours. This seems confirmed by an earlier reference in Gere's accounts to paying Pettit $1.25 for "making Varnish & seating two small Chairs one day." If Pettit worked twelve-hour days when chair framing at piecework rates, the estimated assembly time for one Windsor side chair was one and a half hours, all the "stuff" except the seat blank "formed to hand."[23]

Using averaged figures from table 3 and the retail prices quoted above, and assuming that a hypothetical master chairmaker with his own shop was as efficient, or "clever," a workman as James Pettit, a master's profit can be calculated under stable economic conditions at a good business site. Table 4 establishes daily production rates for the three basic components of chairmaking, using Pettit's high productivity as a guide. The rates are based on a two-week stint, during which period the master produced two dozen Windsor side chairs. Quantity production was essential to achieve maximum efficiency. The master worked at the piece-rate equivalent of $1.50 per ten-hour day for two six-day weeks sometime during the 1820s or 1830s.

Finish work would have been carried out over a number of days or even weeks in normal production. The extra two-thirds of a day realized in the two-week schedule could have been applied to any of several shop-related tasks: cutting timber, going to the sawmill, riving wood, preparing glue or varnish, or grinding paint. Using averaged figures of $1.17½ as the selling price of one chair and 71½¢ as the cost of production, the chairmaker could have realized a 92¢ daily profit above the piecework value of his own labor for a two-week stint. Thus, as his own master, his income could have exceeded that of a journeyman by 61 percent, if conditions were favorable.

REPAIRS, ALTERATIONS, AND DAMAGED MERCHANDISE

Repairs were a mainstay of the chairmaker's business (fig. 3-60). He frequently referred to this service in his public advertisements, especially those dating from the early nineteenth century. Some chairmakers also solicited repair work on the printed labels they affixed to their chairs. In the highly competitive consumer market of the early 1800s some chairmakers offered special enticements to draw customers to their shops, promising repairs "at the shortest notice," "with dispatch," or "in the very best manner." Seymour Watrous of Connecticut was more direct in 1824: "Old Chairs

Table 4. Production Rates for Making Two Dozen Windsor Side Chairs
in the Early Nineteenth Century

One Days' Production	*Twelve Days' Production of Two Dozen Windsor Side Chairs*	
Prepare 4½ sets chair stuff from riven stock	Prepare stuff	5¼ days
or		
Frame 7 chairs	Frame	3⅓ days
or		
Paint, ornament, and varnish 8½ chairs	Finish	2¾ days

repaired, painted and re-gilt so as to look nearly as well as new." In Indiana Mathias Stover promised free repair of his own merchandise if it proved defective. Occasionally notices refer to settee repair, although comparatively speaking the number of long seats in the market was small. Perhaps of equal demand with structural repair was the restoration or replacement of rush seats in kitchen and fancy-painted furniture. The constant maintenance of rushwork in cheap kitchen chairs was one factor that led to the early ascendancy of the plank-bottom Windsor.[24]

Structural repairs to seating were a common call at the chairmaker's shop even before Windsor furniture came into general use, as witnessed in the accounts of chairmaker Solomon Fussell (1738–48) of Philadelphia. By the 1770s Joseph Henzey of that city engaged in "Mending & Painting . . . Windsor Chairs" for "Friend" Norris, possibly Charles Norris, who in 1760 had purchased Windsor seating from Francis Trumble. Several circumstances illuminate the need for repairs, and this work often went hand in glove with repainting: as the wood began to dry, some chairs loosened at the joints; normal wear and tear took its toll; and honest accidents were not uncommon. Alexander Holcomb of East Granby, Connecticut, paid woodworker Oliver Moore 42¢ in 1809 for "mending a Chair [he] broke at Luther Holcombs." Other repairs reflect hard use and even abuse. Work for hotels and steamboats generally belongs in this group (fig. 3-61). During the 1820s chairmakers in New York mended both stools and settees for the steam vessels *Bellona* and *Thistle*. Hotel work frequently was extensive. William White repaired 150 chairs for the Sans Souci Hotel at Ballston Spa, New York, before the summer season of 1821, and two decades later about two-thirds that number required attention at the Baltimore Exchange Hotel. In an 1807 bill for repairs at the Sans Souci chairmaker Miles Beach hinted at a common mishap in public establishments when charging 50¢ for "Putting Back on 1 [Windsor Chair]."[25]

The practice of tipping backward in a chair was common among nineteenth-century American males. Figure 5-46 illustrates a man in this position warming his feet at the stove of a country inn. The result of such abuse—a backless chair—functions nearby as a stool. Lewis Miller pictured Martin Weiser in similar repose at the iron stove in his tavern at York, Pennsylvania (fig. **3-15**). Speaking to similar scenes, Henry Bradshaw Fearon described his arrival at an Albany inn in the winter of 1817–18: "All the fires were surrounded by gentlemen smoking segars, and lolling back on chairs, with their feet fixed against the chimneypiece." The practice of balancing a chair on two legs was so engrained among American men even by 1805 that one traveler carried the habit abroad, much to the amusement of the Europeans. Benjamin Silliman described the event:

> As I was sitting in a chair, [a friend] told me that he should have recognised me as a New-Englander. . . . Upon my inquiring for the peculiarity which marked my origin, he told me that no one except a man educated in New-England, ever leaned back in his

FIG. 3-15 Lewis Miller, *Martin Weiser . . . in His Tavern*, York, Pa., ca. 1815–25, depicting scene of 1810. Ink and watercolor on paper. *(The York County Heritage Trust, PA; Photo, Winterthur Museum.)*

chair, so as to make it stand upon the two hinder feet only. Although I was not in the least aware either that this was a custom peculiar to my country, or that I was then in so awkward a situation, I found that I was so indeed. . . . The incident produced some mirth [and] I am sure I shall never forget again that a chair ought to stand on four legs instead of two.[26]

The modern restorer frequently copes with delicate back bows that have lost their original elasticity, causing cracks and breaks at the bends and joints, whereas early repairers found other tasks common. Rockers are mentioned frequently, although many references represent conversions rather than repairs (fig. 3-73). Entries in accounts that describe "mending Chair rockers" or "a new Rocker on a rocking Chair" are unmistakable, however. George Landon of Erie, Pennsylvania, made extensive repairs in 1819 when replacing "rockers and foot and stretchers on [a] Chair." The price for "rockering," as some craftsmen described it, ranged from about 12¢ to 50¢. The low figure may have reflected the relatively simple task of "fastning rockers to a chair" when the curved pieces came loose.[27]

Stretchers were vulnerable, as the casualty rate suggests. Convenient as footrests, they were broken frequently. In 1818 Benjamin Smith, Jr., brought several chairs to Martin Sampson's shop in Duxbury, Massachusetts, where the craftsman put in nine new "rounds" at a charge of 9¢ apiece. The usual fee appears to have been 6¢ or 6¼¢. John Brown of New York repaired the stretchers of several steamboat settees in 1821 for Captain Vanderbilt at a cost of $1.25. Frequently more radical work was required. On February 20, 1817, Alexander Low of Freehold, New Jersey, "rep[aired] a windsor chaer with feet & a stritcher" for 75¢, the charge equivalent to the cost of some new chairs. Silas Cheney of Litchfield, Connecticut, may have worked more cheaply. He added a new leg and two stretchers to one chair for 17¢ and two legs and three stretchers to another for twice that amount. Sometimes the problem was loosened joints, one easily corrected "by wedging & glueing the legs & rounds." True Currier of Deerfield, New Hampshire, recorded repairs to another form when "put[ting] . . . legs to crickets" (footstools) and painting them.[28]

Windsor-chair seats generally are durable, although planks split on occasion, requiring repairs or replacement. To introduce a new plank the chair was partially disassembled. The labor charge could be substantial: Moyers and Rich of Virginia did this work in 1830 for 25¢; Silas Cheney of Connecticut charged 42¢. Adding a new stretcher raised Cheney's charge to 50¢. Occasionally a craftsman had to undo "home" repairs before proceeding with the work at hand. Cheney spent considerable time "giting . . . nails out of 8 Chairs . . . Seat" in 1820 before tightening the joints in an orthodox manner, smoothing seat surfaces, and repainting at a total charge of $3.60.[29]

Chair backs were as vulnerable as other parts when subjected to abuse and stress. Routine calls are described by Joseph Stone of Rhode Island, who put "one post in a green Chair" in 1795, and Allen Holcomb of rural New York, who in 1822 charged $1.25 for "mending 2 Dining Chairs with ten new sticks in Each Chair." Holcomb actually replaced the entire back of each chair—posts, crest, and spindles—since ten was the correct number of elements in the seven-spindle square-back chair with a single top rod (fig. 3-36). In Maine Paul Jenkins put a new stick in a chair back for 13¢. New sticks and a top were required in 1816 when Titus Preston of Connecticut repaired Captain Phineas Pond's rocking chair. Silas Cheney recorded extensive repairs for Grove Catlin, an innkeeper. He "put . . . backs to 15 Chairs" at 41½¢ apiece and painted the lot. The $10 charge, though less than the price of new chairs, speaks to the cost of maintaining a public house.[30]

Arm assemblies were vulnerable. In 1821 "An arm & standerd" and the skill of William Proud of Providence restored a chair belonging to Asa Bosworth at a charge of 34¢. Charles Robinson made somewhat more substantial repairs to a pair of Windsor chairs brought to his shop in Philadelphia. "Four Elbows & one stick" were required to replace the damaged parts. After "putting new arms on [a] chair" in 1826 for Lieutenant Governor John Taylor, George G. Jewett of Albany proceeded to "Paint & ornament ditto," a frequent complement to repair work. A simple turned arm replacement could cost as little as 8¢ and a "Chair stump," 12½¢. Other records speak of "arming 4 settees," and repairs to rocking-chair arms were not uncommon. A pair of "elbows" for a large rocker could cost from 50¢ to $1, depending on the extent of the damage and whether a fine cabinet wood was required.[31]

References to broken or damaged chair bows are uncommon. William Beesley's account in 1828 for "putting [a] bow in a chair" probably refers to replacing a cross rod in a square-back chair (figs. 3-36, 3-37). Job Danforth of Providence, jobbing for fellow woodworker Samuel Proud in February 1792, made a "chair top" for about 50¢ and three months later produced "a top for a settee" at twice the cost. The charges suggest the "tops" were arched bows for round-back seating, which required bending, surface shaping, boring, and some rather tricky fitting to reframe. The alternative was patching or repairing. A woodworker of Philadelphia described one solution: "To Repairing 7 Chairs with Iren Plates." Whether for Windsors or other types of seating, that repair method was used widely. Some private families sought furniture repairs as frequently as the proprietors of public establishments, as documented in the papers of Dr. Isaac Senter of Newport, Rhode Island, between 1782 and his death in 1799. Joseph K. Ott in sketching the doctor's career and acquisitions of household furnishings noted the "incredible" damage to the family seating furniture: "over ninety-seven chairs were mended . . . and forty-three newly bottomed." In addition, more than 106 chairs were "colored and varnished" (rush-bottom chairs) or painted (Windsor and fancy chairs). Repairs to other furnishings seem to have been in proportion. Documents that illuminate furniture repairs in other families identify this record as the exception rather than the rule.[32]

Because Windsor seating occupied the lower end of the value scale in household furnishings and was more readily expendable in the eyes of both original and later owners, it has been a target for conversion to purposes other than those originally intended. Actual documentation often lies locked in the vague and general language of records; thus visual evidence can be more informative. Prominent are the addition of rockers to a once stationary form and the removal of a section of seat to create a commode chair. In a conversion that took place in April 1834, J. M. Niles of Hartford, Connecticut, paid Philemon Robbins 50¢ for "making hole to large Chair."[33]

References to the addition of rockers abound, although it is usually impossible to determine whether the work replaced worn rockers or introduced new curved pieces to chair legs. Phrases such as "putting Rockers to a chear" or "making rockers to chair" seem to imply the latter. Stronger suggestions occur in several records. Silas Cheney debited Daniel Starr in 1804 at Litchfield, Connecticut, for "mending Char & putin on rockers." Charles C. Robinson, a Windsor-chair maker of Philadelphia, recorded an instance in 1823 of "puting rockers to [an] arm chair." Almost certainly this was a Windsor chair and a new conversion. True Currier of Deerfield, New Hampshire, recorded another conversion two years later when he added rockers to a square-back chair after making a new "bow," or top piece. Toward midcentury the Boston firm of Lawson and Harrington converted a small early nineteenth-century side chair to a rocker and tacked a stuffed covering on the seat and back. When finished, they placed their label on the bottom.[34]

Records describe other alterations. In 1835 Moyers and Rich of southwestern Virginia made "a draw and arm in chair." Two years later David Alling of Newark, New Jersey, altered and repaired four settees, then painted them yellow. The practice of shortening chair legs was uncommon until well into the nineteenth century, although two early references date to 1805. In February a customer deposited a chair at Titus Preston's shop in Wallingford, Connecticut, for the purpose of replacing two rounds and "sawing it lower." The following autumn James Chesney of Albany charged Peter Elmendorf for "cutting off and bottoming two Cottage chairs." This type of alteration was liberally encouraged later in the century by authors H. T. Williams and C. S. Jones in *Beautiful Homes*, much to the dismay of modern furniture collectors and historians:

> There is one comfort for those who desire to furnish . . . [the sitting room] with various kinds of comfortable chairs, and yet have not the well-filled purse . . . which is, that with a few old "Windsor," or cain-bottomed chairs, or even the homely but very comfortable 'splint-bottoms' of the Western States, various cozy and tasteful seats may be made. The very first thing will be to lower the seat, by sawing off two, three or even four inches from each leg, according to the height desired, for what is more uncomfortable than a high chair, or more barren-looking and ungraceful than four long stiff chair-legs?[35]

Although customer complaints about damaged Windsor seating occur infrequently, records leave little doubt that consumers experienced problems. Earliest among these is John Andrews's letter of 1772 from Boston to his brother-in-law William Barrell of Philadelphia complaining about the condition of a pair of chairs that arrived by sailing vessel. He described them as "much defac'd." Carried on deck, one had a split bottom and the other had exchanged its paint for tar. One Windsor among four dozen ordered in Philadelphia for Thomas Jefferson arrived at Monticello in August 1801 with a split bottom. Repairs probably were made at the plantation, perhaps even using "Iren Plates." In New England Thomas Boynton recorded in 1836 the return of a rocking chair with a cracked seat and a broken arm. Among a group of 111 chairs delivered in 1829 to Elisha Harlow Holmes by his brother-in-law Frederick Allen were six described as "Damaged." Although the problem is not identified, the seating probably was bruised, a frequent mishap during transport.[36]

SALE MERCHANDISE

Stock on Hand
In the prerevolutionary days of Windsor production most work was bespoken, that is, made to order. Shops were small, and storage usually was at a premium. The large size of the early Windsor also limited the number of chairs acquired by any one individual, although that production restraint was modified by another factor — the rise of the Windsor as an export commodity. Francis Trumble's advertisement of December 1775 at Philadelphia, itemizing a stock of "Twelve hundred windsor chairs," describes the size of the trade on the eve of the Revolution. Although the chairs were not actually standing in the shop ready to go, large stocks of prepared parts were on the premises available for framing at short notice. This practice is confirmed in a local broadside advertisement of 1808 inscribed as a bill by Gilbert Gaw (fig. 4-17). The printed text reads, in part: "Merchants, Masters of vessels, and others, may be supplied at the shortest notice." In stockpiling parts, a circumstance dictating that construction elements be interchangeable, the industry was only a step away from developing facilities to display finished seating for retail to the public without prior order. The rapid rise of the furniture wareroom in the 1810s has been described in chapter 2.[37]

Before development of that facility, the practice of keeping a small quantity of finished seating furniture in stock slowly gained momentum. In June 1765 Andrew Gautier, probably a shopkeeper rather than a chairmaker, maintained a selection of patterns at New York. Chairmakers Thomas and William Ash advertised in the mid-1780s along similar lines. Labels affixed to seating furniture a decade later by

Ansel Goodrich of Northampton, Massachusetts, state that he stocked and kept "constantly for sale a quantity of warranted chairs." At the craftsman's death in 1803 seating on the premises numbered 39 finished chairs, including dining, children's, and armchairs, with another 56 fan-back chairs in production. The picture changed rapidly. By 1805 Joseph Vail of New York City stocked as many as 587 framed Windsor side chairs, 75 rush-bottom chairs, and several armchairs and settees. The same year Alexander Walker of Fredericksburg, Virginia, had "near 400 CHAIRS finished on hand, double and single square Backs, round ditto, made in the neatest manner and painted different colors." Within a year the number had risen to "one hundred dozen Windsor Chairs of every description." Both men apparently owned or rented storage-display space, although neither identified his facility as a retail store. That step was accomplished by 1812 when Thomas Howard of Providence promoted his "Cabinet warehouse" where "1000 Fancy and Windsor chairs" supplemented a large selection of cabinetwork.[38]

A billhead promoting the firm of Cornwell and Smith of New York describes a typical early nineteenth-century offering in an establishment geared for quantity sales: "An elegant and large assortment of CURLED MAPLE, BRONZE and PAINTED FANCY CHAIRS, likewise an extensive assortment of WINDSOR CHAIRS, SETTEES, &c. of the newest fashions and warranted well finished." As reported in the 1820 manufacturing census, twenty-three chairmakers in Sterling, Massachusetts, produced more than 68,000 chairs annually (fig. 1-6). When geared for production in the 1840s, Walter Corey's factory in Portland. Maine, could turn out 300 to 500 chairs per week. Finished chairs awaiting transportation may have been prewrapped to permit stacking, thus protecting the finish and maximizing storage space.[39]

Sets of Chairs

How many chairs constituted a *set* of Windsors? This term, describing many customer purchases, identifies six side chairs. When "set" is not used in accounts, the number six usually is substituted. Of course, customers were free to purchase as many chairs as needed. General Charles Ridgely of Baltimore acquired twenty-four white and gold fancy chairs in 1797 from William Palmer of New York, although this purchase was the exception rather than the rule. Odd-number lots probably identify replacements, additions, or supplements to existing sets. The records of Nelson Talcott, a chairmaker of Ohio, sometimes describe purchases as "set" fractions: one customer bought "½ Set Dining chairs," another "1½ Set," and a third "1⅔ Set of Green Winsor chairs." Luke Houghton's records describe a four-chair purchase in Massachusetts as a "broken set."[40]

Modifications occurred. Charles C. Robinson, Windsor-chair maker of Philadelphia, often recorded the sale of half a dozen chairs, although he recorded "sets" priced substantially higher. Careful analysis of his accounts suggests that these groups consisted of six side chairs and two armchairs. The combination was not uncommon, as suggested in the inventory of Dr. Isaac Senter of Newport, Rhode Island, which lists among the household seating "5 Sets Green Chairs 8 in a set." Occasionally a set consisted entirely of Windsor armchairs, although these instances are rare. In 1795 Elisha Hawley of Ridgefield, Connecticut, sold a "Set Armd Chairs" priced at 7s. 6d. the chair. Other purchase records list "sets" of six side chairs with companion entries for one or more armchairs, as indicated in an order of chairs placed on shipboard in Philadelphia by Anthony Steel (fig. 4-42). Another example is a bill from John B. Ackley of the city to merchant Samuel Coates itemizing six painted and stuffed bow-back chairs followed by the entry "2 Oval Back Arm Chairs Painted & stuff as the other" (fig. 3-63). Henry Francis du Pont acquired a seven-chair set of Windsors in the 1930s that possibly always contained only one armchair (fig. **3-16**).[41]

At times chairs of several styles from the same shop were intermixed as a "set," as illustrated in two Rhode Island chairs with identical turnings above and below the

FIG. 3-16 Set of bow-back Windsor side chairs and continuous-bow armchair, Rhode Island, 1790–95. White pine (seats, side chairs) with maple, oak, and some hickory and beech (microanalysis), and butternut (seat, armchair) with maple, oak, and ash; side chair: H. 37½", W. (seat) 16¼", D. (seat) 16"; armchair: H. 36", W. (arms) 21⁵⁄₁₆", (seat) 19⅛", D. (seat) 15⅜". *(Former collection, Courtesy, Winterthur Museum.)*

seat (fig. **3-17**). When posting the debits of a customer in October 1803, Solomon Cole of Glastonbury, Connecticut, itemized half a dozen fan-back Windsors and two armchairs, probably of round-back form, all painted in the same two-color finish. Individually the side chairs cost 8*s*. 6*d*., the armchairs, 10*s*.[42]

Several references describe a "set of Chairs & a rocking Chair" as a single purchase. Eunice Warner, probably of Wethersfield, Connecticut, paid Reuben Loomis in 1812 for new seating of this description. A contemporary note from Elizabeth Langdon among the papers of Silas Cheney of Litchfield pertains to a related purchase: "Mr Cheney. Please to send me by Mr Lampson 12 bamboo chairs as we last agreed and the 2 large chairs of the other kind one with rockers."[43]

Secondhand Seating
Though mentioned infrequently, secondhand chairs were available in a number of shops and accepted as trade or barter for new furniture. Public notices appeared from time to time. In 1822 Cornelius J. Tooker of Fayetteville, North Carolina, added as a postscript to a notice: "All kinds of furniture Repaired, Cleaned or Exchanged, as usual." Earlier, Alexander Walker announced at Fredericksburg, Virginia: "New chairs exchanged for old ones." When Phineas B. Wilcox bought a "leaf," or writing, chair in 1819 from Levi Stillman of New Haven, Connecticut, he received credit "by second hand chair & cash." Thomas Boynton of Windsor, Vermont, allowed a Mrs. Silsbee $1.50 credit in 1811 for three old chairs when she purchased nine seating pieces of varied pattern and engaged the craftsman to paint two armchairs and a cricket. One of David Alling's customers at Newark, New Jersey, in 1838 exchanged "4 flat top winsor second handed" for half the price of "4 strait posts chars." Appraisers enumerated "used" furniture at several woodworking establishments. In 1805 eight "Windsor chairs second Hand'd" stood in Joseph Vail's shop at New York. Later, "2 Second hand Settees" were in the possession of Benjamin Love near Philadelphia.[44]

Who purchased this used furniture? Thomas Mulkey of Groton, Connecticut, a farmhand for James Gere in 1829, bought "Six Old Windsor Chairs" for $2. The price was equivalent to two or more days' pay. A year later Simon Smith of Deerfield, New Hampshire, purchased "two kitchen chairs old ones" from True Currier. "Second

FIG. 3-17 Fan-back Windsor side chair and sack-back armchair, Rhode Island, ca. 1792–1800. *(Photo courtesy of David A. Schorsch.)*

hand Flagg seat chairs" cost "Mrs. Swan of Hartford" $3 at Philemon Robbins's shop. Used chairs in good condition probably were better suited to supplementing older sets of seating than shiny new chairs.[45]

Rental Furniture

Scattered references describe the varied uses of rental furniture. Several young ladies attending "Miss Drapers Seminary" at Hartford, Connecticut, rented secondhand "Bureaus" in 1834 from Philemon Robbins for periods of five or six months at a charge of $1. When Mary C. Green set up her school at Windsor, Vermont, that year, Thomas Boynton charged her for "use of the following artickles of mine: 12 chairs 10.00, two tables 7.00." A decade later Boynton allowed one Stephen Hawkins the "use of 1 Doz chairs 1 year" and charged him $1. The proprietors of the Boston Theatre, which flourished from the 1790s into the early nineteenth century, sometimes found it more expedient to rent supplemental seating than to purchase it. By arrangement, they paid John W. Blanchard $9 during the 1828–29 season for the use of an unspecified number of settees.[46]

Men's and Women's Chairs

Distinctions between seating for men and women seldom occur in records, although the concept is implied in the production of certain forms, particularly rocking nurse-chairs and sewing chairs. Silas Cheney of Litchfield, Connecticut, probably referred to seating of this type in 1814: "to 2 women Chairs." The price of $2.83 duplicated that of "2 work Chairs Ornimented" purchased a few weeks earlier, leaving the purpose in little doubt. In 1829 Elisha Harlow Holmes of Essex may have distinguished between household chairs for master and mistress when posting a credit for an outside furniture supplier: "2 Rock[ing] Larg . . . 6 Miss [possibly Missus] Rock[ing]." Nantucket probate records of earlier date indicate that the tall, braced-back Windsor associated with the Island was considered part of the male domain. Inventory entries make the point: "A Mans high Back Chair & Cushion," a "Mans Green Chair," and "1 Great Green Chair & Cushion." Another entry describes a second pattern: "1 Mans Round Chair," presumably a roundabout chair with a rush or wooden bottom.

Eighteenth-century English records often describe these low-back seats as smoking chairs. One known pair of Windsor armchairs, the two chairs of slightly different dimensions, further pursues the theme that variation in physical size can identify seating for individuals of different sex.[47]

Design

PATTERN TERMINOLOGY

Written records identify American Windsor seating in terms ranging from the general to the specific. Basic designations, aside from the word *Windsor* itself, consist of names such as *wood-seat*, *Philadelphia*, and *green* chair and describe, variously, the principal construction unit, the chief production center, and the common color of the early product. The term *plank-seat* chair does not appear in records dating through 1850. Pattern-oriented terms in use during the early production period describe *high-back* (fig. 5-35) and *low-back* chairs (fig. 5-23, as a single seat), designations that focus on the upper structure. *Comb-back*, another name identifying the tall design, is of late nineteenth- or twentieth-century origin. A third armchair of prerevolutionary date was known by several names: *sack-back* chair (fig. 3-17, left), *arched-top* chair, and *round-top* chair. The word *top* describes the curved unit forming a cap above the arm rail, the main structural unit of the back.

Names given to eighteenth-century Windsor side chairs also describe the upper structures. The *fan-back* chair resembles a partially open fan held upright, although in a bill of 1787 directed to the merchant Stephen Girard of Philadelphia, William Cox identified the chair by its "scroole top," or carved crest volutes (fig. 4-18). A second side chair, the back forming an arch, was designated a *bow-back* Windsor (fig. 3-16). Philadelphians often substituted *oval-back*, a name borrowed from contemporary formal seating. Upon occasion *round-back* described the back structure, although that term also identified the continuous-bow armchair (fig. 3-16, center).[48]

Several general terms were in continuous use from the 1780s. The word *dining* identifies a popular function of the Windsor side chair. Starting with the fan-back style and gaining momentum after introduction of the compact bow-back design, the Windsor side chair was accepted universally as the premier dining seat in American households. Painted a color that harmonized with the room and its furnishings and free of the costly maintenance characteristic of upholstered and woven-bottom seating, it was the popular choice. The inexpensive rush-bottom chair still held sway in the kitchen, its design, status, and function expressed in terms such as *slat-back*, *common*, and *kitchen* chair. In the late eighteenth and early nineteenth centuries the word *bamboo* identified both Windsors and fancy chairs with lathe-turned supports that interpreted the Eastern plant (figs. 3-35, 3-64).

Nineteenth-century Windsor styles are titled collectively *square-back* chairs. Moving closer to definite nomenclature are distinctions in the side profiles of the vertical back elements, giving rise to the terms *straight-back* and *bent-back* chair (figs. 3-35, 3-49). Alternatives for the latter were *spring-back* (or *sprung-back*) and occasionally *fall-back*. Until the early 1810s the "new fashioned" seating piece had one or two horizontal sticks in the crest, producing a *single-*, *double-*, or *square-top* chair (figs. 3-34, 3-35). The lateral curve of these members also suggested the names *single-* and *double-bow*. David Pritchard of Connecticut used the rare term *miter top* to describe a variant feature, the ornamental diagonal groove, or "miter," occurring at the bow ends (fig. 3-35). The construction still is square cornered, and the bow caps round tenons at the post tops.[49]

Slat-back Windsor seating, which appeared in the market before the War of 1812, remained popular for several decades. First combined with long spindles, the slats later formed the crests in cross-banister styles (pl. 5; fig. 5-56). Depending on slat depth, the pattern also became a *narrow-* or *broad-top* chair. A Massachusetts inventory described the style as a *mortised-top*, referring to the construction method. A slat also accompanied the ornamental *cross-back* and *ball-back* patterns of the 1810s. The first-named appeared in several areas: Baltimore, eastern New York State (pl. 1), and northern New Jersey, where in 1815–16 David Alling produced *single-* and *double-cross* backs. Chairmakers in several regions framed ball-back chairs (pl. 10). *Fret-back* styles with pierced cross banisters were confined mostly to fancy-painted and formal seating. From the late 1820s many slat-style crests were accompanied by one or two narrow banisters across the center back and sometimes by short spindles (fig. 5-56; pl. 25), producing *double-* or *triple-back* chairs. An arched top modified some slats (pl. 8), and a Pennsylvania fancy *scalloped-top* Windsor is appropriately sawed at the arch center (pl. 20). Chairs with three to five spindles were typical beginning in the late 1810s, when terms such as *three-stick* and *five-rodded* identified the backs (fig. 3-49; pl. 30). *Flat sticks* of "arrow" shape replaced cylindrical spindles in some chairs (fig. 3-38).[50]

Baltimore influence is present in a large tablet-type Windsor crest set on tenons at the post tops (fig. 3-45). At times the name *Baltimore chair* identifies the general style. Other terms describe a *square-top* or a *flat-top* (or *back*) chair. From about the late 1820s *round-top* and *crown-top* chairs with curved-end tablets appeared in records (pls. 21, 27, 32, 33). A turned crest, or roll, was popular from the late 1810s, especially in New York City and State and southern New England. Like many slat-style crests, the *roll top* was combined with one or two cross banisters, and some designs socket short spindles at the lower back (fig. 5-25; pl. 12).[51]

FIG. 3-18 Slat-back rush-bottom armchair, Delaware Valley, 1750–80. Maple and hickory (microanalysis); H. 43", W. 24⅞", D. 20½". *(Courtesy, Winterthur Museum, acc. 67.761.)*

DESIGN SOURCES

American Windsor furniture design derived from four basic sources: eighteenth-century English Windsor furniture; American joined seating influenced by formal English prototypes and design books; painted rush- and cane-bottom fancy seating shaped by high-style furniture; and rush-bottom chairs of the common type. Early high-back American Windsors copied English models closely—in size, height, and use of a bent arm rail and large D-shape saddled seat (fig. 5-35). The principal point of deviation in American construction was the introduction of turned legs and a bold medial stretcher in patterns unlike those common in the English vernacular market. The Delaware Valley slat-back chair was a major influence in this respect (fig. **3-18**). The sequence of turned elements between the arm and ball foot is duplicated beneath the Windsor seat, the length adjusted by shortening the cylinder. Initial placement of the medial stretcher, an adaptation of the front stretcher of the slat-back chair (fig. 3-18), behind the center point of the side braces soon gave way to a balanced arrangement (figs. 5-35, 5-69). For the turned supports beneath the arms, chairmakers copied the elements of the upper legs. Another significant change in early American work occurred with the introduction of a serpentine crest terminated by carved volutes, a successful amalgam of elements drawn from early Georgian design (figs. **3-19**, 5-69). By the 1760s many Windsors had exchanged the complex vase-and-ring turning of the medial stretcher for the simple swell of the side braces.

When developed for American use, the low-back style already was known in English Windsor seating (fig. 5-23), the basic design borrowed from the cabinetmaker's roundabout chair. The turned work of the understructure duplicates that of the tall chair. Rhode Island interpretations of both the low-back and high-back patterns introduced variation in the leg turnings derived directly from English sources, accompanied by cross stretchers similar to those in Rhode Island roundabout chairs

FIG. 3-19 Splat-back armchair, Philadelphia, 1745–55. Mahogany (microanalysis); H. 41¼", W. 32¼", D. 22". *(Courtesy, Winterthur Museum, acc. 60.1039.2.)*

FIG. 3-20 Oval-back armchair, Philadelphia, 1785–95. Mahogany (microanalysis); H. 39½", W. 24⅝", D. 23". *(Courtesy, Winterthur Museum, acc. 52.235.)*

and turned spindles whose profiles mimic the vase-shape slats of banister-back chairs.

The third prerevolutionary armchair, the sack-back Windsor introduced in the 1760s (fig. 3-17, left), again followed an English lead and capitalized on developments that modified the high- and low-back styles. Meanwhile, American chairmakers experimented with several new high-back patterns of smaller size imported from England. One type has a round seat and braced back. Another introduced a shield-shape seat based on the Georgian compass bottom (fig. 3-19). By the late 1760s tapered feet replaced ball-tipped legs (figs. 5-69, 5-35). The new foot introduced production economies and improved structural strength. The large knuckles and ogee-curved arms of Georgian seating also are duplicated in some Windsors (figs. 3-19, 5-69).[52]

Development of a Windsor side chair first occurred in English work in the mid eighteenth century. A production fan-back chair was introduced in the American trade only in the late 1770s. The pattern settled into its well-known classic form in the postrevolutionary years (fig. 3-17, right).

The neoclassical impulse that gained momentum in Europe at midcentury with the discovery of new archaeological sites in Italy and the subsequent circulation of architectural and ornamental designs in the new taste, some by the Adam brothers of England, approached a popular level of interpretation by the Revolution. The transfer of furniture designs in the new mode from London to America was assisted by widely circulated postwar publications, such as Hepplewhite's *Guide* and Sheraton's *Drawing-Book*. One chair design introduced an oval back on curved extensions of the rear legs (fig. **3-20**). The profile, including the extensions, forms a large bow with a pinched waist, a curvilinear shape first introduced in Philadelphia Windsor seating of the mid-1780s (fig. 4-15). Accompanying this entirely new back was turned work in imitation of bamboo, an Eastern plant that had a substantial impact on Western furniture design. It was a simple matter to turn wooden sticks to simulate the exotic material. One unusual interpretation of the new bow back, produced in one or more Philadelphia shops, features an open central back panel marked by pierced cross banisters instead of spindles. The model is found in joined chair work of late Georgian design.[53]

The last Windsor pattern of the eighteenth century was introduced independent of English and Philadelphia influence. The continuous-bow armchair appeared about 1790 in New York City, and shortly thereafter Rhode Island craftsmen inaugurated production (figs. 3-2, 3-16, center). Ansel Goodrich, a Windsor-chair maker of Northampton, Massachusetts, provided the clue to identifying the background of this design in 1795 when he advertised a "Cannopy" chair and noted his working experience "among the French," apparently in New York City. In this context the terms *cannopy* and *bergère* appear interchangeable, the latter term referring specifically to an upholstered chair of high-arched back and forward-sweeping arms. Formal seating in the French taste was produced by 1790 in New York, as confirmed in the records of George Washington and strongly suggested in those of Thomas Jefferson. Both men owned revolving bergère chairs that still exist, purchased that year from cabinetmaker Thomas Burling. There is little doubt that the continuous-bow profile evolved from this high-style design. Initial use of a broad, oval plank "borrowed" from local sack-back production of the 1780s (fig. 3-16) rather than the usual shield-shape seat of this chair reinforces the dating evidence. Goodrich's own continuous-bow Windsor has a broad, shallow plank that interprets rather than duplicates the fully developed New York shield-shape seat. Whether his design is a provincial interpretation or represents a transitional state known to the chairmaker when he worked in the city is unclear.[54]

Design in the new neoclassical taste and the more archaeologically correct "antique style" placed as much emphasis on square as curved shapes. Thus with the start of the new century, the square-back Windsor became fashionable, and angular design in one variation or another held sway for the next half century. Of immediate influence on wooden-bottom seating were contemporary designs for painted fancy chairs, which in turn were reflections of high-style cabinetwork and patterns circulated via design books. The Hepplewhite and Sheraton volumes were augmented by the Continental works of Percier and Fontaine and Pierre La Mésangère, which championed the "antique" style and promoted design based directly on Greek and Roman models rather than conventional shapes with classical ornament grafted to the framework. The London chairmakers' price book issued in 1802 as a guide to manufacturing costs is a compendium of successful marketplace designs. Square-back seating soon received an additional boost in the publication of Thomas Hope's *Household Furniture* and George Smith's *Designs for Household Furniture*. Both works exerted overwhelming influence on American seating. London still was the American fashion focus, as it had been in the mid-eighteenth century when the Windsor was first introduced.[55]

FIG. 3-21 Square-back armchair, New York, 1800–1805. Mahogany; H. 35⅛", W. 22⅜", D. 21⅛". *(Courtesy, Winterthur Museum, acc. 57.835.)*

The cross-rod style (figs. 3-34, 3-35), the first early nineteenth-century square-back design produced in Windsor seating, derived directly from a Baltimore fancy pattern. As demonstrated in Thomas Sheraton's *Cabinet Dictionary* (1803), cross-rod patterns were current in England. A Windsor variation marketed in limited quantity at Salem, Massachusetts, introduced a pronounced serpentine profile to the uppermost of two cross rods. The model was the mahogany shield-back chair popular in American cabinetmaking circles and pictured in Hepplewhite's *Guide*. Following the cross-rod styles in popularity was a crest first produced in Boston shops just before the War of 1812 and later made throughout northern New England (fig. 3-41). This stepped-tablet crest is the painted counterpart of still another local cabinetmaker's design with English roots. Contemporary shops in New York produced rush- and wooden-bottom interpretations of formal cross-back seating popular in the early nineteenth century (pl. 1). Several variations are illustrated in the 1802 London price book, and the feature is an element in the antique style promoted by both Thomas Hope and George Smith.[56]

The arrow-profile spindle, a popular ornament in Windsor chairmaking, was first introduced as a chair banister in Sheraton's *Drawing-Book*, and it soon appeared in high-style furniture at several American centers. The New York chair of figure **3-21**, one of many back variants, is described in *The New-York Book of Prices for Cabinet and Chair Work* of 1802 as "a square back chair . . . With three urn splatts." New York chairmakers likely were the first to adapt the splat for use in Windsor and fancy chairs (fig. 3-49), although Baltimore was a close competitor.[57]

In tracing the origin of other back features in the Windsor, it is notable that small ornamental balls positioned between narrow cross sticks (pl. 10) appear in a design published in Sheraton's *Cabinet Dictionary* (1803). Another engraving pictures a turned roll, an element occasionally used as a Windsor crest (pls. 7, 12). A roll also is pictured in the London price book for 1802, and the feature is an element of American formal and fancy seating. Although known in several regions, the roll-top Windsor was most popular in New York and southern New England. A roll top also caps a New York Windsor that features a cross banister with a central tablet flanked by paired scrolling elements, a pattern peculiar to that city. The design is illustrated in the New York price book of 1817, where it is termed a stayrail "with double Prince of Wales feathers, tied with a gothic moulding." In formal work the banister is carved.[58]

Hepplewhite illustrates a slat set between the back posts of a chair as a crest, although the pattern is more common to the "antique" style promoted by Thomas Hope and George Smith. New York cabinet shops produced formal seating with slat backs as the nineteenth century commenced, which explains why the earliest Windsor slat-type crests appear in New York work (fig. 3-49). Slat-back Windsors documented to the shops of Reuben Odell and Stephen Egbert can be dated securely before 1810. The same crest was used widely in the fancy chair, and it was especially suited to the Grecian-style chair back, with its graceful S curve that rolls backward at the top. Some variant slat-type crests have a small projecting tablet of squared or rounded form, frequently with hollow corners, centered along the top edge. Again the prototypes originated in Hepplewhite and Sheraton designs, the London price book, and high-style and fancy American seating (fig. 3-21).[59]

The top piece that particularly captured the imagination of promoters of the antique style was the large tablet-style crest and its variations. That crest was popular among Baltimore's fancy- and Windsor-chair makers, and the design eventually spread to other areas (figs. 3-45, 3-46). Early tablets were rectangular or angular. Round-end patterns are unknown in American work before the late 1820s, even though two appear in the 1802 London price book. A recognizable crown-top crest, a profile common to the fully developed Boston rocking chair (pl. 27), is included in Mésangère's designs issued periodically from about 1804 until the late 1820s. By that date George Smith had published a comparable design in his *Cabinet-Maker and Upholsterer's Guide* (1826). John Hall's *Cabinet Makers' Assistant* published at Baltimore in 1840 contains another example.[60]

To what extent American woodworking craftsmen owned European design books, especially those of English origin, is difficult to assay, although the close links between products and published designs indicates that these volumes were well known in this country. Fortunately, there is confirming evidence. Ephraim Haines of Philadelphia, son-in-law to Daniel Trotter, acquired from the elder cabinetmaker's estate in 1800 "1 Book Designs Cabinet work." A decade later Jacob Sanderson, one of the well-known cabinetmaking brothers of Salem, Massachusetts, left an estate containing a "Cabinet Makers guide," presumably Hepplewhite's volume, along with an interest in "½ of 3 do [ditto] in Company." Whether the three company volumes were copies of the same design book or other titles is unclear. In any event, the brothers and their circle of artisan business associates were familiar with prevailing design trends. We know that they or another Salem resident owned a copy of Sheraton's *Drawing-Book*, because a set of twelve square-back mahogany chairs made for the Peirce-Nichols house about 1802 almost duplicates a design illustrated in plate 33 of that work. A copy of the London price book of 1802 was available in neighboring Boston—possibly in the possession of Thomas Seymour. Seymour was landlord to Samuel Gragg, who developed an innovative bentwood "elastic" chair and, presumably, the contoured-back Windsor rocking chair, both designs based on direct knowledge of chair backs curved in the "Grecian" manner.[61]

Gregory Weidman documented the presence of four design books in Baltimore, including Hepplewhite's *Guide* and *The Cabinet Maker's London Book of Prices* for 1788 or 1793. A copy of the latter was stolen from cabinetmaker William Camp, demonstrating the recognized importance of owning these works. When Hugh Finlay, partner in the chairmaking firm of John and Hugh Finlay, went abroad in 1810, he sent the firm "a number of Drawings, from furniture in the first houses in Paris and London." Nor were design books confined to metropolitan centers. Miles Benjamin, a cabinetmaker of Cooperstown, New York, recorded in 1824 the sale of "1 Book Architect." Perez Austin of Canterbury, Connecticut, also possessed a book of architecture in 1833 at his death.[62]

Clever craftsmen without access to design books could adapt or copy marketplace designs. Augmenting a wide selection of Windsor and fancy chairs made in America was a selection of seating furniture imported from Europe, particularly England, by merchants and entrepreneurs. One importer was Samuel J. Tuck, a Boston chairmaker and retailer of materials for painting. Along with an assortment of imported paints, he offered the public on October 15, 1803, "London made Chairs, newest fashion" with cane seats, japanned finishes, and gold ornament (fig. **3-22**).

Even with models close at hand, however, success was not always assured. Sheraton addressed this subject in his *Cabinet Dictionary* when commenting on the furniture trade:

> In the chair branch it requires a particular turn in the handling of shapes, to make them agreeable and easy: and the only branch of drawing adapted to assist such, is that of ornaments in general. It is very remarkable, the difference of some chairs of precisely the same pattern, when executed by different chair makers, arising chiefly in the want of taste concerning the beauty of an outline, of which we judge by the eye, more than the rigid rules of geometry.[63]

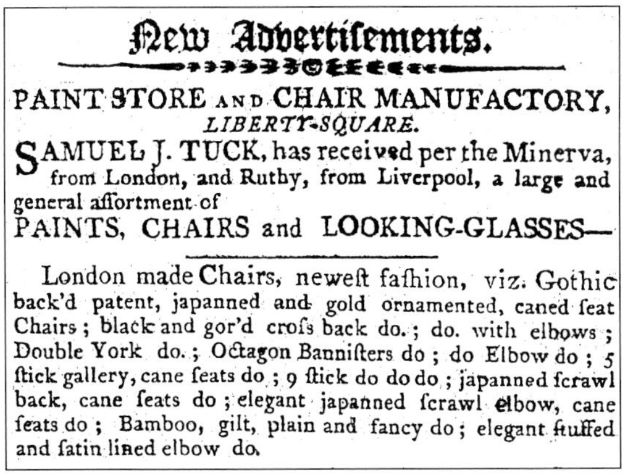

New Advertisements.

PAINT STORE AND CHAIR MANUFACTORY,
LIBERTY-SQUARE.

SAMUEL J. TUCK, has received per the Minerva, from London, and Ruthy, from Liverpool, a large and general aſſortment of

PAINTS, CHAIRS and LOOKING-GLASSES—

London made Chairs, neweſt faſhion, viz. Gothic back'd patent, japanned and gold ornamented, caned ſeat Chairs; black and gor'd croſs back do.; do. with elbows; Double York do.; Octagon Banniſters do; do Elbow do; 5 ſtick gallery, cane ſeats do; 9 ſtick do do do; japanned ſcrawl back, cane ſeats do; elegant japanned ſcrawl elbow, cane ſeats do; Bamboo, gilt, plain and fancy do; elegant ſtuffed and ſatin lined elbow do.

FIG. 3-22 Excerpts from advertisement of Samuel Jones Tuck. From the *Columbian Centinel*, Boston, October 15, 1803.

Surface Treatments

FINISHING WITH PAINT

Painting is an inexpensive method of finishing the exposed surfaces of wooden chairs and other furniture to preserve the material and produce rich effects through the use of color and, frequently, ornament. In its antiquity the use of paint rivals even stick-and-socket construction. Among ornamental techniques practiced in nineteenth-century America, surface decoration in imitation of costly materials and the application of metal leaf have roots dating from at least the classical Egyptian culture. Late Renaissance interest in classical design, which evolved into mannerism and swept Europe from Italy northward, found its way to America in the seventeenth century. Although this decorative style was manifest primarily in carved strapwork ornament and applied moldings, it made considerable use of paint and other coloring materials for accent and contrast.[64]

Other seeds of interest sowed in Europe among designers and decorators bore fruit in America in the early eighteenth century. In chartering the East India Company and allying with Portugal in royal marriage in the seventeenth century, the English opened a vast network of contacts with the East that introduced them to the exotic commodity lacquerware. The invention of a "Japan" varnish in imitation of lacquer occurred as early as 1663 in London. By 1712 a japanner practiced in Boston. Colored japan grounds, some simulating tortoiseshell, with their gilded oriental and fantastic figures, remained popular, though expensive, for many decades. It was this collective transfer of interest in surface ornament from Europe to America over a century or more that laid the groundwork for renewed activity in the postrevolutionary period, when painted ornament became available to the masses.[65]

In the meantime, American householders made extensive use of plain-painted and stained surfaces to protect and enhance furnishings. Prevailing colors were green, blue, blue-green, black, brown, and red, the latter of a brick, brownish, or orange tone. A full range of painted seating was available in prewar styles: slat and banister chairs, vase-back (or fiddle-back) chairs, and Windsors. Contemporary surface ornament that survives on case furniture and interior walls is marked by lively colors and vigorous patterns: geometric forms, delicate scrolling vines, floral subjects in infinite variety, bold tone-on-tone trompe l'oeil work, and imitative wood grain and marble.[66]

A "new" classical impulse swept Europe in the mid- to late eighteenth century stimulated by archaeological excavations at ancient sites and encouraged by scholars, artists, and artisans through the distribution of prints, design books, architectural works, and furnishings. The influence on American domestic arts in the postrevolutionary period was profound. Making timely response were the Windsor-chair makers, many of whom also began to produce the woven-bottom fancy chair newly introduced from England. Hepplewhite described the fancy chair in its particular qualities:

> A new and very elegant fashion has arisen … of finishing [chairs] with painted or japanned work, which gives a rich and splendid appearance. … Several of these designs are particularly adapted to this style, which allows a frame-work less massy than is requisite for mahogany; and by assorting the prevailing color to the furniture and the light of the room, affords opportunity, by the variety of grounds … to make the whole accord in harmony, with a pleasing and striking effect to the eye.

The rich surface treatments common to the fancy chair encouraged Windsor craftsmen to introduce a broad palette of ground color to the wood-seat chair. A line from James Tuttle's advertisement in the *Salem Gazette* for August 19, 1796, illuminates the tone of the times: "warranted work and well painted with different colors as the buyer chooses." Introduced later were the decorative techniques of banding and penciling, freehand painting and stenciling, two-color grounds, and gilded and special ornament—all described in the following pages.[67]

Colors for Surface Finishes
At its introduction in England in the early eighteenth century, the Windsor was used primarily out of doors in gardens and private parks. With its green-painted surfaces, the furniture receded conveniently into the landscape. Green was the color adopted by the early producers of Windsor furniture in America, where the first specific reference to the color occurs in a Philadelphia document of 1754, as indicated in the chart of painted seating colors (chart 1). Based on more than 1,225 references to painted surfaces on Windsor and fancy seating as documented in contemporary records, the chart describes the color explosion that occurred in the postrevolutionary years as classical design introduced from Europe swept America. Although it is not possible to know the precise hue, tint, or shade of colors listed in the records, the terms frequently are descriptive. When amplified by contemporary paint recipes, they provide a reasonably accurate basis for identification. Breaks in chart lines represent lapses between references of more than three years' duration, although these short gaps often reflect the limitations of resource materials rather than the curtailment of a color. As described in the following section, paint of a specific color often was made using any of several pigments and ingredients. A craftsman generally experimented before settling on the recipe that satisfied him best.

GREENS
Green was the popular, if not universal, color of the Windsor in prerevolutionary days, although its use did not end with the war. During a visit to Philadelphia in the 1790s, Moreau de St. Méry described the continuing popularity of "wooden chairs painted green like garden furniture in France." The early Windsor green was made from the pigment verdigris, a copper acetate. Robert Dossie, commenting in his *Handmaid to the Arts*, stated: "Verdigris makes a blue-green colour in paint." The shade was a light one. A recipe "to paint green on winsor chairs," taken from a manuscript volume of "Paints and Receipts for Wooden Work" dating to about 1801, instructs: "Take your verdigrease and g[r]ind it with lin[s]eed oil and A small matter of white lead as to give a Boddy—grind this as thick as you can with the oil and when ground put it in your Paint pot and Stur in as much Common Chair varnish as to thin it Down proper for your Brush—if it does not Brush Smooth enough put in a small matter of Spirrits of turpentine."[68]

Varnish as an ingredient in paint produced a low sheen. As noted by Sheraton in speaking of verdigris, "This green never comes up to its perfect brightness till turpentine varnish be mixed with it." In the *Painter's Guide* of 1830 P. F. Tingry took

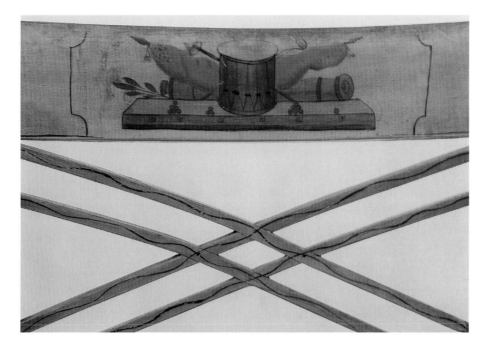

PL. 1 Detail of upper back of slat-back double-cross Windsor side chair, New York, 1810–15. Yellow poplar (seat) with maple and other woods; original surface paint and decoration. *(Courtesy of James and Nancy Glazer; Photo, Winterthur Museum.)*

PL. 2 Detail of upper back of slat-back Windsor armchair, William Bates and Thomas Allen II (label), New Bedford, Mass., ca. 1822–24. White pine (seat) with maple and other woods; original surface paint and decoration. *(Courtesy of The New Bedford Whaling Museum, New Bedford, Mass.; Photo, Winterthur Museum.)*

PL. 3 Detail of upper back of shaped-slat-back Windsor side chair (one of pair), southern Maine, ca. 1828–35. White pine (seat); original surface paint and decoration. *(New York State Historical Association, Cooperstown, NY, acc. N-23.54; Photo, Winterthur Museum.)*

PL. 4 *Maria Rex Zimmerman*, attributed to Jacob Maentel (1778–?), Schaefferstown, Lebanon County, Pennsylvania, ca. 1828. Watercolor gouache, ink, and pencil on paper; 17 × 10½ in. *(Collection American Folk Art Museum, New York. Promised gift of Ralph Esmerian, acc. P1.2001.14a; Photo, Winterthur Museum.)*

PL. 5 Detail of crest of slat-back Windsor side chair, New York, ca. 1809–15. Yellow poplar (seat); original surface paint and decoration. *(Collection of Mr. and Mrs. John T. Walker, Jr.; Photo, Winterthur Museum.)*

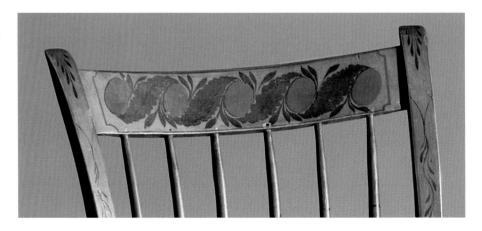

PL. 6 Slat-back Windsor side chair, eastern Pennsylvania, 1825–35. Yellow poplar (seat); H. 33½", (seat) 18⅝", W. (crest) 19", (seat) 16⅜", D. (seat) 15⅜"; original surface paint and decoration. *(Collection of Richard S. and Rosemarie B. Machmer; Photo, Winterthur Museum.)*

PL. 7 Detail of back of roll-top Windsor side chair (one of six), Philadelphia or eastern Pennsylvania, 1830–40. Yellow poplar (seat); original surface paint and decoration. *(Formerly Collection of the late Chris A. Machmer; Photo, Winterthur Museum.)*

PL. 8 Detail of crest of shaped-slat-back Windsor rocking chair, southern New Hampshire, 1820–30. White pine (seat); original surface paint and decoration. *(Private Collection; Photo, Winterthur Museum.)*

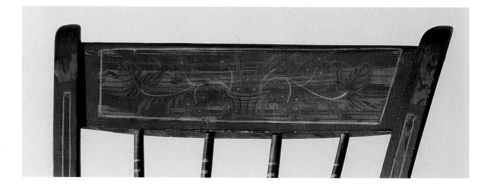

PL. 9 Detail of crest of slat-back Windsor side chair, Worcester Co., Mass., or Maine, 1820–30. Probably white pine (seat); original surface paint and decoration. *(Formerly Hitchcock Museum, Riverton, Conn.; Photo, Winterthur Museum.)*

PL. 10 Detail of upper back of slat-back ball-fret Windsor side chair, Hudson River Valley and environs north of New York City, ca. 1820–28. Yellow poplar (seat, microanalysis); original surface paint and decoration. *(New York State Historical Association, Cooperstown, NY, acc. N-25.54; Photo, Winterthur Museum.)*

PL. 11 Detail of upper back of slat-back Windsor side chair (one of pair), New York, 1810–15. Yellow poplar (seat); original surface paint and decoration. *(Formerly Hitchcock Museum; Photo, Winterthur Museum.)*

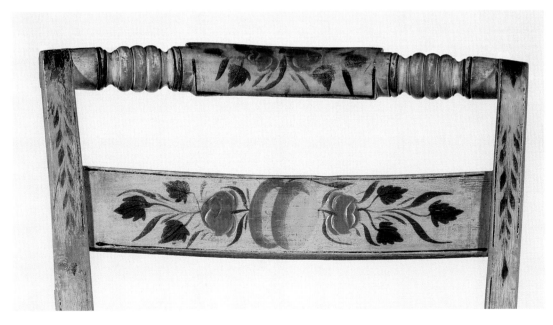

PL. 12 Detail of upper back of roll-top Windsor side chair (one of six), New York, 1820–25. Yellow poplar (seat) with maple and other woods; original surface paint and decoration. *(Collection of Betty and Ted Stvan; Photo, Winterthur Museum.)*

PL. 13 Shaped tablet-top Windsor side chair (one of six), northeastern coastal Massachusetts, ca. 1815–22. Origianl surface paint and decoration. *(Photo courtesy of Frank and Barbara Pollack, American Antiques and Art.)*

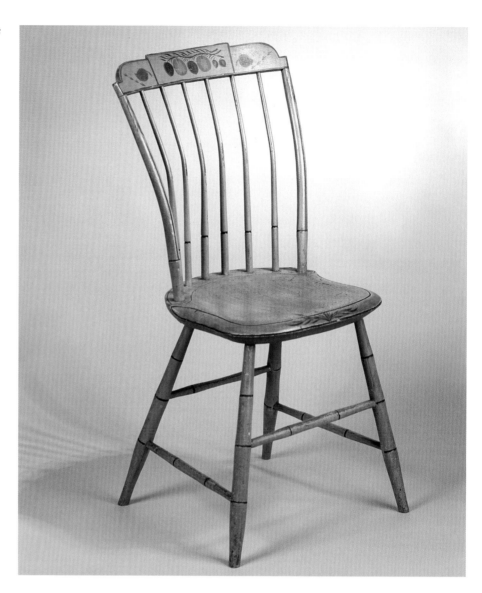

PL. 14 Detail of back of shaped-tablet-top splat-back Windsor side chair (one of six), Pennsylvania, 1850–70. Yellow poplar (seat); original surface paint and decoration. *(Collection of Eugene and Vera Charles; Photo, Winterthur Museum.)*

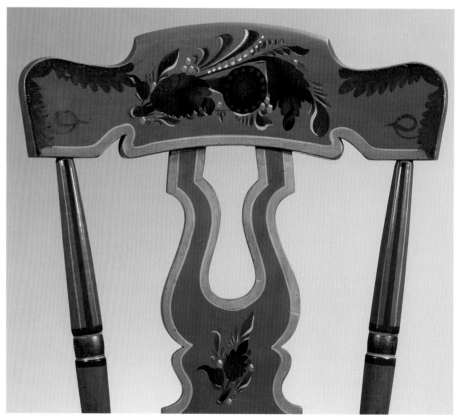

PL. 15 Detail of upper back of slat-back Windsor armchair, southern New Hampshire, 1820–30. Maple and other woods; original surface paint and decoration. *(Private Collection; Photo, Winterthur Museum.)*

PL. 16 Detail of upper back of shaped-tablet-top Windsor side chair (one of two), Maine, 1825–35. White pine (seat); original surface paint and deco-ration. *(Collection of Caroline Von Kleeck Beard; Photo, Winterthur Museum.)*

PL. 17 Detail of upper back of slat-back Windsor armchair (one of pair), New York, 1814–20. Yellow poplar (seat) with maple (microanalysis); original surface paint and decoration. *(Courtesy, Winterthur Museum, Winterthur, Del., acc. 88.2.1.)*

PL. 18 Detail of crest of square-back Masonic Windsor side chair in fig. 5-41, Delaware Valley, 1815–25. Yellow poplar (seat); original surface paint and decoration. *(Collection of Brearley Lodge No. 2, Free and Accepted Masons, Bridgeton, N.J.; Photo, Winterthur Museum.)*

PL. 19 Detail of crest of shaped-slat-back Windsor side chair (one of six), possibly northern Massachusetts, probably southern New Hampshire, 1825–40. Original surface paint and decoration. *(Photo courtesy of Marguerite Riordan.)*

PL. 20 Detail of back of scalloped-top Windsor side chair, central Pennsylvania, 1835–45. Yellow poplar (seat); original surface paint and decoration. *(Collection of Eugene and Vera Charles; Photo, Winterthur Museum.)*

Chart 1. Colors of paint used to cover the wooden surfaces of Windsor and fancy seating furniture made between 1750 and 1850

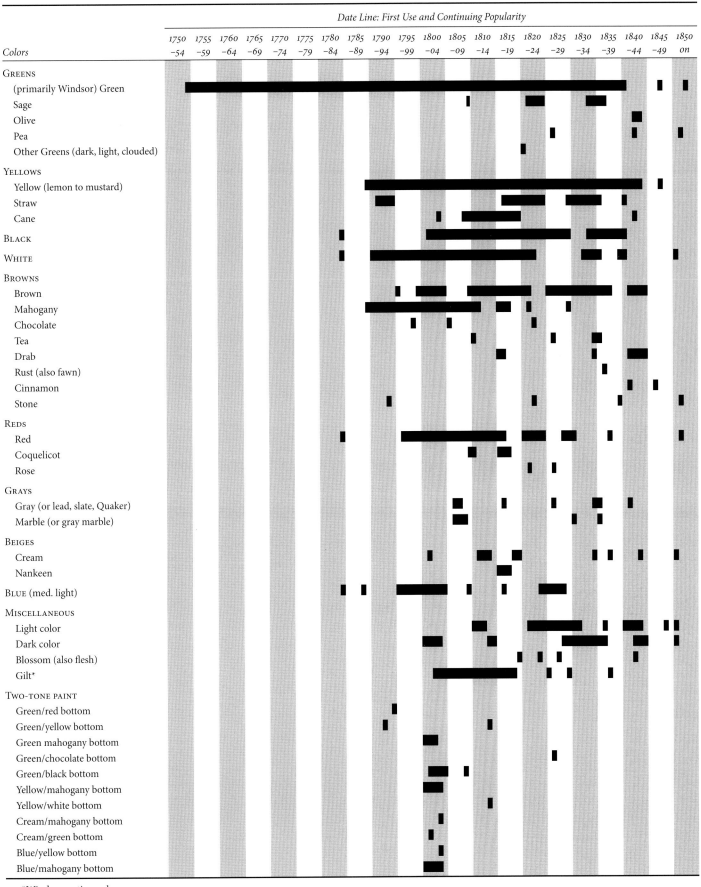

Date Line: First Use and Continuing Popularity

Colors	1750 -54	1755 -59	1760 -64	1765 -69	1770 -74	1775 -79	1780 -84	1785 -89	1790 -94	1795 -99	1800 -04	1805 -09	1810 -14	1815 -19	1820 -24	1825 -29	1830 -34	1835 -39	1840 -44	1845 -49	1850 on

GREENS
(primarily Windsor) Green
Sage
Olive
Pea
Other Greens (dark, light, clouded)

YELLOWS
Yellow (lemon to mustard)
Straw
Cane

BLACK

WHITE

BROWNS
Brown
Mahogany
Chocolate
Tea
Drab
Rust (also fawn)
Cinnamon
Stone

REDS
Red
Coquelicot
Rose

GRAYS
Gray (or lead, slate, Quaker)
Marble (or gray marble)

BEIGES
Cream
Nankeen

BLUE (med. light)

MISCELLANEOUS
Light color
Dark color
Blossom (also flesh)
Gilt*

TWO-TONE PAINT
Green/red bottom
Green/yellow bottom
Green mahogany bottom
Green/chocolate bottom
Green/black bottom
Yellow/mahogany bottom
Yellow/white bottom
Cream/mahogany bottom
Cream/green bottom
Blue/yellow bottom
Blue/mahogany bottom

*Windsor seating only

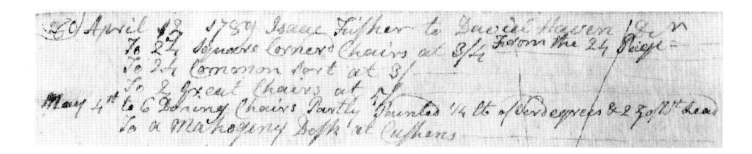

FIG. 3-23 Isaac Fisher account, May 4, 1789, in David Haven account book, Framingham, Mass., 1785–1800. *(Winterthur Library.)*

issue with first grinding verdigris in oil, which he said deteriorated the color, and recommended instead grinding it in turpentine varnish to preserve its "delicacy." On Cape Cod chairmaker Samuel Wing's recipe for green paint, acquired from Obed Faye, a Nantucket chairmaker, emphasized the use of drying agents in the varnish. Before grinding, verdigris required slaking, or heating. James Claypoole of Philadelphia advertised verdigris in 1750, although the pigment was available there earlier. In 1795 Thomas Timpson acquired a pound already ground from a New York City supplier. Verdigris, Spanish white, and lampblack were the coloring materials found in the shop of Windsor-chair maker Ansel Goodrich in Northampton, Massachusetts, at his death in 1803 in the full bloom of his career. David Haven of Framingham hinted in 1789 at the quantity of paint required to finish a set of Windsors when recording: "To 6 Dining Chairs Partly Painted ¼ lb of Verdegrees & 2 oz of Wt Lead" (fig. **3-23**).[69]

Ebenezer Swift perhaps referred to paint from the Nantucket formula in 1799 when directing Samuel Wing to "give them [new] chairs a good Green coler as you can." A year earlier Windsor chairs "finished Green" were part of Francis Trumble's shop stock at Philadelphia. For more than a decade his contemporaries Joseph Henzey and William Cox had sold green Windsors to merchant Stephen Girard for his lucrative export trade, and part of the seating listed in a bill from John B. Ackley to Samuel Coates in 1800 was painted green (fig. 3-63). The color so dominated the seating trade that the term *green chair* was synonymous everywhere with the Windsor. In 1789 William Blake of Boston produced "Warranted Green Windsor chairs . . . painted equally well as those made at Philadelphia," and green Windsors were chosen in 1796 by legislative bodies at Hartford and New York. Cornwell and Cowperthwaite's sale in 1820 of "six Green windsor Chairs" at New York documents the color's longevity, although by then other green pigments were in use.[70]

Sage is the second green mentioned for seating furniture in early records (chart 1). Eight sage chairs are recorded in an inventory of 1809 from Chester County, Pennsylvania. At the death of Windsor-chair maker Benjamin Love in 1821 near Philadelphia appraisers described "eight Sage Coulered Winsor Chairs (2 of them arm)" among his personal possessions. Related references appear in probate documents originating in New Jersey towns along the Delaware River, suggesting that sage-color furniture was used principally in the Delaware Valley. As to the actual hue, it was a grayish green tending toward a blue cast. A fourteenth-century recipe describes sage as a mixture of white lead and terre verte (literally green earth), a mineral still available in the nineteenth century. Another recipe of about 1801 suggests using yellow ocher (another early mineral), indigo blue, and umber, the latter a brown earth that toned the color.[71]

To make the pea green color of the 1820s and later, nineteenth-century painters mixed verdigris and white lead in the proportion of one to ten, achieving a light green tint (chart 1). By midcentury Rufus Porter described pea green as a mixture of white lead and Paris green, one of the new chemically compounded pigments available. Early references to the color occur in the Philadelphia area, although the presence of "Pea green cane seat chairs" in Lambert Hitchcock's household in Connecticut describes a geographic range greater than that of sage. Philadelphia sources also itemize chairs painted olive or dark olive color. Those in the inventory of chairmaker Charles Riley, drawn in 1842, were made in the ball-back and Baltimore styles. A contemporary inventory originating nearby in Chester County describes "6 Chairs olive green." A recipe dating from the early nineteenth century recommends mixing lampblack and yellow ocher to achieve this color. At midcentury Rufus Porter substituted the synthetic pigment chrome yellow, but he also gave a formula that blended blue, red, and yellow pigments. The dark green chairs mentioned in the 1820s and later may have been painted with a mixture of chrome green and Prussian blue. Light green may have been one of various tints; pea green is a good candidate. "Clouded" green probably refers to a surface of mottled appearance. Chairs identified only as "green" from the 1820s on probably were painted one of the new hues rather than the old verdigris green.[72]

YELLOWS

In order of popularity as a color for vernacular seating furniture, yellow followed green (chart 1). The general term *yellow* included a range of hues beginning with pale tints and continuing to bright lemon and toned mustard shades. The word sometimes identified *straw* or *cane* color, terms that were interchangeable. Inventories from Chester County, Pennsylvania, employ all three words, although not in the same documents; nor was use of the terms limited geographically. Yellow chairs first were identified in August 1789 in the Philadelphia export trade to the South when John Minnick of Charleston advertised "Green and yellow Windsor chairs" for sale. The "½ doz Patent Yellow dining Chairs" enumerated in carver Edward Cutbush's "Back Parlor" a year later probably were not new. Documents of the 1790s identify chairs of this color in households in Baltimore County, Maryland, and Lancaster County, Pennsylvania, two rising centers with close trading ties to Philadelphia. The yellow Windsors included in the bill illustrated in figure 3-63, dated in 1800 at Philadelphia, represent part of an order probably destined for a market in Maryland. Windsors of similar color were common by then in New York City, and the yellow dining chair probably was known in New England before June 1797, when Solomon Cole of Glastonbury, Connecticut, sold three to a customer. The Ebenezer Tracy, Sr., household in eastern Connecticut contained half a dozen yellow Windsors in 1803, and the shop held a supply of "stone yellow" pigment. When Benjamin H. Hathorne (Hawthorne), a merchant of Boston, made a household accounting in 1800 and listed half a dozen yellow fan-back chairs, the color also was well established in that city.[73]

Straw-colored paint, possibly the "yellow" of 1789, was fashionable in Philadelphia by March 12, 1791, when William Cox dated a bill for "24 Straw colour'd chairs" delivered to Stephen Girard for export (chart 1). The color, identified in modern dictionaries as "yellowish," was made by introducing a small amount of yellow pigment to white. Authorities describe the pigment variously as spruce yellow, English ocher, and chrome yellow; thus the tint was not fixed and varied from a bright to a dull tone, depending on the pigment. During the same year Daniel Rea of Boston used straw-color paint on half a dozen fancy rush-bottom chairs. The original surface on a set of six stuffed-seat bow-back Boston Windsors still together in an institutional collection was straw color, the grooves picked out in green. Thomas Boynton, who was located at Boston in the early 1800s, employed straw color in his later chairwork at Windsor, Vermont. To compound the color he could have used any of the yellow pigments noted in his accounts—yellow ocher, or French, spruce, patent, or stone yellow.[74]

The cane color associated with early nineteenth-century chairs was comparable, no doubt, to the "shining yellow colour" described by Thomas Sheraton in speaking of the "Indian reed" bamboo (chart 1). A Baltimore auction account of 1803 is the

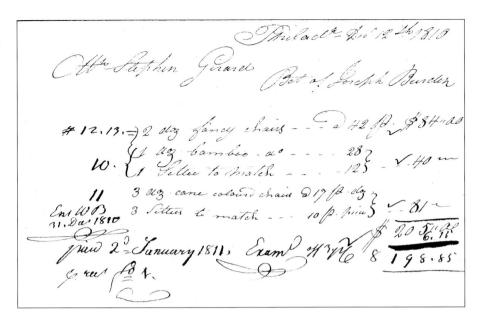

first document to mention cane-colored chairs, although Philadelphia references are about contemporary. Among almost sixteen dozen Windsors shipped in December 1805 by chairmaker Joseph Burden from the Delaware River port to New Orleans were "2 dz Cane coloured double bow Chairs" in the new square-back pattern. Seating of similar hue entered the Charleston, Savannah, and South American markets, the latter shipped by Stephen Girard on December 22, 1810, on board his ship *Rousseau*. The merchant appears to have obtained part of his cargo of cane-colored chairs with settees "to match" from Burden, as itemized in a bill dated December 12 (fig. **3-24**). By the early 1810s Silas Cheney of Connecticut and David Alling of New Jersey also employed cane color to good advantage.[75]

WHITE AND BLACK

An account of Joseph Walker, supercargo on the sloop *Friendship* for a voyage from Philadelphia to Georgia in 1784, identifies white and black as colors suitable for the Windsor market at Savannah, Georgia, although the time lapse between that reference and the next raises questions about the popularity of those colors in Philadelphia at the time (chart 1, fig. 4-39). The earliest white-painted Windsors of domestic record are the two dozen listed in 1790 among the first-floor furnishings of Benjamin Franklin's home at his death, and the color probably was only newly fashionable. In interpreting the word "white" as it relates to seating furniture, it is well to note its double meaning. Some references describe chairs in their unpainted state. Providing illustration are the records of David Haven, a Framingham, Massachusetts, woodworker who made several kinds of seating, including rush-bottom slat-backs. His "White Chair Fraimes" cost less than 2s. apiece; those finished with stain cost 3s. In two entries dating to September 30, 1789, Haven recorded the following Windsor seating: "2 Windsor Chairs finished at 7/6" and "5 Do [Ditto] White at 6/0." When the Windsors were painted, green was the usual color in the Haven shop.[76]

White-painted seating was well established in the retail market before 1800. A "Round Top Settee painted white" was part of John Lambert's stock in 1793 at Philadelphia. The following year General Henry Knox, who patronized William Cox, purchased bow-back chairs of the same color fitted with mahogany arms. John B. Ackley's bill of 1800 to Samuel Coates (fig. 3-63) also lists white-painted chairs as does that of Taylor and King rendered to Stephen Girard the previous year (fig. **3-25**). The color was accepted quickly at Boston, where in 1793 Daniel Rea painted chairs white. The following year the Sanderson brothers of neighboring Salem pur-

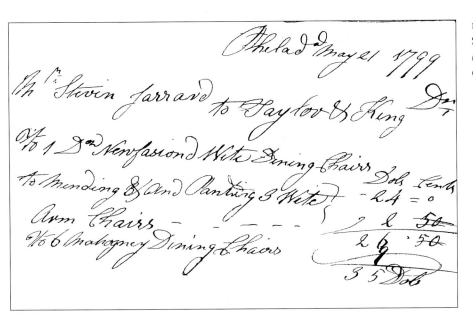

FIG. 3-25 Robert Taylor and Daniel King bill to Stephen Girard, Philadelphia, May 21, 1799. *(Collection of the Board of Directors of City Trusts, Girard College History Collections.)*

chased similar dining Windsors (bow-backs and fan-backs) from chairmaker Micaiah Johnson. White seating had some vogue in New York City, where fancy-chair maker William Palmer completed a set of "Drawing room chairs white & Gold" at the turn of the century. Commercial interests at Philadelphia, New York, and Boston disseminated the fashion along the coast and inland, influencing markets such as the national capital at Washington, western Connecticut, and central Massachusetts.[77]

Painting specialists and chairmakers used either white lead or Spanish white as a pigment in white paint. The first, a carbonate of lead, was sold in its purest quality as flake white. Spanish white, or whiting, came from a clay, or earth. Often both pigments were adulterated with chalk before or after purchase. Of the two, white lead was the better quality, although period documents show extensive use of both. Sheraton directed that to best preserve the color white lead should be mixed with nut oil. For "common purposes" he indicated that linseed oil and turpentine would do.[78]

Lampblack, prepared from the smoke of "woods and resinous substances" or, preferably, linseed oil, was the principal ingredient in black paint and a common additive in compounding and shading other colors. A quality black was made by burning ivory to produce ivory black, although as Sheraton noted, it was "too dear for common chair work." One problem with lampblack was its oily character, which kept it from drying well. Sheraton recommended grinding it in turpentine and then "laying" it on "in white hard varnish, very thin and repeated." As a priming coat he suggested a white ground or a mixture of ingredients, including lampblack and white lead. A little linseed oil or Prussian blue enriched the color. Black and white pigments are listed commonly in period documents because of their broad use in tinting and shading.[79]

Compared with white chairs, black seating had a late start, being marketed about a decade later. An 1801 shipping manifest of Philadelphia origin lists chairs painted black along with other popular colors. Black chairs ordered in the city by Thomas Jefferson that year and again in 1809 were shipped to his residences at Monticello and Poplar Forest. By 1801 Amos Denison Allen had introduced black Windsors to his production in Connecticut to augment a selection of green and yellow chairs. Chairmakers in New York supplied the domestic and export markets with black Windsors, and at Boston William Seaver produced black fancy chairs by 1804. Black "table," or dining, Windsors appear in Nantucket probate records by 1809–10 and likely were relatively new.[80]

BROWNS

The pigments for coloring brown named most often in period records are Spanish brown, prepared by heating native English red ocher; umber, a brown-red earth; and sienna, also an earth (chart 1). The latter two were used in either their raw or burnt states. Umber becomes darker when burnt, and sienna changes from a brownish yellow to a reddish brown. Mixtures of other pigments also produce brown. Browns for Windsor seating were popular by the 1790s, although common slat-back seating of earlier date often was painted brown. Among General Henry Knox's purchases at Philadelphia in the mid-1790s were brown fan-back chairs. Samuel Coates, a local merchant, acquired brown oval-back Windsors a few years later (fig. 3-63), and in 1799 Amos Denison Allen of Connecticut painted a new rocking chair brown. Describing "5 Spanish Brown windsor chairs" in 1810, estate appraisers in Chester County, Pennsylvania, were explicit in naming the coloring agent. In the mid-1810s a notice from Albany and an order from the War Office in Washington for half a dozen "Brown Flat Top Chairs" indicate that brown remained a postwar option.[81]

Mahogany describes the first brown given precise description in Windsor-chair-making records (chart 1). The hue was also the most popular brown from its early appearance in 1789 on painted seating, although house painters already employed mahogany and other browns for interior woodwork. Materials purchased for that purpose at New York in 1773 by William Beekman included "13½ lb Stone Colour," "1 lb Chocolate Colour," and "Mahogany Colour." When in 1789 John Minnick advertised imported mahogany-colored Windsors at Charleston, South Carolina, Francis Trumble and other chairmakers of Philadelphia already were supplying the *overseas* trade with chairs of similar hue. Among Philadelphia suppliers of the 1790s, the firm of Taylor and King did business with Stephen Girard. The "Mahogney Dining Chairs" priced at $1.50 apiece delivered to the merchant in 1799 were Windsor side chairs probably in the bow-back pattern (fig. 3-25). Painted "mahogany" chairs also were marketed successfully into the early 1800s in other areas. A resident of Norfolk, Virginia, bought "Boback mahogany Coloured Chairs" in 1794, and a Winchester chairmaker used the same color in 1803 on his products. When in 1808 a householder of Bordentown, New Jersey, chose mahogany-color paint for chairs, the color was well known as far away as Nantucket. Writing to Philadelphia from Christiana, Delaware, in 1794 Solomon Maxwell directed chairmaker Lawrence Allwine "to send . . . half a dozen good round back windsor Chairs painted mehogany colour."[82]

Chocolate color, a mixture of Spanish brown or Venetian red with lampblack, is identified on Windsor seating in a notice of 1798 from Charleston, South Carolina, offering "An excellent Assortment of Yellow, Green, Mahogany, and Chocolate Colored CHAIRS and SETTEES" from Philadelphia (chart 1). A distinction is made here between mahogany and chocolate: both are red in hue, the former of moderate value, the latter a deep, rich tone. Sometime before 1805 merchant Isaac Kip purchased a dozen "Chocolate Coloured Windsor Chairs" for his home in New York.[83]

Tea, cinnamon, rust, and fawn color were medium shades of brown, the last three of decided red cast, and tea color either of reddish or yellowish hue (chart 1). All are nineteenth-century seating colors. Samuel Coates of Philadelphia paid 50¢ apiece in 1810 to have eight chairs painted "Tea Colour," and fancy and Windsor chairs of the same finish are listed in several estates probated in 1826 in Chester County, Pennsylvania. During the 1830s tea color attracted attention in Hartford, Connecticut, where Philemon Robbins used it for rush, cane, and wooden-bottom seating. He documented the medium intensity of the hue: "to pntng R[ocking] Chair first dark then Tea" and "9 tea collour and 9 best dark col[or] Five rods." Rust, cinnamon, and fawn, colors listed in records dating to the 1830s and 1840s, may refer to a single shade. One recipe describes cinnamon as a mixture of yellow and red ocher. Chairmaker Ebenezer Rose's household at Trenton, New Jersey, contained rust-colored chairs.

Estates in Philadelphia and Chester County list cinnamon and fawn-colored seating. All three hues may have been limited in popularity to the Delaware Valley.[84]

Drab and stone brown were close in color, if not one and the same (chart 1), as indicated in an early nineteenth-century description: "A stone brown is composed of lamp-black, yellow ochre and Venetian red, equal parts: the addition of white to this compound reduces this color to a drab, or light stone color." Further confirmation occurs in 1842 in a bill of sale from eastern Pennsylvania describing "6 S. B. [straight back] drab stone color [chairs]." Stone color as a named chair finish appears as early as 1793 in an accounting of John Lambert's shop at Philadelphia, which identifies "8 Do [chairs] Fan backs Stone Colour." Sporadic use of the term continued until the mid-nineteenth century, when in 1851 Chauncey Strong of Otsego County, New York, recorded the sale of "2 stone chairs." David Alling's reference to drab color in his records for 1815–16 at Newark, New Jersey, suggest the color's currency in New York City as well. Alling possessed the requisite materials for making this paint — stone ocher, lampblack, Venetian red, and white lead.[85]

REDS

The principal pigments for red paint were Venetian red, red lead, and vermilion, in that order (chart 1). The lake pigments, including rose pink, identified with regularity in documents were coloring agents for varnish, distempers, and washes rather than paints. Venetian red, the name loosely associated with the Italian city, was manufactured by artificial means in the eighteenth century and later, primarily through the use of red ocher, or earth. An eighteenth-century author described it as "inclining to the scarlet [yellowish red] rather than the crimson [bluish red] hue." In the manufacturing process red lead was calcinated to the "proper degree of colour, by exposing it with a large furnace to the fire." The derivative color was orange-red. Vermilion is a bright red of crimson hue, not uncommonly adulterated with red lead. Both the English and Dutch products were in the American market. A finer, though more expensive, pigment produced in China is mentioned specifically in the records of Silas Cheney, a furniture craftsman of Litchfield, Connecticut, who in 1818 purchased "½ lb Chinese Vermillion" from Isaac Bull of Hartford.[86]

As with other generic names, it is impossible to know the precise hue or shade designated by the term "red." Chart 1 indicates long use and specific periods of concentrated popularity. Clouding the picture is the practice of referring to some browns as red and the brownish appearance of some colors popularly called red. After 1800 the brighter palette described above likely prevailed. The first mention of red Windsors occurs in the accounts of a Philadelphia supercargo, who commented in 1784 on colors suitable for the Southern market (fig. 4-39). There follows an item in 1796 for "½ Dozen Windsor Chairs (red)" in an inventory from Baltimore County, Maryland, and by 1798 Amos Denison Allen of Connecticut occasionally painted a continuous-bow armchair red. An early nineteenth-century receipted bill originating in Newburyport, Massachusetts, itemizes "red Spring Back Chairs," and a contemporary account book from Gilmanton, New Hampshire, identifies "Bamboo" chairs of this color. The American export trade carried red Windsors from Philadelphia and New York to destinations in the West Indies, South America, and New Orleans. Writing to Salem, Massachusetts, from Brazil in the early 1820s, an unknown commentator remarked on the local chair market: "Common Windsor Chairs are generally Saleable if of high colors, Such as Bright yellow, Green, Red &c."[87]

Coquelicot, a bright poppy red, was rising in popularity in 1809, the date of its first record, when Stephen Girard of Philadelphia shipped a dozen of the orange-red chairs and a settee to South America aboard the *Voltaire* (chart 1). The merchant acquired the furniture from the local chairmaker Isaac M. Bolton (fig. **3-26**). The price identifies fancy seating with woven bottoms, a painted product priced slightly higher than the plank-bottom Windsor. The color may have been devel-

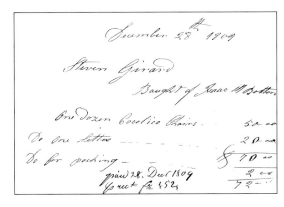

FIG. 3-26 Isaac M. Bolton bill to Stephen Girard, Philadelphia, December 28, 1809. *(Collection of the Board of Directors of City Trusts, Girard College History Collections.)*

oped first in Baltimore, where painted furniture was particularly fashionable. The rare set of red (now darkened) Masonic Windsors from Pennsylvania illustrated in figure 5-38 probably was described as coquelicot color in 1811 when new. James Williams, the painter, apparently migrated north to Lancaster, Pennsylvania, from Washington, where Baltimore influence was strong. Plate 18 illustrates a similarly painted Masonic chair. A notice of May 1809 in a Lexington, Kentucky, newspaper suggests another initial domestic source for the color. Chairmaker William Challen, who boasted "long experience . . . in London and New York," offered local patrons fashionable chairs painted white, black, brown, green, or coquelicot enhanced with gold. Samuel Stibbs from New York may have introduced coquelicot in 1816 to consumers in Cincinnati. Several New York craftsmen had advertised the color in 1810, and another supplied a cargo of "60 Bent Back Coquelicot Winsor Chairs" for the *George and Mary* bound for Buenos Aires from Providence the same year. Across the bay in Newark, Moses Lyon painted and decorated coquelicot chairs for David Alling, probably preparing the bright color from the Venetian red in the shop. Perhaps the rose-colored Windsor seating described in the 1810s in a Chester County, Pennsylvania, estate was of coquelicot hue.[88]

GRAYS AND BEIGES

Gray-painted seating was unknown in the chair market until the early 1800s (chart 1). The surface finish of plate 10 is a light shade. The terms *lead* and *slate* color describe medium and darker tones. Recipes were straightforward. Rufus Porter wrote in *Scientific American* that "several common colours, known as lead-colour, slate-colour &c., are prepared by mixing lamp-black with white lead in different proportions." Before 1810 Samuel Broome furnished a bedroom in his house near Philadelphia with "4 lead coloured wooden chairs," and a home in Chester County contained three. Probably all were plain painted with contrasting color accenting the "bamboo" grooves. William Palmer of New York City made elegant gray and gold fancy chairs with settees en suite in 1815 to furnish the President's House at Washington after the British destruction of the War of 1812.[89]

Two Windsor-chair makers' inventories contain late references to gray chairs. In 1835 John Oldham's estate at Baltimore contained a dozen chairs painted lead color, and Charles Riley stocked slate-colored seating in 1842 at his shop in Philadelphia. The term *quaker* color was current during the mid-1830s at Hartford, Connecticut, when Philemon Robbins did a brisk business in wood-seat and fancy chairs of this finish, although the shade is unknown. References to marble-colored chairs are equally indefinite, as it is unclear whether surface treatments simulated the appearance of the material or duplicated the color only (chart 1). Perhaps belonging to the second group are the six "marble colour" chairs that in 1830 furnished Peter Suplee's home in Honey Brook, Pennsylvania.[90]

Light, yellow-tinted paints were marketed during the early 1800s. A manuscript recipe book of the 1820s identifies cream-color paint as white lead ground in oil with the addition of a small amount of stone yellow (chart 1). "Nankeen" describes the same color, the tint tending toward buff. Popular just after the War of 1812, the name derived from a plain-woven cotton cloth of pale yellow, or natural undyed, fiber originally of Chinese origin. References to nankeen-colored "sofas" and chairs in the slat-back (pl. 11), ball-back (pl. 10), and organ-spindle patterns appear between 1815 and 1817 in the accounts of David Alling of Newark, New Jersey.[91]

Many early references to cream-colored chairs center in Connecticut. In February 1801 Titus Preston of Wallingford completed a set of dining Windsors with cream finish. During the following decade Thomas Safford of Canterbury made cream-colored chairs in the eastern part of the state, and Silas Cheney produced similar seating at his western shop in Litchfield. Philemon Robbins's accounts of the 1830s at Hartford identify cream-colored roll-top chairs. An early reference dating to 1801 from Winchester, Virginia, broadens the geographic range, and there is little doubt that the influence sprang from Baltimore or Philadelphia. A later set of Baltimore-style, tablet-top Windsors of original creamy tan surface is documented to Carlisle, Pennsylvania, near the Maryland border. David Alling of Newark, New Jersey, noted the use of this color only from 1837, although during the late 1820s William Beesley of southern New Jersey had employed cream-color paint.[92]

BLUE

There are few references to blue pigment other than Prussian blue in paint recipes, advertisements, and manuscripts (chart 1). Invented in Berlin at the beginning of the eighteenth century, Prussian blue was manufactured in England less than a quarter century later, and its importation into the colonies is recorded before the mid-eighteenth century. If not properly compounded, the color proved fugitive, turning olive or greenish gray within a short period. Retailers occasionally offered prepared paint for sale. Samuel Wetherill and Sons, manufacturers of Philadelphia, sold Prussian blue paint by the 1780s. A recipe of 1801 directs: "take 2½ lb. of white led to one ounce of Prusian Blue; be very careful to grinde the Prusian blue fine as possible." Oil was the vehicle. Prussian blue, popular for interior woodwork and painted household furnishings, was in moderate demand for Windsor and fancy seating from the post-revolutionary period through the 1820s. In prewar days blue sometimes occurred as a paint or stain on common rush-bottom seating.[93]

In 1784 Joseph Walker, supercargo on a voyage of the sloop *Friendship* out of Philadelphia, advised sending blue paint and a selection of other colors as an accompaniment to Windsor seating destined for Southern markets (fig. 4-39). A year later a public vendue disposed of "Windsor chairs painted blue" from the household of Major James Swan at Boston. Joseph Barrell of neighboring Charlestown paid extra for his special order of a dozen and a half Windsors painted "light blue grey Colour" to match the walls of his summer dining room. He made his purchase in 1795 through his factors in New York. Blue seating "caught on" quickly. A brilliant Prussian blue originally covered all the surfaces except the seats of a set of New England chairs (pl. 34; see also pl. 16). An auction at Beverly, Massachusetts, offered blue fan-back Windsors in 1802, and two years later the Walker family of Sturbridge bought blue dining chairs from the local chairmaker Oliver Wight. The "6 sq[uare] Chairs Blue" sold in 1809 at Silas Cheney's shop in Connecticut were constructed in the narrow-slat or cross-rod pattern. Through the 1810s and 1820s blue-painted fancy seating also remained a domestic and export product of the Delaware Valley.[94]

MISCELLANEOUS AND DUAL COLORS

Two general terms describe surface finishes from the early 1800s through midcentury: *light color* and *dark color* (chart 1). The words identify the brightness or dullness of a hue rather than the color itself. In 1800 Thomas Jefferson referred to chairs of "a very dark colour" when inquiring after a purchase he feared had been misdirected, and a sheriff's inventory of William Seaver's shop compiled in 1804 at Boston itemized "dark" cane-seat chairs. In neighboring Newburyport, Massachusetts, Bernard Foot billed a customer on September 24, 1813, for "One sett of Spring Back Chairs" and "One ditto dark couler." The terms remained in common use in the 1820s, as described in the accounts of Luke Houghton of Massachusetts: "1 doz of straw collar chairs / 1 doz of light collar d[itt]o / ½ doz of dark d[itt]o d[itt]o." Nor were chairs the only form identified in this manner. At midcentury Calvin Stetson of Barnstable on Cape Cod stocked a "Dark Settee Cradle," and Chauncey Strong of New York State retailed a "Light Boston Rocking Chair."[95]

Posing an identification problem is the blossom color first entered in 1819 in the accounts of David Alling of New Jersey (chart 1). More than twenty years later the term reappeared in the shop inventory of Charles Riley at Philadelphia. Perhaps the "winsor chairs flesh color" itemized during the 1820s in two inventories from Chester County, Pennsylvania, were similarly painted. The *Oxford English Dictionary* describes "blossom" as rose or peach color. "Flesh" is identified as pale red, watermelon color, or "light pink with a little yellow." Recipes for colors with the names *peach*, *peach blow*, *peach blossom*, and *dawn* describe pale pink to lilac tints mixed in white lead.[96]

Records frequently identify "Gilt" Windsors, although the word describes decoration rather than surface finish (chart 1). Gilt ornament, which ranged broadly through the paint selection on the chart, will be discussed under decoration. Since some documents focus attention on this feature to the exclusion of the painted finish, however, as for example the item for "12 Dining chairs Gilt" from the inventory of Aaron Boughman of Philadelphia, it is well to note the emphasis.[97]

Apropos to the present discussion is the use of dual paint colors during the early 1800s, a practice that provided colorful contrasts between the painted surfaces of the seat plank and the rest of the chair (chart 1). Use of the decorative technique probably represents the direct influence of upholstered-seat furniture, including the stuffed-bottom Windsor, a fashionable high-priced choice of the 1790s that provided both comfort and visual diversity. Resource materials introduce ambiguities in interpretation, however. For example, the "two dozen Green & Yellow Chairs" shipped in 1792 by chairmaker Thomas Mason from Philadelphia to Charleston could simply have been trimmed with yellow. An appraiser's listing of six "Green [chairs] with Red Bottoms" in a Nantucket estate of 1794 may describe stuffed rather than painted seats; and an item for blue chairs with red bottoms in an estate from New London County, Connecticut, three years later is equally unclear. By the turn of the century Amos Denison Allen of South Windham, Connecticut, was painting fan-back and bow-back side chairs green, blue, or yellow and introducing mahogany-color seats. Green chairs with black bottoms were another option at the shop. There is no mistaking the nature of these references, because Allen identified stuffed-seat chairs as "Cushioned." Titus Preston of Wallingford recorded dining chairs painted cream color with contrasting green bottoms and striped bamboowork for accent. At Winchester, Virginia, in 1803 David Russell painted chairs in several bright combinations: "mazarine blue with mahogany bottoms," "cream coular with magohany [*sic*] bottoms," and "pale blue yellow bottoms." Even as late as 1826 a household in Connecticut contained "½ Doz. Green Chocolate bottom windsor Chairs."[98]

Preparation and Storage of Paint

To commence painting, a chairmaker began by processing the materials. Although some prepared paints were available commercially, the amount of equipment listed in craft inventories establishes the general practice of conducting most of the work in the shop. If his business was substantial, the chairmaker, like the paint seller, could use a paint mill. The first mill recorded was that employed by Thomas Child in Boston during the early eighteenth century and described as a stone globe and oblong trough. Francis Trumble, a Windsor-chair maker of Philadelphia, probably owned grinding equipment of the same general type. Appraisers described the apparatus in 1798 as "1 56 lb Weight & 1 pounding Mortar." Ebenezer Tracy, Sr.'s, "paint pott & 3 balls" served the same purpose in Connecticut. Mechanized equipment sometimes employed "a horizontal stone cylinder revolving in contact with another stone." An eighteenth-century horse-operated English mill of this general type is illustrated in figure **3-27**. A comparable American mill located at New York in 1791 utilized "French Burr Mill Stones." Although John I. Wells did not describe the machinery of his patented mill operated by waterpower at Hartford, Connecticut, about 1809, the capacity of the apparatus is a gauge to its size: "It requires but three gallons of Oil to 112 lbs. White Lead—ground for 112 cents. If desired, can add a portion of Plaister of Paris, which has been frequently the case." Water also may have powered Samuel Ingalls's paint mill at Danbury, Vermont, a few years later.[99]

An early reference to the application of steam power for grinding occurs in a Philadelphia notice of 1798 describing the destruction by fire of a wooden building with its "steam-engine for the purpose of grinding paints." Druggists often used mills for preparing everything from medicines to paints. By 1826 the premises of William Dunlop at New York City was "fitted up with a powerful Steam Engine" for this activity. Elsewhere in the city appraisers described a paint mill at Edward A. Ball's window blind manufactory, which consisted of "One pair Rollers & Machinery" operated by "One Grey Horse (old & Blind)."[100]

Hand-operated paint mills were in use before the Revolution. A notice from 1803 for an "improvement of a Machine or Mill to grind Painters' Colours" noted the ease of the mill's operation: "It grinds with great dispatch, with little exertion of strength." Handmills were popular in New York City, where the estates of three painters contained this equipment. Allen Holcomb, a craftsman of New York State who retailed a grinding apparatus, in 1827 recorded a "premium on 18 paint mills $2 each." Holcomb's sales figures are a testimony to the popularity of the handmill by the early nineteenth century, and other records describe its broad geographic distribution.[101]

Despite its popularity, the paint mill was less common than the paint stone and muller (fig. **3-28**). Specialists relied on stones even when other equipment was available. References in chairmakers' inventories begin in the 1790s and continue for almost a century. Occasionally stones of several sizes appear in a single listing. Some stones are referred to as "flags," identifying the slab material; one was made of marble. The broken stone with its conical muller illustrated in figure 3-28 was used in the Clayton family chair shop at Allentown, New Jersey, beginning about the mid-nineteenth century. A stone used by J. P. Wilder at New Ipswich, New Hampshire, is described as almost 3 feet square and 7 inches thick. The inventory of John Lambert drawn at Philadelphia in 1793 itemizes a complete set of grinding equipment as "1 Paint Stone muller Knife & Brush," the latter possibly for gathering bits of pigment from the pits in the stone's surface. The flexible knife served "to bring the colour scattered over the grinding stone . . . under the muller, or to remove it." Two stones stood on stands in the shop of Ebenezer Knowlton at Boston, and a "Paint Sieve" was part of Silas Cheney's equipment in Connecticut. The sieve separated "bits of straws, fragments of wood, or other foreign bodies" from the "colouring substances."[102]

FIG. 3-27 Horse-powered mill for grinding paints. Broadside advertising sheet, Joseph Emerton, London, ca. 1748. *(Photo: Winterthur Library.)*

FIG. 3-28 Paint stone and muller, New Jersey, used in the Clayton family chair shop at Allentown, Monmouth Co., ca. 1860–70. (Stone) L. 24½", W. 19½", (muller) H. 8", Diam. (base) 5⅛". *(Collection of Monmouth County Historical Association, Freehold, NJ; Photo, Winterthur Museum.)*

A painting manual published at London in 1836 provides directions for the use of hand grinding equipment (fig. 3-32, center top):

> Place upon the stone a small quantity of the colour you are about to grind. . . . The less you grind at a time, the easier will be the process, and the finer the colour. . . . Pour upon it a little of the oil or varnish with which you intend to grind it. . . . Mix the oil and the colour together, then place the muller upon them, and turn it a few times about. If you find there in not oil enough, add a little more, and continue to grind till the colour becomes of the consistence of an ointment. Should the colour spread during the grinding, you must bring it together with your palette-knife. . . . When you have ground it sufficiently fine . . . [and] find the colour completely smooth like butter, without any grittiness, take it off the stone with a palette-knife or spatula, and put it into your pot or pan. . . . Continue grinding in the same manner, till the necessary quantity is ground. It is always desirable to grind, at one time, as much of a colour as is required for the work you have in hand: if you prepare it at intervals, in different quantities, you will often find some difficulty in procuring exactly the same shade or tint. . . . Should any colour happen to be left . . . cover it with water, and deposit it in a cool place.

Silas Cheney ground paint in July 1805 at his cabinet shop in Litchfield, Connecticut. He prepared white lead, Spanish brown, umber, litharge, and verdigris, to which he added "one Paper lamb [lamp] black" and 3⅛ gallons of oil, probably all for house painting. For small jobs Cheney used a "1 quart iron mortar" and "Pestle" purchased at Hartford.[103]

Oil, an essential ingredient of paint, facilitated pigment grinding and thinned the material to the proper consistency for application. Linseed oil, raw or, more commonly, boiled, was preferred. Being "fatty," oils required the addition of drying agents. Rufus Porter in an essay titled "The Art of Painting" directed that litharge and red lead be added to boiling oil and stirred until clear. When preparing white paint, a sulfate of zinc known as white vitriol was required. Boiled oil also was available for purchase at paint shops. The further addition of turpentine to paint, when desirable, prevented "too sharp a gloss" and rendered it "more firm and hard." Prepared by distillation in a still, the volatile liquid was available commercially in several qualities.[104]

Records often list the containers and apparatus employed in paint preparation and storage. For calculating ingredient quantity there were measures, many in sets, some made of "tin." Scales and weights provided finer measurement. A "funnel," "dipper," or "tin scoop" assisted in handling materials, and small and large containers were convenient for storage and marketing. Painting or varnishing was expedited through the use of pots (fig. 3-27), cans, cups, bowls, and dishes. Tin canisters, bottles, jars and jugs, some described as "stone" or "earthen," stored small quantities of paint, varnish, oil, or turpentine. A note directed in 1813 to Silas Cheney by a fellow craftsman of Connecticut states, "I wish you to send by the bearer a Jug of Spts. Terpentine and I will let you have as much." Use of the "paint skins" listed in several documents is explained in a painters' manual of 1836: "Painters and varnishers, who have much business . . . grind . . . quantities of different colours or varnishes, sufficient to serve them for a long while. . . . The best mode of preserving them [is] tied up close in ox or sheep bladders." A cluster of bladders, or skins, hangs at the center top of figure 3-27. Large glass containers stored fluid materials in quantity. The demijohn of figure **3-29** held varnish, japan, turpentine, or oil. The large carboy often contained corrosives, such as "aquafortis" (nitric acid) used in staining. Wickerwork baskets and jackets protected fragile containers from sharp knocks and falling objects. Demijohns enumerated in 1803 in the inventory of Ansel Goodrich at Northampton, Massachusetts, are described "with baskets."[105]

Wooden containers served as storage units for dry, viscous, and wet materials.

FIG. 3-29 Carboy and demijohn, United States, 1825–75. Glass and wickerwork; (*left to right*) H. 21", 15⅝". (*Courtesy, Winterthur Museum, acc. 71.198-.199.*)

A shipping manifest of 1810 describes "one Barrel paint oil" and "one Barrel Spirits Turpentine." A slightly earlier document enumerates "Six Kegs green paint." Casks, tubs, buckets, and pails also served for paint storage (fig. 3-27). Barrels sometimes contained other painting materials, such as rosin and whiting. Small quantities of dry pigment, as used by a decorator, were stored in shop fixtures described as cases or nests of drawers. Jesse Esben's shop near West Chester, Pennsylvania, contained a small painted cabinet with eight 6-inch-square drawers, each labeled with the name of a pigment. Other portable units were described as boxes or trunks. Thomas Boynton of Windsor, Vermont, owned a "Case of Draws & Ornamental Tools" valued at $5 in his estate inventory.[106]

Sources of Painting Supplies
Until near the end of the eighteenth century the principal source of painting materials was Europe. Before 1750 John Humble of New York offered a complete line of pigments and other painter's supplies "just imported from London." His stock included color staples such as red and white lead, Spanish white and brown, Venetian red, English ocher, Prussian blue, verdigris, and umber. Supplementing these materials were gold and silver leaf, brushes and painting tools, white vitriol, and oil. One of Humble's competitors offered materials in bulk: "Paints dry or Ground in Oyl, by the Cask." Paint sellers in Philadelphia were equally active; and even before the Revolution retailers in smaller urban centers, such as Annapolis, could supply the local market.[107]

Following the war there were new emphases in advertising and distribution as some suppliers geared up for volume trade in the expanding backcountry. Many notices were directed in part to rural shopkeepers and artisans. Hugh McDougal, a paint seller of New York, advertised that "Orders from the country . . . shall receive the greatest care and attention, not only with respect to quantity, but a written direction given how to use [materials] to the best advantage." In New England goods flowed inland from Providence, Boston, and lesser ports the size of Norwich, New Haven, and Hartford. Expanding furniture markets also brought increased demand for prepared varnishes—copal, japan, and turpentine. Some dealers made specific note of "Common brown or Chair-Makers Varnish." Many suppliers complied "on the shortest notice" and "in any quantity." John McElwee of Philadelphia mechanized his pigment-grinding operation to handle volume trade by introducing a small steam engine. Cholwell and Summers of New York could offer "4000 gallons of Linseed oil, . . . 5 Tons of dry and ground white lead, in whole, half and quarter casks, 4 Tons of Spanish brown d[itt]o," and other materials in proportion.[108]

House painters and furniture makers with a substantial trade constituted another supply source for craftsmen whose business range was more modest. John B. Jewell of Philadelphia described in a pictorial notice a range of painting supplies, from varnishes to brushes, to meet general needs (fig. 3-30). Large shops often procured raw materials in bulk directly from wholesalers or importers (fig. 3-22). Upon moving from Boston to Vermont in 1812, Thomas Boynton maintained ties with the city by ordering supplies of pigments, some for retail at his new manufactory. His contemporary David Alling of northern New Jersey obtained materials in New York City. Half a century later cabinetmaker Chauncey Strong of rural Otsego County, New York, supplied chairmakers George and Edgar Holcomb with materials, such as boiled oil, varnish, white lead, turpentine, sienna, chrome and French yellow, and rose pink. The death or insolvency of a craftsman in the prime of his career recirculated materials, usually through auction. Chairmakers in Northampton, Massachusetts, had a chance in 1803 to purchase 19 pounds of verdigris, 20 pounds of Spanish white, ⅔ of a barrel of rosin, 48 pounds of gum copal, and 7 papers of lampblack from the estate of Ansel Goodrich. Fourteen years later larger quantities of material were recycled in Philadelphia at Anthony Steel's death: a tub of yellow ocher, a cask

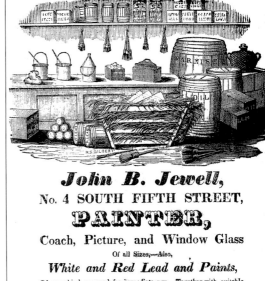

FIG. 3-30 Advertisement of John B. Jewell. From *Desilver's Philadelphia Directory and Stranger's Guide for 1837* (Philadelphia: Robert Desilver, 1837), n. p. *(Winterthur Library.)*

WETHERILL & BROTHERS' *WHITE LEAD MANUFACTORY & CHEMICAL WORKS*

of terrasienna, 43 gallons of linseed oil, 17 gallons of spirits of turpentine, 26 gallons of black japan, 100½ gallons of copal varnish, 154 papers of lampblack, and 2 barrels of gum copal. In the 1830s Benjamin Branson's estate at New York provided painting and gilding tools, bronzes for stenciling, and gold leaf.[109]

During the 1790s Tench Coxe, a leading commentator on American domestic progress, reported that flax cultivation to produce seed for linseed oil was "exceedingly increased" with "oil mills having become more numerous," although domestic supplies by no means met demand. Coxe also noted the presence of ochers, or earth pigments, in Virginia, Connecticut, and other areas and commented that the "patent colours have been imitated with great success." In 1800 chairmaker Lawrence Allwine undertook the manufacture of paint at Philadelphia, "having obtained a Patent from the United States, for a new discovery in the preparation of Paints." The brilliant, durable colors, which dried quickly, were recommended for painting ships, public buildings, and private residences. Allwine continued to sell Windsor chairs "painted with his own patent colours." From these modest beginnings it was possible for James Mease to write within a decade: "Paints of twenty-two different colours, brilliant and durable, are in common use, from native materials. . . . The chromate of lead, that superb yellow colour, is scarcely equalled by any foreign paint."[110]

Tench Coxe also commented about a lead mine in Virginia, although industrial expectations appear to have exceeded reality. The first white lead manufactory in the United States was established in 1809 at Philadelphia by Samuel Wetherill and Son (later Wetherill and Brothers). When the manufactory was completely destroyed by fire about 1812, the works was re-erected, with the addition of "an extensive Chemical laboratory" (fig. **3-31**). Joseph Jones, a chairmaker of Chester County, Pennsylvania, and an aggressive businessman who in 1837 sold woodworking and painting materials, offered "Wetherill's pure white lead by the keg." A second manufactory of white lead established at Philadelphia in 1813 was in the hands of the Lewis family by 1819, when production reached 100 tons annually. In 1830 the firm began the manufacture of linseed oil.[111]

Painting

> Common painting . . . has for its object to produce a uniform and permanent coating upon surfaces, by applying to them a compound, which is more or less opaque. In many cases painting is applied only for ornament, but it is more frequently employed to protect perishable substances from the . . . atmosphere and other decomposing agents.

Previous to the general use of oil paint on seating furniture it was common to introduce inexpensive surface finishes to wood. The options included dyeing, staining, blacking, and coloring. Sometimes a varnish coat followed. The first two terms may at times have been synonymous. Blacking probably refers to rubbing the wood with a dark paste or wax to impregnate the pores. Coloring, the most popular process and one referred to from New England to Philadelphia, is more elusive to define, as it may have identified more than one process. At times the finish was a kind of size coating. A manuscript recipe of unidentified origin dating to about the 1790s and titled "Directions for Making sise for Colouring Chairs, Tables, Desks, Case Draws &c &c &c" describes the process. Ground color of any hue was added to weakened size made of animal-skin parings boiled in water. This was laid on the wood and left to dry. Then full-strength uncolored size was applied, which prevented the final varnish coat from "soaking into the wood." An item dated 1808 in the accounts of Stephanus Knight of Connecticut describes "Painting [coloring] Sizeing and Vernishing 7 common and one grate Chare." Applying ground color in varnish to a wood surface probably also qualified as coloring, although by the 1790s it also might be called japanning.[112]

Most painted seating furniture was primed before the finish was applied. Recipe books direct that greens and blues made of verdigris and Prussian blue be primed with gray. The base for straw color was white "slightly tinged with yellow"; the reds were applied over Spanish brown or a mixture of Spanish brown and red lead. Elijah Eldridge's "receipt" book handwritten at Willington, Connecticut, contains specific directions for priming immediately following a recipe "to paint green" with verdigris: "Take lamp black and white lead made fine. Make a lead color [and] brush this ove[r] the wood once. Then put on the above mentioned paint 2 [twice] over." The purpose of the wood primer was "to fill up the pores, and render the surface smooth."[113]

An early reference to chair priming is found in the accounts of William Gray, a painter of Salem, Massachusetts, who in 1773 charged 8s. for the work. There follows an invoice of knocked-down Windsors shipped by Gillows of Lancashire, England, to Kingston, Jamaica, directing consignees to assemble the chairs before painting. Enclosed was "A little box Conta[ining]: paint & Bruches to paint Do [ditto] over, first Lead Colour & then Green." Chairs described as "primed only" stood in the shops of Francis Trumble and Henry Prall in Philadelphia at their deaths in 1798 and 1802, those of the former designated "oval back" in style. A few years later a dozen primed fan-back chairs were part of the shop stock of Ansel Goodrich at Northampton, Massachusetts. In the early 1800s Silas Cheney of Litchfield, Connecticut, recorded the cost of priming a dozen fancy chair frames as 67¢, while Thomas Boynton's charge for similar work at Windsor, Vermont, was 58¢. Some seating was available with a primer coat only. The purchaser completed the work or specified the finish and decoration. In 1835 William Beesley posted a charge in his accounts for "making & priming a high back Rocking Chr" at his shop in Salem, New Jersey.[114]

Directions for painting published in guides, manuals, encyclopedias, and receipt books of the eighteenth and nineteenth centuries differ little from modern precepts. Because ingredients lacked the homogeneity and stability of present-day materials, the painter was cautioned to mix only what was required for the job at hand and to stir the mixture frequently to "preserve always the same tint." If the mixture thickened, he added oil. To accelerate drying and to prevent blistering, the painter made "the layers as thin as possible," and he allowed each coat to dry thoroughly before applying another. A few colors required only a single coat over the primer, but most called for two. Directions for brush use contained an admonition that the tool not be "overcharge[d] . . . with the colour." As stated in one manual, "The test of the complete workman . . . is to leave no mark of the brush behind him." Weather conditions had to be reckoned with. If cool and damp, a fire was recommended;

otherwise natural air circulation through windows and doors was adequate. Poor drying conditions were responsible for delaying a shipment of Windsor seating from Philadelphia to Boston in June 1795, as noted apologetically by factor Zaccheus Collins to his client.[115]

The brush was the primary painting tool. Period sources describe the head as made of hogs' bristles or the hair of the badger or goat, indicating that the texture could be coarse or fine. The common shape was round (figs. 3-27, 3-30), although by the second quarter of the nineteenth century the flat brush was used in varnishing. Head size in round brushes varied from ¼ inch to 2½ inches. Brush price was determined by size, material, and quality; thus the range was broad — from 7¢ to 75¢. Zadock Hutchins of Pomfret, Connecticut, acquired new brushes at Thomas Walter Ward II's general store. The item "3 bound Brushes" in the inventory of Jacob Fetter, Sr., of Lancaster, Pennsylvania, describes the method of fixing the brush to the stick, or handle. New brushes were best suited for priming; worn ones were preferred for finish work, having become "finer in the points" through use. A workman who regularly employed several paint colors often had brushes for each, or at least some for painting white and others for colors.[116]

Period manuals describe several brush-cleaning methods, starting with wiping the tip with rags followed by water or oil immersion, to cleaning the head with turpentine or washing it in warm water and soap. Two tubs held the brushes of Lodowick Fosdick, a painter of New York City. Rags also kept brush handles clear of oil and paint during use and served to clean the paint stone after mixing color in oil. Rags are specifically identified in two American shops. In the 1790s John Lambert kept a "Green Chest with Cloathes" at Philadelphia, and Boston appraisers found a "Lot old rags" in 1819 on the premises occupied by Benjamin Bass. The twenty-four paintbrushes in Ebenezer Tracy, Sr.'s, estate probated in 1803 in eastern Connecticut suggest the considerable size of his business in painted seating furniture, although that number was modest compared to the more than "60 Brushes Large and small" owned by painting specialist Daniel Rea at Boston.[117]

A painter steadied his work on horses, benches, and tables. The first was unsuited to the chair shop because of the product's size and the interference of stretchers. Benches are delineated clearly in figure 3-32 (top). Probably typical of the trade was the painting equipment in David Alling's chair manufactory at Newark, New Jersey:

> 2 tables in Ornamental Room
> Lot of varnis cans in paint shop
> Lot of paint cups on the shelves
> 1 Keg of Bellvile [probably Bellville on the Passaic River] white lead
> contents on the Bench
> Paint Brushes & Kegs under Bench
> Closets and contents
> . . . .
> 1 High candle stand for paint shop

A trade card for William Buttre's manufactory at New York (fig. **3-32**, top), which depicts three stages in the painting process, illustrates equipment comparable to that described. In the background a workman grinds paint on a stone with a muller, his knife for gathering the color lying nearby. Behind him are a storage jug and a cup to dispense small amounts of pigment and oil. At the left sits the ornamenter, his color cups within easy reach. Stored below the bench are kegs, perhaps containing white lead, as noted in Alling's shop. The workman at the right applies a coat of varnish to the decorated chairs. He dexterously balances one chair leg on a low block or box that permits rotating the chair to any position for fast application of the surface fin-

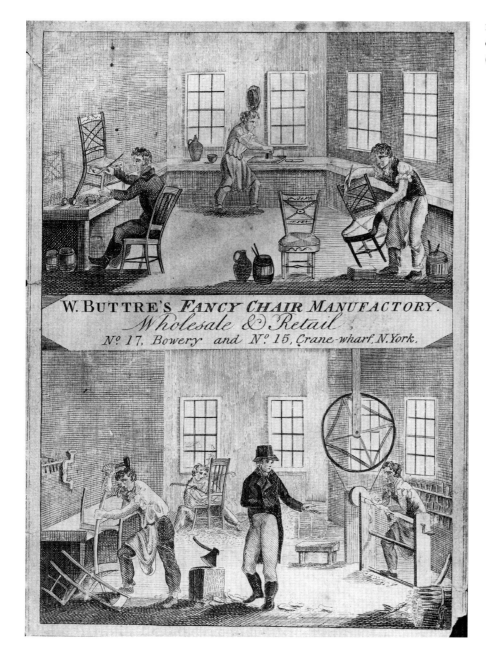

FIG. 3-32 William Buttre trade card, New York, ca. 1813. Engraving; H. 5⅞", w. 4¼" (image). (*Winterthur Library.*)

ish. A trade-card view of James Heaton's shop in New York pictures a similar support the size of a platform. Buttre's round brushes stand in kegs, of which the closest probably contains the coating material.[118]

After being painted, chairs were set aside to dry. In a rural location a clear site out of doors away from road dust served, weather permitting. In the city other solutions were necessary, especially when space was a factor. A detail from Henry J. Megarey's panoramic view of 1849 from the steeple of Saint Paul's Church, New York, pictures buildings along Fulton Street (fig. **3-33**). On the left at the corner of Broadway is Matthew Brady's Daguerrian Miniature Gallery. Several near neighbors were woodworkers, and just out of sight was the establishment of Duncan Phyfe and Son. The tall building right of center labeled "FURNITURE WAREROOMS & MANUFACTORY" housed the chairmakers Daniel and William H. Lee. A close look at the building's roof reveals a group of painted chairs arranged in two rows drying near a covered stairwell. Across the rooftops at the extreme right two chairs stand near a chimney. On the low roof left of the wareroom the presence of several chairs and a long table furnished with a tall bottle and other vessels suggests another use of rooftop space. The general scene is repeated in a daguerrotype dating to about the 1850s: the set-

ting is William Street in New Bedford, Massachusetts. Several low, single or semidetached buildings along the thoroughfare have canopies over the front walkway. One has a second-story porch that supports a row of drying chairs. The signboard on the building facade reads "CHAIR PAINTING" and identifies the establishment of James Scotchler. When promoting his refurbishing services half a century earlier, James Always, a chairmaker of New York, informed the public that he had "good accommodations for drying old chairs, when re-painted."[119]

The absence of significant evidence of payments to workmen for painting new chairs suggests strongly that until the 1820s and the initial movement toward a factory-type system the shop proprietor did most of the work and engaged temporary help as needed. Even during the next quarter century full-time painting specialists probably were limited to large establishments, such as the facility of Lambert Hitchcock in rural Connecticut, the water-powered shops of northern Massachusetts, David Alling's manufactory in New Jersey, and other large urban businesses. Woodworking apprentice Edward Jenner Carpenter noted in Massachusetts that his masters called in a painter-decorator only upon occasion. Many specialists jobbed around at several shops and spent their remaining free time at a related trade or at farming. In his study of central New Jersey chairmaking, William H. MacDonald found that even after 1850 rural craftsmen stockpiled chairs for the painter-decorator's periodic visit. Sometimes chairmakers sold portions of their stock "in the wood" to painters who finished the work and retailed the product on their own accounts. A good example is Jacob Felton of Fitzwilliam, New Hampshire, who supplied unpainted chairs to George Lyman Miller of Boston. An unusual insight from the accounts of Samuel Douglas of Connecticut describes how a shop proprietor even provided "instructions in Painting" to a lay customer for a fee.[120]

Aaron P. Cleveland was a part-time painter for Elisha Hawley of Ridgefield, Connecticut, in October 1788 when he ground pigment and painted chairs. Cleveland's skills ranged further, since he framed chairs, made parts, and felled timber. Some years later Edward Shepard occasionally spent a day painting chairs at Solomon Cole's shop at Glastonbury near Hartford as a complement to his own extensive woodworking activity. Allen Holcomb sometimes supported himself by painting and ornamenting chairs during an itinerancy before settling in Otsego County, New York. He spent parts of the years 1809 and 1810 working for Simon Smith in Troy. His painting accounts document the range of Smith's seating production: dining, bamboo, fancy, cabin (for Hudson River vessels), common, cross-back, spindle-back, and bell-seat chairs. Silas Cheney's records describe a full circle of activity by temporary workmen at Litchfield, Connecticut, including priming, painting, ornamenting, and varnishing. At Newark, New Jersey, from 1815 to 1817 David Alling employed painter Moses Lyon. Records of Lyon's ornamental work serve to identify Alling's production of patterns and special features associated with chairmaking at New York in the early 1800s: slat, ball, cross, double-cross, and wide-top (Baltimore) backs (figs. 3-49, 3-47; pl. 1; fig. 3-45); plain, organ, oval, and flat ("arrow") spindles (figs. 3-41, 3-49); and bamboo-pattern chairs (fig. 3-35).[121]

Records shedding light on what it cost to newly paint a chair are limited, although there are many figures for repainting. The basic problem is identifying the number of coats applied per unit in order to correctly interpret the data. Most figures refer to the side chair, and a general tabulation ranges from 2¢ to 33⅓¢. Undoubtedly figures at the high end include ornamenting. Fortunately some records contain precise data, and the consistent nature of the information suggests the figures are reliable. Putting one coat of paint on a chair cost from 2¢ to about 5½¢, materials excluded. In interpreting the price range it is necessary to recognize the ease and speed of priming compared to applying a basic coat of pigment or the more difficult finish coat. Another consideration is whether chairs were "common" or "fancy." One coat on the former cost Simon Smith 2¢ about 1809 at Troy, New York; Philemon Robbins of Hartford quoted 3¢ in 1834. Single coats on Windsor chairs usually fell into the 3¢ to 4¢ range. Some records mention as many as three coats on a single chair. Another reliable information source is the manuscript "Book of Prices" for cabinetwork and chairwork compiled in 1838 by James C. Helme of Luzerne County, Pennsylvania. Under the heading "Prices for painting & ornamenting chairs" Helme recorded: "For preparing Common Chairs for ornamenting, any required Colour, per half dozen 50[¢]." This works out to 8⅓¢ per chair, although because the surface was readied for ornamenting, both a priming coat and one or more finish coats were applied to the wood. The figure corroborates the others. In apportioning the cost, 2¢ to 3¢ could be assigned to priming and 5⅓¢ to 6⅓¢ to the finish coats.[122]

ORNAMENTATION

The classical revival of the late eighteenth century was responsible for rekindling an interest in ornamenting formal furniture with paint, a decorative technique that had fallen from favor with the passing of japanwork. Generally responsible for this resurgence was Robert Adam, and his commissions for important English clients in 1758 followed his return from study in Rome. So important was the use of painted decoration by the 1790s that Thomas Sheraton saw fit to provide an "accompaniment" to his *Drawing Book* (1791–94) containing "A Variety of Ornaments Useful for Learners to Copy from, but Particularly Adapted to the Cabinet and Chair Branches." American artisans and consumers kept abreast of English developments through furniture importation, the circulation of design books and drawings, and regular transatlantic communication. It was no coincidence that by 1795 John DeWitt and Walter Mac-Bride, Windsor-chair makers of New York, advertised seating furniture "japanned any colour and neatly flowered" or that in 1800 Lawrence Allwine of Philadelphia made "the best windsor chairs, gilt, plain, and variously ornamented." The lucrative export trade from Philadelphia to the South and the Caribbean islands offered both "ornamented" and "common" painted seating to suit the pocketbooks of all purchasers.[123]

With new emphasis on ornament to enhance painted seating, the specialties of chairmaker and ornamental painter often were combined. Barring that circumstance, the chairmaker employed a painting specialist on a full-time or part-time basis as his business warranted. Another convenient arrangement was the partnership enterprise uniting the two specialties. The independent specialist also could purchase seating "in the wood" from area chairmakers to finish and retail on his own account. Representing the epitome of the multifunctional shop was the establishment at Baltimore of John and Hugh Finlay. The brothers' notice of November 8, 1805, amply demonstrates the broad level of expertise realized by a small number of farsighted entrepreneurs:

> CANE SEAT CHAIRS, SOFAS, RECESS, and WINDOW SEATS of every description and all colors, gilt, ornamented and varnished . . . with real Views, Fancy Landscapes, Flowers, Trophies of Music, War, Husbandry, Love &c. &c. Also, A number of new pattern Rush and Windsor Chairs and Settees; Card, Tea, Peir [sic], Writing and Dressing Tables, with Mahogany, Satin-Wood, Painted, Japanned and real Marble Top Sideboards; Ladies' Work, Wash-Stand and Candle Stands; Horse Pole, Candle and Fire Screens; Bed and Window Cornices, the centers enriched with Gold and Painted Fruit, Scroll and Flower Borders of entire new patterns, the mouldings in Japan, Oil and Burnish Gold, with Beads, Twists, Nelson Balls, &c. Likewise Brackets, Girandoles and Try-pods; Ladies' Needle Work, Pictures and Looking Glass Frames; old Frames Regilt; real Views taken on the spot to any dimension, in oil or watercolors; Coach, Flag and Masonic Painting; and particular attention paid to Gold Sign Lettering on Glass, Pannel or Metal.

Apprenticeship records indicate that during the early 1800s the Finlays trained a significant number of young men. Each contract had specific provisions, citing either a specialty in construction or some aspect of finish work, and the progressive youth could familiarize himself with all aspects of the trade before completing his training. Another way of gaining skill in ornamenting was through instruction at a drawing school, the method used by Christian Nestell of New York (fig. 3-42).[124]

By no means were the combined skills of chairmaker and ornamental painter limited during the early 1800s to urban artisans. A growing number of craftsmen in small prosperous regional centers and on the expanding frontier also met the challenges of the changing times. At Northampton, Massachusetts, Luther Davis took great pains "to make the most fashionable kind" of fancy and Windsor chairs and "to gild and ornament them in a neat manner." John Priest of Nashville, Tennessee, also advertised his multiple consumer services. Nor were craft skills limited to new work. The business of refurbishing used furniture was just as extensive. Typical is a notice of 1816 for Joel Brown, who reminded patrons at Raleigh, North Carolina, that he stood ready to "paint and ornament old chairs with Gold, or ornament them to direction." Some craftsmen addressed consumer concern over wear and tear to painted furniture during transport and, like Thomas Henning, Sr., of Lewisburg, West Virginia, recommended painting chairs "where they are to be used." Joel Brown also suggested that he "paint and ornament" chairs on site "so as to suit the rooms" they were to furnish. Apparently holding to the theory that the longer the hauling distance the greater the opportunity for damage, Dockum and Brown of Portsmouth, New Hampshire, importers of Boston chairs, advertised in 1827: "Just received 1000 chairs of various kinds and colours, painted and gilded in this town, by the first rate workmen from Boston."[125]

The cost of ornamenting a chair, or "garnishing" as described in one document, varied from a few cents for picking out grooves in bamboowork to $1.25 for examples with elaborate gilding and bronze-stenciled decoration. James Helme's manuscript book of prices itemizing labor costs in 1838 provides data about price structure in central Pennsylvania, although it is unclear who supplied the materials—presumably the employer. Decorating a Windsor with standard ornament, which involved more than merely coloring grooves, cost 6¼¢ per chair for the straight-back pattern (pl. 4). Bent-backs cost 8⅓¢ apiece because the shaved back posts required special attention (fig. 3-41). Chairs with single mid slats appear to have been similarly priced, but the addition of another cross slat in combination with the roll top advanced the workman's pay by about half a cent a chair. The fancy, or "Stump Back," chair cost the most to decorate, and individual units brought the workman 13½¢. Ornamental settee work was comparable to "6 chairs of the same description." The Helme price book indicates that a varnish coat was considered an integral part of ornamental work. A single application of varnish to a Windsor added about 2¢ to production costs. By contrast, the rate for varnishing a fancy chair equaled that of ornamenting, an indication that the seating received several coats of varnish or colored japan. Within any price structure there likely existed a sliding scale of charges. In a notice published at Chambersburg in 1832 John Denig gave prices for both "gilt" and "Ornamented" chairs of first, second, and third quality.[126]

Striping

The use of fine to broad lines to ornament or accent painted furniture probably constituted the first decorative treatment on Windsor seating. The bamboo turning with its gouge-formed grooves encouraged the use of contrasting color to heighten the effect of the rhythmic divisions. The bold simplicity of this technique is well demonstrated in the portrait *Child Seated in Bamboo Chair* (fig. **3-34**), which also has a striped seat. Thomas Sheraton hinted at the broad popularity of striping by 1803 when commenting in his *Cabinet Dictionary*, "Black chairs look well when ornamented with yellow lines." Thomas Jefferson ordered black chairs with "yellow rings" for his country place near Lynchburg, Virginia, in 1809 as he left the presidency (fig. 5-24). Other colors were just as popular. In the well-known watercolor drawing *Schoolmaster and Boys* the instructor's brick red bow-back chair is striped with yellow. Painters generally ornamented the grooves of bow faces as well. *Striping* was the generic name for the technique; other terms were less common. When ordering Windsors in 1792 for his summer place at Black Point on the Jersey coast, William Bingham instructed that they be painted yellow and "picked out with green." Amos Denison Allen of eastern Connecticut referred to the technique as "edging" and recorded blue, yellow, and black Windsor seating decorated in this manner. Painter Daniel Rea of Boston called the process "creasing" on one occasion but generally used the term "striping."[127]

At first encounter the word *tipping* suggests post-top embellishment in square-back patterns with shaved pillars. The item "Bamboo Chairs painted Mahogany & tipt" from a 1789 invoice of Windsor furniture constructed by Francis Trumble at Philadelphia, long before the shaved-post style was current, identifies the word as an alternative term for striping. The reference may identify the fine tip of the small hair brush used to execute the decoration. "Tipping" was still used as late as 1809, as documented at Schenectady, New York. Over a broad area the ornamental process was described by still another term—*penciling*, a word again springing from the fine hair brush, or pencil, used to execute the decoration. This indispensable tool was made of camel's hair, badger's hair, or "any fine hairs enchased in the pipes of quills of all sizes." Hair length varied from ½ inch to more than 2 inches, depending on the breadth of line required. A painter and glazier of Philadelphia imported this item in 1750. Half a century later appraisers in New York found "6 gro Camels Hair Pencils" on the premises of painter Kenneth McKenzie, which they valued at $15. Allen Holcomb of Otsego County, New York, sold a single brush in 1819 for 12½¢. The same year E. I. du Pont of Wilmington, Delaware, paid chairmaker Jared Chesnut for "painting and penseling 13 fancy winsor chairs." The practice had expanded to include the fine lines that mark some spindle faces (fig. 3-41; pl. 8) and subtly define large and small panels on the crests, posts, banisters, and other elements of fancy and Windsor seating (pls. 2, 6, 17, 20). Sheraton indicates that fine striping was intended initially to simulate inlay, and indeed Solomon Cole of Glastonbury, Connecticut, referred in his accounts for 1804 to "6 fanback Chairs strung." Cole striped

FIG. 3-34 William M. S. Doyle, *Child Seated in Bamboo Chair*, Massachusetts, 1825. Pastel on paper; H. 30", W. 24". *(Former collection of Edgar William and Bernice Chrysler Garbisch.)*

FIG. 3-35 Square-back Windsor side chair (one of three), probably Portland, Maine, 1810–20. H. 35¼", (seat) 18¼", w. (crest) 19¾", (seat) 16⅞", D. (seat) 15¼"; pale mustard beige ground with black and orange red. *(Collections of Maine Historical Society, Wadsworth-Longfellow House; Photo, Winterthur Museum.)*

FIG. 3-36 Anonymous, *Agnes Ackerman*, New Jersey, probably Bergan Co., ca. 1814–15. Pen and watercolor on paper; H. 9", W. 7". *(Philadelphia Museum of Art: The Collection of Edgar William and Bernice Chrysler Garbisch, 1967, acc. 1967-268-10.)*

yellow chairs with green or blue. Other documents describe yellow, white, or black lines on a green ground; yellow, green, blue, or black on white; and of course yellow on black.[128]

For most craftsmen "striping" described the entire process of ornamenting with lines, whether narrow or broad, in grooves or on flat surfaces, or with special embellishments. A square-back bamboo-turned Windsor, one of three from Maine, has unusual striped decoration executed in black on a pale mustard ground (fig. **3-35**). Flanking the painted grooves are single rows of dots further accented adjacent to the creases by a pale, transparent (and worn) orange red band. One is visible near the right end of the lower cross rod. Complementing the bands in color and accent are inverted teardrop motifs on the back posts, cross rods, and lower front legs. This ornament occurs on another chair from Maine labeled by Daniel Stewart. Of similar plan is the sparing use of a leafy motif, similar to that on the square-back Windsor of figure **3-36**.[129]

As the early bamboo style faded, ornamenters employed stripes and bands of varied width in new and different ways: to emphasize vertical or horizontal patterns, to accent a special feature such as a seat-front projection, to simulate reeding, to define panels, or to lighten bulky forms (pls. 7, 14–16; fig. 3-45). Striping often occurred alone as an economical way of producing attractive furniture, whether a chair or a dressing table (fig. 5-56). Striping also had its fashion in other work. Wagons, coaches, and sleighs were striped and otherwise embellished. Thomas Boynton of Windsor, Vermont, even recorded "painting & Pencilling [a] store front." Thomas Sheraton, in describing the square-tipped striping pencil, advised mixing paint pigment in turpentine to the consistency of a paste and then diluting the color with a copal varnish only to the point that the paint began to run freely from the brush. Using the forefinger as a guide along "some straight angle of the work" and holding the pencil between the thumb and first finger, the decorator drew the brush "steadily along." Most authorities cautioned that lines be drawn "with freedom and decision, rather quickly" for best results. Different brush lengths and varying hand pressure determined line breadth. For fine penciling the painter could bring the pencil tip to a point on a flat stone or other surface. In the early 1800s Titus Preston of Wallingford, Connecticut, recorded an embellished variant of the fine line when ornamenting half a dozen green dining (side) chairs, "the striping . . . to be a vine on the front of the bow & legs." Whether the "vine" was merely a wavy line (pl. 1) or decoration relating to that of figure **3-37** is unknown. Preston's note illuminates the flexibility of choice in bespoke work, however, even when the basic product was in the popular domain.[130]

Freehand Decoration

EARLY ORNAMENT

Hand-painted ornament comprising stylized forms drawn from nature, especially blossoms, leaves, and fruits, was first employed on Windsor seating about the turn of the nineteenth century. The "neatly flowered" Windsors made in 1795 by Walter MacBride and John DeWitt are, perhaps, the earliest examples recorded, although their appearance is conjectural. The ornament was simple, given the surface limitations of the round-back style. Figures 3-36 and 3-37 suggest the types of motifs identified. It is worth noting that MacBride and DeWitt also employed the term *japanned* when speaking of "flowered" work. The new decoration likely was a simplification of the high-style japanwork current earlier in the century, as described in 1735 by the ornamental painter Gerardus Duyckinck I: "Lookin-glasses [*sic*] new Silvered and the Frames plain Japan'd or Flowered." Japanning with colored varnishes was current again by 1800, as indicated by Thomas Sheraton, who included a section on "Japanning Window Cornices" in his *Cabinet Dictionary* (1803) and remarked that the usual ornament consisted of "leaves and some kind of trophy, or flowers." The word *flowered* continued in use at least through the following decade. In 1812 a shopkeeper of New Bedford, Massachusetts, offered New York merchandise, including "1 set (of 8) light coloured and flowered sitting Chairs, at a reasonable price."[131]

At least two other words—*figured* and *sprigged*—were alternative terms in the early years of chair ornamentation to describe "flowered" decoration. Both likely originated in the vocabulary of the textile trade. Esther Singleton cites a New York notice of 1808 for chairs "plain and figured." Later, appraisers in New Jersey and Connecticut described "Green figured setting chairs" and "Fig'd dining Chairs." The backs were square. In 1822 "Figured Chairs" painted yellow furnished a household in Chester County, Pennsylvania. Early in the century Silas Cheney had "Sprigged" dining and other chairs at Litchfield, Connecticut. Supplementing the decorative treatments illustrated in figures 3-36 and 3-37 was a larger leaf-and-vine pattern spaced along the faces of both vertical and horizontal members or spiraled up the posts. Another option was the delicate pendent (or upright) vine. A set of fancy chairs with this decoration also contains a crossed-frond motif, as illustrated on the seat front of figure 3-41. This ornament appears to be associated with Boston work.[132]

NEOCLASSICAL DESIGNS

Linked directly with the federal period is ornament of classical orientation, that is, delicate fronds forming guilloche and lattice patterns, drooping vines simulating willow, and swags or drapery with pendent tassels. A harp, urn, or cornucopia sometimes provides a focal point. Some motifs became highly stylized (figs. **3-38**, **3-39**). The illustrated chairs have painted mustard grounds in medium to light hues. The armchair with its companion side chairs forms a set of eight. The white pine seats and late use of the H-plan bracing system suggest an upstate New York or western New England (Massachusetts or Vermont) origin. The side chair of figure 3-39 is one of a suite of six chairs, including a rocking side chair. On the basis of a Holyoke family history associated with a similar chair, now stripped of paint, the set is identified with the Connecticut River Valley in Massachusetts. The penciled work combines black and dark brown, and the primary motifs are brightly painted.

FIG. 3-37 Frederick W. Mayhew, *Mrs. John Harrison and Daughter*, New England, ca. 1823. Oil on canvas; H. 30", W. 24⅞". *(Gift of Edgar William and Bernice Chrysler Garbisch, Image © 2004 Board of Trustees, National Gallery of Art, Washington, acc. 1980.62.17.)*

FIG. 3-38 (left) Slat-back Windsor armchair (one of eight with side chairs), eastern New York State, Vermont, or western Massachusetts, 1810–20. White pine (seat, microanalysis); H. 34½", (seat) 17⅝", W. (crest) 17¾", (arms) 20¾", (seat) 17¾", D. (seat) 15⅝"; medium mustard yellow ground with medium dark green, medium red, and black. *(Private collection; Photo, Winterthur Museum.)*

FIG. 3-39 Tablet-top Windsor side chair (one of six, including a rocking chair), Connecticut Valley in Massachusetts, 1820–30. Basswood (seat, microanalysis); H. 32¼", (seat) 18½", W. (crest) 17¾", (seat) 15⅝", D. (seat) 13"; light mustard yellow ground with black, dark brown, green, red, and mustard. *(Collection of Historic Deerfield, Inc., Deerfield, Mass.; Photo, Winterthur Museum.)*

Construction and Design 167

The trophy, an ornament associated with classical design, accented the crests of some painted chairs and settees in the early 1800s. These compositions, consisting of objects related in use or association, had a long history in Europe, where they appeared in architecture and on maps, prints, ceramics, and textiles. Trophies were popular with Baltimore ornamenters. The Finlay brothers advertised compositions on themes of music, war, husbandry, and love. Plate 1, a detail of a New York chair, reproduces a military trophy with cannon, furled banners, and a drum.[133]

LANDSCAPES

The painted landscape panel was another ornament popular in Baltimore. The Finlays' "Fancy Landscapes" and "Real Views" of area architecture advertised in 1805 were augmented in the trade by subjects that varied from romantic ruins to seascapes and riverscapes, from town views to rural farm buildings and even to scenes containing wild animals (pls. 3, 27). Some scenes were inspired by European prints and book illustrations (fig. **3-40**). The incidence of furniture with painted views was of consequence in the Middle Atlantic region, where known examples represent the work of artisans from Baltimore, rural Maryland, southern Pennsylvania, and New York City and State. Edward Needles still advertised seating with "Landscape . . . Tops" at Baltimore in 1830, and some dozen years earlier two New York firms retailed a similar product. Interest spread to New England, as indicated in a suite of six side chairs and a washstand bearing scenes of a semirural community, and to Ohio by 1816 when Thomas Renshaw carried the Baltimore style to Chillicothe. Baltimore influence also is present in the painted landscape on the crest of a Windsor in the home of Maria Rex Zimmerman at Schaefferstown, Pennsylvania (pl. 4). In structure the chair follows an eastern Pennsylvania pattern (figs. 3-56, 5-11). In surveying the full spectrum of views on painted furniture, it is evident that the work reflects a broad range of talent, varying from the skill of the academic painter to that of the sophisticated ornamenter (pl. 27) and popular practioner (pl. 3).[134]

THE GRAPE AND GRAPEVINE

The grape and grapevine as furniture motifs were current before 1810, being first associated with the double-rod-and-medallion pattern (fig. 5-28, left foreground), and interest continued for several decades. The side chair in figure **3-41**, with its simple yet direct ornament, probably originated in Boston, the city where craftsmen first developed the stepped-tablet top. The central sprig bearing fruits and leaves appears sufficiently stylized to represent the hand of a decorator of individual talent rather than one working within an ornamental school. The interpretation stands midway between a flat decorative style and a natural subject rendering. The accompaniments are typical of the period: the abstract floweret in the crest corners; the meandering vine on the posts; the crossed fronds of Boston origin at the seat front; and the accent lines on the spindle faces, crest, and seat.

David Alling confirmed use of the grape motif in the area of Newark/New York by 1816–17 when he identified chairs ornamented with "Grapes," sometimes in "Nat[ural] Coll[or]." He further recorded decoration of "Fruit" and "Peaches." Expanded versions of the grape motif were popular in the 1820s. Philemon Robbins of Hartford identified the pattern as "grape bush" in the following decade, and he used it to ornament chairs, washstands, and dressing tables, some forming suites. In general the fruit is clustered at the composition center flanked by leaves and wispy tendrils (fig. 3-55). The fruits themselves often are formed by painting through a stencil in color or bronze (as opposed to using powders), while the leaves and tendrils frequently are products of quick, freehand brushstrokes. Because many hands interpreted the motif, spatial organization varies from panels with rectangular, hollow-cornered, or compartmentalized borders to undefined crest surfaces. The grape motif was particularly popular in Massachusetts, which influenced the work of New Hampshire and Maine. In a distinctive interpretation, pendent fruit clusters often fill the flat spindles of ribbon-end-pattern chairs from Maine (pl. 3).[135]

FLORAL AND FRUIT DESIGNS

The most common hand-painted decoration on popularly priced furniture was the floral form; fruit motifs were a second substantial focus. Patterns varied markedly in size, organization, stylization, quality, and specific motif. The first Windsor patterns with surfaces adequate for developing this work were the narrow slat- and tablet-style crests introduced just before the War of 1812. David Alling made note at Newark, New Jersey, in 1817 of a "Flower" design painted on twelve slat-back chairs by workman Moses Lyon. A simple motif often encountered on crests, midback slats, roll tops, and casings of rush-seated chairs is a long narrow horizontal leaf band (pl. 2, mid slat). Both Jacob Maentel and Lewis Miller favored this ornament in their drawings of Pennsylvania subjects (fig. 5-3). A pattern variation substitutes a thick, often undulating, vine. Asahel Powers used a simpler motif in the 1830s when portraying seated Vermont subjects.[136]

Leafy guilloche bands are unusual on Windsor furniture, probably because the fashion was brief and early nineteenth-century chairs with original decoration are uncommon. Nevertheless the motif is important in the vocabulary of painted ornament because of its relationship to high-style design. Two New York chairs made in the early 1810s are enhanced by these continuous interlaced bands (pls. 5, crest, and 11, back posts). At precisely the date of their construction a young apprentice named Christian M. Nestell, a student at an unidentified city drawing school, copied a similar design in his notebook (fig. 3-42). The page bears complete documentation,

FIG. 3-41 Shaped-tablet-top Windsor side chair (one of three), probably Boston, ca. 1812–20. White pine (seat, microanalysis); H. 33½", (seat) 17⅞", W. (crest) 17¾", (seat) 15", D. (seat) 15⅛"; pale mustard orange ground with brown and dark green. *(Private collection; Photo, Winterthur Museum.)*

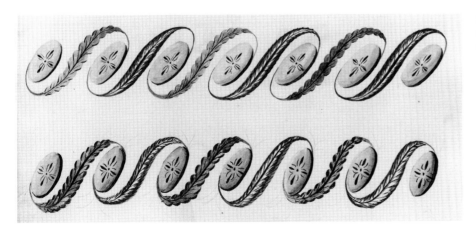

FIG. 3-42 Neoclassical design for a border, Christian M. Nestell drawing/copybook, New York, 1811–12. *(Winterthur Library.)*

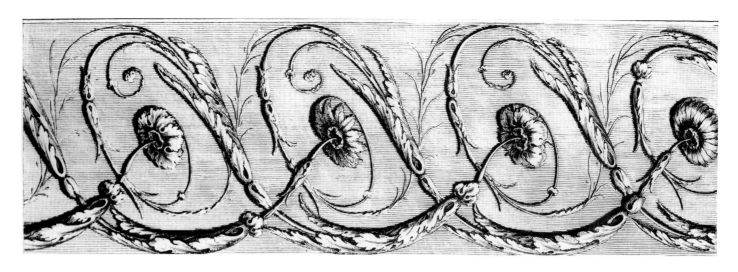

FIG. 3-43 Neoclassical design for a border. From
Thomas Sheraton, *The Cabinet-Maker and
Upholsterer's Drawing-Book* (London: T. Bensley
et al., 1793), accompaniment, pl. 3 (center).
(Winterthur Library.)

comprising date, place, and ownership. Related ornament, painted or inlaid, was
promoted by Thomas Sheraton, who in a special "Accompaniment" to his *Drawing
Book* of 1793 included a guilloche band on a page titled "BORDERS FOR PIER TABLES"
(fig. **3-43**).

Sometime after completing his training, Christian Nestell moved to Providence,
Rhode Island, where beginning about 1820 he specialized in ornamental painting.
An advertisement of 1822 for his "Chair Ware Room" identifies his *fancy* seating
stock of "Newark make." In a telling statement Nestell said of the chairs, "they excell
in finish those made in New York," identifying the painted products of that urban
center as the standard by which ornamental work was measured in the Northeast
(pls. 1, 5, 11, 12). As Nestell gave no indication that his "Windsor . . . Chairs . . . of the
newest patterns" were imported, he probably purchased them locally in the wood or
supervised their construction in his shop, then painted them himself. The decoration of labeled Nestell chairs does not equal the quality of New York work; however,
the craftsman retailed his Windsors "upon the very lowest terms" and, except for
bespoken work, basic ornament had to suffice. Nestell's known decoration, comprising several large motifs forming a central feature, represents still another floral composition found on Windsor furniture. The drawing book does not illustrate
the design, but then the volume dates a decade earlier. Related decoration usually
combines large leaves and a centered blossom or two (pl. 2), centered fruit, such as
a bunch of grapes (fig. 3-55), or occasionally a small animal or abstract motif. Artist Ammi Phillips depicted large, bold decoration on the backs of his sitters' chairs.
Sometimes he painted crossed feathers, a motif recorded in 1815 at Windsor, Vermont, by Thomas Boynton in the note "Ornamenting feathers." Phillips was more
partial to botanical specimens, however, especially the oak leaf, which appears on
many of his works.[137]

Another class of ornament clusters more delicate compositions of foliage and
blossoms, sometimes fruit, to form a central focus. A well-balanced and particularly
graceful design occurs in a Pennsylvania chair (pl. 6). A second regional example
simplifies the decoration to a floral sprig and introduces naturalistic blossoms (pl. 7).
Sometimes the decoration is expanded to fill most of a well-defined panel. Leaves
and floral forms predominate, although there are designs with fruits and, occasionally, vegetables. The crest of a New England rocking chair features a selection of
fruits, including cherries, grapes, peaches, and a pear painted in earth tones touched
with blue and orange red in a composition of distinctive style (pl. 8). Several crests
display a central bowl or basket of fruit. Two unusual designs of this type are illustrated in plates 9 and 10. The first, muted in tone and delicate in execution, makes
effective use of a tan and black grained ground as a contrast to bright red cherries
on wispy vines emanating from a small basket, green leaves and stripes, and yellow

FIG. 3-44 Detail of crest of slat-back Windsor side chair (one of six), southern central Pennsylvania, 1825–35. Green ground. *(Photo, Gail Savage.)*

penciling. The second capitalizes on a medium gray background to present a footed dish supporting fruits and leaves painted in a bright palette that would be gaudy in another context. Figure **3-44**, bold and direct in its brushwork on a green ground, introduces to the central basket a stacked base that appears to be inspired by the flat wreath of twisted silks used beneath a crest in heraldry.

Floral decoration covering most or all of the flat surface it ornaments forms a substantial seating group. Banding when it occurs defines only the outer perimeters of the slat or tablet. This type of decoration appeared relatively early and was inter-regional. A particularly sensitive rendering of the fully decorated slat appears in a New York chair whose white ground lends brilliance to coral red and green decoration (pl. 11). The design's primary motif, a flattened, dotted abstract form, links wavy vines bearing paired leaves that alternate with sylized blossoms. A guilloche band is represented not as a central feature but as a delicate stripe down the face of either post.

A second New York chair balances clustered ornament in a roll top with extended ornament in a cross banister (pl. 12). Although the banister motifs exhibit the same delicate flowing quality of the decoration in plate 11, the ornamenter has substituted two boldly rendered peaches as the primary motif. The yellow ground further accents the composition. Of related motif is the central-panel decoration in the crest of a tablet-top chair of New England origin (pl. 13). Depicting what appears to be two peaches flanked by leaves, the ornamenter has suspended both motifs from an undulating leafy vine, creating a small composition of quite different character. A cream-color ground enhances the decoration. In sharp contrast to these decorative schemes is the dense decoration of grapes and leaves on a cream-color ground that fills the tablet top of a Pennsylvania chair ornamented in rich browns and green balanced by monochromatic grays and bronze banding (fig. **3-45**).[138]

A vigorous floral-type decoration that embellishes equally bold profiles is characteristic of some Pennsylvania-area production from the 1840s and later. Heavy shouldered tablets, often with scallops, projections, and notches, complemented by baluster-shape splats of rounded or angular form, sometimes pierced, require bold banding, lavish gilding, and ornament-filled surfaces to achieve visual balance. The variation is endless. Figure **3-46** with its extensive use of gilding and a sawed rippling effect across the top of the crest is a particularly distinguished example. The tea-colored ground and painted decoration in white and pale yellow are sharply accented by heavy black banding and touches of dark green and coral red in the ornament.

Another Pennsylvania seating group, represented by plate 14, makes effective use of solids and voids defined by heavy banding and accented by modest gilt ornament. Modifying the bold elements of the design are precise flowing floral forms executed in bronze and punctuated by spots of bright red. Innumerable sets of richly ornamented chairs have emerged from homes in central Pennsylvania over the past three-quarters of a century, and the quantity in the marketplace in recent decades has been substantial. Many surfaces are so pristine they appear to have been painted over when in fact they are original. Used in the "best" parlor, which was opened only

FIG. 3-45 Tablet-top Windsor side chair, Pennsylvania, 1830–40. H. 32¾", (seat) 17½", W. (crest) 17⅝", (seat) 15½", D. (seat) 14¼"; cream ground with bronze, gray brown, shaded copper to medium brown, gray, dark green, and black. *(Collection of Harry B. Hartman; Photo, Winterthur Museum.)*

FIG. 3-46 Shaped and scalloped tablet-top Windsor side chair (one of six), central Pennsylvania, possibly Union or Snyder counties, 1855–75. H. 31¾", (seat) 16⅞", w. (crest) 16¼", (seat) 16⅞", D. (seat) 14"; taupe ground with black, medium green, coral red, and gilt (over white). *(Private collection; Photo, Winterthur Museum.)*

FIG. 3-47 Slat-back Windsor armchair (one of four with side chairs), New York, 1815–25. H. 33¾"; black and red grained ground with yellow and green. *(Photo, Nathan Liverant and Son.)*

on special family occasions or for distinguished guests, the furniture was subject to restricted use, and it was decidedly off-limits to juvenile members of the household. When the fashion passed, these relics of former days were relegated to attics and other storage places and thus preserved. Before the Civil War a new manner of decoration gained popularity. Penciling frequently replaced banding, gilded ornament became light and delicate, and floral forms were drawn, colored, and shaded to approximate nature.

SHELLS

Conchological motifs were part of the vocabulary of ornamental design from an early date. The strong interest in shells as decoration in the neoclassical period was a result perhaps of the popularity in Europe of collecting exotic specimens as a pastime. Interest spread to America, where importers offered an interested public "shells from the Pacific Ocean." New England stepped-tablet chairs of the 1810s exhibit some of the first conch shells in American painted furniture. In 1815 Thomas Boynton, a chairmaker of Windsor, Vermont, spoke of ornamenting with shell motifs at his manufactory, and shell-decorated New Hampshire chairs are contemporary. Representing the period from the 1820s to the 1850s are chairs with plain and arched slats, tablet and roll tops, and the shouldered Pennsylvania crest. Sometimes the conch is accompanied by wispy or flowing leafage suggestive of seaweed. At other times the surround consists of broad leaves and even grapelike tendrils. Of naturalistic rendering is the conch on a bed of curling leaves in the crest of plate 15, adorning a New England rocking chair probably of southern New Hampshire origin because of its similarity to the work of Thomas Atwood of Bedford. The coquelicot ground, now dulled with aged varnish, was once a brilliant poppy red. The upright leafy stalks embellishing the spindles and posts ripple with movement suggestive of sea currents interacting with underwater plant life.[139]

Contemporary in date is a chair of New York origin with shell decoration in the crest painted on a vigorously streaked simulated-wood ground (fig. **3-47**). The univalve, probably of the genus *Murex*, relates to that in plate 15, with its spiral top and egg-shape body, although the interpretation here is much bolder and the flanking elongated leaves are curled over at the tips. The shell also is related to one depicted in the drawing book kept by young Christian Nestell in 1811–12 when he attended an unidentified drawing school in New York City (fig. **3-48**). That volume is a compendium of design motifs current in the early nineteenth century. Of entirely different character are the conch shells adorning the ribbon-end crown-type crest of a northeastern New England chair, probably from Maine (pl. 16). These whimsical motifs on a striking blue-green ground banded with brown could almost pass as confectioner's fantasies. The bellflower pendants of the flat spindles, although unusual, appear on other Maine work.[140]

THE CORNUCOPIA

The cornucopia is rare in hand-painted chair decoration, although it was a popular motif with the stencilers. A design of paired cornucopias with floral forms is part of the Nestell drawing book. A colorful interpretation appears on the New York chair illustrated in plate 17. Like other work of that city dating to the 1810s, the decoration is striking. Bronze work, such as that forming the central ribbon and the leafage, was also part of the decorative vocabulary at Newark across New York Bay. On October 13, 1817, David Alling recorded that his ornamenter, Moses Lyon, had completed "[Bronzing] 12 Wide Tops & Scroll Backs (Cornucopia)."[141]

NATIONAL AND OTHER SYMBOLS

On March 24, 1815, Thomas Boynton of Windsor, Vermont, credited a workman with $1.50 for "Lettering National Emblems." Whether the task was chair related is

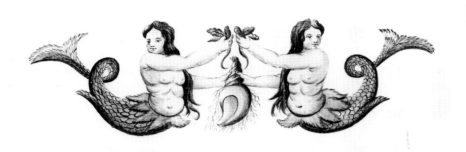

unclear, although it is the last of six consecutive entries of similar date for John Patterson, all pertaining to chair finishing—sizing, gilding, ornamenting, striping, and varnishing. The American eagle, a popular symbol in the arts of the young republic, was employed in chair work from carved to painted examples. Some Windsors of New York origin have an eagle painted on the cross slat at midback following a fancy pattern depicted on a badge worn in 1825 by members of the New York Chairmakers' Society at a Grand Procession to celebrate opening of the Erie Canal. Similar decoration was painted or gilded as a crest motif. Among patriotic designs in the Nestell drawing book, several depict eagles. National heroes had their day. In 1815 David Alling of Newark, New Jersey, credited painter Moses Lyon for finishing "12 Bronzed Double Cross (Decaturs)." The structure of the chair back copied that of plate 1, and the portrait bust was centered in the crest. Stephen Decatur distinguished himself as a naval officer early in the War of 1812 when he captured the British ship *Macedonian*. A decade later in 1824–25 symbols and busts extolling the virtues of the Marquis de Lafayette flooded the market in celebration of the triumphal return of the revolutionary general as the nation's guest. Stenciled ornament adorns a richly decorated commemorative chair bearing Lafayette's name on the seat front (pl. 22). Presidential figures were the subject of other decoration. Nelson Talcott of Ohio listed "Jackson chairs" in his accounts for 1843, and Calvin Stetson of Massachusetts retailed seating that honored the memory of William Henry Harrison (d. 1841).[142]

State and municipal symbols appear in painted, inlaid, and carved form in the decorative arts. A Windsor armchair, one of five from an original purchase for the New Hampshire Statehouse, bears a gilded representation of the state seal centered in the crest. Organizational insigne occur on other furniture. Painted and gilded Masonic ornament decorates two groups of chairs (figs. 5-38, 5-39, 5-41). The contrasting gold and silver leaf of one set is illustrated in a scribe's chair (pl. 18). Personal devices appear from time to time. John Curry, a chairmaker of Bourbon County, Kentucky, advertised in 1818 that he could supply Windsors with gilded initials on the back. Coats of arms and other heraldic devices had some currency. Medallions centered in the double-rod crests of several chairs contain these symbols, although some were added at a later date. Appropriately, Baltimore painters marching in procession in 1788 carried heraldry books as a trade symbol. Decorative work of a religious character is noted occasionally. When Joseph Wilder made a pair of armchairs for a church in southwestern New Hampshire, he grain-painted the surfaces and added as a decorative feature in the crest an open Bible or, perhaps, the stone tablets given to Moses on Mount Sinai (fig. 5-63). One of a pair of side chairs that depicts a mourning scene in the crest was likely part of a larger set commissioned specifically for funerary purposes by a private individual or business (fig. **3-49**). The ground colors are black and medium dull mustard; the decoration is dark green and black. Structural features identify the chair as a product of New York.[143]

FIG. 3-49 Slat-back Windsor side chair (one of two), New York, ca. 1811–17. H. 33⅝", (seat) 17¾", w. (crest) 17⅛", (seat) 16", D. (seat) 15⁵⁄₁₆"; black and medium dull mustard grounds with dark green and black. *(Collection of Steven and Helen Kellogg; Photo, Winterthur Museum.)*

SUMMARY
Hand-painted ornament was the common decoration of Windsor seating through the mid-nineteenth century, surpassing even stenciled work. Floral subjects were the most popular followed by fruit forms, although craftsmen and customers were free to innovate. The possibilities were almost limitless, as suggested in a notice of 1821 from the nation's capital: "Those who are desirous of having Chairs to match their drapery, carpeting, or paper, can have them finished according to order." The customer chose a suitable ground color to which was introduced colored striping or an imitation figure to match a specific room scheme. Nathaniel Whittock, whose *Guide* (1827) was quoted in his own day, went so far as to advise that ornamental borders used by paper hangers serve as inspiration for the chair painter. He cautioned, however, that the workman without particular artistic talents "confine himself to easy subjects, where the lines are graceful and the ornaments tastefully disposed, without representing any definite subject in nature." "Nothing," he declared, "looks so bad as subjects ill-represented; and every person that looks upon them is capable of forming a judgment upon their correctness." He concluded with "another rule . . . in forming patterns": "always . . . have the largest object in the centre, and let the pattern branch from it."[144]

Metallic Work

STENCILING
Decorative painting using cutwork patterns called stencils (also known as theorems or templates) may be an ancient art. By the early nineteenth century furniture decorators were combining the technique with the manipulation of fine metallic powders to produce shaded, glistening ornament, as perfected in Japan to embellish lacquer-work. Stenciling, or *bronzing* as it was commonly called, was a substitute in American painted seating furniture for the metal inlays and mounts popular in European and American formal furniture (fig. 1-16). In 1758 Robert Dossie devoted a section to the subject of bronzing in his *Handmaid to the Arts* (London), a publication with known circulation in America, and the topic is a recurring one in later art manuals. The earliest *published* notices for American bronze work date to 1817, when several chairmakers advertised at New York. A printed billhead for the firm of Cornwell and Smith offering "BRONZE and PAINTED FANCY CHAIRS" probably dates from the start of the partnership the same year. The bronze technique appears to have been well known at the time, as references provide no special explanation. Two of the first notices, published in February 1817, carry dates of the previous year at the bottom of the text.[145]

David Alling's accounts push back the date even further. In April 1815 the chairmaker of Newark, New Jersey, credited Moses Lyon "By Gilding & Bronzing 14 Ball Backs." These were fancy chairs. Subsequent records describe similar ornament on slat-back, double-cross, and wide-top chairs, along with sofas, a table, and a settee. The accounts make specific reference during the next two years to bronzing chairs in patterns such as "Grapes," "Fruit," "Flower," "Peaches," and "Cornucopia." A pair of stenciled cornucopia-back cane-seat fancy chairs in the Newark Museum was once owned by Alling's cousin, John Alling III, a resident of Newark. The roll tops suggest a date in the 1820s. Alling's work predates that of Lambert Hitchcock in Connecticut, which is frequently cited as the earliest stencil-decorated seating in America (fig. 1-16). Interest in stenciled decoration gained momentum. By 1819 A. Clark of Raleigh, North Carolina, was advertising "a new assortment of FANCY & WINDSOR CHAIRS of the latest fashions and various colours, handsomely ornamented, Guilt [*sic*] and Bronze" just "received from New-York." The following year David Bates of Washington, District of Columbia, offered his own assortment of "curled maple, bronze, . . . painted fancy," and Windsor chairs.[146]

Rufus Porter, spokesman on the practical arts and publisher of *Scientific American*, in 1826 described the general technique of stenciling:

> The ground for this work must be varnished with a mixture of copal varnish with an equal quantity of old linseed oil; and whatever figures are to be formed in bronzing, must be represented by holes cut through pieces of paper. Lay these patterns on the work, when the varnish is so dry as to be but slightly adhesive, but not press them down any more than is requisite to keep the paper in place. Then take a piece of soft glove leather, moisten it a little by breathing on it, and dip it in some dry bronze, and apply it to the figure beginning at the edges; tap the figure gently with the leather, and the bronze will stick to the varnish according to the pattern. Thus any figure maybe produced in a variety of shades by applying the bronze more freely to some parts of the work than to others. If some internal parts of the figures require to be more distinct than others, they may be wrought by their peculiar patterns, or coloured paint. . . . The work must . . . have one or more coats of copal or shellac varnish.[147]

Dark-colored grounds were the most effective for bronze-powder stenciling, as they enhanced the contrast achieved by highlighting and shading, although David Alling reported the early use of grounds such as nankeen (buff), satinwood (light wood color), green, and white, in addition to rosewood. Perhaps there was little attempt at first to shade, since bronzing was an inexpensive way to simulate gilding. Esther Stevens Fraser (later Brazer), the twentieth-century pioneer in reviving the art of stenciling, describes grained grounds of black over red and dark brown over light brown as the most common surfaces for stenciling. The decoration also could be placed on a dark panel laid out on the crest of a light-colored chair (pl. 19) or on a dark ground confined to the immediate decorated area. Stencilers cut their patterns from stiff or varnished paper, sometimes using the blank pages of an old account book. A sharp knife and a hard, smooth surface, such as glass or sheet metal, served well. Some craftsmen owned punches of different figures to assist with intricate patterns. "Bronzes" were nothing more than powdered metals. Real gold and silver were the most precious and used sparingly except for the best work. Pulverized tin or zinc substituted for silver. Copper produced reddish tones. Bronze, and gold substitutes such as brass, were available in several shades. Powders identified specifically in documents describe the variety: gold, yellow, silver, white metal, dark, pale, green, copper, and red copper. Figure **3-50** illustrates an unused packet of "Richgold," a composition bronze probably of British manufacture and yellow gold in color. Double wrapped in glossy white paper, the packet was found among the contents of a former chairmaker's shop in central New Jersey. The applicator, called a buff, puff, or pounce, was made of soft leather, according to Rufus Porter, although velvet also was employed. The material was wrapped over a finger or formed into a little stuffed ball, sometimes on a stick. The ornamenter kept several sizes at hand along with some camel's-hair pencils. In 1831 Henry Farley advertised "[Camels-hair] Shades" from his paint store at Concord, New Hampshire.[148]

Stenciling involved a tapping, pressing, or polishing action whereby the applicator containing bronze powder was passed over the tacky ground to be ornamented. Strokes made from the cut edges of the pattern toward the open center gave definition to the figure, and a circular motion concentrating powder in one spot provided highlights. In large motifs the stenciler usually trailed the bronze into total shade on one or more sides of the figure. Early leaf veining generally occurred as highlighting along a shaded, curved line. Later, fine lines were stenciled over or painted on the figure (pl. 25). Combinations of colored powders produced variation, and toward 1850 designs were "occasionally tinged with lacquers, or improved by out lines of opaque paints." Ornamenters created the best stenciled decoration by using individual units fitted together to form harmonious compositions. Most elements were

FIG. 3-50 Package of bronze powder, England, 1840–80. Paper wrapper with metallic powder; L. 4½", W. 3¹/₁₆". *(Collection of Monmouth County Historical Association, Freehold, NJ; Photo, Winterthur Museum.)*

highlighted and then shaded into the background (fig. 1-16). As production demands increased, decorators employed one of two techniques to maximize their time. First, individual figure placement was more random and less carefully composed. Second, larger stencil units combined several design elements. Plate 20 illustrates an example of this working method. The decorator used two large stencils in the crest — one for the center figure containing grapes (?) in a leafy cup and one for the flanking side units composed of larger fruit forms. The side units are oriented in the same direction without reversing the pattern. Telltale evidence that the decorator has used large stencil units is the manner in which the design runs off the crest top. He made do with ornament designed for a larger space, fitting it in as best he could.[149]

Hand-painted work was introduced to stenciled decoration, beginning with tendrils, leaf veins, and colored highlights, and continuing until some compositions contained an equal mixture of stenciled and painted primary figures. The decoration shown in plate 21 intermixes stenciled grapes and leaves of silver and bronze with brightly colored handwork. From the introduction of stenciling, some of the finest decorated examples employed both bronzed and gilded ornament. The final step, as described by Rufus Porter, was to secure painted and ornamented surfaces with one or more varnish coats.[150]

A lidded chest from the Norman Russell Stephens Chair Factory in New York State contains a sampling of typical stencils dating from the 1830s (fig. 3-51). The units are combined to suggest variety of composition, not stock designs, as it was usual to tailor ornament to the surfaces to be covered. Of particular note are the shaded leaf forms and baskets, arabesques, and cornucopias simulating fine cutwork. Delicate, ribbon-like arabesques, represented at the upper left, were used for restricted areas, such as narrow stay rails, seat fronts, and flat post faces. Some designs were executed in mixed media, and the quality of the work varied with the skill of the ornamenter. Plates 19 and 22 introduce special work. The first features a dark crest panel con-

FIG. 3-51 Decorator's work chest, Norman Russell Stephens Chair Factory, Toddsville, Otsego Co., N.Y., 1832. H. 19", W. 41½", D. 17". *(New York State Historical Association, Cooperstown, NY, acc. N-253.92.)*

trasted with yellow surfaces. The composition is well conceived, shaded, and balanced. Hand-painted accents of yellow introduce wispy fronds, top and bottom, and red highlights the blossoms of the central figure. Plate 22, which features a basket in the cross slat, carefully integrates bold shaded and veined stenciling on a black and red grained ground with tooled gilding in the crest and paint-simulated rushwork on the seat. Concealed among the leaves in the upper corners of the slat are small eagle's heads. The stenciled name "LAFAYETTE" on the seat front identifies the chair as a product of the mid-1820s, when the Revolutionary War general returned to America from France for a nationwide tour.

Equally popular as the basket for the central motif in stenciled chair backs were the bowl and the stemmed compote, and, like the basket, they usually contain fruits (fig. 3-51, right top and center bottom). Flanking elements sometimes form sprays. Decoration of compact form, indicative of the early and middle periods of stenciling, usually exhibits good use of the overlapping compositional technique and a considerable degree of shading. By midcentury these techniques gradually gave way to scattered compositions. The best later designs were enhanced with delicate filigrees of scrolling bronze work and pastel varnish tints. Another midcentury technique was to cut large design units from one stencil. Some stencilers in Pennsylvania introduced a compartmentalized technique to define large motifs, sectioning them like units in a stained-glass composition (pl. 23). In New England stenciled scenes sometimes fill the crest pieces of top-of-the-line seating. Subject matter varies from the picturesque to the exotic (pl. 24), and the work often intermixes silver, gold, and copper powders. Occasionally a "train of cars" races across a crest or slat face.[151]

FREEHAND BRONZING

Freehand ornamentation with bronze powders can occur with and be mistaken for bronze stenciling. Two methods were employed:

> The powder is mixed with strong gumwater or isinglass, and laid on with a brush or pencil: or, a coating of gold size, prepared with a due proportion of turpentine, is first applied; and when not so dry as to have still a certain clamminess, a piece of soft leather, wrapped round the finger, is dipped in the powder and rubbed over the work. When the work has, in either of these ways, been all covered with the bronze, it must be left to dry, and any loose powder then cleared away by a hair pencil.

Perhaps both techniques are combined in figure **3-52**, a youth's rocking chair of unique decoration employing both light golden and bronze powders. The seat-front motif probably was outlined to form the guilloche border, then daubed, or pounced, to fill the centers. Although the crest appears to be stenciled, irregularities in the two design halves are apparent upon examination. The heavy, painted scroll motif and the "weeping" foliage of the spindles are almost funerary in concept.[152]

Freehand bronze decoration sometimes augments stenciled and painted ornament. Plate 25 is a prime example. Through the interplay of highlight and deep shadow, the stenciled figures have become three-dimensional, the effect further heightened by the penciled black stems and veining that define rounded surfaces and the light shading surrounding all elements. The light gold powder that accents the bodies of the principal figures is subtle against the pale yellow ground, and the dark bronze of the lobes forming the blossom tops complements painted banding on both flat and turned surfaces. Delicate dots balance spiderlike veining in the blossoms. When new, the bronze banding possessed a lustrous quality enhanced by natural and artificial light. Joseph Jones of West Chester, Pennsylvania, sold drab-colored chairs ornamented with "bronz bands" in 1842 for considerably more than plain seating of the same color.[153]

FIG. 3-52 Youth's slat-back Windsor rocking chair, northeastern New York State, Vermont, or southeastern New Hampshire, 1835–40. Basswood (seat, microanalysis); H. 31½", (seat) 14⅜", W. (crest) 16¾", (seat) 16", D. (seat) 16⅜"; dark and reddish brown grained ground with yellow, black, medium dark green, gold, and bronze. *(Formerly Hitchcock Museum, Riverton, Conn.; Photo, Winterthur Museum.)*

GILDING

In a section titled "Painting Furniture" in his *Guide* of 1827, Nathaniel Whittock stated, "The most beautiful ornament for dark-coloured wood is gold." The many references to painted and gilded seating in the federal period and later proclaim general public agreement with this statement. Although the processes of oil and water gilding were in continuous use from the Middle Ages, the possession of gold- or silver-leaf ornamented furniture was subject to the financial resources of the consumer and the dictates of fashion. In the late eighteenth century, after a lapse in interest of a generation or more, Robert Adam reintroduced gilding to delicate designs in the new classical taste. This was the impulse that traveled to America, where gilding sometimes accented fine cabinetwork but was more successfully employed in popularly priced painted furniture.[154]

Trips abroad and furniture importations in the federal period provided Americans with glimpses of new gilded surfaces and stimulated a taste for the rich decoration. Several references describe the close lines of communication between London and America. In 1789 Henry Hill of Philadelphia imported gilt furniture from that city. His order consisted in part of a set of twelve chairs, "2 pier Tables carv'd & gilt," and a looking glass with an ornamented frame. Early in the 1800s Standfast Smith wrote from Boston to his business associate, John Parker, requesting for Dr. John Warren a dozen London-made rush-bottom drawing room armchairs in white and gilt with cushions. Daniel Rea of Boston had already painted and ornamented six "Chamber Chairs . . . with Gold" for Andrew Craigie, Esq. A few years later William Palmer, advertising at New York as a painter, gilder, varnisher, and japanner, offered fancy chairs and cornices "of the newest London Patterns." Palmer received important commissions for painted and gilded fancy seating during the 1790s and later. His white and gold chairs were most in demand, although black also sold well. In 1797 Palmer shipped a set of twenty-four white chairs with a matching settee to General Charles Ridgely at Baltimore, and black chairs went to the Arnold family of Rhode Island two years later, all with gold enrichment. Nicholas Low, a merchant of New York and owner of the upstate Sans Souci Hotel, purchased six white and gold fancy chairs from Palmer in 1804 and placed them in his drawing room. At $8 apiece the price is the highest recorded for that article. A local member of the Beekman family acquired a large set of ten gilt side chairs and two armchairs a year later. A highlight of Palmer's career was his commission to construct a set of seating furniture for the President's House following the War of 1812. He billed agent George Boyd in December 1815 for eighteen gray and gold chairs and two matching settees. Pleased with the furniture, the Madisons purchased it for their private quarters.[155]

There is little question that the fancy chair occupied a premier position in the gilded-seating market, and the record provides ample evidence that the gilt Windsor was also a popular item. References focusing on plank seating range from the general to the specific, the latter including gilded "bamboo," "fret-back," and "dining" chairs. Most surviving Windsors with gilded surfaces intact originated in Maryland and Pennsylvania (fig. 3-46). Among the former, in particular, ornament is of classical inspiration. Gilded enrichment in Pennsylvania chairs often comprises bold leafy scrolls in shouldered tablets (pl. 26). Of special merit is the chair in plate 27 with its gilt scrolls and banding encircling the crest. Seat-front ornament and accented turnings help to tie the decoration together. A gilded arabesque is featured in the roll top of the Lafayette chair (pl. 22), and a gilded shell and leaf tips define the top of an armchair (pl. 15).

Although William Palmer's customers preferred white and gold chairs, other records show the market dominance of gilded black seating. Green perhaps followed white in popularity, and other options permitted customers to coordinate rich surfaces with household decor. Choices included blue, yellow, brown, coquelicot (red), gray, rosewood graining, and "light color." Metallic leaf decoration also embellished settees and rockers. Household locations of painted and gilded seating included primary living and entertainment areas—the entry, parlor, drawing room, dining room, and principal chamber (bedroom). John Bridges of Washington recorded a commission in 1815 from the Library of Congress for "6 Gilt Windsor Chairs" and a "large Settee" to match (fig. 5-60).[156]

Gilding costs can be determined only generally. William Palmer's fancy-chair prices ranged from $3.25 to $8. Pattern, amount of gilding, additional ornament, and the presence of chair arms all are factors to be considered. In 1808 a workman in Silas Cheney's shop in Connecticut received 33⅓¢ apiece for gilding fancy chairs. The cost of painting and ornamenting versus painting and gilding chairs in the shop was 58⅓¢ and 70⅘¢, respectively. Charges for repainting chairs and either gilding or bronzing them are itemized in a Baltimore Exchange Hotel bill dating several decades later. The charge per chair for gilding was 58⅓¢, for bronzing, 50¢. David Alling's rates at Newark, New Jersey, were comparable. Leaf-decorated work was available in several qualities, as recorded by Philemon Robbins of Hartford who identified "rich gilt," "half rich gilt," and "gilt" seating. John Denig of Chambersburg, Pennsylvania, offered "First rate gilt fancy Chairs" and "Second" and "Third" quality work. Plate 27 and figure 3-46 represent first-quality chairs.[157]

Complementing local sales of painted and gilt furniture was the coastal trade in which Philadelphia was a leading shipper and Charleston, South Carolina, a primary recipient. Gilded woven- and wooden-bottom chairs are mentioned in records along with a gilt settee on occasion. Other pertinent shipments to the South include a consignment to Alexandria, Virginia, and Thomas Jefferson's order of black and gold Windsors for Monticello. In 1801 gilded Philadelphia chairs, some painted green, others black, went by order to John Derby, brother of Elias Hasket Derby, of Salem, Massachusetts. By 1827 Dockum and Brown of Portsmouth, New Hampshire, employed "first rate workmen from Boston" to paint and gild unfinished seating imported from that city.[158]

Foreign markets accounted for other sales of gilt seating. Philadelphia records mention Havana, and in 1816 Stephen Girard, a local merchant, sent "12 Fancy chairs rosewood gilt" to the Isle of France (Mauritius, off Madagascar). A year later a venture to the African coast by Edward Carrington, a Providence merchant, deposited "yellow gilt" and "green gilt" Windsors there or at a stop en route. In 1825 J. H. Stevenson and Company of Philadelphia tested gilt Windsors painted blue, green, or a light color in the Central American market (fig. **3-53**). Chairs described as "Bamboo . . . Gold Leaf" or as gilt over white, brown, or red paint were shipped between 1805 and 1811 from Salem, Massachusetts, New York, and Philadelphia to South American markets. South America also was popular with Baltimore chairmakers. A typical notice reads: "300 DOZEN CANE, RUSH and WINDSOR CHAIRS, made portable, painted in brilliant colours, ornamented in gold, and comprising an ELEGANT ASSORTMENT, suitable for the South American and West India markets."[159]

Records document the availability of gold and other leaf in the retail market. James Claypoole of Philadelphia offered imported gold, silver, and "Dutch metal"

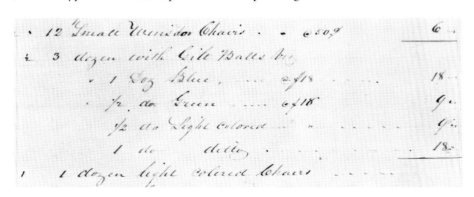

FIG. 3-53 Excerpt of entry for December 24, 1825, from J. H. Stevenson and Co. invoice book, Philadelphia, 1822–26. *(Winterthur Library.)*

FIG. 3-54 Books of gold leaf, probably England, 1800–1830. Laid paper and gold leaf; H. 3⁹⁄₁₆", W. 3¹³⁄₁₆". *(Collection of Monmouth County Historical Association, Freehold, NJ; Photo, Winterthur Museum.)*

(brass) leaf for sale in 1750 along with painters' colors and brushes. After the Revolution painting specialists generally kept a supply of gold leaf on hand. Chairmaker Lawrence Allwine of Philadelphia sold this item in 1800 along with his own patent paints. Thomas West, a chairmaker who always carried "a large and *elegant assortment* of gilt and bronzed Fancy and Windsor chairs" at his shop in Connecticut, marketed silver and gold leaf. During the early 1800s ornamental painters and chairmakers commonly employed leaf in both new production and refurbishing work.[160]

Painters' manuals from the eighteenth century and later contain instructions for gold-leafing on painted furniture. Some volumes even provide patterns of appropriate size to copy. The process can be described in brief: Using thoroughly dry painted surfaces, the ornamenter drew his design(s) in chalk by hand or assisted by a tracing on transparent paper. To transfer the design, a piece of chalked paper was inserted between the pattern and the work, the pattern lines then traced with a pointed instrument. The craftsman coated the chalked areas with gold size (linseed oil boiled with gum animé), sometimes adding varnish and a coloring agent for visual definition. This was applied with a camel's-hair pencil. When the size had dried to a tacky state, it was ready to receive the leaf.

Gold leaf was available commercially in small books interleaved with thin paper (fig. **3-54**). The metal was hand-beaten to form, one ounce producing 1,600 leaves, as reported in 1778. The ornamenter used the interleaves to carry the gold directly to the work or to transfer it to his cushion, a small, stuffed, leather-covered board used to cut leaf to size with a palette knife. He lifted the gold sheet from the cushion to the work by means of a gilder's tip, a thin row of squirrel's or badger's hair fixed between two cards. Static electricity, a trace of oil, or the moisture of human breath caused the leaf to adhere to the brush until placed on the sized pattern. A dabber, or cotton ball, pressed the gold in place. The ornamenter repeated the process until all the sized area was covered with leaf. When the size had dried and hardened, he dusted the gilded surfaces with a large camel's-hair brush to remove the excess. Silver gilding was executed in the same manner; however, leafing with Dutch metal required a common glue size. Shading was introduced with transparent colors in desired tints. The ornamenter detailed veins and other fine markings with opaque paints, especially black and reddish brown, applied with a camel's-hair pencil. Two craftsmen's inventories identify kits used in leafing as a "Gilders ornamenting tool box & contence" and a "Gilding Box."[161]

Wood Graining and Special Surface Effects

Graining has been defined as "a process of painting furniture and woodwork, by which the colour and figure of a more costly wood [is] counterfeited in one of a cheaper kind." Oak and walnut, the first wood imitations to appear in England, were current by the late sixteenth century. A century later a "counterfeit Tortoiseshell," composed of red and black (or brown) pigments, was a popular ground for japanwork furniture. Both japanwork and interior wood graining became fashionable in America, where imitations included cedar, oak, walnut, mahogany, maple, and marble. When John Fendall advertised in the *Maryland Gazette* on June 26, 1760, for a runaway servant and house painter who could "imitate marble or mahogany very exactly," there probably were dozens of colonial workmen proficient in the art of graining.[162]

Records kept by ornamental painters describe postrevolutionary furniture embellished with faux surfaces. Tables resembled marble or combinations of marble and mahogany. Sometimes stools and tables were finished in "Seder Colour," although most wood imitations were of mahogany—a desk and secretary, a large table, a bureau, half a dozen chairs, a bookcase. Interest remained strong well into the 1800s. Writing from New York in 1846, Rufus Porter observed: "Imitation Painting . . . has probably never been so much in vogue as at present. Imitations or pretended imitations of oak, maple, mahogany, or marble, may be seen on three-fourths of the doors of houses in the cities, besides wainscoting, chimney pieces and furniture."[163]

IMITATION ROSEWOOD AND MAPLE GRAINING

Simulated rosewood and maple are the most common grained surfaces on early nineteenth-century painted vernacular seating. About equal in popularity, the ornamental grounds probably were market contemporaries, although two references in 1812 to imitation maple are the earliest by several years. On April 22 the firm of Haydon and Stewart of Philadelphia sold "24 chairs with rush bottoms in imitation of maple" followed on June 27 by "16 fancy chairs maple imitation" with two armchairs en suite. The seating was relatively costly at $4.25 and $6.37½ the chair. A ground coat for painting in imitation maple was a light tint of yellow in oil. Rufus Porter recommended "white lead slightly colored with chrome yellow and yellow ochre." For moderately priced seating simulated maple stripes were applied with a pencil (brush), using darker paint. In plate 28 a Pennsylvania chair with a medium tan or tea-color ground has bold black markings. The penciled borders and foliate decoration are in golden yellow; the floral feature is crimson and medium green accented with white. So popular was this surface that striped, or curled, imitation maple chairs are depicted occasionally in genre portraits. A more subtle version of the imitation ground appears on a New England chair finished completely in monochromatic browns (fig. 3-55). The burled figure of the crest contrasts effectively with the striping of the other surfaces.[164]

Graining methods were detailed in publications throughout the early 1800s. Most recipes for simulated maple describe the sophisticated techniques employed on *interior* woodwork. Clever artisans with special tools could produce highly naturalistic effects, as recommended in manuals. Frequently the graining, or top coat, was distemper, that is, color in a water base, such as ale or sugar water. As that technique is less durable than oil even with protective varnish coats, it was not recommended for seating furniture. Stripes, if not painted on directly, were executed with a brush, feather, or cork drawn through the wet graining coat (or satinwood?; pl. 29). For a bird's-eye figure a flat cork with points cut on the edges was useful, although Nathaniel Whittock described another method:

> The small round specks, with a spot in the centre, are formed by placing the point of a camel-hair pencil on the work, and turning the handle round between the finger and thumb; this will take the . . . colour off the ground, leaving it quite bear [*sic*]: . . . in taking [the brush] off it will leave the dot in the middle of the light.

After the work dried, a workman could pencil in swirling veins with a brush and thin glaze (varnish and color) of burnt umber, if so desired. Varnish coats completed the work. In 1819 David Alling recorded a shipment of "Imitation Curled maple" Windsors from Newark, New Jersey, to New Orleans, and in the mid-1830s he noted the sale of a "small chair with hole pt'd imitation."[165]

Of the rosewood patterns found on furniture, a regular, parallel figure is one basic form. This effect was achieved through the use of homemade or commercial graining combs of metal or wood with thick or slender teeth, uniform or random spacing. A variation was created with waved lines. A quicker approach to pattern development employed broad stripes of grained color, sometimes on the diagonal, applied with a wide, feathered brush (pl. 30). Some seating combined the techniques of combing (or "streaking," as described by William Beesley of New Jersey) and daubing, the latter illustrated in the crest and legs of the Lafayette chair (pl. 22; fig. 5-25). This was nothing more than the tortoiseshell ground of earlier japanwork. In fact, that word occurs in early nineteenth-century terminology, as affirmed in an advertisement of

FIG. 3-55 Shaped-slat-back Windsor side chair, northern Worcester County, Mass., 1820–30. White pine (seat); H. 34⅛", (seat) 17⅜", w. (crest) 17⅜", (seat) 16⅜", D. (seat) 15¼"; pale beige and light brown grained ground with dark brown, orange brown, and shaded dark gray brown. *(Formerly Hitchcock Museum; Photo, Winterthur Museum.)*

1826 from Cincinnati offering fancy flag-bottom and Windsor seating painted and finished in "*Sattin Wood, Tortoise Shell, Coquillico, Green, Cane-Color, Brown, Black,* &c. &c. handsomely gilt and ornamented."[166]

Some Windsor seating exhibits reasonably faithful rosewood graining. Plate 31 illustrates a sweeping figure on the crest, slat, and seat combined with daubing for the turned work. To achieve a realistic effect the grainer was advised to "procure several pieces of veneer, and imitate them as closely as possible." The procedure for reproducing rosewood in oil paints on chairs was described as "very easy": "The ground is red, and should be painted twice over: the black grain is lamp black ground in dryers, with a little boiled oil; this must be put on the red with the flat brush." The grained effect was produced by *removing* some of the black top coat with a dry brush, feather, piece of leather, or the like, permitting the red ground to show through. Graining brushes were available at Thomas W. Ward II's store in Pomfret, Connecticut, during the late 1830s at the substantial cost of 75¢ apiece. Varnish coats followed graining and ornamentation. Rosewood or tortoise grounds were suitable bases for stenciled and painted ornament. David Alling's accounts describe decorative treatments and patterns interpreted in rosewood: bronzed slat backs (1816); fancy chairs with gilt, bronze, and color, including a pineapple motif (1819); rocking chairs and Windsors with bent backs. The craftsman stocked ornamented rosewood Windsors with organ or flat spindles in 1820 along with sewing chairs and fancy seating with fret or diamond-fret backs.[167]

Nathaniel Whittock detailed a more exotic imitation rosewood, directing: "Before the colour is dry, . . . and with great freedom take out the light veins that appear to be part of . . . a knot." Within this light, elliptic-shaped (or other) area the grainer was instructed to pencil lines of Van Dyke brown (pl. 32, splat and crest). The figure was softened with the badger's-hair blender, a tool offered for sale in 1831 by Henry Farley of Concord, New Hampshire. The effect achieved in American work often was striking—less realistic and more whimsical than nature, a figure that another author dubbed "a caricature of the object of which [the painter] attempts to produce a correct resemblance." Related work featuring knots is identified with some production at Walter Corey's factory in Portland, Maine, although the naiveté and verve of the illustrated chair takes it out of mainstream production. Another whimsey here is the free-grained rendering of the scroll seat.[168]

MAHOGANY AND OTHER GRAINING

Mahogany graining is unusual in Windsor and fancy seating, although it is relatively common on painted cabinetwork. The inventory of chairmaker Abraham McDonough, drawn in 1852 at Philadelphia, lists thirty-six "Im[itation] mahog Cain seat chairs." A mahogany-grained Windsor is a rare survival (pl. 33). The graining copies the actual color and figure of the wood, an interpretation David Bates of Washington, District of Columbia, described as "in the European style." To prepare the base coat(s) for mahogany graining, painters' manuals advised grinding white lead in oil with any of several pigments, ranging from the pale yellows through orange brown to red. Most sources agreed that sienna was the coloring agent of the graining coat. Distemper graining was preferred; however, Rufus Porter acknowledged that "graining colors for this work *may* be ground in a mixture of oil and spirits of turpentine, and this is, in some respects, less difficult to manage, than in water staining, though there is less facilitation in the process." The painter used a flat brush to grain, "waving and imitating the veins as they run in any fine piece of mahogany."[169]

Period documents refer to other wood-grained surfaces, although these formed only a small part of the chair market, and few are known today. The most common was satinwood (?; pl. 29). The earliest record is an 1812 bill from the firm of Haydon and Stewart in Philadelphia itemizing "22 Fancy rush bottomd chairs sattin wood imitation plain" with two armchairs to match, priced individually at $3.75 and $5.62½. The chairs still exist, although the original finish does not. David Alling's first record of this surface dates to June 1815, when his workman Moses Lyon grained "2 Satin wood Sew'g Chairs" and a dozen satinwood "slat Backs," which may have been Windsors. Lyon striped and/or bronzed other chairs of similar finish. A reference of 1836 records a fancy rocking chair repainted in satinwood. Imitation oak and walnut also are mentioned in this general period. In 1833 Thomas Ellis of New Bedford, Massachusetts, advertised a selection of ladies' raised-seat (Boston-style) rocking chairs, some painted to resemble oak or curled maple. A dozen cottage, or fancy, chairs painted in "Imitation walnut" represent a purchase of Robert R. Livingston in 1842 from the firm of Bell and Stoneall in New York. The chairs cost about $1.63 apiece.[170]

SPECIAL SURFACE TREATMENTS

Sometimes a Windsor seat plank was grained or patterned to contrast with the plain painted surfaces of the back and support structure. Two sets of late eighteenth-century chairs provide evidence of this treatment. One is a group of fan-back Windsors that descended in the Sowle-Wilbour family of South Dartmouth, Massachusetts, and Little Compton, Rhode Island. The chairs were painted blue-green, although with their aged varnish they appear olive today. On the seats is a ground coat of light, chalky brick red covered with a transparent brown-streaked glaze just visible on all surfaces, especially around the edges. Glazes for interior walls and woodwork were common during the 1790s, when these chairs were made. Plate 34 illustrates a detail from the second set of early Windsors with patterned seats. Here, earth tones contrast with bright Prussian blue on other surfaces, and again the colors are dulled by varnish. The ground coat on the seats is brick red covered with medium light umber. Colored glazes of brick red and dark brown applied next form a looping, streaked pattern on the plank, using the exposed front leg tops as "eyes" and continuing around to the center back in a single loop. Areas of umber flank the loops. In both sets of chairs the spindle platforms at the seat backs are painted the same as the turned and bent parts, while the back edges duplicate the primary seat surfaces. Swirling patterns also have been noted on later chairs.[171]

Several fanciful plank surfaces appear to have been decorated in the medium of distemper, that is, color in a water-soluble base. The colors, usually yellows, browns, and brownish reds, were easily manipulated on a hard oil-base ground through use of a wide range of "tools," including soft leather, cork, sponges, feathers, and the hair blender. Only the limitations of the painter's imagination and dexterity inhibited the figures, which range from swirls and arches to laps and loops, spots and splotches, ripples, fingers, and eyes. Several patterns appear in plate 32. Other seats display small allover spots or splotches of a sponged variety. An uncommon decorative effect was created by smoking tacky surfaces with soot from a candle or lamp flame. Stripes and snakelike patterns are common in this decorative medium.

An unusual surface treatment termed *spotting* dates to the early nineteenth century, when segmental turnings defined chairs of bamboo pattern. In 1804 woodworker William Luther directed a bill to a customer in Salem, Massachusetts, itemizing "six spotted bambues," the $3 unit price only 33¢ less than a "Gilt" bamboo chair. A spotted chair is recorded in a portrait of an elderly lady (fig. **3-56**). As illustrated, small spots and larger "eyes" decorate the turned elements. Similar eyes embellish painted surfaces in a set of English beechwood chairs with bamboo turnings, rush seats, and open tracery backs. The seating, part of a suite of furniture made for actor David Garrick, may have been part of an order supplied about 1770 by Thomas Chippendale. A "spotted wash stand" stood in chairmaker Thomas Boynton's home in Vermont in 1849 at his death, confirming the use of this surface decoration on American forms other than chairs.[172]

FIG. 3-56 Anonymous, *Portrait of Mrs. David Witmar, Sr.*, probably Pennsylvania, ca. 1835. Oil on canvas; H. 35¾", W. 41¾". *(Philadelphia Museum of Art: The Collection of Edgar William and Bernice Chrysler Garbisch, 1970, acc. 1970-254-2.)*

MARBLING

In speaking of "Imitations of marble," Rufus Porter described the usual ground as white or light slate color. The shading colors were ground in oil, "applied immediately to the ground color, and blended therewith before the former [began] to dry." Porter advised painters to furnish themselves with a sample of the stone to imitate. References to marble-painted Windsor seating occur in several documents, the earliest an 1806 "List of Household Furniture in the Dwelling of Saml P Broome at the Marble Quarry in the Township of Whitemarsh, Montgomery County," Pennsylvania. Appropriate for the home of a quarry owner were the "8 wooden Chairs painted like grey marble" in the "Yellow Hall or Eating room." Another household inventory dated two years later itemizes "½ dozen marblebottom Chairs" valued at $6 in the residence of Jacob Chandler, a ship carpenter of Nantucket. Inventories of Chester County, Pennsylvania, origin record other "Marble windsor chairs." No doubt all were something of a novelty. Nathaniel Whittock commented on the subject: "In painting chairs it is sometimes the practice to marble them; nothing can be in worst taste, as no imitation should ever be introduced where the reality could not be applied if persons chose to go to the expense—and who would choose a marble chair?" As an exponent of the ornamental arts, Whittock would have looked more favorably on the imitation marble that embellishes the top of a Windsor stand from Pennsylvania, as it represents the "proper" use of the material. The painter simulated the stone in shades of gray on white.[173]

Staining, Japanning, and Varnishing

Staining is a quick and inexpensive method of giving color to wood. In the seventeenth century the English frequently stained beech to resemble walnut; a century later mahogany was the fashionable color. In America mahogany stain was a common finish on highpost bedsteads. In the eighteenth century cheap slat-back rush-bottom chairs also were tinted with green, black, red, brown, or yellow stain. English chairmakers began to stain Windsor seating perhaps before 1800, and the practice became common during the nineteenth century. Stained Windsors are almost unknown, however, in American production. N. W. Burpee, who offered "A GENERAL assortment of warranted Fancy and Windsor Chairs, Settees &c. Stained and Painted" on January 28, 1826, at Montreal may have produced both English and American-style Windsors to appeal to a broad market. More likely his stained chairs were fancy seating. Thomas West's advertisement at New London, Connecticut, two years later described his stock as "STAIN'D and Painted, Gilt and Bronz'd FANCY AND WINDSOR CHAIRS." Again, some of the fancy chairs probably were stained, but there is no direct indication that the Windsors were finished in this manner. The "high winsor stool stained & varnished" that David Alling of New Jersey made specific note of in 1838 likely was bespoken work because the chairmaker generally painted his Windsor and fancy seating.[174]

Nathaniel Whittock described the English technique to produce cheap stained imitations of rosewood graining for fancy seating:

> The chairs . . . are dipped in a large copper containing the boiling red stain, and then
> taken out, and allowed to dry before they are dipped again. . . . When the red stain is
> sufficiently strong a flat varnish brush, with the hairs separated . . . is dipped in the
> black stain, and drawn over the chairs. . . . It does not take five minutes to give this
> beautiful imitation of rose wood.

In limited production stain was washed over the wood with rags. Chairmaker William Challen, who emigrated from London to New York, stained part of his fancy production, described in 1797 as "dyed" and "japanned" chairs. Consignments of black gilt and "stained" chairs left Philadelphia for Charleston in 1811 on board the *South Carolina Packet*. Similar merchandise stood in Benjamin Bass's shop at Boston in 1819 when appraisers enumerated a "pan for staining chair stuff." Records of the 1820s and 1830s further describe the trade: "Stained fancy chairs" sold at Boston for $2.25 apiece; "maple stain Roll top chairs" and "Hitchcocks stained cane seat chairs" were retailed at Hartford; "low priced Cane Seats, beautifully stained" were an item at Portsmouth, New Hampshire.[175]

Japanwork was the object of a fashion revival in the late eighteenth century. Instructions were available in the Philadelphia edition of the *Dictionary of Arts* (1798), although Robert Dossie had already provided a succinct definition at mid-century: "By japanning is to be understood the art of covering bodies by grounds of opake colours in varnish; which may be either afterwards decorated by painting or gilding, or left in a plain state." A principal variation of the new japanning technique was the elimination of an undercoat of size and whiting. Jacob Bigelow provided a process summary in 1840:

> The article to be japanned is first brushed over with two or three coats of seed lac var-
> nish, to form the *priming*. It is then covered with varnish previously mixed with a pig-
> ment of the tint desired. This is called the *ground color*; and if the subject is to exhibit
> a design, the objects are painted upon it, in colors mixed with varnish, and used in the

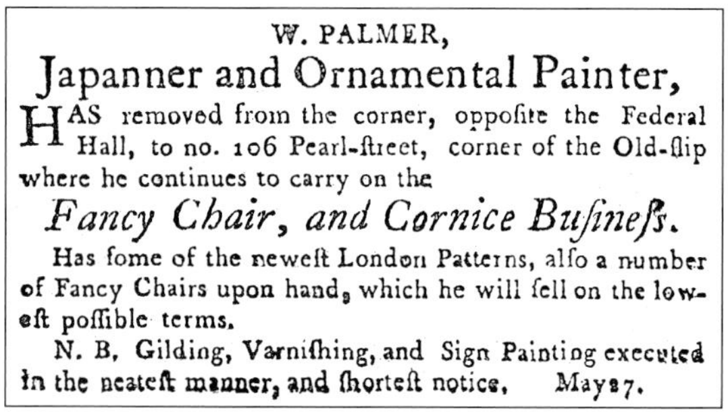
W. PALMER,
Japanner and Ornamental Painter,
HAS removed from the corner, oppoſite the Federal Hall, to no. 106 Pearl-ſtreet, corner of the Old-ſlip where he continues to carry on the
Fancy Chair, and Cornice Buſineſs.
Has ſome of the neweſt London Patterns, alſo a number of Fancy Chairs upon hand, which he will ſell on the loweſt poſſible terms.
N. B. Gilding, Varniſhing, and Sign Painting executed in the neateſt manner, and ſhorteſt notice. May 27.

FIG. 3-57 Advertisement of William Palmer. From *Weekly Museum*, New York, January 6, 1798.

same manner as for oil painting. The whole is then covered with additional coats of transparent varnish, and all that remains to be done, is to dry and polish it.[176]

Japanning was best executed in a warm room to ensure good varnish adhesion and to hasten drying. Pigments suitable for painting in oil could be used in varnish. Colors prepared in shellac varnish were "easiest to work" although, to avoid dulling light colors, a mastic or copal varnish was recommended. When the work was polished, a fine powder, such as pumice, tripoli, or whiting in oil was applied with soft leather. A final oil application was rubbed on with wool. As japanning was time consuming, it was expensive; thus the technique was confined mainly to high-end fancy woven-bottom seating. Many individuals who practiced the art were also Windsor-chair makers.[177]

The new vogue for japanned furnishings was transmitted from England to America, where William Palmer of New York practiced the art by May 1787, when he supplied the merchant Nicholas Low with a dozen "Japan Chairs" priced between $4 and $5 each. "London Patterns" continued to influence Palmer's work through the end of the century (fig. **3-57**). The chairmaker teamed briefly in 1795 with William Lycett as a partner. Only the previous year Lycett had sold a dozen japanned chairs and two settees to Chancellor Robert R. Livingston. It was William Challen, however, who secured the chancellor's patronage in 1798 when Livingston purchased "6 Blue Japan'd Chairs." William Palmer, in turn, sold black and gold chairs to a prominent Rhode Island family. Craftsmen at Philadelphia also practiced the art of japanning, and its diffusion was rapid. By 1805 James Beck "manufacture[d] Windsor-Chairs & Settees . . . agreeable to any pattern" and "painted in different colours, gilt and japanned" at Fredericksburg, Virginia. In the years following, chairmakers at Cincinnati and in Bourbon County, Kentucky, advertised japanned chairs. The commodity proved a salable item in the export trade. Philadelphia customhouse records identify shipments to Havana and Batavia, and chairs from New London, Connecticut, were sent to Martinique. The color range was broad—blue, black, white, red, yellow, and green grounds.[178]

The final step in preparing all but the cheapest painted and stained chairs for sale was to apply a coat of varnish over the ornamented surfaces. Jacob Bigelow described varnishes as resinous solutions "which, after being spread over surfaces, and dried, possess qualities of hardness, brilliancy, and transparency." They gave "lustre and smoothness to painted surfaces" and offered protection "from the action of the air." Varnish resins were dissolved in one of three liquids—oil, turpentine, or spirits of wine (alcohol). The English employed oil varnishes by the sixteenth century, and spirit varnishes had their genesis with the introduction of japanning to England in the following century. Oil varnishes were practical for house painting and heavy-duty use, such as in floorcloths. Chair painting and ornamenting generally were completed with the turpentine and spirit varnishes, which took an excellent polish. The real workhorse was gum copal dissolved in turpentine. Use of this resin in varnish was widespread among American chairmakers. Nathaniel Whittock gave high marks to copal varnish, stating that "so excellent is the resinous quality of copal, that it is now preferred for the finest as well as the more common works."[179]

References to varnish preparation and use of a "copper varnish kettle" are common in chairmaking accounts. Elizabeth Drinker of Philadelphia, a Quakeress and wife of a merchant, wrote on June 24, 1806, in her journal: "We have a Windsor chairmaker [Richard Wall] next door to us, who I think, by the smell, is boiling varnish this day." Joel Brown in advertising for three apprentices to the Windsor chair–making trade at Petersburg, Virginia, five years later stated that instruction in the "Art of Painting, Gilding, and Varnish Making" was part of the training. In some urban areas it was possible to purchase commercially prepared varnishes. Harmon (also Herman) Vosburgh, who owned a "Varnish Manufactory" in 1800 at New York, supplied "all kinds of hard and soft varnishes, gold sizes, lackers and japans." Copal varnish offered for sale at Middletown, Connecticut, in 1815–16 likely was obtained in New York, as was that retailed in 1841 by Frederick Starr at his furniture establishment in Rochester, New York, near the Erie Canal (fig. 4-32). At best, varnish preparation was a hazardous occupation due to the flammable nature of some of the ingredients. Use of a sand bath provided a heat-conducting wall of material between the varnish kettle and the vessel exposed to the fire's flame. Some cities, including Philadelphia, eventually passed ordinances prohibiting the preparation of turpentine and varnish in thickly settled areas unless conducted in an open place thirty feet from other property or in a so-called fireproof building. With the rapid advance of industry in the second quarter of the nineteenth century one author could remark, "The manufacture of [copal varnishes] is now prosecuted to a very respectable extent in this country, especially in Newark, N.J., and in Philadelphia." In 1856 the manufactories in Newark produced varnish annually to the value of almost $300,000.[180]

The practice of varnishing common seating existed long before the advent of the Windsor. The Gaines family of Ipswich, Massachusetts, like other early eighteenth-century chairmakers throughout New England and the Middle Atlantic region, regularly colored, varnished, and bottomed rush-seated chairs. Early Windsor chairmaking records, if available, would illuminate parallel activity. Before 1800 Daniel Rea of Boston repainted, ornamented, and varnished Windsor and other seating on a regular basis. Conversely, in 1798 appraisers at Philadelphia described a group of chairs standing in Francis Trumble's shop at his death as "Not Varnished." After 1800 references to new and maintenance varnishing occur with frequency and variety, as suggested in selected records: at New Bedford, Massachusetts, in 1803 William Russell, Jr., offered "Black Japan and Brown Varnish, suitable for Chairs and other uses, which dries in a few hours" (fig. 3-58); Thomas Gladding recorded "Painting Green & Varnishing sette" in 1828 during refurbishing at the home of Peter Gansevoort in Albany, New York; in the 1830s David Alling made note of varnishing a variety of seating furniture, including a high Windsor stool, long and short settees, a large rocking chair, and several Grecian sewing chairs, at his shop in Newark, New Jersey.[181]

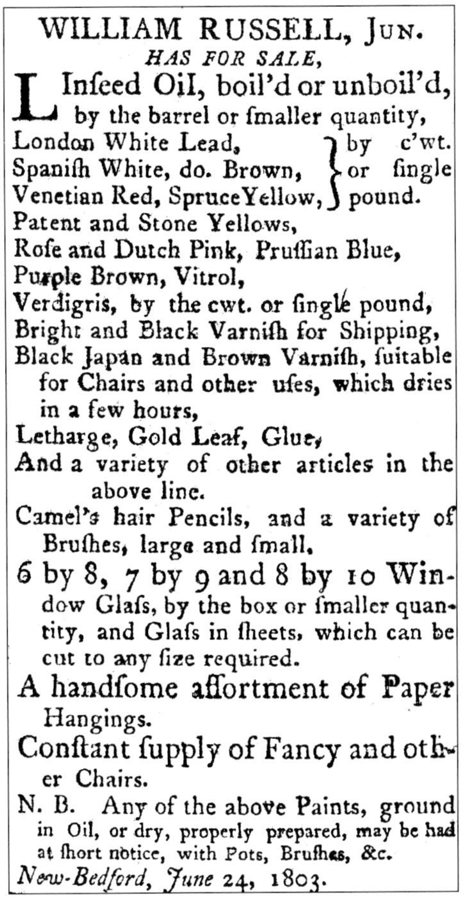

Contemporary instruction on varnishing technique counseled the painter to avoid visible brushstrokes, advising that "the brush be perfectly flat, and as large as the nature of the work will permit." Other directions cautioned against overloading the brush, recommending "as full and flowing a quantity as will remain on a vertical surface without running." Brushing in the direction of the wood grain was essential. Proper maintenance of brushes also was emphasized in manuals. Following use, the tool was cleansed in turpentine or spirits of varnish, as appropriate, and if desired washed in hot water and soap. If varnish dried in the brush, "a few strokes of a hammer or mallet" pulverized and separated the resin and restored pliability. Appraisers in an 1852 enumeration of chairmaker Abraham McDonough's estate at Philadelphia itemized a "Lot Cans, brushes, Varnish benches &c." Other records identify varnish bottles, pots, cups, bowls, demijohns, and barrels. During the 1810s the cost of varnishing new chairs varied from 1¼¢ to 6⅔¢ apiece. Varnishing over ornament fell into the upper price range, indicating that this work was done slowly and carefully. Unit costs remained the same during the next several decades. James Helme's "Book of Prices" for cabinet- and chairwork compiled in Pennsylvania in 1838 placed journeyman pay for "varnishing chairs per ½ Doz" at 12½¢, or 2¹⁄₁₂¢ apiece (fig. 3-59).[182]

Refurbishing

As utilitarian furniture, Windsor seating required periodic freshening in surface finish and sometimes ornament, a circumstance borne out by records and the furniture itself. Minor repairs frequently attended this work. A notice in the *Columbian*

WILLIAM RUSSELL, Jun.
HAS FOR SALE,

Linfeed Oil, boil'd or unboil'd, by the barrel or smaller quantity,
London White Lead, } by c'wt.
Spanish White, do. Brown, } or single
Venetian Red, Spruce Yellow, } pound.
Patent and Stone Yellows,
Rose and Dutch Pink, Prussian Blue,
Purple Brown, Vitrol,
Verdigris, by the cwt. or single pound,
Bright and Black Varnish for Shipping,
Black Japan and Brown Varnish, suitable for Chairs and other uses, which dries in a few hours,
Letharge, Gold Leaf, Glue,
And a variety of other articles in the above line.
Camel's hair Pencils, and a variety of Brushes, large and small.
6 by 8, 7 by 9 and 8 by 10 Window Glass, by the box or smaller quantity, and Glass in sheets, which can be cut to any size required.
A handsome assortment of Paper Hangings.
Constant supply of Fancy and other Chairs.
N. B. Any of the above Paints, ground in Oil, or dry, properly prepared, may be had at short notice, with Pots, Brushes, &c.
New-Bedford, June 24, 1803.

FIG. 3-58 Advertisement of William Russell, Jr. From *Columbian Courier*, New Bedford, Mass., June 24, 1803.

FIG. 3-59 Excerpt from James C. Helme's "Book of Prices for Making Cabinet & chair furnature," Plymouth, Luzerne Co., Pa., August 30, 1838. *(Winterthur Library.)*

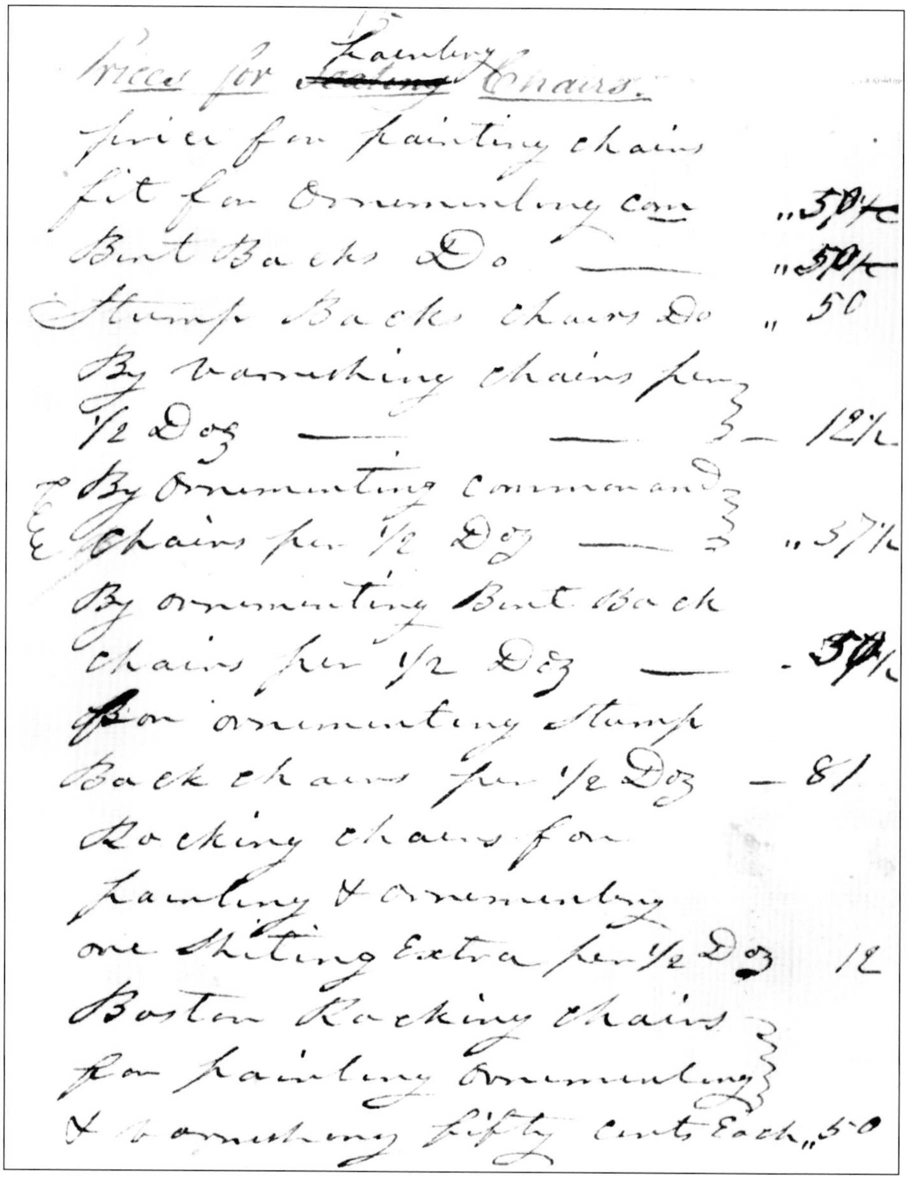

Prices for ~~[illegible]~~ Painting Chairs
price for painting chairs
fit for Ornimenting com ,,50¢
Bent Backs Do — ,,50¢
Stump Back chairs Do „ 50
By varnishing chairs per
1/2 Doz — — 3— 12½
By Ornimenting common and
Chairs per 1/2 Doz — ,,37½
By ornimenting Bent Back
chairs per 1/2 Doz — .50¢
For ornimenting Stump
Back chairs per 1/2 Doz — 81
Rocking chairs for
painting & ornimenting
one Striping Extra per 1/2 Doz 12
Boston Rocking chairs
for painting Ornimenting
& varnishing fifty cents Each,,50

Centinel at Boston for April 17, 1802, stated the general goal: "Chairs repaired and repainted to look as good as new." Work carried out by chairmaker Joseph Henzey of Philadelphia for "Friend Norris" in 1774 included "Mending & Painting 6 Windsor Chairs." Stephen Girard, a merchant prince of Philadelphia, called on local chairmakers between 1787 and 1808 for similar services (fig. **3-60**). Other individuals patronized painting specialists, among them Daniel Rea of Boston. Some records describe Windsor refurbishing in particular terms: "Painting 5 Chares grean and Bottoms Black"; "painting 7 chairs black & striping them"; "Painting 9 Chairs 4 Coats & Ornimenting"; "painting Ornamenting & Varnishing twelve Windsor chairs"; and "mending & painting a settee."[183]

Less commonly noted and generally more extensive was refurbishing undertaken for the business community, because seating in public facilities was subject to greater abuse and wear than that in the home. When the state of Connecticut furnished the new statehouse at Hartford in 1796, "18 Old Chairs belonging to the old Court House" were repainted and recycled. Proprietors of hostelries and hotels were good customers. In the early 1800s Grove Catlin, innkeeper at Litchfield, Connecticut, paid Silas Cheney on a number of occasions to repair, paint, and ornament seating. In 1821, after more than fifteen years' operation, furniture in the Sans Souci Hotel at Ballston Spa, New York, was in considerable need of attention. William White

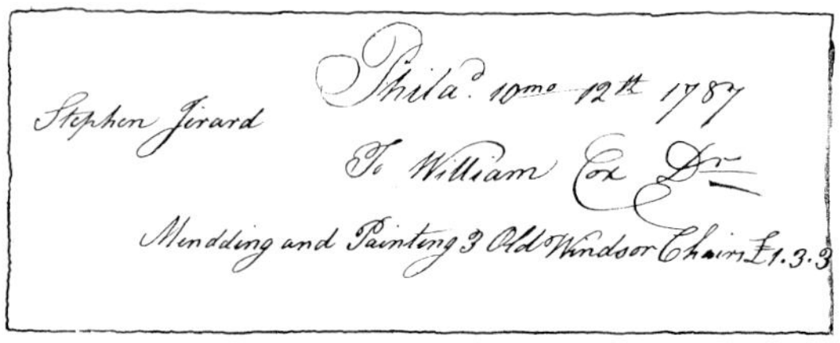

Stephen Girard
Phila. 10mo 12th 1787
To William Cox Dr
Mending and Painting 3 Old Windsor Chairs £1.3.3

FIG. 3-60 William Cox bill to Stephen Girard, Philadelphia, October 12, 1787. *(Collection of the Board of Directors of City Trusts, Girard College History Collections.)*

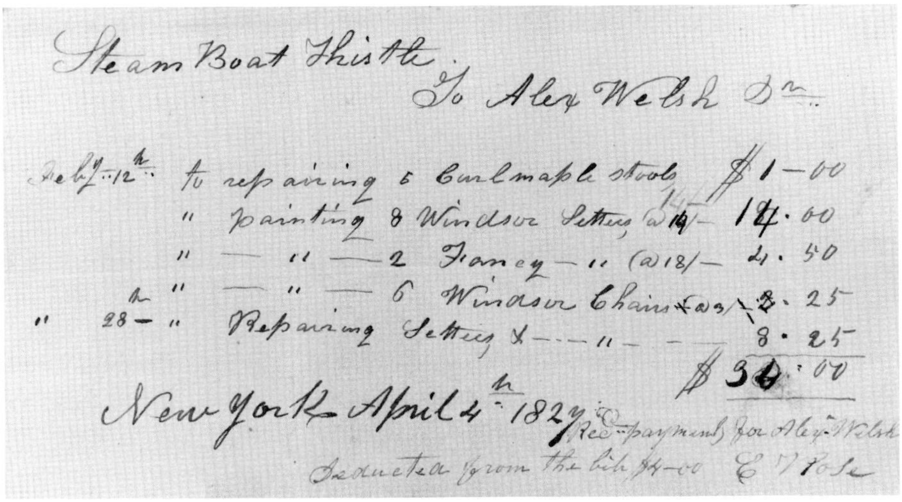

Steam Boat Thistle
To Alex Welsh Dr.

Feby 12th to repairing 5 Curlmaple stools $1—00
" painting 8 Windsor Settees @14/— 14.00
" — " — 2 Fancy — " @18/— 4.50
" — " — 6 Windsor Chairs @3/ 2.25
" 28 — " Repairing Settees & — " — 8.25
$30.00

New York April 4th 1827 Recd payment for Alex Welsh
Deducted from the bill $4—00 E V Rose

FIG. 3-61 Alexander Welsh bill to steamboat *Thistle*, New York, April 4, 1827. *(Winterthur Library.)*

repaired 150 chairs and repainted 469. Similar work at Baltimore's Exchange Hotel in 1843 involved almost 250 seating pieces, including a large rocking chair and a settee. Some fancy furniture required recaning, and redecoration with gold or bronze was specified for other items. All told, Septimus Claypoole refurbished seven "furniture car . . . loads" for the hotel. Steamboat owners had recurring needs: stools, settees, and chairs required repairs and new paint on a continuous cycle. Charles Fredericks and Alexander Welsh, chairmakers of New York, were among those whose shops were patronized for this work (fig. **3-61**).[184]

Craftsmen actively sought commissions for furniture maintenance because the work formed a substantial part of their livelihoods. In a competitive market some offered special inducements for patronage. A familiar promise was that made in 1824 by William Perkins of Connecticut: "Chairs Repaired, Painted, and Gilded, at short notice." Christian Nestell of Providence, Rhode Island, advised that "Families can have their Chairs re-painted and gilt upon fair terms." In 1826 Carman Smith described a complete refurbishing service at Huntington, Long Island: "Old chairs Matted, Mended, Painted and re Gilt or re Bronzed in the neatest manner."[185]

Stuffed Work and Seating Materials

Cushions, pads, and nailed coverings, which introduced a substantial degree of comfort to furniture used for sitting or reclining, had a place in the Windsor seating market. The use of cushions dates to antiquity. Fixed or less portable stuffed work is documented only to medieval England, and it was still uncommon in America into the early 1700s. Although the cushion shared a long life with the Windsor, fast covers for seats were current only in the postrevolutionary years and again during the second quarter of the nineteenth century, when backs also were stuffed.[186]

CUSHIONS

Elegantly embroidered cushions were early symbols of wealth and social position; however, as most cushions were plain, description is limited before the eighteenth century. In Windsor seating three chairs itemized in 1726 in the furnishings of Brigadier General Munden's country home near London had cushions. A decade later Hannah Hodge, widow and shopkeeper of Philadelphia, possessed "3 Elbo Cane Chairs," each with a cushion, and a Windsor. Most prewar American records itemize cushions with unidentified seating, although two inventories drawn at Philadelphia in 1770 list Windsor chairs and cushions. From that date urban references are more common.[187]

Outside Philadelphia a cushion is recorded in the 1760s with a high-back Windsor in the household of William Jevon, a merchant of Lancaster, Pennsylvania. Before 1773 the Reverend Arthur Browne of Portsmouth, New Hampshire, owned a similarly appointed Windsor. On Nantucket listings for Windsor chairs and cushions are relatively common after 1790. In public life cushions provided comfort and served as status symbols for the officials who sat on them, as their cost was substantial. The state of Delaware in 1798 paid $4 apiece for three cushions for "judge's chairs," more than the cost of most painted armchairs. In 1817 cushions served other judges and personnel in the county courthouse at Salem, Massachusetts. Export records of 1798 describe a box of chair cushions shipped from Philadelphia to Havana.[188]

The use of cushions with Windsor furniture was not limited to chairs. Settees frequently had cushions, the practice probably growing out of the earlier custom of placing pads on daybeds, an article of furniture owned primarily by the upper classes. Listed in the estate of Andrew Oliver, Esq., at Boston in 1774 was a "Couch frame Squab & pillow." Late eighteenth-century records of Philadelphia origin contain references to four Windsor settees with cushions, the first dating to 1787. A second settee, described as a "Long Windsor chair & cushion," stood in an upstairs bedroom in the house of merchant Stephen Collins at a time when Captain Thomas Mason furnished his back parlor with a mahogany-colored settee containing a "Matress." In the early 1800s a settee fitted with a cushion stood in Dr. Samuel Lee's home at Windham, Connecticut, for which Amos Denison Allen was a known supplier of Windsor furniture. In the public sector, the Iowa legislature in 1839 introduced a settee and cushion to the capitol furnishings.[189]

Although the appearance of a rocking chair and cushion in a Connecticut estate of 1805 can be considered early, Sarah Anna Emery's recollections of embroidery patterns for rocking chair cushions worked at Newburyport, Massachusetts, predate that record. By the late 1820s cushioned rocking chairs were reasonably commonplace. Maria Foster Brown in recalling her childhood home of the 1830s in Ohio noted a rocking chair "with the most beautiful cushion on it." Another author described his grandmother's rocking chair with its "flat cushion on the seat and a tidy of some sort of needlework on the back." Besides providing comfort, these covers contributed measurably to the preservation of original painted decoration (pl. 27). Cushions were present on still other Windsor forms: A "Close Stool & cushion" and an "easy chair with cushions, hole in seat" date to 1829 and 1833. For the business community there were office chairs with cushions or "extra" cushions and a countinghouse chair with a pad. David Alling of Newark, New Jersey, made a caned barber's chair for a customer in 1838 and furnished it with a "morocco seat cushion."[190]

Cushion materials were varied. For stuffing, rural householders often employed dried grasses or the "husks" (chaff) or straw that remained after threshing grain. Hair or curled hair produced a compact resilient stuffing used extensively. Obtained from the manes and tails of horses and cattle, the material was processed by specialists who twisted their final product "into a kind of rope." As described by Edward Hazen, the upholsterer or cushion maker picked the ropes apart and used the hair in its "curled," or "elastic," state as stuffing. In 1810 John I. Wells of Hartford offered "long Horse and Cattles HAIR" for sale. Feathers were equally popular. Hazen noted their retail by feather merchants whose sources of supply were country merchants, peddlers, and even traveling agents. By the 1830s one New England craftsman offered "First rate live geese feathers, Kentucky and Ohio." Earlier Benjamin Bass of Boston had carried a feather stock of 304 pounds to support his extensive furniture business. Other stuffing materials identified by Hazen include moss, a southern product, and flock, finely chopped wool made from fabric remnants and discarded garments. The secondary cases that received the stuffing were made of inexpensive coarse fab-

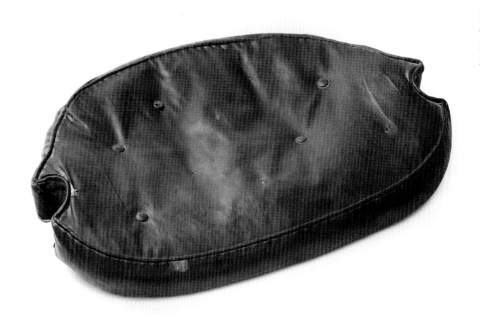

FIG. 3-62 Cushion for Windsor armchair, probably New England, 1810–40. Painted linen or cotton with iron buttons and grass stuffing; w. 21″, D. 16″, thickness 3″. *(Collection of Historic Northampton, Northampton, Mass.; Photo, Winterthur Museum.)*

rics, such as tow cloth, linen, canvas, and ticking, all woven from fibers of the flax plant.[191]

Needlework cushion cases, mentioned frequently in English records, were considerably less common in America. Martha Washington worked a set of a dozen in a shell pattern. Of modified circular form, like the cushion in figure **3-62**, and with fringe around the front, the stuffed pads were fashioned for use on Windsor armchairs. Woven fabrics were popular choices for cushion covers, with moreen and haircloth most in demand. Available in a variety of colors, woolen moreen often was "watered" after weaving to form wavy surface patterns or embossed to introduce flowers and other figures. In 1833 Thomas Ellis, a cabinetmaker of New Bedford, Massachusetts, offered red and green moreen. Woven horsehair coverings were plain or embellished with figures or stripes. Various colors were available, but black was the common choice. Checked fabric, woven in white and any of several colors to form large squares, was of limited popularity. A New York account of 1784 describes the materials needed to cover twelve cushions with "furniture check":

To 12 Cushions at 6/6 [making and stuffing, or recovering]	£3.8.0
To 10½ yds furnerture Check at 2/9	1.8.10½
To 48 yards binding at 5d	1.0.0
To thred & tape	0.6.0[192]

Damask, probably of cotton weave, is specified in 1829 as a cushion cover in an auction at Boston. Durable leather was a good choice, with soft morocco mentioned occasionally. A cheaper substitute was black leatherette (fig. 3-62), an imitation surface on a cotton or linen backing. In this example the interior stuffing probably is grass or straw, and the black-painted iron buttons, ten in number originally, secure the stuffing and introduce a tufted effect to the top surface. Material and technique point to the early nineteenth century, although the profile is that of an eighteenth-century high-back or sack-back Windsor chair seat. George Hepplewhite introduced buttoned surfaces in his *Guide* of 1794 (the plates engraved in 1787), although the technique appears to have been uncommon in America at the time. By 1820 a reference to tufted sofa cushions in the correspondence of the Salisbury family of Worcester and Boston indicates the process was no longer new or unknown. Some cushions were enriched with cord, tassels, or fringes, although these embellishments were more common on fancy seating than on Windsor seating.[193]

STUFFED WINDSOR SEATING

Documentary Evidence
When in 1778 the new American government confiscated the possessions of wealthy Tory sympathizer Joseph Galloway at Philadelphia, "4 Windsor with Hair Bottoms" were enumerated in the estate immediately following an entry for ten mahogany chairs of similar covering. The early date of the notation—some six years before the first "ironclad" reference to Windsors with stuffed seats—opens to question its meaning and validity. The "Hair Bottoms" could have been cushions, yet that identification seems questioned by a similar reference of 1782 in the inventory of Captain Sherman Clarke, a merchant of Newport, Rhode Island, for "One Windsor Chair (Hair Bottom) & Six Hair Bottom Maple Chairs." The practice of stuffing Windsor furniture and coordinating the covering material with that on other household seating appears to have been initiated.[194]

The first public notice of a quasi-upholstery option for Windsor seating dates to October 7, 1784, when the brothers Thomas and William Ash of New York solicited local patrons and "Captains of Vessels": "They have now ready at their Ware-House, a great number of very neat Chairs and Settees, some of which is very elegant, being stuffed in the seat and brass nailed, a mode peculiar to themselves and never before executed in America, and is equal to any mahogany, and comes much cheaper." The following July 4 the local firm of Timpson and Gillihen entered the competition. Among the first Windsors made for stuffing is a round-back armchair of unique pattern, possibly once part of a pair or set, which is labeled by the upholsterer Richard Kip of New York. The chair could date as early as 1786. Another group of stuffed New York Windsors, possessing the rare documentation of both a maker's and an upholsterer's label, comprises a partial set consisting of three bow-back side chairs and two continuous-bow armchairs. The seating probably was ordered by Killian K. Van Rensselaer of Claverack near Albany. The chairs are datable to 1797 through the craftsmen's addresses on the labels. The square-edged seats without a pommel were never painted; the fronts and sides are of rare serpentine form. Stuffed Windsors were then at the height of fashion in New York, as demonstrated in the inventories of two substantial citizens.[195]

The first indication that stuffed Windsor seating was available in Boston shops dates to June 18, 1789, when William Blake advertised "stuff seat chairs" of Windsor construction. Captain Hale Hilton of Beverly may have purchased his padded Windsors shortly thereafter, as the seating was described at his death in 1802 as fan-back chairs rather than the more fashionable bow-backs introduced during the 1790s in the Boston area. Although stuffed-seat Windsors were available in Philadelphia, the only published notice of this service appears to be that of upholsterer [John] Francis Delorme "from Paris." He announced on December 28, 1790, that he stuffed Windsor chairs and settees. Export records also testify to the vitality of the Philadelphia market. Several shipments of stuffed Windsors left the city in 1795 bound for Boston and vicinity, one group identified as mahogany color, another as white. A furniture shipment in 1796 from Joseph Anthony and Company to Elias Hasket Derby at Salem, described as "24 Oval Back Chairs Stuff'd Seats covered with Hair Cloth, 2 Rows Brass Nails at 34/," has been thought through the years to identify either the well-known upholstered and painted feather-back chairs that descended in the family or another unidentified set of fancy seating. Actually, the bill describes Windsor chairs, as determined by the cost. In 1796 another merchant house of Philadelphia recorded the individual price of stuffed Windsor side chairs finished with a single

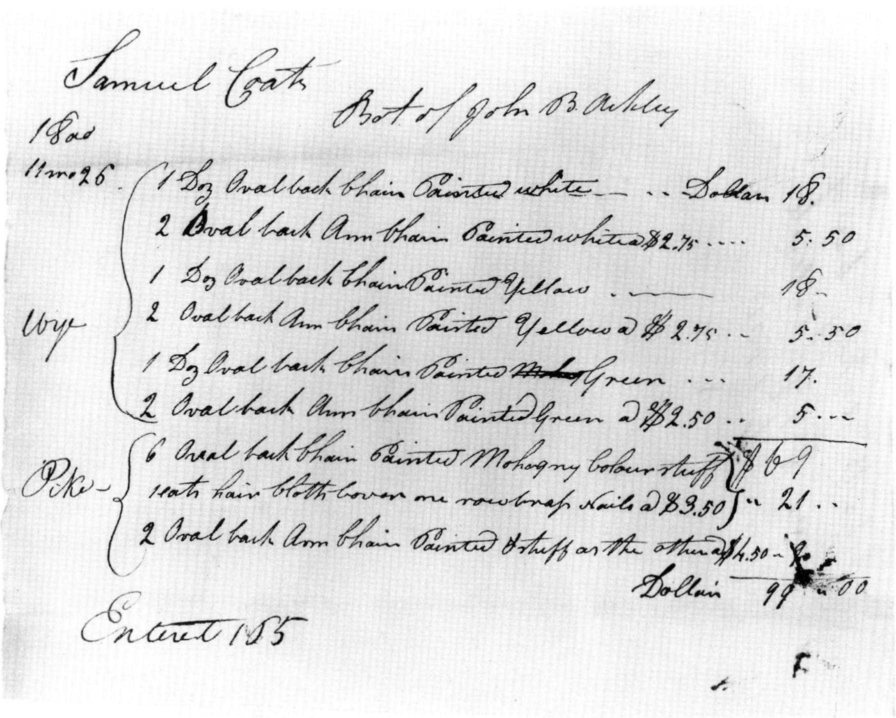
Samuel Coats
Bot of John B Ackley
1800
11mo 26. 1 Doz Oval back Chairs Painted white ... Dollars 18.
2 Oval back Arm Chairs Painted white @ $2.75 .... 5.50
1 Doz Oval back Chairs Painted Yellow ... 18.
Wye 2 Oval back Arm Chairs Painted Yellow @ $2.75 .. 5.50
1 Doz Oval back Chairs Painted ~~Mahog~~ Green ... 17.
2 Oval back Arm Chairs Painted Green @ $2.50 .. 5..
Pike 6 Oval back Chairs Painted Mohogany colour stuff seats hair Cloth Cover one row brass Nails @ $3.50 .. 21..
2 Oval back Arm Chairs Painted & stuff as the other @ $4.50 .. 9
Dollars 99.00
Entered 155

FIG. 3-63 John B. Ackley bill to Samuel Coates, Philadelphia, November 26, 1800. *(Reynell and Coates Collection, Baker Library, Harvard Business School, Cambridge, Mass.)*

row of brass nails as 31*s.* 6*d.*, and the unit cost for Windsor *armchairs* of similar description was 37*s.* 6*d.* Clearly, the Derby chairs fall within the stuffed Windsor price range. Providing additional weight to the argument is brother John Derby's order at Philadelphia five years later for sets of green and black chairs ornamented with gold at a cost of 80*s.* the chair. This was fancy seating of rich gilt, and it appears to have been stuffed.[196]

The accounts of Stephen Collins and Son, merchants, provide penetrating insights into the nature of Philadelphia stuffed Windsor work, as described shortly. The house served as factor between customers and local chairmakers for furniture shipments directed to Boston, Petersburg, Virginia, and probably Saint Croix. Samuel Coates, another local mercantile figure, made extensive purchases of Windsor seating, some stuffed, from John B. Ackley in 1800 in a wide range of colors, as indicated in the chairmaker's bill (fig. **3-63**). A notation at the left of the account, which appears to read "Wye," may identify a Maryland port of call on the Chesapeake Bay where the chairs were to be landed. The previous year "One Doz Chairs Stuff Botoms" were carried to Fredericksburg, Virginia, on the sloop *Friendship*. In Virginia chairmaker James Beck met the competition by advertising his own stuffed Windsors several years later. In 1799 when appraisers evaluated the estate of William Will, a pewterer of Philadelphia, they enumerated "8 Stuffed Winsor chairs" among the furnishings of the "Back parlour," a room used for dining. Philadelphia influence spread inland as well. At Lancaster the prominent lawyer Jasper Yates purchased a dozen yellow Windsors in 1796 from chairmaker Samuel Humes and then took them around to the shop of Conrad Swartz, a saddler, for "stuffing and seating." Presumably the covering was leather. At George Mason's plantation in the Shenandoah Valley of Virginia the parlor contained a large set of twenty Windsors stuffed and covered in green wool moreen.[197]

The new fashion in stuffed seating also found its way to rural southeastern New England, probably through New York sources. In 1794 Ebenezer Tracy, Sr., exchanged ten green stuffed side chairs for store goods from Andrew Huntington at Norwich, Connecticut. As Huntington was engaged in commerce, he probably supplied "stuff" for the "bottoms." At Tracy's death in 1803 his own household contained "8 Cushing'd botomed Chairs," which later were part of his widow's estate. Tracy's son-in-law and

former apprentice, Amos Denison Allen, began making stuffed Windsors at South Windham in spring 1798, when Deacon Samuel Perkins ordered "6 fancy arm'd Chs with cushions in ye bottoms." Fancy was the local name for the continuous-bow Windsor. Jonathan Bright, upholsterer of Hartford, offered stuffed-seat Windsors along with lolling chairs and feather beds. Similar seating was available at neighboring Wallingford and at Providence.[198]

The Seat Plank

Windsor seats designed for stuffing exhibit several treatments in surface and edge preparation. Tracy family chair planks are saucered through the center and finished sufficiently to eliminate the rough wood and tool marks. Cheeks are low at the forward corners, the central pommel is missing, the upper front edge is flat, and the lower edge is sharply chamfered. In the last respect the Tracy seat differs from those of most other areas except, perhaps, some of Rhode Island origin. A full blunt edge without a chamfer is by far more common. The Tracys appear to have stuffed seats principally in the continuous-bow armchair. Marked planks usually bear Ebenezer, Sr.'s, brand ("EB:TRACY"), although a few are stamped by his eldest son, Elijah ("E. TRACY")." Son-in-law Amos Denison Allen's memorandum book clearly indicates he stuffed Windsors of continuous-bow pattern, and he also "cushioned" a set of fanback chairs and several groups of bow-back chairs.[199]

A group of contemporary Rhode Island chairs features thick, blunt-edge seats for stuffing, finished smooth without shaping other than a slight depression worked at the center top (fig. 2-28). The deep edges, which provide a tacking surface for the undercover, also allow for the use of ornamental nails. A pair of bow-back Windsors by James Chapman Tuttle of Salem, Massachusetts (fig. **3-64**), relates to Rhode Island work in general plank shape, although the seats bear visible adze marks on the

FIG. 3-64 Bow-back Windsor side chair with seat for stuffing (one of two) and detail of brand, James Chapman Tuttle, Salem, Mass., ca. 1798–1805. White pine (seat); H. 38¹⁄₁₆", (seat) 17⅜", W. (seat) 17⅜", D. (seat) 16⅞". *(Private collection; Photo, Winterthur Museum.)*

FIG. 3-65 Detail of seat plank of bow-back Windsor side chair in fig. 3-64 showing adzed top surface.

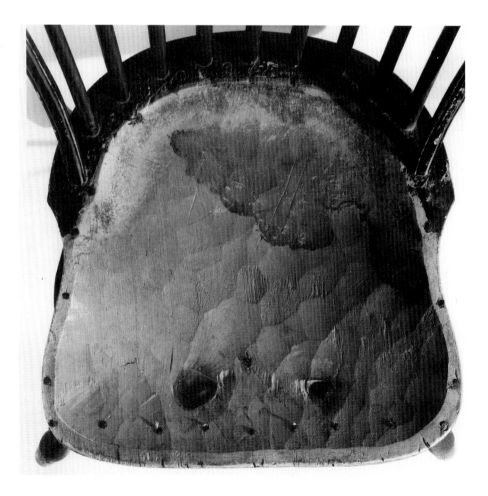

top surface (fig. **3-65**). Armchairs of Philadelphia and New York origin have broad seats of shield form (figs. **3-66**, 3-70). The plank in the Philadelphia chair, which is rounded at the top edge, was only partly stuffed over the front edge, as tack holes indicate. An incised line along the lower edge coordinates with similar ornament on the bow face, arms, and arm posts. Other examples from Philadelphia have thick, blunt forward edges, and a labeled pair of New York bow-back chairs exhibits tool marks on the top surface.[200]

In tracing the general sequence of events, stuffed Windsor work appears to have originated in Philadelphia, moved quickly to New York, then advanced to New England, where workmen in Connecticut and Rhode Island introduced the feature first and Boston craftsmen followed. Quite a different approach to the stuffed seat appears in a later Windsor made in 1819 for use in the New Hampshire Statehouse. The seat is framed in four pieces forming a broad outside rim with an open center supported from the bottom by strips of interlaced webbing, a technique more correctly defined as upholstering. The construction introduced a seat of large size without the expense of purchasing wide plank. Only a year later Robert McKim of Richmond made a dozen stuffed-seat Windsors to furnish a city courtroom. Whether the Virginia chairmaker duplicated the construction process of the New Hampshire chairs is unknown.[201]

Stuffing Materials and Practice
The materials of the stuffed Windsor seat frequently duplicated those of the cushion. The common stuffings were horsehair, dried grasses, and tow, sometimes used in combination. In 1793 John Lambert, a Windsor-chair maker of Philadelphia, stocked "3½ lbs Curled Hair" valued at about $1. The cotton batting sometimes found in old stuffing is not of the early period. To secure the stuffing, workmen used a coarse, plain-woven undercover of natural linen. The finish fabric covered this, and again woven horsehair, wool moreen, leather, and furniture check are all mentioned in the records. The two earliest references to stuffed Windsors describe "Hair Bottoms." Elias Hasket Derby's oval-back chairs ordered in 1796 from Philadelphia also were covered in haircloth, and some customers of the merchant Stephen Collins of that city requested the same fabric. John B. Ackley's bill of 1800 itemizes mahogany-colored Philadelphia Windsors with haircloth seats (fig. 3-63). At that date city retail shops offered "Plain, striped and Figured Hair Seatings." A later document of Connecticut origin identifies horsehair in three widths — 16, 22, and 24 inches. Horsehair and moreen also were popular as seat coverings for mahogany furniture. In 1797 Windsor chairs covered in moreen were part of George Mason's plantation furnishings in western Virginia. When ordering moreens from London in 1784, Stephen Collins used the term "Windsor green," and through the years he also purchased blue, pink, and crimson cloth. Black is mentioned elsewhere. Twice moreen-covered Windsors were ordered by Collins's distant clients. During the 1790s the yard price was 4s. (about 50¢ to 65¢) on Long Island.[202]

Leather-covered Windsor seating was fashionable, particularly at Baltimore, where James Zwisler and Company manufactured "Morocco and other Leather." Apparently the firm purchased Windsor seating locally or imported it from Philadelphia. In summer 1793 they offered "A Variety of Arm and other Windsor Chairs, and Settees, the seats neatly stuffed, and covered with red, green, yellow, blue, and black Morocco coloured leather" of their own manufacture. Jasper Yates of Lancaster, Pennsylvania, took his Windsors to a local saddler for leather covers three years later. In New England Louisa Crowninshield Bacon recalled the leather-covered Windsors in her grandparents' parlor at Danvers, Massachusetts. She described the seats as brown but suggested they once had been green. Checked coverings perhaps formed slipcases as well as fast covers for Windsors. An item in the inventory of Dr. John Baker's household taken in 1797 at New York suggests a nailed covering

FIG. 3-66 Bow-back Windsor armchair with seat for stuffing, John B. Ackley (brand "I•B•ACKLEY"), Philadelphia, 1785–90. Yellow poplar (seat) with maple, oak, and hickory (microanalysis); H. 36⁵⁄₁₆", (seat) 16½", W. (arms) 20⁵⁄₁₆", (seat) 20⁵⁄₁₆", D. (seat) 17⅝". *(Courtesy, Winterthur Museum, acc. 65.3021.)*

for seating in the dining room: "9 Mahogony Chairs stuff bottoms yellow Check furniture, . . . 4 Windsor Chairs same furniture."[203]

Business records and visual evidence indicate there were several levels of stuffed work in Windsor seating. Least expensive was a cover drawn under the seat front and tacked. At the spindle platform, where it is impossible to conceal the fasteners, plain nails were painted to match the seat covering (fig. 3-70). Amos Denison Allen described this kind of "Cushioned" seating in his records: "8 Dining Chs green, cushions green." The next level of work added a row of closely spaced brass nails to the bottom edge of the seat front (fig. 3-69) and a row at the spindle platform, the latter sometimes widely spaced (fig. 3-65, spindle platform). This treatment is mentioned in the Ash brothers' early advertisements at New York and by the local partnership of Timpson and Gillihen. A Boston client of the Collins firm of Philadelphia ordered haircloth and brass nails in 1795. The Ackley bill of 1800 to Samuel Coates describes the embellishment precisely as "one row brass Nails" (fig. 3-63).[204]

A bill from John B. Ackley to the merchant house of Stephen Collins and Son dated August 13, 1796, describes top-line stuffed Windsor seating:

8 Oval Back Chairs Painted Yellow stuff seats covered with morean	
1 Row Brass Nails and Fring @ 31/6	£12.12.0
1 Oval back mohagny Arm Settee Painted and stuff as the Chairs	£ 7.13.0
	£20.05.0

In Connecticut Titus Preston made a set of eight Windsors in 1801 for which the customer supplied the haircloth and fringe. Green fringe ornamented the faded leather on the Windsors in the home of Louisa Bacon's grandparents in Massachusetts. The vogue for fringed trim on Windsors originated with upholstered formal furniture. Joseph Stewart's well-known portrait of the Reverend Eleazer Wheelock, first president of Dartmouth College, pictures the cleric seated on an upholstered "easy" chair finished at the bottom edge with brass nails and fringe. The draped window hanging also is fringed. A double row of brass nails in lieu of fringe produced an equally rich effect.[205]

A Windsor chair of dark-colored seat, probably leather, fully garnished with brass nails and fringe forms a strong secondary focus in William Sidney Mount's interior view of an artist's studio (fig. 3-67). The bulbous chair turnings reflect the New York style. The stuffed work undoubtedly is original, although the padding has worked its way forward, forming an unusually large hump at the front. John Brewster made a colorful rendering of another stuffed Windsor in his portrait *Comfort Starr Mygatt and his Daughter Lucy* (pl. 35). The eighteenth-century grass-green paint is contrasted with a red bottom, possibly representing the woolen fabric moreen. The union of cloth and wood is punctuated by a row of shinny brass nails augmented by compatible green fringe. Brewster probably was familiar with the stuffed-seat Windsor through contemporary work of the Tracy family in his native eastern Connecticut, although its appearance in the Danbury portrait may reflect the influence of New York production on the local market. Certainly the peaked end of the crest visible in the chair back is associated with work from neighboring New Haven.[206]

A clever simulation of the brass-nailed stuffed Windsor seat is a distinctive feature of a painted chair from Baltimore or southern Pennsylvania (fig. 3-68). The "cushion" bottom is carefully rounded at the edges to represent stuffing and depressed slightly at the center, as if from long use. The regularly spaced "nails" around the "seat frame" secure the imaginary cover. Dark brown paint contrasts with cream and medium brown decoration. A landscape typical of Baltimore work adorns the crest, and the cuffs on the front ankles, which bear traces of gilt, probably simulate ornamental metal mounts.

In studying the exposed rough planks of a group of Windsor chairs, it is apparent that the undercover securing the stuffing materials was drawn over the top margin of the seat and nailed widely on either the bottom of the plank or the flat vertical edges (figs. 3-69, 3-70). Sometimes there also was a bottom cover, or sack, which lay against the top surface of the wood and with the undercover formed a large linen pocket. The presence of this extra cloth layer is indicated in several examples by the appearance of a spaced row of handwrought nails, or nail holes, on the top surface of the plank an inch or less inside the edge. The nails further anchored the stuffed unit, as illustrated in figure 3-65. Another use of nails around the top edges of some chair planks was to secure a narrow, snakelike, stuffed roll that created a well for the stuffing, better defined the forward profile, and provided rigidity to the completed seat at a point of stress (fig. 3-70). Here the original edge roll consists of long, stiff reeds secured with blue and white twill-woven ticking closely nailed along a raw cloth edge at the front and a raw edge folded back on itself on the seat top. The front nailing line of the undercover is beneath the seat. The finish fabric was pulled firmly over the stuffed interior of the plank and nailed in place behind the undercover. The closely spaced holes that appear as dark dots within circles along the lower plank edges of several chairs mark the tight row of ornamental brass nails that originally

FIG. 3-68 Tablet-top Windsor side chair, Baltimore or southern Pennsylvania, 1825–30. Yellow poplar (seat, microanalysis); H. 35⅛", (seat) 18", W. (crest) 18½", (seat) 18", D. (seat) 15⅛"; dark brown ground with cream, medium brown, and gold. *(Collection of the late Milton E. Flower; Photo, Winterthur Museum.)*

FIG. 3-69 Detail of seat plank of bow-back Windsor side chair in fig. 3-64 showing tacking lines for undercover (*center*) and row of ornamental brass nails (*bottom*).

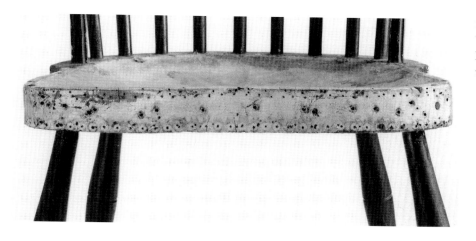

FIG. 3-70 Detail of seat plank and original stuffing material of continuous-bow Windsor armchair, New York, 1790–1800. Yellow poplar (seat); w. (seat) 17½", D. (seat) 17⅜". *(Courtesy of James and Nancy Glazer; Photo, Winterthur Museum.)*

embellished the work (figs. 3-69, 3-70). Their distinct outlines indicate that the original coverings were in place a long time. The holes near the upper edge of figure 3-69 appear to have been made at a later date.

Original nailing lines also are pictured in detail views of a Windsor stool (fig. 3-71). The dark curled horsehair stuffing is clearly visible at the top. Large original nails centered in the side surface mark the place where the coarse linen undercover was secured, and indeed a nail hole appears in the cloth, as pictured below. Originally the outer, or finish, cover was drawn under the seat and nailed at one of two tacking lines on the plank. A row of ornamental brass nails likely finished the lower edge of the seat, although with many holes there now, the evidence is not entirely clear. Seat contours in stuffed Windsors appear to have formed low, somewhat flattened, crowns with just enough padding at the upper plank edges to prevent sharp corners from breaking through. Formal chairs illustrated in Hepplewhite's *Guide* (1794) picture this profile. During the late nineteenth century many standard Windsor planks were converted to stuffed seats by covering the top surface with a fast cushion. Some conversions employed brass-headed nails of large size or incorrect tacking patterns. The Victorians also seemed fond of padding arm tops.[207]

Slipcovers

Throughout the eighteenth century it was common English practice to protect fine upholstery with washable cases, or slipcovers, for general household use, removing them only for special occasions. That practice also prevailed in America (fig. 5-8) and extended even to the stuffed Windsor. A bow-back armchair, the seat covered by a slipcover with a deep flounce, was part of the parlor funishings in the home of Doctor Whitridge of Tiverton, Rhode Island, at the turn of the nineteenth cen-

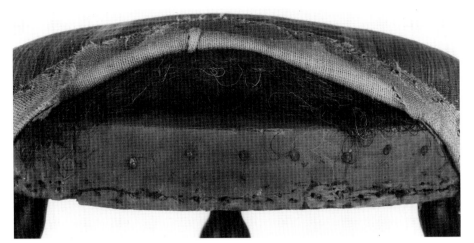

FIG. 3-71 Details of seat plank and original interior stuffing of medium-high Windsor stool, Boston, 1795–1800. Birch (seat, microanalysis). *(Collection of Ledlie I. Laughlin, Jr.; Photo, Winterthur Museum.)*

tury (fig. **3-72**). Related coverings are described in various records. Henry Hill of Philadelphia imported elegant gilt seating in 1789 from London along with cotton "Callico Covers for Chairs," the fabric possibly printed with a pattern. Aaron Burr's home in New York City was furnished in 1797 with "Mahogany chairs Hair Bottoms & Chintz covers" and "6 Stuffed Back chairs (dimity covers)." In 1820 Hugh Finlay and Company of Baltimore, fancy-furniture manufacturers, described moreens, chintzes, and fringes among the "raw materials of the trade." It was chintz covers that protected the horsehair cushions on the green and gold chairs standing in 1806 in Samuel Broome's home in Whitemarsh, Pennsylvania.[208]

Other Stuffed Forms
From time to time specialized Windsor forms were stuffed. In 1796 the Philadelphia firm of Stephen Collins and Son purchased "8 windsor chairs and a sopha stuffed" from John B. Ackley to ship to a client. Stools of all heights had stuffed tops. Crickets, or footstools, often were stuffed and covered with haircloth or carpet. Elisha Harlow Holmes of Essex, Connecticut, recorded in 1829 an instance of "making [and] triming two Crickets." Several years later Isaac Wright of Hartford identified a "high stool" with a hair seat. Beginning in the late 1820s the stuffed rocking chair received considerable attention. In 1827 Henry W. Miller, chair manufacturer of Worcester, Massachusetts, sold a "Rocking Chair Lin'd with Hair Cloth." The design probably was close to that of the chair in figure 4-28, whose contoured back posts and spindles form the framework supporting the stuffing and cloth. Haircloth and moreen continued in popularity, although both were substantially challenged during the 1830s by the new textile "plush," a wool velvet. In 1830 Samuel Beal advertised from his Boston furniture and feather store that he carried a stock of "Spring Seat Plush and

FIG. 3-72 Joseph S. Russell, *North Parlor of Dr. Whitridge*, Tiverton, R.I., ca. 1848–53, depicting scene of 1814. Watercolor on paper; H. 7¹⁄₁₆", W. 9½". *(Collection of New Bedford Whaling Museum, New Bedford, Mass.)*

Hair Cloth Rocking Chairs." Some spring cushions likely were supported on plank bottoms. Plush colors included green, red (crimson), yellow, salmon, blue, and purple. An elegant covering was the "Green Medalion fig[ure]d plush" on the rocking chair purchased from William Hancock of Boston by Mrs. Stephen Salisbury I of Worcester. The Salisbury mansion also contained several crickets covered in plush. Additional coverings for the rocking chair included crimson velvet, described in 1831 in a Boston auction catalogue, morocco leather, and "damask" (probably wool or cotton), used for the "back & seat cushions" of a "large curl Maple Rocking chair" sold in 1835 by Philemon Robbins at his store in Hartford.[209]

Like painted surfaces, cloth covers required periodic renewal; however, because of the expense they were dealt with less frequently. The Greene family of Providence sent a set of chairs to John Hopkins in 1835 for "repairing, painting, & recovering." A few years earlier Isaac Bronson of New York had paid Samuel Perry to "take the covering from & clean the seats of 3 chairs." A more detailed account of this work and its cost is part of the records of Daniel Wadsworth of Hartford. A craftsman's bill for refurbishing green armchairs describes the materials as curled hair, tow cloth (coarse linen), green moreen, fringe, and brass nails (fig. **3-73**). When a Beekman family member sent a rocking chair to the firm of Browne and Ash in New York for repairs and "cleaning," it was directed that "New Marrocco Leather" be placed on the seat and back.[210]

WOVEN, NATURAL SEATING MATERIALS

Rush

Rushing, or matting, chair seats using the pliable stems of freshwater marsh plants, called rushes or flags, was a seating method transplanted from Europe to America during the seventeenth century. Although the technique was popular over a long period, it generally was relegated to common chair work (fig. 3-18) until the introduction of fancy seating (fig. 5-9). A notable exception is the use of rush in cased-seat chairs constructed in the Queen Anne and Chippendale styles.

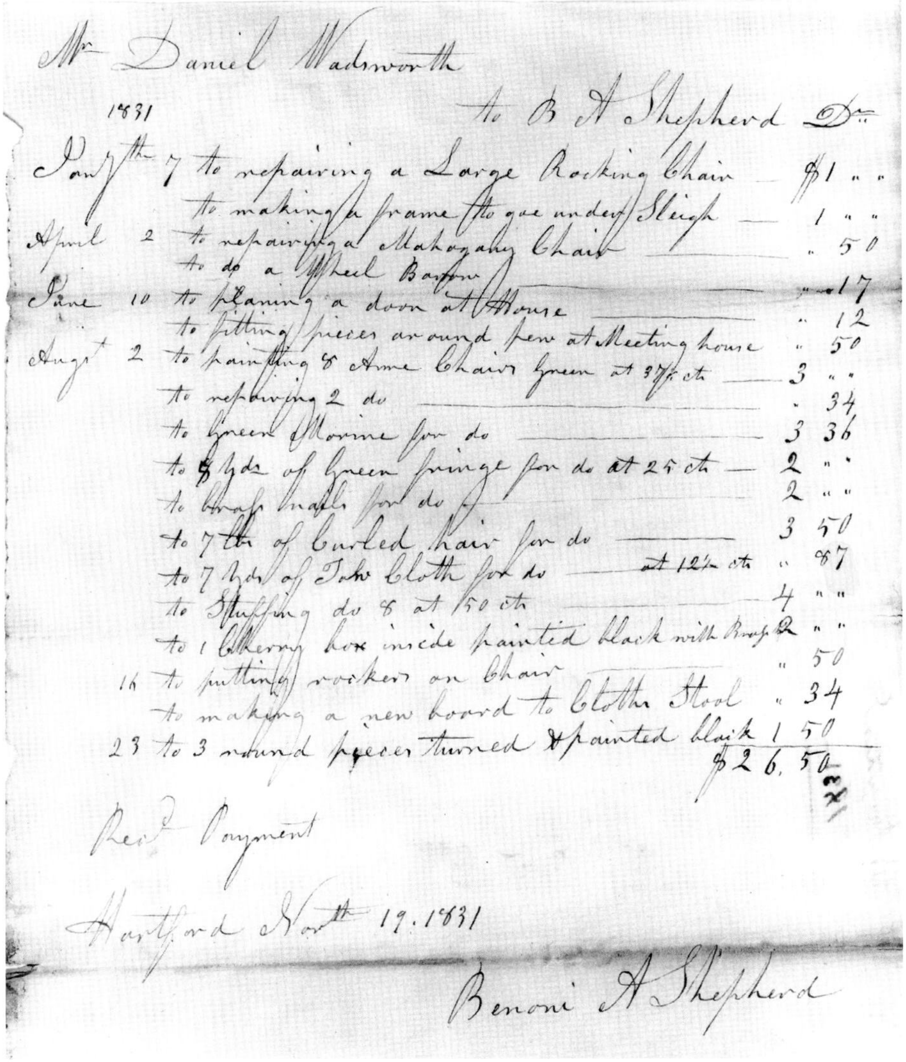
Mr Daniel Wadsworth

1831 to B A Shepherd Dr

Jany 7th 7 to repairing a Large Rocking Chair $1 " "
to making a frame to go under Sleigh 1 " "
April 2 to repairing a Mahogany Chair " 50
to do a Wheel Barrow " 17
June 10 to planing a door at House " 12
to fitting pieces around pew at Meeting house " 50
Augt 2 to painting 8 Arm Chairs Green at 37½ cts 3 " "
to repairing 2 do " 34
to Green Morine for do 3 36
to 8 yds of Green fringe for do at 25 cts 2 " "
to brass nails for do 2 " "
to 7 lb of Curled hair for do 3 50
to 7 yds of Tow Cloth for do at 12½ cts " 87
to Stuffing do 8 at 50 cts 4 " "
to 1 Cherry box inside painted black with Brass 2 " "
16 to putting rockers on Chair " 50
to making a new board to Clothes Stool " 34
23 to 3 round pieces turned & painted black 1 50
$26.50

Recd Payment

Hartford Novr 19.1831

Benoni A Shepherd

FIG. 3-73 Benoni A. Shepherd account of Daniel Wadsworth, Hartford, Conn., 1831. *(Daniel Wadsworth Papers, The Connecticut Historical Society Museum, Hartford, Connecticut.)*

Rush harvesting took place at summer's end in swamps or marshy areas bordering rivers and lakes. The bundled material was hauled with team and wagon to the shop, where the bundles were opened and cured in the sun. When dry the rush, or flag, was rebundled for storage pending use or sale. Among prerevolutionary shop masters, Daniel Jones of Philadelphia, a slat-back-chair maker, had a stock in 1766 of about 300 bundles. His contemporaries Thomas and John Larkin of Charlestown, Massachusetts, lost 700 and 500 bundles, respectively, in 1775 when the British burned the town. David Finch, a nineteenth-century fancy-chair maker of Bridgeport, Connecticut, anticipated brisk business with his supply of "725 Bundles Rush." More modest were Thomas Kinsela's expectations, as in 1822 appraisers counted a mere "53 Bundles flags" at his facility in Schenectady, New York. Among raw materials tabulated in the 1820 manufacturing census are 300 bundles of flag consumed annually in a Cincinnati shop and 1,000 in a New York establishment. The cost of a bundle of flag is difficult to pinpoint, since figures vary from 2¢ to 50¢. No doubt bundle size, and the quality and age of the material, had considerable bearing on the figure. When William Perkins of Connecticut purchased "50 bundles flagg" in 1824 from Elizur Barnes, the charge was 8¢ per bundle.[211]

A *Weekly Museum* notice in 1797 at New York advised local chairmakers that Captain Van Voorhis had "a large quantity of Rushes in bundles" on board his sloop at Coenties Slip (fig. **3-74**). A later record pinpoints the origin of some cargoes. In August 1812 the sloop *Grey Hound* carried 100 bundles of rush to the city from New

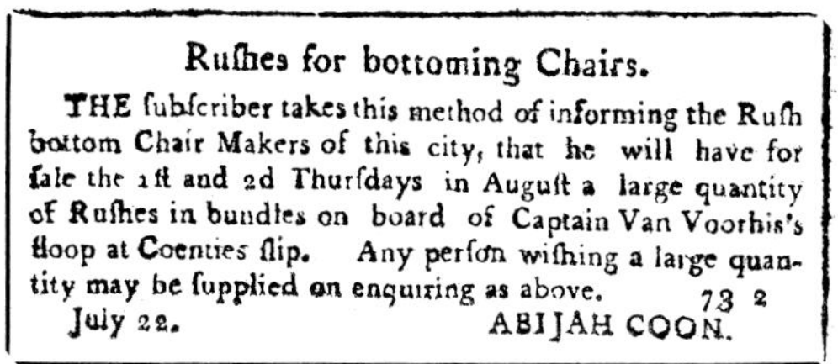
Rufhes for bottoming Chairs.

THE fubfcriber takes this method of informing the Rufh bottom Chair Makers of this city, that he will have for fale the 1ft and 2d Thurfdays in Auguft a large quantity of Rufhes in bundles on board of Captain Van Voorhis's floop at Coenties flip. Any perfon wifhing a large quantity may be fupplied on enquiring as above. 73 2

July 22. ABIJAH COON.

FIG. 3-74 Advertisement of Abijah Coon. From *Weekly Museum*, New York, July 29, 1797.

Brunswick, although New Jersey was only one of many areas that abounded with lakes and lowland rivers where natural seating materials grew. The cost of rush to seat one chair was reasonably low in the nineteenth century — about 4¢ to 6¢. Labor was higher. The complete job, including materials and labor, varied from 20¢ to 50¢, depending on seat size and fineness of work. Elizur Barnes of Middletown, Connecticut, charged 33¢ in 1821 for "Seating Cheir." Because flag seats were highly "destructible under wear & pressure & needed frequent repair or entire replacement," the business was a brisk one. Thomas West of New London, like hundreds of fellow chairmakers, advertised his services in bottoming chairs "with flags on the shortest notice." The perishable nature of rush seats was a decided factor in the rapid ascendancy of the wood-seat Windsor in the vernacular seating market prior to the Revolution.[212]

The rushing process began with dampening a quantity of material to make it soft and pliable. The worker then took several strands of moist rush, attached them to a seat frame, twisted the fibers, and began making the "mat." Before a strand ran out new pieces were twisted in, making the fiber continuous. Fineness of work depended largely on the amount of twist given the fiber. When weaving was complete, the matter stuffed the seat interior with discarded material, using a stick flattened at one end to permit insertion between the woven strands. The worker sat on a low seat or on the floor (figs. 2-5, 3-32, bottom). Even under good conditions matting was a dusty, dirty job.[213]

To prolong the life of a rush seat, it was common to paint it. As Thomas Sheraton recommended:

> Rush-bottom chairs ought always to have their seats primed with common white lead, ground up in linseed oil, and diluted with spirits of turpentine. This first priming preserves the rushes, and hardens them; and, to make it come cheaper, the second coat of priming may have half Spanish white in it, if the price require it. The third coat should be ground up in spirits of turpentine only, and diluted with hard varnish, which will dry quick; but should not be applied till the priming be perfectly dry. Of this, probably the seats may require to have two lays, to make the work firm.

About 1810, when Allen Holcomb worked as a journeyman in Troy, New York, he painted seats in new fancy chairs. Whether all the coats recommended by Sheraton were employed regularly is open to question. Periodically old rush-bottom chair seats were refurbished or strengthened with an additional coat of paint. Specialist Stephanus Knight of Enfield, Connecticut, recorded "Painting Chare bottoms" in 1800 for a client. A few years later Silas Cheney of Litchfield scraped six chair seats before repainting them. Charges ranging between 8⅓¢ and 19⅓¢ seem to have been normal for repainting, and some surfaces likely received more than one coat. White was the most common color, although in 1822 Elizur Barnes of Middletown painted "8 Seats yellow." On April 13, 1832, William Beesley of Salem, New Jersey, recorded the sale of "1 lb yellow for Chair seats." Commenting on central New Jersey chairmaking, William H. MacDonald has stated, "Seats were usually painted yellow." There also is record of "Varnishing . . . Chair Botoms."[214]

Bark Strips and Splints

Narrow strips of wood cut to a thin dimension and woven on an open chair frame to any of several patterns served as another seating material for common chairs. In the 1740s chairmaker Solomon Fussell of Philadelphia referred to these seats as "Checkt bottom[s]." Other craftsmen described the seating material rather than the weaving pattern. Thus in 1794 Elisha Hawley of Ridgefield, Connecticut, spoke of "Bottoming [a] Chair with Bark." The use of wood strips for seating was considerably less common than rush, although in the Boston area Stephen Whipple noted on one occasion that he had reseated "3 chairs 2 of them with bark & the other with flags."[215]

In harvesting wood strips for seats, the chairmaker chose a small tree of 12-inch diameter or less. One modern builder of traditional chairs who uses hickory shaves off the outer bark finely with a drawknife, marks lengthwise strips on the inner bark with a sharp knife, and peels off thin ribbons of material that are coiled and stored for use. The material was soaked briefly in water before use. Some chairmakers used splints of white oak or ash. Peeled from trimmed sections of trunk, they sometimes required pounding to loosen the fibers. The same material served in basketmaking. The naturalist François André Michaux, commenting on the black ash during his American travels, noted that the wood could be "separated into thin, narrow strips" and was "selected in the country for chair-bottoms and riddles." Edward Jarvis of Concord, Massachusetts, commented further on "basketwork" seats in his nineteenth-century reminiscences, noting that "though sufficiently strong & durable," they "were rough and destructive to the garments of the sitters."[216]

Cane

Canework for seating achieved popularity during the reign of Charles II. Light, durable, and free of vermin, it remained in vogue in England until the start of the eighteenth century. The fashion lingered longer in America, where as late as 1720 judge Samuel Sewall of Salem, Massachusetts, ordered two dozen cane chairs and a couch from England. By 1734 Philadelphia had its own resident cane-chair maker, but by that date the fashion also was waning in America.[217]

Renewed interest in canework among English and American furniture makers emerged in the late eighteenth century and continued for almost a century (fig. 1-16). Advertisements by the Finlay brothers of Baltimore in 1805 specifically identify cane-seat fancy chairs. Before the decade's end American cane-seat fancy chairs were imported regularly into Charleston, South Carolina, and even shops in small towns such as Redding, Connecticut, offered the new work to customers. At New York chairmaker Asa Holden described still another dimension of the trade when stating in 1812 that his cane seats were "warranted to be American made, which are well known to be much superior to any imported from India" (fig. **3-75**). The knowledge that seats were prewoven for inserting into chair frames as early as 1812 predates by several decades present information on the practice.[218]

The New York shop that reported using 1,000 bundles of rush annually in the manufacturing census of 1820 identified a parallel consumption of 50 bundles of cane. A Baltimore notice of 1828 offering 27 bales already split for chairmakers' use describes the availability of the eastern commodity (fig. **3-76**). That figure is dwarfed by the recorded sale in 1837 of two lots of cane, both numbering over 1,000 bundles, at 7¢ and 7½¢ the bundle in the accounts of Jacob Felton of New Hampshire. In light of Felton's interaction with the Boston chair market, that city likely was the supply source. David Alling of Newark was already a longtime user of cane. A supplier credit for "14 hundred cane seat side pieces" in 1839 addresses the scope of this branch of his business. As described by Thomas Sheraton, the best cane was "of a fine light straw colour," and that tint was found to be "the most agreeable contrast to almost every colour it is joined with."[219]

Seat caning was a clean process compared with rushing. Through the 1830s caning constituted men's work, but by midcentury women and even children skillfully executed the woven patterns. Walter Corey's factory in Maine employed women for the task by that date, and a piecework cottage industry flourished in northern Worcester County, Massachusetts. The cane weaver sat on a low stool close to the work using only a few simple tools—a knife, pegs to secure the cane, a mallet to drive the pegs, and an awl-like device to clean out clogged holes in seat frames.

FIG. 3-75 Advertisement of Asa Holden. From *New-York Evening Post*, New York, August 4, 1812.

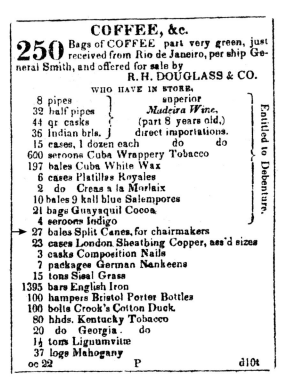

FIG. 3-76 Advertisement of R. H. Douglass and Co. From *American and Commercial Daily Advertiser*, Baltimore, October 30, 1828.

Preparation of cane for weaving usually was the province of men and consisted of trimming joints, splitting stalks, removing pith, and cutting small strips to weaving width. At first chair seats were laboriously drilled by hand to receive woven cane, but eventually machines speeded production. After 1850 another remarkable revolution occurred in the American industry when power looms were introduced to weave continuous webs of cane and automatic channeling machines cut grooves in seats to receive webs cut to shape. The web was installed wet and held fast by splints and glue.[220]

NOTES

1. William G. Beesley daybook, 1828–41, Salem County Historical Society, Salem, N.J. The author is indebted to Frank G. White for his observations on the Daniel's planer.

2. Michael Dunbar, *Make a Windsor Chair with Michael Dunbar* (Newtown, Conn.: Taunton Press, 1984), pp. 6–23; Leigh Keno, "The Windsor Chairmakers of Northampton, Massachusetts, 1790–1820" (Historic Deerfield Summer Fellowship Program paper, Deerfield, Mass., August 1979), p. 29. The author is indebted to John D. Alexander, Jr., for reading the construction section of this chapter and making critical comment.

3. Silas E. Cheney daybook, 1802–7, Litchfield Historical Society, Litchfield, Conn. (hereafter cited LHS; microfilm, Joseph Downs Collection of Manuscripts and Printed Ephemera, Winterthur Museum and Library, Winterthur, Del. [hereafter cited DCM and WL]); use of the travisher in J. Geraint Jenkins, *Traditional Country Craftsmen* (London: Routledge and Kegan Paul, 1965), pp. 117, 119, fig. 26; L. J. Mayes, *The History of Chairmaking in High Wycombe* (London: Routledge and Kegan Paul, 1960), p. 11, fig. 9.

4. Miles Hart receipt, 1816, and Sidney Twidel account of Silas Cheney, 1819, Miscellaneous Papers, Superior Court Records, Litchfield Co., Conn., Connecticut State Library, Hartford (hereafter cited CSL); Silas E. Cheney daybook, 1807–13, LHS (microfilm, DCM); James Gere ledger, 1822–52, CSL; Thomas Boynton ledger, 1811–17, Dartmouth College, Hanover, N.H. (hereafter cited DC; microfilm, DCM); Nelson Talcott daybook, 1839–48, DCM; Josiah Prescott Wilder daybook and ledger, 1837–61, privately owned, as transcribed in Charles S. Parsons, Wilder Family Notes, Visual Resources Collection, WL (hereafter cited VRC). The additional information on seat shaping is from George Craft and Mr. Barnes taped interviews, 1950s, High Wycombe Library, High Wycombe, England. The men were among the last craftsmen in Buckinghamshire to labor within a semi-industrial framework little changed from nineteenth-century practice. Drew Langsner has indicated to the author that elm wood, the choice of English chairmakers for chair seats, is harder and more difficult to adze than American pine and yellow poplar, and it is prone to splinter.

5. Edward Hazen, *The Panorama of Professions and Trades* (Philadelphia: Uriah Hunt, 1836), p. 227; Ebenezer Tracy, Sr., estate records, 1803, Lisbon, Conn., Genealogical Section, CSL; Elijah Babcock account book, 1785–1822, CSL; Parsons, Wilder Family Notes.

6. Barnes taped interview; Talcott daybook. A seat-boring gauge is at the High Wycombe Chair Museum, High Wycombe, England (hereafter cited HWCM). John Henry

Hill, "The Furniture Craftsmen in Baltimore, 1783–1823" (master's thesis, University of Delaware, 1967), p. 119; John Lambert estate records, 1793, as quoted in William MacPherson Hornor, Jr., *Blue Book: Philadelphia Furniture* (1935; reprint, Washington: Highland House, 1977), pp. 300, 311; Dunbar, *Make a Windsor Chair*, pp. 44–53.

7. The Tracys' incised circumferential notch was formed in a lathe. During framing, as the slightly oversize leg tenon was driven into the mortise, it deformed the end-grain fibers of the mortise, pushing them toward the bottom of the socket. As the seat dried, the end-grain fibers of the mortise straightened, returned to their original position, and formed a locking circumferential ridge inside the tenon notch.

8. Dunbar, *Make a Windsor Chair*, pp. 26–27, 62–71; L. J. Mayes, "The Windsor Chairmaker's Tools" (leaflet), HWCM; Ebenezer Bryant accounts of Silas Cheney, 1815 and 1819, Cheney court records. Tenon drying is discussed in the following: Jenkins, *Traditional Country Craftsmen*, p. 120; Barnes taped interview; David Sawyer, "Spoon Bits," and John D. Alexander, Jr., "The Incredible Duckbill Spoon Bit Joint," *Fine Woodworking*, no. 43 (November–December 1983): 71–72; John D. Alexander, Jr., *Make a Chair from a Tree: An Introduction to Working Green Wood* (Newtown, Conn.: Taunton Press, 1978), pp. 8, 11, 31–33, 68–85; Henry Hammond Taylor, *Knowing, Collecting, and Restoring Early American Furniture* (Philadelphia: J. B. Lippincott, 1930), p. 143.

9. William H. MacDonald, *Central New Jersey Chairmaking of the Nineteenth Century* (Trenton, N.J.: By the author, 1960), p. 15; Dunbar, *Make a Windsor Chair*, pp. 65–67; Alexander, *Make a Chair*, pp. 68–77; Thomas Hennell, "The Windsor Chair Maker," *Architectural Review* 90, no. 540 (December 1941): 179–80.

10. Dunbar, *Make a Windsor Chair*, pp. 68–71; Taylor, *Knowing Early American Furniture*, pp. 76–77; wedge making described in Barnes taped interview. R. W. Symonds in "The Windsor Chair," *Apollo* 22, no. 128 (August 1935): 68, commented on the use of wedges in Italian stools dating from the Middle Ages, and he stated, "Continental chairs, dating from the XVIIth century, were also made in this way, and it was a construction that was not unknown to the English joiner of the Jacobean period."

11. Stephanus Knight account book, 1795–1809, Connecticut Historical Society, Hartford (hereafter cited CHS); James Gere ledger, 1809–29, and account book, 1809–39, CSL; Wilder daybook and ledger.

12. Dunbar, *Make a Windsor Chair*, pp. 94–99. For Rhode Island chairs with vase-turned spindles, see Nancy Goyne Evans, *American Windsor Chairs* (New York: Hudson Hills Press, 1996), figs. 6-1, 6-2. Mr. McNiel account with Silas Cheney, 1810–11, Cheney court records.

13. Taylor, *Knowing Early American Furni-*

ture, p. 75. The information is based in part on exhibits at the High Wycombe Chair Museum and conversations with L. J. Mayes. Francis Trumble estate records, 1798, City and County of Philadelphia, Pa., Register of Wills; "The Contence of the Book Paints and Receipts for Wooden Work," *Connecticut Historical Society Bulletin* 9, no. 2 (January 1943): 14.

14. Bryant account of Silas Cheney; Talcott daybook.

15. Alexander, *Make a Chair*, pp. 65–67, 95–99; Talcott daybook; Twidel account of Silas Cheney; Gere ledger, 1822–52.

16. Dunbar, *Make a Windsor Chair*, pp. 72–79.

17. Trumble estate records; Henry J. Harlow, "The Shop of Samuel Wing, Craftsman of Sandwich, Massachusetts," *Antiques* 93, no. 3 (March 1968): 374; Daniel and Samuel Proud ledger, 1782–1825, Rhode Island Historical Society, Providence (hereafter cited RIHS).

18. Dunbar, *Make a Windsor Chair*, pp. 82–93; "Paints and Receipts for Wooden Work," p. 15.

19. Dunbar, *Make a Windsor Chair*, pp. 80–81, 100–125.

20. For Rhode Island low-back chairs with the features described, see Evans, *American Windsor Chairs*, fig. 6-2.

21. James C. Helme book of prices, 1838, DCM. Helme could have copied or modeled his price sheets after a scale of wages for cabinetwork and turned seating drawn in Philadelphia during the early 1830s when the city experienced considerable labor unrest. William Butler account with Silas Cheney, March 26, 1808, Cheney court records.

22. Striping is mentioned in the Boynton ledger and Allen Holcomb account book, 1809–28, Metropolitan Museum of Art, New York.

23. Gere ledger, 1822–52.

24. Seymour Watrous, *Connecticut Courant* (Hartford), March 2, 1824, as illustrated in John Tarrant Kenney, *The Hitchcock Chair* (New York: Clarkson N. Potter, 1971), p. 56; Mathias Stover, *South Bend Free Press* (South Bend, Ind.), April–July 1838, as quoted in Betty Lawson Walters, *Furniture Makers of Indiana, 1793 to 1850* (Indianapolis: Indiana Historical Society, 1972), p. 201.

25. Solomon Fussell account book, 1738–48, Stephen Collins Collection, Library of Congress, Washington, D.C. (hereafter cited LC; microfilm, DCM); Henzey in Hornor, *Blue Book*, p. 301; Charles Norris account book, 1739–70, Norris of Fairhill Manuscripts, Historical Society of Pennsylvania, Philadelphia (hereafter cited HSP); Oliver Moore account book, 1808–19, CHS; Benjamin and Elijah Farrington and Alexander Welsh bills to steamboats *Bellona* and *Thistle*, August 2, 1828, and February 1827, DCM; Miles Beach bill to Nicholas Low, October 9, 1807, and William White bill to

Samuel Hicks, Jr., agent for Nicholas Low, April 20, 1821, Nicholas Low Collection, LC; Septimus Claypoole bill to Jerome N. Bonaparte for Commercial Exchange Co., March 10, 1843, Baltimore Exchange Hotel Collection, Maryland Historical Society, Baltimore (hereafter cited MdHS).

26. Henry Bradshaw Fearon, *Sketches of America*, 2d ed. (London: Longman et al., 1818), p. 130; Benjamin Silliman, *A Journal of Travels in England, Holland, and Scotland, and of Two Passages over the Atlantic in the Years 1805 and 1806*, 2 vols. (Boston, 1812), 1:303–4, as quoted in Wendell Garrett, ed., "Clues and Footnotes," *Antiques* 107, no. 6 (June 1975): 1158.

27. Rocker repairs in Abner Taylor account book, 1806–32, DCM; new rocker in Holcomb account book; rocker and support replacements in George Landon account book, 1813–32, DCM; fastening rockers in Titus Preston ledger, 1811–42, Sterling Memorial Library, Yale University, New Haven, Conn. (hereafter cited Yale).

28. Martin Sampson account book, 1812–30, DCM; John D. Brown bill to Captain Vanderbilt, April 1821, DCM; Alexander Low account book, 1784–1826, Monmouth County Historical Association, Freehold, N.J.; Cheney daybook, 1807–13; wedging and gluing in Preston ledger; True Currier account book, 1815–38, DCM.

29. Thomas J. Moyers and Fleming K. Rich account book, 1834–40, DCM; Silas E. Cheney daybooks, 1807–13 and 1813–21, LHS (microfilm, DCM).

30. Joseph Stone account of William Arnold, 1793–95, A. C. and R. W. Greene Collection, RIHS; Holcomb account book; Paul Jenkins daybook, 1836–41, DCM; Preston ledger; Cheney daybook, 1807–13.

31. Daniel and Samuel Proud daybook and ledger, 1810–34, RIHS; Charles C. Robinson daybook, 1809–25, HSP; George G. Jewett bill to Lt. Gov. John Taylor, June 12, 1826, Taylor-Cooper Papers, New York Public Library, New York (hereafter cited NYPL); Holcomb account book; settee and rocker arms in David Alling ledger, 1803–53, and daybook, 1836–54, New Jersey Historical Society, Newark (hereafter cited NJHS; microfilm, DCM).

32. Beesley daybook; Job Danforth ledger, 1788–1818, RIHS; Richard Alexander account of Mrs. Francis, 1817–22, Cadwalader Papers, Gen. Thomas Cadwalader, HSP; Joseph K. Ott, "Recent Discoveries among Rhode Island Cabinetmakers and Their Work," *Rhode Island History* 28, no. 1 (February 1969): 23.

33. Philemon Robbins account book, 1833–36, CHS.

34. Rocker references in Danforth ledger and Jenkins daybook; Cheney daybook, 1802–7; Robinson daybook; Currier account book. For the Lawson and Harrington chair, see Evans, *American Windsor Chairs*, fig. 7-34.

35. Moyers and Rich account book; Alling ledger, 1803–53; Titus Preston ledger, 1795–1817, Yale; James Chesney bill to Peter E. Elmendorf, November 19, 1805, Sanders Papers, New-York Historical Society, New York (hereafter cited NYHS); Henry T. Williams and Mrs. C. S. Jones, *Beautiful Homes, or Hints in House Furnishing* (New York, 1878), pp. 224–25, as quoted in Wendell Garrett, ed., "Clues and Footnotes," *Antiques* 109, no. 5 (May 1976): 1074.

36. John Andrews letter to William Barrell, June 22, 1772, Andrews-Eliot Papers, Massachusetts Historical Society, Boston (hereafter cited MHS); Thomas and Edward Kindred receipt to Gibson and (George) Jefferson, August 21, 1801, Papers of Thomas Jefferson, MHS; Thomas Boynton ledger, 1817–47, DC (microfilm, DCM); Elisha Harlow Holmes ledger, 1825–30, CHS.

37. Francis Trumble, *Pennsylvania Gazette* (Philadelphia), December 27, 1775; Gilbert Gaw broadside bill to Stephen Girard, October 20, 1808, Girard Papers, Board of Directors of City Trusts, Girard College History Collections, Philadelphia, Pa. (microfilm, American Philosophical Society, Philadelphia, Pa.).

38. Andrew Gautier, *New-York Gazette, or Weekly Post-Boy* (New York), June 6, 1765; Thomas and William Ash, *New-York Packet* (New York), October 7, 1784. For Goodrich labels, see Evans, *American Windsor Chairs*, fig. 6-243. Ansel Goodrich estate records, 1803, Hampshire Co., Northampton, Mass., Registry of Probate; Joseph Vail inventory, 1805, DCM; Alexander Walker, *Virginia Herald* (Fredericksburg), April 26, 1805, and March 14, 1806, citation file, Museum of Early Southern Decorative Arts, Winston-Salem, N.C. (hereafter cited MESDA); Thomas Howard, *Providence Gazette* (Providence, R.I.), May 9, 1812 (reference courtesy of Susan B. Swan).

39. Richard Cornwell and Jacob Smith printed billhead, 1817–19, inscribed in 1820 by Richard Cornwell and Job(?) Cowperthwaite, DCM; records of the 1820 United States Census of Manufactures, state of Massachusetts; Earle G. Shettleworth, Jr., and William D. Barry, "Walter Corey's Furniture Manufactory in Portland, Maine," *Antiques* 121, no. 5 (May 1982): 1201.

40. Ridgely in Hill, "Furniture Craftsmen in Baltimore," p. 14; Talcott daybook; Luke Houghton ledger C, 1834–76, Barre Historical Society, Barre, Mass. (hereafter cited Barre; microfilm, DCM).

41. Robinson daybook; Senter in Ott, "Recent Discoveries," p. 25. For a set of Rhode Island armchairs, see Evans, *American Windsor Chairs*, fig. 6-78. Elisha Hawley account book, 1781–1800, CHS.

42. Solomon Cole account book, 1794–1809, CHS.

43. Reuben Loomis account book, 1793–

1836, CHS; Elisabeth Langdon note to Silas Cheney, n.d., Cheney court records.

44. Cornelius Tooker, *Fayetteville Gazette* (Fayetteville, N.C.), May 15, 1822, as quoted in James H. Craig, *The Arts and Crafts in North Carolina, 1699–1840* (Winston-Salem, N.C.: Old Salem, 1965), pp. 203–4; Alexander Walker, *Virginia Herald*, April 26, 1805, citation file, MESDA; Levi Stillman account book, 1815–34, Yale; Boynton ledger, 1811–17; Alling, daybook; Vail inventory; Benjamin Love estate records, 1821, City and County of Philadelphia, Register of Wills (microfilm, DCM).

45. Gere ledger, 1822–52; Currier account book; Robbins account book.

46. Robbins account book; Boynton ledger, 1817–47; John W. Blanchard bill to Proprietors of Boston Theatre, May 1, 1829, Boston Theatre Papers, Boston Public Library, Boston.

47. For the nurse and sewing chairs, see Evans, *American Windsor Furniture: Specialized Forms* (New York: Hudson Hills Press, 1997), figs. 1-27, 1-56. Cheney daybook, 1813–21; Holmes ledger; Mary Pease, Jonathan Burnell, Peter Coffin, and Henry Clark estate records, 1793, 1799, 1800, and 1801, Nantucket Co., Nantucket, Mass., Registry of Probate. For a Nantucket chair and the man's/woman's chairs, see Evans, *American Windsor Chairs*, figs. 6-235, 6-120.

48. William Cox bill to Stephen Girard, May 9, 1787, Girard Papers.

49. David Pritchard, Jr., ledger, 1800–10, Mattatuck Museum, Waterbury, Conn.

50. "Mortised top" in Peter A. Willard estate records, 1842–43, Worcester Co., Worcester, Mass., Registry of Probate. For a Baltimore cross-back chair, see William Voss Elder III, *Baltimore Painted Furniture, 1800–1840* (Baltimore: Baltimore Museum of Art, 1972), p. 45. David Alling ledger, 1815–18, NJHS (microfilm, DCM). For fret-back and scalloped-top chairs, see Evans, *American Windsor Chairs*, figs. 5-46, 5-47, 7-17, 3-138.

51. "Flat back" in Benjamin Bass estate records, 1819, Suffolk Co., Boston, Mass., Registry of Probate (microfilm, DCM).

52. For high-back chairs of smaller size and their English prototypes, see Evans, *American Windsor Chairs*, figs. 3-19 to 3-21, 1-23, 3-29, 3-34, 1-21.

53. [George] Hepplewhite, *The Cabinet-Maker and Upholsterer's Guide* (1794; reprint, New York: Dover Publications, 1969); Thomas Sheraton, *The Cabinet-Maker and Upholsterer's Drawing-Book* (1793; reprint, New York: Dover Publications, 1972). For chairs with pierced cross banisters and a formal Philadelphia prototype, see Evans, *American Windsor Chairs*, figs. 3-53, 3-54.

54. Ansel Goodrich, *Hampshire Gazette* (Northampton, Mass.), September 16, 1795. For the Jefferson revolving bergère chair, see Evans, *American Windsor Chairs*, fig. 6-242.

55. Charles Percier and Pierre François Fontaine, *Recueil de décorations interieures* (Paris, 1801); Pierre La Mésangère, *Collections des meubles et objets de goût* (Paris, 1802); *The London Chair-Makers' and Carvers' Book of Prices for Workmanship* (London, 1802); Thomas Hope, *Household Furniture and Interior Decoration* (1807; reprint, New York: Dover Publications, 1971); George Smith, *A Collection of Designs for Household Furniture and Interior Decoration* (1808; reprint, New York: Praeger, 1970).

56. For a Baltimore cross-rod prototype, a serpentine-rod chair and shield-back prototype, and a stepped-tablet prototype crest, see Evans, *American Windsor Chairs*, figs. 3-117, 7-44, 7-45, 7-37. Thomas Sheraton, *Cabinet Dictionary*, 2 vols. (1803; reprint, New York: Praeger, 1970), 1: pl. [30, right]; Hepplewhite, *Guide*, pls. 1–7; *London Book of Prices* (1802), pls. 3 and 6, no. 9; Hope, *Household Furniture*, pl. 11; Smith, *Designs for Household Furniture*, pl. 53.

57. Sheraton, *Drawing-Book*, pl. 33, right; *The New-York Book of Prices for Cabinet and Chair Work* (New York: Southwick and Crooker, 1802), p. 56, as quoted in Charles F. Montgomery, *American Furniture: The Federal Period* (New York: Viking Press, 1966), p. 115; Elder, *Baltimore Painted Furniture*, p. 28.

58. Sheraton, *Cabinet Dictionary*, 1: pls. [30], 31; *London Book of Prices* (1802), pl. 3, fig. 6. For a New York cross-banister chair and a formal example, see Evans, *American Windsor Chairs*, figs. 5-49, 5-47. *The New-York Book of Prices for Manufacturing Cabinet and Chair Work* (New York: J. Seymour, 1817), as quoted in Montgomery, *American Furniture: Federal*, p. 104.

59. Hepplewhite, *Guide*, pls. 9, 12–13. For the Odell and Egbert chairs, see Evans, *American Windsor Chairs*, figs. 5-34, 5-36. For a Grecian-style chair, see Evans, *Specialized Forms*, fig. 1-35.

60. *London Book of Prices* (1802), pl. 3, figs. 3, 4. For a Boston rocking chair, see Evans, *Specialized Forms*, fig. 1-42. La Mésangère, *Collections des meubles*; George Smith, *The Cabinet-Maker and Upholsterer's Guide* (London: Jones, 1826), pl. 119; John Hall, *The Cabinet Makers' Assistant* (Baltimore: John Murphy, 1840), fig. 188.

61. Daniel Trotter estate records, household goods taken by Ephraim Haines at the appraisment, December 31, 1800, DCM; Jacob Sanderson inventory, 1810, Sanderson Family Manuscripts, Peabody Essex Museum, Salem, Mass. (hereafter cited PEM); Sheraton, *Drawing-Book*, pl. 33, right; illustration of a Peirce-Nichols chair and note on 1802 London price book in Montgomery, *American Furniture: Federal*, figs. 23, 38. For Gragg's "elastic" chair and a contoured-back rocking chair, see Evans, *Specialized Forms*, figs. 1-34, 1-38.

62. Gregory R. Weidman, *Furniture in Maryland, 1740–1940* (Baltimore: Maryland Historical Society, 1984), pp. 77, 94 (n. 81); Miles Benjamin daybook and ledger, 1821–29, New York State Historical Association, Cooperstown (hereafter cited NYSHA; microfilm, DCM); Perez Austin estate records, 1833, Canterbury, Conn., Genealogical Section, CSL.

63. Sheraton, *Cabinet Dictionary*, 1:145–46.

64. Helena Hayward, ed., *World Furniture* (New York: McGraw-Hill, 1965), pp. 10–18, 20–24, 26–34, 36–39, 57–60; Jonathan L. Fairbanks and Robert F. Trent, *New England Begins: The Seventeenth Century*, 3 vols. (Boston: Museum of Fine Arts, 1982), 3:368–79, 501–3, 517–36.

65. Gertrude Z. Thomas, *Richer Than Spices* (New York: Alfred A. Knopf, 1965), pp. 17–26, 76–92; Hayward, *World Furniture*, pp. 87–90.; Percy Macquoid and Ralph Edwards, *The Dictionary of English Furniture*, 3 vols. (1924–27; reprint of 2d ed., rev. Ralph Edwards, Woodbridge, England: Barra Books, 1983), 3:13–14.

66. Dean A. Fales, Jr., *American Painted Furniture, 1660–1880* (New York: E. P. Dutton, 1972), pp. 32–83, 254–57; Brock Jobe and Myrna Kaye, *New England Furniture: The Colonial Era* (Boston: Houghton Mifflin, 1984), pp. 136–38, 223–26, pl. 2; Scott T. Swank et al., *Arts of the Pennsylvania Germans* (New York: W. W. Norton, 1983), pp. 137, 145, pls. 1-2, 4, 7, 9, 12-15.

67. Hepplewhite, *Guide*, p. 2; James C. Tuttle, *Salem Gazette* (Salem, Mass.), August 19, 1796, as quoted in Mabel M. Swan, *Samuel McIntire, Carver, and the Sandersons, Early Salem Cabinet Makers* (Salem, Mass.: Essex Institute, 1934), p. 30.

68. Kenneth Roberts and Anna M. Roberts, trans. and eds., *Moreau de St. Méry's American Journey, [1793-1798]* (Garden City, N.Y.: Doubleday, 1947), p. 264; Robert Dossie, *The Handmaid to the Arts*, 2 vols. (London: J. Nourse, 1758), 1:104–5; "Paints and Receipts for Wooden Work," pp. 12–13.

69. Sheraton, *Cabinet Dictionary*, 2:328; P. F. Tingry, *The Painter's and Colourman's Complete Guide*, 3d ed. (London: Sherwood, Gilbert, and Piper, 1830), pp. 88–89; Obed Faye paint recipe sent to Samuel Wing, n.d., Samuel Wing Papers, Old Sturbridge Village, Sturbridge, Mass (hereafter cited OSV); Richard M. Candee, "Housepaints in Colonial America: Their Materials, Manufacture, and Application," "Part 3: Nomenclature of Painters' Materials," *Color Engineering* 5, no. 1 (January–February 1967): 40–41; James Claypoole, *Pennsylvania Gazette*, June 14, 1750; Timpson in anonymous account book, 1794–95, DCM; Goodrich estate records; David Haven account book, 1785–1800, DCM.

70. Ebenezer Swift note to Samuel Wing, May 18, 1799, Wing Papers; Trumble estate records; Joseph Henzey and William Cox bills to Stephen Girard, 1786–93, Girard Papers; William Blake, *Independent Chronicle* (Boston), June 18, 1789, as quoted in Esther Stevens Fraser, "Painted Furniture in America, Part 1," *Antiques* 5, no. 6 (June 1924): 306; John De Witt bill to the Corporation of the City of New York, October 1796, New York City Vouchers, Historical Documents Collection, Queens College, Flushing, N.Y.; John Wadsworth bill to Connecticut Statehouse, Hartford, June 8, 1796, CHS; Richard Cornwell and Job(?) Cowperthwait bill addressed to No. 139 Broadway, January 3, 1820, DCM.

71. Margaret Berwind Schiffer, *Chester County, Pennsylvania, Inventories, 1684–1850* (Exton, Pa: Schiffer Publishing, 1974), pp. 104, 108; Love estate records; New Jersey references in James Dorman inventory, 1824, DCM, and Ebenezar P. Rose estate records, 1836, Archives and History Bureau, New Jersey State Library, Trenton (hereafter cited NJSL); Cennino D'Andrea Cennini, *The Craftsman's Handbook*, trans. Daniel V. Thompson, Jr. (New York: Dover Publications, 1933), p. 33; "Paints and Receipts for Wooden Work," p. 12.

72. "Elijah Eldredges Book of Receipts for Painting & Staining Wood," ca. 1821–29, DCM; Hezekiah Reynolds, *Directions for House and Ship Painting* (1812; facsimile reprint, Worcester, Mass.: American Antiquarian Society, 1978), pp. 10–11; Rufus Porter, "The Art of Painting," *Scientific American* 1, no. 6 (October 2, 1845): 2, and no. 5 (September 25, 1845): 3; Schiffer, *Chester County Inventories*, pp. 104, 108; Lambert Hitchcock estate records, 1852, Farmington, Conn., Genealogical Section, CSL; Charles Riley estate records, 1842, City and County of Philadelphia, Register of Wills (microfilm, DCM); light, dark, and clouded green in David Alling account book, 1801–39, NJHS (microfilm, DCM).

73. Schiffer, *Chester County Inventories*, pp. 104, 106, 108; John Minnick, *City Gazette, or the Daily Advertiser* (Charleston, S.C.), August 15, 1789, citation file, MESDA; Cutbush in Hornor, *Blue Book*, p. 298; Nathaniel Smith inventory, 1793, Baltimore Co., Baltimore, Md., Register of Wills (microfilm, DCM); Doris Devine Fanelli, "The Building and Furniture Trades in Lancaster, Pennsylvania, 1750–1800" (master's thesis, University of Delaware, 1979) p. 16; Cole account book; Tracy estate records; Benjamin H. Hathorne account of house furniture, March 14, 1800, Ward Family Papers, PEM.

74. William Cox bill to Stephen Girard, March 12, 1791, Girard Papers; Porter, "Art of Painting," October 2, 1845, p. 2; Reynolds, *Directions for Painting*, p. 10; Daniel Rea daybook, 1789–93, Baker Library, Harvard University, Cambridge, Mass. (hereafter cited BL). For the set of chairs originally painted straw color, see Evans, *American Windsor Chairs*, fig. 6-211. Thomas Boynton ledgers, and shop account, 1817–35, DC (microfilm, DCM).

75. Thomas Sheraton, *Cabinet Dictionary*, 1:29; Nicholas Ridgely account at auction, March 18, 1803, Ridgely Papers, MdHS; manifests of brig *Union* and schooner *Eliza*, December 21, 1805, and December 3, 1811, Philadelphia

Outward Coastwise Entries, U.S. Custom House Records, National Archives, Washington, D.C. (hereafter cited NA); Veree and Blair, *Charleston Courier* (Charleston, S.C.), February 18, 1807, citation file, MESDA; Stephen Girard invoice of goods on ship *Rousseau*, December 22, 1810, in invoice book, 1802–11, Girard Papers; Cheney daybooks, 1802–7 and 1807–13; Alling account book.

76. Joseph Walker invoice book, 1784, Independence Seaport Museum, Philadelphia, Pa.; Benjamin Franklin estate records, 1790, City and County of Philadelphia, Register of Wills (photostat, DCM); Haven account book.

77. John Lambert estate records, 1793, City and County of Philadelphia, Register of Wills; William Cox bill to Gen. Henry Knox, July 29, 1794, Papers of Henry Knox, Maine Historical Society, Portland; Rea daybook; Micaiah Johnson account of Elijah and Jacob Sanderson, 1794–95, Papers of Elijah Sanderson, PEM; William Palmer bill to Nicholas Low, January 4, 1804, Low Collection, LC; Nicholas L. Quinn (?) bill to George Boyd "for the President's House," May 25, 1815, Treasury Records, Miscellaneous Treasury Accounts of the First Auditor, no. 29,494, NA; Cheney daybook, 1807–13; Luke Houghton ledger A, 1834–76, Barre (microfilm, DCM).

78. Candee, "Housepaints in Colonial America, Part 3," pp. 39–40; P. F. Tingry, *The Painter and Varnisher's Guide* (London: G. Kearsley, 1804), pp. 286–87, 289–92; Jacob Bigelow, *The Useful Arts*, 2 vols. (Boston: Thomas H. Webb, 1840), 1:169; Sheraton, *Cabinet Dictionary*, 2:418.

79. Candee, "Housepaints in Colonial America, Part 3," pp. 37–38; Tingry, *Painter and Varnisher's Guide*, pp. 347–50; Bigelow, *Useful Arts*, 1:168–69; Porter, "Art of Painting," October 2, 1845, p. 2; Sheraton, *Cabinet Dictionary*, 1:53–54.

80. Anthony Steel shipping manifest, Philadelphia, December 1, 1801, Philadelphia Custom House Records, HSP; Adam Snyder bill to Thomas Claxton, agent for Thomas Jefferson, July 31, 1801, and Thomas Jefferson letter to George Jefferson, March 10, 1809, Jefferson Papers; Amos Denison Allen memorandum book, 1796–1803, CHS; William Ryder inventory, 1806, DCM; William Ash bill to Captain Randall, July 3, 1802, Wendell Papers, BL; David Tilden lawsuit vs. William Seaver, 1804, Colonial Court Records, Social Law Library, Boston (reference courtesy of Charles A. Hammond and John T. Kirk); Wicklief Chadwick and Lydia Pinkham estate records, 1809 and 1810, Nantucket Co., Mass., Registry of Probate.

81. R. D. Harley, *Artists' Pigments* (New York: American Elsevier Publishing, 1970), pp. 83–84, 137–39; brown slat-back seating in John Gaines II account book, 1712–50, DCM; William Cox bill to Gen. Henry Knox, May 19, 1795, Knox Papers; Allen memorandum book;

Schiffer, *Chester County Inventories*, p. 108; Buttre in J[oseph] Fry, comp., *Albany Register, and Albany Directory, for 1815* (Albany, N.Y.: H. C. Southwick et al., 1815), p. 33 (reference courtesy of Anne Ricard Cassidy); Thomas Adams bill to U.S. War Office, December 8, 1814, Treasury Records, Miscellaneous Treasury Accounts of the First Auditor, no. 29,475, NA.

82. Morris Earle bill to William Beekman, June 4, 1773, White-Beekman Papers, NYHS; John Minnick, *City Gazette, or the Daily Advertiser*, November 13, 1789, citation file, MESDA; Trumble mahogany chairs in Isaac Hazlehurst invoice of cargo, December 1, 1789, and bill of disbursements, December 12, 1789, Constable-Pierrepont Papers, NYPL; H. Richardson bill to Richard Blow, June 2, 1794, Richard Blow Papers, Swem Library, College of William and Mary, Williamsburg, Va.; David Russell account book, 1796–1806, Handley Library, Winchester, Va. (reference courtesy of Neville Thompson); New Jersey reference in John Sagar daybook, 1805–17, HSP; Alexander Gardner, John Clasby, and Davis Coleman estate records, 1803 and 1805, Nantucket Co., Mass., Registry of Probate; Solomon Maxwell note to Lawrence Allwine, August 25, 1794, Hollingsworth Collection, Business Papers, HSP.

83. Reynolds, *Directions for Painting*, p. 18; Porter, "Art of Painting," October 2, 1845, p. 2; Hopkins and Charles, *City Gazette and Daily Advertiser* (Charleston, S.C.), March 7, 1798, citation file, MESDA; Isaac A. Kip inventory, ca. 1805, DCM.

84. Robert Taylor bill to Samuel Coates, August 1, 1810, Coates Reynell Papers, Business Papers, HSP; Schiffer, *Chester County Inventories*, pp. 105, 108, and p. 104; Robbins account book; "Paints and Receipts for Wooden Work," p. 11; Rose estate records; cinnamon-colored chairs in Riley estate records.

85. Porter, "Art of Painting," October 2, 1845, p. 2; Margaret Berwind Schiffer, *Furniture and Its Makers of Chester County, Pennsylvania* (Philadelphia: University of Pennsylvania Press, 1966), p. 134; Lambert estate records; Chauncey Strong daybook, 1841–52, NYSHA; David Alling account book, daybook, and receipt book, 1824–42, NJHS (microfilm, DCM).

86. Candee, "Housepaints in Colonial America, Part 3 (continued)," *Color Engineering* 5, no. 2 (March–April 1967): 32–34, including quotes from Dossie, *Handmaid to the Arts*; Harley, *Artists' Pigments*, pp. 108–17; Isaac D. Bull bill to Silas Cheney, November 17, 1818, Cheney court records.

87. Walker invoice book; Robert Casey estate records, 1796, Baltimore Co., Md., Register of Wills (microfilm, DCM); Allen memorandum book; spring-back chairs in Bernard Foot account of Ebenezer Pearson, 1813–14, Pearson Family Papers, PEM; bamboo chairs in James Chase account books, 1797–1812, in Charles S. Parsons, New Hampshire Notes, VRC; mani-

fest of schooner *Amity*, June 27, 1804, Philadelphia Outward Foreign Entries, U.S. Custom House Records, NA; Arthur Greland and Robert Wilson account of cargo sales of ship *Montesque*, December 4, 1811, Girard Papers; cargo account of ship *George and Mary*, April 7, 1810, as quoted in Joseph K. Ott, "Still More Notes on Rhode Island Cabinetmakers and Allied Craftsmen," *Rhode Island History* 28, no. 4 (November 1969): 121; account of chair shipment, March 25, 1820, in David Alling invoice book, 1819–20, NJHS (microfilm, DCM); memorandum of goods suitable for the Brazilian market, ca. 1822–25, Waters Family Papers, PEM.

88. Invoice of goods on ship *Voltaire*, December 28, 1809, Girard invoice book, Girard Papers; William Challen, *Kentucky Gazette* (Lexington), May 8, 1809, as quoted in Mary Jane Elliott, "Lexington, Kentucky, 1792–1820: The Athens of the West" (master's thesis, University of Delaware, 1973), p. 34; Stibbs and Stout, *Liberty Hall and Cincinnati Gazette* (Cincinnati, Ohio), September 30, 1816, as quoted in Jane E. Sikes, *The Furniture Makers of Cincinnati, 1790 to 1849* (Cincinnati, Ohio: By the author, 1976), p. 230; William Buttre in *Longworth's American Almanac, New-York Register, and City Directory* (New York: David Longworth, 1810), n.p.; Patterson and Dennis, *New-York Evening Post* (New York), January 2, 1810 (reference courtesy of Michael Brown); cargo account of Ship *George and Mary*, April 7, 1810, as quoted in Ott, "Still More Notes on Rhode Island Cabinetmakers," p. 121; Alling ledger, 1815–18; Schiffer, *Chester County Inventories*, p. 108.

89. Porter, "Art of Painting," October 2, 1845, p. 2; Samuel P. Broome inventory, 1806, DCM; Schiffer, *Chester County Inventories*, p. 104; William Palmer bill to George Boyd, agent for the President's House, December 1815, Treasury Records, Miscellaneous Treasury Accounts of the First Auditor, no. 29,494, NA.

90. John Oldham estate records, 1835, Baltimore Co., Md., Register of Wills (microfilm, DCM); Riley estate records; Robbins account book; Schiffer, *Chester County Inventories*, p. 104.

91. "Elijah Eldredges Book of Receipts for Painting"; Florence Montgomery, *Textiles in America, 1650–1870* (New York: W. W. Norton, 1983), p. 308; Alling ledger, 1815–18. For an organ-spindle chair, see Evans, *American Windsor Chairs*, fig. 5-43, pl. 19.

92. Preston ledger, 1795–1817; Thomas Safford ledger, 1807–35, CSL; Cheney daybook, 1813–21; Robbins account book; Virginia reference in Russell account book. For the set of Carlisle chairs, see Evans, *American Windsor Chairs*, fig. 3-159. Alling daybook; Beesley daybook.

93. Candee, "Housepaints in Colonial America, Part 3 (continued)," p. 36; Samuel Wetherill and Sons ledger, 1777–88, University of Pennsylvania, Philadelphia (microfilm,

DCM); "Paints and Receipts for Wooden Work," p. 12; blue rush-bottom chairs in William Barney estate records, 1774, Baltimore Co., Md., Register of Wills (microfilm, DCM). Blue chairs were popular in Stonington, Conn., as indicated in Minor Myers, Jr., and Edgar deN. Mayhew, *New London County Furniture, 1640–1840* (New London, Conn.: Lyman Allyn Museum, 1974), p. 11. Scientific analysis of original surface finishes has determined that Prussian blue was in use on painted case furniture originating in the Connecticut River Valley in Massachusetts as early as the 1710s, as detailed in Philip Zea and Suzanne Flynt, *Hadley Chests* (Deerfield, Mass.: Pocumtuck Valley Memorial Association, 1992), pp. 18, 19, 28.

94. Walker invoice book; James Swan vendue, *Massachusetts Centinel* (Boston), April 23, 1785 (reference courtesy of Wendy Cooper); Joseph Barrell letter to John Atkinson, March 1, 1795, in letter book, 1791–97, MHS (microfilm, DCM); Hale Hilton estate sale, April 9, 1802, Nathan Dane Papers, MHS; Oliver Wight bill to Josiah Walker, November 2, 1804, Walker Family Collection, OSV; Cheney daybook, 1807–13; James Mitchell bill to James J. Skerrett, December 19, 1817, Loudoun Papers, Papers of James J. Skerrett, HSP; Schiffer, *Chester County Inventories*, p. 105; J. H. Stevenson and Co. invoice book, 1822–26, DCM; manifest of ship *Lancaster*, April 26, 1825, Philadelphia Outward Coastwise Entries, U.S. Custom House Records, NA.

95. Thomas Jefferson letter to George Jefferson, July 19, 1800, Jefferson Papers; Tilden-Seaver lawsuit; Foot account of Pearson; Houghton ledger A; Calvin Stetson account book, 1843–57, DCM; Strong daybook.

96. Alling invoice book; Riley estate records; Schiffer, *Chester County Inventories*, pp. 104, 108; "Paints and Receipts for Wooden Work," p. 11; Porter, "Art of Painting," October 2, 1845, p. 2; "Elijah Eldredges Book of Receipts for Painting."

97. Aaron Boughman estate records, 1813, City and County of Philadelphia, Register of Wills.

98. Manifest of sloop *Samuel*, October 11, 1792, Philadelphia Outward Foreign and Coastwise Entries, U.S. Custom House Records, French Spoliation Claims, NA; Oliver Spencer estate records, 1794, Nantucket Co., Mass., Registry of Probate; Myers and Mayhew, *New London County Furniture*, p. 11; Allen memorandum book; Preston ledger; Russell account book; William Chappel estate records, 1826, Lyme, Conn., Genealogical Section, CSL.

99. Stone globe and trough in Candee, "Housepaints in Colonial America," "Part I: The Preparation, Storage, and Sale of Colors," *Color Engineering* 4, no. 5 (September–October): 26, and "The Editor's Attic," *Antiques* 54, no. 6 (December 1948): 443; Trumble and Tracy estate records; Bigelow, *Useful Arts*, 1:157; G. Speth,

Daily Advertiser (New York), June 8, 1791, as quoted in Rita Susswein Gottesman, comp., *The Arts and Crafts in New York, 1777–1799* (New York: New-York Historical Society, 1954), p. 345; John I. Wells, *Connecticut Courant*, April 11, 1810, and *American Mercury* (Hartford, Conn.), November 2, 1809, as quoted in Phyllis Kihn, comp., "Connecticut Cabinetmakers, Part 2," *Connecticut Historical Society Bulletin* 33, no. 1 (January 1968): 30–31; 1820 Census of Manufactures, state of Vermont.

100. John McElwee, *Pennsylvania Packet* (Philadelphia), June 30, 1798, as quoted in Alfred Coxe Prime, comp., *The Arts and Crafts in Philadelphia, Maryland, and South Carolina, 1786–1800* (Topsfield, Mass.: Walpole Society, 1932), p. 304; Dunlop in *Longworth's American Almanac, New-York Register, and City Directory* (New York: Thomas Longworth, 1826), n.p.; Edward A. Ball inventory, 1832, DCM.

101. Alexander Stenhouse, *Maryland Gazette* (Annapolis), August 2, 1764, as quoted in Alfred Coxe Prime, comp., *The Arts and Crafts in Philadelphia, Maryland, and South Carolina, 1721–1785* (Philadelphia: Walpole Society, 1929), pp. 301–2; G. Duyckinck, *New-York Gazette, or Weekly Post-Boy*, November 18, 1754, as quoted in Rita Susswein Gottesman, comp., *The Arts and Crafts in New York, 1726–1776* (1938; reprint, New York: Da Capo Press, 1970), p. 354; Caleb Greene, *Daily Advertiser*, March 24, 1803, as quoted in Rita Susswein Gottesman, comp., *The Arts and Crafts in New York, 1800–1804* (New York: New-York Historical Society, 1965), pp. 274–75; New York City handmills in Kenneth McKenzie, Elijah Warner, and Lodowick Fosdick inventories, 1804, 1821, and 1819, DCM; Holcomb account book.

102. Flags in Godfrey Cole inventory, 1804, as quoted in Hill, "Furniture Craftsmen in Baltimore," p. 119; marble stone in Thomas Kinsela estate records, 1822, Schenectady Co., Schenectady, N.Y., Surrogate Court; Wilder stone described in Parsons, Wilder Family Notes; Lambert estate records; Tingry, *Painter's Guide*, p. 215; Ebenezer Knowlton inventory, 1811, Suffolk Co., Mass., Registry of Probate (microfilm, DCM; document brought to author's attention by Page Talbott); Silas Cheney estate records, 1821, Litchfield, Conn., Genealogical Section, CSL; Tingry, *Painter and Varnisher's Guide*, p. 438.

103. *The Painter's, Gilder's, and Varnisher's Manual* (London: M. Taylor, 1836), pp. 101–3; Cheney daybook, 1802–7; Bull bill to Cheney.

104. Porter, "Art of Painting," September 25, 1845, p. 3.

105. Daniel Huntington note to Silas Cheney, February 9, 1813, Cheney court records; *Painter's, Gilder's, and Varnisher's Manual*, p. 104; Goodrich estate records.

106. Manifests of schooner *Hannah Loretta* and brig *Amazon*, May 1810 and August 8, 1799, Philadelphia Outward Foreign Entries, U.S.

Custom House Records, NA, the latter a French Spoliation Claim; Esben pigment cabinet described in Clarence W. Brazer, "Rare Windsor Candlestands," *Antiques* 6, no. 4 (October 1924): 194; Thomas Boynton estate records, 1849–50, Windsor Co., Woodstock, Vt., Registry of Probate.

107. John Humble, *New-York Gazette, or Weekly Post-Boy*, September 26, 1748, and Obadiah Wells, *New-York Evening Post*, January 11, 1748, as quoted in Gottesman, *Arts and Crafts, 1726–1776*, pp. 350, 352; James Claypoole, *Pennsylvania Gazette*, June 14, 1750; John Boyd, *Maryland Gazette*, May 27, 1773, as quoted in Prime, *Arts and Crafts, 1721–1785*, p. 304.

108. Hugh McDougal, *New-York Gazette and General Advertiser* (New York), December 8, 1797, and varnish notice of William Drewit Smith, *New-York Gazette, and the Weekly Mercury* (New York), April 3, 1780, as quoted in Gottesman, *Arts and Crafts, 1777–1799*, pp. 343, 346; John McElwee, *Pennsylvania Packet*, June 30, 1798, as quoted in Prime, *Arts and Crafts, 1786–1800*, p. 304; Cholwell and Summers, *Commercial Advertiser* (New York), June 3, 1800, as quoted in Gottesman, *Arts and Crafts, 1800–1804*, p. 271.

109. Boynton ledger, 1811–17, and shop account; Alling account book; Chauncey Strong daybook, 1852–69, NYSHA; Goodrich estate records; Anthony Steel estate records, 1817, City and County of Philadelphia, Register of Wills; Benjamin Branson estate records, 1831–35, DCM.

110. Tench Coxe, *A View of the United States of America* (Philadelphia: William Hall et al., 1794), pp. 140–41; Lawrence Allwine, *Aurora* (Philadelphia), May 3, 1800, as quoted in Prime, *Arts and Crafts, 1786–1800*, pp. 165–66; James Mease, *Picture of Philadelphia* (Philadelphia: B. and T. Kite, 1811), p. 75.

111. Coxe, *View of the United States*, p. 141; Thomas Porter, *Picture of Philadelphia from 1811 to 1831*, 2 vols. (Philadelphia, 1831), 2:122–23; Joseph Jones, *Village Record* (West Chester, Pa.), May 17, 1837, as quoted in Schiffer, *Furniture of Chester County*, p. 134; *The Manufactories and Manufacturers of Pennsylvania of the Nineteenth Century* (Philadelphia: Galaxy Publishing, 1875), p. 307.

112. Bigelow, *Useful Arts*, 1:163–64; anonymous recipe for size, ca. 1790, OSV; Knight account book.

113. Reynolds, *Directions for Painting*, pp. 10–11; Candee, "Housepaints in Colonial America, Part 3 (continued)," p. 34; "Elijah Eldridges Book of Receipts," p. 4; *Dictionary of Arts, Sciences, and Miscellaneous Literature*, 18 vols. (Philadelphia: Thomas Dobson, 1798), 13:649.

114. William Gray ledger, 1774–1814, PEM (microfilm, DCM); Gillows cash book, 1764–74, Gillows Papers, Westminster Libraries, London, England (microfilm, DCM). Lead-

color priming in a well-preserved state is occasionally confused for the original finish coat on eighteenth-century Windsors. Trumble and Goodrich estate records; Henry Prall estate records, 1802, City and County of Philadelphia, Register of Wills; Cheney daybook, 1807–13; Boynton ledger, 1811–17; Beesley daybook.

115. *Dictionary of Arts*, 13:649, 652; *Painter's, Gilder's, and Varnisher's Manual*, p. 113; Zaccheus Collins letter to Joseph Blake, June 15, 1795, Stephen Collins and Son letter book, 1794–1801, Collins Collection, LC.

116. *Painter's, Gilder's, and Varnisher's Manual*, pp. 9–11; Tingry, *Painter's Guide*, p. 266; Tingry, *Painter and Varnisher's Guide*, p. 524; Thomas Walter Ward II account book, 1824–25, Ward Papers, American Antiquarian Society, Worcester, Mass. (hereafter cited AAS); Fetter inventory, 1777, as quoted in Fanelli, "Building and Furniture Trades in Lancaster, Pennsylvania," p. 16.

117. *Painter's, Gilder's, and Varnisher's Manual*, p. 108; Tingry, *Painter's Guide*, pp. 265–66; Reynolds, *Directions for Painting*, p. 8; Fosdick inventory; Lambert, Bass, and Tracy estate records; Rea stock quoted in Mabel M. Swan, "The Johnstons and the Reas—Japanners," *Antiques* 43, no. 5 (May 1943): 212.

118. David Alling estate records, 1855, NJSL; Heaton trade card illustrated in David C. Winslow, "Trade Cards, Catalogs, and Invoice Heads," *Pennsylvania Folklife* 19, no. 3 (Spring 1970): 22, fig. 18.

119. Location data relative to the Megarey view is from New York City directories; the New Bedford daguerreotype is at the Old Dartmouth Historical Society, New Bedford, Mass.; James Always, *Weekly Museum* (New York), February 28, 1801, as quoted in Gottesman, *Arts and Crafts, 1800–1804*, p. 136.

120. Winifred C. Gates, "Journal of a Cabinet Maker's Apprentice, Part 2," *Chronicle of the Early American Industries Association* 15, no. 3 (September 1962): 35; MacDonald, *Central New Jersey Chairmaking*, pp. 19–20; Jacob Felton account book, 1836–38, OSV; Samuel Douglas and Son account book, 1810–58, CSL.

121. Hawley, Cole, and Holcomb account books; Cheney daybook, 1807–13; Alling ledger, 1815–18.

122. Smith in Holcomb account book; Robbins account book; Helme book of prices.

123. "Painted Furniture" in Macquoid and Edwards, *Dictionary of English Furniture*, 3:13–14; Clifford Musgrave, "England, 1765–1800," in Hayward, *World Furniture*, pp. 138–44; Sheraton, *Drawing-Book*, pp. 205–31; John DeWitt, *New-York Weekly Chronicle* (New York), June 18, 1795, and Walter MacBride, *Weekly Museum*, July 18, 1795, as quoted in Gottesman, *Arts and Crafts, 1777–1799*, pp. 138–44; Lawrence Allwine, *Aurora*, May 3, 1800, as quoted in Prime, *Arts and Crafts, 1786–1800*, pp. 165–66; manifest of ship *Rousseau*, March 18, 1809, Philadelphia

Outward Foreign Entries, U.S. Custom House Records, NA.

124. John and Hugh Finlay, *Federal Gazette and Baltimore Daily Advertiser* (Baltimore, Md.), November 8, 1805, as quoted in Elder, *Baltimore Painted Furniture*, p. 11; Hill, "Furniture Craftsmen in Baltimore," pp. 71–72, 368, 375, 377–78, 381–83, 385, 389, 395.

125. Luther Davis, *Hampshire Gazette*, March 6, 1808, as quoted in Keno, "Windsor Chair Makers of Northampton," p. 47; John Priest, *Impartial Review and Cumberland Repository* (Nashville, Tenn.), March 24, 1808; Joel Brown, *Star, and North-Carolina State Gazette* (Raleigh), July 5, 1815, citation file, MESDA; Thomas Henning, Sr., *Lewisburg Chronicle* (Lewisburg, W.Va.), February 12, 1852 (reference courtesy of Anne C. Golovin); Joel Brown, *North Carolina Star* (Raleigh), March 29, 1822, as quoted in Craig, *Arts and Crafts*, p. 202; Samuel M. Dockum and Edmond M. Brown, *Portsmouth Journal* (Portsmouth, N.H.), December 18, 1827, as quoted in Parsons, Wilder Family Notes.

126. Helme book of prices; John Denig, *Franklin Repository* (Chambersburg, Pa.), July 1821 (reference courtesy of the late William Bowers).

127. Sheraton, *Cabinet Dictionary*, 2:425; *Schoolmaster and Boys* illustrated in Nina Fletcher Little, *The Abby Aldrich Rockefeller Folk Art Collection* (Boston: Little, Brown, 1957), pl. 77; William Bingham letter to Nicholas Low, June 23, 1792, William Bingham letter book, 1791–93, HSP; Allen memorandum book; Daniel Rea daybooks, 1772–1800, 1789–1802, BL.

128. Trumble in Hazlehurst invoice and bill of disbursements; John Winans (Schenectady) bill to John Sanders, May 22, 1809, and James Chesney (Albany) bill to Peter E. Elmendorf, November 19, 1805, Sanders Papers, NYHS; *Dictionary of Arts*, 13:648; James Claypoole, *Pennsylvania Gazette*, June 14, 1750; McKenzie inventory; Holcomb and Cole account books; Jared Chesnut account of E. I. du Pont, 1818–19, Longwood Manuscripts, Hagley Museum and Library, Wilmington, Del.; Sheraton, as quoted in Zilla Rider Lea, ed., *The Ornamented Chair* (Rutland, Vt.: Charles E. Tuttle, 1960), p. 116.

129. For the Stewart chair, see Evans, *American Windsor Chairs*, fig. 7-117.

130. Boynton ledger, 1817–47; Sheraton, *Cabinet Dictionary*, 2:425–26; Nathaniel Whittock, *The Decorative Painters' and Glaziers' Guide* (London: Isaac Taylor Hinton, 1827), pp. 76, 80; Preston ledger, 1795–1817.

131. MacBride, *Weekly Museum*; DeWitt, *New-York Weekly Chronicle*. There is some question that the word *flowered* refers to wood graining, since light veins that cross the grain, as in oak, were called "flowers," according to Whittock, *Decorative Painters' and Glaziers' Guide*, p. 21. Gerardus Duyckinck, *New-York*

Weekly Journal (New York), January 6, 1735, as quoted in Gottesman, *Arts and Crafts, 1726–1776*, p. 129; Sheraton, *Cabinet Dictionary*, 2:426–27; Caleb Greene, *New-Bedford Mercury* (New Bedford, Mass.), January 3, 1812, as quoted in Elton W. Hall, "New Bedford Furniture," *Antiques* 113, no. 5 (May 1978): 1116, n. 25.

132. Esther Singleton, *The Furniture of Our Forefathers* (Garden City, N.Y.: Doubleday, Page, 1913), p. 539; David Miller inventory (Morris Co., N.J.), 1815, DCM; Samuel Lee estate records, 1815, Windham, Conn., Genealogical Section, CSL; Schiffer, *Chester County Inventories*, p. 104; Cheney daybook, 1802–7; a chair of pendent-vine decoration is illustrated in Fales, *American Painted Furniture*, p. 147, fig. 240.

133. For John and Hugh Finlay, *Federal Gazette and Baltimore Daily Advertiser*, November 8, 1805, and painted Baltimore furniture featuring trophies, see Elder, *Baltimore Painted Furniture*, pp. 11, 18, 20, 28–29, 33–36, 39, 45, 56–57.

134. John and Hugh Finlay, *Federal Gazette and Baltimore Daily Advertiser*. For identification of some of the Finlays' "Real Views," see Lance Humphries, "Provenance, Patronage and Perception: The Morris Suite of Baltimore Painted Furniture," in *American Furniture 2003*, ed. Luke Beckerdite (Milwaukee, Wis.: Chipstone Foundation, 2003), pp. 138–92. Edward Needles, *Baltimore Patriot and Mercantile Advertiser* (Baltimore, Md.), January 11, 1830; Dean and Fredericks, *New-York Courier* (New York), February 18, 1817; Wheaton and Davies, *New-York Evening Post*, June 14, 1817 (reference courtesy of Michael Brown). For the New England chairs and washstand, see I. M. Wiese advertisement, *Antiques* 117, no. 1 (January 1980): 147, and Stacy C. Hollander, *American Radiance* (New York: Harry N. Abrams for the American Folk Art Museum, 2001), pl. 68a–c. May and Renshaw, *Scioto Gazette and Fredonia Chronicle* (Chillicothe, Ohio), February 29, 1816 (reference courtesy of John R. Grabb).

135. Alling ledger, 1815–18; Robbins account book.

136. Alling ledger, 1815–18; Nina Fletcher Little, *Asahel Powers, Painter of Vermont Faces* (Williamsburg, Va.: Colonial Williamsburg Foundation, 1973).

137. Christian Nestell, *Providence Patriot* (Providence, R.I.), August 28, 1822 (reference courtesy of Robert P. Emlen). For a decorated Nestell chair, biographical data on Nestell, and a comprehensive analysis of the Nestell drawing book, see Nancy Goyne Evans, "The Christian M. Nestell Drawing Book: A Focus on the Ornamental Painter and His Craft in Early Nineteenth-Century America," in *American Furniture 1998*, ed. Luke Beckerdite (Hanover, N.H.: University Press of New England for the Chipstone Foundation, 1998), pp. 99–163. Boynton ledger, 1811–17.

138. Some controversy concerning origin

surrounds the chair with the shaped-tablet crest in pl. 13, which is one of a set of six. The seat bottom of each chair in the set bears two initial inscriptions or a name and initial inscription in white chalk. Most prominent are the name "S Noyes" and the initials "SN." Also present on each chair are the initials "PR." All inscriptions are of nineteenth-century origin. S. Noyes has been identified as Samuel Noyes, a cabinetmaker of East Sudbury, Mass., or as the chair dealer Henry Noyes of Belfast, Maine, who advertised that he obtained his stock in Boston. Actually, four of the six Noyes name or initial signatures have been written *over* the "PR" inscription, thus negating an attribution to either Noyes. Whether P.R. was the original maker or, like Noyes, an early owner is unknown. See advertisement of Frank and Barbara Pollack, *Antiques* 126, no. 4 (October 1984): 750, and the news release "Sotheby's to Sell American Folk Art Collection" in *Antiques and the Arts Weekly* (Newtown, Conn.), July 30, 2004, p. 14. (Henry Noyes information courtesy of Edwin A. Churchill, Maine State Museum, Augusta.)

139. L. D. Chapin, *Providence Patriot and Columbian Phenix* (Providence, R.I.), July 13, 1825; Boynton ledger, 1811–17.

140. Evans, "Nestell Drawing Book."

141. Evans, "Nestell Drawing Book," p. 119; Alling ledger, 1815–18.

142. Boynton ledger, 1811–17. For a New York chair with a painted eagle, a badge from the New York Chairmakers' Society, and a chair with a gilded eagle in the crest, see Evans, *American Windsor Chairs*, figs. 5-52, 5-51, 4-11. Evans, "Nestell Drawing Book," pp. 140–41; Alling ledger, 1815–18; Talcott daybook; Stetson account book.

143. For a New Hampshire Statehouse chair, see Evans, *American Windsor Chairs*, fig. 7-87. John Curry, *Western Citizen* (Paris, Ky.), 1818, as noted in Edna Talbott Whitley, *A Checklist of Kentucky Cabinetmakers from 1775 to 1859* (Paris, Ky.: By the author, 1969), p. 23; Baltimore procession, *Gazette of the State of Georgia* (Savannah), June 12, 1788, citation file, MESDA.

144. David Bates, *Daily National Intelligencer* (Washington, D.C.), March 13, 1821, as quoted in Anne Castrodale Golovin, "Cabinetmakers and Chairmakers of Washington, D.C., 1791–1840," *Antiques* 107, no. 5 (May 1975): 909; Whittock, *Decorative Painters' and Glaziers' Guide*, pp. 76–77.

145. "Japanning and Lacquer," "Painted Furniture," and "Papier Mâché" in Macquoid and Edwards, *Dictionary of English Furniture*, 2:266–71, 3:13–15; Janet Waring, *Early American Stencils* (New York: William R. Scott, 1937), pp. 89–92; James M. Koenig, "Decorative Stencil Cutting," *Chronicle of the Early American Industries Association* 32, no. 1 (March 1979): 12; Kenney, *Hitchcock Chair*, pp. 65–66; Kenneth

Jewett, "A Brief Treatise on the History and Execution of Bronze Stenciling" in Edwin A. Churchill, *Simple Forms and Vivid Colors* (Augusta: Maine State Museum, 1983), p. 29; Dossie, *Handmaid to the Arts*, part 3, chap. 3; Elisha Van Brunt, and Dean and Fredericks, *New-York Courier*, February 18, 1817, and Wheaton and Davies, *New-York Evening Post*, September 13, 1817; Cornwell and Smith printed billhead.

146. Alling ledger, 1815–18. For an Alling cornucopia-back fancy chair, see Don C. Skemer, "David Alling's Chair Manufactory: Craft Industrialization in Newark, New Jersey, 1801–1854," *Winterthur Portfolio* 22, no. 1 (Spring 1987): 9. A. Clark, *Raleigh Minerva* (Raleigh, N.C.), April 23, 1819, citation file, MESDA; David Bates, *Daily National Intelligencer,* December 13, 1820, as quoted in Golovin, "Cabinetmakers and Chairmakers of Washington," p. 906.

147. Rufus Porter, *Select Collection of Valuable and Curious Arts*, 5th ed. (Concord, N.H., 1826), as quoted in Esther Stevens Brazer, *Early American Decoration*, 2d ed. (Springfield, Mass.: Pond-Ekberg, 1947), p. 256.

148. Alling ledger, 1815–18; Esther Stevens Fraser, "The Golden Age of Stencilling," *Antiques* 1, no. 4 (April 1922): 162–66, and Esther Stevens Fraser, "Painted Furniture in America, Part 2," *Antiques* 6, no. 3 (September 1924): 141–46; Waring, *Early American Stencils*, pp. 88, 102; Koenig, "Decorative Stencil Cutting," p. 12; Rufus Porter, "The Art of Painting," *Scientific American* 1, no. 9 (November 13, 1845): 2; Henry Farley, *New-Hampshire Patriot* (Concord), May 14, 1831, as quoted in Parsons, New Hampshire Notes.

149. Fraser, "Painted Furniture in America, Part 2," pp. 143–44; Porter, "Art of Painting," November 13, 1845, p. 2; Waring, *Early American Stencils*, pp. 87–133.

150. Fraser, "Painted Furniture in America, Part 2," pp. 143–44; Porter, "Art of Painting," November 13, 1845, p. 2; Waring, *Early American Stencils*, pp. 87–133.

151. For a train of cars stenciled on a fancy-chair slat, see Lea, *Ornamented Chair*, p. 104.

152. *Painter's, Gilder's, and Varnisher's Manual*, p. 148.

153. Joseph Jones bill to Benjamin Sharpless, May 13, 1842, as quoted in Schiffer, *Furniture of Chester County*, p. 134.

154. Whittock, *Decorative Painters' and Glaziers' Guide*, p. 80; "Gilding" in Macquoid and Edwards, *Dictionary of English Furniture*, 2:241–43.

155. Henry Hill invoice of imports on ship *Pigou*, September 28, 1789, Society Miscellaneous Collection, HSP; Standfast Smith letter to John R. Parker, June 2, 1803, DCM; Daniel Rea daybook, 1794–97, BL; William Palmer, *Weekly Museum*, October 15, 1798, and January 6, 1798, as quoted in Gottesman, *Arts and Crafts,*

1777–1799, p. 140; Ridgely purchase recorded in Hill, "Furniture Craftsmen in Baltimore," p. 14; William Palmer bill to Steven Arnold, May 24, 1799, Greene Collection, RIHS; Palmer bill to Low; William Palmer bill to Mr. Cox, June 15, 1805, White-Beekman Papers, James W. Beekman; Palmer bill to Boyd. Because of the near destruction of the White House by the British in August 1814, the presidential residence in 1815 was located at 19th Street and Pennsylvania Avenue (Betty C. Monkman, *The White House: Its Historic Furnishings and First Families* [New York: Abbeville Press for the White House Historical Association, 2000], p. 43).

156. John Bridges bill to Library of Congress, August 11, 1815, Treasury Records, Miscellaneous Treasury Accounts of the First Auditor, no. 31,432, NA.

157. Butler account with Cheney; Cheney daybook, 1813–21; Claypoole bill to Bonaparte for Baltimore Exchange Hotel; Alling ledger, 1815–18; Robbins account book; John Denig, *Franklin Repository*, May 14, 1822 (reference courtesy of the late William Bowers).

158. Manifests of brig *Austides* (for Charleston), March 11, 1802, sloop *Hiland* (for Alexandria, Va.), July 2, 1803, schooner *Judith* (for Boston), February 15, 1806, and ship *South Carolina Packet* (for Charleston), March 9, 1811, Philadelphia Outward Coastwise Entries, U.S. Custom House Records, NA. For Charleston import notices listing gilt chairs, see *Charleston Courier*, August 11 and October 16, 1806, January 16, December 12 and 13, 1807, February 3, 1808, December 22, 1809, February 14 and 26, July 21, and November 7, 1810; *Times* (Charleston, S.C.), December 15, 1808, June 27 and July 20, 1810, citation file, MESDA. Snyder bill to Claxton for Thomas Jefferson; manifest of brig *Morning Star* (for Salem, Mass.), December 10, 1801, Derby Family Papers, vol. 25, PEM; Dockum and Brown, *Portsmouth Journal*, December 18, 1827.

159. Manifests of sloop *Catharine* (for Havana), September 20, 1798, brig *Beaver* (for Havana), February 7, 1801, schooner *Republican* (for St. Thomas), November 15, 1806, and schooner *Fly* (for Havana), March 12, 1807, Philadelphia Outward Coastwise and Foreign Entries, U.S. Custom House Records, NA, some French Spoliation Claims; invoices of ships *North America* (for Isle of France), July 9, 1816, and *Montesque* (for Valparaiso), December 4, 1811, Girard Papers; Carrington Windsor furniture venture with Thomas Howard, Jr., in Eleanore Bradford Monahon, "Providence Cabinetmakers," *Rhode Island History* 23, no. 1 (January 1964): 16; Stevenson and Co. invoice book; Richard Austin account of Jacob Sanderson, 1805–6, as quoted in Swan, *Samuel McIntire*, pp. 27–28; cargo account (New York) of ship *George and Mary*, April 7, 1810, as quoted in Ott, "Still More Notes on Rhode Island Cabinetmakers," p. 121; Matthew McColm, *Ameri-*

can and Commercial Daily Advertiser (Baltimore, Md.), October 6, 1825.

160. James Claypoole, *Pennsylvania Gazette*, June 14, 1750; Lawrence Allwine, *Aurora*; Thomas West, *Republican Advocate* (New London, Conn.), April 28, 1824 (reference courtesy of Wendell Hilt).

161. Whittock, *Decorative Painters' and Glaziers' Guide*, pp. 74, 80–83; *The Cabinet-Maker's Guide* (London, 1825; reprint, Greenfield, Mass.: Ansel Phelps, 1825), pp. 61–63, 67, 71; Bigelow, *Useful Arts*, 1:177; Porter, "Art of Painting," November 13, 1845, p. 2; Francis Phipps, *The Collector's Complete Dictionary of American Antiques* (Garden City, N.Y.: Doubleday, 1974), pp. 152–53; Branson estate records; Henry Farley estate records, 1839, Merrimack Co., Concord, N.H., Registry of Probate.

162. "Graining" and "Japanning" in Macquoid and Edwards, *Dictionary of English Furniture*, 2:250, 268; Fales, *American Painted Furniture*, pp. 32–33; Frank Welsh, "The Art of Painted Graining," *Historic Preservation* 29, no. 3 (July–September 1977): 33–37; John Fendall, *Maryland Gazette*, June 26, 1760, as quoted in Prime, *Arts and Crafts, 1721–1785*, p. 300.

163. Gray ledger; George Davidson waste book, 1793–99, OSV; Daniel Rea daybooks, 1772–1800, 1789–93, and 1794–97; Rufus Porter, "The Art of Painting," *Scientific American* 1, no. 17 (January 8, 1846): 2.

164. Haydon and Stewart bills to Levi Hollingsworth, April 22 and June 27, 1812, Harrold E. Gillingham Collection, HSP; Porter, "Art of Painting," January 8, 1846, p. 2.

165. Rufus Porter, "The Art of Painting," *Scientific American* 1, no. 17 (January 8, 1846): 2; Whittock, *Deocrative Painters' and Glaziers' Guide*, pp. 43–44; Alling invoice book and daybook.

166. Kenney, *Hitchcock Chair*, p. 65; Whittock, *Decorative Painters' and Glaziers' Guide*, pls. 2, 5; Beesley daybook; Samuel Stibbs and Jonathan Stout, *Liberty Hall and Cincinnati Gazette*, September 30, 1816, as quoted in Sikes, *Furniture Makers of Cincinnati*, p. 230.

167. Whittock, *Decorative Painters' and Glaziers' Guide*, pp. 40, 73; Thomas Walter Ward II inventory book, ca. 1838–45, DCM; Alling ledger, 1815–18, and invoice book.

168. Whittock, *Decorative Painters' and Glaziers' Guide*, p. 40; Henry Farley, *New-Hampshire Patriot*, May 14, 1831, as quoted in Parsons, New Hampshire Notes; *The Laws of Harmonious Colouring* (London, 1847), as quoted in Fales, *American Painted Furniture*, p. 154; *Cabinet-Maker's Guide*, pp. 43–44.

169. Abraham McDonough estate records, 1852, City and County of Philadelphia, Register of Wills (microfilm, DCM); David Bates, *Daily National Intelligencer*, March 13, 1821, as quoted in Golovin, "Cabinetmakers and Chairmakers of Washington," p. 906; Whittock, *Decorative Painters' and Glaziers' Guide*, pp. 34–36; Porter,

"Art of Painting," January 8, 1846, p. 2; Reynolds, *Directions for Painting*, pp. 18–19; William Butcher, *Smith's Art of House-Painting* (London: Richard Holmes Laurie, 1821), p. 28.

170. Haydon and Stewart bill to Reuben Haines, December 12, 1812, as illustrated in Anthony A. P. Steumpfig, "William Haydon and William H. Stewart," *Antiques* 104, no. 3 (September 1973): 454, fig. 4; Alling ledger, 1815–18, and daybook; Thomas Ellis, *New-Bedford Mercury*, June 28, 1833, as quoted in Hall, "New Bedford Furniture," p. 1121; Bell and Stoneall bill to Robert R. Livingston, July 15, 1842, Robert R. Livingston Papers, NYHS.

171. The Sowle family chairs are now divided between the Newport and Little Compton, R.I., Historical Societies. An ink inscription on the bottom of one written in 1893 by a great-grandson of the presumed original owner lends credence to the tradition.

172. William Luther bill to Benjamin Goodhue, September 14, 1804, Papers of Benjamin and Stephen Goodhue, vol. 3, PEM; Maurice Tomlin, *Catalogue of Adam Period Furniture* (London: Victoria and Albert Museum, 1972), p. 125. A painted utilitarian chest of drawers with simulated-bamboo moldings and eye-centered spotted decoration, which dates to the early nineteenth century, is part of the collection at Hardwick Hall, Derbyshire, England, as described and illustrated in Christopher Gilbert, *English Vernacular Furniture, 1750–1900* (New Haven, Conn.: Yale University Press, 1991), p. 85. Boynton estate records.

173. Porter, "Art of Painting," January 8, 1846, p. 2; Broome inventory; Jacob Chandler estate records, 1808, Nantucket Co., Mass., Registry of Probate; Schiffer, *Chester County Inventories*, pp. 104, 108; Whittock, *Decorative Painters' and Glaziers' Guide*, p. 77. For the stand with simulated marble top, see Evans, *Specialized Forms*, fig. 3-28, left, pl. 31.

174. "Staining" in Macquoid and Edwards, *Dictionary of English Furniture*, 3:144–45; N. W. Burpee, *Canadian Courant* (Montreal, Que.), January 28, 1826, as quoted in Elizabeth Collard, "Montreal Cabinetmakers and Chairmakers, 1800–1850," *Antiques* 105, no. 5 (May 1974): 1138; Thomas West, *New-London Gazette* (New London, Conn.), February 27, 1828; Alling ledger, 1803–53.

175. Whittock, *Decorative Painters' and Glaziers' Guide*, p. 72; William Challen, *New-York Gazette and General Advertiser*, February 22, 1797, as quoted in Gottesman, *Arts and Crafts, 1777–1799*, p. 113; manifest of ship *South Carolina Packet*, March 9, 1811, Philadelphia Outward Coastwise Entries, U.S. Custom House Records, NA; Bass estate records; Boston reference in Israel Lombard cash book and journal, 1825–26, furniture account with Samuel Beal, 1826, AAS; Hartford references in Robbins account book; Edmund M. Brown and Alfred T. Joy, *New Hampshire Gazette* (Portsmouth),

August 29, 1837, as quoted in Parsons, Wilder Family Notes.

176. Whittock, *Decorative Painters' and Glaziers' Guide*, pp. 90–103; *Dictionary of Arts*, 9: 72–76; Dossie, *Handmaid to the Arts*, as quoted in Macquoid and Edwards, *Dictionary of English Furniture*, 2:266; Bigelow, *Useful Arts*, 1:175.

177. Bigelow, *Useful Arts*, 1:175–76.

178. William Palmer bill to Nicholas Low, May 26, 1787, Low Collection; William Lycett and William Challen bills to Robert R. Livingston, 1794 and April 26, 1798, Livingston Papers; Palmer bill to Arnold; Philadelphia reference in William Buckley account of William Parkinson, 1799–1801, DCM; James Beck, *Virginia Herald*, March 19, 1805, citation file, MESDA (reference courtesy of Margaret Beck Pritchard); Alexander Gibson, *Western Spy* (Cincinnati, Ohio), December 15, 1815, as quoted in Sikes, *Furniture Makers of Cincinnati*, p. 108; John Curry in Whitley, *Kentucky Cabinetmakers*, p. 23; manifests of ship *Diana* (for Havana), January 14, 1799, ship *Sally and Hetty* (for Batavia), June 13, 1806, brig *Trident* (for Havana), October 25, 1820, and brig *Maine* (for Havana), October 29, 1821, Philadelphia Outward Foreign and Coastwise Entries, U.S. Custom House Papers, NA, some French Spoliation Claims; manifest of schooner *Hope* (for Martinique), March 18, 1805, New London Outward Foreign Entries, U.S. Custom House Records, Federal Archives and Records Center, Waltham, Mass.

179. Bigelow, *Useful Arts*, 1:173–75; "Varnishes," in Macquoid and Edwards, *Dictionary of English Furniture*, 3:362; Whittock, *Decorative Painters' and Glaziers' Guide*, pp. 83–90.

180. Varnish kettles in Steel estate records, and James Whitaker estate records, 1822, City and County of Philadelphia, Register of Wills; Henry D. Biddle, ed., *Extracts from the Journal of Elizabeth Drinker* (Philadelphia: J. B. Lippincott Co., 1889), p. 401 (reference courtesy of Karol A. Schmiegel); Joel Brown, *Petersburg Intelligencer* (Petersburg, Va.), March 26, 1811, citation file, MESDA; Harmon Vosburgh, *Republican Watch-Tower* (New York), September 13, 1800, as quoted in Gottesman, *Arts and Crafts, 1800–1804*, pp. 272–73; Dickinson and Badger, *Middlesex Gazette* (Middletown, Conn.), May 2, 1816; *Cabinet-Maker's Guide*, pp. 31–32; Mease, *Picture of Philadelphia*, p. 131; production statistics in Edwin T. Freedley, *Leading Pursuits and Leading Men* (Philadelphia: Edward Young, 1856), p. 169.

181. Gaines account book; Thomas Pratt account book, 1730–68, DCM; William Barker account books, 4 vols., 1750–97, RIHS; Fussell account book; Caleb Emlen accounts in Hornor, *Blue Book*, pp. 293–94; Rea daybook, 1794–97; Trumble estate records; William Russell, Jr., *Columbian Courier* (New Bedford, Mass.), June 24, 1803, as quoted in Hall, "New Bedford Furniture," p. 1116, n. 25; Thomas Gladding account

of Peter Gansevoort, 1827–31, Gansevoort-Lansing Collection, Papers of Peter Gansevoort, NYPL; Alling ledger, 1815–18, and daybook, and David Alling receipt book, 1844–56, NJHS (microfilm, DCM).

182. *Painter's, Gilder's, and Varnisher's Manual*, p. 122; Rufus Porter, "The Art of Painting," *Scientific American* 1 (October 9, 1845): 2; Tingry, *Painter and Varnisher's Guide* p. 525; *Cabinet-Maker's Guide*, pp. 35–36; McDonough estate records; Helme book of prices.

183. Unidentified notice, *Columbian Centinel* (Boston, Mass.), April 17, 1802, as quoted in Fraser, "Painted Furniture in America, Part 1," p. 304n; Henzey in Hornor, *Blue Book*, p. 301; William Cox, John B. Ackley, and Gilbert Gaw bills to Stephen Girard, October 12, 1787, July–August 1796, and October 20, 1808, Girard Papers; Rea daybook, 1794–97, and Daniel Rea ledgers, 1764–99 and 1773–94, BL. Reference miscellany: Knight account book; Preston ledger, 1795–1817; Cheney daybook, 1813–21; Gere ledger, 1822–52; Robinson daybook.

184. Wadsworth bill to Connecticut Statehouse; Cheney daybook, 1807–13; White bill to Hicks for Nicholas Low; Claypoole bill to Bonaparte for Baltimore Exchange Hotel. Steamboat bills: Brown bill to Captain Vanderbilt; Welsh bill to steamboat *Thistle*; B. and E. Farrington bill to steamboat *Bellona*; Charles Fredericks bill to steamboat *Bellona*, March 14, 1826, DCM.

185. William Perkins and Co., *Middlesex Gazette*, November 17, 1824 (reference courtesy of Wendell Hilt); Christian M. Nestell, *Providence Patriot*, August 28, 1882 (reference courtesy of Robert P. Emlen); Carman Smith, *The Portico* (Huntington, N.Y.), January 20, 1826, New York State Cabinetmakers File, NYSHA.

186. "Upholstery" in Macquoid and Edwards, *Dictionary of English Furniture*, 3:355–56.

187. Hollis S. Baker, *Furniture in the Ancient World* (London: Connoisseur, 1966), pp. 89–90; "Cushion" in *Oxford English Dictionary* (Oxford, England: Clarendon Press, 1933), 2:1280; "Cushions" in Macquoid and Edwards, *Dictionary of English Furniture*, 2:199–200; printed catalogues of the household furnishings of Brig. Gen. Munden, March 28 and July 18, 1726, Chancery Masters' Exhibits, C-107, no. 287, Public Record Office, London; Hannah Hodge, Samuel Cheesman, and Robert Jones estate records, 1770, City and County of Philadelphia, Register of Wills.

188. William Jevon inventory, 1767, Lancaster, Pa., Lancaster County Historical Society, Lancaster, Pa.; Arthur Browne inventory, 1773, Portsmouth, N.H., as quoted in Jane C. Giffen (Nylander), "A Selection of New Hampshire Inventories," *Historical New Hampshire* 24, nos. 1, 2 (Spring–Summer 1969): pp. 54–55; estate records, Nantucket Co., Mass., Registry of Probate; Treasurer's Account, 1798, Sussex Co. Levy Court, State of Delaware, Division of Historical and Cultural Affairs, Dover, Del.; "Inventory of County Property in the Court House," 1817, Salem, Mass., Timothy Pickering Papers, PEM; manifest of sloop *Catherine*, September 20, 1798, Philadelphia Outward Foreign and Coastwise Entries, U.S. Custom House Records, French Spoliation Claims, NA.

189. Andrew Oliver inventory, 1774, Boston, Mass., as quoted in Alice Hanson Jones, *American Colonial Wealth*, 3 vols. (New York: Arno Press, 1977), 2:970; settee and cushion references as quoted in Hornor, *Blue Book*, p. 312, including Capt. Thomas Mason.; Stephen Collins inventory, 1794, Philadelphia, Pa., Daniel Parker Papers, HSP; Lee estate records; Lynch and Trask bill to Iowa Territory Legislature, April 15, 1839, as reproduced in Margaret N. Keyes, "Piecing Together Iowa's Old Capitol," *Historic Preservation* 26, no. 1 (January–March 1974): 40.

190. Capt. Soloman Ingraham inventory, 1805, Norwich, Conn., as quoted in Phyllis Kihn, "Captain Solomon Ingraham," *Connecticut Historical Society Bulletin* 29, no. 1 (January 1964): 26; Sarah Anna Emery, *Reminiscences of a Nonagenarian* (Newburyport, Mass.: William H. Huse, 1879), p. 33; Harriet Connor Brown, *Grandmother Brown's Hundred Years, 1827–1927* (New York: Blue Ribbon Books, 1929), p. 27; Walter A. Dyer and Esther Stevens Fraser, *The Rocking-Chair, An American Institution* (New York: Century Co., 1928), pp. 70, 99; Henry W. Miller account book, 1827–31, Worcester Historical Museum, Worcester, Mass.; Peter Wood bill to Arthur Bronson, December 1839, Bronson Papers, Papers of Isaac Bronson, NYPL; N. T. Morse account of Richard W. Greene, 1845, Greene Collection, RIHS; Alling account book and daybook.

191. Hazen, *Panorama*, p. 224; John I. Wells, *Connecticut Courant*, April 11, 1810; "live geese feathers" in Thomas Ellis, *New-Bedford Mercury*, June 28, 1833, as quoted in Hall, "New Bedford Furniture," p. 1121; Bass estate records.

192. Several needlework cushions worked in wool yarns on canvas are in the collection of the Chester County Historical Society, West Chester, Pa., as illustrated in Margaret B. Schiffer, *Historical Needlework of Pennsylvania* (New York: Charles Scribner's Sons, 1968), p. 124 (bottom), pl. 5. Martha Washington cushion illustrated in Helen Maggs Fede, *Washington Furniture at Mount Vernon* (Mount Vernon, Va.: Mount Vernon Ladies' Association, 1966), p. 59; Montgomery, *Textiles in America*, pp. 254–55, 300, 302–3; Thomas Ellis, *New-Bedford Mercury*, June 28, 1833, as quoted in Hall, "New Bedford Furniture," p. 1121; John Brower bill to Robert R. Livingston, January 12, 1784, Livingston Papers.

193. *Catalogue of . . . Furniture*, August 28, 1829 (Boston: Dorr and Allen, 1829), lot 76; Hepplewhite, *Guide*, pls. 18, 21; Mrs. Josiah Salisbury letter to Mrs. Stephen Salisbury I, July 23, 1820, Salisbury Family Papers, AAS.

194. Joseph Galloway inventory, 1778, as quoted in Thomas Lynch Montgomery, ed., *Pennsylvania Archives*, sixth series, vol. 12 (Harrisburg, Pa.: Harrisburg Publishing Co., 1907), p. 511; Capt. Sherman Clarke inventory, 1782, Newport, R.I., Registry of Probate (microfilm, DCM).

195. Thomas and William Ash, *New-York Packet*, October 7, 1784; Timpson and Gillihen, *New-York Packet*, July 4 and 11, 1785, as quoted in Gottesman, *Arts and Crafts, 1777–1799*, p. 129. For the Kip chair, see Evans, *American Windsor Chairs*, fig. 5-20. Joe Kindig III, "Upholstered Windsors," *Antiques* 62, no. 1 (July 1952): 52–53; the chairs are labeled by John De Witt and William W. Galatian. Thomas West and Dr. John Baker inventories, 1795 and 1797, DCM.

196. William Blake, *Independent Chronicle*, June 18, 1789, as quoted in Fraser, "Painted Furniture in America, Part 1," p. 306; Hale Hilton inventory, [1802], Nathan Dane Papers, MHS; Francis Delorme, *General Advertiser* (Philadelphia, Pa.), December 28, 1790, Prime Cards, WL; manifests of brig *West Point* and ship *Three Brothers*, January 7 and August 6, 1795, Philadelphia Outward Foreign and Coastwise Entries, U.S. Custom House Papers, NA; Derby references as quoted in Montgomery, *American Furniture: Federal*, p. 78; John B. Ackley and William Cox bills to Zaccheus Collins, August 13, 1796, and May 20, 1795, Collins Collection, LC.

197. Collins Collection, LC; Zaccheus Collins receipt book, 1794–1831, Daniel Parker Papers, HSP; manifest of sloop *Friendship*, August 25, 1799, Philadelphia Outward Coastwise Entries, U.S. Custom House Records, NA; James Beck, *Virginia Herald*, March 19, 1805, citation file, MESDA; William Will inventory, 1799, DCM; Yates in Fanelli, "Building and Furniture Trades in Lancaster, Pennsylvania," pp. 16–17; George Mason inventory, 1797, Rockbridge Co., Lexington, Va., Registry of Probate (reference courtesy of Margaret Beck Pritchard).

198. Andrew Huntington ledger C, 1780–94, Leffingwell Inn, Norwich, Conn.; Ebenezer Tracy, Sr., estate records; Annavery Tracy estate records, 1807, Lisbon, Conn., Genealogical Section, CSL; Allen memorandum book; Jonathan Bright, *American Mercury*, June 7, 1798 (reference courtesy of Wendell Hilt); Preston ledger, 1795–1817; William Brown, *Providence Gazette*, September 11, 1802, as quoted in Wendell D. Garrett, "Providence Cabinetmakers, Chairmakers, Upholsterers, and Allied Craftsmen, 1756–1838," *Antiques* 90, no. 4 (October 1966): 515.

199. For a Tracy family chair with a seat for stuffing, see Evans, *American Windsor Chairs*, fig. 6-109. Allen memorandum book. A small number of bamboo-turned continuous-bow chairs made by Ebenezer Tracy, Sr., follow a New York pattern. The side and front edges are thick and blunt without a chamfer, and the pro-

files are squared and serpentine. Chairs of this seat pattern have been offered occasionally in the dealer market.

200. For a Rhode Island chair with a seat for stuffing, see Evans, *American Windsor Chairs*, fig. 6-75. For labeled New York chairs by Thomas and William Ash and upholsterer J. Byles, see Wendy Cooper, "The Purchase of Furniture and Furnishings by John Brown, Providence Merchant," *Antiques* 103, no. 2 (February 1973): 335.

201. For a New Hampshire Statehouse chair, see Evans, *American Windsor Chairs*, fig. 7-87. Giles Cromwell, "Andrew and Robert McKim, Windsor Chair Makers," *Journal of Early Southern Decorative Arts* 6, no. 1 (May 1980): 17–18.

202. Lambert estate records; hair seating in John McElwee, *Federal Gazette* (Philadelphia, Pa.), November 4, 1794, as quoted in Prime, *Arts and Crafts, 1786–1800*, pp. 212–13; haircloth widths in Frederick W. Parrott and Fenelon Hubbell insolvency records, 1835, Bridgeport, Conn., Genealogical Section, CSL; first references to stuffed Windsor chairs in Galloway and Clarke inventories, 1778 and 1782; Derby reference in Montgomery, *American Furniture: Federal*, p. 78; Mason inventory; Stephen Collins and Son letter book, daybook, 1786–94, and invoice book, 1783–84, Collins Collection, LC; black moreen mentioned in Robert Underwood account book, 1795–1804, private collection (photostat, DCM); moreen priced in John Green account book, 1790–1803, DCM.

203. James Zwisler and Co., *Maryland Journal and Baltimore Advertiser* (Baltimore), July 12, 1793, Prime Cards, WL; Fanelli, "Building and Furniture Trades in Lancaster, Pennsylvania," p. 17; Louisa Crowninshield Bacon, *Reminiscences* ([Salem, Mass.]: By the author, 1922), pp. 22–23; Baker inventory.

204. Allen memorandum book; Thomas and William Ash, *New-York Packet*, October 7, 1784; Timpson and Gillihen, *New-York Packet*, July 11, 1785; Cox bill to Collins, May 20, 1795.

205. Ackley bill to Collins, August 13, 1796; Preston ledger, 1795–1817; Bacon, *Reminiscences*, p. 22; Wheelock portrait illustrated in Nina Fletcher Little, *Paintings by New England Provincial Artists, 1775–1800* (Boston: Museum of Fine Arts, 1976), pp. 162–63.

206. For a New Haven chair with peaked crest tips, see Evans, *American Windsor Chairs*, fig. 6-177; see also fig. 6-179.

207. Hepplewhite, *Guide*, pls. 2, 3, 6, 7, 16, 17.

208. Hill invoice of imports; "The Furnishings of Richmond Hill in 1797, the Home of Aaron Burr in New York City," *New-York Historical Society Quarterly Bulletin* 11, no. 1 (April 1921): 17, 19; 1820 Census of Manufactures, state of Maryland; Broome inventory.

209. John B. Ackley receipt to Zaccheus Collins, August 30, 1796, in Collins receipt book; Holmes ledger; Isaac Wright account book, 1834–37, CSL; Miller and Robbins ac-

count books; Samuel Beal, *Daily Evening Transcript* (Boston, Mass.), July 24, 1830; David H. Conradsen, "The Stock-in-Trade of John Hancock and Company," in *American Furniture 1993*, ed. Luke Beckerdite (Hanover, N.H.: University Press of New England for the Chipstone Foundation, 1993), pp. 43, 44, 49, 53; William Hancock letter to Mrs. Stephen Salisbury I, November 27, 1830, Salisbury Papers; *Catalogue of Cabinet Furniture*, March 10, 1831 (Boston: Jabez Hatch, Jr., 1831), lots 141, 222; Montgomery, *Textiles in America*, pp. 325–26.

210. John G. Hopkins account of Albert C. Greene, 1834–35, Greene Collection, RIHS; Samuel Perry bill to Isaac Bronson, May 1827, Bronson Papers; Browne and Ash bill to Mr. Beekman, November 1840, White-Beekman Papers.

211. H. L. Herrick, "From Pond Side to Chair Bottom," *Antiques* 6, no. 2 (August 1924): 82; MacDonald, *Central New Jersey Chairmaking*, pp. 9, 10, 18, 46; Kenney, *Hitchcock Chair*, pp. 295–97; Jones and Kinsela estate records; Thomas and John Larkin claims for loss, 1775, as quoted in Mabel M. Swan, "Furniture Makers of Charlestown," *Antiques* 46, no. 4 (October 1944): 205; David Finch insolvency records, 1829–30, Bridgeport, Conn., Genealogical Section, CSL; 1820 Census of Manufactures, states of Ohio and New York, schedules of Jacob C. Roll and an anonymous fancy and Windsor-chair maker; Elizur Barnes account book, 1821–25, Middlesex Historical Society, Middletown, Conn. (microfilm, CHS).

212. Notices for rushes, *Weekly Museum* (July 22, 1797), as quoted in Gottesman, *Arts and Crafts, 1777–1799*, pp. 136–37; manifest of sloop *Grey Hound*, August 18, 1812, Perth Amboy, N.J., Inward and Outward Entries, U.S. Custom House Records, NA; Barnes account book; Edward Jarvis, "Traditions and Reminiscences of Concord, Massachusetts, or a Contribution to the Social and Domestic History of the Town 1779 to 1878," p. 139, Concord Free Public Library, Concord, Mass.; Thomas West, *Connecticut Gazette* (New London), February 10, 1810.

213. In Kenney, *Hitchcock Chair*, p. 39, there is illustrated a long trough raised on stick legs that could have served to soak rush. Herrick, "From Pond Side to Chair Bottom," p. 82; William H. MacDonald, "Central New Jersey Chairmaking of the Nineteenth Century," *Chronicle of the Early American Industries Association* 3, nos. 6 and 7 (January, April 1946): 57, 60.

214. Sheraton, *Cabinet Dictionary*, 2:422–23; Holcomb, Knight, and Barnes account books; Cheney daybooks, 1802–7 and 1813–21, and Silas E. Cheney ledger, 1816–22, LHS (microfilm, DCM); Beesley daybook; MacDonald, *Central New Jersey Chairmaking*, pp. 10, 23; Davidson waste book. The technique of rush seating is demonstrated and described in Drew

Langsner, *The Chairmaker's Workshop* (Asheville, N.C.: Lark Books, 1997), pp. 128–34.

215. Fussell and Hawley account books; Stephen Whipple account book, 1803–11, Ipswich Historical Society, Ipswich, Mass.

216. Alexander, *Make a Chair*, pp. 103–10; George B. Emerson, *A Report on the Trees and Shrubs . . . in the Forests of Massachusetts*, 2 vols. (Boston: Little, Brown, 1894), 2:382–83; François André Michaux, Jr., *The North American Sylva*, 3 vols. (Philadelphia: J. Dobson, 1841), 3:113; Jarvis, "Reminiscences," p. 40. The technique of splint seating is demonstrated and described in Langsner, *Chairmaker's Workshop*, pp. 125–28.

217. "Caning" in Macquoid and Edwards, *Dictionary of English Furniture*, 1:202; Thomas, *Richer Than Spices*, chap. 5, pp. 73–75.

218. John and Hugh Finlay, *Federal Gazette and Baltimore Daily Advertiser*, January 31, 1803, and November 8, 1805, as quoted in Elder, *Baltimore Painted Furniture*, p. 11; cane-bottom chairs in import sale notices, *Charleston Courier*, November 17, December 12 and 31, 1807, February 3, 1808, and December 22, 1809, citation file, MESDA; Connecticut notice in Chapman and Merrit, *Connecticut Herald* (New Haven), April 18, 1809 (reference courtesy of Wendell Hilt); Asa Holden, *New-York Evening Post*, August 4, 1812.

219. 1820 Census of Manufactures, state of New York, anonymous fancy and Windsor-chair maker; R. H. Douglass and Co., *Baltimore American and Commercial Advertiser* (Baltimore, Md.), October 30, 1828 (reference courtesy of Arlene Palmer Schwind); Felton account book; Alling account book, ledger, 1803–53, receipt book, 1824–42, and daybook; Sheraton, *Cabinet Dictionary*, 1:126.

220. Shettleworth and Barry, "Walter Corey," p. 1201; Duane Hamilton Hurd, ed., *History of Worcester County, Massachusetts*, 2 vols. (Philadelphia: J. W. Lewis, 1889), 1:831–34; William D. Herrick, *History of the Town of Gardner* (Gardner, Mass.: By the committee, 1878), pp. 178–80.

Part Two

MERCHANDISING AND CONSUMERISM

CHAPTER 4

Marketing and Markets

The business of selling Windsor chairs was confined largely to a few local areas in the early years of production, but as the practical and economic virtues of stick-and-socket construction became more widely recognized, the Windsor emerged as a highly merchantable commodity. Entrepreneurs gradually channeled Windsor seating into new and expanding markets overland and overseas, beginning in the immediate prerevolutionary years, continuing through the rise of the new nation, and peaking in the 1850s after five decades of technological development that revolutionized manufacturing techniques and transportation.

Victor S. Clark identified the circumstance that encouraged colonial American manufactures as a "rapid expansion of [the] domestic market through [the] extension of settlement and growth of population." He further elaborated:

> These conditions continued after the inauguration of the Republic. . . . During the first quarter century . . . conditions of settlement that arose as . . . colonial pioneers struck inland from the seaboard were repeated, but on a larger scale and with more rapid effect than previously. The territory of a State was industrially subdued in the time formerly required to clear and populate a county, and the number of American consumers in 1800 was already double the number at the outbreak of the Revolution and was nearly to double again during the following decade.[1]

The commercial sphere of the Windsor-chair maker was limited initially to the immediate Delaware Valley—Chester, Bucks, and Philadelphia counties, northern Delaware, and southwestern New Jersey. Even before the Revolution, however, maritime, familial, and religious ties served to extend production to New York City and Newport, Rhode Island. Meanwhile, Philadelphia expanded its trade in Windsors into the Chesapeake Bay region. Production at Newport gradually had an impact on Providence and eastern Connecticut, and New York extended its regional scope up the Hudson, into the communities of western Long Island, and along both shores of Long Island Sound. In time the northern and southern coastal trade provided further merchandising opportunity for all three prerevolutionary centers. Jedidiah Morse described the commercial prospects of the American coaster in the postrevolutionary period: "The vast extent of sea coast, . . . the number of excellent harbours and sea-port towns, the numerous creeks and immense bays, which indent the coast, and the rivers, lakes and canals, which peninsulate the whole country, added to it agricultural advantages and improvements, give this part of the world superior advantages for trade." Rhode Island, alone, is reputed to have had 352 vessels in the coasting trade from Newfoundland to Georgia before the Revolution. Thus the potential for introducing Windsor seating throughout the length of coastal America was tremendous even before the colonies achieved independence.[2]

The West Indian trade also was prominent in early American commerce. Maritime interests increased their mercantile efforts in that region after the Revolutionary War, although Caribbean markets shifted with changing political and military conditions in Europe. A Philadelphian commenting on the commercial scene of

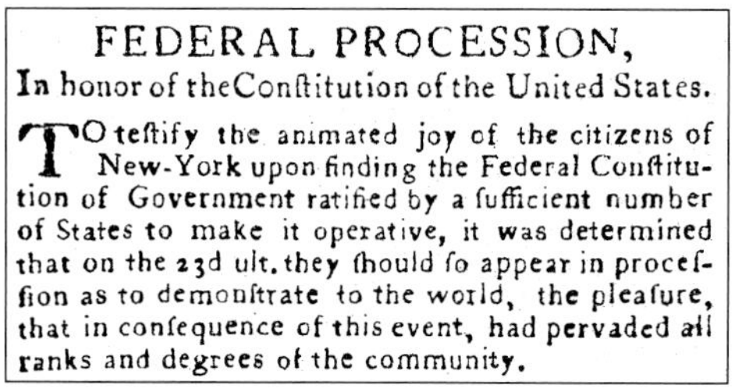
FEDERAL PROCESSION,
In honor of the Conſtitution of the United States.

TO teſtify the animated joy of the citizens of New-York upon finding the Federal Conſtitution of Government ratified by a ſufficient number of States to make it operative, it was determined that on the 23d ult. they ſhould ſo appear in proceſſion as to demonſtrate to the world, the pleaſure, that in conſequence of this event, had pervaded all ranks and degrees of the community.

FIG. 4-1 Announcement of a Federal Procession in New York City on July 23, 1788, in honor of ratification of the Constitution. From *Impartial Gazetteer*, New York, August 9, 1788.

about 1800 described the "carrying trade" between the United States and the West Indies as a "fruitful source of life to the commercial interests of Philadelphia." Even in 1775 Dr. Robert Honyman, a Scotsman who had settled in Virginia, identified Philadelphia as "famous for its extensive trade." Making a survey, he walked "along the wharfs from one end to the other . . . & took a particular view of the shipping." Wheat and lumber were the "principal articles of trade," and he saw in addition "immense quantities of shingles, boards, scantling &c. lying upon all wharfs." Only five years later the Marquis de Chastellux found the seaport with its two hundred quays well recovered from the effects of war, as he counted about three hundred vessels in the harbor.[3]

Rhode Island too was into the West Indian trade, shipping principally lumber and livestock. By 1764 Providence's fifty-four vessels on the seas comprised fourteen coasters and "40 sail . . . Used [in] the West India and other Trade." New York harbor was "one of the best in the world, being sheltered from every wind, having excellent anchoring ground, and sufficient depth of water for ships of the line," and the port was relatively free of ice in winter. Jedidiah Morse commented in 1789 that New York commanded "the trade of one half New Jersey, most of . . . Connecticut, and part of . . . Massachusetts; besides the whole interior country, which is penetrated by one of the largest rivers in America." Next to Philadelphia, noted the duc de la Rochefoucauld Liancourt, New York is "the place of the greatest trade in the United States." Ship entrances and clearances were registered at the Tontine Coffee House at the corner of Wall and Water streets (fig. 5-45).[4]

American merchants began a limited trade with South and Central America after the war as other avenues of commerce opened. China, the East Indies, India, and the western coast of America became new and profitable markets, and the long-enduring European trade still had its attractions. American chairmaking interests sought every opportunity to distribute Windsor seating to the four corners of the earth. Waterborne commerce was the lifeblood of many an American chairmaker in the late eighteenth century, as demonstrated by the Federal Procession held at New York in 1788 to celebrate state and national ratification of the Constitution (fig. **4-1**). The chairmakers, headed by Thomas and William Ash, bore a standard "representing a large manufactory shop, with a number of workmen . . . ; in front of the shop a view of the river, several vessels bound to different parts, taking in chairs, boys carrying them to the wharfs." The motto: "Free Trade. The federal states in union bound, O'er all the world our chairs are found." When Tench Coxe surveyed the state of American exports six years later, he named among "established" commodities the Windsor chair. Coxe provided statistics — at best incomplete — for American goods exported between October 1, 1790, and September 30, 1791. The front-runner in the furniture category with 5,134 items shipped was the Windsor chair. By comparison, rush-bottom chairs numbered 738 items, desks 78, and chests 705. A survey of other commodities describes a brisk trade in staples and livestock. During the early years of the republic various states and the federal Congress provided protection for manufactures by imposing duties on certain imports, among them "cabinet ware" and popularly priced chairs.[5]

Although a commercial upswing occurred in the 1790s, there also were difficulties. First England then France deliberately ignored the neutral rights of American shipping as the two European powers continued their struggle for supremacy on land and sea. For their part American merchants and masters, in their relentless effort to circumvent trade restrictions, were only too willing to tempt fate. The files of the National Archives are filled with French spoliation claims, some dating to the 1780s, which constitute a rich treasure trove of information on the American shipping trade. Thomas P. Cope, a Philadelphia businessman, commented during a visit to Virginia in 1802 on the long-range effects of this piracy: "The merchants of Alexandria have been grievous sufferers by French spoilations [*sic*] & trade here participates largely in the general langour to which American commerce has been latterly reduced." The deprivations continued, and President Jefferson finally answered with an embargo on overseas commerce beginning December 22, 1807. The Embargo Act was exceedingly unpopular, causing widespread suffering in the shipping and related industries and extending even to the inland farmers who sold crops for overseas distribution. Cope noted again on May 20, 1808, that "the continuance of the Embargo has become very oppressive." Repeal finally came on March 15, 1809, and once more trade flourished briefly.[6]

Hard on the heels of the embargo came the War of 1812, affecting both the overseas and coastwise trades. So confining were restrictions that tedious overland routes were developed between New England and the South. British commercial interests were desperate and "ran cargo after cargo into their eastern provinces" in Canada. From there the merchandise "passed across the border and [was] taken South by ox teams." These two situations—the embargo and the war—served as substantial stimuli to encourage men of means to invest their monies in new ways. In New England, where manufacturing had been particularly slow to take hold, the groundwork was laid for a textile industry that matured during the second quarter of the century. Meanwhile a depression of almost national scope, commencing about 1819, followed postwar prosperity. Western banks failed due in part to overspeculation, and eastern and other markets were glutted with British goods. The next major financial reverse began in 1837 and was labeled a "Panic."[7]

The first great era of western expansion in America dates from the early 1800s. The migratory trickle to the West in the immediate postrevolutionary period became a flood with the turn of the century. By 1810 more than a million "Americans" were residents of the "West." Passing through western Pennsylvania in 1817 on his way to Illinois, Morris Birkbeck, an English settler, observed: "Old America seems to be breaking up, and moving westward. We are seldom out of sight . . . of family groups behind and before us." Henry Fearon, traveling about the same date between Chambersburg and Pittsburgh, passed sixty-three wagons with families, comprising former residents of Massachusetts, Maine, New Jersey, Connecticut, Maryland, Pennsylvania, England, Holland, and Ireland. Other individuals were on horseback or foot. One family in a wagon was returning from Cincinnati "disappointed," a rare circumstance though by no means unknown.[8]

As early as 1793 Gilbert Imlay noted of the distant Indiana Territory that "all the trades, immediately necessary to the promotion of the comforts of new settlements, are to be found here." A quarter century later William Darby commented specifically on the western furniture trade: "Tables, chairs, and bedsteads are made in all the large towns in the valleys of Ohio and Mississippi, with all the requisite qualities of elegance and strength." Henry Fearon was careful to note the "state of *mechanic arts*" during his American visit. Those trades that flourished, he observed, were the ones that received protection from European competition and enjoyed "the combined benefit of immigrant and native ingenuity." As for imported goods, eastern merchants found in the West a new area for commercial expansion and profit. During his American travels of the mid-1790s the duc de la Rochefoucauld Liancourt commented on trade with the interior, and his observations were still timely two decades later: "There is no part of the United States, however remote, even in the woods, in which one store, and frequently more, may not be found. There are established warehouses for foreign goods, which are emptied and filled twice in the year, and of which the proprietors make a rapid fortune."[9]

Improvements in transportation proved a great impetus in moving people and commodities to the western territories and encouraged the establishment of towns and cities west of the Alleghenies. In 1829 river trade downstream from Pittsburgh to Cincinnati took three days. To Saint Louis the trip required a week, and the journey to New Orleans consumed a fortnight or more. Construction of the Erie Canal and

steamboat travel opened a northern settlement route across Lake Erie. Commanding statistics illuminate the state of emigration and commerce in the area during the
1830s. Buffalo was the stopover for sixty thousand emigrants and travelers to the
West in 1833, a figure that increased by twenty thousand a year later. In 1836 almost
a thousand each of sailing and steam vessels visited the Cleveland waterfront. On a
single day in 1838 at Sandusky "285 wagons drove into that lake port from Ohio's rich
wheatlands and unloaded produce destined for the eastern cities." Emigrants to Chicago regularly landed on a sandbar at the mouth of the Chicago River, where they
and their goods were floated ashore. The community with its "frontier" population
of 150 in 1832 leaped to "city" size by 1838 with 8,000 inhabitants.[10]

An *early* improvement in interior transportation that stimulated communication and trade was the construction of turnpike roads for vehicles and mounted or
foot traffic. Connecticut in particular was active, chartering its first turnpike in 1792,
which was built between Norwich and New London. In Pennsylvania the Philadelphia and Lancaster Turnpike was established the same year. By 1811 New York State
alone had 137 chartered road corporations. Other roads followed by the hundreds
through the 1830s. The new roadways were eminently successful, attracting considerable traffic and popularizing stagecoach travel as never before. Then as today tolls
were charged, and gates were erected at intervals to collect fees. The turnpike roadways were reasonably smooth and maintained, unlike many other public routes of
the day.[11]

Before the advent of the steamboat, sloops served eastern waterways as local
freight and passenger carriers. Where rivers and streams were of insufficient depth to
admit these vessels, flat-bottom boats took over — above Troy on the Hudson, north
of Trenton on the Delaware, and along the Susquehanna. From the day in 1807 when
Robert Fulton made a successful steam-powered journey up the Hudson, the steamboat captured the public imagination and revolutionized travel. Whereas Fulton's
Clermont labored from New York to Albany in 32 hours in 1807, the same trip took
only 10½ hours, including stops at landing places, twenty-five years later. By 1840 at
least one hundred steamboats vied for passengers on the Hudson alone. The country
was becoming decidedly smaller. Even by 1814 William Bentley, a cleric of Salem,
Massachusetts, marveled at the transformation: "Travel was formerly very rare & a
man who had been by land through our States or any one of them was consulted as
an Oracle. But now it is rare to find a man who has not been at the springs or some
place of resort, & many have passed the whole length of our Atlantic coast."[12]

On the western waters the early workhorses were keelboats, vessels pointed at
each end and sometimes equipped with sail, and flatboats, whose blunt prows were
unsuited for upriver travel. The latter often were of temporary construction to be
knocked apart at their destination and sold for lumber. Migrating families frequently
employed another kind of flatboat called an arc, on which they could erect a log
cabin. Keelboats and flatboats alike carried freight, provisions, and passengers along
the highways of the West — the Ohio, Wabash, Missouri, and Mississippi — to their
downriver destinations. Henry Bradshaw Fearon, touring America in 1817–18, noted
the number of boats in port at Natchez, Mississippi: "twenty-five flats, seven keels,
and one steam-vessel." Steamboats were new on the western rivers in 1813 when an
almanac stated: "The steam boat business is an establishment of the first importance.
It opens new sources of trade, new modes of navigation over our extensive water
courses; and its immense saving of manual labour, is in itself a consideration not
easily . . . estimated. . . . The steam power, as now applied in the United States, is one
of the greatest and most important discoveries that has been made for at least the last
century." For the upriver return a keelboat required laborious poling by the keelmen.
The 1,350-mile journey from New Orleans to Louisville, Kentucky, could take three
months. Some early steamboats cut that time to less than half, and at midcentury the
Eclipse covered the same distance in about 4½ days. By that date Mississippi steam

FIG. 4-2 *View of Cincinnati, Ohio*, drawn by
Edwin Whitefield, 1846, printed by Jones and
Newman, New York, 1848. Color lithograph; H.
16½", w. 37⅞" (image). *(The Mariners' Museum,
Newport News, VA)*

freight had already reached 10 million pounds annually. Western steamboats, unlike their eastern counterparts, had flat bottoms to better navigate the region's shallow channels. In 1836 more than 550 vessels plied the "Western Waters." Wheeling, West Virginia, recorded about 800 arrivals during the course of that year, Louisville 1,700, Saint Louis almost 1,400, and New Orleans just under 1,300. In 1848, when Edwin Whitefield published his view of the Cincinnati waterfront (fig. **4-2**), more than 4,000 steamboats anchored along that Ohio shoreline annually.[13]

Meanwhile canal fever had long since swept the country. The great era of canal building commenced after the War of 1812, although a canal dug earlier around the James River falls at Richmond, Virginia, contributed substantially to the rise of that southern center. The father of all artificial waters was the Erie Canal. Begun in 1817 and completed in 1825, it linked Buffalo, New York, on Lake Erie with Albany on the Hudson. The opening in October was celebrated with jubilation along the entire 363-mile length and down the Hudson to New York. A Northern Canal of 63 miles also connected Fort Edward on the upper Hudson with Whitehall at the southern extremity of Lake Champlain, giving access to the Saint Lawrence River. A large basin of 4,000 feet constructed at Albany provided a place for canal boats to receive and discharge cargoes. Statistics for 1825, the first partial year of operation on the Erie Canal, describe "9594 arrivals and departures . . . at Albany, with 165,000 barrels of flour, and near 16 million feet of plank and boards; 23,292 tons of merchandise also, went north and west." The next year one town along the western route reported nineteen thousand passing boats, and it was not uncommon for fifty craft to leave Albany for the West in a single day. The Erie Canal was a tremendous stimulus to commerce and migration. Rural outposts sprang into cities almost overnight, and Lake Erie came alive with activity. Throughout the country the Erie Canal became the symbol of success for dozens of more modest endeavors.[14]

Canal boats on the Erie were long low conveyances of up to 70 feet (fig. 4-30) drawn over their ribbonlike course by trotting horses. Passenger vessels contained a room for the ladies and a dining room that became sleeping quarters for the men at night. Newspapers and a small library provided amusement, and travelers could view the passing scenery, although they were cautioned against standing on the upper deck because of the many low bridges along the waterway.[15]

The canal era also coincided with the early years of railroad construction. Two roads completed during the 1830s were the Baltimore and Ohio, extending 250 miles to Pittsburgh, and the Massachusetts, which connected Boston and Albany, New York. There were over 30,000 miles of track in the country before the Civil War. Clark has summarized the importance and impact of railroads in emancipating American society "from topography and climate" by describing their salient features—directness, speed, and continuity—conditions that profoundly affected manufactures.[16]

Prerevolutionary Evidence of Exportation

FOREIGN TRADE

There is no way of identifying by type the eighteen chairs carried to Jamaica from Philadelphia in 1749 on the ship *Ruby*; however, the reference documents the existence of a Caribbean trade in seating furniture by the mid-eighteenth century. As early as 1741 Francis Trumble, a cabinetmaker who later made Windsor chairs, had shipped a dozen mahogany chairs to Barbados on consignment. Definite evidence of the introduction of the Windsor to the Caribbean marketplace occurs in a record dated October 4, 1752, when the snow *Charming Polly* carried a cargo of foodstuffs and three Windsor chairs from Philadelphia to Barbados. This voyage was followed by the transfer of a dozen Windsors between the same ports on December 20 as part of the snow *Hannah*'s cargo. The vessel, laden primarily with provisions, also carried staves and headings for casks, barrels, or hogsheads, the common shipping containers of the day. Six chairs in a cargo from Philadelphia to New Providence, the Bahamas, in October 1755 are not further identified. Neither is there a clear picture of the "Duzen of vearry Good house Chears" or the "Duzen of Round Back Greate Chears" ordered in Providence, Rhode Island, on August 5, 1758, by John Wheaton, captain of the *Ann*, on behalf of the governor of Santo Domingo (Dominican Republic) through the merchants Obediah and Nicholas Brown. Despite the scarcity of other early shipping documents, circumstantial evidence points to a gradual rise in the Windsor trade, as suggested in part by Lord Adam Gordon in 1765 in his description of the commerce of Philadelphia with the West Indies: "Everybody in Philadelphia deals more or less in trade. Here they build ships and export timber of all sorts and for all purposes; many timber frames for the West India planters' houses are shipped from thence, their intercourse with Jamaica and all the Leeward and Windward Caribbee Islands being very considerable."[17]

The brig *Mansfield*, a Philadelphia vessel, entered Jamaican waters in November 1760 carrying "24 Chairs," a number suggesting they could have been Windsors. Definite evidence of a burgeoning trade in Windsors to the Indies during the 1760s begins in December 1763 when the ship *Grape* transported "12 high back Chairs," or Windsors, to Petit-Goâve, Haiti. The remaining cargo was typical for the period— foodstuffs, 10,000 feet of boards, 6,000 staves, 2,500 barrel hoops, and specie. Twice in 1767 the 70-ton brig *Morning Star* from Philadelphia carried Windsor chairs to Basseterre, Saint Christopher (Saint Kitts), in the Leeward Islands. Both cargoes were of mixed domestic and foreign origin—flour, bread, "Indian Corn," hams, fish and beef, spermaceti candles, soap, bar iron, shingles, and Madeira wine. Two December sailings, that of the *Mercury* in 1767 and the *Hannah* in 1768, resulted in the deposit of several dozen Windsor chairs in Barbados and Montserrat, respectively. The *Mercury* completed her passage in 5½ weeks. Harrold E. Gillingham, who made a study of early Windsor exportations from Philadelphia, recorded a total of 437 chairs destined for Barbados between July 1766 and June 1768, the number possibly representing several patterns. Missing from the list, however, is the sailing vessel *Industry*, which left Philadelphia on March 30, 1767, and arrived in Barbados on June 3, carrying 96 chairs in addition to 24 "Chair Bottoms" and "Two Barrels chair

Work," that is, turned, sawed, and shaved parts. To date this is the earliest known reference to the shipment of unassembled Windsor chairs.[18]

The Jamaican market experienced renewed activity during the late 1760s, when shipping returns for a two-year period document the entry of almost two hundred chairs. Other records provide glimpses of direct activity by craftsmen in Philadelphia. On November 17, 1768, Benjamin Randolph, cabinetmaker turned entrepreneur, credited Francis Trumble with £10.6.0 worth of merchandise, probably Windsor chairs, for an intended "Voyage to Jamaica." In parallel activity Randolph credited the account of Windsor-chair maker/cabinetmaker Jedidiah Snowden with £18 for an "Adventure to Honduras." The first known New England trade in Windsor chairs to the Caribbean occurred on a voyage to Jamaica and the Bay of Honduras in August 1767 when John Newdigate, master of the brig *Charlotte*, left Newport, Rhode Island, with "12 Round Green Chairs." The next month Captain John Peters loaded a similar cargo aboard the brig *Industry* for the same destinations. Both men were in the employ of merchant Aaron Lopez, who customarily provided his captains with voyage instructions. Those for Newdigate follow:

> The Brig Charlote now under your Comand being ready fitted for the seas, you are to embrace the first fair wind & proceed direcly for Witywood [Withywood] on the Island of Jamaica, where . . . you are to deliver Mr Abm. Per'a. Mendes [Abraham Pereira Mendes, son-in-law to Lopez] such part of your Cargo as he shall demand of you, after which you are to receive of him what effects he thinks proper to consign you on my accot for the Bay of Honduras, where you are to proceed . . . & there dispose of all the goods comited to yr address for the most you Can; which . . . you are to Invest their proceeds in good & sound, Large Logwood.[19]

Directions for John Peters of the *Industry* were about the same. In a separate letter to Abraham Mendes at Jamaica, Lopez also spoke of sending a schooner to the Caribbean with coopers aboard to set up casks for a return cargo. Other Caribbean markets of interest to Lopez and partners were Surinam (Dutch Guiana), a small country on the northeast coast of South America, where in 1768 the brig *Sally* deposited both straw- and wooden-bottom chairs, and the island of Hispaniola (Haiti), which in 1773 received four Windsor chairs from the cargo of the sloop *Betsey*. General chair exports from Rhode Island between January 1, 1771, and January 1, 1772, numbered 84 items. In the same period Philadelphia shipped 462 chairs.[20]

COASTAL TRADE

Philadelphia dominated the coastal Windsor market during the 1760s. There were perhaps no Windsor-chair makers working in New York City on December 6, 1762, when Perry, Hayes, and Sherbrooke, storekeepers in that city, advertised "Philadelphia made Windsor chairs." Three years later Andrew Gautier offered a large and varied selection of Windsor seating, although he too was a dealer only. Gautier illustrated his advertisement with a ball-foot, high-back chair indistinguishable from a contemporary Philadelphia Windsor. Influence from Philadelphia continued to persist. John Kelso and Adam Galer, chairmakers who advertised in 1774, had either apprenticed or worked in Philadelphia. Galer sought to imitate Philadelphia practice, stating that "any gentlemen or masters of vessels may be supplied with a neat assortment upon reasonable terms." Kelso reminded customers that "laying-out as much of our money as possible at home, serves to keep the balance of trade in our favour," a broad hint at the formidable competition from Philadelphia. Thomas Ash I, who in his advertisement of March 1774 illustrated a sack-back chair (fig. **4-3**), expressed the same thought. Not all waterborne commerce from New York was part of the sea trade. Considerable freight was sent up the Hudson to Albany and points

FIG. 4-3 Advertisement of Thomas Ash I. From *Rivington's New-York Gazetteer*, New York, March 31, 1774.

between either on order or on venture. Richard Smith, traveling up the Hudson by sloop in 1769, offered information about the river trade: "Our Skipper says there are at Albany 31 Sloops all larger than this, which carry from 400 to 500 Barrels of Flour each, trading constantly from thence to York and that they make Eleven or 12 Trips a year each."[21]

The New England market was less reliable for the Windsor interests of Philadelphia. A cargo arrived occasionally in Rhode Island, including the "Six winsor Chaires" shipped on June 27, 1771, to Samuel and William Vernon of Newport on the sloop *Retrieve*. Windsors are reported entering Boston from Philadelphia, possibly on New England–owned ships, as early as 1763–64, a time when the northeastern rush-bottom chair with a banister, slat, or vase back still offered formidable competition. Other shipments of Windsors from Philadelphia to Boston occurred in the early 1770s when William Barrell supplied his brother-in-law John Andrews, who also accommodated his friends. Joseph Henzey, a chairmaker of Philadelphia, participated. At decade's end Stephen Salisbury of Worcester sought Philadelphia "Green Chairs" for his brother-in-law at Boston.[22]

Philadelphia's best markets lay to the south, however. From the early 1760s the greater Chesapeake Bay region was a steady source of orders. In a notice of April 1763 A. J. Alexander of Annapolis referred to either Philadelphia or English seating: "Elegant imported double chairs [settees] for sale." In 1765 the Philadelphia firm of Adams and Hollingsworth shipped 8 Windsors on order to the community. Port registers for Annapolis dating several years later record the regular delivery of Windsors from Philadelphia, starting in November 1768 with 6 chairs on board the ship *Esther*. Between September 1769 and December 1774 almost 150 additional chairs can be accounted for. In summer 1771 James Brice, a merchant of Annapolis, ordered "11 Windsor chairs for [a] passage" from a Philadelphia agent, recording their arrival and freight charges in his ledger on September 7. November 22, 1768, marks the first recorded entry of Philadelphia Windsors on the Eastern Shore of the Chesapeake at Oxford, Maryland. Oxford had for some years been a lucrative market for New England joined furniture and chairs, especially Boston imports.[23]

Several members of the mercantile community at Philadelphia, the Hollingsworth family in particular, had commercial interests at Head of Elk (Frenchtown, near Elkton, Maryland), a distribution point for the northern Chesapeake Bay. Consignments were placed on board small river vessels at Philadelphia and conveyed down the Delaware River to Wilmington on the Christina Creek or to New Castle a few miles below. From Wilmington vessels continued up the Christina, past Newport, to Christiana Bridge (Christiana, Delaware). From there or from New Castle wagons hauled the freight overland a dozen miles or more to the Elk River. One craftsman of Philadelphia who supplied chairs for this trade was Francis Trumble. His first known transactions, dating to 1764 and 1766, were with the Philadelphia merchant Zebulon Rudolph, a sometime partner of Levi Hollingsworth, who appears to have acted as agent for merchants at Head of Elk. Rudolph's accounts charge Trumble with freight and credit him with chair sales made by Tobias Rudolph at Elk. There are specific references to a child's chair and high-back Windsors. Freight charges listed by Rudolph confirm the route and methods of transportation. "Cash pd in Phila" covered the water passage down the Delaware and up the Christina Creek. The overland freight charge for "27 Chairs to Elk from Xteen" (Christiana Bridge) was 13*s.* 6*d.*[24]

Levi Hollingsworth, a flour merchant of Philadelphia, also had dealings with Francis Trumble. On "down freight" runs his river shallops often carried furniture consignments to the Chesapeake Bay. Hollingsworth favored Trumble in 1772 with orders for "Round top Windsor Chairs @ 14/" and "One high back D[itt]o" similarly priced. Purchases of sack-back and fan-back chairs are recorded for 1786. Hollingsworth also patronized Joseph Henzey, another chairmaker of Philadelphia. Earlier, in 1765, an anonymous craftsman had supplied Hollingsworth with eight Windsors shipped to William Thomas of Annapolis and a dozen chairs apiece sent to William Lux, a Baltimore merchant, and to Thomas Campbell.[25]

Also supplying the lower Chesapeake Bay with Windsors from Trumble was the merchant house of Clement Biddle. In January 1774 the company charged four chairs to Thomas Richardson and Company at Georgetown on the Potomac. Six high-back chairs had been shipped earlier to Andrew Leitch of nearby Bladensburg. Biddle's letter book also records an inquiry about chair prices from Thomas Contee residing near Georgetown. The firm replied that Windsors cost from 10s. to 15s., depending on the style of the chair. The company had already shipped Contee "2 arm chairs" priced at 15s. apiece. Another lower bay waterway giving access to the inland regions of Virginia and Maryland was the Patuxent River. Biddle and Company shipped several consignments of goods in 1770 to David Cranford of "uper Marlboro" on the river's northern reaches. Each of three cargoes contained Windsors, the total amounting to twenty chairs. One group had round-backs, another comprised "new fashion" seating. A notation scrawled on one invoice suggests that Francis Trumble produced at least one order. The Biddle trade was completely by water. Company vessels sailed south through Delaware Bay, around the Delmarva Peninsula, and north into Chesapeake Bay. Though greater in distance, the water passage probably was no more expensive than the Hollingsworth route, since overland transportation was more costly.[26]

The sloop *John* from Philadelphia entered York River, south of the Patuxent and Potomac rivers, in March 1768 with a dozen Windsor chairs for Virginia consumers. A like number entered neighboring Hampton in June 1774, followed a year later by other seating on a vessel from New York. A similar cargo from Philadelphia arrived in the upper James River district. Rhode Island's presence in the Bay is documented in the Lopez papers when the sloop *Florida* sailed for Maryland in July 1768 with a cargo of low-back and high-back Windsors and "straw bottom'd" chairs.[27]

By 1761 Charleston, South Carolina, was an important market for Philadelphia Windsor chairs. On June 6 the *South Carolina Gazette* carried a notice of the brig *Hannah*'s cargo, which consisted of flour, bar iron, copper stills, and Windsor chairs. Later that month another local firm offered "a parcel of neat *Windsor Chairs*" just imported in the "LAST VESSEL FROM PHILADELPHIA." Scattered references followed for 1762, the count over 300 chairs. One cargo alone contained 150 chairs. Windsor settees from Philadelphia are first mentioned in December 1765, and children's chairs arrived in January 1766 on the brig *Harrietta* as part of a cargo of 180 Windsors. Sheed and White advertised a range of Windsor seating in June (fig. **4-4**), itemizing three patterns and identifying several specialized forms—settees and children's furniture—along with Windsors constructed of walnut. The Philadelphia Windsor was firmly entrenched in the South Carolina market.[28]

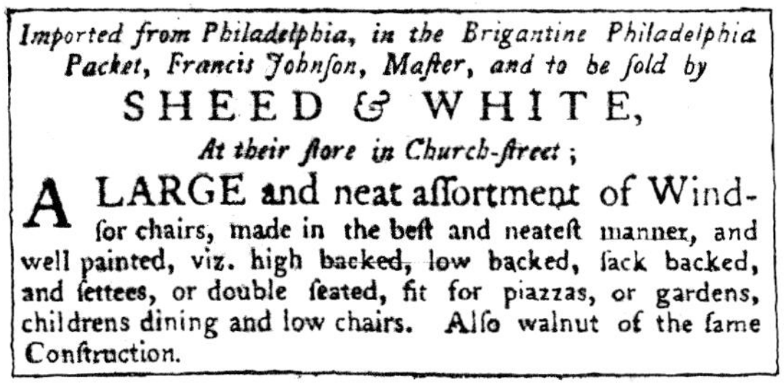

On May 1, 1770, when William Sykes announced from his Charleston store the receipt of "Windsor Chairs of a new Fashion," he referred either to the fan-back side chair or, more likely, to chairs with the support structure converted from the ball-foot leg to a tapered foot. Subsequent notices are silent on the subject of fan-backs, but there are references to the round-top, or sack-back, Windsor, known primarily as a tapered-foot chair. A prewar advertisement of James Bentham and Company first identified "Green Windsor Chairs."[29]

Fourteen Windsors transshipped from Charleston to Georgia on the schooner *Fanny* in 1766 entered the Savannah River in October, following a direct shipment of thirty Windsors in June from Philadelphia. The following year Captain John Hyer, bound for the Caribbean from Rhode Island on the brig *Sally*, undertook to sell the ship's cargo of mahogany and maple desks, maple tables, and green chairs on the mainland, as per instructions from Aaron Lopez of Newport: "Inclosed you have Invo[ice] of sundrys to your address, of which please to dispose on y[ou]r arrival

Imported from Philadelphia, in the Brigantine Philadelphia Packet, Francis Johnson, Master, and to be sold by

SHEED & WHITE,

At their store in Church-street ;

A LARGE and neat assortment of Windsor chairs, made in the best and neatest manner, and well painted, viz. high backed, low backed, sack backed, and settees, or double seated, fit for piazzas, or gardens, childrens dining and low chairs. Also walnut of the same Construction.

FIG. 4-4 Advertisement of Sheed and White. From *South-Carolina Gazette and Country Journal*, Charleston, June 24, 1766.

at Georgia, and what you cant sell there you may (in case you proceed to Jamaica) carry down with you."[30]

Still another southern market that figured in the coastwise Windsor trade was Saint Augustine in East Florida, a region under English control (formerly a Spanish territory) during the late 1760s when several pertinent entries are recorded in district returns. Although the four chair cargoes listed in a shipping volume dating from 1765 to 1769 came from Charleston, South Carolina, it is safe to say they originated in Philadelphia. In June 1767 the schooner *Mary* arrived at Saint Augustine carrying twelve Windsor chairs, and the vessel returned with another dozen chairs in August. The following spring more chairs were deposited by the schooner *Brouton Island Packet*, a vessel owned by statesman Henry Laurens. In March 1769 the *Packet* returned to unload two dozen Windsors.[31]

British trade statistics for the American colonies constitute the best source of commercial data for the prerevolutionary years, although they are incomplete due to trade loopholes, careless record keeping, and a perennial traffic in illegally entered goods. The information is compiled in such a way that figures for household furniture, and specifically chairs, can be extracted and studied independently, providing insights into the domestic seating trade after the Windsor chair had been in the market for more than two decades and at a time when the colonial economy flourished. Table 5 is a record of American coastwise imports and exports from 1768 through 1772 compiled by the British Board of Customs and Excise. When reviewing the table it is important to keep in mind three points: (1) the statistics include all kinds of chairs—joined, rush-bottom, and Windsor; (2) there was no production of Windsor furniture in New England, Rhode Island excepted, or the southern ports at this date; (3) British chairs also entered American colonial ports but in numbers far less than the native product. Figures for the Canadian districts have been omitted as being irrelevant to the study at this period.[32]

It is clear that New Hampshire, with its low importation rate, was reasonably self-sufficient in chair production. In fact, the Piscataqua region experienced a brisk export business in "sitting," or "common" rush-bottom, chairs to coastal markets during the 1760s, as documented in other commercial records. Massachusetts already had a substantial trade in leather-bottom joiner's chairs, called simply "Boston chairs" in documents, and the demand continued. Salem and Marblehead as neighboring maritime communities took advantage of the same trade. The outward chair commerce of Rhode Island probably comprised a mixed offering of rush-bottom chairs and Windsors. The sizable number of chairs imported into the region likely reflects continuing activity on the part of Boston's cabinetmaking community and the entrepreneurship of other coastal shippers. The chair industry of Connecticut was and remained focused primarily on the local market, although much unrecorded business was carried out by a multitude of coasters who regularly sailed in and out of the coves and rivers dotting the shoreline. Chairmakers in New York apparently had a legitimate complaint about competition from imported seating (fig. 4-3), as chairs brought into the colony outnumbered those exported by 2½ to 1. The ascendancy of the Windsor at Philadelphia is well documented in the tabulation. A great part of the production was sent to the South, which from the statistics was a profitable market for other northern trading centers as well. When given, southern exportation figures represent for the most part transshipped merchandise.

British records also permit insight into the growing importance of the prewar chair trade to the West Indies (table 6). Many points made in the previous paragraph hold true. Chair cargoes from New Castle, Delaware, almost certainly represent Philadelphia merchandise. It was common practice for vessels from Philadelphia engaged in the overseas trade to stop downriver on the Delaware before proceeding to Delaware Bay. Additional supplies were boarded in New Castle, and frequently

Table 5. American Coastwise Imports and Exports of Chairs, 1768–1772

Place of Export/Entry	1768 Imports	1768 Exports	1769 Imports	1769 Exports	1770 Imports	1770 Exports	1771 Imports	1771 Exports	1772 Imports	1772 Exports
Maine										
Falmouth		8		12		54		48	6	
New Hampshire							48	423	25	276
Piscataqua		217	6	795	6	354				
Massachusetts	13	1,635	121	1,288						
Boston	13	1,043	107	828	45	1,102	46	813	93	1,165
Salem and Marblehead		584	14	448	15	354	6	857	18	606
Rhode Island	52	540	125	588	21	434	260	395	95	430
Connecticut	21	10	59	34						
New London	9	10	40	28	26		19	12	19	
New Haven	12		19	6			15	24		
New York	95		168	65	1	26	139	153	461	90
New Jersey	56									
Perth Amboy	56						12		6	
Pennsylvania		972	29	768						
Philadelphia		972	29	768		930	27	900		1,724
Maryland	390	30	784	7						
Pocomoke	120		24		19	6	114		132	
Patuxent	108	30	624		487	7	530	6	491	6
Chester	6									
North Potomac	156		136	7	228		364		581	
Virginia	247		879							
Accomac	132		168		44		78		84	
South Potomac			48				24		60	
Rappahannock			4		44		11		12	
York River			48		88		144			
James River (lower)	115		264		74		92	6	204	18
James River (upper)			347		184		258		108	
North Carolina	294		619	18						
Currituck	24		6		18		36		36	
Roanoke	144		366		216		314	36	300	
Bath Town	36		108	18	8		72		180	
Beaufort	84		55		40		114		46	
Brunswick	6		84		31		128		61	
South Carolina	99	49	315	106						
Winyaw Bay (Georgetown)	36		28		36		18		138	
Charleston	63	49	281	106	536	54	234	24	434	36
Port Royal			6							
Georgia	114		126							
Savannah	108		66		242		362		253	
Sunbury	6		60		108		48			
Florida	126									
Saint Augustine	108		88		18		10		24	
Pensacola	18				36	18				

From Ledger of Imports and Exports: America, 1768–73, Board of Customs and Excise, Public Record Office, London.

Table 6. Chair Exports from North America to the British and Foreign West Indies, 1770–1772

Place of Exportation	1770	1771	1772
New Hampshire and the Piscataqua District	298	462	900
Salem and Marblehead, Mass.	96	12	
Boston, Mass.		49	6
Rhode Island	42	84	102
New London, Conn.		7	
New York City	2		17
Philadelphia, Pa.	688	462	529
New Castle, Del.	196	12	
The South (Pocomoke, Md.; lower James River, Va.; Charleston, S.C.; Savannah, Ga.)	12	26	93

From Ledger of Imports and Exports: America, 1768–73, Board of Customs and Excise, Public Record Office, London.

the ship's captain joined the vessel at that point. Southern figures have been lumped together, since they represent transshipped merchandise.[33]

Postrevolutionary Eighteenth-Century Trade: Coastal

The Treaty of Paris, which officially ended the war with Britain on September 3, 1783, marked the start of renewed, escalating activity in painted seating furniture by American shippers, with cargoes eventually sent to almost one hundred ports or landings (map 2). Andrew Redmond, a turner of Charleston, South Carolina, alluded to the revived coastal trade on October 14 when he advertised Philadelphia-style Windsor chairs of his make "as neat as any imported." Redmond also constructed common rush-bottom, slat-back seating and any turned chairs that "gentlemen may want." A cargo of 120 chairs, probably Windsors, left Philadelphia the previous July for New York, and more followed. Wood-seat chairs from Philadelphia also continued to be marketable in New England, where in 1783–84 cargoes were landed in Beverly and Boston, Massachusetts, and Rhode Island. Illuminating particulars of the trade are the merchant activities of Stephen Collins and Son of Philadelphia, who in September 1786 purchased half a dozen "Fan Back Dining windsors chairs" from William Cox, placed them on board the sloop *Friendship* bound for Boston, and charged Captain Daggit with their delivery to Ebenezer Hall. It was the more lucrative southern trade, however, that captured and held the attention of shippers and craftsmen. Fortunately a comprehensive body of records provides insights and statistics. Advertisements like that placed in 1784 by Benjamin Freeman and Andrew Houck of Philadelphia set an eager accommodating tone (fig. 4-5).[34]

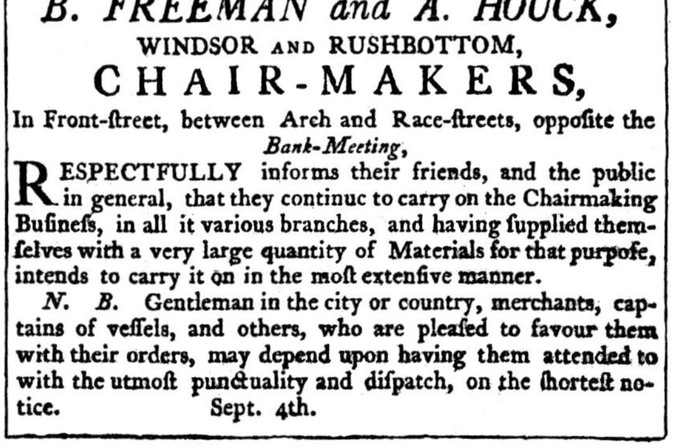

In his study of Philadelphia Windsor export records, Harrold E. Gillingham provided raw material from which it is possible to draw general statistics for the southern chair trade between mid-1783 and mid-1786. Although many entries do not identify chair types, internal evidence such as shippers' names and cargo size tips the balance substantially in favor of the Windsor. According to Gillingham, almost 475 chairs went to North Carolina, 640 to Georgia, and in excess of 2,100 to South Carolina, principally Charleston. Even so Gillingham's figures are deficient. A survey of customhouse papers from Philadelphia identifies a number of vessels and cargoes not listed in that compilation, such as the brig *Hunter*, which left port in May 1785 bound for Charleston with ten dozen Windsor chairs. Several chairmakers of

B. FREEMAN and A. HOUCK,
WINDSOR AND RUSHBOTTOM,
C H A I R - M A K E R S,
In Front-ftreet, between Arch and Race-ftreets, oppofite the
Bank-Meeting,
RESPECTFULLY informs their friends, and the public in general, that they continue to carry on the Chairmaking Bufinefs, in all it various branches, and having fupplied themfelves with a very large quantity of Materials for that purpofe, intends to carry it on in the moft extenfive manner.

N. B. Gentleman in the city or country, merchants, captains of veffels, and others, who are pleafed to favour them with their orders, may depend upon having them attended to with the utmoft punctuality and difpatch, on the fhorteft notice.　　　　Sept. 4th.

FIG. 4-5 Advertisement of Benjamin Freeman and Andrew Houck. From *Pennsylvania Journal*, Philadelphia, September 4, 1784.

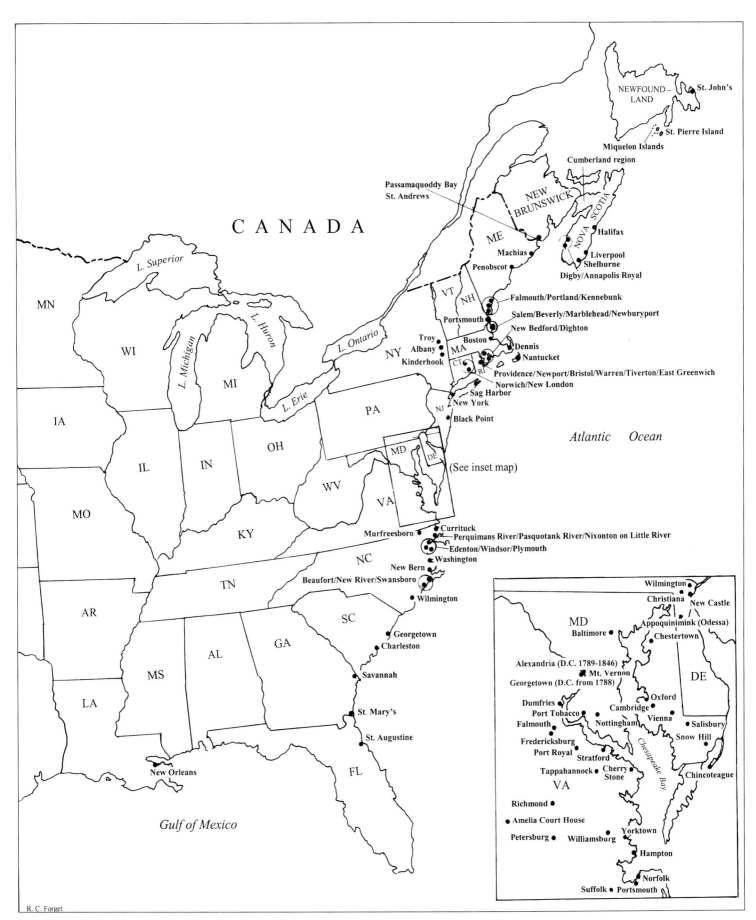

MN

WI

MI

L. Superior

L. Michigan

L. Huron

L. Ontario

L. Erie

CANADA

NEWFOUND–
LAND

St. John's

St. Pierre Island

Miquelon Islands

Cumberland region

Passamaquoddy Bay
St. Andrews

NEW
BRUNSWICK

NOVA SCOTIA

Halifax

ME

Machias

Penobscot

Liverpool
Shelburne

Digby/Annapolis Royal

VT

NH

Falmouth/Portland/Kennebunk

Portsmouth

Salem/Beverly/Marblehead/Newburyport

New Bedford/Dighton

IA

MO

AR

MS

LA

IL

IN

OH

KY

TN

AL

GA

PA

NY

Troy

Albany

Kinderhook

Boston

MA

Dennis

Nantucket

CT

RI

Providence/Newport/Bristol/Warren/Tiverton/East Greenwich

Norwich/New London

Sag Harbor

New York

Black Point

NJ

MD

DE

(See inset map)

WV

VA

Atlantic   Ocean

Murfreesboro

Currituck

Perquimans River/Pasquotank River/Nixonton on Little River

Edenton/Windsor/Plymouth

Washington

New Bern

Beaufort/New River/Swansboro

Wilmington

NC

SC

Georgetown

Charleston

Savannah

St. Mary's

St. Augustine

FL

New Orleans

Gulf of Mexico

Wilmington

Christiana

New Castle

MD

Baltimore

Appoquinimink (Odessa)

Chestertown

Alexandria (D.C. 1789-1846)

Mt. Vernon

Georgetown (D.C. from 1788)

DE

Dumfries

Port Tobacco

Falmouth

Cambridge

Oxford

Vienna

Salisbury

Snow Hill

Nottingham

Fredericksburg

Port Royal

Stratford

Tappahannock

Cherry
Stone

Chesapeake Bay

Chincoteague

VA

Richmond

Amelia Court House

Petersburg

Williamsburg

Yorktown

Hampton

Norfolk

Suffolk   Portsmouth

R. C. Forget

MAP 2   Coastal destinations of American Windsor furniture cargoes, 1783–1800

Philadelphia are linked directly with shipments made during the 1780s. A manifest for the *Commerce* dated June 11, 1783, identifies Richard Mason as the consignor of sixty chairs in a cargo sent to Georgia. In February 1785 Ephraim Evans received payment from merchant Joseph Carson for two dozen fan-back chairs shipped in the brig *Jenny* for a coastal destination. The following year entrepreneur Stephen Girard and his brother John twice purchased Windsor chairs from William Cox for export to Charleston. Three dozen side chairs bought in April and six dozen acquired in November all are identified as "dining," or side, chairs (fig. **4-6**). As the decade closed, the brig *Charleston* arrived with some of "Trumble's Philadelphia made windsor chairs, of various kinds and the newest fashions." The mere mention of Francis Trumble's surname to identify quality merchandise is a tribute to the venerable craftsman whose woodworking career approached half a century. Trumble sold to shippers and also exported in his own name.[35]

At times southern shipping records list special seating, such as stools, settees, and children's chairs. When at Charleston in 1784, the master of the ship *Clementina* offered "Settees of six feet long." Occasionally newspapers at Charleston carry sales notices for Windsor riding chairs. Other advertisements go so far as to describe "Yellow, mahogany color, and green Windsor chairs." At Portsmouth, Virginia, where Blow and Barksdale relied on Daniel Tyson to dispatch goods from Philadelphia, shipments sometimes included one or two dozen Windsors, although the firm was not alone in selling Philadelphia chairs. When the sloop *Dispatch* arrived in autumn 1784 carrying six dozen Windsor chairs, only one-sixth of the cargo was consigned to Blow and Barksdale. Norfolk, a commercial neighbor, recorded a steady stream of Windsor imports in 1789, a year for which records survive. In the upper Chesapeake Bay Francis Trumble tested the Baltimore market in 1786 when consigning "Six Dozen Green Windsor Chairs" to a firm in that rising seaport. Sometimes private individuals placed orders on their own account. George Washington made furniture purchases in Philadelphia through Clement Biddle, his agent. After returning home following a visit to the city in May 1784, the general thought better of an order directed to Biddle: "Upon second thoughts a dozn. and an half of Windsor Chairs will be suffict. (I think my Memm. requested two dozn)."[36]

Summarizing the scope and extent of the coastal trade in Windsors from Philadelphia during the 1780s are records from several sources. Documents account for more than 1,000 Windsors, including settees and children's chairs, shipped from August 20 to December 19, 1789, in schooners, brigs, sloops, and ships to ports extending from Charleston, South Carolina, to Salem, Massachusetts. Annual figures for overseas and domestic shipments combined place the number of exported Windsors from Philadelphia in 1786 at 5,118 and in 1787 at 5,731. Even Wilmington, located downriver on the Delaware, could report the exportation of 1,000 Windsors between June 1788 and June 1789, although many chairs may have originated in Philadelphia.[37]

Other regional participation in the coastal chair trade during the 1780s was limited. Jacob Vanderpool of New York directed a notice of December 1783 in part to

"Captains of vessels" who "by leaving their orders shall have them executed with fidelity." The following year Thomas and William Ash repeated the message in a notice illustrated by the sack-back woodcut Thomas used before the war (fig. 4-3). The brothers enjoyed reasonable success. In 1789 the schooner *Columbia* carried 150 of their Windsors to a consignee in Charleston. Nephew Gabriel Leggett's chair business was located on "Crugars-wharf" convenient to the waterfront, where in March 1786 he stood ready to supply shippers "on very reasonable terms, for cash or produce." Within two months the brig *Rockahock* landed a cargo from New York at Savannah, Georgia, composed in part of Windsor chairs and settees. By late summer Saint George Tucker of Williamsburg, Virginia, had received an order of adult and children's Windsors from the Ashes. The Windsor trade from New York continued to expand, although the exportation of 1,132 chairs reported in the journal of the New York State Assembly for 1788 represents a fraction of the commerce in chairs from Philadelphia.[38]

Records associated with the Windsor trade of New England in the 1780s focus principally on Rhode Island. Joseph K. Ott's studies of Providence and Newport furniture exportations identify its scope. Although Ott found that West Indian and other foreign markets were important to the commercial life of Rhode Island, it is clear that the coastal markets were more stable. Newport had considerable commerce with New York City, as reflected both in records and in the design of its Windsor seating. Boston and New London, Connecticut, were other regional ports of call. Through the 1780s vessels from Rhode Island carried chairs to southern ports, such as Baltimore, Charleston, and Alexandria. Although few cargoes are as well documented as the four dozen Windsors that entered Charleston on the ship *Union*, identification is possible in other ways. Use of the term *dining* to describe seating shipped to Baltimore on the brig *Providence* almost certainly pinpoints Windsor construction, since wood-seat side chairs frequently were used for this purpose. Many entries identify Windsor seating through color, as the "four Green Chairs" shipped in September 1788 from Newport to Georgia. At Boston, where chairmaker Ebenezer Stone and others produced "Warranted Green Windsor CHAIRS" before the end of the 1780s, importation was a more pressing consideration than exportation. Stone in a notice of 1786 voiced his concern over competition when he asserted that his chairs were "painted equally as well as those made at Philadelphia."[39]

During the 1790s coastwise trading patterns continued in part as they had through the 1780s, and Philadelphia remained the front-runner. Now there was more activity among craftsmen in New York as that city moved into its golden age of Windsor-chair making. Parts of New England beyond Rhode Island awakened to the Windsor's potential as a trade commodity. In the South, Baltimore emerged as a rising seaport. Chair exportations from Philadelphia probably well exceeded the 5,000 mark most years, depending on the extent of depredations by the French and English on the high seas. Chairmakers themselves shipped increasing numbers of cargoes without benefit of middlemen, and the number of small markets grew, especially in the South. Records contain more detailed information about cargoes and consignments than formerly.[40]

Documents affirm that ships from Philadelphia carried Windsor furniture to more than fifty coastal destinations during the 1790s, including many northern centers of Windsor-chair making (map 2). Charleston still was the most important southern outlet. Georgetown in the District of Columbia and Baltimore were among several developing markets. An extensive general activity centered in Virginia and North Carolina, although the Norfolk-Richmond region remained the most productive. The map details the complete coastal market served by Philadelphia and other suppliers.[41]

Chairmakers in Philadelphia were a particularly aggressive group during the 1790s, plying the home market and the coastal and overseas trade and acting at times as their own agents in establishing and maintaining contact with retailers in other cities. Records identify at least ten chairmakers who became agent-entrepreneurs. The leaders were Lawrence Allwine, William Cox, and Michael Murphy, each with more than twenty-five independent chair consignments to his credit. A distant fourth-ranking participant with eight consignments was Thomas Mason. One to three known contacts are credited to Francis Trumble, Joseph Burr, Richard Mason, John Mason, Anthony Steel, and James Pentland. One man, Richard Mason, also was well known in Philadelphia as an "engine" maker, having constructed vehicles for firefighting since before the Revolution. Mason's four dozen chairs shipped to Charleston on the brig *Philadelphia* in June 1790 were accompanied by "four garden engines," presumably irrigation devices. For the most part, chairmakers shipped their merchandise to private consumers or business establishments located in population centers. The outstanding market was Charleston, which received forty-eight independent lots from Philadelphia chairmakers. A second market of note was Norfolk, which entered twenty-five cargoes. The largest single consignment, totaling forty dozen chairs, was deposited with Hopkins and Charles of Charleston by Lawrence Allwine. In general, consignments averaged about five dozen chairs.[42]

Collectively, shipping records provide additional insights into the Windsor-chair trade from Philadelphia, supplying information about form, color, pattern, consumers, and arrangements. Chairs, the most common article, were supplemented from time to time by settees, stools, and children's seating, although the latter two were few in number. Two settees at most accompanied a chair consignment, and the figures suggest at times that all formed one or two suites of furniture. Among chair patterns, which rarely are mentioned, the "oval back'd," or "Bow back'd," style is named most often. Another lot described in 1795 as "Four Dusin & half fan back Chairs" was placed on board the sloop *Polly* bound for Norfolk. Straw color is identified as the finish on a consignment of bow-back side and armchairs shipped in 1791 to Charleston by William Cox. Other paint choices were yellow, green, green and yellow, chocolate, and white. Two elegant groups of chairs shipped to Boston in 1795 were mahogany "colored" and had stuffed seats.[43]

Shipping manifests outline only broad voyage plans. Particulars were spelled out in consumer orders or instructions to captains from ship owners, neither of which have survived in great number. Sometimes it is possible to read between the lines and to identify stops made en route to stated destinations. Material relating to the Cheaspeake Bay region provides insights into distribution and marketing practices in the coastal trade of the Middle Atlantic states. The stated destination of several vessels entering the Potomac was Alexandria, although it appears that stops were made along the river. When the sloop *Polly* left Philadelphia in June 1790, her cargo consisted in part of "one Dozen Wanser Chears" consigned to an individual at Port Tobacco. This landing place, near present day La Plata, stood at the tip of a finger in the river almost midway in the ascent to Alexandria. Five years later the sloop *Nancy* left the Delaware for the Potomac carrying 1½ dozen Windsor chairs shipped by and consigned to Henry Lee, Esq. Captain Thomas Gardiner probably had orders to deposit the furniture on the landing at Stratford, of which Henry Lee (Light-Horse Harry) was then proprietor. Other delivery arrangements are described in a letter of 1796 written by President Washington to his manager at Mount Vernon after purchasing twenty-four Windsor chairs from the Gaw brothers at Philadelphia: "By a Vessel which says she will sail from hence to Alex'a on Wednesday next, I shall send two dozn Windsor Chairs which the Captn has promised to land as he passes Mount Vernon. Let them be put in the New Room." No doubt this procedure was repeated several years later when Clement Biddle, Washington's Philadelphia agent, shipped "Seven Cases furniture" to Mount Vernon on the sloop *Harmony*, whose ultimate destination was Alexandria.[44]

Vessels navigating the Rappahannock engaged in something of the same business.

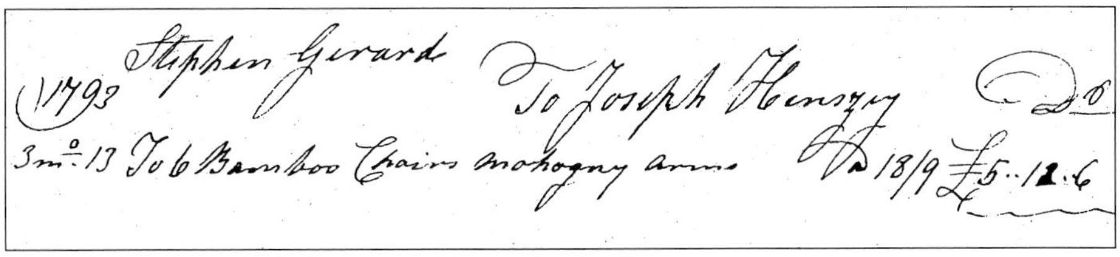

FIG. 4-7 Joseph Henzey bill to Stephen Girard, Philadelphia, March 13, 1793. *(Collection of the Board of Directors of City Trusts, Girard College History Collections.)*

A dozen Windsor chairs shipped from Philadelphia in March 1798 and consigned at Port Royal probably were unloaded there before the schooner proceeded to its destination at Fredericksburg. A year later the *Ann* sailed to the same place, perhaps landing first at Falmouth, on the north bank opposite Fredericksburg, where the captain delivered two dozen Philadelphia Windsor chairs consigned to Dunbar and Voss. The James River was the avenue of access for furniture from Philadelphia ordered in 1791 by Stephen Cocke of Amelia County, Virginia. At Petersburg the firm of William and James Douglas forwarded the pair of gilt pier glasses, four highpost bedsteads, and two dozen green Windsor chairs by wagon to Woodlands, Cocke's new home near Amelia County Court House. Illustrating how some orders were initiated is a letter from a Christiana, Delaware, resident directed in August 1794 to chairmaker Lawrence Allwine of Philadelphia:

> I wish you to send me half a dozen good round back windsor Chairs painted mehogany colour — deliver them to Levi Hollingsworth & Son with the bill which they will pay you on shewing them this letter — I want the Chairs Immediately.
>
> Solomon Maxwell[45]

Providing insights on the coastal furniture trade from the situation of the merchant-factor are excerpts from the papers of two leading houses in Philadelphia, those of the rising merchant-prince Stephen Girard and the Quakers Stephen Collins and Son. Girard's schooner *Thomas* left Philadelphia on March 10, 1791, bound for Petersburg, Virginia, with four dozen Windsor chairs. Although the cargo cannot be linked in records with a specific craftsman of Philadelphia, related information strongly suggests the maker was William Cox, with whom Girard had business dealings beginning in 1786 (fig. 4-6). Only two days after the ship departed, Girard purchased "24 Straw colour'd chairs" from Cox. There followed in 1792 and 1793 two lots of expensive "Bamboo windsor Chairs with mohogny arms" priced at 18s. 9d. apiece from Joseph Henzey (fig. **4-7**). In 1796 Girard also had business dealings with John B. Ackley, and in 1799 he patronized Taylor and King. The partners supplied round-back, mahogany-colored dining chairs and "1 Doz Newfashioned Wite Dining Chairs" (fig. 3-25). The term "Newfashioned" may refer to the serpentine-top rod-back Windsor introduced about this time.[46]

Records of the Stephen Collins firm are enlightening in other ways. The Collinses also had business dealings in Petersburg, Virginia. When they put together a furniture order for Samuel Cheesman of that place in autumn 1792, they patronized the shop of John Mullen, a newcomer to the Windsor trade. Mahogany furniture from John Douglas followed. On October 25 the factors placed the orders on board the schooner *Sans Souci* and received a shipping receipt for the merchandise from Captain Samuel Crozier: "one box — Twelve windsor chairs — and the following mahogany furniture, vizt: Two card tables — two end tables — one dining table, one Pembroke table, & one Bureau table." The following day a Collins clerk recorded the shipment of Cheesman's order in the company daybook, making note of the mahogany furniture, some law books (probably placed in the "box"), and "12 Windsor chairs bot of John Mullen moreen bottoms — stuffed — 20/3." The total price of the Windsors was over £12. The extra labor required to stuff the seats and cover them with woolen moreen greatly advanced the cost from ordinary Windsor seating. In good business fashion the Collinses wrote their client advising that the order had been shipped and remarked, "The Windsor chairs are of the cheapest kind, yet neat and fashionable."[47]

Several years later the Collins firm oversaw a special order of Windsor furniture for a Boston client. In May 1795 the factors received a bill for twenty-two mahogany-colored bow-back armchairs from chairmaker William Cox. Four chairs were stuffed with haircloth, and the rest had plain wooden bottoms, although the frames were enhanced with real mahogany arms. The total bill with wrapping came to just over £25. As this sum was more than Joseph Blake had anticipated paying, Zaccheus Collins went to great pains to examine Cox's shop accounts and to reassure the Bostonian that the price was fair. Collins's commission at 5 percent was £1.5.1. When Zaccheus Collins paid William Cox on June 15, the chairmaker signed Collins's receipt book and noted that he had placed the chairs "onboard the schooner [*Hannah*] Capt Adams for Boston."[48]

Coastal activity in the 1790s by chairmakers at New York is indicated in the notices of two leading craftsmen. John DeWitt offered to supply "Masters of vessels" with Windsor seating "in large or small quantities, at the shortest notice." Thomas Timpson added "low terms for cash or produce" as an inducement. Shipping records confirm that interests at New York enjoyed a substantial waterborne traffic in Windsor seating and suggest the trade's scope. Within the region there were deliveries at Kinderhook, Troy, and Sag Harbor. The South was a good market; Charleston led the way with Savannah close behind. Small towns along the North Carolina coast were good for an occasional cargo, and merchants in Norfolk and Richmond, Virginia, were active. Some merchants at Baltimore dealt in New York seating, even with the local chairmaking trade on the rise. In 1799 the sloop *Christian*'s captain brought five dozen chairs into port. Two years earlier William Palmer, a fancy-chair maker of New York, had been favored with an order from General Charles Ridgely. Palmer supplied the Maryland resident with a set of twenty-four white and gold japanned fancy chairs and a settee en suite at a cost of well over £33. This was a lucrative sale and a promising contact that Palmer was anxious to pursue further:

> N. York Oct 10, 1797
> Sir,
> I have this day Ship'd your chairs &c. On board the Sloop Sea Hour Cap'n Wilson for Balto. All in Godd [*sic*] Order and well Packet I believe perfectly agreeable to your Orders—Should you want anything els in my line; or any of your friends, I hope you will please to Recolect My address where your favors will be most thankfully received and Punctually Executed.
>
> William Palmer[49]

A special order shipped from New York in summer 1792 was one arranged between the merchant Nicholas Low and the wealthy Philadelphian William Bingham, who had purchased a country seat on the northern Jersey coast at Black Point near Long Branch. The dwelling was to be ready for occupancy by July, and in expectation of removing his family there for the summer Bingham shipped household furniture and freight from Philadelphia by way of New York City, where Nicholas Low took charge. In late June Lowe received on board the sloop *Salem* from Philadelphia fourteen Windsor chairs and "Two Sophas" (settees), which he transshipped for the short run to Black Point on the sloop *Good Intent*. Captain David Lewis promised upon his "safe arrival to Black Point [to] deliver said Articles to Mr William Lloyd," Bingham's manager. Bingham made a second request of Low: "Will you . . . purchase . . . four dozen handsome Windsor Chairs to be sent at the same time. If they were painted Straw Colour & picked out with green, I should prefer it."[50]

New England was another market for New York, and contacts extended well north to include occasional intercourse with Digby and Shelburne in British Nova Scotia. At best, however, the chair trade to New England was scattered and limited. An exception was Newport, where communication from New York was frequent. Initiative in the chair trade stood mainly on the side of Rhode Island, and the commerce followed a well-defined pattern. From a study of one hundred chair consignments it can be determined that ship captains from Rhode Island conducted 57 percent of this business. Making frequent runs along Long Island Sound in their little coasting vessels, these small-time entrepreneurs frequently returned to Newport with half a dozen to eighteen or more chairs purchased on their own initiative or to the order of a fellow townsman. The sloops *Aurora*, under the command of Cahoone family members, and *Peggy*, with Captain Thomas W. Bliss on board, were active during the 1790s. A notable exception to the usual pattern was the coastal run of the sloop *Semiramus* in August 1800 when Captain Benjamin Marshall ventured a cargo of two hundred Windsor chairs for local distribution or transshipment after his return to Newport (fig. **4-8**). Newport merchants commanded another 33 percent of the trade, and some New Yorkers are identified. One was a Mr. Sprusen, probably John Sprosen, a chairmaker who in October 1796 sent "Six Green Chairs" to Newport.[51]

The New York to Newport painted seating trade of the 1790s numbered well over 1,600 items, identified as "chairs," "Green Chairs," or "Windsor Chairs." Occasionally the destination was a town in the Narragansett region — Tiverton, Bristol, or Warren. Contact with East Greenwich, also on the bay, is documented through the Greene family papers. In spring 1792 James Bertine shipped fifteen Windsor chairs from his shop in New York to the family. Circumstances such as these help to explain why some Rhode Island Windsors in the continuous-bow and bow-back patterns are almost indistinguishable from their counterparts made in New York. John Brown, a merchant of Providence, sent a cargo of one hundred chairs to Newport in 1799 on the sloop *Sally*, but whether of local manufacture or transshipped from New York is not indicated. The Ash brothers of New York, active as direct shippers to Newport, also had other connections in New England. In 1794 they sent forty-eight Windsors to Norwich, Connecticut.[52]

Not all chairs imported into Newport from New York during the 1790s appear to have been retained for local consumption. Newport along with Providence had a modest furniture trade with the South and occasionally the West Indies. Their southern markets were scattered, and few Windsor cargoes are identified. Those that are include green chairs sent to Norfolk in 1791 and Charleston in 1793. "Six Green Chairs" were carried to Boston in 1794 as a customer purchase or a speculation of the

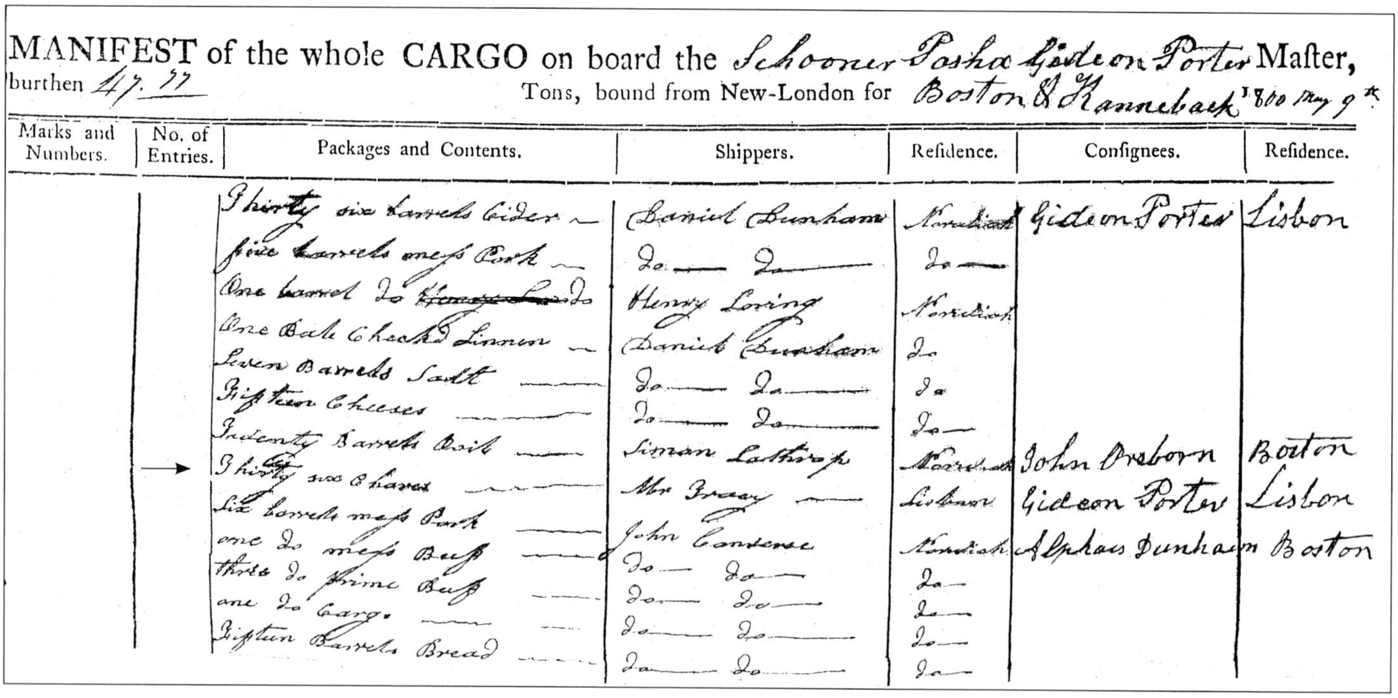

MANIFEST of the whole CARGO on board the *Schooner Pasha Gideon Porter* Master, burthen *47 77* Tons, bound from New-London for *Boston & Kannebank* 1800 May 9

Marks and Numbers.	No. of Entries.	Packages and Contents.	Shippers.	Residence.	Consignees.	Residence.
		Thirty six barrels Cider	Daniel Dunham	Norwich	Gideon Porter	Lisbon
		five barrels mess Pork	Do Do	do		
		One barrel do ~~[illegible]~~ do	Henry Loring	Norwich		
		One Bale Checks Linnen	Daniel Dunham	do		
		Seven Barrels Salt	do do	do		
		Fifteen Cheeses	do do	do		
		Twenty barrels [illegible]	Simon Lathrop	Norwich	John Osborn	Boston
		Thirty six Chairs	Mr Tracy	Lisbon	Gideon Porter	Lisbon
		Six barrels mess Pork				
		one do mess Beef	John Converse	Norwich	Alpheus Dunham	Boston
		three do prime Beef	do do	do		
		one do Cargo	do do	do		
		Fifteen barrels Bread	do do	do		
			do do	do		

FIG. 4-9 Detail of cargo manifest of schooner *Pasha*, New London, Conn., May 9, 1800. *(U.S. Custom House Records, French Spoliation Claims, National Archives, Washington, D.C.)*

sloop *Lucy*'s captain, although Boston appears to have been a better market for chair shippers from neighboring New London, Connecticut.[53]

Several lots shipped from New London to Boston numbered 1½ dozen chairs or more. One group of a dozen "Dining Chairs" went consigned to Gurdon Avery, and in 1794 another Avery family member at Roxbury near Boston received a writing chair. "Mr. Tracy" (Ebenezer) of "Lisbon" shipped thirty-six chairs to the city on May 9, 1800, on the schooner *Pasha*, although after the stop at Boston the vessel proceeded to Kennebunk, Maine, leaving in doubt the actual destination of the Windsor furniture (fig. **4-9**). The district of Maine was a good market for New London vessels. In 1793 Machias near the Canadian border recorded the arrival of three groups of Windsors totaling five dozen chairs. Along the southern Maine coast two dozen chairs were landed in Kennebunk in 1798 by the well-named sloop *Speculator*. Captain Job Harrington of the schooner *Eliza* found a market in December 1799 at Liverpool, Nova Scotia, for a dozen Windsor chairs from New London. The town's southern markets comprised Charleston and Savannah, although chairmakers from Philadelphia and New York had little to fear. Once in autumn 1799 the schooner *Laurel* carried two hundred chairs to Georgia; however, there seem to have been no repeat cargoes, and individual entries at Charleston were modest. When Horace Wadsworth was in Charleston in 1800, his brother John of Hartford sent fifteen Windsors down the Connecticut River and around to New London to make the southern voyage. An "Abstract" of American goods exported from October 1791 to September 1792 credits interests in Connecticut with shipping 1,652 Windsor chairs to various destinations.[54]

Liverpool, Nova Scotia, was primarily a Boston market. Between 1791 and 1801 a steady flow of goods from the Massachusetts capital entered that port. Seating lots varied from half a dozen to three dozen chairs. Other markets for Boston in eastern Canada included Halifax and the Cumberland region of Nova Scotia. Pressing even more northerly, the schooner *Argo* left Boston on December 11, 1801, with six Windsor chairs in her hold for delivery at Saint John's, Newfoundland, just west of the Grand Banks, a location well known to New England fishermen. Timothy Dwight remarked in the mid-1790s that although the commerce of Boston was extensive, its coasting trade was inferior to that of New York, a statement borne out in existing records.[55]

Salem, the sister seaport of Boston, also tapped the furniture market at Liverpool, although the American South was more lucrative to both. The enterprising cabinetmaker-merchants Elijah and Jacob Sanderson, with others, shipped quantities of furniture and chairs to destinations ranging from Baltimore to Savannah. Chair numbers and terms identify Windsor furniture: eight dozen chairs for Norfolk in July 1792; "six Green Chairs" to Savannah later that year; seventy-five chairs in 1794 on the schooner *Edmond* bound for Hampton, Virginia; and six green chairs the following year to Alexandria. The schooner *Sally*'s cargo list for Wilmington, North Carolina, in May 1799 is explicit: "Three doz Winsor Chairs." Sanderson company records provide further insights. Following a voyage in July 1794 to Virginia, the firm had difficulty collecting monies from Gregory and Fox, consignees of a furniture invoice totaling some £90. Included with the mahogany bedsteads, tables, desk and bookcase, and clock case were several groups of Windsor chairs priced from 7s. to 10s. apiece, some with arms. With the account still unsettled in November, the Sandersons placed its collection in the hands of one Benjamin Bullock. Bullock was able to negotiate a satisfactory conclusion to the affair, and the following June 8 the brothers penned their final receipt. When the Sandersons put together the cargo for Virginia, they patronized the local shop of Micaiah Johnson, who from February 22 through June 9 supplied "dyning" chairs, some unpainted, and several "round top chairs." Indications are that the Sandersons advanced the retail prices by a half to a full shilling per chair.[56]

Despite northern competition, a few chairmakers at Baltimore entered the competitive export market of the 1790s. Caleb Hannah described the proportions of the trade in a 1799 notice: "Merchants and captains of vessels may be supplied for shipping to the amount of one hundred dozen more or less." The best domestic chair markets for Baltimore craftsmen were the city, rural Maryland, the western shore of the Potomac, the lower Chesapeake Bay, and northern North Carolina. In coastal Carolina Harmon Vosburgh and John Dunbibin formed a partnership at Wilmington in 1798 to conduct the chair business in "an extensive manner" and promised to prepare "orders for Exportation . . . with the greatest dispatch." Port records itemizing cargoes of Windsors at Savannah, Georgia, indicate that seating was transshipped occasionally from that port to other districts in Georgia, such as Saint Marys and Sunbury, or to nearby Saint Augustine in East Florida.[57]

Postrevolutionary Eighteenth-Century Trade: Foreign

THE CARIBBEAN

Introduction and the English Trade
Between 1750 and 1830 control of individual islands or island groups in the Caribbean varied from war to war in Europe, subjecting the region to changing trade restrictions. Indisputably this underdeveloped area was of vital commercial importance both to its collective owners and to the peoples of continental North America. A vast array of produce and products, ranging from horses to wheat to house frames, poured out of American seaports on vessels, large and small, headed for the warm southern waters. As early as 1752 American Windsor furniture was deemed a suitable commodity for the Caribbean market. Although the Windsor's rise to popularity was not meteoric, the chair achieved some standing in the Caribbean by the outbreak of the Revolution. In the postwar period the product rose to the status of a staple (map 3).[58]

Between 1750 and 1800 part of the Caribbean market for the American Windsor was shared with the English plank-seat chair. Early in 1772 the London factor John

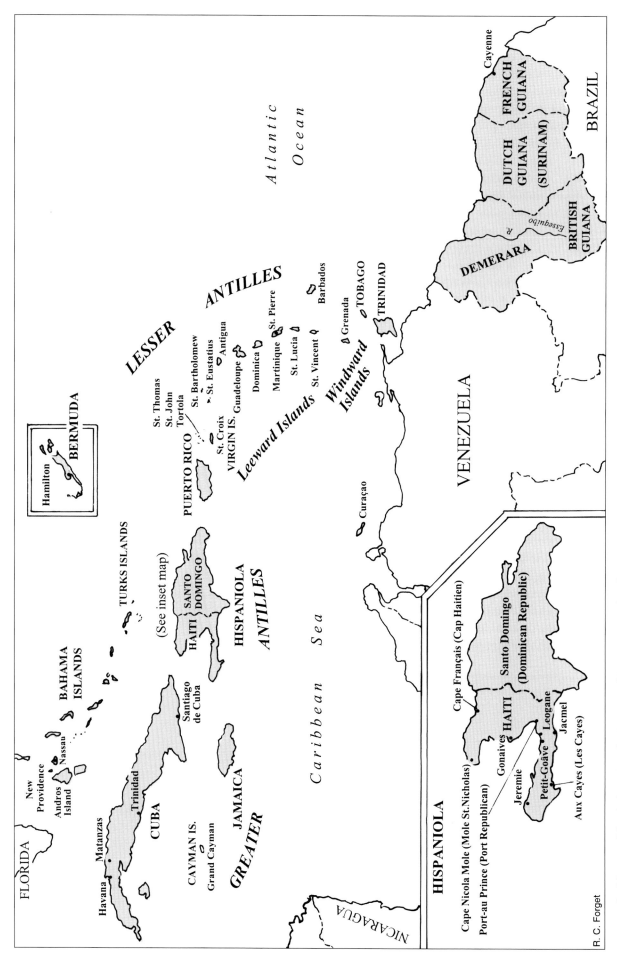

FLORIDA

New
Providence

Havana
Matanzas
CUBA

Trinidad

Santiago
de Cuba

CAYMAN IS.
Grand Cayman

JAMAICA

Andros
Island
Nassau

BAHAMA
ISLANDS

TURKS ISLANDS

(See inset map)

HAITI
SANTO
DOMINGO

HISPANIOLA

GREATER

ANTILLES

Caribbean   Sea

BERMUDA
Hamilton

St. Thomas
St. John
Tortola

St. Bartholomew

St. Eustatius

St. Croix
VIRGIN IS. Guadeloupe

PUERTO RICO

Antigua

Dominica

Martinique St. Pierre

St. Lucia

St. Vincent

Leeward Islands

*Windward
Islands*

Grenada

LESSER

ANTILLES

*Atlantic

Ocean*

Barbados

TOBAGO

TRINIDAD

Curaçao

VENEZUELA

DEMERARA

BRITISH
GUIANA

R.
Essequibo

DUTCH
GUIANA
(SURINAM)

FRENCH
GUIANA

Cayenne

BRAZIL

NICARAGUA

HISPANIOLA

Cape Nicola Mole (Mole St.Nicholas)

Port-au-Prince (Port Republican)

Cape Français (Cap Haïtien)

Gonaïves HAITI

Jeremie

Léogane

Petit-Goâve

Jacmel

Aux Cayes (Les Cayes)

Santo Domingo
(Dominican Republic)

R. C. Forget

MAP 3 Caribbean and South American destinations of American Windsor furniture cargoes, 1783–1800

FIG. 4-10 Francisco Oller (1833–1917), *El Velorio*, Puerto Rico, ca. 1893. Oil on Canvas; H. 96", W. 156½". *(Collection of the Museum of Anthropology, History and Art of the University of Puerto Rico, Río Piedras.)*

Parkinson sent two consignments totaling forty-two "high Backd Green Windsor Chairs" to the care of Martin Williams, Esq., in Jamaica. The Gillow furniture firm of Lancashire also was reasonably active. The company directed at least four invoices of mahogany and Windsor furniture to the islands in 1774—two to Jamaica and one each to Grenada and Barbados/Antigua—all consigned either to the ships' masters or island merchants. In 1776 the Gillow books record a further cargo of Windsors sent to Grenada. John Parkinson continued active in the Caribbean trade, shipping a large furniture order that included high-back Windsors to Mrs. Sarah Parkinson at Westmoreland, Jamaica. He directed low-back chairs the following year to Martin Williams in Montego Bay.[59]

Activity by English shippers continued during the 1780s as American entrepreneurs reveled in their newly established independence. The competition mounted in 1784 when the brig *Jenny* from Lancaster, England, landed six "Parcels" of Windsors—probably twelve chairs—at Barbados. Philadelphia Windsors recorded in the same customhouse that year numbered 132. Grenada and Dominica were other destinations for English chairs. London chancery court papers include an "Inventory and Appraisement of the Goods and Effects of the late Doctor George Rutherford," who died in Antigua about 1797. The doctor was well acquainted with Windsor seating; his household contained twelve low-back and five high-back chairs. But who can say for certain whether they were of English or American manufacture? There is, however, no mistaking the stature of the English Windsor in the West Indian trade. A painting depicting a common, nineteenth-century interior in the Caribbean clearly illustrates an eighteenth-century English Windsor armchair and a child's "campeche" chair as part of the furnishings (fig. **4-10**).[60]

Philadelphia continued to outdistance its American trade competitors in foreign markets in the late eighteenth century. Tench Coxe, in reporting on the commercial progress of the new United States, commented specifically on the Caribbean trade of his home city, stating, "Our vessels make as many West-India voyages as those of the two other principal seaports of the middle states," namely New York and Baltimore.[61]

For purposes of this study the West Indian trade has been divided into four parts. Beginning with Bermuda, which actually lies outside Caribbean waters, the discussion continues with the three major geographic divisions of the Indies themselves: the Bahama Islands; the Greater Antilles, comprising principally Cuba, Hispaniola (Haiti and the Dominican Republic), Jamaica, and Puerto Rico; and the Lesser

Antilles, divided into two main island groups, the Leewards and the Windwards, and including the southernmost island of Trinidad along with westerly Curaçao.

Bermuda and the Bahamas

Bermuda was a minor market in the American Windsor trade (map 3). Minimal activity occurred following the Revolution and again at the turn of the century. Upon leaving Philadelphia on May 15, 1784, the sloop *Adventure* headed for the island carrying six dozen Windsors. Another 8½ dozen chairs were shipped in three vessels from the Delaware River the next year. Due to crippling trade restrictions, American commerce with British possessions was rarely straightforward. Raw materials were welcomed, but Britain expected to supply its colonies with manufactured goods. The restrictions seem to have been uppermost in the minds of several New York shippers in 1798–99 when describing disassembled seating sent to Bermuda as "Two hundred unmanufactured Chairs." In 1801 interests at New Haven sent a cargo of one hundred chairs in the schooner *Rover*.[62]

Customs papers record greater activity in Windsor seating for the Bahamas, including the islands of New Providence (containing the capital of Nassau), Turks, and possibly Andros. Philadelphia, New York, Providence, Newport, and Boston all participated to a limited extent. One cargo of five dozen Windsors shipped from New York in 1785 was carried to New Providence in the British sloop *Little John* registered in Bermuda. Undoubtedly numbers of American chairs entered Caribbean waters in "foreign" ships. In general, vessels employed in the island trade were larger than the sloops common to coastal commerce. Schooners are named frequently; other listings are for brigs and ships (fig. **4-11**). Cargoes of record to the region from Philadelphia and New York were generally of modest size — a dozen to 1½ dozen chairs. One shipment of "Chair stuff," or unassembled chairs, left New York in 1792 for New Providence. Shippers in New England appear to have been more active. Providence, Rhode Island, had a sporadic commerce in furniture with Turks Island(s), shipping "Greene Chairs" in 1794, cabinetware valued in excess of $450 and "Ten Doz of Dineing Chairs" (bow-backs) in 1799, and in 1801 334 "Windsor Chairs" on the ship *Rising States*. In 1792 Newport sent fourteen "Dining" chairs to the Bahamas. Nine dozen chairs in two shipments in 1801 were transferred from Boston to Saint Andres (probably Andros Island).[63]

The Greater Antilles

The postrevolutionary chair trade with the Greater Antilles (map 3) began by December 8, 1784, when the ship *Charming Molly* left Philadelphia with "48 Chairs" for the island of Jamaica. Jamaica, one of the sugar islands and a British possession, was off limits to American shipping by terms of the Treaty of Paris, and this is the only recorded cargo of American chairs shipped in the late eighteenth century. Occasionally materials of a basic sort were permitted entry, such as the 43,900 white oak and 80,000 red oak staves for barrels and containers received in 1789 from Philadelphia.[64]

The leading chair market in the Caribbean from 1786 through the end of the century was the island of Hispaniola, comprising Haiti and Santo Domingo (now the Dominican Republic). Evidence indicates that most important American coastal centers participated in the trade, with Philadelphia the undisputed leader. The history of Hispaniola was one of prosperity followed by turmoil. Until 1795 Haiti was a French possession, and Spain owned Santo Domingo; however, a treaty of that date gave the entire island to France. Meanwhile the basic principles of the French Revolution (1792) — liberty and equality — encouraged the free black population of Haiti and then the slaves to rise against white colonial domination and the plantation system. In 1795 the unrest spread to Santo Domingo. Blacks controlled the island by 1801, and following several exchanges of power between France and native

SLOOP OF 1776

TWO-MASTED SCHOONER

SNOW RIG

BRIG

BARK

SHIP OF 18TH CENTURY

FIG. 4-11 Principal types of American sailing vessels engaged in the overseas and coastal trades, 1750–1840. Composite from Charles G. Davis, *Shipping and Craft in Silhouette* (Salem, Mass.: Marine Research Society, 1929), figs. 8, 17, 23, 28, 51. *(Courtesy Peabody Essex Museum, Salem, Mass.)*

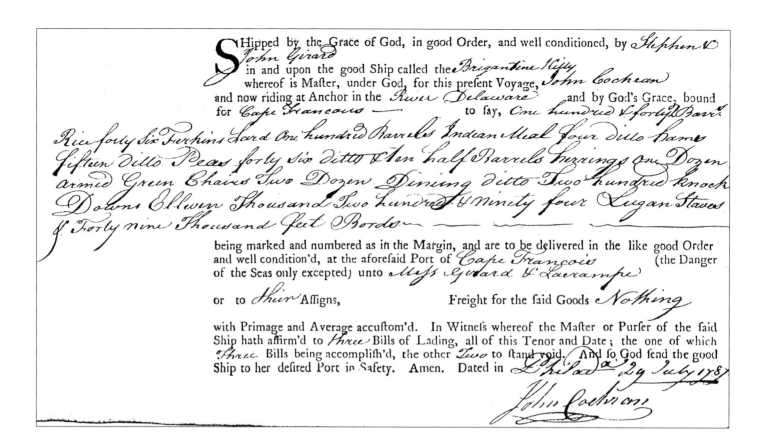

Shipped by the Grace of God, in good Order, and well conditioned, by *Stephen &* *John Girard* in and upon the good Ship called the *Brigantine Kitty* whereof is Master, under God, for this present Voyage, *John Cochran* and now riding at Anchor in the *River Delaware* and by God's Grace, bound for *Cape Francous* to say, *One hundred & forty Barr[els]* *Rice forty Six Firchins Lard One hundred Barrels Indian Meal four ditto hams* *fifteen ditto Peas forty Six ditto & ten half Barrels herrings one Dozen* *armed Green Chairs Two Dozen Dining ditto Two hundred knock* *Downs Eleven Thousand Two hundred & Ninety four Lugan Staves* *& Forty nine Thousand feet Bords*

being marked and numbered as in the Margin, and are to be delivered in the like good Order and well condition'd, at the aforesaid Port of *Cape François* (the Danger of the Seas only excepted) unto *Mess Girard & Lacrampe*

or to *their* Assigns, Freight for the said Goods *Nothing*

with Primage and Average accustom'd. In Witness whereof the Master or Purser of the said Ship hath affirm'd to *Three* Bills of Lading, all of this Tenor and Date; the one of which *Three* Bills being accomplish'd, the other *Two* to stand void. And so God send the good Ship to her desired Port in Safety. Amen. Dated in *Philad[elphia] 29 July 1787*

John Cochran

FIG. 4-12 Stephen and John Girard bill of lading for brig *Kitty*, Philadelphia, July 29, 1787. (*Collection of the Board of Directors of City Trusts, Girard College History Collections.*)

forces, Haiti in 1804 declared its independence. Despite the turbulence of the post-1795 years, the American trade in chairs continued at about half the earlier volume, probably due in a large part to the American policy of maintaining friendly relations with the native leaders in power.[65]

The majority of shipping records for Hispaniola differentiate between Haiti and Santo Domingo, and many name the expected port of entry. Chair cargoes from Philadelphia were divided about eight to one between the western and eastern ends of the island. Many entries were made at the Haitian ports of Port-au-Prince (also Port Republican), Cape Nicola Mole (Môle Saint Nicholas), Leogane, Petit-Goâve, Gonaives, Jeremie, Jacmel, Aux Cayes (Les Cayes), and Cape Français (Cap-Haitien). Substantially fewer entries are recorded for Santo Domingo. Cape Français was a favorite destination in the 1780s and early 1790s for Stephen Girard's vessels. The cargoes illuminate the general trade: flour, rice, Indian meal, hams, beef, herring, lard, castile soap, shingles, barrel staves and hoops, boards, young trees, and seeds. Girard's seating furniture cargoes ranged in size from a dozen to nine dozen chairs, described variously as "Windsor," "green," or "dining" chairs. The brig *Kitty* carried "one Dozen armed Green Chairs [and] Two Dozen Dining ditto" (side chairs) in summer 1787 to Cape Français (fig. 4-12). One day prior to sailing William Cox presented his bill to Stephen and John Girard, charging 13*s*. apiece for the large chairs and 7*s*. 3*d*. for the side chairs (fig. 4-13). A later furniture cargo for Haiti boarded on the Girard brig *Polly* was entered on July 7, 1791, in the custom records as "Eighteen Green dineing Chairs & five arm'd d[itt]o with one Settie." On that date chairmaker Joseph Henzey billed Girard for the settee and six dining chairs. William Cox supplied the remaining dining chairs, one dozen in number, and the armchairs.[66]

Collectively, shipping documents for Hispaniola account for more than 3,500 chairs and 30 settees (also called sophas) transported between 1786 and 1802 from Philadelphia alone. The figure represents, at best, only a portion of the original Windsor trade. For the most part the trade was conducted in schooners or vessels of larger size, especially the square-rigged brig (fig. 4-11). Manifests identify two chairmakers of Philadelphia as direct chair shippers, and in both cases the merchandise may have been consigned to the captains. On June 2, 1802, four dozen chairs from the shop of James Pentland left Philadelphia on the brig *Nancy*. Two years earlier the brig *Amazon* transported eight dozen chairs for Anthony Steel. Both cargoes were destined for Cape Français. Large cargoes of eight dozen Windsors or more were not uncommon in the Hispaniola trade as, for example, sixteen dozen for Port-au-Prince in December 1789 on the ship *Betsy*; ten dozen in August 1794 on the ship *Hope*; "Thirteen doz Windsor Chairs / Four Windsor Settees" in May 1795 for Santo Domingo on the brig *Fair American*; and "Two hundred & twenty four painted Chairs" in July 1799 on the schooner *Harriet* for Santo Domingo. Two manifests identify chair cargoes by pattern. On July 13, 1796, the brig *Nymph* carried "Six Doz Fan back chairs / One D[itt]o Arm D[itt]o" from Philadelphia. Seven weeks later the brig *Delaware*'s cargo consisted in part of "Twelve Dozen Oval [Bow] Back Chair[s]." Occasionally Windsor seating was part of a passenger's baggage. One individual sailed on March 2, 1802, from Philadelphia aboard the schooner *Olive Branch* bound for Cape Français with possessions in tow: two trunks of wearing apparel, an old pianoforte in a box, a mahogany bedstead, fourteen Windsor chairs and one settee, and a "bundle" of books.[67]

The trade in New York chairs to Hispaniola began in 1790, if not earlier, when two vessels with Spanish masters and probably of Spanish registry carried mixed seating to Santo Domingo: four dozen unidentified chairs, six dozen Windsors, four dozen "Green Chairs" probably of Windsor construction, five "Sophias," and "Eight dozends of straw Bottom Chairs." If the straw-bottom seating represented fancy chairs rather than common slat-back chairs, the record documents an early date for fancy-chair production in New York City. Toward the end of the decade the brig *Rebecca* carried six dozen Windsor chairs to Gonaives, Haiti, and almost 200 chairs were entered at Santo Domingo. After 1800 several vessels transported an additional 480 Windsors, more than half unassembled, to Aux Cayes (now Les Cayes) and Port-au-Prince (also Port Republican).[68]

Chair exportations from New England to Hispaniola, like those from New York, were sporadic. Rhode Island perhaps supplied the greatest number. Early activity dates to June 1787, when a vessel from New Haven, Connecticut, carried eight hogsheads of chair parts to Cape Français, Haiti. Twice that number of containers left New London in 1792 for the same destination. A transaction of more particular description began in June 1788 when the sloop *Nabby*, owned in part by John Williams of Norwich, sailed for Port-au-Prince with a large cargo consisting of bricks, hoops and staves, "77 Shaken H[ogs]h[ea]ds," naval stores, and foodstuffs consigned to the captain. Also on board were two dozen "Green" chairs valued at 10s. and 12s. apiece ($1.66 and $2.00). As usual, Captain Elisha Coit had instructions for commodity disposition. At Port-au-Prince he was to obtain a cargo of molasses and French rum. In anticipation of the former, the coopers on board were to "get the Casks ready." If the workmen were unable to supply the requisite number in time, the captain had leave either to "employ other Coopers or exchange . . . Shaken Hhds [hogsheads] for Hhds that are trimmed & pay the difference." In accounting for the Windsors, Coit noted that five had been damaged in transit. In a cargo of three dozen green chairs shipped on July 7, 1801, from New Haven to Aux Cayes, the chairs were valued at $1.50 apiece.[69]

Joseph K. Ott found that in 1792–93 quantities of chairs were shipped from Providence to Hispaniola, some without particular description, others identified as green chairs. The sloop *Union* left port in November 1792 with 24 Windsor chairs; six months later the sloop *Nautilus* accounted for 90 "House Chares" in its island cargo along with maple and cherry case furniture. The Newport chair trade to Hispaniola may have begun in June 1799 when the schooner *William and Margaret* carried a large cargo of 250 Windsors to Cape Français. Chair and settee shipments to Hispaniola from Boston in the late 1790s probably represent Windsor furniture.[70]

Just after 1795 there was a flurry of activity in the chair trade from Baltimore to Haiti and Santo Domingo. The ports of Cape Nicola Mole, Jacmel, Gonaives, and Aux Cayes were destinations for cargoes of Windsor and fancy chairs, and settees. Most lots were of modest size. Exceptions were a cargo of 1796 on the ship *Friendship*, comprising ten dozen Windsors worth $1 apiece, and the schooner *Liberty's* "Six Hundred Winser Chair Stuff" of May 1798 worth $550 unassembled. Either a chairmaker was on board the *Liberty* or the shipper had an appropriate contact in Aux Cayes. The belligerency of the times was foremost in the minds of the schooner *Betsy and Patsy's* owners when preparing her manifest, which itemizes settees for "the Mole." Written at the bottom is the terse note: "6 men no Guns."[71]

The American trade in painted seating to Cuba, the largest of the Caribbean islands, began in 1797 with a lone shipment of one dozen Windsors from Philadelphia on the schooner *Jane*. This voyage was the modest prelude to a veritable commercial explosion that occurred during the years through the turn of the century. Cuba, under Spanish rule, was not open to foreign traders until the 1790s. Even then a Spanish alliance with England against France between 1793 and 1795 permitted only selected neutrals to enter Cuban ports, with Americans excluded from that number. Finally in 1797, with war conditions taking their toll on the provisioning trade, local authorities opened the island to general shipping, a policy that continued with and without the permission of the Spanish monarch until 1818, when Ferdinand VII established a permanent free foreign commerce.[72]

Shipping documents covering the four-year period from 1798 through 1801 record the exportation to Cuba, principally Havana, of forty-five chair cargoes from Philadelphia, twenty-four from New York, twenty-one from Rhode Island, and eight and nine from Boston and Baltimore, respectively. Looking first at Philadelphia records, the size of the furniture trade is best appreciated on compiling available figures, although these numbers represent only a portion of the commerce that existed. Fifty-two high-style mahogany chairs are recorded, one group priced at $8.38 the chair en suite with an upholstered sofa valued at $50. A cargo of "12 Gilt Chairs & 1 Sopha," or fancy rush seating, accompanied by "1 Box of Chair Cushions" was shipped in September 1798 from the Delaware River aboard the sloop *Catharine*. Several months later thirty-three "Japan'd" chairs were exported on the ship *Diana*. Windsors identified by name account for a substantial 7,424 chairs. If, however, seating lots exceeding one hundred items and described only as "chairs" or "painted chairs" are added to this figure, the grand total for the Windsors is 9,151. Some individual lots were of extraordinary size. Single cargoes of twenty-five dozen chairs or more were not uncommon. On December 3, 1798 the brig *George* carried forty dozen chairs and five settees from Philadelphia. The following February the ship *Eagle* sailed with forty-five dozen side chairs and two dozen armchairs. A record forty-nine dozen chairs and thirteen settees were loaded on the ship *Fair American*, which left port on May 8, 1800, and the trade continued. All told, seventy-seven settees are recorded.[73]

The ship *Fair American* made additional voyages to Havana under her captain J. C. Brevoor. For a trip that began on October 14, 1800, the vessel loaded a modest five dozen "small" chairs. The following January proved favorable for another voyage, as the Delaware River was sufficiently free of ice for the ship to make her way to the bay and the open sea. The *Fair American* carried a seating cargo described only as "a parcel of Windsor Chairs." The voyage was ill fated, however, and in a later document prepared by the shipper, Stephen Dutilh of Philadelphia, the "parcel" was described as "Forty seven dozen of Windsor chairs assorted" valued at $1,025.66. Accompanying the Windsors were twenty-four mahogany chairs, two sofas, and a selection of merchandise that included flour, clothing, German looking glasses, and

Nuremberg toys. Dutilh explained the reason for the inventory in a letter dated April 1, 1802. On January 19, 1801, seventeen days after sailing, the "French Republican Privateer LaPorto Ricaine [sp?], François Boulerin Commander," captured the *Fair American*, although a commercial convention had been signed by France and the United States the previous September 30 at Paris. On the way to the French island of Guadeloupe, the prize was recaptured from the French by the British "Ship of Line Leviathon" and sent instead to Martinique, a French island then in possession of the British. The *Fair American* and its cargo were sold "by decree of the Court of Vice Admiralty." Whether Dutilh ever received satisfaction for his claim against the original French captors is unknown. The incident was only one of many similar seizures that plagued American shipping during the early years of the republic. No doubt the *Fair American*'s 564 Windsor chairs were sold at auction in Martinique, demonstrating that despite trade restrictions it *was* possible for American seating furniture to enter markets where it was normally banned.[74]

Because many cargoes transported to Cuba are priced, the average cost per chair at destination can be computed at $1.54, a figure that includes middleman charges at Philadelphia. One exceptional lot of 1801 carried in the brig *Beaver* and described as "8 Black & Gold Windsor Chairs" was priced at $7 the chair. These extraordinary Windsors probably had arms, stuffed seats with embellishments, and decoration that made use of gold leaf. Two varnish coats likely protected the surfaces. Two Philadelphia Windsor-chair makers are among the direct shippers associated with the Cuban trade. In May 1800 Robert Gaw placed forty-two chairs on board the sloop *Cicero*. During the following year Anthony Steel shipped sixteen dozen side chairs, three dozen armchairs, and five settees on the ship *Hope*. A manifest bearing Steel's name describes chairs of three patterns and four colors (fig. **4-14**). All chairs shipped to the island from Philadelphia during this period were directed to Havana except for one cargo sent to Santiago de Cuba on the island's southeastern coast. Occasionally boxes of furniture, some identified as tables, were aboard the same vessels.[75]

The chair trade from New York to Cuba began on or before February 2, 1798, when the bark *Leonora* transported 60 Windsors to Havana, the principal port of entry. Of twenty-four recorded cargoes to Cuba all but three were bound for that place. Records list Matanzas on the north coast near Havana as the destination of two vessels. "Trinidad in Cuba" was the landing place of the brig *Georgia Packet* laden with eight dozen chairs valued at $120 and "forty-Seven furniture pieces" listed at $511.25. Shipping records account for 1,648 Windsors. Most of the other 2,806 "chairs" in the trade also had wooden seats, as indicated by lot size. The total of the two figures is about half that of the Windsor exports from Philadelphia, although the average volume per trip was about the same for the two cities. Chair production at New York reached its stride during the 1790s. Particularly large cargoes are recorded beginning in June 1800, when the ship *Fair American* carried fifty dozen chairs to Havana. The *Eliza* followed in December with 404 Windsor chairs. A high point in local volume may have been established when the ship *Catharine* landed 794 chairs and eight settees valued at $1.25 and $8 apiece, respectively, after an October 1801 sailing.[76]

Any direct commerce in chairs to Cuba from Connecticut was small, if indeed it existed at all. By contrast, the combined chair trade from Providence and Newport, Rhode Island, about equaled that of New York in number of voyages, although the volume was only somewhat more than half the New York figure. Some chairs shipped from Rhode Island may have comprised New York seating acquired in the coastal trade, as suggested by a large cargo of 200 chairs transported in 1800 on the sloop *Semiramis* from New York to Newport (fig. 4-8). Other chairs exported from Providence may have been obtained in the New London–Norwich area because "Connecticut" was given as the source of 100 chairs listed in the ship *Dolphin's* manifest on May 2, 1799, when she sailed for Havana. Windsors and "green chairs" listed

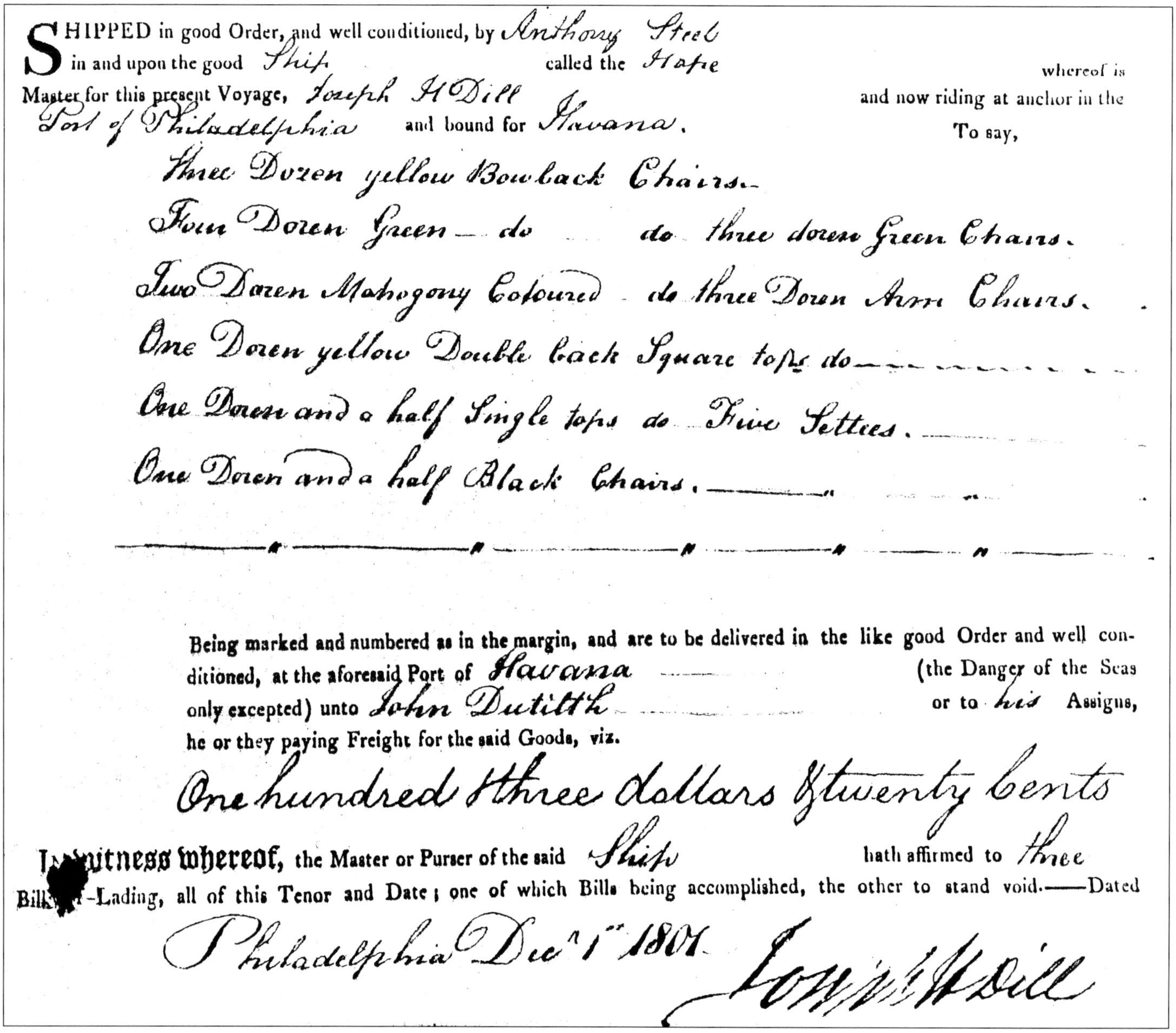

SHIPPED in good Order, and well conditioned, by *Anthony Steel* in and upon the good *Ship* called the *Hope* whereof is Master for this present Voyage, *Joseph M Dill Jr* and now riding at anchor in the Port of *Philadelphia* and bound for *Havana*. To say,

Three Dozen yellow Bowback Chairs.

Four Dozen Green — do   do three dozen Green Chairs.

Two Dozen Mahogony Coloured — do three Dozen Arm Chairs.

One Dozen yellow Double back Square tops do

One Dozen and a half Single tops do Five Settees.

One Dozen and a half Black Chairs.

Being marked and numbered as in the margin, and are to be delivered in the like good Order and well conditioned, at the aforesaid Port of *Havana* (the Danger of the Seas only excepted) unto *John Dutillh* or to *his* Assigns, he or they paying Freight for the said Goods, viz.

One hundred & three dollars & twenty Cents

In witness whereof, the Master or Purser of the said *Ship* hath affirmed to *three* Bills of-Lading, all of this Tenor and Date ; one of which Bills being accomplished, the other to stand void.——Dated

Philadelphia Dec 1st 1801.   Jos M Dill

FIG. 4-14 The Historical Society of Pennsylvania (HSP), Anthony Steel bill of lading for ship *Hope*, Philadelphia, December 1, 1801, Society Miscellaneous Collection. Philadelphia.

in records from Rhode Island number over 1,000 items. Undesignated seating swells the number to 2,867, with some lots containing 300 or more chairs. All shipments were directed to Havana.[77]

Recorded voyages from Boston and Baltimore to Cuba were moderate compared with those from other areas. Shippers in both cities favored Havana; however, their vessels also entered the port of Santiago de Cuba. One cargo from Boston was landed at Matanzas. Most of the eight shipments recorded for Boston between 1799 and 1801 appear to have consisted of fancy seating, judging by the valuations, although the "Quantity" of chair material valued at $500 and shipped in December 1800 aboard the schooner *Hero* probably represented unassembled Windsor-chair parts. Baltimore records identify many lots as Windsors. Compiled from nine recorded voyages in 1798 and 1799, the total of 2,184 chairs is impressive. Baltimore also recorded the largest single cargo in the trade—962 chairs, more than eighty dozen, along with twelve settees—shipped on December 19, 1799, to Havana in the schooner *Sally* The unit value of $1.26 suggests that the chairs were shipped assembled. They were unpainted, however, as a large quantity of paint and oil for finishing on site accompanied the seating. Another document from Baltimore identifies one group of chairs by pattern. Loaded onto the schooner *Weymouth* for Havana in June 1799 were "Three & an half dozen Single Back Windsor Chairs." This is a particularly early reference to the single-rod square-back style (fig. 3-34).[78]

Two chair shipments to Puerto Rico are recorded in the late eighteenth century. As a Spanish possession the island was subject to trade restrictions similar to those in force at Cuba, although local authorities appear to have been less bold and aggressive in their determination to enjoy the benefits of free trade until the early nineteenth century. On August 25, 1796, a cargo of five dozen chairs left Baltimore in the Spanish schooner *Saint Carlos*. In February following, the brig *Florida*, likely of English registry, transported two dozen Windsor side chairs and an armchair from Philadelphia to the Spanish island. The market staple in Philadelphia Windsor seating of this decade was the bow-back chair with simulated bamboo turnings (fig. 4-15). The schooner *Esther* out of Boston in 1799 ventured a cargo of fifty-six chairs (probably Windsors at $1 apiece) to Grand Cayman, a small British possession south of Cuba. Perhaps the vessel was of British registry.[79]

The Lesser Antilles
Scattered records dating from 1783 to 1802 document 213 cargoes of painted chairs in the American trade to the islands of the Lesser Antilles (map 3). Comprising this chain of small tropical, often volcanic-formed, islands extending in an arc from Puerto Rico to the northern coast of South America are the Virgin Islands (part of the larger Leeward group), the Windward Islands, Trinidad, and Curaçao. First among these markets was Saint Croix. Martinique ranked second, followed by Saint Thomas and Saint Eustatius. Of lesser importance, although the destination of ten to twelve cargoes apiece, were Trinidad, Guadeloupe, Barbados, and Antigua, in that order.

The Virgin Islands group — Saint Croix, Saint Thomas, Saint John, and Tortola — formed the largest American chair market in the southern Caribbean, especially Saint Croix and Saint Thomas. All except Tortola were Danish possessions, and they were reasonably free of trade restrictions. Thirty-seven percent of the chair commerce to the lower Caribbean was concentrated in this area, and Philadelphia commanded the greater portion of it, or 62 percent. The first chair-laden vessel of record to sail from the Delaware River for the Virgin Islands was the *Fanny* bound for Saint Croix on August 23, 1783, carrying six dozen Windsors. A steady exchange ensued. Thirty-two cargoes of record through 1802 account for a total of 1,064 chairs, most described as Windsors, and six settees. Philadelphia chairs also dominated other markets in the Virgin Islands. Eleven cargoes are recorded for Saint Thomas and four for Saint John. Two lots of Philadelphia chairs, a quantity of New York seating, and a cargo from the Patuxent River, Maryland, all entered Tortola, a British possession, between 1783 and 1785 in vessels of Tortola or Bermuda registry. Although the traffic to the Virgin Islands was not of the magnitude of the Cuban chair trade, it began early and was of long duration. The largest single lot of Philadelphia chairs landed was a cargo of twenty dozen Windsors carried in June 1802 to Saint Thomas on the ship *Maria*. Other records identify patterns: fan-back Windsors entered Saint Croix in 1791; bow-back chairs destined for the same market are recorded in 1798. Green and mahogany are documented colors. Baltimore was responsible for a cargo of 120 Windsor chairs shipped in September 1799 in the schooner *Peggy* for a market in Saint Thomas.[80]

Further illuminating the southern Caribbean trade are records of the merchant-factors Stephen Collins and Son of Philadelphia, who occasionally acquired Windsor seating and household furniture from local suppliers at the request of overseas customers. In a letter of September 8, 1796, to John C. Heineken, Esq., probably at Saint Croix, Zaccheus Collins described typical mercantile problems:

FIG. 4-15 Bow-back Windsor side chair, M(assey?) Ackley (brand "M·ACKLEY"), Philadelphia, ca. 1800. Yellow poplar (seat) with maple, oak, and hickory (microanalysis); H. 36½", (seat) 16½", W. (seat) 17⅛", D. (seat) 16". *(Courtesy, Winterthur Museum, Winterthur, Del., acc. 67.621.)*

Your accot is credited with . . . 100 dollars rec'd of Capt Keeler also with the barrel of sugar. . . . It is debited with the easy chair sent by Capt Keeler £9.7.6 & with the windsor chairs now on board the brig Planter Capt Hawkins £20.5/. . . . Capt K was to have taken the chairs & they were sent down on the wharf, but his mate . . . during his absense & while I was out of town refused to take them in. . . . Enclosed you will find Capt Hawkins's rec't for the chairs.

Zaccheus Collins purchased the easy chair in the shop of John Douglas. He ordered the Windsors from John B. Ackley. The chairmaker's bill, as recorded in the merchant's letter book, describes the Windsors as "eight oval back chairs painted yellow, stuft seats covered with moreen, one row of brass nails & fringe." A settee of similar color with stuffing and mahogany arms completed the suite. Each side chair cost 31s. 6d., or $5.25 apiece, and the settee was valued at about $25.50. The grand total for the nine pieces without freight charges was $67.50. To place this substantial purchase in its proper perspective, a journeyman craftsman working in Philadelphia at this date earned $1 a day.[81]

The chair trade between New York and the Virgin Islands, which was concentrated in Saint Croix and Saint Thomas, did not begin until the 1790s. The fifteen recorded cargoes were modest in number compared with the Philadelphia trade. The largest shipment, numbering three hundred chairs, was loaded on the brig *Rising States*, which cleared New York on October 31, 1801, for Saint Thomas. At times other types of furniture complemented the painted seating. A notable cargo on the brig *Tethill* to Saint Croix in June 1799 comprised "3½ Dzn Windsor Chairs, . . . 1 Mahogney Book Case, . . . 6 Setts Venetian Window Blinds," and "1 pr Hall Looking Glasses." Late that year the brig *Atlanta* loaded seven dozen Windsor chairs and three settees for a voyage to Saint Thomas.[82]

Records of the chair trade from New England to the Virgin Islands are scattered and few; just eleven pertain to Saint Croix and Saint Thomas. Of four recorded shipments from Connecticut, a cargo from New Haven for Saint Thomas in 1796 describes "Chair Timber" only, a reference to unassembled chairs. One hundred assembled Windsors had left port in February 1793 for the same destination. New Haven also recorded the earliest cargo of New England Windsors to the Virgin Islands—thirty in April 1787 to Saint Croix. Beginning in 1789 shippers at New London and Providence sent small numbers of "green Chares" on consignment to Saint Croix. Only five voyages from Boston between 1793 and 1801 list chair cargoes. One shipment of twenty-five dozen chairs went to Saint Thomas in 1801 on the brig *Francis*; four small cargoes were directed to Saint Croix.[83]

Late eighteenth-century marketing in other islands of the Leeward group—Saint Eustatius, Saint Bartholomew, Guadeloupe, Antigua, and Dominica—accounts for another 22 percent of the seating trade in the lower Caribbean. The last two islands were British possessions, and trading with them was light due to well-enforced restrictions. Guadeloupe was a French colony and, although open to direct American shipping, presented difficulties. Beginning in 1793 the British attempted to wipe out commerce between the United States and the French possessions in the Caribbean by seizing American ships entering French waters, and Guadeloupe was occupied by the British for several months. These circumstances led to a hiatus of chair marketing in the area by American interests between 1793 and 1796. Some slack seems to have been taken up through commerce with Saint Bartholomew, a Swedish possession whose commercial restrictions were minimal. The largest market in the Leewards was Saint Eustatius, a Dutch colony, although war between France and Holland, which resulted in the occupation of Saint Eustatius by the French navy in 1795, put an end to the chair trade there.[84]

Philadelphia sent more chairs to the Leewards than any other American supplier, although the sum total of its trade there was small. Saint Eustatius received only ten lots, the largest comprising six dozen chairs, and not all cargoes were carried in American bottoms. Merchandise and provisions loaded in 1785 on the brig *Don Unzaga* are typical. Besides 18 Windsors chairs, the ship carried flour and bread. The chair trade from Philadelphia to Saint Bartholomew was even smaller. Four cargoes are recorded from 1795 to 1799, the largest containing 108 Windsor chairs shipped on the brig *Eliza*. As few as two groups of Philadelphia chairs may have entered Guadeloupe through 1801. One lot of 12 green chairs left the Delaware River in March 1785. A second departure is recorded in November 1801, when the brig *Molly* sailed with seven dozen Windsors. The chair trade from Philadelphia to British Antigua was concentrated in seven voyages in 1783–84, a period when trade restrictions mandated by the Treaty of Paris of September 1783 were in the initial stages of enforcement. Small seating lots prevailed, except for a cargo of 216 Windsor chairs shipped on March 19, 1784, aboard the *Charleston Packet*. A voyage of the schooner *Jane* elucidates travel time. The vessel left Philadelphia on April 14, 1784, and arrived in Antigua sixteen days later.[85]

Participation by New York in the chair trade of the Leeward Islands was limited. In 1793 one cargo of two dozen chairs entered Saint Bartholomew. Twelve chairs and two settees transported to Antigua in 1797 may have been carried on a British merchantman. The greatest activity in the Leeward market occurred in 1801–2 when three vessels left for Guadeloupe. Two ships carried six dozen chairs each. The schooner *Nancy*'s cargo of twenty-eight chairs and two sofas valued at $150 appears to have been fancy furniture and may have represented bespoke work. Four cargoes of the 1790s document southern participation in the Leeward trade. Three vessels sailing from Baltimore deposited chairs in Saint Eustatius, Guadeloupe, and Antigua. A cargo of seventy Windsor chairs was transferred from Alexandria, Virginia, to Saint Bartholomew.[86]

The New England market in the Leewards also was small and scattered. A few cargoes for Saint Eustatius left Providence, New Haven, and Boston. Connecticut and Massachusetts are recorded as having supplied one cargo each for Saint Bartholomew, the former shipping in 1799 "3 Hhd [hogsheads] chair Timber." Interests at Rhode Island sent "green chairs" to Guadeloupe. Of three cargoes from Connecticut to this island, the one containing twelve hogsheads of chair parts transported in 1792 from New London by the brig *Recovery* was the largest. Area chairmakers also were responsible for supplying fourteen hogsheads of chair stuff in 1800 for Antigua, and a shipper at Boston in June 1795 loaded nine chairs valued at $11 on the schooner *Betsy* for Dominica.[87]

Southerly from the Leeward Islands the Windward group extends from Martinique to Tobago. These islands, including Barbados, Grenada, Saint Vincent, and Saint Lucia, accounted for another 21 percent of the lower Caribbean chair trade. Except for Martinique, all were British possessions; thus the chair trade was light and occurred early. Philadelphia provided most cargoes. The trade to Barbados of 1784–85 exhibits the greatest activity. Several vessels sailed regularly to the island from the Delaware River, and records illuminate voyage length. The schooner *Harrison,* with 2½ dozen chairs, left Philadelphia on July 1, 1784, and entered Barbados after thirty days at sea. The following year the brig *Barbados Packet* arrived only after a voyage of more than six weeks. The delay may have been the result of becalming, storms, or a brief stop along the way. Cargoes were modest, the largest shipment, recorded in the 1780s, numbering 6½ dozen chairs. The seven dozen Windsors carried to Barbados from Savannah, Georgia, in the 1790s on the brig *Maria* probably also originated in Philadelphia, as Savannah constituted a sizable market for vessels trading from the Delaware River.[88]

Grenada received a few chair cargoes between 1784 and 1787 from Philadelphia. The largest recorded was that on the brig *Speedwell* in September 1785, comprising six dozen chairs and two settees. Records for 1785–86 credit Saint Vincent and

FIG. 4-16 Entry of September 18, 1792, from James Brobson shipping record book, Wilmington, Del., 1790–1805. *(Winterthur Library, Winterthur, Del.)*

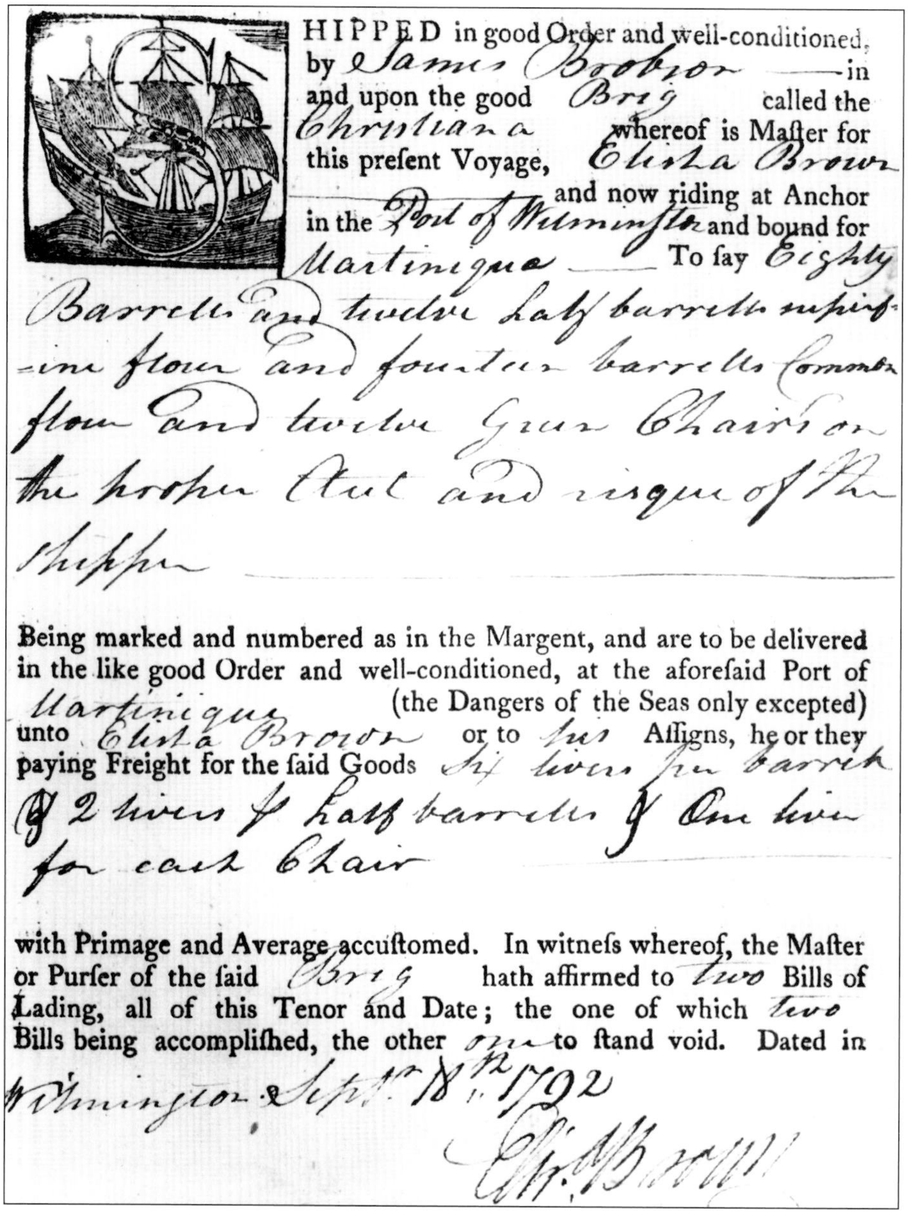

HIPPED in good Order and well-conditioned, by *James Brobson* in and upon the good *Brig* called the *Christiana* whereof is Mafter for this prefent Voyage, *Elisha Brown* and now riding at Anchor in the *Port of Wilmington* and bound for *Martinique* To fay *Eighty Barrells and twelve half barrells fuperfine flour and fourteen barrells common flour and twelve Green Chairs on the proper Cost and risque of the Shipper*

Being marked and numbered as in the Margent, and are to be delivered in the like good Order and well-conditioned, at the aforefaid Port of *Martinique* (the Dangers of the Seas only excepted) unto *Elisha Brown* or to *his* Affigns, he or they paying Freight for the faid Goods *Six livers per barrell @ 2 livers per half barrells & One liver for each Chair*

with Primage and Average accuftomed. In witnefs whereof, the Mafter or Purfer of the faid *Brig* hath affirmed to *two* Bills of Lading, all of this Tenor and Date; the one of which *two* Bills being accomplifhed, the other *one* to ftand void. Dated in *Wilmington & Septr. 18th 1792*

Eli. Brown

Tobago with receiving six and eight dozen chairs, respectively, from Philadelphia. Shippers at Providence, Rhode Island, had a contemporary trade with Tobago. Only Fairfield, Connecticut, and Beverly, Massachusetts, are identified as shippers of seating furniture to Saint Lucia. When the schooner *Union* sailed from Connecticut in January 1791, she carried four hundred Windsor chairs and seven settees to that island.[89]

Shipping papers from Philadelphia record little activity in the chair trade to Martinique. The notable voyage is that of the brig *Sally*, which sailed in May 1793 with 5½ dozen Windsors. Two small cargoes of "green" chairs shipped in 1792–93 from the small downriver port of Wilmington, Delaware, by flour merchant James Brobson were either Philadelphia Windsors or Wilmington chairs in the Philadelphia style (fig. 4-16). Connecticut shippers exhibited the most activity. They sent fifteen chair lots from 1789 until 1793, when the British seized the island from the French. Several cargoes left Fairfield, and New London records identify a shipment in 1792 of five hogsheads of chair parts. The eleven cargoes from New Haven apparently were similar, as parts for more than 2,500 chairs are reported along with twenty-two settees. The largest cargo consisted of "600 Loop Chairs," or bow-backs, placed on the sloop *Sally* for a March 1792 voyage to Saint Pierre, the only named island port. Further cargoes shipped from New London in 1799–1800 include six hundred chairs carried by the *Yankee* and thirteen hogsheads of "Raw Materials for chairs" loaded on the schooner *Henry and Gustavus*. Martinique was Connecticut's Caribbean chair market. In fact, Connecticut chairs outnumbered the combined total of all others shipped there. Exporters at Boston and New York were responsible for one cargo apiece of record. The latter sent $1,200 worth of seating parts in 1802 on the brig *Brutus*. Apparently these late cargoes were found acceptable by the British, who controlled the island from 1793, because chair parts could be classified as "unmanufactured" goods.[90]

Trinidad, an island comprising 1,750 square miles, lies below the main Windward group near the northern coast of Venezuela. It was a French possession in the 1780s and early 1790s when American interests ventured modest quantities of painted seating furniture. The British took over in 1797. The schooner *Recovery* made five annual voyages from Philadelphia to Trinidad between 1789 and 1793, depositing three or four dozen Windsors each trip. A late shipment on the brig *Sally* in April 1800 comprised "Five Dozen Windsor Chairs" and "One Dozen bow back d[itt]o." Valuations of $1 and $2.33 the chair identify Windsors with and without arms in the bow-back style (fig. 3-66). Perhaps these were chair parts, or unmanufactured chairs, although local needs for seating furniture may have been sufficient that officials "looked the other way" when assembled chairs were landed. Interests at New Haven, Connecticut, sent five cargoes to Trinidad, and Massachusetts sent one. A manifest dated in New Haven in December 1786 records parts to construct 150 chairs.[91]

By the late eighteenth century Curaçao, a Dutch colony, was not the American market it had been before the Revolution. Only four chair cargoes are recorded. Jacob Rivera and Joseph Lopez, merchants of Newport, tried a consignment of "Twelve Green Windsor Chairs" in August 1785 along with provisions, spermaceti candles, and pine boards. Merchandise from New York, identified as a "parcell winsor chair Stuff," followed in 1791 on the brig *Betsey*. Baltimore tested the market twice in 1799, the cargoes totaling fourteen dozen chairs and two settees.[92]

Thirteen percent of the vessels clearing American ports for the Caribbean laden with chairs listed their destination only as the West Indies, an indication that the captains probably sought the best market for the general merchandise on board. Sometimes a stop was made en route at a southern American port, frequently Charleston, to learn about current opportunities in the tropical markets from returning vessels. Well over four hundred chairs of record, most described as Windsors, and twelve settees were shipped from Philadelphia between 1785 and 1795 to uncertain Caribbean destinations. Twice in 1792 Captain John Burrows of the sloop *Lark* ventured cargoes on his own account, totaling forty-eight Windsor chairs and four settees. Gilbert Gaw and other Philadelphia chairmakers stood ready to supply merchants and masters of vessels with Windsor chairs for the West Indies "at the shortest notice, at the current prices, for cash or approved notes." Gaw's advertising piece of figure 4-17 dates between 1798, when he and his brother Robert dissolved their partnership, and 1806, when a city directory listed his business address as 84 North Front Street.[93]

Shippers in Connecticut sent almost 250 chairs identified as "green" or "Windsor" seating to unnamed Caribbean markets between 1792 and 1796. In September 1794 the brig *Sally* also carried "1 Windsor Riding Chair." Captain Elijah Clark of the well-named sloop *Negotiator* was responsible for transporting a "Buro," two mahogany tables, and one "Suit Curtains" along with 30 "Green" chairs and other merchandise. Captains sailed under one of several business arrangements. During a visit to New London about 1796 the duc de la Rochefoucauld Liancourt commented on two practices: "The captain has a certain monthly hire, but no share in the profits of the freight; only, when he is interested with the charge of the sale . . . , he then receives five per cent commission." Liancourt further observed that the town's exports were sent "almost all, to the West India isles." At some ports, including Salem, Massachu-

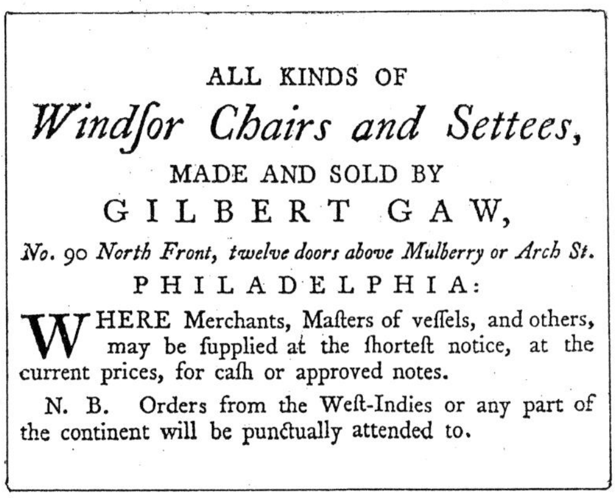

ALL KINDS OF
Windſor Chairs and Settees,
MADE AND SOLD BY
GILBERT GAW,
No. 90 North Front, twelve doors above Mulberry or Arch St.
PHILADELPHIA:
WHERE Merchants, Maſters of veſſels, and others, may be ſupplied at the ſhorteſt notice, at the current prices, for caſh or approved notes.
N. B. Orders from the Weſt-Indies or any part of the continent will be punctually attended to.

FIG. 4-17 Advertising piece of Gilbert Gaw, Philadelphia, printed 1798–1806, inscribed as bill October 20, 1808. *(Collection of the Board of Directors of City Trusts, Girard College History Collections.)*

setts, the master usually received as part pay a "captain's privilege" whereby a small fraction of freight space was reserved for his use to store venture cargo.[94]

SOUTH AMERICA

Chair merchandising on the South American continent before 1800 was confined almost entirely to the Guianas (map 3), with New England engrossing about 69 percent of the trade from 1783 to 1800. The commercial centers were Surinam, Demerara (also Demerary), and Cayenne. Surinam, a river and district of Dutch Guiana, was a leading sugar producer. The colony experienced good trade with America until its occupation by the British in 1799 and the concurrent rise of Cuba as a leading sugar exporter. Demerara, a seacoast county of British Guiana, was a Dutch possession until 1796, when the British occupied it. Cayenne is the coastal island capital of French Guiana.[95]

Of the three Guianian centers, Surinam and Demerara were the most popular commercially. Ships from Connecticut, which accounted for the greatest number of regional voyages, favored Demerara over Surinam and did little or no business with Cayenne. Connecticut was rivaled in the chair trade to Surinam by Philadelphia, although interests from Rhode Island, Massachusetts, and New York were close behind. In 1796 Baltimore was responsible for one cargo of "Twenty Five Chares." "Green Windsor chairs" from Rhode Island were first sent to Surinam about 1783, and shipments continued intermittently until 1798. Philadelphia began to participate about 1786 when the *Harriett* sailed from the Delaware River with 4½ dozen chairs. More than a decade elapsed before two substantial cargoes left the city in 1798. The ship *Thomas Chalkley* set out in February for Surinam carrying three dozen Windsors, a settee, a crib, two armchairs, and two children's chairs. The *Spy* followed in December with eleven dozen Windsors. Three Philadelphia cargoes shipped to Surinam in 1799 contained between them 485 chairs, of which at least twelve dozen were unassembled and accompanied by "Six Kegs green paint" for finishing.[96]

Most chair cargoes of record from Connecticut to Surinam originated at New London between 1792 and 1800 and were of modest size. Except for the twelve dozen Windsors placed on board the brig *Samuel* in 1792, chair lots ranged from only two dozen to five dozen per voyage, many described simply as "green" chairs. The unit price varied from a low of 75¢ to a high of $1.42. Boston's contribution to the trade in 1797 and 1799 may have consisted entirely of fancy rush-bottom seating, since prices averaged about $2 per chair. Of the four recorded chair cargoes from New York to Surinam in the late 1790s, three are identified as Windsor seating and the fourth appears to have been fancy furniture. The whole amounted only to 128 chairs.[97]

Philadelphia apparently abstained from the chair trade to Demerara, although the "130 Green Chairs" sent from Savannah, Georgia, to the colony in 1793 could have been transshipped seating from Philadelphia. Chair exporters at New London, Connecticut, were more than twice as active at Demerara as at Surinam. The shipping papers of Joseph Williams of Norwich record two voyages to the Dutch colony, the first in 1786. The sloop *Nabby* sailed in July, with Elisha Coit as supercargo, laden with foodstuffs, livestock, saddles, plank, and "12 Table Chairs" valued at 10s. ($1.67) apiece. In Demerara Coit's contact was Captain Elisha Lathrop, and his instructions for the voyage directed that he load by November 10 for the return trip. If a suitable cargo was unavailable, Coit was advised to proceed to Saint Bartholomew, Saint Eustatius, Saint Martin, or even Turks Island in the British Bahamas for a return freight, although Williams cautioned him to keep a sharp lookout for the British cruisers at Turks Island. Coit apparently did not leave Demerara until November 28, the date of a memorandum listing unsold items left in the care of Lathrop, including the chairs.[98]

Joseph Williams's next recorded venture to Demerara occurred in March 1789, when his brig *Polly* sailed for the Essequibo River with his brother Isaac in command. To a general cargo of the previous type were added bricks, staves and hoops, linseed oil, kettles and pans, and candles. The furniture cargo was more extensive than earlier. Some, if not all, of the furniture was obtained from Felix Huntington, a cabinetmaker and chairmaker of Norwich. The invoice lists two desks, a bureau, two mahogany sideboards, three dozen "Green Chairs" (also called Windsors elsewhere), six "Writing Chairs," and an easy chair ordered by one S. B. Gilbert and directed to be "stuff'd with something soft." The entire cargo was consigned to Messrs. Lathrop and Luke, "Merchants" of Demerara. The *Polly* returned to New London on August 6. Cargoes tabulated in fourteen later voyages from New London to Demerara total 482 chairs and one unnumbered seating lot, all described as Windsor or "green" chairs. One group referred to in 1799 as "Dining Chairs" probably was constructed in the bow-back pattern. Individual prices varied from 6*s.* to 7*s.*[99]

Chairs sent from Boston to Demerara between 1792 and 1796 were divided between fancy and Windsor seating, judging by the valuations. The largest group, shipped in the brig *Hannah and Mary* to the Essequibo River, totaled eight dozen chairs priced at $1.50 apiece. Newport, Rhode Island, rather than Providence showed minor interest in the market at Demerara. Shipped in December 1791 on the sloop *Dolphin* were 12 green chairs and seven spinning wheels. Earlier in the year chair merchants at New York had tested this market by sending 48 Windsor chairs and four settees on the brig *Venus*, although there appears to have been no follow-up to the region until a decade later when shippers there loaded three cargoes of Windsor chairs for Cayenne, French Guiana. The brig *Abigail* made two voyages. On the first she carried 62 chairs at $1 apiece, and in December 1801 she transported 110 chairs and seven cases of tables. A month earlier the brig *Peacock* had left for Cayenne with about the same number of chairs and eleven cases of mahogany furniture. The only other cities showing interest in this chair market were Providence and Boston.[100]

COASTAL AFRICA AND THE EASTERN ATLANTIC ISLANDS

From the late eighteenth century the American chair trade extended beyond the Western Hemisphere to the shores of Africa (map 4). One cargo was landed at the "Cape," and others were destined for Senegal on the northwestern coast. Most shipments, however, were bound for markets on the Atlantic islands west of the continent. The largest outlet was Madeira, a Portuguese possession thirty-five miles long located west of Morocco. With small bays for access, a salubrious climate, and mountain steeps advantageously cultivated, the island was attractive to traders. Its chief crop was the grape and its product, Madeira wine. Joseph K. Ott has noted the shipment of many *common* chairs in 1787 and 1794 from Providence to Madeira. The term identifies either rush-bottom slat-back seating or Windsors. Three dozen chairs sent to the island from Philadelphia in September 1789 probably were Windsors. This seating was well known on the island by June 1796, when the ship *Four Friends* sailed from the Delaware River carrying "Twelve Windsor Chairs" for consignee Bertolde Francisco Gomia. Two years earlier a Portuguese or Spanish brig carried a like number of Windsors from New York to Madeira. Records of later cargoes for this market date in 1802, when the brig *Boa Amizado* and the ship *Columbus* carried several dozen chairs apiece from New York.[101]

Only one chair cargo is recorded for the more northerly, Portuguese-owned Azores in the late eighteenth century. In July 1798 the *Mary* left New York for Fayal, an island within that group. The ship's manifest identifies two seating units: one lot comprised "Twelve Chairs," the other consisted of "Six Bundles with 12 Chairs / One Bbl Colouring Stuff." The coloring material was stain or japan for slat-back chairs or paint for Windsors. The rugged Azores, while productive in their vineyards, citrus

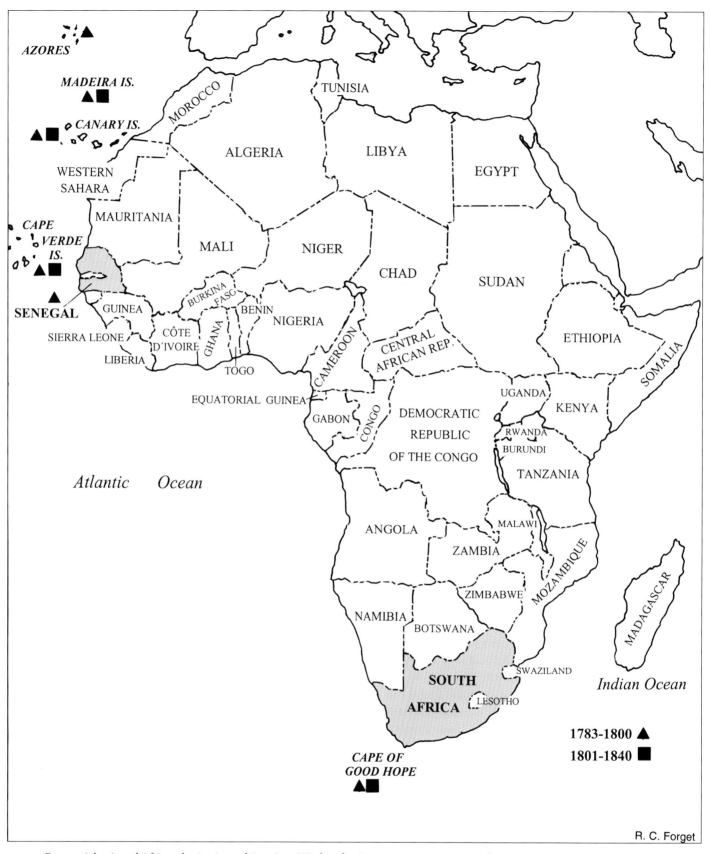

AZORES ▲

MADEIRA IS. ▲■

CANARY IS. ▲■

WESTERN SAHARA

MOROCCO

ALGERIA

TUNISIA

LIBYA

EGYPT

MAURITANIA

MALI

NIGER

CHAD

SUDAN

CAPE VERDE IS. ▲■

SENEGAL ▲

GUINEA

BURKINA FASO

BENIN

NIGERIA

ETHIOPIA

SIERRA LEONE

CÔTE D'IVOIRE

GHANA

TOGO

CAMEROON

CENTRAL AFRICAN REP.

SOMALIA

LIBERIA

EQUATORIAL GUINEA

GABON

CONGO

DEMOCRATIC REPUBLIC OF THE CONGO

UGANDA

RWANDA

BURUNDI

KENYA

TANZANIA

Atlantic Ocean

ANGOLA

ZAMBIA

MALAWI

MOZAMBIQUE

MADAGASCAR

ZIMBABWE

NAMIBIA

BOTSWANA

SWAZILAND

SOUTH AFRICA

LESOTHO

Indian Ocean

1783-1800 ▲
1801-1840 ■

CAPE OF GOOD HOPE ▲■

R. C. Forget

MAP 4 Eastern Atlantic and African destinations of American Windsor furniture cargoes, 1783–1800 and 1801–1840

groves, and other cultivation, suffered from a lack of good harbors, which probably accounts for their low commercial standing among American merchants.[102]

The Canary Islands, a Spanish possession, lie south of Madeira. Although they too supplied wine, they were not as popular with American shippers as Madeira. The sloop *Sally* left Newport, Rhode Island, on August 18, 1787, for Teneriffe, the usual stop for American vessels in the Canaries. On board were a dozen "Green" chairs, ten desks, and two tables. In July 1792 the schooner *Charming Betsey* from Philadelphia introduced another eighty-four Windsors to local households. Shippers at New York ventured a large cargo of twelve dozen Windsors in 1801 on the brig *Star*.[103]

More productive as a chair market for American commercial interests were the Cape Verde Islands ("Cape de Verds"), located south of the Canaries off the coast of Senegal. This Portuguese colony was particularly attractive to Rhode Island merchants. Ott reports more chairs shipped from Providence to the Cape Verdes between 1785 and 1789 than to any other port. An absence of trees on the island appears to have encouraged shipments of other wooden items as well: desks, tables, seamen's chests, wheelbarrows, and boats. One of Ott's tabulated cargoes probably was that of the brig *Harmony*, which carried eight dozen chairs and thirty chests on one outward voyage. In a later venture of 1797 the ship *Maria* deposited chairs, bowls, a maple desk, and tables. Two cargoes of the mid-1790s from Massachusetts introduced additional chairs and bedsteads, and in March 1800 shippers at Middletown, Connecticut, sent sixty Windsor chairs valued at $1 apiece. Beyond the islands the French mainland colony of Senegal was an alternative market for American vessels in African waters. During the 1790s commercial interests at Boston produced at least two Windsor chair cargoes for Senegal. The brig *Polly* sailed from Richmond, Virginia, in 1793 after loading two dozen Windsors at Boston. The same number of wooden chairs entered the colony on the sloop *Maria* five years later. Wharf hands at New York stowed twelve bundles of chairs on the schooner *Maryet* before she sailed from the harbor on January 27, 1802, headed for "Senegal, Coast of Africa."[104]

The Cape of Good Hope in South Africa became the market for a large venture of Windsor chairs whose original destination was Bombay, as stated on the ship's invoice. The *Canton*, owned in part by William Constable of New York City, was outfitted in 1789 at Philadelphia by Isaac Hazelhurst and Company for a voyage to Bombay and China. Hazelhurst's account of disbursements sent to the *Canton*'s owners identifies workmen and suppliers: Michael Owner, ship joiner; Edward Cutbush, carver; John Davis, upholsterer; John Cornish, turner; and Francis Trumble, chairmaker (fig. **4-18**). Trumble was paid £7.10.0 of record, although that sum does not begin to cover the cost of the seating furniture on board, comprising eight dozen Windsor chairs priced by the dozen:

FIG. 4-18 Fan-back Windsor side chair, Francis Trumble (brand "F.TRUMBLE"), Philadelphia, ca. 1778–85. Yellow poplar (seat) with maple, black walnut, oak, and hickory (microanalysis); H. 35¾", (seat) 18", W. (crest) 23½", (seat) 18¼", D. (seat) 19¼". *(Courtesy, Winterthur Museum, acc. 71.281.)*

4 [Doz]	Plain Dining Chairs 70/	14.0.0 [uncarved fan-backs]
½ "	Scroled Arm D[itt]o 150/	3.15.0 [knuckle-arm sack-backs]
½ "	Plain Armed D[itt]o 135/	3.7.6 [flat-arm sack-backs]
½ "	Bamboo Chairs painted Mahogany & tipt 110/	2.15.0 [penciled-groove bow-backs]
½ "	D[itt]o Plain 100/	2.10.0 [plain-painted bow-backs]
½ "	Scrolled Dining Chairs 75/	1.17.6 [carved-scroll fan-backs, fig. 4-18]
1 "	Common D[itt]o	3.10.0 [uncarved fan-backs]
½ "	D[itt]o D[itt]o 60/	1.10.0 [as above]

Other freight included iron, pine plank, tar, turpentine, and porter. The invoice bears the words "to Bombay," the intent being to sell the goods there and pick up a new cargo suitable for trade with the Chinese at Canton. The *Canton* left Philadelphia in early December and by March 30, 1790, was at the Cape of Good Hope, where Cap-

tain Thomas Truxton disposed of cargo to advantage for Spanish currency. Some 158,563 feet of plank sold for $6,342; the Windsors sold for $180.[105]

Preceding the *Canton* to the Orient by a year was Constable's ship *America*, which sailed about December 1788 from New York. Disbursements during its construction at New York include payments to John and Simeon Skillin for carver's work and Malcolm McEuen, a sometime pewterer, for plumber's work. Payments for provisions and goods were made to "Rich'd Kip Upholster & Ash chair maker" together totaling £47.4.2. Bow-back side chairs were in the New York market by this date, and several can be identified with the Ash shop (fig. **4-19**). There is no indication that the seating furniture from New York was sold before it reached the Far East.[106]

THE FAR EAST

Evidence of minor chair sales in the Orient occurs in Massachusetts shipping records beginning in 1795 (map 5), when Boston and Salem were premier commercial centers for this market. Boston alone had twelve vessels engaged in the East India trade. A dozen "Green" chairs loaded onto the ship *Neptune* on December 9, 1795, left Boston for an unspecified destination in the region. In March following, the *Grand Turk II*, owned in Salem by Elias Hasket Derby, voyaged from Boston with a large cargo of eight dozen chairs valued at just over $2 apiece. The vessel's stated destination was Canton, although other goods on board suggest there were intervening stops, making it impossible to know how far the chairs traveled before they found a buyer. The *George Washington* sailing from Salem in 1801 may have carried the "Seventy Sitting Chairs" in its hold valued at $103.66 to the manifest's stated destination, Fort Marlborough, Sumatra. That island in the Malay Archipelago was partially under Dutch control. Return cargoes frequently included pepper, mace, and nutmeg.[107]

Early Nineteenth-Century Trade: Coastal

PHILADELPHIA EXPORTS

Although Philadelphia did not control American shipping in the early nineteenth century, it continued to dominate the export trade in painted seating furniture. Thus the Delaware River remains a central focus in discussing domestic and Caribbean chair markets. Standing ahead of Philadelphia in general trade in 1810 were New York City, whose shipping volume of 268,548 tons was second only to that of London among English-speaking peoples, and Boston with its 149,121 tons. Philadelphia ranked third among American seaports with 125,258 tons to its credit, and Baltimore, a city on the rise, had already achieved fourth place with 103,444 tons annually. Only half that figure was realized by fifth-place Charleston, which carried southern agricultural products to many markets. The size and scope of the chair trade from Philadelphia is indicated in a notice of November 16, 1805, for John Connelly, auctioneer: "This morning, At 10 o'clock precisely, wil[l] be sold in Water street near Pine street, about 50 or 60 dozen Windsor Chairs, new and in complete order for shipping." The next year testimony relating to manufactures and trade at Philadelphia presented in a court suit by the cordwainers of the city cited among exports to the West Indies and the southern states "coaches and other pleasurable carriages [and] windsor chairs." In a statement on industrial progress and the arts published in 1814, Tench Coxe's list of eighty "Manufactures of the United States Most Frequently Exported in 1810" names "Windsor chairs." The reported value of the city's painted chair industry in 1811 was $124,000. That figure can be compared with the contemporary average daily wage of $1 for skilled labor.[108]

The opening years of the nineteenth century were fruitful for American chair-

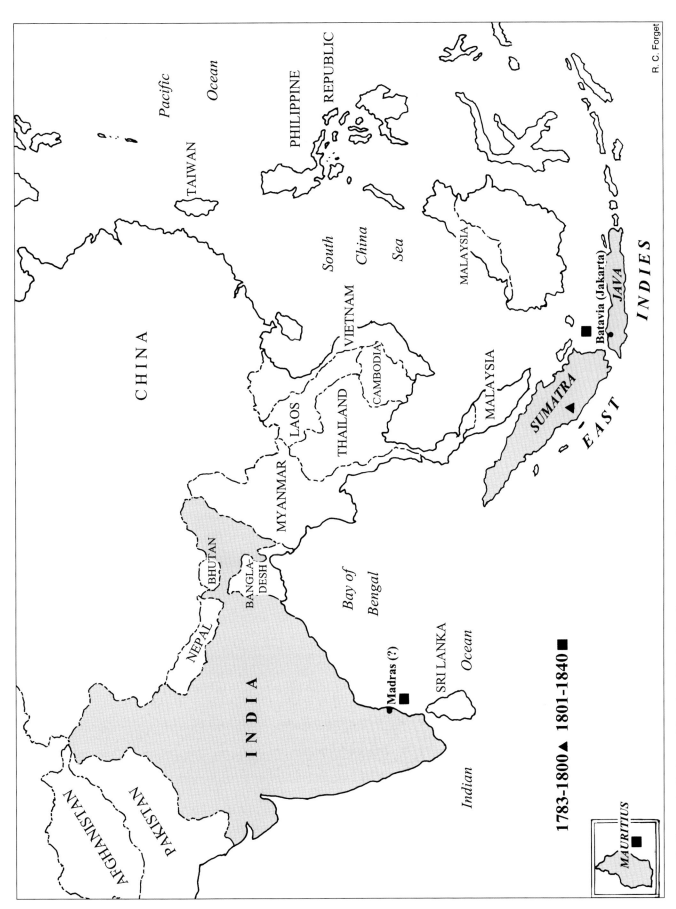

CHINA

Pacific

Ocean

TAIWAN

PHILIPPINE

REPUBLIC

South

China

Sea

VIETNAM

CAMBODIA

THAILAND

LAOS

MYANMAR

MALAYSIA

MALAYSIA

SUMATRA

JAVA

Batavia (Jakarta)

EAST

INDIES

NEPAL

BHUTAN

BANGLA-

DESH

INDIA

Bay of

Bengal

AFGHANISTAN

PAKISTAN

Indian

Ocean

SRI LANKA

Madras (?)

MAURITIUS

1783-1800 ▲ 1801-1840 ■

MAP 5   Far-Eastern destinations of American Windsor furniture cargoes, 1783–1800 and 1801–1840

makers and shippers, particularly those at Philadelphia, whence commercial interests profitably marketed painted seating up and down the American coast and west into the Gulf region (map 6). Charleston was still the leading consumer and Savannah, Georgia, remained a strong market, although Boston now stood second to Charleston in number of chair cargoes received from Philadelphia. From 1800 until 1808 at least thirty-six lots of Philadelphia chairs entered the Massachusetts port, posing a constant source of competition for local craftsmen. The best *regional market* for Philadelphia was Virginia, particularly if trade to Washington and Georgetown is included. Within the area Norfolk, Richmond, and Alexandria were steady consumers, and commerce continued with smaller communities such as Petersburg and Fredericksburg. The North Carolina coast remained a limited, scattered market.[109]

From 1800 to 1807 no fewer than twenty-five chairmakers or chairmaking firms in Philadelphia acted as direct shippers without benefit of middlemen. The craftsmen accounted for 212 of the 422 consignments tabulated for this period and 15,966 of the 25,212 Windsor and fancy chairs carried in the trade, although at best these are incomplete figures. Based on chair numbers, craftsmen appear to have controlled about 63 percent of the coastal export trade in Philadelphia seating; however, there is no evidence that they formed a consortium or acted other than independently.[110]

Chairmakers at Philadelphia conducted their export business in several ways. Small numbers of chairs were shipped "to order" (4 percent) or consigned to ship's captains (5 percent). A majority (84 percent) was consigned to individuals or firms in other cities known to the craftsmen through direct or indirect contacts. Several craftsmen actually accompanied their shipments to distant locations at times, overseeing immediate sales or setting up shop temporarily to retail chairs of their own make and those shipped to them by other craftsmen. Some chairs were shipped unassembled and required framing.

David Moon spent considerable time in Charleston, South Carolina, between autumn 1801, when he left Philadelphia with chairs and chair parts, and February 1804, by which time he had formed a partnership with fellow Philadelphian Edward Prall. Shortly thereafter the two began to consign their merchandise to James Cotton of the southern city. John Wall accompanied a large shipment of more than twenty-six dozen chairs, settees, and stools to Savannah about March 24, 1804, when the brig *Eliza and Sarah* left Philadelphia, and Michael Murphy continued to receive supplies from Philadelphia after he resettled permanently in Norfolk, Virginia. Murphy likely commissioned the captain of the schooner *Winfield Packet* in March 1800 to acquire and ship the "one thousand chair sticks five barrels Glue" on board the vessel when it left Philadelphia. William Haydon and James Whitaker, fancy- and Windsor-chair makers, appear to have established contacts in Charleston before 1803 when each elected to accompany cargoes there. Whitaker, who left about March 16 on the schooner *Nancy*, carried "Twenty Dozen Chairs one Keg Nails one Chest and one Dem[i]john." Haydon followed the next month with fifty-two chairs. A year earlier he had tested the Norfolk market with ten dozen chairs. Haydon also sent shipments to Richmond, Baltimore, Boston, and New Orleans, although Charleston constituted his primary market. From 1800 through 1807 he sent forty cargoes of record to that city, the largest number from one craftsman, save for forty-five sent by James Whitaker. Charleston maintained the greatest popularity among chairmakers.[111]

Markets tapped occasionally by other individuals include New York, Baltimore, Boston, and the national center at Washington, Georgetown, and Alexandria. The old Spanish settlement at Saint Augustine received one lot of twenty-four Philadelphia Windsors in summer 1804 when the sloop *Union* anchored. Accompanying some Windsor chair cargoes were settees, stools, children's chairs, and a few Windsor cradles. Other articles rounding out the shipments include cabinet furniture,

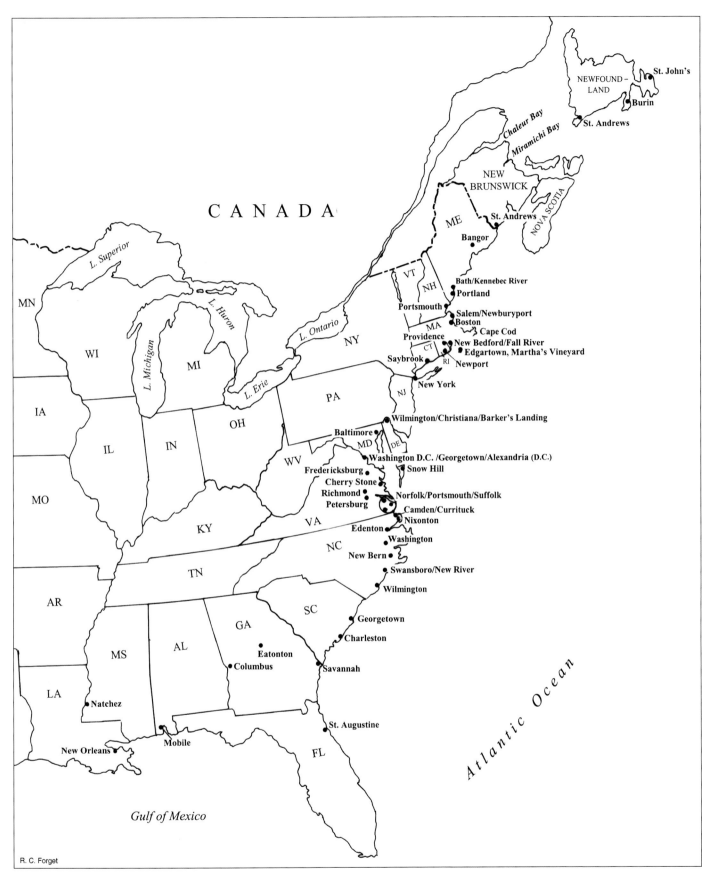

MAP 6 Coastal destinations of American Windsor furniture cargoes, 1801–1840

buckets, horse carts, varnish, kegs of nails, baskets, bread and crackers, soap, beer, and paper.[112]

Manifests occasionally describe exported chairs in detail. One record of note, dated at Philadelphia on December 21, 1805, is that of the brig *Union*. Bound for New Orleans, the vessel carried fifteen dozen Windsor chairs shipped by chairmaker Joseph Burden:

> 5 dozen yellow oval Back Chairs [bow-backs]
> 2 dozen Black double bow Chairs [fig. 3-35]
> 1 doz & four Bamboo Chairs [single-rod chairs, as in fig. 3-34, or fancy seating]
> 2 dz Green Oval back Chairs
> 2 doz & Six Black oval back Chairs
> 2 dz Cane coloured double bow Chairs

Chairmaker John B. Ackley also placed a consignment of twelve dozen and eight chairs on the same vessel. A note of fancy seating occurs in the trade from time to time, as when William Haydon shipped "Forty eight Gilt Chairs with Rush & Cain Bottoms & four Settees Ditto" to a Charleston consignee in 1805 on the schooner *Rising Sun*. Earlier he had sent "Eighty black & Gold Chairs" to the same individual. A newspaper notice at Charleston in 1807 lists among merchandise received from Philadelphia "Fashionable (black and gold) Chairs and Settees."[113]

Spot checks of domestic export records at Philadelphia postdating Jefferson's embargo focus on the years 1810–11, 1815–16, 1820, 1825, 1831, and 1837, amplified by supporting material. There was little if any diminution in independent shipping among the city's chairmakers in these twenty-seven years, when thirty-seven or more craftsmen participated. The markets, numbering ten or more, were much the same as earlier. Charleston, still the most popular destination, received between 75 and 80 percent of the chairmakers' direct consignments. By comparison Savannah, Norfolk, Boston, and Washington-Alexandria received only about 4 percent each of the chairmaker-generated trade. Chairs exported by other shippers accounted for only a small fraction of the trade. Kathleen M. Catalano in her study of the Philadelphia furniture industry between 1820 and 1840 found that domestic coastwise chair exports, mainly of painted seating, numbered about 17,846 items.[114]

Although Charles C. Robinson's name does not appear in shipping manifests, an entry in his accounts dating to May 23, 1812, indicates that he participated in the trade indirectly: "Cash Dr To ½ dozn Windsor Chairs Bot By Captain of Vessel." The "captain" paid $8. Besides the side and armchairs that formed the core of the trade, shippers consigned settees of various sizes, children's seating, and a few rocking chairs and counting-room stools. Merchants Matthew and Richard Brenan of Charleston, who had many Philadelphia contacts, advertised imported seating in November 1810 as they did business with chairmakers John Huneker and James Whitaker: "Just received from Philadelphia, and for sale, a few sets of very handsome Drawing Room Chairs, gilt and ornamented, with Settees to suit, both cane and rush bottoms; plain Windsor Chairs and Settees, with children's Table Chairs." The firm of Sass and Gready advertised in 1816 along the same lines. Their seating was supplied by William Lee, William Haydon, and William H. Stewart. Lee also conducted a periodic business association that year with chairmaker John Mere. On January 2 he placed ten dozen chairs aboard the ship *General Wade Hampton* for Charleston and consigned them to Mere. When the ship still had not sailed on February 5, probably because of ice in the Delaware River, Lee added another twenty dozen chairs to the original stock, consigning them to Butler and Mere. Fifteen dozen chairs followed on the ship *Terrier* at the end of the month. Mere was perhaps in Charleston retailing his own seating furniture, and conducting business for Lee may have enabled him to cover part of his expenses. A cargo shipped by Mere on August 3 from Philadelphia

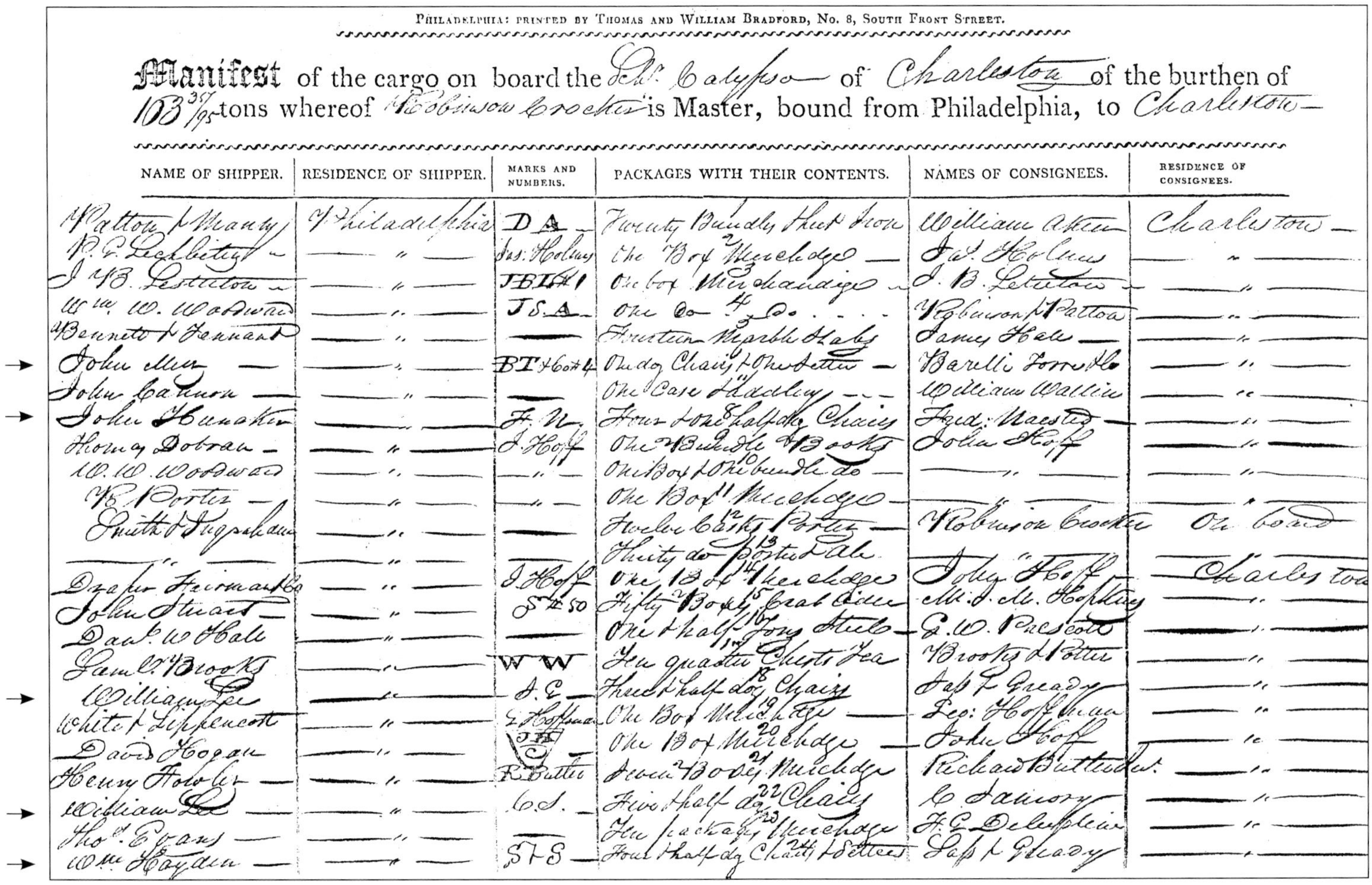

FIG. 4-20 Cargo manifest of schooner *Calypso*, Philadelphia, August 3, 1816. *(U.S. Custom House Records, National Archives.)*

on the schooner *Calypso* went consigned to the firm of Barrelli and Torri of Charleston (fig. 4-20). Also on board were nine dozen chairs from William Lee for two consignees. Two other chairmakers who participated, as indicated on the manifest, were John Huneker and William Haydon. Each consigned 4½ dozen chairs to Charleston firms, and Haydon's chairs were supplemented by several settees.[115]

Joseph Burden had various outlets for his products. In May 1816 he shipped "fifteen bundles Chair rounds" on the sloop *Unity* to Alexandria for Henry R. Burden in Washington, probably his son. Burden made occasional consignments to individuals and firms at Charleston, Savannah, Norfolk, and Baltimore. A shipment to the latter city in 1825 comprised "a quantity of chair rounds" for John Hodgkinson, who operated a chair factory on Liberty Street. Before midcentury Abraham McDonough's business contacts extended from New York to New Orleans and west to Missouri.[116]

NEW YORK AND NEWARK EXPORTS

The character of waterfront life in America's largest seaport, or in any large coastal center in the early nineteenth century, was captured by John Lambert in 1807 in his description of New York trade:

The port was filled with shipping, and the wharfs were crowded with commodities of every description. Bales of cotton, wool, and merchandize; barrels of pot-ash, rice, flour, and salt provisions; hogsheads of sugar, chests of tea, puncheons of rum, and pipes of wine; boxes, cases, packs and packages of all sizes and denominations, were strewed upon the wharfs and landing-places, or upon the decks of the shipping. All

FANCY CHAIR STORE.
....
WILLIAM BUTTRE,

*No. 17, Bowery-Lane, near the
Watch-House, New-York,*
HAS CONSTANTLY FOR SALE,
A large assortment of elegant, well-made,
and highly finished Black, White, Brown, Coquelico, Gold
and Fancy Chairs, Settees, Conversation, Elbow, Rocking,
Sewing, Windsor, and Children's Chairs of every description, and on the most moderate terms.
Orders from any part of the continent
will be attended to with punctuality and despatch. A liberal
allowance made to Shippers, &c.
☞ *Old Chairs repaired, varnished, and
re-gilt.*

FIG. 4-21 Advertisement of William Buttre. From *Longworth's American Almanac, New-York Register, and City Directory* (New York: David Longworth, 1810), n.p. *(Winterthur Library.)*

was noise and bustle. The carters were driving in every direction; and the sailors and labourers upon the wharfs, and on board the vessels, were moving their ponderous burthens. . . . The merchants and their clerks were busily engaged in their counting-houses, or upon the piers. The Tontine coffee-house [fig. 5-45] was filled with underwriters, brokers, merchants, traders, and politicians; selling, purchasing, trafficking, or insuring. . . . The coffee-house slip, and the corners of Wall and Pearl-streets, were jammed up with carts, drays, and wheelbarrows; horses and men were huddled promiscuously together, leaving little or no room for passengers to pass.[117]

Although painted seating furniture ranked lower in commerce at New York than Philadelphia, activity in the early 1800s was reasonable and involved local chairmaker-shippers. An exportation notice of Thomas Hays dating to 1801 describes a substantial trade: "Masters of vessels or Merchants, can be supplied with from 1 to 1000 chairs in one hour." Chairs in small lots could be purchased framed. For the shipper interested in large quantities, parts were ready, waiting in bundles or barrels.[118]

Cabinetmaker John Hewitt tapped still another local chair market before sailing in 1800 for Savannah. He purchased painted seating furniture across the bay in Newark at the shop of David Alling, although he later discovered that the chairs had not received a final coat of varnish. Despite occasional shortcomings, Windsor and fancy seating was quite salable at Savannah, whether of Philadelphia, Newark, or New York make. G. and F. Penny received "an assortment" of "handsome" chairs from New York in 1808 via the *Liverpool Packet*.[119]

Public notices at Charleston announcing the arrival of chairs from New York indicate that not all cargoes were unloaded for sale. The brig *Consolation* had Windsor chairs *on board* for retail or wholesale in March 1804, and the practice continued. Norfolk received several shipments from New York before the War of 1812. Three New York cargoes from Perth Amboy, New Jersey, contained a total of 544 chairs. One vessel also carried four settees and "9 Misses Stools," possibly for a young ladies' academy in the southern community. The largest cargo, twenty-five dozen chairs, was shipped in 1811 on the sloop *Elouisa* and consigned to Reily and Tunis, who were "on board." Later at Norfolk, John Tunis advertised a "large assortment" of fancy and Windsor chairs just received from New York on the schooner *Washington* after a passage of only five days.[120]

The prewar chair trade at New York also exported in other directions. As city chairmakers, including William Buttre, pledged punctuality and offered "a liberal allowance . . . to Shippers" (fig. **4-21**), sailing vessels carried their chairs to New England markets. Small sets of Windsors were shipped to New Bedford and the surrounding area. Members of the Greene or Arnold families living near Providence received a quantity of seating in 1808 from Charles Cluss in New York. The craftsman's bill itemizes two dozen "Fancy Gilt Chairs" at $51, a dozen green Windsors at $11.25, and half a dozen black Windsors for $5.25, the total amounting to $67.50. Among the Greene family papers an undated loose account sheet for Alice Arnold contains an item reading: "Charles Kluss bill for Chares 42.00." Initially this appears to refer to a second bill, but further study indicates that if Alice Arnold purchased only one dozen fancy chairs—a reasonable number for most households—and all the Windsor chairs, her bill would have totaled $42. A later group of fancy and Windsor chairs itemized in the Greene family papers originated in the shop of Charles Fredericks of New York, who on November 8, 1827, billed the seating to S. Larned, Esq., of Providence. Larned apparently had retired from his post at the American legation in Chile and was refurnishing his American home.[121]

Chairmaker John Smith of New York took a chair cargo to Providence in summer 1802, where he advertised: "One Hundred of the newest-fashioned WINDSOR CHAIRS, which he will sell as low as can be bought in New-York. He will remain here but a few Days." As late as 1826 the New York product still had commercial stature in the city, as indicated by Rhodes G. Allen, a cabinetmaker who was "daily receiving, Chairs of all descriptions, from the best manufactory in New-York, for sale at a small advance." Another large regional market open to the commerce of New York before the War of 1812 extended from Long Island and northern New Jersey to the Hudson River Valley and westward along the Mohawk to Lake Ontario and the Finger Lakes.[122]

Following the war the coastal trade from New York revived quickly, encouraging several chairmakers to export their products. On May 23, 1815, Thomas Ash II placed "Seventy one Bundles of Chares" on the brig *Savannah Packet*. A later cargo of October 1817 originating with William Brown was carried on the schooner *Ariadne* to a Savannah consignee. On the same vessel was a furniture cargo consisting of six boxes and one bundle shipped by cabinetmaker Duncan Phyfe. Several small North Carolina communities merchandised New York chairs after the war. Cheshire and Cox of Edenton had just received their fall and winter goods from New York in 1818 when they advertised "a few dozen superior quality *Windsor Chairs*." The next spring A. Clark of Wilmington offered "a new assortment" of fancy and Windsor chairs from New York in "the latest fashions and various colours, handsomely ornamented, Guilt [*sic*] and Bronze." A dry goods retailer from New Bern returned from the northern city in 1820 with Windsor and fancy chairs among his merchandise. Shipping returns in 1815 and 1817 for Perth Amboy, adjacent to Staten Island, account for seating cargoes sent to Fredericksburg and Richmond, Virginia. The brisk trade of the postwar years slackened considerably by 1820, however, as a national recession blanketed the country. A chairmaker of New York responding to a query in the 1820 manufacturing census noted that his production through the years had been "more fore the suthren market than at home."[123]

David Alling of Newark, New Jersey, enjoyed a good trade in the South. Chairs transported on the ship *Hamlet* in 1821 to Natchez, Mississippi, grossed $345. The market was still profitable for Alling in 1833, when he shipped fancy roll-top and Grecian seating along with rocking chairs for children and women. In a contemporary order for Mobile, Alabama, he sent cane-seat and rush-seat roll-top chairs, classified by quality as "inferior" and "better," accompanied by Grecian, children's, and Windsor seating. New York shippers also sent the ship *Catharine* to Mobile in 1832 to deposit 252 chairs. Alling's business contacts extended to several markets in Georgia. Three firms in Columbus ordered fancy seating, some with roll tops, others with fret (pierced) backs and crown tops. Most chairs were painted; a few were made of curled maple. A rocking chair, children's furniture, and chairs with cushions completed the orders. Although Columbus is located inland, it was accessible from the Gulf by small steamboats traveling up the Apalachicola River to Lake Seminole and up the Chattahoochee. Another order was sent to Fort Burnap at Eatonton, a more remote location. Alling shipped the "doz. curl maple flush seat" chairs to Batildwin and Company of Savannah, who directed them up the Savannah River to Mason and Raule of Augusta. The final journey was overland.[124]

NEW ENGLAND EXPORTS

The chair trade was not nearly as prominent a component of domestic New England commerce in the early nineteenth century as that of Philadelphia and New York. Established craftsmen such as Cyrus Cleaveland of Providence advertised "Liberal Credit . . . to those who may want large Quantities of Windsor Chairs or other Furniture for Exportation," although even this incentive produced little action at times. Activity in the export chair market of New England was thin until the 1820s. The small traders who worked the coast, buying and selling as they could, dealt in only modest numbers of chairs. Interests at Philadelphia and New York made substantial inroads into the chair custom of New England, as indicated in notices from Boston: "Philadelphia fancy chairs; bamboo and straw bottomed ditto" (1817) and "Elegant New York Fancy chairs" (1833). Evidence, however, documents modest activity along the East Coast by New England. New Bedford customhouse records for 1808 list a dozen chairs in supplement to a cargo of molasses and cherry boards shipped to Edgartown, Martha's Vineyard. Samuel M. Dockum, cabinetmaker of Portsmouth, New Hampshire, had for sale in 1825 twenty dozen Boston chairs. Boteler and Donn at Washington, the nation's capital, retailed seating in 1833 from both Boston and New York along with chairs of their own production. In 1832 Savannah, Georgia, was an outlet for chairs made by David Partridge of Paxton, Massachusetts, hinting at new trade dimensions realized by internal improvements, such as turnpike roads, canals, and in time the railroad. Nor is this an isolated example of Worcester County work for the southern market. A low-back chair branded by Samuel S. Howe of Gardner is clearly stenciled on the bottom by the retailer, William H. Muir of Alexandria, Virginia.[125]

Reasonable activity occurred from 1801 to 1818 at New London, Connecticut, when about twenty chair shipments of modest size were exported to markets such as Maine, Cape Cod, Norfolk, Richmond, Savannah, and Charleston. South Carolina led as a consumer. Six cargoes are linked with chairmakers, the earliest a shipment in November 1801 of "16 Chairs & other Furniture" made by "Col E[benezer] Tracy (Lisbon)" and consigned to Giles L'Hommedieu, ship captain at Saybrook, probably for reexportation. Less than two years later George Packard, a craftsman of New London, placed five boxes of furniture and forty-two chairs on the sloop *Industry* bound for Norfolk, Virginia. Watson, Wood and Company of Hartford made a shipment to the South in 1805 via New London, consigning sixty fancy chairs to Michael McGrath of Charleston, the recipient a year later of a large cargo of "one thousand chair bottoms" placed on board the ship *Columbia* by Porter and Holbrook of New London. Speculation suggests that the wooden seats from New London may have complemented turnings shipped from New York, Philadelphia, and elsewhere. Indeed, researchers at the Museum of Early Southern Decorative Arts in Winston-Salem, North Carolina, have found Windsor seating with family histories in the coastal South whose features exhibit "mixed" regional characteristics.[126]

Other references for New London date more than a decade later. In a transaction of 1817 Amos Denison Allen of Windham, Connecticut, shipped cabinet furniture, chairs, and settees to Frederick Tracy, his young brother-in-law and agent at Savannah, Georgia, a primary sales outlet for the firm (fig. **4-22**). The shipping manifest is typical of those originating in small coastal New England centers where mixed foodstuffs were a mainstay of the trade. A year later Park Avery of Preston sent six boxes of furniture and two hundred chairs to Charleston consigned to a family member. Another transaction occurred in 1818 when a March family member shipped ninety chairs to Thomas M. March, chairmaker of Baltimore, on the sloop *Humbird*. Communication between Baltimore and New London was excellent by that date, as there was regularly scheduled steamboat service via New York.[127]

Lambert Hitchcock of western Connecticut began his independent woodworking career about 1818 perhaps as a maker of chair parts shipped to Charleston, although no formal record of the trade has surfaced. By 1831 the entrepreneur advertised an annual production of about fifteen thousand chairs, some furnished to shipping merchants and southern traders. The rising scope of production in early nineteenth-century Boston is outlined in an advertisement of the auctioneers Nolan and Gridley, who in February 1811 announced a wareroom stock of three thousand chairs described as "a very complete assortment, from the best workmanship and finest touch of the pencil to the most common, from 7 to 6 dlls. per doz. all which they will pack in shipping order and in the most careful manner."[128]

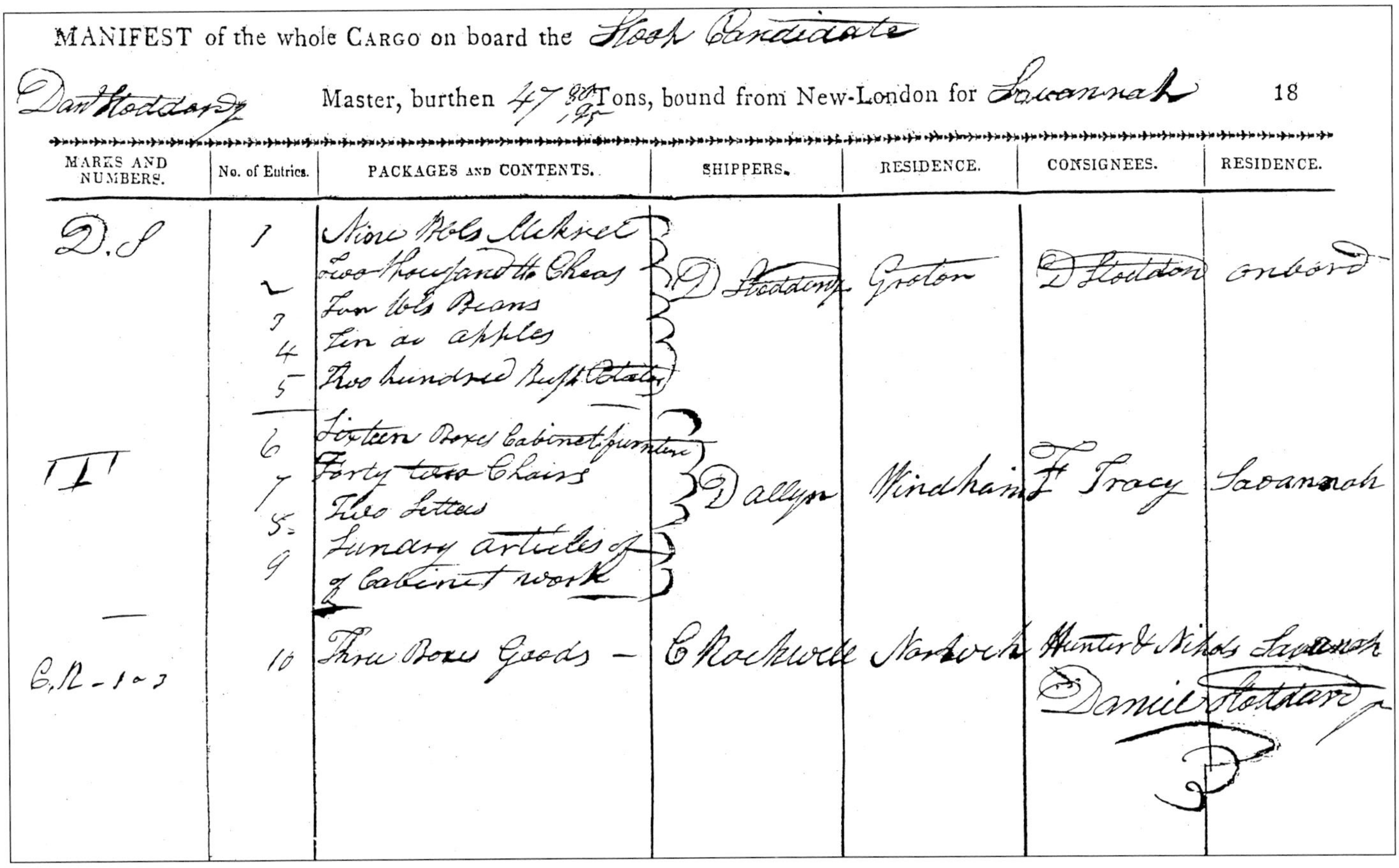

MANIFEST of the whole CARGO on board the *Sloop Candidate*

Dan Stoddard Master, burthen 47 90/95 Tons, bound from New-London for *Savannah* 18

MARKS AND NUMBERS.	No. of Entries.	PACKAGES AND CONTENTS.	SHIPPERS.	RESIDENCE.	CONSIGNEES.	RESIDENCE.
D.S	1	Nine bbls Mackrel Two thousand lb Cheas	D Stoddard	Groton	D Stoddard	onboard
	2	Four bbls Beans				
	4	Ten ao apples				
	5	Two hundred bush Potato				
T	6	Sixteen Boxes Cabinet furniture	Dallyn	Windham	Tracy	Savannah
	7	Forty two Chairs				
	8	Two Settees				
	9	Sundry articles of of Cabinet work				
C.R-1~3	10	Three Boxes Goods —	C Rockwell	Norwich	Hunter & Nihols Daniel Stoddard	Savannah

The Sanderson brothers, Elijah and Jacob, of Salem, Massachusetts, who became active furniture merchants in the coastal and foreign trade in the postrevolutionary years, sometimes shipped painted chairs as a complement to their more valuable consignments of cabinetware. On a voyage of the schooner *Madocawando* to North Carolina in 1812 four "bamboo" rocking chairs and forty-two "kitchen" chairs priced at $1 each shared cargo space with a sideboard, candle stands, washstands, bureaus, portable desks, and tables. The valuation of the kitchen chairs suggests they were Windsors rather than rush-bottom seating. James Odell, Jr., master of the vessel, outlined his instructions from Jacob Sanderson at the bottom of the invoice:

> Receiv d the above on board which I am to carry to the abovenamed place and sell them to the best advantage for which I am to receive 5 per ct Commission, returns to be in such produce . . . as will in my opinion pay the best freight home for which I am to receive Customary freight.
> Salem February 10th 1812.

Sanderson suggested a suitable return freight: "I wish for you to fetch a little Corn, Rise [Rice] and Flour if you can."[129]

Merchandising was not always so cut-and-dried, as Elias Grant, another sea captain, explained in a letter of April 11, 1803, from Richmond, Virginia, to his temporary employers, the Sandersons:

> Dear Sir, As I have not Recev'd any letter from you as I expected I have taken a freight for Yourop [Europe] & shall send your money home. . . . The goods are not sold as yet. . . . I have tried them twice at vendue but sold Very Little and what is sold is Very Lo. . . . But they will be Sold this week I expect as I shall try all in my Power to git them Sold. The Reason they don't sell quick there is Ben a Vessel here from New York with

FIG. 4-22 Cargo manifest of sloop *Candidate*, New London, Conn., October 25, 1817. (*U.S. Custom House Records, Federal Archives and Records Center.*)

FIG. 4-23 Detail of Augustus Mathiot billhead, Baltimore, Md., 1854. *(Winterthur Library.)*

furniture & sold it very lo. . . . There is no way of selling goods here but by Vendue & I shall make a great loss for times is Very dull at present here.

By midcentury the picture had changed completely. The national territory and population were expanding at a rapid rate, creating new markets and consumers. New directions in American industry and trade are reflected in the rise of large factory complexes, such as the furniture manufactory operated by Walter Corey at Portland, Maine, where an entire acre of space was devoted just to one portion of the business.[130]

THE SOUTH AND CANADA

In the early nineteenth century southern craftsmen faced substantial competition in wooing local consumers, merchants, and shippers away from northern seating. Chairmakers in the small seaboard towns experienced further difficulty in having to compete with large southern commercial centers as well. Alexander Walker of Fredericksburg, Virginia, is a case in point. His notice of August 12, 1803, pinpoints one source of retail problems, offering "a large quantity of Windsor Chairs & Settees, Equal if not superior to any manufactured in Baltimore, and at the same prices." Describing the extent of the competition are advertisements from Baltimore placed by Matthew McColm, who offered "75 dozen Chairs, Suitable for exportation," and Francis Younker, who stated that "any quantity can be supplied and delivered on the shortest notice." About 1817, after a short residency in Baltimore, Henry Bradshaw Fearon observed, "It is a commercial city of great importance; and, though not at present of the first rank, is rising with a rapidity almost unparalleled." A decade later local chairmakers still vied to attract local shippers. Patronage remained strong at midcentury when A. and J. B. Mathiot, proprietors of a chair manufactory in Gay Street, advertised "*Shipping Chairs of all kinds*" and pictured their facility on billheads and directory notices (fig. **4-23**).[131]

Although information on Canadian shipping is limited, returns for Nova Scotia from 1811 to 1820 provide some insight on the chair trade. Halifax was the departure point, and the principal destination was Newfoundland. The chair trade to New Brunswick was half the size, perhaps because Saint John and Fredericton were already making substantial progress as commercial centers. Indeed from 1816 on New Brunswick shipped chairs and furniture to Nova Scotia. An occasional consignment from Nova Scotia reached Quebec. Many seating lots were small, varying from half a dozen to three dozen chairs; a few reached seven to nine dozen. Precise destinations often are not given, especially for Newfoundland, suggesting that captains sought markets on their own at entry points in the southern part of the island. Saint John's, located in the east and the capital city, had a sheltered harbor; Burin on the south shore in Placentia Bay had a good harbor and was involved in the fisheries; Saint Andrew's (in New Brunswick?) is in the southwest. The ship *Messenger* carried a typical cargo on September 21, 1811, when it cleared Halifax for Newfoundland: coffee, sugar, flour, tar and pitch, spars, scantling (boards), a box of medicines, corn, hops, and six chairs.

Miramichi Bay was a favored stop in northeastern New Brunswick. Access was easier from Halifax than from Saint John or Fredericton in the southern part of the province. Another destination in New Brunswick (or Newfoundland?) was Saint Andrews at the Saint Croix River on Passamaquoddy Bay adjacent to northern Maine. The community was a lumber and shipbuilding center. On a voyage in July 1817 to "Bay Chaleur," north of Miramichi Bay on the New Brunswick–Quebec boundary, the schooner *Prudence* deposited a dozen chairs. All told the Nova Scotia trade accounted for more than nine hundred chairs, none described any more explicitly. The early nineteenth-century American and Canadian markets along the East Coast are delineated in map 6.[132]

The population of New Orleans numbered somewhat over five thousand in 1794 when William Strickland noted: "A considerable trade is just now opening between New York and New Orleans, the capital of the Spanish territories at the mouth of the Mississippi." The city continued under Spanish rule until 1800, when it was conveyed to the French, the original founders. In 1803 the French ceded New Orleans to the United States as part of the Louisiana Purchase. Even as Strickland wrote of the United States' interest in the southern city, Philadelphia entrepreneurs were casting a commercial eye in that direction. The first American painted chairs of record entered the city in October 1796 from New York, however—nineteen on the brig *Iphigenia*. There followed from the Hudson River port in 1798 two dozen chairs and two settees, and subsequent ventures placed another twenty-seven dozen New York chairs in this southern market. Meanwhile, interest arose in other quarters. Samuel Knap, captain of the schooner *Experiment* from Baltimore, apparently met with success in several ventures in 1797–98 to New Orleans. Each of two voyages in 1798 conveyed "Twenty four arm'd Windsor Chairs" and two settees priced at $3 and $10 apiece to the Gulf port.[133]

New England demonstrated interest in this southern market by the turn of the century. As expected the cabinetmaker-adventurers of Salem sent a cargo of handsome mahogany furniture worth $2,100 in October 1799 and followed it with another cargo of similar value the next year on the brig *Speedwell*. Marked along the margin of the *Speedwell*'s manifest of February 1, 1800, are the shippers' initials and their numbered packing cases. Included are the initials of "IA" for Josiah Austin, who supplemented his cabinetware with twelve Windsor side chairs and four armchairs, each group valued at $12. More than sixteen dozen painted chairs of record were sent to New Orleans in 1801 from neighboring Boston, including one lot initiated by a merchant of Providence, Rhode Island. Philadelphia was represented in the New Orleans chair trade by 1799 when two cargoes totaling twenty-one dozen Windsors left the Delaware River for the Gulf. Eighteen dozen more chairs followed in 1801, although none was consigned directly by a chairmaker of Philadelphia.[134]

During a visit with his daughter at New Orleans in 1801 John Pintard of New York took note of household accommodations in that prosperous business community. His comments confirm that American furniture makers were leaving their mark on the community:

> The Houses facing the levée . . . are . . . two Stories with a gallery in front. . . . The family resides on the 2d floor. . . . Rooms are neatly disposed and furnished, . . . Glass windows or doors opening in the middle down to the floor for the benefit of air in this warm climate. The chimney peices [sic] differ from ours—are highly gilt with different colours—the mantlepeice [sic] always set out with five china tea & coffee cups & saucers a la francaise. . . . The furniture . . . is very plain—But American manufactured Chairs & tea tables are getting into vogue.[135]

Following acquisition of New Orleans by the United States, when the city's population was eight thousand, there occurred a substantial upswing in general commerce. Documents from Philadelphia for the four years from 1804 through 1807 list forty chair lots exported to the city, twenty-seven by the chairmaker-merchants. The group merchandised 78 percent of the 4,317 chairs in the shipments. First to venture into the new market was chairmaker John B. Ackley, who placed a cargo on the ship *John* in January 1804, the year New Orleans became an American port of entry. His example was followed on April 19 by James Pentland and Anthony Steel, who between them sent 318 Windsor chairs and 2 settees on the brig *Hiram*. The schooner *Eliza Tice* left the city the same day laden in part with three dozen chairs shipped by William Haydon. Other chairmaker-shippers were William Mitchell, William Smith, and Joseph Burden. Ackley was the undisputed leader in this trade with thirteen consignments. Joseph Burden was well behind with only four recorded lots. Both men shipped several substantial cargoes. Ackley's first consignment contained twenty dozen chairs, two settees, thirty boxes of soap, and "Eight large boxes Cabinet ware." As Ackley is not known to have been a cabinetmaker, he probably obtained the furniture from another woodworker of Philadelphia. Even the captain of the *John*, James M. Tallman, ventured five dozen chairs, possibly purchased from Ackley. For a July voyage Ackley added a dozen rush-bottom fancy chairs and nine settees to his Windsor cargo. In 1807 Joseph Burden exported twenty-five dozen Windsors in one lot.[136]

During the embargo and war years trade to New Orleans slackened considerably. Eight dozen chairs were shipped in 1809 from Perth Amboy, New Jersey, and a like number in 1816. Modest cargoes left Philadelphia in 1810 and 1811. By that date the population of New Orleans stood above seventeen thousand, more than double the figure at the Louisiana Purchase. The war with Britain came home to New Orleans on January 8, 1815, when General Pakenham's forces attacked the city from Lakes Ponchartrain and Borgne. Pakenham, however, was roundly defeated by the Americans under General Andrew Jackson. With the peace came changes for the city wrought by new technology. The steamboat made it possible to move goods conveniently up the Mississippi for the first time. Whereas storekeepers Bracken and Smith of Natchez, Mississippi, received their Windsor chairs and merchandise in 1811 by keelboat from New Orleans or knew the expense of having it freighted from Pittsburgh, James Turnbull could advertise fancy chairs in 1819 at Natchez as part of a furniture cargo he had accompanied under sail from Philadelphia to New Orleans and transshipped upriver by steam power. John Bristed, writing about 1818, described the change succinctly:

> Until lately the exports far exceeded the imports . . . such were the labour, time, and expense, necessary to ascend the rapid stream of the Mississippi, the nature of whose banks . . . precludes the possibility of towing paths. So that whilst the greater part of the produce of the immense country watered by the Mississippi and its tributary streams, was, of necessity, exported through . . . New-Orleans, the importations of a considerable portion of that country were supplied from the Atlantic seaports by water and land communications. But *now* steam-boats carry merchandise and men from New-Orleans up to the Falls of Louisville, on the Ohio, a distance of seventeen hundred miles. . . . There is a portage of less than two miles at the Ohio falls, whence steamboats ply regularly to Pittsburgh, a distance of seven hundred miles; thus ensuring to the Western Country and its great outlet, New-Orleans, a rapidity of growth in wealth, power, and population.[137]

Several excerpts from the New Orleans trade in the postwar years to the 1830s provide a focus on the nature of the chair cargoes shipped from the North and the rigors of the sea voyage to the Gulf. In October 1819, as the brig *Catharine* conveyed four boxes of furniture and six bundles of chairs from New London, Connecticut, to New Orleans, David Alling, a chairmaker-entrepreneur of Newark, New Jersey, was active in the same trade. Four cargoes shipped in 1819–20, all consigned to Nathan Bolles, are recorded in Alling's accounts. The first lot of twelve dozen chairs appears to have consisted entirely of fancy seating. Prices varied from $2.25 to $4.17 per item. Included were painted chairs of rosewood finish "Gilt & bronsed," and curled maple seating also "Gilt." Some chairs had "Slat backes"; others had "organ Spindles." The second cargo was more extensive, consisting of twenty-nine dozen chairs divided between fancy and Windsor seating. The fancy furniture introduced "fret backs" (pierced slats) and was framed with either "Strait" or "bent front feet." There were organ-spindle chairs and others with ball backs; a dozen chairs had "dimond front rounds." The Windsors consisted of children's high chairs and "little" chairs in brown or green, adult seating with "bent backs" painted yellow, green, or rosewood, and organ-spindle chairs in brown.[138]

Most of Alling's third shipment to Bolles, comprising twelve dozen chairs on the brig *Nancy* in March 1820, consisted of Windsor seating. Ornamentation is noted in particular. Green and "read" bent-backs with "Gilt" were $33 and $35 the dozen; green bent-backs "with Coulers" only were $27. Ornamented organ-spindle Windsors had ground colors of rosewood, green, yellow, or brown. A final chair shipment introduced still other Windsor patterns. Some of the most expensive at $30 the dozen were described as "Rose wood Gilt flat [arrow] Spindles winsor." Green and brown chairs of the same pattern without gilt were cheaper. Other chairs described as "Square seats winsor" were available in several colors—rosewood, light green, and dark green. Yellow slat-backs rounded out the wooden-bottom seating. Fancy chairs introduced both "oval" and "dimond" fret backs. Rosewood sewing chairs and small seats for children painted yellow completed the consignment.[139]

The rigors of a winter trip to New Orleans were recorded some years later by John H. Pile, mate of the brig *Galen* on a voyage from New York: "January the 5th 1835. Wind at N.N.W. Monday. Fresh Breezes with a great deal of ice in the river which Prevented our sailing. At 2 PM Received on board 4 Cases and 12 Bundles of Chairs and 50 Boxes of soap as freight. At Midnight very cold." The *Galen* left the Hudson River on January 15; however, continued icing in local waters caused the captain to seek shelter and anchor until the next day. Pile recorded the vessel's arrival at New Orleans on February 24. A few days later he wrote: "This morning freezing with showers of Hail. Discharged 30 Bales of Hay, 4 Cases of Chairs and 12 Bundles, and 50 Boxes of Soap." The vessel's main cargo was stone. When the *Galen* left New Orleans on March 14 she sailed across the Gulf to Sisal, Yucatan, possibly to pick up a cargo of hides, sugarcane, or dyewood.[140]

Early Nineteenth-Century Trade: Foreign

THE CARIBBEAN

American trade with the Caribbean islands continued unabated during the early nineteenth century (map 7). Changes occurred principally as markets shifted due to war, native uprisings, and variable trade restrictions. Hispaniola, an excellent market in the 1790s, was seldom visited again by the chair merchants until the 1820s. The star of the Greater Antilles chair trade by the late 1790s was neighboring Cuba. Somewhat more activity than earlier may be noted for Puerto Rico, and in the Virgin Islands, Saint Thomas replaced Saint Croix as the principal chair market or distribution point. Within the remaining Leeward group Saint Eustatius dropped out of the picture, but modest activity continued at Saint Bartholomew and Guadeloupe. Martinique in the Windwards had comparable trade, and British Barbados became a more active participant; however, trade in the lower Caribbean did not reach former levels. Philadelphia remained the most active supplier of painted seating, as observed about 1810 by the chevalier Felix de Beaujour. The importance of the Caribbean trade to the woodworking and shipping interests of Philadelphia can be measured in figures compiled between 1820 and 1840, when a staggering 108,485 chairs were shipped to the region. Combined with coastwise figures, the total exports numbered 126,331 chairs.[141]

Chairmakers at New York were alert to opportunity, as well. In October 1801 James Hallet, Jr., offered "5,000 windsor chairs of various patterns, prepared for a Foreign market of the very best materials and workmanship." Even Canadian ship-

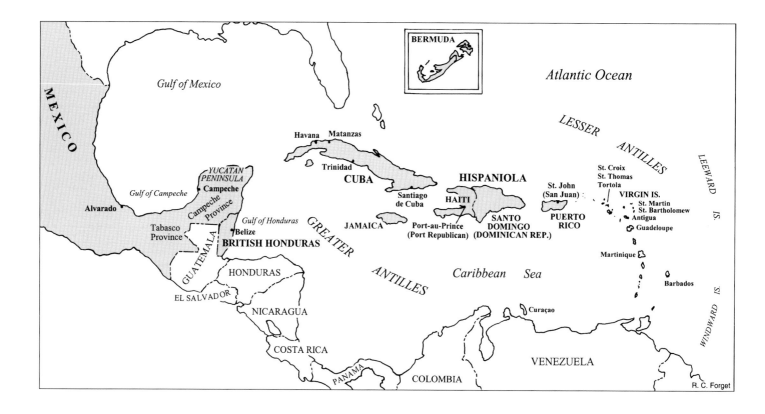

MAP 7 Caribbean and Central American destinations of American Windsor furniture cargoes, 1801–1840

pers were active. A November 1804 notice of Jay Humeston, a transplanted American in Nova Scotia, alerted captains bound for the West Indies that he had chairs available for exportation "by the dozen or by the gross." By midcentury, when large factories were replacing small shops, sizable markets were critical to business. At Portland, Maine, Walter Corey still found one of his two best markets in the West Indies at a time when William Tweed of New York advertised chairs for the "Spanish and West Indian Markets."[142]

Havana and Santiago de Cuba were the leading American chair markets on the island of Cuba before the War of 1812, with Trinidad on the southern shore an occasional destination. Again many chairmakers from Philadelphia participated directly in the trade. Chair lots generally ranged in size from about one to twelve dozen, some accompanied by one or more settees, although there is record of larger consignments, such as the thirty dozen chairs exported on April 1, 1809, by Anthony Steel in the ship *Columbus*. The substantial trade in unassembled chairs is well illustrated in the size of some cargoes. George Halberstadt was particularly active. One hundred dozen (1,200) chair bottoms accompanied his largest shipment of turnings in March 1809 on the brig *Isabella*. The same vessel carried a similar consignment containing 1,130 chair seats from another shipper, and the captain himself ventured ten dozen chairs. Stated Windsor prices are variable, ranging from a low of $1 to a high of $1.93, no doubt reflecting both construction features and degree of ornamentation. Accounts of William Trotter, a merchant of Philadelphia, permit close examination of a typical cargo. On March 16, 1807, Trotter in association with chairmaker George Halberstadt placed on board the schooner *Republican* for consignee George Alcorn of Havana a box containing "4 large mahogany dining tables" and two containers enclosing 106 chairs and two settees, as follows:

3 dozen small chairs	$36
2 dozen round back ditto [bow-backs]	30
3 dozen double bowed ditto [square-backs]	60
½ dozen single d[itt]o ditto [square-backs]	9

| 4 arm ditto | 10 |
| 2 Settees double d[itt]o | 24[143] |

The continuing marketability of the bow-back chair in the opening years of the nineteenth century is no surprise, since this round-back pattern was produced in huge numbers, and demand would have continued for the purpose of augmenting sets purchased earlier (fig. 4-15). At this date leg turnings were grooved to form four rather than three "bamboo" segments, and box-style stretchers replaced the older H-plan bracing system. On the same voyage to Havana the *Republican* carried eighty-six chairs and seven settees shipped by William Haydon. A manifest of merchandise shipped in 1805 from Salem, Massachusetts, to Havana lists consignments of furniture by eight local craftsmen, among them the chairmaker-cabinetmaker James Chapman Tuttle, who supplied ten cases of furniture, each marked on the outside with his initials "I*C*T." There is no indication, however, whether any case contained Windsor chairs.[144]

Only single references document the chair trade to Haiti and Santo Domingo. One cargo was shipped by Robert Taylor of Philadelphia, whose double-bow chair of figure **4-24** is illustrative of the new square-back styles that became fashionable after 1800. Nine cargoes entered Puerto Rico through 1812, with the port of Saint John (San Juan) mentioned several times. The William Trotter Company was responsible for a February 1812 shipment to San Juan comprising Windsors and a quantity of cloth on the schooner *Phoebe and Jane.* Instructions to the supercargo directed that he use the proceeds from the cloth sale to purchase a "new crop [of] green coffee" and stated that "the proceeds of the 6 doz. chairs will also have a separate Invoice." George Halberstadt probably supplied the chairs. Records for April 9, 1810, document the craftsman's sale of "8 Dozen Winsor Chairs / 10 Arm Do" to the company for $150.50. The seating was shipped two days later on the schooner *Active Trader* by Nathan Trotter, a member of the firm, who added a $3 freight charge.[145]

A single shipment of two dozen Windsors in 1806 from Philadelphia represents the Jamaican trade, while port records for Bermuda in 1809 list arrivals of the schooner *Mercator* from Bath, Maine, and the sloop *Argo* from New Haven, Connecticut. Both vessels carried provisions and "chair stuff." The seating cargo of the *Argo* was thirty boxes and "800 chair & Settee Bottoms."[146]

Trade in the upper Caribbean approached the prewar level soon after the War of 1812, and by 1819 area commerce expanded again to Hispaniola. Although years of turmoil on the island had destroyed the sugarcane crop, the coffee culture survived. A sheet of "Prices Current" printed in English at Havana on March 29, 1816, gives the wholesale value of Windsor chairs in Cuba as $22 the dozen but indicates that the commodity was subject to a duty of $37. The generally high valuations for Windsors in manifests for the island appear to reflect this charge. Although trade was good in the upper Caribbean, direct participation by chairmakers at Philadelphia decreased substantially after the war. Robert Gaw produced one cargo, and newcomers John Wall and Philip Halzel each initiated another. A few fancy-chair makers ventured cargoes. Only Joseph Burden pursued this market with vigor, shipping both framed and unframed Windsors. His largest recorded cargo consisted of nine dozen chairs and three settees sent in October 1821 to Port-au-Prince, Haiti, on the brig *Buck.* Halzel placed fourteen dozen chairs on the same vessel. The largest single shipment to the region numbered sixty-four dozen chairs carried in December 1821 by the ship *Pennsylvania.* Four cargoes for Cuba, Puerto Rico, and Santo Domingo were initiated between 1820 and 1826 by William R. Boone, a merchant of Philadelphia. The firm's patronage of John Wall suggests a source.[147]

Records from New England account for two chair cargoes in 1821 to Matanzas, Cuba, and a voyage in January 1825 to Haiti by the brig *General Jackson* of Providence. The vessel had a burden of more than 127 tons and carried a crew of seven. Its

FIG. 4-24 Square-back Windsor armchair, Robert Taylor (label), Philadelphia, 1801–7. Probably yellow poplar (seat) with maple, mahogany (arms), and other woods; dimensions unknown. *(Independence National Historical Park, Philadelphia.)* Part of a set possibly made for the director's room of the First Bank of the United States, Philadelphia.

cargo on the Haitian voyage, valued at $5,391, consisted of cotton goods, soap, food-stuffs, four dozen chairs worth $42, crockery, hardware, and gunpowder. The cotton sheetings, shirtings, stripes, and checks on board appear to have been of Rhode Island manufacture, specialties of the rising domestic textile industry.[148]

In substance the trade to the Virgin Islands was no different than that to the Greater Antilles, although there are no references to unassembled chairs. The chair-maker-shippers of Philadelphia were well represented, especially between 1803 and 1807. New to the list were Lawrence Allwine, William Cox, and Benjamin Freeman. After the war Anthony Steel was the only holdover. He was joined by Joseph Burden and by Ebenezer P. Rose of Trenton, New Jersey. The regional chair trade was centered in Saint Thomas, a Danish island, aside from three cargoes recorded for Saint Croix and two for Tortola (one from Halifax, Nova Scotia). The data for Saint Thomas fall between 1803 and 1807 and from 1815 and later because the British were in temporary possession of the island in 1801–2 and again from 1807 to 1815. Once a producer of cotton, Saint Thomas successfully turned to sugarcane culture when the Napoleonic wars eliminated many other Caribbean sources. As the trade from Philadelphia suggests, it was profitable to exchange chairs for sugar. Highlights of the Saint Thomas trade include cargoes shipped independently by William Cox and Benjamin Freeman in summer 1803 on the brig *Rover*, numbering fourteen dozen Windsors; a dozen each of "Green" and "Red" Windsors sent in 1804 from Philadelphia; 437 chairs and sixteen settees shipped in three lots in 1806 by Gilbert Gaw; and William Haydon's sixty-two "Fancy Gilt Chairs" exported the same year. Shipping returns for Saint Thomas from 1808 to 1810, when the island was in British hands, document the receipt of large chair lots transshipped from Antigua and Puerto Rico and the arrival of others from London and Lancaster, England. In 1811 the schooner *Connecticut* from New York ventured into Saint Thomas with foodstuffs and seven dozen chairs. Merchant William R. Boone shipped cargoes from Philadelphia in the 1820s totaling forty-two dozen chairs.[149]

Collectively the remaining Leeward group—Saint Bartholomew, Guadeloupe, Saint Martin, and Antigua—received only modest numbers of chairs, and most cargoes were sent to the first two. Fewer Philadelphia craftsmen were directly associated with the commerce. Joseph Burr shipped 64 chairs and a trunk of shoes to Guadeloupe in August 1806, six days prior to placing another cargo on a schooner for Havana. George Halberstadt's venture of eight dozen Windsors and five kegs of sausages in April 1809 left for Great Bay, Saint Martin. The following September Halberstadt sent a case of furniture and chairs to Saint Bartholomew, and twenty dozen chairs from Anthony Steel arrived at year's end. In 1804 other sources at Philadelphia had provided a "Parcel [of] Ovel Back Chairs" for Saint Bartholomew and two dozen "Bamboo Chairs" for Guadeloupe. Levi Hollingsworth and Son, an old mercantile firm of Philadelphia, also directed a large shipment of twenty dozen Windsor chairs and twenty settees to Guadeloupe that year. Valuations for two lots of Windsors carried on the schooner *Amity* provide a price comparison of eight dozen "Gilt" chairs at $400 and eight dozen "Common" chairs at $160. A Connecticut adventurer from New London placed 25 "Green" chairs in the Antigua market. After the war another Connecticut vessel, the brig *Greyhound* from New London, carried 315 chairs valued at $1 apiece into Guadeloupe.[150]

Chair shipments to the Windward Islands were confined to Martinique and Barbados, French and British colonies, respectively. Some shipments for Martinique originated at New London, Connecticut. Manifests dated between November 1801 and March 1806 record cargoes such as "22 Hhds Lumber for chairs," "28 japand chairs," and Windsor or fancy chairs with settees en suite. During the same period Philadelphia contributed 458 chairs, two settees, and sixteen children's chairs. Trade with Martinique had reopened in 1801 after a period of British occupation and for the same reason closed again between 1809 and 1814. Upon return of the island to the French after the war, chairmaker Anthony Steel of Philadelphia ventured a modest Windsor cargo of "Four dozen Broad Back Chairs" (slat-backs) and "Four doz. Double [Back Chairs]" (double-rod-backs), the latter accompanied by eight armchairs. The brig *Diamond* from New London deposited six dozen Windsor chairs.[151]

The turmoil of the Napoleonic Wars disrupted Europe's provisioning trade with its Caribbean colonies, and many islands were further handicapped by trade restrictions. Under these conditions ports normally closed to foreign commerce, including Barbados, opened periodically to American shipping. The chairmaking interests quickly seized the opportunity. James Brobson, a merchant of Wilmington, Delaware, initiated a series of seven voyages to Barbados from April 1803 to April 1805. He supplemented provisions on the brig *Eagle* and the schooners *Concord* and *Sea Flower* with two to six dozen chairs, sometimes described as "green" or "bamboo." As several voyages coordinate with shipping returns for Barbados, it can be determined that some cargoes were obtained in Philadelphia and investors besides Brobson shipped Windsor seating on the same vessels. The Barbados returns further hint at the entrepôt character that prevailed in the Caribbean trade because one chair cargo on the *Eagle* was sold for re-exportation. In January 1804 "14 Hogsheads [of] unmanufactured Chair Stuff" arrived from New London, the origin of other cargoes of green, fancy, and Windsor chairs. New England vessels also entered Barbados from Portland, Maine, and Portsmouth, New Hampshire, and occasionally a ship arrived from England. The Philadelphia chair trade was modest. The brig *Tryphena* carried the largest cargo of record, comprising 166 Windsors. Within a few years war between the United States and Britain again closed British ports to American shipping, a condition that continued following the peace. The British sought to supply the islands completely from the homeland and the Canadian provinces, a policy that was unpopular in the United States and the Caribbean colonies and brought hardship to the islands, as described in 1816:

> The Colonial Legislature of Antigua has addressed a memorial to the British government in which they deprecate in strong terms the policy now pursued toward American vessels in their not being admitted to entry in any of the British West Indies. They report the impossibility of their colonies in America [Canada] furnishing the West Indies with adequate supplies and assert that the supplies which reach them through the depot of St. Bartholomew come charged at treble the amount at which they could be landed there direct from America — while on the other hand that Island is so glutted with the articles allowed to be exported from the British Islands as to produce a serious depreciation in their value, &c.[152]

Curaçao, a Dutch island near the Venezuelan coast, was but a minor port of call for the chair-merchandising interests of Philadelphia in the early nineteenth century. Nevertheless, both Anthony Steel and Joseph Burr sent cargoes in 1804 of six and ten dozen Windsor chairs. The brig *Mary* entered the same year with seating described in part as "Oval Back" (fig. 4-15) and "Double Back" (fig. 4-27) chairs. A "Settee Chare," probably large enough to seat three or four persons judging by its $12 valuation, accompanied the lot.[153]

CENTRAL AND SOUTH AMERICA

Although trade along the eastern coast of Central America filled the holds of American sailing vessels with mahogany, logwood, cochineal (a dyestuff), fruits, sugarcane, coffee, and animal skins in exchange for northern-grown foodstuffs, cloth, candles, gunpowder, ironware, and other necessities, calls for furniture were limited (map 7). Modest activity centered in the gulfs of Honduras and Campeche (Campeachy).

On a voyage from Boston in December 1799 the brig *Rover* carried six dozen chairs valued at $1 each to the "Bay of Honduras." Whether the destination was prearranged or the captain sought the best market for selling and buying is not stated. About a decade later shipping returns for British Honduras record a visit of the brig *Ambition* from Portland, Maine, with a cargo of lumber, fish and other foodstuffs, thirteen pieces of furniture, and thirty-seven chairs. Whether the furniture originated in Maine or was acquired en route in coastal Massachusetts or elsewhere is not indicated. The nature of the cargo suggests that the *Ambition* put in first at Belize, capital of the British colony.[154]

A second group of documents referencing the Central American chair trade focuses on southern Mexico around the Yucatan Peninsula. Campeche, the province or the seacoast town, was the destination in November 1805 of the ship *Indiana* from Philadelphia. The ninety-dollar valuation given the two dozen Windsor chairs and accompanying settee on board suggests the furniture was well ornamented rather than "common." Another cargo from Philadelphia for Campeche was shipped by a Dutch firm in spring 1819 on the *Eclipse*. The seven dozen Windsor chairs priced at $20 the dozen were still well above average in cost. Export records of the Philadelphia firm of J. H. Stevenson and Company, which date a few years later, shed light on the Mexican trade between 1823 and 1825/26, shortly after the country declared its independence from Spain (1821). The first voyage to record Windsor seating was that of the schooner *Iris* for Campeche. The voyage of the brig *Susan*, commencing in March 1825, took the vessel first to Alvarado, a small coastal town on the Gulf of Campeche south of Vera Cruz, where she landed three settees and other goods. The *Susan* then proceeded to Tabasco, a province between Vera Cruz and Campeche, and landed two dozen Windsor chairs directed to John A. McPhail, a merchant. The venture to Alvarado proved profitable and provided local contacts for future voyages (fig. **4-25**). The Stevenson Company's last recorded voyage of interest began in December 1825 when the brig *Emeline* sailed for Alvarado and Tabasco with a substantial invoice of furniture (fig. 3-53):

6 dozen Knock down Chairs	@ $10 p. doz	$ 60.00
4 Settees	@ $5 each	20.00
2 Bureaus	@ $18½ d[itt]o	37.00
1 Pair Card Tables	@ $18½ pair	18.50
3 Wash Stands	@ $5 each	15.00
. . . .		
1 Sopha		35.00
11 Small fancy Chairs	@ 1.00¢	11.00
1 Sopha		35.00
12 Small Windsor Chairs	@ 50¢	6.00
3 dozen with Gilt Balls viz		
1 Doz Blue	@ $18	18.00
½ d[itt]o Green	@ $18	9.00
½ d[itt]o Light colored		9.00
1 d[itt]o ditto		18.00
1 dozen light colered Chairs		10.00
. . . .		
4 Plane field Bedstead & Bottoms	@ $7.50 ea	30.00
1 Twisted field Post		8.00[155]

Trading along the Central American coast had its risks, aside from those of an economic or political nature. Tropical storms took their toll, as Spanish conquistadors had learned centuries earlier. Another threat was that of pirates, who menaced Caribbean shipping as late as 1840. Samuel Eliot Morison cites the case of the brig *Mexican* from Salem, Massachusetts, "plundered of her specie in 1832." Only the intervention of a gale "prevented the pirate crew from executing their captain's order — 'Dead cats don't mew.'"[156]

The chair trade to the Guianas on the northern coast of South America (map 8) was of modest size in the mid-1790s and dwindled to nothing for several years following British occupation of the Dutch colonies of Demerara (1796) and Surinam (1799). A brief revival between 1803 and 1805 probably was due to the prolonged war in Europe. Surinam attracted the most activity. The schooner *Charles* from Philadelphia carried fourteen dozen Windsor chairs and three settees to that market in July 1803, and another 48 chairs followed at year's end. A cargo of six dozen Windsors loaded in October 1804 in the Delaware River on the brig *Harriet* perhaps was sold in Cayenne, French Guiana, before the vessel proceeded to Surinam. Other activity is recorded in 1804 at Surinam. On May 18 the *Industry* arrived from Boston with 48 chairs, followed on the twenty-fifth by the *Performance* from New York, which unloaded seven boxes of furniture and 165 chairs. Other vessels entered from Newburyport and Gloucester, Massachusetts. Surinam records also describe the entry of seating on vessels of English, Prussian, and Dutch origin. Records for Demerara are few. In 1804 Anthony Steel of Philadelphia shipped seven dozen Windsor chairs valued at $79 on the brig *Esperanza*. A vessel from Halifax, Nova Scotia, landed a dozen chairs.[157]

The South American ports that replaced the Guianas as furniture markets were located both west and east in the future countries of Venezuela and Brazil, with token activity recorded for Colombia (map 8). The earliest references date to 1798.

Puerto Cabello
La Guaira
Maracaibo
Cartagena
Caracas
Ciudad Bolívar (Angostura)
VENEZUELA
Cayenne
COLOMBIA
SURINAM
FRENCH GUIANA
ECUADOR
BRITISH GUIANA
(DEMERARA)
PERU
BRAZIL
PERNAMBUCO
REGION
Lima
São Salvador
(Bahia)
BOLIVIA
Pacific Ocean
PARAGUAY
CHILE
Río de Janeiro
ARGENTINA
Atlantic Ocean
URUGUAY
Valparaiso
Buenos
Aires
Rio de la Plata

R. C. Forget

MAP 8 South American destinations of American Windsor furniture cargoes, 1801–1840

During visits to La Guaira the ships *General Wayne* and *Henrietta* deposited 327 Windsor chairs from New York on the Venezuelan coast at a point only twelve miles from the inland town of Caracas, and that port of entry remained popular with furniture shippers for more than a decade. Baltimore followed in summer 1798 when the snow *Maryland* deposited twenty-eight dozen chairs. Activity by shippers from Philadelphia between 1805 and 1810 introduced additional quantities of seating to this Spanish provincial market, as no cargo numbered less than 8½ dozen chairs. Although a devastating earthquake almost destroyed La Guaira in 1812, the market appears to have recovered by 1822, when Colonel William Duane visited the seaport and passed along some timely advice to shippers:

> Mercantile men . . . should not send articles which are not transportable by mules, but in such boxes or packages as that two shall not exceed 250 pounds weight, which may be carried to Caracas for two dollars, more or less. . . . Articles of modern taste do not appear to advantage; an elegant sofa alongside a coarse plank table; . . . a mahogany toilette table and swinging glass with a joint-stool, the seat of which is higher than the table, are ill-assorted; and the best chair to be found anywhere is that which is called the Windsor Chair . . . very scarce in any part of South America till the revolution of 1810 opened the market.[158]

Even before the earthquake Philadelphians tapped several new coastal and inland Venezuelan markets. The first was Puerto Cabello, situated west of La Guaira on the Gulf of Triste, where the schooner *Mary Ann* deposited nine dozen Windsors following a June 1807 sailing from Philadelphia. The schooner *Courtney Norton* out of Perth Amboy, New Jersey, followed in 1810 with fancy chairs and settees. Perhaps David Alling's shop in Newark supplied the furniture. A postwar port was Maracaibo, located on a narrow strait linking Lake Maracaibo with the sea. In 1815 the schooner *Sylvia Ann* landed 145 Windsor chairs from Philadelphia. Five years earlier a first contact for similar trade was made at Angostura (Ciudad Bolívar) on the Orinoco River. Although 240 miles from the sea, the commercial center was accessible to navigation, as the tidal river at that point was more than sixty-five fathoms deep. A vessel from Philadelphia carried 142 chairs and three settees upriver from the sea, a journey that took three weeks. Only in 1821, the year of Venezuelan independence from Spain and the visit of the schooner *Gold Hunter*, was another cargo of chairs from Philadelphia recorded. Exchange goods at the Venezuelan ports were similar to those in the Central American trade. A single cargo of chairs recorded for Colombia entered the market at Cartagena, a port on the northern coast near present day Panama. In autumn 1805 John Thompson, master of the schooner *Aurora*, ventured a modest "parcel" of two dozen Philadelphia chairs on his own account.[159]

The opening of South American ports to American shipping in the late eighteenth century was a direct result of the continuing Napoleonic Wars in Europe. Normally South American commerce was carefully controlled, and American shipping was excluded. Portuguese Brazil officially welcomed foreign trade only in 1808 by order of the Portuguese regent, John VI, who fled Lisbon with the royal family in the face of Napoleon's advancing army. References to American merchantmen visiting Brazil appear in shipping papers well before that date, however. Among identified ports of entry Río de Janeiro was the most popular. Here, after sailing from New York in 1800, the ship *Maria* deposited the first American chairs of record in Brazil. The ship *Catharine* from Boston followed the next July with furniture, clocks, and chairs to the value of almost $2,000. Another vessel from Massachusetts, its destination identified only as the "Coast of Brazil," sailed in 1803 from Salem laden with furniture produced by ten furniture makers in the community and consigned by Elijah Sanderson to Jeremiah Briggs, captain of the brig *Welcome Return*. The fifty cases of mahogany furniture and "3 Cases Containing 41 Bamboo Chairs . . . on Deck" were valued at just over $2,900. Sales at Brazil totaled more than $5,000, almost a 100 percent profit before expenses for each participant. The record does not indicate who made the fancy bamboo chairs, but the list of adventurers includes the names of Richard and Josiah Austin and William Luther, all known chairmakers. When consigning the furniture to Briggs, Sanderson provided special instructions for his own merchandise and in so doing shed light on the practice of branding furniture:

> It often happens that furniture shipt by different people on board the same vessel is invoiced at different prices . . . [for] the same kind and quality and sometimes there is a difference in the goodness of the work and stock and when the whole is sold together at a particular rate for the invoice and all the different invoices sold together, it is a disadvantage to those whose furniture . . . is of a quality to have it sold together — therefore I wish you to sell mine by itself — not to mix it in a bargain with others and let me have the benefit of the sale of my own — you will find that my furniture is all marked with a brand ES on the back of each piece.

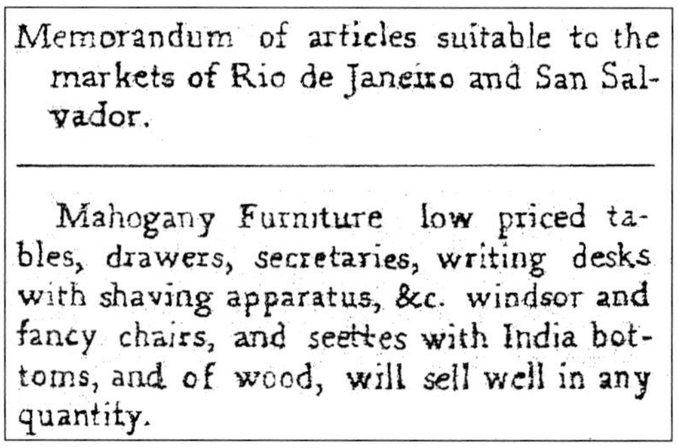

Memorandum of articles suitable to the markets of Rio de Janeiro and San Salvador.

Mahogany Furniture low priced tables, drawers, secretaries, writing desks with shaving apparatus, &c. windsor and fancy chairs, and seettes with India bottoms, and of wood, will sell well in any quantity.

FIG. 4-26 Memorandum of merchandise suitable for the Brazilian market. From *Hope's Philadelphia Price-Current, and Commercial Record*, Philadelphia, April 3, 1809.

Although Sanderson referred to cabinetware, the same purposes were served in marking Windsor seating — identification and advertisement.[160]

In sending the *Welcome Return* to a general Brazilian market, Elijah Sanderson may have followed advice similar to that written in 1809 by an American trader at Río de Janiero. The author, probably from Providence, advised making several coastal stops before arriving at Río "as one port might probably afford a better market for some particular article than the other." Among furniture forms best suited to the Río trade, he suggested "Sofas with and without Cushions & with Chairs to match." Six dozen chairs formed a suitable venture. With reference to the Windsor, he observed, "Common or Windsor chairs & Sofas, are now also abundant in the market, but when a sale is made, it is generally at a very handsome price." Furniture usually sold "at an advance of 75 to 80 per % from the first cost." Coffee, sugar, and hides were leading Brazilian commodities of exchange.[161]

Hope's Philadelphia Price-Current, and Commercial Record offered furniture shippers to "the Brazils" similar advice, suggesting that low-priced mahogany furniture and painted seating, such as Windsor and fancy chairs and settees with India bottoms (caned), were highly marketable (fig. **4-26**). Stephen Girard of Philadelphia pursued this policy, sending his ships to China by way of South America. The *Voltaire*, which left the Delaware River in 1809, carried cabinet furniture and "One Dozen Cocolico Chairs" with a fancy settee to match. The brilliant scarlet-orange (coquelicot) of the corn poppy well suited this market. Girard's ship *Rousseau* followed a year later. With twenty-eight dozen chairs on board, including black and cane-colored seating, the chair trade was lucrative. Two suppliers are identified from Girard's records. The coquelicot-color fancy chairs and matching settee came from the shop of Isaac M. Bolton (fig. 3-26), and Joseph Burden supplied another two dozen fancy chairs at $84.[162]

Still other manifests of Philadelphia origin record activity in the Brazilian chair trade: the ship *Active* departed for Río with a cargo of 51½ dozen chairs on December 8, 1809, the year Jefferson lifted the embargo; the *George* sailed for Canton via Brazil the same month carrying more than sixty-eight dozen Windsors and a settee of similar construction; the ship *Juliana* transported fifteen dozen chairs to Brazil in February 1819 and then proceeded to the Cape of Good Hope. Later in 1819 the *Waterloo* from Nova Scotia entered the lists for Brazil. In 1821, of the 270 chairs placed on several vessels at Philadelphia for Brazil, one lot was shipped by chairmaker John Wall. That was the year John VI left Brazil for Portugal, naming as regent in his stead his son Dom Pedro. At Lisbon the Portuguese assembly elected to rescind reforms carried out in the colony, leading the Brazilians to proclaim independence the following year and to crown Dom Pedro emperor.[163]

Two stops in Brazil on the way to Río recommended in 1809 by the Rhode Island trader were Pernambuco, the most easterly province, and São Salvador (also San Salvador or Bahia), a city on the coast at the entrance to All-Saints Bay. The brig *Three Brothers* left the Delaware River in 1809, sailing for "Pernambuco & A market." On board were six cases of furniture shipped by John Aiken, a cabinetmaker, and seating furniture from chairmaker Anthony Steel, comprising eight dozen side chairs, ten armchairs, and three settees. A memorandum dating about 1821/22 in the Waters family papers at Salem, Massachusetts, describes trade at "St. Salvador or Bahia Brazils," a shipbuilding center, and cites furniture in particular: "Common Windsor Chairs are generally Saleable if of high colours, Such as Bright yellow, Green, Red &c.—chairs of a higher cost, will not answer." The bright red chairs probably were painted coquelicot, the color of those shipped by Girard to South America a decade earlier. Local taste was further described in commentary about case furniture: "Bureaus will often answer, they should be of the common kind, high Polish and Handsome brasses as the Portuguese pay more attention to these superfluities, than the real value of the work."[164]

The Río de la Plata (River Plate), today forming a boundary between Argentina and Uraguay, was an area disputed by Argentina and Brazil when American traders visited in the early nineteenth century (map 8). Vessels entering the river proceeded to Buenos Aires or Montevideo to exchange American goods for Argentine products, although all was not smooth sailing. The first American vessels appear to have traded in 1798, and a brisk exchange followed for several years, primarily due to conditions in Europe. By 1802 the Spanish enforced their old regulations, and the climate changed. Some would-be traders even found themselves thrown into prison. Trading was revived about 1807, but the embargo and war interfered temporarily. Meanwhile the Argentine provinces revolted from Spain in 1810, and internal disorder followed. Records of the chair trade at "La Plata" reflect in part these varying conditions. Earliest knowledge of American painted seating in the region dates to December 8, 1798, when the brig *Rose* left Philadelphia for "River La Plata" carrying two dozen chairs shipped by the captain. The next direct reference appears in the Brazilian "Observations" of 1809, which identify as suitable articles for the market wines, Spanish oil, dry goods, cabinetware, and chairs. In exchange Argentine hides were a good commodity.[165]

Two voyages to Río de la Plata are recorded in 1810. One is that of the brig *Deborah and Jane*, which transported four dozen Windsor chairs from Philadelphia in the spring. The *George and Mary* sailed from Providence, Rhode Island, for Buenos Aires and carried in her hold a superior assortment of cabinet furniture accompanied by fancy and Windsor chairs:

3 Dozen white and gold chairs @ $3	$108.00
3 d[itt]o single cross @ $2.67 [fig. 3-32, top center]	99.00
1 ditto Brown and Gold chairs @ $2.25	27.00
1 d[itt]o Double cross @ $3 [fig. 3-32, top right and left]	36.00
72 Bent[?] Back Winsor chairs @ $1.38	99.36
72 Straight d[itt]o @ $1.25	90.00
12 Wh[it]e fancy ditto @ $3	36.00
1 Settee	18.00
96 Chairs @ $1.25	120.00
. . . .	
60 Bent Back Coquilicot Winsor Chairs @ $1.25	75.00
12 d[itt]o Yellow d[itt]o @ $1.25	15.00
72 Bamboo Coquilicot d[itt]o @ $1.12	81.00
144 Yellow, Brown, and Red d[itt]o @ $1	144.00
. . . .	

FIG. 4-27 Square-back Windsor side chair, Robert Gaw (brand "R.GAW"), Philadelphia, 1800–1810. Wood; dimensions unknown. *(Independence National Historical Park.)*

12 Black Winsor chairs @ $1.50	18.00
18 " " " @ $1.50	27.00

Comparison reveals substantial price differences between the fancy and Windsor seating. Of more particular note, however, are the invoice charges, which indicate that the furniture originated in New York rather than Rhode Island. The *George and Mary* apparently slipped down Long Island Sound to the city and picked up the cargo before proceeding south:

Paid Truckage furniture to the packet in New York	3.75
Paid labourers putting goods on board packet ditto	1.28
90 Boxes for and packing furniture	95.00
Matting chairs [wrapping with woven mats]	10.00
Freight of Cordials, furniture, etc. from New York	220.00

Whereas large cargoes were mainly for speculation, small lots often were ordered goods. Samuel Eliot Morison noted that members of several leading New England families removed to Argentina in these years to conduct business, and many remained to found distinguished Argentinian families.[166]

As North American merchants pressed farther south, it was only a matter of time before they cast an envious eye on western Latin America, known already to the sealers and whalers and traders to the Orient (map 8). One historian has noted that before there were diplomatic representatives American commission houses were located in Valparaiso, Lima, Guayaquil, and elsewhere. Because England, France, Russia, and Spain maintained armed vessels in the southern Pacific, the United states sent a warship to the region in 1818 to protect American shipping.[167]

The Girard Papers describe an initial contact for furniture sales at Valparaiso, Chile. The ship *Montesque* left Philadelphia in December 1810 bound for China via South America with almost eleven dozen fancy and Windsor chairs in her hold. Painted finishes ranged from cane color to "Red Gilt" and "Brown Gilt," and some sets had settees en suite. Among the lots were a dozen fancy "Bamboo Chairs" and a settee. Chairmakers' bills directed to Stephen Girard identify Joseph Burden as the maker of the bamboo chairs and the cane-colored Windsors with accompanying settees (fig. 3-24). The Philadelphia chair illustrated in figure **4-27** probably identifies the pattern of the cane-colored Windsors. John Mitchell supplied the red gilt and brown gilt chairs. The *Montesque* arrived in Valparaiso by December 4, 1811, when both the supercargo and the captain signed and dated an account of sales. The vessel's cargo of cabinet and seating furniture was sold, with the exception of four boxes "Presented to the Governor of Valpa," obviously a move to ensure a welcomed return. The presentation furniture included two bureaus, a pair of card tables, and two dozen fancy chairs.[168]

War with Britain in 1812 curtailed activity in western South America, but following the conflict a brisk general trade was revived, despite the risks. Not all problems were created by belligerents in coastal waters, however, as indicated by E. T. Jenckes in letters from Valparaiso to his uncle Samuel Nightingale at Providence. Jenckes spoke of the frequency of earth tremors in Chile. In a letter dated December 14, 1822, he also described an incident relative to a Chilean government decision to raise the tariff, pinpointing how Yankee and Latin attitudes were worlds apart:

> Since my last, the Government have given us time to amuse ourselves . . . as they have taken into their heads that we worked more than was for their profits. They . . . with the utmost coolness, shut up the Custom House and public offices while . . . deliberating on the best method of getting more duties. It would surprise one of our driving Yankees . . . to observe how little they think of stopping all commerce for a couple

of months, considering it a matter of little consequence & wonder at our getting into a passion about it—This state of things has been since the middle of September. . . . They do not permit a package to be carried from one town to another or to be landed or shipped. Some vessels have been waiting near 2 mo. to land & others 6 weeks for permission to sail.[169]

A later record of the Chilean trade dates to 1825, when the ship *Providence* left Rhode Island for Valparaiso carrying household goods to be deposited with the American consul for delivery to Samuel Larned, Esq., secretary of the American legation to Chile at Santiago, the inland capital ninety miles distant. Eight boxes on board contained mahogany furniture, household furnishings, and clothing. "Six packages" held twelve fancy chairs. Thomas Howard, a leading cabinetmaker of Providence, supplied the furniture.[170]

Other evidence of trade with western South America occurs in an invoice of furniture shipped in September 1826 by Levi Stillman, a cabinetmaker and chairmaker of New Haven, Connecticut, to New York for transfer to Lima. Peru had achieved its independence from Spain only two years earlier. The consignment, directed to Horace A. Augur, contained two mahogany and haircloth sofas, a dressing bureau with glass, three "Pillar & Claw feet work Tables," a "Time Piece," and nineteen dozen chairs divided between cane and wooden bottoms. "Frett back" (pierced midback cross slat) and "Slat back" (slat crest) describe the Windsor patterns; one group was "Gilded." The price range of $17 to $36 the dozen and the use of gilt indicate the chairs were shipped framed and decorated. Accompanying the boxed cabinetwork was a quantity of sandpaper, glue, and copal varnish. An additional inventory shipped to Augur on the same date included hardware, brass ornaments, shellac, and turpentine. Clearly the man was a woodworker, and he probably was a relative of William H. Augur, a craftsman of New Haven. Augur likely received the cabinet furniture in a nearly finished state and readied it for retail. Levi Stillman's statement for the 1820 Census of Manufactures, which describes a slackened export market in furniture, probably refers to the American South, although it also appears relevant to the Lima transaction. Poor trade conditions in one area provided incentive for craftsmen to seek new opportunities, and the Central and South American markets helped to fill the need. It seems doubtful that the Peruvian market was profitable in the long run, however, as by 1827 the duty on furniture was set at 80 percent ad valorem.[171]

Some vessels sailed for South America without naming specific destinations. The brigs *Hannah and Rebecca* and *Emma Matilda* left Philadelphia in 1821 for general trade in southern waters laden with thirty-eight and twenty-one dozen chairs, respectively, for sale at the best prices. As the South American continent moved toward political stability, the market increased in size, and trade assumed a definite pattern. Victor S. Clark wrote that "a single day's sailings from Baltimore in 1827, carried 12,000 chairs of all descriptions to points around the Horn, besides an equal value of mahogany furniture." One or more furniture establishments in Portsmouth, New Hampshire, named South America as a market in an 1832 schedule of manufactures. Trade to the southern continent was still profitable at midcentury, when the Poughkeepsie Chair Manufactory, which employed three hundred hands, produced $60,000 worth of chairs annually, most for shipment to South America.[172]

THE EASTERN ATLANTIC ISLANDS

Madeira remained a focus for Americans trading in African waters during the early nineteenth century (map 4). Funchal, the port of entry and capital, was a regular destination of the brig *Saunders* of Philadelphia from March 4, 1803, to May 25, 1807. The vessel made eight voyages of record, usually depositing three to five dozen Windsor chairs per trip. Two larger lots of eight and ten dozen also are recorded. The voyages fall into three- or four-month cycles, although unpredictable circumstances could alter the pattern: unfavorable conditions at sea, ship repairs, temporary commodity gluts in the island market, or illness of the captain. Joseph Y. Singleton, master during some voyages of the *Saunders*, is also recorded as sailing for Madeira and India as master of the ship *Bramin*. The ten Windsor chairs on board probably were sold on the first leg of the trip. Invoices for these and other voyages value the Windsor cargoes at $16 to $30 the dozen, a broad range that reflects complexity of construction and quality of finish. The ship *Elizabeth*, which sailed for Madeira on July 29, 1809, carried three hundred chairs, the largest cargo of record.[173]

When Edward Carrington, merchant of Providence, pursued business in African markets after the War of 1812, his brig *Vipor* may have traveled by way of Madeira. Aboard in 1818 were ten "yellow gilt" and a dozen "green gilt" Windsor chairs consigned by Thomas Howard, Jr., a furniture maker known to have imported painted seating from Tunis and Nutman of Newark, New Jersey.[174]

Other eastern Atlantic markets of the late eighteenth century remained occasional destinations for chair-laden vessels during the early 1800s (map 4). The brig *Superior*, which carried chairs made by Robert Taylor of Philadelphia (fig. 4-24) to Madeira in 1810, continued to Teneriffe in the Canary Islands and may have deposited seating in that market as well. Sometimes foreign vessels carried Windsor chairs in their return cargoes. For example, the Spanish ship *Eugenia* on a voyage from Philadelphia to Teneriffe in 1811 put into the port of Charleston "in distress," necessitating the sale of her cargo, which included Windsor chairs and a settee originally intended for a consignee or general market in the Canaries. Earlier the schooner *Friendship*, clearing from Philadelphia, voyaged to the Cape Verdes, where stops at the islands of Saint Iago and Mayo likely disposed of three dozen Windsors. A late island contact is recorded in the papers of the Waters family of Massachusetts. John Clifton, owner of the brig *Syren*, shipped furniture from Boston on November 8, 1841, comprising 665 chairs, two cases of clocks, twelve bedsteads, and twelve stands and tables.[175]

EUROPE: THE LATE EIGHTEENTH AND EARLY NINETEENTH CENTURIES

References to painted chairs placed on vessels bound for European ports are rare (map 9), nor is there any assurance that these cargoes actually reached their stated destinations. During long voyages trading vessels commonly made one or more stops to take on supplies or pick up and discharge portions of their cargoes. Sometimes the choices were left to the captain, who might chance upon news about profitable markets. American customhouse records identify two southern Spanish ports as the destinations of chair-laden vessels. The Spanish ship *Saint Juan Bautista* cleared New York on October 6, 1795, for Málaga, a Mediterranean city east of Gibraltar, with "Twelve Windsor Chairs" on board. The captain may have slipped down the American coast to the Carolinas to pick up a cargo of naval stores before making the Atlantic crossing, and once out at sea he may have stopped in the Azores or at Madeira. In any of these locations he could have exchanged the chairs for specie or another commodity. David Callaghan of Philadelphia, who was responsible for the freight of the schooner *John* on its outward voyage to Cádiz in July 1797, collected a varied cargo, ranging from barrel staves to pine boards, rice, flax, and two dozen Windsor chairs. After loading, the *John* probably headed eastward, and Madeira was a likely stop en route. Only the previous year Callaghan had shipped Windsor chairs on consignment to the island. The staves when assembled as containers perhaps transported the wine of Madeira or Cádiz. Still another small lot of Windsors bound for "Cadiz & a market" left Philadelphia in December 1802 on the ship *Maria*.[176]

A manifest listing a dozen chairs boarded on the *Lady Washington* of Boston

for Amsterdam in 1791 is the sole contemporary record of painted seating for that European commercial center, although the vessel could have sailed north or south along the New England coast to deliver the chairs locally before heading out to sea. As early as December 14, 1784, the Danish-registered brig *Goodlookout* loaded food-stuffs, plows, wine, gin, salt, and "26 doz chairs, 4 Settees" at Philadelphia for a voyage to Hamburg. In view of the size of the furniture cargo, there is good reason to believe that the American or Canadian coast provided the market. Still, opportunities for direct interaction with German ports, and specifically Hamburg, became common at the close of the eighteenth century. Charles N. Buck, an emigrant from Hamburg to Philadelphia in 1797 and a successful merchant in German goods, later described the commercial scene at the turn of the century:

> The trade with Hamburg was never more flourishing. The continued French revolution, prevented direct [German] trade with British as well as French or Spanish colonies. The United States was filled with colonial produce, and immense numbers of vessels from Hamburg & Bremen were dispatched to the United States. Baltimore seemed at the time to gain a pre eminence of the linen trade. I remember that I have seen in the years 1798 & 1799 as many as 24 vessels from Hamburg and Bremen, all in port at once, which had arrived full of cargoes of German linens, to new establishments in Baltimore.[177]

There were many opportunities for German shipmasters to carry American Windsor chairs to the homeland. Plank-bottom seating was not native to northern Germany, and the novelty of the form may have intrigued more than one mariner. The euphoria generated by German commerce was short-lived, however. As Buck

noted, the Elbe River was blockaded after 1800, and trade became almost impossible. In time peace returned to the Continent, and commercial ties were reestablished. Confirming that German-American trade encouraged some exportation of American Windsors is a remark by a German schoolmaster who lived in Pennsylvania from 1822 to 1825. On returning to northern Germany via Hamburg, Johann Heinrich Jonas Gudehas commented about American furniture: "One has a kind of wooden chair on which the seat is made of one single piece of wood which is so fashioned that one sits on it especially comfortably and which are so light that one can ... carry two of the same in each hand. A distinguished businessman in Hamburg had half a dozen of such chairs brought ... with him from Philadelphia which I saw during the unloading of the ship in Hamburg."[178]

The single reference to American seating exported to England probably is an isolated example. In correspondence with the merchants Charles Humberston and Company of Liverpool in October 1828, the firm of John Doggett and Company at Boston, looking-glass manufacturers, noted:

> In the morning we shall have put on board the Amethyst, in charge of the mate of said vessell, a Rocking Chair ordered by Mr S. Frodsham. The price of the Chair will be 22 dollars, the same as the other. ... Mr Hancock feels uncertain whether the curve of the back will exactly suit, but if it does not suit in every respect, you will please return it or sell it on his account, and any alteration he [Mr. Frodsham] may suggest shall be strictly attended too [*sic*] in the execution of another one.[179]

The Mr. Hancock of the letter probably was William Hancock, an upholsterer and furniture dealer of Boston. Reference to the chair's back curve and the price of $22 suggests the rocker was tall and bore stuffing throughout—the seat, the arm tops and panels, and the entire back. A general model exists in the rocking chair of figure 4-28, dated between 1829 and 1833 through Hancock's label address. The hybrid design clearly exhibits Windsor construction from the wood seat down. Above the plank the "scroll elbows" (arms) update a pattern published in 1811 in the second supplement to the *London Chair-Makers' and Carvers' Book of Prices*. That pattern with the scroll resting directly on the side seat rails was duplicated in the 1817 *New-York Book of Prices*. Later the *London Chair-Makers' ... Book of Prices* for 1823 modified the design by introducing the turned "stump" found here. The chair back, here stripped of its fabric, is basically a high Windsor-style support complete with six long, contoured spindles, flattened posts to receive upholstery tacks, and a rectangular tablet top with forward "wings" to accommodate a head roll that retains its stuffing of curled horsehair. The irony of this American rocking chair that combines formal, fancy, and Windsor features partly inspired by English design is its placement in a domestic British setting. The attraction may have been the tall reclining feature of the stuffed contoured back and the relatively sophisticated interpretation of the form, permitting its use in the parlor as well as the bedroom.[180]

THE PACIFIC AND THE FAR EAST

Another instance of differences between stated destinations and actual markets occurs in clearances for "the North West Coast of America," a region inhabited by the primitive Nootka Indians. The first American voyage to this region began in 1787 when captains Gray and Kendrick of the ship *Columbia-Redidiva* and sloop *Washington* sailed from Boston on a trip sponsored by merchant Joseph Barrell and associates. Island stops for provisioning included Saint Iago in the Cape Verdes, the Falklands, and Juan Fernandez off the coast of Chile, all potential sites for marketing trade goods. Addressing the hazards of navigation, Barrell cautioned the captains to keep a sharp eye out for the Spanish at Juan Fernandez and to be cautious of the "indraft of wind that Blowes in on the Coast" when sailing north because of the many islands in their path and the danger of shoals as far north as the Californias. At Nootka Sound (Vancouver Island) Barrell's instructions were to "purchase as much furs as possibal of the Native and in perticular the Sea otter." These were the prized trading goods for Canton, the ultimate destination of the vessels. The Northwest Indians happily exchanged their pelts for firearms, ammunition, chisels, blankets, and items pleasing to the eye, such as copper bangles and pearl shells, which they called "riches." The voyage established for the Americans a pattern of trading furs for the luxuries of the Orient—teas, silks, nankeens, and porcelains. The voyage also created new opportunities for furniture manufacturers and shippers to provide goods for trade along the way, as a vessel provisioned or exchanged one cargo for another at a profit. Although Boston led the way in the Northwest trade, other cities soon followed.[181]

Particularly intriguing are cargoes of the ships *General Washington*, a Brown and Ives vessel, and the *Tyre* recorded in 1800 during outward voyages from Providence, Rhode Island, to "the North West Coast of America." Each vessel carried an invoice of furniture valued at $2,656 and $3,051, respectively. The *General Washington* alone held twenty-five hogsheads of "Shaken Chairs" worth more than $700, 613 additional chairs valued slightly higher, and two "Sette Chairs" worth $10 apiece. Formal furniture consisted of twenty-six tables, eighteen desks, two chests of drawers, two bureaus, two secretaries, two sofas, sixteen chairs, ten tea urn stands, three sideboards, and a washstand. The furniture cargo of the *Tyre* was comparable; she carried 547 chairs. These were not trading goods for the Nootka Indians! The market possibilities were threefold: the Caribbean, whose premier port was Havana; the River Plate on the eastern coast of South America, where Providence vessels were active; and the western coast of South America, where "whalers, sealers, and ships bound for the Columbia River . . . occasionally put in . . . for supplies, repairs, and as much trading as could be managed." In view of the amount of furniture on board each vessel, all three markets could have been tapped. Cargoes to western South America sometimes were exchanged for copper and silver.[182]

Another prominent figure in the early China trade was Elias Hasket Derby, whose ship *Grand Turk I* was the first vessel from Massachusetts to reach Canton. She sailed from Salem in the mid-1780s for the Isle of France (Mauritius), east of Madagascar (map 5), then on to Canton. Three years and one voyage later Derby's son and namesake sold the aging vessel to a willing Frenchman at Mauritius for twice the value on his father's books. Records of a Canton voyage by the new *Grand Turk II*, beginning at Boston in March 1796, identify a cargo of foodstuffs, cloth, iron, oars, and eight dozen chairs for sale at one or more of the scheduled stops on the eastern route to China. Potential markets were the Cape, India, and Mauritius. India produced muslins and calicoes that were popular in the home market. Mauritius in particular became an important "way-station" for the "mid-exchanges" necessary in preparing suitable cargoes for Canton. In 1787 the French opened the island to American shipping on terms similar to those of their own citizens. In exchange for their cargoes American adventurers obtained coffee, pepper, hides, and East India manufactured goods.[183]

Philadelphia vessels also exchanged commodities in the eastern islands. The brig *Dominick* may have carried eight dozen Windsors in 1805 all the way to Mauritius, its stated destination. Stephen Girard transacted business there some years later. Placed on board his ship *North America* for a voyage to "Isle of France" in July 1816, with intermediate stops at Lisbon and Marseille, were foodstuffs, spirits, sheet and bar metal, tobacco, earthenware, candles, dry goods, cordage, and pine boards besides almost eleven dozen fancy chairs valued at $608. Most if not all of the chairs reached the Isle of France (Mauritius), where they were consigned to Martin Bickham, a merchant of Port Louis. More than half the chairs were painted to resemble rosewood; some had decoration of gilt or bronze. One small lot had "Scrowl" (probably "Grecian") backs; a larger group painted cane color had bent backs. Bickham supplied Girard with sugar, coffee, pepper, and ninety-one ebony logs. In a letter dated January 20, 1817, Bickham commented that the chairs were high priced for the island market, which by that time was under British rule. From Isle of France the *North America* proceeded to the neighboring island of Bourbon (now Réunion), then on to India and Batavia.[184]

Batavia (present day Jakarta, Java) first received visits from American merchantmen after the Revolutionary War. Elias Hasket Derby sent the *Astrea* in 1789 on her way to Canton. Thomas Handasyd Perkins, the supercargo, later founded his own merchant empire. Activity by Philadelphians commenced after 1800. When the ship *Camilla* sailed from the Delaware River for the East Indies on April 15, 1805, she carried two dozen "Lacqurd ware Chairs" (japanned) and two settees to match, all valued at $185. The *Sally and Hetty* followed a year later with a dozen japanned armchairs. Seventeen "Setts" of fancy chairs and five dozen Windsors were on board the ship *Bramin* when she sailed on May 30, 1807, for Batavia, although some freight probably was sold along the way. William Haydon, a chairmaker of Philadelphia, supplied seating furniture valued at $678.40 for the brig *Hyperion* on a voyage to Batavia in 1818 sponsored in part by merchant Robert Waln, Jr.[185]

Inland Distribution and the Dissemination of Furniture Design

THE EIGHTEENTH CENTURY

Considerably less is known about the movement of furniture from production centers to inland points than about seaborne trade, as these goods were not subject to registration at a customhouse. Within the radius of a short wagon trip, out-of-town deliveries were common via the consumer's or producer's vehicle or a hired conveyance. When available, local water transport usually was cheaper than land carriage and provided greater range. The rivers and bays of the East Coast afforded good opportunities for local distribution: from the Potomac and Chesapeake to the Delaware; from the Hudson and eastern Mohawk to Long Island Sound; from Narragansett Bay to the Connecticut River. Chairs transferred from one community to another could influence production in their new location. Large cities such as Philadelphia and New York supplied a sizable regional territory, a circumstance well documented in a portrait of Colonel Elie Williams executed in 1789 by Charles Willson Peale (fig. **4-29**). The young man, who served as clerk of the court for Washington County, Maryland, at its center in Hagerstown, is seated in a fan-back Windsor side chair that originated in Philadelphia. Williams probably ordered the chair, likely one of a set, during a visit to Philadelphia or through a factor. The delivery method from Philadelphia was either by sailing vessel to Baltimore, where wagons forwarded the furniture to Frederick and beyond, or by wagon west from Philadelphia over the Great Wagon Road through Lancaster and York then south to Frederick or Hagerstown.

Craftsmen in second-size communities operated in much the same way but on a more limited scale. At Wilmington, Delaware, in 1789 Sampson Barnet welcomed "orders from the country," complying "at the shortest notice . . . the work done on the most reasonable terms." When fellow craftsman Israel Stalcup first manufactured Windsor chairs a decade later, he too solicited "commands from the country," advising that orders could be "left at Thomas Spackman's, junr. near the Friends' Meeting-House," a central location known to Wilmington-area residents. Alexander Walker of Fredericksburg, Virginia, promised rural customers to take "every possible care . . . to convey Furniture without injury," and across the state at Lynchburg, William

Dicks guaranteed rural customers chairs framed "in a neat and masterly manner," according to his usual standards.[186]

Craftsmen who migrated from one area to another often carried patterns with them. Thus bits and pieces, if not whole designs, emerged in new environments. Philadelphia design spread north and south. John Biggard removed to Charleston, South Carolina, before the Revolution; William Cocks followed late in the century. Ephraim Evans made "Philadelphia" chairs in Alexandria, Virginia, before 1790, and Michael Murphy framed chairs in Norfolk from parts shipped from Philadelphia. David and Samuel Moon of Bucks County, Pennsylvania, were influenced by fashions from Philadelphia even before they worked in the city. Samuel further interacted with consumers in nearby Chester County during a brief residency, and David made several business trips to Charleston. David Stackhouse served an apprenticeship in Philadelphia in the 1770s and then returned to Bucks County to practice his trade. Andrew McIntire, active in Chester County in the same period, later went to Philadelphia before migrating to Pittsburgh late in the century. His one known Pittsburgh chair duplicates a rare Philadelphia pattern. George Young left the city in 1798 to practice chairmaking downriver at Wilmington, Delaware, two years after

Thomas Crow had removed farther south to Baltimore. Even before the Revolution two Windsor craftsmen with experience in Philadelphia emigrated to New York City. John Kelso and Adam Galer illustrated their advertisements of 1774 with cuts of fashionable Windsor chairs in Philadelphia patterns. After the war John Sprosen also left Philadelphia for this rising city on the Hudson, although his marked chairs indicate that he soon fell in step with emerging chair design in the "New York style."[187]

The influence of New York was particularly strong in northern New Jersey. Several craftsmen moved back and forth, among them Joseph Hampton, partner in the New York firm of Hampton and Always in the mid-1790s, and Isaac Kitchell from Elizabeth. Several men moved north into West Chester County, New York, after gaining experience in New York City. Gabriel Leggett, Jr., left in 1793 for White Plains and David Coutant in 1798 for New Rochelle. The city also *attracted* craftsmen. Sometime after 1786 Joseph Vail moved from Millbrook in the Hudson Valley. Craftsmen from New York and New Jersey also migrated to New England. Stacy Stackhouse moved from New York City to Hartford, Connecticut, in 1784, and Alpheus Hewes left Salem, New Jersey, before 1787 for New Haven. In 1795 Stackhouse relocated again — to Claverack, New York, south of Albany. Omar Boden of Burlington, New Jersey, later pushed farther west, settling at Cooperstown.

Other removals occurred in Connecticut. In 1799 Thomas Cotton Hayward left Pomfret for Boston and Charlestown, although he returned to his native state in the mid-1820s after retiring from business. Lewis Sage and William Shipman of Middletown moved up the Connecticut River in the 1790s to Northampton and Hadley, Massachusetts, respectively. At the turn of the century Shipman's nephew Henry Titus Shipman migrated from Saybrook on the Connecticut to Coxsackie on the Hudson, where he constructed Windsor chairs that are hybrids of Connecticut and New York design. Joseph Adams divided his career between Litchfield and Boston during the 1790s at a time when Julius Barnard of Northampton, Massachusetts, found local competition challenging, prompting him to move in 1801 to Hanover, New Hampshire. Eventually he pushed on to Montreal. Samuel Hemenway's motivation for leaving Shrewsbury, Massachusetts, about 1792 for Shoreham, Vermont, near Lake Champlain, was to join other family members who had settled there.[188]

Migrating craftsmen usually capitalized on their backgrounds to establish themselves in new locations. Training or experience in a major production center had its impact. Oliver Pomeroy of Northampton advertised in 1795 that he had worked for two or three years in Philadelphia, whereas Julius Barnard informed local consumers that previous experience had placed him "with the most distinguished workmen in New York." Chairs exported from major production centers influenced design well beyond the region of manufacture. Chairmaking in Philadelphia had a strong impact on Boston design. As early as 1789 William Blake compared his product with Windsor seating from Philadelphia. A few years later Samuel J. Tuck announced that his work was "as well executed as that which arrives from Philadelphia or New-York." Fellow townsman William Seaver proclaimed he could "make as good work, as can be imported from any place whatsoever" and lived up to that claim. His work, especially that produced while in partnership with Nathaniel Frost, achieved a high level of excellence in craftsmanship and design. In neighboring Salem customers of James Chapman Tuttle pressed him "for chairs made in the Philadelphia style," which he was able to supply by August 1796. Influence from New York was especially strong in eastern Connecticut and Rhode Island. Allyn and Huntington of Norwich priced their chairs "as cheap as can be had from New-York or else where." Chairmaker Daniel Lawrence of Providence took another tack and merchandised his product as "beautifully painted, after the Philadelphia mode."[189]

PL. 21 Shaped-tablet-top Windsor side chair (one of six with matching settee), central Pennsylvania, 1850–70. Yellow poplar (seat); H. 33¹⁄₁₆", (seat) 17¹⁵⁄₁₆", W. (crest) 17", (seat) 15⅝", D. (seat) 14⅝"; original surface paint and decoration; foot-glides modern. *(Collection of Eugene and Vera Charles; Photo, Winterthur Museum.)*

PL. 22 Roll-top Windsor side chair in fig. 5-25 (one of pair), eastern New York State or western New England, ca. 1824–25. White pine (seat); original surface paint and decoration. *(Collection of Claire and Ridgley Cook; Photo, Winterthur Museum.)*

PL. 23 Detail of crest of balloon-back Windsor side chair (one of pair), Pennsylvania, 1855–70. Yellow poplar (seat); original surface paint and decoration. *(Private collection; Photo, Winterthur Museum.)*

PL. 24 Detail of crest of rounded-tablet-top Windsor side chair, Walter Corey (stencil), Portland, Maine, ca. 1844–55. Basswood (seat) with beech and birch; original surface paint and decoration. *(Collection of the Maine State Museum, Augusta. Gift of Earle G. Shettleworth, Jr.)*

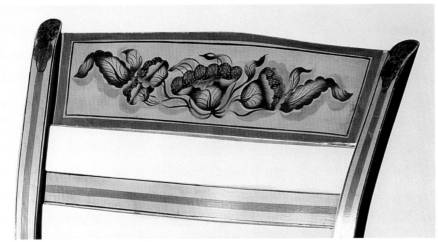

PL. 25 Detail of upper back of slat-back Windsor side chair (one of four), Silas Buss (brand), Sterling, Mass., ca. 1820–27. White pine (seat); original surface paint and decoration. *(Courtesy of the Marblehead Museum & Historical Society, Marblehead, MA; Photo, Winterthur Museum.)*

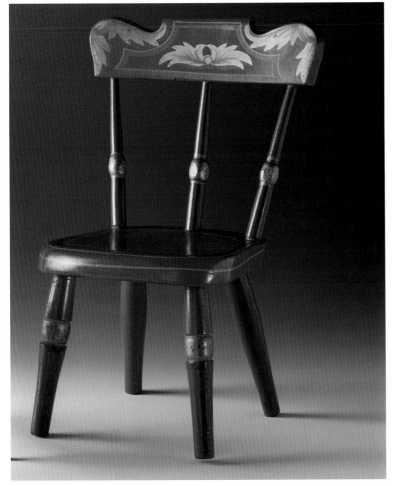

PL. 26 Miniature shaped-tablet-top Windsor side chair, Pennsylvania, 1855–65. Yellow poplar (seat); H. 15⅛", W. (crest) 10½", (seat) 8", D. (seat) 8"; original surface paint and decoration. *(Collection of Richard S. and Rosemarie B. Machmer; Photo, Winterthur Museum.)*

PL. 27 Boston-type Windsor rocking chair, western New England or New York State, 1840–50. Mahogany (arms) and other woods; H. 41½", seat 15⅝", w. (crest) 25¾", (arms) 25¼", (seat) 21¼", D. (seat) 21½"; original surface paint and decoration. *(Formerly Hitchcock Museum; Photo, Winterthur Museum.)*

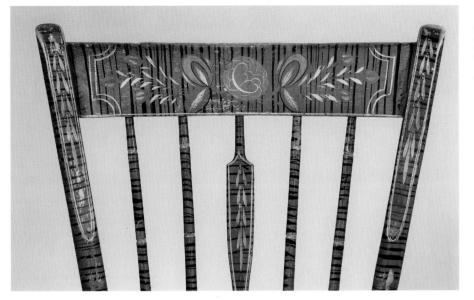

PL. 28 Detail of upper back of slat-back Windsor side chair, eastern Pennsylvania, 1820–25. Yellow poplar (seat); original surface paint and decoration. *(Collection of Richard S. and Rosemarie B. Machmer; Photo, Winterthur Museum.)*

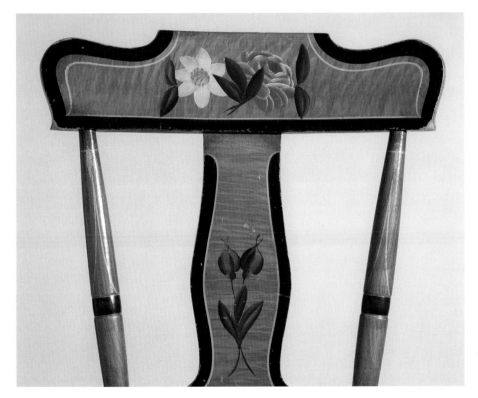

PL. 29 Detail of back of shaped-tablet-top splat-back Windsor side chair (one of six), Pennsylvania, 1850–70. Yellow poplar (seat); original surface paint and decoration. *(Collection of Richard S. and Rosemarie B. Machmer; Photo, Winterthur Museum.)*

PL. 30 Detail of crest of slat-back Windsor side chair, Pennsylvania, probably Lancaster or Lebanon counties, 1820–35. Yellow poplar (seat); original surface paint and decoration. *(Collection of Eugene and Vera Charles; Photo, Winterthur Museum.)*

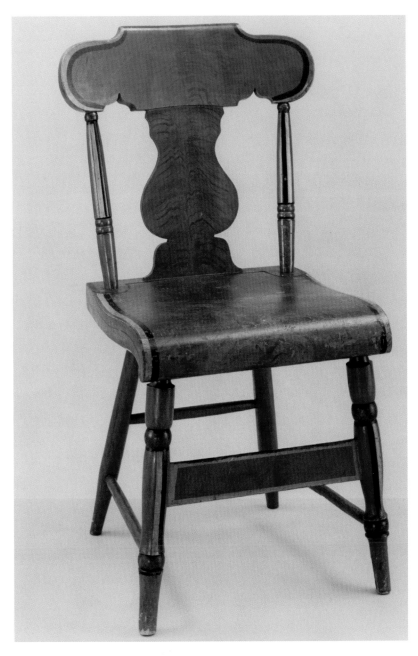

PL. 33 Shaped-tablet-top splat-back Windsor side chair, Baltimore or adjacent southern Pennsylvania, 1840–50. H. 33¼"; original surface paint and decoration. *(Abby Aldrich Rockefeller Folk Art Museum, Colonial Williamsburg Foundation, Williamsburg, VA, acc. 1972.2000.3.)*

PL. 34 Detail of seat of bow-back Windsor side chair (one of six), Connecticut–Rhode Island border region, ca. 1797–1805. White pine (seat) with birch and ash (microanalysis); original surface paint and decoration. *(Courtesy, Winterthur Museum, Winterthur, Del., acc. 69.1563.2.)*

PL. 35 John Brewster, Jr., *Comfort Starr Mygatt and His Daughter Lucy*, Danbury, Conn., 1799.
Oil on canvas; H. 54″, W. 39¼″. *(Photograph Courtesy of Sotheby's, Inc. ©1988.)*

The Middle Atlantic Region

Information amplifying the patterns and scope of inland trade and the assimilation of seating styles from region to region is more plentiful for the nineteenth century. North, south, and west of Philadelphia chairmakers in small communities kept an eye on developments in that major chairmaking center, then constructed comparable seating for local consumption. Storal Hutchinson of Bucks County and John McClintic of Chambersburg, Franklin County, produced chairs in the new square-back styles from Philadelphia at the beginning of the century (fig. 4-27). Burchall and Wickersham and Joseph Jones, practicing in the 1820s in Chester County, copied slat-back styles made in the city (pl. 4). Still later, craftsmen across the state imitated tablet-top designs produced by chairmakers in Philadelphia, who themselves were inspired by work produced at Baltimore (figs. 3-45, 3-46). Direct influence from Baltimore also was substantial in the Susquehanna Valley, where interpretations of the rectangular tablet embellished with gilt decoration produced many handsome examples of *fancy* Windsor seating, even though some chairmakers, like John Hastey, still claimed "long experience in Philadelphia." By the 1820s river and overland commerce from Philadelphia was supplemented by an emerging canal trade. In 1826 an estimated thirty-two tons of furniture passed along the waterway of the Schuylkill Navigation Company to Pottsville, gateway to the anthracite coal fields, and points between. By 1829 Philadelphia Windsors were being sold in Pottsville. Meanwhile, craftsmen in small communities across Pennsylvania actively solicited the country trade as well.[190]

Chairmaking in western Pennsylvania advanced considerably during the 1810s. In April 1819 George Landon, a craftsman of Erie, recorded a consignment of six chairs sent to one R. S. Reed "at Mackenaw . . . Caridge paid." Although Mackinaw in northern Michigan lies more than five hundred miles from Erie, transportation by sailing craft or steamboat was possible: west on Lake Erie to a passage along the Detroit River, through Lake Saint Clair and into the Saint Clair River to Lake Huron, then on to the northern destination. The commercial promise of Erie faded quickly after the Erie Canal transformed the lake port of Buffalo, New York, into the entrepôt for the upper Midwest. Even as William E. Willis of Erie claimed in 1832–33, "I will always have the latest fashions," he faced the facts, stating that his chairs were "as cheap for cash, as work of the same quality . . . purchased in Buffalo or any other place in the western country." South of Erie, Pittsburgh on the Ohio became the gateway to the southern and central regions of the Midwest. In 1819 when Henry Bheares advised that he filled orders from a distance "with articles of workmanship equal, if not superior to any made here, and perhaps on more moderate terms," his market, like that of George Landon at Erie, was considerably larger than those enjoyed by most state chairmakers, save at Philadelphia. Dockhands at Pittsburgh loaded riverboats with foodstuffs, whiskey, and local manufactures — window glass and bottles, cabinetwork and chairwork, nails, and farming utensils — along with dry goods and other merchandise brought overland in wagons during the summer months from Philadelphia and Baltimore. As described by Thaddeus M. Harris in 1803, the trading boats floated down the river "stopping at the towns on its banks to vend the articles." He continued: "In a country, so remote from commerce, and of so great extent, where each one resides on his own farm, and has neither opportunity nor convenience for visiting a market, these trading boats contribute very much to the accommodation of life, by bringing to every man's house those little necessities which it would be very troublesome to go a great distance to procure." Produce received in exchange was sent to New Orleans, sold, and the proceeds remitted by ocean vessel to merchants in Philadelphia and Baltimore who had supplied many of the trading goods — a domestic triangular trade.[191]

East of Pennsylvania, New Jersey was still primarily rural, its inhabitants oriented to trade with either Philadelphia or New York. A strong tradition of common rush-bottom chairmaking lingered in the country villages until well past midcentury. Local consumption absorbed most production, the surplus going to retailers in small towns like Flemington, Trenton, Freehold, and New Brunswick. Some few common chairs even entered the New York market. Windsor chairs documented to shops in New Jersey follow prototypes from either Philadelphia or New York. At Trenton the work of Ebenezer P. Rose, who trained with Benjamin Love of Philadelphia, imitated the Philadelphia product. Similarly, David Alling's substantial production at Newark, if identifiable, would prove indistinguishable from that of New York. Alling through vigorous merchandising, particularly in southern markets, overcame the competition of a major urban center at his threshold and enjoyed a highly successful business career that spanned half a century. The firm of Tunis and Nutman in Newark also did reasonably well. By 1813 they supplied Windsor and fancy seating to Thomas Howard, Jr., of Providence, Rhode Island, for retail at his cabinet warerooms.[192]

New York City was the hub of a circle of influence that extended well beyond Newark to the shores of Long Island Sound, the rivers and bays of northern New Jersey, the Hudson and Mohawk rivers, and even the Great Lakes. So extensive was the intercommunication that in 1811 Timothy Dwight, a keen observer of customs and commerce, stated, "The coasting vessels of the Hudson, New England, and New Jersey appear to the eye to be numberless." Like their neighbors at Newark, craftsmen in the "village" of Brooklyn worked in the very shadow of the City. John Hildreth opened a chair wareroom on Hicks Street in 1836 to sell cabinetware and chairs, although he continued his insurance agency and peripheral enterprises as backups. Upstate chairmakers countered the intrusion of merchandise from New York City by offering chairs comparable in pattern, price, and quality. Even so, some householders *preferred* furniture from the City. Gerrit Wessel Van Schaick of Albany purchased yellow and gilt fancy seating from Alexander Patterson, who noted their delivery mode on the bill: "Sent on board Genl Trotters sloop Columbia Capt Windell[?] 2 June 1814."[193]

Gilbert Ackerman of Albany may have given up chairmaking for merchandising by 1825 when he purchased property at the new Albany pier and basin. The city-constructed anchorage along the riverfront comprised a 4,323-foot pier parallel to the shore enclosing a basin of thirty-two acres. Drawbridges provided wagon and foot passage to the pier, and locks provided controlled access for shipping. Ackerman acquired two pier "lots" for which he paid $1,200 each, including the "privilege and franchise of dockage, wharfage, and canal tolls." Construction of the basin coincided with the opening of the Erie Canal, whose eastern terminus was just upriver at Watervliet-Cohoes. The Champlain Canal system began at the same point, giving access to the northern lake of that name and the city of Montreal beyond the lake. These were perfect facilities for a shipping merchant, and with Ackerman's background in chairmaking, seating furniture may have comprised part of his cargoes.[194]

Figure **4-30** illustrates activity at the terminus of either the Champlain or the Erie Canal. The store above the lock wall carries a sign that reads "Z. BELKNAP." Zebina (or Zabina) Belknap is listed in Albany directories from 1834 through at least 1860. The boat passing through the lock below the store carries household goods, probably personal possessions rather than new merchandise considering that the Windsor chairs have been tumbled in helter-skelter. Open boats were less than satisfactory in inclement weather. Better, though not perfect, is the tentlike frame protecting the boat in the right foreground. The enclosed vessels at the left may combine freight and passenger facilities. In the stern of the distant vessel a woman passenger is seated on a Windsor chair.

FIG. 4-30 John W. Hill, *Unidentified Town and Canal Locks*, upper Hudson River, probably Cohoes where the Erie Canal meets the Hudson River/Champlain Canal or Fort Edward where the Champlain Canal turns inland toward Whitehall and Lake Champlain, ca. 1838–50. Aquatint proof; H. 9½", W. 13½". *(Collection of The New-York Historical Society, New York.)*

Westward along the Erie Canal James C. Gilbert, proprietor of the Utica Chair Store, countered the threat posed by merchandise from New York City in the local market with a vigorous advertising campaign. In 1842 by way of emphasizing his credentials he informed readers that he had "been employed in the manufacturing of Chairs for these thirty-five years past." He further offered "a general assortment of Chairs of the latest New York patterns" and said that he employed "the very best workmen from the city of New York." As if this were not enough, Gilbert took "special care to select the best and richest wood of curled and birds-eye Maple the country can produce" for his fancy seating. His advertisement, directed to "the citizens of Utica, and his friends in the country," also advised: "COUNTRY DEALERS supplied at Wholesale or Retail." Several decades earlier John Melish had noted the potential of Oneida County when stating, "Trade with the back country is secure to a very large extent, and provisions must be for ever cheap at Utica." Even then the area supported some industry, including several glassworks, paper mills, cotton and woolen factories, and fulling mills, suggesting there also was a sizable consumer market for seating furniture. Located farther west on the canal, Syracuse was noted for its manufacture of salt from the local saline springs. Ashley and Williston operated a seating manufactory there at midcentury, and they also stocked chairs of "Eastern manufacture," referring to work produced in either Albany or New York. Buffalo, the western terminus of the canal, was growing and thriving at that date, although as early as 1817 its future status was predicted: "Buffalo possesses natural advantages for trade, equal, if not superior, to any internal place in the United States; having at present a ship navigation for 1000 miles west, through lakes Erie, Huron and Michigan, and with little expense, in improving the navigation at the entrance into Lake Superior, may be extended to a distance much further to the west."[195]

With water transportation relatively inexpensive, chairmakers along the canal capitalized on the opportunity to ship chairs to markets in the West. Nor were long distances a deterrent to commercial interests in New York City. An auction notice of April 1845 announced the sale of "the entire stock of a fancy chair maker declining business" and noted: "In the sale will be found 100 Windsor chairs, suitable for shipping and western merchants." The impact of the inland water route on New York trade is readily apparent in the state census of 1855, which lists cabinetmakers and furniture dealers collectively by county. In tracking by map those counties that reported a hundred or more operatives, it becomes apparent that they form a pathway extending up the Hudson, across the canal route, and down Lake Erie. No county without access to this water course reported as many furniture specialists. An alternative water route to the West directed merchandise from New York along the southern coast into the Gulf and up the Mississippi.[196]

New England

The influence of New York chair production was extensive in southern New England. Craftsmen in Connecticut especially were conscious of the competition for their markets, and many voiced concern in public notices. James E. Kilbourn of Norwalk, a cabinetmaker and chairmaker, stated clearly in 1823 that his furniture was "made after the N. York fashions, of superior materials." Inland at Redding, Chapman and Merrit met the competition by offering work "at New-York prices and warranted." Local markets up the Connecticut River fared no better. In 1807 Sylvester Higgins of East Haddam noted the incursions of merchandise from New York. As early as 1800 John I. Wells, a furniture maker of Hartford, had commented: "It is possible that much trouble and the extra expense, attending the purchase of such articles as he offers for sale, in New-York, might be saved by calling at his shop, near the Bridge." Benjamin Doolittle, a resident of Litchfield, met the competition in 1819 by manufacturing "Fancy, Bamboo, & Windsor CHAIRS, of every description . . . from a choice selection of materials . . . [in] the latest New-York patterns." This was the merchandising territory that Lambert Hitchcock soon made his own.[197]

The influence of chairwork from New York was no less considerable at Providence, Rhode Island. In fact, the impact of production at New York on craftsmen in Rhode Island occurred as early as the 1790s, and the urban product remained a formidable presence. Thomas Howard, Jr., and Rhodes G. Allen of Providence were importers of Newark (New York) chairs, although by the 1820s other suppliers were competing for the market at Providence. Charles Scott alluded to that fact in 1822 when he guaranteed his work "equal to any that may be bought in Boston, New-York, or elsewhere." By then Christian Nestell, who had trained in New York as an ornamental painter and possibly as a chairmaker, had seized the opportunity and settled in Providence to produce chairs in the New York style. Features originating in New York also appear in chairs made at the inland shop of Zadock Hutchins in Pomfret, Connecticut, and as far east as New Bedford, Massachusetts.[198]

In western and northern New England, Boston design had a significant impact. In a notice of 1824 Daniel Munger promised customers at Greenfield, Massachusetts, "as good work and as cheap as can be had in Boston or New York." Walter Corey repeated this message at Portland, Maine. Advertising from Salisbury in 1806, Levi Bartlett pinpointed the major source of competition for chairmakers in southern New Hampshire when offering "Windsor and Bamboo CHAIRS of the latest fashions . . . warranted good, which will be sold as cheap as can be bought in Boston, or at any shop in New-Hampshire." Indeed Timothy Dwight noted during a journey to Lake Winnipesaukee that "the trade of New Hampshire is principally carried on with Boston, and to some extent with Hartford, Newburyport, Portsmouth, and Portland."

The commercial interaction between Boston and New Hampshire is evident in the painted seating furniture of the two areas. Pierced slats, which first appeared before 1810 in Boston work, made their appearance in New Hampshire a few years later. The long rectangular medallion, or tablet, of the "double-bow" chair crest copied in Boston from chairs made at Philadelphia (fig. 5-41) occurs in the work of the Wilder family of New Ipswich. The stepped tablet crest, introduced in Boston by 1810 (fig. 3-41), was popular throughout northern New England. The Wilders made chairs of this pattern in New Hampshire, and Daniel Stewart of Farmington, Maine, framed similar seating. Among later patterns the large rectangular hollow-cornered tablet top made by 1820 in Boston was imitated in New Hampshire. Another tablet-style Boston pattern, the crown-top, was widely copied in northern and southern New England (pl. 27).[199]

Country trade was as vital to commercial life in New England as it was to commerce in other regions. Typically, chairmakers John Wadsworth and Eli Wood of Hartford promised that orders from the country or "neighboring towns" would be "duly attended to." When advertising in 1809 and 1822 Asa Jones and R. and W. Swift made similar statements at Northampton and New Bedford, Massachusetts. Jonas Child, a chairmaker of Packersfield, New Hampshire, was willing to take "many kinds of produce . . . in payment." A notice of Low and Damon at Concord in February 1816 further amplifies the varied methods of communication: "All orders by Post-Riders or otherwise strictly attended to, and every favor gratefully acknowledged."[200]

The markets pursued by chairmakers in nineteenth-century New England were varied and widespread. Some craftsmen made a living providing furniture parts to shops that specialized in framing, painting, and retailing chairs. Several accounts illustrate the scope of operations. Early in 1840 Josiah Prescott Wilder began to ship chair parts from his manufactory at New Ipswich, New Hampshire, to Edwin Stewart in New York City. The New York firm later became Wilder (Calvin R.) and Stewart (Edwin). In February 1841 J. P. Wilder noted the transport of 4,500 pieces of chair stock weighing 1,893 pounds "By freight to Boston" at a charge of $8.51. This leg of the journey was perhaps entirely by land, although wagons could have traveled through Groton, Massachusetts, and on to Lowell, where locks and canals on the Merrimack River made navigation possible to Newburyport on the coast followed by water passage to Boston. There the materials were shipped to New York on board the schooner *Jasper*, which followed a regular schedule. Carl David Arfwedson had previously noted the importance of the Merrimack to the Boston-Lowell trade, and J. P. Wilder was no stranger to Lowell, a prosperous mill town where he sold framed chairs.[201]

Inland markets for chairs and chair parts from New England extended to still other states and regions. A schedule of manufactures drawn up in 1832 by the federal government is particularly enlightening in this respect. Berkshire County, Massachusetts, was home to an active group of craftsmen who often vended their wares in neighboring New York State. As a gauge to production, two turning establishments at Lee together merchandised "90,000 sets chair stuffs" annually. Information of earlier date in papers relating to Silas Cheney of Litchfield, Connecticut, describes a brisk trade south of the border as well. When not employing horse-drawn wagons, the suppliers merchandised their wares north and south on the Connecticut River. Several shipped part of their production to furniture entrepreneur Philemon Robbins at Hartford. That community also engrossed a substantial share of the river commerce via sailing vessel, steamboat, and scow. Railroads began to take over in the late 1830s. East of the river in Worcester County, Massachusetts, craftsmen enjoyed a varied market in framed chairs and parts extending to Boston and Providence.[202]

Lambert Hitchcock and William Moore, Jr., of Barkhamstead in western Connecticut identified their chair markets as Connecticut and adjoining states when responding to the 1832 schedule. A more particular description occurs in Hitchcock's insolvency records of 1829, which list a factory stock of 1,500 chairs in the Hartford store of Barzillai Hudson and 500 more chairs with Joel Atwater and Sons of New Haven. William Moore's failure in 1830, probably as a direct result of Hitchcock's financial difficulties, identified assets comprising over 400 chairs scattered in various markets. One hundred were in transit to Philadelphia, and another 30 were in the hands of a retailer at New York. Vendors in Massachusetts in the communities of Northampton, Chester, Blanford, East Granville, Springfield, and West Springfield held the remainder. Later information following Lambert Hitchcock's business reorganization names other outlets in the home territory. The Scovel general store in neighboring Colebrook served as a distribution point for consignments to Sandisfield, New Marlborough, South Lee, and Tyringham in western Massachusetts along with New Hartford and South Canaan in western Connecticut. Philemon Robbins, a furniture maker and dealer of Hartford, was another outlet. Hitchcock himself looked over the western market in 1835 when he journeyed by horseback, stagecoach, and foot to Detroit, Chicago, and Saint Louis. During the third quarter of the century market potential increased dramatically as the national population grew and settlement advanced westward. Technological improvements enhanced production, and new developments in transportation assured access to distant markets. Chair manufacturers in Worcester County, Massachusetts, a region with superior waterpower and steam power capabilities, opened outlets around the country — in Boston, Providence, New York, Philadelphia, Baltimore, Chicago, San Francisco, and later Los Angeles and Portland, Oregon.[203]

The South and Midwest

Except for Baltimore craftsmen, southern chairmakers realized more business from local and inland trade than from exportation. Notices soliciting rural merchants are common. In 1800 William Snuggrass of Baltimore advised that "any commands from the country by land or water will be attended to — the best work will be forwarded, and the commands of such gentlemen as wish to favour him with their custom shall be executed with fidelity and dispatch" (fig. 4-31). Other notices describe the flexibility of arrangements. Jacob Kurtz of Staunton, Virginia, accepted "all kinds of country produce . . . in payment for work," and at the nation's capital David Bates proposed supplying country merchants "at a very short notice and at 90 days, adding the interest." Joel Brown made an unusual offer in 1822 at Raleigh, North Carolina: "Gentlemen in the country, who may wish to have their homes painted, and also Chairs or articles of furniture in his line, can be supplied, as he will furnish the Chairs, and take them to the distance of 30 or 40 miles either from Raleigh or Fayetteville, and paint and ornament them at the house of the person ordering them, so as to suit the room and prevent their being injured by carriage over rough roads." Inland at Lewisburg, West Virginia, Thomas Henning, Sr., anticipated a brisk regional business in February 1852 when he advertised that he could "furnish from 3 to 5 or 600 chairs per month, and would be glad to receive orders from gentlemen who want or will want a lot of Chairs, either now or in the Spring."[204]

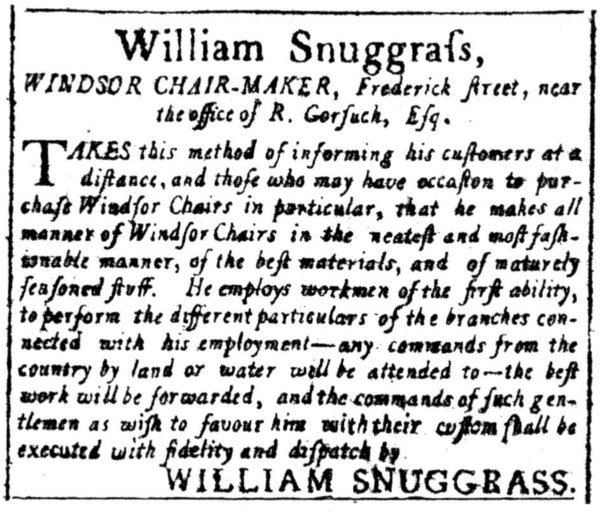
William Snuggraſs,

WINDSOR CHAIR-MAKER, Frederick ſtreet, near the office of R. Gorſuch, Eſq.

TAKES this method of informing his cuſtomers at a diſtance, and thoſe who may have occaſion to purchaſe Windſor Chairs in particular, that he makes all manner of Windſor Chairs in the neateſt and moſt faſhionable manner, of the beſt materials, and of maturely ſeaſoned ſtuff. He employs workmen of the firſt ability, to perform the different particulars of the branches connected with his employment—any commands from the country by land or water will be attended to—the beſt work will be forwarded, and the commands of ſuch gentlemen as wiſh to favour him with their cuſtom ſhall be executed with fidelity and diſpatch by

WILLIAM SNUGGRASS.

FIG. 4-31 Advertisement of William Snuggrass. From *American and Daily Advertiser*, Baltimore, March 28, 1800.

As demonstrated in discussion relating to the coastal trade, southern markets were prime outlets for northern chairs. Pennsylvania, New York, and Baltimore commerce exerted the greatest influence on southern chairmakers. Several craftsmen at Petersburg, Richmond, and New Bern focused particularly on their ability to meet New York prices. During the 1790s and early 1800s bow-back and square-back patterns from Philadelphia were influential in shaping southern design, although bamboo turnings in southern chairs are somewhat more vigorous than in the prototypes. Philadelphia remained a strong force in the chair market, as demonstrated in John Cooper's notice of 1825 at Salisbury, North Carolina, stating that "he has received from Philadelphia, the latest fashions for chairs and bedsteds, and intends to keep pace with all the changes of fashions." Many southern chairs made after the War of 1812 have mixed features. Chairs made in Virginia by Seaton and Matthews at Petersburg and Johnson and Hardy at Lynchburg have slat-type crests of Pennsylvania origin, and sometimes the seats are centered with a front projection in the Baltimore style. Chairs made in Wheeling, West Virginia, also exhibit heavy influence from Pennsylvania and Baltimore.[205]

The Ohio River, with Pittsburgh as its gateway, was the great highway of the West during the early nineteenth century. In 1811 John Melish observed, "Besides the supply of the town and country round with manufactures, Pittsburg has a vast export trade, principally down the Ohio." At first the main carriers were keelboats and flatboats, which in a good run traveled from Pittsburgh to Louisville in ten days and to the mouth of the river at present-day Cairo, Illinois, in fifteen days. Then came the steamboats, which proliferated rapidly until by 1836 there were more than 550 on the western waters. In addition wagons carried goods throughout the West. Wheeling, West Virginia, located downriver from Pittsburgh, was also a place of considerable trade. Statistics for 1851 document a workforce that included twenty-two chairmakers who produced seating furniture to an annual value of almost $19,000, a figure that exceeded requirements for local consumption.[206]

Philadelphia and Baltimore were the principal suppliers of manufactured goods to the upper Midwest, a circumstance that explains eastern influence on regional chairwork. The route between those cities and Pittsburgh was overland. The impact of New York was modest before construction of the Erie Canal because the nine-hundred-mile route from New York City to Pittsburgh was three times the distance from Philadelphia or Baltimore. The early water passage from New York followed the Hudson, Mohawk, and other rivers and passed through parts of Lakes Oneida, Ontario, and Erie, with a final passage down the Allegheny River.[207]

Farther inland Cincinnati became the great entrepôt of the Midwest early in the century. John Melish, visiting in 1811, found the city "next to Pittsburg, the greatest place for manufactures and mechanical operations on the river, and the professions exercised . . . nearly as numerous as at Pittsburg." In 1836 Cincinnati's chairmakers did an annual business of more than $94,000. Like their eastern counterparts, they solicited orders from the country, and regional competition was a concern. Cincinnati craftsmen warranted their work as "superior in taste and elegance to any manufactured in the western country" and cited a body of satisfied customers. Jacob Roll, a leading chairmaker of the city until the depression of the 1820s, sent chairs to retailers in Louisville, Kentucky. In 1831 Winthrop G. Orr and Company had "1300 chairs assorted suitable for the downriver trade." Louisville was a natural stopping place because the Ohio River shallows prevented large vessels from passing. Goods traveling beyond that point were unloaded and reshipped. A bill of lading for the steamboat *Guyandotte* dated in 1835 also documents the transport of "One Set of Chairs" eastward on the river from Cincinnati to Guyandotte, now part of Huntington, West Virginia. By midcentury the chair factory of George W. Coddington at Cincinnati had an annual production of 180,000 chairs, a measure of the vast proportions of the river trade. Charles Cist further commented on the Coddington enterprise: "All the painting and gilding to the chairs is in the south and southwest, although they find customers throughout the west and northwest. In the south they have entirely driven out the eastern article, their quality and price rendering them more acceptable."[208]

In Indiana, where it was common to accept "Country produce . . . at market prices, in payment for Chairs," craftsmen felt competition keenly from several midwestern sources. Hartley, Wheat and Company of Brookville, adjacent to the Ohio border, identified an obvious competitor in 1838 when advertising chairs "of every description, and of the latest Cincinnati fashions." Levi McDougle of New Albany on the Ohio River named another source in 1826 when stating, "He flatters himself that his work will not be inferior to any made in Louisville." The furniture trade flourished in other centers, large and small. Lexington, Kentucky, and environs could support five chairmakers and five cabinetmakers in 1817, when the city's population was about five or six thousand. Saint Louis, Missouri, which traded on the Ohio, Mississippi, and Missouri rivers, had thirty or more steamboats in its harbor at any given time during the 1830s, all with full freight. The population in 1831 stood at about six thousand, and by 1836 the figure rose to about fifteen thousand. Samuel Williams and Company of Nashville, Tennessee, met the competition in 1818 by employing "several of the best workmen from . . . shops in New-York and Philadelphia." At Knoxville in the east James Bridges announced that he "spared no pains or expense in procuring from New York, Philadelphia, Baltimore, and Washington city Workmen of the first description." Even as late as 1830 John Rudisill of Jackson profited by importing "a large assortment of WINDSOR CHAIRS, manufactured at Pittsburgh, of various patterns and colors." Henry May and Thomas Renshaw, partners in Chillicothe, Ohio, whose work was "equal to any imported," capitalized on Renshaw's experience at Baltimore by offering Baltimore-style chairs featuring "Broad Tops with landscapes" (fig. 3-68).[209]

CANADA AND THE COMPETITION OF AMERICAN IMPORTS

Previous sections have touched on the overseas chair trade of the Canadian Maritimes with the Caribbean, inward clearances of American seating at Canadian ports, and exchanges between the Maritimes and Upper and Lower Canada. Several points remain to be addressed, including that of English imports. Most current evidence derives from inference only. Jay Humeston, a transplanted American chairmaker working in Nova Scotia by 1804, spoke of making Windsor chairs and settees "equal to the best British manufacture." Whether the "British" chairs were imported articles or simply seating furniture produced by provincial chairmakers is unclear. Two years later at Montreal in Lower Canada (now Quebec), Henry Corse, chairmaker and paint seller, reproduced fancy chairs and other furniture on short notice "after any particular pattern, and warranted equal in strength and beauty to any ever imported from Europe." Military and government personnel, arriving bag and baggage, perhaps brought with them some utilitarian as well as formal furniture. Due to the problems and expense of transporting bulky goods to inland sites, however, publications discouraged British immigrants to the New World from bringing any but the most select furnishings. If "Common Windsor chairs" sold for an average 5s. apiece in 1831, as noted by Adam Ferguson, this seating was much cheaper purchased in Canada than transported from England to the Canadian wilderness.[210]

Throughout eastern Canada the impact of American seating was substantial, except in the French-speaking settlements. American Loyalists and others who sought new opportunities in Canada after the Revolution brought their woodworking skills or furnishings with them. Chairmaker Nathan Oaks (d. 1797) of Gondola Point, Saint John, New Brunswick, perhaps resided in Deerfield, Massachusetts, in 1786, and an unnamed woodworker emigrated from Rhode Island, as indicated by the character of his work that remains. Samuel Park of New England began his Canadian career in 1797 in Montreal. Migration brought other craftsmen to Canada's eastern provinces: Thomas Read to Montreal in 1803 from Boston; Jay Humeston to Halifax, Nova Scotia, about 1804 from Charleston, South Carolina; Julius Barnard to Montreal about 1812 from Windsor, Vermont; Thomas Lewis Hutchings by 1814 to Saint John, New Brunswick, from Maine; and Amos Hagget to Fredericton, New Brunswick, by 1817 from Charlestown, Massachusetts. Two examples of reverse migration date to the 1830s and 1840s when Henry Billings of Brockville, Ontatio, moved across Lake Ontario to Rochester, New York, and Samuel Church of Toronto settled near Buffalo.[211]

A greater influence on the painted seating furniture of Canada was the substantial traffic in chairs and chair parts from the United States. The impact of New York State was paramount, probably followed by that of Vermont and New Hampshire. John Melish remarked on the commerce of Vermont and Canada in 1806 when he visited New England. The value of American exports sent across the border the previous year had been $169,402. Commenting specifically on the Champlain trade into Lower Canada, John Lambert noted that most lake towns in Vermont were almost entirely dependent on the lake trade. Burlington in particular was of "growing importance." Sloops of 100 to 150 tons could "navigate with ease" the seventy miles to Saint Johns (Saint-Jean). As most of the vessels were American, "a double advantage was derived from the trade." The commerce included oak and pine timber, staves, pot and pearl ashes, livestock, provisions, and maple sugar. In exchange there were Canadian pelts, salt, and specie, but the balance was "in favor of the States." Also engaged in considerable trade with northern New England and Canada at this date was Troy, New York, on the upper Hudson. Jefferson's embargo, however, interrupted inland commerce with Canada as effectively as it halted the overseas trade. Several years after the embargo's repeal Timothy Dwight commented that a road had been opened between the upper Connecticut River and Quebec for trade.[212]

A new phase of American-Canadian trade, focusing on Lakes Ontario and Erie, began in the postwar years. An early record is the 1½ dozen American spinning wheels imported in 1817 into Niagara, Ontario. Kingston, at the eastern end of Lake Ontario, was the outlet for chairs from the inland towns of Carthage and Canandaigua, New York, two years later. From its location on the navigable Black River, Carthage had access, past Watertown, to the lake. Canandaigua's access to Lake Ontario from the Finger Lakes is noted in the reminiscences of Captain Hosea Rogers of Genesee River (later Rochester): "The merchants of Canandaigua, about 1804, cut a road to the mouth of the Genesee, which was their shipping port for western trade." Passing through the region in 1820, Thomas P. Cope of Philadelphia remarked, "From the Genesee [River] westward, the produce has been heretofore carried principally down the St. Lawrence to Montreal." Importation records for Toronto (York) along western Lake Ontario document the entry of five hundred "Chair Bottoms" and two dozen framed chairs in 1811 from the United States. The 1820 manufacturing census notes that a cabinetmaker of Erie, Pennsylvania, exported part of his production via the lake to southern Ontario, and other western Pennsylvania chairmakers likely followed suit.[213]

The commercial boom that swept across central New York following completion of the Erie Canal had a direct effect on the American seating trade to Canada. Towns and cities that sprang up almost overnight along the waterway had the advantage of tapping several markets, including the adjacent countryside, the western settlements, and the vast regions of Upper Canada (Ontario). The area attracted both new and seasoned craftsmen, many from New England. This number included members of the Robinson family, who are said to have emigrated to Rochester from Connecticut. Charles T. Robinson, like fellow craftsman Frederick Starr who advertised in 1840–41 for "orders from the country or Canada" (fig. 4-32), knew the power of printed communication. By 1851 his firm produced fifty thousand chairs a year. As early as 1829 Alexander Drummond of Toronto gave voice to the impact of American imports on production in Ontario when offering "a large assortment of Fancy and Windsor chairs warranted to be of the best quality and finished in the latest New York fashions." In the years that followed, trade in American chairs and chair parts flourished at Toronto. Between 1838 and 1846 Richard French led city chairmakers

FIG. 4-32 Advertisement of Frederick Starr. From *King's Rochester City Directory and Register, 1841* (Rochester, N.Y.: Welles and Hayes, 1840), n.p. *(Collection of Local History Division, Central Library of Rochester and Monroe County, Rochester, N.Y.)*

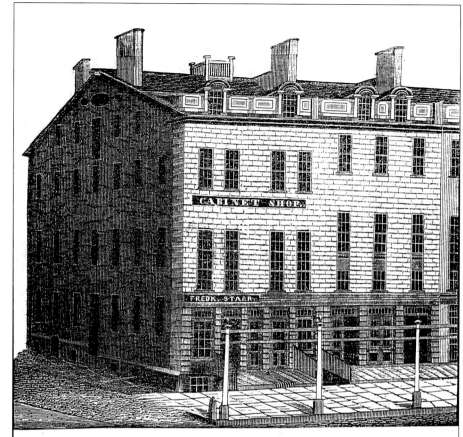

FREDERICK STARR,

At his old stand, No. 45, Main-street, near the Rail-Road, Rochester, continues to manufacture, and has constantly on hand for sale, a very large and general assortment of

CABINET FURNITURE & CHAIRS,

of the best materials and workmanship, and of the newest New York Fashions; among which are the following of a great variety of patterns and prices, viz:—

Sofas,	Book Cases,	Dining Tables,	Mahog'y Grecian Ch's,	French Bedsteads,
Tabauretts,	Bureaus,	Work Tables,	Painted Boston Rock's,	High Bedsteads,
Ottomans,	Dressing Bureaus,	Basin Stands,	do. Fancy Cane Seats,	Field Bedsteads,
Foot Benches,	Pier Tables,	Cloak Stands,	do. do. Flagg Seats,	Trundle Bedsteads,
Piano Stools,	Side & Centre Tables,	Mahogany Rock. Ch's,	do. Cottage, do do.	Cots—Cribs,
Sideboards,	Marble Top do.	do. French Chairs,	do Winsor,	Cradles; Coffins of all
Secretaries,	Pembroke Tables,	do. half French do.	Grecian Bedsteads,	sizes and qualities.

with almost every other article usually found in a Furniture and Chair Shop. Also, a large assortment of MA-HOGANY, WALNUT, HOLLY, ZEBRA & BORE WOOD. VENEERS, with MAHOGANY Boards, Plank, and Scantling, suitable for Furniture, Stair-rails, Banisters, Newells, &c., together with Hair Cloth, Sofa Webb, Sofa Tassels, Sacking bottoms, and many more articles of Cabinet Hard-Ware, Bench Screws, Hand Screws, and the best

COPAL VARNISH,

by the barrel or gallon, at a small advance from New-York prices. Cabinet Makers or others wishing to purchase any of the articles, are invited to call at his Ware Rooms and Mahogany Yard, No. 45, Main-st,, near tho Rail-Road, and examine quality and price for themselves.

All orders from the country or Canada, will be promptly attended to.

Rocheser, Jan. 1841.

in the importation of American chair "stuff," comprising "bottoms," caned seats, and "fittings" packaged in bundles and boxes.[214]

American competition for the Ontario market reached formidable proportions during the 1830s and 1840s. Chair factories from Buffalo to Utica advertised in Canadian newspapers and followed the notices with shipments of chairs and parts to dealers and craftsmen. Some firms even established outlets in Canada. One example is the Rochester company of Edwin Brown, which maintained a showroom during part of 1840 at the Royal Exchange Hotel in Kingston, a prosperous lake town near the Saint Lawrence River. The company offered a general assortment of chairs "consisting of curled maple, cane seats, scroll top with either plain or banister backs; also imitation rosewood cane bottom, gilded and bronzed with either slat or roll tops, together with Boston rocking, sewing, nurse and a superior article of office arm chairs."[215]

The competition often was disastrous for Canadian producers. Chester Hatch of Kingston declared bankruptcy in 1847 after more than three decades in business. Ironically, he had migrated to Canada from the United States. During the prosperous 1820s Hatch even opened a showroom in Toronto (York). It was he who spearheaded a petition to the Assembly of Upper Canada in 1830 after failure of an earlier proposal requesting legislative restraints on imported manufactures from America. This and other petitions fell on almost deaf ears, however. In later years Hatch returned to business with his son Wilson. Making the best of conditions, they imported quantities of parts from American suppliers, probably finding that by framing and finishing chairs themselves they could slightly undersell imported ready-made seating. Stuff, bottoms, backs, and rockers were ordered from factories at Cape Vincent and Clayton, New York, towns across the Saint Lawrence River.[216]

Oswego, New York, on Lake Ontario's eastern shore, was another source of chair parts for Canadian craftsmen. In 1843 a "parcel of chair rails" was sent to Kingston. During the next decade production at the firm of J. M. Wright, which in 1857 became the Oswego Chair Factory, reached an annual figure of 150,000 chairs. The seating was framed without glue, finished, and disassembled for shipment to customers in Canada and the American West. By midcentury Niagara Falls and Buffalo at the western end of the lake were centers of chair production, and other facilities developed as settlement pushed farther west. Detroit was a recognized competitor in Canadian chairmaking circles by the 1840s, as indicated by Robert Smith of Chatham, near Windsor, Ontario, who retailed Windsors by the set for $3.00 to $3.50, stating that the chairs were of his own manufacture and "not imported from Detroit." A decade later a resident of London, Ontario, northeast of Detroit, commented on the continuing influence of American furniture in Canadian retail circles, noting that the American merchandise comprised three-quarters of local sales and the supply did not equal the demand.[217]

In summary, from the 1790s, when the Windsor attained the status of a merchantable commodity, through the technological and commercial advances of the first half of the nineteenth century, the American painted seating industry achieved a truly national market. Improvements in communication and transportation, free trade among the states, and the flexibility of exchanging produce for manufactured articles permitted the development of systematic distribution methods and cemented business relations between the far-flung regions of the nation.[218]

Sales Techniques

DIRECT, CONSIGNMENT, AND COMMISSION SALES

The standard method of retailing chairs and other merchandise in the eighteenth and early nineteenth centuries was by direct sale or order at the shop, manufactory, or retail wareroom. The medium of exchange varied from cash to produce to services. A common supplement to direct merchandising was the distribution of goods on consignment for commission sales. The export trade to the South is a good example of this practice. The shipper placed his goods in the hands of a supercargo or sea captain to sell as he could for the best prices, or he directed the merchandise to an individual or firm at a specific location by prior arrangement. When the merchandise was sold, or in the case of large consignments partially sold, the consignee remitted the monies due, deducting for commissions, expenses, and other charges. Depending on market location and speed of travel, the consignor could wait from two to twelve months for a return — providing there were no complications, disasters, adverse economic conditions, or other problems. Bad debts of over $100 listed in 1852 in the estate of chairmaker Abraham McDonough of Philadelphia suggest that they were remittances due for chair consignments. His distribution range was broad: New Orleans, Missouri, Virginia, New York.[219]

Ebenezer P. Rose of Trenton, New Jersey, tested local consignment sales in 1807 when he distributed spinning wheels to area businesses: "the store of William Ridgeway, in . . . Burlington, and . . . Henry Crusen's near Rowley's Mill, on the Trenton and New-Brunswick turnpike road." The locations had heavy commercial and consumer traffic. Another chairmaker of New Jersey, Charles Cluss of Newbridge, formerly of New York, stocked chairs for sale at his house in 1828 and at Jasper Westerfelt's cabinet store in Hackensack. Westerfelt may have acted as an agent for Cluss rather than as a commission merchant, although the business methods would have been similar. Joseph Jones, a chairmaker of West Chester, Pennsylvania, kept "an assortment of Chairs . . . on hand at WILLIAM MAJOR's near Manor Meeting House" in Chester County. This site, like those selected by Ebenezer Rose, was along a well-traveled highway.[220]

Levi Stillman of New Haven, Connecticut, who enjoyed a good trade in cabinetwork and chairs, retailed merchandise in several ways. The local firm of Sherman Blair sold a selection of Stillman's seating, comprising settees, rockers, and chairs, on commission in 1821–22, the patterns described as bamboo and rolltop. Farther afield, Stillman established a contact with Andrew Sweeney of Richmond, Virginia, for similar sales. The chairmaker also advertised locally, commenting on the general abuse of words such as *cheap* and *cheaper* and the deceptions practiced by retailers who employed these tactics. Stillman assured customers of "fair dealing" at his shop.[221]

Lambert Hitchcock, chairmaker of western Connecticut, sold much of his production through regional dealers. In 1829 business associate John Dewey of Litchfield offered "a large assortment of FASHIONABLE CHAIRS on consignment from L. Hitchcock's Manufactory." Seating lots ranging from 500 to 1,500 chairs were also in the hands of merchants at Hartford and New Haven. The next year Hitchcock's neighbor William Moore, Jr., of Barkhamstead distributed small quantities of his chairs to local stores in western Massachusetts, and other seating was consigned in New York City. Craftsmen also worked out special agreements. One plan was negotiated in 1834 by Hitchcock with Isaac Wright, a cabinetmaker and dealer of Hartford: "Receved of L. Hitchcock to be sold on commission 24 wood seat chairs at 92. cents each at 10 per cent commission." Wright also bought "6 Fancy flagg Seat chairs" at 9s. ($1.50) apiece and received a 10 percent discount. Direct sale was the retailer's preferred method of doing business, as payment (or credit) was immediate and goods were not returned unsold. Due north at Heath, Massachusetts, Lysander Ward and Company received two chair lots in 1841 from H. F. Dewey of Bennington, Vermont, for commission sales. The profit was pegged at 12 percent for the sale of each of eighty-three "Cane seat" and forty-four "maple" chairs. The merchandise retailed for between $1.25 and $1.75 the chair.[222]

Frederick Allen constructed chairs at Essex on the lower Connecticut River in 1828–29 for retail through his brother-in-law Elisha Harlow Holmes. Along with charges for raw materials, Holmes posted debits for "Commissions on sales." One account entry covers commissions on "Sales from March 12th to April 10 — $1.56," indicating that the monies Holmes received for his retail services for one month amounted to something more than a day's pay. The figure fluctuated from month to month. At New Bedford, Massachusetts, the partners William Swift and William Ottiwell retailed "*On Consignment*—400 Fancy and Windsor CHAIRS, of various patterns and prices" along with their own cabinet furniture (fig. **4-33**). The firm probably anticipated little difficulty in disposing of so sizable a lot, as New Bedford was a principal supplier of the area's fishing villages and islands. By contrast, the chairs sold at Essex by Holmes numbered about one-quarter that figure.[223]

CABINET FURNITURE.

SWIFT & OTTIWELL have constantly on hand a good assortment of Cabinet Furniture, manufactured in the best manner, from the newest patterns.

On Consignment—400 Fancy and Windsor CHAIRS, of various patterns and prices.—Also, a few dozen German LIQUOR CASES.

☞ The public are invited to call and examine the above; all of which will be sold on the most reasonable terms. [40—tf.]

FIG. 4-33 Advertisement of William Swift and William Ottiwell. From *New-Bedford Mercury*, New Bedford, Mass., May 22, 1829.

Agents were individuals or firms who distributed the products of a second party. They were paid a fee, commission, or both. This type of business arrangement was announced in April 1813 by Tunis and Nutman of Newark, New Jersey, who appointed Thomas Howard, Jr., cabinetmaker-merchant of Providence, "their sole Agent for the Sale of CHAIRS of their Manufactory" and stated "their Intention to keep a constant Supply of CHAIRS and SETTEES, of the first quality, in Mr. Howard's Furniture Ware-House." The relationship continued until at least January 11, 1823, when Howard offered "4000 fancy and Windsor chairs of superior quality with handsome patterns 50¢ to 5 dollars." The association's long duration speaks to its success. Besides retailing the New Jersey chairs in area markets, Howard tapped the overseas trade by doing business with several shipping houses in Providence. In one case he exported yellow gilt and green gilt Windsors on a ship bound for Africa. Rhodes G. Allen, a local cabinetmaker, may have followed in Howard's footsteps. Although notices do not identify him as an agent, he stocked chairs of "Newark make" in 1824 and "Chairs of all descriptions, from the best manufactory in New-York" two years later.[224]

Barzillai Hudson of Hartford was a distributor for Lambert Hitchcock. In 1828–29 chairs in stock numbered from 200 to 1,500, and the selection included cane, flag, and wood-seat types, all "warranted well made." Several years later, as first announced on January 22, 1835, Charles Ingalls served as agent for Franklin Howe in Vermont: "FRANKLIN HOWE offers for sale at Windsor, Vermont, by his agent Charles Ingalls, a large assortment of the most fashionable Chairs, ever offered . . . in this vicinity, . . . cheap as any ever sold in this country." Howe's manufactory may have been at Grafton, about thirty miles to the southwest. Some seating arrived at Windsor unfinished, as there are entries for painting, ornamenting, and varnishing chairs under Howe's account in the local furniture records of Thomas Boynton. Boynton and agent Ingalls exchanged services as well. The duration of the agency can be gauged in part by the accounts. On November 1, 1836, Boynton debited the "Agency for selling chairs"; the following May 30 he recorded "2 days work varnishing Howes Chairs." Furniture agencies were common by 1850, as small shops gave way to large factories "where a more efficient organization and supervision of the workers and the application of machinery left old handicraft methods hopelessly behind." The manufactories employed dozens, even hundreds of workers and found their sales outlets in furniture stores.[225]

AUCTIONS AND PEDDLERS

Chairs shipped in quantity on sailing vessels often were disposed of at auction. This was especially true in the large southern centers of Charleston and Savannah. Vendues usually produced quick though sometimes disappointing returns, and too many held close together could glut the market. Joseph Walker, supercargo of the sloop *Friendship* on a voyage in 1784 from Philadelphia to Savannah, remarked on the general commercial atmosphere of the community five years before it achieved the status of a city: "Much of the business here is done by Vendues, and altogether by that way with any article that becomes a Drug, for if One Article is offered for Sale by two or three . . . people, the merch[ants] immediately cry out a Glut & will not give you half the Original Cost, because they say in a few days it will be sold at Vendue on their terms. . . . But sometimes Goods sell Very well at Vendue if they have not been hawked about." David Alling of Newark, New Jersey, used this method several decades later in 1821 at Natchez, Mississippi, although whether he realized financial success is unknown. An auction of chairs from Richmond in the inland community of Lynchburg, Virginia, in 1814 may have served principally to introduce residents to

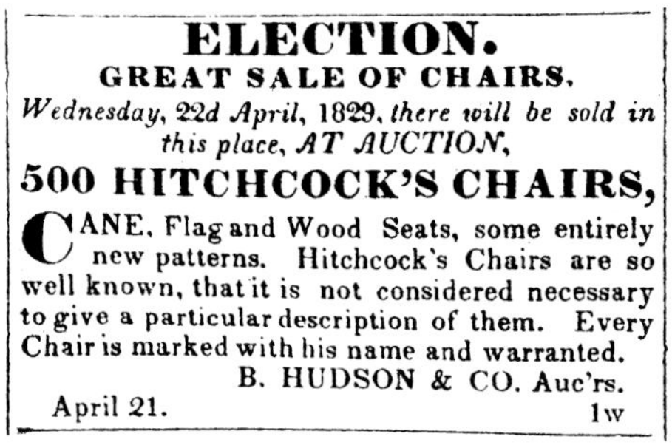
ELECTION.
GREAT SALE OF CHAIRS.
Wednesday, 22d April, 1829, there will be sold in this place, AT AUCTION,
500 HITCHCOCK'S CHAIRS,
CANE, Flag and Wood Seats, some entirely new patterns. Hitchcock's Chairs are so well known, that it is not considered necessary to give a particular description of them. Every Chair is marked with his name and warranted.
B. HUDSON & CO. Auc'rs.
April 21. 1w

FIG. 4-34 Notice of Barzillai Hudson for auction of chairs consigned by Lambert Hitchcock. From *Connecticut Courant*, Hartford, April 21, 1829.

seating made in the port city. Nathan Pierce, shopkeeper and chair dealer of Greenfield, Massachusetts, pursued similar goals a year later when he promoted a public auction in the country town of Colrain. He carefully chose a site "at the house of Charles Thompson, Inn Holder" for the sale of "one hundred good dining Chairs." At midcentury Washington G. Henning, a newcomer in business at Lewisburg, West Virginia, chose this sales method to distribute over nine hundred chairs of his own manufacture "as samples of [his] future." He wisely chose "the first day of May Court next" as the date of the event.[226]

Rhodes G. Allen held an auction in spring 1823 at Providence, Rhode Island, to dispose of "his entire stock of CABINET FURNITURE," including fancy and children's seating. His reason was to make "new arrangements in . . . business," that is, to rebuild his furniture manufactory. In 1809 Allen Holcomb of Greenfield, Massachusetts, gave notice of a vendue to dispose of "a large number of new CHAIRS." To encourage sales Holcomb extended "a short credit . . . for good security" to purchasers. By way of explanation he stated that he was leaving Greenfield and wished "to dispose of his CHAIRS, and other furniture, in the quickest and best manner." Holcomb moved to Troy, New York, where he worked briefly before settling permanently at New Lisbon, Otsego County.[227]

Because volume sales were necessary to keep his new factory in operation, Lambert Hitchcock of Barkhamstead (now Riverton), Connecticut, turned to the auction as a means of retailing mass-produced chairs in quantity. The first auction of record was on September 26, 1827, when Barzillai Hudson and Company, auctioneers and dealers of Hartford, placed "800 HITCHCOCK's fancy flag-seat Chairs" on the block. The seating was to be sold "in lots to suite [the] purchasers," who were free to examine the stock before the auction at eleven sites, two in Hartford and the others in communities surrounding the city. John T. Kenney, Hitchcock's biographer, estimated that the 800 chairs represented "about two and a half weeks production." The auction proved a success, as Hudson followed it with another in April 1829 when he offered 500 chairs. In commenting on the merchandise, Hudson stated: "Hitchcock's Chairs are so well known, that it is not necessary to give a particular description of them. Every Chair is marked with his name and warranted" (figs. **4-34**, 1-16). Still another sale of chairs took place on May 30, 1830, "in front of the State-House."[228]

A limited method of merchandise distribution, although not as common to the seating trade as to the clock industry, was peddling. In 1838 the accounts of Josiah Prescott Wilder of New Ipswich, New Hampshire, document two peddling trips. Wilder sponsored one; the other probably was an independent endeavor. Upon completion of the first trip in February, Wilder made note:

Chairs sold on a peddling excursion, out two nights	
12 chairs 4/	8.00
6 " 3/6	3.50
3 Nurse d[itt]o 4/6	2.27
2 Rocking d[itt]o 10/6	1.75
2 Crickets 1/	.33
24 Small chars	10.00
2 Table d[itt]o 4/	1.50
	27.35

The peddler may have been James Smith, Jr., whose account was debited with part of the same merchandise. In April an individual identified only as a "Pedler" purchased eighteen "Common Chairs," night and nurse chairs, two small chairs, and two crickets. He paid $13.41 in cash.[229]

About 1844 Edward Jenner Carpenter, an apprentice in the cabinet shop of Joel Lyons and Isaac Miles at Greenfield, Massachusetts, noted with interest in his journal, "Russel Warren the tin peddler was here today & bought a butternut table and a couple of rocking chairs." Another craftsman's experience with peddlers was far from pleasant. Amos Denison Allen's only known advertisement, dated April 12, 1813, at Windham, Connecticut, concentrates on the subject entirely:

> The subscriber is informed that his name is made use of in this and the neighbouring towns, by Hawkers and Pedlers of chairs, representing that their chairs were made at his shop, &c. And having been called upon to answer for frauds practiced by them, he takes this method to inform the publick, that although he makes a business of manufacturing and selling CABINET WORK and CHAIRS of almost every description at his shop, he never has sent any furniture abroad to be hawked and pedled in the streets, and shall not consider himself amenable for the frauds and falshoods of Pedlers.[230]

Payment for Goods and Services

The desirable medium of exchange was cash, either in specie or negotiable paper. The shortage of both in America into the early nineteenth century, especially in nonurban areas, led to a variety of accommodations in the transaction of day-to-day business. A description of the prevailing system was given in the 1790s by a pair of visiting Frenchmen:

> They are reciprocally furnished in the country with what they are in want of, without the interference of money. The taylor, shoemaker &c. exercise their professions in the house of the husbandman who has occasion for their commodities, and who, for the most part, furnishes materials, and pays for the workmanship in provisions, &c. . . . Each of these people write down what they receive and give, and at the end of the year they close an account consisting of an infinity of articles, with a very small sum.

When cash exchanged hands, the transaction often was uncommon enough to warrant a special notation. Amos Denison Allen, of Windham, Connecticut, recorded in 1799 that fellow chairmaker Theodosius Parsons had agreed to pay for chairs he had bought from Allen "in cash in the month of January 1800." At Greenfield, Massachusetts, Daniel Clay stated in 1809 that he accepted "most kinds of Produce . . . and Cash not refused." More often than not when cash exchanged hands it covered only part of the obligation, the rest made up in goods, produce, or services. From time to time craftsmen accepted used furniture in partial exchange for new work. John Mehargue of Halifax, Pennsylvania, allowed a customer $1 for a rocker in 1826, an exchange that helped to offset the $2 expense of a new chair. Out-and-out credit without an immediate exchange frequently required "approved security," unless the customer was well known to the retailer.[231]

The exchange of produce or manual labor for goods and services, which was within reach of most consumers, was a primary method of doing business. Grain, flour, foodstuffs, spirits, and at times an unusual item, such as "5 lb Eales" (eels), were acceptable substitutes for money. Livestock for slaughter or domestic and business use was welcomed, but the debt had to be sufficiently large. In exchange for making and repairing furniture for lawyer Tapping Reeve at Litchfield, Connecticut, Silas Cheney acquired a three-year-old colt, an animal that served for general transport and hauling. Allen Holcomb of central New York State received a hog and a cow in 1813–14 as part pay for sign-painting and chairmaking services. Closely related to this type of exchange was access to pasture land. Farmers also provided labor in exchange for furniture. Martin Dudley paid Titus Preston of Wallingford, Connecticut, for a Windsor chair in 1797 by "threshing oats." Often a woodworker rented the building in which he conducted business, as in the case of Luke Houghton, a furniture maker of Barre, Massachusetts. From July 1823 to May 1825 he was indebted to the widow Sally Bussel in the sum of $47.90 for the rent of his facility. In return she received cabinet services.[232]

An exchange of miscellaneous skills and home or craft products was an especially popular way to pay for furniture or woodworking services. Among women customers cloth weaving and seamstress work were skills utilized to advantage. Polly Smith paid for the Pembroke table she bought in 1798 from Amos Denison Allen of South Windham, Connecticut, "in spining & weaving." Another female customer exchanged tow cloth for a bureau and four dining chairs. Across the state at Litchfield, Sally Munger bought a "Soing Chair" from Silas Cheney in 1817 and "paid" for it "by making Panterloons & Shirt." Closely related to the need for cloth and clothing was that for leather products, shoes in particular. A customer at Joseph Griswold's shop in Buckland, Massachusetts, in 1804 paid for his new bedstead with shoe repairs and a "lathe strap." Amos Denison Allen received shoes in payment for furniture. The needs of a single family could be substantial, as demonstrated in Wait Stoddard's supply of the Allen family with almost three dozen pairs of boots and shoes along with repairs during a three-year period. To close out an account in 1820 George Landon of Erie, Pennsylvania, accepted as a final payment for chairs a quantity of feathers and tallow (fig. 4-35).[233]

Metalwork was in considerable demand, and woodworkers were happy to exchange services with the local blacksmith or coppersmith. Critical jobs performed by Frink and Chester for A. D. Allen include mending a pitchfork, sharpening plow irons, providing a linchpin for the wagon, shoeing his horse, and mending a chisel. Allen reciprocated with a secretary-bookcase and chairs. At Windsor, Vermont, one of Thomas Boynton's patrons provided a lathe crank in 1827 and shoed the chairmaker's horse. Spoon bits and spokeshave irons came from another source. One company reciprocated with a tallow lamp and a copper boiler, the latter possibly similar to the "long boiler for Chair stuff" acquired by James Gere in 1823 from a Connecticut metalworker who also repaired his teakettle spout. A more sophisticated series of exchanges was recorded by Thomas Boynton in 1815–16 when the local firm of Johonnot and Smith supplied silver tablespoons, a pen, a steel purse, and snuffbox repairs to compensate for Boynton's work in painting, gilding, and shading their shop sign and making a "label" reading "Walk In." Later Boynton added a painted and gilded watch to the shop sign. Medical care is listed in some accounts. In exchange for furniture construction and repairs, including mending a rocking chair, Titus Preston of Wallingford, Connecticut, received medical services and medicines between 1802 and 1808 from Doctor Brandin.[234]

Wood was an important commodity to the furniture maker. It was easily supplied, and both craftsman and customer benefited. Some craftsmen owned woodlots, although frequently their sources were local patrons and sawmills. Woodworkers, such as William Rowzee of Salisbury, North Carolina, regularly advertised their willingness to accept "lumber suitable for the Business . . . in payment for Work," although not all material was destined for furniture making. Some cordwood provided energy for heating and cooking; other lumber was used in carpentry. Allen Holcomb of Otsego County, New York, struck a bargain in 1825 with a customer

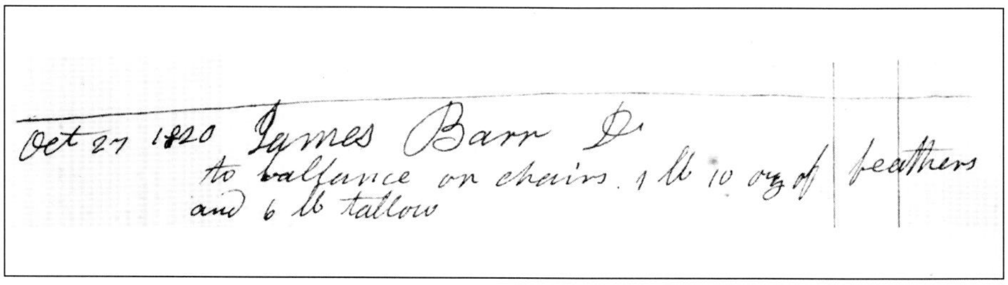

FIG. 4-35 James Barr account, October 27, 1820, in George Landon account book, Erie, Pa., 1813–32. (Winterthur Library.)

who acquired "6 Dining Chairs for which he is to Deliver at my Shop 7 three quarters Bunches of Shingles." References to maple, a common material for turned work, occur with frequency. Between 1814 and 1819 Captain Eneas Morgan exchanged a maple log and other wood with James Gere of Groton, Connecticut, for a set of dining chairs and wagon-wheel hubs. Windsor seat plank was a commodity in demand. In 1806 Silas Cheney of Litchfield credited a customer with "350 ft Bass plank Deliverd at the mill" valued at $2 per 100 feet. Cheney was less pleased with stock from another customer, which he described as "Badly Cracked & shakey." A. D. Allen received 500 feet of unspecified plank from a customer in Colchester as payment for cabinetwork and half a dozen continuous-bow Windsor armchairs. At Framingham, Massachusetts, David Haven credited a customer with "Plank for Chair Bottoms for 10 Chairs." A more involved transaction was effected at Saratoga, New York, on August 8, 1841, when Ransom Cook received a request from a business acquaintance: "Pleas let the bearer . . . have a half dosen Chairs & I wil pay you in wood plank or other lumber this fall as you & I shall agree when I shal see you & Charge the amount to your friend.   Coles Goldin."[235]

Other raw and processed materials used in the trade entered the chairmaker's shop in the course of business, including glue, paint pigments, linseed oil, varnish, nails, and flag and cane for fancy-chair seats. Some chairmakers, among them Elisha Hawley of Connecticut and Jacob Felton and True Currier of New Hampshire, credited several customers with bottoming flag-seat chairs, an example of a minor skill put to good use. Felton employed seven local women who were paid in chair frames to bottom and retail on their own accounts. Wooden seats for Windsor chairs were supplied to some shops by semiskilled workmen who had access to timberlands and did the work as a sideline to farming and other occupations to gain extra buying power. Elisha Hawley credited James Sturgis with "27 Chair Bottoms" in 1793 as part payment for a set of Windsors and a table. David Pritchard, Jr., of Connecticut exchanged "fan bac[k]" chairs for wooden seats. In New Jersey William G. Beesley accepted ninety-eight "feet" (legs) from turner Nathaniel Swing in 1834 in part payment for half a dozen "broad top Chairs." When D. Burton painted chairs for H. F. Dewey in Vermont, he received as pay a large rocking chair "in the white" (unpainted).[236]

Product exchanges between furniture makers were common. From 1800 through 1802 Simon Stockwell deposited twenty-seven "Read" rush-bottom chairs with Solomon Sibley at Ward (Auburn), Massachusetts, in return for "dining" and "Green" Windsors and a "riting" chair. John Parmeter's two sets of dining chairs only partially paid for the bureau and tea table he took home from William Mather's shop at Whately. After several years of exchanges in the early 1830s David Pritchard, Jr., and Hiram White of Waterbury, Connecticut, balanced their books with White supplying twenty-four clock cases. Among the furnishings White had received from Pritchard were a sideboard, crown-top chairs, a dressing table, and a rocking chair.[237]

Three-way exchanges of goods and services were common. If a prospective customer could not provide payment acceptable to a producer, a third party might effect the transaction. The third party could be a debtor of the would-be consumer or a creditor of the prospective producer. To close the transaction the third party's trading goods had to be acceptable to the producer or the consumer's products agreeable to the third party. Sometimes a producer accepted goods he did not need but could hold for future transactions. For example, Miles Benjamin of Cooperstown, New York, sold chairs made by one "Cory" to customer Daniel French in 1824 and in the bargain gained basswood plank needed in his own chairmaking business. Jesse Bedent wiped out a debt to Ames Standish in 1830 when he directed James Gere of Groton, Connecticut, to deliver Standish "6 Roll Top Chairs." A similar transaction occurred in the shop of Luke Houghton at Barre, Massachusetts:

Templeton Octr 22nd 1830

Mr. Luke Houghton

Sir please to let Mr. Bryant such Articles of furniture as he wants & I will pay you for the same in Chairs.

Jonathan Holman

When Jeduthern Avery, a cabinetmaker of Bolton-Coventry, Connecticut, acquired chairs in sets from Daniel W. Badger between 1828 and 1832, he distributed them to five customers.[238]

Occasionally records provide insights into unusual exchanges among craftsmen. Ira Hubbard worked briefly in 1806 for Solomon Cole of Glastonbury, Connecticut, for the express purpose of acquiring a silver watch that Cole was willing to trade for skilled labor. The agreed value of the timepiece was £5.2.0. At the prevailing daily wage of about 6s. ($1), the watch was equal to seventeen days' labor. In payment Hubbard agreed to "get up 24 fanback Chairs at one shilling each and 12 square top with double bows at 1/3 each and make one Desk like Leonard Wells omitting the middl drawer in the head and . . . to pay 10/ per week while making the desk for bord—the making the Desk . . . to bee eight Dollars." The remaining balance was equal to a note Hubbard held against Cole and agreed to endorse. Two exchanges in the accounts of Thomas Boynton for 1837 involved a printer and a tavernkeeper of Windsor, Vermont. As part of his promotion of "stamp painting," a new branch of business, Boynton prepared a "treatise" on the subject that Preston Merrifield printed and bound. Merrifield's press also produced handbills for distribution. Through the years the printer acquired stools and spit boxes for shop use. Samuel Patrick in payment for furniture repairs and painting at his tavern supplied the Boynton family with "a turkey for thanksgiving."[239]

In summary, the operation of a successful shop depended in part on a craftsman's ability to negotiate simple day-to-day business transactions in a society where coin and paper currency were scarce. Excerpts from the accounts of Allen Holcomb of Otsego County, New York, dating from 1822 to 1825 demonstrate the range of versatility. On one occasion Holcomb exchanged a "little" chair for shoemaking services, and on another he gained a clock case worth $17 in return for a set of chairs and turned work for bedsteads. He traded rocking chairs for payments as varied as a quantity of grain or "the newspapers [for] one year." Sometimes a "Sett of Chairs" commanded a range of commodity payments, among them cider, apples, wheat, and oats, with some cash to boot.[240]

Transportation and Packaging

WATER CARRIAGE

Domestic Trade

Water transport to regional or distant markets was cheaper than hauling goods overland by wagon until the railroad was established. Local waterways with shallow beds or impediments, such as shoals and rocks, employed shallow-draft, open craft like the Durham boat of the upper Delaware River and the gundelow and Moses boats of New England. Even canoes served as conveyances for furniture, as a notice of 1762 suggests: "Taken up on Mr. Tilghman's Island [in the Chesapeake Bay near Saint Michaels] . . . a large Pine Canoe about 23 feet long. She had in her 14 Rush Bottom Chairs, a small Black Walnut Table, and a Pair of oyster Rakes." Shallops, propelled by oar or sail, were larger open craft for obstacle-free river travel. These vessels were common on the Chesapeake Bay and the lower Delaware and Hudson rivers. Larger conveyances on the same waterways were the single-masted sloop and two-masted schooner, common trade vessels (fig. 4-11).[241]

A location close to a navigable watercourse was a benefit cited in 1825 by the firm of John Rand and Ephraim Abbott when the partners decided to dispose of their Bedford, New Hampshire, cabinet shop "near Merrimack river, where furniture may be easily and very cheaply transported to Boston by water." Small boats would have been employed. On the Hudson, where sailing craft normally carried freight between Albany and New York, Christian Schultz noted that from two to five days were required for the upriver passage, depending on the breezes. Freight charges for bulky merchandise were set at 40¢ per 100 pounds and on heavy articles at 20 to 25 percent less. Freight landed at Albany for inland distribution in the precanal days was portaged 15 miles over a turnpike road to Schenectady at a cost of 16¢ per 100 pounds. Water passage from Schenectady to Utica, a distance of 104 miles, was possible in poled boats even before the Erie Canal opened. The charge for this leg of the inland journey was 75¢ a hundred lot. Schultz explained that "the carriage by land is the same . . . oweing to the great number of wagons, loaded with produce, which enter the cities of Albany and Schenectady, where, after having discharged their loads, rather than return empty and earn nothing, they are glad to take a freight at the rate of water-carriage."[242]

Furniture shipments up the Hudson are recorded in the papers of two New York families. John Bleecker, Jr., of Albany purchased a dozen chairs, probably of the fancy type, during a visit to New York in 1803 and shipped them north for the use of Geritt Wessel Van Schaick at a cost of 25¢ apiece. Van Schaick acquired other New York seating eleven years later from chairmaker Alexander Patterson, who charged him $1.50 to pack a dozen yellow and gilt chairs placed on board the sloop *Columbia*. Robert R. Livingston's freight charges for eighteen chairs shipped from New York City to a destination along the lower Hudson in 1817 were about $2.22. When Robert Carter, a chairmaker of New York, signed the receipt book of Frederick Rhinelander of West Chester County in 1800, he noted a $3 allowance "for a Chair lost," presumably during shipment upriver.[243]

Water transport by small boat was common on the Connecticut River below and above Enfield Falls. Some river commerce was initiated on the coast at New Haven, where in 1820 Levi Stillman shipped twenty-five Windsor chairs valued at $37.50 to Hartford at freight charges of $1.81. By 1830 steamboats were common on the waterway, and a canal at Enfield gave access to the upper river. The Farmington Canal, with its southern terminus at New Haven, provided a parallel inland route through Connecticut to Northampton, Massachusetts. Contemporary records of an unnamed freight company based in New Haven provide further insights into the hauling business. The company's steamboat *General Sheldon* made runs along the coast, up the Connecticut River, and down the Sound to New York and the Hudson River. Freight rates were based on weight and bulk. Carriage of twenty-two chairs from New Haven to Chester on the river cost $2.25, a fee that may have included cartage to and from the boat at both ports. A resident at Middletown paid "Packet charges" of $1 for a settee shipped from New Haven in 1830. The same freight line may have operated a craft on the canal, as suggested in the item "Cartage to Canal Boat." Lambert Hitchcock shipped furniture via the Farmington Canal in the 1840s when he opened his Unionville factory.[244]

Twelve white fancy chairs retailed in 1810 at Boston by Samuel Gridley and wrapped in mats for transport at a charge of $3 were turned over to Aaron Purback for a water passage to neighboring Salem. Joshua Ward, the purchaser, paid freight charges of $1 and wharfage fees of 24¢, together amounting to about one-quarter the cost of one chair. Ward may have been attracted to the Gridley firm due to its inventory or attention to detail, as a notice of 1811 suggests: "Nolan and Gridley have for sale at their ware room, Nos. 27 and 28 Cornhill—3,000 Chairs, comprising a very

complete assortment, from the best workmanship and finest touch of the pencil to the most common, from 7 to 6 dlls. per doz. all which they will pack in shipping order and in the most careful manner." Fourteen chairs packed in mats and forming seven bundles were purchased from Gridley's establishment two years later by Benjamin H. Hathorne (Hawthorne), who paid $1.19 for freight and 28¢ for wharfage. Seating transported to Daniel Rogers, Jr., at Gloucester in the late 1820s from Salem or Boston at charges of 4¢ for chairs and 6¢ or 8¢ for a large, bulky rocking chair probably also was conveyed in light bundles. This type of packaging was a far cry from the four cases built to carry twenty-four chairs shipped on the steamboat *Boston* in January 1834 to merchant Sullivan Dorr at Providence. The substantial charge of $19.31 probably included case building and carriage.[245]

Further insights into the calculation of freight charges for seating in the coastal trade occur in a miscellany of New York records. In the late eighteenth century fourteen Windsor chairs cost William Bingham almost $3, or about 21¢ a chair, for the short water passage from the city to Black Point on the northern Jersey coast. The charge may have included packing and materials. Bingham paid for boxed freight in the same cargo at the rate of almost 10¢ per foot. Two dozen white and gold japanned chairs "well Packet" and sent by William Palmer to General Charles Ridgely of Baltimore several years later were charged at the rate of 16¢ per chair. When Joseph Dean, a sawmill owner of Taunton, Massachusetts, purchased a dozen chairs in 1818 for $15, the freight cost from New York for the shorter haul was $1.50, or 10¢ a chair. Dean could have patronized any of more than five dozen chair shops and stores. The shop of Thomas Ash II at 33 John Street (fig. **4-36**) was just one. Ash's trade card depicts an advantageous location near the waterfront from which flatbed carts conveyed purchases or consignments anywhere in town or to nearby slips for loading onto sailing craft, such as the vessel lying in the background.[246]

David Alling's records expand on waterborne commerce. In January 1825 the chairmaker of Newark, New Jersey, paid Tompkins, Tucker and Company "fifty Cents for freight don in the last year in the Sloop." This was followed in summer by a $2 payment to another business "for freighting a lot of white wood plank from N York to N Ark dock." Deliveries of flag (rush) by water are noted between 1829 and 1847, once on the steamboat *Newark*. Twice in 1839 Alling went to New York to purchase mahogany chairs, suggesting he did not make formal seating. His travel expenses on the first trip were 63¢, and he paid $1.09 for freighting ("fetching up by

Boat") two dozen chairs. Expenses for the second trip included a 12½¢ charge for carting his purchases to the dock.[247]

Another expense hinted at in the Alling records is insurance. John Pintard, a businessman of New York, also touched on this subject in October 1827 when he wrote to his daughter, Eliza Davidson of New Orleans, telling her of a gift he was sending for her new house:

> I begged yr brother to . . . go to the best Cabinet makers & purchase a dozen fashion-
> able mahogany Chairs, black horse hair bottoms, . . . I have been to look at them, just as
> they were preparing to box them to be sent on board the *Talma* tomorrow morning & I
> have called at Capt Holmes to have then stowed in a dry part of the ship. The chairs are
> of the very best quality & I think they will please. Price $9 [apiece] $108 [total], 2 Boxes
> $4, make $112, the set, freight & insurance I shall pay besides. . . . It is best to insure in
> case of accident, although at this season, there is very little hazard.

Freight charges came to $10.13, which Pintard paid, noting that Eliza would incur only the expense of "cartage to yr door." The generous father followed the gift of chairs with a sofa a year later, which he saw "carefully cased to go on board the *Talma*."[248]

The South was the destination of much furniture freighted from Philadelphia. Furnishings for Stephen Cocke's house in Amelia County, Virginia, traveled by water to Petersburg in 1791 and then overland. Although two marble hearths of 22 feet total length cost 6*s.* ($1) to ship, the charge for two dozen Windsor chairs and four dis-assembled bedsteads was £1.5.6. ($4.25), again indicating that bulk not weight was the principal factor in determining rates. Settees were unpopular with freighters, as indicated in charges paid in 1817 by John Lloyd at Alexandria. For each 12 inches of his 14-foot bench he paid freight at the rate of 12½¢. The total charge was $1.75 with an additional 10¢ for wharfage. Regarding the last fee, rates varied from port to port, making it wise for captains to own a copy of the *Commercial Directory*, which gave details. At Charleston, South Carolina, vessels paid 50¢ to 75¢ a day to unload, excepting coasters, and $1 a day if "lying idle." Wharfage charges to land case furni-ture, such as desks and chests of drawers, were 12½¢ per item; sofas and settees were 8¢. Tables and small furniture, probably chairs, cost 6¼¢. The charge explains why many captains who ventured chair cargoes to the city preferred to make their sales on board, because the purchaser paid the wharfage when he removed the furniture. Captains unfamiliar with city ordinances could purchase a copy from the harbor-master for $2. At Savannah, Georgia, sofas and settees cost 25¢ to land, the same as a dozen Windsors. Good wharfage rates existed at New Haven, Connecticut, where the fee for chairs was 1½¢ per item.[249]

Insights into the trials of shipping and receiving merchandise occur in the records of Thomas Jefferson. On May 10, 1800, the vice president visited the shop of John Letchworth in Philadelphia and ordered half a dozen Windsor chairs. Jefferson placed the business in the hands of his Philadelphia agent, John Barnes, and appar-ently had word sometime in June that the chairs had been shipped. Writing from his Virginia home in July to his cousin and southern agent, George Jefferson, in Rich-mond, he noted a delay in the delivery and provided explicit information about the chairs' appearance (fig. **4-37**):

> Monticello July 19. 1800.
> I find that our friend Barnes has made some mistake about the stick chairs. He
> received and paid for half a dozen for me. They were painted a very dark colour & were
> in this style [sketch]. Perhaps, if you saw those forwarded to Col Cabell you will recol-
> lect whether they were in this form, And may judge whether they were mine. If not,
> then Mr Barnes has not forwarded mine at all.

FIG. 4-37 Detail of letter from Thomas Jefferson to George Jefferson, Monticello, Charlottesville, Va., July 19, 1800. *(Courtesy of the Massachusetts Historical Society, Boston.)*

On the twenty-first George Jefferson replied, "I did not take particular notice of the chairs, but from my recollection of them do not think they can be yours." At Richmond George Jefferson probably forwarded the seating and other merchandise when it arrived by riverboat to a point where the statesman's wagon could conveniently receive and convey the goods overland to Monticello.[250]

Transportation on the western waters was remarked on by every traveler who recorded his experiences in the western country. The two-thousand-mile watercourse from Pittsburgh to New Orleans, formed by the Ohio and Mississippi rivers, was the main thoroughfare of commerce and travel. A journey from the first to the second point in 1803 took six or seven weeks by keelboat, and the return trip against the current consumed several months. The tide began to turn about 1812 as the application of steam power to navigation radically changed the face of the West. Twenty years later the English barrister Henry Tudor exclaimed in wonder how the "inventive genious and mechanical enterprise of man" had overcome the natural obstacle of the swift river current: "The exhalation arising from a few tea-kettles full of boiling water has triumphed over opposing winds and tides, and has served, in the figurative language of the poet, to 'annihilate space and time.'"[251]

Pittsburgh served as the first warehouse for the West. Commission merchants received wagons laden with credit goods from Philadelphia, paid carriage, and when the rivers were full of water forwarded the goods by boat to retailers and distributors along the waterways, receiving 5 percent commission. Louisville, below Cincinnati, marked the point at which goods were transferred for the lower river journey until a canal circumvented the rapids located at that point. Freight from Louisville to New Orleans in 1817 cost 56¢ to 75¢ per hundredweight and took twelve days to descend by steam vessel or twenty-eight by flatboat. The charge for freight on the return to Louisville was $3 to $3.75 per hundred. The journey required thirty-six days by steamboat, when the "machinery" did not "meet with an accident," and ninety by poled boat. Commenting in 1833, Carl David Arfwedson noted that among the hundreds of steamboats on the western rivers the greatest number were of 200 to 300 tons burden. Among the largest vessels the *Mediterranean* could carry a freight of 700 tons. Some vessels had two decks, the upper one for cabin passengers and the lower one for deck passengers, the ship's machinery, and "such goods as could not be stowed in the hold." Many deck passengers on the upriver run were flatboatmen who had deposited their goods and vessels in New Orleans and were returning home. Arfwedson noted that they could travel for a small expense "if they engaged to assist the crew in taking in firewood at various stations."[252]

Overseas Trade

Greater concerns attended the overseas trade. Several months often were required to outfit, freight, and provision a vessel, especially a large one. Freight was collected over a period of time, and some required storage until the assemblage was complete. The accounts of the brig *Rising Sun* owned by Christopher Champlin of Newport, Rhode Island, are pertinent. Planning began in October 1800 when the ship engaged dock space at Benjamin Fairbanks's wharf at a daily rate of 1s. 6d. after its return from a voyage to Rotterdam. When the vessel sailed 126 days later, the bill for wharfage was $31.50. Because storage charges are itemized and some accompanied by rates, it is possible to determine storage time. Eight casks of ham were on the docks for eight days before loading and 6,000 feet of pine boards for two days less. In addition the vessel took on board 100 barrels of potatoes, 300 firkins of lard, 191 boxes of cheese, and "300 Green Chairs," for which item the wharfage was $2. Although the storage rate for the seating is not given, the period appears to have been short, no more than a few days. The total wharfage for all commodities was $44.54. The *Rising Sun* left Fairbanks's dock on February 6, 1801, bound for Havana, where it arrived between February 28 and March 4 after a good passage. Not infrequently vessels entering or leaving port were impeded by unfavorable or sudden changes in weather conditions, as reported in 1829 by John Doggett of Boston, who noted that "the prevailing westerly winds" had prevented the arrival of the packet ships from England.[253]

Other documents shed further light on the export business, among them the papers of the ship *George and Mary*. The vessel left Providence, Rhode Island, in April 1810 for a voyage to Buenos Aires, stopping at New York City to pick up a furniture cargo that included Windsor and fancy seating. Charges recorded at New York list expenditures for matting chairs and boxing furniture, furniture truckage to the wharf, the payment of laborers to load goods, and freight costs from New York to Argentina. In another transaction Levi Stillman's invoice of Windsor and other furniture shipped in 1826 from New Haven to Lima, Peru, lists additional charges for an insurance policy and commissions to people who expedited the sale of goods. Stillman gave the consignee a 10 percent discount. Following usual practice, the Sanderson brothers of Salem, Massachusetts, provided ship captains with specific directions concerning their cargoes and the charges. Instructions for the voyage of the schooner *Prince*, laden with thirty-eight cases of furniture in June 1806, are typical:

> Capt Taylor Sir — you having the consinement of the above invoice — you will sell the same for the most they will fetch and conduct with the proceeds as you are directed in the Order given for this Voyage — it is agreed that the above Invoice is equal to one hundred and seven Barrels in bulk for which you may Deduct Two Dollars pr Barrel for the freight ought [out] to the medarias — one Dollar will be alowd Pr Barrel or that proposhion from the madeiras to the West Indies — the freight from the West Indies home as Customary — your Commitions also as Customary on such a voyage.

The equation of thirty-eight cases of furniture with 107 barrels, the more usual containers, in terms of bulk illuminates the process of determining charges for merchandise carried in special containers. The statement further provides a clear picture of the substantial space requirements of some furniture shipments made by American craftsmen to overseas and domestic markets.[254]

Packaging

The simplest and cheapest method of shipping framed chairs was loose, although the furniture was not usually tumbled into a storage space as illustrated in figure 4-30. On shipboard small items filled in between, above, and around other cargo. Specific data from records provide a better focus on the mechanics of packing, or lack thereof, and the problems encountered under the worst and even the best conditions. An early reference in the Boston-Philadelphia correspondence of John Andrews and William Barrell describes two methods of shipping. Andrews wrote on June 22, 1772, from Boston:

> If you have not ship'd the chairs before this comes to hand, should be glad you'd desire the people on board to take good care of 'em, as the others were much defac'd, one with the bottom splitt, and the other being tar'd and ye paint wore off by being lash'd over ther stern, if they could be brot in the cabbin it would be best.

Evidently there was little attempt at wrapping inexpensive painted chairs for transport at this early date, although placement of the furniture in a "cabbin" area rather than on deck subjected it to normal rather than extraordinary wear and tear.[255]

There were relatively inexpensive packaging procedures for seating furniture that ensured a better passage. A wrapping method of minimal cost and effort covered vulnerable chair parts with straw or "haybands." Whether the technique was current in this country before the early 1800s is unknown; however, an English document of 1792 records its use. D. Watson and Son of London prepared a dozen "Round top'd

FIG. 4-38 Glenister chair wagon, High Wycombe, Buckinghamshire, England, ca. 1880–1915. (Collection of High Wycombe Library, High Wycombe, England.)

Green Painted Elbow Chairs" (Windsor armchairs) for shipment using haybands and other "Packing," possibly mats. The same winding technique may have been used at David Alling's shop in Newark, New Jersey. In 1846–47 the chairmaker made payments for a total of 630 bundles of straw. This was not rush for seating, although the material may have been for stable use. Having an extensive trade, Alling kept a number of horses and wagons for deliveries. Levi Stillman of New Haven, Connecticut, in accounting for Windsor and fancy chairs shipped to Richmond, Virginia, in December 1826 for commission sales listed a charge of $1.50 for "Winding with Straw." The following March "Winding & Packing" costs were part of consignment expenses to the same place. Hay- or straw-wrapped chairs loaded for wagon carriage are illustrated in a photograph of English origin dating to the late nineteenth or early twentieth century (fig. 4-38), and the practice perpetuated a long tradition. Close inspection reveals that the load was composed of pairs of chairs nested seat to seat and piled five chairs high. In some bundles only the backs appear to have been wrapped. In protecting this area, a chair's most important surface, the straw also minimized damage to the leg fronts of its mate, since when nested those two areas were in close contact. Traditional craft practice, which lingered into the twentieth century in England, asserts that one man could wrap three dozen side chairs in an hour. Sometimes paper was used for the same purpose, although in America that material was not plentiful until the nineteenth century.[256]

Once the first novelty of Windsor seating had worn off, customers residing at a distance from the source began to demand chairs in good condition. The packing technique mentioned most frequently is matting, or wrapping a chair with a coarse piece of fabric woven of straw or bast fiber. The same material was employed frequently as a floor covering in warm climates. When closing out a line of matting in

1829, John Doggett of Boston offered it to a customer wholesale: "We have from 75 to 100 Rolls matting 25 Yard pieces. . . . [It] is 4 feet 8 inches wide. . . . We will engage freight as low as possible and make no charge for putting it on board."[257]

The exact function of mats is not always detailed. When William Ash I of New York City shipped two sets of chairs in 1802 to Portsmouth, New Hampshire, he included a charge of 16s. for "matts." Other references identify their use in wrapping chairs in bundles, also referred to as parcels, packs, or packages. Specific information occurs in a shipping record of John Mere, a chairmaker of Philadelphia, who in 1805 exported to Boston "Two Bundles of windsor chairs 2 in Each bunds." Other documents contain supporting data: "Six Bundles with 12 Chairs" from New York to the Azores (1798); "Twelve packages contg Twenty four Chairs" from Philadelphia to Baltimore (1801); "eighteen packs Thirty-six chairs" from Philadelphia to the West Indies (1819).[258]

Matting was used by English chairmakers for many years. A bill prepared in 1777 by the London firm of Ayliffe and Company lists "6 Rout Chairs" and "3 Large Mats & pack'g D[itt]o." The practice dates far earlier, however. In 1746 Gillow of Lancashire, England, already employed this wrapping for case and seat furniture. The earliest American reference to chairs wrapped in mats dates to 1785, when nine packages from Philadelphia were landed in Virginia. Mats were still in use in 1867 when A. H. Brick of Gardner, Massachusetts, advertised "chairs carefully packed in Boxes or bundles for transportation." Inside the packages vulnerable surfaces could be further wrapped with straw or hay, although special care was not always the rule, as noted in 1797 by Vosburgh and Childs of Wilmington, North Carolina: "How far preferable chairs must be manufactured in the state . . . to those . . . imported, which are always unavoidably rubbed and bruised."[259]

Two side chairs, Windsor or fancy, nested together with seats joining and perhaps cushioned between with straw normally stand about 3½ feet high. Wrapped around they require a piece of matting 2½ or 3 yards in length, including an overlap. John Doggett cited material measuring 4 feet 8 inches in width — enough to provide end extensions of 6 or 7 inches as fold-overs to prevent the chairs from slipping out. Wrapping cord twice around and lengthwise, the loops at right angles, resulted in a sturdy package. Settees and other forms also could be wrapped in mats, as suggested in two items: "forty-two Bundles Chairs & Settees" shipped from Philadelphia to Boston (1805); "1 Matt for Rocking Chair" charged a Boston customer of William Hancock (1833). Mats also protected chairs shipped unassembled and without paint, as noted in a memorandum of goods for Grenada prepared in 1776 by Gillow of Lancashire, England: "Two Matts and a small Box Contng. 12 neat Windsor chairs also paint & Brushes to paint 'em twice over after they are put together."[260]

Painted chairs of fine quality warranted protection in boxes. Thomas Sheraton commented on this packing method in his *Cabinet Dictionary* of 1803, and American chairmakers probably followed similar practice. Sheraton described how "light japanned chairs for bed-rooms" were "generally packed in slightly skeleton [open] cases, after being papered over," that is, individually wrapped. There were two packing plans. In the first, three chairs were placed side by side in a long case on a hanging batten to which each was secured with two screws at either side seat rail. The batten was positioned so as to elevate the feet slightly above the case bottom. Another line of three chairs were secured to a second batten and inverted within the case, the seats of both groups almost touching. Crosswise stays reinforced the long battens. In the second arrangement six chairs were placed on crosswise battens in the case, two by two, the front rails parallel with the case ends. For gilt or "richly finished" chairs, Sheraton recommended "a close case of full half inch deal" (fir or pine).[261]

Many references to chair boxes and cases involve the overseas trade. When the ship *Lydia* left Philadelphia on September 1, 1752, she carried "4 Cases Chairs" to Jamaica, although these were likely of walnut or mahogany construction rather than

Windsor design. Much later, in 1803, the brig *Welcome Return* left Salem, Massachusetts, for the "Coast of Brazills" carrying "3 Cases Bamboo Chairs on Deck Vizt 41 Chairs." Although exposing the cases to sea washings and the elements was far from an ideal situation, the anticipated profits in retailing forty-one chairs may have been sufficient to hazard their arrival in salable condition. A contemporary Massachusetts manifest of the *Topsham Beauty* describes a similar cargo: "9 Boxes cont'g 72 Chairs." Sheraton specified only six chairs to a case. These carried eight and may have required additional internal bracing.[262]

Rare among references is a packing item listed in an "Invoice of Furniture" shipped in 1826 by Levi Stillman of New Haven, Connecticut, to Lima, Peru. All the furniture, including two mahogany sofas, a dressing bureau, three worktables, a "Time Piece," and nineteen dozen fancy and Windsor chairs, apparently was contained in "19 Boxes for furniture" supplied at a cost of $26 for material and labor. Immediately following the charge for boxes is the item "517¾ Yds Cotton Sheeting" at 13½¢ the yard. Aside from sandpaper, varnish, and glue, there are no other commodities on the list. The sheeting appears to have been used to wrap the furniture contained within the boxes. At Lima the cloth was reused or sold for the best price it would bring.[263]

Other insights into the trade in cased seating furniture emerge from documents of Philadelphia origin. In 1807 Halberstadt and Trotter sent three furniture containers to Havana on the schooner *Republican*. One held mahogany dining tables. The other two carried between them 8½ dozen round- and square-back side chairs, four armchairs, and two double-seated settees. Given the number, there is little doubt that the seating furniture traveled partly or totally disassembled. In the 1810s Stephen Girard shipped boxed fancy chairs to Valparaiso and the Isle of France. The seating, handsomely painted in "rosewood Gilt," "Bronze," "Cane Colour," "Brown gilt," and "Red gilt," required the protection of boxes if it was to arrive in good order.[264]

Unassembled Seating

Despite the extensive use of bundles and cases for packaging, another technique fairly dominated the furniture export trade — the shipment of chairs, and sometimes other seating forms, unassembled. Chairs in pieces could be placed in compact units to save space and, thus, expense. Hamilton and Fardon of Baltimore, who were prepared to "put up" chairs "in a manner for shipping," calculated "a saving of at least one third the usual freight" by this method. Chairs exported in parts are identified by several names, the most common being *chair stuff*. Next in popularity were the terms *shooks* and *shaken chairs*, language derived from the cooper's craft. It was common practice to transport staves for barrels and hogsheads loose for setup at a ship's destination, where the containers were filled with produce and other commodities on the return trip. In the trade loose staves were called *shakes* (for shaken barrels) or *shooks*. The same language identified unassembled chairs shipped in pieces. The term *knockdowns* has a similar background. Chairs were completed to the gluing stage and then disassembled or "knocked down" for easy carriage. The term was popular at Philadelphia. Other names applied to unassembled chairs include chair sticks or timber, lumber for chairs, loose chairs, unmanufactured chairs or stuff, a quantity of materials, unmade chairs, raw materials for chairs, chairs in bulk, and chairs made portable. Undoubtedly, cargoes containing hundreds of chairs, even many dozens, comprised unassembled seating.[265]

The practice of shipping chairs in pieces for assembly at their destination was not peculiar to American commerce. At the start of the eighteenth century English merchants shipped chairs to American colonial markets to be framed and caned upon receipt. References in the accounts of Gillow of Lancashire for 1757 speak of hogsheads of "open Back" chairs with leather bottoms (seats) shipped to Barbados. Company invoices for consignments to Jamaica in 1774 describe partly assembled seating: "Three Mats Conta[ining] eighteen Windsor Chairs (the legs and rails [stretchers] sent loose to save room); paint sent in a Little Box . . . to paint em when togather."[266]

American exporters shipped unassembled chairs by 1767 when the *Industry* sailed to Barbados from Philadelphia with "Twenty four Chair Bottoms" and "Two Barrels of Chair Work," although the practice was limited in America before the Revolution. In the 1780s Joseph Walker, supercargo of the sloop *Friendship*, in remarking on the "Savannah Trade" described a still uncommon procedure:

> Have a quantity of Windsor chairs set up then knock'd down again having every piece particularly marked in such a manner that no mistake can be made. The bottoms may be stowed loose in the hole and the rounds pack'd up. And mind to have a sufficient copy of paint of every kind; Viz green, blue, red, purple, white, black in order to soot [suit] the different tastes of the inhabitants, tho' I believe the customary colors with us will be most in demand. P. S. Be sure and take a workman along with you In order to [put] the Chairs together for there are no Macanicks here [fig. **4-39**].

This may be the earliest direct reference in American records addressing the need to send along a workman to reassemble the chairs. Little more than a decade later circumstances had changed, and among Philadelphia chairmakers the practice of accompanying shipments of chair parts to other cities had become more routine. Even after removing from Philadelphia to Norfolk, Virginia, Michael Murphy received "one thousand chair sticks, five barrels Glue" by the schooner *Winfield Packet*.[267]

Chair parts, or knockdowns, were shipped in several ways. In 1809 the schooner *Mercator* from Bath, Maine, carried "2 Hogsheads and 4 boxes Chair Stuff" to Bermuda. Also clearing inward at the island that year was the *Argo*, whose cargo

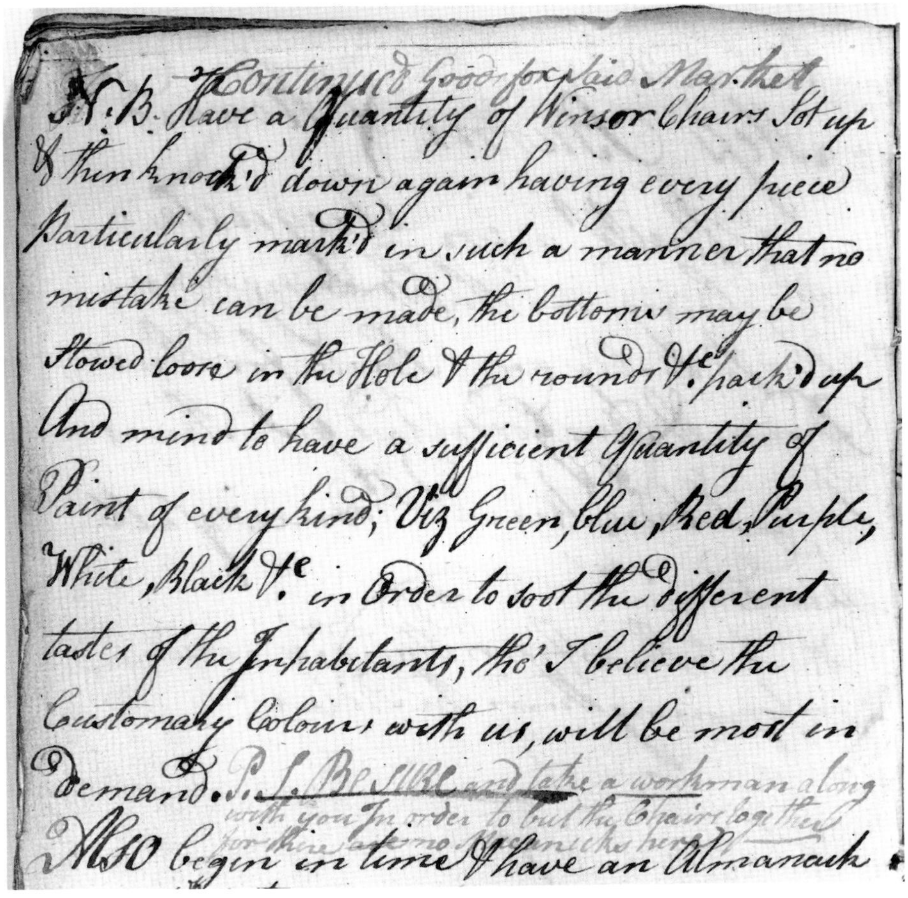
Continued Good for said Market
N.B. Have a Quantity of Winsor Chairs Set up
& then knock'd down again having every piece
Particularly mark'd in such a manner that no
mistake can be made, the bottoms may be
Stowed loose in the Hole & the rounds &c. pack'd up
And mind to have a sufficient Quantity of
Paint of every kind; Viz Green, blue, Red, Purple,
White, Black &c. in Order to soot the different
tastes of the Inhabitants, tho' I believe the
Customary Colours with us, will be most in
Demand. P. S. Be sure and take a workman along
with you In order to put the Chairs together
for there are no Macanicks here
Also begin in time & have an Almanack

FIG. 4-39 Entry from Joseph Walker invoice book, Philadelphia and Savannah, Ga., April–May 1784. *(Independence Seaport Museum, Philadelphia.)*

included "30 Boxes chair stuff, 800 chair & Settee Bottoms," the latter likely loose. Barrels and tierces also held "loose chairs." When Richard Blow shopped for Windsor seating at Norfolk in 1794, he acquired a "Chest Boback Mahogany Coloured Chairs," prepainted but possibly only partly assembled. Records identify chair parts other than "bottoms." David Moon, who was in Charleston briefly in 1803, received "Six Cases chairs . . . a Quantity of Chair Backs" from chairmaker Joseph Burr. "Some Bows in Bulk" and "Two Bundles Settee Bows" from Providence and Philadelphia, respectively, arrived in the early 1800s at Havana. Joseph Burden of Philadelphia shipped "fifteen bundles Chair rounds" in 1816 to Henry Burden at Washington.[268]

Sources other than shipping records provide insights into the trade in unassembled chairs. In the 1830s Cornelius Briggs of Boston advertised "Chairs boxed to go safe to any part of the country" at a time when contemporaries Matthew McColm and John Robinson of Baltimore each stocked "a very SPLENDID ASSORTMENT OF CHAIRS, the greater part of which are made portable." Reminiscing in the 1860s, Walter Barrett described the business practice of chairmakers Tweed and Bonnell, partners at New York between 1823 and 1843, who "used to ship on their own account to South America the Windsor chair, plain and knock down. That is, they were packed in boxes of twelve each." A wholesale price list of 1867 for Prentice P. Gustine of Philadelphia describes the prepackaged stuff more particularly: "Windsor chair stock (all but the seat), bored, tenoned and mortised, bows and slats got out, 100 chairs in a box." Seats were a separate purchase.[269]

The system was not without its problems. As early as 1803 Standfast Smith, a Boston importer, commented on the difficulties encountered with chairs received from his London supplier:

> Those in Bundles may answer — those in pieces packt in boxes are handsome chairs but not sufficiently so (in my opi[ni]on) for the price — the legs of them have not been squared off and some of them are an inch longer than others. I have to give 18/ sterling per doz for putting together and they occasion more trouble than I had an idea of — upon the whole I believe we had better drop that article altogether, as I fear we shall not gain much credit by the sale of them — they are very slight and will prove to the purchasers an unprofitable speculation.

In the same letter Smith further elaborated on assembly when ordering drawing-room chairs for his client Doctor John Warren. He directed that the chairs be "carefully packt in parts as those we received, but markd more distinctly so that there may be no difficulty in putting them together."[270]

The brisk trade in "portable" seating stimulated business beyond chairmaking circles. Tench Coxe of Philadelphia, in assessing the American commodities market of 1810, wrote: "The coopers and carpenters' packages for exported goods alone, probably exceed 2,200,000 in number. To these may be added as many more for home use." As indicated in the chair trade of Tweed and Bonnell, Prentice Gustine, and others, the demand for containers grew by leaps and bounds. The export chair market achieved international proportions by the mid-nineteenth century, when American shippers looked to the Caribbean Islands, Central and South America, and Canada for continuing markets. The English, meanwhile, were finding a new outlet in their Australian colonies.[271]

LAND CARRIAGE

Wagons, Carts, and Sleds
Some chairmaking craftsmen did not own a vehicle, some not even a horse, although most had access to transportation to meet personal and business needs. The business

conveyances mentioned most frequently in records dating between 1750 and 1850 are wagons, carts, and sleds, in that order. Several Europeans who visited or settled in America made comment. John Lambert described the wagon that carried his baggage to Troy, New York, in 1807 as a "long narrow cart upon four wheels . . . drawn by two horses abreast," and he indicated that these conveyances were "common in the States." Besides a passenger function, he cited the vehicle's common use in carrying provisions to market and transporting goods. Several decades earlier Hector Saint John de Crèvecouer, who settled on an Orange County, New York, farm before the Revolution, spoke at length on the all-essential wagon. His remarks are equally appropriate to the chairmaking business:

> Our two-horse wagons . . . are extremely well-contrived and . . . answer with ease and dispatch all the purposes of a farm [or business]. . . . [The] length . . . is sixteen feet including the . . . tongue. We have room in . . . their bodies to carry five barrels of flour. We commonly put in them a ton of hay and often more. . . . We can lengthen them as we please, and bring home the body of a tree twenty or thirty feet long. We commonly carry . . . eighteen hundred pounds, with which we can go forty miles a day with two horses. On a Sunday it becomes the family coach. We then take off the common, plain sides and fix on it others which are handsomely painted. . . . If it rains, flat hoops . . . are placed in mortises, and a painted cloth is spread and tied over the whole. Thus equipped, the master of a family can carry six persons either to church or to meetings. When the roads are good we easily travel seven miles an hour. In order to prevent too great shakings, our seats are suspended on wooden springs—a simple but useful mechanism. . . . We generally pay . . . from fifty to sixty dollars.[272]

A survey of thirty-seven documents listing vehicles, the majority probate records dating between 1807 and 1881, provides general insights into the ownership and use of business vehicles among woodworking craftsmen. Of the seventy-two wagons listed, forty are not further identified save for occasional use of adjectives such as "old," "second hand," or "horse wagon." Likely most followed the general description of "common spring wagon." Within the second group are terms of note, the most common one *lumber wagon* followed by *pleasure wagon*, also called an *easy* or *fancy wagon*. Both one- and two-horse conveyances are noted along with one reference each to a team wagon and a four-horse team wagon. The latter two belonged to Elisha Harlow Holmes of Windham, Connecticut, who by 1843 was dabbling in several mercantile ventures (fig. **4-40**). The "furniture Car" in the possession of John

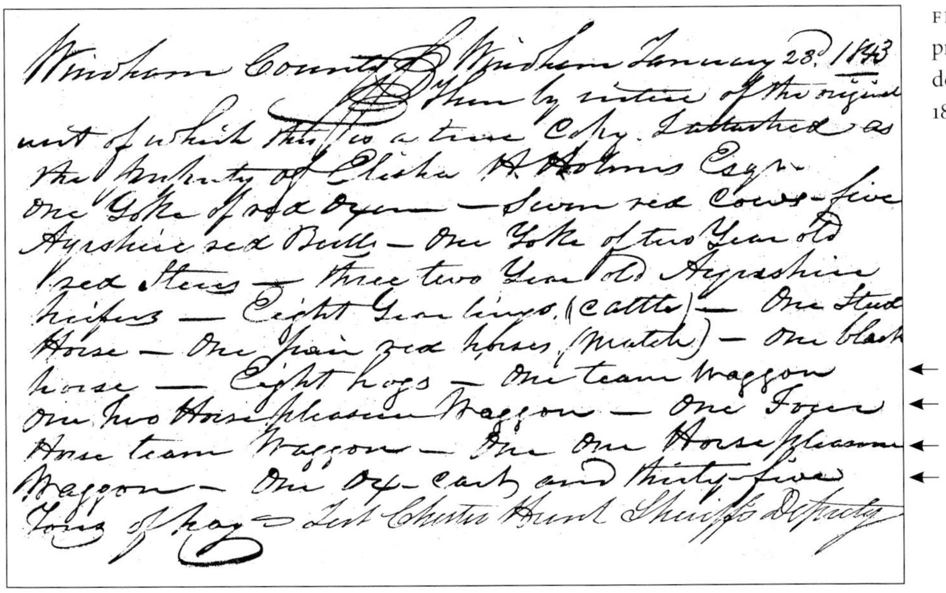
Windham County ss Windham January 28th 1843
Then by virtue of the original
writ of which this is a true Copy I attached as
the property of Elisha H Holmes Esqr
One Yoke of red Oxen — Seven red Cows — five
Ayrshire red Bulls — One Yoke of two Year old
red Steers — three two Year old Ayrshire
heifers — Eight Yearlings (cattle) — One Stud
Horse — One pair red horses (Match) — One black
horse — Eight hogs — One team Waggon
One two Horse pleasure Waggon — One Four
Horse team Waggon — One One Horse pleasure
Waggon — One Ox-cart and thirty-five
Tons of hay — Test Charles Hunt Sheriffs Deputy

FIG. 4-40 Entry from Elisha Harlow Holmes property attachment listing livestock and vehicles, detail, New London County, Conn., January 23, 1843. *(Connecticut State Library, Hartford.)*

E. Hartman of Chester County, Pennsylvania, probably was the same type of vehicle. Several other specialty wagons are noted: Samuel Stuart and Peter A. Willard of Sterling, Massachusetts, owned business vehicles described as a "one horse wagon & chair rack" and a "Large chair Waggon," respectively. A "Furniture wagon" in Joseph Bachelder's West Waterville, Maine, estate was valued at $75. The "excellent new big-road Wagon" offered for sale in Charlotte, North Carolina, in 1826 by chairmaker William Culverhouse may have been of the same general type. During the 1840 annual inventory at Thomas Walter Ward II's general store in Pomfret, Connecticut, two covered wagons were valued at $112 each, a figure that may have included the horses and complete harness. Two partly enclosed vehicles in the survey were a Dearborn owned by Samuel Lobach of Berks County, Pennsylvania, and a "Buggy Waggon" listed in the estate of Edward Shepard at Wethersfield, Connecticut. A few wagons described as "new" were valued between $30 and $80. When Lambert Hitchcock, who had an extensive overland chair trade, declared his insolvency in 1829, his "Carriages, Wagons, Horses, [and] Harnesses" were valued at $605.90. In later years his furniture wagon carried "ropes and padding" as part of its equipment.[273]

A few carts appear on the vehicle list, including some designated for use with oxen. Both sleds and sleighs are mentioned, sometimes in the same document, indicating that the two were distinct. The first was a working conveyance, the second a pleasure or general business vehicle. Special accessories included sleigh bells and buffalo robes. The incidence of formal vehicles is uncommon. Benjamin F. Heywood of Gardner, Massachusetts, owned a gig, and Samuel Lobach used a carriage in Pennsylvania. At Newark, New Jersey, David Alling got about town in a "Light one seat Carriage." The "waggonhouse" mentioned in Peter Willard's estate is of rare occurrence. The shelter probably housed his "Large chair Waggon," which when loaded at night was safe from the elements and ready to leave Sterling, Massachusetts, at the crack of dawn. A wagon shed also stood on the factory site at Unionville, Connecticut, occupied in 1852 by Lambert Hitchcock.[274]

Other documents enlarge on the day-to-day business use of a wagon. In a 1759 agreement between Robert Crage (Craig), spinning-wheel and furniture maker of Leicester, Massachusetts, and "Esqr Campbell of Oxford," Crage agreed to transport "4 foot wheels . . . to [Campbell's] house if he sells them." Teamsters at Philadelphia had brisk business in settling Secretary of War General Henry Knox into new quarters in December 1790 after the federal government moved to the city. James Davison carried nineteen loads of household furniture "from the Vessel" to Knox's store on Mifflin's Wharf, charging about 1s. per load. Eight days later another teamster hauled "two Loads of Office articles to Carpenters Hall" and two loads of furniture to the general's house in Second Street; still other loads followed. Several years later Anthony Morris prepared for a longer move from Philadelphia to his new house at Whitemarsh, about sixteen miles distant. He engaged one Accuff to haul the first three "waggon load of furniture," paying at the rate of £1.2.6 per load. Most if not all goods were boxed, since Morris paid Francis Trumble, cabinetmaker and Windsor-chair maker, the substantial sum of £8.4.9 "for packing Cases." When in 1832 Hamilton and Kevan, merchants of Petersburg, Virginia, advised Humberston Skipwith of Clarksville that they were sending "by the waggons all the remaining furniture from Baltimore and other Articles as pr statement," they noted, "We have been particular in the Loading of both Waggons—that all the Boxes and other articles are properly put in and well secured with cords—and we hope will reach home, all well."[275]

Selected woodworking accounts provide insights on traffic between the craft shop and the domestic setting. Common practice placed the responsibility and cost of moving furniture from the shop on the householder until well into the nineteenth century. Thus in 1830 Edward Tuckerman of Boston queried his sister, Mrs. Stephen Salisbury I of Worcester: "Mr. Hancock has completed your Sofa and squabs, and

FIG. 4-41 Detail of Shaker wagon loaded with spinning wheels. From Joshua H. Bussell, American, 1816–1900, *The Shaker Village at Alfred, Maine* (detail), about 1848. Pen, ink, and watercolor on paper; 53.3 × 174.0 cm (21 × 68½ in.). (*Museum of Fine Arts, Boston. Gift of Dr. J. J. G. McCue, acc. 1978.461. Photograph © 2004 Museum of Fine Arts, Boston.*)

they are packed and ready to be sent. Will You have the order given from Worcester or shall I look for a Team?" When practice varied, the craftsman usually noted it. Titus Preston of Wallingford, Connecticut, charged Doctor Brandin in 1804 with "Carrying home furniture," and David Haven of Framingham, Massachusetts, noted in a customer account: "to 6 Joyner Chairs . . . Sent to your House." Upon "mending, painting, & ornamenting . . . Six windsor Chairs" in 1831 for George Harvey of Preston, Connecticut, James Gere of Groton charged him 1s. for "Carting home the same." Knowledge of trip cost and distance and a craftsman's daily wage permits an estimate of the time involved. Silas Cheney transported chairs in 1808 from Litchfield to Farmington, a distance of about twenty-three miles. The 42¢ charge suggests that the craftsman was able to make the trip in half a day — one that probably began shortly after dawn.[276]

Thomas Boynton of Windsor, Vermont, made elaborate preparations in 1816 and 1818 before shipping furniture to two customers. Twelve gilt fancy chairs sent to Robert Davis of Hanover, New Hampshire, were boxed at a charge of $2; transportation, probably by public conveyance, was $1.50. When other furniture and chairs destined for Montreal were packed, boxed, and readied for loading, Boynton arranged for provending the team before the wagon was on its way. The charges were $8.38, more than a week's pay for most craftsmen. Two decades later the Grayson Spring Company paid handily at $5 a load for three wagons of furniture hauled to the spring from the shop of Moyers and Rich at Wythe Court House (Wytheville), Virginia. The route possibly was a mountainous one. Night trips existed well before modern technology made the task easy. Edward Carpenter, an apprentice cabinetmaker at Greenfield, Massachusetts, in the mid-1840s, remarked one evening in his journal, "Miles & Lyons sent off tonight a load of furniture to North Adams for H. L. Dawes, consisting of a Sofa, 2 tables, a Pillar Work table, Dress Table, wash Stand, 3 Bedsteads, a Set of chairs & a Rocking chair." A contemporary Shaker drawing conveys a general image of the woodworking craftsman or teamster in his "two-horse wagon" distributing goods as part of his occupational routine (fig. **4-41**). Creative license probably explains why the spinning wheels are fully assembled rather than taken apart and wrapped to endure the rigors of the road. A wagon on the grounds of David Dexter's manufactory at Black River, New York (fig. 2-30), is loaded with upright chairs, suggesting that they were being transported between buildings for finishing, drying, or packing.[277]

Long trips and large loads became more common in the second quarter of the nineteenth century as the chair shop gave way to the "manufactory," the immediate forerunner of the highly mechanized factory of the next quarter century. Gradual acceleration can be tracked in records of the Boston trade. In 1827 when Henry W. Miller opened his Worcester "Chair Factory," he noted several charges for items such as "Transportation of a Box of Chair Stuff from Boston." By the mid-1830s Jacob

Felton of Fitzwilliam, New Hampshire, engaged teamsters to cart from 225 to 325 unpainted chairs in a single load *to* Boston at the rate of 6¢ (later 4½¢) per chair and 10¢ for rocking chairs. There may have been little wrapping, since the chairs were painted at Boston. Josiah Prescott Wilder of neighboring New Ipswich conducted a majority of his business in the Lowell market. After the periodic demands of that rising textile center were met, Lowell middlemen likely forwarded surplus chairs via the Merrimack River to Boston and sold others in the countryside. Wilder usually freighted his own merchandise, thus economizing on transportation charges. A load averaged from 116 to 126 chairs, and he calculated that carriage per chair was 2.2¢ to 2.5¢. From the 1830s northern Worcester County, Massachusetts, was the scene of considerable activity. By midcentury "huge wagons drawn sometimes by six horses" transported chairs to Boston in two-day journeys. Hotel barns en route were "especially large so that these 'chair racks' could be driven in." The wagon load in figure 4-38 approaches although does not equal those on the wagons from Worcester County.[278]

Carts were open, two-wheeled vehicles smaller than a wagon and used for general business and heavy work. A cart without permanent sides was a dray. While visiting New York in 1817, Henry Fearon described the cart as "long and narrow, drawn by one horse" (fig. 4-36). The bed was flat and of a size sufficient to meet the needs of city craftsmen and most country operatives. When necessary the cartman could place stakes, sometimes roped, around the outside to secure a load. Deliveries to the congested waterfronts in large cities were accomplished more easily with a horse and cart than a wagon, as indicated by Francis Guy in his view of the Tontine Coffee House at New York (fig. 5-45). Undoubtedly this was the vehicle used in 1793 by Anthony Steel at Philadelphia when delivering six bow-back Windsor side chairs and an armchair "on board the brig *Lavinia*" (fig. **4-42**). The wharves also were alive with the hustle and bustle of the porters with their wheelbarrows. Moreau de Saint Méry reported twenty-four such individuals at New York in the mid-1790s, identified by their copper neckpieces "Stamped with their initials and a number." Waterfront life would have been quieter on Cape Cod, where in 1803 Samuel Wing carted six green chairs "down to the vessel" for delivery to a neighborhood customer. The following year he loaned his "hos Cart" to Josiah Keen "to go to Yermoth sixteen milds [miles]" and charged him 4s.[279]

As a furniture maker and farmer, Ebenezer Tracy, Sr., of Lisbon, Connecticut, employed two carts, and a set of "cart boxes" permitted him to change vehicle size to suit the job. On several occasions at his suburban shop in Philadelphia Charles C. Robinson carefully noted Windsor chairs "Taken to town." In time, the inland cities on the western waterways also were alive with activity as substantial as that in the East. In 1833 Carl David Arfwedson described how the "bustle of hundreds of

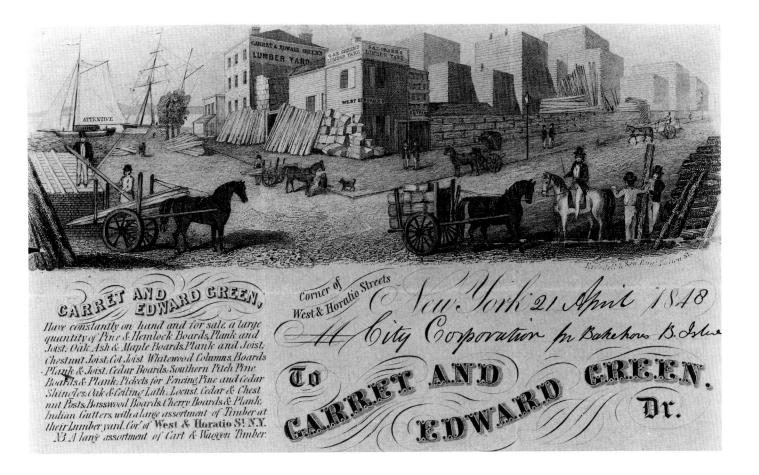

waggons and carts" contributed measurably to the "really . . . extraordinary sight" of
Cincinnati. Pittsburgh also was a "vast hive" where twelve thousand wagons from
Philadelphia and Baltimore came and went in the course of a year. Many streets
leading to the waterfront were wide to accommodate the vehicles arriving constantly
to transfer loads to the keelboats lining the banks of the Monongahela.[280]

To maintain a supply of cordwood and lumber, carts (and sleds where the climate permitted) were essential to the woodworker, especially in the country. In the
1770s Nathaniel Heath of Warren, Rhode Island, found that "carting . . . Bords at 1
. . . Shillin [per] Hund" was a service he could obtain in exchange for furniture. The
contemporary records of Major John Dunlap contain many entries for "going after"
boards or "halling Boards" from a Bedford, New Hampshire, sawmill. The method
is suggested by the entry "to one pair of oxen to John orrs Mill after Boards." As a
newcomer to the woodworking trades in the late 1790s, Amos Denison Allen relied
on his uncle Elijah Babcock for assistance in assembling and maintaining the materials necessary to pursue his trade. Entries in Babcock's accounts, such as "Oxen one
day to Cart from Sawmill," emphasize the importance of adequate transportation
and accessibility to a mill. To supply a growing demand, lumber yards of modest size
existed in the large commercial centers before the mid-eighteenth century, although
they were a far cry from the sprawling establishments of a hundred years later, like
that owned by Garret and Edward Green at New York (fig. 4-43). Here the builder,
furniture maker, and wagon maker could obtain needed materials and engage a
teamster to carry the stock to his door, if he did not transport it himself. Visible in
the foreground and middle ground of this view are no fewer than four carts, two
loaded with boards. The vehicles are the same as those pictured in Thomas Ash II's
advertisement (fig. 4-36), with the addition of corner staves to support the load.[281]

During the winter sleds often were more practical than wagons and carts for
heavy work, especially in New England and New York State. At Ridgefield, Con-

necticut, a customer of Elisha Hawley sledded timber in exchange for furniture and chairs. Silas Cheney knew the same service at Litchfield. He credited a customer in 1806 with "sledding one Lode slitwork." In 1830 a "Lumber Sleigh" was part of William Moore, Jr.'s, insolvency assignment at Barkhamstead.[282]

The Business of Hauling and Marketing
Woodworking accounts yield specific data relative to hauling supplies. In rural Windsor, Vermont, Thomas Boynton noted the loan of a horse in August 1816 from one Calvin Carlton "to get flaggs" for rushing. Production at Nelson Talcott's chair manufactory in Portage County, Ohio, was sufficiently large by the 1840s that he found it convenient to own "Horses & [a] Waggon" to haul timber. He used the same conveyance to transport rattan from Cleveland.[283]

Sometimes woodworkers hired out their horses, oxen, wagons, and carts to gain extra income. Robert Crage of Leicester, Massachusetts, charged Ebenezer Lock, Jr., 1s. 4d. in 1758–59 when Lock used Crage's "oxen and cart to fetch his Chest of drawers from Town." Later, in 1801, Wait Stoddard, a cordwainer of Windham, Connecticut, credited chairmaker Amos Denison Allen for "use [of] your Waggon 28 mile at 2½ d" the mile. Fees for wagon use were based on several factors—mileage, length of service, wagon size, and use of the owner's horse. Allen Holcomb charged 72¢ in 1823 for the nine-mile wagon trip from Cooperstown to Laurens, New York. Eight years later at Barre, Massachusetts, the expense of a sixty-mile round trip to New Ipswich, New Hampshire, in Luke Houghton's wagon over hilly terrain was $1.60. Urban craftsmen, including James Williams of Washington, District of Columbia, sometimes advertised their "furniture wagon for hire."[284]

By the early nineteenth century, as competition was taking its toll, urban and rural furniture makers turned to the enticement of free delivery to gain an edge. An early notice is that of James Always at New York, who promoted his refurbishing services in 1803 by offering to pick up chairs for painting from any part of town and return them in good order. Competition was especially keen in the South, where chairmakers vied with each other for customers and fought the encroachment of imported seating. Martin C. Phifer of Lincolnton, North Carolina, made potential customers a handsome offer in 1824 when promising to send chairs "to any of the neighboring counties within a reasonable distance, without any additional expense to purchasers." Phifer stood to gain in making the offer as he also repaired vehicles, and one activity could complement the other. A craftsman's offer of free delivery often was a measure of the area he served or targeted for expansion. Thomas Ellis of New Bedford, Massachusetts, advised "purchasers in Fairhaven and Oxford villages" that they could "have their furniture delivered at their houses free of expense." In 1850 William Sweney of West Chester, Pennsylvania, demonstrated another method of bidding for patronage. With tongue in cheek he stated that his chairs were quite "a bit cheaper than at any other establishment in the State" and added, "If you don't believe it come and see for yourselves. It is worth a quarter to look at the variety; and there is no charge for looking. You will always find the proprietor in a good humor and ready to give all the information necessary in reference to prices." The good-humored proprietor did business "at the sign of the AMERICAN FLAG," in itself an eye-catcher.[285]

Rough roads and constant use took their toll on business and pleasure vehicles. Repair work or new conveyances were required periodically, as documented in Connecticut records. In 1810 Amos Denison Allen's wagon needed a linchpin for a wheel. A year later Captain Phineas Pond of Wallingford called on Titus Preston for extensive work. Boards were replaced, and Preston installed "a chair with a framed bottom without legs" to which he "fix[ed] springs" to provide comfort. A new vehicle was Timothy Marsh's objective in 1821 at Windsor when he and Oliver Moore of Granby exchanged services: "Oliver Moore is to make a slay or waggon for sd Marsh at the market prices and receive his pay in Chairs at the market price sd chairs to be taken by sd Moore at Marshes shop in Windsor and sd Waggon or slay to be taken by sd Mars[h] at Moores shop in Granby." Silas Cheney of Litchfield and Daniel Foot of Lee, Massachusetts, agreed that Cheney would make a new wagon priced at $24 to haul the "chair stuff" Foot made and distributed to area shops. A "Waggon Chair" cost $2 more. A later agreement between Thomas Boardman, bank cashier at East Haddam, Connecticut, and wheelwright Azel G. Snow for a $30 "Lumber Waggon" set explicit standards, stating that "the Waggon . . . be painted and Varnished in a good workmanlike manner."[286]

Careful packing was as essential to overland transportation as to exportation, and craftsmen found it advantageous to capitalize on this point in their advertisements. In 1809 William Challen of Lexington, Kentucky, packed his chairs "to send to any part of the state, without injuring." Andrew L. Haskell packaged furniture "for transportation" in 1827 at Dover, New Hampshire. Jonathan Mullen boxed chairs at Cincinnati in a manner "to be conveyed with perfect safety, over the roughest roads." Some chairs were sent knocked down in boxes, similar to export merchandise. Thomas Henning, Sr., had his doubts about the effectiveness of even the best packing and suggested to his customers in West Virginia that he "deliver chairs unpainted, and paint them where they are to be used." Freighting by general carriers posed other problems. John Doggett and Company of Boston, dealers in looking glasses and other merchandise, noted their difficulty in collecting a debt in 1827 as a result of a misunderstanding on a customer's part or questionable activity by the forwarding agent:

> Merrit & Ashby are not our agents and have never been entrusted by us in any way. —
> We delivered our bill *not receipted* to the *driver* of the *Waggon* to be handed to you
> with the glass, but we never authorized him to receive the money nor did we authorize
> him to employ Merrit & Ashby to receive it. As you were to pay for the carriage of the
> article, neither the driver nor his employers, Meritt & Ashby can be considered as our
> agents in any light whatever.[287]

Perhaps the misunderstanding could have been avoided had communication been better. James Greenleaf took particular care at Boston to draw an agreement in advance when conveying goods to Rhode Island. He wrote on July 15, 1796, to his friend Doctor Peter Turner of East Greenwich:

> I have taken the Liberty to address to your care under the guidance of Messrs Guild &
> Fuller Waggoners — Two Waggon Loads of household Furniture Trunks &c — which I
> request you would have the goodness to receive and have placed in my house at East
> Greenwich — Messrs Guild & Fuller guarantee from all damage from bad weather and
> breaking down — you will please therefore to note particularly any damage that may
> have arisen & you will oblige me by writing a line by return of the Waggoners, address-
> ing to me at Mrs Grammon's, Providence where I shall be on Monday Evening & on
> Wednesday. . . . A list . . . is inclosed.

On the reverse Greenleaf noted Doctor Turner's place of residence as "Near the Court House" so as to avoid confusion.[288]

Railroad Transportation
Development of a comprehensive system of railroads by the mid-nineteenth century brought substantial change to the chair industry, opening a vast new potential for distribution. The railroad permitted the factory system to grow and endure. Through the influence of Levi Heywood the Fitchburg Railroad, which opened in 1854, included Gardner, Massachusetts, on its route and gave the Heywood Chair

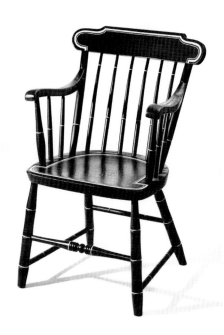

FIG. 4-44 Rounded-end tablet-top Windsor armchair, William O. Haskell (stencil), Boston, 1855. Mahogany (arms) and other woods; H. 34⅜", (seat) 16½", W. (crest) 23¼", (arms) 22¾", (seat) 19", D. (seat) 17½"; paint and decoration modern. *(Collection of Portsmouth Athenæum, Portsmouth, N.H.)*

Company and other businesses of the area new outlets for their products and "access to the lumber regions of New Hampshire and Vermont." Within twenty years cars of the Boston, Barre, and Gardner Railroad were loaded at the factory platform, introducing economies in shipping and maintaining better control over packing. By 1849 J. P. Wilder of New Ipswich, New Hampshire, described chair shipments for Lowell, Massachusetts, as "forwarded by Railroad." The initial freight charge per chair was slightly more than 1½¢; by 1855 the figure had risen to 3½¢. Wilder likely hauled chairs by wagon to the neighboring town of Mason to make the connection for Lowell.[289]

In a rare example a group of Windsor chairs shipped by railroad in 1855 from Boston to Portsmouth, New Hampshire, can be identified by maker, dealer, carrier, and consumer (figs. **4-44**, **4-45**, **4-46**). Typical of contemporary practice, these Boston chairs of late tablet-top design bear a producer's stencil on the plank bottom: "WM. O. HASKELL,/MAKER/141 NORTH st./BOSTON" (fig. 4-44). Haskell, who had been in business almost twenty years, probably was one of several chairmakers who supplied dealers Blake, Ware and Company with seating furniture. Chairs of similar pattern and detail are branded by chairmaker John C. Hubbard. After J. M. Tredick placed the order on behalf of the Portsmouth Athenaeum, Blake, Ware and Company packed the chairs in twelve bundles and sent them to the railroad depot (fig. 4-45). The bill identifies the unit price as $3.75 and indicates that two stools accompanied the order. The Eastern Railroad shipped the chairs about October 31 (fig. 4-46). The waybill lists freight charges of $2.47 with an additional 25¢ fee for carting, probably from the Portsmouth depot to the Athenæum. Earlier, Ransom Cook of Saratoga, New York, had shipped eleven bundles of chair seats and two boxes of chair backs on the Saratoga and Schenectady Railroad for $5.45.[290]

Connecticut chairmakers also enjoyed the benefits of railroad transportation. The New Haven and Hartford line was operational by 1840, and within a few years trains ran from New Haven to Plainville and from Bridgeport up the Naugatuck Valley. These advances meant prosperity for some but proved disastrous for Lambert Hitchcock. In relocating at Unionville, near Farmington, he had counted on cheap canal transportation to move his goods to market. When the Farmington Canal closed in 1847 after years of problems, his fate was sealed. Plainville was far enough away to make land carriage difficult and costly in a highly competitive market. For every failure, however, there were many successes, and on the whole railroad transportation was beneficial to most businesses. At Baltimore, Maryland, J. Creamer and Son, lumber merchants, enjoyed wide distribution by 1842 via "*Vessel* or *Rail Road.*" Frederick Starr, who operated a furniture manufactory at Rochester, New York, noted in 1841 that his location on Main Street was "near the Rail-Road" (fig. 4-32). Canadian woodworkers also prospered from improved transportation. In 1863 the *Canadian Illustrated News* noted the special arrangement of the Bowmanville Cabinet Factory with the Grand Trunk Railway Company, which permitted the firm to ship furniture and chairs "at a low rate of freight."[291]

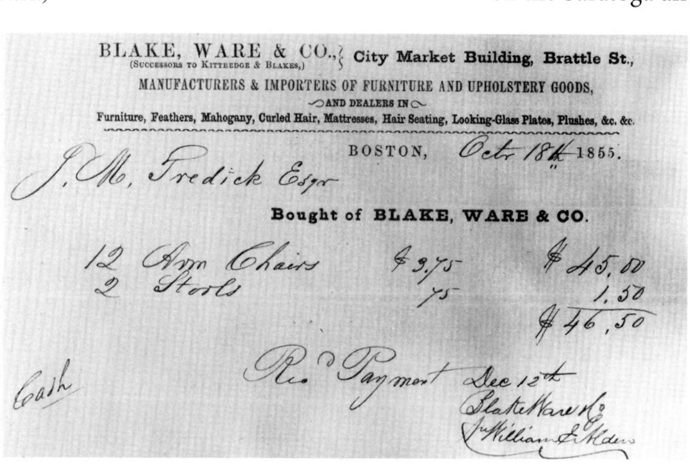

BLAKE, WARE & CO., (Successors to Kittredge & Blakes,) City Market Building, Brattle St.,
MANUFACTURERS & IMPORTERS OF FURNITURE AND UPHOLSTERY GOODS,
AND DEALERS IN
Furniture, Feathers, Mahogany, Curled Hair, Mattresses, Hair Seating, Looking-Glass Plates, Plushes, &c. &c.
BOSTON, Octr 18th 1855.
J. M. Tredick Esqr
Bought of BLAKE, WARE & CO.
12 Arm Chairs $3.75 $45.00
2 Stools 75 1.50
$46.50
Cash
Recd Payment Dec 12th
Blake Ware & Co

FIG. 4-45 Blake, Ware and Company bill to J. M. Tredick for the Portsmouth Athenæum, Boston, October 18, 1855. *(Collection of Portsmouth Athenæum.)*

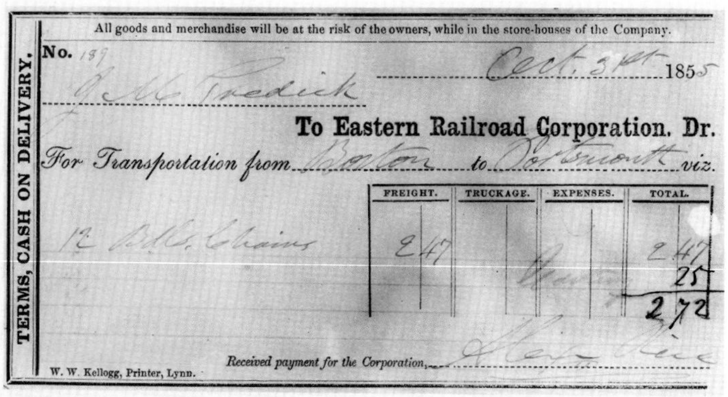

All goods and merchandise will be at the risk of the owners, while in the store-houses of the Company.
TERMS, CASH ON DELIVERY.
No. Oct. 31st 1855
J. M. Tredick
To Eastern Railroad Corporation. Dr.
For Transportation from Boston to Portsmouth viz.

	FREIGHT.	TRUCKAGE.	EXPENSES.	TOTAL.
12 Bdls Chairs	2 47			2 47
				25
				2 72

Received payment for the Corporation,
W. W. Kellogg, Printer, Lynn.

FIG. 4-46 Eastern Railroad Corporation bill to J. M. Tredick for the Portsmouth Athenæum, Boston, October 31, 1855. *(Collection of Portsmouth Athenæum.)*

1. Victor S. Clark, *History of Manufactures in the United States*, 3 vols. (1929; reprint, New York: Peter Smith, 1949), 1:354.

2. Jedidiah Morse, *American Geography* (Elizabethtown, N.J.: Shepard Kollock, 1789), p. 82; William B. Weeden, *Economic and Social History of New England, 1620–1789*, 2 vols. (Boston: Houghton Mifflin, 1891), 2:761.

3. Abraham Ritter, *Philadelphia and Her Merchants as Constituted Fifty and Seventy Years Ago* (Philadelphia: By the author, 1860), p. 19; Philip Padelford, ed., *Colonial Panorama, 1775: Dr. Robert Honyman's Journal* (San Marino, Calif.: Huntington Library, 1939), p. 14; Marquis de Chastellux, *Travels in North-America in the Years 1780, 1781, and 1782*, 2 vols. (London: G. G. J. and J. Robinson, 1787), 1:325–26.

4. Weeden, *Economic and Social History*, 2:757; J. F. D. Smyth, *A Tour in the United States of America*, 2 vols. (London: G. Robinson et al., 1784), 2:375; Morse, *American Geography*, p. 256; duc de la Rochefoucauld Liancourt, *Travels through the United States of North America*, 2 vols. (London: R. Phillips, 1799), 2:455; Marshall B. Davidson, *New York: A Pictorial History* (New York: Charles Scribner's Sons, 1977), p. 72.

5. Federal Procession notice, *Impartial Gazetteer* (New York), August 9, 1788, as quoted in Rita Susswein Gottesman, comp., *The Arts and Crafts in New York,1777–1799* (New York: New-York Historical Society, 1954), p. 109; Tench Coxe, *A View of the United States of America* (Philadelphia: William Hall et al., 1794), pp. ix, 25, 405–7; impost data in "Information respecting Laws passed in any of the United States of America affecting the Commerce or property of his Majesty's Subjects," Board of Trade, American Trade Volume, 1784–91, Public Record Office, London (hereafter cited PRO).

6. Samuel Eliot Morison and Henry Steele Commager, *The Growth of the American Republic*, 2 vols., 4th ed. (New York: Oxford University Press, 1950), 1:354–58, 370–73; Eliza Cope Harrison, ed., *Philadelphia Merchant: The Diary of Thomas P. Cope, 1800–1851* (South Bend, Ind.: Gateway Editions, 1978), pp. 110, 228.

7. Samuel Eliot Morison, *The Maritime History of Massachusetts, 1783–1860* (London: William Heinemann, 1923), p. 206; Sarah Anna Emery, *Reminiscences of a Nonagenarian* (Newburyport, Mass.: William H. Huse, 1879), p. 275.

8. "Morris Birkbeck's Notes," in John W. Harpster, ed., *Pen Pictures of Early Western Pennsylvania* (Pittsburgh: University of Pittsburgh Press, 1938), pp. 274–75; Henry Bradshaw Fearon, *Sketches of America*, 2d ed. (London: Longman et al., 1818), p. 196.

9. Gilbert Imlay, *A Topographical Description of the Western Territory of North America* (London: J. Debrett, 1793), p. 93, and William Darby, *The Emigrant's Guide to the Western and Southwestern States and Territories* (New York: Kirk and Mercein, 1818), p. 217, as quoted in Betty Lawson Walters, *Furniture Makers of Indiana, 1793 to 1850* (Indianapolis: Indiana Historical Society, 1972), p. 11; Fearon, *Sketches*, p. 385; La Rochefoucauld Liancourt, *Travels*, 2:583.

10. "Pittsburgh in 1829," in Harpster, *Pen Pictures*, p. 295; T. V. Olsen, "The Great Lakes: Gateway to the Heartland," in Western Writers of America, *Water Trails West* (Garden City, N.Y.: Doubleday, 1978), pp. 101–2.

11. J. Hammond Trumbull, *Memorial History of Hartford County, Connecticut, 1633–1884*, 2 vols. (Boston: Edward L. Osgood, 1886), 1:553; Marshall B. Davidson, *Life in America*, 2 vols. (Boston: Houghton Mifflin, 1951), 2:198, 203.

12. Davidson, *Life in America*, 2:226; Carl David Arfwedson, *The United States and Canada*, 2 vols. (1834; reprint, New York: Johnson Reprint Corp., 1969), 1:47; *The Diary of William Bentley*, 4 vols. (Salem, Mass.: Essex Institute, 1905), 4:257.

13. Robert T. Smith, "The 'Father of Waters,'" and Robert West Howard, "The Ohio River: Throughway 'For the West,'" in Western Writers of America, *Water Trails West*, pp. 20, 44–45, 48–49, 50; Fearon, *Sketches*, p. 267; *Cramer's Pittsburgh Almanac for . . . 1813* (Pittsburgh, Pa.: Cramer, Spear and Eichbaum, 1812), pp. 49–50; Davidson, *Life in America*, 2:232, 235; William G. Lyford, *The Western Address Directory* (Baltimore, Md.: J. Robinson, 1837), p. 166; Louis C. Hunter, *Steamboats on the Western Rivers* (Cambridge, Mass.: Harvard University Press, 1949), pp. 645–46.

14. Clark, *History of Manufactures*, 1:338–39; Morse, *American Geography*, p. 382; Cadwallader D. Colden, *Memoir Prepared at the Request of a Committee of the Common Council of the City of New York and Presented to the Mayor of the City at the Celebration of the Completion of the New York Canals* (New York: W. A. Davis, 1825), pp. 148, 157, 210–11; Henry Tudor, *Narrative of a Tour in North America*, 2 vols. (London: James Duncan, 1834), 1:180–81; [Theodore Dwight, Jr.], *The Northern Traveller*, 2d ed. (New York: A. T. Goodrich, 1826), pp. 48–49; Davidson, *Life in America*, 2:218, 221; Davidson, *New York*, p. 94.

15. [Dwight], *Northern Traveller*, p. 50; Arfwedson, *United States and Canada*, 2:278.

16. Arfwedson, *United States and Canada*, 2:262, 265; Clark, *History of Manufactures*, 1:351.

17. Entries for ship *Ruby*, June 13, 1749, snows *Charming Polly*, October 4, 1752, and *Hannah*, December 20, 1752, and sloop *Charming Peggy*, October 23, 1755, Shipping Returns: Jamaica, 1752–53, Barbados, 1728–53, and Bahamas, 1753–57, Colonial Office, PRO; Trumble reference in Nancy A. Goyne (Evans), "Francis Trumble of Philadelphia, Windsor Chair and Cabinetmaker," in Milo M. Naeve, ed., *Winterthur Portfolio 1* (Winterthur, Del.: Winterthur Museum, 1964), p. 233; John Wheaton memorandum to Obediah and Nicholas Brown, August 5, 1758, Papers of Obediah Brown, Rhode Island Historical Society, Providence (hereafter cited RIHS); "Journal of Lord Adam Gordon," in Howard H. Peckham, ed., *Narratives of Colonial America, 1704–1765* (Chicago: R. R. Donnelley and Sons, 1971), pp. 262–63.

18. Entry for brig *Mansfield*, November 20, 1760, Shipping Returns: Jamaica, 1760–69, Colonial Office, PRO; bill of lading, ship *Grape*, December 15, 1763, Bills of Lading, principally William Bishop and Thomas Riche, Historical Society of Pennsylvania, Philadelphia (hereafter cited HSP); manifests of brig *Morning Star*, May 29 and August 14, 1767, and vessels *Hannah*, December 3, 1768, *Mercury*, December 14, 1767, and *Industry*, March 30, 1767, Philadelphia Customhouse Papers, vols. 6, 7, 10, HSP; Harrold E. Gillingham, "The Philadelphia Windsor Chair and Its Journeyings," *Pennsylvania Magazine of History and Biography* 55, no. 3 (October 1931): 310–11.

19. Entries for ships *Mercury*, March 30,1767, and *Speedwell*, May 13, 1768, Shipping Returns: Jamaica, 1760–69, Colonial Office, PRO; Benjamin Randolph account book, 1767–87, New York Public Library, New York (hereafter cited NYPL; microfilm, Joseph Downs Collection of Manuscripts and Printed Ephemera, Winterthur Museum and Library [hereafter cited DCM and WL]); Goyne, "Francis Trumble," p. 236; invoices of brigs *Charlotte*, August 21, 1767, and *Industry*, September 28, 1767, in Aaron Lopez outward bound invoice book, 1763–68, Newport Historical Society, Newport, R.I. (hereafter cited NHS); Aaron Lopez to John Newdigate, August 20, 1767, in Aaron Lopez letter book, 1767, NHS.

20. Aaron Lopez to John Peters and Abraham Mendes, September 28 and 27, 1767, in Lopez letter book; invoice of brig *Sally*, November 20, 1768, Lopez outward bound invoice book; invoice of sloop *Betsey*, February 15, 1773, Aaron Lopez shipping book, 1771–73, NHS; Rhode Island and Philadelphia exports in Mabel Munson Swan, "Coastwise Cargoes of Venture Furniture," *Antiques* 55, no. 4 (April 1949): 279.

21. Perry, Hayes, and Sherbrooke, *New-York Mercury* (New York), December 6, 1762 (reference courtesy of Susan B. Swan); Andrew Gautier, *New-York Gazette, or Weekly Post Boy* (New York), June 6, 1765; John Kelso, *New-York Gazette and the Weekly Mercury* supplement (New York), September 5, 1774; Adam Galer, *Rivington's New-York Gazetteer* (New York), September 2, 1774; "Richard Smith [Journal]," in Roland Van Zandt, ed., *Chronicles of the Hudson: Three Centuries of Travelers' Accounts* (New Brunswick, N.J.: Rutgers University Press, 1971), p. 75.

22. Bill of lading for sloop *Retrieve*, June 27, 1771, Wetmore Papers, vol. 6, Massachusetts Historical Society, Boston (hereafter cited MHS); entries for sloop *Deborah*, September 13, 1763, and schooner *Jane*, December 27, 1764, Shipping Returns: Massachusetts, 1752–65, PRO; John Andrews–William Barrell correspondence, 1772–73, Andrews-Eliot Papers, MHS; William Barrell memorandum and account book, 1772–76, and daybook, 1772, Stephen Collins Collection, Library of Congress, Washington, D.C. (hereafter cited LC); Samuel Barrett to Stephen Salisbury, April 1, 1779, Salisbury Papers, American Antiquarian Society, Worcester, Mass. (hereafter cited AAS).

23. A. J. Alexander, *Maryland Gazette* (Annapolis), April 5, 1763, as quoted in Henry J. Berkley, "A Register of Cabinet Makers and Allied Trades in Maryland, as Shown by the Newspapers and Directories, 1746 to 1820," *Maryland Historical Magazine* 25, no. 1 (March 1930): 9; Adams and Hollingsworth account of William Thomas, 1765–66, Hollingsworth Manuscripts, Business Papers, HSP; Annapolis Port of Entry Books, vol. 1 (1756–75), Maryland Historical Society, Baltimore (hereafter cited MdHS); James Brice ledger, 1767–1801, privately owned (microfilm, Maryland Hall of Records, Annapolis; reference courtesy of Karen E. Peterson); Oxford Port of Entry Account Books, vol. 1759–73, Inward Entries, MdHS.

24. Goyne, "Francis Trumble," p. 234.

25. Goyne, "Francis Trumble," pp. 234–35.

26. Goyne, "Francis Trumble," p. 235; Clement Biddle letter book, 1769–70, Thomas A. Biddle Co., Business Books, HSP.

27. Sloop *John* entry, *Virginia Gazette* (Williamsburg), March 31, 1768; sloops *Success* and *Lucretia* entries, *Virginia Gazette, or Norfolk Intelligencer* (Norfolk), June 23, 1774, and February 23, 1775, citation file, Museum of Early Southern Decorative Arts, Winston-Salem, N.C. (hereafter cited MESDA); schooner *Peggy* entry, *Virginia Gazette*, February 3, 1774; invoice of sloop *Florida*, July 20, 1768, in Lopez outward bound invoice book.

28. Brigs *Hannah* and *Harrietta* notices, *South Carolina Gazette* (Charleston), June 6, 1761, and *South-Carolina Gazette and Country Journal* (Charleston), January 21, 1766, Prime cards, WL; Philadelphia vessel, *South Carolina Gazette*, June 27, 1761, and Thomas Shirley notice, *South-Carolina Gazette and Country Journal*, December 17, 1765, citation file, MESDA; Charleston entries, 1762, in "South Carolina Naval Office Lists from March 25, 1736, to January 5, 1764," Colonial Office, PRO.

29. William Sykes, John James, and Sykes and Lushington notices, *South Carolina Gazette*, May 1, 1770, December 7, 1771, May 14 and July 2, 1772, and September 12, 1774, citation file, MESDA, and Prime cards, WL; James Bentham notice, *South Carolina and American General Gazette* (Charleston), March 10, 1775.

30. Entries for schooners *Fanny* and *Ogeeche*, October 11 and June 19, 1766, Shipping Returns: Georgia, 1752–64, Colonial Office, PRO; invoice of brig *Sally*, December 24, 1767, Lopez outward bound invoice book, and Lopez to John Hyer, December 24, 1767, Lopez letter book.

31. Entries for schooners *Mary* and *Brouton Island Packet*, June 1 and August 20, 1767, April 14, 1768, and March 9, 1769, Shipping Returns: East Florida, 1765–69, Colonial Office, PRO.

32. Ledger of Imports and Exports: America, 1768–73, British Board of Customs and Excise, PRO.

33. Ledger of Imports and Exports, British Board of Customs and Excise, PRO.

34. Andrew Redmond, *South Carolina Gazette and General Advertiser* (Charleston), October 14, 1783, Prime cards, WL; exports to New York and New England in Gillingham, "Philadelphia Windsor Chair," pp. 312, 314–15; William Cox bill to Stephen Collins, and Stephen Collins to Ebenezer Hall, September 27, 1786, Stephen Collins and Son letter book, 1786–87, Collins Collection, LC.

35. Gillingham, "Philadelphia Windsor Chair," pp. 318–27, including vessel *Commerce*; manifest of brig *Hunter*, May 12, 1785, Philadelphia Customhouse Papers, Outward Entries, 1785–86, HSP; Joseph Carson receipt book, 1783–86, HSP; William Cox bills to Stephen and John Girard, April 28 and November 10, 1786, Girard Papers, Board of Directors of City Trusts, Girard College History Collections, Philadelphia, Pa. (microfilm, American Philosophical Society, Philadelphia); brig *Charleston* notice, *City Gazette, or the Daily Advertiser* (Charleston, S.C.), September 15, 1789, citation file, MESDA.

36. Gillingham, "Philadelphia Windsor Chair," pp. 320, 322, 325–26; ship *Clementina* notice, *South Carolina Gazette and General Advertiser*, June 17, 1784, Prime cards, WL; manifests of schooner *Success* and brig *Philadelphia*, August 20 and 22, 1789, Philadelphia Outward Coastwise Manifests, U.S. Custom House Records, National Archives, Washington, D.C. (hereafter cited NA); riding chair notice, *Charleston Morning Post* (Charleston, S.C.), January 22, 1787, Prime cards, WL; notices mentioning paint colors (Charleston, S.C.): *Columbia Herald*, March 31 and August 10, 1785, and January 20, 1786, *Charleston Evening Gazette*, June 23, 1786, *Charleston Morning Post*, April 9, 1787, and *City Gazette, or the Daily Advertiser*, August 15 and November 13, 1789, Prime cards, WL, and citation file, MESDA; bills of lading for sloops *Dispatch*, October 23, 1784, and *Nancy*, April 16, 1785, Richard Blow Papers, Swem Library, College of William and Mary, Williamsburg, Va. (hereafter cited WM); manifest of sloop *Dispatch*, October 23, 1784, Philadelphia Customhouse Papers, Outward Entries, 1784–85, HSP; book of inward entries,

district of Elizabeth River, port of Norfolk, Va., 1789, Virginia State Library, Richmond; Francis Trumble bill of lading for schooner *Friendship*, May 3, 1786, private collection; Washington information in Helen Maggs Fede, *Washington Furniture at Mount Vernon* (Mount Vernon, Va.: Mount Vernon Ladies' Association, 1966), pp. 30, 33.

37. Gillingham, "Philadelphia Windsor Chair," pp. 327–29; broadside, "Port of Philadelphia, Exports 1786," Hagley Museum and Library, Wilmington, Del. (photostat, DCM); 1787 Philadelphia export figures in Morse, *American Geography*, p. 334; *The American Museum, or Universal Magazine* 6 (1789): 108.

38. Jacob Vanderpool, *Town and Country Journal* (New York), December 11, 1783, and Gabriel Leggett, *Daily Advertiser* (New York), March 20, 1786, as quoted in Gottesman, *Arts and Crafts, 1777–1799*, pp. 123, 130; Thomas and William Ash, *New-York Packet* (New York), October 7, 1784; manifest of schooner *Columbia*, September 25, 1789, New York Outward Entries, U.S. Custom House Records, French Spoliation Claims, NA; brig *Rockahock* notice, *Gazette of the State of Georgia* (Savannah), May 11, 1786, citation file, MESDA; Thomas Ash I and William Ash I bill to St. George Tucker, August 8, 1786, Tucker-Colemen Papers, WM; "General Account of Exports, from the Port of New-York," 1788, in *Journal of the Assembly of the State of New-York, at Their Twelfth Session, Begun and Holden at the City of Albany, the Eleventh Day of December, 1788 [to 2 March, 1789]* (Albany, N.Y.: Samuel and John Louden, [1789]), p. 71.

39. Joseph K. Ott, "Exports of Furniture, Chaises, and Other Wooden Forms from Providence and Newport, 1783–1795," *Antiques* 108, no. 1 (January 1975): 135–41; Swan, "Coastwise Cargoes," pp. 278–80; manifest of brig *Seven Brothers*, September 24, 1788, "Registry of Newport Vessels, 1785–90," RIHS; Ebenezer Stone, *Massachusetts Gazette* (Boston), September 11, 1787, and *Independent Chronicle* (Boston), April 13, 1786.

40. "Port of Philadelphia, Exports 1786"; Morse, *American Geography*, p. 334; *The American Museum, or Universal Magazine* 8 (1790): 11, 115.

41. Gillingham, "Philadelphia Windsor Chair," pp. 330–32; Philadelphia Outward Entries, 1790–99, U.S. Custom House Records, some French Spoliation Claims, NA.

42. Gillingham, "Philadelphia Windsor Chair," pp. 330–32; Philadelphia Outward Entries, 1790–99, U.S. Custom House Records, some French Spoliation Claims, NA.

43. Gillingham, "Philadelphia Windsor Chair," p. 331; Philadelphia Outward Entries, 1790–99, U.S. Custom House Records, some French Spoliation Claims, NA; specialized Windsor furniture advertised in *Charleston City Gazette and Daily Advertiser* (Charleston,

S.C.): settees, May 15, 1798, and April 17, 1799, children's cribs, September 12, 1798, counting-house stools and children's high chairs, December 11, 1799, Prime cards, WL; chocolate-color chairs in *City Gazette and Daily Advertiser* (Charleston, S.C.), March 7, 1798, citation file, MESDA.

44. Manifests of sloops *Polly*, June 28, 1790, *Nancy*, November 7, 1795, and *Harmony*, February 5, 1799, Philadelphia Outward Entries, U.S. Custom House Records, the first a French Spoliation Claim, NA; Mary Tyler Cheek, "Stratford Hall, the Virginia Home of the Lees," *Antiques* 119, no. 3 (March 1981): 642–48; George Washington to William Pierce, May 1, 1796, as quoted in Fede, *Washington Furniture*, p. 58.

45. Manifests of schooners *Pt. Royal*, March 1798, and *Ann*, April 12, 1799, Philadelphia Outward Coastwise Entries, U.S. Custom House Records, NA. Stephen Cocke account book, 1791, Virginia Historical Society, Richmond (hereafter cited VaHS, reference courtesy of Helen S. T. Reed); see also Helen Scott Townsend Reed, "Woodlands, a Virginia Plantation House," *Antiques* 119, no. 1 (January 1981): 228–29. Solomon Maxwell to Lawrence Allwine, August 25, 1794, Hollingsworth Manuscripts, Business Papers, HSP.

46. Bill of lading for schooner *Thomas*, March 10, 1791, William Cox bill to Stephen Girard, March 12, 1791, Joseph Henzey bill to Stephen Girard, September 20, 1792, John B. Ackley accounts of Stephen Girard, 1796, and Taylor and King bill to Stephen Girard, May 21, 1799, all in Girard Papers. For a serpentine-top rod-back chair, see Nancy Goyne Evans, *American Windsor Chairs* (New York: Hudson Hills Press, 1996), fig. 3-112.

47. Capt. Samuel Crozier shipping receipt to Stephen Collins and Son, October 25, 1792, Stephen Collins and Son, daybook, 1786–94, and letter book, 1792–1801, all in Collins Collection, LC.

48. William Cox bill to Zaccheus Collins, May 20, 1795, and Zaccheus Collins to Joseph Blake, June 15, 1795 (two), Stephen Collins and Son letter book, 1794–1801, Collins Collection, LC; Zaccheus Collins receipt book, 1794–1831, Daniel Parker Papers, HSP.

49. John DeWitt, *New-York Weekly Chronicle* (New York), June 18, 1795, and Thomas Timpson, *The Diary, or Loudon's Register* (New York), May 11, 1792, as quoted in Gottesman, *Arts and Crafts, 1777–1799*, pp. 115, 129; manifests of sloops *Olive Branch*, December 18, 1795, *Commerce*, December 10, 1795, and *Nancy*, October 8, 1793, New York Outward Entries, U.S. Custom House Records, French Spoliation Claims, NA; New York Outward Entries, 1790–99, U.S. Custom House Records, French Spoliation Claims, NA; William Palmer to Gen. Charles Ridgely, October 10, 1797, as quoted in John Henry Hill, "The Furniture Craftsmen in

Baltimore, 1783–1823" (master's thesis, University of Delaware, 1967), pp. 14–15.

50. William Bingham to Nicholas Low, June 23, 1792, William Bingham letter book, 1791–93, HSP; see also Margaret L. Brown, "Mr. and Mrs. William Bingham of Philadelphia," *Pennsylvania Magazine of History and Biography* 61, no. 3 (July 1937): 301, and Robert C. Alberts, *The Golden Voyage: The Life and Times of William Bingham, 1752–1804* (Boston: Houghton Mifflin, 1969), pp. 222–23. Owners of sloop *Salem* bill of freight to Nicholas Low, June 30, 1792, Nicholas Low Collection, LC.

51. New York Outward Entries, 1790–99, U.S. Custom House Records, French Spoliation Claims, NA; Newport Inward and Outward Entries, 1790–1800, U.S. Custom House Records, Federal Archives and Records Center, Waltham, Mass. (hereafter cited FRC-Waltham).

52. New York Outward Entries, 1790–99, U.S. Custom House Records, French Spoliation Claims, NA; James Bertine bill to Dean Sweet, May 8, 1792, A. C. and R. W. Greene Collection, RIHS; Newport Inward and Outward Entries, 1790–1800, U.S. Custom House Records, FRC-Waltham.

53. Joseph K. Ott, "Rhode Island Furniture Exports, 1783–1800, Including Information on Chaises, Buildings, Other Woodenware and Trade Practices," *Rhode Island History* 36, no. 1 (February 1977): 2–13; Newport Inward and Outward Entries, 1790–1800, U.S. Custom House Records, FRC-Waltham.

54. New London Outward Entries, 1792–1801, U.S. Custom House Records, French Spoliation Claims, NA; Coxe, *View of the United States*, p. 414.

55. Boston Outward Entries, 1790–1801, U.S. Custom House Records, French Spoliation Claims, NA; Timothy Dwight, *Travels in New England and New York*, 4 vols., ed. Barbara Miller Solomon (Cambridge, Mass.: Belknap Press, 1969), 1:363.

56. Salem-Beverly Outward Entries, 1790–1800, U.S. Custom House Records, French Spoliation Claims, NA; Elijah and Jacob Sanderson account current with Benjamin Bullock, November 22, 1794, to June 8, 1795, and Micaiah Johnson account of Elijah and Jacob Sanderson, 1794–95, Papers of Elijah Sanderson, vol. 1 (1785–1809), Peabody Essex Museum, Salem, Mass. (hereafter cited PEM).

57. Caleb Hannah, *Federal Gazette and Baltimore Daily Advertiser* (Baltimore, Md.), December 2, 1799, citation file, MESDA; Baltimore Outward Entries, 1792–99, U.S. Custom House Records, French Spoliation Claims, NA; Vosburgh and Dunbibin, *Hall's Wilmington Gazette* (Wilmington, N.C.), May 31, 1798, citation file, MESDA; Savannah Outward Entries, 1792–96, U.S. Custom House Records, French Spoliation Claims, NA.

58. Entry for snow *Charming Polly*, October

4, 1752, Shipping Returns: Barbados, 1728–53, Colonial Office, PRO.

59. Invoices of merchandise, January and February, 1772, February 8, 1776, and December 17, 1777, John Parkinson invoice book, 1772–79, Chancery Masters' Exhibits, C-108, no. 42, PRO; invoices of merchandise, March 3, October, and December 1774, and waste book, 1776, Gillow Papers, Westminster Libraries, London (microfilm, DCM).

60. Shipping Returns: Barbados, 1783–1804, Grenada, 1783–88, and Dominica, 1764–91, Colonial Office, PRO; Dr. George Rutherford estate records, 1797, Chancery Masters' Exhibits, C-104, no. 25, PRO.

61. Coxe, *View of the United States*, p. 72.

62. Manifest of sloop *Adventure*, May 15, 1784, and voyages of other vessels on July 18, August 1 and 16, 1785, Philadelphia Customhouse Papers, Outward Entries, 1784–85, HSP; manifests of sloops *Three Sisters*, February 19, 1798, and *Cato*, May 20, 1799, New York Outward Entries, Custom House Records, French Spoliation Claims, NA; manifest of schooner *Rover*, August 6, 1801, New Haven Outward Foreign Entries, Custom House Records, French Spoliation Claims, NA.

63. Gillingham, "Philadelphia Windsor Chair," p. 324; Philadelphia Customhouse Papers, Outward Entries, 1784–85 and 1785–86, HSP; New York, 1790–1801, Providence, 1792–1801, Newport, 1792–1801, and Boston, 1791–1801, Outward Entries, U.S. Custom House Records, French Spoliation Claims, NA; entry for sloop *Little John*, November 4, 1785, Shipping Returns: Bahamas (1784–1813), Colonial Office, PRO.

64. Manifest of ship *Charming Molly*, December 8, 1784, Philadelphia Customhouse Papers, Outward Entries, 1784–85, HSP; manifest of ship *John*, December 3, 1789, Philadelphia Outward Foreign Entries, Custom House Records, NA.

65. Earl C. Tanner, "Caribbean Ports in the Foreign Commerce of Providence, 1790–1830, Part 1," *Rhode Island History* 14, no. 4 (October 1955): 105–7; La Rochefoucauld Liancourt, *Travels*, 2:263.

66. Philadelphia Outward Foreign Entries, 1789–1800, U.S. Custom House Records, some French Spoliation Claims, NA; Stephen Girard bills of lading, brigs *Kitty*, July 29, 1787, and *Polly*, July 7, 1791, Girard Papers; William Cox bill to Stephen and John Girard, July 28, 1787, and bill to Stephen Girard, July 7, 1791, and Joseph Henzey account of Stephen Girard, 1796, all in Girard Papers. Positive identification that the Cox chairs were part of the *Kitty*'s cargo on July 29, 1787, occurs in entries titled "Adventure to Cape francois" in a Girard journal, 1786–90, and a waste book, 1786–88, Girard Papers.

67. Gillingham, "Philadelphia Windsor Chair," p. 331; Dutilh and Wachsmuth invoice of goods, October 23, 1790, DCM; Philadel-

phia Customhouse Papers, Outward Entries, 1785–86, HSP; Philadelphia Outward Entries, 1791–99, U.S. Custom House Records, French Spoliation Claims, NA; Philadelphia Outward Foreign Entries, 1789–1801, U.S. Custom House Records, NA; Stephen Girard bills of lading, brig *Kitty*, April 28 and July 29, 1787, and ca. 1793, schooners *Caroline*, October 14, 1786, and *Industry*, November 20, 1788, ship *Barnada*, July 27, 1789, and brig *Polly*, April 30 and July 7, 1791, Girard Papers.

68. Manifests of schooner *Del Carmer*, October 3, 1790, sloops *Trinity*, October 26, 1790, and *John*, May 18, 1797, brigs *Rebecca*, May 23, 1797, and *Lucy*, December 6, 1799, and other New York Outward Foreign Entries, 1800–1802, U.S. Custom House Records, French Spoliation Claims, NA.

69. New Haven and New London Outward Entries, 1786–1801 and 1792–1801, U.S. Custom House Records, French Spoliation Claims, NA; invoice of cargo for sloop *Nabby* and orders to Capt. Elisha Coit, June 11, 1788, Joseph Williams Papers, Mystic Seaport Museum, Mystic, Conn. (hereafter cited MSM).

70. Ott, "Rhode Island Furniture Exports," p. 6; Providence, 1792–1801, Newport, 1798–1801, and Boston, 1791–1801, Outward Entries, U.S. Custom House Records, French Spoliation Claims, NA.

71. Baltimore Outward Entries, 1792–99, U.S. Custom House Records, French Spoliation Claims, NA.

72. Manifest of schooner *Jane*, December 6, 1797, Philadelphia Outward Entries, U.S. Custom House Records, French Spoliation Claims, NA; Tanner, "Caribbean Ports, Part 2," *Rhode Island History* 15, no. 1 (January 1956): 15–19.

73. Philadelphia Outward Entries, 1797–1803, U.S. Custom House Records, some French Spoliation Claims, NA.

74. Philadelphia Outward Foreign Entries, 1789–1803 and 1799–1801, U.S. Custom House Records, the first a French Spoliation Claim, NA; Stephen Dutilh inventory of cargo, ship *Fair American*, ca. January 2, 1801, and letter, April 1, 1802, DCM.

75. Philadelphia Outward Entries, 1797–1803, U.S. Custom House Records, some French Spoliation Claims, NA.

76. New York Outward Entries, 1798–1802, U.S. Custom House Records, French Spoliation Claims, NA.

77. Providence and Newport Outward Entries, 1798–1801, U.S. Custom House Records, French Spoliation Claims, NA.

78. Boston and Baltimore Outward Entries, 1799–1801 and 1798–99, U.S. Custom House Records, French Spoliation Claims, NA.

79. Manifest of schooner *St. Carlos*, August 25, 1796, Baltimore Outward Entries, U.S. Custom House Records, French Spoliation Claims, NA; manifest of brig *Florida*, February 21, 1797, Philadelphia Outward Entries, U.S. Custom

House Records, French Spoliation Claims, NA; manifest of schooner *Esther*, May 10, 1799, Boston Outward Entries, U.S. Custom House Records, French Spoliation Claims, NA.

80. Gillingham, "Philadelphia Windsor Chair," pp. 318, 324, 326–27; Philadelphia Customhouse Papers, Outward Entries, 1784–85 and 1785–86, HSP; Philadelphia Outward Entries, 1791–1801, U.S. Custom House Records, French Spoliation Claims, NA; Philadelphia Outward Entries, 1789–1802, U.S. Custom House Records, NA; Shipping Returns: Virgin Islands (Tortola), 1784–86, Colonial Office, PRO; port of Patuxent, Md., outward entry, sloop *Kitty*, July 12, 1783, Otho Holland Williams accounts, 1773–96, MdHS; manifest of schooner *Peggy*, September 23, 1799, Baltimore Outward Entries, U.S. Custom House Records, French Spoliation Claims, NA.

81. John B. Ackley bill to Zaccheus Collins, August 13, 1796, and Zaccheus Collins letter and account to John C. Heineken, St. Croix, September 8, 1796, Collins Collection, LC.

82. New York Outward Entries, 1790–1802, U.S. Custom House Records, French Spoliation Claims, NA.

83. New Haven and New London Outward Entries, 1786–1801 and 1792–1801, U.S. Custom House Records, French Spoliation Claims, NA; "Return of Goods, Wares & Merchandizes exported from district of New London, State of Connecticut commencing 1 Ap: end'g 30 June 1793" (for the Danish West Indies), New London, Conn., Outward Foreign Manifests, 1789–1831, FRC-Waltham; Ott, "Rhode Island Furniture Exports," pp. 5–6; Providence and Boston Outward Entries, 1792–1801 and 1790–1801, U.S. Custom House Records, French Spoliation Claims, NA.

84. Tanner, "Caribbean Ports, Part 1," pp. 102–3; "Part 2," pp. 11–14.

85. Gillingham, "Philadelphia Windsor Chair," pp. 325–26; Shipping Returns: Antigua and Montserrat, 1784–1814, Colonial Office, PRO; Philadelphia Customhouse Papers, Outward Entries, 1784–85 and 1785–86, HSP; Philadelphia Outward Entries, 1792–1801, U.S. Custom House Records, French Spoliation Claims, NA; Philadelphia Outward Entries, 1789–1803, U.S. Custom House Records, NA.

86. New York and Baltimore Outward Entries, 1790–1802 and 1792–99, U.S. Custom House Records, French Spoliation Claims, NA; Alexandria Outward and Inward Entries, 1792–99, U.S. Custom House Records, French Spoliation Claims, NA.

87. Ott, "Rhode Island Furniture Exports," p. 6; New Haven and New London Outward Entries, 1786–1801 and 1792–1801, U.S. Custom House Records, French Spoliation Claims, NA; Boston Outward Entries, 1790–1801, U.S. Custom House Records, French Spoliation Claims, NA.

88. Gillingham, "Philadelphia Windsor

Chair," p. 324; Shipping Returns: Barbados, 1783–1804, Colonial Office, PRO; Philadelphia Customhouse Papers, Outward Entries, 1784–85 and 1785–86, HSP; Savannah Outward Entries, 1792–96, U.S. Custom House Records, French Spoliation Claims, NA.

89. Philadelphia Customhouse Papers, Outward Entries, 1784–85 and 1785–86, HSP; Shipping Returns: Granada, 1784–88, Colonial Office, PRO; Ott, "Rhode Island Furniture Exports," p. 6; Fairfield-Bridgeport Outward Entries, 1789–92, U.S. Custom House Records, French Spoliation Claims, NA; manifest of schooner *Patty*, October 26, 1801, Salem (and Beverly) Customhouse Records, PEM.

90. Philadelphia Outward Entries, 1792–93, U.S. Custom House Records, French Spoliation Claims, NA; James Brobson shipping record book, 1790–1805, DCM; Fairfield-Bridgeport, 1789–92, New London, 1792–1801, and New Haven, 1786–1801, Outward Entries, U.S. Custom House Records, French Spoliation Claims, NA; Boston and New York Outward Entries, 1790–1801, U.S. Custom House Records, French Spoliation Claims, NA; Tanner, "Caribbean Ports, Part 1," pp. 103–5.

91. Gillingham, "Philadelphia Windsor Chair," p. 329; Philadelphia Outward Entries, 1792–95, U.S. Custom House Records, French Spoliation Claims, NA; Philadelphia Outward Entries, 1789–1803, U.S. Custom House Records, NA; New Haven and Boston Outward Entries, 1786–1801 and 1790–1801, U.S. Custom House Records, French Spoliation Claims, NA.

92. Bill of lading, sloop *Betsey*, August 19, 1785, Jacob R. Rivera and Joseph Lopez shipping book, 1785–86, NHS; New York and Baltimore Outward Entries, 1791–1801 and 1792–99, U.S. Custom House Records, French Spoliation Claims, NA.

93. Philadelphia Customhouse Papers, Outward Entries, 1785–86, HSP; Philadelphia Outward Entries, 1791–95, U.S. Custom House Records, French Spoliation Claims, NA; Philadelphia Outward Entries, 1789–1803, U.S. Custom House Records, NA; Gilbert Gaw, *The True American and Commercial Advertiser* (Philadelphia, Pa.), July 10, 1798, Prime cards, WL.

94. New London Outward Entries, 1792–1801, U.S. Custom House Records, French Spoliation Claims, NA; La Rochefoucauld Liancourt, *Travels*, 1:511–12.

95. Tanner, "Caribbean Ports, Part 1," p. 103; "Part 2," pp. 14–15.

96. Baltimore Outward Entries, 1792–99, U.S. Custom House Records, French Spoliation Claims, NA; Ott, "Rhode Island Furniture Exports," p. 6; Gillingham, "Philadelphia Windsor Chair," p. 326; Philadelphia Outward Entries, 1797–1801, U.S. Custom House Records, French Spoliation Claims, NA.

97. New London, 1792–1801, Boston, 1790–1801, and New York, 1790–1802, Outward En-

tries, U.S. Custom House Records, French Spoliation Claims, NA.

98. Savannah Outward Entries, 1792–96, U.S. Custom House Records, French Spoliation Claims, NA; invoice of cargo, sloop *Nabby*, July 1786, orders to Capt. Elisha Coit, July 21, 1786, and memorandum of Elisha Coit, November 28, 1786, Williams Papers.

99. Invoice of cargo and memorandum of cargo, brig *Polly*, March 31, 1789, Williams Papers; New London Outward Entries, 1792–1801, U.S. Custom House Records, French Spoliation Claims, NA.

100. Boston and New York Outward Entries, 1790–1801 and 1790–1802, U.S. Custom House Records, French Spoliation Claims, NA; Newport Inward and Outward Entries, 1790–1800, U.S. Custom House Records, FRC-Waltham; Ott, "Rhode Island Furniture Exports," pp. 6, 9.

101. Ott, "Rhode Island Furniture Exports," p. 6; Gillingham, "Philadelphia Windsor Chair," p. 327; manifest of ship *Four Friends*, June 24, 1796, Philadelphia Outward Entries, U.S. Custom House Records, French Spoliation Claims, NA; New York Entries, 1790–1802, U.S. Custom House Records, French Spoliation Claims, NA.

102. Manifest of ship *Mary*, July 11, 1798, New York Outward Entries, U.S. Custom House Records, French Spoliation Claims, NA.

103. Manifest of sloop *Sally*, August 18, 1787, "Registry of Newport Vessels, 1785–90"; manifest of schooner *Charming Betsey*, July 26, 1790, Philadelphia Outward Foreign Entries, U.S. Custom House Records, French Spoliation Claims, NA; manifest of brig *Star*, June 24, 1801, New York Outward Entries, 1792–93, U.S. Custom House Records, French Spoliation Claims, NA.

104. Ott, "Rhode Island Furniture Exports," p. 6; Providence Outward Entries, 1792–1801, U.S. Custom House Records, French Spoliation Claims, NA; Swan, "Coastwise Cargoes," p. 279; Boston Outward Entries, 1790–1801, U.S. Custom House Records, French Spoliation Claims, NA; manifest of sloop *President*, March 19, 1800, Middletown Outward Entries, U.S. Custom House Records, French Spoliation Claims, NA; manifest of schooner *Maryet*, January 27, 1802, New York Outward Entries, U.S. Custom House Records, French Spoliation Claims, NA.

105. Isaac Hazelhurst invoice of cargo and bill of disbursements for ship *Canton*, December 1 and 12, 1789, and Capt. Thomas Truxton to Isaac Hazelhurst and Co., March 30, 1790, Constable-Pierrepont Papers, NYPL.

106. Capt. Thomas Truxton bill of disbursements for ship *America*, ca. December 1788, Constable-Pierrepont Papers.

107. La Rochefoucauld Liancourt, *Travels*, 1:475–76; manifests of ships *Neptune*, December 9, 1795, and *Grand Turk*, March 12, 1796, Boston Outward Entries, U.S. Custom House Records, French Spoliation Claims, NA; manifest of ship *George Washington*, December 9, 1801, Salem Customhouse Records, PEM.

108. Shipping figures in John Bristed, *America and Her Resources* (1818; reprint, New York: Research Reprints, 1970), p. 45; John R. Commons et al., eds., *A Documentary History of American Industrial Society*, 11 vols. (Cleveland, Ohio: Arthur H. Clark, 1910), 3:136–37; John Connelly, *United States Gazette* (Philadelphia, Pa.), November 16, 1805; Tench Coxe, *A Statement of the Arts and Manufactures of the United States of America for the Year 1810* (Philadelphia: A. Cornman, Jr., 1814), p. xiv; *Census Directory for 1811* (Philadelphia: Jane Aitken, 1811), p. 470.

109. Philadelphia Outward Coastwise Entries, 1800–11, U.S. Custom House Records, NA.

110. Independent craftsmen-shippers include John B. Ackley, Lawrence Allwine, Joseph Burden, Joseph Burr, Burr (Joseph) and Moon (David), William Cox, Gilbert Gaw, Robert Gaw, William Hayden, Thomas Higbee, Thomas Mason, John Mere (Meer), William Mitchell, David Moon, Moon (David) and Prall (Edward), Michael Murphy, James Pentland, John Rea, William Smith, Adam Snyder, Anthony Steel, Robert Taylor, John Wall, Robert Wall, and James Whitaker.

111. Philadelphia Outward Coastwise Entries, 1800–11, U.S. Custom House Records, NA; Philadelphia Outward Foreign Entries, 1803–5, U.S. Custom House Records, NA (includes New Orleans).

112. Philadelphia Outward Coastwise Entries, 1800–11, U.S. Custom House Records, NA; Philadelphia Outward Foreign Entries, 1803–5, U.S. Custom House Records, NA (includes St. Augustine).

113. Manifest of brig *Union*, December 21, 1805, Philadelphia Outward Coastwise Entries, 1805–6, U.S. Custom House Records, NA; manifests of schooners *Hiram* and *Rising Sun*, April 27 and August 23, 1805, Philadelphia Outward Coastwise Entries, 1805, U.S. Custom House Records, NA; merchandise notice, *Charleston Courier* (Charleston, S.C.), January 16, 1807, citation file, MESDA.

114. A partial list of postwar craftsmen-shippers includes Thomas Ashton, Aaron Boughman, Joseph Burden, William Hayden, Hayden (William) and Stewart (William H.), John Huneker, Charles W. James, William Lee, John Mere, John Mitchell, John W. Patterson, John Rea, Charles Riley, William H. Stewart, John Wall, and James Whitaker. Philadelphia Outward Coastwise Entries, 1811–37, U.S. Custom House Records, NA; Philadelphia Outward Foreign [and Coastwise] Entries, 1810–19, U.S. Custom House Records, NA; Kathleen M. Catalano, "Cabinetmaking in Philadelphia, 1820–1840: Transition from Craft to Industry," in Ian M. G. Quimby, ed., *Winterthur Portfolio 13* (Chicago: University of Chicago Press, 1979), pp. 85, 91–138. The independent craftsmen-shippers of the 1820s and 1830s also include George Apple, Samuel Bailey, Benjamin Booth, Daniel Enston, Robert Gaw, Philip Halzel, William Kennedy, I. H. Laycock, Lentner (George) and Patterson (John), David Lyndell, Abraham Mcdonough, James Mitchell, William Mitchell, Edward Prall, Simons (Stephen) and Baris (Samuel), Joseph Snyder, Stewart (John) and James (Charles), Stewart (John) and Sanderson (William), Daniel Teas, Enock Tomlin, and John White.

115. Charles C. Robinson daybook, 1809–25, HSP; Matthew and Richard Brennan, and Sass and Gready, *Charleston Courier*, November 7, 1810, and May 22, 1816, citation file, MESDA; Philadelphia Outward coastwise entries, 1811–37, U.S. Custom House Records, NA, including manifests of ship *General Wade Hampton*, January 2 and February 15, 1816, and ship *Terrier*, February 26, 1816.

116. Philadelphia Outward Coastwise Entries, 1811–37, U.S. Custom House Records, NA; Abraham McDonough estate records, 1852, City and County of Philadelphia, Pa., Register of Wills.

117. John Lambert, *Travels through Canada and the United States of North America*, 2 vols. (London: C. Cradock and W. Joy, 1813), 2:62–64.

118. Thomas Hays, *Daily Advertiser*, April 8, 1801, as quoted in Rita Susswein Gottesman, comp., *The Arts and Crafts in New York, 1800–1804* (New York: New-York Historical Society, 1965), p. 144.

119. John Hewitt to Matthias Bruen, January 4, 1801, DCM; G. and F. Penny, *Columbian Museum and Savannah Advertiser* (Savannah, Ga.), January 22, 1808, as quoted in Mrs. Charles M. Theus, *Savannah Furniture, 1735–1825* (Savannah, Ga.: By the author, 1967), p. 89.

120. Brig *Consolation* and sloop *Schoharie* notices, *Charleston Courier*, March 3, 1804, and October 23, 1815, citation file, MESDA; Perth Amboy Inward and Outward Entries, 1809–17, U.S. Custom House Records, NA; John Tunis, *Norfolk Gazette and Publick Ledger* (Norfolk, Va.), June 12, 1812, citation file, MESDA.

121. Buttre in *Longworth's American Almanac, New-York Register, and City Directory* (New York: David Longworth, 1810), n.p.; New Bedford Inward and Outward Entries, 1807–8, U.S. Custom House Records, FRC-Waltham; Charles Cluss bill of chairs, May 23, 1808, Arnold family account sheet, ca. 1808, and Charles Fredericks's bill to Samuel Larned, November 8, 1827, Greene Collection, RIHS.

122. John Smith, *Providence Gazette* (Providence, R.I.), September 11, 1802, and Rhodes G. Allen in *Providence Directory* (Providence, R.I.: Carlisle and Brown, 1826), as quoted in Wendell D. Garrett, "Providence Cabinetmakers, Chairmakers, Upholsterers, and Allied Craftsmen, 1765–1838," *Antiques* 90, no. 4 (October 1966): 515, 519; Dwight, *Travels*, 3:326.

123. Manifests of brig *Savannah Packet* and schooner *Ariadne*, May 23, 1815, and October 13, 1817, Savannah Entries, U.S. Custom House Records, NA (photostat, DCM). Katharine Gross in tabulating coastwise chair imports at Savannah for the period from 1800 through 1815 recorded almost 5,000 units, some representing packages containing more than one item; named Windsor chairs account for almost 2,000 of that number. Thirty-seven additional cargoes contained unspecified numbers of chairs; see Katharine Wood Gross, "The Sources of Furniture Sold in Savannah, 1789–1815" (master's thesis, University of Delaware, 1967), pl. 9. Cheshire and Cox, *Edenton Gazette* (Edenton, N.C.), May 12, 1818, A. Clark, *Raleigh Minerva* (Raleigh, N.C.), April 16, 1819, and Thomas W. Pittman, *Carolina Sentinel* (Newbern, N.C.), November 18, 1820, citation file, MESDA; Perth Amboy Inward and Outward Entries, 1809–17, U.S. Custom House Records, NA; anonymous New York chairmaker, Records of the 1820 Census of Manufactures, state of New York, NA (microfilm, DCM).

124. David Alling account book, 1801–39, and ledger 1815–18, New Jersey Historical Society, Newark (hereafter cited NJHS; microfilm, DCM); manifest of ship *Catharine*, September 26, 1832, New York Outward Entries, U.S. Custom House Records, with French Spoliation Claims, NA.

125. Cyrus Cleaveland, *Providence Gazette*, October 3, 1801, as quoted in Garrett, "Providence Cabinetmakers," p. 516; Boston notices, *New England Palladium* (Boston, Mass.), August 16, 1817, and *Independent Chronicle and Boston Patriot* (Boston, Mass.), June 5, 1833, as quoted in Esther S. Fraser, "Painted Furniture in America, Part I: The Sheraton Fancy Chair, 1790–1817," *Antiques* 5, no. 6 (June 1924): 304; manifest of schooner *Freedom*, July 13, 1808, New Bedford Outward Entries, U.S. Custom House Records, FRC-Waltham; Samuel Dockum, *New Hampshire Gazette* (Portsmouth), April 15, 1825 (reference courtesy of Joseph Hammond); Boteler and Donn, *Daily National Intelligencer* (Washington, D.C.), July 1, 1833, as quoted in Anne Castrodale Golovin, "Cabinetmakers and Chairmakers of Washington, D.C., 1791–1840," *Antiques* 107, no. 5 (May 1975): 908–9; Partridge in *Documents Relative to the Manufactures in the United States Collected and Transmitted to the House of Representatives in Compliance with a Resolution of January 19, 1832, by the Secretary of the Treasury*, 2 vols. (Washington, D.C.: Duff Green, 1833), 1:528–29. For the Samuel S. Howe chair, see Evans, *American Windsor Chairs*, fig. 8-3.

126. New London Outward Coastwise Entries, 1801–21, U.S. Custom House Records, FRC-Waltham. Giles L'Hommedieu probably was a connection of Grover L'Hommedieu, brother-in-law to Ebenezer Tracy, Sr.

127. New London Outward Coastwise Entries, 1801–21, U.S. Custom House Records, FRC-Waltham; steamboat information in Fearon, *Sketches*, p. 341.

128. Mrs. Guion Thompson, "Hitchcock of Hitchcocks-ville," *Antiques* 4, no. 2 (August 1923): 74; *The American Advertising Directory, Manufacturers and Dealers in American Goods for the Year 1831* (New York: Joceylyn, Darling, 1831), p. 56; Nolan and Gridley, *Columbian Centinel* (Boston, Mass.), February 16, 1811, as quoted in Zilla Rider Lea, ed., *The Ornamented Chair* (Rutland, Vt.: Charles E. Tuttle, 1960), p. 63.

129. Invoice of cargo, schooner *Madocawando*, February 10, 1812, Papers of Elijah Sanderson, vol. 2 (1785–1822), PEM.

130. Grant letter, as quoted in Mabel M. Swan, *Samuel McIntire, Carver, and the Sandersons, Early Salem Cabinet Makers* (Salem, Mass.: Essex Institute, 1934), p. 11; Earle G. Shettleworth, Jr., and William D. Barry, "Walter Corey's Furniture Manufactory in Portland, Maine," *Antiques* 121, no. 5 (May 1982): 1201.

131. Alexander Walker, *Virginia Herald* (Fredericksburg), August 12, 1803, Matthew McColm and Francis Younker, *American and Commercial Daily Advertiser* (Baltimore, Md.), May 12, 1809, and September 12, 1810, citation file, MESDA; Fearon, *Sketches*, p. 340; representations of the Mathiot establishment appear in *Matchett's Baltimore Director[y]* (Baltimore, Md.: R. J. Matchett, 1840, 1847, and 1855).

132. Shipping Returns: Nova Scotia, 1811–20, Colonial Office, PRO.

133. William Strickland, *Journal of a Tour in the United States of America, 1794–1795*, ed. J. E. Strickland (New York: New-York Historical Society, 1971), p. 64; Philadelphia, 1793–95, New York, 1790–1802, and Baltimore, 1792–99, Outward Entries, U.S. Custom House Records, French Spoliation Claims, NA.

134. Salem, 1789–1800, Boston, 1790–1801, and Philadelphia, 1799–1801, Outward Entries, U.S. Custom House Records, French Spoliation Claims, NA; John Innes Clark invoice book, 1801–8, DCM.

135. David Lee Sterling, ed., "New Orleans, 1801: An Account by John Pintard," *Louisiana Historical Quarterly* 34 (July 1951): 224–25, as quoted in Wendell Garrett, ed., "Clues and Footnotes," *Antiques* 104, no. 5 (November 1973): 877.

136. Philadelphia Outward Coastwise and Foreign Entries, 1803–7, U.S. Custom House Records, NA.

137. Perth Amboy, Inward and Outward Entries, 1809–17, U.S. Custom House Records, NA; Philadelphia Outward Coastwise Entries, 1810–11, U.S. Custom House Records, NA; Bracken and Smith, *Weekly Chronicle* (Natchez, Miss.), March 12, 1810, and James Turnbull, *Mississippi Republican* (Natchez), January 26, 1819 (references courtesy of Milly McGehee); Bristed, *America and Her Resources*, p. 31.

138. Manifest of brig *Catharine*, October 13, 1819, New London Outward Coastwise Entries, U.S. Custom House Records, NA; David Alling invoice book, 1819–20, NJHS (microfilm, DCM). For chairs with organ spindles, fret backs, or diamond stretchers, see Evans, *American Windsor Chairs*, figs. 5-43, 5-41, 5-35.

139. Alling invoice book.

140. Brig *Galen* log, 1833–37, MSM.

141. Le chevalier Felix de Beaujour, *Sketch of the United States of North America . . . from 1800 to 1810*, trans. William Walton (London: J. Booth et al., 1814), p. 90; Catalano, "Cabinetmaking in Philadelphia," pp. 82, 85–86.

142. James Hallet, Jr., *New-York Gazette and General Advertiser* (New York), October 22, 1801, as quoted in Gottesman, *Arts and Crafts, 1800–1804*, p. 143; Jay Humeston, *Nova Scotia Royal Gazette* (Halifax), November 23, 1804, as quoted in George MacLaren, "The Windsor Chair in Nova Scotia," *Antiques* 100, no. 1 (July 1971): 124; Shettleworth and Barry, "Walter Corey," p. 1201; William Tweed printed billhead, 1850–57, inscribed in 1857, as illustrated in Leo Hershkowitz, "Early Trade Bills of New York City," *Antiques* 113, no. 1 (January 1978): 231.

143. Philadelphia chairmakers who participated directly in the trade to Cuba and other islands include John B. Ackley, Joseph Burden, Joseph Burr, Gilbert Gaw, Robert Gaw, George Halberstadt, William Haydon, John Huneker, Thomas Mason, Anthony Steel, Robert Taylor, Richard Wall, and James Whitaker. Philadelphia Outward Foreign Entries, 1803–10, U.S. Custom House Records, NA; William Trotter and George Halberstadt invoice of cargo, schooner *Republican*, March 16, 1807, Nathan Trotter Collection, Baker Library, Harvard University, Cambridge, Mass. (hereafter cited BL).

144. William Gray, Jr., invoice of cargo, brig *Massafeuro*, May 4, 1805, DCM.

145. Philadelphia Outward Foreign Entries, 1803–10, U.S. Custom House Records, NA; William Trotter invoice of cargo, schooner *Phoebe and Jane*, February 21, 1812, and George Halberstadt bill to Nathan Trotter, April 9, 1810, Trotter Collection, BL.

146. Manifest of brig *Fame*, January 2, 1802, Philadelphia Outward Foreign Entries, 1805–7, U.S. Custom House Records, NA; entries for schooner *Mercator* and sloop *Argo*, June 21 and August 3, 1809, Shipping Returns: Bermuda, 1807–10, Colonial Office, PRO.

147. Tanner, "Caribbean Ports, Part 1," p. 108; Havana Price Current, March 29, 1816, Papers of Benjamin Pickman, Jr., PEM; Philadelphia Outward Foreign Entries, 1815–21, U.S. Custom House Records, NA; William R. Boone bills of lading, brigs *Flora*, April 10, 1824, *Hamlet*, April 17, 1826, and *Zeno*, October 20, 1820, and account of sales, brig *Hamlet* at Puerto Plata, Jeremiah Boone Papers, HSP.

148. New London, Conn., Outward Foreign

Entries, 1820–21, U.S. Custom House Records, FRC-Waltham; Earl C. Tanner, "Early 19th-Century Providence Exports to the Caribbean," *Rhode Island History* 19, no. 2 (April 1960): 48.

149. Philadelphia Outward Foreign Entries, 1803–7 and 1815, U.S. Custom House Records, NA; entry for sloop *Barton*, November 15, 1816, Shipping Returns: Nova Scotia, 1816–20, Colonial Office, PRO; Tanner, "Caribbean Ports, Part 2," p. 13; Shipping Returns: St. Thomas, 1808–14, Colonial Office, PRO; William R. Boone bills of lading, brigs *Hamlet*, November 23, 1820, and April 19, 1821, and *Zeno*, March 12, 1821, Boone Papers.

150. Philadelphia Outward Foreign Entries, 1803–10 and 1819–20, U.S. Custom House Records, NA; manifests of schooner *Dispatch* and brig *Greyhound*, December 26, 1801, and December 2, 1820, New London Outward Foreign Entries, U.S. Custom House Records, FRC-Waltham.

151. New London Outward Foreign Entries, 1801–6 and 1816, U.S. Custom House Records, FRC-Waltham; Philadelphia Outward Foreign Entries, 1803–7 and 1815, U.S. Custom House Records, NA.

152. Brobson shipping record book; Shipping Returns: Barbados, 1781–1810, Colonial Office, PRO; New London Outward Foreign Entries, 1801–6, U.S. Custom House Records, FRC-Waltham; Philadelphia Outward Foreign Entries, 1803–7, U.S. Custom House Records, NA; West Indies notice, *Providence Phenix* (Providence, R.I.), February 24, 1816, as quoted in Tanner, "Caribbean Ports, Part 1," pp. 100–101.

153. Philadelphia Outward Foreign Entries, 1803–7 and 1821, U.S. Custom House Records, NA.

154. Manifest of brig *Rover*, December 4, 1799, Boston Outward Entries, U.S. Custom House Records, French Spoliation Claims, NA; entry for brig *Ambition*, November 10, 1811, Shipping Returns: British Honduras, 1807–12, Colonial Office, PRO.

155. Manifests of ships *Indiana*, November 16, 1805, and *Eclipse*, April 17, 1819, Philadelphia Outward Foreign Entries, 1805–7 and 1819, U.S. Custom House Records, NA; J. H. Stevenson and Co. invoice book, 1822–26, DCM.

156. Morison, *Maritime History of Massachusetts*, p. 270.

157. Philadelphia Outward Foreign Entries, 1803–5, U.S. Custom House Records, NA; Shipping Returns: Surinam, 1804–8, Colonial Office, PRO; entry for brig *Harriet*, April 15, 1817, Shipping Returns: Nova Scotia, 1816–20, Colonial Office, PRO.

158. Manifests of ships *General Wayne*, May 19, 1798, and *Henrietta*, February 15, 1798, New York Outward Entries, U.S. Custom House Records, French Spoliation Claims, NA; manifest of snow *Maryland*, June 6, 1798, Baltimore Outward Entries, U.S. Custom House Records,

French Spoliation Claims, NA; Philadelphia Outward Foreign Entries, 1805–7 and 1810, U.S. Custom House Records, NA; Col. William Duane, *A Visit to Colombia in the Years 1822 and 1823* (Philadelphia, 1826), pp. 27–28, as quoted in Eleanor H. Gustafson, ed., "Clues and Footnotes," *Antiques* 113, no. 4 (April 1978): 868.

159. Philadelphia Outward Foreign Entries, 1805–7, 1815, and 1821, U.S. Custom House Records, NA; manifest of schooner *Courtney Norton*, July 4, 1810, Perth Amboy, Inward and Outward Entries, 1809–17, U.S. Custom House Records, NA.

160. Earl C. Tanner, "South American Ports in the Foreign Commerce of Providence, 1800–1830," *Rhode Island History* 16, no. 3 (July 1957): 66; manifest of ship *Maria*, December 5, 1800, New York Outward Entries, 1791–1801, U.S. Custom House Records, French Spoliation Claims, NA; manifest of ship *Catharine*, July 20, 1801, Boston Outward Entries, 1790–1801, U.S. Custom House Records, French Spoliation Claims, NA; invoice of cargo, brig *Welcome Return*, 1803, Sanderson Papers, vol. 2; Swan, *Samuel McIntire*, p. 9.

161. "Observations made and collected at Río de Janeiro," 1809, RIHS (microfilm, DCM).

162. *Hope's Philadelphia Price-Current, and Commercial Record* (Philadelphia, Pa.), April 3, 1809, p. 4 (reference courtesy of Anne C. Golovin); Stephen Girard invoices of cargoes, ships *Voltaire*, December 28, 1809, and *Rousseau*, December 22, 1810, and Isaac M. Bolton and Joseph Burden bills to Stephen Girard, December 28, 1809, and December 12, 1810, Girard Papers.

163. Philadelphia Outward Foreign Entries, 1809–10, 1815, 1819, and 1821, U.S. Custom House Records, NA; entry for brig *Waterloo*, July 6, 1819, Shipping Returns: Nova Scotia, 1816–20, Colonial Office, PRO.

164. Manifest of brig *Three Brothers*, December 9, 1809, Philadelphia Outward Foreign Entries, 1807–9, U.S. Custom House Records, NA; memorandum of goods suitable for the Brazilian market, ca. 1821–22, Waters Family Papers, PEM; Earl C. Tanner, "Early 19th-Century Providence Exports to Brazil," *Rhode Island History* 19, no. 3 (July 1960): 91–93.

165. Tanner, "South American Ports," pp. 68–69; manifest of brig *Rose*, December 8, 1798, Philadelphia Outward Entries, 1797–99, U.S. Custom House Records, French Spoliation Claims, NA; "Observations made and collected at Río de Janeiro."

166. Manifest of brig *Deborah and Jane*, March 14, 1810, Philadelphia Outward Foreign Entries, 1810, U.S. Custom House Records, NA; invoice of cargo, ship *George and Mary*, April 7, 1810, as quoted in Joseph K. Ott, "Still More Notes on Rhode Island Cabinetmakers and Allied Craftsmen," *Rhode Island History* 28, no. 4 (November 1969): 121; Morison, *Maritime History of Massachusetts*, pp. 181–82.

167. Davidson, *Life in America*, 1:339.

168. Stephen Girard invoice of cargo, ship *Montesque*, December 13, 1810, and Joseph Burden and John Mitchell bill to Stephen Girard, December 12, 1810, and account of sales, ship *Montesque*, December 4, 1811, Girard Papers.

169. Tanner, "South American Ports," pp. 75–76.

170. George Larned invoice of cargo, n.d., and manifest of ship *Providence*, March 23, 1825, Greene Collection, RIHS.

171. Levi Stillman invoice of furniture, September 20, 1826, in account book, 1815–34, Sterling Memorial Library, Yale University, New Haven, Conn. (hereafter cited Yale); 1820 Census of Manufactures, state of Connecticut, p. 52; Tanner, "South American Ports," p. 78.

172. Manifests of brigs *Hannah and Rebecca* and *Emma Matilda*, August 3 and December 15, 1821, Philadelphia Outward Foreign Entries, 1821, U.S. Custom House Records, NA; Clark, *History of Manufactures*, 1:472: *Documents Relative to Manufactures*, 1:602–3; J. H. French, *Gazetteer of the State of New York* (Syracuse: R. Pearsall Smith, 1860), p. 175.

173. Philadelphia Outward Foreign Entries, 1803–10 and 1820, U.S. Custom House Records, NA.

174. Eleanore Bradford Monahon, "Providence Cabinetmakers," *Rhode Island History* 23, no. 1 (January 1964): 12–16.

175. Manifests of schooner *Friendship*, April 10, 1806, and brig *Superior*, February 26, 1810, Philadelphia Outward Foreign Entries, 1806 and 1810, U.S. Custom House Records, NA; ship *Eugenia* notice, *Charleston Courier*, April 3, 1811, citation file, MESDA; John Clifton bill of lading, November 8, 1841, Waters Family Papers.

176. Manifest of ship *St. Juan Bautista*, October 6, 1795, New York Outward Foreign Entries, 1795, U.S. Custom House Records, French Spoliation Claims, NA; manifests of schooner *John*, July 18, 1797, and ship *Maria*, December 10, 1802, Philadelphia Outward Foreign Entries, 1790–1802, U.S. Custom House Records, NA; manifest of ship *Four Friends* (to Madeira), June 24, 1796, Philadelphia Outward Entries, 1795–97, U.S. Custom House Records, French Spoliation Claims, NA.

177. Manifest of brig *Lady Washington*, November 23, 1791, Boston Outward Entries, 1790–1801, U.S. Custom House Records, French Spoliation Claims, NA; manifest of brig *Goodlookout*, December 14, 1784, Philadelphia Customhouse Papers, Outward Entries, 1784–85, HSP; Charles N. Buck, "Memoirs of Charles N. Buck . . . 1791–1841," p. 65, HSP.

178. Buck, "Memoirs," p. 127; Johann Heinrich Jonas Gudehus, "Journey to America," trans. Larry M. Neff, in *Ebbes fer Alle-Ebber, Ebbes fer Dich* (Something for Everyone, Something for You), Publications of the Pennsylvania

German Society, vol. 14 (Breinigsville: Pennsylvania German Society, 1980), p. 305.

179. John Doggett and Co. to Charles Humberston and Co., October 31, 1828, John Doggett letter book, 1825–29, DCM.

180. *The Second Supplement to the London Chair-Makers' and Carvers' Book of Prices for Workmanship* (London: T. Sorrell, 1811), pl. 1, no. 7. For the illustration from *The New-York Book of Prices for Manufacturing Cabinet and Chair Work* (New York: J. Seymour, 1817), see Charles F. Montgomery, *American Furniture: The Federal Period* (New York: Viking Press, 1966), p. 104. *The London Chair-Makers' and Carvers' Book of Prices for Workmanship* (London: T. Sorrell, 1823), pl. 6, no. 10.

181. Dean A. Fales, Jr., "Joseph Barrell's Pleasant Hill," in *Publications of the Colonial Society of Massachusetts: Transactions*, vol. 43 (Boston: By the society, 1966), p. 375; Alexander Laing, *Seafaring America* (New York: American Heritage Publishing, 1974), pp. 94–97; memorandum of voyage, ship *Columbia*, 1787–90, Joseph Barrell (?) to Capt. Robert Gray, n.d., and John Hoskins (supercargo), "Memo. of the trade at Nootka sound," n.d., all in Ship *Columbia* Papers, MHS.

182. Manifests of ships *General Washington*, November 22, 1800, and *Tyre*, December 18, 1800, Providence Outward Foreign Entries, 1799–1801, U.S. Custom House Records, French Spoliation Claims, NA; Tanner, "South American Ports," pp. 68–69, 71; Laing, *Seafaring America*, p. 30.

183. Laing, *Seafaring America*, pp. 87–88; manifest of ship *Grand Turk II*, March 12, 1796, Boston Outward Foreign Entries, 1795–96, U.S. Custom House Records, French Spoliation Claims, NA; Weeden, *Economic and Social History*, 2:826–27.

184. Manifest of brig *Dominick*, October 23, 1805, Philadelphia Outward Foreign Entries, 1805, U.S. Custom House Records, NA; Stephen Girard invoice of cargo and bill of lading, ship *North America*, July 9, 1816, and Martin Bickham to Stephen Girard, January 20, 1817, Girard Papers.

185. *Astrea* voyage in Weeden, *Economic and Social History*, 2:822; Philadelphia Outward Foreign Entries, 1805–7, U.S. Custom House Records, NA; Robert Waln, Jr., account book, 1816–20, DCM.

186. Sampson Barnet and Israel Stalcup, *Delaware Gazette* (Wilmington), October 10, 1789, and March 24, 1798, as quoted in Charles G. Dorman, *Delaware Cabinetmakers and Allied Artisans, 1655–1855* (Wilmington: Historical Society of Delaware, 1960), pp. 12, 76; Alexander Walker, *Virginia Herald*, October 16, 1798, citation file, MESDA; William Dicks, *Lynchburg and Farmer's Gazette* (Lynchburg, Va.), August 1, 1795 (reference courtesy of Catherine Lynn).

187. For the Andrew McIntire chair, see Evans, *American Windsor Chairs*, fig. 3-113.

188. For an H. T. Shipman chair, see Evans, *American Windsor Chairs*, fig. 5-24.

189. Oliver Pomeroy and Julius Barnard, *Hampshire Gazette* (Northampton, Mass.), April 8, 1795, and December 2, 1795, as quoted in Leigh Keno, "The Windsor Chair Makers of Northampton, Massachusetts, 1790–1820 (Historic Deerfield Summer Fellowship Program paper, Deerfield, Mass., August 1979), pp. 5–6, 47; William Blake, *Independent Chronicle*, June 18, 1879, as quoted in Fraser, "Painted Furniture in America, Part 1," p. 306; Samuel J. Tuck and William Seaver, *Columbian Centinel*, October 3, 1795, and April 20, 1796, Prime cards, WL. For examples of William Seaver's work, see Evans, *American Windsor Chairs*, figs. 6-203, 6-207, 6-209, 6-213, and 6-214. James C. Tuttle, *Salem Gazette* (Salem, Mass.), August 19, 1796, as quoted in Swan, *Samuel McIntire*, pp. 29–30; Allyn and Huntington, *Chelsea Courier* (Norwich, Conn.), June 7, 1797; Daniel Lawrence, *United States Chronicle* (Providence, R.I.), July 19, 1787, as quoted in Irving Whitall Lyon, *The Colonial Furniture of New England* (Boston: Houghton Mifflin, 1924), pp. 180–81.

190. Illustrations of documented chairs made by Storel Hutchinson, John McClintic, Burchall and Wickersham, and Joseph Jones are in the author's study files. John Hastey, *Carlisle Herald* (Carlisle, Pa.), April 18, 1806 (reference courtesy of the late Milton Flower); Schuylkill Navigation Co. and chairs for sale in Pottsville in Catalano, "Cabinetmaking in Philadelphia," p. 87. Pennsylvania craftsmen soliciting the country trade include the following: David Gosner, *American Eagle* (Easton, Pa.), June 11, 1808 (reference courtesy of Jonathan Cox); James and Emor Jefferis and John White, *Village Record* (West Chester, Pa.), January 20, 1830, and September 7, 1831, as quoted in Margaret Berwind Schiffer, *Furniture and Its Makers of Chester County, Pennsylvania* (Philadelphia: University of Pennsylvania Press, 1966), pp. 128, 247; George W. Lea and Michael Stoner, *Lancaster Journal* (Lancaster, Pa.), January 6, 1815, and June 23, 1809, advertisement file, Lancaster County Historical Society, Lancaster, Pa.

191. George Landon account book, 1813–32, DCM; William E. Willis, *Erie Observer* (Erie, Pa.), April 20, 1833 (reference courtesy of Wendell Hilt); Henry Bheares, *Pittsburgh Gazette* (Pittsburgh, Pa.), May 11, 1819 (reference courtesy of Marilyn M. White); "Journal of Thaddeus M. Harris," in Harpster, *Pen Pictures*, pp. 243–44.

192. William H. MacDonald, *Central New Jersey Chairmaking of the Nineteenth Century* (Trenton, N.J.: By the author, 1960), pp. 16, 42, 53. For a chair by E. P. Rose, see Evans, *American Windsor Chairs*, fig. 4-40. Tunis and Nut-

man in Monahon, "Providence Cabinetmakers," pp. 12, 14, 19.

193. Dwight, *Travels*, 3:330; Hildreth in *Brooklyn Directory, for 1832–33* (Brooklyn, N.Y.: William Bigelow, 1832), p. 99; Alexander Patterson bill to Gerrit Wessel Van Schaick, June 1, 1814, Van Schaick Papers, NYPL.

194. Gilbert Ackerman property records, 1825, and Rawdon, Clark and Co., "Map of the ALBANY Pier and Basin," ca. 1825, Albany Co., Albany, N.Y., Registry of Deeds.

195. Gilbert in William Richards, comp., *The Utica Directory: 1842–'43* (Utica, N.Y.: John P. Bush, 1842), p. 133; John Melish, *Travels through the United States of America*, 2 vols. (Philadelphia: By the author, 1815), 2:388–89; Ashley and Williston, *Syracuse Weekly Journal* (Syracuse, N.Y.), May 14, 1851 (reference courtesy of Wendell Hilt); Samuel R. Brown, *The Western Gazetteer, or Emigrants Directory* (Auburn, N.Y.: H. C. Southwick, 1817), p. 344.

196. Jacob Platt, *New-York Evening Post* (New York), April 22, 1845 (reference courtesy of David Kiehl); French, *Gazetteer of New York*, p. 152.

197. James E. Kilbourn, *Norwalk Gazette* (Norwalk, Conn.), September 2, 1823, and Chapman and Merrit, *Connecticut Herald* (New Haven), April 18, 1809 (references courtesy of Wendell Hilt); Sylvester Higgins, *Connecticut Gazette* (New London), January 7, 1807, as quoted in Ethel Hall Bjerkoe, *The Cabinetmakers of America* (Garden City, N.Y.: Doubleday, 1957), p. 124; John I. Wells, *Connecticut Courant* (Hartford), July 21, 1800; Benjamin Doolittle, *Litchfield Republican* (Litchfield, Conn.), October 11, 1819, as quoted in John F. Page, *Litchfield County Furniture* (Litchfield, Conn.: Litchfield Historical Society, 1969), p. 121.

198. Charles Scott, *Providence Gazette*, August 28, 1822, as quoted in Garrett, "Providence Cabinetmakers," p. 519.

199. Daniel Munger, *Franklin Herald and Public Advertiser* (Greenfield, Mass.), September 28, 1824, advertisement file, Historic Deerfield, Deerfield, Mass. (hereafter cited HD); Corey in Harlowe Harris, *The Portland Directory, for 1841* (Portland, Maine: Arthur Shirley and Son, 1841), p. 158; Levi Bartlett, *New Hampshire Gazette*, September 5, 1806, Decorative Arts Photographic Collection, Visual Resources Collection, WL (hereafter cited VRC); Dwight, *Travels*, 4:117.

200. John Wadsworth, *American Mercury* (Hartford, Conn.), March 1, 1804 (reference courtesy of Wendell Hilt); Eli Wood, *Connecticut Courant*, July 7, 1800; Asa Jones, *Hampshire Gazette*, September 6, 1809; R. and W. Swift, *New-Bedford Mercury* (New Bedford, Mass.), November 19, 1822, as quoted in Elton W. Hall, "New Bedford Furniture," *Antiques* 113, no. 5 (May 1978): 1126; Jonas Child, *New Hampshire Sentinel* (Keene), June 22, 1805, as quoted in Charles S. Parsons, New Hampshire Notes,

VRC; Low and Damon, *New-Hampshire Patriot* (Concord), February 6, 1816, as quoted in Donna-Belle Garvin, James L. Garvin, and John F. Page, *Plain and Elegant, Rich and Common: Documented New Hampshire Furniture, 1750–1850* (Concord: New Hampshire Historical Society, 1979), p. 149.

201. Josiah P. Wilder and George B. Gardner account book, 1839–41, as quoted in Charles S. Parsons, Wilder Family Notes, VRC; Arfwedson, *United States and Canada*, 2:248.

202. *Documents Relative to Manufactures*, 1:146–47; West and Hatch bills to Silas Cheney, 1814, Miscellaneous Papers, Superior Court Records, Litchfield Co., Conn., Connecticut State Library, Hartford (hereafter cited CSL); Philemon Robbins account book, 1833–36, Connecticut Historical Society, Hartford (hereafter cited CHS); W. DeLoss Love, "The Navigation of the Connecticut River," *Proceedings of the American Antiquarian Society*, new series, vol. 15, pt. 3 (April 29, 1903): 429.

203. *Documents Relative to Manufactures*, 1:990–91, 1019; John Tarrant Kenney, *The Hitchcock Chair* (New York: Clarkson N. Potter, 1971), pp. 108, 112, 136, 143, 308–10; Robbins account book; William D. Herrick, *History of the Town of Gardner* (Gardner, Mass.: By the committee, 1878), p. 174; Heywood-Wakefield Co., *A Completed Century, 1826–1926* (Boston: By the company, 1926), p. 11.

204. Jacob Kurtz, *Staunton Eagle* (Staunton, Va.), August 14, 1807, citation file, MESDA; David Bates, *Daily National Intelligencer*, June 28, 1820, as quoted in Golovin, "Cabinetmakers and Chairmakers of Washington," p. 906; Joel Brown, *North Carolina Star* (Raleigh), March 29, 1822, as quoted in James H. Craig, *The Arts and Crafts in North Carolina, 1699–1840* (Winston-Salem, N.C.: Old Salem, 1965), p. 202; Thomas Henning, Sr., *Lewisburg Chronicle* (Lewisburg, W.Va.), February 12, 1852 (reference courtesy of Anne C. Golovin).

205. William H. Russell, *Petersburg Intelligencer* (Petersburg, Va.), September 22, 1815, and Robert McKim, *Richmond Commercial Compiler* (Richmond, Va.), November 25, 1818, citation file, MESDA; Frederick W. Parrott, *Carolina Sentinel*, December 6, 1833, and John Cooper, *West Carolinian* (Salisbury, N.C.), March 22, 1825, as quoted in Craig, *Arts and Crafts*, pp. 211, 232; Nancy Goyne Evans, "Design Transmission in Vernacular Seating Furniture: The Influence of Philadelphia and Baltimore Styles on Chairmaking from the Chesapeake to the 'West,'" in *American Furniture 1993*, ed. Luke Beckerdite (Hanover, N.H.: University Press of New England for the Chipstone Foundation, 1993), pp. 75–116.

206. Melish, *Travels*, 2:56; Lyford, *Western Address Directory*, pp. 66, 461; Oliver I. Taylor, *Directory of the City of Wheeling and Ohio County* (Wheeling, W.Va.: Daily Gazette, 1851), p. 11.

207. Christian Schultz, Jr., *Travels on an Inland Voyage*, 2 vols. (1810; reprint, Ridgewood, N.J.: Gregg Press, 1968), 2:11–12.

208. Melish, *Travels*, 2:127; Lyford, *Western Address Directory*, p. 294; Stibbs and Stout and others in Jane E. Sikes, *The Furniture Makers of Cincinnati, 1790 to 1849* (Cincinnati, Ohio: By the author, 1976), pp. 48, 53, 84–85, 141–42, 216–17, 230; Samuel Stibbs in Donna Streifthau, "Cincinnati Cabinet- and Chairmakers, 1819–1830," *Antiques* 99, no. 6 (June 1971): 904–5; Jacob Roll in McSwiney and Barnes, *Louisville Public Advertiser* (Louisville, Ky.), February 19 and March 1, 1820, citation file, MESDA; Arfwedson, *United States and Canada*, 2:124; Charles Cist, *Sketches and Statistics of Cincinnati* (Cincinnati, Ohio, 1851), p. 205, as quoted in Sikes, *Furniture Makers of Cincinnati*, pp. 84–85.

209. Levi Cobb in Arthur Whallon, "Indiana Cabinetmakers and Allied Craftsmen, 1815–1860," *Antiques* 98, no. 1 (July 1970): 119; Hartley, Wheat and Co., *Indiana American* (Brookville), September 14, 1838, and Levi McDougle, *Indiana Recorder and Public Advertiser* (New Albany), January 6, 1826, as quoted in Walters, *Furniture Makers of Indiana*, pp. 107, 140; Brown, *Western Gazetteer*, pp. 92–93; Lyford, *Western Address Directory*, pp. 398–99; Samuel Williams and Co., *Clarion and Tennessee State Gazette* (Nashville), January 6, 1818, citation file, MESDA; James Bridges, *Knoxville Register* (Knoxville, Tenn.), August 24, 1819, and John Rudisill, *Jackson Gazette* (Jackson, Tenn.), May 15, 1830, as quoted in Ellen Beasley, "Tennessee Cabinetmakers and Chairmakers through 1840," *Antiques* 100, no. 4 (October 1971): 613, 620; May and Renshaw, *Scioto Gazette and Fredonia Chronicle* (Chillicothe, Ohio), February 29, 1816, as quoted in John Grabb to author, December 3, 1978.

210. Jay Humeston, *Nova Scotia Royal Gazette*, November 23, 1804, as quoted in MacLaren, "Windsor Chair in Nova Scotia," p. 124; Henry Corse, *Montreal Gazette* (Montreal, Que.), August 11, 1806, as quoted in Elizabeth Collard, "Montreal Cabinetmakers and Chairmakers: 1800–1850," *Antiques* 105, no. 4 (May 1974): 1138; Adam Ferguson, *Practical Notes Made during a Tour in Canada* (Edinburgh: W. Blackwood, 1833), as quoted in Jeanne Minhinnick, "Canadian Furniture in the English Taste, 1790–1840," *Antiques* 112, no. 1 (July 1967): 86.

211. For work of the unknown Rhode Island chairmaker, see Evans, *American Windsor Chairs*, figs. 8-44, 8-45.

212. Melish, *Travels*, 1:104; Lambert, *Travels*, 1:239–40; 2:34–35, 502, 511; Dwight, *Travels*, 3:296; 4:117.

213. W. John McIntyre, "Arms across the Border: Trade in Chairs and Chair Parts between the United States and Upper Canada," in *Victorian Furniture: Essays from a Victorian Society Autumn Symposium*, ed. Kenneth L. Ames, published as *Nineteenth Century* (Victorian Society in America) 8, nos. 3, 4 (1982): 59; George H. Harris, "Early Shipping on the Lower Genesee River: Reminiscences of Captain Hosea Rogers," in *Publication Fund Series* (Rochester, N.Y.: Rochester Historical Society, 1930), 9:91–109; Harrison, *Diary of Thomas P. Cope*, p. 359; William Barton in 1820 Census of Manufactures, state of Pennsylvania, p. 216.

214. Joan Lynn Schild, "Furniture Makers of Rochester, New York," *New York History* 37, no. 1 (January 1956): 98–100; Starr in *King's Rochester City Directory and Register, 1841* (Rochester, N.Y.: Welles and Hayes, 1840), n.p.; Alexander Drummond, *Upper Canada Gazette* (Toronto, Ont.), 1829, as quoted in Joan Mackinnon, *A Checklist of Toronto Cabinet and Chair Makers, 1800–1865*, National Museum of Man Mercury Series (Ottawa: National Museums of Canada, 1975), p. 42; McIntyre, "Arms across the Border," pp. 59, 61.

215. Edwin Brown and Co., *Upper Canada Herald* (Kingston, Ont.), July 28, 1840, as quoted in Joan Mackinnon, *Kingston Cabinetmakers, 1800–1867*, National Museum of Man Mercury Series (Ottawa: National Museums of Canada, 1976), p. 45.

216. Mackinnon, *Kingston Cabinetmakers*, pp. 30, 45–48; Mackinnon, *Toronto Cabinet Makers*, p. 68; McIntyre, "Arms across the Border," pp. 60–61.

217. Mackinnon, *Kingston Cabinetmakers*, p. 69; McIntyre, "Arms across the Border," p. 60; Jeanne Minhinnick, *At Home in Upper Canada* (Toronto: Clarke, Irwin, 1970), p. 181.

218. Clark, *History of Manufactures*, 1:360.

219. McDonough estate records.

220. Ebenezer P. Rose, *Trenton Federalist* (Trenton, N.J.), November 30, 1807 (reference courtesy of James B. Seibert); Charles Cluss, *Sentinel of Freedom* (Newark, N.J.), November 25, 1828, as quoted in *Early Furniture Made in New Jersey, 1690–1870* (Newark, N.J.: Newark Museum, 1958), p. 49; Joseph Jones, *Village Record*, November 9, 1825, as quoted in Schiffer, *Furniture of Chester County*, p. 133.

221. Stillman account book; Levi Stillman, *Connecticut Herald*, September 11, 1821, as quoted in Phyllis Kihn, comp., "Connecticut Cabinetmakers, Part 2," *Connecticut Historical Society Bulletin* 33, no. 1 (January 1968): 22.

222. Kenney, *Hitchcock Chair*, pp. 101–2, 108, 112; Isaac Wright account book, 1834–37, CSL; H. F. Dewey account book, 1837–64, Shelburne Museum, Shelburne, Vt. (microfilm, DCM).

223. Elisha Harlow Holmes ledger, 1825–30, CHS; Swift and Ottiwell, *New-Bedford Mercury*, May 22, 1829, as quoted in Hall, "New Bedford Furniture," p. 1126.

224. Thomas Howard, Jr./Tunis and Nutman, *Providence Gazette*, April 3, 1813, as quoted in Garrett, "Providence Cabinetmakers," p. 517;

Thomas Howard, Jr., *Providence Journal* (Providence, R.I.), January 11, 1823, and other material in Monahon, "Providence Cabinetmakers," pp.12–17, 19; Allen in *Providence Directory* (Providence, R.I.: Brown and Danforth, 1824), p. 33, and *Providence Directory* (1826), n.p.

225. Kenney, *Hitchcock Chair*, pp. 101–2; Franklin Howe/Charles Ingalls, *Democratic Statesman* (Windsor, Vt.), November 12, 1835, the advertisement itself dated January 22 (reference courtesy of Wendell Hilt); Thomas Boynton ledger, 1817–47, Dartmouth College, Hanover, N.H. (hereafter cited DC; microfilm, DCM); Clive Day, *The Rise of Manufacturing in Connecticut, 1820–1850*, Tercentenary Commission of the State of Connecticut, no. 44 (New Haven, Conn.: Yale University Press, 1935), p. 23.

226. Joseph Walker invoice book, 1784, Independence Seaport Museum, Philadelphia; Alling ledger; Lynchburg notice, *Lynchburg Press* (Lynchburg, Va.), August 25, 1814, citation file, MESDA; Nathan Pierce, *Franklin Herald* (Greenfield, Mass.), October 3, 1815, as quoted in Peter Rippe, "Daniel Clay of Greenfield, 'Cabinetmaker'" (master's thesis, University of Delaware, 1962), p. 46; Washington G. Henning, *Lewisburg Chronicle*, February 24, 1853 (reference courtesy of Anne C. Golovin).

227. Rhodes G. Allen, *Providence Gazette*, May 17, 1823, as quoted in Garrett "Providence Cabinetmakers," pp. 514–12; Allen Holcomb, *Greenfield Gazette* (Greenfield, Mass.), May 15, 1809, advertisement file, HD.

228. Barzillai Hudson and Co., *Connecticut Courant*, August 25, 1827, and April 13, 1829, as quoted in Kenney, *Hitchcock Chair*, pp. 101–2; Barzillai Hudson and Co., source unknown, 1830, as quoted in Carl W. Drepperd, *Pioneer America: Its First Three Centuries* (Garden City, N.Y.: Doubleday, 1949), p. 264.

229. Josiah P. Wilder daybook and ledger, 1837–61, Parsons, Wilder Family Notes.

230. Winifred C. Gates, "Journal of a Cabinet Maker's Apprentice, Part 2," *Chronicle of the Early American Industries Association* 15, no. 3 (September 1962): 35; Amos D. Allen, *Windham Herald* (Windham, Conn.), April 15, 1813, as quoted in Phyllis Kihn, comp., "Connecticut Cabinetmakers, Part 1," *Connecticut Historical Society Bulletin* 32, no. 4 (October 1967): 103.

231. Jacques Pierre Brissot de Warville and Etienne Clavière, *The Commerce of America with Europe* (New York: T. and J. Swords, 1795), p. 33n; Amos Denison Allen memorandum book, 1796–1803, CHS; Daniel Clay, *Greenfield Gazette*, July 24, 1809, as quoted in Rippe, "Daniel Clay," p. 32; John E. Mehargue account book, 1825–48, DCM.

232. Eels and colt in Silas Cheney ledger, 1799–1817, and daybook, 1807–13, Litchfield Historical Society, Litchfield, Conn. (hereafter cited LHS; microfilm, DCM); Holcomb in William Bentley ledger, 1812–15, DCM; Titus

Preston ledger, 1795–1817, Yale; Luke Houghton ledger A, 1816–27, Barre Historical Society, Barre, Mass. (hereafter cited Barre; microfilm, DCM).

233. Allen memorandum book; Cheney ledger; Joseph Griswold ledger, 1804–13, private collection (microfilm, DCM); Allen in Wait Stoddard ledger, 1798–1810, Windham Historical Society, Willimantic, Conn. (hereafter cited WHS); Landon account book.

234. Andrew Frink and Jonathan Chester ledger, 1806–ca. 1817, WHS; Boynton ledger, 1817–47, and Thomas Boynton ledger, 1811–17, DC (microfilm, DCM); James Gere ledger, 1822–52, CSL; Preston ledger.

235. William Rowzee, *Carolina Watchman* (Salisbury, N.C.), March 29, 1834, as quoted in Craig, *Arts and Crafts*, p. 234; Allen Holcomb account book, 1809–ca. 1828, Metropolitan Museum of Art, New York; James Gere ledger, 1809–29, CSL; Cheney ledger, and Silas E. Cheney daybook, 1802–7, LHS (microfilm, DCM); Allen memorandum book; David Haven account book, 1785–1800, DCM; Margaret Coffin, "Ransom Cook, Saratoga Chairmaker (1794–1881)," *The Decorator* 31, no. 2 (Spring 1977): 21.

236. Elisha Hawley account book, 1781–1800, CHS; Jacob Felton daybook, 1836–38, Old Sturbridge Village, Sturbridge, Mass. (hereafter cited OSV); True Currier account book, 1815–38, DCM; David Pritchard, Jr., ledger, 1800–10, Mattatuck Museum, Waterbury, Conn. (hereafter cited Mattatuck); William G. Beesley daybook, 1828–41, Salem County Historical Society, Salem, N.J.; Dewey account book.

237. Solomon Sibley account book, 1793–1840, OSV; William Mather account book, 1808–25, HD. For "read chairs" (red), see Robert Trent, *Hearts and Crowns* (New Haven, Conn.: New Haven Colony Historical Society, 1977), pp. 70–71. David Pritchard, Jr., account book, 1827–38, Mattatuck.

238. Miles Benjamin daybook and ledger, 1821–29, New York State Historical Association, Cooperstown (microfilm, DCM); Gere ledger, 1822–52; Luke Houghton ledger B, 1824–51, Barre; Jeduthern Avery account book, 1811–55, CHS.

239. Solomon Cole account book, 1794–1809, CHS; Boynton ledger, 1817–47.

240. Holcomb account book.

241. Canoe notice, *Maryland Gazette*, January 21, 1762, as quoted in Alfred Coxe Prime, comp., *The Arts and Crafts in Philadelphia, Maryland, and South Carolina, 1721–1785* (Philadelphia: Walpole Society, 1929), p. 188; Carl Bridenbaugh, *The Colonial Craftsman* (Chicago: University of Chicago Press, 1961), pp. 38, 57.

242. Rand and Abbott, *New-Hampshire Patriot*, October 15, 1825, as quoted in Parsons, New Hampshire Notes; Schultz, *Travels*, 1:2–3.

243. John Bleecker, Jr., and Alexander Pat-

terson bills to Gerritt W. Van Schaick, May 30, 1803, and June 1, 1814, Van Schaick Papers; Jacob Ring bill to Robert R. Livingston, June 2, 1817, Robert R. Livingston Papers, New-York Historical Society, New York (hereafter cited NYHS); Frederick and Philip Rhinelander receipt book, 1795–1800, Rhinelander Family Collection, NYHS.

244. Stillman account book; anonymous freight boat account book, 1830–31, CHS; Kenney, *Hitchcock Chair*, pp. 156, 160, 306.

245. Samuel Gridley and Aaron Purbeck bills to Joshua Ward, February 5 and 9, 1810, and Benjamin Archer bill to Benjamin H. Hathorne, June 19, 1812, Ward Family Manuscripts, vol. 14, PEM; Nolan and Gridley, *Columbian Centinel*, February 16, 1811, as quoted in Lea, *Ornamented Chair*, p. 63; William Dexter bills to Daniel W. Rogers, July 12, 1827, and June 3, 1829, Papers of Daniel Rogers, Jr., PEM; Sullivan Dorr account book, 1830s, as quoted in Jane L. Cayford, "The Sullivan Dorr House in Providence, Rhode Island" (master's thesis, University of Delaware, 1961), p. 144.

246. Owners of sloop *Salem* bill to Nicholas Low for William Bingham, 1792, Low Collection, LC; Ridgely purchase in Hill, "Furniture Craftsmen in Baltimore," pp. 14–15; Joseph Dean loose sheet of accounts, 1818, in account book, 1804–39, OSV.

247. Alling account book, and David Alling receipt book, 1824–42, NJHS (microfilm, DCM).

248. Dorothy C. Barck, ed., *Letters from John Pintard to his Daughter*, 4 vols. (New York: New-York Historical Society, 1940–41), 2:372–73; 3:35. Pintard purchased the furniture from a Mr. Young, probably Stephen or Moses.

249. William and James Douglas account of Stephen Cocke, [1791], VaHS (reference courtesy of Helen Scott Townsend Reed); John Hand, Jr., bill to John Lloyd, May 3, 1817, John Lloyd Collection, LC; *Commercial Directory* (Philadelphia: J. C. Kayser, 1823), pp. 7–8, 11, 13, 31–32, 40–43.

250. Thomas Jefferson to George Jefferson, July 19, 1800, and George Jefferson to Thomas Jefferson, July 21, 1800, Papers of Thomas Jefferson, MHS; Fiske Kimball, "Thomas Jefferson's Windsor Chairs," *Pennsylvania Museum Bulletin* 21, no. 98 (December 1925): 58–60.

251. Dorothy Smith Coleman, "Pioneers of Pittsburgh, the Robinsons," *Western Pennsylvania Historical Magazine* 42, no. 1 (January 1959): 69; Tudor, *Narrative*, 2:37.

252. Fearon, *Sketches*, pp. 231, 246; Arfwedson, *United States and Canada*, 2:82–84.

253. Benjamin Fairbanks's account of wharfage for brig *Rising Sun*, October 3, 1800, to February 6, 1801, Shepley Papers, vol. 2, RIHS (reference brought to author's attention by the late Joseph K. Ott); invoice of brig *Rising Sun*, February 7, 1801, Christopher Champlin invoice book, 1769–1804, RIHS; John Doggett

to Charles Humberston and Co., January 1, 1829, Doggett letter book.

254. Invoice of ship *George and Mary*, April 7, 1810, as quoted in Ott, "Still More Notes on Rhode Island Cabinetmakers," p. 121; Levi Stillman invoice of furniture to Horace A. Augur, September 20, 1826, Stillman account book; Captain Taylor's orders in Swan, *Samuel McIntire*, p. 12.

255. John Andrews to William Barrell, June 22, 1772, Andrews-Eliot Papers.

256. D. Watson and Son bill to James Duff, May 17, 1792, Trade Card Collection, Guildhall Library, London; Alling receipt book; Stillman account book; wrapping notes from taped interview with retired chair packer, 1957, High Wycombe Chair Museum, High Wycombe, England.

257. Abraham McDonough, *Public Ledger* (Philadelphia, Pa.), March 25, 1836; John Doggett to Henry Andrew, April 20, 1829, Doggett letter book.

258. William Ash bill to Captain Randall, July 3, 1802, Wendell Papers, BL; manifests of schooner *Sally*, April 23, 1805, ship *Mary*, July 11, 1798, brig *Newton*, March 10, 1801, and ship *Laconia*, April 6, 1819, Philadelphia and New York Outward Entries, U.S. Custom House Records, 1798–1819, some French Spoliation Claims, NA.

259. Ayliffe and Co. bill to the Reverend Mr. Drake, August 26, 1777, Collection of Billheads, Tradecards, Etc., British Library, London (microfilm, DCM); Gillow Company waste book, 1742–54, Gillow Papers; manifest of the *Nancy*, November 11, 1785, as quoted in Gillingham, "Philadelphia Windsor Chair," p. 325; A. H. Brick, source unknown, 1867, as quoted in Drepperd, *Pioneer America*, p. 265; Vosburgh and Childs, *Hall's Wilmington Gazette*, February 9, 1797, citation file, MESDA.

260. Manifest of brig *Cyrus*, November 19, 1805, Philadelphia Outward Coastwise Entries, 1805-6, U.S. Custom House Records, NA; William Hancock account of C. G. Loring, 1832–33, Landauer Collection, NYHS; Gillow Company waste book, 1776, Gillow Papers.

261. Thomas Sheraton, *Cabinet Dictionary*, 2 vols. (1803; reprint, New York: Praeger, 1970), 2:279–80.

262. Entry for ship *Lydia*, September 1, 1752, Shipping Returns: Jamaica, 1752–53, Colonial Office, PRO; invoice of cargo, brig *Welcome Return*, 1803, Sanderson Papers, vol. 2; entry for *Topsham Beauty*, August 18, 1804, Shipping Returns: Surinam, 1804-8, Colonial Office, PRO.

263. Stillman invoice of furniture to Augur in account book. Reinforcing the use of cloth for packing purposes is the item "To forty yards Ozenburg for Packing" in an account rendered by Jacob Sass, a cabinetmaker of Charleston, S.C., to John Singleton, a customer who lived at a distance from the city; see Bradford L. Rauschenberg and John Bivins, Jr., *The Furniture of Charleston, 1680–1820*, 3 vols. (Winston-Salem, N.C.: Museum of Early Southern Decorative Arts, 2003), 3:1205. Ozenburg (Osnaburg), originally associated with the town of Osnabrück in northern Germany, is a coarse, unbleached linen used for common purposes.

264. Invoice of schooner *Republican*, March 16, 1807, Trotter Collection, BL; account of sales, ship *Montesque*, December 4, 1811, and invoice of cargo, ship *North America*, July 9, 1816, Girard Papers.

265. Hamilton and Fardon, *American and Commercial DailyAdvertiser*, January 18, 1827 (reference courtesy of Susan B. Swan).

266. Open-back chairs in Gillow Company daybook, 1756–62, and invoice of cargo on *Maria*, December 1774, in Gillow Company cash book, 1764–74, Gillow Papers.

267. Manifest of ship *Industry*, March 30, 1767, Philadelphia Customhouse Papers, vol. 6, HSP; Walker invoice book; manifest of schooner *Winfield Packet*, March 8, 1800, Philadelphia Outward Coastwise Entries, 1799–1800, U.S. Custom House Records, NA.

268. Entries for schooner *Mercator* and sloop *Argo*, June 21 and August 3, 1809, Shipping Returns: Bermuda, 1807–10, Colonial Office, PRO; H. Richardson bill to Richard Blow, June 2, 1794, Blow Papers; manifests of schooner *Dispatch*, May 19, 1803, brig *Neptune*, September 15, 1810, and sloop *Unity*, May 4, 1816, Philadelphia Outward Entries, 1802–3, 1810, 1816, U.S. Custom House Records, NA; manifest of schooner *Sally*, December 1, 1801, Providence Outward Entries, 1799–1801, U.S. Custom House Records, French Spoliation Claims, NA.

269. Matthew McColm and John Robinson, *American and Commercial Daily Advertiser*, October 6, 1825; Cornelius Briggs, source unknown, 1830s, as quoted in Carl W. Drepperd, *Handbook of Antique Chairs* (Garden City, N.Y.: Doubleday, 1948), p. 256; Walter Barrett [Joseph Alfred Scoville], *The Old Merchants of New York City* (New York: Worthington Co., 1863), p. 142; Prentice P. Gustine price list, p. 3, as quoted in Page Talbott, "Cheapest, Strongest and Best Chairmaking in 19th-Century Philadelphia, Part 1," *Chronicle of the Early American Industries Association* 33, no. 2 (June 1980): 30.

270. Standfast Smith to John R. Parker, June 2, 1803, DCM.

271. Coxe, *Arts and Manufactures*, p. xvi; L. J. Mays, *The History of Chairmaking in High Wycombe* (London: Routledge and Kegan Paul, 1960), p. 52.

272. Lambert, *Travels*, 2:26–27; Hector Saint John de Crèvecoeur, *Sketches of Eighteenth-Century America*, ed. Henri L. Bourdin et al. (New Haven, Conn.: Yale University Press, 1925), pp. 138–39.

273. Elisha H. Holmes property attachment, 1843, Superior Court Records, New London Co., Conn., CSL; John E. Hartman property attachment, 1842, as quoted in Schiffer, *Furniture of Chester County*, pp. 108–9; Samuel Stuart and Peter A. Willard estate records, 1829, and 1842/43, Worcester Co., Worcester, Mass., Registry of Probate; Joseph Bachelder estate records, 1881, Kennebec Co., Augusta, Maine, Registry of Probate; William Culverhouse, *Catawba Journal* (Charlotte, N.C.), October 10, 1826, as quoted in Craig, *Arts and Crafts*, p. 214; Thomas Walter Ward II inventory book, ca. 1838–45, DCM; Samuel Lobach estate records, 1847, Berks Co., Reading, Pa., Register of Wills; Edward Shepard estate records, 1862, Wethersfield, Conn., Genealogical Section, CSL; Kenney, *Hitchcock Chair*, pp. 113, 321.

274. Benjamin F. Heywood estate records, 1843, Worcester Co., Mass., Registry of Probate; Lobach estate records; David Alling estate records, 1855, Archives and History Bureau, New Jersey State Library, Trenton; Willard estate records; Kenney, *Hitchcock Chair*, p. 321.

275. Robert Crage account book, 1757–81, OSV; James Davison, Lewis Emory, and William Booth receipts to Samuel Hodgdon for Gen. Henry Knox, December 2, 10, and 16, Papers of Henry Knox, Maine Historical Society, Portland; Anthony Morris daybook, 1794–99, DCM; Hamilton and Kevan to Humberston Skipwith, May 8, 1832, Peyton Skipwith Papers, WM.

276. Edward Tuckerman to Mrs. Stephen Salisbury I, July 13, 1830, AAS; Preston ledger; Haven account book; Gere ledger, 1822–52; Cheney daybook, 1807–13.

277. Boynton ledgers; Thomas J. Moyers and Fleming K. Rich account book, 1834–40, DCM; Gates, "Journal of a Cabinet Maker's Apprentice, Part 2," p. 35.

278. Henry Wilder Miller account book, 1827–31, Worcester Historical Museum, Worcester, Mass.; Felton daybook; Wilder daybook and ledger, and Charles S. Parsons's synopsis, Parsons, Wilder Family Notes; Heywood-Wakefield Co., *Completed Century*, p. 7.

279. Fearon, *Sketches*, p. 6; Anthony Steel bill to Andrew Clow and Co., September 18, 1793, DCM; Kenneth Roberts and Anna M. Roberts, eds. and trans., *Moreau de St. Méry's American Journey [1793-1798]* (Garden City, N.Y.: Doubleday, 1947), p. 163; Samuel Wing account books, 1800–1808, OSV.

280. Ebenezer Tracy, Sr., estate records, 1803-8, Lisbon, Conn., Genealogical Section, CSL; Robinson daybook; Arfwedson, *United States and Canada*, 2:127; "Birkbeck's Notes" and "Pittsburgh in 1829," in Harpster, *Pen Pictures*, pp. 275, 291.

281. Nathaniel Heath account book, 1767–91, RIHS; Charles S. Parsons, *The Dunlaps and Their Furniture* (Manchester, N.H.: Currier Gallery of Art, 1970), pp. 189, 221; Elijah Babcock account book, 1785–1822, CSL.

282. Hawley account book; Cheney daybook, 1802-7; William Moore, Jr., insolvency

records, 1830, Barkhamstead, Conn., Genealogical Section, CSL.

283. Boynton ledger, 1811–17; Nelson Talcott daybook, 1839–48, DCM.

284. Crage account book; Stoddard ledger; Holcomb account book; Houghton ledger B; James Williams, *Daily National Intelligencer*, June 1, 1839, as quoted in Golovin, "Cabinetmakers and Chairmakers of Washington," p. 921.

285. James Always, *Weekly Museum* (New York), February 28, 1801, as quoted in Gottesman, *Arts and Crafts, 1800–1804*, p. 136; Martin C. Phifer, *Catawba Journal*, November 16, 1824, as quoted in Craig, *Arts and Crafts*, p. 209; Thomas Ellis, *New-Bedford Mercury*, February 4, 1825, as quoted in Hall, "New Bedford Furniture," p. 1120; William Sweney, *Village Record*, February 19, 1850, as quoted in Schiffer, *Furniture of Chester County*, p. 227.

286. Allen in Frink and Chester ledger; Preston ledger; Oliver Moore account book, 1809–21, CHS; Silas E. Cheney daybook, 1813–21, LHS (microfilm, DCM); Thomas C. Boardman agreement with Azel G. Snow, July 11, 1844, Papers of Thomas Boardman, CHS.

287. William Challen, *Kentucky Gazette and General Advertiser* (Lexington), May 9, 1809, citation file, MESDA; Andrew L. Haskell, *Dover Gazette* (Dover, N.H.), December 1, 1827, Parsons, New Hampshire Notes; Mullen in *Robinson and Jones' Cincinnati Directory for 1846* (Cincinnati, Ohio: Robinson and Jones, 1846), p. 469; Thomas Henning, Sr., *Lewisburg Chronicle*, February 12, 1852 (reference courtesy of Anne C. Golovin); John Doggett and Co. to Benjamin L. Oliver, November 28, 1827, Doggett letter book.

288. James Greenleaf to Dr. Peter Turner, July 15, 1796, Rhode Island Manuscripts, John Hay Library, Brown University, Providence, R.I.

289. Heywood-Wakefield Co., *Completed Century*, p. 7; Herrick, *History of Gardner*, p. 183; Wilder daybook and ledger, and Parsons's synopsis, Wilder Family Notes.

290. Coffin, "Ransom Cook," p. 19.

291. Day, *Rise of Manufacturing in Connecticut*, p. 29; Kenney, *Hitchcock Chair*, p. 160; Creamer and Son in *Matchett's Baltimore Director[y], or Register of Householders* (Baltimore, Md.: Baltimore Director[y] Office, 1842), p. 11; Minhinnick, *At Home in Upper Canada*, p. 195.

CHAPTER 5

The Role of Windsor Seating in American Life

Beginning in the late 1720s Windsor furniture was an occasional, then a moderately common, household furnishing in America. Eventually it was employed in every part of the home. Owners of Windsor furniture represented almost the entire spectrum of society, from the day laborer to the prosperous merchant. Urban, village, and rural dwellings alike benefited from the economy and utility of the ever stylish Windsor. Sometimes household Windsors were limited in number; at other times chairs of this type comprised almost the entire seating of the home. In the 1790s forty-nine Windsor chairs furnished the dwelling of Doctor John Baker in New York City, the locations ranging from the dining room and "pantry" to the staircase hall, bedrooms, and "Work Shop."[1]

Joining the average householder in the use of Windsor furniture were individuals of national prominence, ranging from the statesman Benjamin Franklin to the naval hero Stephen Decatur. Out of doors the Windsor served as seating on the piazza and terrace and in the garden. Windsor furniture was prominent at social gatherings, whether routs or theater parties. Fraternal societies, clubs, libraries, and public grounds benefited from the practical qualities of the Windsor, which met organizational needs without sacrificing aesthetic merit. In the world of business and commerce chairs, stools, and settees proved suitable for counting rooms and offices, stores and shops, taverns and hotels, and shipboard accommodation. Windsor seating also was ideal for public facilities, including schools, statehouses and courthouses, and various departments of the national government. In short, the ubiquitous Windsor gained universal acceptance.

Domestic Use

Initial use of Windsor seating in America centered in the home. Patrick Gordon, lieutenant governor of Pennsylvania from 1726 to 1736, owned five Windsor chairs of English manufacture. The chairs furnished a second-story bedroom, which also served as a private dining area, a secondary function common at the period. Between the governor's death in 1736 and 1750, probate records for Philadelphia residents further document early Windsor use in household locations such as "the Street Parlor" (entry level), "the Little Back Room South," "the Parler Below" the back garret (second floor), "the Nursery," and the "back Chamber" (bedroom).[2]

American production of Windsor seating began in the 1740s at Philadelphia. In the next quarter century the new type of chair rose steadily in popularity, achieving preeminence in the Middle Atlantic region by the Revolution and along the remaining eastern seaboard in the 1780s. In reminiscing, Edward Jarvis of Massachusetts identified the factors that enabled the Windsor to capture a market held for more than a century by the traditional rush-bottom, slat-back chair:

> The chairs of the kitchen had four perpendicular posts.... There were 4 or 5 flat strips behind ... fixed into the posts at each end ... against which the sitter leaned. These

frames were coarsely made of oak, maple, ash, or other hard and strong wood often unpainted and generally unvarnished. Their seats . . . were usually woven of flags [rush], which were very destructible under wear and pressure and needed frequent repair or entire replacement. . . . Some of these . . . chairs had seats of split wood or basket work [splint]. These, though sufficiently strong and durable, were rough and destructive to the garments of the sitters.

Jarvis continued by describing the Windsor's superior qualities and its suitability for sitting rooms, parlors, and chambers:

These usually had wooden seats made of plank . . . somewhat hollowed for ease of sitting. They were of hard wood, of the nicer kinds, maple, birch, &c. The legs and the other parts were turned, sometimes elegantly. The legs were inserted into the bottom of the seat . . . generally inclining outward, so as to give the chair a wider base on the floor, than the seat. . . . These chairs were painted of various colors and varnished, and sometimes striped with other colors.[3]

Moreau de Saint Méry, while in Philadelphia during the 1790s, commented on the broad role of Windsors in American life: "Almost all Philadelphia houses—and this is also the case with all houses in the United States—have the simplest of furniture, usually consisting of several pieces of mahogany, chairs of the same wood with seats covered with horsehair in the case of wealthy people. Other classes have walnut furniture and wooden chairs painted green like garden furniture in France."[4]

The physical divisions of the colonial and federal house are familiar to most visitors of historic properties, although the actual disposition of space by former occupants is less clear. In letters penned by Susanna Dillwyn to her father in England shortly after her marriage to Samuel Emlen, the young bride provided insights on space utilization in a prosperous middle-class home and described how this use was modified as physical design and family needs varied. The Emlens' first home was in Keys Alley, Philadelphia, near the Friends Meeting House, of which society they were members. Susanna wrote in January 1796:

I will . . . give . . . some kind of an idea how we have disposed of the different rooms of the house. I almost wish the alteration proposed . . . had been made, of taking the front entry into the little parlour, but S Emlen does not much like the house. . . . That room [is] too small for much company and too distant from the kitchen when we are alone. . . . The furniture consists of eight chairs, a round pier table under a glass and a small Sopha cover'd as the chairs with black hair. In our entry stand two chairs and a large dining table. . . . The back parlour . . . is furnished with eight chairs painted green [probably Windsors], as is the paper, two large armchairs for our senior visitors with stuff'd backs &c and cover'd with green worsted, a side board, a small dining table and a tea table under a glass between the two windows.

Susanna further identified the chamber located over the back parlor as the room where she and her husband slept. The hired man lodged over the kitchen, and a servant woman and young girl slept on the third story. The front rooms on the second and third floors were guest chambers. Between them and the back rooms were "Sammy's" library and, upstairs, Susanna's "store room."

By May 1797 the Emlens had moved to even smaller quarters near the Delaware River in Burlington, New Jersey, where Susanna had spent her childhood. She described their new situation:

The front room on the right hand of the entry . . . is our parlour; to the left a long narrow room contains Sammys books, papers, Secretary &c. The entry opens into a

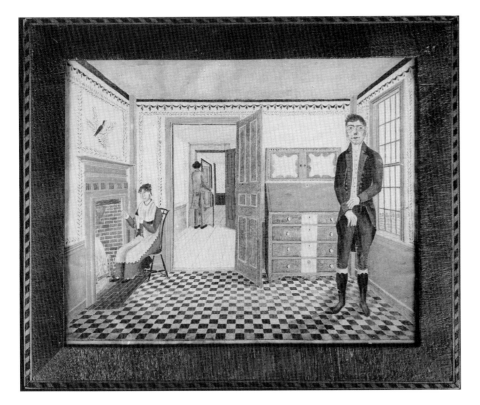

FIG. 5-1 Joseph Warren Leavitt (1804–1833), *Interior of John Leavitt's Tavern*, Chichester, Merrimack County, New Hampshire, ca. 1825. Watercolor, ink, and pencil on paper, in original maple frame; 6½ × 8⅝ in. sight (8⁹⁄₁₆ × 10½ × ½ in. framed). *(Collection American Folk Art Museum, New York. Promised gift of Ralph Esmerian, acc. P1.2001.18; Photo, the late Nina Fletcher Little.)*

little hall where we dine, and shall I suppose often sit. . . . Into a small room back of the parlour . . . I have put a bed, for want of more chambers. . . . [Upstairs] open four chambers, one is a spare room, one occupied by ourselves, . . . the western back room is our two Hannahs [servants], and in the other . . . is a closet, large and roomy, which serves me for a store room.[5]

These living arrangements continued until the Emlens built their own house nearby at Oxmead. Work began in 1798, despite the fact that the Philadelphia property remained unsold "owing to the embarrased state of things in that City." The barn and orchard were in place when Samuel Emlen described the first-floor plan to his father-in-law as "40 feet Square . . . two parlours on the South side, towards Oxmeed; & the Kitchen, Stairs and a small room for Books &c on the north Side next the Barn." The second floor rooms were comparable except for a "Store Room over the front . . . Entry." The lawn that surrounded three sides of the house was to be planted with trees and shrubs.[6]

The new house was ready for occupancy in July 1799. After the young couple had settled in, Susanna wrote to her father from a small room "furnished with shelves for Books, a book case and desk, a table . . . and two chairs," which appears to have been the north room on the first floor that was Sammy's office. Of reasonable comparison is a public room in Leavitt's tavern in Chichester, New Hampshire, where the innkeeper's bookcase desk is prominent and a woman of the family sews while seated at the hearth in a square-back Windsor chair with "double bows" (fig. **5-1**). The decor of the room in New Hampshire is more lively than was common in a Quaker household.[7]

The Emlens' accommodations were above average. Many families of larger size made do with quarters smaller than those in the Burlington house. Life in frontier settlements and other developing areas was far different still. Even in 1844 when Lois Card wrote from Onondaga, New York, to her brother Francis Peabody of North Stonington, Connecticut, living conditions in the new region were far from adequate or comfortable. The Cards, proprietors of a cloth factory, struggled to make their venture a success, and their living accommodations were modest: "You wished me to write you what furniture I had in my house. I have not got much yet. . . . I have two sets of chairs — one cost 3 shillings a piece the other $5, two highpost Bedsteads cost 2 dollars apiece, one table 2 dollars and a half, one bookcase 2 dollars, one large rocking chair 2 dollars, one stand 2 dollars. One set of chairs was flag botom furniture [and] is very cheap up here. My bedsteads are as good as yours that you gave 4 dollars for. One is light the other red. I have tried to get along with as little as I could."[8]

THE ENTRY

The space encountered first on entering the colonial or federal home was the entry. Some areas were small; others formed sizable halls. The staircase to the upper levels usually rose from this point, and sometimes a narrow back passage gave access to rooms at the rear of the house. Upstairs, the second- and third-floor "entries" often contained enough space to house furniture besides providing a passage to the chambers. The first-floor entry frequently served as a reception area for guests and household members. Windsor seating was common here, and it may have served in part to receive outer garments shed when the wearers came indoors. Other furnishings generally were sparse. In the 1750s the entrance in the home of Abraham Lodge, a prosperous attorney of New York, was furnished with four high-back Windsor chairs and two lanterns. Lighting devices occurred frequently in this area. The "Entry lamp with fixtures" in the house of Whitehead Fish at New York was part of a reasonably sophisticated setting in 1819 that comprised a Windsor settee, a stair and "Entry carpet," and "1 Willards Patent Clock" (banjo type). Fish was cashier (director) of the Mechanics Bank in Wall Street.[9]

Carpeting occurred with frequency in other entries furnished with Windsors, especially those of nineteenth-century date. In 1803 a carpet in the entry of James Barron, a merchant of New York, accompanied "9 Green Chairs Winsor & Sophia d[itt]o"; four fire buckets were stored there for emergencies. Carpeting and "wires" (rods) covered Andrew Oliver's stairway in Boston, where twenty-three pictures hung on the walls. Painted floorcloths were particularly favored for entries. Another identified covering was the "Rag Carpet." In 1833 one accompanied a settee in the entry of Thomas Ogden, a cabinetmaker of West Chester, Pennsylvania. Before 1818 an entire suite of Windsor seating, comprising a settee, six side chairs, and three armchairs, filled the entrance and hall of tanner William Corbit's brick mansion house in the Delaware village of Odessa. In Wilmington, Doctor Henry Latimer furnished two entries in his four-story residence on Market Street with settees. One was located just inside the front door; the other stood on the third story. In 1800 four settees filled the "Hall," or "front room," of Thomas Mifflin's Philadelphia house. These bow-back seats painted white with contrasting varnished mahogany arms were made in the shop of John Letchworth.[10]

Use of the term *passage* to describe the entry and its accompanying hall was common in the South. As early as 1770 Mann Page, a tobacco grower of Fredericksburg, Virginia, ordered "1 dozn Windsor Chairs for a Passage" from his London agent John Norton and Sons, suppliers of many Virginia families. Just a year later James Brice wrote from Annapolis, Maryland, to Philadelphia for seating of similar description. By 1781 Fielding Lewis's residence in Fredericksburg, Virginia, was furnished with Windsor chairs in the downstairs "passage," an area that several decades later was also the location of "Five large Windsor arm chairs" in the Williamsburg estate of Joseph Prentis.[11]

Many inventories describe more extensive entry furniture, and some refer to the area as the "hall." An increase in furnishings frequently signaled an expansion of use. Probate records from the Sprague family of Dedham, Massachusetts, chronicle the changing emphasis in the "Lower front Entry" within a single household during sixteen years of successive occupation by three family members. At the death of Doctor John I in 1797 this area, including the stairs, was carpeted and furnished with two glass lamps, three Windsor and "other" chairs, a "couch & cushions," and a "Marble slab & frame." The area was used as a sitting room on occasion. The house was next occupied by the physician's son, Doctor John II, and his wife. At the death of John II in 1812 minor changes were recorded. Everything was in place except the couch and the "other" chairs. A fourth Windsor had joined the original three, probably for "balance," and all had cushions. The area probably served for reception only. Within a year and a half Rebecca Sprague followed her husband to the grave. In the meantime, she had removed the slab table and replaced it with a three-piece dining table, thereby broadening the room's function. For seating, the area now contained "6 Green Windsor chairs." An adjacent room also was fitted for dining, and its numerous furnishings, which included a sideboard and half a dozen yellow Windsors, suggest a new emphasis on entertaining. This supposition is further strengthened by the title "Great Entry" given to the former modest hall.[12]

Documentation of the entrance hall as a dining area occurs in various records, including an Emlen letter. The hall in the home of Nathaniel Coleman, another resident of Burlington, New Jersey, functioned in this manner several decades later and also housed a settee. Modest dining furniture was part of the "Large Entry" at Captain Jonathan Dalton's home in Newburyport, Massachusetts. Accompanying a 4-foot mahogany table protected by an "oil Cloth" were two armchairs and "1 high green Chair." The presence of a "Writing Desk," which contained a sextant, suggests the room served several functions. Another dual-purpose hall was recorded in 1778 in the home of John Knowles at Ridley in southeastern Pennsylvania. An oval walnut dining table, six Windsor chairs, and a bookcase desk were supplemented by an "Arch'd face Eight day Clock," a walnut chest, a pier glass, a map of Philadelphia, and a lantern.[13]

Records from New York City indicate that large entrance halls in the homes of Doctor John Baker (1797) and Johannah Beekman (1821) served primarily for social gatherings, including dinner parties, although both houses also contained a dining room with appropriate furnishings. Windsor chairs provided seating in the halls of both houses, and carpets covered the floors. Mahogany dining tables were accompanied by a pair of card tables at the Baker house and by two tea tables in the Beekman home. Baker also managed to fit in a "small Mahogany sideboard" as a complement to a "large" one in the dining room. On it was a "butlers Tray"; beneath it stood a "Large Wine Cooler." In the Beekman house a map of New York, "Hall Lamp," and "thermometer" completed the room. The presence of a scientific instrument on the wall recalls the painting of Elizabeth Fenimore Cooper, mother of the author, portrayed about 1816 in the hall of her spacious Cooperstown, New York, home, where a weather indicator is displayed prominently in the foreground (fig. 5-2). The view clearly delineates yellow Windsor chairs and a large drop-leaf dining table. The chintz-covered sofa, handsome carpet, and "greenhouse" at one end of the room suggest that the wallpapered hall was a pleasant place for socializing and general entertainment presided over by Elizabeth Cooper herself.[14]

Halls also functioned as sitting rooms. A selection of wooden-bottom seating, including green Windsor chairs, two rockers, and a yellow settee, stood in Samuel Townsend's carpeted New York hall in 1826, accompanied by a tall clock in a cherry case. Townsend appears to have been a machinist. Utilization of the hall as a second parlor during the summer months was a practical necessity in southern households. When traveling in Virginia in the mid-1790s, Isaac Weld described the area as a "favourite apartment, during the hot weather . . . on account of the draught of air through it, and it is usually furnished similar to a Parlour, with sofas, &c."[15]

Several records serve to document the *miscellaneous* use of the hall and areas connected to it via the stairway. Upon entering the Philadelphia home of Joseph

FIG. 5-2 George Freeman, *Elizabeth Fenimore Cooper*, Cooperstown, N.Y., 1816. Watercolor on paper; H. 17¹/₁₆", W. 22⅜". *(Fenimore Art Museum, Cooperstown, NY, acc. N-145.77.)*

Galloway, whose fortune was calculated at £70,000 sterling in 1776, the visitor found two Windsor chairs. Otherwise, the area was devoted to the storage of china, silver, and glassware, probably in built-in cupboards, since no furniture is itemized. Galloway had been the powerful Speaker of the Pennsylvania Assembly and then a member of the First Continental Congress until his Tory sympathies led in 1778 to the confiscation of his property. In 1824 the Isaac Pennock home in neighboring Chester County contained similar storage. The movables comprised a tallcase clock and nine Windsor chairs, two with arms; "29 Yds Domestic Carpet" were on the floor. Sometimes upper stairhalls also served as storage, and if space permitted, the area became a supplemental bedroom or lounge. In 1778 the second-floor entry in Samuel Shoemaker's home at Philadelphia contained Windsor and walnut chairs, "2 Settles, 1 Matrass, [and] 2 Pillows," supplemented by pictures on the walls. Another couch with bedding provided supplemental lodging in the second floor "Chamber Entry" of the John Sprague house in Dedham, Massachusetts. When not serving as sleeping quarters, the area functioned as a lounge furnished with seven Windsor chairs and a tallcase clock.[16]

Perhaps the most sophisticated entrance hall of its day was that of millionaire William Bingham, whose mansion stood at Third and Spruce streets, Philadelphia. Of broad, spacious proportions, the room had a central, white marble staircase and a mosaic-pattern marble floor. When the contents of the house were sold at auction following Bingham's death in 1804, the "CATALOGUE" listed the "Hall" furnishings: "Large Lamp / 3 Composition Pedestals / 3 Marble ditto with busts of Voltaire and Rosseau / 4 Bronze figures / 1 Female figure composition stone / A Dial on Composition pedestal / 2 Marble medallions in gilt frames / 3 Busts of Franklin." Heading the list were one dozen Windsor chairs, their sculptural simplicity and appropriate white paint, perhaps touched with gilt, subtle complements to the neoclassical elegance of the room. Another instance of busts used with Windsor furniture in a front entry occurred three decades earlier at Andrew Oliver's home in Boston. Standing near the entrance was Oliver's "walking Cain mounted with Gold," a symbol of social status and position to be carried in the "outside world" when the door closed on his private castle.[17]

Various names described the area for taking meals before the term *dining room* achieved acceptance in the nineteenth century. Frequently only knowledge of a room's contents allows us to identify its purpose. In Pennsylvania, the greater Delaware Valley, and the South the word *hall* was used from an early date to denote a confined area employed for dining. The term is not to be confused in meaning with the same word applied to an entrance area, where the space was less defined in its boundaries. In 1753 the family of John Coxe, Esq., at Trenton, New Jersey, used the "Back Hall" as a parlor and the "front Hall" as a dining facility. The room included a large round dining table of walnut and smaller tables for informal dining and tea drinking. The seating consisted of six New England chairs (probably leather-covered Boston or Boston-style seating) and one Windsor. The "china" appears to have been stored in wall cupboards, as no movable storage furniture occurs in the listing. A decade later the dining area in the Reading, Pennsylvania, home of William Bird, a Berks County ironmaster, served a dual function under the title "Compting Room." Prominent were a "Writing Desk & Ink stand," although other furnishings describe the room's broader purpose. Large and small walnut dining tables were covered with carpets, an old-fashioned practice at this date, and there was also an old joint stool. The rest of the seating—six rush-bottom chairs and four Windsors—was relatively up to date. A tea table and tea chest describe other room functions. Gracing the walls were five "Glass Pictures" and a looking glass. Another piece of furniture placed here, a bookcase desk, was to become a fairly standard form in Delaware Valley dining rooms through the end of the century.[18]

After the 1750s the term *hall* faded from use to denote a center for taking meals. During the hiatus before *dining room* became the accepted name for this area, there were various substitutes, many descriptive of location rather than function. Thus in inventories dating into the nineteenth century rooms furnished for dining were identified as the "Lower Story Southwest Room," the "west front room down stairs," the "Back Room," or the "Back Parlour." At Philadelphia, in particular, the "parlor" or "back parlor" often denoted a dining or dining-sitting room.[19]

Analysis of a group of twenty comprehensive inventories of Delaware Valley origin dating between 1774 and 1799 provides a pattern for Windsor-furnished rooms devoted mainly to dining. The similarities of furnishings are greater than the differences, even though the owners' occupations varied considerably: merchant, lawyer, woodworker, farmer, blacksmith, silversmith, gunpowder maker, baker, shopkeeper, and pewterer. In general, the Windsors shared dining space with mahogany, walnut, or rush-bottom chairs. Dining tables constructed of walnut somewhat exceeded in number those made of mahogany. One at least had "Claw feet"; another was made of poplar, and one was painted. Tallcase clocks stood in about half the rooms, and all but one room contained a looking glass. More than three-quarters of the rooms were furnished with at least one large case piece, more often than not a desk or bookcase desk made of walnut, mahogany, or cherry. Other large forms included a walnut clothespress in a German household and furniture for reclining—two couches and two bedsteads with bedding—all in the Chester County, Pennsylvania, homes of farmers. In 1778 a "Side Board" stood in a "Back Room" in Philadelphia used for dining by attorney Joseph Galloway. This was not the well-known federal form but a serving piece probably like that described as a "Marble Slab Side board" in an inventory taken at neighboring Graeme Park in Horsham the same year. Small items of furniture included stands, tea tables, and card tables.

Of particular note are the framed pictures on the walls of eight houses and the

FIG. 5-3 Lewis Miller, *Dr. John Rause and Family,*
York, Pa., ca. 1815–25, depicting scene of 1807. Ink
and watercolor on paper. *(The York County
Heritage Trust, PA; Photo, Winterthur Museum.)*

"Landscape" in another. Prints and maps, including one of Philadelphia, are mentioned. Almost half the rooms had cupboards built into the walls. All held ceramics and, occasionally, other items. Enhancing the "Back Parlour" at the home of Stephen Carmick, a merchant of Philadelphia, was a "Small Wilton Carpet" complemented by "Furniture Check" at the windows, which probably matched the removable "Check Covers" on six mahogany chairs with "Damask Bottoms." Records in four instances (three outside the sample) identify the colors of Windsor "dining Chairs" as green, "Patent Yellow," mahogany, and white. Windsors located in the dining room of pewterer William Will of Philadelphia had "stuff'd" bottoms. The room also contained a settee.[20]

Changes in dining room furnishings in the Delaware Valley occurred in the early nineteenth century. Although many householders in Philadelphia turned to fancy or more sophisticated seating, the Windsor was still the common dining chair in rural areas and small towns such as Wilmington, West Chester, and Trenton. It was less common to mix Windsors with other seating. Instead sets were made larger to provide the requisite number of seats. Mahogany and cherry dining and breakfast tables prevailed, almost to the exclusion of walnut construction, and the appearance of the tall clock in this setting was less frequent. Use of the looking glass remained popular. The desk virtually disappeared from the dining area, the space occupied now by a settee and cushion or a sideboard, which served both storage and service functions. The sideboard in the home of attorney William Hemphill of West Chester held a tea service. Wall pictures remained popular. Floor coverings were more common, consisting generally of carpeting, one described as "Ingrain." Matting and green floorcloths also were present. Blinds, some described as "venetian," were in greater use, and closets or corner cupboards were still repositories for dinnerware, teaware, and utensils.[21]

Visual materials depict Windsor dining furniture. Two views from eastern Pennsylvania illustrate three seating forms and two early nineteenth-century patterns (figs. **5-3, 5-4**). Large families were common, and that of Doctor John Rause at York was no exception (fig. 5-3). The family is dining on noodle soup at the noon meal, a Pennsylvania German favorite. The scene is somewhat later than the 1807 date assigned by the artist, Lewis Miller (b. 1796), given the large rectangular tablet crests of the Windsors. Low stools used at the table for small children extended the function of this form and made sense during their growing years, when a high chair was too small and an adult-size seat unsatisfactory. This type of table seating was not peculiar to Pennsylvania, however, for on December 20, 1814, Wait Garret billed a customer at New Hartford, Connecticut, for "two Table Stools." The second family scene, depicting a small child drawn close to the table in a high chair as it would have been for dining, is by another German American artist, John Lewis Krimmel (fig.

FIG. 5-4 John Lewis Krimmel, *Christmas Eve*, southeastern Pennsylvania, 1812–13. Ink, ink wash, and pencil on paper; H. 4⅛", W. 6³⁄₁₆". From sketchbook 2, southeastern Pennsylvania, 1812–13. *(Winterthur Library, Winterthur, Del.)*

5-4). A German family from the Philadelphia area celebrates the secular traditions of the Christmastide. The square back of the high chair is a pattern developed about 1800 in the city.[22]

The contents of the room used for dining in the 1770s by Frederick Wollffe, proprietor of a "Painters Shop" in New York, were similar to those found in contemporary Philadelphia residences: a corner cupboard, desk, looking glass, small dining table, stand, two Windsor and nine rush-bottom chairs, and four pictures. Extending the range of activities were a mahogany card table and two tea tables. By the end of the century furniture styles and practices in New York were changing. The mahogany dining table occasionally had a "Cover," and some rooms contained a new furniture form, the sideboard. Formal chairs accompanying Windsor seating in this room often had haircloth bottoms. Green cloth covered the mahogany and Windsor dining chairs in the home of John Pell. A well-furnished house among members of the professions was that of Doctor John Baker, who before 1797 used his entry as a second dining area. Appointments in the main dining room were handsome and complete: "9 Mahogany Chairs stuff bottoms yellow Check furniture / 4 Windsor Chairs same furniture / 2 Mahogany ends for a dining table / 1 small Mahogany table claw feet / 1 large Mahogany side board / 2 Mahogany Knife Cases / 3 Venetian Window blinds / 1 small Oval Glass gilt frame / 1 Clock made by Webb / 1 Scotch Carpet / 1 Franklin Stove [and fire tools] / 3 Wedgwood flower pots." Like the Pells' Windsors, Doctor Baker's chairs had stuffed seats, a treatment that doubled or tripled the price and placed the cost within the range of plain mahogany seating. Windsor colors in dining rooms of the early federal period at New York suggest schemes that harmonized with other furniture, textiles, or painted woodwork. Those mentioned are chocolate, green, black, and yellow.[23]

Rooms in some prosperous middle-class Boston households of the 1770s contained furnishings surprisingly similar to those found in Philadelphia and New York, although local Windsor production had yet to begin. Samuel Parker's "Back lower Room" contained half a dozen black walnut chairs with leather seats for use at a 4-foot round mahogany table. Two "painted Windsor Chairs" provided extra seating as needed. A large looking glass hung on one wall; an eight-day clock in a veneered case stood against another. There were two painted pine tables, and a wall cupboard served as storage. A "Canvas painted floor Cloth" provided a central focus, serving to integrate furnishings and architecture. Parker's Windsors likely originated in Philadelphia, a trade documented in other records and a supposition strengthened by Parker's ownership of "a Sloop & Appurtenances."[24]

Windsor furniture ranked first in New England painted seating by the 1790s. Ansel Goodrich of Northampton, Massachusetts, advertised dining Windsor chairs (bow-backs) and other patterns. In summer 1797 Amos Denison Allen, a craftsman

FIG. 5-5 Joseph S. Russell, *Dining Room of Dr. Whitridge*, Tiverton, R.I., ca. 1848–53, depicting scene of 1814–15. Watercolor on paper; H. 7¹⁄₁₆", W. 9½". *(Courtesy of The New Bedford Whaling Museum, New Bedford, Mass.)*

of South Windham, Connecticut, first recorded an order for "Dining Chairs." Most customers bought seating in sets of six, sometimes nine, chairs, although Allen noted the sale of a set of twelve chairs or odd groups numbering fewer than half a dozen. Some chairs had a pair of extra spindles forming back "braces." Green, yellow, and black paint were popular. Some production was of fancy quality, including Windsors with "cushions," or stuffed seats. The price was double that of plain chairs, and the usual fabric color was green. More popular were painted combinations, such as mahogany-color "bottoms" contrasted with green or yellow surfaces. Some dining chairs were "edged" ("penciled" with fine lines) in an accent color. The chairmaker mentioned yellow and black.[25]

Dining chairs of the bow-back type made by A. D. Allen and other chairmakers in the 1790s and later are illustrated in the dining room of Doctor William Whitridge of Tiverton, Rhode Island, as the room appeared in 1814–15 (fig. **5-5**). The furnishings are sparse by modern standards but typical of the colonial and early federal periods. A rush-bottom chair in the corner, the seat covered by a pillow with a flounce, is earlier than the Windsors. The dining table with leaves extended appears to be set for about six people. Breakfast consists of "Pot-Apple pie." A white tablecloth commonly covered the dining surface at meals, but it was out of sight at other times when the table was folded and pushed against a wall with the chairs. Bare floors still were more common than those covered with carpets. The doctor perhaps has been out of doors tending to morning chores, as he now warms his feet near the Franklin stove while reading. He uses a small tea table or candle stand as a book support. The map on rollers above the doctor's head probably depicts the local area.

Another Windsor-furnished dining room in New England was that of Joseph Barrell, a wealthy merchant of Boston. Barrell's "Pleasant Hill," designed by Charles Bulfinch and erected in 1792–93 at Charlestown, Massachusetts, was "the most outstanding private residence built in America" during the 1790s. The site was a prom-

FIG. 5-6 Joseph S. Russell, *Dining Room of Abraham Russell*, New Bedford, Mass., ca. 1848–53, depicting scene of 1810–14. Watercolor on paper; H. 5½", W. 8⅞". *(Courtesy of The New Bedford Whaling Museum.)*

ontory overlooking the Charles River and Boston. From the bow-front east facade of the house there was a view of lawns, trees, gardens, and terraces. Inside, the bow front formed part of Barrell's elegant oval room, where the architecture and appointments were sumptuous yet tasteful. The entrance hall contained an extraordinary divided flying staircase.[26]

Within this house Barrell furnished the hall and summer dining room with Windsor furniture. On March 1, 1795, he wrote to his New York agents, the merchants John and Francis Atkinson, requesting: "18 of the handsomest windsor Chairs fit for Dining & my Hall. I would have them with arms, rather less in the Seat than larger than Common, as they will thereby accomodate more at table. I would have them painted of light blue grey Colour, the same as my summer dining Room if you can remember. Let them be strong and neat." The contemporary New York armchair was the continuous-bow Windsor (fig. 3-16, center). As Barrell requested strong construction and cost was of little consequence, the chairs probably had back braces. Barrell was anxious to have the furniture, noting, "The Chairs also I shall be made glad to receive when they are ready." The previous year he had "determined to have a carpet for [his] Summer Room instead of a canvas" and had written to Benjamin Joy, his future son-in-law, requesting him to "send for a Brussels Carpet" of about 22 feet 6 inches by 19 feet. Barrell suggested a plain ground "covered with handsome Bunches of flowers." No doubt the new floor covering was intended to complement a large French tapestry that Barrell had transferred to the summer dining room from the sitting room. The textile, a bucolic scene, was one of only a few furnishings the merchant had saved during the Revolution.[27]

In sharp contrast to Barrell's summer room, to say nothing of his formal dining room, was the stark simplicity of the dining area in the Quaker household of Abraham Russell at New Bedford depicted by his son Joseph Shoemaker Russell as it looked in the early nineteenth century (fig. **5-6**). The double-rod and medallion-back Windsors may have been made locally. Otherwise they were ordered from

Philadelphia, where the family had business connections and kin. As a whaling town New Bedford also had close ties with Nantucket, which was not far distant. There merchant Andrew Myrick's dining room was comfortably furnished before the Revolution with "open d back" and "Common" chairs complemented by "2 high Back Green Chairs" (Windsors) and a "low round" one. Fringing the "Turkey Carpet" were a maple desk and a black walnut table supporting a mahogany case for knives and forks. A looking glass hung on the wall. Nantucket inventories dating into the 1800s document the continued use of "Green Chairs," some of "bow Back" pattern, with and without "Braces." From about 1800 mahogany-colored Windsors appear in the records with considerable frequency. Black chairs also are mentioned and occasionally a cushion.[28]

Windsor seating sometimes furnished dining rooms containing a sideboard, a new form in the federal period, although the cost, limited storage, and function of this case piece was too restrictive for many middle-class households. Furnishings owned by America's merchant princes, such as Elias Hasket Derby of Salem, Massachusetts, were another matter. Appointments in Derby's "South East Parlour," used for dining, were relatively new in 1800 when he died. A sideboard, appraised at $40, held two knife cases with silver flatware. A looking glass and set of eight mahogany chairs each commanded a similar high figure. Two lolling chairs were costly at $36. Crickets, or footstools, accompanied two Windsor armchairs. A cupboard, part of the interior architecture, contained a considerable amount of china. Window curtains and cornices provided finishing touches.[29]

In the 1840s Lambert Hitchcock's dining room at Unionville, Connecticut, contained a sideboard and other typical furnishings. His rocking chairs were a relatively new item for this setting, and there was another rocker for a child. These were accompanied by Windsor chairs and three "Pea green cane seat chairs." Small items in some number and variety, from "Block tin" lamps to vinegar cruets, began to appear in homes about midcentury, the general date of a dining corner in the home of a typical American citizen (fig. **5-7**). The walls, furniture, and hearth held some of the many accessories today considered part of a normal household. Windsor seating continued to play an important role in dining, and the medium-high stool still provided seating for the family children.[30]

THE PARLOR

Records and reminiscences confirm that, in meeting the needs of family and guests to socialize, the late colonial and federal parlor sometimes was a dining facility. Sara Josepha Hale, writing from New England in 1827, recalled her youthful days when describing the function of the "best" room in the house: "The parlor . . . was seldom used, except on important occasions. . . . The furniture . . . consisted of a mahogany sideboard and table, a dozen handsome chairs, a large mirror, the gilt frame covered with green gauze to prevent injury from dust and flies; and on the floor was a . . . home-manufactured carpet, woven in a curious manner, and blended with all the colors of the rainbow."[31]

In 1815 a mahogany sideboard, secretary, birch table, and twelve green chairs were the major furnishings of the "South West sitting Room" in George Frost's home at Portsmouth, New Hampshire. The "Back Parlour" of Christopher Marshall, Jr's., home at Philadelphia also served on occasion for taking meals, as identified by the "Dining Table with semicircular ends" standing there. Seating consisted of Windsor and mahogany chairs. The presence of a sofa and cover, pier looking glasses, mantel ornaments, and a floor carpet identify the room's alternative use as a social center. A description of Cedar Grove, on the eastern shore of Virginia, as it looked about 1840 recalls a parlor of large, square, "airy" form with windows that opened on a world of exterior bloom and greenery:

It had no carpet, but the floor was painted a deep lemon-color, and twelve high-backed, hard-seated, long-legged Windsor chairs, of the same tender tint, were ranged in regimental order against the walls. A tall mahogany side-board, much carved and ornamented, stood in a prominent place, and displayed an old-fashioned silver tea-service . . . and a quantity of ancient eggshell china, with quaint glass pitchers and mugs. . . . Over the mantel-shelf . . . hung a group of . . . profile portraits. . . . In the wide open fireplace was the huge bow-pot filled with great branches of roses and feathery sprays of asparagus.[32]

During the colonial period and later it was not uncommon for the parlor to function as a bedroom besides serving as a sitting and dining area. An inventory of the John Coxe home at Trenton, New Jersey, taken in 1753 identifies the dual function of the "back hall," or parlor, as a sitting area and occasional bedroom. The tradition continued later in rural and developing areas than in urban locations. When Alice Cary described her Ohio "neighborhood" of the early nineteenth century, she concluded her remarks by stating, "Everybody who has been in western country houses, knows that the parlor is also the spare bedroom":

The walls were bare, but white-washed; the floor was covered with a home-made carpet striped alternately with green and red and yellow; six black windsor chairs stood in a straight line against the wall; a bed with a white muslin tester was in one corner; and an old-fashioned bureau . . . and a breakfast table, covered with a green and red oil-cloth, completed the furniture, except that the windows were shaded with highly-colored wallpaper. On one side of the chimney was a cupboard with glazed doors, originally designed for china, but filled with a variety of coverlids [coverlets].[33]

As early as the 1750s the sophisticated Berks County ironmaster William Bird furnished the "parlour" of his Reading, Pennsylvania, townhouse purely as a social area. A "Table Carpet" covered his dining-size walnut table, where a "Japan Server," plates and custard cups, and "18 Glasses of different sorts" were used to serve light refreshment. A Windsor and six leather-bottom chairs were moved about as required. Otherwise the room contained a tallcase clock, a stand, two looking glasses, and "9 Glass pictures." The "Front Room below Stairs" in the Woodstown, New Jersey, home of Joseph James served in the same manner a decade later. The rush-bottom chairs and "Low backed" Windsors in the room could be drawn around either a large walnut table or a tea table as needed. Social gatherings probably seldom numbered more than half a dozen people, since there were only six "China Cups and Saucers" and "6 Silver Tea Spoons" in the room. A looking glass and maple chest of drawers, possibly to hold linens, completed the furnishings.[34]

Written and visual materials dating from the Revolution to the early 1800s further illuminate the appointments of the Windsor-furnished parlor in its dual capacity as a family sitting room and place of entertainment. In the 1770s some furnishings of the "front parlour" in the Philadelphia home of mariner Joseph Brown dated from an earlier period—the "sconce looking glass," the "old" tea table, and the "leather bottomed" chairs. The stark walls were relieved by fourteen pictures and an eight-day clock placed against one surface. A "tea Chest" and "sugar box" testify to the regular use of the area. A few years later in neighboring Chester County a front room furnished with a tea table had as a special attraction a "perspective glass and prints" for the pleasure of young and old on social occasions. Evening entertainments in the home of the bachelor Spanish ambassador at Philadelphia appear to have been common following the war. The "Front Room" contained no fewer than six mahogany card tables, one at least covered in baize. The twenty-four mahogany chairs and eight Windsors accompanying the tables describe the room size.[35]

The card table became an increasingly common parlor furnishing during the

1790s. A card table in the "Front Room" of George Shaw, a Philadelphia joiner, was accompanied by half a dozen Windsor chairs "without arms." Similar seating complemented two mahogany card tables in the Boston home of cabinetmaker John Cogswell before 1818, and as late as the 1830s Daniel Proud, a cabinetmaker of Providence, kept tables of this description in his "North Parlour," which also housed a "Wood settee." More elegant in its internal appointments was the late eighteenth-century house at Philadelphia of the Quaker merchant Stephen Collins. His second-story "front room" was furnished with two card tables, a breakfast table, and an upholstered sofa possibly covered in "morine," the fabric of the three window curtains. Other seating consisted of eight mahogany chairs and two Windsors. Two superb looking glasses hung on the walls complemented by a picture. An expensive carpet covered the floor, and the mantel held a "Set of China Jars & Glass Candlesticks." The appraised value of this room alone was £110. Compared with the average daily wage of a working man with a trade, computed at about 6s. in the 1790s, this was truly a rich and handsome room.[36]

Use of Windsor seating with the sofa in the early nineteenth-century parlor is recorded in prosperous households such as that of William Hemphill, a West Chester, Pennsylvania, attorney, Doctor Henry Latimer of Wilmington, Delaware, and Ann Lewis, a Philadelphia widow who in 1825 kept her pianoforte in the same room. Appraisers noted that Mrs. Lewis's sofa had a "Cover." This protective cloth probably was not unlike the "wash cover" that draped upholstered sofas at Otsego Hall (fig. 5-2) and Eleutherian Mills, an early du Pont family residence at Wilmington (fig. **5-8**). The sofa in the du Pont home, equipped with a large ruffled pillow and accompanied by Windsor chairs, was an agreeable place for the daughters of the family to gather for afternoon readings.[37]

The presence of a "Writing Table" and a "Mahogany Box for Papers" in the parlor of Charles Ward Apthorp's residence in the village of Bloomingdale, New York, just prior to 1800 describes still another room function. The area also contained a "Round Tea Table" and a set of eight Windsor chairs painted "yellow & green." Recalling the days of his young manhood in the 1810s is a sketch by Joseph Shoemaker Russell of the Tiverton, Rhode Island, parlor of Doctor William Whitridge with its fallfront desk accompanied by Windsor chairs. The walls are enlivened with patterned wallpaper, and pictures and floral bouquets serve as accessories (fig. 3-72). More up-to-date than Whitridge's desk was the secretary that stood in William Ryder's New York parlor in company with a card table, mahogany breakfast table, and nine black Windsor chairs in 1806, a time when the place of the Windsor in the parlor was being challenged. Chairmakers in metropolitan centers already offered handsome fancy painted seating with woven bottoms described as "Elegant white, coquilico, green, . . . and gilt drawing room chairs" or "gilt and ornamented" chairs "with Settees to suit, both cane and rush

FIG. 5-9 John Collins, *Mr. and Mrs. Nathaniel Coleman in House Interior*, Burlington, N.J., 1854. Photographic duplicate of watercolor on paper; H. 6", W. 8½". *(John Collins Collection of Drawings, Burlington County Historical Society, Burlington, N.J.)*

bottoms." In this respect the parlor of Thomas Marston at New York appears to have been à la mode in 1814 in its use of "12 Straw Bottom chairs with Gilt Backs." The furniture stood on or around a "handsome Wilton carpet" accompanied by six yellow Windsors, mahogany card tables, and a tea table. Less pretentious rooms had "homespun carpet" on the floor.[38]

Household inventories occasionally itemize a "work stand" in the sitting room, or parlor. Undoubtedly many more were present among the numerous small tables listed without particular description. The Eliakim Prindall parlor at Gloucester, Massachusetts, contained a work stand, breakfast table, half dozen Windsors painted yellow, and a rocking chair in 1824 at Prindall's death. A comparable assemblage stood in the back parlor of Nathaniel Coleman's residence at Burlington, New Jersey (fig. **5-9**). The fashionable painted side chairs with rush seats are accompanied by a late eighteenth-century Windsor armchair that serves the master of the house, a local silversmith. Mrs. Coleman appears to be sewing in her 1830s high-back rocking chair, her worktable across the room below the old-fashioned looking glass. The Coleman parlor, although large, is sparsely furnished, as was typical of the early nineteenth century. Other appointments represent objects noted in contemporary inventories. Beneath a side table are a footstool and a large japanned waiter for tea service. The floor covering probably is a flat-woven "ingrain" carpet; a Venetian blind hangs at the window.[39]

During the 1820s the rocking chair became a common fixture in many American parlors. The Colemans' crown-top rocker is contemporary with the scene. Confirming that this painted chair was an integral part of domestic life in other parts of the nation are Maria Foster Brown's recollections of her girlhood days in the 1830s at Athens, Ohio. She described the family's "best room":

The chairs were of the kind called Windsor — the bottoms solid, the backs round. In that room too was one large rocking-chair with the most beautiful cushion on it. I think the chairs must have been of cherry — perhaps mahogany; they were red [probably grain painted]. And in one corner stood a large bureau — the most work on it! — big claw feet, glass knobs. The walls of this room were painted white. The floor had a rag carpet. . . . [The] window shades were made of . . . green paper. We had thin white curtains over the shades. No pictures.

In another section of the country during the 1830s Joseph H. Davis depicted chairs of contoured back, crown top, and fancy decoration (fig. **5-10**). John and Abigail Montgomery of Strafford Ridge, New Hampshire, spend a typical quiet Sunday afternoon seated in the matched rocking chairs that furnish their parlor. The setting suggests that the family enjoyed relatively comfortable circumstances. A lively pattern decorates the floor, the grain-painted table exceeds the ordinary, and the basket on the table contains the fruits of the productive family farm pictured in the wall view.[40]

THE KEEPING ROOM

Written and pictorial records describe the range of social interaction associated with the "keeping room," where Windsor furniture again filled a need for durable, economical seating. In the 1770s this multifunctional room served for limited food and beverage service in Benjamin Coats's home at Boston. A desk further expanded the range of activity. Keeping rooms at Newport in the same decade accounted for green Windsors, leather-bottom black walnut chairs, rush seating, and easy chairs. Early in the nineteenth century Daniel Danforth, a storekeeper of Hartford, Connecticut, used his keeping room in much the same manner as Benjamin Coats, although the presence of many dishes in the cupboards and the use of half the room for cooking purposes speak to an expanded dining function. During the early 1800s keeping room furnishings appear to have kept pace with the times. At the Hartford home of pianoforte maker Isaac Wright there were "Wood seat sewing Chairs" and rocking chairs with cushions. Other functions served by Wright's room are indicated by the presence of a large dining table, a worktable, a secretary containing books, and a center table with a marble top. A "map of Solomon's Temple" suggests that Wright was a Mason. Down at the heels but giving evidence of a brighter future is the keeping room depicted on the cover of a Pennsylvania German calendar for 1837 (fig. 5-11). Ostensibly a promotion for abstinence from strong drink, the view depicts an area furnished for cooking, dining, and socializing, where a set of slat-back Windsor chairs provided the primary seating and a long backless bench probably served as both a seat and a stand.[41]

Views of New England interiors painted in the late nineteenth century by Eastman Johnson show that cooking as a primary activity in multipurpose rooms gave way occasionally to more quiet pursuits, such as sitting by an open fire or reading from the family Bible. In the Middle Atlantic states authors and artists captured other scenes from daily life in Windsor-furnished settings. A fraktur from Northumberland County, Pennsylvania, dating after 1808 illustrates a family scene with ladies spinning and paring apples. Elizabeth Calder Rock described a Christmas Eve celebration at Cherry Valley, New York, in 1835 when a yule log, evergreens, spiced posset, and bread and cheese were accompaniments to carol singing and dancing. John Lewis Krimmel's Pennsylvania genre scenes depict family gatherings, games of blindman's buff, and country weddings amid cupboards, trunks, laundry baskets, tubs, brooms, and other domestic paraphernalia (fig. 5-12). Of necessity, the frontier cabin was a keeping room of a basic sort, as depicted in prose and sketch.[42]

FIG. 5-11 Pennsylvania keeping room scene. From Carl F. Egelmann, *Pennsylvanischer Massigkeits-Calender auf das Jahr unfers herrn 1837* (Philadelphia: G. W. Mentz and Son, [1836]), front cover. *(Winterthur Library.)*

THE CHAMBER, OR BEDROOM

The word "stark" is appropriate in describing the colonial and federal bedroom. Walls were usually bare and floors generally uncovered. Furniture was sparse and frequently outmoded. Rooms for "lodging" or sleeping were termed *chambers*, although appraisers often described these areas by location only. Although a few Windsor chairs were used in homes before 1750 in the Delaware Valley, their presence in sleeping quarters anywhere was uncommon before the Revolution. The seating still was new enough to find a place on the first floor, and either common rush-bottom or outdated joiner's seating filled comparable needs on other floors. "Kitchen chambers" (a room *above* the kitchen) and garrets often served as sleeping quarters for hired help. Apprentices and live-in journeymen probably also found lodging there. These rooms often contained more than one bedstead with appropriate bedding but little else.

FIG. 5-12 John Lewis Krimmel, study for *The Country Wedding*, southeastern Pennsylvania, ca. 1813. Pencil and watercolor on paper; H. 3⅝", W. 5¹/₁₆". From sketchbook 2, southeastern Pennsylvania, 1812–13. *(Winterthur Library.)*

When Windsors were introduced to bedrooms in the Delaware Valley after the Revolution, this seating still was of limited appearance and often mixed with other types of chairs. A survey of regional inventories containing Windsor furniture dating between 1777 and 1833 provides thirty complete chamber listings and insights into common furnishing practice. Bedrooms furnished with Windsor seating usually were not considered the "best" in the house. The bedstead, or wooden framework upon which the "bed" and linens were placed, was rarely described in its particulars, although appraisers cited a few mahogany frames. The presence of a suit of curtains identifies a bedstead with high posts. In 1794 two Windsor-furnished bedrooms out of eight chambers in merchant Stephen Collins's Philadelphia home contained curtained mahogany frames. A bedstead in the "East" room, second floor, at Owen Jones's residence was hung with printed cotton curtains. At Frankford, near Philadelphia, in 1821 a pair of highpost bedsteads in a chamber at chairmaker Benjamin Love's home had calico (printed) curtains. A pair of lowpost bedsteads occupied another chamber. A turned frame and a maple field bedstead appear in other documents; trundles are rare.

From one to as many as eight Windsors might have furnished a single chamber. During the early 1800s the use of *sets* was on the rise. As early as 1784 six green Windsors furnished a chamber containing the "Best bed & furniture" in the home of William Levis, a miller of Chester County, Pennsylvania. A "Long" Windsor chair, or settee, with a cushion stood in Stephen Collins's "first chamber 2nd Story" a decade later at Philadelphia. Unfashionable by his death in 1793 were Owen Jones's low-back Windsors, which furnished a bedroom. By contrast, chairmaker Timothy Hanson had two up-to-date "bamboo" (bow-back) armchairs in his "Front Chamber up stairs" at Wilmington, Delaware. A half dozen white chamber Windsors were enumerated in 1808 in the estate of cabinetmaker Samuel Claphamson at Blockley near Philadelphia.

All but a few rooms surveyed in the sample contained some piece of storage furniture in the Windsor-furnished chamber. The case, or chest, of drawers, sometimes described as "high," was the eighteenth-century form. A walnut bookcase and an "old desk" served in two instances. The Stephen Collins inventory of 1794 introduced a "bureau" made of mahogany. A bureau in the West Chester home of attorney William Hemphill had a "cover" in 1817, about the date that Benjamin Love of Frankford owned a cherrywood bureau. The table was more common in the chamber than the stand, many apparently recycled from the "better" household rooms. In fact, the appearance of the washstand as a form in this sample is relatively uncommon. There were dressing and tea tables, dining, breakfast, and card tables. Walnut, mahogany, maple, and painted woods are represented.

In half the rooms a looking glass was deemed a necessary fixture. Most hung on a wall; a few were on a tabletop or chest. Prints or "pictures" adorned the walls of only four rooms. Window curtains were more common by the end of the eighteenth century than earlier. Three rooms even had paper curtains, and one featured a cornice above cloth hangings. In about a quarter of the sample a carpet covered the chamber floor, but only a rag example was noted. Carpeted rooms usually had curtains at the windows. Few chambers held fireplace equipment, although one had a warming pan. Either the utensils were shared between rooms or fires simply were not made in sleeping areas unless the occupant's health warranted the excess. Doctor Henry Latimer of Wilmington installed a "sheat-iron stove" on the third floor, possibly in a room he occupied before his death, as the area contained two "Cases Surgeons instruments," a large easy chair, and two small chests with tea. Trunks and boxes were stored in a number of chambers, and some may have held the linens or wearing apparel itemized there. The austere appearance of the typical Delaware Valley bedchamber during the federal period is captured in a simple drawing of family life in the du Pont home at Eleutherian Mills on the Brandywine River (fig. **5-13**). The

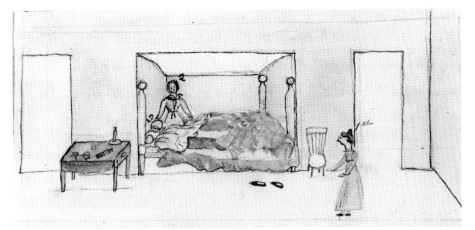

FIG. 5-13 Sophie M. du Pont, bedroom scene from "One Day on the Tancopanican," Wilmington, Del., 1827. Pencil and watercolor on paper; H. 2", w. 4". (Collection of Hagley Museum and Library.)

alcove bed has no curtains, and a single chair, table, and perhaps a chest of drawers were considered sufficient to meet other basic needs.[43]

Several southern household inventories itemized by room describe bedchamber furnishings in families of substantial means. In the period of the Revolution a downstairs bedroom in Landon Carter's plantation house in Virginia contained sleeping furniture, a mahogany desk that probably served for storage, a looking glass, a closestool, a Windsor, and other chairs. Joseph Prentis of Williamsburg, who died in 1809, furnished a more complete downstairs chamber. There was a bookcase desk, a bedstead, and a clothespress to provide storage. The seating, which was relatively expensive, also speaks to room size. Complementing a large armchair and a dozen mahogany seats were an easy chair and a "green stick chair." A variety of accessories indicate a room of greater dimension. Georgia appraisers in the early 1790s enumerated the stylish contents of George Basil Spencer's home at Savannah. One chamber contained six Windsor chairs, a mahogany bedstead, a chest of drawers, and a dressing glass. The windows may have been hung with curtains.[44]

Post-1800 advertisements by New York chairmakers make it clear that householders also purchased new furniture for bedrooms, and they indicate that Windsor seating was considered suitable. In 1810 Patterson and Dennis advised that their stock consisted of "a large and very elegant assortment" of "white, coquilico, green, &c. and gilt drawing room chairs with cane and rush seats" together with handsome groupings "of dining and bed room chairs." The implication is that the last-named furniture had wooden seats. The stylish arrays of seating found in city inventories suggest that New Yorkers needed little urging to buy.[45]

Doctor John Baker made liberal use of Windsor seating in the bedrooms of his New York house during the late eighteenth century. Four or five Windsors stood in each of two large chambers furnished with mahogany four-post bedsteads dressed with white cotton counterpanes and hung with printed "furniture," presumably to match the calico window curtains. A mahogany bureau, probably supporting a dressing glass, stood in each chamber. Completing the list of joined furniture was a pine toilet table in one room and a "mahogany double Chest of drawers," a night table, a "Washhand stand," and an easy chair in the other. Smaller bedrooms in the house also contained Windsors. In contrast to Baker's Windsor-furnished *best* bedrooms was merchant William Constable's choice several years later of ornamental "Japannd" chairs for the chambers of his New York home. Windsor seating was relegated to lesser quarters—the small "Back Bed Room Up Stairs" and the servant's rooms.[46]

Inventories drawn in New York in the early 1800s document chair colors favored locally for bedchambers. Yellow and black are mentioned, and green continued in use. Convertible furniture added another dimension to sleeping accommodations in the postwar years. By 1818 Bates and Johnson of Albany offered "Johnson's Patent Portable Settees, convenient for sitting or lodging for two persons." The rush bottoms of the early seats later shared favor with wooden planks. Perhaps the "Sofa Bedstead" that appraisers described in 1833 when enumerating the contents of the "Back room Third Story" of Gerard Beekman's home at New York was a convertible settee. During the same decade Windsor and fancy rocking chairs often were selected for bedrooms. Robert Troup, a New York lawyer, owned one of each. A Boston rocker stood on the matted floor in the "Front Bed room Second Story" of the Beekman home, its $10 value an indication it was still relatively new.[47]

Windsor seating first furnished the New England bedchamber in the 1770s. An anonymous account of furnishings dated 1775, probably for a house in northeastern Massachusetts, describes a "Green Chamber" containing a Windsor chair and a "Green Harrateen easy chair"; the "Blue Chamber" held another Windsor. The source of the Windsors at this early date is speculative. Philadelphia, New York, and Rhode Island are candidates. Governor William Wanton of Newport placed half a dozen "greene Chairs" in the chamber above his keeping room a few years later.[48]

Appraisers could just as easily have called the "South East Chamber" in Elias Hasket Derby's Salem mansion the "Green Room" in 1800 when they evaluated the deceased merchant's estate. The mahogany four-post bedstead was hung with green damask curtains, and the "Silk Bottoms" of eight mahogany chairs in the room likely were similar. An "Easy Chair & Covering" may have been part of the same suite. The "Two Green Chairs" valued at $1.50 apiece probably were Windsors. The furniture, which stood on a Brussels carpet, was supplemented by a bureau, chest-on-chest, "Stand Table," and an elegant $70 looking glass. The chamber furnishings of Jacob Sanderson, cabinetmaker-entrepreneur of Salem, as appraised in 1810, were modest by comparison. His four-post mahogany bedstead had no hangings, and his mahogany chairs were covered with haircloth. An easy chair and some or all of the dozen "bamboo Chairs" valued at slightly more than $1 apiece probably stood in the same room. Whether the bamboo chairs were of fancy or Windsor construction is not specified.[49]

As in New York households, New England bedchambers often included rocking chairs as part of their furnishings in the nineteenth century. Jonas Heywood, a farmer of Middlesex County, Massachusetts, introduced a pair to a bedroom still furnished in 1831 with fan-back chairs. At about the same date rocking chairs fitted with "coverings" stood in the "West" chamber of the Samuel Proud home at Providence complemented by a half dozen yellow side chairs. The addition of a "box-stove & pipe" and a carpet made a comfortable, if not cozy, room for sitting and sleeping.[50]

THE KITCHEN

Windsor furniture probably was common to kitchens in the Delaware Valley only after the Revolution, when the newly introduced side chair made the price more attractive, although the kitchen remained a depository for old-fashioned and worn examples from other rooms in the house. In New England, however, the rush-bottom chair remained the traditional kitchen, or common, seat until much later. The rocking chair appeared in this room by the second quarter of the nineteenth century. In the 1830s Samuel Proud of Providence fitted his kitchen rocker with a cover.[51]

Tables were kitchen fixtures, many described as "old" or made of "pine." Built-in closets were part of some rooms, although the freestanding "dresser" was common to Pennsylvania homes. The placement of a couch in the kitchen on occasion makes sense because this was the warmest area for napping during the winter months. The settee or "wooden settee" sometimes served the same purpose. Occasionally a bench provided seating. One with board ends stands in the keeping room illustrated in figure 5-11. By the early 1800s a looking glass and/or a clock were introduced to some kitchens. A shelf timepiece is prominent in figure **5-14**. Metalwares of great variety were housed in the kitchen, and closets held an assortment of tablewares. The well-ordered, cleanly work space depicted in figure 5-14 was the ideal kitchen of the 1840s. The variety of cooking utensils, storage containers, and implements for food preparation anticipates that newfound freedom realized later in the century as household chores were lightened by a range of labor-saving gadgetry. The mantel lamp is one of several lighting devices named in kitchen inventories; others are candlesticks and lanterns. The rush-bottom chair had given way by this date to the Windsor.[52]

The frequent enumeration of flatirons, or "smoothing" irons, in the kitchen addresses another basic activity frequently performed in this area. Supplementary accoutrements of the laundry ranged from "Cedar washing Tubs" to horses "for drying cloths" to the "Ironing table." A reel, "big wheel," and "Bunch of Yarn" in a Pennsylvania inventory describe another kitchen function. The presence of a child's chair in a New York kitchen is a reminder that along with her other duties the housewife or servant was responsible for child care.[53]

THE STUDY AND MISCELLANEOUS AREAS

Rooms used as studies, or libraries, are seldom identified by name in household inventories. The mansion Elias Hasket Derby built at Salem, Massachusetts, in the 1790s included a library upstairs in the "South West Room." Itemized here in his estate were "Two Mahogany Book Cases contain'g about Seven Hundred & Seventy Volumes" valued at $1,400. Among other room furnishings were two "Semi circular Tables," a pair of globes, and six green Windsor chairs. The "Study" in the home of Joseph Prentis at Williamsburg, Virginia, may have held an equally substantial book collection, as appraisers itemized two presses, or bookcases, and a mahogany "writing desk." The seating was "two green stools," presumably for use at the tall desk, and a "stick settee" painted the same color.[54]

Two interior views illustrating studies, or libraries, depict rooms with late eighteenth- and early nineteenth-century furnishings (figs. **5-15, 5-16**). One represents the study of William White, first Episcopal bishop of Pennsylvania, as painted in 1836 by John Sartain after White's death (fig. 5-15). The room, located on the second floor of White's Walnut Street home in Philadelphia, is as the Bishop left it. Three

FIG. 5-14 Kitchen scene. From Mrs. Esther Allen Howland, *The New England Housekeeper and Family Receipt Book* (Worcester, Mass.: S. A. Howland, 1847). Also published in 1845. *(Winterthur Library.)*

FIG. 5-15 John Sartain, *Bishop White's Study*, Philadelphia, 1836. Oil on canvas; H. 18 ½", W. 24⅜". *(Independence National Historical Park, Philadelphia.)*

mahogany presses inherited from his father flank the doorway to the bedroom where the Bishop died. Pine shelving, painted to match, expands the storage. Straw matting covers the floor, and a collection of prints hangs above the fireplace. At left center is a mahogany table that served as a stand for a portable reading desk. The seating mixes styles and construction, typical of general furnishing practice. The set of Philadelphia straight-legged "Chippendale" chairs is divided between the study and the bedroom. An upholstered mahogany chair of nineteenth-century date and curved Grecian back served for reading and writing at the mahogany table, whose offset drawer ensured sufficient legroom. The low stool elevated the Bishop's feet above the floor drafts. The mahogany-arm, bow-back Windsor chair at the left with similar paint was made for the Bishop in the 1790s by chairmaker John Letchworth, who branded his work. The loose green cushion matches the color of the slip seats in the mahogany chairs. Perhaps Letchworth also supplied the pair of square, medallion-back Windsors in the room before 1805, when he left Philadelphia.[55]

The second view (fig. 5-16) forms the cover of a diary kept by Isaac Mickle, Esq., during his young manhood in Camden, New Jersey. The room contains Mickle's law library along one wall with his writing desk sandwiched between the well-filled shelves. Above are placed a philosopher's (or poet's) head and a painted coat of arms or national shield. Mickle has drawn himself reading in a lounging chair. Nearby is a Windsor side chair constructed in a late 1810s or early 1820s Pennsylvania pattern. The table behind Mickle has tapered federal-style legs. The terrestrial globe prominent in the foreground is complemented by a large regional map on the wall. In lighter moments Mickle could take down his violin and bow from the wall and enjoy a musical interlude. Typical of the 1830s is the bold floral pattern on the floor, whether woven or painted (fig. 5-10).

Any corner of a room could serve as a "study," as illustrated in a sketch made at Hartford, Connecticut, in 1821 (fig. 5-17). The subject is Barzillai Hudson, co-owner

FIG. 5-18 Eastman Johnson, *Little Girl with Golden Hair*, New York or New England, 1870–1900. Oil on canvas. *(© Shelburne Museum, Shelburne, Vermont, acc. 27.1.1-185.)*

from 1779 to 1815 of the *Courant*, a local newspaper. The old, spectacled gentleman reads from the history of Charles V using an eighteenth-century candle stand as a book rest (see fig. 5-5). His continuous-bow Windsor dates to the 1790s and probably was made locally. Hudson has draped the back of the chair and his knees with cloths to keep off drafts, a practice probably more common than generally noted in records (see fig. 5-20). His walking stick is cleverly anchored in the chair to be handy when needed.

Occasionally inventories list rooms and structures of limited or specialized function that contained Windsor furniture. A rarity in the 1830s was the indoor bathroom, complete with shower, tub, and water closet, in Catherine Chew's home at Philadelphia. Windsor chairs and a painted table were the movables. At Doctor John Baker's New York City property in 1797 a workshop heated by a Franklin stove held four Windsor chairs. As the small building also served for storage of garden tools, the Windsors could have been used on the grounds. Some years later the City property of Thomas Marston contained a "distill house" furnished in part with two "large windsor chairs" painted yellow. Two small chairs of similar construction "for Children" were located in an upstairs bedroom of the main house. A few inventories, like that of 1799 for the Boston residence of merchant James Cutler, identify a separate nursery furnished with Windsor chairs. Several decades later the low-seated adult rocking chair became "an excellent article" for nursery or bedroom use by mothers and nurses. Eastman Johnson's portrait *Little Girl with Golden Hair* (fig. **5-18**) describes the affluence of American society after 1850, when separate play areas for children became part of many households and child-size furnishings in great variety were accessible and affordable.[56]

Well before 1750, when Nicholas Scull and George Heap issued their *Map of Philadelphia and Parts Adjacent*, prosperous Philadelphians began to build country places, or "plantations," in the city environs — along the Schuylkill and Delaware rivers, west to Germantown, and north into Bucks County. The mapmakers included about 150 rural sites in their delineation. At first most retreats were small and best suited to short visits or daytime excursions, often to escape the summer heat in the city. Orchards and gardens were planted. By midcentury several prominent citizens had retired from business in the city to develop new country seats or to enlarge and improve older ones. Among the early country gentlemen was William Penn's secretary, James Logan, builder of Stenton in Germantown. There followed Chief Justice William Allen at Mount Airy, his brother-in-law Governor James Hamilton at Bush Hill, and the Quaker merchant Isaac Norris II at Fairhill. Doctor Thomas Graeme and his wife occupied Graeme Park, the vast country seat at Horsham built by Mrs. Graeme's father, Sir William Keith, which featured lakes, vistas, and a 300-acre deer park. Building continued until the Revolution. Pennsbury, the proprietor's rural manor erected before 1700 on the Delaware near Bristol, likely sparked initial interest in developing country estates in the Delaware Valley. The rural aristocracy that evolved before the Revolution developed "the most nearly perfect replica of English country life that it was possible for the New World to produce."[57]

Early evidence of the Windsor in Philadelphia-area plantation houses dates from the 1750s. Appraisers of Israel Pemberton's estate located two Windsors "at the Plantation called Evergreen." His contemporary, the physician Lloyd Zachary, furnished the parlor of his rural retreat with "Ten Windsor Arm Chairs." In 1760 half a dozen low-back chairs were enumerated at Green Spring, the seat of William Masters. By that date Lynford Lardner, lawyer and confidant of the Penn family, had built Somerset Farm north of the city along the Delaware River. Lardner furnished two parlors with Windsor furniture that included a double-seated settee. Before the British burned Oswald Peel's estate during the war, it housed as many as eighteen Windsors in the front entry, stairhall, and upper hall. The "6 old fashion'd windsor Chairs" in merchant Samuel Neave's country parlor are a reminder that outmoded furniture was common at plantations. As one Philadelphian noted in 1763 in her diary, "Our tables and chairs that do not meet approval have been sent to the country."[58]

At a later date the Delaware River at Gunner's Run in Kensington was the site of Strawberry Hill, a house used as a country retreat by Commodore John Barry, head of the United States Navy in 1803 at his death. A green Windsor "sopha" and six chairs, probably painted "to suit," provided the seating in one room. The "Best Parlour," which contained "14 new Winsor Chairs," may have been recently decorated. North along the Delaware River the farm later named Andalusia became the property in 1795 of merchant John Craig, who in 1796–97 provided a suitable house. Windsor chairs stood in the parlor, joining several mahogany and japanned tables and a "Gilt framed looking Glass." Andalusia later was remodeled twice, the second time under the direction of Thomas U. Walter, who added Greek Revival piazzas. About this time the British traveler Mrs. Trollope passed through the Delaware Valley, noting the "succession of gentlemen's seats" along the river above Philadelphia.[59]

William Bingham, a wealthy merchant of Philadelphia, established a summer residence outside the Delaware Valley. In summer 1791 he purchased a property of 200 acres on the Jersey coast near the mouth of the Shrewsbury River on a promontory known as Black Point. From its elevated situation the house overlooked the surrounding countryside and the sea. Renovations and improvements were sufficiently well in hand for the family to spend time there the next summer. In anticipation of this event Bingham sent furniture by boat from Philadelphia to New York City, directing Nicholas Low, his agent there, to send the household goods on to Black Point. On June 23 Bingham also requested Low to purchase for him "four dozen handsome Windsor chairs to be sent at the same time. If they were painted Straw Colour & picked out with green, I should prefer it."[60]

Country estates and farms of varied size dotted Manhattan Island and environs from about 1750, many owned by descendants of early Dutch settlers. During a visit in 1759 Hannah Callender found the local seats worthy of praise, but she noted "they have no gardens in or about New York which come up to ours of Philadelphia." The inventory of John Aspinwall, Esq., who died in 1774, identifies a town residence and a country house in Flushing (Queens). At the rural site appraisers listed a range of seating, from out-of-date caned, leather-bottom, and "Old" black walnut chairs, to more contemporary styles including Windsors, cheap straw-bottom chairs, and mahogany chairs with red upholstery. Callender, who included Flushing on her itinerary, found it "a pleasant place."[61]

Bloomingdale on Manhattan Island, "three miles distant from Federal-Hall," was a choice site for a country house, being both picturesque and convenient to the city. In 1769 James Beekman traveled the 4½ miles to his rural seat with his "fast Trotters" in just twenty-eight minutes. Reluctantly, he parted with the horses because they were "too spirited" for his children. Some estates developed at Bloomingdale were substantial. One offered for sale in 1804 had two parlors with marble fireplaces, eight bedrooms, two kitchens, a coach house and other substantial outbuildings, an orchard, a vegetable garden, and a gardener's residence.[62]

Bloomingdale inventories confirm that the rural economy revolved around light farming into the early nineteenth century. Before 1797 Charles Apthorp had a number of slaves who tended his land. His "small parlor" held eight Windsor chairs painted yellow and green. A quarter century later the estate of John Cornelius Vanden Heuvel, Esq., contained a suite of green Windsor furniture, comprising thirteen chairs and five large and small settees, complemented by mahogany and fancy-painted seating. Card and tea tables served for social occasions. Mrs. Trollope was impressed with Bloomingdale in the 1820s during her visit: "The luxury of the New York aristocracy is not confined to the city; hardly an acre of Manhattan Island but that shows some pretty villa or stately mansion. . . . Among these, perhaps, the loveliest is one situated in the beautiful village of Bloomingdale."[63]

Some New Yorkers established country places substantially closer to the business center. Greenwich (now Greenwich Village), described as a "quiet dreamy village" in a "pleasant and healthy location," was accommodated with stagecoach service from Federal Hall five times a day. Abraham Brinckerhoff kept a dwelling house there that he furnished extensively with fancy seating. The front entry held eight Windsor chairs complemented by two settees, one with a rush bottom.[64]

Other New York residents preferred a rural setting well away from the city. Isaac Clason acquired a farm in Westchester County. He, like Brinckerhoff, was partial to fancy-painted seating and used it to furnish many areas of the farmhouse, including the two principal rooms on the main floor. One of these functioned as a dining area. The "Octagon Room," with its fancy sofa and fourteen chairs, was reserved for card playing and light refreshment served from the sideboard. The upstairs back bedroom, which contained Windsor seating, held two field bedsteads, a tea table, washstand, and looking glass. George Clinton, Jr.'s, farm along the Hudson River in Orange County was furnished in 1809 with an assortment of chairs, including ten Windsors.[65]

Southern inventories shed light on country seats in Virginia. When he died in 1767 Philip Ludwell owned three estates near Williamsburg. On the premises at "Green Spring" were "12 old Windsor chairs," probably English. Later, Charles Young of Norfolk had a place "up the Country" furnished in part with twelve green Windsor chairs. In western Virginia, Windsors were obtained almost as easily as along the seacoast. Thirty-six green side and armchairs served dining and other needs at George Mason's plantation near Lexington. A special group of eighteen Windsors in the parlor stuffed with green moreen complemented two stuffed sofas. The same room held a marble slab on a rich gilt frame, two large gilt-framed looking glasses, and a "new Wilton Carpet."[66]

THE PIAZZA, STOOP, AND GARDEN

The first Windsors made in England were used out of doors. From his London shop in 1730 John Brown advertised "WINDSOR GARDEN CHAIRS" either painted green or "in the wood." Green paint was a conscious choice, as it harmonized with the landscape. English source materials from the 1720s onward abound with references to the use of Windsor seating out of doors. Green also was the primary finish of the American Windsor from its introduction until after the Revolution. The first American document to identify the Windsor's outdoor function "for Piazza[s] or Gardens" is an advertisement dated April 18, 1765, placed by Andrew Gautier of New York. The Charleston firm of Sheed and White offered imported Philadelphia Windsors for similar purposes the following year (fig. 4-4), and thereafter notices of this type appeared regularly through the end of the century. Customers were supplied at New York by Timpson and Gillihen, in New Haven by Alpheus Hewes, at Baltimore by merchant Chandless, and in Albany by James Chesney. William Williams's conversation piece of 1772 depicting the Denning family in the garden of their Wall Street home is the first American representation of Windsor seating employed in this manner.[67]

The piazza, a covered walkway located immediately adjacent to the house and also called a porch, portico, or veranda, served several functions. In warm climates and during hot weather in other regions a piazza on the southern front shaded the house, as noted in 1808 by John Lambert in South Carolina. Lambert further remarked on the "convenience of walking therein during the day," a circumstance that was attractive to Susanna Emlen in her new house near Burlington, New Jersey, particularly in wet weather. A traveler in Pennsylvania in 1806 visited a "plantation" along the Schuylkill River where he "found the family sitting in the shade of the piazza, in the front of the house." Earlier, Charles N. Buck, a merchant of Philadelphia, completed renovations to a farmhouse on the Oxford Road, which he converted to a summer residence. Exterior improvements included new plantings, fences, outbuildings, and a large piazza at the back of the house to complement one at the front. Buck discovered that "the sum total cost a very great deal of money," and in later years he remarked, "I soon found like many others before me, that country seats are absolute pickpockets." In 1828 Mrs. Basil Hall described a house in South Carolina with a piazza off the drawing and dining rooms. Steps led down to a "delightful garden filled with all sorts of flowers in full bloom."[68]

The earliest direct reference to the use of Windsor seating on the piazza dates to 1760, when Robert Bolling of Buckingham County, Virginia, pressed his suit for marriage with Anne Miller of Blandford near Petersburg. She was a guest in a James River home at Flower de Hundred when young Bolling, seeking to have a word with her, found her "seated in a large Windsor Chair in the Piazza." Years later in 1797 Windsor seating furnished the porch at Prestwould, the Virginia seat of Sir Peyton Skipwith in Mecklenberg County. The "2 Portico Settees" supplemented his order for household Windsors purchased from area craftsman David Ruth. About this date Vosburgh and Childs, Windsor-chair makers from New York, relocated to the South and advertised their "elegant settees of ten feet in length or under, suitable to either halls or piazzas." Settees of considerably smaller size were placed on the front

piazza at the Morrisville, Pennsylvania, seat of General Jean Victor Moreau, a French exile, as drawn in 1809 by his countrywoman the baroness Hyde de Neuville (fig. **5-19**). The baroness also drew a large settee in a distant view of the piazza at Mount Vernon when she delineated the tomb of Washington on the adjacent grounds.[69]

In the absence of a piazza for enjoying the evening breezes or the pleasures of a spring day, householders could repair to the front stoop, a small porch either open or ceiled. The structure and the custom of sitting on the stoop were European in origin. John Macky in passing through the village of Stratford, a summer retreat outside London, remarked in 1714, "I thought my self here in *Holland* again, the Houses having all Rows of Trees before their Doors, with Benches to sit on, as there, and little Gardens behind." When traveling in the New World at midcentury, Peter Kalm made a similar observation at New Brunswick, New Jersey: "Before each door is a veranda to which you ascend by steps from the street; it resembles a small balcony, and has benches on both sides on which people sit in the evening to enjoy the fresh air and to watch the passers-by." The custom prevailed at Philadelphia, as confirmed in 1788 by J. P. Brissot de Warville when pronouncing the practice a "bad custom, as the evening air is unhealthful." Nevertheless, the stoop was a favorite Middle Atlantic retreat. Charles Willson Peale drew Nathan Sellers at his Pennsylvania home about 1818 seated in a Windsor chair on the front stoop overlooking the meadows (fig. **5-20**). Suggesting that the season was still early is the draped cloth that covers the sitter's legs. In Bloomingdale on Manhattan Island the baroness Hyde de Neuville took a view of the Cruger residence the following year, delineating a narrow, columned portico, or stoop, a chair standing prominently in the open doorway. Another artist rendered a street scene in New York City, giving prominence to the Bull's Head Tavern in the right middle ground. The front stoop is furnished with Windsor chairs and settees for the convenience of patrons or passersby (fig. **5-21**). Other stoops are visible along the street.[70]

There were still other ways of enjoying the summer breezes. At Wyck in Germantown, outside Philadelphia, the Reuben Haines family converted a through hall joining two older houses into a kind of conservatory in 1824 by installing large sliding

FIG. 5-19 Baroness Hyde de Neuville, French, active in United States, about 1779–1849, *The Moreau House*, Morrisville, Pa., July 2, 1809. Bursh and brown wash over graphite on paper; sheet: 18.6 × 32.8 cm (7⁵⁄₁₆ × 12¹⁵⁄₁₆ in.). *(Museum of Fine Arts, Boston. The M. and M. Karolik Collection of American Watercolors, Drawings, and Prints, 1800–1875, acc. 58.920. Photograph © 2004 Museum of Fine Arts, Boston.)*

FIG. 5-20 Charles Willson Peale, *Nathan Sellers at Mill Bank*, southeastern Pennsylvania, ca. 1818–20. Pencil, ink, and watercolor on paper; H. 14½", W. 15½" (sight). *(Formerly collection of the late Charles Coleman Sellers; Photo, Frick Art Reference Library, New York.)*

doors with multiple panes at the front and back of the room to admit sunlight in the
winter and cooling air in the summer. The Frenchman Charles LeSueur sketched the
hall in August, detailing family and friends in the open room seated around a table
on double-cross-back fancy chairs purchased a dozen years earlier from William
Haydon and William Henry Stewart, chairmakers of Philadelphia. Thomas Birch
captured the beauty of the Delaware Valley in 1818 in a river view from the terrace of
Point Breeze near Bordentown, New Jersey, the estate of Joseph Bonaparte, brother
of Napoleon (fig. **5-22**). A mixed group enjoys the afternoon air from the comfort of
light-colored, square-back Windsor chairs of single- and double-bow pattern.[71]

Although the use of Windsors and other seating in English gardens is well documented in records and views, American practice is not as easily interpreted. Garden
seating in America probably was more common than evidence indicates, however.
An advertisement of 1758 identifies a New York surveyor who designed "all Sorts
of Buildings" and small features, including "Seats for Gardens." Garden structures
probably contained seating, as found on English estates. Public notices for "Gar-
den-Chairs" dating through the end of the century, such as those of Thomas Ash in
1774 at New York and Daniel Lawrence in 1787 at Providence, help to support this
conclusion. Other records occur. An inventory of the Reverend Arthur Browne's
property at Portsmouth, New Hampshire, compiled in 1773 lists "1 Gardner Winzor
[chair] & Cushion" located in the front parlor. The basement of Tazewell Hall, John
Randolph's Virginia residence, provided storage in 1775 for "5 green windsor chairs
and a green settee for the summerhouse." Thomas Bringhurst billed Charles Wistar
of Philadelphia for "Bottoms for three Garden Chaires" at the start of the following
century. These may have been made of wood because rush seating was impractical
for use out of doors.[72]

FIG. 5-22 Thomas Birch, detail of *Point Breeze on the Delaware*, Bordentown, N.J., 1818. Oil on canvas; H. 39⅞", W. 56". *(Private collection; Photograph courtesy of Hirschl & Adler Galleries, New York.)*

Substantially more evidence in visual records documents the appearance of Windsor seating in American gardens, although little dates to the eighteenth century. Early views picture the Denning family in their New York garden and members of the Ramsey Polk family on their estate near Charlestown, Maryland, as painted by James Peale (fig. **5-23**). The Polk property, on the Northeast River at Carpenter's Point, was located on a finger in the upper Chesapeake Bay. The distant view with sailing vessels in the river and storage sheds and barrels of fish on the point describes the mercantile pursuits of the family. Nineteenth-century scenes with Windsor garden seating are more common. At Wareham, Massachusetts, Dorcas Fearing used silk yarns to work an outdoor family portrait with Windsors early in the century. Later, the Charles Hawkins family posed outside their Onsted, Michigan, area farm home, and in this view Windsor chairs are scattered throughout the side yard.[73]

USE BY HISTORIC FIGURES

George Washington

"General Washington . . . is certainly a very great character — but the common people don't know how to admire without adoring him" wrote a young Susanna Dillwyn (Emlen) from Philadelphia in May 1787 as delegates assembled for the Constitutional Convention. During the years that followed, the man who later was called the "Father of his Country" had little time to devote to the affairs of Mount Vernon, and as a consequence the housekeeping suffered. The Englishman Isaac Weld visited in 1795 and commented on the house and its condition: "The rooms . . . are very small, excepting one, which has been built since the close of the war for . . . entertainments. All . . . are very plainly furnished, and in many of them the furniture is dropping to pieces." When the Washingtons resumed residency at Mount Vernon in 1797, conditions improved. The family enjoyed "A Republican State of Living" — one free of ostentation yet reflecting "dignified good taste."[74]

Washington first occupied Mount Vernon in the early 1750s as a young bachelor. He enlarged the house to 2½ stories in 1758, and the following year he married Martha Dandridge Custis. By then he had begun to order furnishings from England through his factor, a practice that continued for many years. In 1764 the young householder acquired his first stick furniture of record, "6 Windsor Chairs painted Green,"

FIG. 5-23 James Peale, *The Ramsey-Polk Family*, Charlestown, Md., ca. 1793. Oil on canvas; H. 50", W. 40". *(Photograph courtesy of Hirschl & Adler Galleries, New York.)*

through Edward Polhill, an upholsterer of London, who also supplied leather-bottom chairs. At the outbreak of hostilities with England in the mid-1770s, Washington was in the midst of adding two wings to the house, one at the north to serve as a reception or banquet room and another at the south to house a study and bedchamber. Washington probably made no additional purchases of Windsor seating for Mount Vernon until after the war, when Clement Biddle became his Philadelphia agent. Following a visit to the city in 1784 Washington wrote to Biddle saying, "Upon second thoughts a dozn. and an half of Windsor Chairs will be suffict. (I think my Memm. requested two dozn.)." The date is early for bow-back seating; however, two sack-back Windsors at Mount Vernon with general family associations could have been part of the group. One is a high chair, which likely proved useful when the Washingtons took in the two youngest children of Martha's son, John Park Custis, who died in 1781. The surviving armchair resembles the work of Joseph Henzey. Shell-pattern cushions worked by Martha Washington could well have been made for these chairs. The Washingtons were in residence at Mount Vernon for almost five years before the general assumed the presidency.[75]

While in Philadelphia to attend the Constitutional Convention in 1787 Washington acquired a "Fan Chair," a term interpreted to identify a chair with a superstructure to accommodate a fan activated by a treadle. Washington's next recorded purchase of painted seating occurred the year before his retirement from the presidency. A personal account dated May 14, 1796, documents the payment of $42 to the Gaw brothers of Philadelphia "for 24 ovel Back Chairs at 13/9." Although the price was substantial for side chairs, it was in line with contemporary purchases. In July 1794 General Henry Knox paid William Cox 11s. 3d. apiece for oval-back (bow-back) chairs. The following May similar seating cost Knox 12s. 6d., an increase of slightly more than 11 percent. By the time Washington purchased his chairs a year later, the cost had leaped another 11 percent. It would seem that living at the seat of government had its price. Washington immediately shipped the chairs by boat to Mount Vernon and notified his manager of their pending arrival. Although the Windsors were first placed in the "New Room," or banquet hall, at Washington's death in 1799 they were located at the back of the house on the piazza overlooking the Potomac. Three more Windsors purchased in November 1796 may have gone down to Mount Vernon only after Washington closed his Philadelphia residence early the following year. A high-back Windsor chair with tapered-foot, baluster-style turned legs is thought to have once stood in the presidential mansion at Philadelphia.[76]

During the last several years of Washington's life at Mount Vernon, Windsor seating furnished several areas besides the piazza. When Joshua Brookes visited early in 1799, he commented on the furnishings of the small back parlor "with the chimney in the corner" where he saw ten "yellow bottom windsor chairs." The color appears to identify cushions, in particular the shell-patterned set worked by Martha Washington. Because the cushions were of a size and shape made for use on armchairs (fig. 3-62), it seems likely that sack-back Windsors filled the room. Complementing the chairs were a settee, tea table, and looking glass. The harpsichord of Nellie Custis, the Washingtons' granddaughter and ward, also stood in the room. Stick chairs standing in a small chamber containing a dressing table and glass, washstand, and bedstead may have rounded out the Windsor seating.[77]

Thomas Jefferson
The Windsor furniture purchases of the man who became third president of the United States were ongoing almost to the extent of his personal building projects. Jefferson's initial acquisition may have been the large, revolving high-back chair now in Philadelphia at the American Philosophical Society. The future president probably ordered the chair during the mid-1770s when in Philadelphia to attend sessions of the Continental Congress or to help draft a Declaration of Independence. The chair

remained at Monticello during the 1780s, a period when the statesman spent most of his time in France in the service of his country. Later, as secretary of state under President Washington in the first federal government, Jefferson resided in New York in 1789–90 until the national seat was moved to Philadelphia. A furniture purchase while in New York was a group of thirty "green Chairs," which provided an economical, yet fashionable, solution to the social needs of a ranking member of government. Jefferson may have taken some or all of the chairs with him to Philadelphia.[78]

Jefferson's Windsor purchases continued until 1809. In May 1791 he wrote from Philadelphia to his daughter Martha Jefferson Randolph, who resided near Monticello, telling her he was sending packages containing books and furnishings along with "Some Windsor chairs if the vessel can take them." The chairs appear to have been for Jefferson's own use. A record of April 1793 documents Jefferson's purchase of a dozen Windsors from Francis Trumble, who also repainted other chairs. The statesman twice paid portage at Philadelphia for "loads of furniture to Waterside." Another visit to Trumble's shop in August probably added three chairs to the original purchase. After resigning federal office on December 31, 1793, Jefferson did not reside again at the seat of government until 1797, when he was vice president under John Adams. He made other purchases of Windsor seating in spring 1798, acquiring chairs at Philadelphia from the estate of Joseph Henzey and patronizing Lawrence Allwine for a custom-made "stick sopha and mattras." This low bench with incurved ends and six bamboo-style turned legs braced by stretchers was used with each of Jefferson's two revolving chairs—the Windsor purchased at Philadelphia in the 1770s and a bergère-type armchair of mahogany and leather probably constructed in 1790 by Thomas Burling, a cabinetmaker of New York.[79]

Jefferson acquired three groups of Windsor seating between 1800 and 1809. He purchased half a dozen double-bow, square-back Windsors painted "a very dark color" in 1800 at the shop of John Letchworth in Philadelphia (fig. 4-37). There followed in 1801 another order for "4 Dozen of Armd Chairs Black & Gould" purchased through his agent Thomas Claxton from chairmaker Adam Snyder. Claxton forwarded the bill of lading to Jefferson at Monticello on August 5, probably as the chairs were en route from Philadelphia to Richmond consigned to the firm of Gibson and Jefferson (George). From Richmond the chairs went by local carrier to a destination near Monticello, as described in the waybill signed by Edward Kindred: "Richmond 21st. August 1801 Received of Gibson & Jefferson four dozen Chairs, one barrel, one keg, and two small boxes which I promise to deliver in good order to Thomas Jefferson esquire at Milton he paying the freight. *The bottom of one chair split." Before the end of the month Claxton wrote again to Jefferson asking "whether the trunk with the plated ware went safe, and without being defaced, and also how the chairs look." By then Jefferson probably had placed many of the chairs in the entrance hall at Monticello.[80]

Jefferson's last recorded purchase of Windsors dates to 1809, when he ordered seating for Poplar Forest, his octagonal Palladian country "retreat" near Lynchburg. Concluding his second term in office, Jefferson wrote from Washington to his agent and kinsman George Jefferson in Richmond (fig. **5-24**) asking him to procure "3 dozen stick chairs, of the kind marked in the margin, painted black with yellow rings, & forward them for me to Lynchburg." The chairs were to be sent by boat up the James River, which was navigable by shallow craft to Lynchburg. The accompanying sketch clearly indicates the retiring president wanted bow-back chairs, probably to complement seating already in the Bedford County house. Plans did not proceed smoothly, however. Writing from Richmond on June 19, George Jefferson indicated there had been delays: "If you go to Bedford as soon as you contemplate, you will be surprised I expect at not finding the 3 dozen Chairs there, which you ordered several months ago. The first person who engaged to make them disappointed us altogether, & the next one has been a long time about them. They are however at last

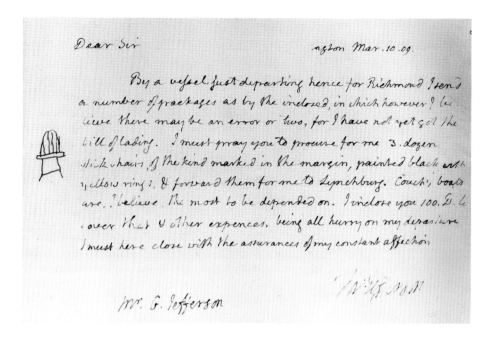

ready and shall be forwarded by the first safe boat to the care of Sam'l Harrison." At Lynchburg Harrison would have notified Thomas Jefferson of the chairs' arrival so that Jefferson could dispatch a wagon to fetch them. The construction delay likely was due to Jefferson's selection of a pattern reasonably out of date by 1809 and the problem of bending the long bow that forms the back. Square-back chairs with short bent elements were then fashionable, and many chairmakers probably lacked the proper equipment to complete the work Jefferson wanted. Constructing the chairs also meant stopping regular production and losing time—even though the order was for the former president of the United States.[81]

Other Presidents, Statesman, and Public Figures
Following the close of Jefferson's second term as president, the Madisons faced the problem of occupying a "President's House" (White House) devoid of furnishings. Congress had not seen fit to decorate the executive mansion, and it had been up to the occupants to find their own furnishings. Congress at last appropriated monies, and early in 1809 the Madisons appointed architect Benjamin Henry Latrobe, surveyor of public buildings, to oversee the interior appointments. Latrobe made drawings for cane-bottom seating based on a neoclassical, tablet-top klismos design published in 1807 at London by Thomas Hope and sent a set to the Finlay brothers at Baltimore. Because the new American nation aligned itself in spirit with the ancient Greek republic, there was much sympathy with the classical ideal in architecture, domestic arts, place-names, and modes of dress. The Finleys, John and Hugh, did themselves and the designer proud. On September 18, 1809, they shipped part of the order to Georgetown on board the sloop *Olive Branch*. Their bill to Latrobe describes the cargo as "36 Cane Seat Chairs made to a Grecian Model, painted, gilded & varnished, with the United States arms painted on each"; the charge was $20 per chair. To this cost the brothers added itemized charges for packing, freight by water, and insurance at 1 percent of valuation. About September 20 four settees, also called "window Seats" in several documents, and two sofas to match, priced at $40 and $80, respectively, plus additional shipping charges, followed by wagon and cart. The Finlay's complete itemized bill to Latrobe, "agent for furnishing the president's House," came to $1,111, which upon payment they signed and receipted at the bottom: "Received the Contents in full of B Henry Latrobe." When the suite was installed in the oval drawing room, the chairs had red velvet cushions with tassels, complementing the room-high window hangings. A pair of mirrors hung on the

walls. At Washington Irving's visit in 1811 he was dazzled upon entering "the blazing splendor of Mrs. Madison's Drawing Room." The glory of the room was short-lived, however, because on August 24, 1814, the British put the mansion to the torch.[82]

New furnishings were needed for the president's temporary quarters after the fire. The fancy seating bought in spring 1815 at $5 and $6 the chair was more restrained than Latrobe's furniture. John Finlay of Baltimore supplied a dozen chairs, although they are not described. William Palmer, a chairmaker of New York, received an order for eighteen chairs with two settees "to match," the finish identified as "Gray & Gold." A note at the bottom of the receipt indicates the Madisons were pleased with the chairs and retained them for their own use. George Boyd, agent for furnishing the President's House, turned to local supplier George Worthington for case pieces, tables, bedsteads, and half a dozen chairs priced at $1.50 apiece. It seems likely these were Windsors. The dozen "white" chairs Boyd acquired at auction for $19.20 may have been of a fancy pattern.[83]

James Monroe was in office when the White House was ready for reoccupancy. He bought a quantity of mahogany furniture, although as a young man he had been acquainted with Windsor seating. A sack-back chair from the late 1780s owned at Fredericksburg, Virginia, by the James Monroe Memorial Library is said to have been used by Monroe at his law office. The chair originated in New York, one of the northern cities that pursued an active export trade to the South after the Revolution. At the other extreme in style is the nineteenth-century low-back Windsor that in 1843 supported John Quincy Adams, sixth president of the United States, when posing for a daguerreotype. Adams probably was seated in the parlor of his family home at Quincy, Massachusetts. During a visit to the homestead a decade earlier, the young Swede Carl David Arfwedson described it as having "altogether the appearance of a common farm-house . . . shaded only by a few venerable trees."[84]

One of the many facets of Benjamin Franklin's personality was a love of socializing, and the inventory of his home reflects that focus. At the statesman's death in 1790 "18 new Mahogany Chairs" and "24 white Windsor Chairs" stood in the parlor, although the furniture probably represented the seating of both this room and the dining room. The Windsors were relatively new, as white was one of the colors introduced in the mid-1780s with the bamboo-turned, bow-back chair. The grooves probably were "picked out" suitably in a contrasting color. The intimacy of the parlor was enhanced by portraits and prints, curtains, and a carpet. On April 21 Jacob Hiltzheimer of Philadelphia noted the passing of the great man in his diary: "The body was conveyed to Christ Church grounds on Arch Street. I never saw so many people attend a funeral before."[85]

John Penn, grandson of the founder of Pennsylvania and a contemporary of Franklin, died only a few years later in 1795. He owned several local properties, including a country estate called Lansdowne built in 1773 on 200 acres along the Schuylkill River. An undated inventory of furnishings, which lists twenty-seven "green chairs" in several chambers, the garrets (also furnished with beds), and the servants' sleeping quarters, may have been made at Penn's death. Sold about that time were the contents of another house furnished in several bedrooms with "Windsor Chairs." The housekeeper's small sitting room in the same house held five more Windsors, a walnut breakfast table, and a looking glass. The seating may have been part of a group of twenty-eight chairs and two settees that Penn acquired in August 1792 from Windsor-chair maker John Wire.[86]

The venerable Charles Carroll of Carrollton, last surviving signer (d. 1832) of the Declaration of Independence, apparently used Windsor seating in his home. On May 21, 1796, he wrote to his Baltimore agent about a set of chairs he had paid for but never received. Another signer, Roger Sherman of Connecticut, may have purchased the low-back Windsor armchair depicted in his portrait by Ralph Earl when in Philadelphia in September 1774 at the convening of the First Continental

Congress. Two "green winsor chairs," part of the estate of Patrick Henry, a fellow member of the Continental Congress, are listed in an inventory drawn in 1799 at his home at Red Hill in Charlotte County, Virginia. Another inventory, one compiled in 1797 when Aaron Burr leased Richmond Hill, his Greenwich, New York, house, to Sir John Temple, British consul general to the United States, lists a dozen Windsor chairs in the entry in company with a painted floorcloth and several sections of a dining table. The transaction occurred seven years before the infamous duel. During the period of the Revolution, Windsor furniture was employed in the household of another figure of notoriety, Benedict Arnold. Several naval heroes used Windsor seating: John Barry furnished a country seat near Philadelphia, and Stephen Decatur bought Windsors for a townhouse bedroom in Washington.[87]

The Celebration of Lafayette

In 1824, almost fifty years after he volunteered his services in the cause of liberty, the Marquis de Lafayette returned to America at the invitation of the United States Congress for a national tour. Prior to his arrival a Philadelphia newspaper reported that "the public mind is so highly excited by the arrival of Lafayette, that ten thousand persons have visited his portrait at the Coffee House." The general sailed into New York harbor on August 16 aboard the *Cadmus* escorted by the steamboat *Robert Fulton*. He landed at Castle Garden amid pealing bells, cannon fire, and the well wishes of nearly fifty thousand citizens. Everywhere he traveled Lafayette was feted. There were processions and receptions, collations and dinners, military salutes and rocket displays, illuminations, arches and festoons, ringing bells and roaring cannons. At Newburyport, Massachusetts, Major David Emery was a marshal the day Lafayette visited. In recounting the event years later, his wife stated that Mr. James Prince's "elegant mansion was put in readiness to receive the distinguished guest."[88]

Everywhere the excitement of Lafayette's visit was in the air. In Washington Anne Newport Royall commented on the national spirit of anticipation, and even the entrepreneurism, that prevailed: "The whole city rung with acclamations of joy. . . . The newspapers furnished daily accounts of his movements, and long before he arrived we had the La Fayette ribbons, La Fayette waistcoats, La Fayette feathers, hats, caps, &c.; everything was honored by his image and superscription." In light of this enthusiasm, it is not surprising to find that several examples of seating furniture made to mark this great national event have survived. The back of a fancy side chair in the collection of the York County Heritage Trust of Pennsylvania is mounted with a lead relief bust of Lafayette and an American eagle. The Baltimore Museum of Art owns a fancy, cane-seat tablet-top side chair displaying in the crest a painted polychrome bust of Lafayette surrounded by gilt foliage. Similar decoration occurs on a painted table now in the Moses Myers House at Norfolk, Virginia.[89]

Each of a pair of handsome and unusual Windsor chairs grain-painted in dark brown and brick red and ornamented with shaded gold stenciled decoration bears the name "LAFAYETTE" across the seat front within a "penciled" rectangular panel (fig. 5-25; pl. 22). The seat tops, painted with fine lines of golden mustard yellow forming four triangles converging at the center accompanied by faux wood blocks at the front corners above the legs, simulate woven rush. The squared back posts and slim roll tops suggest an eastern New York or western New England origin. The paint is in excellent condition, indicating that the chairs were little used beyond the special purpose for which they were intended. It is conceivable that they were part of a large set commissioned for the use of public officials and important guests at a Lafayette entertainment and afterward distributed among participating dignitaries. As cherished souvenirs, the chairs probably were stored in a garret or placed in a "best" parlor that was used only on special occasions.

FIG. 5-25 Roll-top Windsor side chairs (pair), eastern New York State or western New England, ca. 1824–25. White pine (seat); H. 34⅞", (seat) 17¾", W. (crest) 17", (seat) 16¾", D. (seat) 16⅛"; dark brown and brick red grained ground with golden mustard yellow, reddish brown, shaded gold, and black. *(Collection of Claire and Ridgely Cook; Photo, Winterthur Museum.)*

Use by Cultural and Social Groups

Well before the mid-eighteenth century American society was sufficiently stable to encourage citizens, particularly those of moderate or greater income, to seek recreational pursuits during leisure hours, especially in urban centers. John Bristed reported even as late as 1818 that "theatrical exhibitions, balls, routs, the sports of the field and turf, and the pleasures of the table are the chief amusements of [the] people." A major supplementary activity among American men was membership in clubs, some whose function was purely social and others whose underlying principles were fraternal and benevolent. As cities grew, more attention was given to the development of parks, promenades, and pleasure grounds. The country folk had rural festivals and frolics. Recreational seating, whether for small or large groups, varied with the nature of the activity.[90]

THEATERS AND HALLS

The theater was a popular diversion of the late colonial and federal periods, despite moral objections from religious and other groups. In the mid-eighteenth century touring companies from Europe struggled to keep their shows open amid restrictive local ordinances, financial problems, and poor performing conditions. After the Revolution, however, theater in America began to come into its own. Jacob Hiltzheimer of Philadelphia joined a group in January 1793 composed of the governor and legislature that inspected the "new play house at [the] Northwest corner [of] Sixth and Chestnut Streets" and found the handsome Palladian-style Chestnut Street Theatre "nearly ready for performances." The German merchant Charles N. Buck, who settled in Philadelphia in 1797, may have patronized this theater; he certainly had a taste for such entertainment, which some citizens still considered "outlandish," that is, morally wrong. In 1804 after his engagement to Betsy Smith, a local girl, Buck arranged a family outing to a different theater in Baltimore, where the party, comprising Betsy, her father, and her cousin, had stopped on their return from Alexandria. Buck never suspected there would be any objection when he purchased the tickets: "On returning to our hotel, I joyfully reported my success ... when [the ladies] looked at each other in some confusion and expressed their doubts that Mr Smith (an elder of the [Presbyterian] church) would give his consent. But Mr Smith, who ... came in, declared with great liberality, that if his daughter would marry a german, there could be no objection in following his outlandish amusements, and had no objections to go himself." The box secured by Buck may have contained movable chairs, while the open areas of the theater likely had benches fixed in place.[91]

As the Chestnut Street Theatre rose in Philadelphia, another facility was under construction in Boston after designs by Charles Bulfinch. On February 3, 1794, the Boston, or First Federal Street, Theatre opened for performances. The large rectangular brick and stone building had an auditorium whose color scheme was azure blue, lilac, and straw color embellished with gilding. Crimson silk draped the fronts of the upper and lower tiers of boxes, which held cushioned benches. Benches without cushions probably furnished the gallery and pit, and all were likely of board construction. Records identify Windsor seating elsewhere in the building. Left of the front entry was a "Hall" in the Ionic order, extending 36 feet along one side of the building. In June 1797 the room held "70 Green fan Backed Chairs." Ten more chairs identified as "Broak" describe the heavy use of the area. The Windsors comprised two lots acquired in 1794 from local chairmaker William Seaver (fig. **5-26**). Joseph Russell, a theater trustee, handled the purchase. Also standing in the room was a "Long wooden Bench." Other movables included eleven "Small pine Tables Covered with Green Baze" and a like number of "Ticket Boxes," probably stored there when not in use. A fireplace and a "Small Iron Stove" provided heat, and seven "Large tin hanging Candlesticks" supplied light after dark. The three Scotch carpets on the floor probably could be taken up as activity required.[92]

Across the "Great Entry" from the "Hall" were two parlors, also called tea, coffee, or card rooms, leased as a restaurant. Upstairs the assembly room used for concerts and subscription balls was a handsome area with a vaulted and compartmented ceiling and Corinthian columns and pilasters. The furnishings included "24 Long wooden Benches," crimson festoon curtains, and a pair of large gilt looking glasses, which on festive evenings reflected a blaze of light from the room's three glass chandeliers, fourteen girandoles, and "20 tin hanging Candlesticks."[93]

A theater in New York reopened in autumn 1804 after extensive refurbishing. The Corinthian columns under the dome were painted to imitate marble or lapis lazuli. The white and gold boxes were "lined with pink paper, and ornamented with crimson drapery and cushions." By contrast, an opera house that opened in the city in 1833 had owner-decorated private boxes with varied seating:

Box No. 2. Interior lined with gros de Naples silk, fluted, Wilton carpeting, taleurets [tabourets, low stools or chairs], gilt mouldings, &c. . . .

No. 4. No ostentatious display in this box — plain Windsor chairs, ingrain carpeting, walls whitewashed and colored blue. . . .

No. 14. Walls covered with satin damask of a light fawn color, enriched with gilt moulding, inside damask curtain to the door, light Italian chairs, with Venetian carpet. . . .

No. 20. A *Bijou*, walls covered with satin damask, mirrors and gilt mouldings, pyramid of oriental cushions, quite a Sultana's boudoir.[94]

Of less pretentious character than the theater or concert hall was the lecture room. Discourse in the eighteenth century treated many subjects in whatever accommodations came to hand—a room in a library or courthouse. In the nineteenth century the country embraced the lyceum movement, which "all but covered the nation with lecturers who spoke on every conceivable subject to large and tireless audiences." An Englishman described how workingmen and factory girls rushed from their long day's toil to the crowded lecture room of an evening. By midcentury chairmakers regularly advertised their products for use in "Halls" and "Lecture Rooms." Even in the 1820s the proprietors of Boston's Second Federal Street Theatre rented settees during the season from John W. Blanchard, a furniture dealer, to accommodate the various activities of the establishment. Samuel Horton, Jr., a Boston druggist, owned the "Pantheon," a hall furnished with thirty settees, a cut glass chandelier and Grecian lamps, and a cast-iron stove. Among related entertainment was that which relied on dexterity of the hand rather than facility of the tongue. When Mathew Carey of Philadelphia published the eleventh edition of Henry Dean's *Hocus Pocus, or the Whole Art of Legerdemain in Perfection* in 1795, the frontispiece carried a representational practitioner plying his art accompanied by "props" that included a cloth-covered table and a bow-back Windsor chair.[95]

TEA PARTIES, DANCING ASSEMBLIES, AND BALLS

Early evening gatherings, called teas or routs, are described as seated affairs in written accounts. Windsor seating was prominent at these events, as indicated in Auguste Hervieu's drawing of a rout at Cincinnati (fig. 5-27). The chairs depicted show strong influence of Baltimore design in the tablet-style crests. The rout chair is identified at Hartford, Connecticut, where in 1835 Philemon Robbins recorded the sale of "12 best curld Maple root chairs." It was the custom in America for men and women to be seated separately at these entertainments. The ladies, observed Mrs. Trollope, engaged in small talk and studied each other's dresses. After refreshments were served, they returned to the drawing room, where they "remained together as long as they could bear it, and then [rose] *en masse*, cloak, bonnet, shawl, and exit[ed]." Altogether she pronounced the gatherings "supremely dull." In touring New England the Basil Halls had occasion to attend a country wedding near Mount Holyoke, Massachusetts, and they found the ritual not much different: "The company were seated according to the American fashion as if they were pinned to the wall, and

FIG. 5-27 Auguste Hervieu, *Cupid at a Rout*, Cincinnati, Ohio, 1830. Pencil, ink, and watercolor on paper; H. 9½", W. 11⁷⁄₁₆". *(Cincinnati Art Museum, Gift of Elsie Holmes Warrington.)*

The Role of Windsor Seating in American Life 373

FIG. 5-28 John Lewis Krimmel, *Country Frolic and Dance*, southeastern Pennsylvania, 1820. Watercolor, pencil, and ink on paper; H. 8¼", W. 11¹⁄₁₆". *(Library of Congress, Washington, D.C.)*

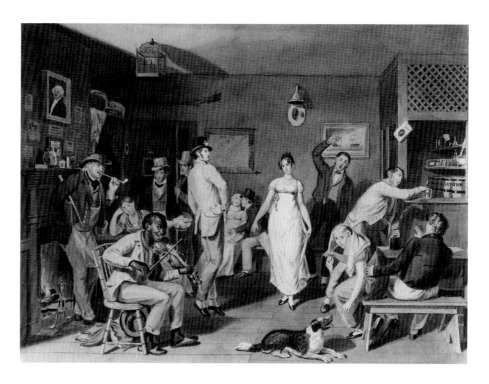

the gentlemen divided from the ladies." In another respect the rout conformed to British custom, prompting John Bristed to observe that Americans also crammed "a hundred people into a room not large enough to contain fifty."[96]

Dancing assemblies and public and private balls flourished in major American cities among the upper classes from the 1750s or earlier; consequently dancing masters, many of them Frenchmen, were in considerable demand. In 1794 Pierre Duport leased the Windsor-furnished "Hall" at the First Federal Street Theatre in Boston as a dancing school and was given leave to use the assembly room on the second floor every other week "for the practice of his schollars." Here, students and weary dancers could rest on the long benches. George Labottiere ran a dancing school in Portland, Maine, several years later, furnishing it with black fan-back Windsors, chairs of "Light Colour," and a settee. When cosmopolitan Francisco de Miranda arrived in Philadelphia in winter 1784 he found a dancing assembly held every other week at City Tavern. Activity began at seven o'clock and lasted "until two or three in the morning." Those who did not dance played cards "on tables prepared for that purpose in near-by rooms." The Marquis de Chastellux observed that "towards midnight" dancing stopped temporarily for "a supper, served in the manner of coffee, on several different tables."[97]

Assemblies also were held outside large urban centers in the nineteenth century. Sarah Anna Emery described the monthly winter series held about 1810 at the New Washington Hall in Newburyport, Massachusetts, where "the young people danced contra dances, four-handed and eight-handed reels, while their elders amused themselves at the card tables spread in the ante rooms." The "lofty and spacious" ballroom was on the second floor: "Large windows draped with red faced on either side; at the upper end was a gallery for musicians; opposite were two fireplaces where huge logs crackled and sparkled. Round the sides was a platform, slightly raised above the spring floor, upon which stood rows of yellow wooden settees. Two glittering chandeliers were suspended from the ceiling. Upon the mantels and orchestra stood glass candelabra and candlesticks." Commentary by Nellie Parke Custis in 1798 following an assembly at Alexandria, Virginia, described the seating as "very roughly done, wooden & small . . . benches."[98]

In rural districts a local home or barroom of a neighborhood tavern substituted as an assembly room. Some entertainment was spontaneous; other events were planned, as depicted in William Sidney Mount's *Rustic Dance after a Sleigh Ride* and Christian Mayr's *Kitchen Ball at White Sulphur Springs*. Moreau de Saint Méry spoke of an annual "Melon Frolic" at the Red Lion Tavern north of Philadelphia that brought together "the neighboring people to eat watermelons and dance." In 1766 Jacob Hiltzheimer attended a "cider frolic at Greenwich Hall" in the city. Impromptu rustic entertainment is captured in John Lewis Krimmel's *Country Frolic and Dance* painted near Philadelphia (fig. 5-28). The black fiddler sits on a light-colored Windsor with the bamboowork "picked out" in a contrasting dark color; the small crest medallion bears a leafy accent. A similar chair, drawn to the table in the right foreground, is partly visible; elsewhere board benches are in use. The almanac for 1819 hanging at the bar pinpoints the period. Other appointments are typical. The pictures include a local map, a print of George Washington, and a naval battle, probably an encounter in the War of 1812. Urn-top andirons stand in the fireplace far below a bird and cage hung out of harm's way near the ceiling. Equipment for beverage service is in evidence: glassware in the bar and on the mantel; a pewter mug and a lusterware pitcher decorated with an American eagle above the hearth; punch bowls in the hands of a patron and behind the bar. The barkeeper has his hands full, as the uncorked, heady local brew is dousing his patrons.[99]

PUBLIC DINNERS AND INFORMAL GATHERINGS

Both Jacob Hiltzheimer and the Reverend William Bentley attended public dinners where large numbers of people sat down together to sup. Hiltzheimer noted in September 1776 that a group of Philadelphia gentlemen gave a dinner in the statehouse (Independence Hall) for "the Delegates now sitting in Carpenters' Hall," who comprised the Continental Congress. Sawhorses and boards to form tables along with cloth covers could be borrowed. Seating may have been assembled from the furniture that served the bodies and groups occupying the premises. On two occasions in 1790 William Bentley of Salem, Massachusetts, participated in dinners given for the local militia. On October 13 "nearly 200 dined at the tables" set up in the courthouse. Benches, if only boards on low supports, no doubt were available from various town groups on these occasions. English prints show this type of seating employed for large groups, even royal banquets. John Lewis Krimmel's *Fourth of July Celebration in Centre Square, Philadelphia*, drawn in 1819, further develops the subject. In the right foreground a woman seated on a bow-back Windsor chair distributes printed broadsides. A group at the left seated within a tent around a cloth-covered table supported on sawbucks employs long board benches, although a fiddler at the entrance sits on a Windsor chair.[100]

Small informal gatherings used whatever seating was available. A quilting party painted by an anonymous artist illustrates slat-back rush-bottom chairs, a board bench, and wooden-bottom stools. Late nineteenth-century artists occasionally depicted groups of older men gathered at a local store or shop to reminisce or discuss current events. Eastman Johnson titled one scene *The Nantucket School of Philosophy* and gave prominence to an eighteenth-century Windsor armchair in the foreground. Public rooms for billiards, bowling, or cards were furnished with Windsor seating. A lithographic view of the Waverly Bowling Saloon on Chestnut Street in Philadelphia printed about 1854 depicts low-back Windsors of mid-nineteenth-century date distributed around small tables where patrons enjoyed refreshment from the bar.[101]

SOCIETY IN THE ISLANDS

As indicated, card playing often accompanied a ball or an assembly, although this entertainment also was pursued for its own sake independent of other activity. A

FIG. 5-29 William H. Meyers, *Cards*, Cuba, 1838. Watercolor on paper. From William H. Meyers diary, Philadelphia to West Indies, 1838–39. *(Manuscripts and Archives Division, The New York Public Library, Astor, Lenox and Tilden Foundations, New York.)*

self-portrait depicts William Meyers, a Philadelphia sailor, playing cards in 1838 with two Cuban señoritas while puffing contentedly on a "principe" during a West Indian voyage (fig. **5-29**). Of the principe he confided to his journal, "I varily beleive [*sic*] I could die on such tobaccy happy." In typical sailor fashion he found the Spanish ladies "beautiful in the extreme." Meyers's liberal interpretation of the Windsor chairs seating the group precludes identification of their coastal American origin; however, their presence underscores the impact of the American seating trade on Caribbean culture. While in Havana Meyers also visited "Antoines Billiard room," where he probably met with more American wooden seating.[102]

Earlier, the Windsor had a serious brush with ignominy in the islands. Returning to England from a tour of duty in Jamaica, Abraham James collaborated in 1803 with a London print publisher to produce caricatures of island life, beginning with "THE TORRID ZONE, OR, BLESSINGS of JAMAICA." Not the least of the "blessings" was the "YELLOW FEVER" with its accompanying "SORE THROAT" and "DRY GRIPES." On the brighter side was the "SEGAR SMOKING SOCIETY in JAMAICA!" (fig. **5-30**), a highly sociable group. Members were dedicated to cigars, sangaree, and a happy informality — the latter a little too carefree to be quite innocent. Among the furnishings artist James has drawn a large group of low-back Windsor chairs. The cigar-smoking scene recalls a passage from the diary of Quaker merchant Thomas Cope, president of the Board of Guardians of the Poor at Philadelphia in the early nineteenth century and responsible for placing orphans with respectable foster parents. He was conscientious in his duty, as related in his diary:

> Some years ago it was the practice of females, called Ladies of pleasure, to visit Havana in the autumn, spend the winter there & return to the U.S. at the approach of warm weather. They were the cause of so much jealousy & bickering between the Spanish Grandees & their wives as to induce the interference of the public authorities who, by ordinance, prohibited the landing of single women in their City. Married women were not excluded. The forbidden class found the means of evading the prohibition. They possessed themselves of children & thus gained admission. In the selection, female

SEGAR SMOKING SOCIETY in JAMAICA!

infants were preferred, as they could be inducted into the same infamous course of their foster mothers.

Cope went on to describe the visit of an "elegant" young "widow" anxious to "procure an orphan child . . . to console her in her sad bereavement."[103]

PUBLIC GARDENS AND PLEASURE GROUNDS

Public gardens and entertainment centers in imitation of those in London were part of the American scene before the Revolution, and some of the earliest sites were located in New York City. Inexpensive seating was common, and the variety was much the same as found in other public facilities. Esther Singleton described the Ranelagh and Vauxhall gardens of the lower Manhattan suburbs, named for their London counterparts, as the "two famous establishments." From colonial days visitors could dine, attend concerts, dance in a "commodious hall in the garden," socialize in the "drawing rooms," view fireworks, drink beverages, and partake of tarts and cakes. On July 4, 1800, Elizabeth de Hart Bleecker (McDonald) recorded a "handsome display of fire works from Vauxhall and Mount Vernon Gardens." At a later date she and her husband went to a friend's "to go on the top of his House to see a Balloon that was launch'd from Mount Vernon Garden." Occasionally Elizabeth and friends or family stopped at Vauxhall to eat ice cream. The Englishman John Lambert described the place about 1807 as "a neat plantation, with gravel walks adorned with shrubs, trees, busts, and statues. In the centre is a large equestrian statue of General Washington. . . . A small theatre [is] situate in one corner of the gardens: the audi-

FIG. 5-30 Abraham James, *Segar Smoking Society in Jamaica*, published by William Holland, London, November 12, 1802. Etching and aquatint with hand-coloring; H. 11¹³/₁₆", W. 18⁹/₁₆" (image). *(Courtesy of the Lewis Walpole Library, Yale University, Farmington, Conn., acc. 802.11.12.1.)*

ence sit in what are called the pit and boxes, in the open air. The orchestra is built among the trees, and a large apparatus is constructed for the display of fire-works." Another garden was Niblos. Writing to his daughter in 1831, John Pintard remarked, "The young folks went to the Niblos to see the panorama of Bonaparte."[104]

Castle Garden at the Battery, or fort, on the tip of Manhattan Island was "the pride of New-York." Anne Newport Royall strolled its "large green lawn, handsomely paled in, and planted with trees" in 1824, the year General Lafayette landed there to begin his national tour. From its acres the stroller could view the bay, fortifications, and shipping, and the sea breezes were refreshing. Royall had one criticism: "[It] would be the most delightful spot on earth, on a sultry day, if it was provided with seats." A watercolor view of the grounds taken from a nearby building with a large veranda actually shows the encircling porch furnished with long, backless, board benches.[105]

North along the Hudson the grounds at West Point were a popular attraction. Among the many views of this military site is a watercolor drawing picturing a promontory from which strollers view the scenery in reasonable comfort seated on stick-leg wooden benches. Across the river from New York City the Elysian Fields at Hoboken, New Jersey, were accessible by steamer. On a visit in 1832 the English actress Fanny Kemble described an "Italianish-looking" café. Other entertainment consisted of woodland walks, "brightly painted [row] boats," yellow gondola swings, and a circular course called the "pleasure railway" with vehicles of half-carriage, half-bicycle form. A lithograph details the surrounding grounds where visitors could stroll or rest on chairs and stick-leg benches.[106]

Philadelphia's popular retreat was Gray's Ferry Gardens. On an afternoon in July 1787 Jacob Hiltzheimer and others went "to Mr Gray's ferry [and] saw the great improvements made in the garden, summer houses, and walks in the woods. General Washington and a number of other gentlemen of the [Constitutional] Convention came down to spend the afternoon." The duc de la Rochefoucauld Liancourt described the setting with its ferry tollhouse as accented by "large points of rock . . . trees scattered here and there amongst them." At the river were "a considerable number of sailing vessels belonging to an adjoining inn." The tavern was a "place of general resort" in the summer and one frequented in the winter "by the young people of Philadelphia, who travel there in sledges, dine, and sometimes pass the night there in dancing." A contemporary inventory of Gray's Ferry itemizes "12 Stool winsor chears" on the property.[107]

Another garden enjoyed by residents and visitors stood behind the statehouse (Independence Hall). Henry Wansey found it "the pleasantest walk at Philadelphia." In 1799 William and Thomas Birch published a view of the grounds picturing children, adults, Indians (Native Americans), and animals intermingled in the shady retreat of the elm trees (fig. 5-31). John Fanning Watson stated that the Englishman Samuel Vaughan, who moved to Philadelphia, developed the statehouse gardens about 1783–84 "as an embellishment to the city." He concluded that Vaughn had succeeded "in a very tasteful and agreeable manner": "The trees and shrubbery which he . . . planted were very numerous and in great variety. When thus improved, it became a place of general resort as a delightful promenade. Windsor settees and garden chairs were placed in appropriate places."[108]

Southern citizens also enjoyed the pleasures of the public garden. The Hay Market at Richmond had good seasons in 1800 and 1801, offering "Barbaques, Dinners, Relishes, and breakfast" on special order along with parties "under cover, or in the Gardens." There was music for dancing, a gallery with an organ, and a building for "theatrical exhibitions." Baltimore had four pleasure grounds in 1800. Chatsworth featured a summerhouse, serpentine walks, and shady groves, and the grounds provided "every other rural appearance." Spring Gardens was "a place of resort for those fond of fishing," complete with a house to accommodate the fishing parties. In 1812 a

FIG. 5-31 William Birch and Son, *Back of the State House, Philadelphia*, Philadelphia, 1799. Engraving; H. 10⅞", w. 13" (plate). From William Birch and Son, *The City of Philadelphia* (Philadelphia: William Birch, 1800), n.p. *(Winterthur Library.)*

garden "on an eminence commanding a fine view" opened in Lexington, Kentucky. A special attraction was "a handsome pavillion in the center for large parties." All the gardens provided indoor and outdoor seating, as the sale of refreshments was one of the proprietors' sources of income.[109]

Informal gatherings in rural settings brought friends and families together for picnics. A typical English painting by George Morland, *The Anglers Repast*, shows gentlemen seated on the ground around an open cloth while the ladies sit in lightweight, cane-bottom chairs. A scene titled *Pic Nick* painted about 1850 at Camden, Maine, by Jerome G. Thompson details more considerable preparation. Long tables are spread with white cloths and laid with a substantial repast. Several participants sit on wooden boxes. Others appear to be using Windsor stools of medium height, and a seat of that description in the foreground is tucked handily under the end of one table.[110]

VEHICULAR USE

In many sections of the country removable, as opposed to fixed, wooden and rush-bottom seating was used in carts and wagons. The "traditional" view in figure **5-32** is a 1925 reenactment of life on Nantucket Island. Originally the "tip cart," as illustrated, was used at shearing time to bring in wool, although it probably served for other farm chores as needed. When cleaned out and supplied with a house chair or two the cart became a kind of carriage and conveyed families to the shearing place at Miacomet Pond. (This view also shows a Windsor on the front stoop of the house at the left, representative of another tradition of earlier days.) Elsewhere in Massachusetts, Sarah Anna Emery of Newburyport commented on the use of loose chairs in wagons about 1816 when she observed "a party of Quakers on their bridal tour, who came to the village in a large Dutch wagon, which had been cleaned and furnished with chairs for the accommodation of the bride and her sister."[111]

At neighboring Salem the Reverend William Bentley described an eccentric gentleman from Rowley who came to market "with a chair in his cart until the waggons

FIG. 5-32 H. Marshall Gardiner, *Nantucket "Tip Cart"*, Nantucket, Mass., 1925, reviving a tradition of the late eighteenth and nineteenth centuries. Photolithograph; H. 3¼", W. 5¼". *(Private collection.)*

were introduced." Travel of this general type seems to have been regular fare in New York State. When journeying to Troy in 1807 John Lambert hired a wagon such as that "used by the country people to carry their provisions to market, or to transport goods" and noted that "when used as a stage for travelling, a couple of chairs are placed in it." The traveler needed "excellent nerves to endure the shaking and jolting of such a vehicle over bad roads," for the wagons had no springs. When the going was really rough the passengers "were *waggon'd* most unmercifully." Many vehicular seats were double chairs for two people, which probably lent greater stability to the "perch" and lessened the chances of body and chair being pitched to the ground. On one occasion Lambert and companions procured double chairs, which were placed forward in the wagon behind the driver. The passengers were all wrapped in buffalo robes and greatcoats, as "the morning was excessively cold, and the snow fell in abundance." When in the area of Albany, Thomas Cope, a Philadelphia businessman, also took note of pleasure wagons with "chairs . . . placed in them for seats."[112]

CLUBS, FISHING CLUBS, AND FISHING EXCURSIONS

Windsor seating was a natural choice for clubs, especially in the postrevolutionary period, when mass production of durable stick furniture made it readily available and economical (fig. **5-33**). Clubbing became a popular leisure activity among

FIG. 5-33 *The Delphian Club Celebrating Their First Anniversery*, Baltimore, 1817. From Delphian Club minutes, Baltimore, 1817. *(Collection of Maryland Historical Society, Baltimore.)*

FIG. 5-34 Matthew Swett, *The Castle of the State in Schuylkill*, printed by Pendleton Kearney and Co., Philadelphia, 1830. Lithograph; H. 8¼", W. 9". *(Courtesy, Winterthur Museum, Winterthur, Del., acc. 75.244.)*

upper-class men by the third quarter of the eighteenth century and in time included individuals of lesser social rank. The purposes of these organizations were varied — conviviality, political and literary discussion, or benevolent and charitable pursuit. Representative of the small groups that enjoyed evenings of light literary diversion and wit was the Delphian Club of Baltimore. Organized with seven members in 1816, the group met at private homes on Saturday evenings. Upon the successful completion of a year's good fellowship, the Delphians assembled on September 2, 1817, at a "place of celebration three miles from the city." Here at five o'clock in a room furnished with Windsor chairs "the sons of Apollo sat down to a good dinner — well seasoned with the ambrosial condiments of wit and good fellowship." The artist of the group captured the spirit of enthusiasm with which this festive repast was consumed.[113]

Other groups of patent convivial pursuit include two fishing clubs established in Philadelphia by the mid-eighteenth century, namely the Schuylkill Fishing Company of the State in Schuylkill and the Fishing Company of Fort Saint Davids. The former was organized in 1732 as the Colony in Schuylkill. After the Revolution the group adopted the name State in Schuylkill. The Fort Saint Davids Club was formed about 1750 and five years later erected a timber meetinghouse on a rock foundation at the falls of Schuylkill. The club had a museum of "natural and artificial curiosities" and furnishings of some significance, including several large pewter platters bearing the Penn coat of arms, presumably presented to the Fishing Company by the Penn family. During the Revolution the club secured its movables elsewhere, a fortunate step in view of the building's near destruction. Toward the end of the century the club elected to join forces with the State in Schuylkill and took their possessions with them.

The Schuylkill Fishing Company first erected a clubhouse, later known as the "castle," in 1748 in "a wilderness" along the Schuylkill. A new building was constructed in 1812, which after three moves and some modifications still stands today (fig. **5-34**). The stick stools depicted out of doors may simply have been deemed "suitable" by the artist. Indoors the Company furnished the castle with round and square-back Windsor seating dating to the 1790s and early 1800s, and that furniture continues in use today. Originally the Schuylkill abounded with fish. When erection of the waterworks at Fairmount effectively halted upriver fishing, the Company relocated the castle below the dam. Later pollution of the Schuylkill led to two more moves along the Delaware River.

The chair of honor occupied until recent decades by the club "governor" at gatherings of the Schuylkill Fishing Company was a high-back Windsor of stately pro-

FIG. 5-35 High-back Windsor armchair (The Governor's Chair, State in Schuylkill, Andalusia, Pennsylvania, destroyed by fire, December 22, 1980), possibly by Jedidiah Snowden, Philadelphia, ca. 1754–60. H. 47¾", (seat) 17⅛", w. (crest) 24¾", (arms) 31¾", (seat) 31½", D. (seat) 17⅛". (Photo, Winterthur Museum.)

FIG. 5-36a, b Details of fig. 5-35. Arm and seat scrolls; carved shell in crest. The crest suffered damage in the loss of the top of the arch and shell. (Photos, Winterthur Museum.)

portions (fig. **5-35**). It is datable through several features to the early 1750s: the plank of flat-chamfered edge is double-grooved inside the spindle platform, the arm rail dips noticeably across the center back, and the bold William-and-Mary-style medial stretcher is positioned behind the center point between the front and rear legs. The particular embellishments that distinguish this chair as a unique product of the Windsor-chair maker's art are the horizontal scrolls carved into the arm terminals complemented by similar carved projections at the front corners of the seat and the carved "Queen Anne"–style shell centered in the damaged serpentine-profile crest (fig. **5-36**).[114]

Although the State in Schuylkill had its own clubhouse by 1748, it is likely that the governor's chair came into its possession through merger with the Fort Saint Davids Fishing Company. Modern tradition states that the chair was a Penn family gift. Indeed in 1864 in preparation for the Great Central Fair in Philadelphia, the committee charged with furnishing the "William Penn Parlor" asked to borrow the Penn armchair and the "large pewter dish." The Fort Saint Davids group owned a special chair occupied by the governor during the early fishing days, as confirmed by John Goodman, who recalled that as a boy he often visited the Fish House before the Revolution. Goodman remembered a long table where "the Governor of the

Institution had his seat at the South end ... elevated above the rest, a light canopy hung suspended over his seat, much in the east indian style." Although this could have been a different chair altogether, several names on a company membership list dating to 1763 encourage speculation. Among them are those of two Philadelphia cabinetmakers active in the 1750s—Jonathan Shoemaker and James James. Of even greater interest is the name of Jedidiah Snowden, cabinetmaker and Windsor-chair maker of Philadelphia. Snowden's membership dates as early as 1754—the period of the chair. His brother Isaac also was a member of the company. Both men, Isaac in particular, were prominent public officials during the Revolution and later. Of further note are the Fort Saint Davids records for 1763, when the Company voted its thanks "To Miss Clifton ... for making the Government Cushion." The "Government," of course, rested with the governor! Club records are silent on the subject of the governor's chair, however, or any link with the Penn family. Either the club purchased the Windsor from Snowden or another chairmaker in the early 1750s or Snowden himself made and donated the seat to the Company.[115]

Fishing, a transplanted European pastime, was enjoyed by individuals and groups outside the club experience, especially in the postwar period, when travel conditions made substantial advances. Reasonably common, especially with ladies present, was the practice of placing inexpensive chairs for their accommodation in the small boats used for this activity (fig. 5-37). Resort areas, including those in eastern upstate New York, offered fishing as a regular attraction. Theodore Dwight noted that Lakes George and Saratoga were well "supplied with accommodations for fishing parties" and if "wind and weather [were] favourable," the visitor could "expect good sport in fishing."[116]

Neighboring Ballston Lake, although smaller, offered similar recreation. Jacob Barker's memoirs describe an incident in 1807 that illustrates the pleasures and hazards of the sport. A fishing party composed of several ladies and Barker left the landing amid directions from shore not to return without a whale. The party met with success at the upper end of the lake, but in the excitement of the catch one of the ladies lost her balance and toppled into the lake headfirst along "with the chair on which she was sitting." She became caught in tall grass and did not come up. "Fortunately, her foot was entangled in the chair, which, although submerged, was within an arm's length" and was the means of her recovery. As the boat could not land because of the grass, the lady was unable to reboard and had to cling to the gunwale during the return. As the fishing party approached shore, the gentleman on

FIG. 5-37 Robert Pollard, *Angling from a Punt*, England, ca. 1823 (original). Facsimile engraving; H. 4³⁄₁₆", W. 13¾". *(Department of Printing and Graphic Arts, Houghton Library, Harvard College Library, Cambridge, Mass.)*

FIG. 5-38 Masonic master's and wardens' square-back Windsor armchairs, Frederick Fetter and Jacob Fetter III, Lancaster, Pa., 1811. (*Center and right*) H. 42¾", 41½", (seats) 19", W. (crests) 23⅝", 22½", (arms) 22¾", 21½", (seats) 21¼", 19⅝", D. (seats) 18¼", 17¼"; coral pink (coquelicot) ground with golden yellow and gilt. (*Collection of Lodge No. 43, Free and Accepted Masons, Lancaster, Pa.; Photo, Winterthur Museum.*)

board "had great difficulty in repressing a disposition . . . to call out, 'I have got the whale.'"[117]

FREEMASONRY

Of intercolonial and later national scope was the fraternal and benevolent association of Freemasons established in America by the early 1730s, when lodges existed at Philadelphia and Boston. Although modern Freemasonry grew out of the intellectual milieu of seventeenth-century England, the ancient stonemason's craft provided the symbolism that became associated with the ritual and principles of the brotherhood. Within a few years of a procession of Freemasons in Philadelphia on Saint John's Day in 1755, lodges were making their appearance in increasing numbers along the Atlantic seaboard. By the Revolution the order had many prominent members—George Washington, Benjamin Franklin, Paul Revere, and John Hancock, to name a few. Among the fifty-five delegates to the Constitutional Convention at Philadelphia in 1787, thirty-two were Masons. Most objects associated with Masonry in the prewar period were used exclusively in the ritual. That circumstance changed following the war, when "Masonic imagery . . . permeate[d] American culture almost as Christian symbolism permeated the art of the Middle Ages." Products available in the market represented a fusion of Masonic symbolism and doctrine and the new classicism that swept the nation in the federal era. Today the body of objects associated with Masonry from the fifty years preceeding 1830 constitutes a rich cultural heritage comprising many materials. The furniture includes individual chairs and several sets of painted seating dating from the early 1800s, all made for lodge use.[118]

A set of chairs of striking design was commissioned and used in Pennsylvania by Lancaster Lodge No. 43; the chairs retain their original coquelicot ground and painted decoration. The three principal chairs in the group of nine are those of the master at the center and the senior and junior wardens (fig. 5-38). The chair of the first officer stands about 1¼ inches higher than the other two and bears in its oval crest medallion the painted "Eye of Providence, the great superintendent of all the works of the universe, and Masonry" (fig. 5-39a). The master's emblem, the compass and square on the front stretcher, symbolizes a life "on the square" and within bounds, or "compass." The same emblem, or the square alone, crafted of silver was often worn suspended from the neck of the master on a ribbon as a "jewel" at meeting times and on special occasions. In one of chairmaker Thomas Boynton's exchanges in 1824 with local tradesmen at Windsor, Vermont, he gained "a masonic Jewell," although the office it represented is not specified. Common to all nine chairs at Lancaster is the lodge identification, "No 43," painted on the spindle medallions. Decorating the front stretchers of the Windsors flanking the master's chair are the triangular level and vertical plumb, representing the offices of senior and junior warden, respectively. Complementary symbols in the crests include the beehive of industry and the radiant sun of the master Mason "standing in the east, and setting the men to work." Also of note is the design of the arms and handgrips (figs. 5-39b, 3-7). Scrolled terminals are unusual in straight arms. To provide a grip of suitable size the chairmaker increased the width beyond that of the turned arm itself. The profile, rounded connection, and carved knuckle reflect earlier design, although the effect could have been heightened by using the undulating arm of the 1790s (fig. 3-66). Accompanying the chairs originally were one or more long benches. A now backless ten-legged settee stands on bamboo-turned legs of the same slender profile as the chairs.[119]

Lodge No. 43, Free and Accepted Masons, of Lancaster was chartered on April 21, 1785. As customary among new groups, the members met for some years in a room provided at a local tavern, although that arrangement had its drawbacks. In 1798 when the borough contemplated erecting a new market house at Center Square, a committee of Masons approached the burgesses with a plan to undertake the expense of adding a second story to the building to house permanent lodge rooms. The group occupied the new premises in 1800, although the illustrated chairs date from 1811, when the lodge engaged Frederick Fetter and Jacob Fetter III to construct the furniture. The brothers' charge for the master's and wardens' chairs was $16 (fig. 5-40). Ornamenting and varnishing cost another $10. The decorator, James Williams, may have worked independently in the Fetter shop, and he may be the same man who apprenticed in 1806 to chairmaker Thomas Adams of Washington. Williams would have completed his training and achieved journeyman status by the date of the Lancaster chairs. The region from Washington to Lancaster was highly influenced by chairmaking at Baltimore, where in 1805 the leading craftsmen, John and Hugh Finlay, advertised "Coach, Flag and Masonic Painting." To complement the Lancaster lodge chairs, Valentine Hoff made three velvet cushions stuffed with horsehair and trimmed with binding and fringe at a charge of $13.40.[120]

A mixed set of coquelicot-painted Windsors with Masonic decoration, now comprising seven chairs and four settees, was made during the 1810s and 1820s for use by two lodges in Bridgeton, New Jersey. The furniture represents three pattern variants of which two are similar. Comparable in structure and decoration are three armchairs, identified by their symbols as those of a master and two wardens, and a side chair ornamented with crossed pens above an open Bible, emblematic of a scribe or chaplain (fig. 5-41, right and center; pl. 18). The pierced crest boards are an unusual interpretation of the double-rod-and-medallion pattern. The seats of blunt, con-

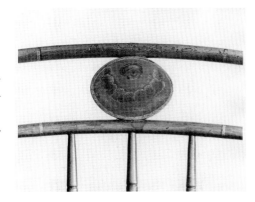

FIG. 5-39a, b Details of fig. 5-38. "Eye of Providence" crest decoration and arm terminal from master's chair (center). (*Collection of Lodge No. 43, Free and Accepted Masons; Photos, Winterthur Museum.*)

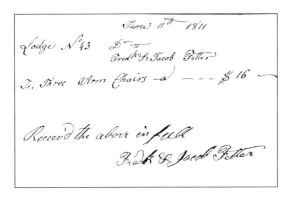

FIG. 5-40 Frederick Fetter and Jacob Fetter III, bill to Lodge No. 43, Free and Accepted Masons, Lancaster, Pa., June 11, 1811. (*Collection of Lodge No. 43, Free and Accepted Masons; Photo, Winterthur Museum.*)

FIG. 5-41 Masonic square-back Windsor armchairs, side chair, and settee, Delaware Valley, 1815–25. Yellow poplar (seats); (chairs, *left to right*) H. 34¾", 33⅝", 35", (settee) 33⅝", w. (seats) 17¾", 18", 21⅞", (settee) 48"; dark wine red grounds with gilt, black, silver, and white (chairs) and bright yellow (settee). *(Collection of Brearley Lodge No. 2, Free and Accepted Masons, Bridgeton, N.J.; Photo, Winterthur Museum.)*

toured edge reflect both Philadelphia and Baltimore design, and the cylinder-tipped arms and structure beneath them relate to fancy seating. The sprigged decoration is executed in gilt with dark accents except for the silver gray (now indistinct) corner ornaments in the crest tablets. The "No 9" flanking the officers' symbols identifies the chairs as from the Brearley Lodge of Free and Accepted Masons, a basic order, or "Blue Lodge," founded in 1790. The plank shapes indicate the seating could date as late as 1820. Comparable in pattern and decoration are three armchairs of smaller size (fig. 5-41, left). The pierced crests are coarser than those of the first group, the flat outward-scrolled arms are sawed rather than turned, and the planks vary in outline. The decoration is gilt and silver gray, the latter accented with white and dark gray. The triangle in the decoration identifies the seating as the property of the Royal Arch Masons, Brearley Chapter No. 6, an advanced-degree order organized in 1815 that met in the same building and shared some members in common with Lodge No. 9. Four settees, two with six legs and two with eight, round out the furnishings (fig. 5-41, right rear). The settees are painted coquilicot color but are undecorated. The plank ends are close in design to those of the Royal Arch chairs, and the large tablet-type crests are in the Baltimore style.

Masonic furniture with original paint is rare today but probably no less so than written accounts describing lodge-room appointments in the federal period. The Reverend William Bentley commented that upon entering his lodge at Salem, Massachusetts, for an installation he found the "brethren [seated] on the wall benches." The cleric's description of the newly constituted Mount Lebanon Lodge of Boston, where he attended an investment in 1801, hints at the richness of meeting rooms in large urban centers: "The Hall . . . was superbly decorated. In the east was a rich painting. In the south a beautiful representation of the Urn of Washington, & in the west a Crescent in bronze. . . . An elegant glass chandelier illuminated well the arch of the building. The Master sat in an arch upon columns decorated, & in the keystone an eye motto, He seeth in secret." Several contemporary Boston painters provided Masonic decoration. The firm of Rea and Johnston billed Colonel Paul Revere in August 1786 for "painting the backs of Masonick chairs." Revere was active in Masonry, serving as grand master of Massachusetts from 1794 to 1797. A debit of

1791 in the accounts of Daniel Rea charged the firm of Winship and James for "Painting and Gilding three Large Carv'd Candlestick for the Free masons use." During Revere's tenure as grand master, the Boston painter George Davidson was paid by a customer for "Painting a Masons Badge of Masonery" on canvas.[121]

FUNERALS

Funerary ritual expanded in scope and opulence during the eighteenth century in accord with English custom. Women laid out the corpse until well into the following century, although by the mid-eighteenth century families could turn over funeral arrangements to an outsider. Upholsterers often advertised undertaking services, and sometimes they and the furniture makers kept "a convenient hearse to hire, at reasonable Rates." Coffins varied from simple pine boxes to elaborate mahogany cases.[122]

Even before the Revolutionary War, steps were taken to curb the excesses of mourning custom. The Quakers were the first to revolt against ostentatious celebration, even condemning the erection of tombstones over graves. In 1776 the Quakers at Philadelphia acquired "6 Windsor chairs for the Use of the burial Ground" from Joseph Henzey, probably to provide graveside seating for the elderly and infirm. Prior to interment the coffin and corpse were supported on a raised, flat surface—a table, bench, bier, or even stools. When members of the Delphian Club of Baltimore held a mock funeral in the early 1800s for a fictitious member, the coffin was supported on a stick-leg bench while members, all carrying large onions, shed appropriate tears for their departed comrade. Inventories of several woodworkers of Philadelphia describe funerary equipment kept for rental, presumably to accompany coffins of their own construction: John Gillingham owned "two Coffin stools" (1794); Francis Trumble and George Halberstadt could supply a pair of "Coffin Stools and Boards" (1798, 1812). Other documents itemize biers. The side chair illustrated in figure 3-49, with its mourning scene in the crest, was probably part of a set also associated with the funerary ritual.[123]

Several visual representations of the dead laid in their coffins illustrate the use of stick-leg stools to support the box. Johnny Newcome's career in Jamaica was short-lived (fig. **5-42**). After an encounter with "Musquitoes" upon his arrival, he had his first bilious attack. Recovering, he found amusement in drinking sangaree and smoking cigars, but his time was short. The "Yellow Claw of Febris" soon gave him "a mortal nip." Johnny sent for "Mr Codicil & bequeth[ed] his Kit," and then it was all over. On a more serious note is a woodcut depicting the Harbaugh triplets of Adams County, Pennsylvania, laid in their coffin (fig. **5-43**). The broadside text tells of the infants' death on February 4–5, 1820, after thirty-one days of life. The traditional, angular-sided box is supported on a pair of bow-back Windsor side chairs as a bereaved mother looks on. The bird perched on the chair back carried the children's souls to heaven.[124]

Commercial Use

DINING, DRINKING, AND LODGING IN PUBLIC HOUSES

Eighteenth Century

The tavern, inn, or hotel of colonial and federal America was a multifunctional institution—a social and cultural center, a place of business and political activity, a post office and communications center, a transportation depot, a restaurant and barroom, a place of lodging, and a shelter for beasts of burden. It served both local

FIG. 5-42 Abraham James, detail from *Johnny New-Come in the Island of Jamaica*, published by William Holland, London, 1800. Aquatint. *(Collection of the late Gordon W. Colket; Photo, Winterthur Museum.)*

FIG. 5-43 Detail of broadside *Eine wahre Gischichte*, commemorating the deaths of the Harbaugh (Herbach) triplets of Adams County, Pa., ca. 1820. Woodcut; H. 3⅜", W. 5½". *(The York County Heritage Trust, PA; Photo, Winterthur Museum.)*

and transient populations. The innkeeper often was more than just a publican. In colonial days he frequently pursued a trade or farmed his land. In the new republic he sometimes served as a "magistrate, the chief of a battallion of militia, or even a member of a state legislature," as related by James Fenimore Cooper. The words *tavern* and *inn* were interchangeable, describing an establishment that dispensed food and drink and often took lodgers. Accommodations of early date often were cramped, crude, and without privacy; however, by the late 1700s there was new emphasis on expanded lodging spaces and comfort as transportation improved and a greater number of women traveled. Barracks-like sleeping areas consisting of several large rooms gave way, except in remote rural and frontier areas, to individual quarters. The concept that led to the modern hotel had taken hold, and before 1800 some large establishments assumed that name.[125]

In the years before the Revolution the average traveler often found accommodations wanting in fresh linens, cleanliness, palatable meals, privacy, and comfort. In some regions these conditions prevailed well into the nineteenth century. The "pleasure of withdrawing apart" often was denied lodgers during daylight hours as well, since even when eating and drinking one was "compelled to be among all sorts of company." In better taverns, especially those in large urban centers, dinners could be prepared to order, although many establishments served an "ordinary," that is, a daily public meal of fixed price, menu, and hour. Locally, these often were frequented by single men. James Flint of Ohio stated that "in such promiscuous parties, the governor of a state, or a general of the militia, may be seen side by side with the waggoner." For better or worse, democracy prevailed. Despite their shortcomings American inns were licensed and for the most part well regulated.[126]

An early reference to a Windsor-furnished tavern is that of 1769 in the inventory of George Gilbert, an innholder in the Northern Liberties of Philadelphia. Citations follow in other local inventories, among them one of 1774 for Henry Ireland. Here, items listed under the heading "Barr" serve to amplify Webster's early nineteenth-century definition of this specialized area of the facility as "the inclosed place of a tavern . . . where the landlord or his servant delivers out liquids, and waits upon customers." Ireland's bar contained decanters, tumblers, wineglasses, bottles, "delf bowles," a scale and weights, pewter measures, "lime squeezers," a punch spoon, and sundry earthen and stoneware jugs. The bar occupied only a section of one room. Careful reading of the inventory indicates that the facility was part of the "Parlor," the only area appropriately furnished to receive patrons. The furniture included sixteen rush-bottom chairs, two Windsors, a walnut tea table, and three other small tables. Two corner cupboards stored pewter, earthenware, and "China." A walnut "desk & drawers" probably served primarily for the owner to keep his accounts. On the walls hung eight pictures, two sconces, and a large looking glass. Andrew Heath's "Bar Room" in the Germantown section of the city contained seventeen Windsor chairs in the late 1770s at a time when a "high Back d" Windsor stood in David Jones's "Beer House, near the Dock."[127]

Philadelphia also had better establishments. After the war one lodger described the Indian Queen as "a large pile of buildings" kept "in an elegant style." The servants wore livery, and the rooms were handsome. Manasseh Cutler found his quarters "furnished with a rich field bed, bureau, table with drawers, a large looking-glass, neat chairs, and other furniture." The window faced the Delaware River. Offering competition was the City Tavern, built just prior to the Revolution and furnished in the "style of a London tavern." It became a popular center of social activity.[128]

An early reference to Windsor seating in a New England inn is one of 1777 in the estate of James Dwyer of Portsmouth, New Hampshire. Documents describe a "Setting Room" furnished with six side chairs and one armchair, all of Windsor construction. Painted furniture was not necessarily the rule for inn furnishings, however. The Marquis de Chastellux described a New Hampshire tavern where on a rainy day in 1782 he received warm hospitality: "We dried ourselves by a good fire, in a very handsome apartment, adorned with good prints, and handsome mahogany furniture."[129]

A Baltimore probate record provides further insights into the business of tavern keeping. Appraisers who drew Elijah Tull's inventory in 1784 placed strong emphasis on the beverage stock and recreational facilities of the establishment. The former consisted of fifty dozen bottles of porter, six dozen bottles of claret, 1¼ and two casks, respectively, of Madeira and Teneriffe wine, a cask of punch brandy, two casks of cherry rum, and three hogshead of plain rum, together valued at almost £177. While tippling or dining, patrons could enjoy billiards at a table complete with "Tacks & balls" or backgammon at one of two tables. Eighteen Windsor chairs were part of the seating. The proprietor maintained the establishment with the help of four African slaves — two women and two men. A hostelry of good accommodation in Alexandria, Virginia, was remarked on in 1802 by Thomas P. Cope, a businessman of Philadelphia: "Gadsby keeps a good inn & is a civil, obliging man." John Gadsby's "tavern" had taken on the aspect of a hotel; indeed it was called the City Hotel during his tenure from 1796 to 1808. Patrons found the accommodations "elegant" to the extent that some had to seek less expensive quarters after an initial stay. The building had more than a dozen bedrooms, a ballroom, barroom, utilitarian rooms, servants' quarters, and the proprietor's lodging room. Painted chairs valued at $1 apiece in 1802 comprised the seating throughout; probably all were Windsors.[130]

Catering to a more modest clientele was Ann Cross's tavern in postwar Charleston, South Carolina. Mrs. Cross probably took in boarders rather than transients, and she derived additional income from operating a public room to dispense "gin, brandy, beer, and rum by the glass." At the opposite extreme were the rural ordinaries, also termed "extraordinaries" by John Bernard, found in southern and frontier regions:

> They were mostly log-huts, or a frame weatherboarded; the better sort consisting of one story and two rooms; the more numerous having no internal divisions, with a truly sociable character placing all upon a level. . . . One corner of the rooms would be occupied by a "bunk" containing the family bed; another by a pine-wood chest, the family clothes-press and larder; a third . . . railed off for a bar, containing a rum-keg and a tumbler. The rest of the furniture consisted of two chairs and a table, all in the last stages of palsy. . . . You might always know an ordinary, on emerging from the woods, by an earthen jug suspended by the handle from a pole . . . or a score of black hogs luxuriating in the sunshine and mud before the door.

Thomas Birch of Philadelphia drew a tavern of close to this description in the early nineteenth century, appropriately identified by the Sign of the Pig, as a visual statement warning of the consequences of intemperance (fig. **5-44**). The scene, intentionally dramatizing both human and environmental decay, further documents the common use of Windsor seating in public establishments. The illustrated square-back pattern was one current from about 1800.[131]

Records of the Golden Tun Tavern of Philadelphia and the Tontine Coffee House of New York provide glimpses of the appointments and operation of two prominent public houses in the 1790s. Samuel Fraunces, proprietor of the Tun Tavern, began his American innkeeping career in New York in the mid-1750s after emigrating from the West Indies, and within a few years he had established the inn at Broad and Pearl streets today housing the Fraunces Tavern Museum. At one time the entrepreneur also operated the Vauxhall Gardens. In 1789 he became steward to George Washington, the newly elected president, and the following year he moved his family to the new seat of government at Philadelphia. Fraunces continued with the Washington

FIG. 5-44 Thomas Birch, detail of *Virtue and Vice, Sobriety and Drunkeness*, Philadelphia, ca. 1830. Ink and watercolor on paper; H. 10¹⁄₁₆", W. 14⁷⁄₁₆". *(Courtesy, Winterthur Museum, acc. 67.131.)*

family until 1794, when he returned to innkeeping. He operated the Golden Tun Tavern in 1795 at his death.[132]

Had Samuel Fraunces lived a few years longer, the Golden Tun likely would have achieved lasting prominence as a genteel establishment. Fraunces's natural talents and experience as an innkeeper and the house furnishings suggest that was his plan. His estate inventory details a substantial and well-appointed hostelry containing twelve bedsteads and a couch to provide sleeping accommodation for family and lodgers, five rush-bottom chairs and assorted cooking utensils to equip the kitchen, and fashionable furnishings to fill the public areas. Six dozen Windsors and twelve mahogany chairs with "Worked" bottoms itemized near the beginning of the list comprised the general seating. Interpretation of the public rooms remains indefinite due to the limitations of the inventory, although it appears that there were three or four main areas on the first floor beyond the entry, which contained a "Hall lamp" and a "Windsor bench." Kym Rice, who conducted extensive research on American taverns, suggests that one area served as a coffee room, such as found in the nearby City Tavern. The hypothesis seems substantiated by items such as two tin biggins (drip-type coffee urns), a caddy, and a coffeepot. The furnishings here were painted, including tables, a bar, and five "boxes" described elsewhere as "Wooden Stalls." The room was lighted at night by "3 Side tin lamps" supplemented by the brass, tin, or "2 high iron Candlesticks" listed elsewhere in the house. The seven "Green Curtains & rods" probably covered the windows and stalls.[133]

Other first-floor areas had more sophisticated appointments. The mahogany furnishings consisted of tables, some in sets, sideboards, card tables covered with green baize, and pier tables. Two cases containing white-handled knives and forks probably also were mahogany. Enhancing the decor were pairs of large and small gilt looking glasses, four large pictures, and plated sconces, chandeliers, and candlesticks. A "square pattern" painted floorcloth may identify another small public room on the ground floor that contained a "pr of Wooden Stalls," several mahogany tables, and spitting boxes placed about the floor. Perhaps this is where gentlemen smoked some of the "2500 Segars" Fraunces stocked and used some of the establishment's seventy-six packs of playing cards. A "Bar & Shelves," the location unidentified, may have stood at the back of the entrance hall, as it is preceded in the inventory by an 11½-foot "Entry Cloth" and "a small painted floor Cloth." The bar housed a variety of utensils appropriate to its function. A selection of tablewares was available for food service — green-edged and blue-edged wares, Queen's ware, and blue English China. Typical silver and plated forms were an epergne, coasters, mustard pot, and "tipd" knives and forks.[134]

The use of Windsor furniture at the Golden Tun was no accident. Painted seating was cheap yet colorful. Some chairs may have had a mahogany finish, a popular choice in the 1790s for settings with fine cabinetwork. Fraunces probably used Windsors as early as the 1760s to furnish his inn at Broad and Pearl streets in New York. This is suggested by an apparent close friendship with the Huguenot shopkeeper Andrew Gautier, since the innkeeper named one of his sons Andrew Gautier Fraunces. Gautier was the first American retailer to illustrate a published notice with a Windsor chair.[135]

New York's Tontine Coffee House, a three-story brick structure with a raised portico erected in 1792–93, functioned as a coffeehouse until 1834 (fig. **5-45**). More than mere taverns, coffeehouses were centers of business, modeled in general after London prototypes. On the first floor, as Henry Wansey described it, was "a large public room which is the Stock Exchange of New York, where all bargains are made. Here are two books kept, as at Lloyd's, of every ship's arrival and clearing out." Outside, the streets "were jammed up with carts, drays, and wheelbarrows; horses and men were huddled promiscuously together, leaving little or no room for passengers to pass." This was the scene painted by Francis Guy about 1803–4 at the intersection of

Water and Wall streets, a few short blocks from the waterfront. The Coffee House is the imposing structure at the left of the view.[136]

Other public areas in the building were a dining room, bar, and card or tea room on the first floor, and a "Long Room" for balls on the second story. Several cabinetmakers supplied mahogany furniture. Other craftsmen provided chandeliers, looking glasses, and a timepiece. The seating furniture probably was confined to Windsor chairs. Thomas and William Ash received the lucrative contract for £87.4. About a decade later 122 chairs stood on the premises. Thomas P. Cope of Philadelphia took note of the Coffee House in 1801: "There are no houses in N. York which answer to the Inns in Philada. for the accommodation of travellers, excepting the Tontine Coffee House."[137]

Nineteenth Century
The small, less formal taverns that dotted city and countryside by the early nineteenth century ran the gamut from simple barrooms to establishments for dining and lodging. John Lambert commented on accommodations in general when stopping for the night at Granville, New York, a village on the Vermont border: "One large room upstairs contained above a dozen beds, so that we each had a separate one; a thing not always to be met with . . . in the States. But the practice of putting two or three in a bed is now little exercised, except at very indifferent taverns, and they are chiefly confined to the back parts of the country. Within the last twenty years the States have been so much improved, that good inns are established in almost every town . . . along the principal roads."[138]

For drinking and dining the unpretentious Bloomingdale facility kept in 1802 by innkeeper Moses Oakley near New York was of good size, in view of the twelve pine

FIG. 5-45 Francis Guy, *The Tontine Coffee House*, New York, ca. 1803–4. Oil on canvas; H. 43", W. 65". *(Collection of The New-York Historical Society, New York.)*

FIG. 5-46 John Lewis Krimmel, *Village Tavern*,
southeastern Pennsylvania, 1813–14, oil on canvas;
16⅞ × 22½ inches. *(Toledo Museum of Art,
Purchased with funds from the Florence Scott
Libbey Bequest in Memory of her Father, Maurice
A. Scott, 1954.13.)*

tables scattered throughout the public rooms surrounded by some of the four dozen
Windsor chairs in the house. A mahogany dining table and tables for "Breakfast"
and tea extended the services in a modest way. John Douglass, named a tavern and
ferry house keeper in the New York directory of 1804, ran a more extensive business along the East River where a "Shuffle Board" was an attraction. Pine and "common" tables with Windsor and fancy seating filled several rooms. The parlor was
more imposing with its gilt looking glass and mahogany furniture. The presence of
"china" and playing cards identifies part of its function. Across the river in Brooklyn
Selah Smith kept a substantial Windsor-furnished tavern. His stables contained a
"coachee," seven riding chairs, and a "pleasure sleigh" for hire.[139]

John Douglass was one of a number of tavernkeepers in New York and elsewhere
who worked in wood. His "Work shop in the Garden" at Corlear's Hook contained
"2 work Benches & a quantity of Carpinar plains." John Brown of the Bowery aban-
doned his occupation of bellows and card maker about 1802 for that of tavernkeeper.
Charles Trute from London eventually settled in Wilmington, Delaware, to join his
cousin from the mid-1790s until 1807 in making pianofortes. He also was proprietor of the Swan Inn, furnished in part with ten Windsor chairs in the barroom. At
Chillicothe, Ohio, James Phillips gave up chairmaking in 1818 for tavernkeeping. He
maintained the business for about eleven years before his house and tavern furnishings were sold at sheriff's sale.[140]

John Lewis Krimmel captured much of the conviviality of the American inn in
1813 in a painted interior scene (fig. **5-46**). Conversation was never in short supply.

Locals and transients could catch up on news and events from a selection of newspapers hanging on the wall near the door. In a back corner the innkeeper provided a writing desk, stool, and paper for patrons wanting to attend to business or correspondence. Still other activity of the inn is illuminated in contemporary documents. The German American appraisers of John Heintzelman's estate betrayed their regional origin when describing an attraction of the Manheim, Pennsylvania, hostelry as a "Gacker [checker] Board." Also on the premises was a "Ten plated Stoff & Pipe," which made the inn a comfortable lounging place in cold weather. A "spoy [spy] Glass" offered amusement to others.[141]

Foreign travelers found rural inns fairly similar from region to region. About 1837 Frederick Marryat recorded his impressions: "The way-side inns are remarkable for their uniformity; the furniture of the bar-room is invariably the same: a wooden clock, map of the United States, map of the State, the Declaration of Independence, a looking-glass with a hair-brush and comb hanging to it by strings; . . . sometimes [there is] the extra embellishment of one or two miserable pictures, such as General Jackson scrambling upon a horse, with fire or steam coming out of its nostrils, going to the battle of New Orleans."[142]

Written documents and painted views by Krimmel provide further insight on the appointments of the inns (figs. 5-28, 5-46). Pewter mugs were common, and John Douglass introduced japanned tea trays for serving. Itemized in the inventory of John Brown of New York are typical contents of a modest barroom: "1 Looking Glass / 1 Comon Dineing Table / 1 Small pine Table / 9 Winsor Chairs / 2 Benches / 18 Quart & pint Muggs / 1 Lott of Tumblers & wine Glasses / 2 Large Earthen Dishes / 1 knife Box, knives and forks / 1 Lott keggs & Bottles &c." Nor can the rocking chair be overlooked as a tavern fixture. John Heintzelman kept one in 1804 at his Pennsylvania hostelry, although the greatest popularity of the chair occurred several decades later. As Europeans were little familiar with the form, some visitors, including Harriet Martineau, found the practice of rocking disagreeable, particularly at small inns where it seemed excessive. Perhaps Carl David Arfwedson's account of a visit to a Georgia inn describes Martineau's own experience: "On entering the only room I perceived two other travellers warming themselves at a large fire. . . . Rocking backward and forward on wooden chairs, they had fixed their dirty feet against the fire-place, almost in a horizontal direction with their eyes, and amused themselves with spitting continually in the fire."[143]

The accounts of several early nineteenth-century woodworkers contain specific references to seating furniture supplied for tavern use, among them the records of Silas E. Cheney of Litchfield, Connecticut. The craftsman probably first became acquainted with innkeeper Grove Catlin in winter 1801 when he boarded for several months. Through the years Cheney sold Catlin chairs and other items, such as fire boards for empty hearths and spit boxes to fill with sand and place about the floors of the public rooms. Cheney made fancy side chairs for Catlin in 1812 at $2.50 apiece; armchairs to match were $1 more. Understandably, a considerable amount of Cheney's work for Catlin dealt with mending, repainting, and ornamenting used chairs. Some repairs were major, as when Cheney put new backs in fifteen Windsor chairs (see fig. 5-46 for a backless Windsor). He completed the job by giving each chair three coats of paint for durability. At Catlin's death in 1829 the house seating consisted of "18 Bamboo Chairs / 2 Settees / 24 Old Fancy Chairs" and "30 Common d[itt]o."[144]

In the years following the War of 1812 Thomas Boynton of Windsor, Vermont, provided handsome seating for Frederick Pettes's inn. The furniture supplied in 1815 consisted of half a dozen "gilt fancy bamboo chairs," a dozen "rush bottom elegant f[an]cy ch[airs]," a "B[oar]d top" rocker, and six "round top Chairs." Furniture repairs occurred with some regularity: a portable desk, a cricket, a light stand. Late the same year Boynton charged Pettes for painting and hanging a sign identifying the tavern as a "Stage House." In 1840, toward the end of his career, Boynton performed work for the Windsor Tavern Company. He varnished floors and decorated the second- and third-floor entry halls, dining room, and sitting room, using his newly perfected "stamp painting" technique. He followed this work with bell hanging, lettering and numbering doors, and painting a sign reading "Windsor House." In neighboring New Hampshire Josiah P. Wilder of New Ipswich supplied a seat called a "Barr room" chair in the 1830s and later, selling it to customers in Townsend, Lowell, and Boston, Massachusetts. By midcentury Chauncey Strong of Otsego County, New York, made chairs of similar description. Several decades earlier at Erie, Pennsylvania, George Landon had sold half a dozen chairs at $2 apiece to "Mr Davison the tavern keper."[145]

HOTELS

By 1800 the American urban hotel had passed from a poor imitation of its European counterpart to a mature institution. Oeller's Hotel, which flourished in Philadelphia before its destruction by fire in 1799, was praised as an establishment of superior accommodation by the Frenchman Moreau de Saint Méry. The house had a large and elegant assembly room with a music gallery and paper hangings "after the French taste." An advertisement of March 1802 for the City Hotel on Broadway in New York describes the general operation of similar establishments as to boarding arrangements, refreshments, and meals (fig. 5-47). The Basil Halls, traveling in the late 1820s, found similar family arrangements in the better boarding houses and inns. At Boston they were well pleased with their accommodations and commented, "Instead of being all crammed into one room for dinner like so many pigs in a sty, we had a separate, neat, small dinner for ourselves."[146]

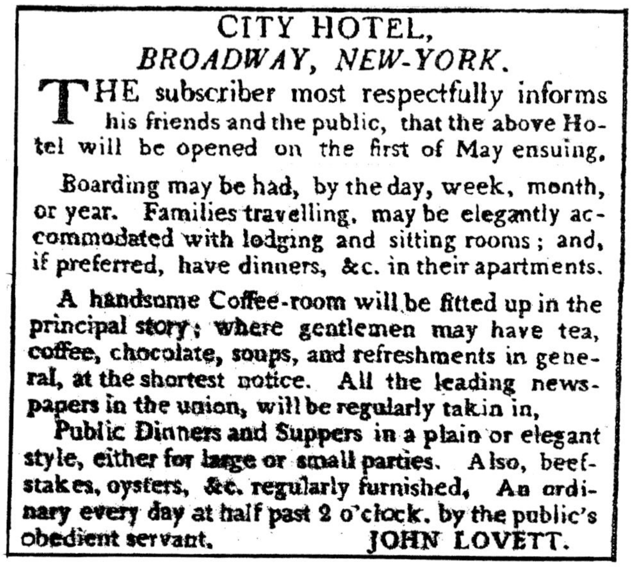

Carl David Arfwedson was less enthusiastic when describing single lodgings in American hotels: "The bed-rooms are invariably too small. . . . They are often so diminutive, that from his bed the tenant may step out of the window. Had Sir John Falstaff lived in our times, his bulky frame would, unquestionably, have got entangled between the wall and the bed. The walls . . . are . . . only whitewashed, and the furniture consists of a few rattan [cane-seat] chairs and a table; but they are always carpeted." These lodgings were of less concern to Americans, Arfwedson noted, as most were rarely in their rooms except at night. Bedrooms in country hotels were more spare. The lodgings of newlyweds William and Frances Thackara on Martha's Vineyard, Massachusetts, in 1820 were devoid of furniture except for a lowpost bedstead and chair. Yet having been aboard ship for six days, they found the room "spacious" and were delighted it was "*motionless and tranquil*."[147]

Substantial strides were made in the design, facilities, and appointments of American hotels in the early nineteenth century. By 1808 the Boston Exchange Coffee House, designed by Asher Benjamin, had a neoclassical facade with pilasters and Venetian windows. The structure housed a merchants' exchange, six-story atrium, reading room, Masonic hall, dining room for three hundred, shops, and a two-story ballroom, besides lodgings. The Tontine in New Haven was more modest. The brick building had "a spacious dining hall, cotillion room, 8 private and public parlours, and lodging chambers [for] 80 to 100 guests." Traveling in the Midwest in 1817 Henry Bradshaw Fearon found Washington Hall and the Indian Queen Hotel at Louisville, Kentucky, "both upon a very large scale." Sleeping areas were dormitory style, and an open yard with a cistern, towels, and an attendant served as a community washroom. Among the public areas were a dining room, bar, newsroom, and boot room.[148]

CITY HOTEL, BROADWAY, NEW-YORK.

THE subscriber most respectfully informs his friends and the public, that the above Hotel will be opened on the first of May ensuing.

Boarding may be had, by the day, week, month, or year. Families travelling, may be elegantly accommodated with lodging and sitting rooms ; and, if preferred, have dinners, &c. in their apartments.

A handsome Coffee-room will be fitted up in the principal story ; where gentlemen may have tea, coffee, chocolate, soups, and refreshments in general, at the shortest notice. All the leading newspapers in the union, will be regularly taken in,

Public Dinners and Suppers in a plain or elegant style, either for large or small parties. Also, beef-stakes, oysters, &c. regularly furnished, An ordinary every day at half past 2 o'clock. by the public's obedient servant.   JOHN LOVETT.

FIG. 5-47. Advertisement of City Hotel, New York. From *New-York Evening Post*, March 30, 1802.

By midcentury William Chambers found that American hotels exceeded expectations. Some large metropolitan establishments were a source of astonishment, and Chambers could not help but compare their advanced state with more conservative European facilities. In particular he spoke of Astor House on Broadway in New York adjacent to City Hall Park and next door to Saint Paul's Chapel (fig. **5-48**). He noted, as had others, that American hotels actually were boardinghouses with "two distinct departments" — large rooms for ladies and families, and smaller quarters for single gentlemen. All paid a specified daily charge whether they attended meals or not. Chambers found the lobbies filled with porters and chairs for lounging. Special facilities included a coat check, bootblack, washroom, barbershop, laundry, suites of baths, a room service bell system, mail service, and a dining room with a printed bill of fare. The bar at Astor House occupied the central court, and "a number of chairs [were] scattered about" a central fountain. Newspapers from the "principal cities in the Union" were available, as were cigars. Some residents and guests retired to the parlors after meals to read newspapers, write letters, or lounge on the sofas. Completing some facilities were shops and stores on the ground floor fronting the street. The presence of these small businesses prompted Chambers to exclaim, "An American hotel is not a house: it is a town."[149]

By the 1820s and 1830s appointments in urban establishments of moderate size were about the same from one area to another. Furnishings of the City Hotel at Saint Louis, Missouri, auctioned in 1828 included "very large superb Gilt framed Mantel and pier Looking Glasses." The fine cabinet furniture consisted of two large "Patent slide dining tables," each seating about thirty persons, a large mahogany sideboard, dining, tea, card, and worktables, a number of "Superb gilt rosewood Chairs," and two dozen four-post cherrywood bedsteads with frames for mosquito netting. Kitchen tables, twelve dozen Windsor chairs, and a large settee were among the painted furnishings.[150]

A sizable body of information describes the furnishing and later refurbishing of the Baltimore Exchange Hotel, a facility that occupied the west wing of the central-domed Baltimore Exchange building. The wing was erected in 1833–34 when Jerome N. Bonaparte was president of the Exchange Company. Hotel size is detailed in an 1842 inventory: 111 guest bedrooms; 5 parlors, several containing a dining table, sideboard, and chairs; a salon and an ordinary for the ladies, the latter furnished with forty-eight armchairs valued at $2.50 apiece; a gentlemen's dining room containing seventy-five armchairs of lesser value at $1.75 each; a barroom, reading room, bathhouse, barber and bootblack shop; and servants' quarters, storage areas, and service facilities. Also filling the public spaces were looking glasses, ingrain and turkey carpets, lamps, and Venetian blinds. The Baltimore Patent Floor Cloth Manufactory supplied "oil cloth carpet" for stairs and passages, some pieces of marble pattern. Paper hangings covered the walls of several rooms. Heating needs were met in part by eighteen Franklin stoves and ten pairs of andirons. The cost of the looking glasses was substantial. Two gilt pier glasses purchased in Baltimore for $37 were priced modestly when compared with the $713.50 paid for eleven glasses acquired from Thomas Natt of Philadelphia, who also supplied "3 Framed Sporting Prints" with "Bevel gilt Frames." John and James Williams of Baltimore made case furniture, tables, and upholstered items costing almost $2,500. Furniture of note included extension tables, columned and "Round Centre" sideboards, center tables with marble tops, a cherry wardrobe, a French maple bedstead, "pilaster" bureaus, and butlers' trays. Barry and Krickbaum of Philadelphia shipped six dressing bureaus, a work stand, sofas, and pillows. Thirty painted tables were made locally.[151]

Except for three dozen cabinetmaker's chairs purchased from the Williams firm for $7.92 apiece, only painted seating is identified in the hotel bills. Two craftsmen in the vicinity of the new facility supplied these chairs. Jacob Hiss, Jr., provided 60 fancy side chairs with caned seats at $24 a dozen. Another 272 painted side and

FIG. 5-48 Astor House Hotel on Broadway, New York. From John W. Barber and Henry Howe, *Historical Collections of the State of New York* (New York: S. Tuttle, 1841), p. 334. *(Winterthur Library.)*

armchairs came from John H. Gordon at unit costs ranging from 79¢ to $1.67. These Windsor "slat chairs" were framed either with a crest set between the back posts in the Philadelphia style or a cross slat at midback and a tablet top (figs. 3-44, 3-68). Gordon also supplied a dozen "old" chairs, presumably destined for the servants' quarters and service areas.[152]

When the hotel appointments were reasonably complete in the late 1830s, the Commercial Exchange Company leased the premises to Joseph Jewett. The lease continued until October 1842, when Jewett became bankrupt. An inventory identifies furnishings typical of a better-class hotel, as described for "Bedroom No. 70": a bureau, washstand, table, looking glass, bedstead, and three chairs valued at 50¢ apiece. The floor was carpeted, and a mosquito net covered the bed.[153]

Following the bankruptcy, the Exchange Company initiated a "thorough repair" of the premises that included work on the hotel furniture. Jerome Bonaparte engaged chairmaker Septimus Claypoole to refurbish the seating. When the chairmaker submitted his bill on March 10, 1843, he itemized charges for painting and mending 105 armchairs and painting 116 cane chairs. A dozen of the latter were "finished in Gold," the others in "Bronze." Claypoole painted two large caned rocking chairs after replacing the upper structure of one. He recaned fifteen chair seats and repainted a caned settee. Claypoole's charge also covered rental of a "furniture car" to transport seven loads of furniture at 28¢ the load between the two premises. The complete bill came to just over $110.[154]

The hotel refurbishing pointed up the need for additional seating. With a substantial pool of chairmakers located in Baltimore, it is strange that Bonaparte looked to Tweed and Bonnell of New York to supply his needs. Upon completion of the work the partners wrote on February 22, 1843, to Bonaparte: "We have this day shipped you pr Schr Mary Bright one hundred cane seat arm chairs which we trust will reach you in good condition." An enclosed bill indicates the unit cost was $3. Freight charges for fifty bundles, each containing two chairs, were $18.75.[155]

A landlord's warrant sworn in New York on August 18, 1841, by John G. Coster against John Cotter, proprietor of the Washington Hotel, for arrears in rent totaling $4,131.72 was occasion for drawing an inventory of the premises. Heading the list are furnishings of the barroom, where patrons sat on twenty-two Windsor chairs placed around an extension table or "4 marble Top Tables," which in view of their modest valuation were merely painted imitations of stone. The barroom patrons may have divided their time between that area and the basement, where the management provided a billiard table and benches. Although ladies would have been out of place in these rooms, they would have moved freely about the parlor, where two card tables were part of the furnishings.[156]

An assortment of mahogany and pine tables, some of the latter painted in imitation of marble, filled the carpeted dining room. Thirty-two chairs provided seating. The spacious size of the ballroom is suggested by the "Platform, staging and steps" located there in company with forty settees. Of fourteen chairs in the room, seven may have provided seating for an orchestra. An area adjacent to the ballroom probably was used for collations, receptions, and other gatherings. There was no seating, only a "Circular Table top" and other accoutrements for serving refreshments.[157]

Private accommodations at the Washington Hotel included several dozen bedrooms, large and small. The cheaper rooms apparently had no chairs. Of the few private sitting rooms available, No. 15 had a sofa, four chairs, and a rocking chair. William Chambers noted the latter form at Astor House, where doors to the "sitting-apartments" generally were kept wide open and the passerby could see "highly-dressed ladies reposing on satin couches, or lolling in rocking-chairs." By the 1840s chairmakers in or near population centers were finding hotels major customers for their products.[158]

FIG. 5-49 O. H. Throop, *Sans Souci Hotel,*
Ballston Spa, N.Y., 1826–28. From Theodore
Dwight, Jr., *The Northern Traveller,* 6th ed. (New
York: John P. Haven, 1841), facing p. 82. *(Winter-*
thur Library.)

RESORT HOTELS

The resort hotel became part of the American social scene at the beginning of the
nineteenth century, although it achieved its greatest development and widest popularity after 1850. Among resorts of status by the 1830s were Saratoga Springs in
upstate New York, Nahant near Boston, and White Sulfur Springs in West Virginia.
Their stars were still in their ascendency when that of Ballston Spa, probably America's first developed resort, was already on the wane. The mineral springs for which
Ballston, New York, became renowned in the early 1800s were known before the
Revolution; however, not until the early 1790s was there much attempt to capitalize
on the natural resource. Several modest guesthouses with adjacent bath facilities
were erected, one by Nicholas Low, a merchant of New York City. On the advice of
his agents, Low laid out village lots on land he owned adjacent to the springs and
began to promote the site. By 1800 the small community was established. Low then
turned his attention to planning and building a large resort hotel.[159]

The Sans Souci opened to guests in summer 1805. The three-story frame structure, painted white with green shutters, had a 160-foot facade on Front Street with
a piazza across the first story and a balustrade at the roofline (fig. **5-49**). Two long
wings extending behind the main building terminated in small pavilions. The first
floor contained the dining room, a "large, airy and pleasant" public parlor, a ladies'
private parlor, and a ballroom. Elkanah Watson, who visited in August, commented
on the scenes of elegance and gaiety: "We seated ourselves at a sumptuous table, with
about one hundred guests of all classes, but generally . . . of the first respectability.
. . . This is the most splendid watering-place in America, and scarcely surpassed in
Europe in its dimensions and the taste and elegance of its arrangement. The building contains almost one hundred apartments, all respectably furnished. The plan
upon which it is constructed, the architecture, the style of the outbuildings, and the
gravel walks girded with shrubbery—all are on a magnificent scale." The auxiliary
buildings Watson referred to included both utilitarian and public structures, the latter comprising a bathhouse, tavern, billiard and game rooms, and a "temple" with
benches for sitting. Touring in 1805, the Englishman John Melish termed the Sans
Souci "uncommonly superb."[160]

At the time the hotel was rising Nicholas Low and George White, his agent in
Ballston, corresponded about the furnishings. Local craftsmen in Ballston and
neighboring Milton participated in the work. Elihu Alvord constructed all the bedsteads, using cherrywood or beech for the ninety-seven single and forty-two double
frames. He also supplied 101 Windsor side chairs of "round back" (bow-back) pat-

FIG. 5-50 Lewis Miller, *The Party at Supper and Breakfast at Chapman's Springs*, White Sulphur Springs, Eggleston, Va., 1853. Ink and watercolor on paper. From Lewis Miller, *Sketch Book of Landscapes in the State of Virginia*, 1853–67, p. 44, lower portion. *(Abby Aldrich Rockefeller Folk Art Museum, Colonial Williamsburg Foundation, Williamsburg, VA, acc. 1978.301.1.)*

tern "neatly painted" at a cost of 7s. 6d. apiece. William Stillwell of Ballston supplied fifty cherrywood tables, probably for bedroom use, and two of pine for the "shower hous[e]." Another local man, Miles Beach, was favored with two Windsor orders totaling 425 chairs, although difficulties arose over the quality of some chairs in the first group. Beach's Windsors differed in pattern from those of Alvord, comprising 350 fan-backs, 50 square-backs, and 25 armchairs of unspecified design. The large Windsor purchase, 526 chairs in all, suggests the seating was used throughout the building—in the bedrooms and dining room, on the piazzas, and even in the parlors and other public rooms. Before the hotel opened Elihu Alvord also supplied "a small high Chair." In later years orders for new furnishings and repairs often were the responsibility of the hotel's manager, Andrew Berger, who in 1811 added seventy-six washstands. Eleven years later he purchased 60 new chairs for the ballroom. There was a lengthy session of repairs in spring 1821. William L. White mended 150 chairs and painted a total of 469. Hotel furniture was well used.[161]

Seven miles distant at Saratoga Springs the superiority of the waters at Congress Spring gave the community a decided edge by the 1820s. Ransom Cook, who worked in Saratoga as a journeyman between 1813 and 1822 after training with his father, opened shop in 1822, an opportune moment in community development. In 1825 he made eighteen Windsor chairs for Joel Sadler's tavern, having previously constructed two hundred chairs for the new United States Hotel, a three-story brick building with a long colonnade at the front. At Congress Hall, the most fashionable hotel in the community, Cook was employed on occasion to repair, paint, and varnish chairs, some fitted for rocking.[162]

A quarter century later Lewis Miller of York, Pennsylvania, described in pen and watercolor a trip to a resort in the mountains of western Virginia (fig. **5-50**). His party of men and women set out from Christiansburg on a summer morning in July 1853 bound for Chapman's White Sulphur Springs high in the Appalachians. The twenty-five-mile trip over mountains and through valleys in open buggies and on horseback took most of the day. When the party arrived at the springs (Eggleston), members of the group perhaps rested on the piazza of Doctor Chapman's large white-painted hotel overlooking the New River. The seating furniture probably consisted of painted chairs of the same tablet-top pattern used around the dinner table. A Baltimore-inspired design, the rectangular-top Windsor was popular from eastern Pennsylvania to Virginia. The scene at supper is described by a modern historian: "When the supper bell rang . . . the large table was quickly surrounded by the

FIG. 5-51 John Lewis Krimmel, *Cabin of a Sailing Vessel*, southeastern Pennsylvania, 1812–13. Ink, ink wash, and pencil on paper; H. 4⅜", W. 6¼". From John Lewis Krimmel sketchbook 2, southeastern Pennsylvania, 1812–13. *(Winterthur Library.)*

jolly company. It was July, and the flies were there ahead of the guests; but large fans, suspended from the ceiling and kept in motion by a Negro maid, shooed the pests away with moderate success. In that day hearty appetites were not discouraged by so common an annoyance as flies."[163]

SAILING SHIPS AND STEAMBOATS

Sailing Vessels

Shipboard furnishings were by no means sparse or crude. William Hogarth's *Lord George Graham in His Cabin*, for example, portrays Graham with pipe in hand, dressing cap on head, enjoying a musical interlude with friends. The spacious shipboard room is richly paneled and accented with Ionic pilasters. On the floor a large punch-filled bowl rests on a handsome figured carpet near a cloth-draped dining table. The party sits on cabriole-leg joiner's chairs. By contrast, John Lewis Krimmel's sketch on shipboard depicts simple utilitarian painted furniture in a common room that served for dining and sleeping (fig. **5-51**). The scene recalls a note penned in 1788 by Susanna Dillwyn (Emlen) to her father in England during a return voyage to America following a visit: "We were eight collected at the breakfast Table. . . . I staid at the Table where I am now writing. . . . The wind is now quite a fresh breeze & the water is rough. . . . The chairs and things begin to ship about so that I cant write much longer."[164]

American business papers also describe cabin furnishings. When Richard Mills of Philadelphia billed William Barrell in 1768 "for work Done for your Ship," he itemized jobs such as "Turning 12 Pillars & fluting them" and "Fixing [securing] 2 Chairs in Cabin." Mills also supplied a "Large Tabel" for 35s. and "6 Cabin Chairs" at 8s. apiece. The price, date, and supplier suggest slat-back rush-bottom armchairs. Rush seating was reasonably common on shipboard at this period. A few years later chairmaker Joseph Vickary of Newport, Rhode Island, delivered "three Cabbing Chairs" to Christopher Champlin and charged him for "2 Bunshes of flages" (rush). Champlin's sloop *Adventure* was about to sail for Africa with Robert Champlin at the helm. From time to time the term *cabin stool* is encountered. Alexander Edward delivered half a dozen to Grant Webster at Boston in 1772 along with a "Cabben tabl[e]." The stools probably had rush seats and may have had low backs formed by one or two cross slats.[165]

Windsor construction began to ease out rushwork for economical shipboard seating in the 1780s as Elias Hasket Derby's ship *Grand Turk I* acquired new equipment and furnishings. Basic purchases at Salem, Massachusetts, included a logbook, lamps, "Doctors Box," "Spying Glass," "Sett of Colours," and marking irons. Among the furnishings were "Green Chairs," tables, and a "large chest for Cash." The table equipment ranged from cloths and napkins to flatware, wineglasses, and dishes. Among the latter was "A small Tea Set of China for company." Preparations for the schooner *Nancy*'s voyage to Edenton, North Carolina, from Boston in summer 1791 found the owners replenishing the cups, saucers, and linens and purchasing "7 Fan back Chairs" for 6s. apiece. This type of activity was routine in shipping circles as vessels prepared for new voyages. The sale of a vessel or even a part interest usually prompted an inventory of the ship's fixtures, tools, and furnishings. Documents relating to John Cochran's sale of a half interest in the 153½-ton brig *Sally* to Stephen Girard at Philadelphia note especially a "New Table" and "2 Windsor Chairs" before the closing summary: "The Cabin Furniture Compleat besids Curtains in the Cabin State Rooms & Carpet — with a number of other articles as She Came from Sea the 2d of September 1792." Together the new owners fitted the *Sally* for a voyage to Cape François. Also active briefly in the West Indian trade as master of the *Saint Croix Packet* was Captain James Josiah, painted by Charles Willson Peale in 1787 on shipboard on the eve of the mariner's first voyage to the Orient in another command (fig. **5-52**). In the cabin of the *Saint Croix Packet* Josiah sits on a Windsor side chair in the newly fashionable bow-back pattern surrounded by the "tools of his trade" — a chart and dividers, and a compass overhead.[166]

New York craftsmen were particularly active in the outfitting market. Andrew Norwood, primarily an upholsterer, opened a furniture warehouse where he supplied many items needed for refurbishing vessels — mattresses, bed curtains, fancy and Windsor chairs, carpets, and cushions. The market was broad. Accounts of the brig *Rowena* out of Newport note disbursements at New York in 1801 for the purchase of "3 Cabbin Chairs" at $1 apiece. Probably the most elegantly appointed contemporary American vessel was George Crowninshield's private yacht, the hermaphrodite brig *Cleopatra's Barge*, launched in 1816 at Salem, Massachusetts. Upon visiting the vessel in the harbor, William Bentley found her "fitted for sea in a manner never before observed in this Town," her "naval Architecture . . . the best," and the equipment of the latest improvement and patent. Furnishing the dining room, which measured 20 by 19 feet, were lyre-back settees made of mahogany and bird's-eye maple with ornamental brasswork, velvet cushions, and an edging of gold lace. "Splendid" looking glasses hung at either end of the room, and suspended from the center was a "magnificent" chandelier. A rich Brussels carpet covered the floor. Bentley particularly noted "buffets [wall cupboards] loaded with plate . . . & the best glass & porcelain" and remarked the "chairs with descriptive painting." Many items from the barge have survived, including the fancy rush-seat chairs mentioned by Bentley, their broad back panels painted with landscape scenes.[167]

Domestic Travel and the Steamboat

Water transport for domestic travel came into its own after the Revolution. Brissot de Warville praised the cleanliness and good order of the packet boats in 1788, noting that towns of any size along the southern New England coast, such as New Haven and New London, had regular service to New York. When John Lambert booked Hudson River passage on the *Experiment* two decades later, sloop travel on local waters was common. The 130-ton vessel was "built expressly for carrying passengers between Hudson and New York." Quarters for ladies were in the stern, and a general room lined with berths amidships served the gentlemen. There was beverage and food service.[168]

In another decade the steamboat replaced the sloop for passenger service. When

FIG. 5-52 Charles Willson Peale, *Capt. James Josiah*, Philadelphia, 1787. Oil on canvas; H. 30", W. 25". *(Private collection; Photo, Frank S. Schwarz and Son.)*

John Melish traveled on the Hudson by this new conveyance late in 1811, he found the cabin "sufficiently large to accommodate 80 or 100 people." Berths with "clean bedding" were concealed behind drapery, and a "good stove" stood in the room. His praise was echoed by Paul Svinin, a contemporary Russian visitor to America. Often there was a tent on the upper deck to shade travelers from the sun, and every-where there were "comfortable seats" for the passengers. The steamboat continued as a source of fascination and wonderment to foreign visitors. Henry Fearon in 1817 described the *Chancellor Livingston* on the Hudson River as "a floating palace" and reported the vessel's dimensions as 175 by 50 feet. There were 160 berths on board and "accommodation for 40 more by settees." But all was not quite the rosy picture painted by visitors from abroad. Traveling on the *Paragon* in July 1820, Thomas P. Cope of Philadelphia found it crowded with passengers, some received on board and discharged during frequent halts through the night. Not surprisingly, he complained that "the noise from this cause, from the machinery & the trampling overhead were illy calculated to insure sleep."[169]

The steamboat appeared before 1813 on the western waters. By the 1820s builders were adding two stories above the main deck surrounded by promenades, and passengers were divided into cabin and deck classes, the latter shifting for themselves as best they could around the freight and machinery. Mrs. Basil Hall and party, traveling in the West in the late 1820s, "heard magnificent tales of the splendour and good cheer on board the Mississippi boats while . . . still at a distance from them." The experience did not entirely live up to expectations, although Mrs. Hall commented on the spaciousness of their quarters and noted that the crimson curtains and gilt mirrors had an "imposing look." These appointments, however, were "not altogether of a piece with the . . . tin basins chained to the board which . . . the passengers . . . [had] to wash in." Mrs. Trollope actually found American steamboats superior to those she knew in Europe. Steaming from Cincinnati to Wheeling on the *Lady Franklin*, she found "an ample balcony" fronting the ladies' cabin sheltered by an awning and furnished with "chairs and sofas" (settees). The saloon, or ballroom, was a point of ostentatious display in the western steamboat, especially in vessels of the first class. Rich furniture and carpeting, lustrous mirrors and chandeliers, crimson velvet curtains, imitation marblework, gilded ornament, and even frescoes were considered essential elements in creating the spectacular decor thought necessary to attract public patronage in an increasingly competitive business. Much of the elegance was mere veneer, however—a thin disguise for flimsy construction.[170]

Ladies' parlors on shipboard, which were furnished with chairs and, frequently, sofas, were deemed incomplete in the 1830s if they did not include a complement of rocking chairs. Charles Dickens, touring America in 1842, even found a rocking chair in his cabin on a small steam vessel in the East when traveling on the Connecticut River from Springfield to Hartford. The chair well filled the room, since Dickens likened the tiny apartment to "the parlour of a Lilliputian public-house, which had got afloat in a flood or some other water accident."[171]

Chairmakers, particularly those in the West, pursued the steamboat market as avidly as they sought the hotel trade. In 1820 McSwiney and Barnes of Louisville, Kentucky, advised in a notice: "Steam Boats can be furnished with Chairs and Settees. United States, Kentucky, Indiana, and Ohio notes received in payment." Within several years Cincinnati chairmakers supplied steamboat seating on "the shortest notice" and on "accommodating terms." In 1844 William Galligan of Buffalo promoted his "PATENT STEAMBOAT STOOL" to the Lake Erie trade. A later notice carries a small cut of the stool, consisting of a tall chair base, scroll seat, and low upper structure of rounded-tablet crest with lunettes cut along the lower edge. "Oak Bent Rim Steamboat Chairs" ("Captain's" chairs, as styled in modern times) were in vogue by 1855 when W. D. Rand and Company offered them at Louisville. Similar chairs of low continuous rail appear in a gouache view of a Mississippi vessel titled the *Main Cabin or Saloon of the Steamboat Princess*, drawn in 1861 by A. Persac.[172]

Several accounts further illuminate the steamboat furnishing trade. A record kept in 1818 by John H. Piatt, a Cincinnati merchant, details a payment to chairmaker Samuel Stibbs "For 1 Settle [settee] for Steam Boat." Piatt also acquired fourteen fancy chairs and four stools from the firm of Roll and Deeds, although their intended use is not indicated. A group of New York accounts dating to the 1820s records furniture and other furnishings purchased for four East Coast steamboats. Two vessels, the *Thistle* and the *Emerald*, operated between New Brunswick, New Jersey, and New York City. The firm of Fredericks and Farrington made seating for both vessels. A bill of May 1824 lists six Windsor chairs for the cabin of the *Thistle*. Within weeks Alexander Welsh billed the same owners for seating furniture amounting to over $141 (fig. **5-53**). Listed are thirteen settees divided between fancy curled-maple and Windsor construction. The maple settees had five matching chairs. Eight stools on the list were expensive at $3 apiece. Other bills for furnishing the *Thistle* record the purchases of a round table and baize (a table covering), two candle stands, and a sideboard. When two dozen flint glass tumblers and a blue tureen were added in

September 1828, Alexander Welsh had already repaired five curled maple stools and many of the ship's settees and repainted ten fancy and Windsor settees and half a dozen Windsor chairs.[173]

The *Emerald* probably was put into service in 1826. In April the owners purchased a quantity of Brussels carpeting and green baize at Henry Andrews's store in Broadway. There followed a large furniture order from Alexander Welsh, consisting of curled maple cane-seat settees, stools, and chairs and a group of "30 wooden bottom Settees." The long Windsor seats were priced at $7 apiece. Welsh also varnished the interior of the vessel. He used 19½ gallons of finish and spent thirty-one days on the job at charges ranging from $1 to $2 per day. By September the steamboat owners had called on the new firm of Benjamin and Elijah Farrington to make a dozen stools.[174]

Some craftsmen who supplied furnishings for the *Thistle* and *Emerald* made furniture for the steamboat *Bellona*. Leading the way in August 1824 were Fredericks and Farrington with half a dozen Windsor settees. Later Charles Fredericks repaired and painted what may have been the same settees. He performed similar work on two rush-bottom settees and painted half a dozen stools. In 1828 Benjamin and Elijah Farrington made other settee repairs. By all appearances steamboat furniture was subjected to hard use. The fourth steam vessel named in New York accounts was the *Swan*. William Gibbons, owner, patronized Alexander Welsh in April 1827 for curled maple furniture, consisting of settees, stools, and chairs, to the amount of $138.50. The same month Captain Vanderbilt (Jacob or Cornelius) acquired a "high stool" for the vessel from chairmaker Philip I. Arcularius. Cabinetmaker Stephen B. Young supplied "one pair Claw tables." An extensive bill of upholstery from John Voorhis itemizes damask upholstery fabric, moreen curtains, and a sofa cushion among a long list of items. Lighting fixtures and supplies rounded out the purchases.[175]

The Vanderbilt name is associated with other furniture bills. In July 1827 the captain bought a dozen "Steamboat Stools" from Benjamin and Elijah Farrington, probably for the *Swan*. Earlier, in 1821, one of the Vanderbilts sought the services of John D. Brown to paint and repair four settees and six stools. Cornelius appears to have acted as a go-between in 1828 when he sold a Captain Brooks twenty stools for $12.50. Half a dozen similar seats made by William G. Beasley of Salem, New Jersey, the same year for the local steamboat *Essex* were close in price at 56¢ apiece. During the next three decades mechanization advanced sufficiently in the woodworking trades to permit Joel W. Mason to sell "5 Doz 18 inch wood Stools" to the steamboat *Keyport* for $15 in 1858 from his chair factory in New York.[176]

An agreement and bond involving another New York artisan illuminates particulars in the construction and design of steamboat seating. The document was drawn in 1832 between Smith Ely, chairmaker, and Gurdon H. Montague, warden of the Connecticut State Prison at Wethersfield. Ely agreed to purchase seating furniture made by prison inmates at stipulated prices listed on an annexed schedule. Two items are pertinent. Ely paid $3 each for "Steam Boat Settees," described as "6 feet in Length, 14 in wide from outside to outside, to be made from Curled Maple Stuff 1¼ in thick all round." The second item was a steamboat stool with rounded corners at $4 per dozen.[177]

Canal boat travelers found physical arrangements and furnishings compact but otherwise similar to the simplest steamboat accommodations. The ladies slept in berths hung with curtains in a carpeted cabin. The dining room doubled as the men's quarters, where by day tables stood parallel to seating built along either wall. At night mattresses converted the seating to beds, and two rows of cots suspended from the ceiling provided additional places. Neither arrangement was particularly satisfactory. The Cope family traveled on a canal boat built to lodge ten or twelve passengers and overcrowded with twenty-one. The men "spread themselves on settees & on the floor."[178]

Chairmakers along the Erie Canal actively merchandised their specialty wares. At Troy David McKelsey capitalized on two opportunities in promoting his "Steam and Canal Boat work made to order, on the shortest notice." A. and E. Brown, cabinet and chair wareroom owners at Rochester, advertised their "Stools & Settees For Boats." Views of nineteenth-century canal packets detail roofs filled with wooden settees and chairs of varied construction to seat passengers in clear weather. The tillerman stood ready in the stern with his trumpet to warn of approaching low bridges.[179]

COUNTINGHOUSES, OFFICES, AND GENERAL BUSINESS USE

Men of substance, including merchants, traders, and manufacturers, usually reserved an area or small building, called a counting room or house, at their store, wharf, or production site to conduct business and keep accounts. Commercial papers provide glimpses of the physical settings of these miniature centers of capitalism. In 1800 Elias Hasket Derby's "Counting Room" at Salem, Massachusetts, was on or near "the Wharf." The furnishings included a "Lanthorn" to light the room after sundown, hearth equipment, a "Spy Glass," a "Writing Desk," and "6 Green Chairs." There is no mention of a tall stool. The desk either was used with standard seating or while standing.[180]

Furnishings of other description stood in the New York countinghouse of John Eastmond and Benjamin Armitage a few years later. Both men could work simultaneously at their "double Writing desk & benches," comprising a large box on a frame with two opposing slanted surfaces. The desk held a pair of seals and a "Copying Machine," a mechanical device that produced a duplicate letter as the original was written. A bookcase stood against one wall, and a stove provided heat. Counting rooms facing the morning or afternoon sun sometimes employed Venetian blinds in summer to moderate the seasonal heat, as at John Slesman's Philadelphia property. Humphrey Hathaway occupied spacious quarters at New Bedford, Massachusetts, in the stone building he erected in 1819 at the head of Rotch's Wharf (fig. 5-54). A long pipe vented the stoves standing in the front and back rooms. Each area contained a tall double desk of slanted writing surface positioned perpendicular to the east wall. Beneath the clock near the opposite wall were one or two cases, probably supporting open shelves containing ledgers and account books. A settee of slat-back pattern forward of the cases is contemporary with the building, whereas the baluster-turned seating around the stove was constructed more than a quarter century earlier. On the table behind the chairs rests "a spyglass used to recognize vessels entering and leaving the harbor."[181]

FIG. 5–54. Edward S. Russell, *Office of Humphrey Hathaway, at the Head of Rotch's Wharf*, New Bedford, Mass., ca. 1873, depicting scene of 1819 and later. Pencil sketch on paper. From Horatio Hathaway, *A New Bedford Merchant* (Boston: Merrymount Press, 1930). *(Collection of Estate of Thomas S. Hathaway; Photo, New Bedford Whaling Museum.)*

Some businessmen set up counting rooms in their homes. A tall stool stood in front of the pine desk used in the early 1800s by Isaac Clason of New York at his Broadway home, and a pine bookcase held his records. Clason, who operated a store in Front Street, owned four sailing vessels. In Broome Street John P. Mumford occupied the "Lower Back Room" of his house as a business center. A "counting Room Stool" was part of the furnishings. William Smith's Philadelphia home contained substantial business quarters: a "Compting House Desk" and stool were complemented by a book rack and a "Compting house Table." Five chairs stood in the room, which was heated by a "small stove" and lighted by three candlesticks. For convenience a "Spitt Box" sat on the floor.[182]

High seats were popular accompaniments of the tall business desk. In 1794 cabinetmaker John Gillingham of Philadelphia owned "two writing stools." Thomas West, a contemporary dealer in dry goods at New York, kept a "Compting house Stool" at his store in Water Street. Imported Philadelphia seats of similar description found a good market in the early 1800s at Charleston. When Silas Cheney of Litchfield, Connecticut, made a business sign for a customer in 1821, he followed it with a "Seat for writing before [a] Desk." Records of contemporary date kept by Henry W. Miller of Worcester, Massachusetts, name a "Desk Chair" and "Desk Stool," probably terms for two different forms. The former may have had a complete chair back and seat supported on long legs. Like other painted specialty seating, the tall desk stool had broad distribution. In 1830 David Alling of Newark, New Jersey, charged 87½¢ for this form. Five years later a customer at the shop of Philemon Robbins in Hartford, Connecticut, purchased six "high stools," apparently to expand his business, and simultaneously acquired "1 Sett black walnut book shelves large." The records

FIG. 5-55 Lewis Miller, *The Shop of William Spangler, Tobacconist*, York, Pa., ca. 1814–20, depicting scene of 1811. Ink and watercolor on paper. *(The York County Heritage Trust, PA; Photo, Winterthur Museum.)*

of H. F. Dewey, a chairmaker of Bennington, Vermont, describe both tall stools and chairs for use at high desks. By midcentury "Counter and Desk Stools" were regular fare in the Midwest.[183]

The terms *office* and *counting room* were of parallel meaning by 1830, although seating for the two facilities could be different. At New Ipswich, New Hampshire, chairmaker Josiah P. Wilder continued to make a few tall counting stools in the 1830s and later, but his larger trade was in "Office Chairs." He sent quantities of "Stuff" for this type of seating to the New York firm of Wilder and Stewart. Dual production of business seating also is recorded in the shop of Charles Riley at Philadelphia. At his death in 1842 estate appraisers identified both countinghouse stools and "Swivell Office Chairs." A cushion made the latter more comfortable. Richard W. Greene of Providence acquired four office chairs at $1.75 apiece in 1845 and then paid $1.50 for a cushion. Edwin Freedley, a contemporary commentator, noted that Philadelphia supported "several manufactories and warerooms of *Office* and *Counting-house Furniture* exclusively." He explained that "articles of this description [were] both supplied to order, and kept on hand in large quantities." The statement appears to have been applicable to other large urban centers.[184]

Records identify several forms of seating used at business locations other than the counting room and office. Retail stores head the list. A record of 1772 indicates that Joseph Henzey, a chairmaker of Philadelphia, provided William Barrell with "2 Windsor chairs for the Store" in return for dry goods and other items. Silas Cheney of Litchfield, Connecticut, debited a local account in the early 1800s for "2 Seats for Store" at 3s. 9d. apiece. The description and price suggest the seats were stools, a form that appears in engraved views of store interiors. Stools of several types were popular for stores after 1800, including the "high Seat" and the "curld counter stool" of maple.[185]

Chairs and stools commonly furnished small shops and craft establishments. References from the 1750s to a "Seat for the Shop" in the accounts of William Barker of Providence, Rhode Island, refer to rush-bottom furniture. In the following decades the Proud family craftsmen continued to produce this form locally. Wooden-bottom seating probably is represented in 1819 in a customer purchase of "2 seats for shop" from Silas Cheney of Connecticut and Charles Wistar's acquisition of a "Shop stool" in the 1830s at Philadelphia. A scene in the tobacco shop of William Spangler at York, Pennsylvania, depicts nine working hands in 1811 rolling cigars while seated on Windsor stools of chair height (fig. **5-55**). Barbers required chairs with adjustable headrests. Sometimes the seat height was that of a normal chair; at other times the legs were extended.[186]

Scattered references describe the use of wooden-bottom seating in other walks of business and professional life. In the early 1800s six red Windsor chairs, an armchair, and a settee were sufficient to convert the law office of William Hemphill at West Chester, Pennsylvania, to a sitting or meeting room as occasion dictated. Hemphill had a "Small Desk & Case" at which he worked, a stove for warmth in cold weather, and a clotheshorse for coats. On the walls hung a variety of prints and maps. Tapping Reeves made a contemporary purchase of a "seat 8 feet long for office" from Silas Cheney for his Litchfield, Connecticut, law office.[187]

Banking needs were well served by Windsor seating. Five square-back chairs with mahogany arms scrolling forward and double-bow crests centered by a medallion were by tradition part of a set used in the early 1800s in the Director's Room of the First Bank of the United States (fig. 4-24). One chair bears the label of its Philadelphia maker, Robert Taylor. A slat and ball-spindle chair of later date has original mustard yellow paint and a tradition of ownership by a bank in southeastern Pennsylvania at West Chester (fig. **5-56**). An old hand-printed label on the bottom reads: "Director's Chair / Bank of Chester County / 1837." The restrained decoration consists of black penciling, black and gilt banding on the slats and seat front, and bronze banding in other areas. In 1814 Silas Cheney supplied a "large table for the bank" at Litchfield, Connecticut. A suite of fancy seating made in the 1830s by Philemon Robbins for the Hartford Exchange Bank comprised "15 flagg seat drab chairs." The work complemented two "Large counting room Desk[s]," small desks "to sett on counter," a large mahogany table, and a desk covered with cloth, possibly baize. A year later Robbins supplied the Hartford Fire Insurance Company with a high stool and two "Roll top wood seat Chairs."[188]

Just as Windsors were carried out of doors for use in private gardens, so they served commercial interests in exterior settings. William Birch's 1799 view of Second Street, Philadelphia, near Christ Church illustrates a group of produce sellers seated in Windsor and rush-bottom chairs outside the arched portal of the old courthouse (fig. **5-57**). Charles C. Robinson of the city hinted at the use of a "small Windsor Chair" purchased in 1812 by Joseph Harlin when he identified the man as the "Watchman at the Bridge." Several years later Silas Cheney of Connecticut was called on to repair a "Chair for toolhous" (tollhouse), a building where fees were collected for the right to use a "turnpike road." By the time Richard Caton Woodville

FIG. 5-56 Slat-back Windsor armchair, southeastern Pennsylvania, ca. 1837. Maple and other woods; H. 33½", (seat) 17¾", W. (crest) 18⅞", (arms) 23", (seat) 19¼", D. (seat) 17¼". (Collection of Chester County Historical Society, West Chester, Pa. Gift of the National Bank of Chester County; Photo, Winterthur Museum.)

FIG. 5-57 William Birch, detail of *Second Street North from Market St. wth Christ Church*, Philadelphia, 1799. Engraving; H. 11⅛", W. 13⅛" (plate). From William Birch and Son, *The City of Philadelphia* (Philadelphia: William Birch, 1800), n.p. *(Winterthur Library.)*

painted *Waiting for the Stage* in 1851, board benches and plank-bottom chairs were common sights in public waiting rooms.[189]

Vernacular seating filled business needs in industrial America. On September 30, 1795, the Providence firm of William Almy and Moses Brown, proprietors of the Warwick Spinning Mills, paid William Barker for "bottoming 2 Chairs for [the] factory." Perhaps these were the same "2 Shop Chairs" supplied in spring 1791 by Samuel Proud. Samuel and his brother Daniel made another chair for the factory in 1795, and they were suppliers of spinning equipment: turned cylinders, buttons, whorls, and spindles. The brothers made frequent repairs to chairs and chair seats, suggesting that seating furniture was scattered throughout the mill for the workers. In Massachusetts Luke Houghton of Barre produced sixteen stools in February 1830 for J. and D. Dunbar. The order was supplemented in May by "1 doz of high stooles" and six low seats. These purchases and Houghton's work at lettering the words "no admittance" on the premises suggest a factory site, possibly a textile mill. J. P. Wilder of New Ipswich, New Hampshire, supplied the Columbia Manufacturing Company with seventy-four stools and a match factory with two stools. As late as 1884 the American Watch Company seated its workers on rows of tablet-top Windsors at long tables in the Pinion Room. Heavy industry is represented by the Hopewell Furnace of southeastern Berks County, Pennsylvania, whose representative purchased six Windsors in 1812 from the local chairmaker William Bird.[190]

THE MORAVIANS

American Moravian communities found in Windsor seating economical and functional qualities that met their domestic needs and filled the demands of their commercial and educational programs. The Episcopal Unity of Brethren, which traced its roots to continental Europe in pre-Reformation days, established its first *permanent* American settlement in 1741 and named it Bethlehem. A highly organized community life permitted the Pennsylvania settlement to flourish. A second village founded at Lititz followed in the mid-1750s, and a community was established in 1766 at Salem, North Carolina. Thomas Anburey, who visited Bethlehem in 1781, commented on several aspects of Moravian life: the tavern erected for the convenience of travelers; the farms "interspersed around the settlement"; the highly developed state of "all manner of trades and manufactures"; and the accommodations and occupations of the single members of the community. He described the house of the single women, or sisters, as "a spacious stone building, divided . . . into large chambers [and,] after the German mode, heated with stoves." Aside from their domestic duties, some sisters were employed "in fancy and ornamental [needle] work," for which the Moravians were justly acclaimed. Anburey observed in all the "apartments . . . various musical instruments." The refectory was a "large hall" that also served as a chapel. Thus the "handsome organ" and the "scripture pieces" on the walls were appropriate. The single men engaged in trades or assisted with farming. In the town center was a "great church." Each Moravian community had its *Gemeinhaus*, a common building that served several functions, those of meeting place, school, and pastoral accommodation.[191]

An inventory of the *Gemeinhaus* at Bethlehem taken in 1802 describes the seating furniture common to these buildings: "3 grüun Arm Stulln" (three green armchairs) in the meeting room on the second floor; a red cane-seat chair in the "little Saal," or worship room. Windsor seating furnished many private living quarters in the building. Eight side chairs, half painted green, half yellow, and a green armchair were in "Schaafs Room," and the "South" chamber occupied by Brother and Sister Van Vleck contained two yellow Windsors. The room set aside for John Francis Peter, a musician, contained two Windsor chairs painted green. By 1791 the meeting hall in the *Gemeinhaus* at Salem housed a dozen green chairs. Later furnishing lists also describe the private rooms. Those occupied by Charles G. Reichel during his ministry from 1802 to 1811 contained ten green Windsor side chairs and an armchair. Furnishings for Christian Frederick Schaaf, who arrived in 1819 as associate minister, included a suite of one dozen Windsor side and armchairs made by the Moravian chairmaker Karsten Petersen. During the pastorate of Brother and Sister Andrew Benade from 1822 to 1829, the couple's rooms were furnished with sixteen green Windsors.[192]

The chairs followed patterns popular in the federal period. Slat-back Windsors probably were first used by the Moravians during the 1820s. An 1837 inventory of congregational property at Bethlehem identifies the seating as scroll-top, bent-back, and "plain" chairs. Probably all terms refer to the side profiles of the back posts. The first-named pattern probably was of Grecian, or S-curved, form, the post tops scrolled backward. The seats probably were woven. The plain and bent-back chairs had straight or steamed and angled posts, each type set at a slight cant in the wooden seat. Records describe yellow, red, brown, and green surfaces. Several settees complemented the side and armchairs.[193]

THE SUN INN, 1758.

FIG. 5-58 *The Sun Inn, 1758*, Bethlehem, Pa. From William C. Reichel, *The Old Sun Inn at Bethlehem, Pa., 1758* (Doylestown, Pa.: W. W. H. Davis, 1876), frontispiece. *(Collection of Moravian Archives, Bethlehem, Pa.; Photo, Winterthur Museum.)*

When Hannah Callender and friends from Philadelphia visited Bethlehem in summer 1761, the community was already a wayside stop on a well-traveled route to New York State and New England. As the party approached Bethlehem, it passed the old Crown Tavern on the south side of the Lehigh before crossing the river into town and engaging accommodations at the newly built Sun Inn, a substantial stone building of steep gable roof with jerkin-head ends (fig. **5-58**). On his visit to Bethlehem two decades later Thomas Anburey found the inn built "upon an exceeding good plan, and well calculated for the convenience and accommodation of travellers." On the main floor off a central hall were a public room, kitchen, innkeeper's quarters, and a suite of three rooms. Three more suites and a large dining room filled the second story, and four large dormitory-type sleeping rooms divided the attic. Inventories of inn furnishings made in 1763, 1772, and 1781 describe the seating seen by Hannah Callender and Thomas Anburey as several dozen rush-bottom chairs. From at least 1772 these were supplemented by four benches, probably located in the public room.[194]

Sometime between 1781 and 1800 the inn converted to Windsor seating. An inventory of 1805 lists forty-five green chairs valued at 5s. apiece, and five more worth 6s. The same number of green chairs with similar valuations appears on an inventory of 1800 written in German. Other furnishings of this period include a twenty-four-hour clock, an eight-day timepiece, a "moldit [molded] dresser with glass windows," cherry and walnut dining tables, "4 Benches in the public Roome," and "34 sundrie Chairs part moldit." The "molded" chairs may have included most, if not all, of the "30 Schriner Stuhle," or cabinetmaker's chairs, listed in 1816. The number of Windsors on the premises had increased to eighty-two by that date, two dozen described as "new." A rocking chair was now part of the group. During the Revolution and later the inn had a steady stream of notable visitors, among them Governor John Penn, General Horatio Gates, John Adams, the Marquis de Lafayette, John Hancock, Richard Henry Lee, Baron von Steuben, George Washington, John Jay, and Alexander Hamilton. Few could fail to have been impressed by the community's substantial buildings, well-tended gardens and fields, highly developed handicrafts, and rich cultural life. Those visitors who put their thoughts on paper also remarked on the inn's excellent cuisine, a surprise to many in the midst of a rural wilderness. By 1801 area roads were sufficiently improved that the innkeeper could note the arrival of "a gentleman in a Windsor [riding] chair."[195]

An inn for travelers also was considered a necessary part of the community structure at Salem. Inventories of record begin in 1787, when "woven-bottom" chairs were itemized. Windsor, or green, chairs made their appearance in 1789, although for a while their number was modest, varying from six to nine seats. In 1809 eighteen new

FIG. 5-59 Long-legged Moravian Windsor seating, Lititz, Pa., 1790–1805. Yellow poplar (seats) with maple and other woods; *(left to right)* H. 45⅛", 44½", 47½", (seat) 24⅛", 24", 27½", W. (seat) 19¼", 19¼", 32¼". *(Collection of Moravian Congregation, Lititz, Pa.; Photo, Winterthur Museum.)*

Windsors joined the old ones, and by 1819 the number had reached eighty-eight. The common chairs numbered fifty. Karsten Petersen was credited with making sixty-six of the Windsors. Chairs constructed by John Daniel Siewers were added in 1839. During the 1840s the total number of chairs stood at about 150. The "common" chairs had splint seats.[196]

Music was an important part of Moravian life. Thomas Anburey commented on seeing an organ in the "large hall" of the Sisters' House at Bethlehem, and Hannah Callender's party heard the organ played at the neighboring Moravian village of Nazareth. The Saal of the *Gemeinhaus* at Lititz had an organ, and the walls were hung with oil paintings depicting the life of Christ executed by the Moravian artist Valentine Haidt. Tin sconces with candles provided light at the Sunday evening service. In 1765 both an orchestra and a choir were organized.[197]

By tradition a group of long-legged Windsor side chairs of fan- or bow-back design was used in the Moravian communities of Bethlehem and Lititz (fig. **5-59**). Called "trombone chairs" in modern times, their function probably was that of seats for the trombone players. As the trombones of the day were slide instruments without valves, the extension required to play the instrument was substantial. One "high green chair," probably a seat of this kind, is itemized in an 1837 inventory of the small meeting room in the church at Bethlehem. At Lititz an ensemble of trombonists, known as the "trombone choir," was organized about 1771, the year the group made its first public appearance during the Christmas Eve vigil. The "choir" comprised soprano, alto, tenor, and bass instruments, which produced "soft, blending tones."[198]

The patterns represented in the trombone chairs place their initial use in the 1790s. The chairs exhibit several peculiarities of design associated with Pennsylvania German Windsor craftsmanship: broad seats, squared and channeled bows, distinctive beaded and carved scroll-end crests, simple turned back posts, spindles pinched together at the base, conical- and swelled-tip stretchers, dual leg patterns, and baluster forms sharply tapered at the base. One bow-back trombone chair bears the stamped initials "HGR" on the plank bottom. The letters suggest an association with Henry Gottlieb Rudy (1781–1818), a faithful church member who lived near Lititz. Although farmer Rudy was a jack-of-all-trades, the chair is too sophisticated to have been made by an amateur, and Rudy is not known to have been a member of the trombone choir or orchestra. Plugged holes in the faces of the front legs indicate that a footrest was once in place, although it may have been a later addition, since the chairs illustrated in figure 5-59 are without this feature.[199]

The tall, two-seated settee that accompanies the chairs in figure 5-59 has several design features copied directly from Philadelphia work, namely, a crowned bow face, forward-scroll arms, a rounded shield-shape seat, and early bamboo turnings with cup-shape swells in the lower legs and stretchers. The profiles of the post turnings are German American. The bench was thought to have been used with the Tannenberg organ put into service in 1787 at the Lititz church; however, restoration of the instrument has shown that was impossible. The bench may have been used at musical functions. The footrest, probably not original, has been in place long enough to exhibit wear. The depressions seem greatest near either end, suggesting the seat often held two people.[200]

Institutional Use

LIBRARIES AND RELATED INSTITUTIONS

The earliest documented use of Windsor seating by an institution was recorded on September 14, 1759, when the Philadelphia merchant Samuel Emlen credited the account of chairmaker Thomas Gilpin with "12 Windsor Chairs given to the Hospital @ 16/ £9.12." The furniture was made for the Manager's Room of the Pennsylvania Hospital. The date and placement of the chairs in a meeting room suggest the high-back pattern. Because Gilpin branded some of his work, his chairs can be distinguished from those produced by other craftsmen in the city's small, early Windsor-chair-making community. Following the hospital seating in date are the dozen Windsors acquired by the Redwood Library at Newport, Rhode Island, after a meeting on September 26, 1764, when a levy was voted to raise funds for the purchase of a dozen chairs. When the Yale College commencement exercises of September 1782 were held in a meetinghouse at New Haven, the "Presid't & two Fellows sat in the Pulpit; the rest of the Fellows with the Professor of Div'y sat in Windsor Chairs upon a Platform or Stage 18 feet square before the Pulpit . . . covered with a Turkey Carpet."[201]

Records of the Library Company of Philadelphia identify the purchase of two groups of Windsor seating during the eighteenth century. The Company, founded by Benjamin Franklin and friends in 1731, rented temporary quarters during the early years before moving to the west wing of the statehouse (Independence Hall) for several decades. In 1773 with membership and collections growing, the library rented expanded quarters on the second floor of the new building erected by the Carpenters' Company less than two blocks away. Upon occupying the premises the organization ordered a dozen Windsor chairs from Joseph Henzey. At 15s. apiece the seating had arms and was of high-back or sack-back pattern. The question of suitable quarters arose again after the Revolutionary War, this time resolved by the construction of Library Hall in 1789–90 on Fifth Street facing the statehouse yard. Two years later, as the library expanded with an addition, it ordered another dozen chairs from Henzey. Changing fashion prescribed bow-back Windsors with forward-scroll arms and simulated bamboo legs (fig. 3-66). Later seating is delineated in a pair of interior views drawn in 1879 by Colin C. Cooper, Jr. Nineteenth-century tablet-top and low-back armchairs are prominent in the foreground, although standing at the back of the room is an eighteenth-century high-back chair.[202]

American trade and mechanic organizations, which appear to have found inspiration in the European guild system, began organizing to promote educational and charitable objectives in the postwar years, although these organizations were not unknown before the Revolution. One of the oldest groups is the Carpenters' Company of the City and County of Philadelphia, founded in 1724. Many eighteenth-century members practiced their craft as more than mere carpenters. The term "builder" is appropriate today, and a few individuals even rose to the level of builder-architect. After almost forty years of existence, the Company looked for a site to erect a meeting hall. A suitable lot was acquired on Chestnut Street near the Pennsylvania Statehouse. Construction was sufficiently advanced to receive the Library Company in 1773 as a second-floor tenant. Early the next year the Carpenters' Company was ready to acquire furniture for its own use on the first floor. Several members agreed to make tables, and a subscription was raised to pay for chairs. At least one group of seating was purchased from Joseph Henzey. The chairs probably were in the sack-back style and may have matched those acquired by the Library Company. A Philadelphia chair of this pattern branded on the seat bottom with the name "J.OGILBY," presumably for Joseph Ogilby, a member of the Carpenters' Company, was in the antiques market some years ago.

A second acquisition of seating furniture by the Carpenters' Company in 1774 is indicated by the reimbursement of one member "in full for Chares" at a cost of £10.5. Another transaction recorded in June 1781 between the Company and chair-maker Jedidiah Snowden may describe the purchase of still a third group of chairs, although by the 1780s Snowden is referred to in other documents as a shopkeeper. Early in 1779 the organization decided to place an identifying mark on its possessions. Accordingly, the Company directed Joseph Rakestraw "to have a Brand Made with the words Carpenters Co. thereon and to brand the Chairs and other Articles belonging to the Comp'y and to Draw on the Master for the pay for the brand." The varied use of the building may have prompted the move. Beginning in 1774 the ground floor had a succession of illustrious occupants. The Provincial Assembly, the First Continental Congress, and the Constitutional Convention all convened in Carpenters' Hall, and during the war the building was used as a hospital by American and British forces. Further record of new furnishings for the building occurs in 1857 when William Sanderson supplied six settees probably supplemented by chairs. An interior view of the main hall after refurbishing shows late tablet-top settees, eighteenth-century sack-back chairs, and several early nineteenth-century square-back Windsors with double bows centering a crest medallion (fig. 4-24).[203]

Many mechanics' organizations supported libraries where members and apprentices could borrow books or read during free hours. By 1822 the Providence Association of Mechanics and Manufacturers, founded in 1789, established a facility of this type. A committee was formed part of whose responsibility was "to prepare . . . a Library Room for the reception of the Books, by Whitewashing, papering, or Painting the same [they papered], and to furnish the same with Book cases or shelves, Tables and Chairs, or other necessary furniture." As a number of chairmakers and cabinetmakers were members of the organization, it is likely that one or more were patronized for the furnishings. The Association often rented its hall, and on one occasion it also collected rent when it loaned the "Benches & Settees used at Commencement."[204]

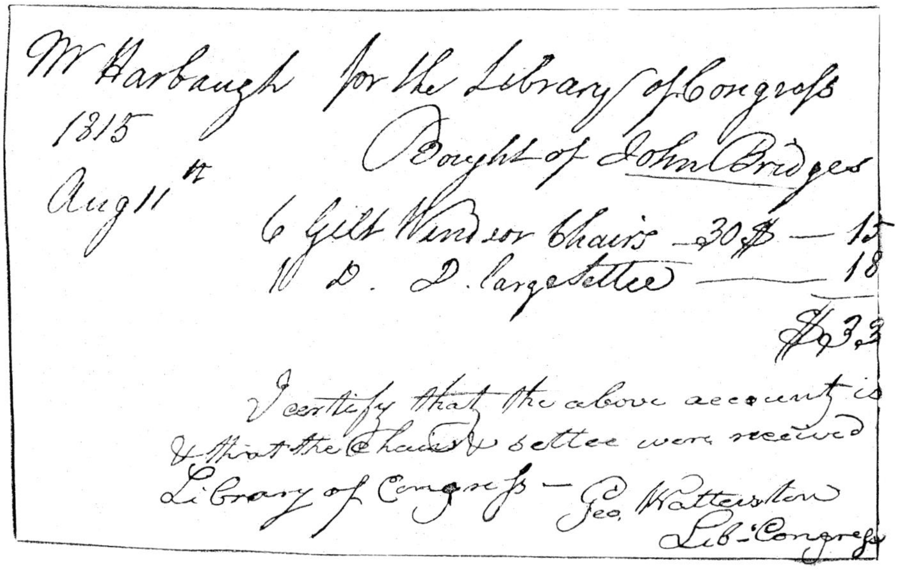
Mr Harbaugh for the Library of Congress
1815 Bought of John Bridges
Aug 11th
6 Gilt Windsor chairs 30$ — 15
1 D. D. large Settee —— 18
$33
I certify that the above account is
& that the Chairs & settee were received
Library of Congress — Geo. Watterston
Lib. Congress

FIG. 5-60 John Bridges bill to Library of Congress, Washington, D.C., August 11, 1815. *(Treasury Records, Miscellaneous Treasury Accounts of the First Auditor, National Archives, Washington, D.C.)*

The founding of private libraries took a new turn in the nineteenth century with the development of the athenæum. Established as literary centers housing current periodicals and selected titles, some institutions also collected objects for display. The Athenæum of Philadelphia, founded in 1814, acquired its first seating furniture of record in 1822 at the chair shop of Philip Halzel. Described only as a dozen Windsor chairs, these seats may be the "bamboo"-turned slat-back side chairs still among the Athenaeum's furnishings. The pattern was popular in eastern Pennsylvania (pl. 4). Other Windsors in the library's collection, framed with and without arms and embellished with arrow-type spindles ("flat sticks"), could well date earlier than the 1847 Italianate building on Washington Square for which they are thought to have been acquired. Later chairs with low backs and heavy scroll arms or "bent rims" forming arms are contemporary with the building.[205]

Other libraries recorded the purchase of painted seating. In 1822 a committee at the Boston Athenaeum engaged chairmaker Samuel Gragg to build furniture. Described only as "Bamboo" seating, the construction featured either plank or woven seats. The suite consisted of sixty-four chairs, some with arms, a settee, and six "window stools," at a cost of just over $120. Boston chairs of a later pattern were ordered in 1855 for the Portsmouth Athenaeum from Blake, Ware, and Company, who acquired the seating from chairmaker William O. Haskell. The chairs were shipped to New Hampshire via the Eastern Railroad (figs. 4-44 to 4-46).[206]

The national library at Washington had a rebirth at the beginning of the athenæum movement. Following destruction of the facility when British troops set fire to the Capitol on July 24, 1814, Congress enacted a statute directing that "the President of the United States be . . . authorized to cause a proper apartment to be immediately selected and prepared for a library room, and to cause the library lately purchased from Thomas Jefferson, to be placed therein during the insuing recess of Congress." Jefferson offered the national government his select collection of books from the library at Monticello following the fire, and in due course the purchase was effected. The Capitol was located temporarily in a three-story brick building at the corner of Seventh and E streets, which also housed the Post Office and Patent Office. George Watterston, librarian of Congress, wrote to President Madison on March 25, 1815, suggesting that "in the third story of the present Capitol, a room sufficiently commodious and convenient might, at a small expense, be prepared." Outfitting of the temporary "Congressional Library room" began almost immediately. Carpentry, plastering, and painting were completed by summer. The bill for painting specifically mentions the color green. Meanwhile, orders had been placed for the furnishings.

FIG. 5-61 Sack-back Windsor armchair, Boston, 1791. White pine (seat); H. 37", (seat) 17¾", W. (arms) 24⅜", (seat) 20⅜", D. (seat) 14¾". *(Courtesy of the Massachusetts Historical Society; Photo, Winterthur Museum.)*

Workmen installed 77½ yards of carpeting, tacked a "piece [of] paper Bordering" to the walls, and hung five Venetian blinds strung with green cords at the windows. Green baize covered two desks and a "Large table." One desk probably was that purchased in June from H. V. Hill for $25. John Bridges supplied the seating furniture. His bill for $33 dated August 11 itemizes gilt Windsor chairs and a large settee to match (fig. **5-60**).[207]

Of plainer finish but earlier date were the Windsors acquired in 1791 by the newly formed Massachusetts Historical Society for use in the library and the museum room. At the third meeting of the organization on June 30 it was "*Voted*, That the Treasurer be desired to purchase twelve chairs (Windsor, green, elbow); a plain pine table, painted, with drawer and lock and key; an inkstand, &c." As the society maintained its collection in rented rooms during the early years, the seating and other furnishings along with the books and artifacts were packed and moved periodically. Therefore it is remarkable that at least two chairs survive. The Society owns one (fig. **5-61**), and another is in private hands. Fixed to the bottom of the latter is a large, discolored paper label of nineteenth- or early twentieth-century date hand-printed in black ink with the legend: "One of the / Twelve Windsor Chairs / purchased by the / Mass. Historical Society / in / 1791." The "labeled" chair is identical to that illustrated in figure 5-61, although the seat is in better condition and displays a definite pommel at the center front. The turnings of the chairs are of excellent design.[208]

CHURCHES AND RELIGIOUS GROUPS

Sarah Anna Emery remarked on the use of single chairs to supplement fixed pews and movable benches in American churches or meetinghouses in the eighteenth century and later, and a variety of documents provide corroborating evidence. Emery noted the "large, square pews . . . furnished with one or two high-backed chairs . . . commonly of rich wood, handsomely carved, with flag seats. These chairs were . . . usually occupied by elderly ladies. Besides the chairs, there was generally one or more high stools, for the accommodation of the more infantile portion of the congregation." Emery's commentary reflects her childhood before 1800 in Newburyport, Massachusetts. In supplement to these recollections is a note describing the square pews in the church at Newent, New London County, Connecticut, as "large enclosures made of high wainscoted walls, against the sides of which seats were ranged and within which were frequently two or three chairs." Further notations occur in furniture accounts. On several occasions during the 1780s and 1790s David Haven of Framingham, Massachusetts, sold slat-back rush-bottom chairs "to set in the Meeting House" at a recorded price of 3*s*. Of similar date and cost are chairs made for meetinghouse use by Major John Dunlap of Bedford, New Hampshire. Moody Carr of neighboring Rockingham County billed a customer a few years later for "a red Chaire for your Pew."[209]

Of rare survival is an eighteenth-century baluster-turned Windsor armchair with ecclesiastical associations (fig. **5-62**). By tradition the chair was used during visits to Saint John's Church in Bridgeport, Connecticut, by the Reverend Doctor Samuel Seabury (d. 1796) of New London, first Episcopal bishop of Connecticut and Rhode Island. The imposing arm terminals and center back spindle indicate the chair was made for special use. Seabury appears to have acquired the chair in the Connecticut–Rhode Island border region, where flat-chamfered seat edges were relatively common until about 1800. Other features associated with this region include the large-headed baluster and spool profiles, the subtle swell of the feet, the bold spindle nodules, the pronounced blocked bow tips, and the well-carved flowerets defining the arm scrolls, now missing their scroll returns.[210]

Nineteenth-century references to furniture made for church use are more common. About 1811–12 Sarah Emery described the furnishings of the Belleville meet-

FIG. 5–62. Sack-back Windsor armchair and detail of arm terminal (lower part of terminal scroll missing), Rhode Island or New London County, Conn., ca. 1785–96. H. 41¾", (seat) 17¼", W. (arms) 28¼", (seat) 22⅛", D. (seat) 16⁹⁄₁₆". *(Collection of Seabury Society for the Preservation of the Glebe House, Inc., Woodbury, Conn.; Photo, Winterthur Museum.)*

inghouse near Newburyport, Massachusetts, which she called "a good-sized edifice, with galleries, and a tall and graceful spire" : "The pulpit . . . was in the style of the period [with] a sounding-board. Upon [the pulpit desk] rested a green velvet cushion. . . . The seats of the three yellow, oval-backed, wooden chairs which stood beneath it were covered to match. A mahogany communion table occupied the platform in front, and two handsome glass candelabra were placed either side of the sacred desk. There was no chandelier, but the sconces for candles were hung around the walls."[211]

Not all recorded church seating is identifiable. Some was rush bottomed (common or fancy), and the rest was mostly of Windsor construction. A chair priced at $2.50 and delivered to the "meting hous" in 1816 by Silas Cheney of Litchfield, Connecticut, appears to have had fancy paint, a rush-bottom seat, and arms, judging by comparable entries in Cheney's accounts. In Windsor, Vermont, at that date chairmaker Thomas Boynton made "a Settee for the meeting house," probably of Windsor construction, for $4. In neighboring Cornish, New Hampshire, Andrew Tracy's estate records of a few years later list among the deceased's personal property "a chair at the meeting house" of unidentified construction. Tracy was the brother

of Connecticut chairmaker Ebenezer Tracy, Sr., and the father of Stephen, who then resided in New Hampshire.[212]

Also from New Hampshire is a pair of Windsor armchairs with shaped tablet tops made in the New Ipswich shop of Joseph Wilder for an area church dedicated in 1821 (fig. **5-63**). The painted crest decoration is said to represent the stone tablets given to Moses on Mount Sinai; however, the form is more like that of a book—perhaps the holy scriptures. Wilder's knowledge of Boston work is evident in the structural features: the lower crest arch, arm scrolls, seat shape, and ornamental front stretcher. Later references to church furniture include an 1834 account of Philemon Robbins at Hartford, Connecticut, who provided "2 Curl maple Chairs" at $7 for the Ecclesiastical Society of neighboring Andover. Isaac Wright sold "1 pine stool for church" in Hartford, and John G. Hopkins supplied the Greene family of Providence, Rhode Island, with "one pare of Crickets for pew." By the 1850s Boston furniture houses regularly supplied seating furniture for churches and vestries.[213]

References from several sources document the ecclesiastical work of chairmakers outside New England. At Cincinnati, Ohio, "Brother" Samuel Stibbs received payment in 1820 for chairs supplied to the Methodist Episcopal Church. Toward the end of the following decade David Alling billed Doctor J. B. Jackson for "12 Chairs for [the] Second Presbyterian Church" of Newark, New Jersey. In southerly Cape May County Samuel Fithian Ware supplied a customer in 1843 with a "foot stool for the Church" at a modest 50¢. Chairmakers also provided furniture for peripheral church activity. Early in the nineteenth century the Philadelphia Society of Friends patronized John Chapman when purchasing a dozen Windsor chairs for committee rooms in the new Mulberry Street meetinghouse. Chapman also received an appointment as caretaker of the premises. John Oldham, a member of the Light Street Methodist Church of Baltimore, was chosen in 1819 to supply a dozen chairs for the church parsonage. A few years later in August 1834 the Episcopal Church Society of Hartford, Connecticut, paid Philemon Robbins 50¢ for the "use of furniture for commencement."[214]

Closely affiliated with the religious community in the nineteenth century was the camp meeting, or revival, especially in the South and West. This form of mass worship, frequently held in rural outdoor settings, attracted large crowds of people, some of whom came from a distance, pitched tents, and stayed for several days. A lithograph published by Kennedy and Lucas in the early 1830s illustrates a scene with worshippers both sitting and kneeling on long stick-legged benches. Another event is described in a Charles Town, West Virginia, newspaper notice of June 1810 by the owner of a square-back Windsor chair painted black who sought to recover his property taken "from the grove where preaching was on Sunday last." A year earlier Benjamin Henry Latrobe had sketched a camp meeting in Virginia depicting men seated on rush-bottom slat-back chairs. Private family devotions, which sometimes are pictured in paintings or prints, generally show adults kneeling at chairs, some of Windsor construction, and children at low stools.[215]

SCHOOLS

Alice Morse Earle wrote of the American schoolroom, "The furnishing was meagre." Even at the end of the eighteenth century George G. Channing of Newport, Rhode Island, found the low, second-floor chamber where he received his early schooling mostly devoid of furniture. There were a desk and some chairs for the use of the teacher and an occasional visitor, but the children "were furnished by their parents with seats made of round blocks of wood, of various heights." Even when better quarters became available, "the furniture was of the most ordinary stamp": "The desks and benches . . . used for the writing exercises, had leaden inkstands in the centre; and their surface was more or less disfigured with rude indentures. . . . The benches without backs, were so tall and shaky as to be very uncomfortable, especially to the shortest boys, whose legs had to be suspended."[216]

References to school benches appear in documents of several types. On the eve of the Revolution schoolmaster Oliver Dale's estate at Charleston, South Carolina, contained "12 school Benches" and "3 writing Tables" for students and a desk for the master. In New England when a special program accompanied the closing of a school term "the audience were seated on the benches of the schoolroom," suggesting that the furniture was movable rather than fixed. Benches of stick or panel construction are not uncommon in artists' renderings of rooms depicting instruction for small children or evening and painting classes for young ladies. A notice from New York in 1800 directed "To Teachers" advised that "a quantity of excellent new School Furniture" consisting of "Writing Desks and Benches little used" was for sale. A new school bench from the shop of Job E. Townsend at Newport, Rhode Island, could cost as little as 2s. 6d. One supplied by Job Danforth of Providence was more expensive at 6s. 8d. The material for this type of seat is recorded in January 1795 in the accounts of the Sanderson brothers of Salem, Massachusetts, as "[Pine Stuff] for 2 school bentches about 8ft each." Illuminating design is an agreement of 1830 made between John Cooper, joiner, and the selectmen of Newburyport. Cooper agreed to construct "forty writing benches and seats for the use of Scholars . . . of good seasoned clear Stuff." The "benches" actually were panel-end desks 30 inches high with a slanting top and an inside shelf "for the purpose of lying in books slates &c of the Scholars." The desk front was enclosed by a panel from the top to a point 16 inches above the floor, where there was a fixed seat 9 inches deep with paneled ends to accommodate the "scholar" at the next forward desk. Interior braces strengthened the structure.[217]

Within a few decades the long school settee with arms and a back had become a commercial article. John C. Hubbard of Boston advertised in 1860 as a manufacturer of settees "FOR HALLS, SCHOOLS, VESTRIES, ETC.," and there is record that Josiah P. Wilder constructed ninety-two long seats for the Appleton Academy at New Ipswich, New Hampshire. A single chair for students also was an important piece of furniture by this date. The *Illustrated London News* commented on a display of New England furniture at the Great Exhibition in 1851, noting particularly "a set of the desks and chairs used in the . . . common schools" and stating, "The chairs are a great improvement on the system of benches." Some chairs had pedestal bases fixed to the floor. Those that stood on four legs sometimes had a leaf for writing or a small box attached at one side for books.[218]

There appears to have been little use of individual seats in American schools before the 1800s except by the schoolmaster. Acquired for the new schoolhouse erected in 1797 at Barkhamstead, Connecticut, were a "plain square table" and a "large fiddle-back chair, painted blue." A school chair supplied in 1808 by William H. Reed of Hampden, Maine, probably also was rush-bottomed. The "chair fraim for the school house" constructed that year at Buckland, Massachusetts, by Joseph Griswold describes the type. For several decades during the early 1800s common rush-bottom seating for schoolhouses appears to have been favored among New England officials, who kept a watchful eye on the town pocketbook, as demonstrated in the accounts of various chairmakers.[219]

Gradually during the 1790s the Windsor chair began to gain popularity for schoolroom use. Representations of the bow-back side chair occur in some renderings of these facilities. One of the best known is Jacob Maentel's portrait of a schoolmaster instructing two young boys in the Bible. Behind the master is a brick red bow-back Windsor with straw-colored penciled "creases." A Baltimore tablet-top Windsor of later date is prominent in a classroom scene forming the frontispiece of the 1818 and 1820 editions of *The Youth's Guide* (fig. **5-64**). Well-appointed urban classrooms of that date offered instruction in social as well as mathematical sciences, and coeduca-

FIG. 5-64 Schoolroom interior. From Mordecai Stewart, *The Youth's Guide* (Baltimore: By the author, 1818), frontispiece. *(Photo courtesy of Special Collections Department, Enoch Pratt Free Library, Baltimore, MD; Photo, Winterthur Museum.)*

tion was part of some curriculums. In the frontispiece illustration a schoolmistress offers the young ladies seated on a bench at the back of the room advice in the execution of their needlework, as the schoolmaster conducts a lesson for boys in the foreground. A tablet-top chair of fancy klismos form appears in a book of penmanship published about 1831 by Carl Friedrich Egelmann at Reading, Pennsylvania, under the title *Deutsche & Englische Vorshriften für die Jugend*. A young female student sits at a table practicing her letters; a bookshelf is on the wall behind her.[220]

Windsor chairs for schools are named in the accounts of several woodworkers. In 1828 James Gere made a schoolhouse chair at Groton, Connecticut. Two years later Caleb Hobart, Jr., billed similar work to town officials at Hingham, Massachusetts: "The Building committee for schoolhouses to C Hobart Jr Dr to 2 Chairs one for the west & one for the east schoolhouse $2.50." Of close date were payments made at Northfield, Vermont, by the military academy, styled Norwich University, to John B. Southmayd for 166 chairs, some called "straight Back." Southmayd also made four book racks for the library, painted a blackboard, and turned seven pairs of drumsticks. Some craftsmen made repairs; legs, stretchers, and arm posts were common replacements.[221]

Several documents provide insights on schoolroom appointments. Schoolmaster Dale of Charleston, South Carolina, owned "a parcel of Reading & School Books" in 1774, which he stored in a bookcase. About the room stood writing tables and a dozen benches accompanied by a desk, probably the master's own. Sarah Anna Emery described the schoolhouse near Newburyport, Massachusetts, that she attended during the 1790s as a small child: "Passing through an entry, furnished with high and low rows of wooden pegs, you entered the school-room. On the left, extended the fire-place; beyond stood the teacher's desk; in front rose tier after tier of clumsy, unpainted desks, front of these, and around the walls were ranged low forms. Six good sized windows lighted the apartment." Emery spoke elsewhere of the teacher's chair as "flag-seated." Lewis Miller, the nineteenth-century chronicler of York, Pennsylvania, drew a comprehensive interior view of the old Lutheran schoolhouse as it appeared early in the century when his father was schoolmaster. Miller's visual description complements the others. Present are three long rectangular tables with plain legs and stretchers. At the end of one stands a pail and drinking cup, a broom propped alongside. The seating consists of three long, backless board benches with panel ends shaped in curves in the German manner. A lone chair occupies a place at one table end. A hanging shelf supports an hourglass. Books and ink pots with quill pens stand on the tables.[222]

The accounts of several New England craftsmen provide a broader look at the boarding and day school of the early nineteenth century. In 1792 Miss Sarah Pierce began a private school for young ladies in her home at Litchfield, Connecticut, which flourished for forty years. The curriculum appears to have been reasonably comprehensive, including studies in the social sciences, grammar, and ciphering, complemented by instruction in the gentle arts—painting and drawing, music, drama, needlework, and dancing. Silas Cheney debited the Pierce account in 1807 for "two embroydery frames," and an embroidery frame on stand followed. Repairs made in the next decade included new seat casings and paint for a settee. Cheney also was patronized by Betsey Collins, who either ran a school or boarded students. In 1820 Cheney debited Collins for the cost of a "Chair with [an] arm to write on & rockers" made for George Jacobs, who is identified as a "Student at Mrs Collins's."[223]

When Miss Mary C. Green set up a school in 1833 in Windsor, Vermont, she found able assistance in the person of Thomas Boynton, a local woodworker. Green purchased eight washstands and tables from Boynton and rented two additional tables, a dozen chairs, and fireplace equipment. The craftsman set up a clock and installed a looking glass. Some students boarded with Boynton, and on one occasion

FIG. 5-65 Baroness Hyde de Neuville, *Female Student at the Economical School*, New York, ca. 1810–14. Pencil on green paper; H. 7½", W. 5¾". *(Collection of The New-York Historical Society, acc. 1953.274.)*

he provided "2 meals for woman to clean school room and a quart of soap washing school room window curtains."[224]

An extensive group of school records originating in New York City in the early 1800s details information about several facilities, of which the earliest was the Economical School founded in 1810 by the baron and baroness Hyde de Neuville for the purpose of instructing children of French refugees from Cuba and Santo Domingo. Other students were admitted, as indicated by a bill of tuition sent to Timothy Green for schooling his daughter Mary during fall and winter 1810–11. Mary Green probably was the young woman who later set up school in Vermont. The bill directed to Timothy Green includes charges for "classical books" and "wood for the winter." During the baroness's tenure at the Economical School, she drew a student working on her copybook while seated on a Windsor chair at a writing table (fig. **5-65**). The chair, of rare flat cross-rod pattern, resembles a Windsor labeled by Reuben Odell, whose Duane Street shop was within blocks of the school.[225]

Curiously the mother of Mary Green, also named Mary, became a school proprietress after the death of her husband, although city directories list her only as a "widow." Identification comes from a group of bills, the earliest dating to 1823 when Mary Green was living in Chambers Street. The contents of Abraham Acker's bill suggest that Mrs. Green was just commencing her new venture:

A Black Board, in a frame	$ 6-50
An Atlass frame	$ 5-50
2 Globe stands @ $2	$ 4-00
1 Double Desk, for 4 young Ladies	$ 6-50
4 Swinging Desks @ $3	$12-00
1 Table D[itt]o	$ 6-00
3 Benches @ $1⅓	$ 4-00
A Tree to hang the young Ladies things on	$ 5-00
	$49-50

Beginning in 1828 Mary Green patronized the firm of William and Jonathan Osborn, where she acquired additional school seating. The purchase of twenty-one stools was followed in 1829 by the acquisition of three Windsor chairs. Repairs to four stools were necessary by 1833.[226]

One of the most complete tabulations of an instructional facility comes from the inventory of Lewis Bancel, who is listed in New York directories between 1821 and 1827 as a "teacher." The document identifies Bancel as owner of "4 Houses in Provost St.," a sizable complex. The premises contained fifty "Cotts with their Covers," a greater number without covers, and almost two dozen broken units, numbers that speak to the size of the boarding school, even without counting day students. Appraisers tabulated a substantial 354 seats. Represented were more than seven dozen "wooden," or Windsor, chairs painted green, yellow, red, or black. The "72 Green bed chairs part Damaged at 3/" apiece may have been cheap Windsors or rush seating with slat backs, although another item identifies thirty-three "Straw" chairs by name. Extending the seating were a large number of wooden seats, some described as "long class benches." Eighty other board-seated units are identified as "red seats or stools" and "Benches for school or Seats." Some were used at the seven "writing tables of 6 places" listed following an entry for two "masters Desks." The school had a number of classrooms because items for large tables and master's desks occur several times in the thirteen-page listing.

Several inventory entries describe the facility. There was a playroom. At mealtime students ate together or in turns at the "long school dining table." Many rooms had window curtains, and carpets covered some floors. More than two dozen glass-globe lamps, some japanned, lighted the premises. Blooming plants in "Sundry flowers Pots from the Green house" lent a cheery atmosphere. The "Fire Engine" owned by the school may have seen double duty as a garden machine.[227]

GOVERNMENTAL USE

Local and County Governments
The durability and economy of the Windsor suggested its use in public facilities and by bodies politic. Although documentation is uncommon, existing references support the practice. Tradition holds that John Letchworth, a chairmaker of Philadelphia, made bow-back Windsors for the local council. A lineal descendant came into possession of a branded chair "about 1898 at Tinicum Quarantine Station, down the Delaware [River], where the old furnishings of the Council Chamber had been stored." William Hornor, Jr., set the chair's date at 1791 and identified its place of use as the new city hall at Fifth and Chestnut streets. Downriver the burgesses of Wilmington, Delaware, cast their lot with Windsor seating at an early date. Borough minutes for October 1775 record a payment to "John Ferriss for 6 Windsor Chairs & Sundries." When the same body furnished the new town hall a quarter century later, municipal leaders turned to Samuel Nichols for chairs. These may have been bow-

back Windsors, although in 1803, when Nichols formed a partnership with George Young, the firm also produced square-back "Bamboo Chairs."[228]

Records of the Common Council of New York chronicle changes in municipal furnishings over a period of 100 years. The earliest purchase was recorded in April 1711 when the municipal body acquired "Eighteen Rush bottom Chairs and an Ovel Table." The seating sufficed until 1722, when the council ordered eighteen "leather chairs" augmented by "a handsome large table" covered by a "fine green broadcloth" purchased in London. Further charges occurred in 1765 when the council acquired twenty-four mahogany chairs for $39 from Andrew Breestead. Five years later the governing body "Cause[d] to be made two large Chairs for the Common Council Chamber the one for the Mayor and the other for the Recorder," described as "2 large Mohogony Arm'd Chairs Carv'd with Compass Backs, Calf skin Bott[om]s." Within two years additional seating augmented the Breestead chairs. A purchase of "3 Windsor Chairs for the Corporation" in 1784 from Thomas and William Ash probably provided seating for council clerks or quarters apart from the council chamber. Not until 1812 were council furnishings changed again. Charles-Honoré Lannuier received $409 to construct mahogany chairs in the neoclassical style. Each council member had a table or "Desk to himself," probably made by William Mandeville, the furniture arranged counterclockwise by wards. The council appears to have moved to quarters in the new city hall designed by John McComb, Jr. Other charges include sums for upholstery, gilding, and two rugs. A year later William Ash supplied forty-eight Windsors at $1 apiece for the new building, and Asa Holden made fancy chairs totaling $103.50.[229]

Courts and other county bodies were substantial consumers of Windsor seating. Following the Revolution Jacob Fetter II supplied the county courthouse at Lancaster, Pennsylvania, with nineteen chairs, as recorded in 1786 by the county treasurer. At almost 8s. apiece the chairs were Windsors rather than rush seating. The furniture was placed in the new courthouse on Centre Square, where in February 1787 the county court took possession of the entire ground floor. At the north end of the room a platform supported the judges' bench. Above it in a gilt frame hung the Pennsylvania coat of arms by the local painter Jacob Eicholtz. The Fetter Windsors may still have been in the courtroom in 1814 when the county commissioner recorded the purchase of "three chairs for Judges," the seats stuffed in linen and covered with red morocco. Certainly, by 1820 the furniture made by Jacob Fetter in 1786 was old and worn and inadequate to fill the needs of an active public facility. The commissioners turned to Elizabeth Weaver (also Weber), who operated the Windsor-chair making business of her late husband, John. The acquisition of "chairs for the court" at a cost of $78 was followed by the purchase for $22 of an additional two dozen chairs. Assuming the chairs were of like pattern and finish, the entire group numbered about 109 chairs. The purchase occurred as the courtroom was being refurbished. By 1852 the old facility was inadequate, and the county commissioners drew plans for a new structure at the corner of Duke and King streets. Local and Philadelphia suppliers provided seating furniture for the new building, designed by Samuel Sloan of Philadelphia.[230]

Across the Susquehanna River the principal town in York County served a rural population, like its neighbor. The carpenter-artist Lewis Miller has left a visual record from the early 1800s of the court of quarter sessions and common pleas in his native York (fig. **5-66**). Prominent in the foreground are almost a dozen green bow-back Windsor chairs. The judges sit elevated above floor level on the "bench" beneath the Pennsylvania coat of arms and flanked by "tipstaves" (bailiffs), identified by their official "poles" to keep order. The lawyers sit within the "bar," the space enclosed by the railing. The jury occupies a long bench at the left, and the court crier is elevated in a box at the right. The clerk of the court occupies a small table in the left rear corner of the bar; the balancing table at the right is that of the witness, who appears

FIG. 5-66 Lewis Miller, *Court of Quarter Sessions and Court of Common Pleas*, York, Pa., ca. 1814–20, depicting scene of 1801. Ink and watercolor on paper. *(The York County Heritage Trust, PA; Photo, Winterthur Museum.)*

FIG. 5-66 Lewis Miller, *Court of Quarter Sessions and Court of Common Pleas*, York, Pa., ca. 1814–20, depicting scene of 1801. Ink and watercolor on paper. *(The York County Heritage Trust, PA; Photo, Winterthur Museum.)*

to be swearing in. The judges have hung their hats on pegs in the tabernacle frame (paneling) above the bench. Isaac Weld, an Englishman interested in the American judicial system, provided insight in the mid-1790s on the conduct of the rural Pennsylvania court:

> On entering into the courts, a stranger is apt to smile at the grotesque appearance of the judges . . . and at their manners on the bench; but . . . there is no country, perhaps, in the world, where justice is more impartially administered. . . . The judges in the country parts of Pennsylvania are . . . plain farmers. . . . The laws expressly declare that there must be, at least, three judges resident in every county; now as the salary allowed is but a mere trifle, no lawyer would accept the office, which of course must be filled from amongst the inhabitants, who are all in a happy state of mediocrity, and on a perfect equality with each other.[231]

Originating closer to Philadelphia is a document dated in March 1825 that identifies Joseph Jones of West Chester as supplying a chair for the local Chester County Courthouse. The craftsman also repaired fourteen chairs. A scene depicting a circuit court session in New York State painted by A. Wighe demonstrates that even at mid-century some isolated rural areas still held public hearings in makeshift quarters. The scene is a barn interior with adults seated on benches, blocks of wood, Windsors, and rush-bottom chairs. Children romp in the haymow.[232]

Rhode Island, the first center of Windsor-chair making in New England, led in the early use of wooden-bottom seating in regional facilities. The area's five county courthouses served on a rotating basis as colony/statehouses, and a considerable number of chairs were required. Timothy Waterhouse supplied the courthouse at Newport (now Colony House) in 1774 with a dozen chairs. In 1783, after the war, the Rhode Island General Assembly directed the sheriffs of Newport and Washington counties to purchase "Three good large Windsor or stick-back chairs, with resting Elbow-Pieces and also Two Dozen of good common Windsor chairs" for their respective courthouses to be funded from the general treasury. Sheriff William Davis of Newport County procured two dozen "Green chears" and a "Large" one with a "high back." Because the twenty-seven "Green Windsor Chairs" acquired for Washington County were purchased in the Newport shop of Joseph Vickary, the Newport County chairs likely came from the same source. General Assembly records also describe Windsor purchases for the Providence Courthouse. Three high-back chairs acquired from Martin Seamans and Henry Bacon in 1769 were accompanied by a dozen armchairs of sack-back or low-back form. Jonathan Cahoone probably supplied the dozen chairs added in 1773. Not until 1797 was this seating supplemented by the purchase of two dozen Windsors for $48 from Kingsley Carpenter.[233]

Rare evidence documenting the *complete* furnishings of a New England county facility dates to 1817, when Essex County officials made an inventory of "County property in the Court House" at Salem, Massachusetts. The seating consisted of six chairs with cushions—five for judges and one for the attorney general, twelve armchairs for the bar, and a selection of general seating that included ten settees and fifty-four painted chairs. The clerk and reporter also had cushions for their seats. Nine tables accommodated the judges, clerk, bar, attorney general, sheriff, and crier. One or more inkstands furnished each. A tall "tree" held hats, and twelve spitting boxes stood on the floor. The fireplace was fully equipped. Two lanterns and twenty-eight candlesticks provided artificial light.[234]

Several decades later, in 1842, H. F. Dewey of Vermont supplied Bennington County with a dozen Windsor side chairs and four matching armchairs at a total cost of $18. The following year Calvin Stetson, a woodworker of Barnstable, Massachusetts, repaired a courthouse chair on Cape Cod. Of interest elsewhere in the state is the survival of a large group of Windsor furniture sold at auction in 1974 from the old Middlesex County Superior Court Building at Cambridge. The structure, erected in 1814, was enlarged, renovated, and refurnished in 1848. John C. Hubbard of Boston received the seating contract, as documented by his stamp on the seats. The order consisted of at least eighty side chairs and a like number of armchairs. At a later date the seats were covered with cushions or stuffed. The accompanying settees of plain tablet top were constructed in part to fill a two-tiered gallery of curved plan (fig. 5-67). Of necessity the seat planks were of segmental form, curved front and back. Four curved settees, each about 10 feet, filled either arced tier. Across the back of the room on a third tier stood three 15-foot settees with straight planks. In Woodstock, Vermont, thirty-eight long settees with legs set chairwise placed in the town hall and county courthouse probably during the 1840s were products of the local shop of John White.[235]

Evidence of Windsor furnishings in southern courthouses begins with Delaware, a border state, where a levy court docket for Sussex County records a series of purchases during the 1790s. Two expenditures posted in November 1794 document the acquisition of "24 good Windsor stools" and "3 arm chairs with cushions," the cushions loose or fixed. Four years later the county purchased three cushions for judges' chairs. At Wake County, North Carolina, court minutes for 1807 record a payment to chairmaker David Ruth for providing "two Arm chairs & cuting the Bench in the Court House." Similar records originating in Davidson County, Tennessee, in 1813 document Joseph Saunders's sale of a dozen Windsors to the county for courtroom use. Court records for Richmond, Virginia, identify services performed in spring 1820 by Windsor-chair maker Robert McKim, who furnished the court with a dozen chairs fitted with "stuffed seats." Each chair cost more than $5, reflecting the extra labor and materials required for stuffing and suggesting the chairs had arms.[236]

Midwestern and Canadian records point to a similar pattern of furnishing public facilities with Windsor seating. At Chillicothe, Ohio, James Phillips was in business

about four years in 1802 when the court of general quarter sessions called on him to supply twenty-four Windsor chairs at $2 each. Chillicothe was the governmental center of the Northwest Territory, and the courthouse had just been completed. W. D. Rand's midcentury advertisement for his "STEAM CHAIR FACTORY" at Louisville, Kentucky, lists seating furniture for many uses and makes specific reference to outfitting "Public Offices." Windsor benches are said to have been prevalent in New Brunswick, Canada, where they were used "in County Court Houses, Lodge rooms, and other public places."[237]

State Governments
Almost nowhere in American public life was the Windsor more popular than in the statehouse. Capitol buildings from New Hampshire to Georgia to Iowa employed Windsor seating successfully, especially during the early years of statehood. Philadelphia records document the use of Windsor furniture by the Pennsylvania Assembly prior to statehood. On October 18, 1775, this representative body ordered that "one Dozen and a half of Windsor Chairs be immediately procurred for the Use of the House." Rush-bottom seating of earlier date probably then furnished the provincial chambers. These first Windsors of record for the Pennsylvania Statehouse (now Independence Hall) came from the shop of Francis Trumble, who received payment the following March for a dozen chairs and two tables. The furniture may have been used initially in an upstairs committee room.[238]

When Philadelphia was occupied by British forces during the Revolution, between September 1777 and June 1778, the statehouse served as a prison and hospital. There was general destruction of the furnishings and premises. In July 1778, after the British evacuation, the Pennsylvania Supreme Executive Council, the state governing body, directed that the building be "cleansed . . . for the reception of Council." Upon finding "that there are no Chairs therein," the body "Ordered, that the Secretary procure eighteen Windsor Chairs for the Council Room." Within a month the council had received nineteen Windsors made by Francis Trumble for its second-floor quarters. A week later Trumble received payment on behalf of the House of Representatives for a new group of Windsors, which cost comparison identifies as twenty-five chairs. This order was followed by twenty Windsors in November. Hornor describes all of

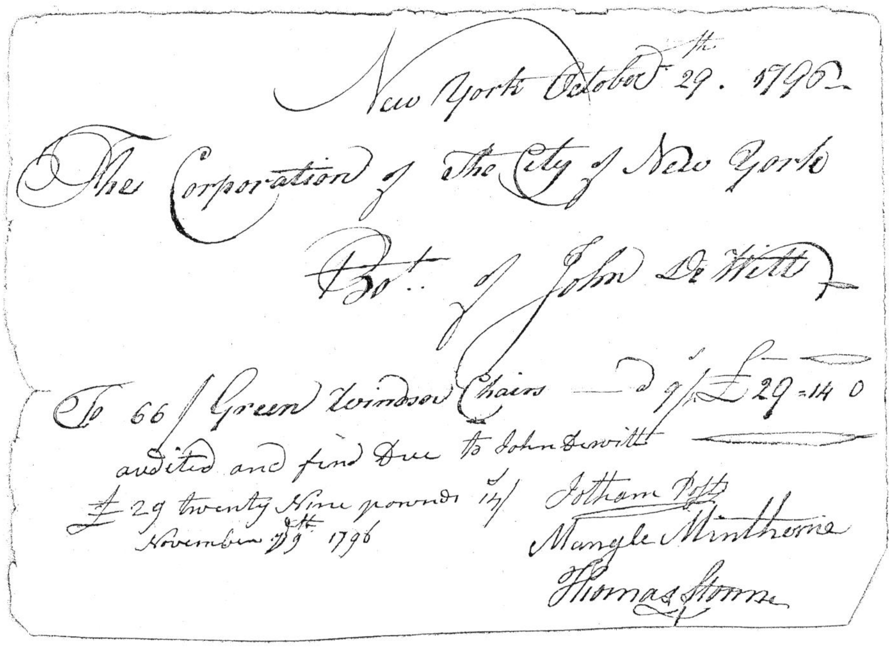
New York October 29th. 1796

The Corporation of the City of New York

Bot. of John DeWitt

To 66 Green Windsor Chairs — 9/ £29=14 0

audited and find Due to John Dewitt

£29 twenty Nine pounds 14/ Jotham Post

November 7th 1796 Mangle Minthorne

Thomas Storm

FIG. 5-68 John DeWitt bill to the Corporation of the City of New York, October 29, 1796. *(Historical Documents Collection, Queens College, Flushing, N.Y.)*

the seating supplied by Trumble in 1778 as low-backs and sack-backs, the latter of plain or "Scrol" arm. Michael Kurtz had by this date been paid for making benches, although as he was not a Windsor-chair maker, the seats probably were of board-end construction. John Pinkerton, who made two settees in July 1779 for the statehouse courtroom, filled a similar order for the house of representatives the next January. A dozen years elapsed before the number of statehouse seats was increased. In 1791 the state senate made a large purchase at a cost of £61.5 from Joseph Henzey. Neither pattern or unit price is given, but if the chairs were bow-backs with arms—the prevailing fashion—and priced at 12*s.* apiece, their number would have exceeded 100. If side chairs, the total could have reached 150.[239]

I. N. Phelps Stokes has amplified the use of furniture by the state government of New York. Joseph Powell of New York City made two bookcases and a large table in 1768 for the General Assembly. In the postwar years the city's Common Council minutes record a mayoral warrant of November 14, 1796, on the city treasurer authorizing the payment of £29.14 to "John DeWitt for Windsor Chairs for [the] Senate & Assembly Rooms," then located in city hall. Miraculously, DeWitt's original bill of October 29 for sixty-six green Windsors priced at 9*s.* apiece survives (fig. **5-68**).[240]

John Wadsworth made Windsor furniture the same year for the new Connecticut Statehouse at Hartford. The first floor housed a courtroom and offices for state officials, including the governor. The second story contained small quarters for the secretary of state and two large chambers to seat the house of representatives and senate. Lemeul Adams and Samuel Kneeland, cabinetmakers of Hartford, independently constructed mahogany and cherry furniture for the senate—seating, tables, a desk, and two "vote boxes." Windsor-chair maker John Wadsworth made and refurbished furniture for the representatives' chamber. Newton Brainard has written that the house speaker presided from a platform on the north wall of the room and the representatives sat on green-painted settees facing a central aisle. Twenty-five long seats made by Wadsworth may have supplemented settees brought from the old courthouse. One dozen new "Green painted Chamber Chairs" listed in the bill possibly were dispersed throughout the building for use by officials, judges, and others. Wadsworth also painted eighteen chairs belonging to the old county courthouse, which may have been returned to the facility in the new building. In 1797 the craftsman supplied another three dozen chairs. The unit price of $1.42 equaled the individual charge of 8s. 6d. for the first dozen, suggesting the new chairs were similar. Brainard also illustrates a side chair branded on the bottom with the state seal. The double-rod square-back pattern suggests the chairs were acquired in the early 1800s.[241]

More than a decade later another New England statehouse furnished its rooms with painted seating. The Concord, New Hampshire, firm of William Low and Benjamin Damon billed "The State of New Hampshire" in 1819 for a large group of seating furniture comprising 182 chairs, three cushions, and eleven settees. Half a dozen of the Windsors had arms, and the substantial unit price of $2.75 reflects the sum of their special features: a painted state seal in the crest, fancy spindles and front stretcher, mahogany arms, and a framed, webbed, and upholstered seat. Porter Blanchard, a local cabinetmaker, also supplied furniture for the statehouse, including two large circular tables for the senate chamber and several desks for state officials.[242]

Chairmakers in southern capitals knew considerable business from state contracts. In Dover, Delaware, Christopher Horton, a woodworking enigma, was named in records in autumn 1791 when the state was completing its facility, and then he mysteriously disappeared. The craftsman rendered bills for two dozen Windsor chairs for the house of representatives, each priced at 6s. 10d., and eighteen for the senate at 11s. 3d. apiece. Clearly, one group had arms and the other did not. Both legislative chambers were located on the second floor of the new Capitol. Evidence for the use of Windsor seating in the Maryland Statehouse at Annapolis comes from two sources. In January 1784 a lawyer and businessman of Baltimore shipped five dozen chairs, probably of high-back pattern in view of the 21s. 3d. unit cost, down the bay to Annapolis for use by the legislature. About fifteen years later armchairs of the fashionable bow-back pattern were introduced to the same building. A related side chair is said to have come from an Eastern Shore courthouse at Princess Anne. The Richmond chairmakers Andrew and Robert McKim were solicited by the state of Virginia in 1802 to supply half a dozen Windsor chairs and "2 tall Stools" for the superintendent's office at the Virginia manufactory of arms.[243]

David Ruth's business relationship with the state of North Carolina began in 1795 when he made two dozen chairs for the treasurer's and comptroller's offices in Raleigh. The 13s. 6d. unit cost suggests the chairs had arms. A decade passed before Ruth made ten tables and six wooden sconces and completed odd jobs on state property. Later he supplied another "1 dozen sitting chairs" for the treasurer's office. Tragedy struck in 1810 when Ruth lost his left hand in an accident; however, this did not end his association with the state. He drew pay in 1818 as "Ranger of Public Grounds," and in 1820 he continued maintenance and repair work on the statehouse premises. In the early 1820s C. J. Tooker of Raleigh won the contract "to furnish the Capitol of North Carolina."[244]

Another commission of the early 1800s was John Furlow's work in the Gothic-style Georgia Statehouse erected in 1807 at Milledgeville. A letter written on September 26, 1812, by the chairman of the Board of State Commissioners to the governor identifies the work: "We have to request your Excellency to give Mr. Jno. Furlow another warrant on the Treasury for the sum of eighty four dollars . . . for forty two Windsor chairs at two dollars each in addition to those heretofore made & delivered by him for the use of the Senate & House of Representatives, agreeably to . . . a resolution of the Legislature passed the 15th Decem. 1810 requiring . . . suitable desks & seats in the Senate & Representatives Chambers."[245]

James Phillips, the Chillicothe chairmaker who secured the courthouse commission in 1802, worked for the territorial government the same year constructing three dozen chairs for the Ohio legislature. As reported by the *Indiana Journal* on April 19, 1824, the chamber of the state house of representatives at Indianapolis contained "a painted Windsor chair and a table with a drawer" for each member. Another western government, the territory of Iowa, ordered a large quantity of seating from the Saint Louis firm of Lynch and Trask for its temporary Capitol at Burlington in 1839, seven years before the region achieved statehood. As both cities lie along the Mississippi River, steamboat transport furnished a reliable, economical method of conveying the goods upriver. The order covers a broad range of seating: "Twenty Six Cane Chairs" probably were intended for the house of representatives, which body contained a like number of members. The dozen "flagg Chairs" likely were employed by the twelve members of the senate. The half dozen Windsor chairs may have been for office or courtroom use, and at $2 apiece they were armchairs of contemporary pattern. The two mahogany chairs of the order were suitable for the governor's office, and a rocking chair may have joined them. The settee with cushion was an appropriate seat for a reception area. Also distributed throughout the premises were "Forty Spittoons."[246]

The Federal Government

When the First Continental Congress convened in Carpenters' Hall, Philadelphia, in September 1774, the group made good use of the hall's furnishings, consisting in part of tables made by members of the Carpenters' Company and Windsor chairs, probably in the sack-back style, purchased from Joseph Henzey earlier in the year. Sack-back chairs in the Company's possession today bear the branded name "CAR-PENTERS.CO." on the plank bottoms, made by an iron purchased in 1779. A pair of long-legged high-back chairs is similarly marked (fig. **5-69**). By tradition these chairs were used by the Continental Congress, a legend strengthened by a nineteenth-century gilt inscription printed on the crest faces, which reads "Continental Congress. / 1774." John Fanning Watson, a local nineteenth-century antiquarian, commented on the same chairs in describing Carpenters' Hall: "In the first story the first Continental Congress assembled, and among the furniture preserved that was in use by Congress are two very high-backed quaint arm-chairs." There was enough time prior to the convening of Congress on September 5 for the Carpenters' Company to have acquired these "special" chairs for use by that body. As early as August 30 John Adams described Carpenters' Hall as the place "where Congress is to sit," although the "official" choice between that building and the statehouse had yet to be made. A week's time would have been sufficient to construct the two chairs. As the Carpenters had dealt earlier with Joseph Henzey, he would have been the logical choice, and reasonable similarities exist between the tall chairs and Henzey's regular high-back production. Because the tall chair seats are 25¼ inches from the floor, they were used with a footstool or low bench. Peyton Randolph was chosen president of Congress, and Charles Thomson secretary. Whether the secretary would have used a tall chair is debatable. During the upheaval of the Revolution, the Carpenters apparently removed their furnishings from the hall.[247]

When the delegates returned to Philadelphia for the Second Continental Congress in spring 1775, they met on the first floor of the statehouse. The Pennsylvania Assembly is said to have moved across the hall to the supreme court room during the remainder of their session, leaving furnishings and equipment behind for the use of Congress. The nature of the seating in the assembly room at this date is uncertain, as Francis Trumble had not yet begun his Windsor work. It is likely that in 1775 the assemblymen still sat on rush-bottom chairs. State records show payments to Thomas Ackley in 1760 and 1761 for a total of two dozen rush chairs priced at 5s. apiece. The seating was on the premises when Congress met, as indicated by a payment in 1776 to John Fiss for rebottoming six chairs. A large number of tables, probably covered with baize, were arranged around the room, and an elevated platform supported the presiding officer. The tables had writing equipment and lighting devices for night sessions, and a chandelier possibly hung in the center of the room.

FIG. 5-69 Long-legged high-back Windsor armchair (one of pair), Philadelphia, ca. 1774. H. 53⅞", (seat) 25¼", W. (crest) 25¹⁄₁₆", (arms) 26", (seat) 23", D. (seat) 17½". *(Collection of The Carpenters' Company of the City and County of Philadelphia; Photo, Winterthur Museum.)*

Popple's large map of North America dominated one wall. In cold weather two ten-plate, cast-iron stoves and pipes supplemented the heat from a pair of fireplaces. From the 1740s curtains hung at the windows to alleviate the echo in the high-ceiled room. Behind the speaker's platform hung the carved arms of the Penn family. The Second Continental Congress met in a split session from May 10 to August 1 and again from September 5 to December 30. When the Pennsylvania Assembly reconvened in the autumn, it was not in the supreme court room but in the cramped quarters of a small upstairs committee room. Francis Trumble supplied two tables and twelve Windsor chairs for their use.[248]

A distinguished national body occupied the assembly room of the statehouse in 1776, with John Hancock its elected "President," or speaker. The furnishings probably had not changed significantly, as only a few months had elapsed since the close of the Second Continental Congress. One small piece of furniture introduced to the room was a table-top "Desk for congress" purchased by John Hancock for 25s. from David Evans. Another colorful addition hung suspended over the door. It was a naval standard of yellow ground bearing "a lively representation of a rattlesnake . . . in the attitude of going to strike, and [the] words . . . 'Don't tread on me.'" What occurred on July 4 and the events leading to and following adoption of the Declaration of Independence by the Continental Congress are historical fact. Less clear are the origin and date of a painted canvas that depicts members of the Continental Congress seated in sack-back Windsor chairs in the assembly room (fig. **5-70**). *Congress Voting Independence* may be a painting begun by Robert Edge Pine (d. 1788), who emigrated from England in 1784, although some sources say that canvas was destroyed by fire. Edward Savage either completed the Pine work or produced another.[249]

Whether Windsor chairs were in the assembly room when Congress voted independence is open to question. The Pennsylvania Assembly had acquired Windsor chairs from Francis Trumble in autumn 1775, although presumably the members placed them on the second floor of the statehouse for their own use. Evidence already outlined suggests there were only rush-bottom chairs downstairs where Congress met. When Robert Edge Pine arrived from England in 1784, the seating in place at the time of the historic vote had all been destroyed or carried off during the British occupation of the city (September 1777 to June 1778). It was following the occupation that Trumble supplied several more groups of Windsors, some in the sack-back style. These are the chairs that Pine or Savage would have seen during visits to the statehouse. Still, the sack-back chair with *bamboo supports*, as depicted, is rare if not unknown in Philadelphia Windsor work. This new leg style of the mid-1780s was actually the support of the bow-back armchair. Given the small size of the canvas and the amount of detail, however, bamboowork was a logical "artistic" choice. Trumble's sack-back Windsors ordered in 1778 and the tall mahogany "Speaker's" chair made by John Folwell the following year comprised the seating that members of the Federal Constitutional Convention found in place in the statehouse assembly room on May 14, 1787, when they convened at Philadelphia.

The new United States government, when formed, settled temporarily in New York City, where the First Congress was in session by early April 1789. Washington was inaugurated as the nation's first president on April 30, taking the oath on the balcony of a newly renovated and renamed Federal Hall at Broad and Wall streets. Little is known about the structure's furnishings aside from a body of high-style mahogany and upholstered furniture in the French and English tastes, which tradition says was used there. A contemporary description of the building interior touches on the furnishings in noting the sophistication and elegance of several public rooms. The representatives sat in an octagonal chamber decorated in the Ionic order. Separate chairs and desks were ranged in two semicircular rows in front of a raised Speaker's chair. Curtains and upholstery were of light blue damask. The senators sat on "26 stuffed Chairs," possibly of crimson damask to match the window curtains and a canopy above the "President's" chair. Painted seating probably was placed in the library, lobbies, committee rooms, and guards' quarters that completed the facility.[250]

In 1790 the First Congress met in its third session at Philadelphia on Statehouse Square in a building erected as a county courthouse, now known as Congress Hall. The House of Representatives occupied the first floor, where Henry Wansey noted a seating plan of three semicircular rows, similar to that in New York, with "every member . . . accommodated for writing by . . . a circular . . . desk." Furnishing bills describe desks and armchairs of mahogany. Carpeting was on the floor, Venetian blinds at the windows. Stoves provided heat. The Senate chamber was more elaborate. Another document dated November 17, 1790, titled "Articles of Furniture Necessary to be provided for the Committee-rooms and Clerk's Office of the House of Representatives" provides insights into the furnishings of the auxiliary rooms in Congress Hall. Provision was made for "1 dozen Chairs" for each committee room. Appended to the entry is the name "Wm. Coxe," a local Windsor-chair maker. Each group of chairs was placed around a "pine table covered with green baise, 8 feet long by 3½ feet in width" on which stood a "complete wooden inkstand." Also planned for each committee room was a "double Book press" (bookcase) of pine "with sliding divisions." Another dozen of Cox's Windsors were ordered for the clerk's office and adjoining room. Three smaller tables were acquired for this suite along with two double bookcases and "3 pewter Ink pieces."[251]

When the federal government moved in 1800 to its permanent home at Washington, the city was still in its infancy, and construction moved slowly. Thomas P.

Cope of Philadelphia was pleased with the Capitol, although it was incomplete. He remarked on the "symmetry, elegance & architectural magnificence" of the Senate chamber, where crimson moreen upholstery contrasted with white walls and ceiling. Hardly less rich in appearance was President and Mrs. Madison's drawing room with its elegant painted furniture made by the Finlay brothers of Baltimore for the White House ("President's House"). Less costly but rich in effect were the gilt Windsor chairs and settee ordered for the new congressional library room after destruction of that facility during the War of 1812 (fig. 5-60).[252]

Many government offices and departments required furnishing, and a practical solution was painted seating. Philadelphia shipping records for 1800–1801 describe several furniture freights for the Navy Department. In June 1800 the schooner *Olive Branch* carried a table, writing desk, and seventeen Windsor chairs to Georgetown for delivery to the capital. The following year "Eighteen packages Fancy Chairs" (probably thirty-six) were shipped as per "Secret[ar]y of the Navy's Order — Wash[ington]." The Department of War made a series of local purchases in 1814 beginning with an upholstered mahogany stool supplied by William Worthington in May. There followed in the autumn six tables and four desks, three of the latter no more than slant-top boxes for table use, judging by the cost. Late in the year the department acquired two groups of seating from chairmaker Thomas Adams of Georgetown. Described as "Single Tops" and "Flat Tops" at $1.50 and $2 apiece, the patterns probably followed Philadelphia and Baltimore Windsor designs.[253]

One department that remained in Philadelphia after the government moved to Washington was the United States Mint, where David Rittenhouse was the first mintmaster. The facility on Seventh Street between Market and Arch was occupied in summer 1792. Movable furniture included twelve Windsor chairs "in the clerks rooms" bought in March 1794 from Joseph Burden for 7s. 6d. apiece. In October Sims and Barnitt provided a desk and table "for the Director and Assayer's Office."[254]

Another branch of government that was a consumer of painted seating was the military. Within months of the Louisiana Territory purchase on December 20, 1803, the brig *Hannah* sailed from Philadelphia carrying "military stores for the Posts at New Orleans." "One Settee" was part of the cargo. In another setting a watercolor view of Fort Smith, Arkansas, taken in 1821 by Samuel Seymour of Philadelphia depicts a male figure lolling on a Windsor side chair in front of a barracks-like wooden building. Canadian records also describe the use of inexpensive seating at military sites. Kingston on Lake Ontario became a principal naval base for the British during the War of 1812, and as a result the facility was considerably enlarged and improved. In 1814 the military sought the services of a contractor to build one hundred tables each for the barracks and officers and "200 cane or rush bottomed Chairs, painted black." The following year the commissariat office in York (Toronto), at the western end of the lake, advertised to fill similar needs for "the Barracks Department."[255]

NOTES

1. Dr. John Baker estate records, 1797, New York, Joseph Downs Collection of Manuscripts and Printed Ephemera, Winterthur Museum and Library, Winterthur, Del. (hereafter cited DCM and WL).

2. Patrick Gordon estate records, 1736, City and County of Philadelphia, Pa., Register of Wills; William Bell estate records, 1745, City and County of Philadelphia, Register of Wills (microfilm, DCM; reference courtesy of Wendy Kaplan); William Fishbourne, Samuel Coates, and Samuel Powell estate records, 1742, 1748, and 1750, Philadelphia, as quoted in Arthur W. Leibundguth, "The Furniture-Making Crafts in Philadelphia, ca. 1730–1760" (master's thesis, University of Delaware, 1964), p. 43; Matilda Oliver estate records, 1746, City and County of Philadelphia, Register of Wills (microfilm, DCM; reference courtesy of Arlene Palmer Schwind).

3. Edward Jarvis, "Traditions and Reminiscences of Concord, Massachusetts, . . . 1779 to 1878," ca. 1878–84, Concord Free Public Library, Concord, Mass. (hereafter cited CFPL).

4. Kenneth Roberts and Anna M. Roberts, eds. and trans., *Moreau de St. Méry's American Journey, [1793–1798]* (Garden City, N.Y.: Doubleday, 1947), pp. 263–64.

5. Susanna Dillwyn Emlen letters to William Dillwyn, January 11, 1796, and May 20, 1797, Dillwyn Correspondence, 1770–1818, Historical Society of Pennsylvania (on deposit from the Library Company of Philadelphia [hereafter cited LCP]), Philadelphia (hereafter cited HSP).

6. Samuel Emlen letters to William Dillwyn, January 22, April 2, and July 6, 1798, Dillwyn Correspondence.

7. Susanna Dillwyn Emlen letter to William Dillwyn, May 4, 1800, Dillwyn Correspondence.

8. Lois A. Card letter to Francis S. Peabody, September 29, 1844, DCM.

9. Abraham Lodge estate records, 1758 (1750?), New York, as quoted in Esther Singleton, *Social New York under the Georges, 1714–1776* (New York: D. Appleton, 1902), p. 66, and Irving Whitall Lyon, *Colonial Furniture of New England* (1891; reprint, Boston: Houghton Mifflin, 1924), p. 177; Whitehead Fish estate records, 1819, New York, DCM.

10. James Barron estate records, 1803, New York, DCM; Andrew Oliver estate records, 1774, Boston, Mass., as quoted in Alice Hanson Jones, *American Colonial Wealth*, 3 vols. (New York: Arno Press, 1977), 2:966–71; Thomas Ogden property assignment, 1833, Chester Co., Pa., as quoted in Margaret Berwind Schiffer, *Furniture and Its Makers of Chester County, Pennsylvania* (Philadelphia: University of Pennsylvania Press, 1966), pp. 180–82; William Corbit and Dr. Henry Latimer estate records,

1818 and 1820, New Castle Co., Del., DCM; Thomas Mifflin estate records, 1800, Philadelphia, as quoted in William MacPherson Hornor, Jr., *Blue Book: Philadelphia Furniture* (1935; reprint, Washington, D.C.: Highland House, 1977), p. 312.

11. Mann Page letter and invoice to John Norton and Sons, February 22, 1770, as quoted in Frances Norton Mason, ed., *John Norton and Sons Merchants of London and Virginia* (Richmond: Dietz Press, 1937), pp. 123–25; James Brice ledger, 1767–1801, privately owned (microfilm, Maryland Hall of Records, Annapolis; reference courtesy of Karin E. Peterson); Fielding Lewis, Sr., estate records, 1781, Fredericksburg, Va., Kenmore Association, Fredericksburg (reference courtesy of Betsy Connell); Joseph Prentis estate records, 1809, Williamsburg, Va., Swem Library, College of William and Mary, Williamsburg (hereafter cited WM).

12. Drs. John Sprague I and II, and Rebecca Sprague estate records, 1797, 1812, and 1813, Dedham, Mass., John Sprague Papers, American Antiquarian Society, Worcester, Mass.

13. Nathaniel Coleman estate records, 1842, Burlington, N.J., DCM; Capt. Jonathan Dalton estate records, 1803, Newburyport, Mass., Papers of James Locke, Peabody Essex Museum, Salem, Mass. (hereafter cited PEM); John Knowles estate records, 1778, Chester Co., Pa., as quoted in Margaret Berwind Schiffer, *Chester County, Pennsylvania, Inventories, 1684–1850* (Exton, Pa.: Schiffer Publishing, 1974), pp. 319–22.

14. Baker estate records; Johannah Beekman estate records, 1821, New York, DCM.

15. Samuel Townsend estate records, 1826, New York, DCM; Isaac Weld, *Travels through the States of North America*, 2 vols. (London: John Stockdale, 1800), 1:156.

16. Joseph Galloway and Samuel Shoemaker estate records, 1778, Philadelphia, as quoted in Thomas Lynch Montgomery, ed., *Pennsylvania Archives*, sixth series, vol. 12 (Harrisburg, Pa.: Harrisburg Publishing Co., 1907), pp. 511–16, 721–29; Isaac Pennock estate records, 1824, Chester Co., Pa., as quoted in Schiffer, *Chester County Inventories*, pp. 202–3, 346–47; Dr. John Sprague I estate records.

17. Robert C. Alberts, *The Golden Voyage: The Life and Times of William Bingham, 1752–1804* (Boston: Houghton Mifflin, 1969), pp. 162, 467; Andrew Oliver estate records.

18. John Coxe estate records, 1753, Trenton, N.J., DCM; William Bird estate records, 1763, Berks Co., Reading, Pa., Register of Wills.

19. Inventory terms found in the following: James Gilpin estate records, 1798, Wilmington, Del., Ferris Collection, Friends Historical Library, Swarthmore College, Swarthmore, Pa.; William Jones estate records, 1789, Chester Co., Pa., as quoted in Schiffer, *Chester County Inventories*, pp. 328–29; Galloway estate re-

cords; Edward Cutbush estate records, 1790, Philadelphia, as quoted in Hornor, *Blue Book*, p. 298.

20. Inventory analysis based on the following: Jones estate records; William Miller, Rees Peters, Thomas Potts, and Thomas Pim, Sr., estate records, 1781, 1784, 1785 and 1786, Chester Co., Pa., DCM; Joseph Richardson, Bernard Shomo, and William Will estate records, 1784, 1794, and 1799, Philadelphia, DCM; Joseph Galloway, Alexander Bartram, Oswell Eve, Melchoir Meng, Samuel Shoemaker, John Clark, John Turner estate records, 1778–80, Philadelphia, as quoted in Montgomery, *Pennsylvania Archives*, sixth series, vol. 12, pp. 504–782; Stephen Carmick and Joseph Frazer estate records, 1774, Philadelphia, and Andrew Caldwell estate records, 1774, Kent Co., Del., as quoted in Jones, *American Colonial Wealth*, 1:232–46, 269–72, 370–74; Robert Smith estate records, 1777, Philadelphia, Robert Smith Estate, American Philosophical Society, Philadelphia, Pa. (hereafter cited APS); Gilpin estate records. Dining chair colors are also given in Hornor, *Blue Book*, pp. 298–99. Graeme Park inventory, 1778, Philadelphia Co., as quoted in Montgomery, *Pennsylvania Archives*, pp. 647–60.

21. William Hemphill estate records, 1817, Chester Co., Pa., as quoted in Schiffer, *Chester County Inventories*, pp. 337–42.

22. Wait Garret account book, 1810–58, Connecticut State Library, Hartford (hereafter cited CSL).

23. Frederick Wollffe and John Pell estate records, 1776 and 1804, New York, DCM; Baker estate records.

24. Samuel Parker estate records, 1773, Suffolk Co., Boston, Mass., Registry of Probate (microfilm, DCM). For a discussion of the Philadelphia trade in Windsors to Boston in the 1770s, see Nancy Goyne Evans, *American Windsor Chairs* (New York: Hudson Hills Press, 1996), pp. 244–45.

25. Ansel Goodrich, *Hampshire Gazette* (Northampton, Mass.), September 16, 1795; Amos Denison Allen memorandum book, 1796–1803, Connecticut Historical Society, Hartford (hereafter cited CHS).

26. Frank Chouteau Brown, "The Joseph Barrell Estate, Sommerville, Massachusetts, Charles Bulfinch's First Country House," *Old-Time New England* 38, no. 3 (January 1948): 53–62; Dean A. Fales, Jr., "Joseph Barrell's Pleasant Hill," in *Publications of the Colonial Society of Massachusetts* 43 (Boston: By the society, 1966), pp. 373–90.

27. Fales, "Pleasant Hill," pp. 373–90; Joseph Barrell letter book, 1791–97, Massachusetts Historical Society, Boston (hereafter cited MHS; microfilm, DCM).

28. Andrew Myrick estate records, 1783, Nantucket Co., Nantucket, Mass., Registry of Probate.

29. Elias Hasket Derby estate records, 1799–1805, Essex Co., Salem, Mass., Registry of Probate.

30. Lambert Hitchcock estate records, 1852, Farmington, Conn., Genealogical Section, CSL.

31. Sara Josepha Hale, *Northwood, or Life North and South* (Boston, 1827), as quoted in Eleanor H. Gustafson, ed., "Clues and Footnotes," *Antiques* 114, no. 5 (November 1978): 958.

32. George Frost estate records, 1815, Rockingham Co., Exeter, N.H., Registry of Probate; Christopher Marshall, Jr., estate records, 1807, Philadelphia, Daniel Parker Papers, HSP; Cedar Grove in *The Aldine* 4 (April 1872), as quoted in Wendell Garrett, ed., "Clues and Footnotes," *Antiques* 105, no. 4 (April 1974): 921.

33. Coxe estate records; Alice Cary, *Clovernook, or Recollections of Our Neighborhood in the West* (New York, 1854), as quoted in Wendell Garrett, ed., "Clues and Footnotes," *Antiques* 8, no. 3 (September 1975): 456–57.

34. Bird estate records; Joseph James estate records, 1767, Woodstown, N.J., DCM.

35. Joseph Brown estate records 1774, Philadelphia, as quoted in Jones, *American Colonial Wealth*, 1:259–60; Will Moore estate records, 1783, Chester Co., Pa., as quoted in Schiffer, *Chester County Inventories*, pp. 322–25; Spanish ambassador in Hornor, *Blue Book*, pp. 147, 298.

36. George Shaw estate records, 1792, City and County of Philadelphia, Register of Wills (photostat, DCM); John Cogswell estate records, 1818, Boston, DCM; Daniel Proud estate records, 1833, Providence, R.I., as quoted in William Mitchell Pillsbury, "The Providence Furniture Making Trade, 1772–1834" (master's thesis, University of Delaware, 1975), p. 124; Stephen Collins estate records, 1794, Philadelphia, Parker Papers.

37. Hemphill and Latimer estate records; Ann Lewis estate records, 1825, City and County of Philadelphia, Register of Wills (microfilm, DCM).

38. Charles Ward Apthorp estate records, 1797, Bloomingdale, N.Y., DCM; William Ryder estate records, 1806, New York, DCM; M. and R. Brenan, *Charleston Courier* (Charleston, S.C.), November 7, 1810, citation file, Museum of Early Southern Decorative Arts, Winston-Salem, N.C. (hereafter cited MESDA); Alexander(?) Patterson and Joshua(?) Dennis, *New-York Evening Post* (New York), September 9, 1810 (reference courtesy of Michael Brown); Thomas Marston estate records, 1814, New York, DCM; homespun carpet in Philip P. Tunison estate records, 1813, Somerville, N.J., DCM.

39. Eliakim Prindall estate records, 1824, Gloucester, Mass., Papers of Daniel Rogers, Jr., PEM; Nathaniel Coleman biography in Carl M. Williams, *Silversmiths of New Jersey, 1700–1825* (Philadelphia: George S. MacManus, 1949), pp. 25–31.

40. Harriet Connor Brown, *Grandmother Brown's Hundred Years, 1827–1927* (New York: Blue Ribbon Books, 1929), p. 27.

41. Benjamin Coats estate records, 1774, Boston, as quoted in Jones, *American Colonial Wealth*, 2:907–9; Nicholas Lechmere, Capt. Linn Martin, Col. Joseph Wanton, Jr., and William Wanton estate records, 1779, Newport, R.I., Rhode Island State Archives, Providence (hereafter cited RISA; photostats, DCM); Daniel Danforth and Isaac Wright estate records, 1808 and 1838, Hartford, Conn., Genealogical Section, CSL.

42. Pennsylvania fraktur by Carl Münch in National Gallery of Art, Washington, D.C.; "Reminiscences of Mrs. Elizabeth Calder Rock" (b. 1828), privately owned, as quoted in Wendell Garrett, ed., "Clues and Footnotes," *Antiques* 104, no. 6 (December 1973): 1101.

43. Inventory analysis based on the following: Hugh Ferguson and John Roberts estate records, 1778, Philadelphia Co., as quoted in Montgomery, *Pennsylvania Archives*, pp. 511–16, 653–60, 710–21; Peters, Smith, Will, Galloway, Latimer, Hemphill, and Collins estate records; Owen Jones(?) estate records, ca. 1793, Philadelphia, Owen Jones Papers, HSP; Timothy Hanson estate records, 1798, Wilmington, Del., State of Delaware, Division of Historical and Cultural Affairs, Hall of Records, Dover (hereafter cited DDHCA); William Levis estate records, 1784, Chester Co., Pa., James Dorman estate records, 1824, Woodbury, N.J., and Samuel Claphamson estate records, 1808, Philadelphia Co., Pa., DCM; Charles Willing and James Jefferis estate records, 1799 and 1822, Chester Co., Pa., as quoted in Schiffer, *Chester County Inventories*, pp. 331–33, 337–42, 397–98; Benjamin Love estate records, 1821, Philadelphia Co., Pa., Register of Wills (microfilm, DCM); Ogden property assignment.

44. Landon Carter estate records, 1779, Sabin Hall, Va., WM; Prentis estate records; George Basil Spencer estate records, 1791, Savannah, Ga., as quoted in Mrs. Charleton M. Theus, *Savannah Furniture, 1735–1825* (n.p.: By the author, ca. 1967), pp. 17–18.

45. Patterson and Dennis, *New-York Evening Post*, September 9, 1810 (reference courtesy of Michael Brown).

46. Baker estate records; William Constable estate records, 1803, New York, DCM.

47. Bates and Johnson in B. Pearce, *The Albany Directory* (Albany, N.Y.: E. and E. Hosford, 1819), n.p.; Gerard Beekman estate records, 1833, New York, DCM; Robert Troup estate records, 1832, New York, Papers of Robert Troup, New York Public Library, New York (hereafter cited NYPL).

48. "Account of Sund'y Articles Left at Ashford March ye 1st 1775," prob. Massachusetts, DCM; William Wanton estate records.

49. Derby estate records; Jacob Sanderson estate records, 1810, Salem, Mass., Sanderson Family Manuscripts, PEM.

50. Jonas Heywood estate records, 1831, Middlesex, Mass., CFPL; Samuel Proud estate records, 1835, Providence, R.I., as quoted in Pillsbury, "Providence Furniture Making Trade," pp. 120–21.

51. Samuel Proud estate records.

52. Inventory analysis based on the following: Smith, Galloway, Turner, Hanson, Dalton, Jefferis, Rebecca Sprague, and Samuel Proud estate records; John Aspinwall and Thomas West estate records, 1774–86 and 1795, New York, DCM; Benjamin Barnard estate records, 1789, Nantucket Co., Mass., Registry of Probate; Joseph Hobson estate records, 1797, Chester Co., Pa., as quoted in Schiffer, *Chester County Inventories*, pp. 394–95; Capt. William Harris estate records, 1809, New London, Conn., Genealogical Section, CSL; Abraham McDonough estate records, 1852, City and County of Philadelphia, Register of Wills; David Alling estate records, 1855, Newark, N.J., Archives and History Bureau, New Jersey State Library, Trenton.

53. Inventory terms found in the following: West, Hanson, Hobson, McDonough, and Prentis estate records. A comprehensive discussion of the multifunctional role of the kitchen in the federal period occurs in Nancy Goyne Evans, "Everyday Things: From Rolling Pins to Trundle Bedsteads," in *American Furniture 2003*, ed. Luke Beckerdite (Milwaukee, Wis.: Chipstone Foundation, 2003), pp. 27–94.

54. Derby and Prentis estate records.

55. Charles G. Dorman, "Room with a View," *The University Hospital Antiques Show Catalogue* (Philadelphia: University Hospital Antiques Show, 1970), pp. 95–97; Friends of Independence National Historical Park, *Newsletter* 2, no. 2 (May 1974): 2.

56. Elisabeth Donaghy Garrett, *At Home: The American Family, 1750–1870* (New York: Harry N. Abrams, 1990), p. 132; Baker and Marston estate records; James Cutler estate records, 1799, Boston, DCM.

57. Carl and Jessica Bridenbaugh, *Rebels and Gentlemen: Philadelphia in the Age of Franklin* (New York: Oxford University Press, 1962), pp. 191–93; Carl Bridenbaugh, *Cities in Revolt: Urban Life in America, 1743–1776* (New York: Alfred A. Knopf, 1955), pp. 145, 338–39.

58. Israel Pemberton estate records, 1754, City and County of Philadelphia, Register of Wills; Lloyd Zachary estate records, 1757, Philadelphia, as quoted in Lyon, *Colonial Furniture*, p. 176; Jack L. Lindsey, "Lynford Lardner's Silver: Early Rococo in Philadelphia," *Antiques* 153, no. 4 (April 1993): 608–15; Hornor, *Blue Book*, pp. 107, 297, 299, 308, 312; J. Stogdell Stokes, "The American Windsor Chair," *Antiques* 9, no. 4 (April 1926): 225.

59. Commodore John Barry estate records, 1803, Philadelphia, DCM; John Craig estate records, 1807, City and County of Philadelphia, Register of Wills; Nicholas B. Wainwright, "Andalusia, Countryseat of the Craig Family and of

Nicholas Biddle and his Descendants," *Pennsylvania Magazine of History and Biography* 101, no. 1 (January 1977): 2–69; Frances M. Trollope, *Domestic Manners of the Americans*, 2 vols. (London: Whittaker, Treacher, 1832), 2:184.

60. Alberts, *Golden Voyage*, pp. 222–23; William Bingham letter book, 1791–93, HSP.

61. Hannah Callender, as quoted in Bridenbaugh, *Cities in Revolt*, p. 145; George Vaux, ed., "Extracts from the Diary of Hannah Callender," *Pennsylvania Magazine of History and Biography* 12 (1888): 441, 444–45; Aspinwall estate records.

62. Bridenbaugh, *Cities in Revolt*, p. 341; house for sale, *New-York Evening Post*, July 27, 1804, as quoted in Rita Susswein Gottesman, comp., *The Arts and Crafts in New York, 1800–1804* (New York: New-York Historical Society, 1965), pp. 184–85.

63. Apthorp estate records; John C. Vanden Heuvel estate records, 1826, New York, DCM; Trollope, *Domestic Manners*, 2:215.

64. Alice Morse Earle, as quoted in Elise L. Lathrop, *Early American Inns and Taverns* (New York: B. Blom, 1968), p. 36; Abraham Brinckerhoff estate records, 1823, New York, DCM.

65. Isaac Clason estate records, ca. 1815, New York, DCM; George Clinton, Jr., estate records, 1809, Orange Co., N.Y., DCM.

66. "Appraisement of the Estate of Philip Ludwell Esqr Decd," *Virginia Magazine of History and Biography*, vol. 21 (1913; reprint, New York: Kraus Reprint Corp., 1968), pp. 395–416; Charles Young estate records, 1804, Norfolk, Va., Mary Cam Young Papers, Virginia State Library, Richmond; George Mason estate records, 1797, Rockbridge Co., Lexington, Va., Registry of Probate (reference courtesy of Margaret Beck Pritchard).

67. For the Brown, Gautier, and Hewes advertisements, a discussion and illustration of English Windsors used out of doors, and the Denning family portrait, see Evans, *American Windsor Chairs*, pp. 38–50; figs. 1-12, 1-16, 1-19, 1-30, 5-1, 6-128, and 5-2; Thomas Timpson and William Gillihen, *New-York Packet* (New York), July 11, 1785; (?) Chandless, *Baltimore Daily Repository* (Baltimore, Md.), January 9, 1791; James Chesney, *Albany Chronicle* (Albany, N.Y.), April 10, 1797.

68. John Lambert, *Travels through Canada and the United States of North America*, 2 vols. (London: C. Cradock and W. Joy, 1813), 2:207; Susanna Dillwyn Emlen letter to William Dillwyn, May 4, 1800; Robert Sutcliffe, *Travel in Some Parts of North America in the Years 1804, 1805, and 1806* (York, England, 1811), p. 247, as quoted in Wendell Garrett, ed., "Clues and Footnotes," *Antiques* 103, no. 1 (January 1973): 104; Charles N. Buck, "Memoirs of Charles N. Buck . . . 1791 to 1841," HSP; *The Aristocratic Journey: Being the Outspoken Letters of Mrs. Basil Hall*, ed. Una Pope-Hennessy (New York: G. P. Putnam's Sons, 1931), p. 219.

69. Robert Bolling, "A Circumstantial Account of Certain Transactions . . . 1760," Tucker-Coleman Collection, WM (reference courtesy of Leo Lemay); David Ruth bill to Sir Peyton Skipwith, November 6, 1797, Peyton Skipwith Papers, WM; Harman Vosburgh and (?) Childs, *Hall's Wilmington Gazette* (Wilmington, N.C.), February 9, 1797, citation file, MESDA; Beatrix T. Rumford, ed., *American Folk Paintings . . . from the Abby Aldrich Rockefeller Folk Art Center* (Boston: Little, Brown, 1988), cat. 18.

70. [John Macky], *A Journey through England*, 2d ed (London: J. Hooke, 1722), pp. 24–25; Adolph B. Benson, ed., *Peter Kalm's Travels in North America*, 2 vols. (New York: Dover Publications, 1966), 1:121; J. P. Brissot de Warville, *New Travels in the United States of America* (Dublin: P. Byrne et al., 1792), p. 314; the Hyde de Neuville watercolor drawing is titled (and depicts) the *Home of Mr. and Mrs. Cruger at Bloomingdale, N.Y., Sept. 1819*, as illustrated in *American Drawings, Pastels, and Watercolors, Part 1* (New York: Kennedy Galleries, 1967), p. 31.

71. For a description and illustrations of the through hall at Wyck, see Sandra Mackenzie Lloyd, "Wyck," *Antiques* 124, no. 2 (August 1983): 276–83.

72. Theophilus Hardenbrook, *New-York Mercury* (New York), October 2, 1758, and Thomas Ash, *Rivington's New-York Gazetteer* (New York), February 17, 1774, as quoted in Rita Susswein Gottesman, comp., *The Arts and Crafts in New York, 1726–1776* (1938; reprint, New York: Da Capo Press, 1970), pp. 110, 180–81; Daniel Lawrence, *United States Chronicle* (Providence, R.I.), July 19, 1787, as quoted in Lyon, *Colonial Furniture*, pp. 180–81; Rev. Arthur Browne estate records, 1773, Rockingham Co., N.H., Registry of Probate (reference courtesy of Elizabeth Rhodes Aykroyd); Tazewell Hall reference from Mark R. Wenger, "The Center Passage in Virginia: Evolution of an 18th-Century Living Space" (conference paper, Vernacular Architecture Forum, 1984); Thomas Bringhurst bill to Charles Wistar, July 23, 1808, Charles Wistar Papers, DCM.

73. For the Denning family portrait, see Evans, *American Windsor Chairs*, fig. 5-2. For the Dorcas Fearing needlework, see *The Collection of Edgar William and Bernice Chrysler Garbisch, Part II*, May 8–9, 1974 (New York: Sotheby Parke Bernet, 1974), lot 67. For the Hawkins family, see Robert Bishop, *Centuries and Styles of the American Chair, 1640–1970* (New York: E. P. Dutton, 1972), fig. 785.

74. Susanna Dillwyn (Emlen) letter to William Dillwyn, May 1, 1787, Dillwyn Correspondence; Weld, *Travels*, 1:94; Helen Maggs Fede, *Washington Furniture at Mount Vernon* (Mount Vernon, Va.: Mount Vernon Ladies' Association, 1966), p. 8.

75. Fede, *Washington Furniture*, pp. 10, 14–16, 22, 26, 30, 32–33.

76. Fede, *Washington Furniture*, pp. 33, 58–59. For an illustration and discussion of the fan-chair form, see Nancy Goyne Evans, *American Windsor Furniture: Specialized Forms* (New York: Hudson Hills Press, 1997), pp. 231–32. William Cox bills to Gen. Henry Knox, July 29, 1794, and May 19, 1795, Papers of Henry Knox, Maine Historical Society, Portland; "Washington's Household Account Book, 1793–1797," *Pennsylvania Magazine of History and Biography* 31 (1907): 326; Esther Singleton, *The Furniture of Our Forefathers* (Garden City, N.Y.: Doubleday, Page, 1913), p. 131.

77. Joshua Brookes journal, 1798–1803, as quoted in "A Dinner at Mount Vernon—1799," *Annual Report, The Mount Vernon Ladies' Association of the Union, 1947* (Mount Vernon, Va.: Mount Vernon Ladies' Association, 1947), p. 24; Singleton, *Furniture of Our Forefathers*, pp. 506–7; *Annual Report, The Mount Vernon Ladies' Association of the Union, 1971* (Mount Vernon, Va.: Mount Vernon Ladies' Association, 1971), p. 28.

78. Charles L. Granquist, "Thomas Jefferson's 'Whirligig' Chairs," *Antiques* 109, no. 5 (May 1976): 1056–60.

79. Thomas Jefferson letter to Martha Jefferson Randolph, May 8, 1791, as quoted in Edwin Morris Betts and James Adams Bear, Jr., eds., *The Family Letters of Thomas Jefferson* (Columbia: University of Missouri Press, [1966]), pp. 80–81; Thomas Jefferson expense account book, 1791–1803, NYPL; Granquist, "Jefferson's 'Whirligig' Chairs," pp. 1056–59. For the Burling chair, see Evans, *American Windsor Chairs*, p. 388.

80. Letchworth purchase identified in letters to author from Charles Granquist, March 3 and 24, 1975; Adam Snyder bill to Thomas Claxton, July 31, 1801, Thomas Claxton letters to Thomas Jefferson, August 5, 24, and 27, 1801, and Edward Kindred receipt to Gibson and Jefferson, August 21, 1801, Papers of Thomas Jefferson, MHS; Susan R. Stein, "Furnishings at Monticello," *Antiques* 144, no. 1 (July 1993): 70.

81. Thomas Jefferson letter to George Jefferson, March 10, 1809, and George Jefferson letter to Thomas Jefferson, June 19, 1809, Jefferson Papers.

82. Robert L. Raley, "Interior Designs by Benjamin Henry Latrobe for the President's House," *Antiques* 75, no. 6 (June 1959): 568–71; John and Hugh Finlay papers relating to furniture for the President's House, September 1809, Treasury Records, Miscellaneous Treasury Accounts of the First Auditor, no. 28,634, National Archives, Washington, D.C. (hereafter cited NA). A controversy exists with respect to the actual builder of the furniture for the President's House before it was painted and ornamented. Some authors believe the furniture was constructed in Philadelphia, then shipped to Baltimore for finishing. The Finlay's bill to Latrobe, totaling $1,111, suggests the broth-

ers undertook the complete work. See Jack L. Lindsey, "An Early Latrobe Furniture Commission," *Antiques* 139, no. 1 (January 1991): 215–16; Gregory R. Weidman, "The Painted Furniture of John and Hugh Finlay," *Antiques* 143, no. 5 (May 1993): 745–47; Sumpter Priddy, *American Fancy: Exuberance in the Arts, 1790–1840* (Milwaukee, Wis.: Chipstone Foundation, 2004), pp. 57–60.

83. John Finlay bill to George Boyd, agent, June 5, 1815; William Palmer bill to George Boyd, December 1815; William Worthington account with George Boyd, June 15, 1814–June 14, 1815; and auction bill to George Boyd, May 25, 1815, Treasury Records, Miscellaneous Treasury Accounts of the First Auditor, no. 29,494, NA.

84. James Monroe accounts, 1817–20, Treasury Records, Miscellaneous Treasury Accounts of the First Auditor, no. 43,754, NA. For the Monroe Windsor, see Marshall B. Davidson, ed., *The American Heritage History of Colonial Antiques* (New York: American Heritage Publishing Co., 1967), pp. 240–41. For the Adams daguerreotype, see Evans, *American Windsor Chairs*, fig. 7-41. Carl David Arfwedson, *The United States and Canada*, 2 vols. (1834; reprint, New York: Johnson Reprint Corp., 1969), 1:217.

85. Benjamin Franklin estate records, 1790, City and County of Philadelphia, Register of Wills (photostat, DCM); Jacob Cox Parsons, ed., *Extracts from the Diary of Jacob Hiltzheimer* (Philadelphia: William F. Fell, 1893), p. 161.

86. List of furnishings at Lansdowne, n.d., and "Sales of the furniture of the Hon'bl John Penn," June 9, 1795, DCM; Anthony Butler (agent for John Penn) receipt book, 1788–99, DCM.

87. Charles Carroll purchase in John Henry Hill, "The Furniture Craftsmen in Baltimore, 1783–1823" (master's thesis, University of Delaware, 1967), p. 187. For the Sherman portrait, see Evans, *American Windsor Chairs*, fig. 3-15. Patrick Henry estate records, 1799, Charlotte Co., Va., Patrick Henry Papers, Library of Congress, Washington, D.C. (hereafter cited LC); "The Furnishings of Richmond Hill in 1797, the Home of Aaron Burr in New York City," *The New-York Historical Society Quarterly Bulletin* 11, no. 1 (April 1927): 17–23; Benedict Arnold in Davidson, *Colonial Antiques*, p. 242; Barry estate records; Stephen Decatur estate records, 1820, Washington, D.C., as quoted in "Decatur House," *Historic Preservation* 19, nos. 3–4 (July–December 1967): Appendix I, p. 92.

88. T. Kenneth Wood, "A Lafayette Chair," *Antiques* 10, no. 4 (October 1926): 293–95; John A. H. Sweeny, *Lafayette, the Nation's Guest* (Winterthur, Del.: Winterthur Museum, 1957), pp. 2–3; Sarah Anna Emery, *Reminiscences of a Nonagenarian* (Newburyport, Mass.: William H. Huse, 1879), p. 316.

89. Anne Newport Royall, *Sketches of History, Life, and Manners in the United States* (New Haven, Conn.: By the author, 1826), pp. 175–76; Wood, "Lafayette Chair," p. 293; William Voss Elder III, *Baltimore Painted Furniture, 1800–1840* (Baltimore: Baltimore Museum of Art, 1972), pp. 69–70. The Baltimore Museum's chair may have been part of the furnishings for the "Silver Supper" of 1824 held in Lafayette's honor at the Dancing Assembly Rooms, Baltimore (Lance Humphries, "Provenance, Patronage, and Perception: The Morris Suite of Baltimore Painted Furniture," in *American Furniture 2003*, ed. Luke Beckerdite [Milwaukee, Wis.: Chipstone Foundation, 2003], pp. 167–68).

90. John Bristed, *America and Her Resources* (1818; reprint, New York: Research Reprints, 1970), pp. 450–51; Lambert, *Travels*, 2:100.

91. Bridenbaugh, *Cities in Revolt*, pp. 369–71; Marshall B. Davidson, *Life in America*, 2 vols. (Boston: Houghton Mifflin, 1951), 2:16–22; Parsons, *Jacob Hiltzheimer*, p. 188; Buck, "Memoirs of Charles N. Buck."

92. John Alden, "A Season in Federal Street: J. B. Williamson and the Boston Theatre, 1796–1797," in *Proceedings of the American Antiquarian Society* 65 (Worcester, Mass.: By the society, 1955), pt. 1, pp. 36, 47, 52; Frank Chouteau Brown, "The First Boston Theatre on Federal Street," *Old-Time New England* 36, no. 1 (July 1945), pp. 1–7; Richard Stoddard, "A Reconstruction of Charles Bulfinch's First Federal Street Theatre, Boston," in *Winterthur Portfolio* 6, ed. Richard K. Doud and Ian M. G. Quimby (Charlottesville: University Press of Virginia, 1970), pp. 190–95; William Seaver bills to Joseph Russell, January 21 and October 18, 1794, Boston Theatre Papers, Boston Public Library, Boston, Mass. (hereafter cited BPL).

93. Stoddard, "First Federal Street Theatre," pp. 190–95; Alden, "Season in Federal Street," pp. 36, 47, 52.

94. Theater Notice, *Morning Chronicle* (New York), October 18, 1804, as quoted in Gottesman, *Arts and Crafts, 1800–1804*, p. 458; Opera House description, *New-York Evening Post*, November 1833 (reference courtesy of the late Benno M. Forman).

95. Davidson, *Life in America*, 2:28, 358–59; Bridenbaugh, *Cities in Revolt*, pp. 200–201, 203, 206–8, 416; John W. Blanchard bill to the Proprietors of the Boston Theatre, May 1, 1829, Boston Theatre Papers; Samuel Horton, Jr., estate records, 1828, Suffolk Co., Mass., Registry of Probate (microfilm, DCM); Henry Dean, *Hocus Pocus, or the Whole Art of Legerdemain in Perfection*, 11th ed. (Philadelphia: Mathew Carey, 1795), frontispiece.

96. Philemon Robbins account book, 1833–36, CHS; Marcus Cunliffe, "Frances Trollope, 1780–1863," in *Abroad in America: Visitors to the New Nation, 1776–1914*, ed. Marc Pachter and Frances Wein (Reading, Mass.: Addison-Wesley Publishing Co., 1976), p. 37; Trollope, *Domestic Manners*, 2:132; *Aristocratic Journey*, ed. Pope-Hennessy, p. 81; Bristed, *America and Her Resources*, p. 451.

97. Bridenbaugh, *Cities in Revolt*, pp. 163–65; Stoddard, "First Federal Street Theatre," p. 195; *William Freeman vs. George Labottiere*, September 8, 1808, Cumberland Co., Maine, DCM; *The New Democracy in America: Travels of Francisco de Miranda in the United States, 1783–84*, trans. Judson P. Wood, ed. John S. Ezell (Norman: University of Oklahoma Press, 1963), p. 54; marquis de Chastellux, *Travels in North-America in the Years 1780, 1781, and 1782*, 2 vols. (London: G. G. J. and J. Robinson, 1787), 1:278.

98. Emery, *Reminiscences*, p. 247; Nellie Parke Custis, as quoted in Gretchen Sullivan Sorin and Ellen Kirven Donald, *Gadsby's Tavern Museum Historic Furnishing Plan* (Alexandria, Va.: By the city, 1980), p. 157.

99. For the Mount painting, see Alfred Frankenstein, *Painter of Rural America: William Sidney Mount* (Stony Brook, N.Y.: Suffolk Museum, 1968), p. 15. For the Mayr painting, see Jesse Poesch, *The Art of the Old South: Painting, Sculpture, Architecture, and the Products of Craftsmen, 1560–1860* (New York: Knopf, 1983), p. 292. Roberts and Roberts, *Moreau Journey*, p. 99; Parsons, *Jacob Hiltzheimer*, p. 10.

100. Parsons, *Jacob Hiltzheimer*, p. 32; *The Diary of William Bentley*, 4 vols. (Salem, Mass.: Essex Institute, 1905), 1:204, 215. For the Krimmel watercolor drawing, see Robin Bolton-Smith et al., "Philadelphia: Three Centuries of American Art," *Antiques* 105, no. 1 (July 1976): 140.

101. For *The Quilting Party*, see Rumford, *American Folk Paintings*, cat. 88. For the Johnson painting, see William R. Johnston, "American Paintings in the Walters Art Gallery," *Antiques* 106, no. 5 (November 1974): 858. For the bowling saloon, see Nicholas B. Wainwright, *Philadelphia in the Romantic Age of Lithography* (Philadelphia: Historical Society of Pennsylvania, 1958), p. 231.

102. William H. Meyers diary (journal), 1838–39, NYPL.

103. Eliza Cope Harrison, ed., *Philadelphia Merchant: The Diary of Thomas P. Cope, 1800–1851* (South Bend, Ind.: Gateway Editions, 1978), p. 485.

104. Singleton, *Social New York*, pp. 369–72; Elizabeth de Hart Bleecker diary, 1799–1806, NYPL; Lambert, *Travels*, 2:61; Dorothy C. Barck, ed., *Letters from John Pintard to his Daughter*, 4 vols. (New York: New-York Historical Society, 1940–41), 3:284.

105. Royall, *Sketches*, p. 266. For the *Castle Harbor, View of the Battery, New York*, see John A. H. Sweeney, "Paintings from the Sewell C. Biggs Collection," *Antiques* 119, no. 4 (April 1981): 897, pl. 17.

106. For the *View of West Point*, see *101 American Primitive Water Colors and Pastels*

from the Collection of Edgar William and Bernice Chrysler Garbisch (Washington, D.C.: National Gallery of Art, 1966), fig. 72; Edward Halsey Foster and Geoffrey W. Clark, eds., Hoboken: A Collection of Essays (New York: Irvington Publishers, 1976), pp. 35–36; Marshall B. Davidson, New York: A Pictorial History (New York: Charles Scribner's Sons, 1977), pp. 138–39; Davidson, Life in America, 2:29.

107. Parsons, Jacob Hiltzheimer, pp. 128, 153; duc de la Rochefoucauld Liancourt, Travels through the United States of North America, 2 vols. (London: R. Phillips, 1799), 2:246; Hornor, Blue Book, p. 308.

108. Henry Wansey, An Excursion to the United States of America in the Summer of 1794, 2d ed. (Salisbury, England: J. Easton, 1798), pp. 117, 152; John F. Watson, Annals of Philadelphia and Pennsylvania in the Olden Time, 3 vols. (1830; reprint, rev. Willis P. Hazard, Philadelphia: Leary, Stuart, 1927), 1:397.

109. Hay-Market Gardens, Virginia Gazette and General Advertiser (Richmond), August 22, 1800, and October 23, 1801, citation file, MESDA; Chatsworth, Spring Gardens, and other gardens listed in Warner and Hanna, Baltimore Directory (Baltimore, Md., 1800), citation file, MESDA; pleasure garden, American Statesman (Lexington, Ky.), July 18, 1812, citation file, MESDA.

110. For The Anglers Repast, see George Dawe, The Life of George Morland (London: Dickinsons, 1904), n.p. For A "Pic Nick" Camden, Maine, see Donaldson F. Hoopes, "American Narrative Painting," Antiques 106, no. 5 (November 1974): 818, pl. 1.

111. William Oliver Stevens, Nantucket, the Far-Away Island (New York: Dodd, Mead, 1936), pp. 148–50; Emery, Reminiscences, p. 300.

112. Diary of William Bentley, 4:360; Lambert, Travels, 2:26–27, 30, 514–15; Harrison, Diary of Thomas P. Cope, p. 70.

113. Bridenbaugh, Cities in Revolt, pp. 162–63, 363; Delphian Club Papers, vols. 1, 2, Maryland Historical Society, Baltimore (hereafter cited MdHS).

114. John Patterson Sims, The Fishing Company of Fort St. Davids (Philadelphia: Society of Colonial Wars in the Commonwealth of Pennsylvania, 1951); A History of the Schuylkill Fishing Company of the State in Schuylkill, 1732–1888 (Philadelphia: By the members, 1889); Townsend Ward, "A Walk to Darby," Pennsylvania Magazine of History and Biography 3 (1879): 252–53. The "governor's chair" was destroyed by fire on December 22, 1980.

115. John Goodman letter to William Milnor, March 2, 1830, as quoted in "Notes and Queries," Pennsylvania Magazine of History and Biography 21 (1897): 417–18; Sims, Fort St. Davids, pp. 13, 25–30; Schuylkill Fishing Company, p. 220.

116. [Theodore Dwight, Jr.], The Northern Traveller, 2d ed. (New York: A. T. Goodrich, 1826), pp. 145, 152, 163.

117. Incidents in the Life of Jacob Barker of New Orleans, Louisiana, . . . from 1800 to 1855 (Washington, D.C., 1855), p. 22 (reference courtesy of Eleanor B. Conary).

118. Bridenbaugh and Bridenbaugh, Rebels and Gentlemen, p. 187; Bridenbaugh, Cities in Revolt, pp. 163, 363; Alan Gowans, "Freemasonry and the Neoclassical Style in America," Antiques 77, no. 2 (February 1960): 172–75; Barbara Franco, Masonic Symbols in American Decorative Arts (Lexington, Mass.: Museum of Our National Heritage, 1976), pp. 9–30.

119. Jachin and Boaz, or an Authentic Key to the Door of Free Masonry (Boston, 1817), frontispiece, p. 52; Thomas Boynton ledger, 1817–47, Dartmouth College, Hanover, N.H. (hereafter cited DC; microfilm, DCM).

120. Franklin Ellis and Samuel Evans, History of Lancaster County, Pennsylvania (Philadelphia: Everts and Peck, 1883), pp. 378–79, 488–89; James Williams and Valentine Hoff bills to Lodge No. 43, June 10 and April 23, 1811, Lodge No. 43, Free and Accepted Masons, Lancaster, Pa.; John and Hugh Finlay, Gazette and Baltimore Daily Advertiser (Baltimore, Md.), November 8, 1805, as quoted in Elder, Baltimore Painted Furniutre, p. 11.

121. Diary of William Bentley, 2:403–4, 4:428; Daniel Rea, Jr., and John Johnston ledger, 1773–94, and Daniel Rea, Jr., daybook, 1789–93, Baker Library, Harvard University, Cambridge, Mass.; George Davidson waste book, 1793–99, Old Sturbridge Village, Sturbridge, Mass. (hereafter cited OSV); Franco, Masonic Symbols, pp. 26–27.

122. Bridenbaugh, Cities in Revolt, p. 274; John Hill, Pennsylvania Gazette (Philadelphia), June 12, 1760, and May 15, 1766.

123. J. Thomas Scharf and Thompson Westcott, History of Philadelphia, 1609–1884, 3 vols. (Philadelphia: L. H. Everts, 1884), 2:868; Philadelphia Monthly Meeting of Friends, Committee of Twelve minutes, vol. 1, 1770–95, p. 89 (December 6, 1776), directive to pay Joseph Henzey for chairs, Society of Friends, Philadelphia, Pa. (hereafter cited SF; on deposit, APS); Delphian Club Papers, vol. 4, facing p. 264; John Gillingham, Francis Trumble, and George Halberstadt estate records, 1794, 1798, and 1812, City and County of Philadelphia, Register of Wills.

124. The observation on the bird was made by the Reverend Frederick S. Weiser, who also indicated that the triplets are buried in the cemetery of the Lower Bermudian Lutheran and Reformed Church near East Berlin, Pa.

125. Sorin and Donald, Gadsby's Tavern, pp. 1, 2; Davidson, Life in America, 2:212–13; James W. Miller, The Genesis of Western Culture (1938; reprint, New York: Da Capo Press, 1969), pp. 17–19.

126. Kym S. Rice, Early American Taverns: For the Entertainment of Friends and Strangers (Chicago: Regnery Gateway for the Fraunces Tavern Museum, 1983), p. 105; Miller, Genesis of Western Culture, p. 19; Sorin and Donald, Gadsby's Tavern, p. 3; Bridenbaugh, Cities in Revolt, p. 158; Alice Morse Earle, Stage-Coach and Tavern Days (New York: Macmillan, 1922), p. 85; Timothy Dwight, Travels in New England and New York, 4 vols., ed. Barbara Miller Solomon (Cambridge, Mass.: Belknap Press, 1969), 1:309.

127. George Gilbert estate records, 1769, City and County of Philadelphia, Register of Wills (reference courtesy of Arlene Palmer Schwind); Henry Ireland estate records, 1774, Philadelphia, as quoted in Jones, American Colonial Wealth, 1:209–11; Webster definition (1828), as quoted in Schiffer, Chester County Inventories, p. 196; Andrew Heath estate records, 1778, Philadelphia, as quoted in Montgomery, Pennsylvania Archives, pp. 860–62; David Jones estate records, 1778, Philadelphia, as quoted in Hornor, Blue Book, p. 308.

128. Rice, Early American Taverns, pp. 34–35, 37–38.

129. James Dwyer estate records, 1777, Rockingham Co., N.H., Registry of Probate (reference courtesy of Elizabeth Rhodes Aykroyd); Chastellux, Travels, 2:217.

130. Elijah Tull estate records, 1784, Baltimore Co., Baltimore, Md., Registry of probate (microfilm, DCM); Harrison, Diary of Thomas P. Cope, p. 111; Sorin and Donald, Gadsby's Tavern, pp. 74–75, 217–24.

131. Rice, Early American Taverns, pp. 49–50; John Bernard, Retrospection of America, 1797–1811 (New York, 1811), as quoted in Eleanor H. Gustafson, ed., "Clues and Footnotes," Antiques 117, no. 4 (April 1980): 806.

132. "Samuel Fraunces," in Dictionary of American Biography, ed. Allen Johnson and Dumas Malone (New York: Charles Scribner's Sons, 1931), 7:1; Rice, Early American Taverns, pp. 125–33.

133. Samuel Fraunces estate records, 1795, City and County of Philadelphia, Register of Wills (microfilm, DCM); Rice, Early American Taverns, p. 133.

134. Fraunces estate records.

135. Andrew Gautier, New-York Gazette, or Weekly Post-Boy (New York), June 6, 1765, as illustrated in Evans, American Windsor Chairs, fig. 5-1.

136. Wansey, Excursion, pp. 57–58; Lambert, Travels, 2:63; dating of canvas based on Stiles Tuttle Colwill, Francis Guy, 1760–1820 (Baltimore: Maryland Historical Society, 1981), p. 48; Rice, Early American Taverns, pp. 38–41.

137. Tontine Coffee House account books, 1791–93 and 1791–1816, New-York Historical Society, New York; Harrison, Diary of Thomas P. Cope, p. 67.

138. Lambert, Travels, 2:29.

139. Moses Oakley and John Douglass es-

tate records, 1802 and 1804, New York, DCM; Selah Smith in Louise Hall Tharp, *Mrs. Jack* (Boston: Little, Brown, 1965), p. 5.

140. Douglass estate records; John Brown estate records, 1808, New York, DCM; Charles Trute estate records, 1807, Wilmington, Del., as quoted in Charles G. Dorman, *Delaware Cabinetmakers and Allied Artisans, 1655–1855* (Wilmington: Historical Society of Delaware, 1960), pp. 81–82, 102–3; James Phillips information in letter to author from John R. Grabb, December 3, 1978.

141. John Heintzelman estate records, 1804, Lancaster, Pa., DCM.

142. Frederick Marryat, *A Diary in America*, 2 vols. (London: Longman et al., 1839), 1:102.

143. Douglass, John Brown, and Heintzelman estate records; Harriet Martineau, as quoted in Catherine Fennelly, *Life in an Old New England Country Village* (New York: Thomas Y. Crowell, 1969), p. 107; Arfwedson, *United States and Canada*, 2:12.

144. Silas Cheney daybooks, 1799–1817, 1807–13, and 1813–21, Litchfield Historical Society, Litchfield, Conn. (hereafter cited LHS; microfilm, DCM); Grove Catlin estate records, 1829, Litchfield, Conn., Genealogical Section, CSL.

145. Boynton ledger, 1817–47; Thomas Boynton ledger, 1810–17, DC (microfilm, DCM); Josiah P. Wilder daybook and ledger, 1837–61, Charles S. Parsons, Wilder Family Notes, Decorative Arts Photographic Collection, WL; Chauncey Strong daybook, 1852–69, New York State Historical Association, Cooperstown; George Landon account book, 1813–32, DCM.

146. Rice, *Early American Taverns*, p. 38; *Aristocratic Journey*, ed. Pope-Hennessy, p. 82.

147. Arfwedson, *United States and Canada*, 1:32–33; "A Philadelphian Looks at New England—1820," excerpts from William Wood Thackara, "Journal of a Journey by Sea from Philadelphia to Boston," ed. Robert Donald Crompton, *Old-Time New England* 50, no. 3 (January–March 1960): 62.

148. Boston Exchange Coffee House, as described in Hayden Goldberg, "Two Newly Identified American Views on Historical Blue Staffordshire," *Antiques* 125, no. 1 (January 1984): 281–82; [Gideon Miner Davison], *Traveller's Guide*, 6th ed. (Saratoga Springs, N.Y.: G. M. Davison, 1834), p. 434; Henry Bradshaw Fearon, *Sketches of America*, 2d ed. (London: Longman et al., 1818), pp. 246–47.

149. William W. Chambers, *Things as They Are in America* (Philadelphia: Lippincott, Grambo, 1854), pp. 47, 179–81, 184–87, 189–90; Leo Hershkowitz and Theodore Cohen, *Fine Art, 19th-Century Trade Bills and Images of New York City* (Hempstead, N.Y.: Hofstra University, 2001), fig. 2.

150. Charles van Ravenswaay, *The Anglo-American Cabinetmakers of Missouri, 1800–1850* (St. Louis: Missouri Historical Society, 1958), p. 242.

151. J. Thomas Scharf, *History of Baltimore City and County* (Philadelphia: Louis H. Everts, 1881), pp. 437–38; Baltimore Exchange Hotel bills and inventory for furnishing, 1833–35 and 1842, Baltimore Exchange Hotel Collection, MdHS.

152. John and James Williams, Jacob Hiss, Jr., and John H. Gordon bills to Baltimore Exchange Hotel, 1833–34, Exchange Hotel Collection, MdHS.

153. Trustees of Joseph Jewett agreement with Baltimore Commercial Exchange Co., 1842, and inventory of Baltimore Exchange Hotel, 1842, Exchange Hotel Collection, MdHS.

154. Septimus Claypoole bill to Jerome Bonaparte, March 10, 1843, Exchange Hotel Collection, MdHS.

155. Richard Tweed and Hezekiah Bonnell letter and bill to Jerome Bonaparte, February 22, 1843, Exchange Hotel Collection, MdHS.

156. John G. Coster landlords' warrant against John Cotter, August 18, 1841, and inventory of Washington Hotel, October 19, 1841, Historical Documents Collection, Queens College, Flushing, N.Y. (hereafter cited QC).

157. Inventory of Washington Hotel.

158. Inventory of Washington Hotel; Chambers, *Things as They Are*, p. 182.

159. Nancy Goyne Evans, "The Sans Souci, a Fashionable Resort Hotel in Ballston Spa," in *Winterthur Portfolio 6*, ed. Richard K. Doud and Ian M. G. Quimby (Charlottesville: University Press of Virginia, 1970), pp. 111–26.

160. Evans, "Sans Souci," pp. 111–26.

161. George White letters to Nicholas Low, 1803–5; Elihu Alvord, William Stillwell, and Miles Beach contract, bills, and price list, 1803–5; Avery Swan bill to Nicholas Low, May 11, 1811; Samuel Hicks, Jr., bill to William L. White, April 21, 1821; and Andrew Berger bill to Nicholas Low, September 1822, Nicholas Low Collection, LC.

162. Evelyn Barrett Britten, *Chronicles of Saratoga* (Saratoga Springs, N.Y.: By the author, 1959), pp. 370–73; obituary of Ransom Cook, *Saratoga Sentinel* (Saratoga Springs, N.Y.), June 2, 1881, Historical Society of Saratoga Springs, Saratoga Springs, N.Y.; [Dwight], *Northern Traveller*, pp. 148–49.

163. William M. E. Rachal, "A Trip to the Salt Pond," *Virginia Cavalcade* (Autumn 1952), pp. 22–27. Chapman's White Sulphur Springs, also known as New River White Sulphur Springs and located in the village of Eggleston Springs, Va., was not the same resort as today's White Sulphur Springs, W.Va., about 50 miles distant.

164. For *Lord George Graham in His Cabin*, see Mario Praz, *Conversation Pieces* (University Park: Pennsylvania State University Press, 1971), fig. 57; Susanna Dillwyn letters to William Dillwyn, August 14, 1788, Dillwyn Correspondence.

165. Richard Mills bill to William Barrell, November 30, 1768, Stephen Collins Papers, LC; Joseph Vickary bill to Christopher Champlin, October 18, 1773, Shepley Papers, Rhode Island Historical Society, Providence (hereafter cited RIHS); Alexander Edward account of Grant Webster, 1772–85, Greenough Papers, MHS.

166. "A List of Stores for Ship Grand Turk," n.d., Derby Family Papers, PEM; Winslow Lewis bill to "Owners of the Schooner Nancy," July 30, 1791, Greenough Papers; John Cochran, "Inventory of the Materials &c of the Brig Sally," May 12, 1791, Girard Papers, Board of Directors of City Trusts, Girard College History Collections, Philadelphia, Pa. (microfilm, APS); William Bell Clark, "James Josiah, Master Mariner," *Pennsylvania Magazine of History and Biography* 79, no. 4 (October 1955): 452–84.

167. Andrew Norwood, *New-York Gazette and General Advertiser* (New York), August 27, 1798, as quoted in Rita Susswein Gottesman, comp., *The Arts and Crafts in New York, 1777–1799* (New York: New-York Historical Society, 1954): 150–51; "Account of Sundry disbursements paid for Acct of Brig Rowena at New York," May 1, 1801, Shepley Papers; *Diary of William Bentley*, 4:425; Singleton, *Furniture of our Forefathers*, pp. 554–55, 557; Dean A. Fales, Jr., *American Painted Furniture, 1660–1880* (New York: E. P. Dutton, 1972), pp. 168–69.

168. Brissot de Warville, *New Travels*, p. 150; Lambert, *Travels*, 2:41–42.

169. John Melish, *Travels through the United States of America*, 2 vols. (Philadelphia: By the author, 1815), 2:423; Abraham Yarmolinsky, *Picturesque United States of America: A Memoir on Paul Svinin* (New York: William Edwin Rudge, 1930), pp. 9–10; Fearon, *Sketches*, p. 75; Harrison, *Diary of Thomas P. Cope*, p. 354.

170. *Cramer's Pittsburgh Almanac for . . . 1813* (Pittsburgh, Pa.: Cramer, Spear and Eichbaum, 1813), pp. 49–50; Louis C. Hunter, *Steamboats on the Western Waters* (Cambridge, Mass.: Harvard University Press, 1949), pp. 390–93, 395–98; *Aristocratic Journey*, ed. Pope-Hennessy, pp. 264–65; Trollope, *Domestic Manners*, 1:18, 256.

171. Hunter, *Steamboats*, p. 396; W. De-Loss Love, "The Navigation of the Connecticut River," *Proceedings of the American Antiquarian Society*, new series, vol. 15, pt. 3 (April 29, 1903): 428.

172. G. W. McSwiney and E. Barnes, *Louisville Public Advertiser* (Louisville, Ky.), March 1, 1820, citation file, MESDA; Philip and Corson C. Skinner in *Cincinnati Directory for . . . 1829* (Cincinnati, Ohio: Robinson and Fairbanks, 1829), n.p.; Jonathan Mullen in *Cincinnati Directory for 1836-7* (Cincinnati, Ohio: J. H. Woodruff, 1836), n.p.; William Galligan in Horatio N. Walker, *Walker's Buffalo City Direc-*

tory (Buffalo, N.Y.: Lee Thorp's Press, 1844), n.p., and *J. F. Kimball and Co.'s Eastern, Western, and Southern Business Directory* (Cincinnati, Ohio: J. F. Kimball, 1846), p. 300; W. D. Rand in *Louisville Directory and Annual Business Advertiser for 1855–6* (Louisville, Ky.: W. Lee White, 1855), p. 210. For Mississippi steamboat, see H. Parrott Bacot, "The Anglo-American Art Museum of Louisiana State University in Baton Rouge," *Antiques* 125, no. 3 (March 1984): 645, pl. 8.

173. Jane E. Sikes, *The Furniture Makers of Cincinnati, 1790 to 1849* (Cincinnati, Ohio: By the author, 1976), pp. 206, 232; "The Diary of Samuel Breck, 1823–1827," *Pennsylvania Magazine of History and Biography* 103, no. 1 (January 1979): 99, 101, 104; Charles Fredericks and Benjamin Farrington, and Alexander Welsh bills to owners of steamboat *Thistle*, May 10 and 24, 1824, and April 4, 1827, DCM; Kenan and Mead, and Isaac Graham and Son bills to owner(s) of steamboat *Thistle*, April 24, 1824, and September 14, 1828, DCM.

174. Henry Andrews, Alexander Welsh, and Benjamin and Elijah Farrington bills to owners of steamboat *Emerald*, April 13, May 6, and September 11, 1826, DCM.

175. Charles Fredericks and Benjamin Farrington, Charles Fredericks, and Benjamin and Elijah Farrington bills to owners of steamboat *Bellona*, August 30, 1824, March 14, 1826, and August 2, 1828, DCM; Alexander Welsh, Stephen B. Young, and John Voorhis bills to owner(s) of steamboat *Swan*, April 27, July 5, and May 7, 1827, DCM; Philip I. Arcularius bill to Capt. Vanderbilt, April 19, 1827, DCM.

176. Benjamin and Elijah Farrington and John D. Brown bills to Capt. Vanderbilt, July 30, 1827, and April 1821, DCM; Cornelius Vanderbilt receipt from Capt. Brooks, September 12, 1828, DCM; William G. Beesley daybook, 1828–36, Salem County Historical Society, Salem, N.J.; Joel W. Mason bill to owners of steamboat *Keyport*, July 3, 1858, DCM.

177. Smith Ely schedule of prices and agreement with Gurdon H. Montague, October 2, 1832, DCM.

178. [Dwight], *Northern Traveller*, p. 50; "Aunt Anne" letter to Cornelia N. Bristol, November 29, 1836, DCM; Harrison, *Diary of Thomas P. Cope*, p. 359.

179. David McKelsey in *Troy Directory for 1829* (Troy, N.Y.: John Disturnell, 1829), n.p.; A. and E. Brown in *King's Rochester City Directory and Register, 1841* (Rochester, N.Y.: Welles and Hayes, 1840), n.p.; The Western Writers of America, *Water Trails West* (Garden City, N.Y.: Doubleday, 1978), pp. 86, 89.

180. Derby estate records.

181. John Eastmond account book, 1803–6, NYPL; John Slesman receipt book, 1799–1802, HSP; Horatio Hathaway, *A New Bedford Merchant* (Boston: By the author at the Merrymount Press, 1930), pp. 4–5.

182. Clason estate records; John P. Mum-

ford estate records, 1821, New York, DCM; William Smith estate records, 1830, City and County of Philadelphia, Register of Wills (microfilm, DCM).

183. Gillingham and West estate records; Charleston imports, *Charleston Courier*, November 17, 1807, and July 21, 1810, and *Times* (Charleston, S.C.), December 15, 1808, citation file, MESDA; Cheney daybook, 1813–21; Henry Wilder Miller account book, 1827–31, Worcester Historical Museum, Worcester, Mass. For a tall desk chair and tall desk stools, see Evans, *Specialized Forms*, figs. 3-22 to 3-25. David Alling account book, 1801–39, New Jersey Historical Society, Newark (hereafter cited NJHS; microfilm, DCM); Robbins account book; Henry F. Dewey account book, 1837–64, Shelburne Museum, Shelburne, Vt. (microfilm, DCM); W. D. Rand in *Louisville Directory*, p. 210.

184. Wilder daybook and ledger; Charles Riley estate records, 1842, City and County of Philadelphia, Register of Wills (microfilm, DCM); N. T. Morse account of Richard W. Greene, June-July 1845, A. C. and R. W. Greene Collection, RIHS; Edwin T. Freedley, *Philadelphia and Its Manufactures* (Philadelphia: Edward Young, 1858), p. 274.

185. William Barrell daybook, January–November 1772, Collins Papers, LC; Silas Cheney daybook, 1802–7, LHS (microfilm, DCM); Daniel and Samuel Proud ledger, ca. 1782–1825, RIHS; David Alling daybook, 1836–54, NJHS (microfilm, DCM).

186. William Barker account books, 1750–72 and 1753–66, RIHS; Daniel and Samuel Proud ledgers, ca. 1782–1825 and 1810–34, RIHS; Cheney daybook, 1813–21; William Crout bill to Charles Wistar, 1833, Wistar Papers. For Windsor barber chairs, see Evans, *Specialized Forms*, figs. 1-70 to 1-72.

187. Schiffer, *Chester County Inventories*, pp. 337–38; Silas Cheney ledger, 1816–22, LHS (microfilm, DCM).

188. Cheney daybook, 1813–21; Robbins account book.

189. Charles C. Robinson daybook, 1809–25, HSP; Cheney daybook, 1813–21. For the Woodville painting, see *A Catalogue of the Collection of American Paintings in the Corcoran Gallery of Art*, 2 vols. (Washington, D.C.: Corcoran Gallery of Art, [1966]), 1:116.

190. William Barker account of Almy and Brown, 1793–95, and Samuel and Daniel Proud accounts of Almy and Brown, 1789, 1791–92, and 1796–98, Almy and Brown Papers, RIHS; Luke Houghton ledger B, 1824–51, Barre Historical Society, Barre, Mass. (hereafter cited Barre; microfilm, DCM); Wilder daybook and ledger. For the view of the American Watch Company, see "What's Going On: Exhibits," *History News* 37, no. 7 (July 1982): 28; "Furnishings List of Purchases Noted in Hopewell Records and Documents," Hopewell Village

National Historic Site, Elverson, Pa. (reference courtesy of Margaret R. Burke).

191. Thomas Anburey, *Travels through the Interior Parts of America*, 2 vols. (Boston: Houghton Mifflin, 1923), 2:297–98.

192. Gemeinhaus inventory, April 1802, Archives of the Moravian Church, Bethlehem, Pa. (hereafter cited MA-Pa.); Gemeinhaus inventory, 1791, Archives of the Moravian Church, Southern Province, Winston-Salem, N.C. (hereafter cited MA-N.C.); inventories of the lodgings of Charles G. Reichel, May 1802, Christian F. Schaaf, 1819–22, and Brother and Sister Andrew Benade, 1822, MA-N.C.

193. Inventories of the minister's, warden's, and bishop's houses and various rooms in the church, 1837, MA-Pa.

194. Vaux, "Diary of Hannah Callender," pp. 448–49; Anburey, *Travels*, 2:295; Vernon H. Nelson, "The Sun Inn at Bethlehem, Pennsylvania" (lecture, Bethlehem, Pa., June 21, 1971), pp. 1–3, 11–12, MA-Pa.; inventories of the Sun Inn, 1763–1816, MA-Pa. For elevations and floor plans of the Sun Inn, see Rice, *Early American Taverns*, p. 103.

195. Inventories of the Sun Inn, 1800–16, MA-Pa.; Nelson, "Sun Inn," pp. 5–7; Anburey, *Travels*, p. 296; William C. Reichel, *The Old Moravian Sun Inn, Bethlehem, Pennsylvania, 1758*, 3d ed. (Bethlehem, Pa.: Times Publishing, 1896), p. 36.

196. Inventories of the inn at Salem, 1787–1849, MA-N.C.

197. Anburey, *Travels*, 2:297; Vaux, "Diary of Hannah Callender," p. 450; Mary Augusta Huebner, *History of the Moravian Congregation of Lititz, Pennsylvania* (Bethlehem, Pa.: Times Publishing, 1949), pp. 215–18.

198. Inventory of the church at Bethlehem, 1837, MA-Pa.; Heubner, *History of the Moravian Congregation*, p. 223; Herbert H. Beck, "Lititz as an Early Musical Centre," in *Lancaster County Historical Society Papers* 19, no. 3 (Lancaster, Pa.: By the society, 1915), p. 80.

199. For Pennsylvania German prototype chairs, see Evans, *American Windsor Chairs*, figs. 3-67 to 3-75. Henry Gottlieb Rudy estate records, 1818, Lancaster County Historical Society, Lancaster, Pa. (hereafter cited LCHS).

200. For Philadelphia prototype chairs and Pennsylvania German post turnings, see Evans, *American Windsor Chairs*, figs. 3-51 to 3-66.

201. Samuel Emlen daybook, 1751–67, HSP (on deposit from LCP); Hornor, *Blue Book*, p. 297; "Record Book of the Proceedings of the Annual and Special Meetings of the Redwood Library Company," 1747 and later, Redwood Library, Newport, R.I.; Yale commencement exercises in Franklin Bowditch Dexter, ed., *The Literary Diary of Ezra Stiles*, 3 vols. (New York: Charles Scribner's Sons, 1901), 3:40 (reference courtesy of E. McSherry Fowble). For Gilpin chairs and chairs similar to those made for the

Redwood Library, see Evans, *American Windsor Chairs*, figs. 3-3, 3-4, 6-1, 6-2.

202. Charles E. Peterson, "Carpenters' Hall," "Library Hall: Home of the Library Company of Philadelphia, 1790–1880," in *Historic Philadelphia*, issued as *Transactions of the American Philosophical Society* 43, pt. 1 (1953): 100, 129–31; Bridenbaugh and Bridenbaugh, *Rebels and Gentlemen*, pp. 86–90; Library Company of Philadelphia minute books, vol. 2 (April 24, 1773) and vol. 3 (December 6, 1792), LCP; Edwin Wolf II, "The Library Company of Philadelphia, America's First Museum," *Antiques* 120, no. 2 (August 1981): 360, figs. 15, 16. A Library Company formed in Baltimore in the late eighteenth century ordered Windsor seating from Jacob Daley in 1798 when it occupied space in the building housing the Dancing Assembly Rooms (Humphries, "Provenence, Patronage, and Perception," p. 171).

203. Carpenters' Company account books, 1763–1834, 1769–99, and warden's book, 1769–1831, Papers of the Carpenters' Company, APS; Peterson, "Carpenters' Hall," pp. 96–104, 113–14.

204. "Journal of the Select Committee of the Providence Association of Mechanics and Manufacturers," 1822 and later, RIHS.

205. Robert C. Smith, "The Athenaeum's Furniture, Parts 1, 2," *Athenaeum Annals* 4, nos. 1, 7 (January and September 1958): 1–2, 3; Roger W. Moss, Jr., "The Athenaeum of Philadelphia," *Antiques* 114, no. 6 (December 1978): 1264–79. For low-back chairs from the Athenaeum, see Evans, *American Windsor Chairs*, fig. 3-151.

206. Samuel Gragg bills to Boston Athenaeum, July 1 and August, 1822, Boston Athenaeum, Boston (reference courtesy of the late Joyce Hill).

207. Statute of March 3, 1815, as quoted in Richard Peters, ed., *The Public Statutes at Large of the United States of America* (Boston: Little, Brown, 1854), pp. 225–26; William Dawson Johnston, *History of the Library of Congress* (Washington, D.C.: Government Printing Office, 1904), pp. 66–78, 120–21; John Garther, L. Labelle, John Bridges, and H. V. Hill bills to the Library of Congress, May 16–October 9, 1815, and "Account of Disbursements by Thomas Munroe, Sup't City of Washington, fitting up and furnishing the Congressional Library room," February 1, 1816, Treasury Records, Miscellaneous Treasury Accounts of the First Auditor, no. 31,432, NA.

208. Meetings of the Massachusetts Historical Society, in *Proceedings of the Massachusetts Historical Society* 1 (Boston, 1879), pp. 13, 35, 39, 67.

209. Emery, *Reminiscences*, p. 15; Henry F. Bishop, *Historical Sketch of Lisbon, Conn.* (New York: By the author, [1903]), p. 32; David Haven account book, 1785–1800, DCM; Charles S. Parsons, *The Dunlaps and Their Furniture* (Man-

chester, N.H.: Currier Gallery of Art, 1970), pp. 229, 290, 308; Moody Carr account book, 1800–15, OSV.

210. Anne W. Rowthorn, ed., *Miles to Go before I Sleep: Samuel Seabury's Journal from 1791–1795* (Hartford, Conn.: Church Missions Publishing, 1982).

211. Emery, *Reminiscences*, p. 273.

212. Cheney daybook, 1813–21, and ledger; Boynton ledger, 1810–17; Andrew Tracy estate records, 1820–22, Cheshire Co., Keene, N.H., Registry of Probate.

213. Robbins account book; Isaac Wright account book, 1834–37, CSL; John G. Hopkins bill to Albert C. Greene, 1834–35, Greene Collection, RIHS; William O. Haskell in *Boston Directory for . . . 1856* (Boston: George Adams, 1856), p. 49; John C. Hubbard in *Boston Directory for . . . 1860* (Boston: Adams, Sampson, 1860), p. 80.

214. Sikes, *Furniture Makers of Cincinnati*, p. 231; Alling daybook, 1836–54; Samuel Fithian Ware account book, 1826–49, DCM; Philadelphia Monthly Meeting of Friends, Committee of Twelve minutes, vol. 2, 1795–1817, SF; Oldham in Hill, "Furniture Craftsmen in Baltimore," p. 178; Robbins account book.

215. For the Kennedy and Lucas lithograph, see Davidson, *Life in America*, 2:23. Lost chair notice in *Farmer's Repository* (Charles Town, W.Va.), June 29, 1810, citation file, MESDA. For the camp meeting view, see Edward C. Carter II et al., eds., *Latrobe's View of America, 1795–1820* (New Haven, Conn.: Yale University Press, 1985), fig. 109. For a family devotion view, see Monica Kiefer, *American Children through Their Books, 1700–1835* (Philadelphia: University of Pennsylvania Press, 1948), facing p. 15.

216. Alice Morse Earle, *Child Life in Colonial Days* (New York: Macmillan, 1899), p. 78; George C. Channing, *Early Recollections of Newport, R.I.* (Newport, R.I.: A. J. Ward, 1868), pp. 44, 49.

217. Oliver Dale estate records, 1774, Charleston, S.C., as quoted in Jones, *American Colonial Wealth*, pp. 1500–1501; Earle, *Child Life*, p. 115; school furniture notice in *Commercial Advertiser* (New York), April 29, 1800, as quoted in Gottesman, *Arts and Crafts, 1800–1804*, p. 155; Job E. Townsend ledger, 1794–1802, Newport Historical Society, Newport, R.I. (microfilm, DCM); Job Danforth, Sr., ledger, 1788–1818, RIHS; Mabel M. Swan, *Samuel McIntire, Carver, and the Sandersons, Early Salem Cabinet Makers* (Salem, Mass.: Essex Institute, 1934), p. 15; John Cooper agreement with the selectmen of Newburyport, Mass., March 10, 1830, DCM.

218. Hubbard in *Boston Directory for . . . 1860*; Wilder daybook and ledger; *Illustrated London News* (London, England), August 23, 1851, as quoted in Eleanor H. Gustafson, ed., "Clues and Footnotes," *Antiques* 115, no. 5 (May 1979): 1064. For a child's writing-arm chair,

now missing its original book box, see Evans, *Specialized Forms*, fig. 2-47.

219. Richard G. Wheeler and George Hilton, *Barkhamsted Heritage* (Canton, Conn.: By the American Revolution Bicentennial Steering Committee, 1975), p. 51; William H. Reed account book, 1803–48, DCM; Joseph Griswold ledger, 1804–13, private collection (microfilm, DCM). Other rush-bottom school seating is recorded in Daniel and Samuel Proud ledger, 1810–34; Samuel Davison ledger, 1795–1824, Pocumtuck Valley Memorial Association, Deerfield, Mass. (on deposit at Historic Deerfield, Deerfield, Mass.); Samuel Chapin account book, 1817–28, DCM; Solomon Sibley ledger, 1793–1840, OSV; and Luke Houghton ledger C, 1834–76, Barre (microfilm, DCM).

220. For Maentel's *Schoolmaster and Boys*, see Nina Fletcher Little, *The Abby Aldrich Rockefeller Folk Art Collection* (Boston: Little, Brown, 1957), pl. 77. For the Egelmann engraving, see "So Henn Die Alde Leit Geduh," *Der Reggeboge* (Journal of the Pennsylvania German Society) 16, no. 2 (1982): 47, fig. 3.

221. James Gere ledger, 1809–39, CSL; Caleb Hobart, Jr., bill to the Hingham Schoolhouse Committee, March 3, 1830, DCM; Norwich University invoice book, 1827–28, Vermont Historical Society, Montpelier.

222. Dale estate records; Emery, *Reminiscences*, p. 48. For the Miller school interior, see *Lewis Miller: Sketches and Chronicles* (York, Pa.: Historical Society of York County, 1966), p. 41.

223. Emily Noyes Vanderpoel, comp., and Elizabeth C. Barney Buel, ed., *Chronicles of a Pioneer School from 1792 to 1833* (Cambridge, Mass.: University Press, 1903); Cheney daybook, 1802–7, and ledger.

224. Boynton ledger, 1817–47.

225. Economical School bill to [Timothy Green, Esq.] for Miss Mary Green, December 28, 1810, DCM. For the Odell chair, see Evans, *American Windsor Chairs*, fig. 5-33.

226. Various bills to Mrs. Mary Green, 1823–34, DCM.

227. Lewis Bancel estate records, 1828, DCM.

228. Handwritten label affixed to branded council chair by Arthur Letchworth, as quoted in "Exhibit of 18th-Century Furniture" (typescript catalogue, Society of Descendants of the Signers of the Declaration of Independence, May 17 to September 30, 1952), National Park Service, Philadelphia, Pa., entry no. 20; Hornor, *Blue Book*, p. 297; Dorman, *Delaware Cabinetmakers*, pp. 27, 62.

229. Common Council records, as quoted in I. N. Phelps Stokes, *The Iconography of Manhattan Island, 1498–1909*, 6 vols. (New York: Robert H. Dodd, 1915–28), 4:471, 498–99, 807, 829; 5:1191, 1551; *Minutes of the Common Council of the City of New York, 1784–1831*, 19 vols. (New York: By the city, 1917), 1:34; Scott Graham Williamson, "Extant Furniture Ascribed

to New York's Federal Hall," *Antiques* 33, no. 5 (May 1938): 251–52.

230. Fetter account in William H. Egle, ed., *State of the Accounts of the County Lieutenants during the War of the Revolution, 1777–1789*, in *Pennsylvania Archives*, third series, vol. 3 (Harrisburg: Clarence M. Busch, 1896), p. 399; Franklin Ellis and Samuel Evans, *History of Lancaster County, Pennsylvania* (Philadelphia: Everts and Peck, 1883), pp. 204–7; notes made by the late John Aungst from Records of the Lancaster County Commissioners, LCHS; Fay Follett Kramer, "Lancaster County's Present Court House: A History of Its Construction," *Journal of the Lancaster County Historical Society* 71, no. 1 (1967): 6–7, 39–41, 44, 58–59. For Windsor armchairs made for the Sloan courthouse and attributed to Daniel M. Karcher and Sons, Philadelphia, see Evans, *American Windsor Chairs*, fig. 3-152.

231. The physical appearance of the courtroom in Lancaster was close to that in York, as described in Ellis and Evans, *History of Lancaster County*, pp. 205–6; Weld, *Travels*, 1:130.

232. Joseph Jones bill to Chester County, Pa., March 25, 1825, as quoted in Schiffer, *Furniture of Chester County*, p. 132. For the Wighe painting, see Davidson, *New York*, pp. 180–81.

233. Waterhouse in *Acts and Resolves of the Colony of Rhode Island* (Newport: Solomon Southwick, 1774), 7:127 (reference courtesy of Richard L. Champlin); Newport County resolve, and chairmaker's account, as quoted in Rhode Island Colony Records, October 1783, v. 12, p. 517, RISA (reference courtesy of Keith Morgan); Washington County resolve, as quoted in *Narragansett Historical Register* 2 (1883–84): 314 (reference courtesy of Richard L. Champlin); Providence Courthouse records in Accounts Allowed by the General Assembly, boxes 9–10 (1764–76) and 15 (1796–99) and Rhode Island Colony Records, October 1796, v. 14, p. 843, RISA (references courtesy of Edward F. Sanderson).

234. "Inventory of Property in the Court House, Salem," November 1817, Timothy Pickering Papers, PEM.

235. Dewey account book; Calvin Stetson account book, 1843–57, DCM; Middlesex County Courthouse furniture information in letter to author from Michael Dunbar, October 20, 1974. For a John White settee, see Evans, *Specialized Forms*, fig. 1-95.

236. Levy Court Docket and Public Book, Sussex County, Del., 1794 and 1797, DDHCA (reference courtesy of Ann Baker Horsey); Court Minutes, Wake Co., N.C., August term, 1807, as quoted in James H. Craig, *The Arts and Crafts in North Carolina, 1699–1840* (Winston-Salem, N.C.: Old Salem, 1965), pp. 169–70; Court Minutes, Davidson Co., Tenn., 1813, as noted in Derita Coleman Williams and Nathan Harsh, *The Art and Mystery of Tennessee Furniture and Its Makers through 1850* (Nashville:

Tennessee Historical Society and Tennessee State Museum Foundation, 1988), p. 313; Robert McKim account of the Corporation of Richmond, April 20, 1820, Hustings Court Minute Book No. 7, Richmond, Va., p. 365, citation file, MESDA.

237. James Phillips information in letter to author from John R. Grabb, December 3, 1978; Rand in *Louisville Directory* (1855), p. 210; Huia G. Ryder, *Antique Furniture by New Brunswick Craftsmen* (Toronto: Ryerson Press, 1965), p. 66.

238. Trumble chair purchase and order in *Pennsylvania Archives*, eighth series, vol. 8, p. 7308, and House Cash Book, p. 36, as quoted in "Exhibit of 18th-Century Furniture," p. 1.

239. Statehouse seating purchases in William Henry Egle, ed., *Pennsylvania Archives*, second series, vols. 11 and 12 (Harrisburg: William Stanley Ray, 1897), pp. 535, 558, and p. 4. Journal of the Pennsylvania House of Representatives, 1776–81, p. 298; journal of the Comptroller General, A-1, pp. 85, 96, 119; and journal of the Pennsylvania Senate, 1790, p. 267, as quoted in "Exhibit of 18th-Century Furniture," pp. 1, 2. Hornor, *Blue Book*, pp. 305–6; Henzey record in *Pennsylvania General Assembly, Senate Journal of the Senate of the Commonwealth of Pennsylvania* (Philadelphia: Zachariah Poulson, 1791), pp. 266–67.

240. Common Council records, as quoted in Stokes, *Iconography*, 4:789, 5:1335; *Minutes of the Common Council*, 2:300; John DeWitt bill to the Corporation of the City of New York, New York, October 1796, New York City Vouchers, QC.

241. John Wadsworth bill to Statehouse, Hartford, Conn., June 8, 1796, CHS; Newton C. Brainard, *The Hartford State House of 1796* (Hartford: Connecticut Historical Society, 1964), pp. 17–32. For a statehouse-type highback chair possibly made by Wadsworth, see Evans, *American Windsor Chairs*, fig. 6-187.

242. Donna-Belle Garvin, James L. Garvin, and John F. Page, *Plain and Elegant, Rich and Common: Documented New Hampshire Furniture, 1750–1850* (Concord: New Hampshire Historical Society, 1979), pp. 70–75, including Blanchard quote. For a statehouse armchair, see Evans, *American Windsor Chairs*, fig. 7-87.

243. Christopher Horton bills to the State of Delaware, October 25, 1791, DDHCA; Mark Pringle letter to Daniel of St. Thomas Jenifer, January 13, 1784, State of Maryland, Hall of Records, Annapolis (reference courtesy of William V. Elder III). For a bow-back chair thought to have been used in the Maryland Statehouse, see Evans, *American Windsor Chairs*, fig. 4-2. Giles Cromwell, "Andrew and Robert McKim, Windsor Chair Makers," *Journal of Early Southern Decorative Arts* 6, no. 1 (May 1980): 8–10.

244. David Ruth bills for statehouse furnishings, 1795, 1805–7, 1818, 1820, Treasurer and Comptroller's Papers, State of North Carolina,

citation file, MESDA; David Ruth notice of accident, *Raleigh Register* (Raleigh, N.C.), July 12, 1810, citation file, MESDA; C. J. Tooker, *Raleigh Register*, July 9, 1824, as quoted in Craig, *Arts and Crafts*, p. 208.

245. Georgia Board of State Commissioners, Request for Warrant, September 26, 1812 (reference courtesy of J. L. Sibley Jennings, Jr.).

246. Phillips information in letter to author from John R. Grabb, December 3, 1978; Betty Lawson Walters, *Furniture Makers of Indiana, 1793 to 1850* (Indianapolis: Indiana Historical Society, 1972), p. 31; Lynch and Trask bill to Secretary of the Iowa Territory, April 15, 1839, as illustrated in Margaret N. Keyes, "Piecing Together Iowa's Old Capitol," *Historic Preservation* 26, no. 1 (January–March 1974), pp. 40, 42–43.

247. Peterson, "Carpenters' Hall," p. 102; Watson, *Annals of Philadelphia* 3:278. For a Henzey high-back chair, see Evans, *American Windsor Chairs*, fig. 3-25.

248. Statehouse seating purchase from Thomas Ackley in *Pennsylvania Archives*, eighth series, vol. 6, p. 5272, as quoted in "Exhibit of 18th-Century Furniture," p. 1; Fiss in Hornor, *Blue Book*, p. 304; Charles G. Dorman, "Refurnishing the Assembly Room of the Pennsylvania State House," in *University Hospital Antiques Show Catalogue, 1967* (Philadelphia: University Hospital Antiques Show, 1967), pp. 27–30; Charles G. Dorman, "Philadelphia Furniture: 'Of the Best Sort,'" in John C. Milley, ed., *Treasures of Independence* (New York: Mayflower Books, 1980), pp. 130–31.

249. David Evans account of John Hancock, August 12–October 13, 1776, Collection of Private and Business Papers (Boston), vol. 4, BPL; Frank M. Etting, *An Historical Account of the Old State House of Pennsylvania* (Philadelphia: Porter and Coates, 1891), p. 94; the Pine-Savage painting is discussed in Ann C. Van Devanter *"Anywhere so Long as There Be Freedom": Charles Carroll of Carrollton, His Family and His Maryland* (Baltimore: Baltimore Museum of Art, ca. 1975), pp. 114–15.

250. Williamson, "New York's Federal Hall," pp. 250–52; Common Council records, as quoted in Stokes, *Iconography*, 5:1283–84.

251. Wansey, *Excursion*, p. 98; Edward M. Riley, "The Independence Hall Group," in *Transactions of the American Philosophical Society* 43, pt. 1 (1953): 27–28; U.S. Congress, "Articles of Furniture necessary to be provided," Miers Fisher Papers, HSP.

252. Harrison, *Diary of Thomas P. Cope*, p. 116.

253. Manifests of schooner *Olive Branch*, June 11, 1800, and sloop *Harmony*, December 19, 1801, Philadelphia Outward Coastwise Entries, U.S. Custom House Records, NA; William Worthington, Edward Douglass, James Patterson, and Thomas Adams bills to Department of War, May 18, September 26, October 6, Novem-

ber 9, and December 8, 1814, Treasury Records, Miscellaneous Treasury Accounts of the First Auditor, no. 29,475, NA. For the "single-top" and "flat-top" patterns, see Evans, *American Windsor Chairs*, figs. 3-114, 4-12.

254. Frank H. Stewart, *History of the First United States Mint* (Camden, N.J.: By the author, 1924), pp. 23–27, 65–66, 173, 175, 177.

255. Manifest of brig *Hannah*, June 1, 1804, Philadelphia Outward Coastwise Manifests, U.S. Custom House Records, NA. For the Seymour watercolor, see *American Art from Alumni Collections* (New Haven, Conn.: Yale University Art Gallery, 1968), fig. 40. Joan Mackinnon, *Kingston Cabinetmakers, 1800–1867*, National Museum of Man Mercury Series (Ottawa: National Museums of Canada, 1976), p. 7; Philip Shackleton, *The Furniture of Old Ontario* (Toronto: MacMillan of Canada, 1973), p. 22.

Select Bibliography

Books

Alberts, Robert C. *The Golden Voyage: The Life and Times of William Bingham, 1752–1804.* Boston: Houghton Mifflin, 1969.

Aldrich, Lewis Cass, and Frank R. Holmes. *History of Windsor County, Vermont.* Syracuse, N.Y.: D. Mason, 1891.

Alexander, John D., Jr. *Make a Chair from a Tree: An Introduction to Working Green Wood.* Newtown, Conn.: Taunton Press, 1978.

Atwater, Edward E. *History of the City of New Haven.* New York: W. W. Munsell, 1887.

Belknap, Henry Wyckoff. *Artists and Craftsmen of Essex County, Massachusetts.* Salem, Mass.: Essex Institute, 1927.

Bivins, John, Jr., and Paula Welshimer. *Moravian Decorative Arts in North Carolina.* Winston-Salem, N.C.: Old Salem, 1981.

Brainard, Newton C. *The Hartford State House of 1796.* Hartford: Connecticut Historical Society, 1964.

Brazer, Esther Stevens. *Early American Decoration.* 2d ed. Springfield, Mass.: Pond-Ekberg, 1947.

Bridenbaugh, Carl. *Cities in Revolt: Urban Life in America, 1743–1776.* New York: Alfred A. Knopf, 1955.

———. *The Colonial Craftsman.* Chicago: University of Chicago Press, 1961.

Churchill, Edwin A. *Simple Forms and Vivid Colors.* Augusta: Maine State Museum, 1983.

Clark, Victor S. *History of Manufactures in the United States.* 3 vols. 1929. Reprint. New York: Peter Smith, 1949.

Craig, James H. *The Arts and Crafts in North Carolina, 1699–1840.* Winston-Salem, N.C.: Old Salem, 1965.

Davidson, Marshall B. *Life in America.* 2 vols. Boston: Houghton Mifflin, 1951.

———. *New York: A Pictorial History.* New York: Charles Scribner's Sons, 1977.

Day, Clive. *The Rise of Manufacturing in Connecticut, 1820–1850.* Tercentenary Commission of the State of Connecticut, no. 44. New Haven, Conn.: Yale University Press, 1935.

Dorman, Charles G. *Delaware Cabinetmakers and Allied Artisans, 1655–1855.* Wilmington: Historical Society of Delaware, 1960.

Dow, George Francis, comp. *The Arts and Crafts in New England, 1704–1775.* 1927. Reprint. New York: Da Capo Press, 1967.

Drepperd, Carl W. *Pioneer America: Its First Three Centuries.* Garden City, N.Y.: Doubleday, 1949.

Dunbar, Michael. *Make a Windsor Chair with Michael Dunbar.* Newtown, Conn.: Taunton Press, 1984.

Earle, Alice Morse. *Child Life in Colonial Days.* New York: Macmillan, 1899.

Elder, William Voss, III. *Baltimore Painted Furniture, 1800–1840.* Baltimore: Baltimore Museum of Art, 1972.

Emerson, George B. *A Report on the Trees and Shrubs . . . in the Forests of Massachusetts.* 2 vols. Boston: Little, Brown, 1894.

Etting, Frank M. *An Historical Account of the Old State House of Pennsylvania.* Philadelphia: Porter and Coates, 1891.

Evans, Nancy Goyne. *American Windsor Chairs.* New York: Hudson Hills Press, 1996.

———. *American Windsor Furniture: Specialized Forms.* New York: Hudson Hills Press, 1997.

Fales, Dean A., Jr. *American Painted Furniture, 1660–1880.* New York: E. P. Dutton, 1972.

Fede, Helen Maggs. *Washington Furniture at Mount Vernon.* Mount Vernon, Va.: Mount Vernon Ladies' Association, 1966.

Franco, Barbara. *Masonic Symbols in American Decorative Arts.* Lexington, Mass.: Museum of Our National Heritage, 1976.

Garrett, Elisabeth Donaghy. *At Home: The American Family, 1750–1870.* New York: Harry N. Abrams, 1990.

Garvin, Donna-Belle, James L. Garvin, and John F. Page. *Plain and Elegant, Rich and Common: Documented New Hampshire Furniture, 1750–1850.* Concord: New Hampshire Historical Society, 1979.

Gilbert, Christopher. *English Vernacular Furniture, 1750–1900.* New Haven, Conn.: Yale University Press, 1991.

Goodman, William L. *History of Woodworking Tools.* New York: David McKay, 1964.

Gottesman, Rita Susswein, comp. *The Arts and Crafts in New York, 1726–1776.* 1938. Reprint. New York: Da Capo Press, 1970.

———. *The Arts and Crafts in New York, 1777–1799.* New York: New-York Historical Society, 1954.

———. *The Arts and Crafts in New York, 1800–1804.* New York: New-York Historical Society, 1965.

Herrick, William D. *History of the Town of Gardner.* Gardner, Mass.: By the committee, 1878.

History of Litchfield County, Connecticut. Philadelphia: J. W. Lewis, 1881.

A History of the Schuylkill Fishing Company of the State in Schuylkill, 1732–1888. Philadelphia: By the members, 1889.

History of Worcester County, Massachusetts. 2 vols. Boston: C. F. Jewett, 1879.

Hoadley, R. Bruce. *Understanding Wood.* Newtown, Conn.: Taunton Press, 1980.

Hornor, William MacPherson, Jr. *Blue Book: Philadelphia Furniture.* 1935. Reprint. Washington, D.C.: Highland House, 1977.

Hummel, Charles F. *With Hammer in Hand.* Charlottesville: University Press of Virginia, 1968.

Hunter, Lewis C. *Steamboats on the Western Rivers.* Cambridge, Mass.: Harvard University Press, 1949.

———. *Waterpower in the Century of the Steam Engine.* Vol. 1 of *A History of Industrial Power in the United States, 1780–1930.* Charlottesville: University Press of Virginia, 1979.

Hurd, Duane Hamilton, ed. *History of Worcester County, Massachusetts.* 2 vols. Philadelphia: J. W. Lewis, 1889.

Jenkins, J. Geraint. *Traditional Country Craftsmen.* London: Routledge and Kegan Paul, 1965.

Jobe, Brock, and Myrna Kaye. *New England Furniture: The Colonial Era.* Boston: Houghton Mifflin, 1984.

Johnston, William Dawson. *History of the Library of Congress.* Washington, D.C.: Government Printing Office, 1904.

Jones, Alice Hanson. *American Colonial Wealth.* 3 vols. New York: Arno Press, 1977.

Kenney, John Tarrant. *The Hitchcock Chair.* New York: Clarkson N. Potter, 1971.

Laing, Alexander. *Seafaring America.* New York: American Heritage Publishing, 1974.

Langsner, Drew. *The Chairmaker's Workshop.* Ashville, N.C.: Lark Books, 1997.

Lea, Zilla Rider, ed. *The Ornamented Chair.* Rutland, Vt.: Charles E. Tuttle, 1960.

Lewis, W. David. *From Newgate to Dannemora: The Rise of the Penitentiary in New York, 1796–1848.* Ithaca, N.Y.: Cornell University Press, 1965.

Lyon, Irving Whitall. *The Colonial Furniture of New England.* Boston: Houghton Mifflin, 1924.

MacDonald, William H. *Central New Jersey Chairmaking of the Nineteenth Century.* Trenton, N.J.: By the author, 1960.

Mackinnon, Joan. *A Checklist of Toronto Cabinet and Chair Makers, 1800–1865.* National Museum of Man Mercury Series. Ottawa: National Museums of Canada, 1975.

———. *Kingston Cabinetmakers, 1800–1867.* National Museum of Man Mercury Series. Ottawa: National Museums of Canada, 1976.

Macquoid, Percy, and Ralph Edwards. *The Dictionary of English Furniture.* 3 vols. 1924–27. Reprint of 2d ed., rev. Ralph Edwards. Woodbridge, England: Barra Books, 1983.

Mayes, L. J. *The History of Chairmaking in High Wycombe.* London: Routledge and Kegan Paul, 1960.

Mercer, Henry C. *Ancient Carpenters' Tools.* Doylestown, Pa.: Bucks County Historical Society, 1951.

———. *The Bible in Iron.* 1914. Rev. Horace M. Mann. Doylestown, Pa.: Bucks County Historical Society, 1941.

Miller, James W. *The Genesis of Western Culture.* 1938. Reprint. New York: Da Capo Press, 1969.

Minhinnick, Jeanne. *At Home in Upper Canada.* Toronto: Clark, Irwin, 1970.

———. *Early Furniture in Upper Canada Village, 1800–1837.* Toronto: McGraw-Hill of Canada, 1964.

Montgomery, Charles F. *American Furniture: The Federal Period.* New York: Viking Press, 1966.

Montgomery, Florence. *Textiles in America, 1650–1870.* New York: W. W. Norton, 1983.

Morison, Samuel Eliot. *The Maritime History of Massachusetts, 1783–1860.* London: William Heinemann, 1923.

Morison, Samuel Eliot, and Henry Commager. *The Growth of the American Republic.* 2 vols. 4th ed. New York: Oxford University Press, 1950.

Myers, Minor, Jr., and Edgar deN. Mayhew. *New London County Furniture, 1640–1840.* New London, Conn.: Lyman Allyn Museum, 1974.

Pain, Howard. *The Heritage of Country Furniture.* Toronto: Van Nostrand Reinhold, 1978.

Parsons, Charles S. *The Dunlaps and Their Furniture.* Manchester, N.H.: Currier Gallery of Art, 1970.

Prime, Alfred Coxe, comp. *The Arts and Crafts in Philadelphia, Maryland, and South Carolina, 1721–1785.* Philadelphia: Walpole Society, 1929.

———. *The Arts and Crafts in Philadelphia, Maryland, and South Carolina, 1786–1800.* Topsfield, Mass.: Walpole Society, 1932.

Rice, Kym S. *Early American Taverns: For the Entertainment of Friends and Strangers.* Chicago: Regnery Gateway for the Fraunces Tavern Museum, 1983.

Rock, Howard B. *Artisans of the New Republic.* New York: New York University Press, 1979.

Roe, F. Gordon. *Windsor Chairs.* London: Phoenix House, 1953.

Ryder, Huia G. *Antique Furniture by New Brunswick Craftsmen.* Toronto: Ryerson Press, 1965.

Salaman, Raphael A. *Dictionary of Tools.* London: George Allen and Unwin, 1975.

Schiffer, Margaret Berwind. *Chester County, Pennsylvania, Inventories, 1684–1850.* Exton, Pa.: Schiffer Publishing, 1974.

———. *Furniture and Its Makers of Chester County, Pennsylvania.* Philadelphia: University of Pennsylvania Press, 1966.

Seybolt, Robert Francis. *Apprenticeship and Apprenticeship Education in Colonial New England and New York.* New York: Columbia University, 1917.

Sikes, Jane E. *The Furniture Makers of Cincinnati, 1790 to 1849.* Cincinnati, Ohio: By the author, 1976.

Sims, John Patterson. *The Fishing Company of Fort St. Davids.* Philadelphia: Society of Colonial Wars in the Commonwealth of Pennsylvania, 1951.

Singleton, Esther. *The Furniture of Our Forefathers.* Garden City, N.Y.: Doubleday, Page, 1913.

———. *Social New York under the Georges, 1714–1776.* New York: D. Appleton, 1902.

Sorin, Gretchen Sullivan, and Ellen Kirven Donald. *Gadsby's Tavern Museum Historic Furnishing Plan.* Alexandria, Va.: By the city, 1980.

Stearns, Ezra S. *History of Ashburnham, Massachusetts.* Ashburnham: By the town, 1887.

Stokes, I. N. Phelps. *The Iconography of Manhattan Island, 1498–1906.* 6 vols. New York: Robert H. Dodd, 1915–28.

Sullivan, William A. *The Industrial Worker in Pennsylvania, 1800–1840.* Harrisburg: Pennsylvania Historical and Museum Commission, 1955.

Swan, Mabel M. *Samuel McIntire, Carver, and the Sandersons, Early Salem Cabinet Makers.* Salem, Mass.: Essex Institute, 1934.

Sweeney, John A. H. *Lafayette, the Nation's Guest.* Winterthur, Del.: Winterthur Museum, 1957.

Walters, Betty Lawson. *Furniture Makers of Indiana, 1793 to 1850.* Indianapolis: Indiana Historical Society, 1972.

Waring, Janet. *Early American Stencils.* New York: William R. Scott, 1937.

Weeden, William B. *Economic and Social History of New England, 1620–1789.* 2 vols. Boston: Houghton Mifflin, 1891.

Woodbury, Robert S. *History of the Lathe to 1850.* Monograph Series, no. 1. Cleveland, Ohio: Society for the History of Technology, 1961.

Articles

Beasley, Ellen. "Tennessee Cabinetmakers and Chairmakers through 1840." *Antiques* 100, no. 4 (October 1971): 612–21.

Berkley, Henry J. "A Register of Cabinet Makers and Allied Trades in Maryland, as Shown by the Newspapers and Directories, 1746 to 1820." *Maryland Historical Magazine* 25, no. 1 (March 1930): 1–27.

Candee, Richard M. "Housepaints in Colonial America: Their Materials, Manufacture, and Application." "Part 1: The Preparation, Sale, and Storage of Colors" and "Part 3: Nomenclature of Painters' Materials." *Color Engineering* 4, no. 5 (September–October 1966): 26–34, and 5, nos. 1, 2 (January–February, March-April 1967): 37–43, 32–42.

Catalano, Kathleen M. "Cabinetmaking in Philadelphia, 1820–1840: Transition from Craft to Industry." In *Winterthur Portfolio 13,* ed. Ian M. G. Quimby, pp. 81–138. Chicago: University of Chicago Press, 1979.

Chase, Ada R. "Two 18th-Century Craftsmen of Norwich." *Connecticut Historical Society Bulletin* 25, no. 3 (July 1960): 84–88.

Coffin, Margaret. "Ransom Cook, Saratoga Chairmaker (1794–1881)." *The Decorator* 31, no. 2 (Spring 1977): 18–25.

Collard, Elizabeth. "Montreal Cabinetmakers and Chairmakers: 1800–1850." *Antiques* 105, no. 5 (May 1974): 1132–46.

Cotton, Bill. "Vernacular Design: The Spindle Back Chair and Its North Country Origins." *Working Wood* (Spring 1980): 40–50.

Cromwell, Giles. "Andrew and Robert McKim, Windsor Chair Makers." *Journal of Early Southern Decorative Arts* 6, no. 1 (May 1980): 1–20, frontispiece.

Curtis, John O. "The Introduction of the Circular Saw in the Early 19th Century." *Bulletin of the Association for Preservation Technology* 5, no. 2 (1973): 162–89.

DePuy, Leroy B. "The Walnut Street Prison: Pennsylvania's First Penitentiary." Reprint. *Pennsylvania History* 18, no. 2 (April 1951): 2–16.

Deveikis, Peter. "Hastings Warren: Vermont Cabinetmaker." *Antiques* 101, no. 6 (June 1972): 1037–39.

Dorman, Charles G. "Refurnishing the Assembly Room of the Pennsylvania State House." In *University Hospital Antiques Show Catalogue, 1967,* pp. 27–30. Philadelphia: University Hospital Antiques Show, 1967.

Earl, Polly Anne. "Craftsmen and Machines:

The Nineteenth-Century Furniture Industry." In *Technological Innovation and the Decorative Arts*, ed. Ian M. G. Quimby and Polly Anne Earl, pp. 307–29. Charlottesville: University Press of Virginia, 1974.

Evans, Nancy Goyne. "The Christian M. Nestell Drawing Book: A Focus on the Ornamental Painter and His Craft in Early Nineteenth-Century America." In *American Furniture 1998*, ed. Luke Beckerdite, pp. 99–163. Hanover, N.H.: University Press of New England for the Chipstone Foundation, 1998.

———. "Design Transmission in Vernacular Seating Furniture: The Influence of Philadelphia and Baltimore Styles on Chairmaking from the Chesapeake to the 'West.'" In *American Furniture 1993*, ed. Luke Beckerdite, pp. 75–116. Hanover, N.H.: University Press of New England for the Chipstone Foundation, 1993.

———. "The Sans Souci, a Fashionable Resort Hotel in Ballston Spa." In *Winterthur Portfolio 6*, ed. Richard K. Doud and Ian M. G. Quimby, pp. 111–26. Charlottesville: University Press of Virginia, 1970.

Fales, Dean A., Jr. "Joseph Barrell's Pleasant Hill." In *Publications of the Colonial Society of Massachusetts: Transactions*, vol. 43, pp. 373–90. Boston: By the society, 1966.

Forman, Benno M. "Delaware Valley 'Crookt Foot' and Slat-Back Chairs." *Winterthur Portfolio* 15, no. 1 (Spring 1980): 41–64.

Fraser, Esther Stevens. "The Golden Age of Stencilling." *Antiques* 1, no. 4 (April 1922): 162–66.

———. "Painted Furniture in America, Parts 1, 2." *Antiques* 5 and 6, nos. 6, 3 (June, September 1924): 302–6, 141–46.

Garrett, Wendell D. "Providence Cabinetmakers, Chairmakers, Upholsterers, and Allied Craftsmen, 1756–1838." *Antiques* 90, no. 4 (October 1966): 514–19.

Gillingham, Harrold E. "Benjamin Lehman, a Germantown Cabinet-Maker." *Pennsylvania Magazine of History and Biography* 54, no. 4 (1930): 289–306.

———. "The Philadelphia Windsor Chair and Its Journeyings." *Pennsylvania Magazine of History and Biography* 55, no. 3 (1931): 301–32.

Golovin, Anne Castrodale. "Cabinetmakers and Chairmakers of Washington, D.C., 1791–1840." *Antiques* 107, no. 5 (May 1975): 898–922.

Goyne (Evans), Nancy A. "Francis Trumble of Philadelphia, Windsor Chair and Cabinetmaker." In *Winterthur Portfolio 1*, ed. Milo M. Naeve, pp. 221–41. Winterthur, Del.: Winterthur Museum, 1964.

Grabb, John R. "The Bucksaw and the Sawbuck." *Chronicle of the Early American Industries Association* 29, no. 2 (June 1976): 18–20.

———. "Burning Brands or Marking Irons." *Chronicle of the Early American Industries Association* 31, no. 3 (September 1978): 37–40.

Hall, Elton W. "New Bedford Furniture." *Antiques* 113, no. 5 (May 1978): 1105–27.

Hancock, Harold B. "Furniture Craftsmen in Delaware Records." In *Winterthur Portfolio 9*, ed. Ian M. G. Quimby, pp. 175–212. Charlottesville: University Press of Virginia, 1974.

Harlow, Henry J. "The Shop of Samuel Wing, Craftsman of Sandwich, Massachusetts." *Antiques* 93, no. 3 (March 1968): 372–77.

Howard, Robert W. "The Ohio River: Throughway 'For the West.'" In Western Writers of America, *Water Trails West*, pp. 43–54. Garden City, N.Y.: Doubleday, 1978.

Howe, Florence Thompson. "The Brief Career of Ansel Goodrich." *Antiques* 18, no. 1 (July 1930): 38–39.

Hummel, Charles F. "English Tools in America: The Evidence of the Dominys." In *Winterthur Portfolio 2*, ed. Milo M. Naeve, pp. 27–46. Winterthur, Del.: Winterthur Museum, 1965.

Jenkins, J. Geraint. "A Chiltern Chair Bodger." *Country Life* 118, no. 3063 (September 29, 1955): 684, 686.

Kihn, Phyllis, comp. "Connecticut Cabinetmakers, Parts 1, 2." *Connecticut Historical Society Bulletin* 32 and 33, nos. 4, 1 (October 1967, January 1968): 97–144, 1–40.

Kimball, Fiske. "Thomas Jefferson's Windsor Chairs." *Pennsylvania Museum Bulletin* 21, no. 98 (December 1925): 58–60.

Kindig, Joe, III. "Upholstered Windsors." *Antiques* 62, no. 1 (July 1952): 52–53.

Kirkham, Pat. "Introduction, Part I, Furniture-Makers and Trade Unionism: The Early London Trade Societies." In reprint of *The Cabinet-Makers' London Book of Prices* (London: London Society of Cabinet Makers, 1793), in *Furniture History* 18 (1982): 1–10.

Love, W. DeLoss. "The Navigation of the Connecticut River." *Proceedings of the American Antiquarian Society*, new series, vol. 15, pt. 3 (April 29, 1903): 385–433.

MacLaren, George. "The Windsor Chair in Nova Scotia." *Antiques* 100, no. 1 (July 1971): 124–27.

McIntyre, W. John. "Arms across the Border: Trade in Chairs and Chair Parts between the United States and Upper Canada." In *Victorian Furniture: Essays from a Victorian Society Autumn Symposium*, ed. Kenneth L. Ames, pp. 55–64. Published as *Nineteenth Century* (Victorian Society in America) 8, nos. 3, 4 (1982).

McMillen, Loring. "Sandpaper." *Chronicle of the Early American Industries Association* 8, no. 2 (April 1955): 17–18.

Monahon, Eleanore Bradford. "Providence Cabinetmakers." *Rhode Island History* 23, no. 1 (January 1964): 1–22.

Olsen, T. V. "The Great Lakes: Gateway to the Heartland." In Western Writers of America, *Water Trails West*, pp. 95–112. Garden City, N.Y.: Doubleday, 1978.

Ott, Joseph K. "Exports of Furniture, Chaises, and Other Wooden Forms from Providence and Newport, 1783–1795." *Antiques* 108, no. 1 (January 1975): 135–41.

———. "Recent Discoveries among Rhode Island Cabinetmakers and Their Work." *Rhode Island History* 28, no. 1 (February 1969): 3–25.

———. "Rhode Island Furniture Exports, 1783–1800, Including Information on Chaises, Buildings, and Other Woodenware and Trade Practices." *Rhode Island History* 36, no. 1 (February 1977): 2–13.

———. "Still More Notes on Rhode Island Cabinetmakers and Allied Craftsmen." *Rhode Island History* 28, no. 4 (November 1969): 111–21.

Peterson, Charles E. "Carpenters' Hall" and "Library Hall: Home of the Library Company of Philadelphia, 1790–1880." In *Historic Philadelphia*, issued as *Transactions of the American Philosophical Society* 43, pt. 1 (1953): 96–128, 129–47.

———. "Sawdust Trail." *Bulletin of the Association for Preservation Technology* 5, no. 2 (1973): 84–144.

Salinger, Sharon V. "Artisans, Journeymen, and the Transformation of Labor in Late Eighteenth-Century Philadelphia." *William and Mary Quarterly* 40, no. 1 (January 1983): 62–84.

Saltar, Gordon. "New England Timbers." In *Boston Furniture of the Eighteenth Century*, ed. Walter Muir Whitehill, pp. 254–64. Publications of the Colonial Society of Massachusetts, vol. 48. Boston: Colonial Society of Massachusetts, 1974.

Schild, Joan Lynn. "Furniture Makers of Rochester, New York." *New York History* 37, no.1 (January 1956): 97–106.

Shettleworth, Earle G., Jr., and William D. Barry. "Walter Corey's Furniture Manufactory in Portland, Maine." *Antiques* 121, no. 5 (May 1982): 1199–1205.

Skemer, Don K. "David Alling's Chair Manufactory: Craft Industrialization in Newark, New Jersey, 1801–1854." *Winterthur Portfolio* 22, no. 1 (Spring 1987): 1–21.

Smith, Robert T. "The 'Father of Waters.'" In Western Writers of America, *Water Trails West*, pp. 15–27. Garden City, N.Y.: Doubleday, 1978.

Stokes, J. Stogdell. "The American Windsor Chair." *Antiques* 9, no. 4 (April 1926): 222–27.

Streifthau, Donna. "Cincinnati Cabinet- and Chairmakers, 1819–30." *Antiques* 90, no. 6 (June 1971): 896–905.

Swan, Mabel M. "Coastwise Cargoes of Venture Furniture." *Antiques* 55, no. 4 (April 1949): 278–80.

———. "Furniture Makers of Charlestown." *Antiques* 46, no. 4 (October 1944): 203–6.

Talbott, Page. "Cheapest, Strongest, and Best Chairmaking in 19th-Century Philadelphia, Part 1." *Chronicle of the Early American Industries Association* 33, no. 2 (June 1980): 28–30.

Tanner, Earl C. "Caribbean Ports in the Foreign Commerce of Providence, 1790–1830, Parts 1, 2." *Rhode Island History* 14 and 15, nos. 4, 1 (October 1955, January 1956): 97–108, 11–20.

———. "Early 19th-Century Providence Exports to Brazil." *Rhode Island History* 19, no. 3 (July 1960): 89–94.

———. "Early 19th-Century Providence Exports to the Caribbean." *Rhode Island History* 19, no. 2 (April 1960): 42–49.

———. "South American Ports in the Foreign Commerce of Providence, 1800–1830." *Rhode Island History* 16, no. 3 (July 1957): 65–78.

Tuttle, Donald L., and Joyce Baudin. "James Wilson, a Pennsylvania Chairmaker." *Chronicle of the Early American Industries Association* 32, no. 4 (December 1979): 53–57.

Weil, Martin Eli. "A Cabinetmaker's Price Book." In *Winterthur Portfolio 13*, ed. Ian M. G. Quimby, pp. 175–92. Chicago: University of Chicago Press, 1979.

Welsh, Frank. "The Art of Painted Graining." *Historic Preservation* 29, no. 3 (July–September 1977): 33–37.

Whallon, Arthur. "Indiana Cabinetmakers and Allied Craftsmen, 1815–1860." *Antiques* 98, no. 1 (July 1970): 118–25.

Wolcott, Stephen C. "A Cooper's Shop of 1800." *Chronicle of the Early American Industries Association* 1, no. 9 (January 1935): 1–2, 7.

Travel Journals, Design Books, and Works of Social, Economic, and Technological Commentary

Anburey, Thomas. *Travels through the Interior Parts of America*. 2 vols. Boston: Houghton Mifflin, 1923.

Arfwedson, Carl David. *The United States and Canada*. 2 vols. 1834. Reprint. New York: Johnson Reprint Corp., 1969.

The Aristocratic Journey: Being the Outspoken Letters of Mrs. Basil Hall. Ed. Una Pope-Hennessy. New York: G. P. Putnam's Sons, 1931.

Atwater, Caleb. *The Writings of Caleb Atwater*. Columbus, Ohio: By the author, 1833.

Bacon, Louisa Crowninshield. *Reminiscences*. [Salem, Mass.]: By the author, 1922.

Barber, John W., and Henry Howe. *Historical Collections of the State of New Jersey*. Newark, N.J.: Benjamin Olds, 1844.

Barck, Dorothy C., ed. *Letters from John Pintard to His Daughter*. 4 vols. New York: New-York Historical Society, 1940–41.

Benson, Adolph B., ed. *Peter Kalm's Travels in North America*. 2 vols. New York: Dover Publications, 1966.

Bigelow, Jacob. *The Useful Arts*. 2 vols. Boston: Thomas H. Webb, 1840.

The Book of Trades, or Library of Useful Arts. London, 1805.

Brissot de Warville, J. P. *New Travels in the United States of America*. Dublin: P. Byrne et al., 1792.

Brissot de Warville, Jacques Pierre, and Etienne Clavière. *The Commerce of America with Europe*. New York: T. and J. Swords, 1795.

Bristed, John. *America and Her Resources*. 1818. Reprint. New York: Research Reprints, 1970.

Brown, Harriet Connor. *Grandmother Brown's Hundred Years, 1827–1927*. New York: Blue Ribbon Books, 1929.

Brown, Samuel R. *The Western Gazetteer, or Emigrants Directory*. Auburn, N.Y.: H. C. Southwick, 1817.

Buckingham, Joseph T., comp. *Annals of the Massachusetts Charitable Mechanic Association*. Boston: Crocker and Brewster, 1853.

The Cabinet-Maker's Guide. London, 1825. Reprint. Greenfield, Mass.: Ansel Phelps, 1825.

Campbell, R. *The London Tradesman*. London: T. Gardner, 1747.

Cennini, Cennino D'Andrea. *The Craftsman's Handbook*. Trans. Daniel V. Thompson, Jr. New York: Dover Publications, 1933.

Chambers, William W. *Things as They Are in America*. Philadelphia: Lippincott, Grambo, 1854.

Channing, George C. *Early Recollections of Newport, R.I.* Newport, R.I.: A. J. Ward, 1868.

Chastellux, marquis de. *Travels in North-America in the Years 1780, 1781, and 1782*. 2 vols. London: G. G. J. and J. Robinson, 1787.

Clark, Christopher, ed. "The Diary of an Apprentice Cabinetmaker: Edward Jenner Carpenter's 'Journal,' 1844–45," pp. 303–94. Proceedings of the American Antiquarian Society, vol. 98, pt. 2. Worcester, Mass.: By the society, 1989.

Colden, Cadwallader D. *Memoir Prepared at the Request of a Committee of the Common Council of the City of New York and Presented to the Mayor of the City at the Celebration of the Completion of the New York Canals*. New York: W. A. Davis, 1825.

"The Contence of the Book Paints and Receipts for Wooden Work." *Connecticut Historical Society Bulletin* 9, no. 2 (January 1943): 9–16.

Cooper, John M. *Recollections of Chambersburg, Pa., Chiefly between the Years 1830–1850*. Chambersburg, Pa.: A. N. Pomeroy, 1900.

Coxe, Tench. *An Address to an Assembly of the Friends of American Manufactures*. Philadelphia: R. Aitken and Sons, 1787.

———. *A Statement of the Arts and Manufactures of the United States of America for the Year 1810*. Philadelphia: A. Cornman, Jr., 1814.

———. *A View of the United States of America*. Philadelphia: William Hall et al., 1794.

[Davison, Gideon Miner]. *Traveller's Guide*. 6th ed. Saratoga Springs, N.Y.: G. M. Davison, 1834.

de Beaujour, Le chevalier Felix. *Sketch of the United States of North America . . . from 1800 to 1810*. Trans. William Walton. London: J. Booth et al., 1814.

de Crèvecoeur, Hector Saint John. *Sketches of Eighteenth-Century America*. Ed. Henri L. Bourdin et al. New Haven, Conn.: Yale University Press, 1925.

De Witt, Francis. *Statistical Information Relating to Certain Branches of Industry in Massachusetts for the Year Ending June 1, 1855*. Boston: William White, 1856.

Dexter, Franklin Bowditch, ed. *The Literary Diary of Ezra Stiles*. 3 vols. New York: Charles Scribner's Sons, 1901.

"The Diary of Samual Breck, 1823–1827." *Pennsylvania Magazine of History and Biography* 103, no. 1 (January 1979): 85–113.

The Diary of William Bentley. 4 vols. Salem, Mass.: Essex Institute, 1905.

Dictionary of Arts, Sciences, and Miscellaneous Literature. 18 vols. Philadelphia: Thomas Dobson, 1798.

Documents Relative to Manufactures in the United States Collected and Transmitted to the House of Representatives in Compliance with a Resolution of January 8, 1832, by the Secretary of the Treasury. 2 vols. Washington, D.C.: Duff Green, 1833.

Dossie, Robert. *The Handmaid to the Arts*. 2 vols. London: J. Nourse, 1758.

Duane, Col. William. *A Visit to Colombia in the Years 1822 and 1823*. Philadelphia, 1826.

[Dwight, Theodore, Jr.] *The Northern Traveller*. 2d ed. New York: A. T. Goodrich, 1826.

Dwight, Timothy. *Travels in New England and New York*. 4 vols. Ed. Barbara Miller Solomon. Cambridge, Mass.: Belknap Press, 1969.

Earle, Thomas, and Charles T. Congdon, eds. *Annals of the General Society of Mechanics and Tradesmen*. New York: By the society, 1882.

Emery, Sarah Anna. *Reminiscences of a Nonagenarian*. Newburyport, Mass.: William H. Huse, 1879.

Fearon, Henry Bradshaw. *Sketches of America*. 2d ed. London: Longman et al., 1818.

Freedley, Edwin T. *Leading Pursuits and Leading Men*. Philadelphia: Edward Young, 1856.

———. *Philadelphia and Its Manufactures*. Philadelphia: Edward Young, 1858.

French, J. H. *Gazetteer of the State of New York*. Syracuse: R. Pearsall Smith, 1860.

Gates, Winifred C. "Journal of a Cabinet Maker's Apprentice, Parts 1, 2." *Chronicle of the Early American Industries Association* 15, nos. 2, 3 (June, September 1962): 23–24, 35–36.

Gudehus, Jonas Heinrich. "Journey to America." Trans. Larry M. Neff. In *Ebbes fer Alle-Ebber, Ebbes fer Dich (Something for Everyone, Something for You)*, pp. 185–329. Publications of the Pennsylvania German Society, vol. 14. Breinigsville: Pennsylvania German Society, 1980.

Hall, John. *The Cabinet Makers' Assistant*. Baltimore: John Murphy, 1840.

Harrison, Eliza Cope, ed. *Philadelphia Merchant: The Diary of Thomas P. Cope, 1800–1851*. South Bend, Ind.: Gateway Editions, 1978.

Hazen, Edward. *The Panorama of Professions and Trades*. Philadelphia: Uriah Hunt, 1836.

Hepplewhite, [George]. *The Cabinet-Maker and Upholsterer's Guide*. 1794. Reprint. New York: Dover Publications, 1969.

Hogan, Edmund. *Prospect of Philadelphia*. Philadelphia: Francis and Robert Bailey, 1795.

Hope, Thomas. *Household Furniture and Interior Decoration*. 1807. Reprint. New York: Dover Publications, 1971.

James, Edwin, comp. *Account of an Expedition from Pittsburgh to the Rocky Mountains, Performed in the Years 1819 and '20*. 2 vols. Philadelphia: H. C. Carey and I. Lea, 1823.

"Journal of Lord Adam Gordon." In *Narratives of Colonial America*, ed. Howard H. Peckham, pp. 232–94. Chicago: R. R. Donnelley and Sons, 1971.

"Journal of Thaddeus M. Harris." In *Pen Pictures of Early Western Pennsylvania*, ed. John W. Harpster, pp. 242–45. Pittsburgh: University of Pittsburgh Press, 1938.

Lambert, John. *Travels through Canada and the United States of North America*. 2 vols. London: C. Cradock and W. Joy, 1813.

La Mésangère, Pierre. *Collections des meubles et objets de goût*. Paris: By the author, 1802–1835.

La Rochefoucauld Liancourt, duc de. *Travels through the United States of North America*. 2 vols. London: R. Phillips, 1799.

Lewis Miller: Sketches and Chronicles. York, Pa.: Historical Society of York County, 1966.

The London Chair-Makers' and Carvers' Book of Prices for Workmanship. London, 1802.

The London Chair-Makers' and Carvers' Book of Prices for Workmanship. London: T. Sorrell, 1823.

The Manufactories and Manufacturers of Pennsylvania of the Nineteenth Century. Philadelphia: Galaxy Publishing, 1875.

Marryat, Frederick. *A Diary in America*. 2 vols. London: Longman et al., 1839.

Mease, James. *Picture of Philadelphia*. Philadelphia: B. and T. Kite, 1811.

Melish, John. *Travels through the United States of America*. 2 vols. Philadelphia: By the author, 1815.

Michaux, François André. *The North American Sylva*. 3 vols. Philadelphia: J. Dobson, 1841.

———. *Travels to the West of the Allegheny Mountains*. London: D. N. Shury, 1805.

Minutes of the Common Council of the City of New York, 1784–1831. 19 vols. New York: By the city, 1917.

Montgomery, Thomas Lynch, ed. *Pennsylvania Archives*. Sixth series, vol. 12. Harrisburg, Pa.: Harrisburg Publishing, 1907.

"Morris Birkbeck's Notes." In *Pen Pictures of Western Pennsylvania*, ed. John W. Harpster, pp. 274–77. Pittsburgh: University of Pittsburgh Press, 1938.

Morse, Jedidiah. *American Geography*. Elizabethtown, N.J.: Shepard Kollock, 1789.

Moxon, Joseph. *Mechanick Exercises*. 1703. Reprint. New York: Praeger Publishers, 1970.

The New Democracy in America: Travels of Francisco de Miranda in the United States, 1783–84. Trans. Judson P. Wood, ed. John S. Ezell. Norman: University of Oklahoma Press, 1963.

The New-York Book of Prices for Manufacturing Cabinet and Chair Work. New York: J. Seymour, 1817.

Padelford, Philip, ed. *Colonial Panorama, 1775: Dr. Robert Honyman's Journal*. San Marino, Calif.: Huntington Library, 1939.

The Painter's, Gilder's, and Varnisher's Manual. London: M. Taylor, 1836.

Parsons, Jacob Cox, ed. *Extracts from the Diary of Jacob Hiltzheimer*. Philadelphia: William F. Fell, 1893.

Percier, Charles, and Pierre François Fontaine. *Recueil de décorations interieures*. Paris, 1801.

Porter, Rufus. "The Art of Painting." *Scientific American* 1, nos. 5, 6, 7, 9, 17 (September 25, October 2 and 9, November 13, 1845, and January 8, 1846): 3, 2, 2, 2, 2.

Porter, Thomas. *Picture of Philadelphia from 1811 to 1831*. 2 vols. Philadelphia, 1831.

Report of the Directors and Warden of the Connecticut State Prison. Hartford, Conn.: Hezekiah Howe, 1830.

Report of Gershom Powers, Agent and Keeper of the State Prison at Auburn . . . January 7, 1828. Albany, N.Y.: Croswell and Van Benthuysen, 1828.

Reynolds, Hezekiah. *Directions for House and Ship Painting*. 1812. Facsimile reprint. Worcester, Mass.: American Antiquarian Society, 1978.

Ritter, Abraham. *Philadelphia and Her Merchants as Constituted Fifty and Seventy Years Ago*. Philadelphia: By the author, 1860.

Roberts, Kenneth, and Anna M. Roberts, eds. and trans. *Moreau de St. Méry's American Journey, [1793–1798]*. Garden City, N.Y.: Doubleday, 1947.

Rosenberg, Nathan, ed. *The American System of Manufactures, 1854–55*. Edinburgh, Scotland: Edinburgh Press, 1969.

Royall, Anne Newport. *Mrs. Royall's Southern Tour, or Second Series of the Black Book*. 3 vols. Washington, D.C.: By the author, 1831.

[———]. *Sketches of History, Life, and Manners in the United States*. New Haven, Conn.: By the author, 1826.

Schultz, Christian, Jr. *Travels on an Inland Voyage*. 2 vols. 1810. Reprint. Ridgewood, N.J.: Gregg Press, 1968.

The Second Supplement to the London Chair-Makers' and Carvers' Book of Prices for Workmanship. London: T. Sorrell, 1811.

Sheraton, Thomas. *Cabinet Dictionary*. 2 vols. 1803. Reprint. New York: Praeger, 1970.

———. *The Cabinet-Maker and Upholsterer's Drawing-Book*. 1793. Reprint. New York: Dover Publications, 1972.

Silliman, Benjamin. *A Journal of Travels in England, Holland, and Scotland, and of Two Passages over the Atlantic in the Years 1805 and 1806*. 2 vols. Boston, 1812.

Smith, George. *The Cabinet-Maker and Upholsterer's Guide*. London: Jones, 1826.

———. *A Collection of Designs for Household Furniture and Interior Decoration*. 1808. Reprint. New York: Praeger, 1970.

Smith, James. *Panorama of Science and Art*. 2 vols. Liverpool, England: Caxton Press, [ca. 1816].

Smith, Joseph. *Explanation, or Key, to the Various Manufactories of Sheffield, with Engravings of Each Article*. 1816. Reprint. South Burlington, Vt.: Early American Industries Association, 1975.

Stedman, John Woodhull. "Hartford in 1830: Some Things I Remember about Hartford Sixty Years Ago." *Connecticut Historical Society Bulletin* 14, no. 3 (July 1949): 17–24.

Sterling, David Lee, ed. "New Orleans, 1801: An Account by John Pintard." *Louisiana Historical Quarterly* 34 (July 1951): 224–25.

Strickland, William. *Journal of a Tour in the United States of America, 1794–1795*. Ed. J. E. Strickland. New York: New-York Historical Society, 1971.

Thackara, William Wood. "A Philadelphian Looks at New England—1820." Excerpts from "Journal of a Journey by Sea from Philadelphia to Boston." Ed. Robert Donald Crompton. *Old-Time New England* 50, no. 3 (January–March 1960): 57–71.

Tingry, P. F. *The Painter and Varnisher's Guide*. London: G. Kearsly, 1804.

———. *The Painter's and Colourman's Complete Guide*. 3d ed. London: Sherwood, Gilbert, and Piper, 1830.

Tomlinson, Charles. *Illustrations of Trades*.

1860. Reprint. N.p.: Early American Industries Association, 1972.

Trollope, Frances M. *Domestic Manners of the Americans.* 2 vols. London: Whittaker, Treacher, 1832.

Tudor, Henry. *Narrative of a Tour in North America.* 2 vols. London: James Duncan, 1834.

Van Zandt, Roland, ed. *Chronicles of the Hudson: Three Centuries of Travelers' Accounts.* New Brunswick, N.J.: Rutgers University Press, 1971.

Vaux, George, ed. "Extracts from the Diary of Hannah Callender." *Pennsylvania Magazine of History and Biography* 12 (1888): 432–56.

Wansey, Henry. *An Excursion to the United States of North America in the Summer of 1794.* 2d ed. Salisbury, England: J. Easton, 1798.

Watson, John F. *Annals and Occurrences of New York City and State in the Olden Time.* Philadelphia: Henry F. Anners, 1846.

———. *Annals of Philadelphia and Pennsylvania in the Olden Time.* 3 vols. 1830. Reprint, rev. Willis P. Hazard. Philadelphia: Leary, Stuart, 1927.

Weld, Isaac. *Travels through the States of North America.* 2 vols. London: John Stockdale, 1800.

Whittock, Nathaniel. *The Decorative Painters' and Glaziers' Guide.* London: Isaac Taylor Hinton, 1827.

[Worth, Gorham]. "Albany Fifty Years Ago." *Harper's New Monthly Magazine* 14, no. 82 (March 1857): 451–63.

Unpublished Works

Banyas, Frank A. "The Moravians of Colonial Pennsylvania: Their Arts, Crafts, and Industries." Ph.D dissertation, Ohio State University, 1940.

Clunie, Margaret Burke. "Salem Federal Furniture." Master's thesis, University of Delaware, 1976.

Elliott, Mary Jane. "Lexington, Kentucky, 1792–1820: The Athens of the West." Master's thesis, University of Delaware, 1973.

Erbe, Hellmuth. "Bethlehem, Pa.: Eine kommunisikische hernhuter Kolonie." Ph.D dissertation, as published by the German Foreign Language Institute, Stuttgart, Germany, 1929.

Fanelli, Doris Devine. "The Building and Furniture Trades in Lancaster, Pennsylvania, 1750–1800." Master's thesis, University of Delaware, 1979.

Gross, Katherine Wood. "The Sources of Furniture Sold in Savannah, 1789–1815." Master's thesis, University of Delaware, 1967.

Hill, John Henry. "The Furniture Craftsmen in Baltimore, 1783–1823." Master's thesis, University of Delaware, 1967.

Keno, Leigh. "The Windsor Chair Makers of Northampton, Massachusetts, 1790–1820." Historic Deerfield Summer Fellowship Program paper, Deerfield, Mass., August 1979.

Leibundguth, Arthur W. "The Furniture-Making Crafts in Philadelphia, ca. 1730–1760." Master's thesis, University of Delaware, 1964.

Pillsbury, William Mitchell. "The Providence Furniture Making Trade, 1772–1834." Master's thesis, University of Delaware, 1975.

Rippe, Peter. "Daniel Clay of Greenfield, 'Cabinetmaker.'" Master's thesis, University of Delaware, 1962.

Manuscripts

Manuscripts in private and public archives have been the most important sources of written information in the preparation of this work. The number of documents consulted is large and includes account books of woodworkers and other craftsmen; individual bills, receipts, and accounts; family business and household records; letters and letter books; probate and land records; census and vital records; court, legal, and apprenticeship records; and shipping and export papers. For brevity, the depositories whose holdings have been used are listed here in lieu of the documents, which are identified in the notes. The abbreviations are those used in the notes.

PRIVATE DEPOSITORIES

American Antiquarian Society, Worcester, Mass. (AAS); American Philosophical Society, Philadelphia, Pa. (APS); Antiquarian and Landmarks Society, Hartford, Conn.; Archives of the Moravian Church, Bethlehem, Pa. (MA-Pa); Archives of the Moravian Church, Southern Province, Winston-Salem, N.C. (MA-NC); Baker Library, Harvard University, Cambridge, Mass. (BL); Barre Historical Society, Barre, Mass. (Barre); Bennington Museum, Bennington, Vt. (Bennington); Connecticut Historical Society, Hartford (CHS); Dartmouth College, Hanover, N.H. (DC); Friends Historical Library, Swarthmore College, Swarthmore, Pa.; Girard College, Philadelphia, Pa.; Hagley Museum and Library, Wilmington, Del.; Historic Deerfield, Deerfield, Mass. (HD); Historical Society of Pennsylvania, Philadelphia (HSP); Historical Society of Saratoga Springs, Saratoga Springs, N.Y.; Independence Seaport Museum, Philadelphia, Pa.; Institute for Colonial Studies, State University of New York at Stony Brook; Ipswich Historical Society, Ipswich, Mass.; John Hay Library, Brown University, Providence, R.I.; Lancaster County Historical Society, Lancaster, Pa. (LCHS); Leffingwell Inn, Norwich, Conn.; Library Company of Philadelphia, Philadelphia, Pa. (LCP); Litchfield Historical Society, Litchfield, Conn. (LHS); Maine Historical Society, Portland; Maryland Historical Society, Baltimore (MdHS); Massachusetts Historical Society, Boston (MHS); Mattatuck Museum, Waterbury, Conn. (Mattatuck); Metropolitan Museum of Art, New York; Middlesex Historical Society, Middletown, Conn.; Monmouth County Historical Association, Freehold, N.J.; Museum of Early Southern Decorative Arts, Winston-Salem, N.C. (MESDA); Mystic Seaport Museum, Mystic, Conn. (MSM); New Jersey Historical Society, Newark, (NJHS); Newport Historical Society, Newport, R.I. (NHS); New-York Historical Society, New York (NYHS); New York State Historical Association, Cooperstown (NYSHA); Old Dartmouth Historical Society, New Bedford, Mass.; Old Sturbridge Village, Sturbridge, Mass. (OSV); Historical Documents Collection, Queens College, Flushing, N.Y. (QC); Peabody Essex Museum, Salem, Mass. (PEM); Pocumtuck Valley Memorial Association, Deerfield, Mass.; Redwood Library, Newport, R.I.; Rhode Island Historical Society, Providence (RIHS); Rutgers University Library, New Brunswick, N.J.; Salem County Historical Society, Salem, N.J.; Shelburne Museum, Shelburne, Vt.; Social Law Library, Boston, Mass. (SLL); Society of Friends, Philadelphia, Pa. (SF); Sterling Memorial Library, Yale University, New Haven, Conn. (Yale); Swem Library, College of William and Mary, Williamsburg, Va. (WM); Talbot County Historical Society, Easton, Md. (TCHS); Van Pelt Library, University of Pennsylvania, Philadelphia; Vermont Historical Society, Montpelier; Virginia Historical Society, Richmond (VaHS); Windham Historical Society, Willimantic, Conn. (WHS); Winterthur Museum and Library, Winterthur, Del. (WL), including the Joseph Downs Collection of Manuscripts and Printed Ephemera (DCM) and the Visual Resources Collection (VRC); Worcester Historical Museum, Worcester, Mass.

PUBLIC DEPOSITORIES

County Courthouses and City/Town Halls
Albany Co., Albany, N.Y.; Baltimore Co., Baltimore, Md.; Bennington Co. and Bennington town hall, Bennington, Vt.; Berks Co., Reading Pa.; Berkshire Co., Pittsfield, Mass.; Botetourt Co., Fincastle, Va.; Bristol Co., Taunton, Mass.; Cheshire Co., Keene, N.H.; Chester Co., West Chester, Pa.; Cumberland Co., Portland, Maine; Erie Co., Erie, Pa.; Essex Co., Salem, Mass.; Franklin Co., Greenfield, Mass.; Hampden Co., Springfield, Mass.; Hampshire Co., Northampton, Mass.; Hillsborough Co., Nashua, N.H.; Kennebec Co., Augusta, Maine; Lancaster Co., Lancaster, Pa.; Merrimack Co., Concord, N.H.; Middlesex Co., Cambridge, Mass.; Nantucket Co., Nantucket, Mass.; New Castle Co., Wilmington, Del.; Newport city hall, Newport, R.I.; Philadelphia Co. and Philadelphia city hall,

Philadelphia, Pa.; Plymouth Co., Plymouth, Mass.; Providence city hall, Providence, R.I.; Rensselaer Co., Troy, N.Y.; Rockbridge Co., Lexington, Va.; Rockingham Co., Exeter, N.H.; Schenectady Co., Schenectady, N.Y.; Suffolk Co., Boston, Mass.; West Chester Co., White Plains, N.Y.; Windsor Co., Woodstock, Vt.; Worcester Co., Worcester, Mass.

Federal Archives, Libraries, and Sites
Federal Archives and Records Center, Philadelphia, Pa.; Federal Archives and Records Center, Waltham, Mass. (FRC-Waltham); Hopewell Village National Historic Site, Elverson, Pa.; Library of Congress, Washington, D.C. (LC); National Archives, Washington, D.C. (NA).

State Archives, Libraries, and Other Facilities
Connecticut State Library, Hartford (CSL); Maryland Hall of Records, Annapolis; New Jersey State Library, Archives and History Bureau, Trenton (NJSL); Rhode Island State Archives, Providence (RISA); State of Delaware, Division of Historical and Cultural Affairs, Dover (DDHCA); Virginia State Library, Richmond.

Local Libraries and Other Facilities
Boston Public Library, Boston, Mass. (BPL); Concord Free Public Library, Concord, Mass. (CFPL); Handley Library, Winchester, Va.; New York Public Library, New York (NYPL); Philadelphia Archives, Philadelphia, Pa.

Foreign Depositories
British Library, London, England; Guildhall Library, London, England; High Wycombe Chair Museum, High Wycombe, England; High Wycombe Library, High Wycombe, England; Public Record Office, London, England (PRO); Westminster Libraries, London, England.

Newspapers

Some of the newspapers listed here reflect the ongoing publication of single serials at different periods or under different publishers with varying titles. Complete chronologies for many of these newspapers are given in Clarence S. Brigham, *History and Bibliography of American Newspapers, 1690–1820*, 2 vols. (Worcester, Mass.: American Antiquarian Society, 1947).

CONNECTICUT

American Mercury (Hartford); *American Sentinel* (Middletown); *Chelsea Courier* (Norwich); *Connecticut Courant* (Hartford); *Connecticut Gazette* (New London); *Connecticut Herald* (New Haven); *Litchfield Republican* (Litchfield); *Middlesex Gazette* (Middletown); *New Haven Palladium* (New Haven); *New-London*

Gazette (New London); *Norwalk Gazette* (Norwalk); *Norwich Courier* (Norwich); *Republican Advocate* (New London); *Windham Herald* (Windham).

DELAWARE

Delaware Gazette (Wilmington).

DISTRICT OF COLUMBIA

Daily National Intelligencer (Washington); *Museum and Washington and George-town Advertiser* (Georgetown).

GEORGIA

Augusta Chronicle and Gazette of the State (Augusta); *Columbian Museum and Savannah Advertiser* (Savannah); *Gazette of the State of Georgia* (Savannah); *Milledgeville Journal* (Milledgeville).

INDIANA

Brookville Enquirer (Brookville); *Indiana American* (Brookville); *Indiana Recorder and Public Advertiser* (New Albany); *South Bend Free Press* (South Bend).

KENTUCKY

American Statesman (Lexington); *Argus of Western America* (Frankfort); *Kentucky Gazette* (Lexington); *Kentucky Gazette and General Advertiser* (Lexington); *Louisville Public Advertiser* (Louisville); *Western Citizen* (Paris).

MARYLAND

Baltimore
American and Commercial Daily Advertiser; *American and Daily Advertiser*; *Baltimore American*; *Baltimore American and Commercial Advertiser*; *Baltimore Daily Repository*; *Baltimore Patriot and Mercantile Advertiser*; *Federal Gazette and Baltimore Daily Advertiser*; *Gazette and Baltimore Daily Advertiser*; *Maryland Gazette, or the Baltimore General Advertiser*; *Maryland Journal*; *Maryland Journal and Baltimore Advertiser*; *Maryland Journal and Baltimore Universal Daily Advertiser*; *Niles Weekly Register*.

Other
Maryland Gazette (Annapolis); *Maryland Herald and Hagerstown Weekly Advertiser* (Hagerstown).

MASSACHUSETTS

Boston
Boston Gazette; *Boston News-Letter*; *Columbian Centinel*; *Daily Evening Transcript*; *Independent*

Chronicle; *Independent Chronicle and Boston Patriot*; *Massachusetts Centinel*; *Massachusetts Gazette*; *New England Palladium*.

Other
Columbian Courier (New Bedford); *Franklin Herald* (Greenfield); *Franklin Herald and Public Advertiser* (Greenfield); *Greenfield Gazette* (Greenfield); *Hampshire Gazette* (Northampton); *New-Bedford Mercury* (New Bedford); *Salem Gazette* (Salem).

MISSISSIPPI

Mississippi Republican (Natchez); *Weekly Chronicle* (Natchez).

NEW HAMPSHIRE

Concord Gazette (Concord); *Dover Gazette* (Dover); *New Hampshire Gazette* (Portsmouth); *New-Hampshire Patriot* (Concord); *New Hampshire Sentinel* (Keene); *Portsmouth Journal* (Portsmouth).

NEW JERSEY

Sentinel of Freedom (Newark); *Trenton Federalist* (Trenton).

NEW YORK

New York City
American Citizen and General Advertiser; *Commercial Advertiser*; *Daily Advertiser*; *The Diary, or Loudon's Register*; *Impartial Gazetteer*; *Mercantile Advertiser*; *Morning Chronicle*; *New-York Courier*; *New-York Enquirer*; *New-York Evening Post*; *New-York Gazette*; *New-York Gazette and General Advertiser*; *New-York Gazette, and the Weekly Mercury*; *New-York Gazette, or Weekly Post-Boy*; *New-York Herald*; *New-York Journal*; *New-York Mercury*; *New-York Packet*; *New-York Weekly Chronicle*; *New-York Weekly Journal*; *Republican Watch-Tower*; *Rivington's New-York Gazetteer*; *Town and Country Journal*; *Weekly Museum*.

Other
Albany Chronicle (Albany); *Auburn Daily Advertiser* (Auburn); *Cayuga Patriot* (Auburn); *Gazette* (Buffalo); *The Portico* (Huntington); *Rochester Daily Advertiser* (Rochester); *Saratoga Sentinel* (Saratoga Springs); *Syracuse Weekly Journal* (Syracuse).

NORTH CAROLINA

Raleigh
North Carolina Star; *Raleigh Minerva*; *Raleigh Register*; *Raleigh Register and North Carolina Gazette*; *Raleigh Register and North Carolina State Gazette*; *Star, and North-Carolina Gazette*; *Star, and North-Carolina State Gazette*.

Other
Cape-Fear Recorder (Wilmington); *Carolina Sentinel* (Newbern); *Carolina Watchman* (Salisbury); *Catawba Journal* (Charlotte); *Edenton Gazette* (Edenton); *Fayetteville Gazette* (Fayetteville); *Hall's Wilmington Gazette* (Wilmington); *West Carolinian* (Salisbury); *Wilmington Gazette* (Wilmington).

OHIO

Chillicothe Advertiser (Chillicothe); *Liberty Hall and Cincinnati Gazette* (Cincinnati); *Scioto Gazette* (Chillicothe); *Scioto Gazette and Fredonia Chronicle* (Chillicothe); *Western Spy* (Cincinnati).

PENNSYLVANIA

Philadelphia
Atkinson's Saturday Evening Post; *Aurora*; *Federal Gazette*; *General Advertiser*; *Hope's Philadelphia Price-Current, and Commercial Record*; *Pennsylvania Chronicle*; *Pennsylvania Gazette*; *Pennsylvania Packet*; *Philadelphia Ledger*; *Public Ledger*; *Relf's Philadelphia Gazette and Daily Advertiser*; *The True American and Commercial Advertiser*; *United States Gazette.*

Other
American Eagle (Easton); *American Republican* (West Chester); *Berks and Schuylkill Journal* (Reading); *Carlisle Gazette* (Carlisle); *Carlisle Herald* (Carlisle); *Chester and Delaware Federalist* (West Chester); *Dauphin Guardian* (Harrisburg); *Erie Observer* (Erie); *Franklin Repository* (Chambersburg); *Lancaster Journal* (Lancaster); *Lancaster Union* (Lancaster); *Pittsburgh Gazette* (Pittsburgh); *Reporter* (Washington); *Village Record* (West Chester).

RHODE ISLAND

Providence
Providence Gazette; *Providence Journal*; *Providence Patriot*; *Providence Patriot and Columbian Phenix*; *Providence Phenix*; *United States Chronicle.*

SOUTH CAROLINA

Charleston
Charleston City Gazette and Daily Advertiser; *Charleston Courier*; *Charleston Evening Gazette*; *Charleston Morning Post*; *City Gazette and Daily Advertiser*; *City Gazette, or the Daily Advertiser*; *Columbia Herald*; *South Carolina and American General Gazette*; *South Carolina Gazette*; *South-Carolina Gazette and Country Journal*; *South Carolina Gazette and General Advertiser*; *Times.*

TENNESSEE

Clarion and Tennessee Gazette (Nashville); *Clarion and Tennessee State Gazette* (Nashville); *Impartial Review and Cumberland Repository* (Nashville); *Jackson Gazette* (Jackson); *Knoxville Register* (Knoxville); *Nashville Clarion* (Nashville); *Tennessee Gazette* (Nashville); *Western Cabinet* (Fayetteville).

VERMONT

Democratic Statesman (Windsor); *Vermont Gazette* (Bennington); *Vermont Mirror* (Middlebury).

VIRGINIA

Herald and Norfolk and Portsmouth Advertiser (Norfolk); *Lynchburg and Farmer's Gazette* (Lynchburg); *Lynchburg Press* (Lynchburg); *Norfolk Gazette and Publick Ledger* (Norfolk); *Norfolk Herald* (Norfolk); *Petersburg Intelligencer* (Petersburg); *Petersburg Republican* (Petersburg); *Republican* (Petersburg); *Richmond Commercial Compiler* (Richmond); *Richmond Enquirer* (Richmond); *Staunton Eagle* (Staunton); *Virginia Argus* (Richmond); *Virginia Gazette* (Williamsburg); *Virginia Gazette and General Advertiser* (Richmond); *Virginia Gazette, or Norfolk Intelligencer* (Norfolk); *Virginia Herald* (Fredericksburg); *Virginia Journal and Alexandria Advertiser* (Alexandria).

WEST VIRGINIA

Farmer's Repository (Charles Town); *Lewisburg Chronicle* (Lewisburg); *Martinsburgh Gazette* (Martinsburg).

CANADA

Canadian Courant (Montreal); *Montreal Gazette* (Montreal); *Nova Scotia Royal Gazette* (Halifax); *Upper Canada Gazette* (Toronto); *Upper Canada Herald* (Kingston).

ENGLAND

Illustrated London News (London); *London Chronicle* (London).

Directories

City/town directories published from the late eighteenth century through 1850 can be helpful in identifying branded, stenciled, and handwritten names found on Windsor furniture made before 1850 and in tracking the migratory routes of artisans. Besides names, the volumes provide addresses and occupations. Some include an advertising section. Few communities were sufficiently large or prosperous before the early nineteenth century to support the publication of directories listing local residents, and only Boston, Charleston, New York, and Philadelphia produced annual directories before 1790. In other communities publication was intermittent at best. The following list identifies the specific volumes that have been useful in this study.

Albany, N.Y. (1815, 1819); Auburn, N.Y. (1817); Baltimore, Md. (1800, 1824, 1831, 1837, 1840, 1842, 1847, 1855); Boston, Mass. (1856, 1860); Brooklyn, N.Y. (1832, 1833, 1837); Buffalo, N.Y. (1844); Cincinnati, Ohio (1825, 1829, 1834, 1836, 1846); Louisville, Ky. (1855); New Haven, Conn. (1843); New York City (1795, 1809, 1810, 1813, 1819, 1826, 1840); Philadelphia, Pa. (1811, 1820, 1823, 1840); Pittsburgh, Pa. (1813, 1819); Portland, Maine (1841); Providence, R.I. (1824, 1826); Rochester, N.Y. (1841); Troy, N.Y. (1829); Utica, N.Y. (1840, 1842); Wheeling, W.Va. (and Ohio Co., 1851).

Index

Page numbers in *italics* represent illustrations.

Caribbean trade, *238, 239, 247, 249*; in prerevolutionary Caribbean trade, 222
barber's chairs, 190
Barker, Jacob, 383–84
Barker, William, 406, 408
Barkhamstead (Conn.): schoolmasters' chair purchased in, 417. *See also* Hitchcock, Lambert; Moore, William, Jr.
bark strips and splints, 202–3
Barnard, Julius, 20, 288, 296
Barnes, Elizur, 95, 201, 202
Barnes, John, 309
Barnes and Seaton, 47
Barnet, Sampson, 101, *101*, 286
Barnstable (Mass.), 153, 423
Barre (Mass.): Boston, Barre and Gardner Railroad, 324; Ephraim Wilder, 14, 95. *See also* Houghton, Luke
Barrell, Joseph, 153, 284–85, 346–47
Barrell, William, 134, 224, 311, 399, 406
Barrelli and Torri, 261
Barrett, Walter, 316
Barron, James, 340
Barry, John, 360, 370
Barry and Crickbaum, 395
Barstow, Calvin, 71
Bartlett, Joseph, 7, 10
Bartlett, Levi, 292
Barton, Isaac, 49
Bass, Benjamin: cast-iron stove of, 105; circular saw of, 59; cushion materials of, 190; rags for cleaning paintbrushes, 160; stained chairs in stock of, 185; wood used by, 86, 90
basswood (*Tilia americana*): Canadian chairmakers using, 92; New England chairmakers using, 86, *87*, 88–89; New York State chairmakers using, 85–86
Batavia (Jakarta), *257*, 286
Batcheler, Jacob, 11
Bates, David, 91, 174, 182, 294
Bates, William, Plate 2
Bates and Johnson, 355–56
Bath (Maine), *259*, 271
bathrooms, 359
Bath Town (N.C.), *227*
Batildwin and Company, 263
Beach, Miles, 131, 398
beader (scratch stock), 68
Beal, Samuel, 199
Beasley, William G., 403
Beaufort (N.C.), *227, 229*
Beaujour, Felix de, 269
Beautiful Homes (Williams and Jones), 134
Beck, James, 18, 91, 186, 193
Beck, Joseph, 102
Bedent, Jesse, 305
Bedford (N.H.), 414
Bedortha, Calvin, 48
bedrooms (chambers), 353–56
beech, 86, 91
Beekman, Gerard, 356
Beekman, James, 361
Beekman, Johannah, 341
Beekman, William, 150
Beesley, William: bow repair by, 133; cream-color paint used by, 153; exchange of produce or labor for goods of, 305; paint for rush-bottom

chairs sold by, 202; priming by, 159; seat preparation hired by, 119; on wood graining, 181
beetles (tool), 65
beige-color paint, *145*, 152–53
Belize (British Honduras), *270*, 274
Belknap, Zebina (Zabina), 290
Bell and Stoneall, 183
Bellona (steamboat), 403
belts, leather, 103
Benade, Andrew, 409
bench planes, 68
bench rule, 78
bench stops, 51, 120
"bender," 98
bending: cost of, *129*, 130; equipment for, 56–59; molds, 58–59, *58*
Benjamin, Asher, 394
Benjamin, Miles, 106, 142, 305
Bennett, Abraham, 48–49
Bennett, James, 48–49
Bennington (Vt.): basswood used in, 88–89; Dewey and Woodworth, 19, *19*, 48. *See also* Dewey, Henry Freeman
Bennington County (Vt.): courthouse furniture in, 423. *See also* Bennington
bent-back chairs, 138, 409
Bentham, James, and Company, 225
Bentley, William: on blacks in Salem, 18; on chairs in wagons, 379–80; on Crowninshield's *Cleopatra's Barge*, 400; on fire in Salem, 33; on Masonic furniture, 386; on prison labor, 34; at public dinners, 375; on Quebec wood, 92; on steamboat travel, 220
bent-work construction, 127
Berger, Andrew, 398
Berger, Daniel, 64
bergère chairs, 140
Berks County (Pa.): William Bird, 343, 349, 408; Hopewell Furnace, 408; Samuel Lobach, 318
Berkshire County (Mass.), 16, 293
Bermuda, *238, 239, 240, 270*
Bernard, John, 389
Bertine, James, 235
Bethlehem (Pa.), 49, *49*, 408–9, 410
bevel squares, 78
Beverly (Mass.), 228, 229, 250
Bheares, Henry, 289
Bickham, Martin, 285–86
Biddle, Clement, 225, 230, 232, 366
Bigelow, Jacob, 83, 185–86
Biggard, John, 287
billheads and advertising sheets (pictorial), *46*, 15, 174, 266, *266*
billiard parlors, 375, *376*, 389
Billings, Henry, 297
Bingham, William, 165, 234, 308, 342, 360–61
birch: Canadian chairmakers using, 92; chairmakers using, 82; New England chairmakers using, 86, *87*, 90, 91
Birch, Thomas, 364, *365*, 378, *379*, 389, *389*
Birch, William, 378, *379*, 407, *407*
Bird, William, 343, 349, 408
Birdsey, Joseph, 88
Birge, Edward, 46
Birge, Francis A., 46, 47
Birkbeck, Morris, 219
Bishop White's Study (Sartain), 357, *357*

bits and braces, 72–76
black paint, *145*, 148–49
black Americans, 17–18
black ash (*Fraxinus nigra*), 83
blacking, 159
black maple (*Acer nigrum*), 83, 92
Black Point (N.J.), 165, *229*, 234, 308, 360–61
Black River (N.Y.). *See* Dexter, David
Blair, Sherman, 18, 300
Blake, Joseph, 234
Blake, William, 146, 192, 288
Blake, Ware and Company, 324, 413
Blanchard, John W., 137, 373
Blanchard, Porter, 426
Blauvelt, James, 47
Bleecker, Elizabeth de Hart, 32, 377
Bleecker, John, 307
Bliss, Thomas W., 235
block knives (stock knives), 64
Bloomingdale (Manhattan), 350, 361, 363, 391–92
blossom-color paint, 153–54
blossoms and foliage motif, 170–71, Plate 2, Plate 6, Plate 7, Plate 9, Plate 11, Plate 12, Plate 13, Plate 19, Plate 23, Plate 25, Plate 28, Plate 29, Plate 30
Blow, Richard, 316
Blow and Barksdale, 230
blue paint, *145*, 153, Plate 16
boarding schools, 418–20
Boardman, Thomas, 323
Boden, Omar, 288
Bolles, Nathan, 268–69
Bolling, Robert, 362
Bolton, Isaac M., 151, *151*, 278
Bonaparte, Jerome N., 395, 396
Bonaparte, Joseph, 364
bookcase desks, 341, 343
"Book of Prices for Making Cabinet & chair furniture" (Helme), 128, *129*, 163, 164, 187, *188*
Book of Trades, 100
books of prices. *See* price books
Boone, William R., 271, 272
Booth, Joel, 63, 67
Booth, John, 75, *75*
boots, 23
Bordentown (N.J.), 364, *365*
boring tools, 72–77
Boston: John Andrews, 134, 224, 311; Samuel Beal, 199; William Blake, 146, 192, 288; blue chairs in, 153; Boston Athenaeum, 413; Boston Exchange Coffee House, 394; Boston Theatre, 137, 372; cane for woven seats, 203; chairmakers' shops in, 43; George Davidson, 49–50, 387; John Doggett, 284, 311, 313, 323; domestic use of Windsor chairs in, 345, 346–47, 350, 352; in early nineteenth-century Central American trade, 274; in early nineteenth-century coastal trade, 258, *259*, 264, 267; in early nineteenth-century Eastern Atlantic Islands trade, 282; in early nineteenth-century Far Eastern trade, 285; in early nineteenth-century South American trade, 275; fire of 1760, 31; Freemasonry in, 384, 386–87; Nathaniel Frost, 49, 121, *121*, 288; William Hancock, 200, 284, *284*, 313; Thomas Cotton Hayward, *11*, 50, 70, 77, 288; John C. Hubbard, 324, 417, 423; influence of, 292–93; land carriage from, 319–20; in late-eighteenth- and early-

Davis, Robert, 319
Davis, Samuel, 12, *12*, 22
Davis, William (chairmaker), 65
Davis, William (sheriff), 423
Davison, James, 318
Davison, Samuel, 95, 98, 119
Dawes, H. L., 319
day schools, 418
Dean, Henry, 373
Dean, Joseph, 308
Decatur, Stephen, 173, *337*, 370
Dedham (Mass.), 340–41, *342*
Deeds, Isaac, 96
Deerfield (N.H.), 132, *133*, 136, 305
Deland, Philip, 55, 79
Delaware: in commercial sphere of Windsor-chair
    making, 217; cushions in, 190; Dover, 426;
    in early nineteenth-century coastal trade,
    259; New Castle, 224, 226, 229; Odessa, *229*;
    in postrevolutionary coastal trade, 229; state
    government furniture in, 426; Sussex County,
    423. *See also* Christiana; Wilmington (Del.)
Delaware River, 84, 224, 256, 306
Delaware Valley: bedrooms in, 354; blue chairs in,
    153; brown chairs in, 151; in commercial sphere
    of Windsor-chair making, 217; country seats
    in, 360; dining rooms in, 343–44; kitchens in,
    356; Point Breeze, 364, *365*; sage-color chairs in,
    146; wood used in, 84
Delaware Valley slat-back chair, 139, *139*
delivery charges, 318, 322
Delorme, John Francis, 192
Delphian Club, *380*, 381, 387
Demerara, *238*, 252–53, 275, *276*
demijohns, 156, *156*
de Miranda, Francisco, 374
Denig, John, 49, 92, 165, 179
Denison, Andrew, 94
Denning family, 362, 365
Dennis (Mass.), 229
Derby, Elias Hasket: bedroom furniture of, 356;
    brother John Derby, 179; counting room of,
    404; dining furniture of, 348; in Far Eastern
    trade, 256, 285, 286; *Grand Turk I* refitted,
    400; study of, 357; and stuffed Windsor chairs,
    192–93, 195
Derby, John, 179, 193
design, 138–43; inland trade and dissemination of,
    286–96; pattern terminology, 138–39; sources
    of American, 139–43
design books, xii, 140–43
Designs for Household Furniture (Smith), 141
Detroit, 294, 299
Dewey, Henry Freeman: Bennington County
    courthouse furniture made by, 423; commis-
    sion sales of, 300; desk stools made by, 406;
    exchange of produce or labor for goods of, 305;
    journeyman of, 14; partnership of, 19, *19*; shop
    location of, 48
Dewey, John, 300
Dewey and Woodworth, 19, *19*, 48
DeWitt, Henry, 79
DeWitt, John, 163, 166, 234, 425, *425*
Dexter, David: privy of, 106; shop location of, 49;
    wagon of, 319; waterwheel of, 103; woodwork-
    ing complex of, 93, *93*, 107
Dick, William, 286–87

Dickens, Charles, 402
Digby (Nova Scotia), 235
Dighton (Mass.), *229*
Dillwyn, Susanna, 338–39, 362, 365, 399
dining chairs, 138, 231, 343–48
Dining Room of Abraham Russell (Russell), *347*,
    347–48
Dining Room of Dr. Whitridge (Russell), 346, *346*
dining rooms, xiii, 343–48
dining tables, 343, 344, 346
dinners, public, 375
direct sales, 299
distemper, 182, 183, Plate 32
distributors, 301
District of Columbia. *See* Alexandria (Va.);
    Georgetown (D.C.); Washington, D.C.
division of labor, 107
Dockum, Samuel S., 264
Dockum and Brown, 164, 179
dog (bench clamp), 77
Doggett, John, 284, 311, 313, 323
dog power, 102
Dole, Samuel, 32
domestic trade: water carriage, 306–10. *See also*
    coastal trade; inland trade
domestic use of Windsor chairs, 337–70; in bath-
    rooms, 359; in bedrooms (chambers), 353–56,
    355; in country seats, 360–62; in dining rooms,
    343–48, *344*, *346*, *347*; in entry halls, 340–43,
    342; in gardens, 364–65, *365*; by historic figures,
    365–70; in keeping rooms, 352–53, *353*; in
    kitchens, 356–57, *357*; outdoor uses, 362–65; in
    parlors, 348–52, *351*; in piazzas, 362–63, *363*; on
    stoops, 363, *363*; in studies, 357–59, *357*, *358*
Dominica, *238*, 239, 248, 249
Dominican Republic. *See* Santo Domingo
Dominy, Nathaniel, V, 57, *57*
Dominy family: block knives of, 64; chisels made
    by, 71; daily wage for, 21; pole lathe of, 52; shop
    and residence of, 46; tool handles made by, 79;
    wood used by, 85
Doolittle, Benjamin, 292
Dorr, Sullivan, 308
Dossie, Robert, 144, 174, 185
double-back chairs, 139
double-bow chairs, 138
double-cross-back chairs, 139, 173, Plate 1
double-rod-and-medallion pattern, 168, 173
double-top chairs, 138
Douglas, James, 233
Douglas, John, 233, 248
Douglas, Samuel, 162
Douglas, William, 233
Douglass, John, 392, 393
Douglass, R. H., and Co., *203*
Dover (Del.), 426
Dow, Joseph N., 48
Doyle, William M. S., 165, *165*
drab brown paint, *145*, 151
Drawing-Book (Sheraton), 140, 141, 142, 163, 170,
    170
drawknives, 66–68, 79
drays, 320
dress, 22–24
drilling equipment, 60
Drinker, Elizabeth, 186
Dr. John Rause and Family (Miller), 344, *344*

Drummond, Alexander, 297
dual paint colors, *145*, 154
Duane, William, 277
dubbing, 119
Dudley, Martin, 303
Dumfries (Va.), 229
Dunbar, J. and D., 408
Dunbibin, John, 237
Dunham, Campbell, 56
Dunlap, John, 9, 321, 414
Dunlop, William, 155
Dunn, Justus, 6
du Pont, E. I., 165
du Pont, Henry Francis, 135
du Pont, Sophie M., *350*, 355
du Pont family, 350, *350*, 354–55
Duport, Pierre, 374
Durham boats, 306
Dutch Guiana, 223, *238*, 252
Dutilh, Stephen, 244–45
Duyckinck, Gerardus, I, 166
Dwight, Theodore, 383
Dwight, Timothy, 86, 236, 290, 292, 297
Dwyer, James, 388
dyeing, 159

eagle, American, 173
Earl, Ralph, 369
Earle, Alice Morse, 416
Eastern Atlantic Islands trade, *254*; early
    nineteenth-century, 281–82; postrevolutionary,
    253–55
Eastern Railroad Corporation, 324, *324*, 413
Eastern State Penitentiary (Pa.), 37
East Greenwich (R.I.), 25, 229, 235
Easthampton (Long Island). *See* Dominy family
East Indies, 218, 285–86
Eastman, Robert, 59
Eastmond, John, 404
Eatonton (Ga.), *259*, 263
Eatontown (N.J.), 58, 85
Economical School (New York City), 419, *419*
Edenton (N.C.), 229, *259*, 263
Edgartown (Mass.), *259*, 264
edge roll, 197
Edward, Alexander, 399
Edwards, Benjamin Alvord, 66
Egbert, Stephen, 142
Egelmann, Carl Friedrich, *353*, 418
Eicholtz, Jacob, 421
Eldridge, Elijah, 159
Election Day 1815 (Krimmel), *23*
Eleutherian Mills, 350, *350*, 354–55, *355*
Ellis, Thomas, 183, 191, 322
Elmendorf, Peter, 134
Elwell, Amasa, 47
Ely, Smith, 36, 404
Elysian Fields (Hoboken, N.J.), 378
Embargo Act (1807), 24, 30, 219, 278, 297
Emerald (steamboat), 402, 403
Emery, David, 370
Emery, Sarah Anna, 190, 374, 379, 414–15, 418
Emlen, Caleb, 46
Emlen, Samuel, 338–39, 411
Emlen, Susanna Dillwyn, 338–39, 362, 365, 399
energy. *See* power
Enfield (Conn.), 124, 159, 202

Frankford (Pa.), 9, 46, 84, 136, 146, 354
Franklin, Benjamin, 148, 337, 369, 384, 411
Franklin Institute, 24
Franklin stoves, 104, 346, 359, 395
Fraser, Esther Stevens, 175
Fraunces, Andrew Gautier, 390
Fraunces, Samuel, 389–90
Fraunces Tavern Museum, 389
Fredericks, Charles, 189, 262, 403
Fredericks and Farrington, 402, 403
Fredericksburg (Va.): James Beck, 18, 91, 186, 193;
    domestic use of Windsor chairs in, 340; in
    early nineteenth-century coastal trade, 258,
    259, 263; in postrevolutionary coastal trade,
    229; stuffed Windsor seating in, 193
Fredericton (New Brunswick), 266, 296
free delivery, 322
Freedley, Edwin T., 97, 107, 406
"freedom dues," 10
freehand decoration, 166–74; bronzing, 177;
    cornucopias, 167, 172, Plate 17; early ornament,
    166–67; floral and fruit designs, including
    grape and grapevine motif, 168–72; landscapes,
    168; national and other symbols, 172–73;
    neoclassical designs, 167–68; shell motif, 172
Freeman, Benjamin, 228, 228, 272
Freeman, George, 342
Freemasonry, 173, 384–87, 384, Plate 18
freight charges, 307, 308, 309
freight insurance, 309, 311
French, Daniel, 305
French, Richard, 36, 297–98
French Guiana, 238, 275, 276
fret-back chairs, 139, Plate 10
fret saws (keyhole saws), 63
Friends of American Manufactures, 24
Friends of National Industry, 24
fringe, 196–97
Frink and Chester, 304
froes, 65
Frost, George, 348
Frost, Nathaniel, 49, 121, 121, 288
Frost, "Uncle Jo," 14
fruit and floral designs, 169–72
fuel, 105
Fulton, John, 103
Fulton, Robert, 220
funerals, 387
Furlow, John, 426
furniture patterns, 81, 81
Fussell, Solomon, 79, 94, 131, 202

Gadsby, John, 389
Gaines family, 187
Galer, Adam, 20, 223, 288
Galligan, William, 402
Galloway, Joseph, 192, 341–42, 343
Gansevoort, Peter, 187
gardens: private, 364–65; public, 377–79
Gardiner, Thomas, 232
Gardner (Mass.): Boston, Barre and Gardner
    Railroad, 324; Fitchburg Railroad serving, 323;
    Samuel S. Howe, 264; labor statistics in, 16, 16;
    Asa Nichols, 28, 66; prepared chair stock for, 95
Garret, Wait, 94, 344
Garrick, David, 183
Gautier, Andrew, 134, 223, 390

Gaw, Gilbert: in early nineteenth-century
    Caribbean trade, 272; fire of, 32; in post-
    revolutionary Caribbean trade, 251, 251;
    square-top Windsor settee by, 76; stock on
    hand of, 134
Gaw, Robert, 245, 251, 271
Gaw brothers: Robert Gaw, 245, 251, 271;
    Washington purchases chairs from, 232, 366.
    See also Gaw, Gilbert
Gemeinhaus, 408–9
General Society of Mechanics and Tradesmen,
    24, 25
Georgetown (D.C.): Thomas Adams, 17, 430;
    chairs for new capital shipped to, 430; in early
    nineteenth-century coastal trade, 258, 259;
    in postrevolutionary coastal trade, 229, 231;
    Thomas Richardson and Company, 225
Georgetown (S.C.), 229, 259
Georgia: Augusta, 263; Columbus, 259, 263; in
    early nineteenth-century coastal trade, 259,
    263; Eatonton, 259, 263; Milledgeville, 426; in
    postrevolutionary coastal trade, 228, 229, 230,
    236, 237; in prerevolutionary coastal trade,
    225–26, 227; prison work in, 37; Saint Mary's,
    229, 237; state government furniture in, 426;
    Sunbury, 227, 237. See also Savannah
Gere, James: auxiliary trade of, 28; chair parts sup-
    plied by, 96, 120; chair slat cost, 126; customer
    billed for hauling by, 319; exchange of produce
    or labor for goods of, 304, 305; payment for
    chair framing, 130; Pettit working for, 13; school
    furniture made by, 418; secondhand chairs sold
    by, 136; shaving back posts hired out by, 124
Germantown (Pa.), 360, 363–64, 388
Germany, 283, 283–84
Gibbons, William, 403
Gibson and Jefferson, 367
Gilbert, George, 388
Gilbert, Jabez, 66
Gilbert, James C., 291
Gilbert, S. B., 253
Gilbert and Fairbanks, 86
gilding, 154, 178–80, Plate 15, Plate 26, Plate 27
Gill, Bryson, 29
Gill and Halfpenny, 49
Gillingham, Harrold E., 222, 228
Gillingham, John, 387, 405
Gillow of Lancashire, 239, 313, 314
Gilpin, Thomas, 28, 411
gilt chairs, 154, 178–80, Plate 15, Plate 26, Plate 27
gimlets, 76
Girard, John: in postrevolutionary Caribbean
    trade, 242, 242, 243; in postrevolutionary
    coastal trade, 230
Girard, Stephen: boxes used in packaging by,
    314; cane-colored chairs shipped by, 148, 148;
    coquelicot chairs bought by, 151, 151; in early
    nineteenth-century Far Eastern trade, 285–86;
    in early nineteenth-century South American
    trade, 278, 279, 280; and fan-back chairs, 138;
    gilded chairs exported by, 179; green chairs
    bought by, 146; interest in brig Sally purchased
    by, 400; mahogany-color chairs made for, 150;
    in postrevolutionary Caribbean trade, 242,
    242, 243; in postrevolutionary coastal trade,
    230, 233, 233; refurbishing done for, 188, 188;
    Skinner employed by, 80; straw-color chairs

bought by, 147; white chairs bought by, 148,
    149
Gladding, Thomas, 187
Glastonbury (Conn.). See Cole, Solomon
Gloucester (Mass.), 275, 308
glue, 79, 80, 100–101, 305
glue pots, 79–80
Golden Tun Tavern (Philadelphia), 389–90
Goldin, Coles, 305
gold leaf, 180, 180
Gomia, Bertolde Francisco, 253
Gonaives (Haiti), 238, 242, 243, 244
Goodman, John, 382–83
Goodman, W. L., 64
Goodrich, Ansel: coloring materials of, 146;
    continuous-bow chairs made by, 140; demijohn
    of, 156; dining chairs advertised by, 345; paint-
    ing supplies in estate of, 157; primed chairs in
    stock of, 159; seat preparation contracted by,
    119; seats in inventory of, 98–99; stock in hand
    of, 135; wood used by, 89
Gordon, Lord Adam, 91, 222
Gordon, John H., 396
Gordon, Patrick, 80, 337
Gormly, John, 84
gouges, 71–72
government use of Windsor chairs, 420–30;
    federal government, 427–30; local and county
    government, 420–24; state government,
    424–27
Governor's Chair, 381–83, 382
Graeme, Thomas, 360
Graeme Park, 343, 360
Gragg, Samuel, 142, 413
Grand Cayman, 238, 247
Grand Truck Railway Company, 324
Grand Turk I (ship), 400
Grant, Elias, 265
Grant and Jemison, 11
grape and grapevine motif, 168–69
Gray, William, 159
gray paint, 145, 152
Gray's Ferry Gardens (Philadelphia), 378
Grayson Spring Company, 319
Greater Antilles: in early nineteenth-century
    Caribbean trade, 269, 270; in postrevolutionary
    Caribbean trade, 238, 239, 240–47
Great Exhibition of 1851, 417
Great Fire of New York (1776), 31–32
Great Wagon Road, 286
great wheel lathes, 53, 53, 102
Green, Edward, 321, 321
Green, Garret, 321, 321
Green, John, 67, 119, 120, 128
Green, Mary (mother), 419–20
Green, Mary C. (daughter), 137, 418–19
Green, Timothy, 419
Greene, Richard W., 406
Greene family, 200, 262, 416
Greenfield (Mass.): Boston influencing, 292;
    William Bull blacksmith, 80; Daniel Clay, 63,
    76, 80, 303; Gilbert M. Lyons, 63, 68, 105; Miles
    and Lyons, 9, 14, 47, 302, 319
Greenleaf, James, 323
green paint, xii, 144–47, 145, 362
Green Spring, 360
Greenwich (Manhattan), 361

Hilton, Hale, 192
Hiltzheimer, Jacob, 34, 369, 371, 375, 378
Hingham (Mass.), 102, 418
Hinman, Philemon, 78
Hispaniola: in early nineteenth-century Caribbean
    trade, 269, *270*, 271; in postrevolutionary
    Caribbean trade, *238*, 240–44. *See also* Haiti;
    Santo Domingo (Dominican Republic)
Hiss, Jacob, Jr., 395
historic figures, use of Windsor chairs by, 365–70
Hitchcock, Lambert: auction held by, 302, *302*;
    boring machinery of, 77; center bit charged
    for, 75; dining room of, 348; double tenanting
    machine of, 60; in early nineteenth-century
    coastal trade, 264; employees of, 15; factory
    of, 107; Farmington Canal used by, 307; first
    shop of, 47; in Flag Seating Shop, 36; fuel of,
    105; "India rubbers" of, 23; insolvency of, 30,
    32, 36; journey to midwest, 294; journeyman's
    guarantee signed by, 14; kiln of, 93; lathes of,
    53; on log construction, 45; market of, 293–94;
    and New York style, 292; pea green chairs of,
    146–47; prison contract of, 36; railroad causing
    failure of, 324; regional dealers of, 300, 301; and
    Philemon Robbins, 6, 294; roll-top fancy side
    chair of, 36; screws of, 102; specialist painters
    in shop of, 162; stenciling used by, 174; stove
    purchased by, 104; ups and downs of career of,
    7; wages paid by, 22; wagons and wagon shed
    of, 318; waterpower used by, 59, 103; working
    hours of, 21
Hitchcocksville (Conn.), 32
Hitchcocksville Company, 16
Hobart, Caleb, Jr., 102, 418
Hoboken (N.J.), 378
*Hocus Pocus, or the Whole Art of Legerdemain in
    Perfection* (Dean), 373
Hodge, Hannah, 189
Hodgkins, Thomas, 6–7
Hodgkinson, John, 261
Hoff, Valentine, 385
Hogarth, William, 399
Holcomb, Alexander, 131
Holcomb, Allen: auction held by, 302; bending
    machine made by, 57–58; exchange of produce
    or labor for goods of, 303, 304–5, 306; fees for
    wagon use, 322; as journeyman, 13; migration
    of, 20; painting by, 162–63; paint mills sold by,
    155; repairs made by, 132; rush-bottom chairs
    painted by, 202; shave blade sold by, 67; strip-
    ing brush sold by, 165; wood used by, 86
Holcomb brothers, 6, 157
Holden, Asa, 203, *203*, 421
holdfasts, 77, 120
Holgate, William, and Son, 55, 59–60
holidays, 21
Hollingsworth, Levi, 224–25, 272
Hollingsworth family, 224
Holman, Jonathan, 306
Holmes, Elisha Harlow: as apprentice, 8, 10; candle
    sticks made by, 106; chairs damaged during
    transport, 134; insolvency of, 30; retailing
    chairs for Frederick Allen, 300; stuffed crickets
    made by, 199; toolbox made by, 79; wagons of,
    317, *317*; women's chairs sold by, 137
home ownership, 3
Honduras, Gulf of, *270*, 273–74

Honyman, Robert, 218
Hooper, Joseph, 94
Hope, Thomas, 141, 368
*Hope's Philadelphia Price-Current, and Commercial
    Record*, 278, *278*
Hopewell Furnace, 408
Hopkins, John G., 200, 416
Hopkins and Charles, 232
Hornor, William, Jr., 420, 424–25
horsehair, 195
horsepower, 102, *155*
Horsham (Pa.), 343, 360
Horton, Christopher, 426
Horton, Samuel, 47
Horton, Samuel, Jr., 373
hotels, 394–99; Astor House, New York City, 395,
    395, 396; Boston Exchange Coffee House, 394;
    City Hotel, New York City, 394, *394*; City Hotel,
    Saint Louis, 395; development from taverns,
    388; Exchange Hotel, Baltimore, 179, 189,
    395–96; Indian Queen Hotel, Louisville, 394;
    Oeller's Hotel, Philadelphia, 394; refurbishing
    of chairs from, 188–89, 396; repair of chairs
    from, 131, 398; Tontine Hotel, New Haven, 394;
    Washington Hall, Louisville, 394; Washington
    Hotel, New York City, 396. *See also* resort
    hotels
Houck, Andrew, 228, *228*
Houghton, Luke: exchange of produce or labor for
    goods of, 303–4, 305–6; factory stools made
    by, 408; fees for wagon use, 322; fuel of, 105;
    light and dark chairs in accounts of, 153; as not
    specializing, 28; prepared chair stock for, 13–14,
    95; on set fractions, 135; shop rented by, 44
hours of work, 3, 20–21
Household Furniture (Hope), 141
houses, colonial and federal, 338–40
Howard, Thomas, Jr., 135, 282, 290, 292, 301
Howe, Franklin, 301
Howe, Samuel S., 264
Howland, Mrs. Esther Allen, *357*
H-plan stretcher system, 79, 93, 167, 271
Hubbard, Ira, 306
Hubbard, John C., 324, 417, 423
Hubbardston (Mass.), 16
Hudson, Barzillai: auction of Lambert Hitchcock
    chairs by, 302, *302*; as distributor for Lambert
    Hitchcock, 294, 301; study of, *358*, 358–59
Hudson River: in early nineteenth-century coastal
    trade, 263; Erie Canal, 221; furniture traffic on,
    307; length of voyage to Albany by sailing craft,
    307; shallops on, 306; sloop service on, 400;
    steamboat traffic on, 220, 401
Humble, John, 157
Hume, John, 47
Humes, Samuel, 193
Humeston, Jay, *270*, 296
Huneker, John, 260, 261, *261*
Hunt, Edmond, 15
Hunter, Louis C., 103
Huntington (N.Y.), 189
Huntington, Andrew, 193
Huntington, Felix, 30, 253
Hurford, Samuel, 94
Hutchings, Thomas Lewis, 296
Hutchins, Zadock, 66, 71, 72, 76, 160, 292
Hutchinson, Storal, 289

Hyde de Neuville, Baroness, 363, *363*, 419, *419*
Hyer, John, 225

Illinois, 219, 220, 294
Illustrated London News, 417
Imlay, Gilbert, 219
impressions. *See* brands
India, 218, *257*
Indiana: Brookville, 33; dog-powered lathes in,
    102; Indianapolis, 426–27; William McCracken
    in Knox County, 45; New Albany, 296; in
    nineteenth-century inland trade, 295–96; state
    government furniture in, 426–27; in western
    expansion, 219; wood used in, 92
Indianapolis (Ind.), 426–27
Indian Queen Hotel (Louisville, Ky.), 394
informal gatherings, 375, 379
Ingalls, Charles, 301
Ingalls, Samuel, 155
inland trade: eighteenth-century, 286–88;
    nineteenth-century, 289–96
innkeepers, 388
inns. *See* taverns (public houses)
inscriptions, 267, 271, 427
insolvencies, 29–30, 157
institutional use of Windsor chairs, 411–20; by
    churches and religious groups, 414–16; by
    government, 420–30; in libraries and related
    institutions, 411–15; in schools, 416–20
insurance, freight, 309, 311
Iowa, 20, 190, 427
Ireland, Henry, 388
iron plates, in chair repairs, 133
Irving, Washington, 369

jack planes (fore planes), 68–70, 119
Jackson, Andrew, 173, 268
Jackson (Johnson), Benedict, 17
Jackson, J. B., 416
Jackson, Peter, 17
Jacmel (Haiti), *238*, 242, 244
Jacobs, George, 418
Jacques and Hay, 59, 103–4, 107–8
Jakarta (Batavia), *257*, 286
Jamaica: in early nineteenth-century Caribbean
    trade, *270*, 271; James's caricatures of, 376, *377*,
    387; in postrevolutionary Caribbean trade, *238*,
    239, 240; in prerevolutionary Caribbean trade,
    222–23
James, Abraham, 376, *377*, *387*
James, James, 383
James, Joseph, 349
James, Josiah, 400, *401*
James River, 227, *228*, 233
japanning, 185–86; coloring and, 159; DeWitt and
    MacBride advertising, 163, 166; European
    origins of, 143; wood graining and, 180
Jarvis, Edward, 203, 337–38
Java, *257*, 286
jeans, 23
Jefferson, George, 309, 310, *310*, 367–68
Jefferson, Thomas, 366–68; bergère chair of, 140,
    367; black chairs of, 149; chair damaged in
    transport, 134; on dark chairs, 153; Embargo
    Act of 1807, 24, 30, 219, 278, 297; gilded chairs
    for, 179; library of, xiv, 413; shipping of chairs
    to, 309–10, *310*; striping on chairs of, 165

Lexington (Ky.) *(continued)*
    and Manufacturers of Lexington, 26; public
    gardens in, 378–79
Lexington (Va.), 193, 195, 362
L'Hommedieu, Giles, 264
libraries, 411–14; athenæum movement and, 413;
    Library Company of Philadelphia, 411–12;
    of Massachusetts Historical Society, 414; of
    mechanics organizations, 412; Portsmouth
    Apprentices' Library, 25; Redwood Library,
    Newport, R.I., 411; Washington, D.C., xiv,
    413–14
Library Company of Philadelphia, 411–12
Library Hall (Philadelphia), 412
Library of Congress, xiv, 413–14
lighting, 51, 105–6
Lima (Peru), *276*, 280, 281
Lincolnton (N.C.), 322
Lines, Charles B., 18, 32–33
linseed oil, 156, 157, 158, 305
Litchfield (Conn.): Sarah Pierce's school for young
    ladies, 418; Tapping Reeve, 303, 407. *See also*
    Cheney, Silas
Lititz (Pa.), 410, 411
Little Girl with Golden Hair (Johnson), *359, 359*
Liverpool (England), *283*, 284
Liverpool (Nova Scotia), 229, 236, 237
Livingston, Robert R., 183, 186
Lloyd, John, 309
Lloyd, William, 234
Lobach, Samuel, 318
local and county government, 420–24
Locke, Ebenezer, Jr., 322
Lockwood and Waite, 89
Lodge, Abraham, 340
Logan, James, 360
London (Ontario), 299
London Chair-Makers' and Carvers' Book of Prices,
    284
London price book of 1802, 141, 142
London Tradesman, 7, 9
Long Island: in commercial sphere of Windsor-
    chair making, 217; in early nineteenth-century
    coastal trade, 263; Huntington, 189; oak and
    hickory from, 85; Sag Harbor, 229, 234. *See also*
    Dominy family
long planes (jointer trying planes), 69
looking glasses: in bedrooms, 354, 355, 356; in
    dining rooms, 343, 344, 345, 348; in hotels, 395;
    in kitchens, 356; in parlors, 348, 349, 350
Loomis, Reuben, 64
Loomis, Samuel, 65, 79
Lopez, Aaron, 93, 223, 225
Lopez, Joseph, 251
Lord George Graham in His Cabin (Hogarth), 399
Loring, Joseph F., 47–48
Louisiana. *See* New Orleans
Louisville (Ky.): hotels in, 394; keelboat traffic with
    Pittsburgh, 295; McSwiney and Barnes, 402;
    in nineteenth-century inland trade, 295; W.
    D. Rand, 103, 402, 424; river voyage to New
    Orleans, 220, 268, 310; steamboats supplied
    with furniture at, 402; steamboat traffic at, 221,
    295; steam power in, 103
Love, Benjamin, 9, 46, 136, 146, 354
Love, William, 45
Low, Alexander, 132

Low, Nicholas: Ballston Spa resort hotels
    developed by, 397; as Bingham's agent, 234,
    361; fancy chairs bought from Palmer by, 178;
    japanned chairs bought from Palmer by, 186;
    Sans Souci Hotel promoted by, 6, 20, 22, 397
Low, William, 50, 293, 426
Low and Damon, 50, 293, 426
low-back chairs, 138
Lowell (Mass.), 293, 320, 324
Lower Manhattan, 48
Loyalists, 296
Lucas and Shepard, 70
Ludwell, Philip, 361
Luther, William, 183, 278
Lux, William, 225
Lycett, William, 186
lyceum movement, 373
Lynch and Trask, 427
Lynchburg (Va.), 286–87, 295, 301–2, 367
Lyon, Moses: coquelicot used by, 152; cornucopia
    motif used by, 172; floral and fruit designs used
    by, 169; national heroes depicted by, 173; as
    painter for Alling, 13, 152, 163, 172, 173, 174, 183;
    stenciling done by, 174; wood graining done
    by, 183
Lyons, Gilbert M., 63, 68, 105
Lyons, Joel, 9, 14, 47, 302, 319

MacBride, Walter, 163, 166
MacDonald, William H., 162, 202
Machias (Maine), 229, 236
Mackinaw (Mich.), 289
Macky, John, 363
Madeira, 253, *254*, 281–82
Madison, James and Dolley, 152, 178, 368–69, 413,
    430
Madras (India), *257*
Maentel, Jacob, 169, 417, Plate 4
mahogany (wood): for dining tables, 343, 344; in
    Golden Tun Tavern, 390; mahogany graining,
    182, Plate 33; Pennsylvania chairmakers using
    in arms, 84
mahogany-color: paint, *145*, 150, 390; stain, 185
Maine: American coastwise chair trade, 1768–72,
    227; Bangor, 259; Bath, 259, 271; Camden, 379;
    in early nineteenth-century coastal trade,
    259, 264; Falmouth, *227*, 229; grape motif in,
    169; Kennebunk, 229, 236; Machias, 229, 236;
    Penobscot, 229; in postrevolutionary coastal
    trade, 229, 236; shell motif in, 172; shop signs
    in, 50; wood used in, *87*, 91, 92; yellow birch in,
    92. *See also* Portland
Málaga (Spain), 282, *283*
Malay Archipelago, 256, *257*
mallets, 65
Mandeville, William, 421
mandrels, 77
Manheim (Pa.), 393
manufactory, 43, 107, 319
maple: black maple, 83, 92; Canadian chairmakers
    using, 92; maple graining, 181, Plate 28, Plate
    29, Plate 30; New England chairmakers using,
    87, 89–90, 91; New York chairmakers using, 85,
    86; Pennsylvania chairmakers using, 82–83; red
    maple, 83, 85; Southern chairmakers using, 91;
    sugar maple, 83, 92
maps, 344, 349, *346*

Maracaibo (Venezuela), *276*, 277
marble gray paint, *145*, 152
Marblehead (Mass.), 226, *227, 228*, 229
marbling, 184
March, Thomas M., 264
Maritime Provinces (Canada): in Caribbean trade,
    296. *See also* New Brunswick; Newfoundland;
    Nova Scotia
marketing, 217–324; forms of merchandising, 7. *See
    also* advertisements; packaging; sale of chairs;
    trade; transportation
marking gauges, 78
marking irons (branding irons), *80*, 80–81
marking tools, 78
Marryat, Frederick, 393
Marsh, Timothy, 322–23
Marshall, Benjamin, 235
Marshall, Christopher, Jr., 348
Marston, Thomas, 351, 359
Martha's Vineyard (Mass.), *259*, 264, 394
Martineau, Harriet, 393
Martinique: in early nineteenth-century
    Caribbean trade, 269, *270*, 272–73; in postrevo-
    lutionary Caribbean trade, *238*, 245, 247, 249,
    250–51, *250*
Maryland: Annapolis, 157, 224, 225, 426;
    Cambridge, 229; Charlestown, 365, *365*;
    Chester, *227*; Chestertown, 229; Chincoteague,
    229; in early nineteenth-century coastal trade,
    259; gilded chairs from, 178; Hagerstown,
    84–85, 286; Head of Elk, 224; landscapes as
    popular in, 168; Nottingham, 229; Oxford, 224,
    229; Patuxent, *227*; Patuxent River, 225, 247;
    Pocomoke, *227, 228*; Port Deposit, 84; Port
    Tobacco, 229; in postrevolutionary coastal
    trade, 229; in prerevolutionary coastal trade,
    224–25, *227*; Princess Anne, 426; Salisbury, 229;
    Snow Hill, 229, *259*; state government furniture
    in, 426; Vienna, 229; wood used in, 84–85. *See
    also* Baltimore; Chesapeake Bay
Mason, George, 193, 195, 362
Mason, Joel W., 403
Mason, John, 232
Mason, J. W., 101
Mason, Richard, 230, 232
Mason, Thomas, 10, 154, 190, 232
Mason and Raule, 263
Masonic ornament, 173, 384–87, *384, 385*, Plate 18
Massachusetts: Barnstable, 153, 423; Berkshire
    County, 16, 293; Beverly, 228, 229, 250; blue
    chairs in, 153; Buckland, 304, 417; Colrain,
    302; Concord, 203, 337–38; Dedham,
    340–41, 342; Dennis, 229; Dighton, *229*; in
    early nineteenth-century coastal trade, *259*;
    Edgartown, *259*, 264; Fall River, *259*; in Far
    Eastern trade, 256; Fitchburg, 16; furniture
    production increasing in, 107; Gloucester, 275,
    308; grape motif in, 169; Heath, 300; Hingham,
    102, 418; Hubbardston, 16; industrialization
    of chairmaking in, 15–16; Leicester, 29, 318,
    322; Marblehead, 226, *227, 228*, 229; Martha's
    Vineyard, *259*, 264, 394; Nahant, 397; Paxton,
    264; in postrevolutionary African and Eastern
    Atlantic Islands trade, 255; in postrevolutionary
    Caribbean trade, 249, 251; in postrevolutionary
    coastal trade, 229; in postrevolutionary South
    American trade, 252; in prerevolutionary

coastal trade, 226, *227*; Princeton, 16; prison work in, 37; railroads in, 222; Roxbury, 34; Royalston, 16; Springfield, 48, 294, 402; statistical information relating to industry, 16, *16*; Stockbridge, 16; Westminster, 16, *16*; white chairs in, 149; wood used in, 86, *87*, 89, 90, 91. *See also* Ashburnham; Barre; Boston; Cape Cod; Framingham; Gardner; Greenfield; Lee; Nantucket Island; Newburyport; New Bedford; Northampton; Salem (Mass.); Sterling; Templeton; Weymouth; Worcester County

Massachusetts Charitable Mechanics Association, 24

Massachusetts Historical Society, xiv, 414

master craftsmen, 3–7; apprentices trained by, 3, 7–11; dual and supplementary occupations of, 28–29; in dual capacities as master and employee, 6–7; as entrepreneurs, 3; financial records of, 4–6; households of, 3; journeymen employed by, 3, 11–18; as managers, 6; merchandising by, 7; migration of, 19–20; profits for, 130; renting unused shop space, 6; requirements for setting up as, 11; success attained by, 7

Masters, William, 360

Matanzas (Cuba): in early nineteenth-century Caribbean trade, *270*, *271*; in postrevolutionary Caribbean trade, *238*, 245, 246

materials, 81–102; in exchange for goods and services, 305; fasteners, 101–2; glue, 79, 80, 100–101, 305; master craftsmen acquiring, 6; miscellaneous, 100–102; as requirement for setting up as master, 11. *See also* wood

Mather, William, 305

Mathews, Edward, 75

Mathiot, A. and J. B., 266, *266*

Maule, Thomas, 74, 75

Maule and Brother, 84

Mauritius, 179, *257*, 285

Maxwell, Solomon, 150, 233

May, Henry, 296

May, John, 6

Mayes, L. J., 64, 65, 68, 73

Mayhew, Frederick W., *167*

Mayr, Christian, 375

McClintic, John, 289

McColm, Matthew, 10, 266, 316

McComb, John, Jr., 421

McCracken, William, 45

McDonough, Abraham, 182, 187, 261, 299–300

McDougal, Hugh, 157

McDougle, Levi, 296

McDugal, Levi, 15

McElwee, John, 157

McEuen, Malcolm, 256

McFarland, William, 15

McGarvey, Owen, 49

McGrath, Michael, 264

McIntire, Andrew, 287

McKarahan, Charles, 33

McKeen, Robert, 12–13, 94

McKelsey, David, 404

McKenzie, Kenneth, 165

McKim, Andrew, 426

McKim, Robert: courthouse furniture made by, 423; fires of, 32; in mechanic society, 25; shop of, 44, 49; state government furniture made

by, 426; stuffed Windsor seating made by, 195; supplementary occupation of, 29

McPhail, John A., 274

McSwiney and Barnes, 402

Mease, James, 158

measuring tools, 77–78

mechanical equipment, 59–60

mechanic and manufacturing societies, 24–27, 412

Mechanicks and Manufacturers of Lexington, 26

mechanization: Daniel's thickness planer, 119, *120*; mechanical equipment, 59–60; paint mills, 154–55; seat-shaping machinery, 121; of seat weaving, 16, 203

medical care, in exchange for goods or services, 304

Megarey, Henry J., 161–62, *162*

Mehargue, John, 303

Melish, John, 22, 34, 291, 295, 297, 397, 401

Mendes, Abraham, 223

men's chairs, 137–38

Mercer, Henry C., 66, 71

Mere, John, 260–61, 313

Merrifield, Preston, 306

Merrimack River, 293, 307, 320

metallic work, 174–80; freehand bronzing, 177; gilding, 154, 178–80; stenciling, 174–77

metalwork, in exchange for goods or services, 304

Mexico: Alvarado, *270*, 274; Campeche, *270*, 273, 274; in early nineteenth-century Caribbean trade, *270*, 274

Meyers, William H., 376, *376*

Michaux, François André: on prepared chair stock, 94; on wood for splint seating, 203; on wood used in chairmaking, 81–82, 83, 86, 88, 89, 90, 91, 92

Michigan, 294, 299, 365

Mickle, Isaac, 358, *358*

Middle Atlantic region: in Census of Manufactures of 1820, 15; chairmakers' shops in, 45–46; keeping rooms in, 352–53; landscapes as popular in, 168; mechanic societies in, 25; migration from, 20; in nineteenth-century inland trade, 289–92; wood used in, 82–86. *See also* Delaware; New Jersey; New York State; Pennsylvania

Middlebury (Vt.). *See* Warren, Hastings

Middletown (Conn.): Elizur Barnes, 95, 201, 202; copal varnish sold in, 187; in postrevolutionary African and Eastern Atlantic Islands trade, 255; water transport, 307

Midwest: in Census of Manufactures of 1820, 15; Eastern styles in, 19; Illinois, 219, 220, 294; Iowa, 20, 190, 427; mechanic societies in, 26; Michigan, 294, 299, 365; in nineteenth-century inland trade, 295–96; steam power in, 103; waterpower in, 103; wood used in, 91–92. *See also* Indiana; Kentucky; Missouri; Ohio; Tennessee

Mifflin, Thomas, 340

migration: to and from Canada, 296–97; of chairmakers, 19–20; patterns carried by chairmakers in, 287–88, 296; in western expansion, 219–20, 296

Miles, Isaac, 9, 14, 47, 302, 319

Miles and Lyons, 9, 14, 47, 302, 319

military posts, 430

Milledgeville (Ga.), 426

Miller, Anne, 362

Miller, George Lyman, 162

Miller, Henry W., 6, 7, 95, 199, 319, 405

Miller, Lewis: bench dog of, 77; bench rule of, 78; bench stop of, 51; on Chapman's Springs, Va., *398*, 398–99; compass saw of, 63; *Court of Quarter Sessions and Court of Common Pleas*, xiv, 421–22, *422*; dress of, 24; *Dr. John Rause and Family*, 344, *344*; floral and fruit designs used by, 169; glue kettle and pot stand of, 79–80; hammer of, 66; handsaw of, 62; lighting in shop of, 106; Lutheran schoolhouse depicted by, 418; *Martin Weiser . . . in His Tavern*, 131, *131*; *Self Portrait* in his shop, *50*; *The Shop of William Spangler, Tobacconist*, 406, *406*; tool handles of, 79; trying plane of, 69

Mills, Edward, 75, *75*

Mills, Richard, 399

Milton (N.Y.), 6, 397

Minnick, John, 147, 150

Miramichi Bay, *259*, 266

mirrors. *See* looking glasses

Mississippi. *See* Natchez

Mississippi River, 220–21, 310

Missouri. *See* Saint Louis

Mitchell, John, 280

Mitchell, Thomas, 32, 46

Mitchell, William, 32, 46, 268

miter-top chairs, 138

Mobile (Ala.), *259*, 263

molding planes, 70, *70*

molds, bending, 58–59, *58*

Montague, Gurdon H., 404

Montego Bay, 239

Montgomery, Abigail, 352, *352*

Montgomery, Charles F., 26, *27*

Montgomery, John, 352, *352*

Montpelier (Vt.), 88

Montreal (Quebec): Julius Barnard, 20, 296; N. W. Burpee, 97, 185; Champlain Canal giving access to, 290; in nineteenth-century inland trade, 296

Montserrat, 222

Moon, David, 258, 287, 316

Moon, Samuel, 287

Moore, D. C. Y., 36

Moore, Oliver, 131, 322–23

Moore, William, Jr.: insolvency of, 30, 294; market of, 293–94; property of, 47; sales techniques of, 300; sled of, 322; store of, 29; turning and boring machinery of, 60, 77; waterpower used by, 103

Moravians, 408–11

Moreau, Jean Victor, 363, *363*

Moreau de St. Méry, Médéric-Louis-Élie, 34, 50, 144, 320, 338, 394

moreen, 195, 197, 350, 362

Morgan, Eneas, 305

Morison, Samuel Eliot, 274–75, 280

Morland, George, 379

morocco leather, 190, 191, 195, 200

Morris, Anthony, 318

Morrisville (Pa.), 363, *363*

Morse, Jedidiah, 88, 217, 218

mortise and tenon joints, 71–72, 125–27, *126*, *127*

mortised-top chairs, 139

mortising equipment, 60

Moses boats, 306
Mount, William Sidney, 55, *196, 197*, 348, 375
Mount Vernon (Va.), *229, 232*, 363, 365–66
Mount Vernon Garden (New York City), 377
Moxon, Joseph, 52, 64, 77, 78, 79, 100, 101
Moyers and Rich, 132, 133, 319
Mrs. John Harrison and Daughter (Mayhew), *167*
Muir, William H., 264
Mulkey, Thomas, 136
Mullen, John, 233
Mullen, Jonathan, 323
Mullen and Cowperthwaite, 50
Mumford, John P., 405
Munden, Brigadier General, 189
Munger, Daniel, 292
Munger, Sally, 304
municipal symbols, 173
Murfreesboro (N.C.), *229*
Murphy, Michael, 232, 258, 287, 315
Myers, Moses, 370
Mygatt, Comfort Starr, 197, Plate 35
Myrick, Andrew, 348

Nahant (Mass.), 397
nails, brass, 196–98
nankeen-color paint, *145*, 152
Nantucket Island: black chairs in, 149; Charles
    Chase, 47; cushions in, 190; domestic use of
    Windsor chairs in, 348; dual-color chairs in,
    154; Obed Faye's green paint formula, 146;
    mahogany-color chairs in, 150; marbling in,
    184; in postrevolutionary coastal trade, *229*;
    tip carts in, 379, *380*; Windsor chair associated
    with, 137
narrow-top chairs, 139
Nashville (Tenn.): Kerm swindles residents of, 33;
    mechanic society in, 26; in nineteenth-century
    inland trade, 296; John Priest, 81, 164; Samuel
    Williams and Company, 19, 92–93, 296
Natchez (Miss.), 20, *259*, 263, 268, 301
national and other symbols, 172–73
national heroes, 173
National Trades' Union, 27
Native Americans, 18, 284–85
Natt, Thomas, 395
natural catastrophes, 33
Neave, Samuel, 360
Needles, Edward, 168
Needles, John, 103
needlework cushion cases, 190, 191
neoclassicism, 140, 143, 167–68, 172, 394
Nestell, Christian: American eagle used by, 173;
    brand of, 81; cornucopia motif used by, 172;
    drawing school attended by, 164, 172; mermaid
    design of, *173*; neoclassical design by, 169–70,
    169; New York-style chairs made by, 292;
    ornamentation as specialty of, 170; refurbishing
    done by, 189; renting shop space from Proud
    brothers, 6; shell motif used by, 172, *173*
New Albany (Ind.), 296
Newark (N.J.): L. M. Crane and Company, 103;
    mechanic society in, 25; timber in vicinity of,
    85; Tunis and Nutman, 282, 290, 301; varnish
    production in, 187; wood graining in chairs
    from, 181. *See also* Alling, David
New Bedford (Mass.): Cromwell, Howland, and
    Davis, 19; domestic use of Windsor chairs in,

347–48; in early nineteenth-century coastal
    trade, *259*, 262, 264; Thomas Ellis, 183, 191, 322;
    flowered chairs in, 167; Humphrey Hathaway's
    offices in, 404, *405*; New York influencing,
    292; paint drying in, 162; in postrevolutionary
    coastal trade, *229*; William Russell, Jr., 89, 187,
    187; sales techniques in, 300, *300*; R. and W.
    Swift, 293; William S. Wall, 63, 67
New Bern (N.C.), *229, 259*, 263, 294
New Brunswick: courthouse furniture in, 424; in
    early nineteenth-century coastal trade, *259*,
    266; Fredericton, 266, 296; in postrevolution-
    ary coastal trade, *229*; Saint Andrew's, *229, 259*,
    266; Saint John, 266, 296; yellow birch in, 92
New Brunswick (N.J.), 363, 402
Newburyport (Mass.): chairs in churches in,
    414; John Cooper, 417; dancing assemblies
    in, 374; in early nineteenth-century coastal
    trade, *259*; in early nineteenth-century South
    American trade, 275; fire of 1811, 32; Bernard
    Foot, 153; Lafayette's visit to, 370; loose seating
    in wagons in, 379; mechanic society in, 25; in
    postrevolutionary coastal trade, *229*; rocking
    chair cushions in, 190; schoolhouse furniture
    in, 418
New Castle (Del.), 224, 226, *229*
Newdigate, John, 223
New England: in Census of Manufactures of 1820,
    15; chairmakers' properties in, 47–48; country
    trade in, 293; cushion materials in, 190;
    domestic use of Windsor chairs in, 345–48,
    346, 347, 350–53, *352*, 356–59, *358*; in early
    nineteenth-century coastal trade, 263–66, *265*,
    267; holidays in, 21; keeping rooms in, 352–53;
    kitchen chairs in, 356; landscapes on painted
    seating as popular in, 168; Merrimack River,
    293, 307, 320; migration in, 20, 288; New York
    influencing, 292; in nineteenth-century inland
    trade, 292–94; packet boat service on coast
    of, 400; painting supplies imported by, 157;
    in postrevolutionary Caribbean trade, 240,
    243–52; in postrevolutionary coastal trade, 228,
    234–37; in postrevolutionary South American
    trade, 252–53; prepared chair stock in, 94–95,
    96; in prerevolutionary coastal trade, 224, 226,
    227; public houses (taverns), 388–89; roll-top
    chairs in southern, 139; schoolhouse furniture
    in, 416–19; shell motif in, 172; stenciling in, 177;
    stepped-tablet crest in, 141; stuffed Windsor
    seating in, 193–94, 195; textile industry in, 219;
    wages in, 22; War of 1812 affecting trade of, 219;
    wood used in, 86–91; yellow chairs in, 147. *See
    also* Connecticut; Connecticut River; Maine;
    Massachusetts; New Hampshire; Rhode Island;
    Vermont
Newent (Conn.), 414
Newfoundland: Burin, *259*, 266; in early
    nineteenth-century coastal trade, *259*, 266; in
    postrevolutionary coastal trade, *229*, 236; Saint
    Andrew's, *259*; Saint John's, *229*, 236, *259*, 266
Newgate Prison (Conn.), 36
New Hampshire: Bedford, 414; Boston influencing,
    292–93; Canada influenced by, 297; Chichester,
    339, *339*; Cornish, 415–16; Deerfield, 132, 133,
    136, 305; in early nineteenth-century coastal
    trade, *259*; grape motif in, 169; Keene, 47;
    mechanic societies in, 25; Piscataqua, 226,

227, 228; in postrevolutionary Caribbean
    trade, 228; in postrevolutionary coastal trade,
    229; in prerevolutionary coastal trade, 226,
    227; Salisbury, 47; shell motif in, 172; state
    government furniture in, 173, 426; state symbol
    on chairs in, 173; stuffed Windsor seating in,
    195; wood used in, *87*, 88, 91. *See also* Concord
    (N.H.); Fitzwilliam; New Ipswich; Portsmouth
New Haven (Conn.): American coastwise chair
    trade, 1768–72, *227*; William H. Augur, 11, 281;
    Edward Bulkley, 46, 49, 95; in early nineteenth-
    century Caribbean trade, 271; fire in, 32–33;
    Alpheus Hewes, 288, 362; packet boat service,
    400; painting supplies imported by, 157; in
    postrevolutionary Caribbean trade, 240, 243,
    248, 249, 250, 251; river commerce from, 307;
    Tontine Hotel, 394; Treat & Lines, 18; wharfage
    charges at, 309. *See also* Stillman, Levi
New Haven and Hartford Railroad, 324
New Ipswich (N.H.): Appleton Academy, 417. *See
    also* Wilder, Josiah Prescott
New Jersey: American coastwise chair trade,
    1768–72, *227*; Black Point, 165, *229*, 234, 308,
    360–61; Bordentown, 364, *365*; Bridgeton,
    385–86, *386*, Plate 18; Camden, 358, *358*;
    in commercial sphere of Windsor-chair
    making, 217; cross-back chairs in, 139; in
    early nineteenth-century coastal trade, 263;
    Eatontown, 58, 85; Hoboken, 378; natural
    seating materials growing in, 201–2, *201*; New
    Brunswick, 363, 402; New York influencing,
    288; in nineteenth-century inland trade, 290;
    in postrevolutionary coastal trade, *229*; wood
    used in, 85. *See also* Burlington (N.J.); Newark;
    Perth Amboy; Salem (N.J.); Trenton
New Lisbon (N.Y.). *See* Holcomb, Allen
New London (Conn.): American coastwise chair
    trade, 1768–72, *227*; in early nineteenth-century
    Caribbean trade, 272, 273; in early nineteenth-
    century coastal trade, 264, 268; japanning
    in, 186; packet boat service, 400; Porter and
    Holbrook, 264; in postrevolutionary Caribbean
    trade, 228, 243, 245, 248, 249, 250, 251; in post-
    revolutionary coastal trade, *229*, 231, 236; in
    postrevolutionary South American trade, 252;
    turnpike between Norwich and, 220; Thomas
    West, 24, 29, 180, 185, 202
Newman, Gawen B., 60
New Orleans: David Alling shipping chairs to,
    181, 268; in early nineteenth-century coastal
    trade, 258, *259*, 260, 261, 267–69; military stores
    shipped to, 430; in postrevolutionary coastal
    trade, *229*; river voyage from Louisville, 220,
    268, 310; river voyage from Pittsburgh, 219,
    310; in triangular trade with Philadelphia and
    Baltimore, 289
Newport (R.I.): Jonathan Cahoone, 93, 423; in
    commercial sphere of Windsor-chair making,
    217; in early nineteenth-century coastal trade,
    259; keeping rooms in, 352; local and county
    government furniture in, 422–23; Aaron Lopez,
    93, 223, 225; in postrevolutionary African and
    Eastern Atlantic Islands trade, 255; in postrevo-
    lutionary Caribbean trade, 228, 240, 243–44,
    251; in postrevolutionary coastal trade, *229*,
    231, 235; in postrevolutionary South American
    trade, 252, 253; preparations for sailing from,

310; in prerevolutionary coastal trade, 224; Redwood Library, 411; stuffed Windsor seating in, 192; Joseph Vickary, 399, 423
New Providence (Bahamas), *238*, 240
New River (N.C.), *229*, *259*
Newton, Proctor, 36
Newtown (Conn.), 63, 67
New-York Book of Prices for Cabinet and Chair Work, The (1802), 141
New York Chairmakers' Society, 173
New York City: James Always, 162, 322; American eagle on chairs from, 173; Bell and Stoneall, 183; black chairs in, 149; Bloomingdale, Manhattan, 350, 361, 363, 391–92; Browne and Ash, 200; Thomas Burling, 140, 367; William Buttre, 160–61, *161*, 262, *262*; cane-seat chairs in, 203; chairmakers' shops in, 44, 45–46, 48; chocolate-color chairs in, 150; Cholwell and Summers, 157; City Hotel, 394, *394*; in commercial sphere of Windsor-chair making, 217; Common Council, 421; continuous-bow chairs in, 140; coquelicot chairs in, 152; Cornwell and Cowperthwaite, 146; Cornwell and Smith, 135, 174; countinghouses in, 405; country seats near, 361; craft community of, 3; cross-back chairs in, 141; John DeWitt, 163, 166, 234, 425, *425*; domestic use of Windsor chairs in, 340, 341, 345, 350–51, 355–56, 359; in early nineteenth-century Caribbean trade, 269, 272; in early nineteenth-century coastal trade, 259, 261–63, 263–64, 267, 269; in early nineteenth-century South American trade, 277, 280, 281; in eighteenth-century inland trade, 286; Erie Canal and, 292; Federal Procession of 1788, 218, *218*; fires in, 32; First Congress in, 429; Flushing, Queens, 361; Fraunces Tavern Museum, 389; Charles Fredericks, 189, 262, 403; Fredericks and Farrington, 402, 403; freight charges at, 308; French influence in, 140; Friends of National Industry convention in, 24; Adam Galer, *20*, 223, 288; Andrew Gautier, 134, 223, 390; General Society of Mechanics and Tradesmen at, 25; gilded chairs from, 179; glue production in, 100–101; gray chairs in, 152; Great Fire of 1776, 31–32; James Hallet, Jr., 30, 269; Asa Holden, 203, *203*, 421; hotels in, 394, 396; influence of, 288, 290, 292, 294; insolvencies in, 30; japanning in, 186, *186*; John Kelso, 223, 288; labor strife in, 27; Lafayette's visit to, 370; landscapes as popular in, 168; in late-eighteenth- and early-nineteenth-century European trade, 282; Daniel Lee, 161; William H. Lee, 161, *162*; Lower Manhattan, 48; Lucas and Shepard, 70; mechanics' societies in, 24; migration to, 20; Native American woodworker in, 18; in nineteenth-century inland trade, 290–91, 295; Reuben Odell, 30, 34, 142, 419; outdoor uses of Windsor chairs in, 362, 364, 365; packet boat service, 400; paint dealers in, 157; paint mills in, 154, 155; Patterson and Dennis, 355; Perry, Hayes, and Sherbrooke, 223; population growth of, 3; in postrevolutionary African and Eastern Atlantic Islands trade, 253, 255, 256; in postrevolutionary Caribbean trade, 228, 240, 243, 244, 245, 247, 248, 249, 251; in postrevolutionary coastal trade, 229, 230–31,

234–35; in postrevolutionary South American trade, 252; prepared chair stock for, 96; in prerevolutionary coastal trade, 223, *227*; prison work at, 35; public gardens in, 377–78; public houses (taverns) in, 391–92; red chairs in, 151; roll-top chairs in, 139, 141; Nathaniel S. Rose, 34–35, 46, *46*; sandpaper in, 101; schools in, 419–20; seat planks for stuffing in, 195; shell motif in, 172; ship outfitting in, 400; shipping volume in early nineteenth-century, 256; shop signs in, 50; slat-back chairs in, 141–42; John Smith, 262–63; splat-back chairs (formal) in, 141; steamboat connection with Albany, 220; steamboats supplied with furniture at, 402–3; stoops in, 363, *364*; stuffed Windsor seating in, 192, 195, 197; theaters in, 372; Thomas Timpson, 146, 234; Timpson and Gillihen, 192, 362; Tontine Coffee House, 218, 320, 390–91, *391*; trade of, 218, 261–62; Tweed and Bonnell, 95, 316, 396; Joseph Vail, 135, 136, 288; varnish production in, 186–87; view from steeple of St. Paul's, 161–62, *162*; wages in, 22; Alexander Welsh, 189, *189*, 402, 403, *403*; white chairs in, 149; Wilder and Stewart, 96, 293, 406; wood used in, 81, 85; yellow chairs in, 147. *See also* Ash, Thomas, I; Ash, Thomas, II; Ash, William, I; Brooklyn; Palmer, William
New York Mechanick Society, 43, *44*
New York State: Canadian trade of, 297; Canandaigua, 297; Carthage, 297; chair exportations reported in journal of state assembly, 231; Cooperstown, 6, 106, 288, 305, 341; cross-back chairs in, 139; fishing at resorts in, 383–84; green chairs for legislature of, 146; Kinderhook, *229*, 234; landscapes on painted seating as popular in, 168; migration to, 20; Milton, 6, 397; New York City intruding in upstate markets, 290; Niagara Falls, 299; Orange County, 361; Oswego, 299; in postrevolutionary coastal trade, 229; Poughkeepsie, 103, 281; prison work in, 35–36; Saratoga, 305, 324; Saratoga Springs, 397, 398; seating in wagons in, 380; state government furniture in, 146, 425; stuffed Windsor seating in, 192; turnpikes in, 220; Utica, 86, 291, 298, 307; waterpower in, 103; Westchester County, 361; West Point, 378; wood used in, 85–86. *See also* Albany; Ballston Spa; Black River; Buffalo; Erie Canal; Hudson River; Long Island; New York City; Otsego County; Rochester; Schenectady; Syracuse; Troy
Niagara Falls (N.Y.), 299
Niblos Garden (New York City), 378
Nichols, Asa, 28, 66
Nichols, Horace, 7
Nichols, Samuel, 420–21
Nields, Daniel, 28
Nightingale, Samuel, 280
Niles, J. M., 133
Niles Weekly Register, 24
nippers (pincers), 77
Nixonton (N.C.), *259*
Noble, Matthew, 89
Nolan and Gridley, 264, 307–8
nomenclature of chair parts, 97–98
Nootka Indians, 284–85
Norfolk (Va.): destruction in American

Revolution, 32; in early nineteenth-century coastal trade, 258, 259, 260, 261, 262, 264; mahogany-color chairs in, 150; Michael Murphy, 232, 258, 287, 315; Moses Myers house, 370; in postrevolutionary coastal trade, *229*, 230, 231, 232, 234, 235, 237; tulip trees at, 91; unassembled seating shipped to, 315, 316; Charles Young estate, 361–62
Norris, Charles, 131
Norris, Isaac, II, 360
Northampton (Mass.): Julius Barnard, 288; John Breck hardware dealer, 71, 72, 74; Luther Davis, 76, 164; drawknife suppliers in, 67; Farmington Canal to, 307; Asa Jones, 293; migration to, 20; Oliver Pomeroy, 45, 288; Seth Pomeroy blacksmith, 66, 71; Tontine Building fire in, 32, *32*. *See also* Goodrich, Ansel
North Carolina: American coastwise chair trade, 1768–72, 227; Bath Town, 227; Beaufort, *227*, 229; Brunswick, *227*; Camden, 259; Currituck, *227*, 229, 259; in early nineteenth-century coastal trade, 258, 259, 263, 265; Edenton, 229, 259, 263; Lincolnton, 322; Murfreesboro, 229; New Bern, 229, 259, 263, 294; Nixonton, 259; Plymouth, 229; in postrevolutionary coastal trade, 228, 229, 231, 234, 237; Roanoke, *227*; Salem, 408–10; Salisbury, 295, 304; state government furniture in, 426; Swansboro, 229, 259; Wake County, 423; Washington, 229, 259; Windsor, 229. *See also* Raleigh; Wilmington (N.C.)
Northern Canal, 221
North Parlor of Dr. Whitridge (Russell), 198, *200*, 350
Norton, Jacob, 89
Norton, John, and Sons, 340
Norton, Rufus, 95
Norwalk (Conn.), 292
Norwich (Conn.): Stephen B. Allyn, 63; Allyn and Huntington, 288; Felix Huntington, 30, 253; painting supplies imported by, 157; in postrevolutionary Caribbean trade, 245; in postrevolutionary coastal trade, 229; turnpike to New London, 220; John Williams, 243
Norwood, Andrew, 400
Nottingham (Md.), 229
Nova Scotia: Digby and Shelburne, 235; in early nineteenth-century coastal trade, 259, 266; in early nineteenth-century South American trade, 278; Halifax, 229, 236, 266, 275, 296; Liverpool, 229, 236, 237; in postrevolutionary coastal trade, 229, 235, 236, 237; yellow birch in, 92
Noyes, Joseph, 32
nursery chairs, 137, 359–60
Nutt, John, 17, 32, 107

oak: interregional use in chairmaking, 81, 82, 83; Lake Champlain chairmakers probably using, 85; New England chairmakers using, 91; oak graining, 183; Pennsylvania chairmakers using, 84; red oak, 84, 126; Southern chairmakers using, 91; for spindles, 124. *See also* white oak
Oakley, Moses, 391–92
Oaks, Nathan, 296
Odell, James, Jr., 265
Odell, Reuben, 30, 34, 142, 419

283–84, 362, 371–72; cane used in chairmaking in, 203; Carpenters' Company, 26, 80, 411, 412, 427, *427*; chairmakers' shops in, 43–45, 46, 48; chairs shipped to new capital from, 430; John Chapman, 48, 416; Chestnut Street Theatre, 371, 372; chocolate-color chairs in, 150; in commercial sphere of Windsor-chair making, 217; countinghouses in, 404, 405; country seats near, 360–61; cream-color chairs in, 153; cushions in, 189–90; domestic use of Windsor chairs in, 337, 338, 340, 341–42, 343–45, 349, 350, 353, 354, 357–58, 359, 360–61; in early nineteenth-century Caribbean trade, 269, 270, 271, 272–73; in early nineteenth-century Central American trade, 274; in early nineteenth-century coastal trade, 256–61, 263–64, 267–68; in early nineteenth-century Eastern Atlantic Islands trade, 281–82; in early nineteenth-century Far Eastern trade, 285–86; in early nineteenth-century South American trade, 275, 277, 278, 279, 280, 281; in eighteenth-century inland trade, 286–87; fire insurance company in, 31; fires in, 32; First Congress in, 429; First Continental Congress in, 427; Franklin stoves in, 104; Franklin Institute founded in, 24; Freemasonry in, 384; Friends of American Manufactures organized in, 24; funerary equipment in, 387; Solomon Fussell, 79, 94, 131, 202; Germantown, 360, 363–64, 388; gilded chairs from, 179–80; John Gillingham, 387, 405; Thomas Gilpin, 28, 411; glue production in, 101; Golden Tun Tavern, 389–90; Gray's Ferry Gardens, 378; George Halberstadt, 270, 271, 272, 387; Halberstadt and Trotter, 270, 314; Haydon and Stewart, 181, 182–83, 260, 364; Levi Hollingsworth, 224–25, 272; hotels in, 394; influence of, ix, 287–88, 289, 290, 294–95; japanning in, 186; Daniel Jones, 57, 201; journeymen cabinetmakers' wareroom in, 27, *27*; journeymen labor strife in, 26–27; Krimmel's *Election Day 1815*, 23; in late-eighteenth- and early-nineteenth-century European trade, 282, 283–84; John Letchworth, 46, 48, 309, 340, 357, 358, 420; Library Company of Philadelphia, 411–12; lumber district of, 84; mahogany-color chairs made in, 150; matting used at, 313; Thomas Maule, 74, 75; Maule and Brother, 84; Abraham McDonough, 182, 187, 261, 299–300; John Mere, 260–61, 313; migration from, 20, 287; John Mitchell, 280; Thomas Mitchell, 32, 46; William Mitchell, 32, 46, 268; Michael Murphy, 232, 258, 287, 315; in nineteenth-century inland trade, 289, 295–96; Oeller's Hotel, 394; office chairs made in, 406; ornamented chairs made in, 163; outdoor market in, 407, *407*; outdoor uses of Windsor chairs in, 362, 363, 364; paint dealers in, 157; Philadelphia and Lancaster Turnpike, 220; John Pinkerton ironmonger, 61, 63, 67, 78; plane-making industry in, 70; in postrevolutionary African and Eastern Atlantic Islands trade, 253, 255–56; in postrevolutionary Caribbean trade, 240, 242, 243, 244–45, 247, 248–50, 251; in postrevolutionary coastal trade, 228–34; in postrevolutionary South American trade, 252; in prerevolutionary Caribbean trade, 222, 223, *228*; in prerevolutionary coastal

trade, 223–26, *227*; Price and Harper, 103, *104*; price books from, 26; public dinners at, 375; public gardens in, 378, *379*; public houses (taverns) in, 388, 389–90; red chairs in, 151; sandpaper in, 101; seat planks for stuffing in, 195; Second Continental Congress in, 427–29; shipping volume in early nineteenth-century, 256; shop signs in, 49, 50; simulated bamboo supports in, 26; slave woodworkers in, 17; Samuel Sloan, 421; Jedidiah Snowden, 67, 77, 223, 383, 412; sources of design of chairs from, 139, 140; stained chairs from, 185; state government furniture in, 424–25; steam power in, 103; J. H. Stevenson and Company, 179, *179*, 274, *275*; stoops in, 363; stuffed Windsor seating in, 192, 193, 195, *195*, 196; Taylor and King, 148, 150, 233; teamsters at, 318; trade of, 218; in triangular trade with New Orleans, 289; William Trotter, 270, 271, 314; United States Mint, 430; value of painted chair industry in 1811, 256; varnish production in, 186, 187; wages in, 22; Walnut Street Jail, 33, 37; Waverly Bowling Saloon, 375; Samuel Wetherill and Sons paint manufacturers, 153; James Whitaker, 30, 258, 260; white chairs in, 149; white lead manufacturing in, 158; woodlands near, 84; wood used in, 81, 84; working hours in, 21; yellow chairs in, 147, 148. *See also* Ackley, John B.; Allwine, Lawrence; Burden, Joseph; Coates, Samuel; Collins, Stephen; Cox, William; Gaw, Gilbert; Haydon, William; Henzey, Joseph; Lambert, John (chairmaker); Riley, Charles; Robinson, Charles C.; Steel, Anthony; Taylor, Robert; Trumble, Francis
Philadelphia and Lancaster Turnpike, 220
Philadelphia Monthly Meeting of Friends, 44–45, 48
Philadelphia Society of Journeymen Cabinet-makers, 27
Phillips, Ammi, 170
Phillips, James, 392, 423–24, 426
Phippen, Samuel, 90
Phyfe, Duncan, 7, 79, 161, 263
Piatt, John H., 402
piazzas, 362–63, 366, 398
picnics, 379
piecework wages, xi, 12–13, 22, 26, 94, 203
Pierce, Nathan, 302
Pierce, Peter, 92, 93, 97, 103
Pierce, Sarah, 418
Pile, John H., 269
pillars (arm posts; standards), 127, *128*
pincers (nippers), 77
Pine, Robert Edge, *428*, 428–29
pine, white. *See* white pine
Pinkerton, John (chairmaker), 425
Pinkerton, John (ironmonger), 61, 63, 67, 78
Pintard, John, 267, 309, 378
pirates, 274–75
Piscataqua (N.H.), 226, *227*, *228*
pit saws (whipsaws), 61
Pittsburgh: Baltimore and Ohio Railroad serving, 221–22; as gateway to Midwest, 289, 295, 310; in nineteenth-century inland trade, 289, 295, 310; river voyage to Cincinnati, 219; river voyage to New Orleans, 310; in timber trade, 84, 92; wages in, 22; wagon traffic at, 321; Windsor-chair factories in, 15

Plainville (Conn.), 324
planes, 68–70
plank-seat chairs: English, 237, 239; pattern terminology, 138–39
pleasure grounds, 377–79
pliers, 77
Plymouth (N.C.), 229
Pocomoke (Md.), *227*, *228*
Point Breeze, 364, *365*
pole lathes, 52, *52*, 54, 102
Polhill, Edward, 366
Polk, Ramsey, 365, *365*
Pollard, Jonathan P., 6
Pollard, Robert, *383*
Pomeroy, Oliver, 45, 288
Pomeroy, Seth, 66, 71
Pomfret (Conn.): Zadock Hutchins, 66, 71, 72, 76, 160, 292. *See also* Ward, Thomas Walter, II
Pond, Phineas, 132, 322
poplar (*Populus*), 86, *87*, 89, 90
poplar, yellow. *See* yellow poplar
Portage County (Ohio). *See* Talcott, Nelson
Port-au-Prince (Haiti): in early nineteenth-century Caribbean trade, *270*, 271; in postrevolutionary Caribbean trade, 238, 242, 243
Port Deposit (Md.), 84
Porter, Rufus: "The Art of Painting," 156; on gray paint, 152; on marbling, 184; on olive green paint, 147; on paint preparation, 156; on pea green paint, 146; on stenciling, 175, 176; on wood graining, 180–81, 182
Porter and Holbrook, 264
Portland (Maine): dancing school in, 374; in early nineteenth-century Caribbean trade, 273; in early nineteenth-century Central American trade, 274; in early nineteenth-century coastal trade, 259; fires in, 33; in postrevolutionary coastal trade, 229; prepared chair stock for, 96; wood used in, 81. *See also* Corey, Walter
Portrait of Mrs. David Witmar, Sr. (anonymous), *184*
Port Royal (S.C.), *227*
Port Royal (Va.), 229, 233
Portsmouth (N.H.): Arthur Browne, 190, 364; cushions in, 190; Samuel S. Dockum, 264; Dockum and Brown, 164, 179; domestic use of Windsor chairs in, 348; James Dwyer's public house, 388; in early nineteenth-century Caribbean trade, 273; in early nineteenth-century coastal trade, 259, 264; in early nineteenth-century South American trade, 281; mechanic society in, 25; Portsmouth Apprentices' Library, 25; Portsmouth Athenæum, 413; in postrevolutionary coastal trade, 229; railroad transportation, 324; stained chairs in, 185
Portsmouth (Ohio), 15
Portsmouth (Va.), 229, 230, 259
Portsmouth Apprentices' Library, 25
Portsmouth Athenæum, 413
Port Tobacco (Md.), 229
Post, John, 32
posts, 97–98
Pote, Increase, 96
Potomac River, *227*
Pottsville (Pa.), 289
Poughkeepsie (N.Y.), 103, 281

Powell, Joseph, 425
power, 102–4; dog power, 102; horsepower, 102, *155*; for lathes, 54–55. *See also* steam power; waterpower
Powers, Asahel, 169
Powers, Gershom, 35
Powers, Josiah, 74
Prall, Edward, 258
Prall, Henry, 44, 79, 159
Pratt, Joel, Jr., 6, 91, 108, *108*
Prentis, Joseph, 355, 357
prepared chair stock, 93–97; levels of business with, 93–95; major suppliers and consumers, 95–97
presidents: John Adams, 427; John Quincy Adams, 369; historic figures as ornament, 173; Andrew Jackson, 173, 268; James and Dolley Madison, 152, 178, 368–69, 413, 430; Windsor chairs owned by, 365–69. *See also* Jefferson, Thomas; Washington, George
Preston (Conn.), 71, 264
Preston, Almon, 47, 94
Preston, Titus: alterations done by, 133–34; cream-color chairs made by, 152; customer billed for hauling by, 319; dual-color chairs made by, 154; exchange of produce or labor for goods of, 94, 303, 304; repairs done by, 132; striping done by, 166; stuffed Windsor seating made by, 196; wagon repaired by, 322
Price and Harper, 103, *104*
price books, 26–27; *Cabinet and Chair Maker's Union Book of Prices* of 1828, 106; *Cabinet Maker's London Book of Prices*, 27, 142; Helme's "Book of Prices for Making Cabinet & chair furnature," 128, *129*, 163, 164, 187, *188*; *Journeymen Cabinet and Chair-Makers Philadelphia Book of Prices*, 26; *London Chair-Makers' and Carvers' Book of Prices*, 284; London price book of 1802, 141, 142; *The New-York Book of Prices for Cabinet and Chair Work*, 141
prices, retail. *See* retail prices
Priest, John, 81, 164
priming, 159
Prince, James, 370
Princess Anne (Md.), 426
Princeton (Mass.), 16
Prindall, Eliakim, 351
prints, 344, 354
prison work, xii, 33–37, 404
Pritchard, David, Jr.: apprenticeship agreement of, 14; exchange of produce or labor for goods of, 305; on miter-top chairs, 138; prepared chair stock for, 94, 95
privies, 106
profit, 130
Proud, Daniel: bows in stock of, 127; Colgrew supplying parts for, 94; cost of spindles, 99; daily income of, 21; factory chairs made by, 408; Nestell renting shop space from, 6; parlor of, 350; partnership with brother, 18; repairs made by, 408
Proud, Samuel: bedroom furniture of, 356; bows in stock of, 127; Colgrew supplying parts for, 94; cost of spindles, 99; daily income of, 21; Job Danforth jobbing for, 133; kitchen rocking chair of, 356; Nestell renting shop space from,

6; partnership with brother, 18; repairs made by, 408; shop chairs made by, 408
Proud, William, 132
Proud family, 406
Providence (R.I.): William Barker, 406, 408; Edward Carrington, 179, 282; Cyrus Cleaveland, 48, 52, 65, 263; in commercial sphere of Windsor-chair making, 217; Job Danforth, 105, 133, 417; in early nineteenth-century Caribbean trade, 271–72; in early nineteenth-century coastal trade, *259*, 262–63, 267; in early nineteenth-century South American trade, 279–81; Richard W. Greene, 406; Greene family, 200, 262, 416; Thomas Howard, Jr., 135, 282, 290, 292, 301; Daniel Lawrence, 92, 288, 364; local and county government furniture in, 423; Christian Nestell, 170; in Pacific Northwest trade, 285; painting supplies imported by, 157; in postrevolutionary African and Eastern Atlantic Islands trade, 253, 255; in postrevolutionary Caribbean trade, 218, 240, 243, 245, 248, 249; in postrevolutionary coastal trade, 229, 231; in postrevolutionary South American trade, 253; in prerevolutionary Caribbean trade, 222; price book from, 26; Proud family, 406; tool-making industry in, 70. *See also* Allen, Rhodes G.; Nestell, Christian; Proud, Daniel; Proud, Samuel
Providence Association of Mechanics and Manufacturers, 25, 412
Prussian blue paint, 153
public dinners, 375
public facilities: repair and refurbishment of chairs from, 131, 188–89. *See also* hotels; steamboats
public gardens, 377–79
public houses. *See* taverns (public houses)
Puerto Cabello (Venezuela), 276
Puerto Rico: in early nineteenth-century Caribbean trade, 269, *270*, 271; in postrevolutionary Caribbean trade, *238*, 239, *239*, 247
Purback, Aaron, 307

quaker-color paint, *145*, 152
Quakers (Society of Friends), 44–45, 48, 387, 416
Quebec: woods from, 92. *See also* Montreal
Queen Anne style, 200, 382
quilting parties, 375

racks, slat-bending, 57–58, *57*, *58*
railroads, 323–24; Baltimore and Ohio Railroad, 221–22; Boston, Barre and Gardner Railroad, 324; development of, 221–22; Eastern Railroad Corporation, 324, *324*, 413; Fitchburg Railroad, 323–24; New Haven and Hartford Railroad, 324; river traffic taken over by, 293; Saratoga and Schenectady Railroad, 324; specialization encouraged by, 28
Rakestraw, Joseph, 412
Raleigh (N.C.): Zenos Bronson, 30, 91, 97; Joel Brown, 47, 164, 294; David Ruth, 33, 362, 423, 426; stenciling in, 174; Cornelius J. Tooker, 136, 426; Wesley Whitaker, 10; wood used in, 91
Rand, John, 307
Rand, W. D., 103, 402, 424
Randolph, Benjamin, 223
Randolph, John, 364
Randolph, Martha Jefferson, 367

Randolph, Peyton, 427
Ranelagh Garden (New York City), 377
Rappahannock River, 227, 232–33
Rauch, Charles W., 49, *49*
Rause, John, 344, *344*
raw materials. *See* materials
Rea, Daniel: gilding done by, 178; Masonic accoutrements gilded by, 387; paintbrushes of, 160; refurbishing done by, 188; straw-color paint used by, 147; striping done by, 165; varnish used by, 187; white paint used by, 148
Rea and Johnston, 386
Read, Thomas, 296
recreational seating. *See* cultural and social uses of Windsor chairs
Redding (Conn.), 292, 203
red lead, 151
red maple (*Acer rubrum*), 83, 85
Redmond, Andrew, 228
red oak (*Quercus rubra*), 84, 126
red paint, *145*, 151–52
Redwood Library (Newport, R.I.), 411
Reed, Elbridge Gerry, 59, 67, 75
Reed, R. S., 289
Reed, William H., 50, 417
Reeve, Tapping, 303, 407
refurbishing: of government furniture, 188; of hotel furniture, 188–89, 396; of stuffed Windsor seating, 200; of surface finishes, 187–89
Reichel, Charles G., 409
Reily and Tunis, 262
religious groups, 414–16
Renshaw, James, 28, 80
Renshaw, Thomas S., 19, 168, 296
rental furniture, 137
repairs, 130–33; of factory chairs, 408; of hotel chairs, 131, 398; of stuffed Windsor seating, 200; of wagons and carts, 322. *See also* refurbishing
resort hotels, 396–99; Chapman's Springs, White Sulphur Springs at Eggleston, Va., 398, *397*–99; Congress Hall, Saratoga Springs, 398; Sans Souci Hotel, Ballston Spa, New York, 6, 20, 22, 131, 188–89, *397*, *397*–98; United States Hotel, Saratoga Springs, 398. *See also* hotels
retail prices: for chair tools, 60; for middle-range seating, 130; in Ontario, 299; in price books, 26; for side chairs, 128–30
retail stores, Windsor chairs for, 406
Revere, Paul, 24, 384, 386–87
revivals, religious, 416
Reynell, John, 66
Rhode Island: Bristol, 229, 235; in Chesapeake Bay trade, 225; in coasting trade, 217; construction of early chairs from, 128; continuous-bow chairs made in, 140; in early nineteenth-century coastal trade, *259*; in early nineteenth-century South American trade, 279; East Greenwich, 25, 229, 235; local and county government furniture in, 422–23; New York influencing, 288, 292; in postrevolutionary Caribbean trade, 228, 243, 244, 245–46, 249, *251*; in postrevolutionary coastal trade, 228, 229, 231, 235; in postrevolutionary South American trade, 252; in prerevolutionary Caribbean trade, 218, 223; in prerevolutionary coastal trade, 224, 226, 227; seat planks for

stuffing in, 194; sources of design of chairs from, 139–40; spindle socket boring in, 122; stuffed Windsor seating in, 195; Warren, 229, 235, 321; wood used in, 86, *87*, 88, 89, 90, 91. *See also* Newport; Providence; Tiverton

Rice, Kym, 390

Rich, Solomon, 48

Richardson, Thomas, and Company, 225

Richmond (Va.): auction to sell chairs from, 301–2; canal at, 221; courthouse furniture in, 423; in early nineteenth-century coastal trade, 258, *259*, 263, 264, 265; fire in, 32; George Jefferson, 309, 310, *310*, 367–68; New York influencing, 294; in postrevolutionary African and Eastern Atlantic Islands trade, 255; in postrevolutionary coastal trade, 229, 231, 234; prison work in, 34; public gardens in, 378; wood used in, 81. *See also* McKim, Robert

Ridgefield (Conn.). *See* Hawley, Elisha

Ridgely, Charles, 135, 178, 234, 308

Ridgeway, William, 300

Riley, Charles: bending equipment of, 58; blossom color in inventory of, 153; clamps of, 77; coal owned by, 105; green paint used by, 147; office chairs made by, 406; slate-color chairs in stock of, 152; spokeshaves of, 67; stoves of, 105

Riley, Joseph, 30, 100

Río de Janeiro (Brazil), *276*, 277, 278

Río de La Plata, *276*, 279–80

Rising Sun (brig), 310

Rittenhouse, David, 430

Ritter, Abraham, 32

Rivera, Jacob, 251

road travel. *See* land transportation

Roanoke (N.C.), 227

Robbins, Philemon: altering Windsor chairs, 133; bank chairs made by, 407; churches purchase chairs from, 416; cream-color chairs made by, 152; desk stools made by, 405; furniture rentals by, 137; gilding quality levels of, 179; on grape motif, 169; and Lambert Hitchcock, 6, 294; in nineteenth-century inland trade, 293; on painting costs, 163; quaker-color chairs made by, 152; rout chairs sold by, 373; secondhand chairs sold by, 137; stuffed rocking chair sold by, 200; tea-color chairs made by, 150; white pine used by, 88; Worcester County, Mass., suppliers of, 6

Robinson, Charles C.: altering Windsor chairs, 133; Daniel Carteret, Jr., working for, 13; chairs delivered by, 320; in early nineteenth-century coastal trade, 260; on outdoor use of Windsor chairs, 407; repairs made by, 132–33; sets of chairs sold by, 135; shop and residence combined, 43–44; shop location of, 48

Robinson, Charles T., 297

Robinson, John, 316

Robinson, Joseph, 84

Robinson firm, 35–36

Rochester (N.Y.): A. and E. Brown, 404; in Canadian trade, 298; chair production at, 16; Frederick Starr, 46, 187, 297, *298*, 324; waterpower in, 103

Rock, Elizabeth Calder, 353

rocking chairs: in bedrooms, 356; Boston-type, 98, Plate 27; conversion of Windsor chairs to, 133; crest from shaped-slat-back, Plate 8;

crown-top, 351, Plate 27; cushions for, 190; frame for stuffing, 284, *284*; in kitchens, 356; Montgomerys' matched, 352, *352*; nursery chairs, 137; repairs for, 132; in sets of chairs, 136; on steamboats, 402; stuffed, 199–200; in taverns, 393; youth's slat-back with freehand bronzing, 177, *177*

Rogers, Daniel, Jr., 308

Rogers, Hosea, 297

Rogers, William, 47

Roll, Jacob, 92, 96–97, 295

Roll and Deeds, 402

roll-top chairs: fancy side chair, *36*; Lafayette chairs, 370, *371*, Plate 22; pattern terminology, 139; turned roll as crest, 141, Plate 7, Plate 12, Plate 22

Rooker, Samuel, 55

Rose, Ebenezer P., 49, 150, 272, 290, 300

Rose, Elihu, 46, *46*

Rose, Nathaniel S., 34–35, 46, *46*

Rose, Westal, 14

rose-color paint, *145*, 152

rosewood graining, 181–82, Plate 30, Plate 31

Ross, Stephen, 47

Ross and Geyer, 19

round-back chairs, 138

rounder planes, 76

round-top chairs, 138, 139

Rousham, James, 63

rout chairs, 373

routs (social gatherings), 373–74

Rowena (brig), 400

Rowzee, William, 304

Roxbury (Mass.), 34

Royall, Anne Newport, 37, 370, 378

Royalston (Mass.), 16

Rudisill, John, 296

Rudolph, Tobias, 224

Rudolph, Zebulon, 224

Rudy, Henry Gottlieb, 411

Ruggles and Company, 34

rulers, 78

rush, 200–202; cost of, 202; as impractical in seats of chairs used out of doors, 364; in kitchen chairs, 138, 356; maintenance required for seats of, 131; New York chairmakers using, 85; in school chairs, 417; water deliveries of, 201–2, *201*, 308. *See also* rush-bottom slat-back chairs

Rush, Benjamin, 34

rush-bottom slat-back chairs: at camp meetings, 416; in churches, 414; for Common Council of New York City, 421; from Delaware Valley, 139; in dining rooms, 346; exportation of, 218, factors in Windsor chair capturing market of, 337–38; in kitchens, 138; in New Jersey tradition, 290; mortise-and-tenon joints in, 125; at quilting party, 375; on sailing ships, 399–400; slat-bending clamps for, 57, *57*; as source of American Windsor design, 139; staining of, 185

Russell, Abraham, *347*, 347–48

Russell, David, 154

Russell, Edward S., *405*

Russell, Joseph, 372, *372*

Russell, Joseph Shoemaker, 200, 346, 347, *347*, 350

Russell, William, Jr., 89, 187, *187*

rust brown–color paint, *145*, 150

Ruth, David, 33, 362, 423, 426

Rutherford, George, 239

Ryder, William, 54, 350

sack-back chairs: in advertisements, *20*, 223; bent-work in, 127; of Carpenters' Company of Philadelphia, 411, *412*, 427; hickory in, 83; from Massachusetts Historical Society, 414, *414*; pattern terminology, 138; from Rhode Island, *137*; from Saint John's Church, 414, *415*; at Second Continental Congress, 428–29; sources of design of, 140; of George Washington, 366

Sadler, Joel, 398

Safford, Thomas, 152

Sage, Lewis, 67, 72, 288

sage-color paint, *145*, 146

Sag Harbor (N.Y.), 229, 234

sailing vessels: principal types of American, *241*; schooners, *241*, 307; sloops, 224, *241*, 307, 400; Windsor chairs on, 399–400

Saint Andrew's (New Brunswick), 229, 259, 266

Saint Andrew's (Newfoundland), *259*

Saint Augustine (Fla.): in early nineteenth-century coastal trade, 258, *259*; in postrevolutionary coastal trade, 229, 237; in prerevolutionary coastal trade, 226, 227

Saint Bartholomew: in early nineteenth-century Caribbean trade, 269, *270*, 272; in postrevolutionary Caribbean trade, 238, 248, 249

Saint Croix: in early nineteenth-century Caribbean trade, 269, *270*, 272; in postrevolutionary Caribbean trade, 238, 247, 248

Saint Croix Packet (ship), 400

Saint Eustatius, 238, 247, 248–49, 269

Saint John (New Brunswick), 266, 296

Saint John (San Juan) (Puerto Rico), *270*, 271

Saint John (Virgin Islands), 238, 247

Saint John's (Newfoundland), 229, 236, 259, 266

Saint Lawrence River, 221

Saint Louis (Mo.): City Hotel, 395; Lambert Hitchcock journeying to, 294; Lynch and Trask, 427; river traffic at, 221, 296; river travel from Pittsburgh, 219

Saint Lucia, 238, 249, 250

Saint Martin, *270*, 272

Saint Mary's (Ga.), 229, 237

Saint Pierre, 238, 250–51

Saint Thomas: in early nineteenth-century Caribbean trade, 269, *270*, 272; in postrevolutionary Caribbean trade, 238, 247, 248

Saint Vincent, 238, 249–50

Salaman, Raphael, 67, 81

Salem (Mass.): black woodworkers in, 18; cross-rod chairs in, 141; cushions in, 190; in early nineteenth-century Caribbean trade, 271; in early nineteenth-century Central American trade, 275; in early nineteenth-century coastal trade, 259, 267; in early nineteenth-century Far Eastern trade, 285; in early nineteenth-century South American trade, 277, 279; fires at establishments of Nehemiah Adams, 33; Ebenezer Fox's general store, 97; Freemasonry in, 386; gilded chairs in, 179; William Gray, 159; loose seating in wagons in, 379–80; William Luther, 183, 278; in postrevolutionary Caribbean trade, 251–52; in postrevolutionary coastal trade, 229, 230, 237; in postrevolutionary Far Eastern trade, 256; in prerevolutionary Caribbean

Williams, John (Norwich, Conn.), 243

Williams, Joseph, 252–53

Williams, Martin, 239

Williams, Samuel, and Company, 19, 93, 296

Williams, William, 362

Williamsburg (Va.): Philip Ludwell's estates near, 361; in postrevolutionary coastal trade, 229, 231; Joseph Prentis, 355, 357

Williamson, David, 63

Willis, William E., 289

Wilmington (Del.): Sampson Barnet, 101, *101*, 286; James Brobson, 250, *250*, 273; Jared Chesnut, 76, 165; in early nineteenth-century coastal trade, *259*; in eighteenth-century inland trade, 286; Eleutherian Mills, 350, *350*, 354–55, *355*; Ziba Ferriss, 104; Henry Latimer, 340, 350, 354; local government using Windsor chairs, 420–21; in postrevolutionary Caribbean trade, 250, *250*; in postrevolutionary coastal trade, 229, 230; in prerevolutionary coastal trade, 224; Charles Trute's Swan Inn, 392; George Young, 287–88, 421. *See also* Hanson, Timothy

Wilmington (N.C.): in early nineteenth-century coastal trade, *259*, 263; fire at, 32; John Nutt, 17, 32, 107; in postrevolutionary coastal trade, 229, 237; Vosburgh and Childs, 313, 362

Wilson, James, 45, 104

Wilson, John, 58, 85

Winchester (Va.), 150, 153, 154

Windham (Conn.): Wait Stoddard, 322. *See also* Holmes, Elisha Harlow

Windsor (N.C.), 229

Windsor (Ontario), 299

Windsor (Vt.): basswood used in, 88; Green and Wardner hardware store, 71; Mary C. Green's school, 137, 418–19; Hayes and Hubbard, 29; Charles Ingalls, 301; prison work at, 34. *See also* Boynton, Thomas

Windsor chairs: in American life, 337–430; commercial use of, 387–411; cultural and social uses of, 370–87; domestic use of, 337–70; factors in popularity of, 337–38; institutional use of, 411–20; sets of chairs, 135–36, 346, 354. *See also* armchairs; chairmaking; government use of Windsor chairs; marketing; side chairs

Windsor Tavern Company, 394

Windward Islands: in early nineteenth-century Caribbean trade, 272–73; in postrevolutionary Caribbean trade, *238*, 240, 247, 249–51

Wing, Samuel: auxiliary trades of, 28, 29; bows in stock of, 58, 127; cart of, 320; furniture pattern of, *81*; green paint recipe of, 146; molding planes of, 70, *70*; shop of, 45; slat-bending racks of, 57; tenon tapering tool of, 76

Winship and James, 387

Winsor, Olney, 32

Winyaw Bay, *227*

Wire, John, 369

Wistar, Charles, 364, 406

Witmar, Mrs. David, Sr., *184*

Wollffe, Frederick, 345

women: canal boat accommodations for, 404; cane woven by, 203; at Daniel Churchill's factory, 16; exchanging produce or labor for goods, 304; at Hugh Finlay and Company, 15; hotel accommodations for, 395; ladies of pleasure visiting Havana, 376–77; and mechanization of seat weaving, 16; in schools, 418–20; seated separately at social occasions, 373–74; seating for fishing by, 383, *383*; sloop accommodations for, 400; steamboat accommodations for, 402; traveling by, 388; wages of, 22; Windsor chairs for, 137–38

wood, 81–93; beech, 85–86, 91; butternut, 86, *87*, 89, 90; chestnut, 86, *87*, 89; in exchange for goods or services, 304–5; for fuel, 105; hauling of, 321–22; poplar, 86, *87*, 89, 90; preparation of, 92–93; sycamore, 86, *87*, 89, 90; whitewood, 85, 89. *See also* ash; basswood; birch; hickory; mahogany; maple; oak; timber; walnut; white pine; yellow poplar

Wood, Edwin, 28

Wood, Eli, 9, 48, 293

wood graining, 180–83; mahogany graining, 182; maple graining, 181; rosewood graining, 181–82; satinwood graining, 182–83

woodlots, 48, 64, 304

wood scrapers, 68

wood screws, 102

Woodstock (Vt.), 423

Woodville, Richard Caton, 407–8

Woodworth, Heman, 19, *19*, 48

Worcester County (Mass.): cane weaving in, 203; chairmakers opening outlets around the country, 294; in early nineteenth-century coastal trade, 264; labor statistics for furniture-making trades of, 16, *16*; Henry W. Miller, 6, 7, 95, 199, 319, 405; in nineteenth-century inland trade, 293; prepared chair stock for, 95; wagon traffic in, 320; waterpower in, 55, 103; as wooded, 48; wood used in, 88, 89, 91

workbenches, 50–52

working hours, 3, 20–21

work stands, 351

Worthington, George, 369

Worthington, William, 430

woven, natural seating materials, 200–204; bark strips and splints, 202–3; cane, 85, 203–4. *See also* rush

Wright, Isaac, 199, 300, 352, 416

Wright, J. M., 299

Wytheville (Va.), 132, 133, 319

Yale College, 411

Yates, Jasper, 193, 195

yellow birch, 92

yellow pine, 91

yellow paint, *145*, 147–48

yellow poplar (tulip tree; *Liriodendron tulipifera*; also whitewood): near Albany, 85; Maryland chairmakers using, 85; midwestern chairmakers using, 92; New England chairmakers using, 86, *87*, 89; New York chairmakers using, 85; Pennsylvania chairmakers using, 82, *82*; Southern chairmakers using, 91

York (Pa.): court furniture in, 421–22, *422*; mechanic societies in, 25. *See also* Miller, Lewis

York River, 225, *227*

Yorktown (Va.), 229

Young, Charles, 361–62

Young, George, 287–88, 421

Young, Jonathan, 15

Younker, Francis, 266

Youth's Guide, The (Stewart), 417–18, *417*

Yucatan Peninsula, *270*, 274

Zachary, Lloyd, 360

Zimmerman, Maria Rex, 168, Plate 4

Zwisler, James, and Company, 195